Dictionary of Literary Biography

1. *The American Renaissance in New England*, edited by Joel Myerson (1978)
2. *American Novelists Since World War II*, edited by Jeffrey Helterman and Richard Layman (1978)
3. *Antebellum Writers in New York and the South*, edited by Joel Myerson (1979)
4. *American Writers in Paris, 1920-1939*, edited by Karen Lane Rood (1980)
5. *American Poets Since World War II*, 2 parts, edited by Donald J. Greiner (1980)
6. *American Novelists Since World War II, Second Series*, edited by James E. Kibler Jr. (1980)
7. *Twentieth-Century American Dramatists*, 2 parts, edited by John MacNicholas (1981)
8. *Twentieth-Century American Science-Fiction Writers*, 2 parts, edited by David Cowart and Thomas L. Wymer (1981)
9. *American Novelists, 1910-1945*, 3 parts, edited by James J. Martine (1981)
10. *Modern British Dramatists, 1900-1945*, 2 parts, edited by Stanley Weintraub (1982)
11. *American Humorists, 1800-1950*, 2 parts, edited by Stanley Trachtenberg (1982)
12. *American Realists and Naturalists*, edited by Donald Pizer and Earl N. Harbert (1982)
13. *British Dramatists Since World War II*, 2 parts, edited by Stanley Weintraub (1982)
14. *British Novelists Since 1960*, 2 parts, edited by Jay L. Halio (1983)
15. *British Novelists, 1930-1959*, 2 parts, edited by Bernard Oldsey (1983)
16. *The Beats: Literary Bohemians in Postwar America*, 2 parts, edited by Ann Charters (1983)
17. *Twentieth-Century American Historians*, edited by Clyde N. Wilson (1983)
18. *Victorian Novelists After 1885*, edited by Ira B. Nadel and William E. Fredeman (1983)
19. *British Poets, 1880-1914*, edited by Donald E. Stanford (1983)
20. *British Poets, 1914-1945*, edited by Donald E. Stanford (1983)
21. *Victorian Novelists Before 1885*, edited by Ira B. Nadel and William E. Fredeman (1983)
22. *American Writers for Children, 1900-1960*, edited by John Cech (1983)
23. *American Newspaper Journalists, 1873-1900*, edited by Perry J. Ashley (1983)
24. *American Colonial Writers, 1606-1734*, edited by Emory Elliott (1984)
25. *American Newspaper Journalists, 1901-1925*, edited by Perry J. Ashley (1984)
26. *American Screenwriters*, edited by Robert E. Morsberger, Stephen O. Lesser, and Randall Clark (1984)
27. *Poets of Great Britain and Ireland, 1945-1960*, edited by Vincent B. Sherry Jr. (1984)
28. *Twentieth-Century American-Jewish Fiction Writers*, edited by Daniel Walden (1984)
29. *American Newspaper Journalists, 1926-1950*, edited by Perry J. Ashley (1984)
30. *American Historians, 1607-1865*, edited by Clyde N. Wilson (1984)
31. *American Colonial Writers, 1735-1781*, edited by Emory Elliott (1984)
32. *Victorian Poets Before 1850*, edited by William E. Fredeman and Ira B. Nadel (1984)
33. *Afro-American Fiction Writers After 1955*, edited by Thadious M. Davis and Trudier Harris (1984)
34. *British Novelists, 1890-1929: Traditionalists*, edited by Thomas F. Staley (1985)
35. *Victorian Poets After 1850*, edited by William E. Fredeman and Ira B. Nadel (1985)
36. *British Novelists, 1890-1929: Modernists*, edited by Thomas F. Staley (1985)
37. *American Writers of the Early Republic*, edited by Emory Elliott (1985)
38. *Afro-American Writers After 1955: Dramatists and Prose Writers*, edited by Thadious M. Davis and Trudier Harris (1985)
39. *British Novelists, 1660-1800*, 2 parts, edited by Martin C. Battestin (1985)
40. *Poets of Great Britain and Ireland Since 1960*, 2 parts, edited by Vincent B. Sherry Jr. (1985)
41. *Afro-American Poets Since 1955*, edited by Trudier Harris and Thadious M. Davis (1985)
42. *American Writers for Children Before 1900*, edited by Glenn E. Estes (1985)
43. *American Newspaper Journalists, 1690-1872*, edited by Perry J. Ashley (1986)
44. *American Screenwriters, Second Series*, edited by Randall Clark, Robert E. Morsberger, and Stephen O. Lesser (1986)
45. *American Poets, 1880-1945, First Series*, edited by Peter Quartermain (1986)
46. *American Literary Publishing Houses, 1900-1980: Trade and Paperback*, edited by Peter Dzwonkoski (1986)
47. *American Historians, 1866-1912*, edited by Clyde N. Wilson (1986)
48. *American Poets, 1880-1945, Second Series*, edited by Peter Quartermain (1986)
49. *American Literary Publishing Houses, 1638-1899*, 2 parts, edited by Peter Dzwonkoski (1986)
50. *Afro-American Writers Before the Harlem Renaissance*, edited by Trudier Harris (1986)
51. *Afro-American Writers from the Harlem Renaissance to 1940*, edited by Trudier Harris (1987)
52. *American Writers for Children Since 1960: Fiction*, edited by Glenn E. Estes (1986)
53. *Canadian Writers Since 1960, First Series*, edited by W. H. New (1986)
54. *American Poets, 1880-1945, Third Series*, 2 parts, edited by Peter Quartermain (1987)
55. *Victorian Prose Writers Before 1867*, edited by William B. Thesing (1987)
56. *German Fiction Writers, 1914-1945*, edited by James Hardin (1987)
57. *Victorian Prose Writers After 1867*, edited by William B. Thesing (1987)
58. *Jacobean and Caroline Dramatists*, edited by Fredson Bowers (1987)
59. *American Literary Critics and Scholars, 1800-1850*, edited by John W. Rathbun and Monica M. Grecu (1987)
60. *Canadian Writers Since 1960, Second Series*, edited by W. H. New (1987)
61. *American Writers for Children Since 1960: Poets, Illustrators, and Nonfiction Authors*, edited by Glenn E. Estes (1987)
62. *Elizabethan Dramatists*, edited by Fredson Bowers (1987)
63. *Modern American Critics, 1920-1955*, edited by Gregory S. Jay (1988)
64. *American Literary Critics and Scholars, 1850-1880*, edited by John W. Rathbun and Monica M. Grecu (1988)
65. *French Novelists, 1900-1930*, edited by Catharine Savage Brosman (1988)
66. *German Fiction Writers, 1885-1913*, 2 parts, edited by James Hardin (1988)
67. *Modern American Critics Since 1955*, edited by Gregory S. Jay (1988)
68. *Canadian Writers, 1920-1959, First Series*, edited by W. H. New (1988)
69. *Contemporary German Fiction Writers, First Series*, edited by Wolfgang D. Elfe and James Hardin (1988)
70. *British Mystery Writers, 1860-1919*, edited by Bernard Benstock and Thomas F. Staley (1988)

71 *American Literary Critics and Scholars, 1880–1900,* edited by John W. Rathbun and Monica M. Grecu (1988)

72 *French Novelists, 1930–1960,* edited by Catharine Savage Brosman (1988)

73 *American Magazine Journalists, 1741–1850,* edited by Sam G. Riley (1988)

74 *American Short-Story Writers Before 1880,* edited by Bobby Ellen Kimbel, with the assistance of William E. Grant (1988)

75 *Contemporary German Fiction Writers, Second Series,* edited by Wolfgang D. Elfe and James Hardin (1988)

76 *Afro-American Writers, 1940–1955,* edited by Trudier Harris (1988)

77 *British Mystery Writers, 1920–1939,* edited by Bernard Benstock and Thomas F. Staley (1988)

78 *American Short-Story Writers, 1880–1910,* edited by Bobby Ellen Kimbel, with the assistance of William E. Grant (1988)

79 *American Magazine Journalists, 1850–1900,* edited by Sam G. Riley (1988)

80 *Restoration and Eighteenth-Century Dramatists, First Series,* edited by Paula R. Backscheider (1989)

81 *Austrian Fiction Writers, 1875–1913,* edited by James Hardin and Donald G. Daviau (1989)

82 *Chicano Writers, First Series,* edited by Francisco A. Lomelí and Carl R. Shirley (1989)

83 *French Novelists Since 1960,* edited by Catharine Savage Brosman (1989)

84 *Restoration and Eighteenth-Century Dramatists, Second Series,* edited by Paula R. Backscheider (1989)

85 *Austrian Fiction Writers After 1914,* edited by James Hardin and Donald G. Daviau (1989)

86 *American Short-Story Writers, 1910–1945, First Series,* edited by Bobby Ellen Kimbel (1989)

87 *British Mystery and Thriller Writers Since 1940, First Series,* edited by Bernard Benstock and Thomas F. Staley (1989)

88 *Canadian Writers, 1920–1959, Second Series,* edited by W. H. New (1989)

89 *Restoration and Eighteenth-Century Dramatists, Third Series,* edited by Paula R. Backscheider (1989)

90 *German Writers in the Age of Goethe, 1789–1832,* edited by James Hardin and Christoph E. Schweitzer (1989)

91 *American Magazine Journalists, 1900–1960, First Series,* edited by Sam G. Riley (1990)

92 *Canadian Writers, 1890–1920,* edited by W. H. New (1990)

93 *British Romantic Poets, 1789–1832, First Series,* edited by John R. Greenfield (1990)

94 *German Writers in the Age of Goethe: Sturm und Drang to Classicism,* edited by James Hardin and Christoph E. Schweitzer (1990)

95 *Eighteenth-Century British Poets, First Series,* edited by John Sitter (1990)

96 *British Romantic Poets, 1789–1832, Second Series,* edited by John R. Greenfield (1990)

97 *German Writers from the Enlightenment to Sturm und Drang, 1720–1764,* edited by James Hardin and Christoph E. Schweitzer (1990)

98 *Modern British Essayists, First Series,* edited by Robert Beum (1990)

99 *Canadian Writers Before 1890,* edited by W. H. New (1990)

100 *Modern British Essayists, Second Series,* edited by Robert Beum (1990)

101 *British Prose Writers, 1660–1800, First Series,* edited by Donald T. Siebert (1991)

102 *American Short-Story Writers, 1910–1945, Second Series,* edited by Bobby Ellen Kimbel (1991)

103 *American Literary Biographers, First Series,* edited by Steven Serafin (1991)

104 *British Prose Writers, 1660–1800, Second Series,* edited by Donald T. Siebert (1991)

105 *American Poets Since World War II, Second Series,* edited by R. S. Gwynn (1991)

106 *British Literary Publishing Houses, 1820–1880,* edited by Patricia J. Anderson and Jonathan Rose (1991)

107 *British Romantic Prose Writers, 1789–1832, First Series,* edited by John R. Greenfield (1991)

108 *Twentieth-Century Spanish Poets, First Series,* edited by Michael L. Perna (1991)

109 *Eighteenth-Century British Poets, Second Series,* edited by John Sitter (1991)

110 *British Romantic Prose Writers, 1789–1832, Second Series,* edited by John R. Greenfield (1991)

111 *American Literary Biographers, Second Series,* edited by Steven Serafin (1991)

112 *British Literary Publishing Houses, 1881–1965,* edited by Jonathan Rose and Patricia J. Anderson (1991)

113 *Modern Latin-American Fiction Writers, First Series,* edited by William Luis (1992)

114 *Twentieth-Century Italian Poets, First Series,* edited by Giovanna Wedel De Stasio, Glauco Cambon, and Antonio Illiano (1992)

115 *Medieval Philosophers,* edited by Jeremiah Hackett (1992)

116 *British Romantic Novelists, 1789–1832,* edited by Bradford K. Mudge (1992)

117 *Twentieth-Century Caribbean and Black African Writers, First Series,* edited by Bernth Lindfors and Reinhard Sander (1992)

118 *Twentieth-Century German Dramatists, 1889–1918,* edited by Wolfgang D. Elfe and James Hardin (1992)

119 *Nineteenth-Century French Fiction Writers: Romanticism and Realism, 1800–1860,* edited by Catharine Savage Brosman (1992)

120 *American Poets Since World War II, Third Series,* edited by R. S. Gwynn (1992)

121 *Seventeenth-Century British Nondramatic Poets, First Series,* edited by M. Thomas Hester (1992)

122 *Chicano Writers, Second Series,* edited by Francisco A. Lomelí and Carl R. Shirley (1992)

123 *Nineteenth-Century French Fiction Writers: Naturalism and Beyond, 1860–1900,* edited by Catharine Savage Brosman (1992)

124 *Twentieth-Century German Dramatists, 1919–1992,* edited by Wolfgang D. Elfe and James Hardin (1992)

125 *Twentieth-Century Caribbean and Black African Writers, Second Series,* edited by Bernth Lindfors and Reinhard Sander (1993)

126 *Seventeenth-Century British Nondramatic Poets, Second Series,* edited by M. Thomas Hester (1993)

127 *American Newspaper Publishers, 1950–1990,* edited by Perry J. Ashley (1993)

128 *Twentieth-Century Italian Poets, Second Series,* edited by Giovanna Wedel De Stasio, Glauco Cambon, and Antonio Illiano (1993)

129 *Nineteenth-Century German Writers, 1841–1900,* edited by James Hardin and Siegfried Mews (1993)

130 *American Short-Story Writers Since World War II,* edited by Patrick Meanor (1993)

131 *Seventeenth-Century British Nondramatic Poets, Third Series,* edited by M. Thomas Hester (1993)

132 *Sixteenth-Century British Nondramatic Writers, First Series,* edited by David A. Richardson (1993)

133 *Nineteenth-Century German Writers to 1840,* edited by James Hardin and Siegfried Mews (1993)

134 *Twentieth-Century Spanish Poets, Second Series,* edited by Jerry Phillips Winfield (1994)

135 *British Short-Fiction Writers, 1880–1914: The Realist Tradition,* edited by William B. Thesing (1994)

136 *Sixteenth-Century British Nondramatic Writers, Second Series,* edited by David A. Richardson (1994)

137 *American Magazine Journalists, 1900–1960, Second Series,* edited by Sam G. Riley (1994)

138 *German Writers and Works of the High Middle Ages: 1170–1280,* edited by James Hardin and Will Hasty (1994)

139 *British Short-Fiction Writers, 1945–1980,* edited by Dean Baldwin (1994)

140 *American Book-Collectors and Bibliographers, First Series*, edited by Joseph Rosenblum (1994)

141 *British Children's Writers, 1880–1914*, edited by Laura M. Zaidman (1994)

142 *Eighteenth-Century British Literary Biographers*, edited by Steven Serafin (1994)

143 *American Novelists Since World War II, Third Series*, edited by James R. Giles and Wanda H. Giles (1994)

144 *Nineteenth-Century British Literary Biographers*, edited by Steven Serafin (1994)

145 *Modern Latin-American Fiction Writers, Second Series*, edited by William Luis and Ann González (1994)

146 *Old and Middle English Literature*, edited by Jeffrey Helterman and Jerome Mitchell (1994)

147 *South Slavic Writers Before World War II*, edited by Vasa D. Mihailovich (1994)

148 *German Writers and Works of the Early Middle Ages: 800–1170*, edited by Will Hasty and James Hardin (1994)

149 *Late Nineteenth- and Early Twentieth-Century British Literary Biographers*, edited by Steven Serafin (1995)

150 *Early Modern Russian Writers, Late Seventeenth and Eighteenth Centuries*, edited by Marcus C. Levitt (1995)

151 *British Prose Writers of the Early Seventeenth Century*, edited by Clayton D. Lein (1995)

152 *American Novelists Since World War II, Fourth Series*, edited by James R. Giles and Wanda H. Giles (1995)

153 *Late-Victorian and Edwardian British Novelists, First Series*, edited by George M. Johnson (1995)

154 *The British Literary Book Trade, 1700–1820*, edited by James K. Bracken and Joel Silver (1995)

155 *Twentieth-Century British Literary Biographers*, edited by Steven Serafin (1995)

156 *British Short-Fiction Writers, 1880–1914: The Romantic Tradition*, edited by William F. Naufftus (1995)

157 *Twentieth-Century Caribbean and Black African Writers, Third Series*, edited by Bernth Lindfors and Reinhard Sander (1995)

158 *British Reform Writers, 1789–1832*, edited by Gary Kelly and Edd Applegate (1995)

159 *British Short-Fiction Writers, 1800–1880*, edited by John R. Greenfield (1996)

160 *British Children's Writers, 1914–1960*, edited by Donald R. Hettinga and Gary D. Schmidt (1996)

161 *British Children's Writers Since 1960, First Series*, edited by Caroline Hunt (1996)

162 *British Short-Fiction Writers, 1915–1945*, edited by John H. Rogers (1996)

163 *British Children's Writers, 1800–1880*, edited by Meena Khorana (1996)

164 *German Baroque Writers, 1580–1660*, edited by James Hardin (1996)

165 *American Poets Since World War II, Fourth Series*, edited by Joseph Conte (1996)

166 *British Travel Writers, 1837–1875*, edited by Barbara Brothers and Julia Gergits (1996)

167 *Sixteenth-Century British Nondramatic Writers, Third Series*, edited by David A. Richardson (1996)

168 *German Baroque Writers, 1661–1730*, edited by James Hardin (1996)

169 *American Poets Since World War II, Fifth Series*, edited by Joseph Conte (1996)

170 *The British Literary Book Trade, 1475–1700*, edited by James K. Bracken and Joel Silver (1996)

171 *Twentieth-Century American Sportswriters*, edited by Richard Orodenker (1996)

172 *Sixteenth-Century British Nondramatic Writers, Fourth Series*, edited by David A. Richardson (1996)

173 *American Novelists Since World War II, Fifth Series*, edited by James R. Giles and Wanda H. Giles (1996)

174 *British Travel Writers, 1876–1909*, edited by Barbara Brothers and Julia Gergits (1997)

175 *Native American Writers of the United States*, edited by Kenneth M. Roemer (1997)

176 *Ancient Greek Authors*, edited by Ward W. Briggs (1997)

177 *Italian Novelists Since World War II, 1945–1965*, edited by Augustus Pallotta (1997)

178 *British Fantasy and Science-Fiction Writers Before World War I*, edited by Darren Harris-Fain (1997)

179 *German Writers of the Renaissance and Reformation, 1280–1580*, edited by James Hardin and Max Reinhart (1997)

180 *Japanese Fiction Writers, 1868–1945*, edited by Van C. Gessel (1997)

181 *South Slavic Writers Since World War II*, edited by Vasa D. Mihailovich (1997)

182 *Japanese Fiction Writers Since World War II*, edited by Van C. Gessel (1997)

183 *American Travel Writers, 1776–1864*, edited by James J. Schramer and Donald Ross (1997)

184 *Nineteenth-Century British Book-Collectors and Bibliographers*, edited by William Baker and Kenneth Womack (1997)

185 *American Literary Journalists, 1945–1995, First Series*, edited by Arthur J. Kaul (1998)

186 *Nineteenth-Century American Western Writers*, edited by Robert L. Gale (1998)

187 *American Book Collectors and Bibliographers, Second Series*, edited by Joseph Rosenblum (1998)

188 *American Book and Magazine Illustrators to 1920*, edited by Steven E. Smith, Catherine A. Hastedt, and Donald H. Dyal (1998)

189 *American Travel Writers, 1850–1915*, edited by Donald Ross and James J. Schramer (1998)

190 *British Reform Writers, 1832–1914*, edited by Gary Kelly and Edd Applegate (1998)

191 *British Novelists Between the Wars*, edited by George M. Johnson (1998)

192 *French Dramatists, 1789–1914*, edited by Barbara T. Cooper (1998)

193 *American Poets Since World War II, Sixth Series*, edited by Joseph Conte (1998)

194 *British Novelists Since 1960, Second Series*, edited by Merritt Moseley (1998)

195 *British Travel Writers, 1910–1939*, edited by Barbara Brothers and Julia Gergits (1998)

196 *Italian Novelists Since World War II, 1965–1995*, edited by Augustus Pallotta (1999)

197 *Late-Victorian and Edwardian British Novelists, Second Series*, edited by George M. Johnson (1999)

198 *Russian Literature in the Age of Pushkin and Gogol: Prose*, edited by Christine A. Rydel (1999)

199 *Victorian Women Poets*, edited by William B. Thesing (1999)

200 *American Women Prose Writers to 1820*, edited by Carla J. Mulford, with Angela Vietto and Amy E. Winans (1999)

201 *Twentieth-Century British Book Collectors and Bibliographers*, edited by William Baker and Kenneth Womack (1999)

202 *Nineteenth-Century American Fiction Writers*, edited by Kent P. Ljungquist (1999)

203 *Medieval Japanese Writers*, edited by Steven D. Carter (1999)

204 *British Travel Writers, 1940–1997*, edited by Barbara Brothers and Julia M. Gergits (1999)

205 *Russian Literature in the Age of Pushkin and Gogol: Poetry and Drama*, edited by Christine A. Rydel (1999)

206 *Twentieth-Century American Western Writers, First Series*, edited by Richard H. Cracroft (1999)

207 *British Novelists Since 1960, Third Series*, edited by Merritt Moseley (1999)

208 *Literature of the French and Occitan Middle Ages: Eleventh to Fifteenth Centuries*, edited by Deborah Sinnreich-Levi and Ian S. Laurie (1999)

209 *Chicano Writers, Third Series*, edited by Francisco A. Lomelí and Carl R. Shirley (1999)

210 *Ernest Hemingway: A Documentary Volume*, edited by Robert W. Trogdon (1999)

211 *Ancient Roman Writers*, edited by Ward W. Briggs (1999)

212 *Twentieth-Century American Western Writers, Second Series*, edited by Richard H. Cracroft (1999)

213 *Pre-Nineteenth-Century British Book Collectors and Bibliographers*, edited by William Baker and Kenneth Womack (1999)

214 *Twentieth-Century Danish Writers*, edited by Marianne Stecher-Hansen (1999)

215 *Twentieth-Century Eastern European Writers, First Series*, edited by Steven Serafin (1999)

216 *British Poets of the Great War: Brooke, Rosenberg, Thomas. A Documentary Volume*, edited by Patrick Quinn (2000)

217 *Nineteenth-Century French Poets*, edited by Robert Beum (2000)

218 *American Short-Story Writers Since World War II, Second Series*, edited by Patrick Meanor and Gwen Crane (2000)

219 *F. Scott Fitzgerald's* The Great Gatsby: *A Documentary Volume*, edited by Matthew J. Bruccoli (2000)

220 *Twentieth-Century Eastern European Writers, Second Series*, edited by Steven Serafin (2000)

221 *American Women Prose Writers, 1870–1920*, edited by Sharon M. Harris, with the assistance of Heidi L. M. Jacobs and Jennifer Putzi (2000)

222 *H. L. Mencken: A Documentary Volume*, edited by Richard J. Schrader (2000)

223 *The American Renaissance in New England, Second Series*, edited by Wesley T. Mott (2000)

224 *Walt Whitman: A Documentary Volume*, edited by Joel Myerson (2000)

225 *South African Writers*, edited by Paul A. Scanlon (2000)

226 *American Hard-Boiled Crime Writers*, edited by George Parker Anderson and Julie B. Anderson (2000)

227 *American Novelists Since World War II, Sixth Series*, edited by James R. Giles and Wanda H. Giles (2000)

228 *Twentieth-Century American Dramatists, Second Series*, edited by Christopher J. Wheatley (2000)

229 *Thomas Wolfe: A Documentary Volume*, edited by Ted Mitchell (2001)

230 *Australian Literature, 1788–1914*, edited by Selina Samuels (2001)

231 *British Novelists Since 1960, Fourth Series*, edited by Merritt Moseley (2001)

232 *Twentieth-Century Eastern European Writers, Third Series*, edited by Steven Serafin (2001)

233 *British and Irish Dramatists Since World War II, Second Series*, edited by John Bull (2001)

234 *American Short-Story Writers Since World War II, Third Series*, edited by Patrick Meanor and Richard E. Lee (2001)

235 *The American Renaissance in New England, Third Series*, edited by Wesley T. Mott (2001)

236 *British Rhetoricians and Logicians, 1500–1660*, edited by Edward A. Malone (2001)

237 *The Beats: A Documentary Volume*, edited by Matt Theado (2001)

238 *Russian Novelists in the Age of Tolstoy and Dostoevsky*, edited by J. Alexander Ogden and Judith E. Kalb (2001)

239 *American Women Prose Writers: 1820–1870*, edited by Amy E. Hudock and Katharine Rodier (2001)

240 *Late Nineteenth- and Early Twentieth-Century British Women Poets*, edited by William B. Thesing (2001)

241 *American Sportswriters and Writers on Sport*, edited by Richard Orodenker (2001)

242 *Twentieth-Century European Cultural Theorists, First Series*, edited by Paul Hansom (2001)

243 *The American Renaissance in New England, Fourth Series*, edited by Wesley T. Mott (2001)

244 *American Short-Story Writers Since World War II, Fourth Series*, edited by Patrick Meanor and Joseph McNicholas (2001)

245 *British and Irish Dramatists Since World War II, Third Series*, edited by John Bull (2001)

246 *Twentieth-Century American Cultural Theorists*, edited by Paul Hansom (2001)

247 *James Joyce: A Documentary Volume*, edited by A. Nicholas Fargnoli (2001)

248 *Antebellum Writers in the South, Second Series*, edited by Kent Ljungquist (2001)

249 *Twentieth-Century American Dramatists, Third Series*, edited by Christopher Wheatley (2002)

250 *Antebellum Writers in New York, Second Series*, edited by Kent Ljungquist (2002)

251 *Canadian Fantasy and Science-Fiction Writers*, edited by Douglas Ivison (2002)

252 *British Philosophers, 1500–1799*, edited by Philip B. Dematteis and Peter S. Fosl (2002)

253 *Raymond Chandler: A Documentary Volume*, edited by Robert Moss (2002)

254 *The House of Putnam, 1837–1872: A Documentary Volume*, edited by Ezra Greenspan (2002)

255 *British Fantasy and Science-Fiction Writers, 1918–1960*, edited by Darren Harris-Fain (2002)

256 *Twentieth-Century American Western Writers, Third Series*, edited by Richard H. Cracroft (2002)

257 *Twentieth-Century Swedish Writers After World War II*, edited by Ann-Charlotte Gavel Adams (2002)

258 *Modern French Poets*, edited by Jean-François Leroux (2002)

259 *Twentieth-Century Swedish Writers Before World War II*, edited by Ann-Charlotte Gavel Adams (2002)

260 *Australian Writers, 1915–1950*, edited by Selina Samuels (2002)

261 *British Fantasy and Science-Fiction Writers Since 1960*, edited by Darren Harris-Fain (2002)

262 *British Philosophers, 1800–2000*, edited by Peter S. Fosl and Leemon B. McHenry (2002)

263 *William Shakespeare: A Documentary Volume*, edited by Catherine Loomis (2002)

264 *Italian Prose Writers, 1900–1945*, edited by Luca Somigli and Rocco Capozzi (2002)

265 *American Song Lyricists, 1920–1960*, edited by Philip Furia (2002)

266 *Twentieth-Century American Dramatists, Fourth Series*, edited by Christopher J. Wheatley (2002)

267 *Twenty-First-Century British and Irish Novelists*, edited by Michael R. Molino (2002)

268 *Seventeenth-Century French Writers*, edited by Françoise Jaouën (2002)

269 *Nathaniel Hawthorne: A Documentary Volume*, edited by Benjamin Franklin V (2002)

270 *American Philosophers Before 1950*, edited by Philip B. Dematteis and Leemon B. McHenry (2002)

271 *British and Irish Novelists Since 1960*, edited by Merritt Moseley (2002)

272 *Russian Prose Writers Between the World Wars*, edited by Christine Rydel (2003)

273 *F. Scott Fitzgerald's* Tender Is the Night: *A Documentary Volume*, edited by Matthew J. Bruccoli and George Parker Anderson (2003)

274 *John Dos Passos's* U.S.A.: *A Documentary Volume*, edited by Donald Pizer (2003)

275 *Twentieth-Century American Nature Writers: Prose*, edited by Roger Thompson and J. Scott Bryson (2003)

276 *British Mystery and Thriller Writers Since 1960*, edited by Gina Macdonald (2003)

277 *Russian Literature in the Age of Realism*, edited by Alyssa Dinega Gillespie (2003)

278 *American Novelists Since World War II, Seventh Series*, edited by James R. Giles and Wanda H. Giles (2003)

279 *American Philosophers, 1950–2000*, edited by Philip B. Dematteis and Leemon B. McHenry (2003)

280 *Dashiell Hammett's* The Maltese Falcon: *A Documentary Volume*, edited by Richard Layman (2003)

281 *British Rhetoricians and Logicians, 1500–1660, Second Series*, edited by Edward A. Malone (2003)

282 *New Formalist Poets*, edited by Jonathan N. Barron and Bruce Meyer (2003)

283 *Modern Spanish American Poets, First Series*, edited by María A. Salgado (2003)

284 *The House of Holt, 1866–1946: A Documentary Volume*, edited by Ellen D. Gilbert (2003)

285 *Russian Writers Since 1980,* edited by Marina Balina and Mark Lipovetsky (2004)

286 *Castilian Writers, 1400–1500,* edited by Frank A. Domínguez and George D. Greenia (2004)

287 *Portuguese Writers,* edited by Monica Rector and Fred M. Clark (2004)

288 *The House of Boni & Liveright, 1917–1933: A Documentary Volume,* edited by Charles Egleston (2004)

289 *Australian Writers, 1950–1975,* edited by Selina Samuels (2004)

290 *Modern Spanish American Poets, Second Series,* edited by María A. Salgado (2004)

291 *The Hoosier House: Bobbs-Merrill and Its Predecessors, 1850–1985: A Documentary Volume,* edited by Richard J. Schrader (2004)

292 *Twenty-First-Century American Novelists,* edited by Lisa Abney and Suzanne Disheroon-Green (2004)

293 *Icelandic Writers,* edited by Patrick J. Stevens (2004)

294 *James Gould Cozzens: A Documentary Volume,* edited by Matthew J. Bruccoli (2004)

295 *Russian Writers of the Silver Age, 1890–1925,* edited by Judith E. Kalb and J. Alexander Ogden with the collaboration of I. G. Vishnevetsky (2004)

296 *Twentieth-Century European Cultural Theorists, Second Series,* edited by Paul Hansom (2004)

297 *Twentieth-Century Norwegian Writers,* edited by Tanya Thresher (2004)

298 *Henry David Thoreau: A Documentary Volume,* edited by Richard J. Schneider (2004)

299 *Holocaust Novelists,* edited by Efraim Sicher (2004)

300 *Danish Writers from the Reformation to Decadence, 1550–1900,* edited by Marianne Stecher-Hansen (2004)

301 *Gustave Flaubert: A Documentary Volume,* edited by Éric Le Calvez (2004)

302 *Russian Prose Writers After World War II,* edited by Christine Rydel (2004)

303 *American Radical and Reform Writers, First Series,* edited by Steven Rosendale (2005)

304 *Bram Stoker's* Dracula: *A Documentary Volume,* edited by Elizabeth Miller (2005)

305 *Latin American Dramatists, First Series,* edited by Adam Versényi (2005)

306 *American Mystery and Detective Writers,* edited by George Parker Anderson (2005)

307 *Brazilian Writers,* edited by Monica Rector and Fred M. Clark (2005)

308 *Ernest Hemingway's* A Farewell to Arms: *A Documentary Volume,* edited by Charles Oliver (2005)

309 *John Steinbeck: A Documentary Volume,* edited by Luchen Li (2005)

310 *British and Irish Dramatists Since World War II, Fourth Series,* edited by John Bull (2005)

311 *Arabic Literary Culture, 500–925,* edited by Michael Cooperson and Shawkat M. Toorawa (2005)

312 *Asian American Writers,* edited by Deborah L. Madsen (2005)

313 *Writers of the French Enlightenment, I,* edited by Samia I. Spencer (2005)

314 *Writers of the French Enlightenment, II,* edited by Samia I. Spencer (2005)

315 *Langston Hughes: A Documentary Volume,* edited by Christopher C. De Santis (2005)

316 *American Prose Writers of World War I: A Documentary Volume,* edited by Steven Trout (2005)

317 *Twentieth-Century Russian Émigré Writers,* edited by Maria Rubins (2005)

318 *Sixteenth-Century Spanish Writers,* edited by Gregory B. Kaplan (2006)

319 *British and Irish Short-Fiction Writers 1945–2000,* edited by Cheryl Alexander Malcolm and David Malcolm (2006)

320 *Robert Penn Warren: A Documentary Volume,* edited by James A. Grimshaw Jr. (2006)

321 *Twentieth-Century French Dramatists,* edited by Mary Anne O'Neil (2006)

322 *Twentieth-Century Spanish Fiction Writers,* edited by Marta E. Altisent and Cristina Martínez-Carazo (2006)

323 *South Asian Writers in English,* edited by Fakrul Alam (2006)

324 *John O'Hara: A Documentary Volume,* edited by Matthew J. Bruccoli (2006)

325 *Australian Writers, 1975–2000,* edited by Selina Samuels (2006)

326 *Booker Prize Novels, 1969–2005,* edited by Merritt Moseley (2006)

327 *Sixteenth-Century French Writers,* edited by Megan Conway (2006)

328 *Chinese Fiction Writers, 1900–1949,* edited by Thomas Moran (2007)

329 *Nobel Prize Laureates in Literature, Part 1: Agnon–Eucken* (2007)

330 *Nobel Prize Laureates in Literature, Part 2: Faulkner–Kipling* (2007)

Dictionary of Literary Biography Documentary Series

1 *Sherwood Anderson, Willa Cather, John Dos Passos, Theodore Dreiser, F. Scott Fitzgerald, Ernest Hemingway, Sinclair Lewis,* edited by Margaret A. Van Antwerp (1982)

2 *James Gould Cozzens, James T. Farrell, William Faulkner, John O'Hara, John Steinbeck, Thomas Wolfe, Richard Wright,* edited by Margaret A. Van Antwerp (1982)

3 *Saul Bellow, Jack Kerouac, Norman Mailer, Vladimir Nabokov, John Updike, Kurt Vonnegut,* edited by Mary Bruccoli (1983)

4 *Tennessee Williams,* edited by Margaret A. Van Antwerp and Sally Johns (1984)

5 *American Transcendentalists,* edited by Joel Myerson (1988)

6 *Hardboiled Mystery Writers: Raymond Chandler, Dashiell Hammett, Ross Macdonald,* edited by Matthew J. Bruccoli and Richard Layman (1989)

7 *Modern American Poets: James Dickey, Robert Frost, Marianne Moore,* edited by Karen L. Rood (1989)

8 *The Black Aesthetic Movement,* edited by Jeffrey Louis Decker (1991)

9 *American Writers of the Vietnam War: W. D. Ehrhart, Larry Heinemann, Tim O'Brien, Walter McDonald, John M. Del Vecchio,* edited by Ronald Baughman (1991)

10 *The Bloomsbury Group,* edited by Edward L. Bishop (1992)

11 *American Proletarian Culture: The Twenties and The Thirties,* edited by Jon Christian Suggs (1993)

12 *Southern Women Writers: Flannery O'Connor, Katherine Anne Porter, Eudora Welty,* edited by Mary Ann Wimsatt and Karen L. Rood (1994)

13 *The House of Scribner, 1846–1904,* edited by John Delaney (1996)

14 *Four Women Writers for Children, 1868–1918,* edited by Caroline C. Hunt (1996)

15 *American Expatriate Writers: Paris in the Twenties,* edited by Matthew J. Bruccoli and Robert W. Trogdon (1997)

16 *The House of Scribner, 1905–1930,* edited by John Delaney (1997)

17 *The House of Scribner, 1931–1984,* edited by John Delaney (1998)

18 *British Poets of The Great War: Sassoon, Graves, Owen,* edited by Patrick Quinn (1999)

19 *James Dickey,* edited by Judith S. Baughman (1999)

See also DLB 210, 216, 219, 222, 224, 229, 237, 247, 253, 254, 263, 269, 273, 274, 280, 284, 288, 291, 294, 298, 301, 304, 308, 309, 315, 316, 320, 324

Dictionary of Literary Biography Yearbooks

1980 edited by Karen L. Rood, Jean W. Ross, and Richard Ziegfeld (1981)

1981 edited by Karen L. Rood, Jean W. Ross, and Richard Ziegfeld (1982)

1982 edited by Richard Ziegfeld; associate editors: Jean W. Ross and Lynne C. Zeigler (1983)

1983 edited by Mary Bruccoli and Jean W. Ross; associate editor Richard Ziegfeld (1984)

1984 edited by Jean W. Ross (1985)

1985 edited by Jean W. Ross (1986)

1986 edited by J. M. Brook (1987)

1987 edited by J. M. Brook (1988)

1988 edited by J. M. Brook (1989)

1989 edited by J. M. Brook (1990)

1990 edited by James W. Hipp (1991)

1991 edited by James W. Hipp (1992)

1992 edited by James W. Hipp (1993)

1993 edited by James W. Hipp, contributing editor George Garrett (1994)

1994 edited by James W. Hipp, contributing editor George Garrett (1995)

1995 edited by James W. Hipp, contributing editor George Garrett (1996)

1996 edited by Samuel W. Bruce and L. Kay Webster, contributing editor George Garrett (1997)

1997 edited by Matthew J. Bruccoli and George Garrett, with the assistance of L. Kay Webster (1998)

1998 edited by Matthew J. Bruccoli, contributing editor George Garrett, with the assistance of D. W. Thomas (1999)

1999 edited by Matthew J. Bruccoli, contributing editor George Garrett, with the assistance of D. W. Thomas (2000)

2000 edited by Matthew J. Bruccoli, contributing editor George Garrett, with the assistance of George Parker Anderson (2001)

2001 edited by Matthew J. Bruccoli, contributing editor George Garrett, with the assistance of George Parker Anderson (2002)

2002 edited by Matthew J. Bruccoli and George Garrett; George Parker Anderson, Assistant Editor (2003)

Concise Series

Concise Dictionary of American Literary Biography, 7 volumes (1988–1999): *The New Consciousness, 1941–1968; Colonization to the American Renaissance, 1640–1865; Realism, Naturalism, and Local Color, 1865–1917; The Twenties, 1917–1929; The Age of Maturity, 1929–1941; Broadening Views, 1968–1988; Supplement: Modern Writers, 1900–1998.*

Concise Dictionary of British Literary Biography, 8 volumes (1991–1992): *Writers of the Middle Ages and Renaissance Before 1660; Writers of the Restoration and Eighteenth Century, 1660–1789; Writers of the Romantic Period, 1789–1832; Victorian Writers, 1832–1890; Late-Victorian and Edwardian Writers, 1890–1914; Modern Writers, 1914–1945; Writers After World War II, 1945–1960; Contemporary Writers, 1960 to Present.*

Concise Dictionary of World Literary Biography, 4 volumes (1999–2000): *Ancient Greek and Roman Writers; German Writers; African, Caribbean, and Latin American Writers; South Slavic and Eastern European Writers.*

Dictionary of Literary Biography® • Volume Three Hundred Thirty

Nobel Prize Laureates in Literature, Part 2: Faulkner–Kipling

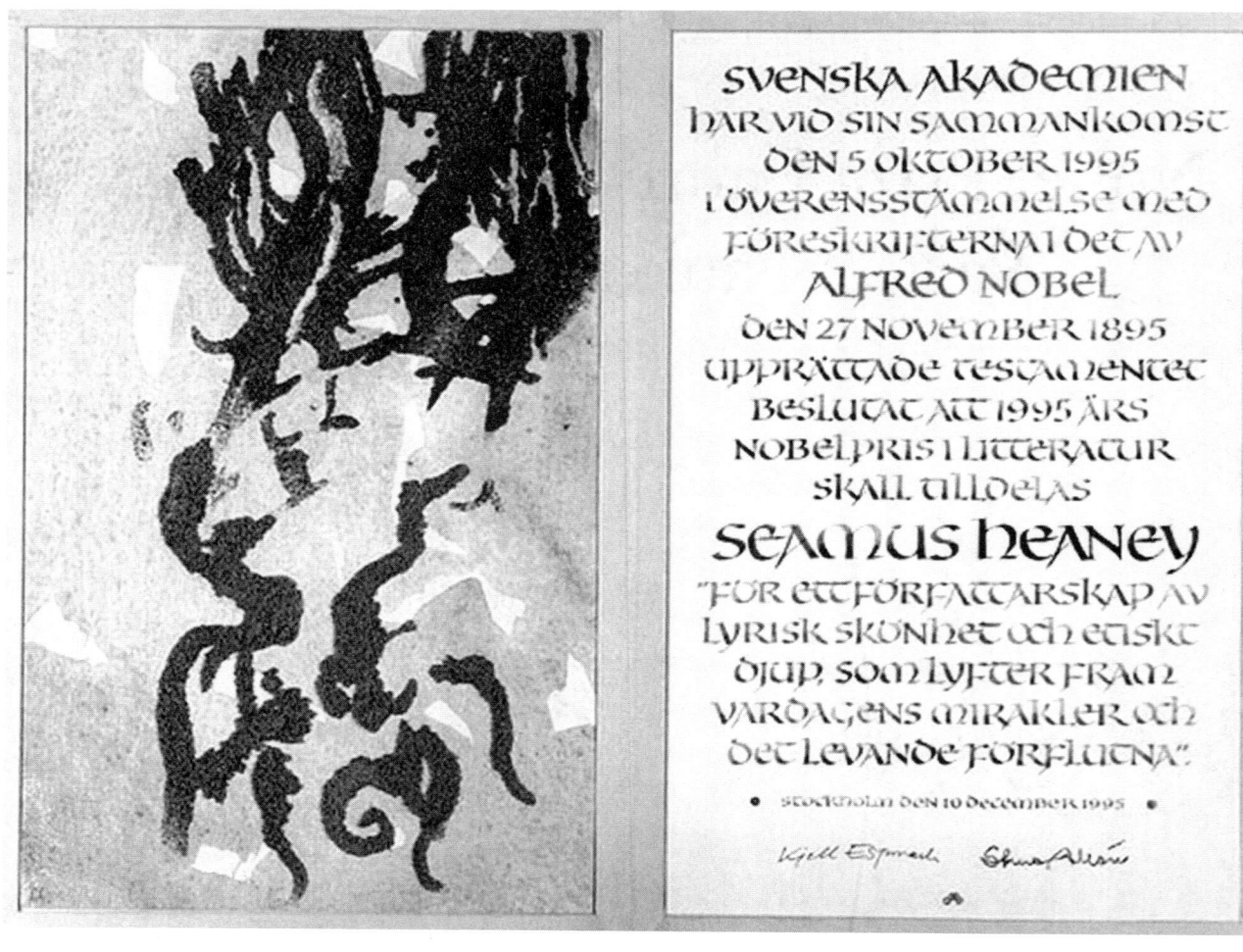

Seamus Heaney's Nobel Prize diploma (art by Bo Larsson, calligraphy by Annika Rucker; © The Nobel Foundation, 1995)

Dictionary of Literary Biography® • Volume Three Hundred Thirty

Nobel Prize Laureates in Literature, Part 2: Faulkner–Kipling

A Bruccoli Clark Layman Book

Detroit • New York • San Francisco • New Haven, Conn. • Waterville, Maine • London • Munich

Dictionary of Literary Biography
Volume 330: Nobel Prize Laureates in Literature, Part 2: Faulkner–Kipling

Advisory Board
John Baker
William Cagle
Patrick O'Connor
George Garrett
Trudier Harris
Alvin Kernan

Editorial Directors
Matthew J. Bruccoli and Richard Layman

© 2007 Thomson Gale, a part of The Thomson Corporation.

Thomson and Star Logo are trademarks and Gale is a registered trademark used herein under license.

For more information, contact
Thomson Gale
27500 Drake Rd.
Farmington Hills, MI 48331-3535
Or you can visit our Internet site at
http://www.gale.com

ALL RIGHTS RESERVED
No part of this work covered by the copyright hereon may be reproduced or used in any form or by any means—graphic, electronic, or mechanical, including photocopying, recording, taping, Web distribution, or information storage retrieval systems—without the written permission of the publisher.

For permission to use material from this product, submit your request via Web at http://www.gale-edit.com/permissions, or you may download our Permissions Request form and submit your request by fax or mail to:

Permissions Department
Thomson Gale
27500 Drake Rd.
Farmington Hills, MI 48331-3535
Permissions Hotline:
248-699-8006 or 800-877-4253, ext. 8006
Fax: 248-699-8074 or 800-762-4058

While every effort has been made to ensure the reliability of the information presented in this publication, Thomson Gale does not guarantee the accuracy of the data contained herein. Thomson Gale accepts no payment for listing; and inclusion in the publication of any organization, agency, institution, publication, service, or individual does not imply endorsement of the editors or publisher. Errors brought to the attention of the publisher and verified to the satisfaction of the publisher will be corrected in future editions.

LIBRARY OF CONGRESS CATALOGING-IN-PUBLICATION DATA

Nobel prize laureates in literature.
　　v. cm. — (Dictionary of literary biography ; v. 329-　)
"A Bruccoli Clark Layman book."
Includes bibliographical references and index.
ISBN-13: 978–0–7876–8147–0 (v. 329)
ISBN-10: 0–7876–8147–4 (v. 329: hardcover : alk. paper)
　1. Literature, Modern—20th century—Bio-bibliography—Dictionaries.
　2. Literature, Modern—21st century—Bio-bibliography—Dictionaries.
　3. Nobel Prizes. 1. Thomson Gale (Firm)
PN171.P75N58 2006
809'.04—dc22
　　[B]

ISBN-13: 978–0–7876–8148–7 (v. 330)
ISBN-10: 0787681482 (v. 330)

2006018605

Printed in the United States of America
10 9 8 7 6 5 4 3 2 1

Contents

Plan of the Series xv

Acknowledgments xvii

William Faulkner (1897–1962) 3
   Hans H. Skei

   1949 Nobel Prize in Literature Presentation Speech 17
      by Gustaf Hellström, Member of the Swedish Academy

   Faulkner: Banquet Speech 19

Dario Fo (1926–) 20
   Andrea Bisicchia

   1997 Nobel Prize in Literature Presentation Speech 37
      by Professor Sture Allén of the Swedish Academy (Translation from the Swedish)

   Fo: Banquet Speech 38

   Press Release: The Nobel Prize in Literature 1997 38

Fo: Nobel Lecture, 7 December 1997 40

Anatole France (1844–1924) 44
   Catharine Savage Brosman

   1921 Nobel Prize in Literature Presentation Speech 63
      by E. A. Karlfeldt, Permanent Secretary of the Swedish Academy

   France: Banquet Speech 66

John Galsworthy (1867–1933) 67
   Sanford Sternlicht

   1932 Nobel Prize in Literature Presentation Speech 82
      by Anders Österling, Member of the Nobel Committee of the Swedish Academy

Gao Xingjian (1940–) 85
   Mabel Lee

2000 Nobel Prize in Literature Presentation Speech 97
      by Professor Göran Malmqvist, Member of the Swedish Academy

   Gao: Banquet Speech 98

   Press Release: The Nobel Prize in Literature 2000 99

Gao: Nobel Lecture, 7 December 2000 100

Contents

Gabriel García Márquez (1927–) 106
Raymond Leslie Williams

    1982 Nobel Prize in Literature Presentation Speech 119
        by Professor Lars Gyllensten of the Swedish Academy (Translation from the Swedish)

    García Márquez: Banquet Speech 120

García Márquez: Nobel Lecture, 8 December 1982 122

André Gide (1869–1951) 125
Catharine Savage Brosman

    1947 Nobel Prize in Literature Presentation Speech 146
        by Anders Österling, Permanent Secretary of the Swedish Academy

    Gide: Banquet Speech 148

Karl Gjellerup (1857–1919) 149
Poul Houe

    1917 Nobel Prize in Literature Presentation 160

    Gjellerup: Autobiographical Statement 163

William Golding (1911–1993) 164
Michael C. Prusse

    1983 Nobel Prize in Literature Presentation Speech 176
        by Professor Lars Gyllensten, of the Swedish Academy

    Golding: Banquet Speech 178

Golding: Nobel Lecture, 7 December 1983 179

Nadine Gordimer (1923–) 184
Rowland Smith

    1991 Nobel Prize in Literature Presentation Speech 198
        by Professor Sture Allén, Permanent Secretary of the Swedish Academy (Translation from the Swedish)

    Gordimer: Banquet Speech 199

    Press Release: The Nobel Prize in Literature 1991 200

Gordimer: Nobel Lecture, 7 December 1991 201

Günter Grass (1927–) 206
Sigrid Mayer

    1999 Nobel Prize in Literature Presentation Speech 222
        by Dr. Horace Engdahl, Member of the Swedish Academy, Secretary of its Nobel Committee

    Grass: Banquet Speech 224

    Press Release: The Nobel Prize in Literature 1999 225

Grass: Nobel Lecture, 7 December 1999 226

Knut Hamsun (1859–1952) 232
Harald Næss

    1920 Nobel Prize in Literature Presentation Speech 246
        by Harald Hjärne, Chairman of the Nobel Committee of the Swedish Academy

    Hamsun: Banquet Speech 248

Gerhart Hauptmann (1862-1946)	249
Roy C. Cowen	
1912 Nobel Prize in Literature Presentation Speech	268
by Hans Hildebrand, Acting Secretary of the Swedish Academy	
Hauptmann: Banquet Speech	269
Hauptmann: Autobiographical Statement	270
Seamus Heaney (1939-)	271
Brendan Corcoran	
1995 Nobel Prize in Literature Presentation Speech	288
by Mr. Östen Sjöstrand, Member of the Swedish Academy (Translation from the Swedish)	
Heaney: Banquet Speech	289
Press Release: The Nobel Prize for Literature 1995	289
Heaney: Nobel Lecture, 7 December 1995	291
Verner von Heidenstam (1859-1940)	298
Ann-Charlotte Gavel Adams	
1916 Nobel Prize in Literature Presentation	307
by Sven Söderman	
Ernest Hemingway (1899-1961)	309
John C. Unrue	
1954 Nobel Prize in Literature Presentation Speech	323
by Anders Österling, Permanent Secretary of the Swedish Academy	
Hemingway: Banquet Speech	325
Hermann Hesse (1877-1962)	326
Joseph Mileck	
1946 Nobel Prize in Literature Presentation Speech	347
by Anders Österling, Permanent Secretary of the Swedish Academy	
Hesse: Banquet Speech	348
Hesse: Autobiographical Statement	349
Paul Heyse (1830-1914)	351
Charles H. Helmetag	
1910 Nobel Prize in Literature Presentation Speech	364
by C. D. af Wirsén, Permanent Secretary of the Swedish Academy	
Heyse: Autobiographical Statement	366
Elfriede Jelinek (1946-)	368
Steve Dowden	
2004 Nobel Prize in Literature Presentation Speech	378
by Professor Horace Engdahl of the Swedish Academy	
Jelinek: Nobel Lecture, 7 December 2004	379

Contents

Johannes V. Jensen (1873–1950) 385
Sven Hakon Rossel

   1944 Nobel Prize in Literature Broadcast Presentation 400

   1944 Nobel Prize in Literature Presentation Speech 402
      by Anders Österling, Permanent Secretary of the Swedish Academy

   Jensen: Banquet Speech 403

   Jensen: Autobiographical Statement 404

Juan Ramón Jiménez (1881–1958) 405
Howard T. Young

   1956 Nobel Prize in Literature Presentation Speech 420
      by Hjalmar Gullberg, Member of the Swedish Academy

   Jiménez: Banquet Speech 422

Eyvind Johnson (1900–1976) 423
Monica Setterwall Wranne

   1974 Nobel Prize in Literature Presentation Speech 434
      by Karl Ragnar Gierow, of the Swedish Academy (Translation from the Swedish)

   Johnson: Banquet Speech 436

Erik Axel Karlfeldt (1864–1931) 437
Paul Norlén

   1931 Nobel Prize in Literature Presentation Speech 447
      by Anders Österling, Member of the Nobel Committee of the Swedish Academy

Yasunari Kawabata (1899–1972) 449
Van C. Gessel

   1968 Nobel Prize in Literature Presentation Speech 460
      by Anders Österling, Ph.D., of the Swedish Academy (Translation from the Swedish)

   Kawabata: Banquet Speech 461

Kawabata: Nobel Lecture, 12 December 1968 463

Imre Kertész (1929–) 469
Éva Forgács

   2002 Nobel Prize in Literature Presentation Speech 477
      by Torgny Lindgren, Writer, Member of the Swedish Academy

   Kertész: Banquet Speech 478

   Press Release: The Nobel Prize in Literature 2002 479

Kertész: Nobel Lecture, 7 December 2002 481

Rudyard Kipling (1865–1936) 485
Donald Gray

   1907 Nobel Prize in Literature Presentation Speech 501
      by C. D. af Wirsén, Permanent Secretary of the Swedish Academy

Nobel Prize Laureates in Literature, 1901–2005 505

Contributors 507

Index 511

Plan of the Series

... Almost the most prodigious asset of a country, and perhaps its most precious possession, is its native literary product—when that product is fine and noble and enduring.

Mark Twain*

The advisory board, the editors, and the publisher of the *Dictionary of Literary Biography* are joined in endorsing Mark Twain's declaration. The literature of a nation provides an inexhaustible resource of permanent worth. Our purpose is to make literature and its creators better understood and more accessible to students and the reading public, while satisfying the needs of teachers and researchers.

To meet these requirements, *literary biography* has been construed in terms of the author's achievement. The most important thing about a writer is his writing. Accordingly, the entries in *DLB* are career biographies, tracing the development of the author's canon and the evolution of his reputation.

The purpose of *DLB* is not only to provide reliable information in a usable format but also to place the figures in the larger perspective of literary history and to offer appraisals of their accomplishments by qualified scholars.

The publication plan for *DLB* resulted from two years of preparation. The project was proposed to Bruccoli Clark by Frederick G. Ruffner, president of the Gale Research Company, in November 1975. After specimen entries were prepared and typeset, an advisory board was formed to refine the entry format and develop the series rationale. In meetings held during 1976, the publisher, series editors, and advisory board approved the scheme for a comprehensive biographical dictionary of persons who contributed to literature. Editorial work on the first volume began in January 1977, and it was published in 1978. In order to make *DLB* more than a dictionary and to compile volumes that individually have claim to status as literary history, it was decided to organize volumes by topic, period, or genre. Each of these freestanding volumes provides a biographical-bibliographical guide and overview for a particular area of literature. We are convinced that this organization—as opposed to a single alphabet method—constitutes a valuable innovation in the presentation of reference material. The volume plan necessarily requires many decisions for the placement and treatment of authors. Certain figures will be included in separate volumes, but with different entries emphasizing the aspect of his career appropriate to each volume. Ernest Hemingway, for example, is represented in *American Writers in Paris, 1920–1939* by an entry focusing on his expatriate apprenticeship; he is also in *American Novelists, 1910–1945* with an entry surveying his entire career, as well as in *American Short-Story Writers, 1910–1945, Second Series* with an entry concentrating on his short fiction. Each volume includes a cumulative index of the subject authors and articles.

Between 1981 and 2002 the series was augmented and updated by the *DLB Yearbooks*. There have also been nineteen *DLB Documentary Series* volumes, which provide illustrations, facsimiles, and biographical and critical source materials for figures, works, or groups judged to have particular interest for students. In 1999 the *Documentary Series* was incorporated into the *DLB* volume numbering system beginning with *DLB 210: Ernest Hemingway*.

We define literature as the *intellectual commerce of a nation:* not merely as belles lettres but as that ample and complex process by which ideas are generated, shaped, and transmitted. *DLB* entries are not limited to "creative writers" but extend to other figures who in their time and in their way influenced the mind of a people. Thus the series encompasses historians, journalists, publishers, book collectors, and screenwriters. By this means readers of *DLB* may be aided to perceive literature not as cult scripture in the keeping of intellectual high priests but firmly positioned at the center of a nation's life.

DLB includes the major writers appropriate to each volume and those standing in the ranks behind them. Scholarly and critical counsel has been sought in deciding which minor figures to include and how full their entries should be. Wherever possible, useful refer-

*From an unpublished section of Mark Twain's autobiography, copyright by the Mark Twain Company

ences are made to figures who do not warrant separate entries.

Each *DLB* volume has an expert volume editor responsible for planning the volume, selecting the figures for inclusion, and assigning the entries. Volume editors are also responsible for preparing, where appropriate, appendices surveying the major periodicals and literary and intellectual movements for their volumes, as well as lists of further readings. Work on the series as a whole is coordinated at the Bruccoli Clark Layman editorial center in Columbia, South Carolina, where the editorial staff is responsible for accuracy and utility of the published volumes.

One feature that distinguishes *DLB* is the illustration policy—its concern with the iconography of literature. Just as an author is influenced by his surroundings, so is the reader's understanding of the author enhanced by a knowledge of his environment. Therefore *DLB* volumes include not only drawings, paintings, and photographs of authors, often depicting them at various stages in their careers, but also illustrations of their families and places where they lived. Title pages are regularly reproduced in facsimile along with dust jackets for modern authors. The dust jackets are a special feature of *DLB* because they often document better than anything else the way in which an author's work was perceived in its own time. Specimens of the writers' manuscripts and letters are included when feasible.

Samuel Johnson rightly decreed that "The chief glory of every people arises from its authors." The purpose of the *Dictionary of Literary Biography* is to compile literary history in the surest way available to us—by accurate and comprehensive treatment of the lives and work of those who contributed to it.

The *DLB* Advisory Board

Acknowledgments

This book was produced by Bruccoli Clark Layman, Inc. Tracy Simmons Bitonti was the in-house editor.

Production manager is Philip B. Dematteis.

Administrative support was provided by Carol A. Cheschi.

Accountant is Ann-Marie Holland.

Copyediting supervisor is Sally R. Evans. The copyediting staff includes Phyllis A. Avant, Caryl Brown, Melissa D. Hinton, and Rebecca Mayo. Freelance copyeditors are Brenda Cabra, Jennifer Cooper, and Dave King.

Pipeline manager is James F. Tidd Jr.

Editorial associates are Elizabeth Leverton, Dickson Monk, and Timothy C. Simmons.

In-house prevetter is Catherine M. Polit.

Permissions editor is Amber L. Coker.

Layout and graphics supervisor is Janet E. Hill. The graphics staff includes Zoe R. Cook.

Office manager is Kathy Lawler Merlette.

Photography editor is Crystal A. Leidy.

Digital photographic copy work was performed by Zoe R. Cook.

Systems manager is James Sellers.

Typesetting supervisor is Kathleen M. Flanagan. The typesetting staff includes Patricia Marie Flanagan.

Library research was facilitated by the following librarians at the Thomas Cooper Library of the University of South Carolina: Elizabeth Suddeth and the rare-book department; Jo Cottingham, interlibrary loan department; circulation department head Tucker Taylor; reference department head Virginia W. Weathers; reference department staff Laurel Baker, Marilee Birchfield, Kate Boyd, Paul Cammarata, Joshua Garris, Gary Geer, Tom Marcil, Rose Marshall, and Sharon Verba; interlibrary loan department head Marna Hostetler; and interlibrary loan staff Bill Fetty and Nelson Rivera.

Dictionary of Literary Biography® • Volume Three Hundred Thirty

Nobel Prize Laureates in Literature, Part 2: Faulkner–Kipling

William Faulkner

(25 September 1897 – 6 July 1962)

Hans H. Skei
University of Oslo

This entry has been expanded by Skei from his Faulkner entry in *DLB 102: American Short-Story Writers, 1910–1945, Second Series*. See also the Faulkner entries in *DLB 9: American Novelists, 1910–1945; DLB 11: American Humorists, 1800–1950; DLB 44: American Screenwriters, Second Series; DLB 316: American Prose Writers of World War I: A Documentary Volume;* and *DLB Documentary Series 2: James Gould Cozzens, James T. Farrell, William Faulkner, John O'Hara, John Steinbeck, Thomas Wolfe, Richard Wright.*

BOOKS: *The Marble Faun* (Boston: Four Seas, 1924);
Soldiers' Pay (New York: Boni & Liveright, 1926; London: Chatto & Windus, 1930);
Mosquitoes (New York: Boni & Liveright, 1927; London: Chatto & Windus, 1964);
Sartoris (New York: Harcourt, Brace, 1929; London: Chatto & Windus, 1932); original, uncut version edited by Douglas Day as *Flags in the Dust* (New York: Random House, 1974);
The Sound and the Fury (New York: Cape & Smith, 1929; London: Chatto & Windus, 1931);
As I Lay Dying (New York: Cape & Smith, 1930; London: Chatto & Windus, 1935);
Sanctuary (New York: Cape & Smith, 1931; London: Chatto & Windus, 1931); unrevised version edited by Noel Polk as *Sanctuary: The Original Text* (New York: Random House, 1981);
These 13 (New York: Cape & Smith, 1931; London: Chatto & Windus, 1933);
Idyll in the Desert (New York: Random House, 1931);
Miss Zilphia Gant (Dallas: Book Club of Texas, 1932);
Salmagundi (Milwaukee: Casanova, 1932);
Light in August (New York: Smith & Haas, 1932; London: Chatto & Windus, 1933);
A Green Bough (New York: Smith & Haas, 1933);
Doctor Martino and Other Stories (New York: Smith & Haas, 1934; London: Chatto & Windus, 1934);
Pylon (New York: Smith & Haas, 1935; London: Chatto & Windus, 1935);

Absalom, Absalom! (New York: Random House, 1936; London: Chatto & Windus, 1937);
The Unvanquished (New York: Random House, 1938; London: Chatto & Windus, 1938);
The Wild Palms (New York: Random House, 1939; London: Chatto & Windus, 1939);
The Hamlet (New York: Random House, 1940; London: Chatto & Windus, 1940; revised, New York: Random House, 1964);
Go Down, Moses and Other Stories (New York: Random House, 1942; London: Chatto & Windus, 1942);
Intruder in the Dust (New York: Random House, 1948; London: Chatto & Windus, 1949);
Knight's Gambit (New York: Random House, 1949; London: Chatto & Windus, 1951);
Collected Stories of William Faulkner (New York: Random House, 1950; London: Chatto & Windus, 1951);
Notes on a Horsethief (Greenville, Miss.: Levee, 1950 [i.e., 1951]);
Requiem for a Nun (New York: Random House, 1951; London: Chatto & Windus, 1953);
Mirrors of Chartres Street (Minneapolis: Faulkner Studies, 1953);
A Fable (New York: Random House, 1954; London: Chatto & Windus, 1955);
Big Woods (New York: Random House, 1955);
Faulkner's County: Tales of Yoknapatawpha County (London: Chatto & Windus, 1955);
Jealousy and Episode: Two Stories (Minneapolis: Faulkner Studies, 1955);
The Town (New York: Random House, 1957; London: Chatto & Windus, 1958);
New Orleans Sketches, edited by Carvel Collins (New Brunswick, N.J.: Rutgers University Press, 1958; London: Sidgwick & Jackson, 1959);
The Mansion (New York: Random House, 1959; London: Chatto & Windus, 1961);
The Reivers (New York: Random House, 1962; London: Chatto & Windus, 1962);
Early Prose and Poetry, edited by Collins (Boston: Little, Brown, 1962; London: Cape, 1963);

William Faulkner (right) receiving the 1949 Nobel Prize in Literature from King Gustav VI Adolf of Sweden, 10 December 1950 (AP World Wide)

Faulkner's University Pieces, edited by Collins (Tokyo: Kenkyusha, 1962; Folcroft, Pa.: Folcroft, 1970);

Essays, Speeches & Public Letters, edited by James B. Meriwether (New York: Random House, 1966; London: Chatto & Windus, 1967);

The Wishing Tree (New York: Random House, 1967; London: Chatto & Windus, 1967);

The Big Sleep [screenplay], by Faulkner, Jules Furthman, and Leigh Brackett (New York: Irvington, 1971);

The Marionettes: A Play in One Act (Charlottesville: Bibliographical Society, University of Virginia, 1975);

Mayday (South Bend, Ind.: University of Notre Dame Press, 1976);

Mississippi Poems (Oxford, Miss.: Yoknapatawpha, 1979);

Uncollected Stories of William Faulkner, edited by Joseph Blotner (New York: Random House, 1979);

To Have and Have Not [screenplay], by Faulkner and Furthman (Madison: University of Wisconsin Press, 1980);

The Road to Glory [screenplay], by Faulkner and Joel Sayre (Carbondale & Edwardsville: Southern Illinois University Press, 1981);

Helen: A Courtship (Oxford, Miss.: Yoknapatawpha, 1981);

Faulkner's MGM Screenplays, edited by Bruce F. Kawin (Knoxville: University of Tennessee Press, 1982);

Elmer, edited by Dianne Cox (Northport, Ala.: Seajay, 1983);

A Sorority Pledge (Northport, Ala.: Seajay, 1983);

Father Abraham, edited by Meriwether (New York: Red Ozier Press, 1983; New York: Random House, 1984);

The DeGaulle Story [screenplay], edited by Louis Daniel Brodsky and Robert W. Hamblin (Jackson: University Press of Mississippi, 1984);

Vision in Spring, edited by Judith Sensibar (Austin: University of Texas Press, 1984);

Battle Cry [screenplay], edited by Brodsky and Hamblin (Jackson: University Press of Mississippi, 1985);

William Faulkner Manuscripts, 25 volumes, edited by Blotner, Thomas L. McHaney, Michael Millgate, and Noel Polk (New York & London: Garland, 1986–1987);

Country Lawyer and Other Stories for the Screen, edited by Brodsky and Hamblin (Jackson: University Press of Mississippi, 1987);

Stallion Road [screenplay], edited by Brodsky and Hamblin (Jackson: University Press of Mississippi, 1989).

Collections: *Three Famous Short Novels* (New York: Random House, 1942)—comprises *Spotted Horses, Old Man,* and *The Bear;*

The Portable Faulkner, edited by Malcolm Cowley (New York: Viking, 1946; revised and enlarged, 1967); republished as *The Essential Faulkner* (London: Chatto & Windus, 1967);

The Faulkner Reader (New York: Random House, 1954);

Snopes: A Trilogy, 3 volumes (New York: Random House, 1964)—comprises *The Hamlet* (revised edition), *The Town,* and *The Mansion.*

PLAY PRODUCTIONS: *The Marionettes,* University, Miss., University of Mississippi, 4 March 1920;

Requiem for a Nun, London, Royal Court Theatre, 26 November 1957; New York, John Golden Theatre, 30 January 1959.

PRODUCED SCRIPTS: *Today We Live,* story and dialogue by Faulkner, motion picture, M-G-M, 1933;

The Road to Glory, by Faulkner and Joel Sayre, motion picture, 20th Century-Fox, 1936;

Slave Ship, story and additional dialogue by Faulkner, motion picture, 20th Century-Fox, 1937;

To Have and Have Not, adapted by Faulkner and Jules Furthman from Ernest Hemingway's novel, motion picture, Warner Bros., 1944;

The Big Sleep, adapted by Faulkner, Furthman, and Leigh Brackett from Raymond Chandler's novel, motion picture, Warner Bros., 1946;

Land of the Pharaohs, by Faulkner, Harry Kurnitz, and Harold Jack Bloom, motion picture, Warner Bros., 1955;

The Graduation Dress, by Faulkner and Joan Williams, television, CBS, 1960.

When William Faulkner was awarded the Nobel Prize in Literature for 1949, he used his Nobel Prize address in Stockholm in December 1950 to address the youth of the world. He spoke of the old verities of the human heart and offered the most direct expressions of the legacy that he wanted to leave behind. His words may sound vague and general; yet, they are a summing up of beliefs central to all his writing:

I believe that man will not merely endure: he will prevail. He is immortal, not because he alone among creatures has an inexhaustible voice, but because he has a soul, a spirit capable of compassion and sacrifice and endurance. The poet's, the writer's, duty is to write about these things. It is his privilege to help man endure by lifting his heart, by reminding him of the courage and honor and hope and pride and compassion and pity and sacrifice which have been the glory of his past. The poet's voice need not merely be the record of man, it can be one of the props, the pillars to help him endure and prevail.

Faulkner's writings are immersed in history; they record minute changes in social structures and in the rules and conventions that regulate human behavior, and they demonstrate the complexity of individual man and of social life.

Faulkner was in many ways a born storyteller, although his apprenticeship period was long and arduous, and when he reached complete mastery of character and narrative voice, critics and readers alike were unappreciative and reluctant to accept the challenge his experimental and modernistic texts presented. Over the years criticism and scholarship have discovered that his genius lies in the ability to portray all types of characters—male and female, white and Indian and black, old and young, normal and mentally handicapped—and in the use of a variety of narrative voices. By letting the characters contribute to the narration, Faulkner also reveals that the same story may mean many things to different people, that truth is relative, and that literature may lead to understanding but more often leads to more questions.

Faulkner was deeply immersed in the culture, the landscape, and the mores and values of the region where he was born and where he spent all of his life: the American South. He is clearly and obviously a "Southern writer," but not in any sense of denigration or limitation. His books transcend the borders of his native region and of what he called in a *Paris Review* interview his own "postage stamp of native soil," since he always rewrites the homeland and lifts his tales to a new level of significance and meaning, not only through his technical brilliance but through a rich and varied imagery that is both local and universal, rural and modernistic, rooted in local custom and in classical literature, and moving between the mimetic rendering of local speech and high modernist prose.

Faulkner scholarship—almost an industry in itself—has little by little sorted out the many factual errors that marred early criticism and research. In some cases Faulkner was himself responsible for factual errors in his biography, because of the stories he told and the different masks he hid behind. As late as in the 1950s critics still referred to Faulkner's experience in World War I and the wounds he suffered there—although he never saw active duty. Furthermore, early critics and readers sought correspondences between Faulkner's life and his fiction, being used to contemporary writers who frequently drew on autobiography in their writing. There are no direct parallels between Faulkner as a person and his characters, with the possible exception of the portraits of the artist that he creates early in his career. In a general sense, Faulkner's fiction derived from the fact that he was descended from a colorful Southern family and from growing up and living in a South that had lost the Civil War but still kept the memory of the glory and gallantry in the war and the humiliation of defeat alive. Although Faulkner may not always have had the facts and details right, he had a profound sense of history. The past would never become only past but would always remain a part of a living now.

He was born William Cuthbert Falkner in New Albany, Mississippi, on 25 September 1897, the first child of Maud Butler Falkner and Murry Cuthbert Falkner. (William Faulkner added the *u* to his last name in 1918.) His paternal great-grandfather, Colonel William Clark Falkner, had a literary reputation, based mainly on his novel *The White Rose of Memphis* (1881), and must be seen as a major influence on his descendant, not the least because of his eventful life, which Faulkner transformed and fictionalized as that of Colonel John Sartoris. William Clark Falkner was killed on the street in Ripley, Mississippi, by his former business partner, and this scene is re-created several times in Faulkner's fiction. Faulkner's paternal grandfather, John Wesley Thompson Falkner, was a lawyer, railroad owner, and banker. He moved his family from Ripley to Oxford, Mississippi, in 1885, and in Faulkner's fiction he is used as a model for Colonel John Sartoris's son, Bayard. Yet, Faulkner's use of family matters is more than simple recollection: it becomes an attempt to understand the meaning of past events in the context of Southern history.

Murry Falkner led a less glamorous life than his father and grandfather. He married Maud Butler in 1896, and they lived in New Albany and then Ripley, where Murry Falkner worked for the family railroad. When the railroad was sold, the family moved back to Oxford in 1902. Faulkner's father participated in various business ventures financed by his father, including a livery stable and a hardware store. He finally became secretary of the University of Mississippi and later the business manager of the university.

Growing up in an area of the United States that was just advancing from frontier land, Faulkner led an adventurous life as the oldest of four boys (his brothers were Murry, born in 1899; John, born in 1901; and Dean, born in 1907), learning to handle guns and to hunt. The boys lived among horses and dogs while their father ran the livery stable, and they had many close playmates. Faulkner was a good student in elementary school, but as he grew older he became more interested in playing football than attending school. He enjoyed writing and drawing and often illustrated the poems and stories he wrote—a practice he continued even after he had established himself as a writer.

Faulkner stopped attending Oxford High School midway through the 1914–1915 school year without completing the last grade. He returned the following fall, mostly to play football, but quit school at the end of the season. He had, however, been reading poetry with Phil Stone, an older friend who was important to Faulkner's development in these early years, and he had already begun showing his own poems to Stone.

Faulkner had several different jobs—ranging from bank clerk to postmaster at the university—during the long period before he began his literary career. He was discontented with his job in his grandfather's bank but formed several important friendships while spending time around the university campus. He met the writer Stark Young, who became one of Faulkner's early mentors, as well as Ben Wasson, who later served as his literary agent. But the friendship with Stone, four years older than Faulkner and a native of Oxford who studied law at the University of Mississippi and went on to Yale Law School, was the most decisive one, since Stone introduced him to much important literature and contributed significantly to Faulkner's literary education.

In 1918 Faulkner's girlfriend, Estelle Oldham, announced her engagement to Cornell Franklin. She and Faulkner had planned to marry, but the parents on both sides forbade the union. Faulkner had no education or profession, while Franklin was an established lawyer. Even though Oldham was willing to elope with Faulkner, he wanted her father's consent. Unhappy also with other aspects of his life in Oxford, he decided to join the military. Unable to meet height and weight requirements for the United States Army, he instead joined the Canadian branch of the Royal Air Force (RAF) and went into training in Toronto in July; however, World War I came to an end before he could complete his flight training. He received a discharge in early December and returned to Oxford, wearing his RAF uniform and telling stories that suggested that he not only had been flying but also had been on active duty in the war. Throughout his life Faulkner remained fascinated with flying and fliers, as seen in several of his short stories and in the novel *Pylon* (1935). The flight training is clearly reflected in Faulkner's first printed prose sketch, "Landing in Luck" (published in the student newspaper *Mississippian,* 26 November 1919), a story about a young cadet's first solo flight, told with humor and a certain amount of technical skill. Despite this attempt at prose fiction, Faulkner was now writing poetry in earnest. He published his first poem in the 6 August 1919 issue of the *New Republic,* but most of his early poetry appeared in the local student newspaper.

In 1919 and 1920 Faulkner attended the University of Mississippi as a special student, taking courses in French, Spanish, and English (studying William Shakespeare) in his first semester but dropping the English course in his second semester. During this period Faulkner also contributed many drawings to the student newspaper. He began a second academic year but quit after a few weeks, officially withdrawing from the university in November 1920. His verse play, *The Marionettes,* produced by hand in six copies, was performed in 1920 at the university but was not published until 1975. He also made a single copy of a collection of his poems, "Visions in Spring," and gave it to Estelle Franklin, who visited in Oxford in 1921. He went to New York, apparently following a suggestion from Young, and there he worked briefly as a bookstore clerk in the Fifth Avenue Doubleday Bookstore, run by Elizabeth Prall, who later married Sherwood Anderson. In late December 1921 he returned to Oxford to become postmaster of the University of Mississippi post office, a position he held from December 1921 to October 1924. Customers' complaints were frequent, and he even got an official government reprimand for the job he did, but he read a great deal—probably including the literary magazines subscribed to by the university professors—and he continued writing poetry. In New Orleans, where he often went on weekends, he met some of the literati who edited the *Double Dealer,* which published his poem "Portrait" in the June 1922 issue. He also wrote book reviews and made his first attempts at writing some of the short stories published in the early 1930s.

Through the financial patronage of his friend Stone, Faulkner's first book, *The Marble Faun,* was published in Boston in 1924. That same year he met Anderson in New Orleans, and for the first half of 1925 Faulkner lived in the city with the Andersons. It was the most formative year in Faulkner's development as an artist: in this decisive year he made an almost complete transition from being a poet to becoming a fiction writer, publishing several pieces of experimental prose in the *New Orleans Times-Picayune* (collected in *New Orleans Sketches,* 1958). Faulkner had planned to embark from New Orleans to Europe, but he stayed on for some time with the Andersons and sailed for Europe aboard the *West Ivis* on 7 July 1925. He traveled in Italy, Switzerland, France, and England before sailing for home on 8 December. Some of his early stories are set in postwar Europe, and his travels also paid off in his later fiction, although the time he spent on a novel titled "Elmer" did not pay off—he had to abandon this work before completion (the material was later turned into a short story, "A Portrait of Elmer," and a 1983 book.)

Faulkner's first published novel, *Soldiers' Pay,* appeared on 25 February 1926, apparently accepted on Anderson's recommendation. In the same year he wrote *Mosquitoes* (1927) in addition to minor work, such as the novelette *Mayday* (not published until 1976) and some poems for Helen Baird, whom he courted at this time; the poems were posthumously published as *Helen: A Courtship* (1981).

Soldiers' Pay is not a remarkable first novel, but it is typical of its time—the aftermath of World War I. It depicts the fortunes of returning war hero Donald Mahon with sympathy and bitterness. The wounded hero does not have a chance of fitting into postwar society, and he heads toward death with little regret. In a later story Faulkner depicts "All the Dead Pilots"—which includes those who survived the war but are at a total loss in a world at peace. The pessimism of Faulkner's first novel was noted by many readers, but it offers interesting stories of several minor characters, such as the enigmatic Margaret Powers, a war widow who marries the dying soldier, making martyrs of them both. *Soldiers' Pay* thus becomes more than a war story or an antiwar novel. It was the first Faulkner book to be translated into any language when a Norwegian version was brought out in 1932.

Mosquitoes was completed in New Orleans, where Faulkner spent most of his time in 1926. It is a book about artists and art, with much discussion of aesthetics and with artists as some of the main characters—Gordon the sculptor and Dawson the writer. Other characters are simply those who want to be with artists, and many of them are losers. The symbolism Faulkner attempts in this book is not consistent, and much of the imagery seems overdone. Yet, he manages to establish an understanding of the power of art to create harmony, even if this harmony is based on unhappiness or grief.

In 1927, dividing his time between Oxford and Pascagoula, Mississippi, Faulkner wrote *Flags in the Dust,* which was accepted only after his friend Wasson cut it severely. It was published as *Sartoris* on 31 January 1929 (the original version was published in 1974), and the reception was mixed. In the meantime, he had abandoned a serious attempt to write a fictional account of a clannish group of people, almost a tribe of their own, who arrived in his fictional world and slowly but surely changed everything there for the worse: the Snopeses. Apparently, Stone had suggested that such people deserved fictional treatment, but Faulkner was unable to pursue his material further than a piece of short-story length, called "Father Abraham" (published in 1983).

Faulkner had high hopes for *Flags in the Dust* and was disappointed when it had to be cut and revised. It was a novel that he had to write, and for which he found much of the story material in the lives of his ancestors and other stories he had picked up. It is Faulkner's first storytelling novel, in which legends, tall tales, and gossip are included. It is also the first "typical" Faulkner novel, because it is located in his part of the South and because it tells the story of a family. Episodes from this novel are reused and retold in subsequent books. A central theme is the brother-sister relationship between Narcissa and Horace Benbow, which is even more developed and thematically important in the uncut version of the book. This kind of relationship, often with dramatic consequences, is at the core of several of Faulkner's best novels, published in the years immediately following the publication of *Sartoris*.

Despite all the diverse work Faulkner did in 1927 and 1928—he also worked sporadically on many short stories—he had a new and clear understanding of what the material for his fictions ought to be. Anderson may have suggested that he ought to use his own landscape and his own people, but Faulkner's discovery is also related to the problem of narrative form. As he struggled against reluctant publishers, bad reviews, and low sales, he discovered his own "postage stamp of native soil," the basis for his fictional Yoknapatawpha County. With *The Sound and the Fury* (1929) a complete transition seems to have occurred. His earlier novels are flawed by self-involvement and lack of distance from his characters; not so in *The Sound and the Fury*. The apprenticeship years had come to an end, and what are undoubtedly the major years of his career began.

In his private life important events also took place: Estelle Franklin divorced her husband and married Faulkner on 20 June 1929. In 1930 they bought an old house, naming it Rowan Oak, and Faulkner began making money from the sales of short stories to the national magazines. Estelle Faulkner had two children from her previous marriage; she and Faulkner had a prematurely born daughter, Alabama, on 11 January 1931, but the child died nine days later. Their daughter Jill was born on 24 June 1933. The house needed much expensive renovation and repair, and after the death of his father in 1932 Faulkner also contributed to the support of his mother. In 1935, when his youngest brother, Dean, died in an airplane crash, Faulkner—who had paid for his flying lessons—felt obliged to support Dean's wife and child. Only income from short-story sales made this responsibility at all possible, but he was unable to sell enough stories to the best-paying magazines, notably *The Saturday Evening Post*, and in May 1932 he went to Hollywood for the first time to secure a steady, monthly income.

Faulkner's early career is interesting and bewildering, and only in retrospect is it at all possible to find unity and continuity in it. His themes, subjects, and narrative methods went in many directions, and they could change abruptly. In different books—*Flags in the Dust* and *The Sound and the Fury*—Faulkner was, to varying degrees, "rewriting the homeplace" and creating the basis for his Yoknapatawpha County. This area appears to have been sharply mapped out in the author's head, including people and events that he could refer to as needed in his fiction.

With the writing of *The Sound and the Fury*, completed in October 1928, Faulkner had gone through a complete transition. He had written an experimental novel, and he had done so without thinking of publication or critics or readers. At the same time he did his best to write and market saleable short stories, since they were more profitable. In the late 1920s Faulkner worked consistently on his short stories, some of which had their origins in sketches and stories written a few years before, and which he now revised, often time and again, until he finally had to abandon a story or sell it for as little as $25 to a magazine. The short-story activity was higher than at any other point in his career, and it is almost incredible that he could write his best and most autonomous short stories—as many as forty of them—in the same period that he was writing *The Sound and the Fury, As I Lay Dying* (1930), *Sanctuary* (1931), and *Light in August* (1932).

Faulkner regarded the short story highly and deemed it the most demanding form after poetry. He worked consistently and conscientiously to perfect his stories—not to suit the needs of a particular market but to satisfy his own artistic demands. This concern is demonstrated in his arduous work on his short-story collections, most notably *These 13* (1931) and *Collected Stories* (1950), in which he tried to superimpose a design or a structure upon the otherwise disparate short stories. He was a dedicated craftsman in all his work, and the seriousness of his short-story writing is demonstrated in the many different manuscripts and typescripts for individual stories, as well as in his correspondence with magazine editors and agents.

Faulkner is often referred to only as a novelist, and his name always brings to mind the titles of his great novels; but his short-story achievement is not to be forgotten, and there are enough outstanding stories among the 120 he wrote to place him among the great American short-story writers of the twentieth century. Many of Faulkner's short stories may be regarded as a concentration of material later developed in novels. Faulkner's material—the immense array of strange local no matter what happens out there tonight, will still be in the family; the skeleton (if it be a skeleton) still in the closet. Or more than that even. She may believe that if it hadn't been for your grandfather's friendship Sutpen could not have got a foothold here and that if he had not got that foothold, he could not have married Ellen. So maybe she considers you partly responsible for what happened to her and her family through him."

Whatever the reason, Quentin thought, the getting to it was taking a long time. Meanwhile, as time passed and as though in inverse ratio to the vanishing of the voice, the invoked ghost of Sutpen, the brother-in-law, with whom at one time she herself had been engaged to marry began to assume a quality almost of solidity, permanence. Itself circumambient and in turn enclosed by its effluvium of hell, its aura of unregeneration, the ogre-shape of Miss Coldfield which, as the voice went on, began to resolve before Quentin out of itself the two half-ogre children, the three of them forming a shadowy background for the fourth, the wraith of the mother, the dead sister Ellen, a Niobe without tears who had conceived to the demon in a kind of nightmare, and who even alive had moved but without life and grieved but without weeping, and who now, had an air of tranquil and unwitting desolation, not as though she had either outlived the others or had died first, but as if she had never lived at all.

Page from a typescript for Faulkner's 1936 novel Absalom, Absalom! *with annotations and emendations by Faulkner and his editor Saxe Commins (University of Virginia Library, Manuscript Department)* characters, hunting stories, and tall tales, and the Southern legacy, including the lost cause, slavery, and aristocratic families—often seemed to require the longer form. Yet, some of Faulkner's novels started in a single image, a central episode, material fit for a short story.

The Sound and the Fury began as a short story, initially titled "Twilight" and focusing on what Faulkner called, in an introduction to the novel (included in *A Faulkner Miscellany,* 1974), "perhaps the only thing in literature which would ever move me very much"—an image of Caddy Compson "climbing the pear tree to look in the window at her grandmother's funeral while [her brothers] Quentin and Jason and Benjy and the negroes looked up at the muddy seat of her drawers." Faulkner said he had to write a novel about Caddy, "my heart's darling," almost in spite of himself. Caddy is a kind of absent center: although none of the four sections of the book presents her point of view, the novel documents and interprets her journey through life. Caddy's brothers—who narrate one section of the novel each—react to her actions. She is in many ways the brave one, the kind one, the beautiful one in the Compson family, the only one who really cares for the mentally handicapped Benjy, who in his turn always associates her name (or the sound of it) with the smell of trees, with the good things in his poor life.

The novel depicts a family disintegrating completely over a period of some thirty years. The Compsons cannot adjust to a changing world: their proud heritage is of no help, and a whining mother and a drinking father with no capacity for compassion or pity provide poor role models for the children. The book also portrays the decline of traditional values and the rise of commercialism in the new South, but everything is presented through the decline of the Compson family. If the book carries a message, it is the timeless one that people must care for each other and that only love makes life bearable.

The Sound and the Fury is a modernist novel in the sense that it tells a story four times, and if one includes the appendix that Faulkner wrote for Malcolm Cowley's *The Portable Faulkner* in 1945, there is even a fifth attempt at telling the story in order to "get it right." The reiterated attempts at telling the story of the Compson family's decline indicates that understanding is possible, although it may be hard to achieve.

The Sound and the Fury was published on 7 October 1929 in a printing of 1,789 copies, and there was no need for a new printing until a year and a half later, despite enthusiastic reviews. Faulkner had ignored the demands of the marketplace and had written only for himself when he began *The Sound and the Fury;* his next book was designed to be "the most horrific tale I could imagine," in order to make money. Faulkner began work early in 1929 on what eventually appeared in 1932 as *Sanctuary,* but the publishers initially found that the manuscript was too shocking. After his marriage and a summer away from Oxford, Faulkner took a job at the university power plant. During this period he wrote *As I Lay Dying,* which was published before *Sanctuary.*

Faulkner always referred to *As I Lay Dying* as a tour de force, a book for which he had such deliberate plans that when he wrote the first word he knew what the last one would be. Accordingly, there was no sense of joy and expectation in the creation of this novel, compared to what he said he had experienced with *The Sound and the Fury.* Yet, *As I Lay Dying* can be paired with *The Sound and the Fury* since these two novels are among Faulkner's most brilliant stylistic experiments and since brother-sister conflicts are central in both novels. Both books are radical deviations from the norms of the well-made novel, but the form of the novels is so much a part of their theme that any kind of straight chronological and authorial narrative is unthinkable. If modernist fiction was understood to be an urban phenomenon, Faulkner in *As I Lay Dying* made modernism rural, through fifty-nine dialogues by fifteen different narrators or observers who enable readers to follow the odyssey of the Bundrens from the backwoods areas of Yoknapatawpha to Jefferson in order to bury Addie, their dead wife and mother, with her people there.

All through the novel there is a precarious balance, not always kept, between the desires of the individual characters and the responsibility they should have to their society. Responsibility and obligation lie behind the macabre journey, since the dying Addie has asked to be buried with her kin. Anse, the incredibly lazy husband, intends to keep his promise, although readers may ultimately become suspicious of his motives. A strong irony is at work in most of the monologues in the novel, revealing Anse and his children with their individual dreams and preoccupations, some of them utterly selfish, others not. A whole range of emotions colors the monologues and hence the novel as a whole, from anger and hatred and fear to loyalty and reverence. Each monologue has the name of the speaker or observer as its title, and some of them are by non-family members, most importantly the neighbors Cora and Vernon Tull, thus letting readers see the grotesque journey with the rotting corpse from new perspectives.

As I Lay Dying was published on 6 October 1930. Again Faulkner surprised his readers with a tale of almost epic stature about poor peasants in a rural world, told with passion and sympathy for the mother figure. But the novel also works through irony and mockery so that readers have difficulty deciding whether the book is comic or tragic. It relies upon a classical structure to create a mock epic, and it indirectly discusses the limits of language and its referential ability; Addie, in her one monologue, also comments on language versus action in a world that has become increasingly strange to her.

Faulkner was now in the midst of his most productive period, and his output was enormous by any standard. Unexpectedly, he received galley proofs for *Sanctuary* shortly after the publication of *As I Lay Dying*. Faulkner asked his publisher not to print the original version, because he now felt that this "horrific tale" was "a shabby thing," but he needed the money and agreed to cut and revise it. Faulkner revised the book, almost to the extent of rewriting it, now focusing the novel on the heroine, Temple Drake.

Sanctuary in the 1931 version has been hailed by critics as a *roman noir* and has been studied together with other examples of crime fiction of high literary merit. The story of Temple Drake is a study in human evil; Faulkner later called it an examination of "the outrage of a potential believer." The gangster Popeye rapes Temple, using a corncob since he is impotent. Popeye has murdered a man to get to Temple, whom he sets up in a brothel. Horace Benbow defends the man who is falsely accused of the murder, but Temple lies when she testifies, so that Popeye goes free and an innocent man is sent to death. Popeye is later executed for a murder he has not committed. Popeye is a deliberate caricature, mechanical, inhuman, and inflexible, and the reader is never allowed to get close enough to even try to understand him. Nor is it simple to understand the motives behind Temple's actions or her psychology; by the end of this story of foreboding and horror, she appears to be as innocent and untainted as any other young woman.

Published on 9 February 1931, *Sanctuary* was a sensation. It sold seven thousand copies by early April, but critics were furious, especially those in the South. Faulkner was somewhat surprised and later had a tendency to disparage this novel, which scholars later have deemed a much more competent novel and more technically adept than its author would admit. He enjoyed the money, including the funds that the movie rights for the controversial 1933 adaptation *The Story of Temple Drake* brought in—all spent on Rowan Oak. The original text of *Sanctuary*, which focuses more on Horace Benbow and filters most of the story through his perspective, was brought out in 1981.

As I Lay Dying had introduced several characters that reappear and become more important in later books. Events that became important narrative kernels in Faulkner's novels in the 1950s were hinted at in the early 1930s, and episodes from short stories were often revised to fit in with the longer narrative of a novel. His first short-story collection, *These 13,* was published in 1931 and received more laudatory reviews than any of his novels had.

When Faulkner put together this collection he had some forty stories from which to choose. One can only guess his motives for selecting the thirteen stories he included in the book, but the resulting volume presents a rather coherent and convincing picture of the world as a wasteland filled with dust and dreams, hopes and frustrations. Faulkner took great care in structuring this collection to achieve unity, moving toward one finale.

His next novel was begun in August 1931 and published on 6 October 1932, and proved to be closer to the conventional narrative than its predecessors had been. *Light in August* is not an experimental novel, although the narrative works by delayed flashbacks and gives readers access to the pasts of major characters through long capsule stories. A strong and moving such narrative is the story of mixed-blood protagonist Joe Christmas's childhood, which may help readers understand Joe's alienation. Joe is one of the loneliest characters in American fiction, always on the run, most of the time from himself and a self-knowledge that he never obtains.

Light in August opens with a description of the pregnant Lena Grove, alone and barefoot on the road from Alabama, searching for the man whom she has known as Lucas Burch. She finds instead the kind and helpless Byron Bunch, who immediately falls in love with her. This story is contrasted to the relationship of Joe Christmas and Joanna Burden, whom he murders, an act for which he is later brutally slain by Percy Grimm, since the Reverend Gail Hightower, living in the dark past of his ancestor's glory in the Civil War, is unable to act until it is too late. *Light in August* is a novel about community and family, about religious fanaticism and lack of humanity, and it may still be a novel about humanity since so many people are called upon to act on behalf of others and to form new relationships that may in the end bring to the community a recognition of its failure and its errors.

Faulkner was working in Hollywood from May through August 1932, and he returned to work there often during the next decades, even though he strongly disliked Hollywood. He needed the money, and he formed a good and productive cooperation with director Howard Hawks. He was on contract with M-G-M the first time he went there and had success with transforming his own short story "Turn About" (first published in *The Saturday Evening Post,* 5 March 1932) into the movie *Today We Live* (1933). In 1935 he worked for 20th Century-Fox to produce *The Road to Glory* (1936). The short story "Golden Land" (first published in

American Mercury, May 1935) demonstrates Faulkner's intense dislike of Hollywood, but he also had happy times there, not the least because of a lasting love affair with Meta Carpenter Wilde, whom he met during work on *The Road to Glory.* Faulkner's marriage deteriorated sharply through the 1930s; both he and Estelle Faulkner drank heavily and fought, but divorce seems to have been out of the question as socially unacceptable for the head of a Southern family.

Faulkner continued publishing short stories after 1932, although his writing of new stories declined drastically. In 1933 Faulkner's second and last collection of poetry, *A Green Bough,* was published. By the time of *Doctor Martino and Other Stories* (1934) he had more stories than he needed for the book, and most of them had been published already. Whereas *These 13* includes seven previously unpublished stories, *Doctor Martino and Other Stories* includes only two. There seems to be no internal organization of the volume, and the stories do not form any discernible pattern. Yet, there is a clear shift from the preoccupation with war, wilderness, and townspeople in *These 13* to a focus on sex, death, and loss in *Doctor Martino and Other Stories.* Faulkner's second short-story collection elicited fewer reviews than the first one, and they were not quite in the same vein. Most Faulkner scholars rightly consider the later volume inferior to *These 13.*

Several of Faulkner's short stories are set in areas far away from Southern rural locales, and with his next novel, *Pylon,* he did the same. *Pylon* has been treated slightly by critics and scholars alike, perhaps because it is a comparably weak book if seen in relation to the books before it and the one to follow, *Absalom, Absalom!* (1936).

Faulkner had long been fascinated with pilots and flying and was taking flying lessons in 1933. He had watched flying circuses, and in *Pylon* he tells the story of three fliers, centering on the strong and tough female character of Laverne Shumann, who works and lives with two men. The narrator is a newspaper reporter who seems to be reliable and trustworthy, but the implications of the story he tells are really beyond his grasp. The fliers lead lives that are too unconventional, too deviant, to be understood by an ordinary citizen. Faulkner admired the stunt pilots and their way of life, saying (in *Faulkner in the University,* 1959) that they were "outside the range of God, not only of respectability, of love, but of God too. Everyone knew that they wouldn't last very long, which they didn't."

Pylon was published on 25 March 1935 to negative reviews. The book was shocking to most critics; the elements of adultery and suicide led Cowley to comment on its "air of unnecessary horror and violence." The writer himself said that he did not care much about the reception of *Pylon,* because by that time he was deeply immersed in writing what many critics and scholars claim is his best novel, *Absalom, Absalom!,* published on 26 October 1936. Confused reviewers still praised *Pylon* for its narrative power and its tragic tone, and *Absalom, Absalom!* is certainly one of the most impressive books in Faulkner's career.

In its presentation of different versions of the same story and an assessment of all kinds of rumors about Thomas Sutpen and his plantation, Sutpen's Hundred, *Absalom, Absalom!* is a probing investigation of the human ability to know or to reach certain knowledge. When a story lacks in detail or cannot be concluded, characters and readers speculate, telling new stories of how it might have been, or how it must have been. Suppositions must replace accurate knowledge. Two characters from *The Sound and the Fury* (who also appear in several short stories), Mr. Compson and his son Quentin, are among the four unreliable narrators. They are joined by the spinster Rosa Coldfield and by Quentin's Canadian roommate at Harvard, Shreve McCannon. When all possible knowledge of facts comes to an end, and Quentin and Shreve have to substitute speculation, some critics have found that Faulkner, for one chapter in the novel, is a postmodern writer.

At the center of the novel lies Sutpen's dream of creating his own world, of realizing a magnificent dream of a plantation created through the exploitation of a group of African Americans and an architect he has taken captive. Sutpen is totally absorbed in his mission and has no regard for other people. His lifestyle offends everyone, and rumors about him are spread all over the countryside. The incest theme is again central, and the title does of course suggest a lament for the relations of father and son. Sutpen had left his first wife and son, Charles Bon, when he discovered that his wife has black blood. Charles reappears and falls in love with his half sister, Judith Sutpen, and is killed by his half brother to avoid the incestuous union. When Thomas Sutpen is finally brought down and viciously killed, it is by one of his greatest admirers, who suddenly discovers who the real Sutpen is. This episode is told in one of Faulkner's strongest short stories, "Wash," written in 1933 and included in *Collected Stories* despite Faulkner's use of it in *Absalom, Absalom!*

In 1934 Faulkner had written the first six stories in a series about the Civil War (the "Bayard-Ringo" stories). Three of these stories were published in 1934, one in 1935, and the last two stories late in 1936. A seventh story, "An Odor of Verbena," was written in order to complete *The Unvanquished* (1938), but Faulkner also made unsuccessful attempts to sell it independently. For *The Unvanquished* Faulkner had to revise these stories, some of them substantially. He considered his Civil War stories "trash" and felt that he sacrificed more important work by writing his romanticized tales about heroic Southern action during the Civil War. But when he undertook the work of revising and transforming the stories into a unified book, more of his genuine concerns were included. In his revisions Faulkner carefully brought the thematic content of the earliest stories in line with the serious direction of the later stories, adding a more mature narrator who could give a clearly retrospective view of the incidents and cruelties of war. The issue of race became more significant, and Faulkner proved that he could make a serious novel out of short fiction he had described as trash. Published on 15 February 1938, *The Unvanquished* was certainly not a mere collection of short stories, although Faulkner's next recycling of a series of stories into a novel, *Go Down, Moses* (1942), resulted in a more important work of fiction.

The Wild Palms, published on 19 January 1939, is an interesting book in Faulkner's career since he blends two stories: one a distinctly Southern story with old mores and values and situated in a flooded landscape, the other a story about modern people who follow their idea of romantic love and who fight against financial constraints and respectability to make it last. The book has a contrapuntal structure, with alternating chapters from the two juxtaposed tales and an ending that is surprising but inevitable.

The two stories are so different that they have been printed separately, as when Cowley used "Old Man" in *The Portable Faulkner.* But Faulkner's intention was clearly to join them, even if they may appear to have little in common. In "Wild Palms" Harry Wilbourne leaves medical school to run away with a married woman, Charlotte Rittenmeyer, in an attempt to find the romantic and idyllic love that she believes in. Later he becomes the bigger romantic, but it all ends in catastrophe when she gets pregnant and he bungles the abortion so that she bleeds to death. He accepts his punishment, because he knows that *"between grief and nothing I will take grief."* In "Old Man" a tall convict in a work gang is assigned the rescue of a pregnant woman from a tree during a raging flood. He saves her, and even cuts the umbilical cord when her baby is born, only to have ten years for attempted escape added to his prison sentence. Prison is for him a safe place from women, and so the two male protagonists are both jailed, and the romantic hero and his opposite are brought together.

In 1938, when Faulkner mapped out his plans for what has become known as "The Snopes Trilogy" (*The Hamlet,* 1940; *The Town,* 1957; and *The Mansion,* 1959), he had reached the maturity and had all the storytelling tools to undertake what he really had begun as early as 1926 with "Father Abraham." His production had been enormous and on a consistently high level, but it had brought him less money than he had expected and wanted. He still struggled to make ends meet, but he knew his worth: at some point during the writing and revisions of *The Hamlet* he added a manuscript note: "By God, I'm the best in America!" *The Hamlet,* in its broad and leisurely narrative so distant from the urgency and experimentation of his early books, proves his point. Following Cleanth Brooks's 1963 assessment, critics now consider it the best of the books in the trilogy, and one of Faulkner's richest and most rewarding works of art.

The Hamlet is one of Faulkner's loosely joined novels because so much of the material had been used in short stories from the late 1920s onward. Faulkner said in a letter to Cowley as the latter was preparing *The Portable Faulkner* (1946) that the book "was incepted as a novel," but that the writing of it only produced short stories. Thus, he created the Snopes clan. On the basis of this material and the character of the sewing machine agent Suratt, later renamed V. K. Ratliff, Faulkner sat down in 1938 and wrote *The Hamlet.* In classroom discussions in Virginia in 1957 Faulkner claimed that he wrote it "in the late twenties," then added that "It was mostly short stories. In 1940 I got it pulled together."

All three books in the trilogy are dedicated to Stone, with good reason, since he had the original idea of what became "Snopesism"—the single-minded drive for property without any human consideration at all. Yet, Faulkner had grown and matured to the point where he could create likeable Snopeses, and finally to a point where even the meanest Snopes, the murderous Mink, also has human traits.

Flem Snopes's rise from poverty to riches begins in the hamlet of Frenchman's Bend, where Varner's store is the center of all talk, gossip, and barter. Flem clerks in Varner's store. He is a shrewd businessman who apparently cannot be beaten, because all his adversaries have some humanity in them. Old Will Varner is the only match for Flem, but he lets Flem marry his youngest daughter, the lazy and beautiful Eula, who is pregnant. To the itinerant sewing machine seller, Ratliff, who observes the couple when they leave for their honeymoon, this union is the real tragedy in the little, lost village: the impotent little man whose only interest is money gets the young and lovely Eula, so rare and exquisite that she is always compared to Helen of Troy. Ratliff sees it as his duty and obligation to stand up against Flem. But he is also fooled, which gives Flem his first foothold in Jefferson. By the end of the novel, Flem has outgrown and exploited everyone, including his own kin, and now seeks greener pastures in the county seat.

One may find a sociological theme at the center of *The Hamlet,* or one may read the novel as an absolute confrontation between opponents—Flem versus Ratliff, or even Snopesism versus humanity. The wide canvas, the rich and varied storytelling, the happy and relaxed humor, and the wild exaggeration of the tall tales included in the narrative, contributed to its positive reception. Although a few contemporary critics condemned the book for moralistic reasons, most were either mildly bewildered or intrigued by this book that is not really a novel but reads like one and thus represents something new.

The trilogy has invariably been read and studied as a trilogy, with less emphasis on the values of the individual volumes. *The Hamlet* easily stands alone as an autonomous work, whereas *The Town* is a much weaker book, relying to a large degree on retelling parts of past events in the history of the Snopeses and thus becoming repetitive and tedious. But Faulkner also brings in new characters and additional perspectives in the second Snopes novel, by using different narrators and by letting his knight of good intentions, the lawyer Gavin Stevens, compete with Manfred de Spain, the mayor, for Eula's attention. Flem is of course able to exploit even Eula's affair with de Spain, to the extent that he becomes president of the bank and hardly reacts when Eula commits suicide. Gavin also protects Eula's daughter, Linda, closely, and in *The Mansion,* when she has returned home from New York after her husband was killed in Spain during the civil war, Linda is given a more prominent role. She is instrumental in getting Mink Snopes released from prison (after thirty-eight years), so that her stepfather, Flem, can be brought down. As is often the case, the middle volume in the trilogy is the weakest one; however, *The Mansion* in almost all respects is a better book than Faulkner criticism and scholarship seems to indicate.

The next book to be published after *The Hamlet* was *Go Down, Moses,* which offers Faulkner's fullest treatment of the lives of African Americans in the South. Not only their endurance is praised; the black characters simply come forth as more stable, more reliable, more just. The stories that in revised form made up *Go Down, Moses* were all written over a relatively short span of time, with almost no other short-story activity intervening. One may thus say that this continuous process resembles the writing of a novel, and it is now commonplace to consider *Go Down, Moses* as a novel and not a collection, although by some editorial mistake it was originally published as *Go Down, Moses and Other Stories.*

Critics consider *Go Down, Moses* one of Faulkner's most convincing artistic creations, a unified volume with tremendous emotional impact, far greater than that of any of the individual stories. The first part of the book centers on the scheming and cheating Lucas Beauchamp and is a light, comic collection of anecdotes, including those about moonshining and "planted" gold coins. Lucas and his wife, Molly, appear as stereotypical blacks, but slowly both people and tone are modified and softened. Faulkner barely avoids melancholy and pathos in the description of the old woman's plight, but Molly becomes the embodiment of all the virtues cherished in her society. After the more loosely integrated story "Pantaloon in Black" come the stories or chapters that center on Isaac McCaslin—"The Old People," "The Bear," and "Delta Autumn."

Important links with the past of Yoknapatawpha are established in *Go Down, Moses,* as readers learn about Ike's formative years and come to understand where he got his knowledge of "the old people" and his deep respect for the untamed wilderness. Sam Fathers, an Indian of mixed ancestry, has been Ike's substitute father and mentor. Ike's renunciation of his inheritance later in life and most of his subsequent behavior may be considered as acts of sacrifice and expiation, but they may also be viewed as acts of weakness and escape.

Ike's three-part saga ends with "Delta Autumn" (first published in *Story,* May–June 1942), set in a wilderness that is slowly being destroyed by civilization. Human beings in conflict with nature and with themselves are presented in a web of ideas and thoughts about race, history, morality, and love. The story provides the last view of Ike McCaslin, "uncle to half a country and father to no one," before the novel is brought to an end with the story of Molly Beauchamp's struggle to get her dead grandson back home to be buried where he belongs. It opens onto a larger world beyond the plantation, beyond Yoknapatawpha, and is thus a fitting conclusion to *Go Down, Moses* as a novel.

Faulkner wrote a whole series of short stories in 1942 in an attempt to avoid having to return to Hollywood, but the stories did not bring in much money, so he spent most of his time between 1942 and 1945 in California. This period resulted in the 1944 movie version of Ernest Hemingway's 1937 novel, *To Have and Have Not,* which Faulkner changed drastically, and in 1946 he wrote the screenplay for Raymond Chandler's 1939 novel, *The Big Sleep,* most likely Faulkner's best movie work ever.

It is possible to maintain that *Go Down, Moses* was Faulkner's last "great" book, and also that his career reached a record low in the years afterward. Most of his books were out of print. The publication of *The Portable Faulkner* in 1946 changed this situation considerably, and with the returning soldiers who now went to colleges and universities, Faulkner's books were suddenly in demand. Abroad, particularly in France, Faulkner was translated and read and commented on by famous writers such as André Malraux, Jean-Paul Sartre, and Albert Camus. And even if his creative powers were not what they had been, he had enough material in a wide range of published and unpublished short stories and new ideas and possibilities with the Snopes material. First he returned to Lucas Beauchamp and made him the major character in a novel of detection and race—*Intruder in the Dust* (1948). Told in the third person, the events of the book are transmitted through Charles Mallison's experiences with Lucas. Gavin Stevens is Charles's uncle, and Faulkner had used these characters in the 1930s and 1940s in several detective stories, which he collected in *Knight's Gambit* (1949). They also figured decisively as actors and narrators in the later Snopes volumes. Faulkner sold the movie rights to *Intruder in the Dust* for $50,000 in July 1948, and his financial worries finally came to an end.

In the late 1940s Faulkner made plans for a collection of his short stories that would include the stories of detection. When *Knight's Gambit* was published as a separate volume, he had an easier task of selecting what finally became forty-two stories. *Collected Stories* as a title is slightly misleading; the author selected the stories he wanted to represent him for posterity. The volume was published in 1950 and received the 1951 National Book Award for fiction.

In November 1950 it was announced that Faulkner had won the 1949 Nobel Prize in Literature. He had known about the possibility of his nomination, and in a 22 February 1950 letter to Joan Williams he had stated that he would rather be a member of the group of American writers who had not been awarded the Nobel Prize, such as Sherwood Anderson and Theodore Dreiser, than join a club that included Sinclair Lewis and "Mrs. Chinahand [Pearl S.] Buck." Yet, he had no problem accepting the prize when it came, although he did not want to travel to Stockholm to receive it. He was persuaded by friends and publishers, and he had an enjoyable stay with his daughter, Jill, in the snow and winter of the Swedish capital. He delivered his acceptance speech so rapidly and in such a low voice that few present knew that they had listened to one of the most memorable of such speeches until they could read it in print.

So far Faulkner had voiced opinions about social and political matters through characters in his books, and he had seldom let his voice be heard outside of his fiction. Following the prize, podiums and lecterns were offered from everywhere, and even though he still carefully guarded his private life and resented the intrusions of journalists, he took his obligations as a Nobel Prize–winning author and public figure seriously. He established a Nobel Prize fund with the money. Now his books sold more than ever before and were translated into more languages, even in countries where he had not been discovered before the Nobel Prize.

Even if he now could afford to slow down, he had unfinished work that needed to be completed. He returned to the Temple Drake story and wrote *Requiem for a Nun* (1951), and he worked with Ruth Ford and others to adapt the story for the stage. It was not produced until 1957 in London and 1959 in New York, whereas Camus's adaptation was produced with success in Paris in 1956.

Another project on Faulkner's mind—and on the roof and walls of his study at Rowan Oak—was *A Fable* (1954), for which Faulkner had high hopes. It won both a National Book Award and a Pulitzer Prize in 1955 but was not well received by critics. The long story of World War I in France was meant to be an affirmative book, and it claims that man must hope and must "believe in belief." Faulkner scholars still disagree about the merits of this novel, although it is generally regarded as one of his less splendid failures.

Much of what Faulkner wrote after the Nobel Prize may be seen as echoes and reminiscences of what he had done before; but he wrote enough good books to refute those critics who think that his career was destroyed by the prize and the fame that followed. Nevertheless, he might have displayed more of his creative genius in the last decade of his life had it not been for the public demands upon his person and his time. All of his major works were written before he became a Nobel laureate and a public figure who was too proud not to carry out what he saw as his duty, even when he hated it.

As a Nobel laureate, Faulkner traveled widely on State Department missions. He spoke to his fellow Southerners on racial issues, for the first time in his career publishing articles and essays more often than he published stories, and he responded to an incredible popularity in Japan by visiting there in 1955. Starting in 1957 he was writer-in-residence at the University of Virginia in Charlottesville, where he purchased a house and settled with his wife (their daughter Jill had married in 1954).

Faulkner wrote commissioned essays and sketches in the 1950s, and one about his own state, "Mississippi" (first published in *Holiday*, April 1954), may well show his best prose of the decade. A volume of Faulkner's hunting stories, *Big Woods*, was brought out in 1955. A collection of mostly earlier material, it also includes one new story, "Race at Morning." Excerpts from forthcoming novels were also printed in magazines and provided extra income. He struggled with the sequels to *The Hamlet* and concluded his long career with *The Reivers*, which appeared only a month before his death.

The Reivers, published on 4 June 1962, is a last nostalgic, optimistic, and good-humored glance at Yoknapatawpha. It is set in 1905 and is a reminiscence of the old days, when cars were scarce and moral standards high. The book includes some of the wildest tall tales and comic episodes Faulkner ever wrote. The simple fictions are woven into a strong and insistent lesson in honor, and the message is that nothing is forgotten and a man can live through anything. The book renders what "grandfather said," and many of the characters are old acquaintances who now appear on the stage for the last time.

In Charlottesville, Faulkner took up horseback riding on a regular basis and was injured in several falls. His final accident came in Oxford, Mississippi, on 17 June 1962; the connection between his injuries and the heart attack from which he died is unclear, but he was taken to a sanatorium on 5 July and died the following day. He was buried in St. Peter's Cemetery, Oxford, near the graves of most of the Falkners.

The biographical facts of a writer's life and career cannot explain how the works were written or what made it possible to write them. William Faulkner's craftsmanship came slowly, and he learned it through practice and stubborn dedication. He was willing to sacrifice most things to get his work done, and he was never in doubt as to the importance of the artist and his work.

Letters:

The Faulkner-Cowley File: Letters and Memories, 1944–1962, edited by Malcolm Cowley (New York: Viking, 1966);

Selected Letters of William Faulkner, edited by Joseph L. Blotner (New York: Random House, 1976);

The Letters, volume 2 of *Faulkner: A Comprehensive Guide to the Brodsky Collection,* edited by Louis Daniel Brodsky and Robert W. Hamblin (Jackson: University Press of Mississippi, 1984);

Thinking of Home: William Faulkner's Letters to his Mother and Father, 1918–1925, edited by James G. Watson (New York: Norton, 1992).

Interviews:

Faulkner in the University: Class Conferences at the University of Virginia, 1957–58, edited by Frederick L. Gwynn and Joseph L. Blotner (Charlottesville: University of Virginia Press, 1959);

Lion in the Garden: Interviews with William Faulkner, 1926–1962, edited by James B. Meriwether and Michael Millgate (New York: Random House, 1968);

Conversations with William Faulkner, edited by M. Thomas Inge (Jackson: University Press of Mississippi, 1999).

Bibliographies:

James B. Meriwether, *The Literary Career of William Faulkner: A Bibliographical Study* (Princeton: Princeton University Library, 1961; Columbia: University of South Carolina Press, 1971);

Linton R. Massey, *William Faulkner: "Man Working," 1919–1962, A Catalogue of the William Faulkner Collections at the University of Virginia* (Charlottesville: Bibliographical Society, University of Virginia, 1968);

Meriwether, "The Short Fiction of William Faulkner: A Bibliography," *Proof,* 1 (1971);

John E. Bassett, *William Faulkner: An Annotated Checklist of Criticism* (New York: Lewis, 1972);

Carl Petersen, *Each in Its Ordered Place: A Faulkner Collector's Notebook* (Ann Arbor, Mich.: Ardis, 1975);

Thomas L. McHaney, *William Faulkner: A Reference Guide* (Boston: G. K. Hall, 1975);

Louis Daniel Brodsky, *The Bibliography,* volume 1 of *Faulkner: A Comprehensive Guide to the Brodsky Collection* (Jackson: University Press of Mississippi, 1982);

John E. Bassett, *Faulkner in the Eighties: An Annotated Critical Bibliography* (Metuchen, N.J.: Scarecrow Press, 1991).

Biographies:

Joseph L. Blotner, *Faulkner: A Biography,* 2 volumes (New York: Random House, 1974);

David Minter, *William Faulkner: His Life and Work* (Baltimore: Johns Hopkins University Press, 1980);

Michel Gresset, *A Faulkner Chronology,* translated by Arthur B. Scharff (Jackson: University Press of Mississippi, 1985);

Frederick R. Karl, *William Faulkner: American Writer* (New York: Weidenfeld & Nicolson, 1989);

Richard J. Gray, *The Life of William Faulkner: A Critical Biography* (Oxford: Blackwell, 1994).

References:

Cleanth Brooks, *William Faulkner: The Yoknapatawpha Country* (New Haven & London: Yale University Press, 1963);

Brooks, *William Faulkner: Toward Yoknapatawpha and Beyond* (New Haven & London: Yale University Press, 1978);

James B. Carothers, *William Faulkner's Short Stories* (Ann Arbor, Mich.: UMI Research Press, 1985);

Deborah Clarke, *Robbing the Mother: Women in Faulkner* (Jackson: University Press of Mississippi, 1994);

Leland H. Cox, ed., *William Faulkner, Critical Collection* (Detroit: Gale Research, 1982);

Joanne V. Creighton, *William Faulkner's Craft of Revision: The Snopes Trilogy, "The Unvanquished" and "Go Down, Moses"* (Detroit: Wayne State University Press, 1977);

Thomas E. Dasher, *William Faulkner's Characters: An Index to the Published and Unpublished Fiction* (New York: Garland, 1981);

Thadious M. Davis, *Faulkner's "Negro": Art and the Southern Context* (Baton Rouge: Louisiana State University Press, 1983);

James Ferguson, *Faulkner's Short Fiction* (Knoxville: University of Tennessee Press, 1991);

Evans Harrington and Ann J. Abadie, eds., *Faulkner and the Short Story: Faulkner and Yoknapatawpha, 1990* (Jackson: University of Mississippi Press, 1992);

Irving Howe, *William Faulkner: A Critical Study,* third edition, revised and enlarged (Chicago: University of Chicago Press, 1975);

M. Thomas Inge, ed., *William Faulkner—The Contemporary Reviews* (Cambridge & New York: Cambridge University Press, 1995);

Richard Marius, *Reading Faulkner: Introductions to the First Thirteen Novels,* edited by Nancy Grisham Anderson (Knoxville: University of Tennessee Press, 2006);

John Matthews, *The Play of Faulkner's Language* (Ithaca, N.Y.: Cornell University Press, 1982);

Stephen Ross, *Fiction's Inexhaustible Voice: Speech and Writing in Faulkner* (Athens: University of Georgia Press, 1989);

Hans H. Skei, *William Faulkner: The Novelist as Short Story Writer* (Oslo: Universitetsforlaget, 1985);

Skei, *William Faulkner: The Short Story Career* (Oslo: Universitetsforlaget, 1981);

Theresa M. Towner and James B. Carothers, eds., *Reading Faulkner: Collected Stories: Glossary and Commentary* (Jackson: University Press of Mississippi, 2006);

Edmond L. Volpe, *A Reader's Guide to William Faulkner* (New York: Farrar, Straus & Giroux, 1964);

Linda Wagner-Martin, ed., *William Faulkner: Six Decades of Criticism* (East Lansing: Michigan State University Press, 2002);

Philip M. Weinstein, ed., *The Cambridge Companion to William Faulkner* (Cambridge, England: Cambridge University Press, 1995);

Eudora Welty, *On William Faulkner* (Jackson: University Press of Mississippi, 2003);

Joel Williamson, *William Faulkner and Southern History* (New York: Oxford University Press, 1993);

Sally Wolff and Floyd C. Watkins, *Talking about William Faulkner: Interviews with Jimmy Faulkner, and Others* (Baton Rouge: Louisiana State University Press, 1996).

Papers:

The William Faulkner Collection at the University of Virginia Library, Charlottesville, is the most important repository of his manuscripts and typescripts. Material related to Faulkner's short stories can also be found in the Henry W. and Albert A. Berg Collection, New York Public Library; the Harry Ransom Humanities Research Center, University of Texas at Austin; and the William Wisdom Collection, Tulane University.

1949 Nobel Prize in Literature Presentation Speech

by Gustaf Hellström, Member of the Swedish Academy, 10 December 1950

William Faulkner is essentially a regional writer, and as such reminds Swedish readers now and then of two of our own most important novelists, Selma Lagerlöf and Hjalmar Bergman. Faulkner's Värmland is the northern part of the state of Mississippi and his Vadköping is called Jefferson. The parallelism between him and our two fellow countrymen could be extended and deepened, but time does not allow such excursions now. The difference—the great difference—between him and them is that Faulkner's setting is so much darker and more bloody than that against which Lagerlöf's cavaliers and Bergman's bizarre figures lived. Faulkner is the great epic writer of the Southern states with all their background: a glorious past built upon cheap Negro slave labour; a civil war and a defeat which destroyed the economic basis necessary for the then existing social structure; a long drawn-out and painful interim of resentment; and, finally, an industrial and commercial future whose mechanization and standardization of life are strange and hostile to the Southerner and to which he has only gradually been able and willing to adapt himself. Faulkner's novels are a continuous and ever-deepening description of this painful process, which he knows intimately and feels intensely, coming as he does from a family which was forced to swallow the bitter fruits of defeat right down to their worm-eaten cores: impoverishment, decay, degeneration in its many varied forms. He has been called a reactionary. But even if this term is to some extent justified, it is balanced by the feeling of guilt which becomes clearer and clearer in the dark fabric at which he labours so untiringly. The price of the gentlemanly environment, the chivalry, the courage, and the often extreme individualism was inhumanity. Briefly, Faulkner's dilemma might be expressed thus: he mourns for and, as a writer, exaggerates a way of life which he himself, with his sense of justice and humanity, would never be able to stomach. It is this that makes his regionalism universal. Four bloody years of war brought about the changes in the social structure which it has taken the peoples of Europe, except the Russians, a century and a half to undergo.

It is against a background of war and violence that the fifty-two-year-old writer sets his more important novels. His grandfather held a high command during the Civil War. He himself grew up in the atmosphere created by warlike feats and by the bitterness and the poverty resulting from the never admitted defeat. When he was twenty he entered the Canadian Royal Air Force, crashed twice, and returned home, not as a military hero but as a physically and psychically war-damaged youth with dubious prospects, who for some years faced a precarious existence. He had joined the war because, as his *alter ego* expressed it in one of his early novels, "one doesn't want to waste a war." But out of the youth who once had been thirsting for sensation and battle, there gradually developed a man whose loathing of violence is expressed more and more passionately and might well be summed up by the Fifth Commandment: Thou shalt not kill. On the other hand, there are things which man must always show himself unwilling to bear: "Some things," says one of his latest characters, "you must always be unable to bear. Injustice and outrage and dishonor and shame. Not for kudos and not for cash—Just refuse to bear them." One might ask how these two maxims can be reconciled or how Faulkner himself envisages a reconciliation between them in times of international lawlessness. It is a question which he leaves open.

The fact is that, as a writer, Faulkner is no more interested in solving problems than he is tempted to indulge in sociological comments on the sudden changes in the economic position of the Southern states. The defeat and the consequences of defeat are merely the soil out of which his epics grow. He is not fascinated by men as a community but by man in the community, the individual as a final unity in himself, curiously unmoved by external conditions. The tragedies of these individuals have nothing in common with Greek tragedy: they are led to their inexorable end by passions caused by inheritance, traditions, and environment, passions which are expressed either in a sudden outburst or in a slow liberation from perhaps generations-old restrictions. With almost every new work Faulkner penetrates deeper into the human psyche, into man's greatness and powers of self-sacrifice, lust for power, cupidity, spiritual poverty, narrow-mindedness, burlesque obstinacy, anguish, terror, and degenerate aberrations. As a probing psychologist he is the unrivalled master among all living British and American novelists. Neither do any of his colleagues possess his fantastic imaginative powers and his ability to create characters. His subhuman and superhuman figures, tragic or comic in a macabre way, emerge from his mind with a reality that few existing people—even those nearest to us—can give us, and they move in a milieu whose odours of subtropical plants, ladies' perfumes, Negro sweat, and the smell of horses and mules penetrate immediately even into a Scandinavian's warm and cosy den. As a painter of landscapes he has the hunter's intimate knowledge of his own hunting-ground, the topographer's accuracy, and the impressionist's sensitivity. Moreover—side by side with Joyce and perhaps even more so—Faulkner is the great experimentalist among twentieth-century novelists. Scarcely two of his novels are similar technically. It seems as if by this continuous renewal he wanted to achieve the increased breadth which his limited world, both in geography and in subject matter, cannot give him. The same desire to experiment is shown in his mastery, unrivalled among modern British and American novelists, of the richness of the English language, a richness derived from its different linguistic elements and the periodic changes in style—from the spirit of the Elizabethans down to the scanty but expressive vocabulary of the Negroes of the Southern states. Nor has anyone since Meredith—except perhaps Joyce—succeeded in framing sentences as infinite and powerful as Atlantic rollers. At the same time, few writers of his own age can rival him in giving a chain of events in a series of short sentences, each of which is like a blow of a hammer, driving the nail into the plank up to the head and securing it immovably. His perfect command over the resources of the language can—and often does—lead him to pile up words and associations which try the reader's patience in an exciting or complicated story. But this profusion has nothing to do with literary flamboyance. Nor does it merely bear witness to the abounding agility of his imagination; in all their richness, every new attribute, every new association is intended to dig deeper into the reality which his imaginative power conjures up.

Faulkner has often been described as a determinist. He himself, however, has never claimed to adhere to any special philosophy of life. Briefly, his view of life may perhaps be summed up in his own words: that the whole thing (perhaps?) signifies nothing. If this were not the case, He or They who set up the whole fabric would have arranged things differently. And yet it must mean something, because man continues to struggle and must continue to struggle until, one day, it is all over. But Faulkner has one belief, or rather one hope: that every man sooner or later receives the punishment he deserves and that self-sacrifice not only brings with it personal happiness but also adds to the sum total of the good deeds of mankind. It is a hope, the latter part of which reminds us of the firm conviction expressed by the Swedish poet Viktor Rydberg in the recitative of the Cantata presented at the Jubilee Degree Conferment at Uppsala in 1877.

Mr. Faulkner—The name of the Southern state in which you were born and reared has long been well known to us Swedes, thanks to two of the closest and dearest friends of your boyhood, Tom Sawyer and Huckleberry Finn. Mark Twain put the Mississippi River on the literary map. Fifty years later you began a series of novels with which you created out of the state of Mississippi one of the landmarks of twentieth-century world literature; novels which with their ever-varying form, their ever-deeper and more intense psychological insight, and their monumental characters—both good and evil—occupy a unique place in modern American and British fiction.

Mr. Faulkner—It is now my privilege to ask you to receive from the hands of His Majesty the King the Nobel Prize in Literature, which the Swedish Academy has awarded you.

[© The Nobel Foundation, 1950.]

Faulkner: Banquet Speech

Introductory remarks by Robin Fåhraeus, Member of the Royal Academy of Sciences, at the Nobel Banquet at the City Hall in Stockholm, 10 December 1950:

Mr. William Faulkner—We heard with great pleasure that you were coming to our country to receive your Prize in person. We are indeed happy to greet you as an eminent artist, as a detached analyst of the human heart, as a great author who in a brilliant manner has enlarged man's knowledge of himself.

Faulkner's speech

I feel that this award was not made to me as a man, but to my work—a life's work in the agony and sweat of the human spirit, not for glory and least of all for profit, but to create out of the materials of the human spirit something which did not exist before. So this award is only mine in trust. It will not be difficult to find a dedication for the money part of it commensurate with the purpose and significance of its origin. But I would like to do the same with the acclaim too, by using this moment as a pinnacle from which I might be listened to by the young men and women already dedicated to the same anguish and travail, among whom is already that one who will some day stand here where I am standing.

Our tragedy today is a general and universal physical fear so long sustained by now that we can even bear it. There are no longer problems of the spirit. There is only the question: When will I be blown up? Because of this, the young man or woman writing today has forgotten the problems of the human heart in conflict with itself which alone can make good writing because only that is worth writing about, worth the agony and the sweat.

He must learn them again. He must teach himself that the basest of all things is to be afraid; and, teaching himself that, forget it forever, leaving no room in his workshop for anything but the old verities and truths of the heart, the old universal truths lacking which any story is ephemeral and doomed—love and honor and pity and pride and compassion and sacrifice. Until he does so, he labors under a curse. He writes not of love but of lust, of defeats in which nobody loses anything of value, of victories without hope and, worst of all, without pity or compassion. His griefs grieve on no universal bones, leaving no scars. He writes not of the heart but of the glands.

Until he relearns these things, he will write as though he stood among and watched the end of man. I decline to accept the end of man. It is easy enough to say that man is immortal simply because he will endure: that when the last dingdong of doom has clanged and faded from the last worthless rock hanging tideless in the last red and dying evening, that even then there will still be one more sound: that of his puny inexhaustible voice, still talking. I refuse to accept this. I believe that man will not merely endure: he will prevail. He is immortal, not because he alone among creatures has an inexhaustible voice, but because he has a soul, a spirit capable of compassion and sacrifice and endurance. The poet's, the writer's, duty is to write about these things. It is his privilege to help man endure by lifting his heart, by reminding him of the courage and honor and hope and pride and compassion and pity and sacrifice which have been the glory of his past. The poet's voice need not merely be the record of man, it can be one of the props, the pillars to help him endure and prevail.

[© The Nobel Foundation, 1950. William Faulkner is the sole author of his speech.]

Dario Fo
(24 March 1926 –)

Andrea Bisicchia
University of Padua

See also the Fo entry in *DLB Yearbook 1997*.

BOOKS: *Teatro comico di Dario Fo* (Milan: Garzanti, 1962)–comprises *La Marcolfa; Gli imbianchini non hanno ricordi; I tre bravi; Non tutti i ladri vengono per nuocere; Un morto da vendere; I cadaveri si spediscono e le donne si spogliano; L'uomo nudo e l'uomo in frak;* and *Canzoni e ballate; L'uomo nudo e l'uomo in frak* translated by Ed Emery as *One Was Nude and One Wore Tails* (London: Theatretexts, 1985);

Legami pure che tanto io spacco tutto lo stesso (Milan: Nuova Scena, 1969)–comprises *Il telaio* and *Il funerale del padrone;*

L'operaio conosce 300 parole, il padrone 1000: per questo lui è il padrone (Milan: Nuova Scena, 1969);

Mistero buffo: Giullarata popolare (Cremona: Tip. Lombarda, 1969; revised edition, edited by Franca Rame, Verona: Bertani, 1974; revised and enlarged edition, Turin: Einaudi, 2003); translated by Emery as *Mistero Buffo: Comic Mysteries*, edited by Stuart Hood (London: Methuen, 1988);

Vorrei morire anche stasera se dovessi pensare che non è servito a niente (Verona: E.D.B., 1970);

Morte accidentale di un anarchico (Verona: Bertani, 1971); translated by Gillian Hanna and adapted by Gavin Richards as *Accidental Death of an Anarchist* (London: Pluto, 1980);

Morte e resurrezione di un pupazzo (Milan: Sapere, 1971);

Tutti uniti! Tutti insieme! Ma scusa, quello non è il padrone? (Verona: Bertani, 1971);

Ordine! Per Dio.ooo.ooo.ooo (Verona: Bertani, 1972);

Pum, Pum! Chi è? La polizia! (Verona: Bertani, 1972; revised edition, 1973);

Guerra di popolo in Cile (Verona: Bertani, 1973);

Ballate a canzoni, edited by Lanfranco Binni (Verona: Bertani, 1974);

Non si paga! Non si paga! (Milan: Collettivo Teatrale La Comune, 1974); translated by Lino Pertile and adapted by Bill Colvill and Robert Walker as *We Can't Pay? We Won't Pay!* (London: Pluto, 1978);

Il Fanfani rapito (Verona: Bertani, 1975);

Dario Fo (left) receiving the 1997 Nobel Prize in Literature from King Carl XVI Gustaf of Sweden (AP World Wide/Ola Torkelsson)

La giullarata (Verona: Bertani, 1975);

La signora è da buttare (Turin: Einaudi, 1976);

Poer Nano, text by Fo, illustrations by Jacopo Fo (Milan: Ottaviano, 1976);

La marijuana della mamma è la più bella (Verona: Bertani, 1976);

Tutta casa, letto e chiesa, by Fo and Rame (Verona: Bertani, 1978; new edition, Milan: La Comune,

1981)–1978 edition comprises excerpts from *Tutta casa, letto e chiesa; L'operaio conosce 300 parole, il padrone 1000: per questo lui è il padrone; Mistero buffo; Vorrei morire anche stasera se dovessi pensare che non è servito e niente; Guerra di popolo in Cile; I piatti; Basta coi fascisti!; Fedayn; Canzonissima;* and *Chi l'ha visto?;*

La storia di un soldato, text by Fo, photographs by Silvia Lelli Masotti (Milan: Electa, 1979);

Storia della tigre e altre storie, edited by Rame and Arturo Corso (Milan: La Comune, 1980)–comprises *Storia della tigre; Il primo miracolo di Gesù Bambino; Dedalo e Icaro;* and *Il sacrificio di Isacco; Storia della tigre* translated by Emery as *The Tale of a Tiger: A Comic Monologue* (London: Theatretexts, 1984);

Clacson, trombette e pernacchi, edited by Rame (Milan: La Comune, 1981)–comprises *Clacson, trombette e pernacchi; Terrorismo di stampa;* and *Alcune ricevute di Soccorso rosso militante; Clacson, trombette e pernacchi* translated by Dale McAdoo and Charles Mann as *About Face: A Farce,* in *Theater,* 14, no. 3 (Summer/Fall 1983): 4–42;

L'opera dello sghignazzo, libretto by Fo, music by Fiorenzo Carpi (Milan: La Comune, 1981);

Storia vera di Piero D'Angera, che alla crociata non c'era, edited by Rame and Sergio Martin (Milan: La Comune, 1981);

Fabulazzo osceno, edited by Rame (Milan: La Comune, 1982)–comprises *Il tumulto di Bologna; La parpàja tòpola; Lucio e l'asino;* and *Io, Ulrike, grido . . .;*

Coppia aperta, by Fo and Rame (Milan: Compagnia Teatrale La Comune, 1984); translated by Emery as *The Open Couple: A One-Act Comedy* (London: Theatretexts, 1984); translated by Stuart Hood as *An Open Couple–Very Open, Theater* [Yale] (Winter 1985): 19–31;

Il ratto della Francesca, edited by Rame, Franca Valsania, and Davide Rota (Milan: La Comune, 1986); translated by Rupert Lowe as *Abducting Diana,* adapted by Stephen Stenning (London: Oberon, 1994);

Manuale minimo dell'attore (Turin: Einaudi, 1987; expanded edition, 1997); translated by Joseph Farrell as *The Tricks of the Trade,* edited by Hood (London: Methuen, 1991; New York: Routledge, 1991);

Parti femminili: Una giornata qualunque, Una coppia aperta, by Fo and Rame (Milan: La Comune, 1987);

La fine del mondo (Valverde: Il Girasole, 1990);

Totò: Manuale dell'attor comico, edited by Liborio Termine (Turin: Aleph, 1991);

Johan Padan a la descoverta de le Americhe, edited by Rame (Florence: Giunti, 1992; bilingual edition, translated by John Rugman, Turin: Abele, 1992);

Parliamo di donne, by Fo and Rame (Milan: Kaos, 1992)–comprises *L'eroina* and *La donna grassa;*

Fabulazzo (Milan: Kaos, 1992);

Il diavolo con le zinne, edited by Rame (Turin: Einaudi, 1998);

Marino libero! Marino è innocente! edited by Rame (Turin: Einaudi, 1998);

Lu Santo Jullàre Françesco, edited by Rame (Turin: Einaudi, 1999);

La vera storia di Ravenna (Modena: Panini, 1999);

L'ascensione di Alessandro Magno portato in cielo da due grifoni (Rome: Sinnos, 2001);

Il paese dei Mezàrat: I miei primi sette anni (e qualcuno in più), edited by Rame (Milan: Feltrinelli, 2002); translated by Joseph Farrell as *My First Seven Years (Plus a Few More)* (London: Methuen, 2005);

22 cose che la sinistra deve fare e non ha ancora fatto, by Fo, Rame, and Jacopo Fo (Italy: Nuovi Mondi, 2002);

Il tempio degli uomini liberi: Il Duomo de Modena, edited by Rame (Modena: Panini, 2004);

Caravaggio al tempo di Caravaggio: In occasione della mostra Caravaggio, una mostraimpossibile, a Roma, Castel Sant'Angelo, edited by Rame (Modena: Panini, 2005).

Collection: *Le commedie di Dario Fo,* edited by Franca Rame, 13 volumes (Turin: Einaudi, 1966–1998)–comprises volume 1, *Gli arcangeli non giocano a flipper; Aveva due pistole con gli occhi bianchi e neri;* and *Chi ruba un piede è fortunato in amore;* volume 2, *Isabella, tre caravelle e un cacciaballe; Settimo, ruba un po' meno;* and *La colpa è sempre del diavolo;* volume 3, *Grande pantomima con bandiere e pupazzi grandi, piccoli e medi; L'operaio conosce trecento parole il padrone mille per questo lui è il padrone;* and *Legami pure che tanto io spacco tutto lo stesso;* volume 4, *Vorrei morire anche stasera se dovessi pensare che non è servito a niente; Tutti uniti! Tutti insieme! Ma scusa, quello non è il padrone?* and *Fedayn;* volume 5, *Mistero buffo* and *Ci ragiono e canto;* volume 6, *La Marcolfa; Gli imbianchini non hanno ricordi; I tre bravi; Non tutti i ladri vengono per nuocere; Un morto da vendere; I cadaveri si spediscono e le donne si spogliano; L'uomo nudo e l'uomo in frak;* and *Canzoni e ballate;* volume 7, *Morte accidentale di un anarchico* and *La signora è da buttare;* volume 8, *Venticinque monologhi per una donna;* volume 9, *Coppia aperta, quasi spalancata e altre quattordice commedie,* by Fo and Rame; volume 10, *Il Papa e la strega; Il Fanfani rapito; Clacson, trombette e pernacchi;* and *Il ratto della Francesca;* volume 11, *Storia vera di Pietro d'Angera, che alla crociata non c'era; L'opera dello sghignazzo;* and *Quasi per caso una donna: Elisabetta;* volume 12, *Non si paga! Non si paga!; La marijuana della mamma è la più bella; Dio li fa e poi li accoppa; Il braccato; Zitti! Stiamo precitando!* and *Mamma! I San-*

culotti! by Fo and Rame; and volume 13, *L'eroina; Grasso è bello!; Sesso? Grazie, tanto per gradire!* and "Appunti e altre storie," by Fo and Rame.

Editions in English: *Female Parts: One-Woman Plays,* by Fo and Franca Rame, translated by Margaret Kunzle and Stuart Hood, adapted by Olwen Wymark (London: Pluto, 1981)—comprises *Waking Up, A Woman Alone, The Same Old Story,* and *Medea;*

We Won't Pay! We Won't Pay! A Political Farce, translated by R. G. Davis (New York: S. French, 1984);

Coming Home: A Comic Monologue, by Fo and Rame, translated by Ed Emery (London: Theatretexts, 1984);

The Mother: A Dramatic Monologue, translated by Emery (London: Theatretexts, 1984);

Trumpets and Raspberries, translated and adapted by R. C. McAvoy and Anna-Maria Giugni (London: Pluto, 1984);

Adult Orgasm Escapes from the Zoo, by Fo and Rame, adapted by Estelle Parsons (New York: Broadway Play Pub., 1985);

Archangels Don't Play Pinball, translated by McAvoy and Giugni (London: Methuen, 1987); translated by Ron Jenkins (New York: S. French, 1987);

Elizabeth, Almost by Chance a Woman, translated by Gillian Hanna, edited by Hood (London: Methuen, 1987); translated by Jenkins (New York: S. French, 1987);

The Open Couple and An Ordinary Day, by Fo and Rame, translated by Hood and Joseph Farrell (London: Methuen, 1990);

The Pope and the Witch, by Fo and Rame, translated by Emery (London: Oberon, 1990)—includes *The First Miracle of the Infant Jesus;* translated by Joan Holden (New York: S. French, 1997);

A Woman Alone & Other Plays, by Fo and Rame, translated by Emery, Hanna, and Christopher Cairns (London: Methuen, 1991)—includes *All Home, Bed and Church; More Stories; Tales of the Resistance;* and *Questions of Terrorism and Repression;*

Plays: One, translated by Emery, McAvoy, Giugni, and Farrell (London: Methuen, 1992)—comprises *Mistero Buffo; Accidental Death of an Anarchist; Trumpets and Raspberries; The Virtuous Burglar;* and *One Was Nude and One Wore Tails;*

Plays: Two, by Fo and Rame, translated by Lino Pertile, Hanna, Hood, and Farrell (London: Methuen, 1994)—comprises *Can't Pay? Won't Pay!; Elizabeth, Almost by Chance a Woman; The Open Couple;* and *An Ordinary Day;*

We Won't Pay! We Won't Pay! and Other Plays, edited by Rame, translated by Jenkins (New York: Theatre Communications Group, 2001);

Johan Padan and the Discovery of the Americas, translated by Jenkins and Stefania Taviano (New York: Grove, 2001);

The Peasants' Bible and The Story of the Tiger, translated by Jenkins (New York: Grove, 2004).

PLAY PRODUCTIONS: *Il dito nell'occhio,* by Fo, Franco Parenti, and Giustino Durano, Milan, Piccolo Teatro, 15 June 1953;

I sani da legare, by Fo, Parenti, and Durano, Milan, Piccolo Teatro, 19 June 1954;

Ladri, manichini e donne nude, by Fo and Georges Feydeau, Milan, Piccolo Teatro, 6 June 1958;—comprised *L'uomo nudo e l'uomo in frak; Non tutti i ladri vengono per nuocere; Gli imbianchini non hanno ricordi;* and *Non andartene in giro tutta nuda!;* later productions substituted *I cadaveri si spediscono, le donne si spogliano* [by Fo] for *Non andartene in giro tutta nuda!* [by Feydeau];

Comica finale, Turin, Teatro Stabile, 10 December 1958;—comprised *Quando sarai povero sarai re; La Marcolfa; Un morto da vendere;* and *I tre bravi;*

Gli arcangeli non giocano a flipper, Milan, Teatro Odeon, 11 September 1959;

Il 999° dei Mille, Milan, Il Globo, September 1959;

Aveva due pistole con gli occhi bianchi e neri, Milan, Teatro Odeon, 2 September 1960;

Chi ruba un piede è fortunato in amore, Milan, Teatro Odeon, 8 September 1961;

Isabella, tre caravelle e un cacciaballe, Milan, Teatro Odeon, 6 September 1963;

Settimo, ruba un po' meno, Milan, Teatro Odeon, 4 September 1964;

La colpa è sempre del diavolo, Milan, Teatro Odeon, 10 September 1965;

La signora è da buttare, Milan, Teatro Manzoni, 15 September 1967;

Grande pantomima con bandiere e pupazzi grandi, piccoli e medi, Cesenà, Casa del Popolo di San Egidio, 25 October 1968; revised as *Morte e resurrezione di un pupazzo,* 1971;

Mistero buffo, Sestri Levante, 1 October 1969;

L'operaio conosce 300 parole, il padrone 1000: per questo lui è il padrone, Genoa, Teatro dello Gioventù, 3 November 1969;

Legami pure che tanto io spacco tutto lo stesso, Genoa, Teatro della Gioventù, 5 November 1969—comprised *Il telaio* and *Il funerale del padrone;*

Vorrei morire anche stasera se dovessi pensare che non è servito a niente, Milan, Capannone di Via Colletta, 27 October 1970;

Morte accidentale di un anarchico, Varese, 5 December 1970; Milan, Capannone di Via Colletta, 10 December 1970;

Tutti uniti! Tutti insieme! Ma scusa, quello non è il padrone? Varese, Casa del Popolo, 27 March 1971;

Fedayn, Milan, Capannone di Via Colletta, February 1972;

Ordine! Per Dio.ooo.ooo, Bologna, Salone de San Lazarro, 18 November 1972;

Pum, Pum! Chi è? La polizia! Rome, Circolo Quarticciolo, 7 December 1972;

Guerra di popolo in Cile, Milan, Teatro Palladio, 1973;

Non si paga! Non si paga! Milan, Palazzina Liberty, 3 October 1974;

Il Fanfani rapito, Milan, Palazzina Liberty, 5 June 1975;

La giullarata, Milan, Palazzina Liberty, 11 November 1975;

La marijuana della mamma è la più bella, Milan, Palazzina Liberty, 2 March 1976;

La storia della tigre e altre storie, Perugia, Quasar a Ellera, 12 June 1977;

Tutta casa, letto e chiesa, by Fo and Franca Rame, Milan, Palazzina Liberty, 6 December 1977;

La storia di un soldato, adapted by Fo from Igor Stravinsky's opera, Cremona, Teatro Ponchielli, 18 November 1978;

Clacson, trombette e pernacchi, Milan, Teatro Cristallo, 14 January 1981;

Discorsi sul terrorismo e la repressione, by Fo and Rame, Milan, Teatro Cristallo, 27 February 1981;

L'opera dello sghignazzo, libretto by Fo, music by Fiorenzo Carpi, Turin, Fabbricone, 1 December 1981;

Patapumfete, Milan, Teatro Cristallo, 3 March 1982;

Il fabulazzo osceno, Milan, Teatro Smeraldo, 1982—comprised *Il tumulto di Bologna; La parpàja tópola; Lucio el'asino;* and *Io, Ulrike, grido . . .;*

Coppia aperta, by Fo and Rame, Milan, Teatro Ciak, 30 November 1983;

Quasi per caso una donna: Elisabetta, Riccione, Teatro Turismo, 7 December 1984;

Hellequin Harlekin Arlekin: Arlecchino, Venice, Teatro Goldoni, 18 October 1985;

Una giornata qualunque, by Fo and Rame, Milan, Teatro Nuovo, 9 October 1986;

Il ratto della Francesca, Trieste, Teatro Sloveno, 3 December 1986;

La parte del leone, Venice, Teatro Toniolo Mestre, 15 September 1987;

Diario di Eva, Milan, Teatro Sala dell'Acqua Potabile, 26 June 1988;

Il Papa e la strega, by Fo and Rame, Novara, Teatro Faraggiana, 31 October 1989;

Zitti! Stiamo precipitando! Milan, Teatro Nuovo, 27 November 1990;

Parliamo di donne, by Fo and Rame, Ravenna, Teatro Rasi, 26 November 1991—comprised *L'eroina* and *Grasso è bello;*

Johan Padan a la descoverta de le Americhe, Bologna, Teatro San Giovanni in Persiceto, late 1991;

Settimo: Ruba un po' meno, n. 2, Cararra, Teatro Animosi, 20 November 1992;

Mamma! I Sanculotti! Carrara, Teatro Animosi, 6 November 1993;

Dario Fo recita Ruzzante, Spoleto, Teatro Nuovo, 8 July 1993;

Sesso? Grazie, tanto per gradire, adapted by Fo and Rame from Jacopo Fo's *Lo Zen e l'arte di scopare,* Rome, Teatro Valle, 28 December 1994;

La Bibbia dell'Imperatore, la Bibbia dei villani, Benevento, Teatro Romano, 6 September 1996;

Il diavolo con le zinne, Messina, Teatro Vittorio Emanuele, 7 August 1997;

Marino libero! Marino è innocente!, Milan, Teatro Nazionale, 16 March 1998;

Lu Santo Jullàre Françesco, Spoleto, Festival di Spoleto, 8 July 1999;

Il grande bugiardo, Milan, Palalida, 10 May 2001;

Da Tangentopoli all'irresistibile ascesa di Ubu-Bas, Milan, Teatro Smeraldo, 9 October 2002;

L'anomalo bicefalo, Varallo, Teatro Civico, 13 November 2003;

Il tempio degli uomini liberi: Il Duomo di Modena, Modena, Piazza Grande, 19 July 2004.

PRODUCED SCRIPTS: *Lo svitato,* by Fo, Fulvio Fo, Augusto Frassinetti, Carlo Lizzani, Massimo Mida, and Bruno Vailati, motion picture, Ente Nazionale Industrie Cinematografiche, 1955;

Souvenir d'Italie, by Fo, Agenore Incrocci, Antonio Pietrangeli, and Furio Scarpelli, motion picture, Athena Cinematografica, 1957;

Rascel-Fifì, motion picture, Vides Cinematografica, 1957;

Il teatro di Dario Fo, television, RAI 2, 1977—included *Settimo: Ruba un po' meno; Parliamo di donne; Ci ragiono e canto;* and *Mistero buffo.*

OTHER: Bianca Fo Garambois, *Una strega, una pizza e un orco con la stizza,* illustrations by Fo (Firenze: FATATRAC, 1995);

Fo Garambois, *Cartigli, infernotti e cronache bislacche,* illustrations by Fo (Firenze: FATATRAC, 1999).

SELECTED PERIODICAL PUBLICATION–UNCOLLECTED: "Il dito nell'occhio," by Fo, Franco Parenti, and Giustino Durano, *Teatro d'Oggi,* 3, no. 2 (1954): 9–17.

For more than fifty years Dario Fo has been a central figure of theater practice, both technically and thematically. His method has been one that has gone from the stage to the text and has embodied the tradition of the commedia dell'arte, a theatrical tradition that did not rely on a written text with lines to be uttered by the actors but only on scenarios (basic written plots with no lines). Fo, however, belongs to the tradition of commedia dell'arte actors who did not perform in the royal courts but preferred the streets and the taverns as their stage. His preoccupation has always been to question and denounce the injustices imposed on human beings around the world. Although his theater has used comedy to expose the corruption, dishonesty, and arrogance of the powerful, he has always provoked serious reactions throughout the world. His ideological stance has always been accompanied by a personal commitment, beyond the theater, to help and support those who suffer.

Fo postponed writing his autobiography until 2002, when he published *Il paese dei Mezàrat: I miei primi sette anni (e qualcuno in più)* (translated as *My First Seven Years (Plus a Few More)*, 2005); before then, however, he released many interviews through which his personal and artistic life are widely documented. He was born in San Giano, Varese, Italy, on 24 March 1926. His father, Felice Fo, was a railway stationmaster and a socialist; his mother, Pina Rota, was an educated woman of peasant origin and tradition. Fo's parents were not insensitive to the appeal of art and culture: his father was an amateur actor, and his mother had written a critically acclaimed autobiographical book, *Il paese delle rane* (The Nation of Frogs), published by the prestigious house Einaudi in 1970. However, the family figure who most influenced the future satirical playwright and actor was probably his maternal grandfather, Giuseppe Rota, better known as "Bristin," which means "red pepper seed" and described his spicy sense of humor. Bristin was a natural-born storyteller and used to take Dario with him on his horse-drawn wagon when traveling to various villages to sell fruits and vegetables. In an interview with Maurizio Cherici for the daily newspaper *Il Corriera della Sera* (2 July 1993), Fo stated that his grandfather, to attract clients, would narrate tall tales and cry out news items, with a preference for licentious affairs, such as:

> Tragedia a Sarzana: Lui esce in mutande dal balcone trascinando la moglie nuda, scoperta con l'amico fedifrago che, fuggendo per le scale, inciampava e si rompeva le gambe. Lo potete ritrovare all'ospedale di Carrara, camera 32. Portategli i fiori, se li merita.
>
> (Tragedy in Sarzana: Husband in his underpants draws his naked wife onto the balcony, while the unfaithful friend with whom she had been surprised falls from the staircase and breaks his legs in the attempt to escape. The poor fellow is now in the Carrara Hospital, Room 32. Bring him flowers, please.)

In the interview Fo traced his own talent for theater and literature to this grandparent. Affection may have led Fo to exaggerate his debt to his beloved grandfather, but there is no doubt that his first schooling as an actor, improviser, and writer for the stage had its roots in the oral tradition of the Val Padana people of the Lombardy region in Northern Italy, especially the craftsmen and fishermen. Most of Fo's childhood was spent moving from one town to another, as his father's postings changed according to railway service needs; but wherever the family went, Fo spent hours sitting in taverns and squares listening tirelessly to the local people, who narrated stories often spiced with political satire.

In 1940 Fo enrolled at the Accademia d'Arte di Brera but was unable to attend his courses because of the outbreak of World War II. This period is nonetheless important, for he befriended intellectuals who later dominated the landscape of Italian culture in the 1960s and 1970s, such as Carlo Lizzani, Elio Vittorini, Carlo Bo, and Gillo Pontecorvo. His family took an active part in the antifascist resistance, and Fo helped his father to smuggle refugees and Allied soldiers to Switzerland, while his mother cared for wounded partisans. After Italy's surrender in 1943, which left half of the country in the hands of the Nazis, Fo was conscripted by force into the army of the Repubblica di Salò, the last rampart of the Fascist Regime in Northern Italy, founded by Benito Mussolini. Fo, however, managed to escape and hid until the end of the war.

After the war, Fo continued his studies in Milan, at the faculty of architecture of the Politecnico, commuting every day from Luino before the rest of the family joined him in Milan. He never completed his curriculum for graduation, but he got a part-time job as an assistant architect and began to draw theater scenes and to exhibit his paintings and drawings (he was a staunch admirer of the Italian surrealist painter Giorgio De Chirico). Moreover, he started to frequent the Milan theatrical milieu, where his encounter with the actor and theater manager Franco Parenti turned out to be decisive for his future career. He became involved in the movement of the "piccoli teatri" (small theaters), where he performed improvised monologues. In 1950 he started to work for a theater company led by Parenti. In 1951 Fo performed "Poer Nano" (Poor Little Thing), a series of satirical monologues, as part of the revue *Sette giorni a Milano* (Seven Days in Milan) at the Teatro Odeon in Milan; it was his first experience in an "official" theater. Parenti also introduced Fo into the Italian State Broadcasting Company, RAI, where Fo performed his monologues on the radio program *Chicchirichi* that year.

Also in 1951 he met a young actress, Franca Rame, whose beauty he had admired on the pages of the magazine *Le Ore*. She was born to a theatrical family: her father, Domenico Rame, was the lead actor and *capocomico* (a sort of combined artistic director and stage director) of an itinerant theater company that performed in towns and villages of the Padana Valley in Northern Italy. Although he is a minor figure in the panorama of contemporary national Italian theater, he was so widely beloved by the local public (mainly for his personal generosity and for the assistance he always gave striking workers and the oppressed in general) that, in Lombardy, Franca Rame is still referred to as "Domenico Rame's daughter," even though she is an international celebrity on her own.

Fo and Rame shared common views on political and social matters; both had socialist parents, and they were also convinced of the need for the artist to become socially engaged. Yet, even if they embraced Marxism, they never believed that art, and particularly theater, should be a pure means of political propaganda. This stance caused the couple many problems when they ventured together in the worlds of cinema, theater, and television, because in addition to the foreseeable attacks from the conservatives, the neofascists, and the clergy, they had to face attacks from the most dogmatic wings of the Left as well. The two became engaged in 1951. Rame had to take the initiative, because Fo, in spite of any encouragement on her part, proved terribly shy and tended to avoid the young woman. The two got married in 1954, and the following year Jacopo, their only son, was born.

In 1953 and 1954, working in collaboration with Parenti and Giustino Durano, Fo was the author and actor of the shows *Il dito nell'occhio* (1953, A Finger in the Eye) and *I sani da legare* (1954, Fit to Be Tied Up), which were staged at the Piccolo Teatro of Milan. *Il dito nell'occhio* is composed of twenty-one sketches on the history of humanity. It is a reexamination of historical events by focusing on common people rather than on the traditional historical characters. For instance, the sketch on the construction of Cheops's pyramids emphasizes the thousands of slaves who died in the effort, while another sketch attributes the idea of the Trojan horse to an unknown soldier and not to the mythical figure of Ulysses. *I sani da legare* opened a year after the critical and commercial success of *Il dito nell'occhio*. This second play consists of twenty-four sketches about life in Milan, even though the name of the city is never mentioned in the play. It depicts the underdogs of Milan and offers a strong political satire against the governing Christian Democratic Party. *I sani da legare* was always sold out, even if staged during the summer months, a period that, traditionally in Italy, is not favorable to theatrical events. Both shows experienced censorship interference.

In 1955 Fo and Rame worked in movie production in Rome. Fo became a screenwriter and worked for many productions, having signed a contract with the Dino de Laurentis Film Company. In 1956 he was the co-author and lead actor of *Lo svitato* (The Duffer), a motion picture directed by Lizzani. It is the story of Achille, ironically nicknamed "pié veloce" (swift foot), an errand man for an important newspaper. He longs to become a journalist, and in order to achieve this end, he continuously invents news from which he draws scoops. Even though this movie established Fo's national fame as an actor, it cannot be said to be fully successful from an artistic point of view, as Fo's personal and improvisational acting style was at odds with the movie medium.

After this experience, he collaborated in the screenwriting of three more motion pictures in 1957: *Souvenir d'Italie* (Souvenir from Italy) and *Nata di marzo* (Born in March), directed by Antonio Pietrangeli, and *Rascel-Fifì*, directed by Guido Leoni. The results of this activity were of mediocre quality. Moreover, Rame grew increasingly dissatisfied with the cinematic medium and urged Fo to return to the stage. In 1959 the Compagnia Fo-Rame was established, and for the next nine years the company opened the theater season at the Odeon in Milan with a new play or show. In addition to taking part in her husband's comedies, Rame took charge of the administration responsibilities of the company, while Fo focused more on playwriting and acting.

Fo's activity as a dramatist had begun in the 1950s, when he wrote seven farcical texts that were collected and performed later under two titles, *Ladri, manichini e donne nude* (1958, Thieves, Dummies and Naked Women) and *Comica finale* (1958, Final Gag). The plots were inspired by real life but evolved into paradoxical and ultimately surreal situations. He wrote his first three "regular" plays between 1959 and 1961: *Gli arcangeli non giocano a flipper* (1959; translated as *Archangels Don't Play Pinball*, 1987), *Aveva due pistole con gli occhi bianchi e neri* (1960, He Had Two Pistols with White and Black Eyes), and *Chi ruba un piede è fortunato in amore* (1961, He Who Steals a Foot Is Lucky in Love). The first play, written for twelve actors who play more than forty roles, is about a gang of scoundrels, always ready to steal, blackmail, and swindle while making silly jokes. The work is noticeable for the songs commenting on the action of the main character, Il Lungo (The Long Man), who is in love with La Bionda (The Blonde). The couple celebrates a fake marriage, much in the style of Luigi Pirandello's *Ma non è una cosa seria* (1919, But It's Nothing Serious), a marriage from which a variety of misunderstandings will stem. Echoes of the European theatrical avant-garde experimentations of the beginning of the twentieth century can also be perceived in this play.

Aveva due pistole con gli occhi bianchi e neri is similar in structure to the former play but tends to evoke more the tones and atmospheres of black comedy. The protagonist is a man who has lost his memory; a host of physicians studies him assiduously in order to determine whether his forgetfulness is caused by a physical problem or is merely a psychological state. Allusions to the comedies of Plautus and Molière are apparent in the text, especially when the protagonist's doppelgänger enters. The "double" is a fugitive gangster, Giovanni Gallina, who controls the activities of a vast organization of pilferers, petty swindlers, and pickpockets. The comedy is built totally on paradoxes and misunderstandings, especially when the group of thieves decides to form a cooperative in order to work with better conditions. This cooperative creates a crisis within the state institutions as it undermines all the jobs and careers (such as police officers, lawyers, judges, and crime journalists) that rely on illegal activities to survive. The comedy reaches its dénouement when the man with amnesia turns out to be a priest and the deputy director of the prison from which the gangster escaped, and who has tried to gather the bewildered people who surround him in order to redeem them. In this play Fo relies heavily, for the first time, on a Chorus, which comments, with fifteen songs, on the action taking place on stage.

Paolo Puppa, in his *Il teatro di Dario Fo: Dalla scena alla piazza* (1978, Dario Fo's Theater: From the Stage to the Piazza), regarded the third comedy, *Chi ruba un piede è fortunato in amore,* as the most bookish of Fo's plays. What strikes one immediately are the reduced number of characters in the play (only eight) and the absence of a Chorus. In *Chi ruba un piede è fortunate in amore* the myth of Apollo and Daphne, deprived of any classical dignity and cast in a farcical light that stresses the popular and possibly vulgar developments of the theme, triggers a freewheeling succession of misunderstandings, gags, and misrepresentations. Daphne is a nymph who is turned into a plant by her own father to prevent Apollo from having sex with her, and Mercury is on the whole a debauchee and a protector of thieves and schemers. The plot involves stealing a foot from a statue of Mercury in a museum and burying it in a building site to blackmail the construction company. (In Italy, when archaeological remains—even if not of great importance—are found at a building site, work can be stopped for years.) The play then becomes a bitter satire of the Italian ruling elite of the 1960s, a world of shrewd and dishonest politicians and businessmen, constantly prone to corruption, all of whom resort to Mafia-like methods in order to raise more money to obtain more power. These early plays represents Fo's willingness to find a personal and original voice in the theatrical panorama of Italian playwriting of the 1960s.

By 1962 Fo had earned such a steady reputation in the Italian world of entertainment that he was asked to direct and host *Canzonissima,* a musical contest associated with the Italian national lottery, which was broadcast on prime time on Saturdays when only one state-owned television channel (RAI 1) existed. It was the most important and expensive RAI variety show; the offer was not only a sign of appreciation for his skills as a comedian and stage writer but also an acknowledgment of his popularity and commercial success. Fo and Rame took the opportunity to spice up this traditional "light entertainment for families" with a heavy dose of political satire, depicting the lives of commoners in their sketches and alluding repeatedly to deeds and misdeeds of the Italian ruling class. The show stirred huge controversies among the public and the press, and censorship was often solicited by conservative and clerical areas of Italian society. Fo was also sued for obscene speech, because during one sketch he hinted at (but did not actually pronounce) the most common Italian slang word for "penis." Another controversial sketch about a journalist killed by the Mafia led some politicians to protest, while Fo and Rame received death threats. RAI intervened by placing the couple under police protection and by cutting and censoring the program script. When the cuts became regular practice, Fo and Rame left the show after thirteen episodes, and the Italian Actors' Union urged its members to refuse to replace them. Fo and Rame did not reappear in any RAI program until 1977 but were at this point considered martyrs of a sort of Italian McCarthyism, which helped increase their popularity throughout Italy.

They continued their work in Teatro Odeon in Milan, and a year after the *Canzonissima* incident they staged a new play, *Isabella, tre caravelle e un cacciaballe* (1963, Isabella, Three Sailing Ships and a Con Man), which angered political right-wing groups and caused violent attacks against the Odeon. To protect the couple, the Italian Communist party supplied bodyguards and security for the theater. *Isabella, tre caravelle e un cacciaballe* is the story of an actor who has been sentenced to death for having staged a forbidden play, Fernando de Rojas's *Celestina* (circa 1495). The plot seems to advance toward a happy ending as, while the preparations for the execution go on, the convict is promised a pardon if he and his company will agree to stage a play about Queen Isabella and Christopher Columbus. So the scaffold is turned into a stage, that is, a place of freedom, but only for a short time, because as the performance ends, the promise is not kept, and the execution takes place. It is obvious that the play recalls Fo's experience with *Canzo-*

nissima at RAI and comments heavily on Italian censorship practices.

In September 1964, with the play *Settimo: Ruba un po' meno* (Seventh: Steal a Little Less), Fo once again dealt with a theme that had always attracted his interest: political corruption. The play was written by Fo specifically for his wife, as the protagonist is a woman. The action starts in a depositary of coffins at City Hall, where four undertakers have just laid a coffin on a catafalque. One of the undertakers is a woman, and the action ensues from her naiveté and gullibility: she is led to believe she possesses special paranormal powers that allow her to talk to the dead, and also that the cemetery is going to be moved because of land speculation on construction developments. The audience soon discovers, however, that the joke played on the woman is in fact real and that corrupt public officials are making illegal deals to have the cemetery moved. The comedy is a pretext to expose the problem of corruption of a political class always ready to betray its public mandate for personal interests.

The next year Fo wrote *La colpa è sempre del diavolo* (1965, It's Always the Devil's Fault), a drama set in Lombardy between the end of the thirteenth century and the first half of the fourteenth, at the time of the prosecution of the Catari, a group of heretics who, in addition to a theological contrast with the official Church, fought for a radical renewal of medieval society, calling for the abolition of privileges held by feudal lords, kings, and the Church itself. Fo was deeply interested in Middle Ages culture, namely in the conflict between the hegemonic culture of the upper classes and the lower-class culture of the common folk, which found its spokesman in the jester. Fo has always perceived himself as a modern jester, one who has self-ascribed the mission to denounce, by means of jokes and mockery, the embezzlements and ideological falsifications to which the modern plebeians (the working class, the unemployed, the poor, women, all the downtrodden of the capitalist era) are exposed. The main character of *La colpa è sempre del diavolo* is Brancaleone, a minor but sentimental devil/dwarf. He is bizarre in his use of speech and deprived of any sort of supernatural aura. He enters the body of the female protagonist, Amalusanta, to achieve his purposes. In this play Fo relies largely on quick-changing disguises and fast rhythm. The action develops without any delays until the farcical ending, when the heretics/communards rebel, claiming their long-denied rights. This play did not receive positive reviews from the critics; as Piero Novelli wrote in *Gazzetta del Popolo* (11 September 1965), it was so overloaded with gags and scene changes that it created genuine confusion on stage.

The political events of 1968 brought major changes to Fo's activity. Events such as the Cultural Revolution in China and the crushing of the so-called Prague Spring period in Czechoslovakia raised much debate among the traditional Italian and European Left. In Italy the leading international role of the Soviet Union Communist Party was questioned, and many members and supporters of the Italian Communist Party (the second political party in the country and the largest communist party in the world outside the Eastern Bloc) abandoned the organization and formed groups and movements whose stances ranged from a strong call for radical reforms in the framework of a "socialismo dal volto umano" (socialism with a human face), to be pursued in a dialectic relationship with the parliamentary area of the Left, to revolutionary projects in overt opposition to the Italian Communist Party, seen as a traitor of the working class and an ally of the bourgeoisie. Though these movements remained a minority in the panorama of the Italian Left, they were extremely active and attracted many trade unionists who were well rooted in the workplace and many important intellectuals as well; moreover, the "New Left," with its idealistic vision of a more just world, naturally exerted a strong appeal for youth. In these years the Italian Communist Party changed its strategy and formulated the "linea del compromesso storico" (line of historical compromise): that is, the proposal of an agreement between the Socialists and the Christian Democrats to govern the country together.

Fo never became a member of the Italian Communist Party, while Rame did, even though he considered these new non-aligned movements with the utmost interest. Fo, however, regarded the Communist Party as a political landmark that could not be relinquished in the historical process of emancipation of the working class. For this reason he decided to start cooperating with ARCI (the Communist Party association for recreation and culture, counting about one million members), and, after dissolving the Compagnia Fo-Rame, he founded the Compagnia Nuova Scena. Thus, the traditional theater halls with their red velvet armchairs were abandoned, and the new company began touring Italy and foreign countries to stage their works in places that reflected its social engagement and its popular bias: circuses, squares, culture clubs and associations (especially the Case del Popolo, sites managed by the communist area trade unions, where the workers could meet, socialize, and discuss political issues), university assembly halls, and factories occupied by striking workers.

During this period Fo staged two new plays, *La signora è da buttare* (1967, Throw the Lady Out) and *Grande pantomima con bandiere e pupazzi grandi, piccoli e medi* (1968, Grand Pantomime with Flags and Small, Middle-

Sized and Large Puppets). The action of both plays is set in circuses, and Fo took full advantage of all the technical and scenic solutions offered by this kind of setting. The lady who should be thrown away is America, with her capitalism, consumerism, racism, drugs, cult for technology, and, most of all, warfare and imperialism. The main target of Fo's satirical attacks was the Vietnam War, seen as a sort of epitome of the (organized) aggression natural to the capitalistic system. Comments made in the play about John F. Kennedy's assassination were considered so outrageous, especially in the United States, that President Lyndon Johnson and American authorities denied Fo a visa to enter the country, a prohibition that remained until 1986. *Grande pantomima con bandiere e pupazzi grandi, piccoli e medi* deals with the theme of the continuity of fascism in the structure of contemporary bourgeois state democracies. This popular farce evolves gradually into political invective against the bourgeoisie, the military, and the Catholic hierarchy. At center stage Fo placed a giant puppet that vomits kings, queens, generals, bishops, and other "authorities" symbolizing the occult powers governing Italy and Europe. With this play Fo moved away from popular farce and progressed decidedly into the realm of pure political farce. He politicized his theater even more in this period, not only through his plays but also by choosing to abandon the traditional theater circuit and present his works in the streets and political halls throughout the country. His theater became didactic.

A crucial year for Fo's art and career was 1969, when he completed the first version of *Mistero buffo* (Comic Mystery), considered his masterpiece, in which he proved both his full maturity as a playwright and his sensitivity and virtuosity as an interpreter. *Mistero buffo*, as the title suggests, is a sort of medieval mystery play organized as a series of monologues centering on episodes adapted from both the Canonic and Apocryphal Gospels, in addition to other literary and popular sources. The point of view is that of a jester, who offers a lively, comic, and often bitterly satiric account of facts surrounding Jesus Christ's life and other topics connected to both Christendom and Catholic religion. The play consists of several parts: "Lauda dei battuti" (The Hymn of the Flagellants), "La strage degli innocenti" (The Slaughter of the Innocents), "Resurrezione di Lazzaro" (The Resurrection of Lazarus), "Passione" (The Passion), "Il matto e la morte" (Death and the Madman), "Moralità del cieco e dello storpio" (The Morality Play of the Blind Man and the Cripple), "Maria viene a conoscere della condanna imposta al figlio" (Mary Learns of Her Son's Sentence), "La crocifissione" (The Crucifixion), "Bonifacio VIII," "Le nozze di Cana" (The Marriage at Cana), "La nascita del giullare" (The Birth of the Jester), "La nascita del villano" (The Birth of the Villain), and "Gioco del matto sotto la croce" (The Mad Man beneath the Cross), some of which were added to *Mistero buffo* over the years in the many revisions Fo has made of this work.

The most important feature of the play is its language, an amusing and charming mix of dialects of Northern Italy, giving way to a strange language that never existed as natural speech but is nonetheless quite comprehensible to any Italian speaker. This result was achieved though some linguistic expedients, such as reiterating the most obscure terms in several different dialects, making the actor's speech rich, redundant, and spectacular (much in the style of François Rabelais's *Gargantua* [1534], an obvious cultural reference for *Mistero buffo*) and allowing the audience to catch words and phrases that make the general meaning perfectly clear. This practice also reflects the working reality of Middle Ages jesters who, traveling from one place to another in a time when differences between local dialects were far deeper than today (typically, a strict dialect could not be understood by people living just a few miles away), were forced to resort to this linguistic mixture to communicate with their audiences; a trace of this jester-like language can still be found among circus artists, especially clowns. Most of the capacity of the play to convey meaning relied on Fo's superb acting skills in mimicry and gesture. Between the scenes taken from the Gospels, parts in the Italian language are interpolated: in these segments the actor covers themes in some way connected to the previous or next scene, extending topics by commenting on or introducing the following action; or he deals with recent events thematically linked to the representation, by partly improvising; or he comments on art, theater, literature, history, in a scholarly way, in order to challenge official and traditional positions and interpretations.

In *Mistero buffo,* Fo also resorted largely to *grammelot* (or *gramelot*), a way of speaking that reproduces the tone and rhythm typical of a specific language or dialect, but is made up almost entirely of invented words; sometimes, no existing idiom is imitated, and *grammelot* becomes a pure sequence of expressive sounds, such as noises, animal sounds, roars, cries, gurgles, or mumbling. The message will be understood anyway, if the actor knows how to manage this difficult technique. In the past *grammelot* was part of the technical toolbox of any comedian, and Fo's example revitalized the tradition among many Italian actors. The revolutionary origin of *grammelot* is apparent: it is a method to communicate in an unequivocal way ideas that cannot be expressly said, because a meaningless sequence of sounds, separated from its theatrical context of gestures and facial expressions, cannot and will not be accepted as evidence in a court case.

Mistero buffo was attacked on grounds of alleged irreverence and blasphemy. But Fo's mockery and satire are directed against those who use religion as an instrument of power and oppression, not against religion in itself. Above all, the attitude of the playwright toward the person of Jesus Christ (whatever Fo's personal stance on religious matters is) is one of respect and sympathy: the presence of the Savior, continuously evoked in the background of the action in the various episodes, emerges as a symbol of human aspiration to a more just world. Moreover, Fo's approach to holy texts did not differ much from those of distinguished churchmen such as John Wycliffe, Jan Hus, or Martin Luther.

The most famous episode, "Bonifacio VIII," is a hard-hitting attack against the papacy and its temporal power, which has as its site Rome, defined in the episode as "the great beast." As the pope is getting dressed with all his ornaments and jewels, symbols of his terrestrial power, Christ arrives looking like a poor beggar, representing the other, more authentic side of the Church. Christ is at odds with Boniface VIII, who at first pretends to be kind toward Christ, offering him his mantle and jewels. Christ sees through his hypocrisy: Boniface is being kind only hoping to be rewarded for his gesture, and he is sent away with a tremendous kick.

The 1970s were an agitated period for Italy and for Fo as well. He soon became at odds with the Communist Party leadership, and his collaboration with ARCI was discontinued. Also, the Compagnia Nuova Scena was dissolved, and he and Rame started their third theater group, the Collettivo Teatrale La Comune. This initiative was conducted with Avanguardia Operaia, the best-organized group of the New Left, which was well established in the factories of Northern Italy and had tens of thousands of members having an active and qualified role in workplaces and trade unions. Fo's productions became more linked to contemporary events and more inspired by militant political attitudes. In addition to *Mistero buffo,* two pieces reflecting Fo's strong political engagement were staged in 1969: *L'operaio conosce 300 parole, il padrone 1000: per questo lui è il padrone* (The Worker Knows 300 Words, the Boss 1000: That's Why He's the Boss), a work based on Italian politician Antonio Gramsci's conception of culture as an instrument for economical and social emancipation; and *Il funerale del padrone* (The Boss's Death), set in a factory occupied by laid-off workers. The central themes of *L'operaio conosce 300 parole, il padrone 1000: per questo lui è il padrone* are culture and knowledge. The protagonists are a group of workers who are dismantling the library in a Casa del Popolo in order for the space to become a recreation hall. The books are put in cases that look like coffins and brought down to the cellar. Suddenly, however, the voices of Vladimir Lenin, Mao Tse-tung, Gramsci, and the Apostles are heard, and these historical characters appear onstage to portray significant episodes of their lives. This play is an invocation to the working class to gain as much knowledge as possible; for Fo, knowledge is the only means to attain freedom. In *Il funerale del padrone* a group of laid-off workers decides to stage the factory owner's funeral in the commedia dell'arte tradition. Fo's writing in this period changed once again as it became less farcical and popular and more politically operative, in the sense that he wanted not only to stimulate reflection on social and political events but also, and more importantly for Fo, to promote political action. Fo's new aesthetic was that of the agitprop method; that is, employing simple and direct language onstage and having the spectators participate in the action of the play.

A dramatic incident at the end of 1969 marked Fo both personally and artistically. A bomb killed nineteen people in a bank in Piazza Fontana, Milan; this brutal anonymous attack started what became known as "the season of bombs," and the word "stragismo" (slaughter policy) made its entry into the vocabulary of the Italian language. The Right and the Left accused each other of being responsible for the increasing number of bomb attacks, killings of activists, and other violence. Rightists argued that the opposite front aimed to create an atmosphere of confusion and mistrust toward the established order to promote an armed Communist revolution; leftists thought that terror and confusion were orchestrated by the conservative establishment itself, in order to justify social antidemocratic measures and, ultimately, the coming back to some form of overtly Fascist regime. Fo was among the staunchest supporters of the thesis of an antidemocratic conspiracy managed by the group of people with leading institutional roles. In 1970 he staged *Morte accidentale di un anarchico* (Accidental Death of an Anarchist), inspired by the Piazza Fontana incident and centering on the death of the anarchist Pino Pinelli at the police headquarters of Milan in 1969. It is believed that the authorities tried to frame the anarchists in order to pass restrictive laws and that Pinelli, who allegedly committed suicide by jumping from the fourth floor of police headquarters, was actually thrown out, thus murdered. This play, like the others produced in this period, were frequently revised by Fo in order to keep pace with the continuously evolving situation: for instance, Pinelli's death gave way to a series of bomb attacks and retaliations as well as controversies regarding trials and convictions connected to those events. These debates are still quite bitter.

Another play Fo extensively revised is the *Grande pantomima con bandiere e pupazzi grandi, piccoli e medi,* staged with the new title of *Morte e resurrezione di un pupazzo* (Death and Resurrection of a Puppet), in response to a

Two of the twenty-five illustrations that Fo distributed to accompany his Nobel lecture. The one on the left reads: "Personally I Owe Much to Master Blowers; Crazily; Explosive"; the one on the right reads: "Thunderous and Solemn the Greeting Arises; Shakespeare; Moliere; Both Disparaged by Know-It-Alls and Wise-Guys" (translated by Faust F. Pauluzzi; provided by Donato Santeramo; courtesy of Dario Fo).

vicious attack in *L'Unità* (the official newspaper of the Italian Communist Party), which in one of its columns had defined Fo as a *pupazzo impazzito* (a maddened puppet). At this point he was attacked by both the Left and the Right, not to mention the clergy. His only solace was that his shows were followed by thousands of devoted spectators.

In *Morte e resurrezione di un pupazzo*, Palmiro Togliatti (second secretary general of the Italian Communist Party and the object of a sort of worship for Party activists) is the target of heavy mockery and parody. Fo seemed, in this period, to be attracted to the formula of the "guerrilla theater," marked by a strong interest in international revolutionary movements; in 1972 he produced *Fedayn*, a play focused on the condition of Palestinians, in which he brought onstage nine actual members of the Palestine Liberation Organization (PLO), who recited monologues and sang songs mostly in Arabic. In the play he also tried to present the PLO members as a continuation of the Italian partisans who fought Nazism. For *Fedayn*, Fo incorporated theater, movies (screens were set up on the stage), and slides.

The plays that followed, *Ordine! Per Dio.ooo.ooo.ooo* (1972, Order, By God!) and *Pum, Pum! Chi è? La polizia!* (1972, Knock, Knock! Who's There? Police!), are both about police repression and brutality. Fo was accused of contempt for the armed forces because of the poster promoting the show *Pum, Pum! Chi è? La polizia!* This play is once again about the Piazza Fontana slaughter and Pinelli's death. The work opens with a voice stressing that what is about to be seen is not fantasy but reality. The action of the play takes place entirely in the office of an executive bureaucrat of the Department of "Reserved Affairs" of the Ministry of Internal Affairs. The executive is seen at work while he creates false evidence in order to accuse and incriminate the anarchists for the massacre and to conceal any involvement by government authorities and military generals in the terrorist action. The responsibility of the slaughter fell on the Left; Pinelli's alibi was undercut, and moderate left-wingers were arrested and presented as terrorists. The play can be considered a pamphlet spectacle and a protest spectacle. More than thirty years have passed since the bomb explosion in Piazza Fontana, and still no one knows why this deadly terrorist attack was carried out.

Late in 1972, political differences with Avanguardia Operaia led Fo to discontinue the collaboration with La Comune. During the previous two years, La Comune had grown to a nationwide cultural organization, with about ninety seats and seven hundred thousand members, becoming a serious competitor for the associations of the same nature that operated under the control of the main Italian political parties. In 1973 Fo's company moved to Cinema Rossini in Milan and sustained raids and censorship. On 8 March 1973 another episode had a profound effect on Fo and Rame: she was kidnapped, beaten, and raped by a gang of neofascists. Yet, only two months later she was onstage again. Also in 1973 *Guerra di popolo in Cile* (A People's War in Chile), a work about the rebellion against the Chilean military government, inspired by the coup that overthrew elected Socialist president Salvador Allende that year, was staged at the Teatro Palladio of Milan. In the play it is suggested that the tactic used in Chile was also being used in Italy to overturn democratic practices. Fo was arrested (but soon released) when he tried to prevent the police from stopping the performance. Later in the year, Fo, Rame, and the members of their theater company occupied an old abandoned building in Milan called Palazzina Liberty. After completely restoring it, including its theater, they opened the new structure in 1974 with *Non si paga! Non si paga!* (translated as *We Can't Pay? We Won't Pay!* 1978).

This play, about a tax protest by housewives, features one of Fo's most famous gags: two women who steal regularly from a supermarket, concealing items under their overcoats as if they were pregnant, suddenly find themselves surrounded by the people in the supermarket when a stolen bottle of mineral water breaks, alarming everyone into believing there is going to be an imminent birth. In the play the idea of "prezzo politico" (political price) is also introduced. The women enter the supermarket and decide at first what they feel is the right price is for each item (half of what is on the price tag) and later decide not to pay at all. It would seem the play inspired many Italians, as for a period of time it was common practice to apply "political prices" in supermarkets, butcher shops, and cinemas in several major Italian cities. Indro Mondanelli, editor of the newspaper *Il Giornale*, called for Fo's arrest because, according to Mondanelli, Fo had instigated the thieves.

The two plays that followed were linked to themes of contemporary interest: *Il Fanfani rapito* (1975, Fanfani Kidnapped) was written against the background of the political election that year, and *La marijuana della mamma è la più bella* (1976, Mother's Marijuana Is the Best) deals with the increasing problem of drug use among young working-class Italians. For both plays, Fo used a scenario, a basic written plot in the commedia dell'arte style, which was extended evening after evening with improvised components. The first play, written in only eight days just before a general election, is a work of political fantasy, being centered on the imaginary kidnapping of senator Amintore Fanfani, an historical leader of the Christian Democratic Party who had been prime minister several times. The crime is perpetrated by gangsters hired by Giulio Andreotti, a party fellow and rival hoping to win more votes for the Christian Democratic Party with this scheme. The setting is surreal, a sort of dream dimension, and the action is a sequence of grotesque and exhilarating scenes connected to the complex political situation of the period.

La marijuana della mamma è la più bella is simpler in structure, for it focuses on a single theme, and the action is set in a house where a family—a grandfather, a mother, and her drug-addicted son—has transformed their living room into a cannabis plantation. The opening scene, centered on the description of the "home plantation," is quite funny, with the presentation of the extemporary greenhouse equipment: wet sheets hanging from the ceiling, a large fan, and a hair dryer provide the plants with an ideal humidity level, while lamps and other common house tools are put to similar use. Fo uses the family microcosm to present a proletarian story and to expose major and minor drug traffickers connected to organized crime and, most of all, the hypocrisy of religious and law-enforcement establishments in regard to the drug problem. The moral of the story is that the rich consume drugs, while the working class is consumed by drugs.

Toward the end of the 1970s Fo began to write for and with Rame a series of one-act plays and monologues about the female condition. In 1977 *Tutta casa, letto e chiesa* (All House, Bed and Church; translated as *Adult Orgasm Escapes from the Zoo*, 1985), which consecrated Rame as a great actress, was staged. Her participation in the writing process of this play was significant: she worked for months collecting material, selecting and adapting it for the stage. The work consists of five monologues by five different women. The choice of using monologues was practical, as it allowed the spectacle to be performed easily in factories and neighborhood social centers. The first monologue, "Una donna tutta sola" (A Woman Alone), is the story of a housewife as it emerges from her conversations with a neighbor living across the street, to whom she describes the solitude, hardships, and unhappiness of a woman who cannot understand male logic but who, in the meantime, is too discouraged to do anything to change her life. Her husband often beats her (saying that he does it because he loves her) or uses her as a sexual object to satisfy his bestial instincts, while she does not respond and remains stiff as a statue during intercourse. What emerges is a theme often confronted by Fo and Rame in this series of works: female frigidity induced by male oppression.

Another monologue, "La mamma fricchettona" (A Hippie Mother), is centered on a leftist/punk housewife trying to find her son, a drug addict who had run away from home. The segment begins with the mother hiding in a church in order to escape the police who are after her. She enters a confessional, where she explains to the priest how she gave up her life for her family. She has disguised herself as a gypsy in order to infiltrate the environment of drug users, where she hopes to find her son. The disguise, however, has made her a new person, as she is seen in a different light. Once she is found by her son, who in the meantime has cleaned up his act, she is unable to return home to play the role of a mother again, as she has adopted a new identity.

The theme of the ways that women experience physical love is tackled by Fo once again in "Abbiano tutte le stessa storia" (We All Have the Same Story), whose protagonist, by interrupting intercourse with her boyfriend, tries to get from her partner a *rapporto* (in Italian, *rapporto* can mean both intercourse and relationship) that is different than usual. This series of one-act plays written for Rame were highly successful, even though Rame stated on opening night that "L'unico limite è che il testo sia stato scritto prevalentemente da Dario Fo, il quale, essendo inequivocabilmente un uomo e nonostante tutti i libri e le opere che gli ho procurato, non ha potuto penetrare fino in fondo le contraddizioni, le umiliazioni, le vessazioni a cui noi siamo sottoposte" (Most of the writing was done by Dario Fo, which is perhaps the only flaw of the work as he is unequivocally a man and notwithstanding all the books and works I have procured him, he was unable to penetrate the contradictions, humiliations and harassments to which we [women] are subject). Notwithstanding this flaw, *Tutta casa, letto e chiesa* was staged all over Europe and in Canada and the United States as well.

In 1976 the new managing board of RAI realized, in the wake of Fo's increasing international fame, that he had been prevented from working on television for far too long. They invited him to tape a program, and in 1977 he accepted but demanded the recording take place at Palazzina Liberty in front of a live audience. The program *Il teatro di Dario Fo*, which included four plays he had written, was a hit; but when the latest version of *Mistero buffo* was presented, a Vatican spokesmen described it as blasphemous, and Italian right-wingers protested. The series was watched by thousands of Italians, and millions tuned in to watch *Mistero buffo*.

As the cooperation in playwriting with Rame had been so fruitful, Fo continued the experience, producing more monologues for actors, such as *Storia della tigre* (translated as *The Tale of a Tiger: A Comic Monologue*, 1984), *Il primo miracolo di Gesù Bambino* (The First Miracle of Jesus as a Child), *Dedalo e Icaro,* and *Il sacrifico di Isacco* (Isaac's Sacrifice), all written between 1978 and 1980 and collected in *Storia della tigre e altre storie* (The Tale of a Tiger and Other Tales) in 1980. These plays are based on the use of metaphor and allegory to convey Fo's message. *Storia della tigre* depicts a soldier wounded during the Chinese Long March who is rescued by a tiger that gives him shelter in her den and takes care of him and of her cub. The man remains with the tigers for some time, and when he departs, the animals follow him and eventually defend him and some farmhands from the repression of a tyrant. The story is based on a Chinese myth, and, as Fo explained, the play is an allegory on the necessity to never give up class struggle. The second play is also metaphorical. It is the story of the infant Jesus, the son of an immigrant southern family who is shunned and mocked by his peers, who call him Palestine. In this story Jesus performs his first miracle, giving life to clay statues in order to have playmates.

In 1978 Fo completed the third version of *Mistero buffo;* he also rewrote and directed *La storia di un soldato* (Story of a Soldier), based on Igor Stravinsky's *The Soldier's Tale* (1918). Later, he also adapted and directed operas from Giocchino Rossini.

Fo could not avoid being interested in the Moro Affair, probably the most shocking political crime in the history of the Italian Republic: in March 1978 a commando of the Red Brigades (a clandestine revolutionary Communist organization) kidnapped Aldo Moro, premier and leader of the Christian Democratic Party. For ransom the kidnappers requested that several political prisoners and common criminals be freed from Italy's prisons. State authorities and Moro's party friends refused to negotiate, and the statesman was murdered after being imprisoned for two months. Many thought Moro had been cynically sacrificed for political reasons, but some went so far as to presume the existence of connections between state authorities and the kidnappers. *La tragedia di Aldo Moro* (The Tragedy of Aldo Moro), published in the periodical *Quotidiano dei lavoratori* in June 1979, embraced the latter thesis; it is an intensely dramatic work, based on the letters Moro wrote from the place where he was kept. In spite of the interest of the theme and the considerable artistic value of the text, the play has never been performed publicly.

In 1981 Fo wrote *Clacson, trombette e pernacchi* (Trumpets and Raspberries; translated as *About Face: A Farce,* 1983), again drawing from Plautus and Molière the motif of the doppelgänger. In this play the man who has trouble with his double is Giovanni Agnelli, also known as "L'Avvocato" (The Lawyer), the richest and most influential Italian entrepreneur, whose family owned FIAT, Italy's biggest car manufacturer. A worker prevents the "false Agnelli" from being kidnapped; the attempted kidnapping will however set in motion all Italian Intelligence Units and special police corps, giving way to a series of humorous situations. Also in 1981 Fo created *L'opera dello sghignazzo* (The Laugh Opera), inspired by John Gay's *The Beggar's Opera* (1728). The following year he staged *Il fabulazzo osceno* (1982, Obscene Fable), a play structured according to the model of *Mistero buffo* in which a single actor alternates fixed texts with partially improvised comments on obscenity. The point of the play is that the concept of obscenity does not coincide with transgression but rather with prohibition, in the sense that everything that is forbidden becomes obscene.

In 1984 American authorities suspended their veto on Fo's entry into the country, and two years later he was eventually free to tour the United States, presenting his works and lecturing in many theaters and universities. Despite worldwide acclaim, there was still trouble for Fo. In 1983 Italian censors decided that *Coppia aperta* (translated as *The Open Couple: A One-Act Comedy,* 1984), another play focusing on the female condition and male oppression (even when masked as open-mindedness), should be restricted to audiences over the age of eighteen. That same year, while touring in Argentina, some performances were disturbed by right-wing and Christian conservative youths who threw stones at the theater hall windows and even threw a tear-gas grenade onto the stage.

In 1986 Fo wrote *Hellequin Harlekin Arlekin: Arlecchino,* as the result of a workshop on Harlequin that became a show; Fo's Harlequin was quite different from Giorgio Strehler's insofar as the use of sources was different. In fact, Fo sought Harlequin's precursors in the tradition of the popular commedia dell'arte character Zannis and not in the codified characters of Carlo Goldoni's theater as Strehler had. In 1989 *Il Papa e la strega* (translated as *The Pope and the Witch,* 1990) was staged. Fo imagines that a reactionary pope has been struck by acute crippling lumbago (in Italian: "colpo della strega," literally "witches' stroke"), and, in order to be cured, he needs the witch's help. The witch has actually been given the task to cure him from serious mental torment, as the pope is haunted by the idea of holding in his arms millions of Third World children who are starving to death. From the encounter with the magic healer, the pope's conversion will take place. He will thus promulgate an encyclical letter in which he supports drug legalization, the use of contraceptives, and, most important, the return of the Church to its original theological poverty. Beyond the pleasures of the paradoxical, the play can be seen as a harsh criticism toward the authorities managing the centers for drug addiction, prevention, and care, and the necessity of legalizing drug use is proposed as a solution to the addiction problem.

After addressing the devastating illegal drug problem, Fo turned to the issue of AIDS, with *Zitti! Stiamo precipitando!* (Quiet! We Are All Falling!) in 1990. The opening act is set in an asylum for the insane, where the inmates are playing war games that recall the first Gulf War operations. The patients are in fact being used as guinea pigs to test new medicines. The main character is an engineer, an erotomaniac (he can never get enough sex) who is quite frustrated. He fears AIDS to such an extent that he has friends' and relatives' blood analyzed (blood samples are drawn by trained mosquitoes). The patients in the asylum, following the injection of an experimental bacillus, seem to have developed AIDS immunity; as it appears that this immunity can be sexually transmitted, a therapy based on intensification of sexual activity is realized. The second act takes place in the engineer's grand country villa, where his wife and daughter, with their respective lovers, are betting on how many people will be murdered daily by the Mafia. This play can be defined as a grotesque situation comedy, in which a concoction of themes is dealt with in a way that enhances the monstrous features of power, even if people have become accustomed to them to a point that they have become unaware of their true nature.

Between 1991 and 1993 Fo wrote *Johan Padan a la descoverta de le Americhe* (translated as *Johan Padan and the Discovery of the Americas,* 2001), which was later adapted as a cartoon, and a performance titled *Dario Fo recita Ruzzante* (1993, Dario Fo Recites Ruzzante). The latter is an adaptation of a collection of works by Angelo Beolco (known as "Il Ruzzante"), an anticlassicist actor and author of the sixteenth century, translated into many modern Northern Italian dialects. The model is the same as *Mistero buffo* and *Fabulazzo osceno:* no theater decor, and one actor who performs a text or lectures or makes improvised digressions on recent events. One of the main themes of the work is war, seen from the perspective of the commoner who finds himself involved by force in a situation he fears and hates. In 1993 Fo also wrote *Mamma! I Sanculotti!* (Mama! The Sans-Culottes!), a metaphorical play that is based on an actual event, an attempted coup d'état in Italy by the military supported by sections of the Secret Service. The purpose of the play was to unveil the schemes of the so-called diverted intelligence services (parts of Italian intelligence suspected of having pursued antidemocratic aims outside institutional control) and other "Italian mysteries" such as bomb attacks, exploding cars, inexplicable fatal accidents, and honest magistrates who become the target of obscure machinations. Beginning with this play, Fo became more interested in problems regarding the Italian justice system, focusing particularly on the pressures exerted against judges who only wish to do their duty.

On 17 July 1995, Fo was disabled and almost lost his sight because of an attack of cerebral ischemia. He survived and recovered within a year. In the meantime, Rame continued to manage their theater company. Rame also took advantage of this year of reduced activity to organize the *Archivo Franca Rame Dario Fo,* a full list of Fo's works with related information, together with comprehensive documentation (photographs, videos, music scores, drawings, playbills, press reviews, scripts, and legal documents) on Fo's career; all these materials can now be accessed on the World Wide Web at <http://www.archivio.francarame.it/home.html>. Fo returned to the stage in 1996 with *La Bibbia dell'Imperatore, la Bibbia dei villani* (The Emperor's Bible, The Peasants' Bible) derived, as the author has stated, from an "illuminated code of the 9th century."

The theme of *Il diavolo con le zinne* (1997, The Devil with Tits) is again corruption and the insidious dangers threatening righteous magistrates. The protagonist is a sixteenth-century judge who, because of his exceptional moral integrity, is hated by powerful people who try to slander and frame him on alleged charges of corruption, misuse of authority, rape, and abuse of defendants. Even Hell itself participates in this attack, as the devil Barlocco is entrusted with entering the judge's body to corrupt him. There are many references to recent events, not the least of which were the attempts on the part of some right-wing interests to deny legal status to the actions many judges were undertaking against fraudulent activities and financial crimes involving top-level politicians.

In 1997 Fo received the Nobel Prize in Literature, which caused an uproar in some intellectual circles in Italy. Aside from the controversial nature of many of his plays, opponents felt that his work was mere clowning and did not have the literary merit to deserve the prize. Fo, delighted by the uproar, turned his Nobel lecture into another performance. With the money from the prize, Fo and Rame founded "Il Nobel per i disabili" (The Nobel for the Disabled), an organization dedicated to assisting the handicapped.

In 1998 Fo presented *Marino libero! Marino è innocente!* (Free Marino! Marino Is Innocent!), another work on justice, dealing with one of the most controversial political trials of Italian history. The matter of this case can be traced back to the Piazza Fontana slaughter and the subsequent deaths of the anarchist Pinelli and of Luigi Calabresi, the police commissioner who had questioned him. In 1988 Leonardo Marino confessed his involvement in the commissioner's assassination and accused Adriano Sofri, former leader of the extreme-left movement Lotta Continua (Continuous Struggle) and a significant political figure in the 1960s and 1970s, as the instigator of the murder. Marino escaped prison for his cooperation, and on the basis of Marino's unreliable testimony, Sofri was sentenced to a twenty-two-year term, sparking large protests.

Fo's next play, *Lu Santo Jullàre Françesco* (Francis the Saint Jester), was staged at the Spoleto Festival in 1999. The protagonist is St. Francis of Assisi, whom Fo regards as the first jester ever known, even if God's jester. Fo follows the well-known biography of the most revered Italian saint, according to the canonical account of Bonaventura da Bognorregio, but sometimes diverges from it to exploit other sources and documents, such as the account of his preaching in Bologna in 1222, when the city was at war with Imola. Fo presents a St. Francis who surprises his audience, because he is expected to preach using the dialect of Umbria (his home region) and to invoke the restoration of peace, whereas he speaks in Neapolitan dialect and praises war. Fo identifies St. Francis as the true prototype of the jester, a man capable of turning his body into word, deeply knowledgeable as to the power of gesture and pantomime. Without betraying his political beliefs and social engagement, Fo has produced a text marked by a less aggressive polemical attitude, as if seen from a more distant and somewhat fabulous perspective.

The themes preferred by Dario Fo, especially in later years, have been those that, above all, address the issues of injustice and discrimination in the world without ever neglecting the formal aspect of theater practice. In fact, he has renewed the theater as a playwright, actor, and producer. More important, he has transformed the "comic stage" from a place of pure entertainment to one of debate and reflection.

Interviews:

Dario Fo parla di Dario Fo, edited by Erminia Artese (Cosenza: Lerici, 1977);

Dario Fo and Franca Rame: Theatre Workshops at Riverside Studios, London, edited by Ed Emery (London: Red Notes, 1983);

Dario Fo, *Dialogo provocatorio sul comico, il tragico, la follia e la ragione con Luigi Allegri* (Rome: Laterza, 1990).

References:

Alberto Abbruzzese, "Dario Fo comico, tragico e prosaico," *Rinascita,* 13 (26 March 1976): 36–37;

Serena Anderlini, "Franca Rame: Her Life and Works," *Theater* [Yale] (Winter 1985): 32–39;

Franca Angelini, *Il teatro del Novecento da Pirandello a Fo* (Bari: Laterza, 1976);

Antonio Attisani, *Teatro come differenza* (Milan: Feltrinelli, 1978);

Alessandro Avanzo, "Lo sghignazzo di Fo," *Sipario,* 407 (December 1981): 20–22;

Tom Behan, *Dario Fo: Revolutionary Theatre* (London: Pluto, 2000);

R. Bianchi, "La teatralizzazione permanente: Happening proletario e rituale della militanza nel teatro politico di Dario Fo," *Biblioteca Teatrale,* 21-22 (1978): 160–180;

Lanfranco Binni, *Attento a te. . . ! Il teatro politico di Dario Fo* (Verona: Bertani, 1975);

Binni, *Dario Fo* (Florence: La Nuova Italia, 1977);

Carlo Brusati, *Dario Fo, politica, provocazione, arte* (Milan: Il Quaderno del Sale, 1977);

Marina Cappa and Roberto Nepoti, *Dario Fo* (Rome: Gremese, 1982);

Ettore Capriolo, "Dario Fo e il nuovo impegno," *Sipario,* 273 (January 1969): 43–44;

Jean Chesnaux, *Il teatro politico di Dario Fo: La censura fallita* (Milan: Mazzotta, 1977);

Elena De Pasquale, *Il segreto del giullare: La dimensione testuale nel teatro di Dario Fo* (Naples: Liguori, 1999);

Marco De Poli, "Dario Fo," *Belfagor,* 1 (January 1976): 83–91;

Joseph Farrell, *Dario Fo and Franca Rame: Harlequins of the Revolution* (London: Methuen, 2001);

Farrell and Antonio Scuder, eds., *Dario Fo: Stage, Text, and Tradition* (Carbondale: Southern Illinois University Press, 2000);

Giorgio Grossi, "Nuova scena: Il teatro della cultura," *Sipario,* 286 (February 1970): 19;

David Hirst, *Dario Fo and Franca Rame* (London: Macmillan, 1989);

Bent Holm, *Il mondo rovesciato: Dario Fo e la fantasia popolare* (Stockolm: Drama, 1980);

Ron Jenkins, *Subversive Laughter* (New York: Free Press, 1994);

Gabriella Matrisciano, *Il teatro di Dario Fo* (Messina: EDAS, 1994);

Roberto Mazzucco, "Il teatro di Fo: Italianità e libertà," *Il ponte,* 12 (December 1967): 1612–1619;

Claudio Meldolesi, *Su un comico in rivolta: Dario Fo il bufalo il bambino* (Rome: Bulzoni, 1978);

Toni Mitchell, *Dario Fo: People's Court Jester* (London: Methuen, 1999);

Italo Moscati, "La libertà di consenso," *Sipario,* 284 (December 1969): 12–15;

Moscati, "Teatro e politica," *Sipario,* 274 (February 1969): 8–10;

Marisa Pizza, *Il gesto e la parola: Poetica, drammaturgia e storia dei monologhi di Dario Fo* (Rome: Bulzoni, 1996);

Alessandra Pozzo, *Grr . . . grammelot: Parlare senza parole. Dai primi balbettii al grammelot di Dario Fo* (Bologna: Clueb, 1998);

Paolo Puppa, *Il teatro di Dario Fo: Dalla scena alla piazza* (Venice: Marsilio, 1978);

Franco Quadri, *Il teatro del regime* (Milan: Mazzotta, 1976);

Quadri, *La politica del regista* (Milan: Edizioni Il Formichiere, 1980);

Tito Saffioti, *I giullari in Italia* (Milan: Xenia, 1990);

Jean-Claude Schmitt, *Il gesto del Medioevo* (Rome-Bari: Laterza, 1990);

O. Sciotto and D. De Angelis, *Il teatro di Dario Fo e Franca Rame: Rappresentazioni all'estero dal 1960 al 1991* (Milan: C.T.F.R., 1992);

Antonio Scuderi, *Dario Fo and Popular Performances* (New York: Legas, 1998);

Michele L. Straniero, *Giullari & Fo* (Rome: Lato Side, 1978);

Chiara Valentini, *La storia di Dario Fo* (Milan: Feltrinelli, 1977);

Franco Vegliani, "Dario Fo teatralmente compromesso," *Sipario*, 220-221 (August–September 1964): 39;

Alessandra Venezia, *Dalla svampita alla rapita: L'evoluzione dei personaggi femminili nel teatro di Dario Fo* (Milan: UMI, 1990);

Claudio Vicentini, *La teoria del teatro politico* (Florence: Sansoni, 1981).

Papers:

The main source for manuscripts, playbills, photographs, newspaper articles, letters, and other documents pertaining to Dario Fo's career is the *Archivo Franca Rame Dario Fo,* <http://www.archivio.francarame.it/home.html>.

1997 Nobel Prize in Literature Presentation Speech

by Professor Sture Allén of the Swedish Academy (Translation from the Swedish)

Your Majesties, Your Royal Highnesses, Ladies and Gentlemen,

To be a jester is, and always has been, a serious matter. Swedish mediaeval laws stipulated that it cost a man smaller fines to lay violent hands on somebody from a neighbouring county than on a man from his own part of the country; but to assault a jester, on the other hand, cost him nothing at all. If a jester is beaten up, says the thirteenth-century law concerning such people, it shall not be counted an offence. If a jester comes to bodily harm, he shall have and suffer what was given him—infamy and injury. "Let him never appeal for more justice than a thral woman lashed on her bare back."

One of Dario Fo's sources of inspiration is exactly these mediaeval jesters, unprotected by any law. According to Fo satire is what makes the most forceful impact on man. Mixing laughter and seriousness is his way of telling the truth about abuses and unrighteousness. For Alfred Nobel literary achievements were important means for fulfilling the fundamental aim of the awards, namely to confer benefit on mankind. The maintenance of human dignity is unquestionably an essential aspect of this.

Fo often refers explicitly to the mediaeval joculatores and their comedy and mysteries. In fact, a central work in his oeuvre, *Mistero buffo*—"The Comic Mysteries"—is based on old material culled from many different quarters. In the scene called "The Birth of the Jester" the crucial moment occurs when a landlord avid for more land violates the wife of the man who is breaking untilled ground. "The Marriage at Cana" is seen from the point of view of the intoxicated wine-drinker. In "The Resurrection of Lazarus" the provocative question is whether Jesus will succeed.

There are several other sources. Furthest away in time we seem to glimpse Plautus and Terence in Rome, who were of renewed interest in fifteenth century Italy. The commedia dell'arte, a creation of the sixteenth century, is of importance with its set-character parts and its oral tradition. It is also possible to catch a sly glance from Bottom the weaver and Sir Andrew Aguecheek. Impulses from our own days come from Maiakovski's epic-satirical poetry and from Brecht's didactic theatre. Incidentally, it was from Maiakovski that Fo borrowed the title "Mistero buffo."

Another major achievement in Fo's large production is "Accidental Death of an Anarchist." The play is about the cross-examining following on the supposed accident. By and by the questioning is taken over, through a brilliantly carried out shift, by a Hamlet-like figure—il Matto—who has the kind of madness that exposes official falsehoods. All in all there are many topical allusions in Fo's plays, but the texts transcend everyday situations and are given a far wider range of application.

One cannot hold it against Fo that he is a first-rate actor. The decisive thing is that he has written plays which arouse the enthusiasm of actors and which captivate his audiences. The texts are chiseled in an interplay with the spectators and have often been given their final shape over a long time. Rapidly changing situations give impetus to the plays and shape the characters. The rhythm of the actors' lines, the witty wording and the aptitude for improvisation combine with strong intensity and artistic energy in the profoundly meaningful, steady flow of his flashes of wit. The printed texts can also give you this feeling if you give free range to your imagination. Fo's work brings to the fore the multifarious abundance of the literary field.

His independence and perspicacity have made him run great risks and right enough he has been made to experience the consequences both at home and abroad. When on one occasion he and his wife, Franca Rame, had been stopped from making an agreed-on appearance abroad, their friends and colleagues arranged a representation which they called "An Evening without Dario Fo and Franca Rame."

Looking backwards in time from Dario Fo, the ninety-fourth laureate for literature, to earlier writers given the award, it is tempting to arrest oneself at George Bernard Shaw, winner of the Prize seventy years ago. On that occasion the Swedish Academy emphasised the laureate's idealism, humanity, and stimulating satire. The two writers are no doubt different from each other, but the same evaluative words can be applied to Dario Fo.

Dear Mr. Fo,

The word *dignity* plays an important part in your oeuvre and is at the centre of the piece called "The Birth of the Jester." The dignity bestowed on you today may have other attributes, but it has the same core. On behalf of the Swedish Academy I congratulate you warmly on the work which has resulted in the Nobel Prize in Literature 1997 and I ask you to step forward to receive the prize from the hands of His Majesty the King.

[© The Nobel Foundation, 1997.]

Fo: Banquet Speech

Fo's speech at the Nobel Banquet, 10 December 1997
(Translated by Paul Claesson)

Even though I don't hold a glass in my hand, I'd like to raise a toast to a great Queen, a Queen of your past: Kristina.

Kristina arrived in Italy in the late 17th century. As someone already mentioned, she came to Rome and there, obviously, she got to know the Pope, Alexander VII. He was a man seeking to restore the city's ruined cultural fabric. The reaction to the Counter-Reformation had peaked a few years earlier. Alexander sought the return to Italy of the men of the theatre that had been driven away by the Counter-Reformation, and through his efforts Queen Kristina became acquainted with Italy's greatest comedians, as they returned to their homeland.

She already loved the theatre; through these actors she became enthralled with it. During a visit to France, she got to know Molière, with whom she began a correspondence on her return to Italy. At one point Molière sent her one of his comedies, *Tartuffe*. It was only a draft.

Kristina asked Molière if she could stage it in Italy, and got the consent of the Pope. The Pope, who had a great sense of humour, said: "What are you trying to do, ruin my reputation with this comedy? These . . . the cardinals will fire me."

But Molière couldn't give the play to Kristina because the King wanted it for himself.

This play, *Tartuffe,* was played for the first time . . . it wasn't completed yet. It was a vicious comedy that with great irony took to task the hypocrisy of the day, in particular the hypocrisy of the Catholics and especially as it expressed itself within the family.

It led to a disaster. It was censured. It was banned for three years in a row. It was played again for a while and then was again banned for several years.

It may be safe to assume that if Molière had given in to Kristina, and had she arranged for it to be played in Rome, no one would have dared to censure it. Kristina enjoyed the protection of the Pope, and who could touch the Pope?

So, I beg You, Queen, and you Princesses that are here this evening: if you love the theatre, give it your support, as Kristina did.

I know . . . ? Did you tell your joke? Eh? You've stolen my punch line! Not yet, not yet? All the better, all the better!

As I was saying, when the theatre is ironic, grotesque, it's above all then that you have to defend it, because the theatre that makes people laugh is the theatre of human reason.

And if you have any problems, seek the support of the Pope. You will no doubt succeed.

Here's to Kristina!

[© The Nobel Foundation, 1997. Dario Fo is the sole author of his speech.]

Press Release: The Nobel Prize in Literature 1997

from the Office of the Permanent Secretary of the Swedish Academy, 9 October 1997

Dario Fo

"who emulates the jesters of the Middle Ages in scourging authority and upholding the dignity of the downtrodden"

Dario Fo, the dramatist and actor, was born at Lago Maggiore, and is 71. His education included studies at the Academy of Arts in Milan. He is married to the actress and writer Franca Rame.

For many years Fo has been performed all over the world, perhaps more than any other contemporary dramatist, and his influence has been considerable. He if anyone merits the epithet of jester in the true meaning of that word. With a blend of laughter and gravity he opens our eyes to abuses and injustices in society and also the wider historical perspective in which they can be placed. Fo is an extremely serious satirist with a multi-faceted oeuvre. His independence and clear-sightedness have led him to take great risks, whose consequences he has been made to feel while at the same time experiencing enormous response from widely differing quarters.

The non-institutional tradition has played a great role for Fo. He often alludes to the mediaeval jesters (joculatores) and their comedy and mysteries. The central work *Mistero buffo* from 1969 is based on such historic material as interpreted by Fo. But commedia dell'arte and 20th century writers such as Mayakovski and Brecht have provided him with important impulses.

Another of the high points in Fo's extensive oeuvre is *Morte accidentale di un anarchico* (Accidental Death of an Anarchist) from 1970. Its background was the right-wing extremist bomb attacks of 1969, which were blamed by the authorities and the press on the anarchists. During interrogations in Milan, an innocent suspect "fell" from a fifth-floor window. The play deals with these interrogations, which are gradually taken over by a Hamlet-like figure (il Matto, the Maniac) who possesses the kind of lunacy that lays bare the lies of officialdom.

Other works that can be singled out are *Non si paga! Non si paga!* (We Can't Pay We Won't Pay!) from 1974 and *Clacson, trombette e pernacchi* (Trumpets and Raspberries) from 1981. The latter is a comedy of errors aimed at participants in the disreputable stratagems in high places. In recent years, together with Franca Rame, Fo has dealt with women's issues in several plays.

Fo's most recent work, *Il diavolo con le zinne* (The Devil with Boobs), received its long awaited première in Messina at the beginning of August. It is a satiric comedy set in the Renaissance and its protagonists are a zealous judge and a woman possessed by the devil. As always with Fo, the work is directed at phenomena in today's society.

Translating Fo's texts with their topical references and use of grammelot, the jesting language that Fo has developed based on dialect and onomatopoeia, offers particular problems. Often translators comment on the approach adopted. One example is Ed Emery, who points out in a note to his translation of *Morte accidentale di un anarchico* that he has chosen to stay close to the original and retain Fo's allusions.

Fo's strength is in the creation of texts that simultaneously amuse, engage and provide perspectives. As in commedia dell'arte, they are always open for creative additions and dislocations, continually encouraging the actors to improvise, which means that the audience is activated in a remarkable way. His is an oeuvre of impressive artistic vitality and range.

[© The Nobel Foundation, 1997.]

Fo: Nobel Lecture, 7 December 1997

Contra Jogulatores Obloquentes
Against Jesters Who Defame and Insult
(Translated from Italian by Paul Claesson)

"Against jesters who defame and insult." Law issued by Emperor Frederick II (Messina 1221), declaring that anyone may commit violence against jesters without incurring punishment or sanction.

The drawings I'm showing you are mine. Copies of these, slightly reduced in size, have been distributed among you.

For some time it's been my habit to use images when preparing a speech: rather than write it down, I illustrate it. This allows me to improvise, to exercise my imagination—and to oblige you to use yours.

As I proceed, I will from time to time indicate to you where we are in the manuscript. That way you won't lose the thread. This will be of help especially to those of you who don't understand either Italian or Swedish. English-speakers will have a tremendous advantage over the rest because they will imagine things I've neither said nor thought. There is of course the problem of the two laughters: those who understand Italian will laugh immediately, those who don't will have to wait for Anna [Barsotti]'s Swedish translation. And then there are those of you who won't know whether to laugh the first time or the second. Anyway, let's get started.

Ladies and gentlemen, the title I've selected for this little chat is "contra jogulatores obloquentes," which you all recognize as Latin, mediaeval Latin to be precise. It's the title of a law issued in Sicily in 1221 by Emperor Frederick II of Swabia, an emperor "anointed by God," who we were taught in school to regard a sovereign of extraordinary enlightenment, a liberal. "Jogulatores obloquentes" means "jesters who defame and insult." The law in question allowed any and all citizens to insult jesters, to beat them and even—if they were in that mood—to kill them, without running any risk of being brought to trial and condemned. I hasten to assure you that this law no longer is in vigour, so I can safely continue.

Ladies and gentlemen,

Friends of mine, noted men of letters, have in various radio and television interviews declared: "The highest prize should no doubt be awarded to the members of the Swedish Academy, for having had the courage this year to award the Nobel Prize to a jester." I agree. Yours is an act of courage that borders on provocation.

It's enough to take stock of the uproar it has caused: sublime poets and writers who normally occupy the loftiest of spheres, and who rarely take interest in those who live and toil on humbler planes, are suddenly bowled over by some kind of whirlwind.

Like I said, I applaud and concur with my friends.

These poets had already ascended to the Parnassian heights when you, through your insolence, sent them toppling to earth, where they fell face and belly down in the mire of normality.

Insults and abuse are hurled at the Swedish Academy, at its members and their relatives back to the seventh generation. The wildest of them clamour: "Down with the King . . . of Norway!" It appears they got the dynasty wrong in the confusion.

(At this point you may turn the page. As you see there is an image of a naked poet bowled over by a whirlwind.)

Some landed pretty hard on their nether parts. There were reports of poets and writers whose nerves and livers suffered terribly. For a few days thereafter there was not a pharmacy in Italy that could muster up a single tranquillizer.

But, dear members of the Academy, let's admit it, this time you've overdone it. I mean come on, first you give the prize to a black man, then to a Jewish writer. Now you give it to a clown. What gives? As they say in Naples: *pazziàmme?* Have we lost our senses?

Also the higher clergy have suffered their moments of madness. Sundry potentates—great electors of the Pope, bishops, cardinals and prelates of Opus Dei—have all gone through the ceiling, to the point that they've even petitioned for the reinstatement of the law that allowed jesters to be burned at the stake. Over a slow fire.

On the other hand I can tell you there is an extraordinary number of people who rejoice with me over your choice. And so I bring you the most festive thanks, in the name of a multitude of mummers, jesters, clowns, tumblers and storytellers.

(This is where we are now [indicates a page].)

And speaking of storytellers, I mustn't forget those of the small town on Lago Maggiore where I was born and raised, a town with a rich oral tradition.

They were the old storytellers, the master glass-blowers who taught me and other children the craftsmanship, the art, of spinning fantastic yarns. We would listen to them, bursting with laughter—laughter that would stick in our throats as the tragic allusion that surmounted each sarcasm would dawn on us. To this day I keep fresh in my mind the story of the Rock of Caldé.

"Many years ago," began the old glass-blower, "way up on the crest of that steep cliff that rises from the lake there was a town called Caldé. As it happened, this town was sitting on a loose splinter of rock that slowly, day by day, was sliding down towards the precipice. It was a splendid little town, with a campanile, a fortified tower at the very peak and a cluster of houses, one after the other. It's a town that once was and that now is gone. It disappeared in the 15th century.

"'Hey,' shouted the peasants and fishermen down in the valley below. 'You're sliding, you'll fall down from there.'

"But the cliff dwellers wouldn't listen to them, they even laughed and made fun of them: 'You think you're pretty smart, trying to scare us into running away from our houses and our land so you can grab them instead. But we're not that stupid.'

"So they continued to prune their vines, sow their fields, marry and make love. They went to mass. They felt the rock slide under their houses but they didn't think much about it. 'Just the rock settling. Quite normal,' they said, reassuring each other.

"The great splinter of rock was about to sink into the lake. 'Watch out, you've got water up to your ankles,' shouted the people along the shore. 'Nonsense, that's just drainage water from the fountains, it's just a bit humid,' said the people of the town, and so, slowly but surely, the whole town was swallowed by the lake.

"Gurgle . . . gurgle . . . splash . . . they sink. . . . houses, men, women, two horses, three donkeys . . . heehaw . . . gurgle. Undaunted, the priest continued to receive the confession of a nun: 'Te absolvi . . . animus . . . santi . . . guurgle . . . Aame . . . gurgle. . . .' The tower disappeared, the campanile sank with bells and all: Dong . . . ding . . . dop . . . plock. . . .

"Even today," continued the old glass-blower, "if you look down into the water from that outcrop that still juts out from the lake, and if in that same moment a thunderstorm breaks out, and the lightning illuminates the bottom of the lake, you can still see—incredible as it may seem!—the submerged town, with its streets still intact and even the inhabitants themselves, walking around and glibly repeating to themselves: 'Nothing has happened.' The fish swim back and forth before their eyes, even into their ears. But they just brush them off: 'Nothing to worry about. It's just some kind of fish that's learned to swim in the air.'

"'Atchoo!' 'God bless you!' 'Thank you . . . it's a bit humid today . . . more than yesterday . . . but everything's fine.' They've reached rock bottom, but as far as they're concerned, nothing has happened at all."

Disturbing though it may be, there's no denying that a tale like this still has something to tell us.

I repeat, I owe much to these master glass-blowers of mine, and they—I assure you—are immensely grateful to you, members of this Academy, for rewarding one of their disciples.

And they express their gratitude with explosive exuberance. In my home town, people swear that on the night the news arrived that one of their own storytellers was to be awarded the Nobel Prize, a kiln that had been standing cold for some fifty years suddenly erupted in a broadside of flames, spraying high into the air—like a fireworks *finale*—a myriad splinters of coloured glass, which then showered down on the surface of the lake, releasing an impressive cloud of steam.

(While you applaud, I'll have a drink of water. [Turning to the interpreter:] Would you like some?

It's important that you talk among yourselves while we drink, because if you try to hear the gurgle gurgle gurgle the water makes as we swallow we'll choke on it and start coughing. So instead you can exchange niceties like "Oh, what a lovely evening it is, isn't it?"

End of intermission: we turn to a new page, but don't worry, it'll go faster from here.)

Above all others, this evening you're due the loud and solemn thanks of an extraordinary master of the stage, little-known not only to you and to people in France, Norway, Finland . . . but also to the people of Italy. Yet he was, until Shakespeare, doubtless the greatest playwright of renaissance Europe. I'm referring to Ruzzante Beolco, my greatest master along with Molière: both actors-playwrights, both mocked by the leading men of letters of their times. Above all, they were despised for bringing onto the stage the everyday life, joys and desperation of the common people; the hypocrisy and the arrogance of the high and mighty; and the incessant injustice. And their major, unforgivable fault was this: in telling these things, they made people laugh. Laughter does not please the mighty.

Ruzzante, the true father of the *Commedia dell'Arte*, also constructed a language of his own, a language of and for the theatre, based on a variety of tongues: the dialects of the Po Valley, expressions in Latin, Spanish, even German, all mixed with onomatopoeic sounds of his own invention. It is from him, from Beolco Ruzzante, that I've learned to free myself from conventional literary writing and to express myself with words that you can chew, with unusual sounds, with various techniques of rhythm and breathing, even with the rambling nonsense-speech of the *grammelot*.

Allow me to dedicate a part of this prestigious prize to Ruzzante.

A few days ago, a young actor of great talent said to me: "Maestro, you should try to project your energy, your enthusiasm, to young people. You have to give them this charge of yours. You have to share your professional knowledge and experience with them." Franca—that's my wife—and I looked at each other and said: "He's right." But when we teach others our art, and share this charge of fantasy, what end will it serve? Where will it lead?

In the past couple of months, Franca and I have visited a number of university campuses to hold workshops and seminars before young audiences. It has been surprising—not to say disturbing—to discover their ignorance about the times we live in. We told them about the proceedings now in course in Turkey against the accused culprits of the massacre in Sivas. Thirty-seven of the country's foremost democratic intellectuals, meeting in the Anatolian town to celebrate the memory of a famous mediaeval jester of the Ottoman period, were burned alive in the dark of the night, trapped inside their hotel. The fire was the handiwork of a group of fanatical fundamentalists that enjoyed protection from elements within the Government itself. In one night, thirty-seven of the country's most celebrated artists, writers, directors, actors and Kurdish dancers were erased from this Earth.

In one blow these fanatics destroyed some of the most important exponents of Turkish culture.

Thousands of students listened to us. The looks in their faces spoke of their astonishment and incredulity. They had never heard of the massacre. But what impressed me the most is that not even the teachers and professors present had heard of it. There Turkey is, on the Mediterranean, practically in front of us, insisting on joining the European Community, yet no one had heard of the massacre. Salvini, a noted Italian democrat, was right on the mark when he observed: "The widespread ignorance of events is the main buttress of injustice." But this absent-mindedness on the part of the young has been conferred upon them by those who are charged to educate and inform them: among the absent-minded and uninformed, school teachers and other educators deserve first mention.

Young people easily succumb to the bombardment of gratuitous banalities and obscenities that each day is served to them by the mass media: heartless TV action films where in the space of ten minutes they are treated to three rapes, two assassinations, one beating and a serial crash involving ten cars on a bridge that then collapses, whereupon everything—cars, drivers and passengers—precipitates into the sea . . . only one person survives the fall, but he doesn't know how to swim and so drowns, to the cheers of the crowd of curious onlookers that suddenly has appeared on the scene.

At another university we spoofed the project—alas well under way—to manipulate genetic material, or more specifically, the proposal by the European Parliament to allow patent rights on living organisms. We could feel how the subject sent a chill through the audience. Franca and I explained how our Eurocrats, kindled by powerful and ubiquitous multinationals, are preparing a scheme worthy the plot of a sci-fi/horror movie entitled "Frankenstein's pig brother." They're trying to get the approval of a directive which (and get this!) would authorize industries to take patents on living beings, or on parts of them, created with techniques of genetic manipulation that seem taken straight out of "The Sorcerer's Apprentice."

This is how it would work: by manipulating the genetic make-up of a pig, a scientist succeeds in making the pig more human-like. By this arrangement it becomes much easier to remove from the pig the organ of your choice—a liver, a kidney—and to transplant it in a human. But to assure that the transplanted pig-organs aren't rejected, it's also necessary to transfer certain pieces of genetic information from the pig to the human. The result: a human pig (even though you will say that there are already plenty of those).

And every part of this new creature, this humanized pig, will be subject to patent laws; and whosoever wishes a part of it will have to pay copyright fees to the company that "invented" it. Secondary illnesses, monstrous deformations, infectious diseases—all are optionals, included in the price. . . .

The Pope has forcefully condemned this monstrous genetic witchcraft. He has called it an offence against humanity, against the dignity of man, and has gone to pains to underscore the project's total and irrefutable lack of moral value.

The astonishing thing is that while this is happening, an American scientist, a remarkable magician—you've probably read about him in the papers—has succeeded in transplanting the head of a baboon. He cut the heads off two baboons and switched them. The baboons didn't feel all that great after the operation. In fact, it left them paralysed, and they both died shortly thereafter, but the experiment worked, and that's the great thing.

But here's the rub: this modern-day Frankenstein, a certain Professor White, is all the while a distinguished member of the Vatican Academy of Sciences. Somebody should warn the Pope.

So, we enacted these criminal farces to the kids at the universities, and they laughed their heads off. They would say of Franca and me: "They're a riot, they come up with the most fantastic stories." Not for a moment, not even with an inkling in their spines, did they grasp that the stories we told were true.

These encounters have strengthened us in our conviction that our job is—in keeping with the exhortation of the great Italian poet Savinio—"to tell our own story." Our task as intellectuals, as persons who mount the pulpit or the stage, and who, most importantly, address to young people, our task is not just to teach them method, like how to use the arms, how to control breathing, how to use the stomach, the voice, the falsetto, the *contracampo*. It's not enough to teach a technique or a style: we have to show them what is happening around us. They have to be able to tell their own story. A theatre, a literature, an artistic expression that does not speak for its own time has no relevance.

Recently, I took part in a large conference with lots of people where I tried to explain, especially to the younger participants, the ins and outs of a particular Italian court case. The original case resulted in seven separate proceedings, at the end of which three Italian left-wing politicians were sentenced to 21 years of imprisonment each, accused of having murdered a police commissioner. I've studied the documents of the case—as I did when I prepared *Accidental Death of an Anarchist*—and at the conference I recounted the facts pertaining to it, which are really quite absurd, even farcical. But at a certain point I realized I was speaking to deaf ears, for the simple reason that my audience was ignorant not only of the case itself, but of what had happened five years earlier, ten years earlier: the violence, the terrorism. They knew nothing about the massacres that occurred in Italy, the trains that blew up, the bombs in the *piazze* or the farcical court cases that have dragged on since then.

The terribly difficult thing is that in order to talk about what is happening today, I have to start with what happened thirty years ago and then work my way forward. It's not enough to speak about the present. And pay attention, this isn't just about Italy: the same thing happens everywhere, all over Europe. I've tried in Spain and encountered the same difficulty; I've tried in France, in Germany, I've yet to try in Sweden, but I will.

To conclude, let me share this medal with Franca.

Franca Rame, my companion in life and in art who you, members of the Academy, acknowledge in your motivation of the prize as actress and author; who has had a hand in many of the texts of our theatre.

(At this very moment, Franca is on stage in a theatre in Italy but will join me the day after tomorrow. Her flight arrives midday, if you like we can all head out together to pick her up at the airport.)

Franca has a very sharp wit, I assure you. A journalist put the following question to her: "So how does it feel to be the wife of a Nobel Prize winner? To have a monument in your home?" To which she answered: "I'm not worried. Nor do I feel at all at a disadvantage; I've been in training for a long time. I do my exercises each morning: I go down on my hands and knees, and that way I've accustomed myself to becoming a pedestal to a monument. I'm pretty good at it."

Like I said, she has a sharp wit. At times she even turns her irony against herself.

Without her at my side, where she has been for a lifetime, I would never have accomplished the work you have seen fit to honour. Together we've staged and recited thousands of performances, in theatres, occupied factories, at university sit-ins, even in deconsecrated churches, in prisons and city parks, in sunshine and pouring rain, always together. We've had to endure abuse, assaults by the police, insults from the right-thinking, and violence. And it is Franca who has had to suffer the most atrocious aggression. She has had to pay more dearly than any one of us, with her neck and limb in the balance, for the solidarity with the humble and the beaten that has been our premise.

The day it was announced that I was to be awarded the Nobel Prize I found myself in front of the theatre on Via di Porta Romana in Milan where Franca, together with Giorgio Albertazzi, was performing *The Devil with Tits*. Suddenly I was surrounded by a throng of reporters, photographers and camera-wielding TV-crews. A passing tram stopped, unexpectedly, the driver stepped out to greet me, then all the passengers stepped out too, they applauded me, and everyone wanted to shake my hand and congratulate me . . . when at a certain point they all stopped in their tracks and, as with a single voice, shouted "Where's Franca?" They began to holler "Francaaa" until, after a little while, she appeared. Discombobulated and moved to tears, she came down to embrace me.

At that moment, as if out of nowhere, a band appeared, playing nothing but wind instruments and drums. It was made up of kids from all parts of the city and, as it happened, they were playing together for the first time. They struck up "Porta Romana bella, Porta Romana" in samba beat. I've never heard anything played so out of tune, but it was the most beautiful music Franca and I had ever heard.

Believe me, this prize belongs to both of us.

Thank you.

[© The Nobel Foundation, 1997. Dario Fo is the sole author of the text.]

Anatole France
(16 April 1844 – 12 October 1924)

Catharine Savage Brosman
Tulane University

This entry has been expanded by Brosman from her France entry in *DLB 123: Nineteenth-Century French Fiction Writers: Naturalism and Beyond, 1860–1900.*

SELECTED BOOKS: *La Légende de Sainte Radegonde, reine de France* (Paris: France Libraire, 1859);

Alfred de Vigny (Paris: Bachelin-Deflorenne, 1868; revised, Paris: C. Aveline, 1923); translated by J. Lewis May and Alfred Allinson in *Marguerite and Count Morin, Deputy, together with Alfred de Vigny and The Path of Glory* (London: John Lane/Bodley Head, 1927);

Les Poèmes dorés (Paris: Alphonse Lemerre, 1873);

Jean Racine (Paris: Alphonse Lemerre, 1874);

Le Livre du bibliophile (Paris: Alphonse Lemerre, 1874);

Racine et Nicole: La querelle des imaginaires (Paris: J. Charavay, 1875);

Les Poèmes de Jules Breton (Paris: J. Charavay aîné, 1875);

Les Noces corinthiennes (Paris: Alphonse Lemerre, 1876);

Jocaste et le Chat maigre (Paris: C. Lévy, 1879); translated by Agnès Farley as *Jocasta and the Famished Cat* (London & New York: John Lane, 1912);

Le Crime de Sylvestre Bonnard, membre de l'Institut (Paris: Calmann-Lévy, 1881); translated by Lafcadio Hearn as *The Crime of Sylvestre Bonnard* (New York: Boni & Liveright, 1890);

Lés Désirs de Jean Servien (Paris: Alphonse Lemerre, 1882); translated by Allinson as *The Aspirations of Jean Servien* (London & New York: John Lane, 1912);

Abeille (Paris: Charavay frères, 1883); translated by Peter Wright as *Bee, the Princess of the Dwarfs* (London: Dent / New York: Dutton, 1912);

Le Livre de mon ami (Paris: Calmann-Lévy, 1885); translated by May as *My Friend's Book* (London & New York: John Lane, 1913);

Nos enfants: Scènes de la ville et des champs (Paris: Hachette, 1887); translated as *Our Children: Scenes from the Country and the Town* (New York: Duffield, 1917);

Anatole France, 1920 (Hulton Archive/Getty Images)

La Vie littéraire, 4 volumes (Paris: Calmann-Lévy, 1888–1892); translated by A. W. Evans as *On Life and Letters,* first series (London & New York: John Lane, 1911); second series translated by Evans (London & New York: John Lane, 1922); third series translated by D. B. Stewart (London & New York: John Lane, 1922); fourth series translated by Bernard Miall (London: John Lane/Bodley Head / New York: Dodd, Mead, 1924); volume 5 of original (Paris: Calmann-Lévy, 1950);

Balthasar (Paris: Calmann-Lévy, 1889); translated by Mrs. John Lane (London & New York: John Lane, 1909);

Notice historique sur Vivant Denon (Paris: P. Rouquette & fils, 1890);

Thaïs (Paris: Calmann-Lévy, 1890; revised, 1920), translated by A. D. Hall (Chicago: N. C. Smith, 1891); translated by B. Gulati, with an introduction by Wayne C. Booth (Chicago & London: University of Chicago Press, 1976);

L'Etui de nacre (Paris: Calmann-Lévy, 1892; revised, 1923) translated by Henri Pène Du Bois as *Tales from a Mother-of-Pearl Casket* (New York: G. H. Richmond, 1896);

L'Elvire de Lamartine: Notes sur M. et Mme Charles (Paris: H. Champion, 1893);

La Rôtisserie de la Reine Pédauque (Paris: Calmann-Lévy, 1893; revised, 1921); translated by Jos. A. V. Stritzko as *The Queen Pedauque* (New York: Boni & Liveright, 1923);

Les Opinions de M. Jérôme Coignard (Paris: Calmann-Lévy, 1893; revised, 1925); translated by Mrs. Wilfrid Jackson as *The Opinions of Jérôme Coignard* (London & New York: John Lane, 1913);

Le Lys rouge (Paris: Calmann-Lévy, 1894; revised, 1921); translated as *The Red Lily* (New York: Brentano's, Macaulay, 1898);

Le Jardin d'Epicure (Paris: Calmann-Lévy, 1894?; revised, 1922); translated by Allinson as *The Garden of Epicurus* (London & New York: John Lane, 1908);

Le Puits de Sainte Claire (Paris: Calmann-Lévy, 1895); translated by Allinson as *The Well of Santa Clara* (Paris: Charles Carrington, 1903); partially republished in *The Human Tragedy* (London & New York: John Lane, 1917);

Poésies: Les Poèmes dorés; Idylles et Légendes; Les Noces corinthiennes (Paris: Alphonse Lemerre, 1896);

Séance de l'Académie française du 24 décembre 1896. Discours de réception d'Anatole France (Paris: Calmann-Lévy, 1897);

L'Orme du mail (Paris: Calmann-Lévy, 1897; revised, 1923); translated by M. P. Willcocks as *The Elm-Tree on the Mall: A Chronicle of Our Own Times* (London & New York: John Lane, 1910);

Le Mannequin d'osier (Paris: Calmann-Lévy, 1897; revised, 1924); translated by Willcocks as *The Wicker-Work Woman* (London & New York: John Lane, 1910);

Au petit bonheur (Paris: Pierre Dauze, 1898); translated as *One Can But Try* (London: John Lane, 1925);

La Leçon bien apprise (Paris, 1898);

L'Anneau d'améthyste (Paris: Calmann-Lévy, 1899); translated by B. Drillien as *The Amethyst Ring* (London & New York: John Lane, 1919);

Pierre Nozière (Paris: Alphonse Lemerre, 1899); translated by May (London & New York: John Lane, 1916);

Filles et garçons: Scènes de la ville et des champs (Paris: Hachette, 1900?); translated as *Girls and Boys: Scènes from the Country and the Town* (New York: Duffield, 1913);

Clio (Paris: Calmann-Lévy, 1900); translated by Winifred Stephens (London: John Lane / New York: Dodd, Mead, 1922);

Jean Gutenberg (Paris: E. Pelletan, 1900);

L'Affaire Crainquebille (Paris: E. Pelletan, 1901); translated by Stephens in *Crainquebille, Putois, Riquet and Other Profitable Tales* (London: John Lane, 1915);

Monsieur Bergeret à Paris (Paris: Calmann-Lévy, 1901); translated by Drillien as *Monsieur Bergeret in Paris* (London & New York: John Lane, 1921);

Funérailles d'Emile Zola (Paris: E. Pelletan, 1902);

Opinions sociales (Paris: G. Bellais, 1902);

Crainquebille: Pièce en trois tableaux (Paris: Calmann-Lévy, 1903); translated by Barrett H. Clark as *Crainquebille* (New York: S. French, 1915); translated by Stephens (New York: Dodd, Mead, 1925);

Discours prononcé à l'inauguration de la statue d'Ernest Renan à Tréguier (Paris: Calmann-Lévy, 1903);

Histoire comique (Paris: Calmann-Lévy, 1903; enlarged, 1930); translated by Charles E. Roche as *A Mummer's Tale* (New York: Dodd, Mead, 1908);

Le Parti noir (Paris: Société Nouvelle de Librairie et d'Edition, 1903);

L'Eglise et la république (Paris: E. Pelletan, 1904);

Sur la pierre blanche (Paris: Calmann-Lévy, 1905); translated by Roche as *The White Stone* (London & New York: John Lane, 1910);

Vers les temps meilleurs (Paris: E. Pelletan, 1906); translated by May as *The Unrisen Dawn* (London: John Lane / New York: Dodd, Mead, 1928); original enlarged as *Vers les temps meilleurs: Trente ans de vie sociale,* 3 volumes, edited by Claude Aveline (Paris: Emile-Paul, 1949); revised, 4 volumes (Paris: Cercle du Bibliophile, 1970);

Les Contes de Jacques Tournebroche (Paris: Calmann-Lévy, 1908); translated by Allinson as *The Merrie Tales of Jacques Tournebroche* (London: John Lane / New York: Dodd, Mead, 1909);

Vie de Jeanne d'Arc, 2 volumes (Paris: Calmann-Lévy, 1908); translated by Stephens as *Joan of Arc* (London & New York: John Lane, 1908);

La Descente de Marbode aux enfers (Paris, 1908);

L'Ile des pingouins (Paris: Calmann-Lévy, 1908); translated as *Penguin Island* (New York: Grosset & Dunlap, 1909);

Le Tombeau de Molière (Paris: Imprimerie Nationale, 1908);

Rabelais (Paris: Calmann-Lévy, 1909); translated by Ernest Boyd (New York: Holt, 1929);

Les Sept Femmes de la Barbe-Bleue et autres contes merveilleux (Paris: Calmann-Lévy, 1909); translated by Stewart as *The Seven Wives of Bluebeard and Other Marvellous Tales* (London & New York: John Lane, 1920);

L'Uruguay et ses progrès (Montevideo: Tipografía y Litografía Oriental, 1909);

Aux étudiants (Paris: E. Pelletan, 1910);

Deux discours sur Tolstoï (Paris: "L'Emancipatrice," 1911);

Les Dieux ont soif (New York: Macmillan, 1912; Paris: Calmann-Lévy, 1912?); translated by Allinson as *The Gods Are Athirst* (London & New York: John Lane, 1913);

La Comédie de celui qui épousa une femme muette (Abbeville: F. Paillart / Paris: Calmann-Lévy/Edouard Champion, 1912); translated by Curtis Hidden Page as *The Man Who Married a Dumb Wife* (New York: John Lane, 1915);

Le Génie latin (Paris: Alphonse Lemerre, 1913; revised, Paris: Calmann-Lévy, 1917); translated by Wilfrid S. Jackson as *The Latin Genius* (London: John Lane, 1924);

La Révolte des anges (Paris: Calmann-Lévy, 1914); translated by Mrs. Wilfrid Jackson as *The Revolt of the Angels* (London & New York: John Lane, 1914);

Sur la voie glorieuse (Paris: E. Champion, 1915; enlarged, 1915); translated by Allinson as *The Path of Glory* (London & New York: John Lane, 1916);

Ce que disent nos morts (Paris: R. Helleu, 1916);

Le Crime de Sylvestre Bonnard [stage version] (Paris: Calmann-Lévy, 1918);

Le Petit Pierre (Paris: Calmann-Lévy, 1918; revised, 1928); translated by May as *Little Pierre* (London & New York: John Lane, 1920);

Marguerite (Paris: A. Coq, 1920); translated by May (London & New York: John Lane, 1921);

Stendhal (Abbeville: F. Paillart, 1920); translated by May (London, 1926);

Histoire contemporaine, 4 volumes (Paris: Calmann-Lévy, 1920–1921)—comprises volume 1: *L'Orme du mail;* volume 2: *Le Mannequin d'osier;* volume 3: *L'Anneau d'améthyste;* volume 4: *Monsieur Bergeret à Paris;*

Le Comte Morin député (Paris: Chez Mornay, 1921); translated by May as *Count Morin, Deputy* (London: John Lane, 1921);

Les Matinées de la Villa Saïd: Propos d'Anatole France, edited by Paul Gsell (Paris: Grasset, 1921); translated by Boyd as *The Opinions of Anatole France* (New York: Knopf, 1922);

Le Miracle de la pie (Paris: F. Ferroud, 1921);

La Vie en fleur (Paris: Calmann-Lévy, 1922); translated by May as *The Bloom of Life* (New York: Dodd, Mead, 1923);

Le Chanteur de Kymé (Paris: Ferroud, 1923);

Frère Joconde (Paris: A. Ferroud/J. Ferroud, 1923);

Mademoiselle Roxane (Paris: F. Ferroud, 1923);

Dernières pages inédites d'Anatole France, edited by Michel Corday (Paris: Calmann-Lévy, 1925);

Les Noces corinthiennes: Poème dramatique en trois parties (Paris: A. Ferroud/F. Ferroud, 1926); translated by Wilfrid Jackson and Emilie Jackson in *The Bride of Corinth* (London: John Lane / New York: Dodd, Mead, 1924);

Prefaces, Introductions, and Other Uncollected Papers by Anatole France, translated by May (London: John Lane, 1927; New York: Dodd, Mead, 1928);

Itinéraire de Paris à Buenos-Ayres (Paris: G. Grès et Cie, 1927);

Le Café Procope (Paris: Au dépens d'un amateur, 1928);

Le Château de Vaux-le-Vicomte (Paris: Calmann-Lévy, 1933); translated by Stephens in *Clio and The Château de Vaux-le-Vicomte* (London: John Lane, 1923).

Editions and Collections: *Œuvres complètes illustrées,* 25 volumes, edited by Claude Aveline and Léon Carias (Paris: Calmann-Lévy, 1925–1935);

Œuvres complètes, 29 volumes, edited by Jacques Suffel (Geneva: Edito Service, 1968–1971);

Œuvres, 4 volumes, edited by Marie-Claire Bancquart (Paris: Gallimard, Bibliothèque de la Pléiade, 1984–1994).

Editions in English: *The Authorized English Translation of the Novels and Short Stories of Anatole France,* 19 volumes, edited by Frederick Chapman, translated by Lafcadio Hearn and others (New York & London: Parke, Austin & Lipscomb, 1890);

The Works of Anatole France in an English Translation, 36 volumes, edited by Chapman, James Lewis May, and Bernard Miall (London & New York: John Lane, 1909–1926);

The Works, 30 volumes (New York: G. Wells, 1918–1924);

Works, 10 volumes (New York: Wise, 1930).

PLAY PRODUCTIONS: *Le Lys rouge,* Paris, Théâtre du Vaudeville, 25 February 1899;

Les Noces corinthiennes, Paris, Théâtre de l'Odéon, 30 January 1902;

Crainquebille, Paris, Théâtre de la Renaissance, 28 March 1903;

Le Mannequin d'osier, Paris, Théâtre de la Renaissance, 22 March 1904;

Au petit bonheur, Paris, Théâtre de la Renaissance, 2 February 1906;

La Comédie de celui qui épousa une femme muette, Paris, Café Voltaire, 21 March 1912;

Les Noces corinthiennes [opera], music by Henri Büsser, Paris, Opéra-Comique, 10 May 1922.

OTHER: *Les Œuvres de J.-B. P. Molière,* with a life of Molière, variants, and glossary by France (Paris: Alphonse Lemerre, 1876);

Bernardin de St.-Pierre, *Paul et Virginie,* notice and notes by France (Paris: Alphonse Lemerre, 1877);

Xavier de Maistre, *Voyage autour de ma chambre,* notice by France (Paris: Alphonse Lemerre, 1877);

Marquis de Sade, *Dorci ou la bizarrerie du sort,* notice by France (Paris: Charavay frères, 1881);

Mme de La Fayette, *L'Histoire d'Henriette d'Angleterre,* preface by France (Paris: Charavay, 1882);

Jean de La Fontaine, *Fables,* notice and notes by France (Paris: Alphonse Lemerre, 1883);

Mme de La Fayette, *La Princesse de Clèves,* preface by France (Paris: Conquet, 1889);

Marcel Proust, *Les Plaisirs et les jours,* preface by France (Paris: Calmann-Lévy, 1896);

Emile Combes, *Une Campagne laïque (1902–1903),* preface by France (Paris: H. Simonis Empis, 1904);

Charles Rappoport, *Jean Jaurès, l'homme, le penseur, le socialiste,* preface by France (Paris: Rouvière, 1915);

Hommage à l'Arménie, text by France (Paris: E. Leroux, 1919);

Paul Louis Couchoud, *Japanese Impressions,* translated by Frances Rumsey, preface by France (London & New York: John Lane, 1921);

"Le Mobilier en bois de rosé," attributed to France, *Revue France-Hongrie,* 71 (November 1961): 63–80; 72 (December 1961): 37–64.

In 1927 poet Paul Valéry delivered his *discours de réception,* or initial speech, to the Académie Française after being elected two years earlier to fill the seat of Anatole France, who had died in October 1924. Resenting the fact that, in 1875, as an editor for one of the famous poetry anthologies titled *Le Parnasse contemporain* (Contemporary Parnassus), France had excluded Stéphane Mallarmé's *L'Après-midi d'un faune* (1876; translated as *The Afternoon of a Faun,* 1956), Valéry, while following the convention according to which the new academician pays homage to his predecessor, damned France with somewhat ambiguous, if not faint, praise, suggesting that his grace, clarity, and ease of style disguised superficiality of content; moreover, while affecting to speak of him, Valéry avoided mentioning his name. (Valéry also disagreed with his politics.) The day France was buried, the surrealists—including Louis Aragon, André Breton, Pierre Drieu La Rochelle, and Paul Eluard—disseminated a harsh pamphlet called *Un Cadavre* (A Corpse), in which they denounced the values France represented—skepticism, irony, and wit—and accused him, in essence, of having been a walking corpse. The same year, the Communist Henri Barbusse, in his magazine *Clarté,* urged his followers to keep their distance. André Gide had already remarked in 1916 that France's work, while elegant and subtle, was "sans inquiétude" (without anxiety)—too clear, too easily understood, never disturbing his readers. In 1897, the year before the first collection of France's *Pages choisies* (Selected Texts) appeared, Charles-Louis Philippe, proclaiming the need for "barbares" (barbarians), had written: "Anatole France est délicieux, il sait tout, il est érudit même; c'est à cause de cela qu'il appartient à une race d'écrvains qui finit" (Anatole France is delightful, he knows everything, he's even erudite; that's why he belongs to a species of writers that is ending).

Yet, in 1921, when France was awarded the Nobel Prize in Literature, Erik Axel Karlfeldt, Permanent Secretary of the Swedish Academy, praised both the substance and style of France's writings as worthy of his great predecessors, including François Rabelais and Voltaire, and called the new laureate the last of the great classicists and the most authoritative contemporary representative of French civilization, to which, Karlfeldt stressed, Sweden and the entire world owed a great debt. By 1921 France's works had been translated into at least a dozen languages; English-speaking readers could read them in a series published by John Lane, and several translations appeared in the Modern Library series, with introductions by such literary notables as James Branch Cabell and Lafcadio Hearn. Biographies of France began to appear that same decade.

Stark differences in artistic judgments are no surprise; literary quarrels, some quite serious and having significant consequences, have marked the French cultural landscape for centuries. While Valéry's dismissal can be attributed to his devotion to Mallarmé, Gide's judgment and even more the surrealists' unfair severity reveal a crevasse between France's concerns and literary practice and those of the intransigent new aesthetics. In a 1979 article, Dushan Bresky observed: "La beauté classique qu'il avait récréé mourut avec lui. Bien avant sa mort l'esthétique littéraire avait suivi de nouveaux canons" (The classical beauty he had re-created died with him. Well before his death literary aesthetics had followed new canons). Indeed, few authors who live to occupy a pontifical position avoid the pitfalls fame brings; as their skills decline, their art rarely meets their own earlier standards and still less frequently the demands created by changing tastes and artistic evolution.

The irony of awarding the Nobel Prize to a writer who had fallen into disfavor among influential French contemporaries was compounded, for those aware of it, by his suspicion of science and its presumption of progress, a suspicion justified fully, he thought, by World War I. Yet, science was the very foundation of Alfred Nobel's wealth, and his belief in the future of mankind had led to the prize endowment, the terms of which required recognizing "the most remarkable work of idealistic tendencies." One wonders which of France's books the judges had examined. Claude-Michel Cluny observed, in the *Figaro Littéraire* in 2001, one hundred years after the first French author (Sully Prudhomme) received the prize, that Nobel selections reflect habits of thought of committees, who often confuse intentions and works and can misread one or both: "Pour ces doctes, l'art se voit tributaire d'impératifs idéologiques, il se doit de porter sur ses épaules 'un idéalisme noble et sain,' de 'donner une image claire de la vie humaine'" (For these learned ones, art must be a tributary of ideological imperatives; it owes itself to bear on its shoulders "a noble and healthy idealism," to "give a clear image of human life"). France's work carries out the second imperative better than the first, its idealism being, in truth, greatly qualified.

After France's death, his reputation continued to decline. His brand of intellectual skepticism and Epicureanism appealed less and less, as the Enlightenment humanism to which he remained faithful fell into disfavor and as the moderate literary values of ornamental beauty and critical reason were widely discarded in favor of radical cultural positions. As Breton put it in his *Manifeste du surréalisme* (1924, Surrealist Manifesto), "L'attitude réaliste, inspirée du positivisme, de Saint-Thomas à Anatole France, m'a bien l'air hostile à tout essor intellectuel et moral" (The realistic attitude, inspired by positivism, from Saint Thomas to Anatole France, seems to me hostile to all intellectual and moral development). To the proponents of *littérature engagée* (committed literature) and left-wing activism between the wars and beyond, France's social critiques seemed tame. (He observed himself that he was too bold for his own time but later would appear timid—the fate of moderates and evolutionaries.) Although substantial scholarly works appeared on him through the 1960s, in subsequent decades Francian scholarship declined, and his works nearly disappeared from anthologies and school syllabi. Late-twentieth-century critics, suspicious of texts that appeal to reason and influenced by deconstructionism, which questions the possibility of literary meaning, overlooked the hidden subversiveness of his work and thus its modernity, even as they identified the critical underside of writings by Honoré de Balzac and Gustave Flaubert. Among outstanding exceptions to this scholarly neglect are the 1984 biography by Marie-Claire Bancquart and her edition of his major works in Gallimard's Bibliothèque de la Pléiade.

France was not merely the superficial observer, the Epicurean, the facile writer for which he has been taken. To adopt reason, with considerable skepticism, as a guide to living and thinking is, for the French, honorable and far from naive: Michel Eyquem de Montaigne, Voltaire, and Denis Diderot illustrate how searching the rationalist position can be. France's suspicion of the dogmatic claims of science was complemented by anticlericalism—rejection of both religious dogma and the church. Yet, he made ample room for human feeling and intuition as well as freedom; his work is often sentimental. To the contention that "l'homme est fait pour comprendre" (man is created to understand), Balthasar, in the story of the same name, replies, "Il est fait pour aimer" (He is made for love). In fact, France seems to suggest that sentiment becomes all the more important as developments in knowledge indicate that one can never be sure of anything.

From this intellectual position, France produced a body of literature that is truly sui generis. His fiction is often realistic, especially in *Les Désirs de Jean Servien* (1882; translated as *The Aspirations of Jean Servien*, 1912) and *Le Lys rouge* (1894; translated as *The Red Lily*, 1898), but he generally eschewed the offshoot of realism, literary naturalism, because of its preoccupation with the sordid and its scientific pretensions. (He was also cool toward the naturalist writers—Edmond and Jules de Goncourt, who had treated him with condescension, and Emile Zola, whose novel *La Terre* [translated as *The Soil*, 1888] he criticized in 1887 but whom, however, he later learned to admire.) He likewise has much in common with the decadents of the 1880s and 1890s, cultivating, like Maurice Barrès, Joris-Karl Huysmans, and Pierre Louÿs, a sensuous prose and often choosing his topics from periods in which old worlds were ending—particularly the late Hellenic period and the transitional time between pagan and Christian Rome. Irony, that marker of modern literature, is rarely far below the surface in his prose, attracting critics such as Wayne C. Booth; but it is less the deep self-doubt and self-hatred visible in works by Charles Baudelaire and Flaubert or the existentialist irony of Søren Kierkegaard and Albert Camus than a cultural irony—the understanding that all customs and all history are subject to revision, and that human perspective is necessarily limited, subjective.

France was born François-Anatole Thibault in Paris, on the Quai Malaquais, overlooking the Seine on the Left Bank, on 16 April 1844, also the birth year of poet Paul Verlaine. His father, François-Noël Thibault, had become a bookseller and minor publisher after having learned to read, it appears, only as an adult, in the service of his patron, Count Henri de La Bédoyère. Following the custom of his native Anjou region, Noël Thibault had shortened his first name to "France"; he then called his bookshop "France-Thibault," and by 1844 his imprint was simply "Noël France" or "France." Anatole, while baptized under the name Thibault, was sometimes known as "Anatole France" as early as grammar school. His choice of name under which to live and write should hence be considered only a half pseudonym. Anatole's mother, née Antoinette Galas, a widow, had married Noël France in 1840. She was the illegitimate offspring of a miller's daughter, who married shortly after Antoinette's birth, then was widowed and remarried; the second stepfather, Jean-Pierre Dufour, a ne'er-do-well, remained, until his death in 1865, a drain on his family and then Noël France's. Anatole, however, perceived Dufour's eccentricities as charming; in his fiction they appear in various guises.

Anatole's early life was molded by the atmosphere of his father's shop, to which writers repaired to exchange ideas, as in eighteenth-century coffeehouses. At the age of eight he composed for his mother a collection of thoughts and maxims. He also began a translation of Virgil's first eclogue, complete with notes and preface. At ten he thought that nothing in life was more beautiful than correcting proofs. Even if he later recognized the inadequacies of his autodidactic father's learning, books formed Anatole's mind, and he would always remain not quite a bookish man but a learned one, a devourer of the printed page, embracing both classics and moderns and accumulating a vast store of knowledge—in short, a preeminent example of the late-nineteenth-century man of letters.

Noël France was not, however, the boy's favorite parent; as the author wrote in his autobiographical work *Le Petit Pierre* (1918, translated as *Little Pierre*, 1920), "En toutes choses, d'instinct, je m'opposais à lui" (I was opposed to him in everything, instinctively). Noël France's royalist loyalties led his son to adopt republican sympathies early in life; and the boy refused to adopt his father's livelihood, insisting instead, over objections, upon pursuing a writer's career (which, at the time, was viewed as somewhat precarious financially and, in some circles, not entirely honorable). Anatole was closer to his mother and, as her only child, was showered with affection. This relationship is painted tenderly in the autobiographical *Le Livre de mon ami* (1885; translated as *My Friend's Book,* 1913), in which Noël France is transformed into a doctor but Antoinette France appears much as she apparently was. This intimate relationship between son and mother foreshadows that depicted by one of France's emulators, Marcel Proust, who almost surely found in *Le Livre de mon ami* encouragement for his own study of a close mother-son relationship and who, at least early in his career, was influenced by France's prose style (the model, it is generally believed, for Bergotte's in *Du côté de chez Swann* [1913; translated as *Swann's Way,* 1922]).

France's father and mother were both traditionalists; his mother attended Mass regularly. France probably enjoyed the beauty of services, for his spokesmen express aesthetic appreciation of the liturgy, but he may have lost his faith early, after the disappointment of his First Communion. He resented being sent to the Collège Saint-Stanislas in 1855, after two years elsewhere. While the priests were not unkind, nor indifferent to belles lettres, France did not flourish under their discipline; his performance received praise and prizes only rarely, when the topic of his lessons interested him. Moreover, he felt at a disadvantage with respect to the other boys, nearly all from much wealthier and socially prominent households. His humiliation at having to carry an old portfolio instead of a proper bookbag is recorded in *Le Livre de mon ami*. A certain awkwardness in his personality, sometimes called obsequiousness, noticeable until he achieved renown, can perhaps be traced to a childhood feeling of inferiority.

France left Saint-Stanislas in 1862, presumably to study independently. Upon receiving his baccalaureate somewhat tardily in 1864, he began earning money from various publishers and embarked on his writing career via journalism (especially in bibliophilic publications) and poetry. Finding a position with Alphonse Lemerre improved his fortunes considerably, for Lemerre soon made him a reader for *Le Parnasse contemporain,* in which France's own poetry was included. At that stage it appeared that he would become chiefly a poet, modeling his work (despite its personal tone) on that of the older Parnassians, especially Charles-Marie-René Leconte de Lisle, known for his impassive, chiseled verse and his cult of antiquity. In 1864 France passed off lines by his own hand as work by André Chénier, a late-eighteenth-century poet. Indeed, France's early verse stands up well in comparison to that of many contemporaries. However, the explosion and disintegration of poetic forms in the twentieth century and the resurgence of a poetry of explicit self-expression have rendered Parnassian poetic values almost antiquarian.

His poetry was nourished by the anguish of unrequited love. From his adolescence he had been unsuccessful with women, from the sisters of family acquaintances to Nina de Callias, a bluestocking, and Elise Devoyod, an actress for whom he long harbored a frustrated passion. Actresses often appear in his works, notably *Histoire comique* (1903; translated as *A Mummer's*

Tale, 1908), inspired by the memoirs of Mlle Clairon, a celebrated eighteenth-century actress.

France also turned to criticism. While somewhat derivative and now outdated, his 1868 book on Alfred de Vigny was for its time a sensitive, if rambling, study of the only would-be impassive and stoic among the Romantics. The book inaugurates the critical style France later made famous in his prefaces and regular columns in the *Univers Illustré* (1883–1896), *Le Temps* (1886–1893), the *Echo de Paris* (1892–1899), and the *Figaro* (1899–1901). A critic's function, according to his celebrated formula, was to recount "les aventures de son âme au milieu des chefs-d'oeuvre" (the adventures of one's soul amid masterpieces). His style was labeled "impressionist" by the then-authoritative critic Ferdinand Brunetière, who intended the term pejoratively because he believed in objective standards for literary judgment and scorned those who thought aesthetic appreciation was necessarily subjective and one might as well acknowledge it. Modern critics, of course, have sided with France.

To augment his small writing income from prefaces, encyclopedia articles, and ghost work for Lemerre, which left him dependent often upon his parents, France obtained employment in 1876 at the Senate library. In 1877 he married Valérie Guérin de Sauville, thirteen years younger than he, in what was at least a half-arranged match. It produced one daughter, Suzanne (born in 1881), on whom France long doted. But France and his wife apparently had little in common besides their daughter, and the marriage was not happy. They were divorced in 1893.

France's first published fiction, *Jocaste,* appeared in 1878 in magazine form, then was collected the following year with *Le Chat maigre* (translated together as *Jocasta and the Famished Cat,* 1912). Unlike many early novels, usually autobiographical, that are weak in craft and substance, *Jocaste* is a mature and nonsubjective work with an impressive command of language and a plot designed for the maximum effect on readers craving sensation. While short, it has more than one vein: it is realistic in its character types (which are worthy of Balzac) and its emphasis on the role of money; it is Romantic in its portrait of mute, idealized love and the powerful effects of unexpressed feelings; it is Gothic in its mystery elements (a deformed, vaguely threatening servant slowly poisons his master and then murders a crafty old forger); and it is melodramatic in its characters' fate (the heroine hangs herself, and the man who loved her, René Longuemare, welcomes the disease that will kill him). Even France's trademark irony and skepticism are not lacking. René professes an almost nihilistic radical scientism, questioning all possibilities for truth–while harboring a timid, idealized love.

The title *Le Chat maigre* refers to a Latin Quarter bar where the characters meet. The disquieting eccentricities of certain figures in *Jocaste* reappear here in harmless form, and the tone is generally humorous rather than tragic. Following Henry Murger and other early realists, the author depicts a Left Bank bohemia of poets, artists, and ne'er-do-wells, to which are added a Haitian politician and his son. The denouement, which brings together the young Creole and the girl he has worshiped and leaves the rest of *la bohème* to its incorrigible ways, imparts a sense of human freedom rather than fatality.

The same is true for France's next fiction, *Le Crime de Sylvestre Bonnard, membre de l'Institut* (1881; translated as *The Crime of Sylvestre Bonnard,* 1890), which was awarded a prize by the Académie Française and was long one of his most admired books. It consists of two parts of unequal length, tied together only by the eponymous narrator. A retired professor, book and manuscript collector, and a member of the French Institute, Bonnard resembles his creator in his timidity and his love of old texts.

In the first part he sends a Christmas gift of firewood, including a Yule log, to a young couple living in misery in the garret above him. Otherwise, his routine of research is broken only by conversations with his housekeeper, memories of visits to Uncle Victor (modeled on Dufour), and a trip to Sicily to buy a coveted manuscript. When he learns that the Sicilian dealer who had promised him the parchment has instead given it to his son, who sells antiques in Paris, Bonnard is both furious and disappointed. His travels are, however, made more pleasant by encounters with a charming Parisian and her husband, Prince Trépof, a collector. Back in Paris, Bonnard attends an auction at which the manuscript is for sale, but he cannot outbid an anonymous competitor. At the end of the year, he receives as a gift a hollow Yule log, cradling the precious manuscript. This O. Henryesque ending is made possible by Princess Trépof, who is none other than the woman in the garret, widowed and remarried into wealth; having learned of Bonnard's disappointment, she has repaid her benefactor generously, with the added drama of surprise. This sentimental ending fits his character–good-hearted, easily moved, and unfit for practical life.

In the second part, Bonnard again exercises charity, this time toward the orphaned granddaughter of a woman he had once loved. His efforts to protect Jeanne and secure her education lead to involvements with a dishonest notary and a mean-spirited, frustrated, calculating headmistress, who attempts to maneuver Bonnard into marriage and, when she fails, turns her ire on the girl. The description of the school and schoolmistress and the episode in which Bonnard successfully spirits Jeanne away are both charming and suspenseful, for, although the reader senses that the basic goodness of the hero and his protégée must triumph, malice and the cruelty of fate form a thematic undercurrent to Bonnard's humanism. He subsequently arranges for Jeanne to receive her due—the completion of her education and, finally, a suitor, a young scholar. The "crime" occurs at this juncture: Bonnard, who has promised to sell his library in order to give her a dowry, "steals" books from those to be sold—books with which he cannot bear to part. No matter; Jeanne is duly and happily married.

The semi-autobiographical *Les Désirs de Jean Servien* apparently offered an outlet for France's bitterness concerning his youth and allowed him to set forth his views on contemporary social issues. Published in 1882, it was, he wrote in his preface to the first edition, composed ten years before (though revised before publication), and thus may be considered a youthful bildungsroman. Some of its themes are found also in Alphonse Daudet's *Le Petit Chose* (1868; translated as *The Little Good-for-Nothing*, 1878) and in Jules Vallès's *Le Bachelier* (1881, The Graduate).

Jean is pained by the misery in which he lives with his aunt and father, a hard-toiling bookbinder less erudite than Noël France, and is sensitive to his plebeian status; but he shows no great gifts and has none of the energy of Stendhal's Julien Sorel, hero of *Le rouge et le noir* (1830; translated as *Red and Black,* 1898). His sometime tutor, the boastful drunkard Baron Tudesco, is a farcical character modeled on Dufour, whose appearances always bode ill for the Serviens' pocketbook, and finally for Jean's life. Although Jean receives his baccalaureate, he has no prospects; society offers few positions for those with liberal educations. Often he does nothing but go to the theater with money filched from his aunt. (Noël France had complained in 1868 that his son just scribbled, accomplishing nothing.) A job as a school proctor humiliates Jean; he is shortly dismissed anyway. Enamored of an actress, he writes to her, follows her, and finally confronts her and kisses her hand in a passionate gesture. Recognizing that he is just a mooning schoolboy, she dismisses him, though not unkindly. He falls into despair, and his love turns bitter.

Jean's private drama becomes part of the larger, historical drama. His politics are different from the author's. Although France's youthful republicanism had set him in opposition not only to his father but also to the Second Empire, he had none of the revolutionary or anarchist in him, and until past middle age he was not involved in political causes. During the last years of Napoleon III's reign, when there was considerable liberalizing of laws governing freedom of association and the press, France became less hostile to the empire, which, he recognized, had wide popular support. After the defeat at Sedan (1870) during the Franco-Prussian War, he served briefly as a reserve soldier, posted in Paris only. The consequences of the war, especially the bloody Paris Commune (March–May 1871), during which he managed to escape, thanks to a forged passport, seemed to him disastrous. It was both the sign and the cause of chaos; it represented the triumph of irrationality over a rational social order. Jean, in contrast, hates the empire and joins those who hope to overthrow it and establish a popular socialist government; the Commune represents the realization of his political dream. He has not forgotten the actress, however. Discovering that she is the mistress of Bargemont, a corpulent bureaucrat from the Ministry of Finances who had been, briefly, his protector, he falls ill from the shock. Later, meeting Tudesco, who has become a colonel of the Commune, he confesses his misfortunes in love. Tudesco, in his drunkenness, imagines that Jean is enamored of Bargemont's wife, and steals her portrait for him. When Jean goes to ask for an explanation, he is arrested by Communard guards as a spy of the Versaillais (the army and the Government of National Defense). He is imprisoned, released, but seized again and shot by a vigilante-type *citoyenne* as personal vengeance against the hated bourgeoisie.

Jean's somber story is thus an indictment of the Commune, for its violence and anarchy, and of women and an uncaring society. In contrast, the main section of France's next work, *Le Livre de mon ami,* is an idealized portrait of himself as a child, called Pierre Nozière. (The second section, "Le Livre de Suzanne," depicts his daughter's childhood.) Inspired by a meditation on Dante's line from the *Inferno,* "Nel mezzo del cammin di nostra vita" (In the middle of our life's road), the narrator looks back with tender and bemused eyes on his mother, father, family friends, even an idealized first love. The work purports to be reminiscences, not fiction, and early biographers leaned heavily on it. However, it and its sequels, *Pierre Nozière* (1899; translated, 1916), *Le Petit Pierre,* and *La Vie en fleur* (1922; translated as *The Bloom of Life,* 1923), doubtless represent considerable retouching of the truth. Long a readers' favorite for its charm, indulgence, and an almost Proustian sensitivity to the Paris setting and the feelings of childhood, *Le Livre de mon ami* lacks the critical dimension now expected in autobiography; moreover, the whole problematics of memory and self-writing are missing, though not all irony. France shows his talent for the nice turn of phrase; for example, when the adolescent hero has just humiliated himself unspeakably by replying "Yes, sir" to a woman whose beauty mesmerizes him, France writes: "Puisque la terre ne s'entrouvrit pas en ce moment pour m'engloutir, c'est que la nature est indifférente aux voeux les plus ardents des hommes" (If the earth did not open up then to swallow me up, it is because nature is indifferent to men's most ardent wishes).

The title story of France's first collection of tales, *Balthasar* (1889; translated, 1909), introduced into his prose the important vein of orientalism. Romantic writers and painters earlier in the century had cultivated what they called the Orient, mostly Egypt (made popular by Napoleon's expedition) and other Near Eastern areas, including North Africa after 1830; but they were preoccupied with the exoticism of their own time. In contrast, France's orientalism, like Flaubert's, includes an historical dimension. He displays particular interest in late Hellenic civilization, Egypt, and the Levant at the time of Christ, which appeared to him, accurately, as a period of change with tremendous historical implications. The heir less of rationalist and serene Greece than of its turbulent sequels, France shows keen interest in the Mediterranean cauldron of cultures and cults in which Christianity was forged, and in competing sects such as Mithraism.

Several of the stories in *Balthasar*, and many later tales, deal with biblical or legendary material. France draws on the Bible, the writings of Flavius Josephus, and hagiography, especially Jacques de Voragine's (Iacopo da Varezze) *La Légende dorée* (published first in Latin as *Legenda aurea*, circa 1474; translated as *The Golden Legend*, 1483), as well as his own imagination. He was also interested in biblical apocrypha, both Jewish and Christian. The material on which he embroiders acquires sometimes an almost mythic character, revealing, under the disguise of history and legend, truths that late-nineteenth-century readers devoted to the ideal of progress refused to acknowledge: the disruptive and yet creative power of sexuality, the violence in human character, the death of empires, and the power and persistence of religious belief, including superstition. By his taste for the Hellenic and medieval periods, France is an heir both of the Romantics, with their Christian mythology, and the Parnassians, especially Leconte de Lisle, with his interest in antiquity and his pessimism. But France is also a forerunner of those twentieth-century authors who had recourse to myth as an alternative to realism in fiction.

There are also parapsychological and fantastic elements. The taste for the occult and the fantastic, which seems incongruous in such a skeptic, was deeply ingrained. France was, as Bancquart puts it, "seduced" by Gnostic sciences, as were certain lesser-known Romantics and many late-nineteenth-century writers; though some are now almost forgotten, their works fascinated many of their contemporaries. It was the era of the Theosophists, the revival of Rosicrucianism, and other manifestations of occultism and Gnostic mysticism, which had been a subcurrent during the Enlightenment and had influenced Balzac and Baudelaire. A principal occultist was Alphonse-Louis Constant, who took the name Eliphas Lévi, author of *La Clef des grands mystères* (1861, The Key to the Great Mysteries). Others were Joséphin Péladan (called the Sâr), Stanislas de Guaïta, and Gérard Encausse (called Papus); the influence of occultism is visible in the prose of Huysmans, Philippe-Auguste de Villiers de l'Isle-Adam, and, later, Guillaume Apollinaire.

Thaïs (1890; translated, 1891), originally called a philosophical tale after Voltaire's manner, is France's first full-length orientalist work. Set to music in 1894 by Jules Massenet, with a libretto by Louis Gallet, it became a successful opera. It was inspired in part by marionette performances in Paris in 1888 that led the author to investigate a corpus of tenth-century hagiographic puppet plays. This source complemented his other readings in hagiography and a long-term interest in the courtesan Thaïs, the topic of an early poem.

In part 1, the hermit monk Paphnuce, leaving his desert cell, undertakes to convert Thaïs, a beautiful and successful courtesan of Alexandria. The prose is sensuous, the visual element powerful. France's anticlericalism sprang in part from the church's denunciation of the pleasures of the flesh, which he accepted as being perfectly natural and thus good. In *Thaïs* the flesh takes keen revenge on those who deny it. Until the end, Paphnuce is blind to the attraction of Thaïs, blind to his own motivations and demons, who, unlike those in Flaubert's *La Tentation de Saint Antoine* (1874; translated as *The Temptation of Saint Anthony*, 1895), an obvious point of comparison, are entirely internal. Throughout, the author suggests the connection between religious and erotic ecstasy, as well as the power of human pride disguised by pious motives.

Part 2 presents a lengthy banquet scene in Alexandria, modeled on Plato's symposium. The form of the philosophical dialogue is used effectively to convey a range of opinions (Stoicism, Epicureanism) among intellectuals who reject religion in the name of nature and the senses and who discuss such topics as the reason for creation, evil, free will, and death. At the close, Paphnuce seems to have triumphed: Thaïs consents to renounce her life of pleasure and immure herself among the female monks of the desert. However, Paphnuce remains obsessed by her. In the last part, a period of extreme asceticism atop a pillar only brings further temptations. The stylite ultimately recognizes that he has been the dupe of God, who led him to deny the only true good: sensual love. He goes to reclaim Thaïs from her hermitage, but it is too late; she is dying, honored as a holy woman.

The wheel of fate, whose turning brings Thaïs to the end—holiness—that Paphnuce had sought for himself, can have both an ancient and a modern interpretation. Venus has had her revenge, as the monk's friend Nicias, a hedonist, had warned him; the constants of destiny, which the Athenian Greeks had identified and whose later Hellenic development is explored in the symposium, have prevailed over the efforts of Christianity to deny and counteract this destiny. In modern terms, the libido has burst through the hypocritical and repressive consciousness of Paphnuce, who lied to himself so thoroughly that he denied his true self.

E. M. Forster cited *Thaïs* for its hourglass construction, by which the fates of the two main characters join briefly only at the center, then diverge again. One can admire it even more for imposing, by means of a lush style, a worldview both alien and yet psychologically provocative, in which France's anticlericalism is grounded not on rationalist impatience with absurdities but on the understanding of the human self. The violent denunciation of the book, a notable success, by a Jesuit priest, Father Brucker, in the periodical *Etudes* may have sprung from his recognition that in Anatole France the church faced not just another anticlerical rationalist but an enemy who proposed a total fulfillment of human potentialities, which could not be countenanced by a church preaching sacrifice and self-denial. The church was not to change its position: in 1922 all of France's work was placed on the Index of Proscribed Books.

The defense of desire expressed in *Thaïs* is significant in view of France's personal life. In 1883 he had begun frequenting the salon of Léontine Arman de Caillavet, a lively and intelligent Jewish woman, a Christian convert, whose husband, Albert Arman, had assumed the particle *de* and his mother's maiden name. France became known as the lion of her gatherings; by 1888 they were lovers. His marriage, long unsatisfactory, deteriorated even further. In 1892, after a quarrel in which his wife insulted him deliberately, France, in dressing gown and slippers, seized his writing materials, walked out of the room, and went to a hotel; he never again resided with her. Later he moved to an apartment. Thenceforth the center of his activities was Mme de Caillavet's residence.

Appearances were always maintained: although he had his room upstairs, it is said that for Mme de Caillavet's receptions he entered through the front door, like the other guests; but he lunched and dined and spent nearly all day there, and their intimate relationship was well known. Mme de Caillavet remained married until her death in 1910; Arman took no visible umbrage at her involvement with the by-then famous writer, and the three traveled together. The Armans' son, Gaston, who became a successful playwright in collaboration with Robert de Flers, was, however, disturbed by his mother's conduct. Mme de Caillavet became freer when in 1893 Gaston married Jeanne Pouquet, a friend of Proust (considered one of the models for Gilberte Swann). France and Mme de Caillavet accompanied the young married couple on a wedding trip to Italy.

The affair between Mme de Caillavet and France was a stormy one, marked by quarrels and reconciliations; but they established a close intellectual companionship. She spurred him to write; it was doubtless she who urged him to compose the preface for Proust's first book, *Les Plaisirs et les jours* (1896; translated as *Pleasures and Days,* 1957). Although she may have been despotic as a muse, France seemed to thrive, and she gave him more confidence in himself than had his wife, always hostile to his career; even public adulation was not as inspiring to him as Mme de Caillavet's presence. On occasions she wrote a column or so for him; but it is excessive to maintain that she composed whole works.

During the late 1880s and 1890s France's books and columns were widely appreciated, and he made money. In 1890 he resigned from his librarian's position at the Senate, a stopgap duty for which he had been unenthusiastic. In 1894 he bought a private townhouse, 5 Villa Saïd. Two years later, after he had satirized the Académie Française in *Les Opinions de M. Jérôme Coignard* (1893; translated as *The Opinions of Jérôme Coignard,* 1913), the institution elected him to the seat vacated when Ferdinand de Lesseps died. The decade was made sadder for France by the death in 1892 of an intellectual master, Ernest Renan, author of *Vie de Jésus* (1863), a recounting of the life of Christ according to the principles of nineteenth-century scientific historiography.

The last decade of the century also marked France's initial involvement in political matters. Temperamentally conservative, fond of order, yet Voltairean in his hatred of fanaticism and obscurantism, he had maintained for years a moderate course. His experience during the Commune and his vast reading concerning the French Revolution had made him particularly wary of anarchism and, what was to him nearly the same, socialism. This wariness is visible in *L'Etui de nacre* (1892; translated as *Tales from a Mother-of-Pearl Casket,* 1896)—stories reprinted from a long periodical publication, "Les Autels de la peur" (The Altars of Fear; *Journal des Débats,* 1884), which portray the brutality and lawlessness during the Reign of Terror. In 1888 France was vaguely interested in the career of the nationalist general Georges-Ernest Boulanger but denounced him when it became clear that he represented a threat to constitutional government.

The Dreyfus Affair changed Anatole France permanently. In 1894, when Captain Alfred Dreyfus was convicted of treason and subsequently condemned to deportation to Devil's Island, the public had no reason to question the justice of the sentence; but evidence later emerged that cast doubt on the captain's guilt as well as the propriety of government conduct. In a November 1897 interview, France said he could not approve of the verdict, since he had been unable to examine the evidence. After Zola published his famous open letter, "J'accuse," in the *Aurore* (13 January 1898) and was charged with defamation, France signed the "Pétition des intellectuels" in his support and then testified at his trial. When Zola was suspended from the Legion of Honor in 1898, France, who had been named to the society in 1884, refused to wear his decoration, and in 1900 he ceased attending Académie Française meetings because of the coolness colleagues showed him as a result of the affair. He pronounced an impassioned eulogy at Zola's funeral in 1902.

For the remainder of his career France remained a Left-leaning liberal, associated on and off with the Socialist Party, which he supported in a public speech in 1904 and to whose paper, *L'Humanité*, he contributed. His socialism was, however, undogmatic, inspired less by economic theory than by the failures of the Third Republic, dominated by a wealthy oligarchy. In the quarrel and subsequent split within the party, he followed Jean Jaurès rather than the intransigent Jules Guesde. His socialism was also an expression of his humanist concern for individuals and in no way represented a radical conversion. In 1921 it was announced that he had joined the Communist Party, but he withdrew his support the next year.

Some of France's best-known prose appeared in the 1890s. *La Rôtisserie de la reine Pédauque* (translated as *The Queen Pedauque,* 1923) and *Les Opinions de M. Jérôme Coignard,* both published in 1893, recall eighteenth-century picaresque novels, philosophical tales, and rambling novels of ideas and conversation. *La Rôtisserie de la reine Pédauque* has three thematic strands. The first is Enlightenment skepticism, the sort associated with Voltaire but visible also in works by such figures as Diderot and Pierre Bayle, whose *Dictionnaire historique et critique* (1697, Historical and Critical Dictionary) helped initiate the eighteenth-century struggle against superstition. The second is orthodox church doctrine, which the author mocks and which is judged morally inadequate but not entirely discredited, especially in comparison to popular superstition.

The third strand is occultism. It too is patently mocked, but France appears interested in it nonetheless. Moreover, since he is suspicious of dogma of any sort, both occultism and religion benefit from the skeptic's recognition that perhaps, after all, one should not rule out certain phenomena simply because one cannot understand them, and from the psychologist's awareness that irrational beliefs may spring from the soul. As Jérôme Coignard says, "Il semble que les vieilles erreurs soient moins fâcheuses que les nouvelles, et que, puisque nous devons nous tromper, le meilleur est de s'en tenir aux illusions émoussées" (It seems that old errors are less harmful than new ones, and, since we must necessarily be mistaken, the best thing is to stay with well-worn illusions).

For *La Rôtisserie de la reine Pédauque,* France drew on a wealth of sources, among them Gnostic texts and *The Arabian Nights,* although his text is not just a compendium. The novel takes its title from a Paris cookshop where the young Jacques Ménétrier helps his father by turning the spit—hence his sobriquet, Tournebroche. Jacques narrates his youthful adventures around 1730 in the company of his tutor, Jérôme Coignard, a priest given to the delights of the flesh, whose fortunes have declined; later they are joined by M. d'Astarac, an alchemist and occultist. The loose structure of the work allows for digressions, but the plot is not merely episodic: France knots its threads successfully to bring about a dramatic denouement.

Coignard represents skepticism (which he imparts to the candid Jacques) in all matters save doctrine, for despite his moral failings, he remains faithful to the core of church dogma, through the mechanism of *credo quia absurdum* ("I believe it because it is absurd," a position France mocks but considers no worse than efforts to prove the existence of God by logic). In worldly matters the priest is a prudent and perspicacious counselor. D'Astarac is the opposite; persuaded that he can overcome the limitations of reason and the senses, he tries to fabricate diamonds, pursues the invisible (in the form of sylphs and salamanders), and conducts other magical experiments. He engages Jacques and Coignard to visit his estate outside Paris to assist him in interpreting Greek Gnostic texts while he works with Egyptian hieroglyphs. His illuminism is contagious: Jacques almost comes to believe in otherworldly beings and nearly expects the beautiful salamander that d'Astarac has promised him. What Jacques meets, however, is no spirit but a living young woman, Jahel, the niece (and probably mistress) of old Mosaïde, a Jew who helps d'Astarac with cabalistic texts. A projection, perhaps, of the author's images of woman, she resembles also many eighteenth-century heroines in her faithlessness and talent for troublemaking.

Jacques and Coignard become embroiled in a farcical scrape in Paris involving Catherine (a luscious creature Jacques had coveted), one of her lovers, and the older "protector" at whose house the group is engaged in revelry during his absence. After the protector's sudden return, there is a scuffle, during which Coignard kills a servant. Jacques, Coignard, and the lover are forced to flee, while Catherine will be shipped off to Louisiana. The three men take temporary refuge on d'Astarac's estate and then head for a hideaway near Lyons, taking with them what they think is one of d'Astarac's valuable diamonds and Jahel, who has meanwhile deserted Jacques for the new arrival, Catherine's former lover. On the road their carriage is wrecked when Coignard utters a magic word, "Agla." Coignard is brutally attacked by Mosaïde, who has pursued them from Paris in a jealous rage. But d'Astarac, who has accompanied him, says it was not Mosaïde who wounded Coignard but the spirits, because he had revealed the secrets of the elves. Coignard dies an edifying death, his sins remitted, according to a local priest, by his repentance in extremis. Sometime thereafter, Jacques returns to Paris and finds work at the bookshop of St. Catherine. While going to visit d'Astarac, he learns that Mosaïde has drowned, and he sees the château burning—the result, doubtless, of an experiment gone awry, with the alchemist himself perched on the flaming rooftop, calling out that he is rising on the wings of fire.

The main characters are memorable. By his erudition, his frank admission of his shortcomings, his vitality, and his appeal to reason, Coignard endears himself to both Jacques and the reader. D'Astarac is impressive by his very lunacy, at once frightening and charming, with even a few grains of wisdom. Jacques, a brother to Voltaire's Candide, appeals by his thirst for knowledge as well as his uninhibited attitude toward young women. The rational and the irrational exist side by side not only thematically but also in the development of the plot—as if France wanted to acknowledge, like Voltaire, the inscrutability of human destiny.

In the sequel, *Les Opinions de M. Jérôme Coignard*, the narrator explains that he found Jacques's manuscript of *La Rôtisserie de la reine Pédauque* in a Montparnasse bookstall; having published it, he now is adding a second text, discovered at the same time. France thus evokes the "found manuscript" trope frequent in eighteenth-century novels. The work consists of conversations between the abbé Coignard and Jacques Tournebroche, chiefly on the topic of government. Coignard here becomes France's spokesman—"le plus sage des moralistes, une sorte de mélange merveilleux d'Epicure et de saint François d'Assise" (the wisest of moralists, a sort of marvelous mixture of Epicurus and Saint Francis of Assisi). Contemporary topics are thinly disguised under a cloak of eighteenth-century references—on the model of Enlightenment texts in which oriental characters and settings are subterfuges for attacks on contemporaneous institutions. Readers had no trouble, for instance, in seeing the Panama Scandal of the 1880s in "L'Affaire du Mississipi [*sic*]," ostensibly concerning the John Law financial scandal (in connection with land in Louisiana) in the early eighteenth century. Parallels between the ancien regime of Louis XV and the republic some one hundred and fifty years later are obvious, as when the priest argues that *raison d'état* (reason of state) cannot justify dishonesty (and this book was written before the Dreyfus Affair broke).

Even more striking is Coignard's implied political philosophy, antirevolutionary because it refutes the Rousseauist principle (so named only in the preface) according to which human beings are perfectible creatures and a government of virtue can be attained. With hindsight, France knew that those who had wished to usher in the reign of virtue had brought instead the Reign of Terror, and that the lofty ideals of the Enlightenment were still far from being realized. He thus has his abbé argue that changing the form of government would do little to improve conditions; the next government might be still worse, and government by the many holds out more possibilities for mediocrity and abuse than government by one. Any progress will be imperceptible. Meanwhile, ministers are all venal and incompetent, and wealth and honors reign over virtue; the only good thing that can be said is that ministers play a minor role in the development of human history, which France identifies as the product of vast forces rather than the action of a few individuals. Under such circumstances true freedom is as yet impossible in the body politic; it should be sought, rather, in the self, in a soul freed from ignorance, superstition, and the vanities of the world.

Le Lys rouge, one of France's best-constructed novels, is in a contrasting vein, that of psychological and social realism. It demonstrates that, contrary to those people, including himself, who thought he was naturally a tale-teller, he had a sense of the novel also, which allowed him to structure a work to make plot and psychology coincide. Almost Jamesian in parts, *Le Lys rouge* is a study in love and jealousy. It is also a portrait of society; like Stendhal before him and Proust afterward, France excels at making social mechanisms not only the background but also an agent of personal development.

Thérèse Martin-Bellème is a sensitive and intelligent woman married to a politically ambitious man, who gives her wide latitude as long as she respects proprieties. In their Parisian salon gather diverse social, artistic, and political figures. Thérèse is also, as she says, a sensual woman; but while a late-nineteenth-century French novelist could, without shocking the public as Zola did with *Nana* (1880; translated, 1880), allow himself, as France does, to refer openly to sexual desire among the upper classes, there are no detailed erotic scenes. When Thérèse's lover, Le Ménil, prolongs a hunting trip, she decides to accept the invitation of Miss Bell, a Pre-Raphaelite poetess, to visit her villa in Florence. Much of the action thus takes place in Italy, where natural beauty competes with some of the most exquisite products of the human eye and hand.

In this setting, where nearly every prospect delights the eye—except cemeteries and other reminders of decay—Thérèse is courted by an artist, Dechartre (who is much like the author). Finally yielding, reluctantly, to his importunate suit, she then finds herself falling in love with him. The scenes of their passionate idyll are overlaid with references to art but also to unhappiness. Le Ménil, receiving no reply to his letters and anxious to retrieve the woman he had taken for granted, arrives in Florence. Each lover discovers the existence of the other and feels betrayed. Back in Paris, where her husband needs her help in promoting his election, Thérèse tries to break with Le Ménil, but he pursues her. Dechartre, already jealous of her past, suspects, wrongly, that Thérèse and Le Ménil are still lovers. His physical and mental sufferings are such that he must end the affair; love has led to its own destruction. At the opera, Thérèse injures her hand on the red lily pin he had designed for her as a sign of their Florentine love, and the blood drips onto her bosom.

The character portraits—including those of the eccentric Miss Bell, her unscrupulous suitor Prince Albertinelli, and the half-mystic, half-calculating poet Coulette (modeled partly on Verlaine in his last years)—match those by other masters of French fiction. Similarly, the social comedy and workings of a salon where contacts are made and political maneuvers prepared are handled skillfully. France excels chiefly, however, at depicting love, especially the impossible desire for total possession of the beloved. While the language, symbolism, and other aspects of the novel follow nineteenth-century conventions, they do not invalidate the work as a keen study of desire and unhappiness.

The reader of *Thaïs, Balthasar,* and famous tales including "Le Jongleur de Notre-Dame" (Our Lady's Juggler, first published in the *Gaulois,* 10 May 1890) and "Le Procurateur de Judée" (The Procurator of Judea, first published in *Le Temps,* 25 December 1891), collected in *L'Etui de nacre* along with stories based on saints' legends, might conclude that France was incurably attracted to the past, precisely because it is unverifiable and thus can give free rein to the imagination. But in the four novels later grouped together as *Histoire contemporaine* (Contemporary History), France revealed himself to be a keen, witty, and accurate painter (sometimes a caricaturist) of contemporary mores, society, and politics. He ranks not far from Proust for his depiction of the social and political mechanisms and currents that dominated the Third Republic just before 1900.

L'Orme du mail (1897; translated as *The Elm-Tree on the Mall: A Chronicle of Our Own Times,* 1910), first published serially, deals with two major opposing forces: the Church, which until the separation law (Emile Combes law) of 1905 was still established and protected; and the republic, built partly on the strictly secular principles of the Revolution and including virulently anticlerical elements. The situation is complicated by the new papal order of *ralliement* (that is, expedient recognition of the legitimacy of the French republic), which the novelist satirizes. Despite a structure that lets some plot threads simply dangle, the work has unity because of the piercing social satire and the convincing tones and phrasing by which France renders the speech, thoughts, and appearances of the characters, major and minor. Deft plot turns mirror the machinations of the church and the unvisionary Third Republic, the very image of government by intrigue.

The main plot centers around who will be named bishop of Tourcoing. The competing candidates and the archbishop are so well individualized that, as Jacques Suffel notes in *Anatole France par lui-même* (1954, Anatole France by Himself), they rival the priests of Stendhal and Balzac. Their unctuousness nearly drips off the page; but under that self-righteousness, their scheming and ambitious ways are as visible as those of their lay counterparts, the politicians who support one candidate or another according to their own—or their wives'—purposes. In the background is the insoluble conflict between an established church that remains royalist in both its pronouncements and sympathies and a republic that is anticlerical through historical reference and has a pathological fear of restoration. An additional focus of the novelist's attention is Jewish influence in French society and the role of Jews as brokers of wealth and power. In a nation where Edouard Drumont's inflammatory tract *La France juive* (1886, Jewish France) had enjoyed widespread favor, the depiction of Jewish politicians involved in naming a bishop was not merely a nice irony. In counterpoint to this main plot and associated intrigues are others, chiefly the story of M. Bergeret. Like Sylvestre Bonnard, he seems dear to the author's heart. A modest professor married to a haughty and somewhat shrewish wife, he is only an observer, not a maker, of political and ecclesiastical intrigue; but, as a Voltairean, neither fanatical nor venal, he can play the role of listener and *raisonneur* (reasoner).

The same characters and intrigues are pursued in *Le Mannequin d'osier* (1897; translated as *The Wicker-Work Woman,* 1910), but politics are minor compared to Bergeret's continuing story. It is essentially a domestic drama, rendered without bathos and with wry humor. Bergeret is portrayed in his triple role of husband, professor, and voice of civic reason. He exercises the latter function often in the local bookshop and during walks with friends, repeating some of Coignard's (that is, the author's) views. As a professor he is not seen at the university but rather at home, with his favorite pupil, M. Roux. Again, the author is clearly interested in the master-disciple relationship, which takes a melodramatic turn: the professor comes home unexpectedly to find his wife and Roux joined in an embrace. If his first reaction is predictable and uncivilized—namely, the impulse to kill them—his next, following immediately upon suppressing the first, is to leave the room and hurl to the courtyard below the effigy of his wife, in the form of her wicker dressmaker's model (a gesture France himself had performed in a rage).

To put the whole thing out of mind and reassert his rights as master of the house, the professor henceforth denies his wife's existence, neither conversing nor having any other commerce with her. Public opinion sides with her (her friends deny the rumors of an affair and see her as victimized, and even those aware of Roux's assiduities tend to blame Bergeret, since cuckolds are always ridiculous); but Bergeret philosophically ignores the mockery and spends his time either with books or friends. By the end he succeeds in driving his wife to return to her mother. This drama is obliquely related to the occasional political concerns, for the domestic conflict reflects that between the conservative aristocracy and upper bourgeoisie and their republican opponents.

In *L'Anneau d'améthyste* (1899; translated as *The Amethyst Ring,* 1919), the bishop is finally named, thanks in part to pressure from three different women—two Jewish, and all involved in illicit affairs—who, for varying reasons, none disinterested, urge the government to choose the crafty abbé Guitrel, who has been helping his own cause. His first official act is to declare that, given the unjust tax burden—from which, according to papal decree, the church should be exempt—the congregations of the diocese will refuse henceforth to comply. In the background is the Dreyfus Affair. What, in the novelist's view, made the original judicial error possible and so hard to rectify is implicit throughout *Histoire contemporaine,* although the series was planned before the affair broke. The aristocracy and upper bourgeoisie, who as a caste wield dominant power in the Third Republic—although some members are royalist—are anti-Semitic, pro-army, and pro-church. The characters' reactions are entirely predictable: the politicians and churchmen say that to doubt the verdict of the military court or call for revision is nothing less than treason, and they point out that charges of judicial error come from Freemasons and Jews. Bergeret, on the contrary, argues that seven judges may indeed have been in error.

Monsieur Bergeret à Paris (1901; translated as *Monsieur Bergeret in Paris,* 1921) is a novel of politics, but not quite a political novel, because the political vision is never called into question and dramatized. Moreover, there is little change in the characters' political understanding, and Bergeret, now a Sorbonne professor, undergoes almost no evolution. His socialist commitment to collective ownership and human solidarity is not the result of personal drama but rather the logical consequence of his views, especially concerning the Dreyfus Affair: "L'Affaire a révélé le mal dont notre belle société est atteinte comme le vaccin de Koch accuse dans un organisme les lésions de la tuberculose" (The affair has revealed the moral evil with which our fine society is afflicted, as the Koch vaccine indicates tubercular lesions). Since it was the government that committed errors, to accuse Dreyfusards of attacking and sabotaging the army and the nation is unjust; they are merely trying to rectify errors, in opposition to those who through conviction or self-interest affirm Dreyfus's guilt and call his supporters subversive.

The strange political alliances created by the affair, related to the deep division between republicans and monarchists, will surprise no one familiar with party politics in France. In the major plot of the book, a staunch royalist wins an election as a nationalist, endorsed eventually by republicans and socialists, whom he despises. Much is made also of the alliances between old aristocrats, often impoverished, and wealthy Jewish families, who adopt anti-Semitic positions in order to secure their social standing. The mobility of French society, which Proust later analyzed brilliantly, is well suggested.

The structure of the novel is imperfect, but the portraits are skillfully done, the conversations lively, and the themes played out in multiple registers, including a sixteenth-century fable introduced through *mise en abyme* (interior reproduction of stories or motifs). What is most important about the volume and the series (in which France proved himself to be, with Stendhal, Balzac, and Zola, one of the major sociologists in nineteenth-century French fiction) is the connection established between fundamental flaws in the

French social and institutional fabric—oppressive, unjust, obscurantist, and benighted—and outward political dramas such as the Dreyfus Affair.

During the first decade of the new century, two major works appeared, *Vie de Jeanne d'Arc* (1908; translated as *Joan of Arc*, 1908) and *L'Ile des pingouins* (1908; translated as *Penguin Island*, 1909), along with many other books, articles, and prefaces. France's literary fame and political notoriety increased; to the conservatives, he was persona non grata. He published in Charles Péguy's *Cahiers de la Quinzaine* (Fortnightly Notebooks) and wrote the preface to *Une Campagne laïque (1902–1903)* (1904, A Lay Campaign [1902–1903]), concerning Combes's campaigns for the separation law. For some years France had traveled extensively in Europe and enjoyed lengthy stays at the country properties of the Arman de Caillavets and friends such as the novelist Gyp (Countess of Martel). After 1900 his travels became even more frequent, involving cruises and extended stays in various European countries. Mme de Caillavet usually accompanied him. But his private life was again turbulent. The marriage of his daughter, Suzanne, in 1901 to Henri Mollin was followed by her scandalous liaison with a student, Michel Psichari, Renan's grandson. The marriage ended in divorce in 1905, and later she married Psichari, after the birth of their son, Lucien. France refused, however, to attend the wedding, and he and Suzanne thenceforth remained estranged.

While traveling in South America in 1909 to lecture, France had an affair with an actress, Jeanne Brindeau; it was not his first infidelity to Mme de Caillavet, but, unlike others, it was broadcast in Parisian scandal sheets. Upon returning home he found that Mme de Caillavet, who had attempted suicide, was gravely ill; he then broke off the liaison with Brindeau. Mme de Caillavet died in January 1910. That same year, he began an affair with Emma Laprévotte, who had traveled with them as Mme de Caillavet's chambermaid, and by December, Laprévotte was living at Villa Saïd. This arrangement did not prevent other liaisons, notably with an American woman, Laura MacAdoo Gagey, who committed suicide in 1911. France finally married Laprévotte in 1920.

Sur la pierre blanche (1905; translated as *The White Stone*, 1910) concerns the knowability of the historical process and the possibility of achieving an ideal society—topics that must be connected in any rational theory of history. The story is set in Rome, where visiting archaeologists gather in the Forum to discuss the past, present, and future. The past and future are evoked by embedded tales; France was fond of frame narratives, although he did not always exploit their possible irony. The first tale is set in the Roman Empire during the first century A.D. Questions of cultural change and the unforeseeability of the future are raised when—like Pontius Pilate in "Le Procurateur de Judée," who does not remember Jesus—Seneca's brother Gallion, the Roman proconsul in Corinth, disdains and misunderstands the implications of the new religion that the apostle Paul, Stephen, and others preach. In ironic contrast, Gallion supposes that the peace of the Empire, over which Nero is about to reign, will endure indefinitely. The conclusion is that human beings are enclosed within cultural solipsism and cannot identify historical process.

The second tale, a dream, deals with a socialist utopia of 2270, presented as only one, not the sole, possible development. Means of production are owned by the state; men and women dress in unisex clothes; the traditional division of labor is blurred; and no single religion dominates. Yet, individualism remains, particularly thanks to art, and the state is not markedly oppressive. France acknowledges, however, both social and individual flaws in even this rational society. Anarchism and illegal dealing persist, as do the constants of the human condition—illness, unhappiness—for human beings are animals and often not reasonable ones. France sees the end of history not as rational synthesis but rather as a process of both social and biological evolution, in which the human species will ultimately be replaced by another.

Doubtless the most famous of France's books in North America, *L'Ile des pingouins* is a cutting satire in the form of an historical fable. The satire is directed chiefly against nationalism and superstition, including Christian hagiography; both, France shows, invite fanaticism and lead to persecutions and other abuses. He exposes the pious veil clothing French history and criticizes the idea of divine omnipotence and omniscience, mocking God's "aveugle clairvoyance" (blind lucidity). The medieval period, he shows, was characterized by brutality, by which private property and aristocratic privilege were established. (The depiction of the origin of private property is almost Rousseauist.) Other critical remarks concern purported French racial purity, American imperialism, the press, and modern-style architecture in "Alca" (Paris). The author spares virtually nothing and no one. His wit is not subtle; perhaps he had concluded that satiric niceties would be ineffective for people capable of stampeding in the streets to pursue Zola when he tried to defend Dreyfus.

In early medieval times, the myopic Saint Maël baptizes by mistake some penguins. A heavenly council decides that the penguins must be turned into men, since the virtue of baptism would otherwise be fruitless, and that would be contrary to Christian theology. Their history is recounted, from the metamorphosis and miraculous hauling of their island to the Breton coast (hence a Celtic flavor) to the great penguin revolution (that is, 1789), thence to the present. Even the future appears, with frightening lucidity: a great war (France was prescient); a polluted, barren, skyscraper-dominated city of 15 million; and a huge tree of smoke created by the energies of radiation.

In most readers' memories, the fable is preeminently the history of the Dreyfus Affair, transposed into the "Affair of the Eighty Thousand Bales of Hay." The themes of superstition, nationalism, the aristocracy, and anti-Semitism are brought together in the episode. Partisans of the army, anti-Jewish nationalists, royalists, and ecclesiastics, never reconciled to the republic, all self-serving, are allied against a handful who think justice has miscarried. The invented controversy closely follows the real one, and contemporary readers had no difficulty identifying the historical figures; Zola appears as Colomban and France himself as Bidault-Coquille. The author jabs constantly at the governments of fanaticism, militarism, and intrigue that had plagued his nation for more than a century. These social vices are not the result of flawed institutions; rather, the institutions derive from and mirror human viciousness. Religion and morality are but a hypocritical cloak; in reality, men are brutes. Clearly, France's view of life had not mellowed after he passed sixty; the Dreyfus Affair and other signs of what he viewed as institutionalized injustice and inequity throughout European society had led to deep pessimism. Whereas *Sur la pierre blanche* evokes a rational and successful (if fanciful) new society, the future in the penguin fable appears somber. The book does propose, however, some possibilities for social amelioration. The forward-looking views of an authorial spokesman who argues for different relationships between men and women, including a new sexual morality, contrast with the double standard, still countenanced then not only by the church but also by such novelists as Marcel Prévost, whose *Les Demi-Vierges* (1894; translated as *The Demi-Virgins*, 1895) extols chastity for women while granting men the privilege of unlimited sexual adventures.

L'Ile des pingouins should be read in connection with France's history of Joan of Arc, published earlier the same year and well received by almost no one. He had been interested for years in the Maid of Orleans and had worked intermittently since 1875 on what became two massive volumes. He was not alone: after Jules Michelet's seminal work, which read the Middle Ages in Romantic terms, Maurice Barrès, Léon Bloy, and Péguy all wrote on the Lorraine heroine. Following 1871 and the loss of the eastern provinces, interest in Joan had increased, and during World War I she played an important role in patriotic iconography and rhetoric. In 1908 she was not yet a saint, however; declared Venerable in 1894, she was pronounced Blessed in 1909 before reaching full canonization in 1920.

France took issue with church conservatives, who interpreted her story in miraculous terms. While concerned to preserve her status as a national heroine, he explained her "voices" and other behavior in rational terms and indulged his anticlericalism by attacking the church for sending her to death. His views are not wholly consistent, however; the task of giving a coherent, nonreductionist explanation was beyond him, given the lacunae in knowledge concerning the period when Joan lived.

After Mme de Caillavet's death, France's existence was filled with activity, although—or perhaps because—he felt her loss keenly. He continued traveling, visiting Algeria and, in 1913, taking his seventeenth (and last) trip to Italy. He knew well and corresponded with many famous figures—the sculptor Auguste Rodin; the socialist Jaurès; the actor Sacha Guitry; the writer Barrès—and he met various others, including Bernard Shaw, Albert Einstein, and Valéry. His support for liberal causes was constantly solicited, and he so often complied that his activity in this decade, joined to that of the previous ten years, justifies calling him one of the first *écrivains engagés,* or committed writers, of the twentieth century.

France's last major fictional works, *Les Dieux ont soif* (1912; translated as *The Gods Are Athirst,* 1913) and *La Révolte des anges* (1914; translated as *The Revolt of the Angels,* 1914), are, like many of his books, novels of ideas, although not *romans à thèse* (thesis novels) in which characters are manipulated to demonstrate the dominant thesis. *Les Dieux ont soif* concerns the Terror of 1793, one of the most repressive regimes in modern history. Although after 1900 the author expressed confidence that a better society could be established and European war eliminated through political and economic reform, this reformist creed was only grafted onto and did not replace his long-held belief that ideals are not sufficient to improve mankind, and especially that power held by the masses leads to anarchy and violence. In *Les Dieux ont soif,* the hero, Evariste Gamelin, an honorable person, devoted to the republic and its principle of popular sovereignty, becomes one of the butchers of the Terror, voting with self-righteous conviction for the execution of scores of compatriots. France shows how the Jacobins' ideological obsession, which makes Gamelin admire Jean Marat and Maximilien de Robespierre and judge the moderate Girondists as treacherous, usurps traditional morality, feeling, and rational thought; they are no better than the tyrants and inquisitors they replaced. Opposed to their fanaticism is the tolerance of Brotteaux, a neighbor who is denounced and then condemned by Gamelin. A reader of Lucretius and an authorial spokesman, Brotteaux illustrates the best of the eighteenth-century philosophes' thought: stoical, he accepts with equanimity the changes in his fortunes; virtuous and moral, although he is an atheist, he willingly assists others. He accepts his end with dignity, while realizing the price of the life he is losing. His friend the abbé Longuemare, a persecuted priest, is as devoted to his Christian faith as Brotteaux is to Lucretian philosophy; it is a measure of France's own tolerance and pity that he makes the abbé die with as much dignity as his friend.

Gamelin's end—upon the guillotine to which he had sent many—brings together poetic and historical justice, since it reflects the fate of the principal Jacobin leaders, which illustrates the author's conviction that persecutions beget further persecutions. The novel also offers intimations of the synthetic process, identified by Karl Marx and later historians, by which the excesses of the Terror and failure of the republic led, through reaction, to the militarism of Napoleon and the empire.

La Révolte des anges, which sold sixty thousand copies within six weeks, is a whimsical, imaginative mock epic on serious matters. Set in modern France, it satirizes mores, politics (including monarchism and anarchism), class structure, religion, and, not least, women. It also retells Western history from antiquity through the Middle Ages, Renaissance, and modern times. Finally, it attacks the Judeo-Christian religious tradition through mockery of sacred teachings and God, or Yahweh, himself. The attack was especially timely, in the author's eyes, in view of what is called the Catholic Renaissance in the early twentieth century in France, which included noteworthy conversions among writers and various manifestations of religious militancy—Ernest Psichari's militarism, Georges Bernanos's call to arms under the sign of Joan of Arc, the ministry of Charles de Foucault in Africa, and the nationalistic Catholicism of Charles Maurras's Action Française movement. The Catholic press did not overlook the offensiveness of *La Révolte des anges:* one review was titled "Un Possédé de Belzébuth" (One Possessed by Beelzebub). France's novel will offend any pious reader who reads enough to see that God is called merely a petty Demiurge, the local, limited, but tyrannical deity of a few primitive Syrian tribes; but it will delight those who appreciate the Enlightenment tradition of biblical and doctrinal criticism by its reductio ad absurdum and arguments appealing to natural law. For nature is the author's great model: natural substance, natural law, and natural impulses are the only truth, and morality is merely a useful artifice devised and prolonged by custom.

The cosmogony and theology of Dante and John Milton and Jacques-Bénigne Bossuet's universal history are the author's negative models, as he ridicules the account of creation and the fall in Genesis, Mosaic law, and the doctrine of redemption, and criticizes the imposition of the new religion in the Roman Empire, the establishment of a state church, monasticism, obscurantism, the Reformation (Martin Luther and John Calvin are worse than the popes), and the Romantics' emotional religion. His fallen angels—who turned against God, descended to live in France, and took on human features—expound the truth about the universe and the Divinity himself and, like Prometheus, propose to assist men, whom they pity. But they also plot a new rebellion against Heaven. They consult with Lucifer, who resides in a comfortable Hades where the shades enjoy the sort of intellectual discourse the author loved. Lucifer's prophetic dream enacts what will happen if Heaven is besieged and God is overthrown: God will be exiled to Hell, a new victim, and Satan will assume divine prerogatives and reign as tyrannically as Yahweh. Thanks to this warning, showing what France thought of political power, the angels abandon their plan.

The fable ends without apology for its irreverence and anthropomorphism, and the novelist leaves his reader with a fraternal sense of the physical world. The work, which shows a tolerant understanding of human foibles, as well as human possibilities, constituted a remarkable feat for a man of seventy years; while its mixture of fantasy and social criticism has led to comparisons with Gide's *Les Caves du Vatican* (1914; translated as *The Vatican Swindle,* 1925), by its vitality it also bears comparison with his farewell to fiction, *Thésée* (1946; translated as *Theseus,* 1948).

World War I confirmed predictions France had made concerning the dangers of industrialized warfare. In September 1914, after he had mentioned publicly the possibility of friendship with Germany after the conflict, he was hounded by accusations of treason—including an attack by Maurras—and calls for punishment. He then asked, at the age of seventy, to be drafted for military service. Pronounced unfit, he left Paris with Laprévotte for a country property, La Béchellerie, which he purchased two years later. Thenceforth he was cautious about making pronouncements that might appear unpatriotic.

In 1917 Michel Psichari was killed at the front, and the next year Suzanne died of Spanish influenza. Three years later, when his first wife (who had remarried in 1900) died, France was declared the guardian of his only grandson, Lucien. After the war he made famous pacifist statements, probably truer to his convictions than the patriotic positions he had taken in wartime. His prestige was tremendous; as Bancquart notes, he was endowed, in the eyes of many, with a "sacerdoce antisacerdotal" (antipriestly priestly authority). In 1919 he received an honorary doctorate from the University of Athens and, two years later, the Nobel Prize in Literature. It is significant that, in what was doubtless a gesture of good will toward the principal belligerents of World War I, the Swedish Academy also honored the rector of the University of Berlin and winner of the 1920 Nobel Prize in Chemistry (which was awarded in 1921), Walther Nernst, whose hand France shook. For the writer's eightieth birthday, an official celebration was held in Paris, attended by representatives from all over the world, and after his death on 12 October 1924 he was granted a national funeral.

During the last two years of France's life, controversy continued to surround him. Much of it stemmed from his Nobel Prize speech, in which he criticized the Treaty of Versailles (1919) as being not "un traité de paix, mais la prolongation de la guerre" (not a treaty of peace, but a continuation of the war). He also called for a new Europe and praised Romain Rolland, who was widely despised for his wartime pacifist writings. As Jacques Suffel notes, most Frenchmen did not yet speak so harshly of the treaty in 1921; to do so appeared pacifistic and pro-German. France's words, widely publicized around the world, confirmed his reputation among his compatriots as an enfant terrible with leftist sympathies. Many observers were outraged. Unfavorable reaction was rapid: the day after his speech, two Paris newspapers expressed displeasure, and echoes of disapproval were heard until his death, reinforced by additional words and gestures of his that appeared pacifistic.

France's work illustrates, in a pleasing style, traits generally admired as most Gallic, as if his mind were in harmony with his name: urbanity, wit, taste, craftsmanship, perspicacity, and rationalism. Not without reason was he called "The Master." Yet, his work presents no great synthesis. He came too late, and was perhaps temperamentally unsuited, for the great, creative, utopian imagination of the Revolution and Romanticism, and he was prejudiced, partly because of the Commune, against its late-nineteenth-century avatars; so that, despite his adoption of liberal views when he was past middle age, his modes of writing and thinking were set and he was unable to go beyond his essentially critical spirit. As for visions of destruction and cataclysm, he was prophet enough to see what risks the twentieth century would run but not enough to imagine fully the moral and spiritual consequences. In short, by the measures of the twentieth century, and even more present ones, France may seem to come up short, his humor and workmanship more ornamental than substantive, his insights superficial—his art like the flitting of the bee in Jean de La Fontaine's sixteenth epistle, the "chose légère" (light thing) that goes from flower to flower and object to object.

Yet, to see France as only a shallow, bourgeois dilettante would be shortsighted. At the risk of alienating friends and readers, he embraced the major liberal cause of the late 1800s and in his social novels attempted to show the flaws in French thought and institutions that made possible the miscarriage of justice for Dreyfus. Like Voltaire, he was determined to instruct—indeed to admonish—as well as to please; he was a relentless *moraliste*. In opposition to contemporary scientism, he argued that the apparent progress of science was illusory, since the horizons of the infinite unknowns merely retreat, and that too much reliance on the intellect was dangerous. He belongs thus to a major tradition in French thought and literature that reappears in later writers such as Camus and Gide. As for the anxiety that Gide found missing, it was not entirely absent. As Bancquart writes in her introduction to volume 4 of the Pléiade edition, in France's last novels "nous entendons des interrogations qui annoncent notre modernité inquiète" (we hear interrogations that announce our disquiet modernity). Reason constantly struggles with the unreasonable, the mystery that mocks the very reason which identifies it, and with the inadequacy of language: "On ne dit rien dans un livre de ce qu'on voudrait dire. S'exprimer, c'est impossible" (One says nothing in a book of what one would like to say. It is impossible to express oneself).

Anatole France lived long enough to see that the twentieth century would bear out his skepticism: although abbé Coignard said that the future was a useful place for building dreams, what the new century brought was not a brave new world but destruction: "Les armées augmentent sans cesse en force et en nombre. Les peuples entiers y seront un jour engouffrés" (Armies are ceaselessly growing in strength and numbers. Whole peoples will one day be engulfed by them). With such a prospect, France cultivated the garden of belles lettres and the mind, for his own pleasure and that of readers.

Letters:

Lettres inédites d'Anatole France à Jacques Lion, edited by Marie-Claire Bancquart (Paris: Société Anatole France, 1965);

Lettres inédites d'Anatole France à Paul-Louis Couchoud et à sa femme, edited by Claude Aveline (Paris: Société Anatole France, 1968);

Lettres inédites d'Anatole France à Paul Grunebaum-Ballin (Paris: Société Anatole France, 1971);

Quelques lettres inédites d'A. France et de Mme A. de Caillavet à Charles Maurras, edited by Philippe Delatte (Paris: Société Anatole France, 1972);

Anatole France à l'Académie française, lettres inédites (Paris: Société Anatole France, 1975–1978);

Anatole France et Madame de Caillavet, Lettres intimes, 1888–1889, edited by Jacques Suffel (Paris: Nizet, 1984);

Anatole France et Robert Dell, une correspondance inédite (1913–1917), edited by G. Corbière Gille (Paris: Société Anatole France, 1992).

Biographies:

Lewis Piaget Shanks, *Anatole France* (New York: Harper, 1919; revised, 1932);

James Lewis May, *Anatole France* (New York: Dodd, Mead, 1924);

Nicolas Ségur, *Conversations avec Anatole France* (Paris: Fasquelle, 1925); translated by May as *Conversations with Anatole France* (London: John Lane / New York: Dodd, Mead, 1926);

Jeanne-Maurice Pouquet, *Le Salon de Madame de Caillavet* (Paris: Hachette, 1926);

Ségur, *Dernières conversations avec Anatole France* (Paris: Fasquelle, 1927); translated by May as *The Opinions of Anatole France* (London: John Lane / New York: Dodd, Mead, 1928);

Pierre Calmettes, *La Grande Passion d'Anatole France* (Paris: Seheur, 1929);

Jacob Alexrad, *Anatole France: A Life Without Illusions* (New York & London: Harper, 1944);

Léon Carias, *Les Carnets intimes d'Anatole France* (Paris: Emile-Paul, 1946);

Jacques Suffel, *Anatole France* (Paris: Editions du Myrte, 1946);

André Vandegans, *Anatole France: Les années de formation* (Paris: Nizet, 1954);

David Tylden-Wright, *Anatole France* (New York: Walker/ London: Collins, 1967);

Géraldi Leroy, ed., *Les Ecrivains et l'Affaire Dreyfus* (Paris: Presses Universitaires de France, 1983);

Marie-Claire Bancquart, *Anatole France: Un sceptique passionné* (Paris: Calmann-Lévy, 1984).

References:

Marie-Claire Bancquart, *Anatole France* (Paris: Julliard, 1994);

Bancquart, *Anatole France, polémiste* (Paris: Nizet, 1962);

Bancquart, *Les Ecrivains et l'histoire d'après Maurice Barrès, Léon Bloy, Anatole France, Charles Péguy* (Paris: Nizet, 1966);

Dushan Bresky, "Cinquante ans de la critique francienne," *Nineteenth-Century French Studies,* 7 (Spring-Summer 1979): 245–257;

Bresky, *The Art of Anatole France* (The Hague & Paris: Mouton, 1969);

Jean-Jacques Brousson, *L'Itinéraire de Paris à Buenos-Ayres* (Paris: Cres, 1927);

David Caute, *The Fellow-Travelers: A Postscript to the Enlightenment* (New York: Macmillan, 1973); revised as *The Fellow-Travellers* (New Haven & London: Yale University Press, 1988);

Barry Cerf, *Anatole France: The Degeneration of the Great Artist* (New York: Lincoln, MacVeagh, 1926);

Haakon Chevalier, *The Ironic Temper: Anatole France and His Time* (New York: Oxford University Press, 1932);

Michel Drouin, *L'Affaire Dreyfus de A à Z* (Paris: Flammarion, 1994);

Europe, 32 (December 1954): 3–67 [group of articles on France];

Carter Jefferson, *Anatole France: The Politics of Skepticism* (New Brunswick, N.J.: Rutgers University Press, 1965);

Jean Levaillant, *Les Aventures du scepticisme: Essai sur l'évolution intellectuelle d'Anatole France* (Paris: Armand Colin, 1965);

Diane Wolfe Levy, *Techniques of Irony in Anatole France: Essay on "Les Sept Femmes de la Barbe-Bleu"* (Chapel Hill: University of North Carolina Department of Romance Languages, 1978);

Le Lys Rouge (Paris: Société Anatole France, 1933–1965, 1969–);

Murray Sachs, *France: The Short Stories* (London: E. Arnold, 1974);

Jean Sareil, *Anatole France et Voltaire* (Geneva: Droz, 1961);

W. Searle, *The Saint and the Sceptics: Joan of Arc in the Work of Mark Twain, Anatole France and Bernard Shaw* (Detroit: Wayne State University Press, 1976);

Jacques Suffel, *Anatole France par lui-même* (Paris: Editions du Seuil, 1954);

Suffel, *Les Ecrivains et l'Affaire Dreyfus* (Paris: Presses Universitaires de France, 1983);

G. Todisco, *Anatole France: Littérature et engagement* (Poggibonsi: Antonio Lalli, 1975);

Reino Virtanen, *Anatole France* (New York: Twayne, 1968);

Loring Baker Walton, *Anatole France and the Greek World* (Durham, N.C.: Duke University Press, 1950).

Papers:

Many of Anatole France's manuscripts, including correspondence and notebooks, are at the Bibliothèque Nationale and the Bibliothèque Historique de la Ville de Paris. Others are held in private collections.

1921 Nobel Prize in Literature Presentation Speech

by E. A. Karlfeldt, Permanent Secretary of the Swedish Academy, 10 December 1921

Anatole France was no longer a young man when, in 1881, he captured the attention of the literary public in France and subsequently in the civilized world with his curious novel, *Le Crime de Sylvestre Bonnard.* He had behind him a long stretch of years during which his development had been carried on without attracting wide attention. But if, during this period of slow growth, his literary efforts had been infrequent and not very energetic, the work to which he had subjected his intellect, his thought, and his taste had been proportionately wider and more vigorous. No immoderate desire for fame moved him. Ambition seems to have played a small role in his life. Indeed, he tells the story that at the age of seven he wanted to be famous. Excited by the legends of saints told to him by his good, pious mother, he wanted to settle in the desert and as a hermit match the glory of St. Anthony and St. Jerome. His desert was the *Jardin des Plantes* where the huge beasts lived in houses and cages, and where God the Father seemed to him to raise his arms to heaven blessing the antelope, the gazelle, and the dove. His mother was frightened by such vanity but her husband soothed her: "My dear, you will see that at twenty he will be disgusted with fame." "My father was not mistaken," France says. "Like the King of Yvetot, I lived quite well without fame and no longer had the least desire to engrave my name on the memory of men. As for the dream of becoming a hermit, I refashioned it every time I believed I felt life was thoroughly bad; in other words, I refashioned it every day. But every day nature took me by the ear and led me to the amusements in which our humble lives pass away." At the age of fifteen the young Anatole France dedicated his first essay, "La Légende de Sainte Radegonde, Reine de France," to his father and his beloved mother. This work is now lost, but even much later, when his faith in saints had vanished, he was still able to write legends with a pen dipped in the gold of haloes.

The poet's star seems to have been illuminated first in that bright constellation bearing the name Anatole France. In the old library of his worthy father, he soon felt a thirst for knowledge, amidst the noble dust of old books. Into this shop, whose proud sign "Aux Armes de France" inspired father and son to take up the literary name, came collectors and bibliophiles to examine the recently acquired treasures and to discuss authors and editions. Thus the young Anatole, always a good listener, was initiated into the mysteries of erudition, a pursuit he considered the highest pleasure of a peaceful life. We need only look at the Abbé Coignard, all beaming as he leaves the grill room of the "Reine Pédauque" where he pays for the material pleasures of this world by giving some lessons to a young spit-turner and by dispensing the treasures of an eloquence full of wisdom, irony, and Christian faith; we see him turn toward the library to feast his spirit free of charge on the latest books arrived from Holland, the country of classical editions. And, bored with domestic tedium, here is Mr. Bergeret, who comes to pass the finest hours of his day in conversation with friends gathered around the library's display shelves. Anatole France is the poet of libraries and bookworms. His imagination revels in the visions of bibliophiles, as when he praises that marvellous *Astaracienne,* a giant collection of books and manuscripts in which a noble cabalist sought proofs to bolster his superstition. "More fervently than ever," says Coignard toward the end of his adventurous career, "I want to sit down behind a table, in some venerable gallery, where many choice books would be assembled in silence. I prefer their conversation to that of men. I have found diverse ways of life and I judge that the best way is to devote oneself to study, to support calmly one's part in the vicissitudes of life, and to prolong, by the spectacle of centuries and of empires, the brevity of our days." Love of intellectual work is a fundamental characteristic of Anatole France's personal religion and just like his Abbé, he prefers, from the height of the ivory tower of knowledge and thought, to turn his gaze toward far-off times and countries. His irony lives in the present, his devotion in the past.

Yet though our existence is fragile, beauty lives everywhere, and for the writer it materializes in form and style. Anatole France's vast studies and great meditation have bestowed a rare solidity on his work, but no less serious is the labour he has devoted to the perfecting of his style. The language which he had to shape is one of the noblest; French is the most richly endowed daughter of the mother tongue Latin. It has served the greatest masters. Now grave, now merry, it possesses serenity and charm, strength and melody. In many places France calls it the most beautiful language on earth and lavishes the most tender epithets on it as to a beloved woman. But as a true son of the ancients, he wishes it *simplex munditis*. He is an artist, certainly one of the greatest, but his art aspires to keep his language, through severe purification, as simple and, at the same time, as expressive as possible. In contemporary Europe, where flourishes a superficial dilettantism, dangerous for the purity of languages, his work is a richly instructive example of what art can do with true resources. His language is the classical French, the French of Fénelon and Voltaire, and rather than contribute new ornaments to it, he gives it a slightly archaic stamp which admirably suits his subjects, often taken from antiquity. His French is so transparent that one would like to apply to it what he said of Leila, daughter of Lilith, one of the luminous and fragile beings sprung from his imagination: "If crystal could speak, it would speak in this fashion."

Let us recall now, for our own pleasure, some of the works which have secured for the name of Anatole France the world-wide renown which he has so little desired but which nevertheless he cannot avoid. By so doing we will often encounter France himself, for he is less inclined than most writers to hide behind his characters and words.

He is recognized as a master of the tale, which he has made a wholly personal genre, in which erudition, imagination, serene charm of style, and depth of irony and passion combine to produce marvellous effects. Who can ever forget his Balthazar? The Negro King of Ethiopia comes to pay a visit to Balkis, the beautiful Queen of Sheba, and soon wins her love. But shortly the fickle queen forgets him to give herself to another. Wounded to death physically and emotionally, Balthazar returns to his country to devote himself to the highest wisdom of the seers, astrology. Suddenly an astonishing and sublime light spreads over the intense gloom of his passion. Balthazar discovers a new star and, high in the heavenly concourse, the star speaks to him, and in the light it sheds he joins with two neighbouring kings. No longer can Balkis hold him. His soul is detached from voluptuousness and he undertakes the pursuit of the star. The star which spoke was no other than the star which led the Three Wise Men to the manger at Jerusalem [*sic*; Bethlehem].

Another time France opens before our eyes a mother-of-pearl casket filled with priceless jewels, chased by the hand of a master of antiquity. We find in it the legend, slightly ironic but most seductive, of Célestin and d'Amyers, of the old hermit and the young faun singing together the Easter Alleluia, the one exalting in the return of Christ and the other in the return of the sun, worshippers communing in a single innocent piety, reunited at last—under the alarmed eye of the historian—in a single sacred tomb. This story shows us France in a realm in which he delights, the realm between paganism and Christianity, where twilight and dawn are mingled, where satyrs meet with apostles, where sacred and profane animals wander, where ample materials are found to exercise his fantasy, his contemplation, and his spiritual irony in all its nuances. One often does not know whether to call it fiction or reality.

Romantic chastity is celebrated in the legends of the saints Oliverie and Liberette, Euphrosine and Scolastica. These are pages taken from the chronicles of saints, literary pastiches perhaps, executed with talent and a sense for the miraculous.

Still another time France takes us to the pits outside of Sienna where, in the spring twilight, a sweet barefooted Carmelite narrates the story of St. Francis of Assisi and St. Claire, the daughter of his soul, and that of the holy satyr who served masters as different as Jupiter, Saturn, and the Galilean, a profound if hardly edifying legend, but recounted by France in the most exquisite style.

In his famous novel *Thaïs* (1890) he enthusiastically penetrates the Alexandrine world at the time when the scourging thorns of Christianity were ravaging among the last effeminate survivors of Hellenic civilization. Asceticism and voluptuousness are at their heights here, mysteries and aesthetic orgies flower side by side, angels and demons incarnate press around the Fathers of the Church and the neo-Hellenic philosophers, disputing over human souls. The story is steeped in the moral nihilism of that era, but it includes beautiful passages such as the magnificent descriptions of the desert solitude in which the anchorites preach from atop their columns or are subject to nightmares in the mummies' tombs.

However, one must put *La Rôtisserie de la Reine Pédauque* (1893) [At the Sign of the Reine Pédauque] in the first rank of Anatole France's novels. There he has sketched a group of true-to-life characters, legitimate or natural offspring of his mind in their own colourful world. The Abbé Coignard is so alive that one can study him as a real character who reveals all his complexity only when one has penetrated his privacy. Perhaps others have had the same experience I had. At first I had but little sympathy for this clumsy, loquacious priest and doctor of theology, who has so little concern for his dignity that sometimes he even steals or commits other equally heinous crimes, which he nevertheless defends with shameless casuistry. But he improves on better acquaintance, and I have learned to love him. He is not only a brilliant sophist, but an infinitely amusing character who exercises his irony not only on others but also on himself. There is profound humour in the contrast between his lofty views and his shabby life, and one must regard him with the smiling tolerance of his creator. Coignard is one of the most remarkable figures in contemporary literature. He is a new and vigorous plant in the Rabelaisian vineyard.

A type at once grotesque and lovable is the cabalist d'Astarac. The crude mystic evidently must be included in a novel dealing with eighteenth-century manners. But the beings this magician evokes are of a singularly ethereal species; freed of earthly bonds, he enjoys the sweet and useful society of salamanders and sylphs. As proof of the talents of these beings, d'Astarac tells how once a sylph obliged a French scholar by arranging delivery of a message to Descartes, who was then living in Stockholm where he was teaching philosophy to Queen Christine. Sworn enemy of superstition that he may be, Anatole France should be grateful to that superstition for all the happy suggestions it has given him for his work.

Admirably rendered is the accent of pious simplicity with which the Abbé's student, the young spit-turner, recounts all these turbulent events. When his master, revered despite everything, after having suffered to his last moments the assault of the powers of darkness, finally dies a holy death in a Church he had never ceased to recognize openly, the student traces in Latin an ingenuous epithet praising the Abbé's wisdom and virtues. The author himself, in a later work, delivers an obituary eulogy for his principal hero. Presenting him as a blend of an Epicurean with a St. Francis, one who scorned men tenderly, France speaks of his benevolent irony and his merciful scepticism. Aside from the religious aspect, this characterization applies equally well to Anatole France himself.

Let us accompany him then without fear in his philosophical strolls in the garden of Epicurus. He will teach us humility. He will say to us: the world is infinitely large and man is infinitely small. What do you imagine? Our ideals are luminous shades but it is in following them that we find our only true happiness. He will say that human mediocrity is widespread, but he will not exclude himself from it. We may reproach him for the sensuality that occupies too large a place in some of his works and for the hedonistic sentiments, for example, which he describes under the sign of the red lily of Florence, and which are not made for serious minds. He will reply, according to the maxims of his spiritual father, that the pleasures of the mind surpass by far those of the flesh, and the serene calm of the soul is the port into which the wise man steers his boat in order to escape the tempests of sensual life. We shall hear him express the wish that time, which deprives us of so many things, may allow us compassion for our fellow man, so that in our old age we do not find ourselves shut up as in a tomb.

Following this inclination Anatole France left his aesthetic seclusion, his "ivory tower," to throw himself into the social fray of his time, to clamour like Voltaire for the restoration of the rights of persons unjustly condemned as well as of his own wounded patriotism; and he has gone into the workers' quarters to look for means of reconciling classes and nations. His old age has not become a walled tomb. The end has been good for him. After having been accorded many sunny years at the court of the Graces, he still throws the glint of gay learning into the idealistic struggle that, at an advanced age, he wages against the decadence of societies and against materialism and the power of money. His activity in this regard does not interest us directly, but we obtain from it the inestimable advantage of being able to fix his literary image against the background of a lofty nobility of sentiments. There is nothing of the careerist about him. His much discussed work on Joan of Arc, which has cost him enormous toil and which was intended to tear the veil of mysticism from the inspired heroine of France and to restore her to nature, to real life, was a thankless enterprise in an era prepared to canonize her.

"The Gods are Athirst!" The great drama of the Revolution unfolds and, as with the battle of ideas, the trivial destinies of men are reflected in blood. Do not believe, however, that France would wish to present this squaring of accounts as being definitive. A century is far too short a period of time to permit delineating distinctly the march of men toward more tolerance and humanity. How have events fulfilled his predictions! Several years after the appearance of this book the great catastrophe occurred. What beautiful arenas have been prepared now for the games of salamanders! The smoke of battles still hangs over the earth. And out of the fog surge gnomes, sinister spirits of the earth. Are these the dead who return? Sombre prophets announce a new revelation. A wave of superstition threatens to flood the ruins of civilization. Anatole France wields the subtle and corrosive weapon which puts to flight the ghosts and the false saints. For our times, faith is infinitely necessary—but a faith purified by healthy doubts, by the spirit of clarity, a new humanism, a new Renaissance, a new Reformation.

Sweden cannot forget the debt which, like the rest of the civilized world, she owes to French civilization. Formerly we received in abundance the gifts of French Classicism like the ripe and delicate fruits of antiquity. Without them, where would we be? This is what we must ask ourselves today. In our time Anatole France has been the most authoritative representative of that civilization; he is the last of the great classicists. He has even been called the last European. And indeed, in an era in which chauvinism, the most criminal and stupid of ideologies, wants to use the ruins of the great destruction for the building of new walls to prevent free intellectual exchange between peoples, his clear and beautiful voice is raised higher than that of others, exhorting people to understand that they need one another. Witty, brilliant, generous, this knight without fear is the best champion in the sublime and incessant war which civilization has declared against barbarism. He is a marshal of the France of the glorious era in which Corneille and Racine created their heroes.

Today, as we in our old Germanic country award the world prize of the poets to this Gallic master, the faithful servant of truth and beauty, the heir of humanism, of the lineage of Rabelais, Montaigne, Voltaire, Renan, we think of the words he once spoke at the foot of Renan's statue—his profession of faith is complete in them: "Slowly but surely humanity realizes wise men's dreams."

Mr. Anatole France—You have inherited that admirable tool, the French language, the language of a noble and classical nation, which is reverently guarded by the famous academy you adorn and is maintained by it in an enviable condition of purity. You have that brilliant tool of piercing sharpness, and in your hand it acquires a scintillating beauty. You have used it masterfully to cut out *chefs-d'oeuvre* very French in their style and refinement. But it is not your art alone that charms us: we revere your creative genius as well, and we have been enticed by the generous, compassionate heart which so many exalted pages of your works reveal.

[© The Nobel Foundation, 1921.]

France: Banquet Speech

France's speech at the Nobel Banquet at Grand Hôtel, Stockholm, 10 December 1921 (Translation)

I have cherished the prospect of visiting in the evening of my life your beautiful country which has brought forth brave men and beautiful women. With gratitude I receive the prize that crowns my literary career. I consider it an incomparable honour to have received this Prize established by a man of noble sentiment and awarded to me by judges so just and competent. Invited by you as a member of the French Academy to give advice on the Nobel Prize in Literature, I have several times had the pleasure of directing your choice. It happened in the case of Maeterlinck, who combines a brilliant style with thought of great independence; it also happened in the case of Romain Rolland, in whom you have acknowledged a lover of justice and peace and who has been able to defy unpopularity in order to remain a good man.

Perhaps I am overstepping the limits of my competence, if I now talk about the Peace Prize of the Norwegian Storting [Parliament]. If I do it, nonetheless, it is to praise the choice that the Storting has made. I may perhaps be permitted to say that in my view you have honoured in [Hjalmar] Branting a statesman impassioned for justice. Would that the destinies of peoples could be guided by such men! The most horrible of wars has been followed by a peace treaty that is not a treaty of peace but a continuation of war. Unless common sense finally finds its place in the council chambers of ministers, Europe will perish. If one cannot with good reason hope for the triumph of union and harmony, among the countries of Europe, I wish at least to believe, gentlemen, that under the influence of brave, just, and loyal men like you the good will sometimes prevail.

In the official record, the following event is reported: After Anatole France had received his Prize from the hands of the King, there occurred an incident which left a strong impression on all present. When the venerable had gone up to the rostrum again, he turned to Professor Walther Nernst, Prize winner in Chemistry, and exchanged a long and cordial handshake with him. The Frenchman, the "last classic," and the German, the great scientist and representative of intellectual sobriety, the citizens of two countries which had for a long time been enemies, were united in a handshake—a profoundly symbolic gesture. The audience applauded, feeling that the two nations, which for years had fought against one another, had just met in reconciliation.

[© The Nobel Foundation, 1921. Anatole France is the sole author of his speech.]

John Galsworthy
(14 August 1867 – 31 January 1933)

Sanford Sternlicht
Syracuse University

See also the Galsworthy entries in *DLB 10: Modern British Dramatists, 1900–1945; DLB 34: British Novelists, 1890–1929: Traditionalists; DLB 98: Modern British Essayists, First Series;* and *DLB 162: British Short-Fiction Writers, 1915–1945;* and *DLB Documentary Series 16: The House of Scribner, 1905–1930.*

BOOKS: *From the Four Winds,* as John Sinjohn (London: Unwin, 1897);

Jocelyn, as Sinjohn (London: Duckworth, 1898); as Galsworthy (Saint Clair Shores, Mich.: Scholarly Press, 1972);

Villa Rubein: A Novel, as Sinjohn (London: Duckworth, 1900);

A Man of Devon, as Sinjohn (Edinburgh & London: Blackwood, 1901);

The Island Pharisees (London: Heinemann, 1904);

The Man of Property (London: Heinemann, 1906; New York & London: Putnam, 1909);

The Country House (London: Heinemann, 1907; New York & London: Putnam, 1907);

A Commentary (London: Richards, 1908; New York & London: Putnam, 1908);

Fraternity (London: Heinemann, 1909; New York & London: Putnam, 1909);

Plays: The Silver Box; Joy; Strife (London: Duckworth, 1909);

A Justification of the Censorship of Plays (London: Heinemann, 1909);

Justice: A Tragedy in Four Acts (London: Duckworth, 1910; New York: Scribners, 1910);

A Motley (London: Heinemann, 1910; New York: Scribners, 1910);

The Spirit of Punishment (London: Humanitarian League, 1910);

"Gentles, Let Us Rest": Reprinted from "The Nation" (London: National Union of Women's Suffrage Societies, 1910?);

The Patrician (London: Heinemann, 1911; New York: Scribners, 1911);

The Little Dream: An Allegory in Six Scenes (London: Duckworth, 1911; New York: Scribners, 1911);

For Love of Beasts (London: Animals' Friend Society, 1912);

The Pigeon: A Fantasy in Three Acts (London: Duckworth, 1912; New York: Scribners, 1912);

Moods, Songs, and Doggerels (New York: Scribners, 1912; London: Heinemann, 1912);

The Inn of Tranquility: Studies and Essays (New York: Scribners, 1912; London: Heinemann, 1912);

The Eldest Son: A Domestic Drama in Three Acts (London: Duckworth, 1912; New York: Scribners, 1912);

The Fugitive: A Play in Four Acts (London: Duckworth, 1913; New York: Scribners, 1914);

The Dark Flower (London: Heinemann, 1913; New York: Scribners, 1913);

The Slaughter of Animals for Food (London: Royal Society for the Prevention of Cruelty to Animals/Council of Justice to Animals, 1913);

Treatment of Animals: Being a Speech Delivered at the Kensington Town Hall on December 15, 1913, at a Meeting Called to Protest against Cruelties to Performing Animals (London: Animals' Friend Society, 1913);

The Mob: A Play in Four Acts (London: Duckworth, 1914; New York: Scribners, 1914);

Memories (London: Heinemann / New York: Scribners, 1914);

Some Slings and Arrows, edited by Elsie E. Morton (London: E. Mathews, 1914);

The Little Man, and Other Satires (New York: Scribners, 1915; London: Heinemann, 1915);

A Bit o' Love: A Play in Three Acts (London: Duckworth, 1915; New York: Scribners, 1915);

The Freelands (London: Heinemann, 1915; New York: Scribners, 1915);

A Sheaf (New York: Scribners, 1916; London: Heinemann, 1916);

"Your Christmas Dinner Is Served!" (London: National Committee for Relief in Belgium, 1916);

Beyond (New York: Scribners, 1917; London: Heinemann, 1917);

John Galsworthy, 1919 (photoprint by Bain News Service, New York City; from the George Grantham Bain Collection, Library of Congress Prints and Photographs Division)

The Land: A Plea (London: Allen & Unwin, 1918);

Five Tales (New York: Scribners, 1918; London: Heinemann, 1918);

Another Sheaf (London: Heinemann, 1919; New York: Scribners, 1919);

The Burning Spear: Being the Experiences of Mr. John Lavender in Time of War, as A. R. P-M (London: Chatto & Windus, 1919); as Galsworthy (New York: Scribners, 1923);

Addresses in America (New York: Scribners, 1919; London: Heinemann, 1919);

Saint's Progress (New York: Scribners, 1919; London: Heinemann, 1919);

Tatterdemalion (London: Heinemann, 1920; New York: Scribners, 1920);

The Foundations: An Extravagant Play in Three Acts (London: Duckworth, 1920; New York: Scribners, 1920);

The Skin Game: A Tragi-comedy in Three Acts (London: Duckworth, 1920; New York: Scribners, 1923);

In Chancery (London: Heinemann, 1920; New York: Scribners, 1921);

Awakening (New York: Scribners, 1920; London: Heinemann, 1920);

The Bells of Peace (Cambridge: Heffer, 1921);

To Let (New York: Scribners, 1921; London: Heinemann, 1921);

Six Short Plays (London: Duckworth, 1921; New York: Scribners, 1921);

The Forsyte Saga (New York: Scribners, 1922; London: Heinemann, 1922);

A Family Man: In Three Acts (London: Duckworth, 1922; New York: Scribners, 1922);

Windows: A Comedy in Three Acts for Idealists and Others (London: Duckworth, 1922; New York: Scribners, 1923);

Loyalties: A Drama in Three Acts (London: Duckworth, 1922; New York: Scribners, 1923);

Captures (London: Heinemann, 1923; New York: Scribners, 1923);

International Thought (Cambridge: Heffer, 1923);

The Forest: A Drama in Four Acts (London: Duckworth, 1924; New York: Scribners, 1924);

On Expression (London: English Association, 1924);

Memorable Days (London: Privately printed, 1924);

The White Monkey (New York: Scribners, 1924; London: Heinemann, 1924);

The Little Man: A Farcical Morality in Three Scenes (London: Duckworth, 1924);

Abracadabra & Other Satires (London: Heinemann, 1924);

Old English: A Play in Three Acts (London: Duckworth, 1924; New York: Scribners, 1925);
Caravan: The Assembled Tales of John Galsworthy (London: Heinemann, 1925; New York: Scribners, 1925);
The Show: A Drama in Three Acts (London: Duckworth, 1925; New York: Scribners, 1925);
Is England Done? (London: Privately printed, 1925);
The Silver Spoon (London: Heinemann, 1926; New York: Scribners, 1926);
Escape: An Episodic Play in a Prologue and Two Parts (London: Duckworth, 1926; New York: Scribners, 1927);
Verses New and Old (London: Heinemann, 1926; New York: Scribners, 1926);
Castles in Spain & Other Screeds (London: Heinemann, 1927; New York: Scribners, 1927);
The Way to Prepare Peace (London: Whitefriars Press, 1927);
Two Forsyte Interludes: "A Silent Wooing" and "Passers By" (London: Heinemann, 1927; New York: Scribners, 1928);
Swan Song (New York: Scribners, 1928; London: Heinemann, 1928);
A Rambling Discourse (London: Mathews & Marrot, 1929);
Exiled: An Evolutionary Comedy in Three Acts (London: Duckworth, 1929; New York: Scribners, 1930);
A Modern Comedy (London: Heinemann, 1929; New York: Scribners, 1929);
The Roof: A Play in Seven Scenes (London: Duckworth, 1929; New York: Scribners, 1930);
Four Forsyte Stories (London: Heinemann / New York: Fountain Press, 1929);
On Forsyte 'Change (London: Heinemann, 1930; New York: Scribners, 1930);
Soames and the Flag (London: Heinemann, 1930; New York: Scribners, 1930);
Two Essays on Conrad (Cincinnati: Privately printed, 1930);
The Creation of Character in Literature (Oxford: Oxford University Press, 1931);
"Literature and Life": A Lecture Delivered April 13, 1931, at Princeton University (Princeton: Princeton University Press, 1931);
Maid in Waiting (London: Heinemann, 1931; New York: Scribners, 1931);
Worshipful Society (New York: Scribners, 1932);
Flowering Wilderness (London: Heinemann, 1932; New York: Scribners, 1932);
Candelabra: Selected Essays and Addresses (London: Heinemann, 1932; New York: Scribners, 1933);
Over the River (London: Heinemann, 1933); republished as *One More River* (New York: Scribners, 1933);
Author and Critic (New York: House of Books, 1933);
Ex Libris John Galsworthy, edited by Galsworthy and Ada Galsworthy (London: Heinemann, 1933);
End of the Chapter (New York: Scribners, 1934; London: Heinemann, 1935);
The Apple Tree (New York: Scribners, 1934);
The Collected Poems of John Galsworthy (New York: Scribners, 1934);
The Winter Garden: Four Dramatic Pieces (London: Duckworth, 1935);
Galsworthy in His Humour (London: Duckworth, 1935);
Forsytes, Pendyces, and Others (London: Heinemann, 1935; New York: Scribners, 1935);
Glimpses and Reflections (London & Toronto: Heinemann, 1937).

PLAY PRODUCTIONS: *The Silver Box,* London, Court Theatre, 25 September 1906;
Joy, London, Savoy Theatre, 24 September 1907;
Strife, London, Duke of York's Theatre, 9 March 1909 (transferred to Haymarket Theatre);
Justice, London, Duke of York's Theatre, 21 February 1910;
The Little Dream: An Allegory in Six Scenes, Manchester, Gaiety Theatre, 15 April 1911; London, Court Theatre, 28 October 1912;
The Pigeon, London, Royalty Theatre, 30 January 1912;
The Eldest Son, London, Kingsway Theatre, 23 November 1912;
The Fugitive, London, Court Theatre, 16 September 1913 (transferred to Prince of Wales's Theatre);
The Mob, Manchester, Gaiety Theatre, 30 March 1914; transferred to London, Coronet Theatre, 20 April 1914;
The Little Man, Birmingham, Birmingham Repertory Theatre, 15 March 1915; London, Everyman Theatre, 21 October 1920;
A Bit o' Love, London, Kingsway Theatre, 25 May 1915;
The Foundations, London, Royalty Theatre, 26 June 1917;
Defeat, Hammersmith, Lyric Theatre, 14 March 1920;
The Skin Game, London, St. Martin's Theatre, 21 April 1920;
The First and the Last, London, Aldwych Theatre, 30 May 1921;
A Family Man, London, Comedy Theatre, 2 June 1921;
Loyalties, London, St. Martin's Theatre, 8 March 1922;
Windows, London, Court Theatre, 25 April 1922;
The Sun, Liverpool, Playhouse, 1 November 1922;
The Forest, London, St. Martin's Theatre, 6 March 1924;
Punch and Go, London, Mary Ward Settlement Theatre, 15 October 1924;
Old English, London, Haymarket Theatre, 21 October 1924;
The Show, London, St. Martin's Theatre, 1 July 1925;

Escape, London, Ambassadors' Theatre, 12 August 1926;

Exiled, London, Wyndham's Theatre, 19 June 1929;

The Roof, London, Vaudeville Theatre, 4 November 1929.

The major literary achievement of John Galsworthy's life was the Forsyte Chronicles, a family epic that includes two novel trilogies as well as several short stories. The Chronicles satirize upper-middle-class and upper-class British society in the Edwardian age and the immediate post–World War I period. As a dramatist whose reputation in his lifetime was second only to that of George Bernard Shaw, Galsworthy was a compassionate reformer who campaigned against long prison terms, harsh treatment of prisoners, class discrimination at the bar of justice, anti-Semitism, the intransigence of capitalists and labor union leaders, and other evils of society. Galsworthy was also a master of the short story. A few of his well-crafted stories continue to serve as models for aspiring writers.

In the early decades of the twentieth century, Galsworthy portrayed traditional English values such as love of the countryside, fair play, integrity in business and other worldly affairs, devotion to justice, respect for women, comity between the sexes, honorable behavior, support for the underdog, and the Victorian/Edwardian code of the gentleman and lady. Modernist writers such as D. H. Lawrence, Virginia Woolf, and James Joyce scoffed at these values when emphasized in literature, for they were seen as unrealistic. But the reading public disagreed. Galsworthy met Lawrence in 1918 when Lawrence had already become famous (or notorious) with *Sons and Lovers* (1913) and *The Rainbow* (1915), and the two writers took an instant dislike to each other. Galsworthy felt that Lawrence's focus on sex and the body was unworthy for a writer. Despite the fact that Woolf considered Galsworthy and other Victorian/Edwardian novelists such as H. G. Wells and Arnold Bennett mere sociologists, there was more respect among modernists for Galsworthy when it came to his vigorous satirizing of the upper middle class, with its philistinism, overpossessiveness, snobbery, jingoism, and indifference to the working class and the poor of the land.

Galsworthy, like his problematic and protean protagonist of the Forsyte Chronicles, Soames Forsyte, was born a "man of property." At the time of his birth, the United Kingdom of Great Britain and Ireland ruled the seas and much of the landmass of the world. And his class ran the nation. London was the largest city in the world, and Great Britain was the richest nation, thanks to the Industrial Revolution. Into that confident if not smug world, John Galsworthy was born on 14 August 1867 at Parkfield, Kingston Hill, Surrey, the second child and first son of John Galsworthy, a solicitor, company director, and property owner, and Blanche Bartleet Galsworthy. Later they had another son and daughter. The infant was christened John because his father, grandfather, and great-grandfather had been likewise christened. When John was still a child, the senior Galsworthy moved the family to a huge Victorian Gothic edifice he had built on a large acreage he had bought called Coombe, near the village of Maldon. He called his house Coombe Warren. Galsworthy's childhood memories of Coombe Warren and the beautiful surrounding countryside influenced the author's portrayal of Robin Hill, the house Soames Forsyte has built for his unhappy wife, Irene, and which is almost a character in the Forsyte novels.

The upper-middle-class Galsworthys descended from yeoman stock in Devonshire, and the family traced its paternal roots back to an Edmund Galsworthy who died in Plymouth in 1598. In 1833 the author's paternal grandfather, a prosperous Plymstock merchant, was the first to settle in the London area. He was a skillful and prudent investor who made his fortune investing in land and houses. His son inherited considerable wealth. He too was a prudent businessman and did not marry until he was forty-five years old. Blanche Bailey Bartleet was twenty-five when she married; she came from an established Worcestershire family of a slightly higher social standing (more time on the land and less in business).

Galsworthy's father was an intelligent, well-read, bewhiskered man who was an easygoing, fond, older parent who made time for his children, especially on weekends. The author always had a deep respect and affection for his father.

Galsworthy's mother was a difficult person, less loving than her husband; she did not choose to spend as much time with her children as she spent in running the many-roomed house. There were usually as many as fourteen servants for her to supervise, and she was obsessed with household cleanliness. When Blanche Galsworthy paid attention to the children, it was to fuss over their clothes and hair. Her offspring did not remember her with much affection. She also seems to have been something of a hypochondriac: she was afflicted with frequent headaches, requiring her to recline on a sofa with black lace over her eyes. There were a great many relatives, and it is apparent that the extended Galsworthy clan influenced the author's character constructs in the Forsyte Chronicles and other novels.

Despite their mother's coldness, and mainly because of their father's warmth, the four Galsworthy children had a happy childhood living in and around the series of three spacious houses built by their house-loving father on a twenty-four-acre estate near Epsom, a suburb of London. Galsworthy was an avid reader from childhood on. His early favorite subjects were boys' adventures and sea stories.

Galsworthy was proud of his heritage. As an adult he invested time and money into researching his family lineage on both the paternal and maternal sides. Furthermore, he always maintained pride in being English. It energized him as it did a great many others in that heady time before the horrors of World War I. The only time Galsworthy ever took umbrage at a newspaper reference to him was when he was falsely identified as an Irishman.

When Galsworthy was nine, he was sent away to Saugeen Preparatory School at Bournemouth. The school was small and family-run. The custom at the time was for upper-middle-class and upper-class English boys to be abruptly detached from home life. John, or Jack as his family and friends called him, was a bright, well-behaved pupil more interested in cricket than reading, although the scope of his reading for pleasure had expanded beyond boys' adventure stories into history. His nearsightedness prevented him from excelling at the English sport, but he remained an avid cricket fan all his life.

In 1881 Galsworthy's father enrolled his first son in one of England's premier public (private) schools, Harrow, for his secondary education. Galsworthy neglected his academic subjects for athletics that were less dependent on a keen eye than cricket, such as gymnastics, running, and football (soccer), and he was popular in his house. His headmaster liked him but could not see any promise of distinction for the amiable but unambitious young man.

For Galsworthy's university education his father chose Oxford, making sure his firstborn son and namesake would have a far superior education to his own. Galsworthy went up to New College, Oxford, in 1886 to study jurisprudence. The senior Galsworthy, always a practical businessperson, envisioned having a barrister in the family, useful for the extensive family business interests. In the same year that Galsworthy entered Oxford, his family moved closer to London with the purchase of a house in Kensington, which became the author's base for holidays and adventures in the capital.

Galsworthy convinced his classmates in New College that he had overstrained his heart and therefore could no longer participate in sports. Instead, he became a dandy, parading in his somewhat foppish clothes on High Street, wearing a monocle over his weak right eye. He adopted the mannerism of inserting the monocle and looking over people he was introduced to, giving the impression that he was cold, aloof, and supercilious, but in fact he was merely straining to see. All his life Galsworthy wore eyeglasses in private. His interest in clothes also continued, and he was always regarded as a stylishly dressed man. Academically, Galsworthy was satisfied with a second-class degree. He took up "studying" racehorses at Oxford, and as a result he was frequently in debt, relying on his indulgent father to bail him out with the bookmakers.

Galsworthy fell in love for the first time while he was at Oxford. Her name was Sybil Carlisle, a young woman he had met while visiting Wales. Sybil was a singing instructor who hoped for a stage career. Nothing came of the relationship. His parents felt she was not suitable for their son because her family was not wealthy. In any case, she was not in love with him, although she and Galsworthy continued to see each other as he received his law degree from Oxford University in 1889 and proceeded to London for advanced studies in jurisprudence. There, on 29 April 1890, Galsworthy was called to the bar as a member of Lincoln's Inn.

Galsworthy, however, showed little interest in practicing law and trying cases despite the fact that his father was a senior partner in a successful firm of solicitors and thus able to bring many lucrative briefs to him. He almost tried one case, but he was talking with his father in the hall outside the courtroom when the case was called, and so one of his colleagues took over for him. He did help his father, however, by writing legal opinions and collecting rents in the slum properties that his father's firm owned. Galsworthy's later reformer bent and sympathy for the poor took seed at this time. The senior Galsworthy, unable to motivate the indulged young man who apparently needed some maturing, sent Galsworthy to Canada, supposedly to investigate a mining company, but really to have a change of scenery and forget his disappointment over Carlisle. The trip to Canada was one of several the senior Galsworthy sent his son on, hoping to interest him in practicing maritime law. Galsworthy even opened modest London law chambers at 3 Paper Buildings, Temple.

In 1891, at a family celebration of the marriage of Galsworthy's cousin Arthur Galsworthy, the author met the woman who came to dominate his entire life. That woman was his cousin's bride. Ada Nemesis Pearson Cooper Galsworthy was the illegitimate daughter of Anna Pearson and the adopted daughter of an obstetrician, Emanuel Cooper of Norwich. Ada was born in 1864, but her mother concealed the actual year of her birth, claiming 1866 so the child could appear to be the legitimate offspring of the marriage between the doctor and herself. Anna Cooper shopped Ada around Europe seeking a wealthy husband for her daughter and finally found Arthur Galsworthy. The marriage was a disaster for Ada Galsworthy, who later claimed that she endured marital rape and beatings. Although Ada Galsworthy became the model for Irene, Galsworthy's greatest heroine in the Forsyte Chronicles, her relationship with the author did not materialize until much later.

Meanwhile, the author's sister Lilian fell in love with the artist painting a portrait of her father. Georg Sauter was a Bavarian-born artist of peasant stock, and he was a liberal. Those "defects," along with the general bourgeois view that all artists were dissolute bohemians, made him unacceptable to the Galsworthys. But despite family objections, Lilian and Georg finally married in 1894. The happy couple remained Galsworthy's closest family members for most of his life. Sauter was the model for the architect Philip Bosinney in *The Man of Property* (1906), the first volume of *The Forsyte Saga*.

Still unsettled in his life, Galsworthy made a trip to the South Seas and visited Australia and New Zealand in 1892. In March 1893, on his way home, Galsworthy took passage out of Adelaide on the clipper ship *Torrens*, whose first mate was the Polish-born Joseph Conrad. During the fifty-six-day voyage to England, Galsworthy and Conrad became friends. Conrad had already started his first novel, *Almayer's Folly* (1895), and later introduced Galsworthy to critics and the editor Edward Garnett, who helped to shape Galsworthy's early novels. Galsworthy, always generous, helped Conrad financially when the latter was in need. The two remained friends until Conrad's death in 1924. The meeting with Conrad gave Galsworthy the idea of becoming a writer, but not the motivation. That came from Ada Galsworthy.

Ada Galsworthy, a beautiful woman, next met Galsworthy in 1893, at the annual Eton-Harrow cricket match. She had a classic profile, lovely brown eyes, and a stately, slender figure. Also, like Irene Forsyte, she played the piano exquisitely. Galsworthy was smitten. She was twenty-six years old; he was twenty-three and much less experienced in matters of love and sex than the married woman. She told him about her miserable marriage, and, full of sympathy for her, he began to share her torment. They started to meet often, usually in the company of a female relative. Then, as planned, they met alone in Paris during Easter week of 1895 and became lovers. As she was at a railway station about to begin her return to England, while Galsworthy was staying on in Paris, she turned to her lover and said: "Why don't you write? You are just the person." As Galsworthy was deeply in love—and really had little else to do between trysts—he took her suggestion as a command.

Her marital status in the Victorian era when marriage was truly for life, her undeniable love for Galsworthy, her beauty, and her courage in entering into an illicit relationship condemned by the society of which they were so much a part proved subject and theme for much of Galsworthy's literary output over his lifetime. Without her, Galsworthy might never have become a great writer. She aided him throughout his career by typing manuscripts, listening to his work, shielding him from unwanted visitors, and lavishing affection on him. She managed their household and handled correspondence and appointments, thus helping Galsworthy to be a prolific writer. Most important of all, Ada Galsworthy was Galsworthy's muse. She was a paragon of beauty in his eyes and the model for many of his heroines, especially those who had beastly first husbands.

Galsworthy and Ada Galsworthy were aware that they had done something quite daring and brave. In retrospect their long-term affair was an act of defiance against conventional morality and Victorian mores. They were in the vanguard of the sexual revolution that was a major social architectonic of the twentieth century. They had their affair, and because of their eventual marriage (in 1905), money, and literary fame, they relatively quickly were allowed—even welcomed—back into respectable society. Simultaneously, however, Ada Galsworthy, perhaps out of a frightened possessiveness, kept her lover, later her husband, on a short tether, requiring unstinting adoration from him and sympathetic attention to her real or imaginary illnesses: asthma, rheumatism, colds, and attacks of flu. His continual ministrations to her illnesses made her feel more secure.

At first only Galsworthy's sisters and a few close friends knew of the affair between him and Ada Galsworthy. When, inevitably, the English social world learned of their relationship, they were ostracized. Galsworthy resigned his club membership and the directorships his generous father had arranged for him. Arthur Galsworthy, a reserve cavalry officer for many years, was called to active duty for two years to serve with the British Army in South Africa when the Boer War broke out in 1899. While her husband was in South Africa, Ada Galsworthy left her marital domicile and rented an apartment in London. Galsworthy had a bachelor apartment nearby. It was imperative that the senior Galsworthy not know of the liaison, for the Victorian gentleman would surely have disinherited his wayward son who had "stolen" his cousin's wife.

Galsworthy passed the time writing. In imitation of Rudyard Kipling he wrote a short-story collection titled *From the Four Winds* (1897), which he published at his own expense under the name John Sinjohn. The well-known novelist and editor Ford Madox Ford and Conrad helped Galsworthy to find a publisher willing to publish his first novel. *Jocelyn* (1898) is the story of a man married to an invalid who is addicted to morphine; he falls in love with a beautiful woman whom he cannot have until his wife dies of an accidental overdose. Already Galsworthy was dealing in the guilt, passion, and pleasure of illicit sexual relations. The novel was dedicated to Conrad. It received some critical praise, but much later Galsworthy thought it too emotional and not well written, and he would not allow republishing when many readers wanted access to his earlier work.

Galsworthy's next novel, *Villa Rubein* (1900), was shaped and promoted by Garnett. The story, based on the love affair of his sister Lilian and Sauter, depicts a sensitive young English woman who falls in love with an Austrian painter over the objections of her grandfather, whose values seem rather Galsworthian. Galsworthy's family was not pleased with this transparent story.

The Garnett-Galsworthy collaboration was important to the development of Galsworthy as a literary and commercial artist. Their association lasted for twenty years, until Galsworthy felt more confident in his own judgment than his friend Garnett's. Galsworthy's next work was another collection of short stories, *A Man of Devon* (1901), dedicated to the senior Galsworthy. In one of the stories, "The Salvation of Swithin Forsyte," Galsworthy introduced the fictional family with which he achieved greatness, although he did not return to the Forsytes for several years.

In 1902, when the elder Galsworthy was almost eighty-five, his wife accused him of making sexual advances to a governess of their grandchildren and left him. By 1904 old John Galsworthy was on his deathbed, and the author felt it was safe to use his own name on his books, something he had been longing to do, for he was proud of his growing literary skills. The first novel to bear his name was *The Island Pharisees* (1904), a satire in which a young, well-born, Oxford-educated lawyer meets a tramp who shows him the world of the hungry and poor, thus shaking up the bourgeois values of the hero. Galsworthy drew upon the impressions of slum life he had garnered while collecting rents for his father's firm. The novel gave Galsworthy the opportunity to criticize the smugness, selfishness, and cruel indifference of middle-class England; the English are the "Island Pharisees." *The Island Pharisees* received mixed reviews ranging from appreciation of its humor to criticism of its moralizing.

On 8 December 1904 old John Galsworthy died at age eighty-seven. He left each of his four children a considerable legacy and lifelong annuities. Galsworthy was now independently wealthy. At last Ada Galsworthy could obtain a divorce, and she and Galsworthy could finally marry. They went publicly to a farm in Manaton, on the edge of Dartmoor, and, as expected, Arthur Galsworthy sent a private detective to observe and report on the couple. Ada Galsworthy was then served with divorce papers, and Galsworthy was cited as corespondent. They left for the Continent shortly afterward to wait out the divorce. Arthur Galsworthy was granted it in two months. Six months later the divorce became absolute and the couple were free to marry, which they did in a private ceremony before the registrar at St. George's, Hanover Square, London, on 23 September 1905.

The couple set up residence in a small house on Addison Road, Kensington, London. As quickly as feasible, Ada Galsworthy led her new husband back into society, for the wealthy, handsome, well-dressed man was surely the least bohemian of writers. But Ada Galsworthy never fully recovered her self-esteem and social confidence from the many slights she had endured for ten years as Galsworthy's mistress.

The Galsworthys slept in separate rooms after their marriage. In the diary Galsworthy kept between 1910 and 1918 he cryptically recorded the times the couple made love. It was not often, and after 1912 the entries stopped. They never had children, perhaps because of Ada Galsworthy's poor health. Instead they lavished affection on dogs. When their spaniel Chris, a favorite for twelve years, died in December 1911, Ada Galsworthy was beside herself with grief. She insisted that their "child" came back to visit her at dinnertime twelve days after he died. Galsworthy wrote a biography of Chris, *Memories* (1914), which remains a favorite of dog lovers.

While the couple was waiting out the divorce on the Continent, Galsworthy had been working hard on the novel that became his greatest single literary achievement as well as the foundation of the Forsyte Chronicles: *The Man of Property*. The novel, set in the year 1886 in London and its suburbs, is another Galsworthy narrative attacking upper-middle-class materialism, and once again he presents agonized lovers trapped by the conventions of bourgeois society and unable to fulfill their love. Galsworthy posted sections to Garnett for his appraisal. Garnett, approving of most of the developing novel, required Galsworthy to rewrite the death scene of the architect Bosinney. Actually, Garnett wanted the architect and Irene Forsyte to run off together with her jewelry, but Galsworthy insisted on the architect's death. He was hurt by Garnett's criticism, and their friendship cooled somewhat, although he dedicated the novel to Garnett.

The Man of Property is Galsworthy's most hard-hitting novel. He despises Soames and many of the Forsytes. There are decent Forsytes: specifically old and young Jolyon, the father who tries hard to reestablish a relationship with his loved but estranged son, and the son once ostracized by the Forsyte clan because he fell in love with and married a mere governess. Young Jolyon, a painter, is the foil to Soames in *In Chancery* (1920) and will rescue Irene and appreciate her as a woman, not a beautiful object.

The public took time to warm up to the novel, and some were put off by its depiction of marital warfare, but the tragic story of the arrogant thirty-one-year-old philistine Soames Forsyte; his beautiful but unhappy wife, Irene, whom Soames eventually rapes; and her ill-fated lover Philip Bosinney, the gifted architect overseeing the construction of the suburban mansion that Soames wants to use to isolate his wife, eventually placed Galsworthy among the best-known writers of the day. Even Lawrence came to praise *The Man of Property*, calling it "really rather noble."

The theater, however, is where Galsworthy's contemporary reputation was made. The production of *The Silver Box*, also in 1906, a realistic courtroom drama of class injustice that allowed the author to use his legal experience, caught the attention of critics looking for playwrights who eschewed melodrama for the naturalism of Henrik Ibsen's social dramas. Galsworthy, with his talent for dramatic situations and scenes, fit right into the emerging modern drama of the Edwardian period, and he turned out thesis plays (dramas that address and debate a social problem) for the next twenty-three years. *Strife* (1909) deals with labor-management conflict. *Justice* (1910) reveals how harsh prison punishment destroys individuals. This play helped change the penal system: Sir Winston Churchill, then home secretary in the cabinet, was deeply moved by the drama and consequently introduced sweeping prison reforms. Galsworthy had chosen the theater as the site in which he would try to raise the social consciousness of the nation.

The Eldest Son (1912) is about young men taking responsibility for the young women they make pregnant. *The Fugitive* (1913) discusses married women in extramarital affairs. *The Mob* (1914), produced as World War I commenced, is about morality and war. *The Skin Game* (1920) shows the conflict between old money and new money. *Loyalties* (1922) exposes the tribalism behind English anti-Semitism. *Escape* (1926) once more delineates the harshness of the penal system. Galsworthy was usually present at rehearsals and helped supervise productions.

Galsworthy also continued to write fiction and followed *The Man of Property* with a novel that some critics, then and now, consider his best work. It is arguably his greatest non-Forsyte story. *The Country House* (1907) deals with the landed gentry in the way that *The Man of Property* treats the moneyed bourgeoisie. It shows them naturalistically as a subculture, and it depicts the class with touches of nostalgia and cruelty. The plot centers on a love affair between a young man, George Pendyce, the elder son of Horace Pendyce, a stubborn and prejudiced squire, and an unhappily married woman, Helen Bellew, a relative who has been invited to the estate. Helen's husband, the reprobate Captain Bellew, has made her life miserable. She and George fall in love, and they go to London together. Bellew plans to sue for divorce, and Horace is horrified that the family name will be sullied. His gentle wife, Margery, daringly goes to London to ask Helen to set her son free. The pusillanimous George has proven to be less of a man than Helen thought, so she acquiesces to Margery's request. Margery also persuades Bellew not to start divorce proceedings. Relenting, he says to the older woman: "You are the only lady I know." Galsworthy, who had been so eager to marry Ada Galsworthy, persisted in seeing passion and married life as incompatible. And he persisted in writing versions of his own great love affair.

In 1908 Galsworthy bought the farmhouse called Wingstone at Manaton on the edge of Dartmoor in Devon, the county of his paternal ancestors. He and his wife had stayed in it before their marriage. Galsworthy loved the place because he associated it with the happiest days of their union, as they enjoyed their passionate, illicit love affair. But Ada Galsworthy now did not like it as much as Galsworthy did, because Manaton was too far from the social whirl of London of which she was fond. Also, she did not care for its lack of indoor plumbing and its dampness. Galsworthy, however, was always able to work well there. He kept the house until 1926, although he and his wife always had a London residence as well.

Galsworthy wrote three more novels in the pre–World War I period: *Fraternity* (1909), the story of a liberal, middle-aged novelist who falls in love with a young woman from the London slums but cannot commit to her for fear of societal disapproval; *The Patrician* (1911), another tale of the landed gentry and a promising son who is in love with an unhappily married woman; and *The Dark Flower* (1913), in which Galsworthy follows the love life of a man from youth to middle age, when he falls in love with an eighteen-year-old girl whom he reluctantly gives up in order to stay with his faithful wife.

This time of success for the author and social acceptance of the couple should have been the happiest for the Galsworthys, but it was marred when the forty-five-year-old Galsworthy had the only known affair of his married life. In 1910, at a theater party for the production of Christoph Von Gluck's *Orpheus and Euridice*,

Galsworthy met a beautiful nineteen-year-old dancer named Margaret Morris, who had choreographed and danced in the show. Morris was still wearing her costume: a simple Greek tunic of cotton crepe. Initially, Galsworthy's interests seemed professional and avuncular. He wanted to help the struggling artist. He used his influence to get her work as an actress, although she had no acting experience. He even brought her home to meet his wife. Galsworthy made no advances at first, but eventually they kissed and then met in Morris's apartment and sat at opposite ends of the room while they conspired to become lovers. Morris naively thought that Ada Galsworthy would accept the relationship after it was consummated. But Ada Galsworthy intuitively knew that something was wrong, and sometime in 1912 she broke down. Galsworthy confessed, stating that his love for the younger woman would never supplant his love for his wife. Ada Galsworthy tried to be understanding, but her health had begun to fail again, and Galsworthy soon realized that he could not have his mid-life love affair with all its promise of renewed energy and creativity without sacrificing Ada Galsworthy's happiness and perhaps her life.

Apparently, Galsworthy decided to break off the affair before he and Morris had made love. He sent her a letter asking her to be brave. The young woman was devastated and kept trying to see Galsworthy again, but he avoided her, although he still tried to help her. Eventually, he sent her money to open a school of dance for children, and later he gave her funds to go to Paris, where she met a painter and married him. Galsworthy never saw Morris again. He used this painful episode as the basis for *The Dark Flower;* apparently much of the dialogue in the novel replicates the conversations that Galsworthy had with Morris.

The Galsworthys fled to the Continent again. Ada Galsworthy quickly revived, and they departed for America, where Galsworthy's plays were doing well in New York. If Ada Galsworthy recovered physically from the shock of the betrayal by her husband, she seems never to have recovered psychologically. She became even more dependent on her husband. Galsworthy was suffering also, as his final letters to Morris indicate. His sexual life with his wife was over by this point, and he was apparently celibate for the rest of his life.

When the Galsworthys returned to London, they gave up their house on Addison Road because of the sad memories of the Morris affair and the death of their dog, Chris. They took a flat at 12 Adelphi Terrace, where J. M. Barrie and his wife also lived. Shortly afterward the Galsworthys traveled to Egypt for a trip through the Western desert by camel. Supposedly, their trips were to improve Ada Galsworthy's health, but they also ensured that Galsworthy would not have the opportunity for another relationship.

World War I was a terrible period for Galsworthy. The late Victorian/Edwardian world he understood and loved was destroyed in the blood of millions dead and the political and economic crises that followed after. Galsworthy was a humanitarian. He believed that people were essentially good. He fought for civil liberties and animal rights. He also wanted to aid his country, but at forty-seven he was too old, and he was opposed to violence. Besides, Ada Galsworthy required his care. He turned over his income from writing—quite a substantial sum—to the war effort during the 1914 to 1918 period. Inspiration came hard for Galsworthy during the war. Events were too distracting. Writing seemed vain or shallow when so many young men were being slaughtered. Nevertheless, Galsworthy kept up the writing discipline of his lifetime. Every morning, regardless of where he was or how he felt, he took up his pen and wrote.

Galsworthy's last novel of social satire, *The Freelands* (1915), was nearly finished when the war began in August 1914. During the period he was writing the novel, his mother was terminally ill, and her suffering was another distraction. He gave his mother, who died on 6 May 1915, immortality by using her as the model for Mrs. Frances Freeland, the mother of four children, one of whom is a novelist. Galsworthy knew that his novel writing in the war period was weak, but he kept on. *Beyond* (1917), written in the winter of 1914–1915, is yet another story of an unhappily married woman, this one married to a Swedish violinist. The American serial rights for this monotonous novel brought in a great sum of money that Galsworthy immediately turned over to a fund for soldiers.

Galsworthy's short-story writing at this time was superior to his novel writing. "The Apple Tree," perhaps his best story, was included in *Five Tales* (1918), in which he also reintroduced the Forsyte family: "Indian Summer of a Forsyte" is an epilogue to *The Man of Property*. Galsworthy admired the short-story form; he liked working in limited space and with precise rising and falling structures. The subjects he chose were beauty, love, hate, injustice, and age. Galsworthy used the short story to convey his respect for the common laborer and his compassion for the poor. The weaknesses in Galsworthy's stories include an abundance of sentimentality and the sameness of female characters, whether high-class ladies, country girls, or prostitutes, who are invariably long-suffering, loving, and selfless.

Galsworthy wrote a considerable amount of poetry, but it is little read today. He was also an ardent and effective essayist. His essays show his good will toward humanity, his lack of malice, his intelligence, and his skill as a literary and dramatic critic. He argued for the abolishment of censorship on the British stage. He battled for legislation opposing the vivisection of dogs, the abuse of horses in mines, and the use of performing animals in shows. Galsworthy advocated women's suffrage and the transformation of the British Empire into the kind of confederation that ultimately became the British Commonwealth. He was an idealist who used his prose skills to attempt to bring about action on the part of the British people and change on the part of the British government.

Galsworthy was now the head of his extended family, and the clan decided to give the British Red Cross their mansion at 8 Cambridge Gate, London, to be used as a club for wounded soldiers. Also, they donated money to outfit it. While he was making the arrangements, an old friend suggested that the Galsworthys could join her in the hospital for French soldiers that she was administering in France. Galsworthy could learn how to be a masseur, and Ada Galsworthy could take charge of the linens. They agreed, because not only was it a way to assuage a little of the suffering in the war, but also their activities would not conflict with Galsworthy's opposition to violence. They worked in France from 13 September 1916 to March 1917.

Galsworthy devoted much effort during the war to helping his beleaguered brother-in-law Sauter. Because Sauter was German-born, he was interned as an enemy alien, even though he had spent most of his adult life in England. Galsworthy petitioned the government for Sauter's release, wrote many letters to people with influence, and called on cabinet ministers for help, but to no avail.

On New Year's Eve 1917 the prime minister, Lloyd George, offered Galsworthy a knighthood. The author turned it down because he thought that award was inappropriate for a literary person. In July 1918 Galsworthy was shocked to find that he was ordered to report for an army physical. The Germans were on the offensive in France once more, and Britain was running out of cannon fodder, so that even fifty-year-olds like Galsworthy were being called for service. Given his antiviolence stance and preachments, the author really did not know if he would be willing to fight for his country. However, he was not called up.

In that same month Galsworthy made one of the most important decisions of his professional life. He conceived of, and began to implement, the idea of making *The Man of Property* the first volume of a trilogy that became *The Forsyte Saga*. "Indian Summer of a Forsyte" already existed as a bridge to the future volumes.

In September 1918 the Galsworthys moved to a new domicile: Grove Lodge in Hampstead. However, with the war over, they began their travel again. Their journeys took them twice to the United States and to Algeria, Austria, Brazil, Italy (including Sicily), Morocco, Switzerland, South Africa, and Tunisia. In 1921 Galsworthy was elected first president of PEN, the international organization of writers, and he and Ada Galsworthy attended PEN congresses in Paris, Brussels, Berlin, Vienna, The Hague, Budapest, and Warsaw.

Revivifying the Forsytes (now the personifications of the diffuse Galsworthy clan), Galsworthy wrote furiously. But first he published *Saint's Progress* (1919), a romance and the only Galworthy novel to deal directly with World War I. The new group of Forsyte pieces consisted of *In Chancery;* the second Forsyte interlude, "Awakening" (published separately as a short book in 1920); and *To Let* (1921). When *The Man of Property,* "Indian Summer of a Forsyte," *In Chancery,* "Awakening," and *To Let* were published in one volume under the title *The Forsyte Saga* in 1922, Galsworthy was astounded at the public reception. More than one million copies were sold in Britain and America within one year. The public sensed that the great family epic of their time, a three-generation work, had been produced. The social history of their parents' generation was recorded. Furthermore, it was thought that something essentially English had been created. And to the relief and gratitude of a nation that had lost 750,000 young men in the recent war, Galsworthy skipped over the years of conflict in *The Forsyte Saga*.

The Forsyte Saga chronicles the life and times of three generations of a large, close-knit, upper-middle-class family, from the turn of the twentieth century to the post–World War I period. The Forsytes' materialistic values are personified in the villain of the saga, the solicitor Soames Forsyte, who views even his beautiful wife, Irene, as his property to be used at will.

In Chancery begins in 1895 and ends in 1901 with the birth of Soames's only child, his daughter, Fleur, by his second wife, Annette, a young French woman whose mother has a restaurant in Soho. As the novel opens, the forty-five-year-old Soames has been on his own during the twelve years since Irene left him the morning after he raped her and the distraught Bosinney was killed in a traffic accident. He decides to marry a young woman who could give him a son. But he cannot do so because he is still legally married to Irene. He has not divorced her because the scandal could have hurt his business, and he still has some hope of recovering his lost property: Irene. When he visits her to discuss a divorce, his passion flares up again, for she is still beautiful.

Irene flees to Paris, where Soames's pursuit drives her into the arms of the compassionate young Jolyon, a widower, and he takes her to Robin Hill, the country house Soames had built for Irene but which is now

TWELVE BOOKS - AND WHY.

By John Galsworthy

Not long ago I was chloroformed into a public declaration of what seemed to me the world's twelve best works of fiction, outside Poetry and Drama. When I came to myself, I began to wonder for what qualities I had chosen that particular twelve; and, for the sake of a clear, or comparatively clear, mind, I here set down the result of my wonderings.

The books were these:-

Cervantes' "Don Quixote,"
Tolstoy's "War and Peace" and "Anna Karenina,"
Dickens's "The Pickwick Papers" and "David Copperfield,"
Turgenev's "Fathers and Children" and "Smoke,"
Dumas's "The Musketeer" series and "The Reine Margot" series (but only when read in their native French).
Dostoievsky's "The Brothers Karamasov,"
Mark Twain's "Tom Sawyer" and "Huckleberry Finn,"
Thackeray's "Vanity Fair".

I added a postscript of doubt concerning "Smoke" the "Reine Margot" series, and "Vanity Fair". But on reflection I do not see with what I should replace them.

First, in my cogitation, I perceived that all of these books were very long, with the exception of the two Turgenev's, and the Mark Twain. Sheer bulk then seemed to be an advantage, following the maxim of the racecourse - not invariably justified -

Setting-copy typescript page for a Galsworthy essay that appeared in The Saturday Review of Literature, *3 December 1927 (The Lilly Library, Indiana University, Bloomington, Indiana)* owned by Jolyon. Soames finally divorces Irene and marries Annette. He is now out of chancery. There is no love between them, but she quickly becomes pregnant. Soames is sure he will have a son, but Fleur is born. Soames now has another unsatisfactory marriage, but he is devoted to his daughter, for he can love her without reservation. Meanwhile, Jolyon and Irene marry. As the novel ends, the reader begins to feel sorry for Soames. His penance has been long and painful and is not over. A subplot of the novel concerns the next generation, as Forsyte cousins, representing the two sides in the feud between Soames and Joylon, begin to take romantic interest in each other.

"Awakening" moves the saga along to 1909. It depicts the early life of Jon Forsyte, son of Irene and young Jolyon. It is an idyll of childhood.

The trilogy ends with *To Let* as the story jumps to 1920. Fleur is nineteen. The entire Edwardian period as well as World War I have been passed over. Soames again engages in battle with Jolyon and Irene over the fact that his daughter and their son, Jon, have fallen in love, ignorant of the feud. The couple had met accidentally in an art gallery. Also involved is a decent young nobleman, Michael Mont, who loves Fleur and who will win her on the rebound after Jon breaks with her because the relationship is too painful to his parents. Jolyon, now past seventy, has a heart attack and dies in the same place as his father, the garden of Robin Hill. Fleur marries Michael, whom she does not love. The widowed Irene and Jon move to Canada. Robin Hill, a rich man's creation to store his beautiful wife, an artist's gift to the woman he loves, the happy home of Irene and young Jolyon, now bears a sign: To Let.

The triumph of *The Forsyte Saga* and the critical and financial success of Galsworthy's play *The Skin Game* made him one of the preeminent living English writers. Honorary degrees began to accrue: St. Andrews (Scotland) in 1922, Manchester in 1927, Dublin in 1929, Cambridge and Sheffield in 1930, and Princeton and Oxford in 1931. Finally, he accepted the Order of Merit in 1929. In the years between the two world wars, famous authors were treated like great celebrities: they were addressed with deference by members of the press clamoring for interviews, and they were met at trains or dockside by throngs of fans as well as government, embassy, and consulate officials. Charities, political organizations, and causes demanded time, writing skill, and money. Among the many causes Galsworthy continued to battle for were the abolition of censorship of plays, a minimum wage, labor exchanges, women's suffrage, divorce law reform, prison reform, animal rights, and slum clearance.

With the success of *The Forsyte Saga*, Galsworthy decided to expand the chronicles with another trilogy: *The White Monkey* (1924), *The Silver Spoon* (1926), and *Swan Song* (1928). These novels continue the story of Soames Forsyte and his daughter, Fleur. The trilogy was republished in one volume as *A Modern Comedy* (1929). The aging Edwardian writer now not only related to contemporary society, he satirized it as well. But this second Forsyte trilogy is less successful than the first, partly because it lacks the anchor of a great work like *The Man of Property*. Reacting to a political shift to the left in 1920s Britain, Galsworthy changes from a critic of the upper middle class and the minor aristocracy to a supporter. Soames now seems a victim. Rather than class satire, *A Modern Comedy* focuses on the archetypal struggle between generations.

In *The White Monkey* Fleur represents the flapper generation: spoiled, selfish, and completely devoted to pleasure. Soames sees a painting of a white monkey, its eyes almost human. It is the symbol of modern man: an aging post–Darwinian primate, left only with a squeezed fruit in its outstretched paw, looking bewildered at its heritage.

Fleur cannot love her doting husband, who has come to realize that he was the runner-up. A young poet, Wilfrid Desert, tries to seduce Fleur, and although she would like the excitement and adventure of an affair, she is too middle-class to give in. The decent Michael suspects what is going on and kindly tells his wife that she must do what she needs to do. That generosity brings Fleur back to him, and she becomes pregnant. A son is born, and Fleur comments: "Isn't he a monkey?"

Soames, meanwhile, saves a company for which he had served on the board of directors. He exposes the company manager as dishonest; but the manager flees the country, and the shareholders have no one to blame, so they attack the directors. The proud, incorruptible Soames resigns. *The White Monkey* is a fair picture of post–World War I Britain, weary of the privations of the four terrible war years and perplexed by the widening gulf between the younger generation and the old Edwardians.

The Silver Spoon opens in the year 1924. Michael has been nominated for a Conservative Party seat in Parliament, where he wants to support a harebrained plan for social reform called Foggartism. Galsworthy is probably satirizing Fabian Socialism, espoused by Shaw and other intellectuals. An aristocratic flapper, Marjorie Ferrar, attacks Fleur's celebrity-chasing and Michael's support of Foggartism. Fleur writes letters commenting on Marjorie's immorality and is slapped with a libel suit. Soames tries to keep his daughter out of court by offering a compromise, but it is refused, and the case goes before a judge. The lawsuit is the heart of the novel. The aristocracy is now battling the upwardly mobile and less reverent upper middle class. Soames has Marjorie's past and present investigated and comes up with enough evidence to prove immorality. Marjorie is cut to pieces in cross-examination, and Fleur wins the case; but her victory is a bitter one, for society now snubs her while Marjorie is more popular than ever.

Fleur wants to get away from England for a while, so Soames takes his daughter on a round-the-world trip. Michael cannot leave Parliament and stays behind with the son who was born with the silver spoon in his mouth. *The Silver Spoon* works better as a satire than *The White Monkey* because Galsworthy, the former barrister, is on surer ground when it comes to courtroom drama. Soames, now seventy, has acted forcefully and heroically in defense of his daughter. The older generation seems stronger and more principled than the younger.

Swan Song is set in the fateful year 1926, when Britain endured its only general strike. The British proved able to survive a test of national character with a minimum of violence. The revolution did not come, although the chasm between the working classes and the other classes remains. The strike brings all the surviving Forsytes into action. To help with the crisis, Michael convinces Fleur to open a canteen for strike-breaking volunteer railway workers. Galsworthy's sympathies are with the government, not the workers. Meanwhile, Jon Forsyte has married in America and has brought his wife and Irene to England. Jon becomes a volunteer worker fighting the strike. When Fleur sees Jon in the canteen, she is sexually aroused and begins planning to have an affair with him. Soames suspects something is up with his daughter and is concerned. Unlike in *The Man of Property,* young lovers are not bravely fighting a hostile society but are dangerous violators of the moral code that upholds society.

Fleur is determined to seduce Jon, and although he has rejected her advances, eventually she contrives to bring him to Robin Hill, where she succeeds. But Fleur realizes that Jon will never love her again, and so her victory is over as soon as it is achieved. Jon goes home to confess to his wife, who first announces that she is pregnant and then states that she instinctively realized what has happened. Jon begs forgiveness and promises that he will never see Fleur again.

At home Fleur's distraught state is obvious to Soames, but he senses that the crisis has passed. Fleur accidentally drops a lighted cigarette in Soames's art gallery, and he soon realizes that his precious gallery is on fire. He rushes down to save his daughter, his grandson, and the servants, and then runs back to save his paintings. He rescues many by throwing them out the window. A large picture that has always reminded Soames of Fleur is left hanging on a window ledge when the choking Soames is dragged down to the lawn by the firemen. Soames sees that Fleur is standing below it. He realizes that she wants to be killed, and he darts forward to push her out of the way as the picture falls and strikes him dead. Soames dies a sacrifice for love as Bosinney did in *The Man of Property*. Soames is a champion in the end. As he breathes his last, Fleur, her life and soul saved, says "Yes Dad; I will be good!"

In the mid 1920s Galsworthy was working far too hard for a man of his age. On top of everything else going on in his busy life, in 1926 he and Ada Galsworthy decided to move. Galsworthy's nephew Rudolf Sauter, an artist, and his wife, Viola, were now a part of the Galsworthy household and frequently traveling companions. Wingstone and Grove Lodge were too small for four people, Galsworthy's writing, and Sauter's painting. Galsworthy first seemed to want a modest country house for the two couples, but soon, to Sauter's dismay—because it was understood that he and his wife were going to have to run the establishment—Galsworthy decided on a Tudor-style mansion: Bury House, located halfway between Pulborough and Arundel in Sussex, with a view of Bury Hill. The house had twenty-two rooms, of which fifteen were bedrooms. Grove Lodge was maintained as the London townhouse for the Galsworthys and the Sauters. Galsworthy had avoided a grand style of life before, but now he seemed to believe that his literary, political, and social position required visible opulence.

Although Galsworthy had finally killed off Soames Forsyte in *Swan Song,* he could not quite leave the Forsyte Chronicles. More Forsyte tales appeared in *Four Forsyte Stories* (1929) and *On Forsyte 'Change* (1930). Now Galsworthy seemed to be working against the clock. He started another trilogy, his third. This time he chose to depict an older and more distinguished clan than the Forsytes. The Charwells (pronounced "Cherrells") are upper-class, whereas the Forsytes are upper-middle-class. While the Forsytes represent the Galsworthys, the Charwells stand for the author's maternal ancestors: Worcestershire landed gentry.

The first Charwell novel, *Maid in Waiting* (1931), is set in 1928. The central figure of the trilogy is Dinny Charwell, a maid-in-waiting in the medieval sense: a woman who serves. She is Galsworthy's ideal upper-class young woman: beautiful, charming, intelligent, plucky, and never disillusioned. She loves her family, the countryside, and her ancestral home. She rejects her suitors because at twenty-four she thinks she is too young to marry. Her brother, Captain Herbert Charwell, killed a man in self-defense and was then charged with murder. The main plot of the story is the way the enterprising Dinny saves her strangely passive brother and the Charwells from disgrace. The novel is slight, and Galsworthy is not at ease with a happy ending, but the female characterization is brilliant.

Flowering Wilderness (1932) is set in 1930. The plot is rather absurd. Dinny, now twenty-six, meets the poet Wilfrid Desert, Fleur's would-be seducer in *The White Monkey*. They fall in love and within ten days are engaged. However, Wilfrid has a seemingly awful secret: in the Middle East, threatened with death, he converted to Islam. He had no belief before or afterward but thought that religion was not worth dying for. In the end the establishment ostracizes the poet for having betrayed his tradition and damaged British prestige, and he slinks away to obscurity in Siam. Dinny must slowly recover her will to live, and Galsworthy has returned to the sad ending. *Flowering Wilderness* was a long-outdated book at the time it was written.

On 13 August 1932, the day before his sixty-fifth birthday, Galsworthy finished *Over the River,* his last novel; it was published posthumously in 1933, and the trilogy was published in one volume titled *End of the Chapter* in 1934. *Over the River* is set in 1931, and the historical background is the Great Depression. Again Galsworthy focuses on a woman who is unhappily married. Dinny's younger sister, Clare, needs to dissolve her brief marriage. Her husband, Sir Gerald Corven, seventeen years older than she, has whipped her and done other things unmentionable in the fiction of the time and place. After leaving her husband in Ceylon, Clare meets an impoverished young man, Tony Croom, on the ship bringing her home to England. He falls in love with her at first sight, but although she enjoys his attention, she holds him off, for she has had enough of what she calls "physiology." In England her husband again demands his marital rights.

Clare and Tony continue to see each other but do not sleep together. Corven has them followed and vindictively sues for divorce, charging adultery and naming Tony as corespondent. Changing her mind, Clare seduces Tony, and they become part of the modern, urbane, sexually free smart set, living together but not marrying. The ending is cynical: the courts and society reward dishonesty and promote hypocrisy.

Meanwhile, Dinny learns that Wilfrid has drowned in Siam, and she falls desperately ill. Recovering, she accepts marriage with a conventional forty-year-old suitor named Eustace, whom she will never love. In the Charwell saga the men are weak unless they are bad, and the women must and do take charge of love and life itself. Galsworthy is mourning the breakup of the society he dissected and damned in his earlier fiction.

As Galsworthy was laboring on *Over the River* he was tired and depressed. He had endured radium treatments for a slightly disfiguring growth on his nose. Still enjoying horseback riding, he had experienced a few recent falls, and he had begun to suffer severe attacks of stuttering, sometimes losing the power of speech. Then Galsworthy began to drag one leg slightly, but, not wanting to distress Ada Galsworthy, he refused to see a doctor.

On 10 November 1932 an announcement arrived from Stockholm that Galsworthy had been awarded the Nobel Prize in Literature. The citation from the Swedish Academy stated that the prize was awarded "for his distinguished art of narration which takes its highest form in *The Forsyte Saga*." Congratulations poured in from all over the United Kingdom and the English-speaking world. He was the second native-born English person to receive the award (Rudyard Kipling was the first, in 1907). Rallying with the news, Galsworthy worked on his acceptance speech as he and Ada Galsworthy planned the trip to Stockholm, but he was stuttering and stumbling so badly that he soon realized that the journey was out of the question and that he could not attend the awards ceremony.

Galsworthy was moved to Grove Lodge to be nearer medical attention. Now the physicians began to suspect a brain tumor. The symptoms became clearer, especially when he revealed that he had been suffering from severe headaches. The Nobel Prize medal was delivered to him at Grove Lodge. King George V asked for news. The prime minister telephoned. The press was at the door, while the world waited. Galsworthy struggled on, but on the morning of 31 January 1933 he died at the age of sixty-five. His body was privately cremated three days later.

A grand memorial service was held in Westminster Abbey. It was expected that his ashes would be placed in the Poets' Corner, but because he was not a religious observant and had not been married in a church, the dean of Westminster Abbey refused interment of his ashes in the Abbey. But Galsworthy had requested that his ashes be scattered on the wind in the countryside, and on 25 March 1933 Sauter fulfilled that request on Bury Hill. Ada Galsworthy lived to a relatively healthy old age. On her death in 1956 she was cremated, and her ashes were also scattered on Bury Hill.

When Galsworthy died in 1933, he was at the height of his popularity. Few other British writers—certainly not any of the modernists—had the power, prestige, or the vast reading public he had. Even his friend and mentor, Conrad, had not achieved such success. King George V had made him a member of the Order of Merit, one of Britain's most valued awards. He had been elected the first president of PEN, the most important organization of international authors, and he served in that capacity for almost twelve years. The British nation exulted in Galsworthy's winning of the Nobel Prize. His fame was worldwide.

It is frequently the case that literary reputations free-fall shortly after the deaths of major writers. Only a few reputations rise to critical prominence later. In Galsworthy's case, the fall was extremely rapid. On learning of Galsworthy's death, Woolf wrote in her diary that she was glad "that stuffed shirt" had died. By 1940 Galsworthy was almost entirely ignored by British and American critics.

On 7 January 1967, one hundred years after Galsworthy was born, and thirty-three years after he died, television history was made when the British Broadcasting Corporation (BBC) began showing episodes of one of the first literary miniseries: *The Forsyte Saga*. The series was based on the two trilogies and three bridging "interludes" from the Forsyte epic. The BBC was so sure of the success of the material—even though Galsworthy's critical reputation, if not his popularity with readers, was at its nadir—that the corporation invested more money in the twenty-six-hour, black-and-white production than had ever been spent on a television show. Public reaction in Great Britain and, commencing in 1969, in the United States, was positive beyond the wildest expectations of the producers. Eventually, forty countries bought rebroadcasting rights, including the former Soviet Union. Millions of viewers have seen and loved the television epic. The success of *The Forsyte Saga* had a double effect: sales of Galsworthy's novels rose to unprecedented heights, and critical opinion, which had classified Galsworthy as a "popular" middlebrow writer, began a reevaluation of Galsworthy's literary achievement to the point that some critics offered positive views similar to those expressed prior to, and leading up to, the award of the Nobel Prize in Literature in 1932.

In April 2002 Granada Television in Great Britain remade the series in ten episodes. The new series was moderately successful in both the United Kingdom and the United States, where it was seen on PBS in October 2002. Again bookstores stocked Galsworthy's fiction, and readers enjoyed another look at British upper-middle-class society in the late nineteenth and early twentieth centuries.

Letters:

Autobiographical Letters of John Galsworthy: A Correspondence with Frank Harris, Hitherto Unpublished (New York: English Book Shop, 1933);

Letters from John Galsworthy, 1900–1932, edited by Edward Garnett (London: Cape, 1934; New York: Scribners, 1934);

Margaret Morris, *My Galsworthy Story, Including 67 Hitherto Unpublished Letters* (London: Peter Owen, 1967);

John Galsworthy's Letters to Leon Lion, edited by Asher Boldon Wilson (The Hague: Mouton, 1968).

Bibliographies:

H. V. Marrot, *A Bibliography of the Works of John Galsworthy* (London: Mathews & Marrot / New York: Scribners, 1928);

Gilbert H. Fabes, *John Galsworthy, His First Editions: Points and Values* (London: W. & G. Foyle, 1932);

E. H. Mikhail, *John Galsworthy the Dramatist: A Bibliography of Criticism* (Troy, N.Y.: Whitson, 1971);

Earl E. Stevens and H. Ray Stevens, *John Galsworthy: An Annotated Bibliography of Writings about Him* (De Kalb: Northern Illinois University Press, 1980).

Biographies:

H. V. Marrot, *The Life and Letters of John Galsworthy* (London: Heinemann, 1935; New York: Scribners, 1936);

M. E. Reynolds, *Memories of John Galsworthy by His Sister* (London: Hale, 1936; New York: Stokes, 1937);

R. H. Mottram, *For Some We Loved: An Intimate Portrait of John and Ada Galsworthy* (London: Hutchinson, 1956);

Dudley Barker, *The Man of Principle: A View of John Galsworthy* (London: Heinemann, 1963; New York: Stein & Day, 1963);

Rudolf Sauter, *Galsworthy the Man: An Intimate Portrait* (London: Peter Owen, 1967);

Catherine Dupré, *John Galsworthy: A Biography* (London: Collins, 1976; New York: Coward, McCann & Geoghegan, 1976);

James Gindin, *The English Climate: An Excursion into a Biography of John Galsworthy* (Ann Arbor: University of Michigan Press, 1979);

Gindin, *John Galsworthy's Life and Art: An Alien's Fortress* (Ann Arbor: University of Michigan Press, 1987).

References:

John Fisher, *The World of the Forsytes* (New York: Universe, 1976; London: Secker & Warburg, 1976);

Alan Fréchet, *John Galsworthy: A Reassessment,* translated by Denis Mahaffey (Totowa, N.J.: Barnes & Noble, 1982);

David Holloway, *John Galsworthy* (London: Morgan-Grampian, 1968);

Sheila Kaye-Smith, *John Galsworthy* (New York: Haskell House, 1972);

Herman Ould, *John Galsworthy* (London: Chapman & Hall, 1934);

Leon Schalit, *John Galsworthy: A Survey* (New York: Scribners, 1928; London: Heinemann, 1929);

J. Henry Smit, *The Short Stories of John Galsworthy* (New York: Haskell House, 1966);

Sanford Sternlicht, *John Galsworthy* (Boston: Twayne, 1987).

Papers:

The principal collection of John Galsworthy memorabilia, portraits, letters, diaries, and manuscripts is in the Galsworthy Memorial Collection, established by Rudolf Sauter, Galsworthy's nephew, at the University of Birmingham in 1962.

1932 Nobel Prize in Literature Presentation Speech

by Anders Österling, Member of the Nobel Committee of the Swedish Academy

When we survey John Galsworthy's authorship, it seems to develop unusually smoothly, pushed on by a conscientious and indefatigable creative impulse. Yet he is not one of those who have turned to the literary career rapidly and without resistance. Born, as the English put it, with a silver spoon in his mouth, that is, economically independent, he studied at Harrow and Oxford, chose the law without practising it, and travelled all over the world. When, at the age of twenty-eight, he began writing for the first time, the immediate reason was the exhortation of a woman friend, and it was to Galsworthy a mere recreation, evidently not without the inherent prejudices of the gentleman against the vocation of writing. His first two collections of tales were published under the pen name of John Sinjohn, and the editions were soon withdrawn by the self-critical beginner. Not until he was thirty-seven did he begin his real authorship by publishing the novel *The Island Pharisees* (1904), and two years later appeared *The Man of Property*, the origin of his fame and at the same time of his monumental chief work, *The Forsyte Saga*.

In Galsworthy's satire against the Island Pharisees, the fundamental feature that was to mark all his subsequent works was already apparent. The book deals with an English gentleman's having stayed abroad long enough to forget his conventional sphere of thoughts and feelings; he criticizes the national surroundings severely, and in doing so he is assisted by a Belgian vagabond, who casually makes his acquaintance in an English railway compartment and who becomes his fate. At that time Galsworthy was himself a cosmopolite returned home, prepared to fight against the old capitalistic aristocratic society with about the same program as Bernard Shaw, although the Englishman, contrary to the Irishman who fought with intellectual arms, above all aimed at capturing feeling and imagination. The pharisaical egoism of England's ruling classes, the subject of Galsworthy's debut, remained his program for the future, only specialized in his particular works. He never tired of fighting against all that seemed narrow and harsh in the national character, and the persistence of his attacks on social evil indicates his strong impressions and deeply wounded feeling of justice.

With the Forsyte type he now aimed at the upper middle class, the rich businessmen, a group not yet having reached real gentility, but striving with its sympathies and instincts toward the well-known ideal of the gentleman of rigid, imperturbable, and imposing correctness. These people are particularly on their guard against dangerous feelings, a fact which, however, does not exclude accidental lapses, when passion intrudes upon their life, and liberty claims its rights in a world of property instincts. Beauty, here represented by Irene, does not like to live with *The Man of Property;* in his bitter indignation at this, Soames Forsyte becomes almost a tragic figure. It seems uncertain if in the beginning Galsworthy thought of a sequel to that first Forsyte novel, which is a masterpiece of an energetic, firm, and independent account of human nature. At any rate it was not until fifteen years later that he again took up his Forsytes, and at this time the effects of the World War had radically changed the perspective. But now this work expanded; *In Chancery* (1920) and *To Let* (1921) and two short story interludes were added, and thus *The Forsyte Saga* proper was completed. Not finished with the younger members of the family, Galsworthy wrote *A Modern Comedy,* a new trilogy whose structure is exactly like that of its predecessor and consists of the three novels, *The White Monkey* (1924), *The Silver Spoon* (1926), and *Swan Song* (1928), united by two short story interludes. These two trilogies together form an unusual literary accomplishment. The novelist has carried the history of his time through three generations, and his success in mastering so excellently his enormously difficult material, both in its scope and in its depth, remains an extremely memorable feat in English literature—doubly remarkable, if we consider that it was performed in a field in which the European continent had already produced some of its best works.

In the foreground of this chronicle is everyday reality, as experienced by the Forsytes, all personal fortunes, conflicts, and tragicomedies. But in the background is visible the dark fabric of historical events. Every reader is sure to remember the chapter describing how Soames with his second wife witnesses the funeral of Queen Victoria in grey weather at the Hyde Park fence, and the rapid survey of the age from her accession to the throne: "Morals had changed, manners had changed, men had become monkeys twice removed, God had become Mammon—Mammon so respectable as to deceive himself." In the Forsyte novels we observe the transformation and the dissolution of the Victorian age up to our days. In the first trilogy comes to life the period that in England effected the fusion of nobility and plutocracy with the accompanying change of the notion of a "gentleman," a kind of Indian summer of wealth before the days of the storm. The second trilogy, no longer called "saga" but "comedy," describes the profound crisis of the new England whose task is to change the ruins of the past and the improvised barracks of wartime into its future home. The gallery of types is admirably complete. Robust businessmen, spoiled society ladies, aunts touching in an old-fashioned way, rebellious young girls, gentlemen of the clubs, politicians, artists, children, and even dogs—these last-mentioned especially favoured by Galsworthy—emerge in the London panorama in a concrete form, alive before our eyes and ears.

The situations recur as a curious documentation of the oscillation and the undulation in a family of given hereditary dispositions. The individual portraits are distinguished, and the law of social life is at work.

It is also instructive, however, to observe in these novels how Galsworthy's view gradually changes. The radical critic of culture rises by degrees to a greater objectivity in his appreciation and to a more liberal view of the purely human. An often cited example of this is his treatment of Soames, this standard national type, at first satirized, but then described with a respect that, reluctantly growing, finally changes into a genuine sympathy. Galsworthy has seized upon this sympathy; his characterization of Soames's personality thoroughly worked out becomes the most memorable feature of the Forsyte saga and the comedy of the descendants. One easily remembers one of those masterly final episodes of *Swan Song,* in which Old Soames, having driven to his ancestors' village on the west coast, finds with the help of an old census map the place where the Forsytes' farm had been situated, where only a single stone marks the site. Something like the ghost of a path leads him down into a valley of grass and furze. He breathes in the fresh, rough sea air which goes a little to his head; he puts on his overcoat and sits musing, his back against the stone. Had his ancestors built the house themselves at this lonely place, had they been the first to settle down here? he wonders. Their England rises before him, an England "of pack horses and very little smoke, of peat and wood fires, and wives who never left you, because they couldn't probably." He sits there a long time, absorbed in his feeling for the birthplace.

"And something moved in him, as if the salty independence of that lonely spot were still in his bones. Old Jolyon and his own father and the rest of his uncles—no wonder they'd been independent, with this air and loneliness in their blood; and crabbed with the pickling of it—unable to give up, to let go, to die. For a moment he seemed to understand even himself."

To Galsworthy Soames thus becomes one of the last representatives of static old England. There was no humbug in him, we are told; he had his trying ways, but he was genuine. The sober prosaic respectability is in this manner duly honoured in Galsworthy's realism, and this has been pointed out as the essential factor in his judgment of human nature. As time passed, and the weary, cynical laxity grew more and more visibly modern, the chronicler found that several traits which under other circumstances had been little appreciated, perhaps really constituted the secret of the British power of resistance. On the whole, Galsworthy's later novels are permeated with a patriotic feeling of self-defence that appears also in his descriptions of the home and studies of nature. Even these last-mentioned are rendered with a more tender and more anxious poetry, with the feeling of protecting something precious yet already shadowed by certain loss. It may be old chambers where people have established themselves as if to remain there forever. Or it may be an English garden park, where the September sun is shining beautifully on bronze-coloured beech leaves and centenary hedges of yew.

Time does not permit me to dwell in the same detail upon other of Galsworthy's works, often quite comparable in quality to the Forsyte series, which surpasses them by virtue of its epic dimensions. It is above all in *The Country House* (1907), in *Fraternity* (1901), and in *The Dark Flower* (1913) that his mature essential character is to be sought. In the novel of the manor he created perhaps his most exquisite female portrait, Mrs. Pendyce, the type of the perfect, unaffected lady with all the modest tragedy which surrounds a truly noble nature, condemned to be restrained if not destroyed by the fetters of tradition. In *Fraternity* he represented, with a discreet mixture of pity and irony, the unfulfilled martyr of social conscience, the aesthete who is tortured by the shadows of the proletarian masses in London, but is not able to take the decisive step and carry out his altruistic impulse of action. There we also meet the old original Mr. Stone, the utopian dreamer with his eternal monologues beneath the night sky, indeed one of Galsworthy's most memorable types. Nor do we forget *The Dark Flower,* which may be called a psychological sonata, played with a masterly hand and based on the variations of passion and resignation in the ages of man. Even in the form of the short story Galsworthy has often been able to evoke an emotional response through contrasts of shadow and light which work rather graphically. He can do this in only a few pages which become animated by his personal style, for example, when he tells about such a simple case as that of the German shoemaker in "Quality," the story of the hopeless struggle of good craftsmanship against low-price industry.

By appealing to education and the sense of justice, his narrative art has always gently influenced contemporary notions of life and habits of thought. The same is true of his dramatic works, which were often direct contributions to social discussion and led to definite reforms at least in one area, the administration of public prisons in England. His dramas show an unusual richness of ideas combined with great ingenuity and technical skill in the working out of scenic effect. When certain inclinations are found, they are always just and humane. In *The Forest* (1924), for example, he brands the inconsiderate spirit of greed that, for crass purposes, exploits the heroism of the British world-conquering mind. *The Show* (1925) represents the defencelessness of the individual against the press in a family tragedy where brutal newspaper curiosity functions like a deaf and unchecked machine, removing the possibility of any one being held responsible for the resultant evil.

Loyalties depicts a matter of honour in which loyalty is tested and impartially examined in the different circles where it is at work, that is, the family, the corporation, the profession, and the nation. The force of these and other plays is in their logical structure and their concentrated action; sometimes they also possess an atmosphere of poetic feeling that is far from trivial. I am thinking especially of *The Pigeon* (1912) and *A Bit o' Love* (1915) which, however, did not meet with such brilliant success on the stage. Although on the whole Galsworthy's plays cannot be rated artistically with his novels, they confirm quite as plainly how strongly he sticks to his early ideal of liberty, that which in Shelley put on the wings and flames of dawn. Even in his rather cool dramatic works we meet a steady enemy of all oppression, spiritual as well as material, a sensitive man who with all his heart reacts against lack of consideration and never gives way in his demand for fair play.

In technique Turgenev is one of his first teachers. As in the charming Russian narrator, we find in Galsworthy a definite musical charm catching and keeping the hidden feelings. His intuition is so infallible that he can content himself with a slight allusion and a broken hint. But then there is Galsworthy's irony, such a singular instrument that even the tone separates him from any other writer. There are many different kinds of irony. One principal kind is negative and can be compared to the hoar-frost of the windows in a house where there is no fire, where the hearth has grown cold long ago. But there is also an irony friendly to life, springing from warmth, interest, and humanity; such is Galsworthy's. His is an irony that, in the presence of tragicomic evil, seems to question why it must be so, why it is necessary, and whether there is nothing to remedy it. Sometimes Galsworthy makes nature herself take part in that ironic play about human beings, to underline the bitterness or sweetness of the incidents with the help of winds, clouds, fragrances, and bird cries. Assisted by this irony he successfully appeals to the psychological imagination, always the best ally of understanding and sympathy.

Galsworthy once formulated his artistic motto in words such as harmony, proportion, balance. They mark his natural turn of mind, a spiritual ideal, now often suspect, perhaps because it is so difficult to reach. We soon discover that this poet who so severely and persistently attacked the typical gentleman of self-sufficiency, himself indisputably succeeded in filling the old notion with new life, so that it preserved its contact with both the immediately human and the unrestricted aesthetic instinct. In the artist Galsworthy flourish exactly those qualities of temper that in English are comprehended in this word: *gentleness*. These qualities are expressed in his works, and in this way they have become a cultural contribution to our own times.

As Mr. Galsworthy has unfortunately been prevented by illness from being here today, as he had wished, to receive personally the Nobel Prize in Literature for 1932, it will now be delivered to the representative of Great Britain here present, Minister Clark Kerr.

Your Excellency—May I ask you to receive from His Majesty's hands the Nobel Prize in Literature, awarded to your famous countryman.

At the banquet, Gunnar Holmgren, Rector of the Caroline Institute, made these remarks: "Finally, we are today paying homage to John Galsworthy. If this our homage is marked by a feeling of very special warmth, it is largely because his noble personality and his exquisite artistic gifts, as displayed in his numerous literary works, have long been famous and highly appreciated all over the world. But the reason is no less to be found in that spirit of idealism, that warm sympathy and true humanity that radiate from all his writings and render him especially worthy to receive a gift from Alfred Nobel's Foundation. We regret very deeply that unfortunate circumstances have prevented John Galsworthy from being present here today. We should have been happy indeed to have had the privilege at the same time of honouring in his person the incarnation of that high-minded and idealistic England which we all love and admire. I beg to request His Excellency the British Minister kindly to convey to him our sincere greetings and heartiest congratulations."

[© The Nobel Foundation, 1932.]

Gao Xingjian

(4 January 1940 –)

Mabel Lee
University of Sydney

This entry has been expanded by Lee from her Gao entry in *DLB Yearbook 2000*.

BOOKS: *Xiandai xiaoshuo jiqiao chutan* (Guangzhou: Huacheng, 1981);

You zhi gezi jiao Hongchunr (Beijing: Beijing Publishing House, 1985);

Gao Xingjian xiju ji (Beijing: Qunzhong, 1985)—includes *Juedui xinhao*, translated by Shiao-Ling S. Yu as *Alarm Signal*, in *Chinese Drama After the Cultural Revolution, 1979–1989*, edited by Yu (Lewiston, N.Y.: Edwin Mellen, 1996), pp. 159–232; *Chezhan*, translated by Yu as *The Bus Stop*, in *Chinese Drama After the Cultural Revolution*, pp. 233–289; also translated by Kimberley Besio as *Bus Stop*, in "*Bus Stop*: A Lyrical Comedy on Life in One Act," in *Theater and Society: An Anthology of Contemporary Chinese Drama*, edited by Haiping Yan (Armonk, N.Y.: M. E. Sharpe, 1998), pp. 3–59; and *Yeren*, translated by Bruno Roubicek as *Wild Man*, in "*Wild Man*: A Contemporary Chinese Spoken Drama," *Asian Theater Journal*, 7, no. 2 (Fall 1990): 184–249;

Dui yizhong xiandai xiju de zhuiqiu (Beijing: China Theater Publishing House, 1988);

Gei wo laoye mai yugan (Taipei: Lianhe, 1988); expanded as *Gao Xingjian duanpian xiaoshuo ji* (Taipei: Lianhe, 2001); six stories translated by Mabel Lee as *Buying a Fishing Rod for My Grandfather: Stories* (New York: HarperCollins, 2004)—comprises "The Temple," "In the Park," "Cramp," "The Accident," "Buying a Fishing Rod for My Grandfather," and "In an Instant";

Lingshan (Taipei: Lianjing, 1990); translated by Lee as *Soul Mountain* (Sydney: Flamingo, 2000; New York: HarperCollins, 2000);

Au bord de la vie (Canières-Morlanwelz: Lansman, 1993);

Shanhaijing zhuan (Hong Kong: Cosmos, 1993);

Gao Xingjian xiju liuzhong, 7 volumes (Taipei: Dijiao, 1995)—includes in volume 1, *Bi'an*, translated by Jo Riley as *The Other Side*, in "*The Other Side*: A Contemporary Drama Without Acts," in *An Oxford Anthology of Contemporary Chinese Drama*, edited by Martha P. Y. Cheung and Jane C. C. Lai (Oxford & New York: Hong Kong University Press, 1997), pp. 149–183; also translated by Gilbert C. F. Fong as *The Other Shore*, in his *The Other Shore: Plays by Gao Xingjian* (Hong Kong: Chinese University Press, 1999); in volume 2, *Mingcheng*; in volume 4, *Taowang*, translated by Gregory B. Lee as *Fugitives*, in *Chinese Writing and Exile*, edited by Lee (Chicago: Center for East Asian Studies, University of Chicago, 1993), pp. 89–138; in volume 5, *Sheng si jie*, translated by Fong as *Between Life and Death*, in *The Other Shore*, pp. 45–79; in volume 5, *Yeyou shen*, translated by Fong as *Nocturnal Wanderer*, in *The Other Shore*, pp. 137–190; and in volume 6, *Duihua yu fanjie*, translated by Fong as *Dialogue and Rebuttal*, in *The Other Shore*, pp. 81–136;

Le Somnambule (Carnières-Morlanwelz: Lansman, 1995);

Ink Paintings by Gao Xingjian, text translated by D. J. Toman and Tom Smith (Taipei: Taipei Fine Arts Museum, 1995; Dumont, N.J.: Homa & Sekey, 2002);

Meiyou zhuyi (Hong Kong: Cosmos, 1996)—includes "Zi xu," "Meiyou zhuyi," "Wo zhuzhang yizhong leng de wenxue," "Wenxue yu xuanxue: Guanyu Lingshan," "Geren de shengyin," "Guanyu Taowang," "Geri huanghua," and "Ling yizhong xiju," all translated by Lee in *The Case for Literature* (Sydney: HarperCollins, 2006); and "Bali suibi," translated by Fong as "Parisian Notes," in *Leng de wenxue: Gao Xingjian zhuzuo xuan / Cold Literature: Selected Works by Gao Xingjian*, bilingual edition, translated by Fong and Lee (Hong Kong: Chinese University Press, 2005);

Zhoumo sichongzou (Hong Kong: New Century, 1996)—includes "Sheng sheng man bianzhou," translated by Fong as "Variation on 'A Slow Slow Tune,'" and "Wo shuo ciwei," translated by Fong as "I

Gao Xingjian delivering his Nobel Prize lecture at the Royal Swedish Academy on 7 December 2000, with one of his paintings in the background (photograph by Henrik Montgomery, Associated Press, Pressens Bild)

Say Porcupine," in *Leng de wenxue/Cold Literature;* title work translated by Fong as *Weekend Quartet,* in *The Other Shore,* pp. 191–254; title work revised as *Quatre quatuors pour un week-end* (Carnières-Morlanwelz: Lansman, 1998);

Goût de l'encre (Paris: Voix Richard Meier, 1996);

Au plus près du réel: Dialogues sur l'écriture (1994–1997), by Gao and Denis Bourgeois (La Tour-d'Aigues: Aube, 1997);

L'Encre et la lumière de Gao Xingjian (Paris: Voix Richard Meier, 1998);

Yige ren de shengjing (Taipei: Lianjing, 1999); translated by Lee as *One Man's Bible* (New York: HarperCollins, 2002);

Gao Xingjian (Hong Kong: Ming Pao, 2000);

Bayue xue (Taipei: Lianjing, 2000); translated by Fong as *Snow in August* (Hong Kong: Chinese University Press, 2003);

Mo yu guang: Gao Xingjian jinzuo zhan / Darkness & Light: An Exhibition of Recent Works by Gao Xingjian (Taipei: Xingzheng, 2001);

Wenxue de liyou (Hong Kong: Ming Pao, 2001)–includes "Xiandai hanyu yu wenxue xiezuo," translated by Lee as "The Modern Chinese Language and Literary Creation," in *The Case for Literature;*

Gao Xingjian juzuo xuan (Hong Kong: Ming Pao, 2001);

Ling yizhong meixue (Taipei: Lianjing, 2001); translated by Nadia Benabid as *Return to Painting* (New York: Perennial, 2002);

Muqin (Taipei: Lianhe, 2001);

Gao Xingjian: Ink Paintings 1983–1993, edited by Curtis L. Carter (Milwaukee: Haggerty Museum of Art, 2003);

L'Errance de l'oiseau (Paris: Seuil, 2003);

Le Quêteur de la Mort (Paris: Seuil, 2003); Chinese translation by Gao published as *Kouwen siwang* (Taipei: Lianjing, 2004);

Pengyou (Taipei: Lianhe, 2004);

Gao Xingjian (Paris: Galerie Claude Bernard, 2004);

Gao Xingjian Experience (Singapore: Singapore Art Museum, 2005).

PLAY PRODUCTIONS: *Juedui xinhao,* Beijing, Beijing People's Art Theater, August 1982;

Chezhan, Beijing, Beijing People's Art Theater, July 1983; University of Michigan, Arena Theater, 2001;

Yeren, Beijing, Beijing People's Art Theater, 1985;

Duo yu, Stockholm, Kungliga Dramatiska Teatern, 1987;

Mingcheng, Hong Kong, Hong Kong Dance Company, 1988;

Sheng sheng man bianzou, New York, Guggenheim Museum, 1989;

Bi'an, Taipei, National Arts College, 1990; Gannon University, Schuster Theatre, 2001; Los Angeles, Sons of Beckett Theater Company, 2003;

Taowang, Stockholm, Kungliga Dramatiska Teatern, 26 May 1991;

Duihua yu fanjie, Vienna, Theater des Augenblicks, 1992;

Sheng si jie, Paris, Renaud-Barrault Théâtre du Rond-Point, 1993; New York, Theater for the New City, 1997;

Yeyou shen, Avignon, Théâtre des Halles, 1999; Davis, Theatre and Dance Department of the University of California, 2003;

Bayue xue, Taipei, National Theater, December 2002;

Zhoumo sichongzou, New York, Play Company, 2003;

Kouwen siwang, Marseille, Théâtre du Gymnase, 2003.

OTHER: "Pulieweier, *Geci ji,*" in *Waiguo xiandai shi* (Beijing: People's Literature Publishing House, 1984);

"Younaisiku, *Tutou genii,*" in *Huangdanpai xiju* (Beijing: People's Literature Publishing House, 1985);

"Wenxue de jianzheng: Dui zhenshi de zuiqiu," translated by Mabel Lee as "Literature as Testimony: The Search for Truth," in *Witness Literature: Proceedings of the Nobel Centennial Symposium,* edited by Horace Engdahl (Singapore: World Scientific, 2002), pp. 113–127;

"Meng bo," translated by Lee as "Dream Waves," in *A Birthday Book for Brother Stone: For David Hawkes, at Eighty,* edited by Rachel May and John Minford (Hong Kong: Chinese University Press, 2003), pp. 305–308.

SELECTED PERIODICAL PUBLICATIONS– UNCOLLECTED: "Contemporary Technique and National Character in Fiction," translated by Mau-sang Ng, *Renditions,* 19–20 (1983): 55–58;

"The Voice of the Individual," translated by Lena Aspfors and Torbjörn Lodén, *Stockholm Journal of East Asian Studies,* 6 (1995): 71–81;

"Without Isms," translated by Winnie Lau, Deborah Sauviat, and Martin Williams, *Journal of the Oriental Society of Australia,* 27–28 (1995–1996): 105–114.

Playwright, novelist, and artist Gao Xingjian was a prominent leader of the avant-garde movement in fiction and drama that emerged in the wake of the Cultural Revolution (1966–1976) in China. In 2000 he received the Nobel Prize in Literature "for an oeuvre of universal validity, bitter insights and linguistic ingenuity, which has opened new paths for the Chinese novel and drama," as the citation read. This decision by the Swedish Academy marked the first time the Nobel Prize had been awarded for a body of writings in the Chinese language. At the time of his award, his major works had also been published in French, Swedish, and English translation; and by the end of 2003, Finnish, Norwegian, Danish, German, Italian, Catalan, Spanish, Portuguese, Japanese, Korean, Thai, and Slovenian editions had been published. Gao's plays have not been publicly performed in China since 1986, but, from 1987, performances have been staged in theaters all over the world.

Gao was born on 4 January 1940 in war-torn Republican China (Ganzhou, Jiangxi Province) during the Japanese invasion and received his formal education in the People's Republic of China, Mao Zedong's New China, established in 1949. Gao, however, had grown up in a liberal family environment and had free access to a sizable family library of Chinese literature as well as many volumes on Western literature and art, and he provided a solid education for himself through reading. From childhood he had wanted to become an artist, and on completing high school he wanted to enroll in an art school. When he realized that it would mean painting propaganda posters, he subsequently chose to study French at the Beijing Foreign Languages Institute, a choice that was crucial in his development as a writer. As more and more Chinese books were banned from the 1950s onward, he was able to continue reading his way through the shelves of French books at the Institute library. Following his graduation with a major in French literature, he was assigned work as a translator and editor at the Foreign Languages Press in Beijing. He continued reading books in French until all books in foreign languages were banned during the course of the Cultural Revolution. Before long, in 1970, along with almost the entire staff of the press, Gao was sent to attend a May Seventh cadre school for "reeducation" through hard labor.

Mao Zedong's guidelines for literature, established in Yan'an in 1942, were rigidly enforced during the Cultural Revolution. In Mao's program for literature and the arts, both Chinese and Western traditions had no place. The value of the individual was negated, and it was decreed that literature and the arts should serve the masses, although it was clearly understood that all creative activity was to serve a hierarchy of political authorities, at the pinnacle of which was Mao Zedong. The implementation of Mao's wishes meant that the author and the reader, as well as the characters in literary works, were divested of psychological, intellectual, and physical autonomy.

Gao had begun keeping a diary soon after learning to write, and by the time he was a young adult he had developed an obsessive desire for self-expression in writing. During the Cultural Revolution, when stringent measures were imposed on writers, many who had begun their careers as early as the 1920s were publicly denounced and punished for what they had written decades earlier. Gao was aware that what he wrote in secret did not conform to Mao's guidelines, and at the height of the Cultural Revolution, he reluctantly burned many manuscripts—ten plays, and several short stories, poems, and essays—rather than risk having them found and used as evidence against him.

After a few months at the May Seventh cadre school, he came under investigation for having led a "rebel" Red Guard group against the "revolutionary pedigree" Red Guard group that was subjecting older colleagues of the Foreign Languages Press to brutal beatings and torture for their alleged antirevolutionary, anti-Party criminal pasts. An officer of the Military Control Commission arrived to incite the masses to denounce Gao at meetings so they could arrest him. Before that happened, Gao succeeded in fleeing to a remote mountain village, where he resigned himself to spending the rest of his life as a peasant.

After a period of working in the paddy fields, he was recruited to teach at the village school, where he again began to write in secret, but not before he had made elaborate preparations. He wrote on thin letter paper that could quickly be stuffed into the hollow bamboo handle of his broom if he were interrupted. Completed manuscripts were wrapped in plastic and put in a lime-laced pot that was placed into a hole dug into the dirt floor of his hut and covered with a heavy water barrel. Even in those bleak times he had a visceral craving to articulate his thoughts in writing. In those extreme times, the fear of punishment coerced people into articulating only what was "correct"; one's political masters manipulated what one thought, spoke, or did. Because it was not possible to share his thoughts with another person, being able to express them on paper was important: the act of writing was an affirmation of his existence.

In 1975 Gao was able to return to Beijing, where he was restored to his position in the Foreign Languages Press. The Cultural Revolution ended with Mao's death in 1976, increasing artistic freedom. From 1980 Gao's short stories, novellas, prose essays, and criticism began to appear regularly for the first time in literary magazines; he was among the first to discuss the developments that had taken place in literary theory and practice in the West. In 1981 he was assigned work as a writer for the Beijing People's Art Theater, and in his spare time he wrote introductory essays on writers including Samuel Beckett, Antonin Artaud, Jean-Paul Sartre, Albert Camus, Eugène Ionesco, and the Polish playwrights Jerzy Grotowski and Tadeusz Kantor. Two of his translations from the French were published in anthologies in Beijing: Jacques Prévert's *Paroles* (1945, Words) was included in *Waiguo xiandai shi* (1984, Foreign Modernist Poetry), and Ionesco's *La Cantatrice chauve* (1950, The Bald Soprano) was included in *Huangdanpai xiju* (1985, Absurdist Plays). In the light of his knowledge of world literature, he also wrote critical assessments of China's rich literary heritage. During the politically volatile times of the early 1980s, Gao's insistence on the importance of the individual in literary creation firmly established his credentials among writers, academics, and ordinary thinking people in China.

Although the Cultural Revolution had ended, the established guidelines for literary creation continued to prevail under the watchful eyes of the Chinese Writers' Association and the Ministry of Propaganda. In 1980 Gao's *Xiandai xiaoshuo jiqiao chutan* (Preliminary Explorations into the Art of Modern Fiction) was serialized in *Suibi Monthly* in Guangzhou. Exercising self-censorship, Gao discussed how modern technology had impacted upon people's appreciation of fiction and how attention to technique and language was important to breathe new life into fiction. The Cultural Revolution guidelines for fiction stipulated that characters should be either unambiguously "good" or unambiguously "bad." The "good" characters were to serve as exemplars for the masses, and anyone behaving like the "bad" characters should be reported to the authorities. Rather than mounting a frontal attack on these guidelines, Gao gently proposed that fiction that preached was not effective, and that for fiction to be effective, freedom was important: for the author and reader as well as the characters. He substantiated his argument by drawing on examples mainly from the great Chinese and Russian novels. The work was published as a book in 1981, but when it was reprinted the following year, Gao came under the scrutiny of the authorities because the book had been applauded by older, established writers in literary publications.

In 1982 Gao also made his debut as a playwright with *Juedui xinhao* (translated as *Alarm Signal*, 1996), which was staged to packed audiences at the Beijing People's Art Theater. The play challenged decades of entrenched socialist-realist practices in the theater, not to mention Mao's dictum that literature and the arts should serve the people. Written again with considerable self-censorship, the story is simple and tells of an attempted train robbery that is thwarted when one of the villains has a change of heart. Gao's innovative techniques—such as flashbacks, different perspectives, and his focus on the psychological dimensions of his characters—had enormous appeal for audiences, but for the authorities the play was problematical and deemed subversive because there was ambiguity in the "good" and "bad" characters. In other words, the members of the audience were encouraged to make up their own minds about the characters.

In 1983 his play *Chezhan* (translated as *The Bus Stop,* 1996, and as *Bus Stop,* 1998) was also performed to packed audiences but incurred the wrath of the authorities; it was stopped after several performances. The play depicts the actions of people waiting at a bus stop, as they watch buses pass without stopping, and as years pass by. Western critics found the play reminiscent of the Theater of the Absurd, but not quite the same. Chinese audiences simply found the play refreshing and totally different from the overtly didactic plays of past decades. Bureaucratic intrusion into the smallest details of people's lives had made waiting a familiar daily event for more than a decade. What was subversive in the play was the freedom it gave audiences to identify with the characters. Only one character, The Silent Man, strides off after a short wait, while the others all choose to remain together. The individualism symbolized by the decisiveness of The Silent Man to act alone was unacceptable to the authorities.

After the banning of *Chezhan,* the actors were recalled by the authorities to put on special performances so that journalists could write criticisms of the play for all the major newspapers. During this period of intense anxiety, Gao was diagnosed with lung cancer, and he resigned himself to imminent death from the disease. Weeks later, another x-ray was taken to determine the extent to which the cancer had spread. When instead it confirmed without doubt that there had been a wrong diagnosis, Gao felt "reborn," with a "fundamentalist" belief in his own human worth. He resolved never again to allow himself to be manipulated by others as he had during the Cultural Revolution. On hearing the rumor that the authorities planned to send him to one of the notorious prison farms of Qinghai Province because of his "pernicious" play, he did not wait to be sent. He took an advance royalty from an editor, who in the previous year had urged him to put his theories on fiction into practice, and immediately fled by train to the remote forests of Sichuan Province. From there he wandered to the source of the Yangtze River and leisurely followed it down to the eastern seaboard.

During his absence from Beijing, Gao was singled out and denounced for promoting the decadent modernism of capitalist Western literature. The Oppose Spiritual Pollution Campaign of 1983 had erupted; Gao and other writers were blacklisted and their works banned from publication. Shock waves reverberated through the literary world, as writers nervously faced the possibility of a return to the not-too-distant Cultural Revolution with its persecution campaigns against writers. Gao traveled more than fifteen thousand kilometers in the Chinese hinterland for five months, until the campaign had petered out and friends informed him that it was safe to return to Beijing. In the early part of his travels, he kept to the borders and margins of society to avoid detection by the authorities. There, with the curiosity of an anthropologist, ethnographer, and archeologist, he observed vestiges of early civilization and ancient folk practices that provided much material for his reflections on human existence, the political nature of how human history is documented, and the function of language, song, and storytelling. The solitude of his long journey also provided much space for him to reflect on his own life, both his present predicament and on the fragments of forgotten memories that had surfaced during his confrontation with death.

Gao had been working on a novel since 1982. Firm in his conviction that the Chinese written language in modern times had lost the vitality and sensuality of the spoken language, he wanted to write a long novel that would enable him to explore the limitations and potential of the written language. He consciously strove to invest his writing with the music and rhythm of the spoken language, and his physical and psychological experiences during his five-month journey filled the pages of this novel, which he completed eight years later in Paris. That novel is *Lingshan* (1990; translated as *Soul Mountain,* 2000).

In the 563 pages of *Lingshan,* Gao indulged himself in a grand-scale experimentation with narrative form and language to create an unusual work of autobiographical fiction. Instead of named characters, the pronouns "you," "she," and "he" are used to scrutinize the narrator's psychological self from various perspectives, while the pronoun "I" is used to recount the narrator's physical journey through China. Most of Gao's short stories had experimented with the use of pronouns as characters; however, in *Lingshan,* Gao demonstrates conclusively that this technique could be sustained in a novel of considerable length. During large sections of his journey the narrator, "I," does not encounter anyone for days. Lonely and perceiving the need to talk with someone, the narrator, "I," creates "you," who is in fact a reflection of the narrator. Naturally, being a reflection of "I," "you" also experiences loneliness and creates "she" for a companion. "You" flirts with "she," who finally succumbs, and the two gratify their sexual lust. "You" and "she" travel together to Soul Mountain, and on the way "you" tells "she" many fascinating tales and legends; "she" is also persuaded to tell her stories. Eventually, "she" tires of the never-ending journey to Soul Mountain, and becomes depressed and morbid. "She" feels betrayed in her relationship with "you." While sex has generated feelings of love in the woman, it has not in the man. In a fit of hysteria "she" attacks "you" with a knife, although "you" succeeds in repelling her. "She" becomes paranoid about "you" wanting to push her over a cliff; yet, it is with reluctance that she departs, leaving "you" to travel alone to Soul Mountain. "You" and "I" have been traveling for quite some time together and have become too close, so the narrator suggests that "you" should go his own way. As "you" walks off, the back of "you" becomes "he." Shamans, grave robbers, bandit chiefs, Daoist priests, Buddhist monks and nuns, reclusive forest rangers, and local cadres and officials populate the novel as they do the regions traversed by the author in reality and in his imagination and memories.

Gao returned to Beijing at the end of 1983, and in the following year he was able to submit works for publication again. However, although a generally more liberal policy was being implemented, there could suddenly also be cycles of repression. Gao found the restrictions on literary expression increasingly intolerable. Even while he carefully exercised self-censorship, his writings continued to cause troubles for him. When his play *Yeren* (translated as *Wild Man*, 1990) was staged in 1985 at the Beijing People's Art Theater, he found that his performers were being taken aside and individually warned not to take part in future productions of his plays. In 1986 his play *Bi'an* (translated as *The Other Side*, 1997, and as *The Other Shore*, 1999) was banned at rehearsal. *Yeren* was the last of Gao's plays to be performed in China. Despite these far from ideal circumstances, Gao nevertheless succeeded in publishing a significant number of plays, short stories, and theoretical works on fiction and dramaturgy in various literary magazines and in book form. His other major works of this time are a novella, *You zhi gezi jiao Hongchunr* (1985, A Pigeon Called Red Beak), *Gao Xingjian xiju ji* (1985, Collected Plays by Gao Xingjian), and *Dui yizhong xiandai xiju de zhuiqiu* (1988, In Search of a Modern Form of Dramatic Representation). However, he was utterly frustrated by having to practice self-censorship and yet still failing to satisfy the censors. It was clear to him that he was the target of an unarticulated harassment campaign.

In late 1987 the opportunity arose for Gao to travel to Germany, and on leaving Beijing he had in mind the thought of seeking to remain in Europe. He wanted the freedom to write without the anxiety and frustration of political interference, and by the end of the year he took up residence in Paris. Prior to leaving China he had compiled a collection of seventeen short stories (written between 1982 and 1986) for publication, but learned in Paris that all the major publishers had rejected it. The collection was published in Taipei in 1989 with the title *Gei wo laoye mai yugan,* the title he later also gave to a six-story collection for translation into foreign languages (translated as *Buying a Fishing Rod for My Grandfather,* 2004). The latter collection includes five stories from the original seventeen-story collection, plus one he had written in Paris, "Shunjian" (1990; translated as "In an Instant," 2004). The story "Shunjian" has since been published alongside the original seventeen stories in a collection with a new title, *Gao Xingjian duanpian xiaoshuo ji* (2001, Short Stories by Gao Xingjian).

In the preface he wrote in Beijing in 1987 for his seventeen-story collection (which is also included in the eighteen-story collection), Gao notes the need for changes in the concepts and techniques employed in fiction. He cautions that he is not announcing a new form of fiction and that his collection simply represents his own quest for a "more pure, more penetrating, and more adequate language" that will facilitate a better understanding of what it means to be human. He also alerts readers that his stories have no plot and that the suspense common in most fiction is absent. Gao sees fiction as a form of linguistic art, as the "actualization of language" rather than the imitation of reality: fiction is interesting because it is capable of evoking genuine feelings and sensations in the reader. The collection represents Gao's experimentation with various techniques that evolved further in his novel *Lingshan*, which he was writing in the same period as the stories of the original collection. In *Xiandai xiaoshuo jiqiao chutan*, Gao had identified many of the basic problems facing narrative fiction since the advent of cinema and television. His short stories and novels represent his ongoing quest to resolve these problems. In his drama and painting, he has adopted the same attitude of continual striving and experimentation to satisfy his artistic impulses.

Gao has a wide knowledge of both Chinese and Western drama and theater. Concerned that theater has seemingly lost its appeal, he calls for a return to what he considers to be the essence of theater: its "theatricality," which is precisely what distinguishes drama from other literary forms. In his view theatricality is largely absent in contemporary plays. Through his analysis of the conventions and techniques of traditional Peking Opera, Gao formulated his notion of the "tripartite actor": the actor as a person, the neutral actor, and the character. To achieve neutrality there must be a sloughing off of the everyday self to enable the actor to observe his or her own acting from a distance. The actor would thus modify his or her acting accordingly. In other words, the actor is to effect a psychological identification with the audience, which will allow the actor to communicate better with the audience. Gao observed in his fiction that additional critical perspectives could be generated when a character addressed himself (or herself) in the second or third person, so he also extended this technique into his plays. The inner mind is what interests Gao, and his exploration of innovative techniques is aimed at providing a fuller articulation of the psychological processes that determine human behavior.

Gao's first three plays had been directed by Lin Zhaohua under highly stressful political conditions in Beijing. In 1988, Lin traveled to Germany to direct a production of *Yeren* at the Thalia Theater in Hamburg. Since then, various eminent directors have produced Gao's plays on five continents. Gao has also taken a keen interest in directing his own plays. His productions include *Duihua yu fanjie* (performed in 1992, published in 1995; translated as *Dialogue and Rebuttal*, 1999) at the Theatre Augenblicks in Vienna in 1992 and at the Theatre Molière in Paris in 1995; *Bi'an* at the Hong Kong Academy for Performing Arts in 1995; *Sheng si jie* (performed in 1993, published in 1995; translated as *Between Life and Death*, 1999) at the Theater for the New City in New York in 1997; and *Bayue xue* (published in 2000, performed in 2002; translated as *Snow in August*, 2003) at the National Theater in Taipei in 2002. For the production of *Bayue xue* he mobilized a group of fifty Peking Opera performers and acrobats, a chorus of fifty singers, and a symphony orchestra with close to one hundred musicians. Through *Bayue xue*, a work based on the life of the illiterate woodcutter Huineng, Sixth Patriarch of Chan Buddhism (commonly known in the Western world as Zen), Gao was able to realize his longtime goal of creating modern operatic theatre on a grand scale. The work is in the style of traditional Peking Opera, with singing, dialogue, action, and martial arts, but Gao's production may be said to have totally changed the genre. He employed international experts for musical composition and stage lighting, and he was able to inspire the actors to understand and apply the principles for performance that he had developed from both Eastern and Western theater.

Gao's uncompromising stance in his creative endeavors is demonstrated by the events surrounding his writing of the play *Taowang* (Fleeing, published in 1990, performed in 1991; translated as *Fugitives*, 1993). Eighteen months after he had settled in Paris, the military crackdown on protesters in Tiananmen Square, Beijing, occurred in the early hours of 4 June 1989. Aghast at the brutal actions of the Chinese authorities, Gao tore up his Chinese passport and applied for political asylum in France; in interviews for French television, the Italian daily newspaper *La Stampa*, and *Le Sud* magazine, he angrily denounced the massacre of student protesters in Tiananmen Square. Soon after, he was commissioned by an undisclosed theater company in America to write a play about the events, and he wrote the two-act play *Taowang*. The company arranged for a translation and consequently suggested changes because there were no student heroes. Gao declined to make any changes, withdrew his manuscript, and paid the translation fee himself. In a speech in Stockholm on 26 May 1991, Gao declared: "In China the Communist Party couldn't make me to revise my works, so there was no question about an American theater group making me do so."

The setting for *Taowang* is just after tanks have rolled into an unnamed square in an unnamed city, and the play begins with a young male student and a woman radio broadcaster who have escaped into an unused warehouse. For those who had for so many weeks watched television news of the student demonstrations in Tiananmen Square, the setting is unmistakably the early hours of 4 June 1989. When the traumatized woman tears off her blood-spattered skirt and the man draws her into his arms to comfort her, feelings of lust arise. The couple is disturbed by the arrival of a middle-aged man, who is the persona of the author. The three characters present different perspectives on the events that have just taken place in the square. The impulsive young student is fired with heroic fervor and had been actively involved in the demonstrations; the radio broadcaster had been urging the citizens of Beijing to support the students; and the middle-aged man had gone into the square in response to the woman's passionate broadcasts. Adopting a heroic stance, the student proclaims that despite this setback, the struggle for democracy would continue, and that victory would finally belong to the students. The middle-aged man is cynical and dismissive: the students had been whipped up by emotional crowd frenzy and were deluded into thinking that they were heroes who, by their collective action of protest, would bring democracy to the nation. It was folly, he says, for the student protesters not to have worked out a fall-back strategy.

The student finally decides to leave the building and urges the other two to follow immediately, because at the crack of dawn the army would be combing the city to arrest anyone who had been in the square. As soon as he goes out the door there is a burst of gunfire, and it is assumed that he has been killed. The middle-aged man and the woman sublimate their terror of imminent death and succumb to the comfort of one another's bodies. The play examines human instincts and behavior arising from the fear of death as well as tribal instincts and mass hysteria induced by frenzied dancing, ghetto-blasters, and the worship of totems (even those as noble as nation, freedom, and democracy).

Taowang was first published in 1990 in the Chinese-language literary magazine *Jintian,* established by Chinese writers stranded in various countries abroad after the events of 4 June 1989. Some of these writers had been associated with the well-known Beijing literary magazine publishing under the same name from 1978 until the authorities closed it down in 1981; strong support also came from prominent members of the international academic and literary world for the resurrection of *Jintian* magazine in Stockholm. In the following year, unexpectedly, *Taowang* was published in China. Endorsed by the Chinese authorities, the first print-run of twenty-five thousand copies of a collection titled *Wangming "jingying": Qi ren qi shi* (The Diaspora "Elite": Who They Are and What They Are Doing) went on the market in May and was reprinted within a couple of months. The aim of the book was to provide incriminating evidence of "reactionary" writings by "unpatriotic," "anti-Party" Chinese living abroad. The book was read eagerly, but apparently not with the intended effect. In the book the full text of *Taowang* was reproduced after a three-page diatribe attacking the play for wrongly alleging that thousands of students had been killed in Tiananmen Square. The moral depravity of the three characters of the play is also condemned, especially the sexual promiscuity of the woman. About the same time, Gao learned from friends that his Beijing apartment had been confiscated and that he had been expelled from the Chinese Communist Party. In response to these developments Gao wrote "Guanyu *Taowang*" (1991, translated as "About Fleeing," 2006), first published in *Lianhebao* Supplement (17 June 1991) and later collected in *Meiyou zhuyi*. In it he makes the wry comment that he had already publicly severed his association with the party in 1989, when the student protesters were brutally suppressed.

In "Guanyu *Taowang*," Gao expresses abhorrence for writers who distort the truth in order to "hitch literature to the war chariot of a political group." While sympathizing with the students' cause, he was keenly aware that *Taowang* would anger the Chinese democracy movement, but truth in literature is his only criterion, and he refused to compromise. In those times of high emotions, he knew that a play that failed to portray the students as heroes, or offered the hint of any criticism of their actions, would be construed as a betrayal of the democracy movement. In the stage instructions for *Taowang,* Gao had explained that from ancient times human existence has been the same unending tragedy, and that *Taowang* seeks to portray the dilemma of modern mankind as a classical tragedy. He stipulates that: "The performance should embody both the declamatory tone of classical Greek tragedy and the ritualistic solemnity of Eastern classical drama. . . . This play is political, philosophical and psychological, and should not be construed as a socialist-realist play that simply reflects a single contemporary political event."

His strategy of presenting *Taowang* as classical tragedy is to induce in the reader/audience a psychological distancing from the emotional trauma of the specific events of 4 June. This distancing would allow for critical thinking and reflection on those events, as well as reinforce the fact that the specific incident under scrutiny is not unique in human history. This strategy also allows Gao as the playwright to retain adequate distance for writing truthfully about the harrowing reality of the specific event that, at the surface level, is ostensibly the theme of the play.

In the process of writing this play, Gao's reflections on literature, politics, and the self began to coalesce. In "Guanyu *Taowang*," Gao makes reference to an observation in *Eloge de la fuite* (1976, In Praise of Flight) by the French physician and philosopher Henri Laborit: once protest becomes organized, the protester is reduced to being a follower of the organizer, and the only escape is to flee. Gao broadens the scope of Laborit's thesis to posit that life is continual fleeing—from political oppression, others, and also from the self: "When the self is awakened, it is this self that cannot be escaped, and this is the tragedy of modern human beings." He argues that there are external pressures such as political pressures, social customs, fashions, and the will of others, but that mankind's misfortunes also derive from the self. The self is not God; it cannot be suppressed, but there is no need to worship it. One cannot escape one's self, and that is humankind's fate. This truth, he maintains, is central to classical Greek tragedy, and for this reason he had written *Taowang* as "pure tragedy."

The allusion to Friedrich Nietzsche is unmistakable. Gao had in fact read in Chinese translation all of Nietzsche's major works during the twelve months preceding his departure from China. The Tiananmen events of June 1989 prompted Gao to complete the final revisions to his novel *Lingshan*, which he had begun in Beijing in 1982. His submitting the manuscript to publishers in September 1989 symbolized his break with China, the country of his birth, where he had spent the first fifty years of his life. He went on to write *Taowang* during October 1989, and over the next few years he wrote a series of essays triggered by the events of Tiananmen and his writing of *Taowang*. Mention of Nietzsche's name, or brief reference to Nietzsche's superman, began to recur consistently in these essays. Collected and published as *Meiyou zhuyi* (1996, Without Isms), these essays display Gao's penetrating analyses of the inroads of politics, patriotism, and nationalism on China's modern literature. In these pieces he also establishes the foundation of what he later referred to as "another kind of aesthetics."

China's modern literature had emerged at the height of a Nietzsche craze during the 1910s and 1920s. Nietzsche's superman and his pronouncement "God is dead!" had fueled an intellectual movement that later came to be known as the May Fourth Movement. Although China had contributed to the war effort of the Allies against Germany during World War I, at the Paris Peace Conference in 1919 it was disclosed that the Allies had secretly agreed to hand over to Japan the German concession of Qingdao in North China. This "sell-out" by the Western democracies outraged all thinking Chinese who for decades had been painfully aware of China's impotence in the modern world. These events united China's youth, and fired by emotional fervor, they demanded radical, thoroughgoing change. They condemned the traditional culture of their predecessors, indicting it as the cause of China's problems. Armed with a smattering of Nietzsche, Chinese youth wrested the mantle of authority from their elders and set about smashing all that was old in order to create from its ashes a new culture that would enable the Chinese people to deal with the problems of modern life.

China's modern literature emerged in these emotion-charged times of patriotic fervor. The classical language was to be abandoned and replaced with a written language based on the vernacular language, and China's new literature was to concern itself with the problems of modern society. A cohort of young writers with a solid grounding in classical Chinese literature, and who had widely read and also translated European, Russian, and Japanese literature, laid the foundations of China's modern literature. During the early years of the 1920s, writers imagined that their works would contribute to the spiritual regeneration of the nation. China would then no longer be forced to suffer humiliation and loss of territorial sovereignty at the hands of the capitalist West and Japan. The individual was extolled, but as the nation was threatened further by Japanese territorial encroachments, political unity was seen to be of vital importance. The heroic fervor of empowered Chinese youth was easily manipulated for patriotic goals. Although Nietzsche's name was familiar to Chinese youth of those times, few had read more than a few essays about Nietzsche plus the prologue and a few essays from Nietzsche's *Also sprach Zarathustra* (1883–1885; translated as *Thus Spake Zarathustra: A Book for All and None,* 1896). Nevertheless, the notion of Nietzsche's superman intoxicated them with the romantic view that they were the heroes who would deliver China from the abyss of national failure.

For Gao, however, Nietzsche's superman is anathema. He sees the writer as a frail individual whose writings cannot change the world. By adopting this stance, he is challenging China's modern literary traditions, down to their Nietzschean foundations. He is critical of the literary and intellectual giant Lu Xun, who had called upon compatriots to cease being bystanders and to become actively involved with solving the problems of China. Gao sees Lu Xun's decision to sacrifice his creative life for politics as a tragedy for Chinese literature. In the essays of *Meiyou zhuyi,* he argues that the writer is merely a bystander who observes, and he maintains that literature has always been so, be it in the East or in the West. Politics, religion, fashion, and crass commercialism have led writers away from the essence of literary creation, and Gao is at pains to restate this point in his proposal that literature is "without isms." These views are reiterated in his Nobel lecture.

In *Ling yizhong meixue* (2001; translated as *Return to Painting,* 2002) Gao systematically outlines "another kind of aesthetics" for literature and art, while attacking the pernicious impact of both Nietzsche and modernity on aesthetics. However, Gao most soundly takes Nietzsche to task in his creative writings. In his novel *Yige ren de shengjing* (1999; translated as *One Man's Bible,* 2002) Gao depicts the insidious distortion of human behavior as having been made possible by individuals seeing themselves as supermen. Mao Zedong is the superman who has allowed his bloated ego to run amok and thinks and acts as if he has replaced God. Also possessing bloated egos, a multitude of lesser supermen believing they are Mao's heroes willingly assist the Great Leader in his project of creating "perfect people" in his own image. *Yige ren de shengjing* is a penetrating examination of how the superman's perception of his own heroism can lead to tyrannical behavior or to the individual's being manipulated by others. *Yige ren de shengjing* is Gao's indictment of Nietzsche's superman for the collective insanity of the nation during the Cultural Revolution. The narrator "you" remarks on his present reality: "And you are not a superman. Since Nietzsche, there has been a glut of both supermen and common herds in the world. You are, in fact, very ordinary, the very epitome of ordinariness."

Cover for a 2000 printing of a 1999 collection of Gao's plays, translated by Gilbert C. F. Fong, with special wraparound calling attention to his Nobel Prize win (Bruccoli Clark Layman Archives)

Like others who had lived through those times, Gao had tried to obliterate from memory the painful events he had witnessed during the Cultural Revolution. Not until after he had become a French citizen in 1997, twenty years after the end of the Cultural Revolution, was he prepared to undergo the excruciating experience of recalling those times in *Yige ren de shengjing,* which is an autobiographical novel. The Cultural Revolution had deprived him of a substantial part of his creative life; having to write in secret and often not being able to do so had caused him protracted anguish. But worst of all was his awareness that he was being manipulated, being forced to articulate thoughts that were not his own and having to act as dictated by his political masters. As an author, however, Gao was also mindful that if he inadvertently allowed himself to adopt a victim mentality in his writing, he would instinctively distort the truth to exonerate himself from complicity in the gross excesses of human cruelty that had taken place.

Yige ren de shengjing explores the psychological dimensions of how "he" came to be manipulated by various groups and ended up hopelessly enmeshed in politics. His ego became bloated by his sense of heroism, and he was inexorably overcome by what "he" perceived to be a sacred mission to defend senior colleagues at his workplace who were being persecuted by Red Guards. He found himself joining a "rebel" Red Guard group, and was soon acknowledged as their leader. However, when the Military Control Commission disbanded the Red Guards, his "rebel" Red Guard activities came under investigation. Rather than face certain detention and punishment, he fled to a remote mountain village in southwest China, volunteering to work as a peasant for the rest of his life.

Yige ren de shengjing also tells the stories of people "he" encounters, in the city and in the countryside. Most poignant are the stories of young women "he" meets: they are the most tragic casualties of the novel. Observed from the present, the narrator "you" indicts "he" for being cowardly and weak. Because "he" feels his own self-interests are at stake, he fails to offer sympathy to these women who in desperation had appealed to him for comfort by offering their bodies to him. By ruthlessly analyzing the behavior of "he" the narrator is by extension proposing how a whole population was manipulated in those extreme times. While autobiographical, the novel is at the same time a deep exploration of the dynamics of power at various levels that is of relevance to all human relationships.

Gao's play *Kouwen siwang* (first published as *Le Quêteur de la Mort,* 2003; Interrogating Death) was presented in Marseille as one of the events for "Gao Xingjian Year," declared by La Ville de Marseille in 2003. In this work he launches into a powerful and sustained attack on Nietzsche and modernity. Spoken words, simple but with much compressed meaning, are reinforced by stark visual representations onstage. The play critiques contemporary art as well as presenting Gao's reflections on life and on death. Two actors dressed in black are presenting a soliloquy from two perspectives, in effect doubling the impact of the ideas expressed. Actor A (a neurotic old man) and Actor B (a somber, older man) comment on the words and actions of one another. They observe one another, but their eyes do not meet. Actor B is actually the inner voice of Actor A's character. Both actors refer to themselves as "you," inviting the audience to identify with them. Actor A has missed his train and has to wait more than an hour for the next one, so he enters a museum of contemporary art and finds that he has been locked inside. Surveying the exhibits of such items as urinals, cigarette butts, and used toilet paper, he thinks that if all this rubbish is displayed, undoubtedly with a catalogue offering critiques using the newest jargon, then he too deserves to be one of the exhibits. Amazed at his own genius for thinking of putting himself on display as a live person, he notes that he will be world news—he would be like a soccer star. He admits to being narcissistic just like anyone else, and considers how he will be listed in art histories, become the subject of analysis, be subjected to repeated deconstruction, and win more acclaim than any of the other "artworks" on display. And he would become the topic of endless discussions by art critics.

Through the lips of this neurotic old man, Gao disparages modernity as having created a continuing dynamic to be a trendsetter, just to be sensational, even if it is to do something futile such as masturbating in front of a camera. He regards this trend of continually subverting one's predecessors and debunking all old things as akin to a father teaching the son to shoot and then the son killing the father so that he can be head of the family. Having pronounced the death of God, afraid of being left behind, everyone charges forward wanting to be God. The old man begins to voice his reflections on life and his desire not to be controlled, even by old age, even by death; and eventually he commits suicide.

When the Swedish Academy announced that he had won the Nobel Prize in Literature in 2000, Gao's life as a reclusive writer was suddenly interrupted by crowds of journalists and television crews that arrived at the door of his modest apartment on the outskirts of Paris. The awarding of the prize to Gao caused a controversy of unprecedented proportions. In the hundred-year history of the Nobel Prize, it had never been awarded to a Chinese writer, so that year a large number of Chinese writers had been nominated. By that time, however, Gao was a French citizen, so the prize in fact had been awarded to a writer for a body of writings in the Chinese language but not to a citizen of China. Gao's writings have been blacklisted in China since 1991 and can neither be published nor marketed, although pirated editions are in circulation. In China there was a media blackout on the 2000 Nobel ceremonies.

Being crowned a Nobel laureate did not distract Gao from his literary and artistic endeavors. For him, the fact that he had been awarded this singular honor did not at all signify that he was the best writer in the world, and in his Nobel lecture, "Wenxue de liyou" (translated as "The Case for Literature," 2000), he acknowledges that many of the great writers of the world had died in obscurity. The Nobel award ceremony seemed to him "like a fairytale" in which he was playing a leading role.

The Nobel Prize money allowed Gao to relocate to an apartment in the center of Paris: it was the first time that his writings had brought him any financial rewards. Prior to that, he had supported himself in Paris by selling his paintings. He had once wanted to create works like the European masters, but on seeing the original paintings when he traveled to Europe in 1978 and 1980 as a translator and then a writer with two delegations, he decided to return to Chinese ink painting. As with his writing, his art is not bound to traditions or conventions; informed by his reading and observations on light and perspective in European painting, he began to explore the aesthetic potential of Chinese ink on rice paper. His first solo exhibition at the Beijing People's Art Theatre in 1985 has been followed by others in France, Germany, Taiwan, Hong Kong, Sweden, the United States, Poland, Belgium, and Spain. Public collections of Gao's paintings are held in Germany by Morat Institut für Kunst und Kuntwissenschaft (Frieburg) and Leibniz Gesellschaft für Kulturellen Austausch (Berlin); in Sweden by Ostasiatiska Museet, the Nobel Foundation (Stockholm), and Krapperrus Konsthall (Malmo); in Taiwan by the Fine Arts Museum and the National History Museum (Taipei); and in France by Maison de la Culture (Bourges), Arotheque (Nantes), Théâtre Molière (Paris), and La Ville de Marseille.

In addition to the 2000 Nobel Prize in Literature, Gao has received many honors for his literary achievements. The most significant include the Chevalier de l'Ordre des Arts et des Lettres (1992), the Premio Letterario Feronia (2000), the Chevalier de l'Ordre de la Légion d'Honneur (2000), and the American Academy of Achievement Golden Plate Award (Dublin, 2002). Gao's health forced him to return to a relatively reclusive life. He collapsed and was hospitalized while in Taipei directing rehearsals for his modernized Peking Opera *Bayue xue* in late 2002, but he recovered sufficiently to direct the premiere performance in December before returning to Paris, where he underwent two bypass operations in February and March 2003. In June of that year, while directing rehearsals for his play *Kouwen siwang,* he collapsed again but was able to direct the play with the assistance of Romain Bonnin at the premiere in Marseille in September.

During most of 2004, prompted by his fragile health and the urging of his doctor, Gao resolved to take stock of his physical well-being, canceling all social commitments and following a strict vegetarian diet rather than face a further major operation. If he tried to read anything serious, his blood pressure immediately rose, but he was able to write poetry and to paint on a daily basis. By early 2005 he began to get stronger and was able to direct a production of *Bayue xue* at

Opéra Marseille and to attend the Gao Xingjian Symposium held at Aix-en-Provence University, at which he received an honorary doctorate from Taiwan National University.

Gao has held several solo exhibitions of his new paintings, including those at Claude Bernard Galerie (Paris, 2004), Centra de Cultura Contemporainia (Barcelona, 2004), Frank Pages Art Galerie (Baden, 2005), and Singapore Art Museum (2005). Several of his artworks were also hung at Foire Internationale d'Art Contemporain (Paris, 2003 and 2004, and Brussels, 2006) and Art Paris (2005).

In 2006, having completed the production of his "cinematic poem" *La Silhouette si non l'ombre*, which was entered as an artistic movie at the Cannes Film Festival, Gao has been preparing a series of four video lectures for the Faculty of the Humanities at Taiwan National University. In these lectures he addresses the topics "Zuojia de weizhi" (The Place of the Writer), "Xiaoshuo de yishu" (The Art of Fiction), "Xiju de keneng" (The Possibilities in Drama), and "Yishujia de meishu" (The Aesthetics of the Artist). His health has improved significantly, and he continues to derive pleasure from writing poetry and painting.

Interview:

Gregory Lee and Noel Dutrait, "Conversation with Gao Xingjian: The First 'Chinese' Winner of the Nobel Prize for Literature," *China Quarterly*, 167 (2001): 738–748.

References:

Geremie Barmé, "A Touch of the Absurd: Introducing Gao Xingjian, and His Play *The Bus Stop*," *Renditions*, 19–20 (1983): 373–378;

Olivier Burckhardt, "The Voice of One in the Wilderness," *Quadrant*, 2 (April 2000): 84–85;

Chan Sin-wai, "Postscript: On Seeing the Play *Bus Stop*: He Wen's Critique in the *Literary Gazette*," *Renditions*, 19–20 (1983): 387–392;

Chen Xiaomei, "A Wildman between Two Cultures: Some Paradigmatic Remarks on 'Influence Studies,'" *Comparative Literature Studies*, 29, no. 4 (1992): 397–416;

Michel Draguet, *Gao Xingjian: Le Goût de l'encre* (Paris: Hazan, 2002);

Noël Dutrail, ed., *L'Écriture romanesques et théâtrale de Gao Xingjian* (Paris: Éditions du Seuil, 2006);

Jeffrey C. Kinkley, "Gao Xingjian in the 'Chinese' Perspective of Qu Yuan and Shen Congwen," *Modern Chinese Literature and Culture*, 14 (Fall 2002): 130–163;

Wendy Larson, "Realism, Modernism, and the Anti-'Spiritual Pollution' Campaign in Modern China," *Modern China*, 15, no. 1 (1989): 37–71;

Mabel Lee, "Gao Xingjian on the Issue of Literary Creation for the Modern Writer," *Journal of Asian Pacific Communication*, 9, no. 1–2 (1999): 83–96;

Lee, "Gao Xingjian's Dialogue with Two Dead Poets from Shaoxing: Xu Wei and Lu Xun," in *Autumn Floods: Essays in Honour of Marián Gálik*, edited by R. D. Findeisen and R. H. Gassman (Bern: Lang, 1998), pp. 401–414;

Lee, "Gao Xingjian's *Lingshan/Soul Mountain*: Modernism and the Chinese Writer," *HEAT*, 4 (1997): 128–143;

Lee, "Nobel in Literature 2000 Gao Xingjian's Aesthetics of Fleeing," *Comparative Literature and Culture: A WWWeb Journal*, 3, no. 1 (March 2003), <http://clcwebjournal.lib.purdue.edu/clcweb03-1/lee03.html>;

Lee, "On Nietzsche and Modern Chinese Literature: From Lu Xun (1881–1936) to Gao Xingjian (b. 1940)," *Literature and Aesthetics: The Journal of the Sydney Society of Literature and Aesthetics* (November 2002): 23–43;

Lee, "Personal Freedom in Twentieth Century China: Reclaiming the Self in Yang Lian's *Yi* and Gao Xingjian's *Lingshan*," in *History, Literature and Society: Essays in Honour of S. N. Mukherjee*, edited by Lee and Michael Wilding (Sydney & New Delhi: Sydney Association for Studies in Culture and Society, 1997), pp. 133–155;

Lee, "Pronouns as Protagonists: Gao Xingjian's *Lingshan* as Autobiography," *China Studies*, 5 (1999): 165–183;

Lee, "Returning to Recluse Literature: Gao Xingjian," in *The Columbia Companion to Modern East Asian Literature*, edited by Joshua Mostow (New York: Columbia University Press, 2003), pp. 610–616;

Lee, "Walking Out of Other People's Prisons: Liu Zaifu and Gao Xingjian on Chinese Literature in the 1990s," *Asian & African Studies*, 5, no. 1 (1996): 98–112;

Lee, "Without Politics: Gao Xingjian on Literary Creation," *Stockholm Journal of East Asian Studies*, 6 (1995): 82–101;

Li Jianyi, "Gao Xingjian's *The Bus-Stop*: Chinese Traditional Theater and Western Avant-garde," dissertation, University of Alberta, 1991;

Lin Manshu, ed., *Jiedu Gao Xingjian* (Hong Kong: Ming Pao, 2000);

Sylvia Li-chun Lin, "Between the Individual and the Collective: Gao Xingjian's Fiction," *World Literature Today* (Winter 2001): 20–30;

Liu Zaifu, "Afterword to *One Man's Bible*," *Modern Chinese Literature and Culture*, 14 (Fall 2002): 237–242;

Liu, *Gao Xingjian lun* (Taipei: Lianjing, 2004);

Liu, *Lun Gao Xingjian zhuangtai* (Hong Kong: Ming Pao, 2000);

Torbjörn Lodén, "World Literature with Chinese Characteristics: On a Novel by Gao Xingjian," *Stockholm Journal of East Asian Studies*, 4 (1993): 17–40;

Julia Lovell, "Gao Xingjian, the Nobel Prize, and Chinese Intellectuals: Notes on the Aftermath of the Nobel Prize 2000," *Modern Chinese Literature and Culture* (Fall 2002): 1–50;

Lovell, *The Politics of Cultural Capital: China's Quest for a Nobel Prize in Literature* (Honolulu: University of Hawaii Press, 2006);

Ma Sen, "The Theatre of the Absurd in Mainland China: Gao Xingjian's *The Bus Stop*," *Issues and Studies: A Journal of China Studies and International Affairs*, 25, no. 8 (1989): 138–148;

Thomas Moran, "Lost in the Woods: Nature in *Soul Mountain*," *Modern Chinese Literature and Culture* (Fall 2002): 207–236;

Quah Sy Ren, "Exploration in Action: Gao Xingjian's Theatre in the Context of 1980s China," *Asian Culture*, 26 (June 2002): 80–103;

Quah, *Gao Xingjian and Transcultural Chinese Theater* (Honolulu: University of Hawaii Press, 2004);

Quah, "Gao Xingjian: The Playwright as an Intellectual," *Natah Journal of Chinese Language and Culture*, 5, no. 1 (2002): 201–242;

Quah, "Performance in Alienated Voices: Mode of Narrative in Gao Xingjian's Theater," *Modern Chinese Literature and Culture*, 14 (Fall 2002): 51–98;

Quah, "Searching for Alternative Aesthetics in the Chinese Theatre: The Odyssey of Huang Zuolin and Gao Xingjian," *Asian Culture*, 24 (2000): 44–66;

Quah, "The Theatre of Gao Xingjian: Experimentation Within the Chinese Context and Towards New Modes of Representation," dissertation, University of Cambridge, 1999;

Josephine Riley and Michael Gissenwehrer, "The Myth of Gao Xingjian," in *Haishi Zou Hao: Chinese Poetry, Drama and Literature of the 1980s*, edited by Riley and Else Unterrieder (Bonn: Engelhard-Ng Verlag, 1989), pp. 129–151;

Carlos Rojas, ""Without [Femin]ism: Femininity as Axis of Alterity and Desire in Gao Xingjian's *One Man's Bible*," *Modern Chinese Literature and Culture*, 14 (Fall 2002): 163–206;

Kwok-kan Tam, "Drama of Dilemma: Waiting as Form and Motif in *The Bus Stop* and *Waiting for Godot*," in *Studies in Chinese-Western Comparative Drama*, edited by Yun-Tong Luk (Hong Kong: Chinese University Press, 1990), pp. 23–45;

Tam, ed., *Soul of Chaos: Critical Perspectives on Gao Xingjian* (Hong Kong: Chinese University Press, 2001);

William Tay, "Avant-garde Theater in Post-Mao China: *The Bus Stop* by Gao Xingjian," in *Worlds Apart: Recent Chinese Writing and Its Audiences*, edited by Howard Goldblatt (Armonk & New York: M. E. Sharpe, 1990), pp. 111–118;

Gang Gary Xu, "My Writing, Your Pain, and Her Trauma: Pronouns and (Gendered) Subjectivity in Gao Xingjian's *Soul Mountain* and *One Man's Bible*," *Modern Chinese Literature and Culture*, 14 (Fall 2002): 99–129;

Hai-ping Yan, "Gao Xingjian's Drama," *World Literature Today* (Winter 2001);

Henry Y. H. Zhao, *Towards a Modern Zen Theatre: Gao Xingjian and Chinese Theatre Experimentalism* (London: SOAS Publications, 2000);

Zhou Meihui, *Xue di chan si: Gao Xingjian zhidao Bayue xue xianchang biji* (Taipei: Lianjing, 2002);

Zou Jiping, "Gao Xingjian and Chinese Experimental Theater," dissertation, University of Illinois, 1994.

2000 Nobel Prize in Literature Presentation Speech

by Professor Göran Malmqvist, Member of the Swedish Academy

Your Majesties, Your Royal Highnesses, Ladies and Gentlemen,

Gao Xingjian's literary output comprises eighteen plays, two great novels, and a number of stories, which all fit in one volume. Born in 1940, he began his career as a writer as early as the sixties. His production would certainly have been much larger had not the conditions of life during the Cultural Revolution forced him to burn all his manuscripts of the sixties and the seventies. He also made very important contributions to the theoretical debate concerning the structure and functions of drama and the novel in China during the eighties. His work as a breaker of new ground relates to the form and structure of a literary work as well as to its psychological foundations.

The novel called *Soul Mountain* (1990) stands out as one of the foremost works in twentieth-century Chinese literature. Among many other things Gao Xingjian deals in it with an existential dilemma: man's urge to find the absolute independence granted by solitude conflicts with a longing for the warmth and fellowship which can be given by "the other," be it he or she. At the same time, however, this enriching companionship threatens the individual's integrity and, without fail, ends in some kind of struggle for power.

The author's vivid sense of alienation in a politics-ridden society made him, in the early eighties, go in search for hidden-away parts of southwestern and southern China, where there still existed traces of primitive cultures, age-old shamanistic rites and Daoist notions. In his portrayal of these cultures, replete with fantastic cock-and-bull stories which bring to the reader's mind the repertoires of traditional storytellers, he also castigates strict Confucian orthodoxy as well as Marxist ideology and their respective demands for obedience and uniformity.

In the course of his pilgrimage to *Soul Mountain*, where he hopes to find the ultimate truth about the meaning of life and the human condition, the author's ego is stricken by loneliness and is forced into creating a *you*, a projection of itself, which, in turn, hit by the same loneliness, creates a *she*. The numerous *he* figures that make their appearance in the novel are likewise projections of the author's ego. With the help of these pronominal projections, the author manages to investigate a wide range of human relationships and their consequences for the individual.

The novel entitled *One Man's Bible* (1999), which Gao Xingjian himself looks upon as a companion novel to *Soul Mountain*, is a novel of confession in which he mercilessly lays bare the three different parts he played during the Cultural Revolution: as a leader of a rebel faction, as a victim and as a silent observer. Again he makes use of the pronouns *you* and *he* in order to distinguish between two different degrees of alienation: *you* stands for the exiled author *here* and *now, he* is the author *there* and *then,* in the China of the Cultural Revolution. The framing chapters, which describe episodes in the author's exiled existence, are as factual and personally revealing as those dealing with his different roles during the Cultural Revolution. It is these framing chapters that enable the author to give his view on the meaning of human existence, the nature of literature, the conditions of authorship and, first and foremost, on the importance of remembering and of imagination for the author's view of reality.

The foundation for Gao Xingjian's pioneering activity as a dramatist was laid in the first half of the nineteen-eighties when he worked as artistic advisor, director of plays and playwright at the People's Art Theatre in Peking, at that time considered to be the country's foremost stage. Gao Xingjian's plays are characterized by originality, in no way diminished by the fact that he has been influenced both by modern Western and traditional Chinese currents. His greatness as a dramatist lies in the manner in which he has succeeded in enriching these fundamentally different elements and making them coalesce to something entirely new.

Dear Gao Xingjian: You did not leave China empty-handed. You have come to look on the native language which you brought with you when you left China as your true and real country. It gives me great joy to offer you, on behalf of the Swedish Academy, our warmest congratulations. I will ask you now to receive, from the hands of His Majesty the King, this year's Nobel Prize for Literature.

[© The Nobel Foundation, 2000.]

Gao: Banquet Speech

Gao's speech at the Nobel Banquet, 10 December 2000:

Vos Majestés, Vos Altesses royales, Mesdames, Messieurs,

L'homme qui est devant vous se souvient encore qu'à l'âge de huit ans, sa mère lui avait demandé de tenir un journal. II s'est ainsi consacré à l'écriture jusqu'à l'âge adulte.

II se souvient encore qu'à son entrée au lycée, un vieux professeur de rédaction avait accroché au tableau une peinture sans en révéler le titre et avait demandé aux élèves de faire une rédaction à son sujet. L'homme qui est devant vous n'aimait pas cette peinture, et il avait écrit des critiques contre elle. Non seulement le vieux maître ne s'était pas mis en colère, mais il lui avait donné une bonne note assortie du commentaire: "Plume vigoureuse." Et c'est ainsi que cet homme n'a plus cessé d'écrire, d'abord des contes pour enfants, puis des romans, de la poésie et du théâtre, et ce jusqu'à ce que la révolution renverse la culture. Là, pris de peur, il a tout brûlé.

Ensuite, il est parti cultiver les rizières pendant de nombreuses années. Mais il écrivait encore en secret et cachait ses manuscrits dans des pots de terre quite qu'il enterrait.

Ce qu'il a écrit ensuite a été interdit.

Plus tard encore, arrivé en Occident, il a continué à écrire, mais sans se soucier d'être édité. Et même quand il fut édité, il ne se soucia pas de connaître les réactions. Soudain, le voilà dans cette brillante salle, qui reçoit cette précieuse récompense des mains de Sa Majesté le Roi.

Alors, il ne peut s'empêcher de demander: Votre Majesté, est-ce la réalité ou un conte ?

Translation by William F. Edmiston

Your Majesties, Your Royal Highnesses, Ladies and Gentlemen,

The man who stands before you still remembers that at the age of eight, his mother had asked him to keep a journal. Thus he devoted himself to writing until an adult age.

He still remembers that upon entry into high school, an elderly composition teacher had tacked to the bulletin board a painting, without revealing the title, and asked his pupils to write a composition about it. The man who stands before you did not like that painting, and he wrote a criticism of it. Not only did the old teacher not get angry, but he gave him a good grade along with the comment "Vigorous pen." And thus this man never stopped writing, first stories for children, then novels, poetry and theater, until the revolution overturned the culture. Then, seized with fear, he burned everything.

Then he went off to cultivate rice fields for many years. But he was still writing in secret and hid his manuscripts in earthen pots that he buried.

What he wrote next was forbidden.

Still later, having arrived in the West, he continued to write, but with no wish to publish. And even when he was published, he cared nothing about knowing the reaction to his work. Suddenly, here he is in this brilliant room, receiving this precious award from the hands of His Majesty the King.

And so, he cannot help asking: Your Majesty, is this reality or a story?

[© The Nobel Foundation, 2000. Gao Xingjian is the sole author of his speech.]

Press Release: The Nobel Prize in Literature 2000

from the Office of the Permanent Secretary of the Swedish Academy, 12 October 2000

The Nobel Prize in Literature for 2000 goes to the Chinese writer Gao Xingjian "for an oeuvre of universal validity, bitter insights and linguistic ingenuity, which has opened new paths for the Chinese novel and drama."

In the writing of Gao Xingjian literature is born anew from the struggle of the individual to survive the history of the masses. He is a perspicacious sceptic who makes no claim to be able to explain the world. He asserts that he has found freedom only in writing.

His great novel *Soul Mountain* is one of those singular literary creations that seem impossible to compare with anything but themselves. It is based on impressions from journeys in remote districts in southern and southwestern China, where shamanistic customs still linger on, where ballads and tall stories about bandits are recounted as the truth and where it is possible to come across exponents of age-old Daoist wisdom. The book is a tapestry of narratives with several protagonists who reflect each other and may represent aspects of one and the same ego. With his unrestrained use of personal pronouns Gao creates lightning shifts of perspective and compels the reader to question all confidences. This approach derives from his dramas, which often require actors to assume a role and at the same time describe it from the outside. I, you and he/she become the names of fluctuating inner distances.

Soul Mountain is a novel of a pilgrimage made by the protagonist to himself and a journey along the reflective surface that divides fiction from life, imagination from memory. The discussion of the problem of knowledge increasingly takes the form of a rehearsal of freedom from goals and meaning. Through its polyphony, its blend of genres and the scrutiny that the act of writing subjects itself to, the book recalls German Romanticism's magnificent concept of a universal poetry.

Gao Xingjian's second novel, *One Man's Bible*, fulfils the themes of *Soul Mountain* but is easier to grasp. The core of the book involves settling the score with the terrifying insanity that is usually referred to as China's Cultural Revolution. With ruthless candour the author accounts for his experiences as a political activist, victim and outside observer, one after the other. His description could have resulted in the dissident's embodiment of morality but he rejects this stance and refuses to redeem anyone else. Gao Xingjian's writing is free of any kind of complaisance, even to good will. His play *Fugitives* irritated the democracy movement just as much as those in power.

Gao Xingjian points out himself the significance for his plays of the non-naturalistic trends in Western drama, naming Artaud, Brecht, Beckett and Kantor. However, it has been equally important for him to "open the flow of sources from popular drama." When he created a Chinese oral theatre, he adopted elements from ancient masked drama, shadow plays and the dancing, singing and drumming traditions. He has embraced the possibility of moving freely in time and space on the stage with the help of one single gesture or word—as in the Chinese opera. The uninhibited mutations and grotesque symbolic language of dreams interrupt the distinct images of contemporary humanity. Erotic themes give his texts feverish excitement, and many of them have the choreography of seduction as their basic pattern. In this way he is one of the few male writers who gives the same weight to the truth of women as to his own.

[© The Nobel Foundation, 2000.]

Gao: Nobel Lecture, 7 December 2000

The Case for Literature
(Translated by Mabel Lee)

I have no way of knowing whether it was fate that has pushed me onto this dais but as various lucky coincidences have created this opportunity I may as well call it fate. Putting aside discussion of the existence or nonexistence of God, I would like to say that despite my being an atheist I have always shown reverence for the unknowable.

A person cannot be God, certainly not replace God, and rule the world as a Superman; he will only succeed in creating more chaos and make a greater mess of the world. In the century after Nietzsche manmade disasters left the blackest records in the history of humankind. Supermen of all types called leader of the people, head of the nation and commander of the race did not baulk at resorting to various violent means in perpetrating crimes that in no way resemble the ravings of a very egotistic philosopher. However, I do not wish to waste this talk on literature by saying too much about politics and history, what I want to do is to use this opportunity to speak as one writer in the voice of an individual.

A writer is an ordinary person, perhaps he is more sensitive but people who are highly sensitive are often more frail. A writer does not speak as the spokesperson of the people or as the embodiment of righteousness. His voice is inevitably weak but it is precisely this voice of the individual that is more authentic.

What I want to say here is that literature can only be the voice of the individual and this has always been so. Once literature is contrived as the hymn of the nation, the flag of the race, the mouthpiece of a political party or the voice of a class or a group, it can be employed as a mighty and all-engulfing tool of propaganda. However, such literature loses what is inherent in literature, ceases to be literature, and becomes a substitute for power and profit.

In the century just ended literature confronted precisely this misfortune and was more deeply scarred by politics and power than in any previous period, and the writer too was subjected to unprecedented oppression.

In order that literature safeguard the reason for its own existence and not become the tool of politics it must return to the voice of the individual, for literature is primarily derived from the feelings of the individual and is the result of feelings. This is not to say that literature must therefore be divorced from politics or that it must necessarily be involved in politics. Controversies about literary trends or a writer's political inclinations were serious afflictions that tormented literature during the past century. Ideology wreaked havoc by turning related controversies over tradition and reform into controversies over what was conservative or revolutionary and thus changed literary issues into a struggle over what was progressive or reactionary. If ideology unites with power and is transformed into a real force then both literature and the individual will be destroyed.

Chinese literature in the twentieth century time and again was worn out and indeed almost suffocated because politics dictated literature: both the revolution in literature and revolutionary literature alike passed death sentences on literature and the individual. The attack on Chinese traditional culture in the name of the revolution resulted in the public prohibition and burning of books. Countless writers were shot, imprisoned, exiled or punished with hard labour in the course of the past one hundred years. This was more extreme than in any imperial dynastic period of China's history, creating enormous difficulties for writings in the Chinese language and even more for any discussion of creative freedom.

If the writer sought to win intellectual freedom the choice was either to fall silent or to flee. However, the writer relies on language and not to speak for a prolonged period is the same as suicide. The writer who sought to avoid suicide or being silenced and furthermore to express his own voice had no option but to go into exile. Surveying the history of literature in the East and the West this has always been so: from Qu Yuan to Dante, Joyce, Thomas Mann, Solzhenitsyn, and to the large numbers of Chinese intellectuals who went into exile after the Tiananmen massacre in 1989. This is the inevitable fate of the poet and the writer who continues to seek to preserve his own voice.

During the years when Mao Zedong implemented total dictatorship even fleeing was not an option. The monasteries on far away mountains that provided refuge for scholars in feudal times were totally ravaged and to write even in secret was to risk one's life. To maintain one's intellectual autonomy one could only talk to oneself, and it had to be in utmost secrecy. I should mention that it was only in this period when it was utterly impossible for literature that I came to comprehend why it was so essential: literature allows a person to preserve a human consciousness.

It can be said that talking to oneself is the starting point of literature and that using language to communicate is secondary. A person pours his feelings and thoughts into language that, written as words, becomes literature. At the time there is no thought of utility or that some day it might be published yet there is the compulsion to write because there is recompense and consolation in the pleasure of writing. I began writing my novel *Soul Mountain* to dispel my inner loneliness at the very time when works I had written with rigorous self-censorship had been banned. *Soul Mountain* was written for myself and without the hope that it would be published.

From my experience in writing, I can say that literature is inherently man's affirmation of the value of his own self and that this is validated during the writing: literature is born primarily of the writer's need for self-fulfilment. Whether it has any impact on society comes after the completion of a work and that impact certainly is not determined by the wishes of the writer.

In the history of literature there are many great enduring works which were not published in the lifetimes of the authors. If the authors had not achieved self-affirmation while writing, how could they have continued to write? As in the case of Shakespeare, even now it is difficult to ascertain the details of the lives of the four geniuses who wrote China's greatest novels, *Journey to the West, Water Margin, Jin Ping Mei*, and *Dream of Red Mansions*. All that remains is an autobiographical essay by Shi Naian and had he not as he said consoled himself by writing, how else could he have devoted the rest of his life to that huge work for which he received no recompense during life? And was this not also the case with Kafka who pioneered modern fiction and with Fernando Pessoa the most profound poet of the twentieth century? Their turning to language was not in order to reform the world and while profoundly aware of the helplessness of the individual they still spoke out, for such is the magic of language.

Language is the ultimate crystallisation of human civilisation. It is intricate, incisive and difficult to grasp and yet it is pervasive, penetrates human perceptions and links man, the perceiving subject, to his own understanding of the world. The written word is also magical for it allows communication between separate individuals, even if they are from different races and times. It is also in this way that the shared present time in the writing and reading of literature is connected to its eternal spiritual value.

In my view, for a writer of the present to strive to emphasise a national culture is problematical. Because of where I was born and the language I use, the cultural traditions of China naturally reside within me. Culture and language are always closely related and thus characteristic and relatively stable modes of perception, thought and articulation are formed. However, a writer's creativity begins precisely with what has already been articulated in his language and addresses what has not been adequately articulated in that language. As the creator of linguistic art there is no need to stick on oneself a stock national label that can be easily recognised.

Literature transcends national boundaries—through translations it transcends languages and then specific social customs and inter-human relationships created by geographical location and history—to make profound revelations about the universality of human nature. Furthermore, the writer today receives multicultural influences outside the culture of his own race so, unless it is to promote tourism, emphasising the cultural features of a people is inevitably suspect.

Literature transcends ideology, national boundaries and racial consciousness in the same way as the individual's existence basically transcends this or that-ism. This is because man's existential condition is superior to any theories or speculations about life. Literature is a universal observation on the dilemmas of human existence and nothing is taboo. Restrictions on literature are always externally imposed: politics, society, ethics and customs set out to tailor literature into decorations for their various frameworks.

However, literature is neither an embellishment for authority or a socially fashionable item, it has its own criterion of merit: its aesthetic quality. An aesthetic intricately related to the human emotions is the only indispensable criterion for literary works. Indeed, such judgements differ from person to person because the emotions are invariably that of different individuals. However, such subjective aesthetic judgements do have universally recognised standards. The capacity for critical appreciation nurtured by literature allows the reader to also experience the poetic feeling and the beauty, the sublime and the ridiculous, the sorrow and the absurdity, and the humour and the irony that the author has infused into his work.

Poetic feeling does not derive simply from the expression of the emotions; nevertheless, unbridled egotism, a form of infantilism, is difficult to avoid in the early stages of writing. Also, there are numerous levels of emotional expression and to reach higher levels requires cold detachment. Poetry is concealed in the distanced gaze. Furthermore, if this gaze also examines the person of the author and overarches both the characters of the book and the author to become the author's third eye, one that is as neutral as possible, the disasters and the refuse of the human world will all be worthy of scrutiny. Then as feelings of pain, hatred and abhorrence are aroused so too are feelings of concern and love for life.

An aesthetic based on human emotions does not become outdated even with the perennial changing of fashions in literature and in art. However, literary evaluations that fluctuate like fashions are premised on what is the latest: that is, whatever is new is good. This is a mechanism in general market movements and the book market is not exempted, but if the writer's aesthetic judgement follows market movements it will mean the suicide of literature. Especially in the so-called consumerist society of the present, I think one must resort to cold literature.

Ten years ago, after concluding *Soul Mountain* which I had written over seven years, I wrote a short essay proposing this type of literature:

> Literature is not concerned with politics but is purely a matter of the individual. It is the gratification of the intellect together with an observation, a review of what has been experienced, reminiscences and feelings or the portrayal of a state of mind.
>
> The so-called writer is nothing more than someone speaking or writing and whether he is listened to or read is for others to choose. The writer is not a hero acting on orders from the people nor is he worthy of worship as an idol, and certainly he is not a criminal or enemy of the people. He is at times victimised along with his writings simply because of other's needs. When the authorities need to manufacture a few enemies to divert people's attention, writers become sacrifices, and worse still writers who have been duped actually think it is a great honour to be sacrificed.
>
> In fact the relationship of the author and the reader is always one of spiritual communication and there is no need to meet or to socially interact; it is a communication simply through the work. Literature remains an indispensable form of human activity in which both the reader and the writer are engaged of their own volition. Hence, literature has no duty to the masses.
>
> This sort of literature that has recovered its innate character can be called cold literature. It exists simply because humankind seeks a purely spiritual activity beyond the gratification of material desires. This sort of literature of course did not come into being today.
>
> However, whereas in the past it mainly had to fight oppressive political forces and social customs, today it has to do battle with the subversive commercial values of consumerist society. For it to exist depends on a willingness to endure the loneliness.
>
> If a writer devotes himself to this sort of writing he will find it difficult to make a living. Hence the writing of this sort of literature must be considered a luxury, a form of pure spiritual gratification. If this sort of literature has the good fortune of being published and circulated it is due to the efforts of the writer and his friends; Cao Xueqin and Kafka are such examples. During their lifetimes, their works were unpublished so they were not able to create literary movements or to become celebrities. These writers lived at the margins and seams of society, devoting themselves to this sort of spiritual activity for which at the time they did not hope for any recompense. They did not seek social approval but simply derived pleasure from writing.
>
> Cold literature is literature that will flee in order to survive, it is literature that refuses to be strangled by society in its quest for spiritual salvation. If a race cannot accommodate this sort of non-utilitarian literature it is not merely a misfortune for the writer but a tragedy for the race.

It is my good fortune to be receiving, during my lifetime, this great honour from the Swedish Academy, and in this I have been helped by many friends from all over the world. For years without thought of reward and not shirking difficulties they have translated, published, performed and evaluated my writings. However, I will not thank them one by one for it is a very long list of names.

I should also thank France for accepting me. In France where literature and art are revered I have won the conditions to write with freedom and I also have readers and audiences. Fortunately I am not lonely although writing, to which I have committed myself, is a solitary affair.

What I would also like to say here is that life is not a celebration and that the rest of the world is not peaceful as in Sweden where for one hundred and eighty years there has been no war. This new century will not be immune to catastrophes simply because there were so many in the past century, because memories are not transmitted like genes. Humans have minds but are not intelligent enough to learn from the past, and when malevolence flares up in the human mind it can endanger human survival itself.

The human species does not necessarily move in stages from progress to progress, and here I make reference to the history of human civilisation. History and civilisation do not advance in tandem. From the stagnation of Medieval Europe to the decline and chaos in recent times on the mainland of Asia and to the catastrophes of two world wars in the twentieth century, the methods of killing people became increasingly sophisticated. Scientific and technological progress certainly does not imply that humankind as a result becomes more civilised.

Using some scientific -ism to explain history or interpreting it with a historical perspective based on pseudo-dialectics have failed to clarify human behaviour. Now that the utopian fervour and continuing revolution of the past century have crumbled to dust, there is unavoidably a feeling of bitterness amongst those who have survived.

The denial of a denial does not necessarily result in an affirmation. Revolution did not merely bring in new things because the new utopian world was premised on the destruction of the old. This theory of social revolution was similarly applied to literature and turned what had once been a realm of creativity into a battlefield in which earlier people were overthrown and cultural traditions were trampled upon. Everything had to start from zero, modernisation was good, and the history of literature too was interpreted as a continuing upheaval.

The writer cannot fill the role of the Creator so there is no need for him to inflate his ego by thinking that he is God. This will not only bring about psychological dysfunction and turn him into a madman but will also transform the world into a hallucination in which everything external to his own body is purgatory, and naturally he cannot go on living. Others are clearly hell: presumably it is like this when the self loses control. Needless to say he will turn himself into a sacrifice for the future and also demand that others follow suit in sacrificing themselves.

There is no need to rush to complete the history of the twentieth century. If the world again sinks into the ruins of some ideological framework this history will have been written in vain and later people will revise it for themselves.

The writer is also not a prophet. What is important is to live in the present, to stop being hoodwinked, to cast off delusions, to look clearly at this moment of time and at the same time to scrutinise the self. This self too is total chaos, and while questioning the world and others one may as well look back at one's self. Disaster and oppression do usually come from another, but man's cowardice and anxiety can often intensify the suffering and furthermore create misfortune for others.

Such is the inexplicable nature of humankind's behaviour, and man's knowledge of his self is even harder to comprehend. Literature is simply man focusing his gaze on his self and while he does a thread of consciousness which sheds light on this self begins to grow.

To subvert is not the aim of literature; its value lies in discovering and revealing what is rarely known, little known, thought to be known but in fact not very well known of the truth of the human world. It would seem that truth is the unassailable and most basic quality of literature.

The new century has already arrived. I will not bother about whether or not it is in fact new but it would seem that the revolution in literature and revolutionary literature, and even ideology, may have all come to an end. The illusion of a social utopia that enshrouded more than a century has vanished and when literature throws off the fetters of this and that-ism it will still have to return to the dilemmas of human existence. However, the dilemmas of human existence have changed very little and will continue to be the eternal topic of literature.

This is an age without prophecies and promises, and I think it is a good thing. The writer playing prophet and judge should also cease since the many prophecies of the past century have all turned out to be frauds. And there is no need to manufacture new superstitions about the future; it is much better to wait and see. It would be best also for the writer to revert to the role of witness and strive to present the truth.

This is not to say that literature is the same as a document. Actually, there are few facts in documented testimonies, and the reasons and motives behind incidents are often concealed. However, when literature deals with the truth the whole process from a person's inner mind to the incident can be exposed without leaving anything out. This power is inherent in literature as long as the writer sets out to portray the true circumstances of human existence and is not just making up nonsense.

It is a writer's insights in grasping truth that determine the quality of a work, and word games or writing techniques cannot serve as substitutes. Indeed, there are numerous definitions of truth and how it is dealt with varies from person to person, but it can be seen at a glance whether a writer is embellishing human phenomena or making a full and honest portrayal. The literary criticism of a certain ideology turned truth and untruth into semantic analysis, but such principles and tenets are of little relevance in literary creation.

However, whether or not the writer confronts truth is not just an issue of creative methodology, it is closely linked to his attitude towards writing. Truth when the pen is taken up at the same time implies that one is sincere after one puts down the pen. Here truth is not simply an evaluation of literature but at the same time has ethical connotations. It is not the writer's duty to preach morality, and while striving to portray various people in the world he also unscrupulously exposes his self, even the secrets of his inner mind. For the writer truth in literature approximates ethics, it is the ultimate ethics of literature.

In the hands of a writer with a serious attitude to writing, even literary fabrications are premised on the portrayal of the truth of human life, and this has been the vital life force of works that have endured from ancient times to the present. It is precisely for this reason that Greek tragedy and Shakespeare will never become outdated.

Literature does not simply make a replica of reality but penetrates the surface layers and reaches deep into the inner workings of reality; it removes false illusions, looks down from great heights at ordinary happenings, and with a broad perspective reveals happenings in their entirety.

Of course literature also relies on the imagination, but this sort of journey in the mind is not just putting together a whole lot of rubbish. Imagination that is divorced from true feelings and fabrications that are divorced from the basis of life experiences can only end up insipid and weak, and works that fail to convince the author himself will not be able to move readers. Indeed, literature does not only rely on the experiences of ordinary life nor is the writer bound by what he has personally experienced. It is possible for the things heard and seen through a language carrier and the things related in the literary works of earlier writers all to be transformed into one's own feelings. This too is the magic of the language of literature.

As with a curse or a blessing language has the power to stir body and mind. The art of language lies in the presenter being able to convey his feelings to others; it is not some sign system or semantic structure requiring nothing more than grammatical structures. If the living person behind language is forgotten, semantic expositions easily turn into games of the intellect.

Language is not merely concepts and the carrier of concepts; it simultaneously activates the feelings and the senses, and this is why signs and signals cannot replace the language of living people. The will, motives, tone and emotions behind what someone says cannot be fully expressed by semantics and rhetoric alone. The connotations of the language of literature must be voiced, spoken by living people, to be fully expressed. So as well as serving as a carrier of thought, literature must also appeal to the auditory senses. The human need for language is not simply for the transmission of meaning; it is at the same time listening to and affirming a person's existence.

Borrowing from Descartes, it could be said of the writer: I say and therefore I am. However, the I of the writer can be the writer himself, can be equated to the narrator, or become the characters of a work. As the narrator-subject can also be he and you, it is tripartite. The fixing of a key-speaker pronoun is the starting point for portraying perceptions and from this various narrative patterns take shape. It is during the process of searching for his own narrative method that the writer gives concrete form to his perceptions.

In my fiction I use pronouns instead of the usual characters and also use the pronouns I, you, and he to tell about or to focus on the protagonist. The portrayal of the one character by using different pronouns creates a sense of distance. As this also provides actors on the stage with a broader psychological space I have also introduced the changing of pronouns into my drama.

The writing of fiction or drama has not and will not come to an end and there is no substance to flippant announcements of the death of certain genres of literature or art.

Born at the start of human civilisation, like life, language is full of wonders and its expressive capacity is limitless. It is the work of the writer to discover and develop the latent potential inherent in language. The writer is not the Creator and he cannot eradicate the world even if it is too old. He also cannot establish some new ideal world even if the present world is absurd and beyond human comprehension. However, he can certainly make innovative statements either by adding to what earlier people have said or else starting where earlier people stopped.

To subvert literature was Cultural Revolution rhetoric. Literature did not die and writers were not destroyed. Every writer has his place on the bookshelf, and he has life as long as he has readers. There is no greater consolation for a writer than to be able to leave a book in humankind's vast treasury of literature that will continue to be read in future times.

Literature is only actualised and of interest at that moment in time when the writer writes it and the reader reads it. Unless it is pretence, to write for the future only deludes oneself and others as well. Literature is for the living and moreover affirms the present of the living. It is this eternal present and this confirmation of individual life that is the absolute reason why literature is literature, if one insists on seeking a reason for this huge thing that exists of itself.

When writing is not a livelihood or when one is so engrossed in writing that one forgets why one is writing and for whom one is writing, it becomes a necessity and one will write compulsively and give birth to literature. It is this non-utilitarian aspect of literature that is fundamental to literature. That the writing of literature has become a profession is an ugly outcome of the division of labour in modern society and a very bitter fruit for the writer.

This is especially the case in the present age where the market economy has become pervasive and books have also become commodities. Everywhere there are huge undiscriminating markets, and not just individual writers but even the societies and movements of past literary schools have all gone. If the writer does not bend to the pressures of the market and refuses to stoop to manufacturing cultural products by writing to satisfy the tastes of fashions and trends, he must make a living by some other means. Literature is not a best-selling book or a book on a ranked list, and authors promoted on television are engaged in advertising rather than in writing. Freedom in writing is not conferred and cannot be purchased but comes from an inner need in the writer himself.

Instead of saying that Buddha is in the heart it would be better to say that freedom is in the heart and it simply depends on whether one makes use of it. If one exchanges freedom for something else then the bird that is freedom will fly off, for this is the cost of freedom.

The writer writes what he wants without concern for recompense not only to affirm his self but also to challenge society. This challenge is not pretence and the writer has no need to inflate his ego by becoming a hero or a fighter. Heroes and fighters struggle to achieve some great work or to establish some meritorious deed, and these lie beyond the scope of literary works. If the writer wants to challenge society it must be through language, and he must rely on the characters and incidents of his works; otherwise he can only harm literature. Literature is not angry shouting and furthermore cannot turn an individual's indignation into accusations. It is only when the feelings of the writer as an individual are dispersed in a work that his feelings will withstand the ravages of time and live on for a long time.

Therefore it is actually not the challenge of the writer to society but rather the challenge of his works. An enduring work is of course a powerful response to the times and society of the writer. The clamour of the writer and his actions may have vanished, but as long as there are readers his voice in his writings continues to reverberate.

Indeed such a challenge cannot transform society. It is merely an individual aspiring to transcend the limitations of the social ecology and taking a very inconspicuous stance. However, this is by no means an ordinary stance for it is one that takes pride in being human. It would be sad if human history is only manipulated by the unknowable laws and moves blindly with the current so that the different voices of individuals cannot be heard. It is in this sense that literature fills in the gaps of history. When the great laws of history are not used to explain humankind, it will be possible for people to leave behind their own voices. History is not all that humankind possesses: there is also the legacy of literature. In literature the people are inventions, but they retain an essential belief in their own self-worth.

Honourable members of the Academy, I thank you for awarding this Nobel Prize to literature, to literature that is unwavering in its independence, that avoids neither human suffering nor political oppression and that furthermore does not serve politics. I thank all of you for awarding this most prestigious prize for works that are far removed from the writings of the market, works that have aroused little attention but are actually worth reading. At the same time, I also thank the Swedish Academy for allowing me to ascend this dais to speak before the eyes of the world. A frail individual's weak voice that is hardly worth listening to and that normally would not be heard in the public media has been allowed to address the world. However, I believe that this is precisely the meaning of the Nobel Prize and I thank everyone for this opportunity to speak.

[© The Nobel Foundation, 2000. Gao Xingjian is the sole author of the text.]

Gabriel García Márquez
(7 March 1927 –   )

Raymond Leslie Williams
University of California, Riverside

See also the García Márquez entry in *DLB 113: Modern Latin-American Fiction Writers, First Series.*

BOOKS: *La hojarasca* (Bogotá: Sipa, 1955); translated by Gregory Rabassa in *Leaf Storm and Other Stories* (New York: Harper & Row, 1972; London: Cape, 1972);

El coronel no tiene quien le escriba (Medellín: Aguirre, 1961); translated by J. S. Bernstein in *No One Writes to the Colonel and Other Stories* (New York: Harper & Row, 1968; London: Cape, 1971);

Los funerales de la Mamá Grande (Jalapa, Mexico: Editorial de la Universidad Veracruzana, 1962); translated by Bernstein as *Big Mama's Funeral* in *No One Writes to the Colonel and Other Stories;*

La mala hora (Madrid: Pérez, 1962); translated by Rabassa as *In Evil Hour* (New York: Harper & Row, 1979; London: Cape, 1980);

Cien años de soledad (Buenos Aires: Sudamericana, 1967); translated by Rabassa as *One Hundred Years of Solitude* (New York: Harper & Row, 1970; London: Cape, 1970);

Isabel viendo llover en Macondo (Buenos Aires: Estuario, 1967);

La novela en América Latina: Diálogo, by García Márquez and Mario Vargas Llosa (Lima: Milla Batres, 1969);

Relato de un naúfrago (Barcelona: Tusquets, 1970); translated by Randolph Hogan as *The Story of a Shipwrecked Sailor* (New York: Knopf, 1986);

La increíble y triste historia de la cándida Eréndira y de su abuela desalmada (Barcelona: Barral, 1972); translated by Rabassa as *Innocent Eréndira and Other Stories* (New York: Harper & Row, 1978; London: Cape, 1979);

Ojos de perro azul (Rosario, Argentina: Equiseditorial, 1972);

El negro que hizo esperar a los ángeles (Rosario, Argentina: Alfil, 1972);

Cuando era feliz e indocumentado (Caracas: Ojo del Camello, 1973);

Chile, el golpe y los gringos (Bogotá: Latina, 1974);

Cuatro cuentos (Mexico City: Comunidad Latinoaméricana de Escritores, 1974);

El otoño del patriarca (Barcelona: Plaza & Janes, 1975); translated by Rabassa as *The Autumn of the Patriarch* (New York: Harper & Row, 1976; London: Cape, 1977);

Todos los cuentos (Barcelona: Plaza & Janes, 1975);

Crónicas y reportajes (Bogotá: Instituto Colombiano de Cultura, 1976);

Operación Carlota (Lima: Mosca Azul, 1977);

Periodismo militante (Bogotá: Son de Máquina, 1978);

De viaje por los países socialistas (Cali, Colombia: Macondo, 1978);

Crónica de una muerte anunciada (Bogotá: Oveja Negra, 1981); translated by Rabassa as *Chronicle of a Death Foretold* (New York: Harper & Row, 1982; London: Cape, 1982);

Obra periodística, 4 volumes, edited by Jacques Gilard (Barcelona: Bruguera, 1981–1984);

El rastro de tu sangre en la nieve; El verano feliz de la Señora Forbes (Bogotá: Dampier, 1982);

Viva Sandino (Managua: Editorial Nueva Nicaragua, 1982);

El secuestro: Relato cinematográfico (Salamanca, Spain: Lóguez, 1983);

El amor en los tiempos del cólera (Barcelona: Bruguera, 1985); translated by Edith Grossman as *Love in the Time of Cholera* (New York: Knopf, 1988);

La aventura de Miguel Littín, clandestino en Chile (Madrid: El País, 1986); translated by Asa Zatz as *Clandestine in Chile: The Adventures of Miguel Littín* (New York: Holt, 1987);

El general en su laberinto (Madrid: Mondadori, 1989); translated by Grossman as *The General in His Labyrinth* (New York: Knopf, 1990);

Primeros reportajes (Caracas: Consorcio de Ediciones Capriles, 1990);

Notas de prensa, 1980–1984 (Madrid: Mondadori, 1991); expanded as *Notas de prensa, 1961–1984* (Barcelona: Mondadori, 1999);

Gabriel García Márquez (left) receiving the 1982 Nobel Prize in Literature from King Carl XVI Gustaf of Sweden (AP Photo/Pool)

Doce cuentos peregrinos (Madrid: Mondadori, 1992); translated by Grossman as *Strange Pilgrims: Twelve Stories* (New York: Knopf, 1993);

Elogio de la utopía (Buenos Aires: El Cronista, 1992);

Del amor y otros demonios (Barcelona: Mondadori, 1994); translated by Grossman as *Of Love and Other Demons* (New York: Knopf, 1995);

Diatriba de amor contra un hombre sentado: Monologo en un acto (Santafé de Bogotá: Arango, 1994);

El ahogado más hermoso del mundo, text by García Márquez, photographs by Hernán Díaz (Santafé de Bogotá: Voluntad, 1995);

Cómo se cuenta un cuento (Santafé de Bogotá: Voluntad Interés General, 1995);

Me alquilo para soñar, by García Márquez and others (Santafé de Bogotá: Voluntad Interés General, 1995);

Noticia de un secuestro (Barcelona: Mondadori, 1996); translated by Grossman as *News of a Kidnapping* (New York: Knopf, 1997);

Cuentos: 1947–1992 (Barcelona & Santafé de Bogotá: Grupo Editorial Norma, 1996);

Por un país al alcance de los niños (Bogotá: Villegas, 1996);

La bendita manía de contar (Madrid: Ollero y Ramos, 1998);

Por la libre, 1974–1995 (Barcelona: Grijalbo Mondadori, 1999);

La luz es como el agua (Santafé de Bogotá: Grupo Editorial Norma, 1999);

María dos Prazeres (Santafé de Bogotá: Grupo Editorial Norma, 1999);

Un señor muy viejo con unas alas enormes (Santafé de Bogotá: Grupo Editorial Norma, 1999);

La siesta del martes (Santafé de Bogotá: Grupo Editorial Norma, 1999);

El último viaje del buque fantasma (Santafé de Bogotá: Grupo Editorial Norma, 1999);

Vivir para contarla (Barcelona: Mondadori, 2002); translated by Grossman as *Living to Tell the Tale* (New York: Knopf, 2003);

Memoria de mis putas tristes (Barcelona: Mondadori, 2004); translated by Grossman as *Memories of My Melancholy Whores* (New York: Knopf, 2005).

Editions in English: *Collected Stories,* translated by Gregory Rabassa and J. S. Bernstein (New York: Harper & Row, 1984; London: Cape, 1991);

Collected Novellas, translated by Rabassa and Bernstein (New York: HarperCollins, 1990).

PRODUCED SCRIPTS: *La langosta azul,* motion picture, 1954;

El gallo de oro, by García Márquez, Carlos Fuentes, Roberto Gavaldón, and Juan Rulfo, motion picture, Clasa Films Mundiales, 1964;

Lola de mi vida, adapted by García Márquez, Juan de la Cabada, and Miguel Barbachano-Ponce from Carlos A. Figueroa's story, motion picture, 1965;

Tiempo de morir, by García Márquez and Fuentes, motion picture, Alameda Films, 1966;

Cuatro contra el crimen, adapted by García Márquez and Alfredo Ruanova from Fernando Galiana's story, motion picture, Producciones Sotomayor, 1968;

Presagio, by García Márquez and Luis Alcoriza, motion picture, CONACINE/Producciones Escorpión, 1975;

María de mi corazón, by García Márquez and Jaime Humberto Hermasillo, motion picture, Clasa Films Mundiales/Universidad Veracruzana, 1979;

El año de la peste, by García Márquez, Juan Arturo Brennan, and José Agustín, motion picture, Conacite Dos, 1979;

Eréndira, motion picture, Atlas Saskia Film, 1983;

Milagro en Roma, by García Márquez and Lisandro Duque Naranjo, motion picture, Elisa Cinematográfica, 1988;

Fábula de la Bella Palomera, by García Márquez and Ruy Guerra, motion picture, Fox Lorber Features/Guerra Filmes, 1988;

Cartas del parque, by García Márquez, Eliseo Alberto, and Tomás Gutiérrez Alea, motion picture, Instituto Cubano del Arte e Industrias Cinematográficos, 1989.

Gabriel García Márquez shares with many Nobel laureates in literature a concern for the common man, an ongoing faith in the human spirit, and a commitment to telling stories that are accessible to a broad audience. His novels, short stories, and journalistic accounts are appreciated by readers and scholars alike. His major and most widely acclaimed novel is *Cien años de soledad* (1967, translated as *One Hundred Years of Solitude,* 1970), and he is recognized for his "magic realist" fiction.

García Márquez's early fiction consisted of a set of novels and short stories located in the invented town of "Macondo" and focused mostly on the common folk of this village. In the late 1940s and early 1950s he began writing his first amateurish fictions and sketches, some of which were set in a small town that eventually evolved into Macondo. His first attempt at writing a novel, titled "La casa" (and never published), centered on a village similar to Macondo. His first published novel, *La hojarasca* (1955, translated as *Leaf Storm,* 1972), is set in Macondo, and this book initiated a "cycle of Macondo" consisting of this first novel, the short novel *El coronel no tiene quien le escriba* (1961, translated as *No One Writes to the Colonel,* 1968), the stories of *Los funerales de la Mamá Grande* (1962, translated as *Big Mama's Funeral,* 1968), the novel *La mala hora* (1962, translated as *In Evil Hour,* 1979), and *Cien años de soledad.*

In his later work, the Nobel laureate explored other types of fiction beyond the geographical sphere of Macondo. His landmark novel *El otoño del patriarca* (1975, translated as *The Autumn of the Patriarch,* 1976) represented a change in his writing, with a vaguely Caribbean physical setting and a new theme: power and dictators. After that novel, most of García Márquez's writing has been an ongoing exploration of new themes and settings, even though his characteristic writing style—with frequent uses of hyperbole and entertaining surprises—has remained essentially the same.

García Márquez was born in the northern Caribbean coastal region of Colombia in the town of Aracataca (the model for Macondo) on 7 March 1927. (Many informed sources have published the incorrect date that García Márquez himself has used on occasion, 6 March 1928.) When he was born, this region of Colombia was at the end of a period of suffering caused by the presence of the United Fruit Company in Colombia: foreign companies had controlled banana production since the end of the nineteenth century in this region. The young García Márquez grew up in Aracataca hearing stories of the lives of working people living under the shadow of a dominant foreign culture. Contrary to the history of many Latin American nations, this period was the only time and the only region in which a foreign power dominated the economy in Colombia; since García Márquez has been a lifelong critic of Western postindustrial capitalism, this segment of Colombia's history is noteworthy.

The son of telegrapher Gabriel Eligio García and Luisa Santiaga Márquez de García, the author was raised by his maternal grandparents, Colonel Nicolás Márquez and Tranquilina Iguarán de Márquez, in Aracataca after his father decided to seek better employment in Barranquilla. He has one brother, born after García Márquez had reached adulthood. García Márquez has explained in many interviews and in his autobiography, *Vivir para contarla* (2002, translated as *Living to Tell the Tale,* 2003), that he grew up in the midst of ghosts and fantastic tales, since his grandmother was an accomplished storyteller. This impoverished and strongly Afro-Colombian region of the country was still immersed in the nineteenth century in many ways, with a strong and vibrant oral culture in which the vast majority of the population was illiterate. National newspapers did not yet circulate in this region, and much of the news from the outside world came to Aracataca and other small towns by means of *vallenatos,* popular music that told tales garnished with real people and events. Thus, during García Márquez's childhood he was immersed in oral tradition, stories, and tales identified in Anglo-American tradition as "tall tales."

As was often the case for boys in Colombia at this time, he was sent to Bogotá in 1940 to study in a private high school. There, he was an avid reader of world literature, and, upon graduation, he decided to pursue the path of many highly literate Colombians: law. His main interest, however, was literature, and as a law student at the Universidad Nacional in 1947 he continued reading voraciously and began writing his own stories. He claims that when he read Franz Kafka and William Faulkner, he decided to become a writer. Now familiar with some of the Western modernists and particularly interested in the zones of the fantastic opened to him by Kafka's *The Metamorphosis* (1915), he created early stories that were amateurish explorations of the fantastic. He was particularly interested in blurring the line between life and death, and he portrayed characters in nebulous zones that might be described as intermediate spaces not exactly in the empirical world of everyday lives or of death. His first story, "La tercera resignación" (The Third Resignation), was his attempt to create a Kafkian text that defies the rational limits of what is normally accepted as everyday empirical reality. It deals with a man who is apparently dead but who seems to function in some gray area between the normal categories of life and death. Some of these stories were published in newspapers in Colombia in the late 1940s and then reappeared, years after García Márquez had become a celebrated writer, in a volume titled *Ojos de perro azul* (1972, Eyes of Blue Dog).

Life changed radically for many citizens of Colombia in 1948, including García Márquez, when political violence broke out in the streets of Bogotá after the assassination of the presidential candidate of the Liberal Party, Jorge Eliécer Gaitán, on 9 April of that year. Partisan violence spread across the nation from 1948 to 1956, and Colombia was in a period of civil war identified as La Violencia, which led to more than three hundred thousand deaths. After completing one year of law studies at the Universidad Nacional, García Márquez moved to a more peaceful setting, the coastal city of Cartagena, where he took a job as a journalist.

From there he moved to the nearby port city of Barranquilla, where he continued to work as a journalist, reporting on a broad range of political, cultural, and literary topics. In Barranquilla, the aspiring writer came into contact with a group of other young intellectuals with a serious interest in literature. Their mentor was José Félix Fuenmayor, a writer who had published innovative fiction in the 1920s and 1930s and had promoted avant-garde literature in a nation that was exceptionally conservative in its literary tastes as well as its institutions. Fuenmayor edited an avant-garde cultural magazine, under the title *Voces* (Voices), that was exceptional in Colombia. The group of young artists included García Márquez, Alvaro Cepeda Samudio, Alfonso Fuenmayor, and Germán Vargas. The only two who wrote fiction were García Márquez and Cepeda Samudio, but they were all avid readers of the masters of international modernism promoted by their mentor Fuenmayor: from James Joyce, John Dos Passos, and Faulkner to Kafka and Robert Musil. For García Márquez, however, the true master was Faulkner, and the American writer was an essential model for the first two decades of the Colombian's literary career. Not only was the society Faulkner portrayed parallel to many aspects of Latin American society, but also the strategies for telling a story were a revelation for the young writer. Thus, his first novel, *La hojarasca,* was directly modeled after *As I Lay Dying* (1930). As García Márquez and his cohorts grew in recognition in Colombia first, and then in Latin America, they became known as the "Group of Barranquilla."

Most of the action in *La hojarasca* takes place from 1903 to 1928, depicting Macondo in the early twentieth century as a decadent town left behind by a foreign company. Of the four main characters, there are three members of a family who narrate and a doctor whose wake is the circumstance of the novel. The first of these narrators is a ten-year-old boy who relates for his father his thoughts and perceptions of the wake. The other narrators are the boy's mother and his grandfather. In this manner, García Márquez provides multiple perspectives on the life of the doctor and the history of the town.

In the mid 1950s, García Márquez moved back to Bogotá, where he came into contact with like-minded writers and intellectuals who began publishing the cultural journal *Mito* (Myth) in 1955. This journal promoted literary and cultural modernism in a nation that was still generally among the most culturally conservative in Latin America. In Bogotá, García Márquez gained employment at the liberal newspaper *El Espectador* (The Spectator). Colombia was not only in the midst of La Violencia but also living under the military dictatorship of Gustavo Rojas Pinilla. The newspaper sent García Márquez to Paris to work as a correspondent, but soon thereafter, Rojas Pinilla ordered *El Espectador* closed down, and the young Colombian became unemployed. During this time, when García Márquez was living in poverty in Paris, he wrote and published several of the stories that later appeared in *Los funerales de la Mamá Grande*. Many of his peers in Colombia were writing bloody accounts of La Violencia in the 1950s, but García Márquez's approach was different: he wrote stories that only alluded to political violence, with political conflict as part of the general context. In this way, García Márquez emphasized the human drama in a more universal way than had been the case in Colombian fiction of the 1950s.

In 1958, García Márquez returned to Latin America, married his childhood sweetheart, Mercedes Barcha, and worked as a journalist in Venezuela and Colombia. The stay in Venezuela was a significant experience, for in that nation he experienced another dictatorial regime: Marcos Pérez Jiménez was in power in the late 1950s. This brutal dictator provided some material that appeared later in the novel *El otoño del patriarca*. During the late 1950s and early 1960s, García Márquez wrote journalistic pieces critical of the U.S. government and celebrating the Cuban Revolution. Like many Latin American intellectuals of this period, García Márquez viewed the Cuban Revolution as a model for the Latin American nations establishing economic and cultural independence from the United States. As a result of these writings, and a visit to Cuba (which led to a lifelong friendship with Fidel Castro), García Márquez has had difficulties most of his adult life in getting easy access to visas to visit the United States; for many years, in fact, he was on a State Department "blacklist" of leftist intellectuals.

El coronel no tiene quien le escriba has been praised frequently by other writers as a masterpiece of the craft of fiction, and even the author himself has claimed on occasion that it is his best novel. Indeed, it is a model of sparse, well-wrought fiction with a minimalist use of language that was rare for literature written in the Spanish language at the time. In the context of a literary tradition that still favored Baroque excess and an ample use of adjectives, *El coronel no tiene quien le escriba*, like the Mexican Juan Rulfo's *Pedro Páramo* (1955), is an exceptional book that includes much understatement, minimalist descriptions, and no hyperbole. García Márquez has often spoken and written about *Pedro Páramo* as a great novel that he has always admired. *El coronel no tiene quien le escriba* is a book of many types of silence—above all, the silence created by political censorship. The protagonist is an aged colonel, and he, as well as the remainder of Macondo's inhabitants, are consistently silent about political matters. (The background, of course, is the period of political repression during and following La Violencia.) Despite the silences, the political situation is the essential and overriding factor in the lives of everyone in the town.

In the short stories of *Los funerales de la Mamá Grande* and the short novel *La mala hora*, García Márquez depicted more of Macondo's ordinary people attempting to survive in the context of the political repression. Two of the stories in the former collection are representative of the author's mastery of the art of fiction. In "Un día de estos" (One of These Days), García Márquez relates an anecdote of the town mayor going to the dentist to deal with a toothache. On the surface, it is a story of a man's suffering in the dentist's chair. Once it is understood that the mayor is a representative of the politically repressive military dictatorship of Rojas Pinilla, however, the story is significantly different. The author's mastery is leaving the political as part of the eerie background and underlining the human conflict involved in this encounter between a representative of authority and a citizen who has the opportunity to question authority.

"La siesta del martes" (Tuesday's Siesta) is the story of a woman who goes to the town where her son has been buried after he was shot as a result of his involvement with petty larceny. In the story it becomes evident that the mother is a person of great dignity who had made every effort to raise her son properly, and that the son had followed her admonition never to steal anything that would leave others hungry. At the end, the local priest offers her a way to cover her face with a parasol as she leaves the town, but she refuses this cover and thus reaffirms her dignity. In these two stories, as well as in *La mala hora*, García Márquez underlines the human drama and reaffirms his faith in the spirit of the common man. In the novel, the author makes the political violence of the period more visible: political repression and violence are part of everyday life during seventeen days in the life of Macondo.

Once *El coronel no tiene quien le escriba* and *La mala hora* had appeared in print, García Márquez believed that his career as a novelist was basically over. Historically, the writing of novels had been more of a passion or personal hobby than a profession for most Latin American writers, and García Márquez's profits from the first years of his fiction-writing career had been negligible. He moved to Mexico with his wife in order to pursue a new career in movie scriptwriting, and he soon befriended the Mexican writer Carlos Fuentes, with whom he wrote a movie script as a joint project. He also participated in the intellectual life of Mexico City's young, progressive, and mostly leftist writers. Much of this cultural activity was led by Fuentes, who hosted weekly Sunday literary soirees in his home, and García Márquez was a regular presence. He has consulted and collaborated with Fuentes in multiple venues throughout his career.

García Márquez was not actually planning (in the early 1960s) to write his celebrated novel *Cien años de soledad*. In the mid 1960s, however, an unexpected series of events led to the creation of this masterpiece. García Márquez had planned a weekend vacation for his family (which now included sons Rodrigo, born in 1959, and Gonzalo, born in 1962) in Acapulco, and they decided to drive a car from their home in Mexico City to Acapulco. During this trip, before arriving at his destination, García Márquez experienced a literary epiphany and turned around, driving back to his home in Mexico City. The essence of this epiphany centered on the realization that, contrary to his earlier beliefs, his novelistic career was not over, for he had a novel to write. This novel was the complete story of Macondo. García Márquez also had a strong sense from the beginning how he wanted to tell the Macondo story: in the same way his grandmother told stories. With this idea in mind, García Márquez returned with his family to Mexico City and was soon in the basement of his home, where he spent most of his time writing obsessively for a period of approximately one year. His wife took charge of all family matters for that year, allowing her husband to concentrate on his writing.

While the determined Colombian was in seclusion in Mexico City, his peers in Latin America were in the public eye in a way never before witnessed by Latin American writers, for the 1960s were the years of the internationally recognized "Boom" of the Latin American novel. The novelists of the Boom included the Mexican Fuentes, the Peruvian Mario Vargas Llosa, the Argentine Julio Cortázar, and García Márquez. They were the celebrity figures of the period, though there were other accomplished novelists in the 1960s writing in Latin America, including the Chilean José Donoso (a lifetime friend of García Márquez), the Cuban exile Guillermo Cabrera Infante, the Cuban exile Severo Sarduy, and the Venezuelan Salvador Garmendia.

This Boom of the Latin American novel in the 1960s was a result of several circumstances, institutions, and individuals. Among these factors were the Cuban Revolution (which bonded Latin American intellectuals), the interest of publishers Harper and Row in the United States and Seix Barral in Spain, the appearance of Spanish literary agent Carmen Balcells (agent for both García Márquez and Fuentes, among many others), the rise of international Latin Americanism as a discipline, the publication of the magazine *Mundo Nuevo* (New World) in Paris by Emir Rodríguez Monegal in the mid 1960s, and the emergence of an accomplished translator, Gregory Rabassa, soon to be followed by Suzanne Jill Levine and Margaret Sayers Peden. As Donoso explains in his *Historia personal del "boom"* (1972; translated as *The Boom in Spanish American Literature: A Personal History,* 1977), Fuentes was central to making these disparate factors work together; he brought together the different strands of personal alliances and institutional support. García Márquez and several other writers were guests at the Fuentes home in the San Angel neighborhood of Mexico City, a grouping that sometimes included Vargas Llosa and Donoso. The Chilean writer, in fact, lived in a bungalow in Fuentes's backyard, using this location to write for three years in the early 1960s.

As García Márquez wrote *Cien años de soledad* in his basement, Fuentes followed closely and supported the writing of his good friend. García Márquez has always liked to chat about his work as it has progressed, and he found Fuentes the ideal dialogic friend in 1965 and 1966, the same period he was joining the Sunday evening soirees in San Angel. Fuentes was one of the few individuals to read the manuscript of this masterpiece before its publication. This Mexican collaborator praised the novel in an article that appeared first in the magazine *Siempre* (29 June 1966) in Mexico, then later in the influential literary organ of the Boom, *Mundo Nuevo,* in Paris.

When García Márquez's novel appeared in print in 1967 with the Argentine publishing house Sudamericana, its impact was swift and broad: critics from Argentina to Spain immediately heralded it as one of the major novels to have been published in recent years. Rarely had a novel published in Spanish received such widespread acclaim and then appeared in so many subsequent editions so quickly: with the publication of *Cien años de soledad* in 1967, the Boom was at its zenith in Latin America and gaining an unprecedented international respect. Soon thereafter, translations began appearing in the major Western European languages, and in the 1970s the novel was named one of the best foreign books by *Time* magazine in the United States. The reasons for this broad appeal have been a matter of speculation among critics over the years, but certainly the strong story line, entertaining characters and situations, and unfailing humor are major factors. Following his literary master Faulkner, García Márquez also leads his readers through the unfolding of a pattern that eventually results in harmony. This pattern (from fragmentation or chaos to harmony) characterizes much of the writing of García Márquez and the other writers of the Boom, particularly in reference to their novels of the 1960s.

Cien años de soledad is the story of a family and a small town, as well as the history of Colombia and of many Latin American nations. When García Márquez finally surfaced from his basement with his completed manuscript, he had also written exactly what he had conceived on his trip to Acapulco: he wrote the complete story of Macondo (a synthesis of many stories in his earlier fiction), and he did it as his grandmother told stories—imitating the oral tradition. In this work, the character José Arcadio Buendía marries his cousin, Ursula; both are the first generation of a seven-generation family. Given their kinship, the pair and all of their descendants live under the constant terror of conceiving a child with a pig's tail. The town of Macondo progresses from a backward village to a modern city after the arrival of the accoutrements of twentieth-century modernity. The town also suffers the vicissitudes of Colombian and Latin American history, however, including many civil wars.

This novel consists of twenty untitled and unnumbered chapters that tell the family story in a basically linear fashion, with frequent diversions into the past or future. The first two chapters offer the historical background of the Buendía family, with the first focusing on José Arcadio Buendía and the crazed methods he imagines as a way of understanding the world. The second chapter moves to the history of the family and explains the foundation of Macondo. This chapter traces the family roots back to the sixteenth century, when the historical figure Sir Francis Drake assaulted the Colombian coast (real history) in the region of Riohacha. Many readers have referred to the key episode of the third chapter—an insomnia plague that afflicts Macondo. With the insomnia comes a villagewide loss of memory. The artist Pietro Crespi arrives in Macondo in the fourth chapter, and many critics have understood his presence in the village as the typical case of the frustrated artist in Latin America. In the chapters that follow, García Márquez rewrites much of the history of Colombia, with special emphasis on its civil wars in the nineteenth century. Among the cyclical events and activities in this novel, the political sphere seems particularly repetitive. When a banana company arrives in Macondo (the equivalent of the United Fruit Company in Aracataca), striking soldiers are massacred by government troops. After one of its particularly long rains Macondo seems to be reborn. At the end of the novel, a child is born with a pig's tail, completing the family cycle as it had been suggested at the beginning of the story.

For many foreign readers, *Cien años de soledad* might initially seem like a book of fantastic tales. For many critics in Colombia and Latin America, as well as García Márquez himself, however, this book is based on the social and political reality of Latin America, as well as its history. It is a strong sociopolitical critique that coincides with the author's politics of the 1960s. Colonel Aureliano Buendía, who engages in many battles in the novel, is based on the late-nineteenth-century figure General Rafael Uribe Uribe, who was a leader of the Liberal Party and who suffered several defeats in the civil wars. The strike of the banana workers, which is related as one of the most fantastic events in the novel, is in fact one of the most historic events. In November 1928, Colombian workers declared a strike against the United Fruit Company. García Márquez and his old friend from the Group of Barranquilla, Cepeda Samudio, were the first to tell this story of the banana workers' strike: it appeared in Cepeda Samudio's novel *La casa grande* (1955, translated 1991) and was then popularized in the nation's consciousness in Colombia with García Márquez's novel.

García Márquez's use of narrative voice in *Cien años de soledad* exhibits the strategies he learned from both the modernists such as Faulkner and the oral storytellers such as his grandmother. The narrator in this novel is third-person omniscient, occasionally revealing what the characters think. The predominant mode, however, is external: the reader observes the characters act and speak. In most of the novel this detached narrator offers seemingly neutral observations about the fictional world of Macondo. Despite the detachment, however, the narrator also functions as if he were a character in the novel. At times the narrator demonstrates an innocence toward the world that is similar to that of the characters (and also similar to that of many oral storytellers). The narrator thinks like the townsfolk of Macondo, at times demonstrating the same prejudices, at others the same primitive ideas and reactions.

One consistently used technique of oral storytelling that García Márquez apparently learned from his grandmother is the use of understatement when describing incredible situations and overstatement or exaggeration when dealing with the commonplace. In the first chapter, for example, the narrator shares the characters' utter amazement at their discovery of ice, and by the end of the chapter the narrator uses the words "mysterious" and "prodigious" to describe what would seem to readers just everyday experience. On the other hand, the narrator regularly reacts to the most wondrous events with absolute passivity. In the first chapter, José and his children experience the disappearance of a man who becomes invisible after drinking a special potion. Neither the narrator nor the characters pay particular attention to this unlikely occurrence.

With respect to García Márquez's use of the oral culture of the Aracataca of his childhood, this novel depicts the transition from orality to various stages of literacy. The process is particularly evident if one compares the early chapters with the later ones. In the early chapters, the mindset of a primary orality (that is, the mindset of an illiterate populace) predominates. In the last chapter, however, the most intricate exercises of a writing culture are carried out. These two extremes are represented by the character of Melquíades, who is of a writing culture from the outside, and by Ursula, who possesses a mindset of orality. The effects of the interplay between oral and written culture are multiple. The traditionalism and modernity of this novel are based on various roles the narrator assumes as oral storyteller in the fashion of the tall tale, as narrator with an oral person's mindset, and as the modern narrator of a self-conscious (written) text. As such, *Cien años de soledad* is not only a culmination of García Márquez's cycle of Macondo but also his master synthesis of oral and written traditions.

García Márquez's fiction after *Cien años de soledad* has displayed a variety of settings, characters, and topics, and most of these new stories are not easily associated with the tales of Macondo. His next book was the volume of short stories published under the title *La increíble y triste historia de la cándida Eréndira y de su abuela desalmada* (1972, translated as *Innocent Eréndira and Other Stories*, 1978), a set of well-wrought entertainments that few critics considered to have the symbolic or social value of many of his novels.

Since the publication of *Cien años de soledad* and its international success, García Márquez has assumed the lifestyle of a celebrity writer and an international jet-setter, with homes on several continents and in the cities of Mexico City, Bogotá, Barcelona, Paris, and Cartagena. Since the 1970s, his primary residence has been in Mexico City, although he travels regularly to Colombia and has often lived there for periods of several months. In the early 1970s García Márquez lived most of the time in Barcelona and Paris, where he socialized with Cortázar and Vargas Llosa and wrote much of his next novel, *El otoño del patriarca*.

During the 1970s García Márquez was fully engaged in leftist politics, supporting progressive causes and writing political essays critical of the U.S. government. He visited Bogotá briefly in 1975, shortly after the publication of *El otoño del patriarca*, and declared to the press that he would not publish another novel until after the fall of military dictator Augusto Pinochet Ugarte in Chile. He did not, in fact, fulfill this promise, but his declaration was typical of García Márquez's sense for the uses of the press: he knows how to catch the headlines in Latin America with a statement that might represent more of a truth of the moment than a permanent, lasting truth.

In the spirit of his declaration, García Márquez did write a novel against Pinochet and all other authoritarian leaders. In the late 1960s and early 1970s the writers of the Boom had been talking socially about a joint project on the subject of the archetypal Latin American dictator. This project never got beyond some good conversations over dinner and drinks in Barcelona and Paris, but these thoughts and serious concerns did lead several of them, including García Márquez, to the completion of their own dictator novels. After a hiatus of eight years since publishing *Cien años de soledad* (a period during which he actively and regularly published journalism), García Márquez came forth with *El otoño del patriarca*, based on the lives and political careers of several Latin American dictators. This novel is perhaps his most refined exhibition of technical virtuosity. García Márquez had begun writing this book during the 1950s at the end of the Pérez Jiménez dictatorship in Venezuela and had witnessed the spectacle of an entire nation celebrating the fall of that regime. The figure of the Venezuelan dictator, however, was merely a point of departure for this novel. García Márquez also began reading histories of dictators; some of these historical accounts included anecdotes that seem more fantastic than the most committed magic realist. In one such anecdote, the Haitian dictator François "Papa Doc" Duvalier ordered all black dogs killed because he was convinced one of his political enemies had transformed himself into a black dog. García Márquez's intention was to create a synthesis of all Latin American dictators in this novel, but especially those from the Caribbean, including Venezuela.

The protagonist of *El otoño del patriarca* is a prototype dictator, known only as "the General," and the physical setting is a vaguely Caribbean nation that is never named. From the days of the Pérez Jiménez regime, García has been fascinated with what he has called the "mystery" of power, and that is the main theme of the novel.

García Márquez often creates striking and memorable openings for his books, and the first chapter of *El otoño del patriarca* begins with the discovery of the General's rotting corpse (the cause of death is unexplained) in his presidential palace. The narrative moves quickly to several stories about the General's life. The most important of these anecdotes is what is identified as his "first death," actually that of his government-appointed double, Patricio Aragonés. The action of the second chapter is centered on the woman with whom the General falls in love, Manuela Sánchez. The politics of power are the focus of the third chapter, and his power seems limitless: he is capable of altering the weather and even signaling with his finger so that men prosper, trees give fruit, and animals grow. In the fourth chapter, the General's power begins to wane, and he suffers from a limited ability to understand this loss and his diminishing contact with empirical reality. His final demise is the subject of the last two chapters. The dictator celebrates his one-hundredth anniversary in

no tengo la dirección de juan b tengo una carta para él

alemán escribo para contestarte el disparate pistolar que a tu vez me escribiste como estoy demasiado ocupado creo que no tendré tiempo de poner puntos comas puntoycomas y demás signos ortograficos en esta carta dificilmente tengo tiempo para poner la letras lastima que no exista la telepatpia para contestarte por elpatico correo que debe ser el mejor puesto que no podria estar sometido a la censura con ya sabes estamos semanalmentehaciendocronica lo que no nos da tiempo para hacer incursiones en busca de yerbajos estupefacientes así que por lo pronto vas a tener que conformarte compicha de caiman comun y corriente mientras quiebra cronica y podemos regresar a nuestros predios del hijo de la noche aurelianobuendía te manda saludes igualmente su hija remedios medb puta que se salió al fin con el vendedor de maquinas singer el otro hijo tobias tambien s metió a policía y los mataron así que solo queda la niña que no tiene nombre ni lo tendrá sino a quien todos llamaran simplemente la niña todo el dia sentada en su mecedor oyendo el gramofono que como todas las cosas de este mundo se dañó y ahora se creo el problema en la casporque lo unico que sabe de herrería en el pueblo es un zapatero italiano que nunca en suvida ha visto ungramofono zapatero va a la casa y trata de martillarcomponerremendar cuerdainutilmente mientras tanto muchachito del agua yendoentrandoechandoaguasilbandopiezas gramofo en cada casa a ido diciendogramofonocoronel aurelianose dañó esa misma tarde gente ha corrio vestirsecerrapuertasponersezapatospeinarse para ir a casa del coronel éste por su parte r esperaba visita pues gente del pueblo no había vuelto a su casa en quince años del cuando se negaron enterrar cadaver gregorio por miedo a la policia y coronel insultó curapueblo copartidarios retiroso concejo yencerrose en su casa de tal suerte que solo quince añs despues cuando se dañáreventacuerda el gramofono la gente vuelve a la casa y coge al corel y a su esposa doña soledad completamente desprevenidos para que niña no llore tiene quecantarle toda la gente del pueblo la canciones del gramofono y doña soledad se sorprende te todo el mundo sepa las piezas del gramofo no sin haber ido a la casa y se descubre que e muchachito del agua quien había ido de casa en casa silbandocantando piezas para que todo mundo las aprendiera también se sabe otras mujeres casavecineantoponiendoido contra partes casa coronel lograron oir piezas gramofono y aprenderlas tu sabes que quince años nadie bia querido enterrar a gregorio que era esclavo del coronel y éste lo enterró solo en el pio bajo el almendro mitadvivomitadmuerto cuando ya el muerto se le habia podrido dentro dea casa pero cerro puertas y gritó cuando alguien venga a esta casa le daré agua envenena y puso dos tinajeros en la sala uno con agua para ellos y otro con agua envenenada para cudo llegaran atrevidas visitas como nadie fue la casa se lleno don el silencio que en quinc años guardaron dentro de ella todas las gentes del pueblo que no fueron y coronel ha jurado unca saldrá de su casa y cuando la casa se estaba cayendo su esposa le dijo aureliano salgaos que la casa se está derrumbando y él dijo no se derrumbará mientras yo esté vivo y su esposa dijo pero si está cayendose y el volvió a decir no se caerá mientras yo esté vivo y muere y lo llevan a enterrar y cuando ya la gente venía de regreso del cementerio la casase cayó y eso está muy bien son vainas durante toda la noche en que se daña en gramofono la ente habla de cosas dentro de la casa y es eso lo que hace que la casa se caiga porque el sencio era tan viejo que estaba duro y lo suficientemente fuerte como para no permitir el so de los ruidos y entonces como los ruidos eran de mucha gente se estableció una lucha se rompieron las paredes entre la gente que está en la casa hay dos carpinteros que discuta a lo largo de cuarenta y siete páginas sonbre cómo se debe hacer una jaula y hay una mujer quien doña soledad la esposa dle coronel no conoce y cada vez que va hablarle alguien sinterpone entonces sucede que la mujer pasa toda la noche en un rincón sin hablar con nadie yuando doña soledad apenada logra llegar donde ella ya está amaneciendo y la gente se vá esa bueno son vainas son vainas tu sabes que como el hijo se mete a policía cuando el entierro del hijo del coronel éste está sentado a la puerta como todos los días y cundo ve venir el entierro le tira las puertas en la casa está bueno son vainas es como si essucediera en mompos bueno eso es para que veas como va el novelon en cuanto a lo demas te ire que german alfonso figurita pasamos la vida hablandoescribiendopensandohaciendocronica ro no ya como antes bebiendoputeandofumandocigarrillosyerba porque la vida no puede seresasi no te gusta virginia te vas al carajo a ramiro le gusta y sabe de novela más que tu así qute vas al carajo dile a ramiro que yo le debo carta pero que me escriba que en diciembre ido vacaciones en cronica y me tiene que guardar puesto en el apartamento don ramón se fue yescribio todos estamos bien tito brinqueit eduard putieit veijo fuenmayor hecho un berraco tos te saludamos y te deseamos felicespascuasprospro año nuevo tu amigo que mucho te estima pito.

Typescript letter written by García Márquez in 1950, in which he describes characters and situations that appeared years later in his 1967 novel Cien años de soledad, *translated in 1970 as* One Hundred Years of Solitude *(Ken Lopez Bookseller)* power, but his reign is decadent in every sense of the word. When the General finally dies, he is unsure of the power he exercised and by which he was tormented in the solitude of his dictatorship. His constant suffering of solitude connects him to many of the characters of the cycle of Macondo.

As a master modernist García Márquez manipulates an external and an internal view of the protagonist. In contrast to the god-like power that the General possesses (allowing him to manipulate the citizenry), a view of the General's psyche consistently emphasizes his pettiness and puerility. This contrast is a basis for much of the humor in the book. Throughout the novel, the General carefully locks an elaborate combination of locks, crossbars, and bolts in his room, thus underlining his paranoia. Despite his supreme self-confidence, the only person allowed to defeat the General in a game of dominoes is his friend Rodrigo de Aguilar.

In *El otoño del patriarca*, García Márquez also presents the maintenance of power as a result of the protagonist's ability to manipulate the visible and the invisible. Once an assassination attempt fails, the General not only orders the responsible party put to death but also orders that the different parts of the assassin's body be put on public display throughout the nation, thus providing a graphic demonstration of the consequences of questioning power. When the General feels the need to exert maximum power, he observes its functioning. This need helps to explain the General's strange behavior each morning: he must watch the milking of the cows he owns.

The question of the visible and the invisible and its relation to the theme of power is also developed by means of the presence of the sea in this novel. As the most important visible object in the General's daily life, the sea is his most treasured "possession." The General's sea, his window, and power become so closely associated that the General insists upon maintaining possession of his window and his sea as persistently as his power. When he begins to realize that he is losing his power, he becomes even more adamant about not losing his sea. The opening of a seen reality into a mixture of the visible and the invisible makes the experience of the novel similar to the principal theme it develops: the multiple illusions of reality and of power.

Following the publication of *El otoño del patriarca*, García Márquez remained actively involved in his lifetime passions: literature, journalism, cinema, and politics. He explored new genres, such as the *testimonio* and the literary memoir, at the same time that he continued writing fiction. He wrote journalistic pieces regularly throughout the 1970s and has even stated more than once that he considers himself primarily a journalist. He has remained close to the world of movies by leading movie-making workshops in Cuba, organizing an annual international festival in Cartagena, and serving in other capacities in the international cinema scene. With respect to politics, García Márquez has also taken a variety of roles, often acting as a de facto ambassador-at-large for the Colombian government and political groups within Colombia. He has often been called upon to serve as an intermediary, for example, with Castro, given the Colombian's relationship with Castro since the early 1960s.

García Márquez's two major novels since 1975 have been *Crónica de una muerte anunciada* (1981, translated as *Chronicle of a Death Foretold*, 1982) and *El Amor en los tiempos del cólera* (1985, translated as *Love in the Time of Cholera*, 1988). The former was his last novel before being awarded the Nobel Prize in Literature in 1982, and the latter was his first novel after this international recognition. Since his early experience as a journalist in Cartagena and Barranquilla, García Márquez had often come across unusual events and individuals that later found a place in his fiction. *Crónica de una muerte anunciada* was inspired by a newspaper account of an assassination in 1951 based on a case of the medieval codes of honor that became part of the colonial legacy and, eventually, codes of contemporary daily life in Colombia. The newspaper account explained that a person named Cayetano Gentile Chimento was brutally killed by two brothers in the Department of Sucre in January 1951 because their sister had claimed that she lost her virginity to Gentile Chimento before her marriage to another man. Holding the belief that the honor of their sister and their family had been ruined by Gentile Chimento, the brothers butchered the man with machetes. García Márquez took this grisly series of events and constructed a parody of a detective novel. The genre of the detective novel had interested García Márquez since his youth, and *Crónica de una muerte anunciada* is his detective novel in reverse: he announces the death and the assassins at the beginning and dedicates the remainder of the novel to keeping the reader intrigued with the details.

The Colombian's mastery of the arresting beginning is not lost in this novel, which opens with the sentence "El día en que lo iban a matar, Santiago Nasar se levantó a las 5:30 de la mañana para esperar el buque en que llegaba el obispo" (On the day they were going to kill him, Santiago Nasar got up at five thirty in the morning to wait for the boat the bishop was coming on). From this first line, the reader follows the details on how the murder takes place. As the novel develops, the exact circumstances surrounding Nasar's death become increasingly incredible: there is so much evidence about what is happening that everyone in the town except Nasar realizes exactly what is transpiring.

The novel consists of five chapters which are hardly a "chronicle" if one holds to a strict definition of the genre—a chronological record of historical events. The first chapter tells of the morning of the assassination by the two brothers, Pedro and Pablo Vicario. The second narrates the background of the relationship between the bride, Angela Vicario, and her groom, Bayardo San Román. The third chapter recounts the evening of the wedding vows—the night before Nasar's death. The fourth chapter jumps ahead in time to relate the events subsequent to the killing, such as Angela's life during the years after the failed marriage. The final chapter returns to the chronology of events surrounding the actual murder, culminating in a detailed and bloody description of the death.

As in much of García Márquez's fiction, there is not an underlying belief system that can provide a rational and coherent understanding of the series of events that comprise this novel. Rather, as in the early fictions of Macondo, life is determined by inexplicable forces and irrational acts. The narrator explains directly that all attempts at rational explanation have failed, and the narrator does not offer speculation as to how things happened as they did.

In the end, *Crónica de una muerte anunciada* leaves more questions than it solves, and one of the author's main strategies for creating ambiguity is to employ detailed particularity concerning irrelevant matters and vague descriptions about points of real importance. This basic procedure is like much journalism that abounds in detailed facts but fails to provide the broad picture of the events at hand. And contrary to what has been announced in the title, this novel is not a chronicle: a narrative situation in which the narrator only relates "versions" of what others have said, in effect, subverts any historical pretension underlying the literariness of this verbal construct.

When García Márquez received the Nobel Prize in Literature in 1982, many critics in Latin America had been speculating that he, Carlos Fuentes, or Octavio Paz might well be chosen. The selection of García Márquez was well received throughout Latin America, and particularly in Colombia, where many intellectuals belonging to the ruling elite had tended to be either distant or openly critical of this leftist writer before 1982. When the Nobel laureate returned from Stockholm to Colombia, he was received by the president, Belisario Betancur, as a national hero, and the entire country celebrated. New editions of his works appeared immediately in Spanish as well as many other languages. Another result of the Nobel Prize was the writer's new role as quasi-diplomat: from 1982 to the late 1990s, he often served as intermediary or spokesperson for President Betancur and for Castro, mostly in issues regarding international politics.

After receiving the Nobel Prize, García Márquez began spending less time in Mexico and more time living and writing in Cartagena, the colonial city where he had begun writing journalism in order to eke out a living as an aspiring writer. The ancient city is still surrounded by the walls that the Spaniards built in the seventeenth century to protect it from the pirates who navigated freely in the Caribbean. This now quaint and picturesque place is the main setting for *Amor en los tiempos del cólera*. More than just an improbable love story, this novel is about aging. In it, an older man returns to the love of his youth (after the death of her husband) and courts her on a steamboat. This romantic tale is the author's most lengthy novel (more than five hundred pages in the original Spanish); yet, this first book after the Nobel Prize does not represent as much of the typical García Márquez as some readers had expected, with relatively little of the magic realism, circular structures, and hyperbole that have characterized his most widely read work. Nevertheless, the ghost of a woman who waves at passing ships and the presence of a parrot who speaks Latin and French do remind the reader fleetingly of the magical world of Macondo. The love story begins as Florentino Ariza, at the age of seventeen, falls in love with Fermina Daza. Fermina's family, however, pressures her to marry the aristocratic Dr. Juvenal Urbino. Fifty years later, Urbino dies; Florentino proposes to the widow; and their love is consummated on a boat going down the Magdalena River. This novel and *El general en su laberinto* (1989, translated as *The General in His Labyrinth*, 1990) have been best-selling entertainments, with occasional touches of magic realism, Latin American history, and political critique. *El general en su laberinto* is García Márquez's rewriting of the history of the liberator of Latin America, Simón Bolívar. This mythical figure in Colombia is presented as suffering much of the solitude of power and confusion of the General in *El otoño del patriarca*.

García Márquez's journalistic background is evident in *Noticia de un secuestro* (1996, translated as *News of a Kidnapping*, 1997), a *testimonio* or semidocumentary account of the real kidnapping of ten Colombian journalists by drug kingpin Pablo Escobar. The author offers a day-by-day account of the violent and tense daily life in Colombia as a nation under constant siege by drug traffickers and armed guerrillas. This book is the culmination of a lifetime dedicated to writing not only fiction but also journalism. His journalistic writing from the late 1940s to the 1990s provides many insights into his interests and strategies as a writer. His nonfiction pieces published from 1948 to 1952 would be of considerable interest even if they had not been written by a future Nobel laureate. They offer first-hand insights into this period in Western history, with acute observations on famous people (such as Harry Truman), the movies of the times, and the invention of the atom bomb. During these years, García Márquez published more than four hundred short pieces, ranging in subject from the cultural to the political.

These early articles also demonstrate that the author's interest in detective novels far predates the writing of *Crónica de una muerte anunciada*. One of his more serious expositions on detective fiction, published in 1952, deals with the enigmas of the genre, and he states that the genre has an attraction that no academic can explain. Always more fascinated with enigmas and ambiguities than coherence and rational explanation, he claims in many of these journalistic pieces that science and reason can only partially explain the human experience.

Best known in much of the world as a magic realist, García Márquez has claimed more than once that he is merely a "realist" who describes the everyday reality of his nation and of Latin America. His claim is true in several ways, even though he has always been more interested in writers who invent reality (Kafka, Faulkner, Jorge Luis Borges) than those who merely describe it. The term "magic realism" actually harks back to the 1920s: German art critic Franz Roh coined the term in 1925. For Roh, it was synonymous with postexpressionist painting (1920–1925) because it revealed the mysterious elements hidden in everyday reality. Magic realism expressed the astonishment some perceive in the wonders of empirical reality. For example, José Arcadio Buendía's amazement over the arrival of ice is an indication why the term "magic realism" seems appropriate in the context of García Márquez. Several critics of Spanish-American literature popularized the term later, in the 1950s.

Today, most critics consider magic realism a blend of reality and fantasy in a literary text. The concept often embodies complex aesthetics. Nevertheless, the combination of real-life descriptions and the fantastic, as well as the use of understatement in conjunction with hyperbole, have become the hallmark characteristics of García Márquez's fiction and the de facto commonly accepted descriptions of magic realism. By the 1980s, almost any Latin American writer offering a strong element of fantasy–from Isabel Allende to Laura Esquivel–has been described as a "magic realist."

García Márquez belongs to a generation of Latin American writers committed to modernizing the literatures of their respective nations. In the 1950s García Márquez and his peers were reading modernist fiction writers such as Joyce, Faulkner, and Marcel Proust and embracing them with great enthusiasm as models for breaking from the tradition-bound past of Latin American literature. García Márquez, Fuentes, and Vargas Llosa have also spoken about one of the most influential figures for Latin American intellectuals of the 1950s: Jean-Paul Sartre. During the Boom years of the 1960s, each of these major Latin American writers regularly cited and paraphrased Sartre's ideas about the writer's role in progressive social change and revolution. They spoke often of Sartre's idea of the *engagé* or politically committed writer. In Colombia, García Márquez collaborated with the cultural magazine *Mito*, which carried out this modernizing agenda in that nation. In Mexico, García Márquez's closest intellectual friends were members of the "Generación de Medio Siglo" (Mid-Century Generation) that had a similar agenda and had started a cultural journal, the *Revista Mexicana de Literatura*. The awarding of the Nobel Prize in Literature to García Márquez in 1982 represented, for many of the writers of this generation, a universal acceptance of the fact that they did successfully modernize Latin American literature during the second half of the twentieth century. Certainly his role in this effort will be a significant part of García Márquez's legacy.

García Márquez has dedicated a lifetime to serving as an agent in favor of progressive social change in Latin America. He has written fictional and journalistic critiques of authoritarian uses of power, including power exercised in a broad range of governmental and ecclesiastic institutions. García Márquez was born and raised in an impoverished region with severe class distinctions and intense political conflict. Given the sociopolitical conditions he experienced as a child, he was seemingly born to be a leftist writer. As he matured with the intellectuals of *Mito* in the 1950s and with the writers of the Boom in the 1960s, he became increasingly strident in his political positions. In the 1970s García Márquez was most vocal about his progressive agenda, financing the leftist political magazine *Alternativa* in Colombia and publishing his highly critical *El otoño del patriarca*. In the 1980s and 1990s he was a more moderate political voice for the disenfranchised, and he promoted dialogue among such diverse political forces as the U.S. government, the Colombian government, Cuban leader Castro, and the French head of state François Mitterrand.

In the later years of his life and career, Gabriel García Márquez has suffered from ill health, but he has written his literary memoirs under the title *Vivir para contarla* and the novel *Memoria de mis putas tristes* (2004, translated as *Memories of My Melancholy Whores*, 2005). Like many of the everyday people of his stories, he has prevailed into old age with dignity and faith in the causes of the common man. As an adolescent reading

Kafka's *The Metamorphosis,* García Márquez decided that if this text was literature, then he wanted to be a writer. In Kafka he saw the writer freely exercising the right of invention. This exploration of the human imagination has been García Márquez's passion for more than a half century. In his later years, when asked about the writer's role in society, he has affirmed more than once that it is simply to tell a good story.

Interviews:

Leopoldo Azancot, "Gabriel García Márquez habla de política y de literatura," *Indice,* 237 (1968): 30–31;

José Domingo, "Entrevista a García Márquez," *Insula,* 259 (1968): 45–47;

Armando Durán, "Conversaciones con Gabriel García Márquez," *Revista Nacional de Cultura,* 29, no. 185 (1968): 23–43;

Rosa Castro, "Con Gabriel García Márquez," in *Recopilación de textos sobre García Márquez* (Havana: Casa de las Americas, 1969), pp. 29–33;

Claude Couffon, "Gabriel García Márquez habla de *Cien años de soledad,*" in *Recopilación de textos sobre García Márquez,* pp. 45–47;

Ernesto González Bermejo, "García Márquez: Ahora doscientos años de soledad," *Triunfo,* 441 (1970): 12–18;

Rita Guibert, *Seven Voices: Seven Latin American Writers Talk to Rita Guibert* (New York: Knopf, 1973), pp. 303–338;

Ramón Oviero, "He sido un escritor explotado," *Ahora,* 656 (1976): 34–39;

Alfonso Rentería Mantilla, ed., *García Márquez habla de García Márquez, 33 reportajes* (Bogotá: Rentería, 1979);

Plinio Apuleyo Mendoza, *El olor de la guayaba* (Barcelona: Bruguera, 1982); translated as *The Fragrance of Guava: Conversations with Gabriel García Márquez* (London: Verso, 1983);

Marlise Simons, "A Talk with Gabriel García Márquez," *New York Times Book Review,* 5 December 1982, pp. 7, 60–61;

Raymond Leslie Williams, "The Visual Arts, the Poetization of Space and Writing: An Interview with Gabriel García Márquez," *PMLA,* 104 (March 1989): 131–140;

Gene H. Bell-Villada, ed., *Conversations with Gabriel García Márquez* (Jackson: University Press of Mississippi, 2005).

Bibliographies:

Margaret Eustalia Fau, *Gabriel García Márquez: An Annotated Bibliography, 1947–1979* (Westport, Conn.: Greenwood Press, 1980);

Fau and Nelly Sfeir de González, *Bibliographic Guide to Gabriel García Márquez, 1979–1985* (Westport, Conn.: Greenwood Press, 1986);

Sfeir de Gonzalez, *Bibliographic Guide to Gabriel García Márquez, 1986–1992* (Westport, Conn.: Greenwood Press, 1994).

References:

Michael Bell, *Gabriel García Márquez: Solitude and Solidarity* (New York: St. Martin's Press, 1993);

Gene H. Bell-Villada, *García Márquez: The Man and His Work* (Chapel Hill: University of North Carolina Press, 1990);

Harold Bloom, ed., *Gabriel García Márquez's One Hundred Years of Solitude: Essays* (Philadelphia: Chelsea House, 2003);

Mary E. Davis, "The Voyage Beyond the Map; 'El ahogado más hermoso del mundo,'" *Kentucky Romance Quarterly,* 26, no. 1 (1979): 25–33;

Wilma Else Detjens, *Home as Creation: The Influence of Early Childhood Experience in the Literary Creation of Gabriel García Márquez, Agustin Yanez, and Juan Rolfo* (New York: Peter Lang, 1993);

Robin Fiddian, ed., *García Márquez* (London & New York: Longman, 1995);

Carlos Fuentes, "Macondo, Seat of Time," *Review,* 70 (1971): 119–121;

Hannelore Hahn, *The Influence of Franz Kafka on Three Novels by Gabriel García Márquez* (New York: Peter Lang, 1993);

Paul M. Hedeen, "Gabriel García Márquez's Dialectic of Solitude," *Southwest Review,* 68 (Autumn 1983): 350–364;

Regina Janes, *Gabriel García Márquez: Revolutions in Wonderland* (Columbia: University of Missouri Press, 1981);

Janes, *One Hundred Years of Solitude: Modes of Reading* (Boston: Twayne, 1991);

William Kennedy, "The Yellow Trolley Car in Barcelona and Other Visions: A Profile of Gabriel García Márquez," *Atlantic Monthly,* 231 (January 1973): 50–59;

Carmenza Kline, *Fiction and Reality in the Works of Gabriel García Márquez,* translated by Daniel Linder (Salamanca, Spain: Universidad de Salamanca, 2002);

Latin American Literary Review, special García Márquez issue, 13 (January–June 1985);

John P. McGowan, "A la recherche du temps perdu in *One Hundred Years of Solitude,*" *Modern Fiction Studies,* 28 (Winter 1982–1983): 557–567;

Bernard McGuirk and Richard Cardwell, *Gabriel García Márquez: New Readings* (Cambridge, U.K.: Cambridge University Press, 1987);

George R. McMurray, *Gabriel García Márquez* (New York: Ungar, 1977);

Kathleen McNerney, *Understanding Gabriel García Márquez* (Columbia: University of South Carolina Press, 1989);

Stephen Minta, *Gabriel García Márquez: Writer of Colombia* (London: Cape, 1987);

Harley D. Oberhelman, *Gabriel García Márquez: A Study of the Short Fiction* (Boston: Twayne, 1991);

Oberhelman, *García Márquez and Cuba: A Study of Its Presence in His Fiction, Journalism, and Cinema* (Fredericton, N.B.: York Press, 1995);

Oberhelman, *The Presence of Faulkner in the Writings of García Márquez* (Lubbock: Texas Tech Press, 1980);

Oberhelman, *The Presence of Hemingway in the Short Fiction of Gabriel García Márquez* (Fredericton, N.B.: York Press, 1994);

Julio Ortega, "*One Hundred Years of Solitude* and *The Autumn of the Patriarch*: Text and Culture," in his *Poetics of Change: The New Spanish-American Narrative* (Austin: University of Texas Press, 1984), pp. 85–95, 96–119;

Ortega and Claudia Elliott, eds., *Gabriel García Márquez and the Powers of Fiction* (Austin: University of Texas Press, 1988);

Constance A. Pedoto, *Painting Literature: Dostoevsky, Kafka, Pirandello, and García Márquez in Living Color* (Lanham, Md.: University Press of America, 1993);

Rubén Pelayo, *Gabriel García Márquez: A Critical Companion* (Westport, Conn.: Greenwood Press, 2001);

Arnold M. Penuel, *Intertextuality in García Márquez* (York, S.C.: Spanish Literature Publications, 1994);

Penuel, "The Sleep of Vital Reason in García Márquez's *Crónica de una muerte anunciada*," *Hispania*, 68 (December 1985): 753–766;

Rosa Simas, *Circularity and Visions of the New World in William Faulkner, Gabriel García Márquez, and Osman Lins* (Lewiston, N.Y.: Edwin Mellen Press, 1993);

Robert Lewis Sims, "The Banana Massacre in *Cien años de soledad*: A Micro-structural Example of Myth, History and Bricolage," *Chasqui*, 8, no. 3 (1979): 3–23;

Sims, *The First García Márquez: A Study of His Journalistic Writing from 1948 to 1955* (Lanham, Md.: University Press of America, 1992);

Mario Vargas Llosa, *Gabriel García Márquez: Historia de un deicidio* (Barcelona: Seix Barral, 1971);

Raymond Leslie Williams, *Gabriel García Márquez* (Boston: Twayne, 1984);

Michael Wood, *Gabriel García Márquez: One Hundred Years of Solitude* (Cambridge & New York: Cambridge University Press, 1990).

1982 Nobel Prize in Literature Presentation Speech

by Professor Lars Gyllensten of the Swedish Academy
(Translation from the Swedish)

Your Majesties, Your Royal Highnesses, Ladies and Gentlemen,

With this year's Nobel Prize in Literature to Gabriel García Márquez the Swedish Academy cannot be said to bring forward an unknown writer.

García Márquez achieved unusual success as a writer with his novel *Cien años de soledad* in 1967 (One Hundred Years of Solitude). The book has been translated into a large number of languages and has sold millions of copies. It is still being reprinted and read with undiminished interest by new readers. Such a success with a single work could be fatal for a writer with less resources than those possessed by García Márquez. He has, however, gradually confirmed his position as a rare storyteller richly endowed with a material, from imagination and experience, which seems inexhaustible. In breadth and epic richness, for instance, the novel *El otoño del patriarca*, 1975 (The Autumn of the Patriarch), compares favourably with the first-mentioned work. Short novels such as *El coronel no tiene quien le escriba*, 1961 (No One Writes to the Colonel), *La mala hora,* 1962 (An Evil Hour), or last year's *Crónica de una muerte anunciada* (Chronicle of a Death Foretold), complement the picture of a writer who combines the copious, almost overwhelming narrative talent with the mastery of the conscious, disciplined and widely read artist of language. A large number of short stories, published in several collections or in magazines, give further proof of the great versatility of García Márquez' narrative gift. His international successes have continued. Each new work of his is received by expectant critics and readers as an event of world importance, is translated into many languages and published as quickly as possible in large editions.

Nor can it be said that any literary unknown continent or province is brought to light with the prize to Gabriel García Márquez. For a long time Latin American literature has shown a vigour as in few other literary spheres. It has won acclaim in the cultural life of today. Many impulses and traditions cross each other. Folk culture, including oral storytelling, reminiscences from old Indian culture, currents from Spanish baroque in different epochs, influences from European surrealism and other modernism are blended into a spiced and life-giving brew. From it García Márquez and other Spanish-American writers derive material and inspiration. The violent conflicts of political nature—social and economic—raise the temperature of the intellectual climate. Like most of the other important writers in the Latin American world, García Márquez is strongly committed politically on the side of the poor and the weak against oppression and economic exploitation. Apart from his fictional production he has been very active as a journalist, his writings being many-sided, inventive, often provocative and by no means limited to political subjects.

The great novels remind one of William Faulkner. García Márquez has created a world of his own round the imaginary town of Macondo. In his novels and short stories we are led into this peculiar place where the miraculous and the real converge. The extravagant flight of his own fantasy combines with traditional folk tales and facts, literary allusions and tangible—at times obtrusively graphic—descriptions approaching the matter-of-factness of reportage. As with Faulkner, the same chief characters and minor persons crop up in different stories. They are brought forward into the light in various ways—sometimes in dramatically revealing situations, sometimes in comic and grotesque complications of a kind that only the wildest imagination or shameless reality itself can achieve. Manias and passions harass them. Absurdities of war let courage change shape with craziness, infamy with chivalry, cunning with madness.

Death is perhaps the most important director behind the scenes in García Márquez' invented and discovered world. Often his stories revolve around a dead person—someone who has died, is dying or will die. A tragic sense of life characterizes García Márquez' books—a sense of the incorruptible superiority of fate and the inhuman, inexorable ravages of history. But this awareness of death and tragic sense of life is broken by the narrative's unlimited, ingenious vitality, which in its turn is a representative of the at once frightening and edifying vital force of reality and life itself. The comedy and grotesqueness in García Márquez can be cruel, but can also glide over into a conciliating humour.

With his stories García Márquez has created a world of his own which is a microcosmos. In its tumultuous, bewildering yet graphically convincing authenticity it reflects a continent and its human riches and poverty.

Perhaps more than that: a cosmos in which the human heart and the combined forces of history time and again burst the bounds of chaos-killing and procreation.

Monsieur García Márquez,

Ne disposant que de quelques minutes, je n'ai pu donner de votre œuvre littéraire qu'une image d'aspect general et assez abstraite. Certes, vos romans et vos nouvelles sont d'ordre general, ce qui revient à dire qu'elles ont une portée et une signification humaines de cet ordre. Mais elles ne sont pas abstraites. Au contraire, vos œuvres se caractérisent par un rendu du vivant peu commun et une concretion realiste auxquels aucun condense abstrait ne saurait rendre justice. Le mieux que je puisse faire, c'est d'exhorter ceux qui ne les ont pas lues à les lire. C'est bien ce que j'ai fait.

Sur ces paroles, je vous presente les felicitations les plus cordiales de l'Académie Suédoise et je vous invite à recevoir le prix Nobel de littérature des mains de Sa Majesté le Roi.

[© The Nobel Foundation, 1982.]

(Translation of the French by Michael Lazare)

Mr. García Márquez:

Having only a few moments to speak, I could only give a general, and rather abstract, view of your literary work. In fact, your stories and your novels have universal reach and human significance—but they are not abstract. On the contrary, they are characterized by an uncommon rendition of life, and a true realism to which no abstract description could do justice. The best I can do is to exhort those who have not read your works to do so. And that is indeed what I have done.

With these words, I bring you the most hearty congratulations of the Swedish Academy, and I invite you to receive the Nobel Prize in Literature from the hands of His Majesty the King.

García Márquez: Banquet Speech

García Márquez's speech at the Nobel Banquet, 10 December 1982

Sus Majestades, Sus Altezas Reales, Amigos:

Agradezco a la Academia de Letras de Suecia el que me haya distinguido con un premio que me coloca junto a muchos de quienes orientaron y enriquecieron mis años de lector y de cotidiano celebrante de ese delirio sin apelación que es el oficio de escribir. Sus nombres y sus obras se me presentan hoy como sombras tutelares, pero también como la evidencia, a menudo agobiante, del compromiso que se adquire con este honor. Un duro honor que en ellos me pareció de simple justicia, pero que en mí entiendo como una más de esas lecciones con las que suele sorprendernos el destino, y que hacen más evidente nuestra condición de juguetes de un azar indescifrable, cuya única y desoladora recompensa suelen ser, la mayoría de las veces, la incomprensión y el olvido.

Es por ello apenas natural que me interrogara, allá en ese transfondo secreto en donde solemos trasegar con las verdades más esenciales que conforman nuestra identidad, cuál ha sido el sustento constante de mi obra, que pudo haber llamado la atención de una manera tan comprometedora a este tribunal de árbitros tan severos. Confieso sin falsas modestias que no me ha sido facil encontrar la razón, pero quiero creer que ha sido la misma que yo hubiera deseado. Quiero creer, amigos, que este es, una vez más, un homenaje que se rinde a la poesía. A la poesía por cuya virtud el agobiante inventario de las naves que enumeró en su Iliada el viejo Homero está visitado por un viento que la empuja a navegar con su presteza intemporal y alucinada. La poesía que sostiene, en el delgado andamiaje de los tercetos del Dante, toda la fábrica densa y colosal de la Edad Media. La poesía que con tan evidente como milagrosa totalidad rescata a nuestra América en Las Alturas de Machu Pichu de Pablo Neruda el grande, el más grande, y donde destilan su tristeza milenaria nuestros mejores sueños sin salida. La poesía, en fin, esa energía secreta de la vida cotidiana, que cuece los garbanzos en la cocina, y contagia el amor y repite las imágenes en los espejos.

En cada línea que escribo trato siempre, con mayor o menor fortuna, de invocar los espíritus esquivos de la poesía, y trato de dejar en cada palabra el testimonio de mi devoción por sus virtudes de adivinación, y por su permanente victoria contra los sordos poderes de la muerte. El premio que acabo de recibir lo entiendo, con toda humildad, como la consoladora evidencia de que mi intento no ha sido en vano. Es por eso que invito a todos ustedes a brindar por lo que un gran poeta de nuestras Américas, Luis Cardoza y Aragón, ha definido como la única prueba concreta de la existencia del hombre: la poesía.

Muchas gracias.

[© The Nobel Foundation, 1982. Gabriel García Márquez is the sole author of his speech.]

Translation by Darrell J. Dernoshek

Your Majesties, Your Royal Highnesses, Friends:

I thank the Swedish Academy of Letters for having honored me with a prize that places me with many of those who guided and enriched my years as a reader and as an ordinary celebrant of that delirium without appeal that is the trade of writing. Their names and works come to mind today only as guardian shadows, but also as the evidence, often exhausting, of the commitment acquired with this honor. A difficult honor that in them it appeared to me to be simple justice, but within myself I understand as one more of these lessons by which destiny usually surprises us, and that make more evident our condition of the playthings of an undecipherable fate, whose sole and devastating rewards usually are, most of the time, incomprehension and obscurity.

It is for that reason, hardly natural, that I ask myself, there in that secret background where we usually go back and forth between the most essential truths that form our identity, what has been the constant sustenance of my work, that could have called the attention of this tribunal of such strict judges in such a compromising manner. I confess without false modesty that it has not been easy for me to find the reason, but I want to believe that it has been the same one that I would have wanted. I want to believe, friends, that this is, once again, a homage paid to poetry. To poetry through whose virtue the exhausting inventory of ships, that old Homer spelled out in his *Iliad,* is visited by a wind that pushes it to sail with its timeless and hallucinated swiftness. The poetry that supports, in the thin scaffolding of the tercets of Dante, all the dense and colossal factory of the Middle Ages. The poetry that with a totality as evident as it is miraculous rescues our America in *The Heights of Machu Picchu* by the great, the greatest, Pablo Neruda, and where its thousand-year-old sadness pours out our best dreams without a way out. Poetry, after all, that secret energy of everyday life that cooks the garbanzos in the kitchen, and spreads love and repeats the images in the mirrors.

In every line that I write I always attempt, with more or less success, to invoke the illusive spirits of poetry, and I attempt to leave in every word the testimony of my devotion for its virtue of prediction, and for its permanent victory against the deaf powers of death. The prize that I have just received I understand to be, in all humility, as the consoling evidence that my intention has not been futile. It is for that reason that I invite all of you to toast what a great poet of our Americas, Luis Cardoza y Aragón, has defined as the only concrete test of man's existence: poetry.

Thank you very much.

García Márquez: Nobel Lecture, 8 December 1982

The Solitude of Latin America

Antonio Pigafetta, a Florentine navigator who went with Magellan on the first voyage around the world, wrote, upon his passage through our southern lands of America, a strictly accurate account that nonetheless resembles a venture into fantasy. In it he recorded that he had seen hogs with navels on their haunches, clawless birds whose hens laid eggs on the backs of their mates, and others still, resembling tongueless pelicans, with beaks like spoons. He wrote of having seen a misbegotten creature with the head and ears of a mule, a camel's body, the legs of a deer and the whinny of a horse. He described how the first native encountered in Patagonia was confronted with a mirror, whereupon that impassioned giant lost his senses to the terror of his own image.

This short and fascinating book, which even then contained the seeds of our present-day novels, is by no means the most staggering account of our reality in that age. The Chronicles of the Indies left us countless others. Eldorado, our so avidly sought and illusory land, appeared on numerous maps for many a long year, shifting its place and form to suit the fantasy of cartographers. In his search for the fountain of eternal youth, the mythical Alvar Núñez Cabeza de Vaca explored the north of Mexico for eight years, in a deluded expedition whose members devoured each other and only five of whom returned, of the six hundred who had undertaken it. One of the many unfathomed mysteries of that age is that of the eleven thousand mules, each loaded with one hundred pounds of gold, that left Cuzco one day to pay the ransom of Atahualpa and never reached their destination. Subsequently, in colonial times, hens were sold in Cartagena de Indias, that had been raised on alluvial land and whose gizzards contained tiny lumps of gold. One founder's lust for gold beset us until recently. As late as the last century, a German mission appointed to study the construction of an interoceanic railroad across the Isthmus of Panama concluded that the project was feasible on one condition: that the rails not be made of iron, which was scarce in the region, but of gold.

Our independence from Spanish domination did not put us beyond the reach of madness. General Antonio López de Santana, three times dictator of Mexico, held a magnificent funeral for the right leg he had lost in the so-called Pastry War. General Gabriel García Moreno ruled Ecuador for sixteen years as an absolute monarch; at his wake, the corpse was seated on the presidential chair, decked out in full-dress uniform and a protective layer of medals. General Maximiliano Hernández Martínez, the theosophical despot of El Salvador who had thirty thousand peasants slaughtered in a savage massacre, invented a pendulum to detect poison in his food, and had streetlamps draped in red paper to defeat an epidemic of scarlet fever. The statue to General Francisco Morazán erected in the main square of Tegucigalpa is actually one of Marshal Ney, purchased at a Paris warehouse of second-hand sculptures.

Eleven years ago, the Chilean Pablo Neruda, one of the outstanding poets of our time, enlightened this audience with his word. Since then, the Europeans of good will—and sometimes those of bad, as well—have been struck, with ever greater force, by the unearthly tidings of Latin America, that boundless realm of haunted men and historic women, whose unending obstinacy blurs into legend. We have not had a moment's rest. A promethean president, entrenched in his burning palace, died fighting an entire army, alone; and two suspicious airplane accidents, yet to be explained, cut short the life of another great-hearted president and that of a democratic soldier who had revived the dignity of his people. There have been five wars and seventeen military coups; there emerged a diabolic dictator who is carrying out, in God's name, the first Latin American ethnocide of our time. In the meantime, twenty million Latin American children died before the age of one—more than have been born in Europe since 1970. Those missing because of repression number nearly one hundred and twenty thousand, which is as if no one could account for all the inhabitants of Uppsala. Numerous women arrested while pregnant have given birth in Argentine prisons, yet nobody knows the whereabouts and identity of their children who were furtively adopted or sent to an orphanage by order of the military authorities. Because they tried to change this state of things, nearly two hundred thousand men and women have died throughout the continent, and over one hundred thousand have lost their lives in three small and ill-fated countries of Central America: Nicaragua, El Salvador and Guatemala. If this had happened in the United States, the corresponding figure would be that of one million six hundred thousand violent deaths in four years.

One million people have fled Chile, a country with a tradition of hospitality—that is, ten per cent of its population. Uruguay, a tiny nation of two and a half million inhabitants which considered itself the continent's most civilized country, has lost to exile one out of every five citizens. Since 1979, the civil war in El Salvador has produced almost one refugee every twenty minutes. The country that could be formed of all the exiles and forced emigrants of Latin America would have a population larger than that of Norway.

I dare to think that it is this outsized reality, and not just its literary expression, that has deserved the attention of the Swedish Academy of Letters. A reality not of paper, but one that lives within us and determines each instant of our countless daily deaths, and that nourishes a source of insatiable creativity, full of sorrow and beauty, of which this roving and nostalgic Colombian is but one cipher more, singled out by fortune. Poets and beggars, musicians and prophets, warriors and scoundrels, all creatures of that unbridled reality, we have had to ask but little of imagination, for our crucial problem has been a lack of conventional means to render our lives believable. This, my friends, is the crux of our solitude.

And if these difficulties, whose essence we share, hinder us, it is understandable that the rational talents on this side of the world, exalted in the contemplation of their own cultures, should have found themselves without valid means to interpret us. It is only natural that they insist on measuring us with the yardstick that they use for themselves, forgetting that the ravages of life are not the same for all, and that the quest of our own identity is just as arduous and bloody for us as it was for them. The interpretation of our reality through patterns not our own, serves only to make us ever more unknown, ever less free, ever more solitary. Venerable Europe would perhaps be more perceptive if it tried to see us in its own past. If only it recalled that London took three hundred years to build its first city wall, and three hundred years more to acquire a bishop; that Rome labored in a gloom of uncertainty for twenty centuries, until an Etruscan King anchored it in history; and that the peaceful Swiss of today, who feast us with their mild cheeses and apathetic watches, bloodied Europe as soldiers of fortune, as late as the Sixteenth Century. Even at the height of the Renaissance, twelve thousand lansquenets in the pay of the imperial armies sacked and devastated Rome and put eight thousand of its inhabitants to the sword.

I do not mean to embody the illusions of Tonio Kröger, whose dreams of uniting a chaste north to a passionate south were exalted here, fifty-three years ago, by Thomas Mann. But I do believe that those clear-sighted Europeans who struggle, here as well, for a more just and humane homeland, could help us far better if they reconsidered their way of seeing us. Solidarity with our dreams will not make us feel less alone, as long as it is not translated into concrete acts of legitimate support for all the peoples that assume the illusion of having a life of their own in the distribution of the world.

Latin America neither wants, nor has any reason, to be a pawn without a will of its own; nor is it merely wishful thinking that its quest for independence and originality should become a Western aspiration. However, the navigational advances that have narrowed such distances between our Americas and Europe seem, conversely, to have accentuated our cultural remoteness. Why is the originality so readily granted us in literature so mistrustfully denied us in our difficult attempts at social change? Why think that the social justice sought by progressive Europeans for their own countries cannot also be a goal for Latin America, with different methods for dissimilar conditions? No: the immeasurable violence and pain of our history are the result of age-old inequities and untold bitterness, and not a conspiracy plotted three thousand leagues from our home. But many European leaders and thinkers have thought so, with the childishness of old-timers who have forgotten the fruitful excess of their youth as if it were impossible to find another destiny than to live at the mercy of the two great masters of the world. This, my friends, is the very scale of our solitude.

In spite of this, to oppression, plundering and abandonment, we respond with life. Neither floods nor plagues, famines nor cataclysms, nor even the eternal wars of century upon century, have been able to subdue the persistent advantage of life over death. An advantage that grows and quickens: every year, there are seventy-four million more births than deaths, a sufficient number of new lives to multiply, each year, the population of New York sevenfold. Most of these births occur in the countries of least resources—including, of course, those of Latin America. Conversely, the most prosperous countries have succeeded in accumulating powers of destruction such as to annihilate, a hundred times over, not only all the human beings that have existed to this day, but also the totality of all living beings that have ever drawn breath on this planet of misfortune.

On a day like today, my master William Faulkner said, "I decline to accept the end of man." I would fall unworthy of standing in this place that was his, if I were not fully aware that the colossal tragedy he refused to recognize thirty-two years ago is now, for the first time since the beginning of humanity, nothing more than a simple scientific possibility. Faced with this awesome reality that must have seemed a mere utopia through all of human time, we, the inventors of tales, who will believe anything, feel entitled to believe that it is not yet too late to engage in the creation of the opposite utopia. A new and sweeping utopia of life, where no one will be able to decide for others how they die, where love will prove true and happiness be possible, and where the races condemned to one hundred years of solitude will have, at last and forever, a second opportunity on earth.

[© The Nobel Foundation, 1982. Gabriel García Márquez is the sole author of the text.]

André Gide

(22 November 1869 – 19 February 1951)

Catharine Savage Brosman
Tulane University

See also the Gide entries in *DLB 65: French Novelists, 1900–1930;* and *DLB 321: Twentieth-Century French Dramatists.*

SELECTED BOOKS: *Les Cahiers d'André Walter,* anonymous (Paris: Didier-Perrin, 1891); translated by Wade Baskin as *The Notebooks of André Walter* (New York: Philosophical Library, 1968; London: Owen, 1968);

Le Traité du Narcisse (Paris: Librairie de l'Art Indépendant, 1891); translated by Dorothy Bussy as *Narcissus,* in *The Return of the Prodigal . . .* (London: Secker & Warburg, 1953);

Les Poésies d'André Walter, anonymous (Paris: Librairie de l'Art Indépendant, 1892);

La Tentative amoureuse; ou, Le Traité du vain désir (Paris: Librairie de l'Art Indépendant, 1893); translated by Bussy as *The Lovers' Attempt,* in *The Return of the Prodigal . . .* (London: Secker & Warburg, 1953);

Le Voyage d'Urien (Paris: Librairie de l'Art Indépendant, 1893); translated by Baskin as *Urien's Voyage* (New York: Philosophical Library, 1964; London: Owen, 1964);

Paludes (Paris: Librairie de l'Art Indépendant, 1895); translated by George D. Painter as *Marshlands,* in *Marshlands and Prometheus Misbound: Two Satires* (New York: New Directions, 1953; London: Secker & Warburg, 1953);

Les Nourritures terrestres (Paris: Mercure de France, 1897); translated by Bussy as *The Fruits of the Earth,* in *The Fruits of the Earth* (New York: Knopf, 1949; London: Secker & Warburg, 1949);

Le Prométhée mal enchaîné (Paris: Mercure de France, 1899); translated by Lilian Rothermere as *Prometheus Illbound* (London: Chatto & Windus, 1919);

Philoctète (Paris: Mercure de France, 1899)–comprises *Philoctète, Le Traité du Narcisse, La Tentative amoureuse,* and *El Hadj; Philoctète* translated by Jackson Mathews as *Philoctetes,* in *My Theater* (New York: Knopf, 1952); *El Hadj* translated by Bussy, in *The*

André Gide (Hulton Archive/Getty Images)

Return of the Prodigal . . . (London: Secker & Warburg, 1953);

Feuilles de route, 1895–1896 (Brussels: Vandersypen, 1899);

Lettres à Angèle, 1898–1899 (Paris: Mercure de France, 1900);

Le Roi Candaule (Paris: Revue Blanche, 1901); translated by Mathews as *King Candaules,* in *My Theater* (New York: Knopf, 1952), pp. 161–235;

L'Immoraliste (Paris: Mercure de France, 1902); translated by Bussy as *The Immoralist* (New York: Knopf, 1930; London: Cassell, 1930);

Saül (Paris: Mercure de France, 1903; enlarged, adding a preface by the author and his "De l'évolution du théâtre," 1904); enlarged edition translated by Mathews as *Saul* and *The Evolution of the Theater*, in *My Theater* (New York: Knopf, 1952), pp. 1–107, 259–275;

Prétextes: Réflexions sur quelques points de littérature et de morale (Paris: Mercure de France, 1903; enlarged, 1913); translated by Angelo P. Bertocci and others as *Pretexts: Reflections on Literature and Morality*, edited by Justin O'Brien (London: Secker & Warburg, 1959; New York: Meridian, 1959);

Amyntas (Paris: Mercure de France, 1906); translated by Villiers David (London: Bodley Head, 1958);

Le Retour de l'enfant prodigue (Paris: Vers et Prose, 1907); translated by Bussy as *The Return of the Prodigal*, in *The Return of the Prodigal . . .* (London: Secker & Warburg, 1953);

La Porte étroite (Paris: Mercure de France, 1909); translated by Bussy as *Strait Is the Gate* (New York: Knopf, 1924; London: Jarrolds, 1924);

Oscar Wilde: In Memoriam (souvenirs); Le "De Profundis" (Paris: Mercure de France, 1910); translated by Bernard Frechtman as *Oscar Wilde: In Memoriam (Reminiscences); "De Profundis"* (New York: Philosophical Library, 1949);

Nouveaux Prétextes: Réflexions sur quelques points de Littérature et de Morale (Paris: Mercure de France, 1911);

C.R.D.N., anonymous (Bruges: Sainte-Catherine, 1911); enlarged as *Corydon* (1920); trade edition, as Gide (Paris: Gallimard, 1924; enlarged, 1929); translated (New York: Farrar, Straus, 1950; London: Secker & Warburg, 1952); republished (Paris: Gallimard, 1977);

Isabelle (Paris: Nouvelle Revue Française/Marcel Rivière, 1911); translated by Bussy, in *Two Symphonies* (New York: Knopf, 1931; London: Cassell, 1931), pp. 1–137;

Bethsabé (Paris: Bibliothèque de l'Occident, 1912); translated by Mathews as *Bathsheba*, in *My Theater* (New York: Knopf, 1952), pp. 109–127;

Souvenirs de la cour d'assises (Paris: Nouvelle Revue Française, 1914);

Les Caves du Vatican, 2 volumes (Paris: Nouvelle Revue Française, 1914); translated by Bussy as *The Vatican Swindle* (New York: Knopf, 1925); translation republished as *Lafcadio's Adventures* (New York: Knopf, 1927); republished again as *The Vatican Cellars* (London: Cassell, 1952);

La Symphonie pastorale (Paris: Gallimard, 1919); translated by Bussy as *The Pastoral Symphony*, in *Two Symphonies* (New York: Knopf, 1931; London: Cassell, 1931), pp. 139–233;

Si le grain ne meurt, 2 volumes (Bruges: Sainte-Catherine, 1920, 1921); translated by Bussy as *If It Die . . .* (New York: Random House, 1935; London: Secker & Warburg, 1950);

Morceaux choisis (Paris: Gallimard, 1921);

André Gide (Paris: G. Crès, 1921);

Numquid et tu . . . ? anonymous (Bruges: Sainte-Catherine, 1922); trade edition, as Gide (Paris: Pléiade/Schiffrin, 1926); translated by O'Brien as *Numquid et tu . . . ?* in *The Journals of André Gide*, volume 2: *1914–1927* (New York: Knopf, 1948; London: Secker & Warburg, 1948), pp. 169–190;

Dostoïevsky (Paris: Plon-Nourrit, 1923); translated by Arnold Bennett as *Dostoyevsky* (London & Toronto: Dent, 1925; New York: Knopf, 1926);

Incidences (Paris: Gallimard, 1924);

Caractères (Paris: A l'Enseigne de la Porte étroite, 1925);

Les Faux-Monnayeurs (Paris: Gallimard, 1925); translated by Bussy as *The Counterfeiters* (New York: Knopf, 1927; London & New York: Knopf, 1928); translation republished as *The Coiners* (London: Cassell, 1950);

Journal des Faux-Monnayeurs (Paris: Eos, 1926); translated by O'Brien as *Logbook of the Coiners* (London: Cassell, 1952);

Voyage au Congo (Paris: Gallimard, 1927); translated by Bussy as *Travels in the Congo*, in *Travels in the Congo* (New York: Knopf, 1929), pp. 1–199;

Le Retour du Tchad: Carnets de route (Paris: Gallimard, 1928); translated by Bussy as *Return from Lake Chad*, in *Travels in the Congo* (New York: Knopf, 1929), pp. 201–375;

L'Ecole des femmes (Paris: Gallimard, 1929); translated by Bussy as *The School for Wives* (New York: Knopf, 1929);

Essai sur Montaigne (Paris: Schiffrin/Pléiade, 1929); translated by Stephen H. Guest and Trevor E. Blewitt as *Montaigne: An Essay in Two Parts* (London: Blackamore / New York: Liveright, 1929);

Un Esprit non prévenu (Paris: Kra, 1929);

Robert (Paris: Gallimard, 1930); translated by Bussy, in *The School for Wives; Robert; Geneviève, or The Unfinished Confidence* (New York: Knopf, 1950; London: Cassell, 1953);

Œdipe (Paris: Gallimard, 1931); translated by John Russell as *Oedipus*, in *Two Legends: Theseus and Oedipus* (New York: Knopf, 1950), pp. 1–43; translation republished as *Oedipus and Theseus* (London: Secker & Warburg, 1950);

Œuvres complètes d'André Gide, 15 volumes, edited by Louis Martin-Chauffier (Paris: Gallimard, 1932–1939);

Pages de journal (1929–1932) (Paris: Gallimard, 1934);

Les Nouvelles Nourritures (Paris: Gallimard, 1935); translated by Bussy as *Later Fruits of the Earth*, in *The Fruits of the Earth* (New York: Knopf, 1949; London: Secker & Warburg, 1949);

Nouvelles pages de journal (1932-1935) (Paris: Gallimard, 1935);

Geneviève (Paris: Gallimard, 1936); translated by Bussy as *Geneviève, or The Unfinished Confidence*, in *The School for Wives; Robert; Geneviève, or The Unfinished Confidence* (New York: Knopf, 1950; London: Cassell, 1953);

Retour de l'U.R.S.S. (Paris: Gallimard, 1936); translated by Bussy as *Return from the U.S.S.R.* (New York: Knopf, 1937; London: Secker & Warburg, 1937); translation republished as *Back from the U.S.S.R.* (London: Secker & Warburg, 1937);

Retouches à mon Retour de l'U.R.S.S. (Paris: Gallimard, 1937); translated by Bussy as *Afterthoughts: A Sequel to "Back from the U.S.S.R."* (London: Secker & Warburg, 1938); translation republished as *Afterthoughts on the U.S.S.R.* (New York: Dial, 1938);

Journal 1889-1939 (Paris: Gallimard, 1939); translated by O'Brien, in *The Journals of André Gide*, volume 1: *1889-1913;* volume 2: *1914-1927;* and volume 3: *1928-1939* (New York: Knopf, 1947-1949; London: Secker & Warburg, 1947-1949);

Découvrons Henri Michaux (Paris: Gallimard, 1941);

Théâtre (Paris: Gallimard, 1942)—comprises *Saül; Le Roi Candaule; Œdipe; Perséphone;* and *Le Treizième Arbre; Perséphone* translated by Mathews as *Persephone*, in *My Theater* (New York: Knopf, 1952);

Interviews imaginaires (Paris: Gallimard, 1942); enlarged as *Interviews imaginaires; La Délivrance de Tunis, pages de journal, mai 1943* (New York: Schiffrin, 1943); translated by Malcolm Cowley as *Imaginary Interviews* (New York: Knopf, 1944);

Pages de journal (1939-1942) (New York: Schiffrin, 1944; Algiers: Charlot, 1944; enlarged edition, Paris: Gallimard, 1946); translated by O'Brien, in *The Journals of André Gide*, volume 4: *1939-1949* (New York: Knopf, 1951; London: Secker & Warburg, 1951);

Poussin (Paris: Au Divan, 1945);

Thésée (New York: Schiffrin, 1946; Paris: Gallimard, 1946); translated by Russell as *Theseus* (London: Horizon, 1948; New York: New Directions, 1949);

Le Retour (Neuchâtel & Paris: Ides et Calendes, 1946);

Et nunc manet in te (Neuchâtel: Richard Heyd, 1947); translated by Keene Wallis as *The Secret Drama of My Life* (Paris & New York: Boar's Head Books, 1951); original French enlarged as *Et nunc manet in te, suivi de Journal intime* (Neuchâtel: Ides et Calendes, 1951); translated by O'Brien as *Madeleine* (New York: Knopf, 1952) and as *Et nunc Manet in te and Intimate Journal* (London: Secker & Warburg, 1952);

Paul Valéry (Paris: Domar, 1947);

Poétique (Neuchâtel & Paris: Ides et Calendes, 1947);

Le Procès; Pièce tirée du roman de Kafka, by Gide and Jean-Louis Barrault (Paris: Gallimard, 1947); translated by Jacqueline and Frank Sundstrom as *The Trial, from the Novel of Franz Kafka* (London: Secker & Warburg, 1950);

Préfaces (Neuchâtel & Paris: Ides et Calendes, 1948);

Rencontres (Neuchâtel & Paris: Ides et Calendes, 1948);

Les Caves du Vatican: Farce en trois actes (Neuchâtel & Paris: Ides et Calendes, 1948);

Eloges (Neuchâtel & Paris: Ides et Calendes, 1948);

Notes sur Chopin (Paris: L'Arche, 1948); translated by Frechtman as *Notes on Chopin* (New York: Philosophical Library, 1949);

Feuillets d'automne (Paris: Mercure de France, 1949); translated by Elsie Pell as *Autumn Leaves* (New York: Philosophical Library, 1950);

Littérature engagée, edited by Yvonne Davet (Paris: Gallimard, 1950);

Journal, 1942-1949 (Paris: Gallimard, 1950); translated by O'Brien, in *The Journals of André Gide*, volume 4: *1939-1949* (New York: Knopf, 1951; London: Secker & Warburg, 1951);

Ainsi soit-il ou les jeux sont faits (Paris: Gallimard, 1952); translated by O'Brien as *So Be It, or The Chips Are Down* (New York: Knopf, 1959; London: Chatto & Windus, 1960);

Ne jugez pas (Paris: Gallimard, 1969);

Le Récit de Michel, edited by Claude Martin (Neuchâtel: Ides et Calendes, 1972);

Les Cahiers et les Poésies d'André Walter, avec des fragments inédits du Journal, edited by Martin (Paris: Gallimard, 1986);

Un fragment des Faux-Monnayeurs: Edition critique du manuscrit de Londres, edited by David Keypour (Sainte-Foy-lès-Lyon: Centre d'Etudes Gidiennes, 1990);

A Naples: Reconnaissance à l'Italie, edited, with an afterword, by Martin (Fontfroide: Fata Morgana, 1993);

Le Grincheux (Fontfroide: Fata Morgana, 1993);

L'Oroscope, ou Nul n'évite sa destinée: Scénario, fac-similé et transcription, edited by Daniel Durosay (Paris: Jean-Michel Place, 1995);

Le Scénario d'Isabelle, by Gide and Pierre Herbart, edited by Cameron D. E. Tolton (Paris: Lettres Modernes, 1996);

Journal, I: 1887-1925, edited by Eric Marty (Paris: Gallimard, 1996);

Journal, II: 1926–1950, edited by Martine Sagaert (Paris: Gallimard, 1997);

Essais critiques, edited by Pierre Masson (Paris: Gallimard, 1999);

Le Ramier, foreword by Catherine Gide, preface by Jean-Claude Perrier, afterword by David H. Walker (Paris: Gallimard, 2002).

Editions and Collections: *Le Théâtre complet d'André Gide,* 8 volumes, edited by Richard Heyd (Neuchâtel & Paris: Ides et Calendes, 1947–1949);

Romans, récits et soties, oeuvres lyriques, edited by Yvonne Davet and Jean-Jacques Thierry (Paris: Gallimard, 1958);

Le Roi Candaule, edited by Patrick Pollard (Bron: Centre d'Etudes Gidiennes, 2000);

Souvenirs et voyages, edited by Pierre Masson, Daniel Durosay, and Martine Sagaert (Paris: Gallimard, 2001).

Editions in English: *The Journals of André Gide,* 4 volumes, translated by Justin O'Brien (New York: Knopf, 1947–1951; London: Secker & Warburg, 1947–1955);

The School for Wives; Robert; Geneviève, or The Unfinished Confidence, translated by Dorothy Bussy (New York: Knopf, 1950; London: Cassell, 1953);

Oscar Wilde (London: Kimber, 1951);

My Theater, translated by Jackson Mathews (New York: Knopf, 1952)—comprises *Saul; Bathsheba; Philoctetes; King Candaules; Persephone;* and *The Evolution of the Theater;*

Marshlands and Prometheus Misbound: Two Satires, translated by George D. Painter (New York: New Directions, 1953; London: Secker & Warburg, 1953);

The Return of the Prodigal, Preceded by Five Other Treatises, with Saul, A Drama in Five Acts, translated by Bussy (London: Secker & Warburg, 1953)—comprises *The Return of the Prodigal; Narcissus; The Lovers' Attempt; El Hadj; Philoctetes; Bathsheba;* and *Saul;*

The Immoralist, translated by Richard Howard (New York: Modern Library, 1983);

Amyntas, translated by Howard (New York: Ecco Press, 1988);

The Immoralist, translated by David Watson (New York: Penguin, 2001).

PLAY PRODUCTIONS: *Le Roi Candaule,* Paris, Nouveau Théâtre, 9 May 1901;

Philoctète, Paris, private performance, 3 April 1919; reading, Paris, Comédie des Champs-Elysées, 16 October 1937;

Saül, Paris, Théâtre du Vieux-Colombier, 16 June 1922;

Le Retour de l'enfant prodigue, Monte Carlo, Théâtre de Monte-Carlo, 4 December 1928; Paris, Théâtre de l'Avenue, 23 February 1933;

Œdipe, Antwerp, Cercle Artistique, 10 December 1931; Paris, Théâtre de l'Avenue, 18 February 1932;

Les Caves du Vatican, adapted by Gide from his novel, Montreux, Société des Belles-Lettres, 9 December 1933; revised, Paris, Comédie-Française, 13 December 1950;

Perséphone, libretto by Gide, music by Igor Stravinsky, Paris, Opéra, 30 April 1934;

Le Treizième Arbre, Marseille, Rideau Gris, 8 May 1935; Paris, Théâtre Charles de Rochefort, 13 January 1939;

Robert ou L'Intérêt général, Tunis, Théâtre Municipal, 30 April 1946.

OTHER: Emmanuel Signoret, *Poésies complètes,* preface by Gide (Paris: Mercure de France, 1908);

Stendhal, *Armance,* preface by Gide (Paris: Champion, 1925);

Antoine de Saint-Exupéry, *Vol de nuit,* preface by Gide (Paris: Gallimard, 1931);

Henry Monnier, *Morceaux choisis,* preface by Gide (Paris: Gallimard, 1935);

Thomas Mann, *Avertissement à l'Europe,* preface by Gide (Paris: Gallimard, 1937);

Henry Fielding, *Tom Jones, histoire d'un enfant trouvé,* edited, with a preface, by Gide (Paris: Gallimard, 1938);

William Shakespeare, *Théâtre complet,* 2 volumes, preface by Gide (Paris: Nouvelle Revue Française, 1938);

Johann Wolfgang von Goethe, *Théâtre,* introduction by Gide (Paris: Nouvelle Revue Française, 1942);

Jean Schlumberger, *Saint-Saturnin,* preface by Gide (Zurich: Oprecht, 1946);

Hermann Hesse, *Voyage en Orient,* preface by Gide (Paris: Calmann-Lévy, 1947);

Stendhal, *Lamiel,* preface by Gide (Paris: Livre Français, 1947);

Taha Hussein, *Le Livre des jours,* preface by Gide (Paris: Gallimard, 1947);

Anthologie de la poésie française, edited, with a preface, by Gide (Paris: Gallimard, 1949; New York: Pantheon, 1949);

Knut Hamsun, *La Faim,* preface by Gide (Paris: Chaix, 1950).

TRANSLATIONS: Rabindranath Tagore, *L'Offrande lyrique (Gitanjali)* (Paris: Nouvelle Revue Française, 1914);

Joseph Conrad, *Typhon* (Paris: Nouvelle Revue Française, 1918);

Walt Whitman, *Œuvres choisies,* translated by Gide and others (Paris: Nouvelle Revue Française, 1918);

William Shakespeare, *Antoine et Cléopâtre* (Paris: Vogel, 1921);

Tagore, *Amal et la lettre du roi* (Paris: Vogel, 1922);

William Blake, *Le Mariage du Ciel et de l'Enfer* (Paris: Claude Aveline, 1923);

Aleksandr Sergeevich Pushkin, *La Dame de pique,* translated by Gide, Jacques Schiffrin, and Boris de Scholezer (Paris: Pléiade, 1923);

Pushkin, *Nouvelles,* translated by Gide and Schiffrin (Paris: Pléiade/Schiffrin, 1928);

Shakespeare, *Hamlet, Acte premier* (Paris: La Tortue, 1930; Brussels: Décagone, 1944);

Johann Wolfgang von Goethe, "Second Faust: Fragment," *Nouvelle Revue Française,* 38 (March 1932);

Anonymous, *Arden de Feversham* (partial translation), *Cahiers du Sud* (June–July 1933);

Shakespeare, *Hamlet,* bilingual edition (New York: Schiffrin, 1944; Paris: Gallimard, 1946);

Goethe, *Prométhée* (Paris: Jonquière, 1951).

André Gide stated in a 1903 lecture (published in his *Œuvres complètes* [1932–1939], volume 4): "L'artiste ne peut se passer d'un public; et quand le public est absent, que fait-il? Il l'invente et . . . attend du futur ce que lui dénie le présent" (The artist cannot do without a public; and when the public is absent, what does he do? He invents it and . . . awaits from the future what the present denies him). Although he had already published strikingly original work and was respected by some of the literary elite, he spoke from the position of one needing still to find, or create, his readership. He is the sort of writer of whom Oscar Wilde spoke (see Gide's memoir in his *Œuvres complètes,* volume 3), whose works remain long misunderstood because they provide answers to questions not yet asked. His renown as an artist and a moral influence—whether healthy or, as many believed, corrupting—gradually grew throughout the first decades of the twentieth century; he had many admirers but also enemies and detractors, some of whom attacked him publicly. When, in 1947, he received an honorary doctorate from Oxford University, and that same year the Swedish Academy awarded him the Nobel Prize in Literature, it was obvious that he had found his audience, or the audience had found him, and that this audience had become international. Detractors remained, calling the honors exaggerated, undue, and his influence pernicious, but his fame remains firmly established as one of the most important French literary figures during the first half of the twentieth century, known for brilliantly crafted and highly original, if unsettling, works.

Gide's long list of published writings demonstrates his creative vigor and the varied, Protean character of both man and work. In addition to fiction (short narratives, usually called *récits* in French, one long novel, and a third type he called *soties*) and drama, his writings include literary criticism, art criticism, an autobiography, a book on the music of Frédéric Chopin, essays on social topics, and works that fit into no genre, including the unclassifiable *Les Nourritures terrestres* (1897; translated in *Fruits of the Earth,* 1949). Perhaps his greatest literary achievement is his journal, kept from 1887 until nearly his death. Both personal diary and writer's notebook, it is a model of incisive prose and keen insight. In addition, he was influential as an editor and a friend to other writers.

The connections between Gide's life and his work were close, the life nourishing the work and the work reflecting back into his life, revealing him to himself involuntarily, unconsciously, as he noted as early as 1891. His career offers an example of the phenomenon his lifetime friend poet Paul Valéry later identified (see Valéry's *Œuvres complètes,* volume 2): "L'oeuvre modifie l'auteur" (The work modifies the author). Notwithstanding these close connections between Gide's life and work, his overriding literary concerns were aesthetic: "L'oeuvre d'art ne doit rien prouver; ne peut rien prouver sans tricherie" (A work of art must not prove anything; cannot prove anything without cheating), he wrote in a letter to Jules Renard, published in *Nouveaux Prétextes* (1911; New Pretexts). In his "Chroniques de l'Ermitage" (1905), published in his *Œuvres complètes,* he asserted that morality was "une dépendance de l'esthétique" (dependent upon aesthetics). He prized style and argued for discipline, difficulty, and formalism in art. In a lecture titled "De l'évolution du théâtre" (On the Evolution of the Theater) in 1904 (*Œuvres complètes,* volume 4), he stated that "l'art naît de contrainte, vit de lutte, et meurt de liberté" (Art is born of constraint, lives on struggle, and dies from freedom). His interest in the particular, or individual, was real; but art, he believed, dealt ultimately with the general. "Il n'y a de vérité psychologique que particulière . . . mais il n'y a d'art que général" (There is only individual psychological truth, but only general art), he wrote in *Les Faux-Monnayeurs* (1925; translated as *The Counterfeiters,* 1927). His works are characterized by great stylization and generalization, or what he called "erosion of contours," characteristic of classicism.

Yet, Gide was also a moralist, in the established French sense—one who both portrays mores and raises moral questions. "Mon rôle," he wrote, "est d'inquiéter" (My role is to disturb). His is not, however, a literature of edification; as he wrote (*Œuvres complètes,* volume 9), "C'est avec les beaux sentiments que l'on fait la mauvaise littérature" (It is with fine sentiments that one makes bad literature). The strong vein of moral rigor and self-searching in his work may reflect the influence of Protestant Christianity. More often, and more favorably, it is an innovative personal ethic, born of individual discipline and directed toward self-development.

Gide's themes include sincerity, happiness, freedom, responsibility and consequences, individualism and self-discovery, desire, destiny, and religion. Passions and other motivations interested him, whether they destroy or enhance human beings. "Je n'aime pas les hommes; j'aime ce qui les dévore" (I do not love men; I love what devours them), says Prometheus in *Le Prométhée mal enchaîné* (1899; translated as *Prometheus Illbound*, 1919). A further characteristic of his writing is self-projection: characters not only speak for the author but serve as varied selves, illustrating his potentialities and contradictions. His major works feature characters with traits that, when not counterbalanced or controlled, take over the personality and lead to extraordinary conduct. "L'oeuvre d'art est une exagération" (The work of art is an exaggeration), he wrote in his journal in 1892. In a letter to Ary Scheffer, published in his *Œuvres complètes* and written soon after Scheffer had spoken in print of Gide's *L'Immoraliste* (1902; translated as *The Immoralist*, 1930), Gide explained one of his ways of proceeding as an artist:

> Que de bourgeons nous portons en nous, cher Scheffer, qui n'écloront jamais que dans nos livres! . . . Mais si, par volonté, on les supprime tous, *sauf un,* comme il croît aussitôt, comme il grandit! . . . Pour créer un héros ma recette est bien simple: Prendre un de ces bourgeons, le mettre en pot—tout seul—on arrive bientôt à un individu admirable.
>
> (How many buds we bear within ourselves, dear Scheffer, which will never blossom except in our books! . . . But if, by design, one suppresses them all, *except one,* how it grows at once, how it gets big! . . . To create a hero my recipe is very simple: Take one of these buds, put it in a pot—all alone—and soon one has an wondrous individual.)

The artist resembles a horticulturalist who removes most of the buds from a stalk in order for those remaining to develop and blossom extraordinarily. Aesthetically, the effect is focus, drama, perhaps tragedy. For the artist, it is something like catharsis. As early as 1893 Gide wrote in *La Tentative amoureuse; ou, Le Traité du vain désir* (translated as *The Lovers' Attempt*, 1953):

> Nos livres n'auront pas été les récits très véridiques de nous-mêmes,—mais plutôt de nos plaintifs désirs, le souhait d'autres vies à jamais défendues, de tous les gestes impossibles. Ici j'écris un rêve qui dérangeait par trop ma pensée et réclamait son existence. . . . Chaque livre n'est plus qu'une tentation différée.
>
> (Our books will not be the accurate accounts of ourselves,—but rather of our plaintive desires, the wish for other lives forbidden always, for all impossible deeds. Here I write a dream that bothered my thought excessively and demanded to exist. . . . Each book is only a temptation postponed.)

Gide's life was one of internal, sometimes external, conflict, the currents of which shaped his entire work and ultimately drew to him a tremendously varied readership. He wrote in the note appended to part one of his autobiography, *Si le grain ne meurt* (1920, 1921; translated as *If It Die . . .*, 1935): "Je suis un être de dialogue; tout en moi combat et se contredit" (I am a being of dialogue; everything in me fights and contradicts itself). One who saw his existence in dramatic terms was the Catholic poet Paul Claudel, long a correspondent despite their disagreements; he wrote in a letter dated July 1926: "Vous êtes l'enjeu, l'acteur et le théâtre d'une grande lutte" (You are the stakes, actor, and theater of a great struggle). In his introduction to Gide's *L'Oroscope* (1995, The Mountain Watcher), critic Daniel Durosay suggests that Gide's existence was "fondée sur le mal-être et son dépassement" (founded on ill-being and its surpassing).

Born on 22 November 1869, André Paul Guillaume Gide was the only child of Paul Gide, a Paris law professor from a southern family, and his wife, Juliette (née Rondeaux), who came from Normandy and had considerable personal wealth. Both parents were of Calvinist lineage, though the Rondeaux family had been Catholic until the late eighteenth century, and a collateral branch reverted to the Roman Church. Gide stressed in *Si le grain ne meurt* his dual and opposing heritage, northern and southern, Catholic and Protestant. In practice, Protestant belief and its severe morality dominated his boyhood and early youth, and, though he struggled against it, in some ways he never freed himself entirely from its legacy, both enriching and burdensome. His highly developed individualistic sense derived in part from belonging to a tiny minority (the French population was approximately 2 percent Protestant around 1900).

Gide was a solitary child, with few playmates, though the famous opening scene from *Si le grain ne meurt* depicts him playing with the concierge's son. From 1877 until late October 1880 he attended the Ecole Alsacienne, a private school, with interruptions (three months' suspension for unseemly conduct and absence for illness). Upon his father's death in late October 1880, when Gide was not quite eleven, his mother took him to Normandy, then Montpellier. Upon their return to Paris, he re-enrolled in the Ecole Alsacienne but was withdrawn shortly because of what were termed nervous troubles. After studying with private tutors, he returned and graduated with a baccalaureate in 1889. He was surrounded by women—mother, aunt, his mother's former governess, and various Norman cousins. Among the latter was Madeleine Rondeaux, slightly older than he. From adolescence on, he favored her for her reserve, tact, and intelligence. By chance, he discovered her mother in the arms of a man not her husband, and then realized that Madeleine was aware of her mother's infidelity and was deeply hurt by it. She became, as he wrote in *Si le grain ne meurt*, "un nouvel orient de ma vie" (a new orientation of my life), and he vowed to protect her thenceforth.

Gide's obvious narcissism was demonstrated early by his fascination with mirrors and by his diary, which, in its published form, dates from 1887. In the eyes of certain psychological critics such as Thomas Cordle, narcissism remained a permanent feature of his psyche. Having no obligation to choose a profession, because of his personal fortune, Gide embarked on a literary career. His talent was recognized early by his elders—including poet Stéphane Mallarmé—and contemporaries, among them Pierre Louis (later Louÿs) at the Ecole Alsacienne, and Valéry, whom he met in Montpellier in 1890. He contributed to little magazines and in 1891 published anonymously, at his expense, his début work, *Les Cahiers d'André Walter* (translated as *The Notebooks of André Walter*, 1968), an overblown first-person confessional narrative in diary form with many retrospective passages. Its purpose was to induce Madeleine Rondeaux to marry him; instead, it apparently frightened her, and she refused his proposal. Only a few copies were sold. Though marked by the influence of earlier works in French and German centered on introspective, idealistic, suffering heroes (usually artists), the *récit* shows originality in its individual voice, its sensitive style that registers nuances of feeling and conveys well affective experiences, and its compositional features, involving symmetry, contrast, and reflexivity. The given name *André* suggests identity between its hero and the author; *Walter,* from the German, echoes Johann Wolfgang von Goethe's *The Sorrows of Young Werther* (1774). The proximity of character to author is increased by the verbatim reproduction of entries drawn from Gide's own diary. Moreover, Walter intends to write a book, "Allain," and incorporates parts of it into his diary—just as Gide included in his notebooks material for future works. This *récit* offers the first of many instances in his fiction of a writer-character and a book-within-the-book, planned or partly realized. Each writer—Gide, Walter in his diary, Allain in his diary—is a double of the others. Walter's book is to deal with the Angel and the Beast, or soul and flesh—which are the crux of Gide's work also.

The book is in two parts, "Le Cahier blanc" (The White Notebook) and "Le Cahier noir" (The Black Notebook). In the first, Walter expresses love for his cousin Emmanuèle (the meaning of which is "God with us") through idealistic reveries, evocations of music, quotations from German and French poets, and lyrical flights. This love is not a sensual one, however; he says that he fears wounding her by desire and aspires to a disembodied purity. In fact, he fears the senses: "Je ne te désire pas" (I do not desire you); he frantically flees women in the street as if they might pollute him. His mother, on her deathbed, has told him his love is "fraternal" and urged him to let Emmanuèle go so that she may marry "T." Consenting to the separation, Walter resolves to drive her away, in order to deserve her all the more: love is proven by sacrifice. In the second part, Walter learns that Emmanuèle is dead. Desires assail him, but he considers all sensuality impure. He dreams of brown-skinned children bathing in the river, and of a woman—Emmanuèle—whose dress is lifted up by a monkey, revealing nothing but darkness. The notebooks close with Walter's insanity and death of cerebral fever.

While Gide acknowledged later the adolescent excesses of the book, he allowed its reprinting. Its themes, motifs, and technical features established precedents for works to come. Not least of these precedents was the expression of profound personal dilemmas for either analysis or catharsis or both. Another was the use of fiction, through the dual narrative levels and an author-within-the-book, to explore the fictional process and reflect the play of the real versus the fictitious, creating what twentieth-century critics called metafiction. There is even an outer level: the notebooks are ostensibly presented (through a footnote creating a frame) by Walter's friend, Pierre C., who is taken to be Pierre Chrysis, a pseudonym of Gide's real friend Louÿs—for informed readers, a clue to the uncertain fictional status of the work. In his journal in 1893 Gide proposed the term *la composition en abyme* ("abyss" structure, or structure in depth) for the compositional device that reproduces a work within itself by miniaturized replication of its themes, motifs, story elements, or structural features, and thus creates reflexivity. This reflexivity may go beyond the fictional limits of the work to include external elements (such as the oblique introduction of Louÿs), in a confusion between what Gérard Genette called the diegesis, or diegetic level—the fictional plane—and the extradiegetic level, outside of the novel. While some of these techniques had been used variously in previous centuries, notably by Denis Diderot, it was

Gide who gave them their modern currency, in advance of their subsequent widespread appearance in works by French New Novelists such as Michel Butor, Alain Robbe-Grillet, and Claude Simon.

The same year, 1891, Gide published *Le Traité du Narcisse* (translated as *Narcissus*, 1953), dedicated to Valéry, who wrote several poems on the theme. The term *traité*, meaning *treatise*, suggests the philosophical character of this short prose work. Abandoning his overblown lyricism under the influence of Mallarmé, whose Tuesday gatherings he attended, and other symbolists, he adopted their aesthetic of refined, ethereal, sometimes hermetic images, chastized style, disdain of contingency, and aspirations toward the absolute. Though he eventually went beyond the symbolist view of literature, its demanding aesthetic remained a benchmark for him, and he honored Mallarmé as a master. The treatise served as an unofficial manifesto for the symbolist aesthetic. The choice of Narcissus—one of many occasions on which Gide turned to Greek mythology—is representative of the inward-turning quality of symbolism as well as the author's narcissism. Even the characteristic structural reflexivity, including the use of notebooks, can be considered an expression of narcissism.

The treatise begins with a restatement of the myth of Narcissus, who seeks to integrate appearance and being, form and idea—that is, the unity and perfection of self. It then moves to the story of Eden (treated as myth, not Holy Writ), in which original perfection is destroyed by a gesture, causing unity to disperse as multiplicity. Since then, man has yearned for the lost perfection, the union of world and idea, fleeting appearance and changeless being. (The influence of Platonism as well as of Arthur Schopenhauer's *The World as Will and Idea* [1819] is visible here.) The poet strives to rediscover this union, using symbols to arrive at truths and essences. The poet, writes Gide, must manifest: "Nous vivons pour manifester" (We live in order to manifest), he had written in *Les Cahiers d'André Walter*. The verb became a motif and key to his artistic endeavors.

Another early work, *La Tentative amoureuse*, is a short "treatise" on love in the form of an understated tale. Its importance is threefold—in plot, tone, and structure. Its story—Luc and Rachel's failure to draw meaning from love or preserve it—reinforces Walter's denial of normal sexuality and is psychologically revealing. Its tone has a new hint of irony, one of Gide's primary modes later. Its structure illustrates again *la composition en abyme*, a term that he adopted in speaking of it.

Le Voyage d'Urien (translated as *Urien's Voyage*, 1964) appeared in 1893 and achieved a small *succès d'estime*. Since the title may be rephrased as "Le Voyage du Rien"—the voyage of Nothing—the work may be said to bear an ironic qualification from the beginning. Nevertheless, it is a richly imaginative tale in which the travels are correlatives of spiritual experiences. It thus carried out the symbolist aesthetic, by which the real was valuable only as an opening onto the ideal. As Gide explained in the preface to the second edition, the landscapes and episodes are the visible equivalents of emotions that cannot be expressed or grasped otherwise. As in traditional quests, the travelers—sailors, in this case, but with chivalric features—must pass through ordeals and temptations, to which some of the party succumb. The first stage is the Pathetic Ocean, where various sensual trials await; the next is the Sargasso Sea, where the voyagers fall into stagnation and ennui; the final stage is the Glacial Sea, representing metaphysical sterility and what Gide calls, sarcastically, "joies théologiques" (theological joys). The few voyagers who escape temptation are not rewarded by the ideal; rather, they find, on the frozen wasteland, only nothingness—a man encased in ice and holding a blank paper.

Mallarmé expressed his relief at learning that Gide's book was not the account of a real voyage, but a parable. Gide's *envoi* (a sort of postface in verse) to the book makes that clear: "Madame . . . nous n'avons pas fait ce voyage. . . . Ce voyage n'est que mon rêve, / nous ne sommes jamais sortis / de la chambre de nos pensées" (Madam, we did not make this voyage. . . . This voyage is only my dream, / we have never left / the room of our thoughts). Replete with features of the most excessive symbolists and decadent writers such as Joris-Karl Huysmans, the tale could read like the symbolist novel par excellence. But it was also a sabotaging of symbolism. Cordle has suggested that the white sheet of paper stands for Mallarmé, whose obsession with blank pages and fascination with abstraction were attested, and mention of a "swan-killing knife" may be an aggressive allusion to him also, since "Le Cygne" (1885, The Swan) was one of Mallarmé's best-known poems. Moreover, beneath the self-consciously literary and philosophic parable lies another level, expressed in abundant sexual images and episodes of carnality involving predatory (and diseased) women. Then there is the sketchy female character "Ellis," the "false"—a momentary temptation—and the "true," who is encountered in the polar snows; the latter ascends into heaven in a wedding gown, expressing plainly the impossibility of pure love on earth. Normal sexuality, whether with a temptress or a cherished figure, is excluded.

All Gide's publications through 1893 suggested failure, whether metaphysical (an unreachable, perhaps false ideal) or personal (impossible love, madness, quest ending in nothing). A developing vein of irony indicated, however, personal evolution; and his artistic skills were amply demonstrated. In October 1894 he left for North Africa, accompanying a friend who had won a traveling fellowship. He did not take his Bible, though he later asked his mother to send it. This journey, the first of many to Algeria and Tunisia, was a watershed in his life. (He later traveled widely elsewhere also.) He began by falling ill of pulmonary infection, probably tuberculosis; the episodes in *L'Immoraliste* concerning the hero's illness are considered a transposition of the author's experience. Having recovered, he was eager for sensations and discoveries. The foreign setting, in which he was surrounded by a subjected people (indigenous Arabs), favored his experimentation. He discarded his inhibitions, broke the Calvinist taboos, and discovered—or admitted to himself—his homosexual desires, of which his early writings bore unmistakable traces. In *Si le grain ne meurt,* the 1893 episode during which he makes love to a small boy on a dune comes late in the account of his boyhood and youth but is the key discovery to which earlier parts are a prelude.

As he wrote in *Si le grain ne meurt,* he had laid the foundation for a lifetime personal ethic, "un idéal d'équilibre, de plénitude et de santé" (an ideal of balance, fullness, and health). Oscillation between belief and nonbelief characterized him for many years, but he subscribed no longer to any doctrinaire Christianity and disliked all organized religion. A solution to his theological dilemma was to deny the validity of all proscriptions based on the Bible and fashion a new image of Christ—a vagabond, a freethinking rebel who promised heaven here and now and denied validity to the law in the name of love. Gide long retained, however, the sense of sin imparted to him by his upbringing. "Je ne suis qu'un petit garçon qui s'amuse, doublé d'un pasteur protestant qui le regarde" (I am just a little boy having fun, doubled by a Protestant pastor watching him), he wrote in his journal in 1907.

Like Protestantism when he was a child, homosexuality set him apart from others; in his new self-consciousness, he was doubly an outsider. He insisted always that he was not a sodomist but a pederast, drawn to boys and adolescents. While he did not announce his sexual anomaly until the 1920s, it continued to appear obliquely in many works, and the desire to "manifest" himself consisted largely, though not wholly, in revealing and justifying his sexuality. (He could not live without such autojustification.) He assigned great importance, both personal and social, to the confessional function of *Si le grain ne meurt* and other works and to his case as exemplary. Certain early critics, hesitant to speak of sexual matters, glossed over intimations of his behavior to the degree possible, or, if hostile, seized upon the suggestions and ultimate confirmation of his pederasty to condemn him as immoral. In contrast, critics of the last decades of the twentieth century and of the twenty-first have shown great interest in Gide's sexual history and its reflection in his work, and many erroneously make sexuality the overriding concern of his entire career.

After returning from North Africa in spring 1894, Gide resumed his literary contacts among the symbolist circles, which stifled him and, by their denial of vitality, gave him, he wrote, a feeling of "estrangement." In the autumn he spent some months in a Swiss village, La Brévine, where he composed *Paludes* (1895; translated as *Marshlands,* 1953). He later gave to this work the generic label *sotie* (foolishness), from the name of a type of medieval farce. In a prefatory note, he calls it "cette satire de quoi?" (this satire of what?). An obvious target is the claustrophobic Paris salons; another is a writer who much resembles himself. To carry out this satire, Gide makes clever use of the *en abyme* structure. The main character, a would-be writer, is at work on a book to be called "Paludes," which will be "l'histoire de qui ne peut pas voyager" (the story of one who cannot travel). He keeps a diary, constituting the text, portraying his mostly valetudinarian friends and recording his modest activities and accomplishments. In the diary are incorporated notes for the "Journal de Tityre, ou Paludes," his work-in-progress; Tityre, he says, is himself. He has a jejune woman friend, Angèle. Her name recalls what French critics call the *angélisme* (disposition or aspiration to act as a pure spirit) of *Les Cahiers d'André Walter,* while her tone, slightly whimsical and also critical, resembles that of the false Ellis. The name Angèle also appears in Gide's *Lettres à Angèle, 1898–1899* (1900), a collection of short pieces that appeared separately during the 1890s. While Angèle cannot be considered simply a projection of Madeleine Rondeaux, she is not entirely divorced from her either. One event of the otherwise colorless plot, which suggests the boredom of Paris literary life, is a duck hunt (with sexual innuendoes), recounted in Angèle's salon; another is a trip to the suburbs. After a week, no progress has been made on the book. The hero sits down instead to begin a new project, "Polders" (unclaimed marshlands).

This circular construction, indicating repetition without progress, contrasts with the actual book, which Gide did finish. Other features call attention to the arbitrariness of any narrative and explicitly invite confusion between the diegetic and extradiegetic levels. An opening note invites readers to explain the book to the "author," that is, an authorial persona, noting that a book is always a collaboration. (Gide thus anticipates "reader reception criticism" by many years.) An *envoi* in verse is followed by an "Alternative" in prose, then by the "Table des phrases les plus remarquables de *Paludes*" (Table of the Most Remarkable Sentences in *Paludes*), which includes two sentences (one concerned with carrying out the ideas the other one raises) and then invites the reader to fill in the rest of the page.

In January 1895 Gide returned to Algiers, where he encountered Wilde. Although Wilde rather frightened him, he helped Gide affirm his homosexuality, in part by introducing him to homosexual brothels. Gide's family, while ignorant of his precise conduct, was nevertheless uneasy. Shortly after his mother's death in May 1895, Madeleine Rondeaux agreed to marry him; his mother had expressed her desire that they wed, and his uncle Charles Gide was among those who considered the marriage a precautionary move. The wedding took place in October of that year. The couple spent a lengthy honeymoon in Switzerland, Italy, and North Africa. The marriage remained unconsummated. Personal writings by Gide and others' testimony indicate that despite the devotion of each to the other, it was an unhappy arrangement; evidence suggests that Madeleine Gide became aware early of her husband's proclivities. Although they traveled together early in their marriage, subsequently they often lived apart in unacknowledged half-estrangement, he traveling or in Paris, she at their estate in Normandy, Cuverville.

In 1897 Gide published *Les Nourritures terrestres,* an eight-part work, chiefly lyrical and hortatory, with interspersed narrative elements. It sold so few copies that booksellers were said to beg for buyers; but it gradually acquired readers and became a favorite of discerning young people, especially after World War I. Novelist Roger Martin du Gard had his young hero Jacques Thibault discover the book and thereby see life in an entirely new light. The work was inspired in considerable part by the author's experiences in North Africa, reflected in scenery and motifs. Normandy also serves as a setting, however. The speaker is often an anonymous Gide-like character who sometimes addresses a young disciple, Nathanaël. Another speaker is Ménalque, who serves as an older model; the name is from Virgil, whose works, along with those of Goethe, were influential on Gide. Certain phrases from *Les Nourritures terrestres* are so often quoted that they have become clichés among educated French.

The work is a call to emancipation and cultivation of the self. First, one must reject impediments to self-development, such as rules and the very idea of sin. "Nathanaël, je ne crois plus au péché" (Nathanaël, I no longer believe in sin); "Commandements de Dieu, vous avez endolori mon âme" (Commandments of God, you have made my soul sorrowful). A vague, lyrical pantheism must replace orthodox Christian belief: "Ne souhaite pas, Nathanaël, trouver Dieu ailleurs que partout" (Do not wish, Nathanaël, to find God elsewhere than everywhere). Social structures also must be rejected: "Familles, je vous hais!" (Families, I hate you!). Bookish learning is to be replaced by sensation: "Il ne me suffit pas de *lire* que les sables des plages sont doux; je veux que mes pieds nus le sentent" (It is not enough for me to *read* that the sands along the beach are soft; I want my bare feet to feel it). Desire, whether fulfilled or unfulfilled, is the key to *ferveur* (fervor), Gide's new watchword, the measure of the soul's authenticity. "L'image de la vie, ah! Nathanaël, est pour moi: un fruit plein de saveur sur des lèvres pleines de désir" (The image of life, ah! Nathanaël, is for me: a fruit full of savor on lips full of desire). The listener or reader must cultivate his own individuality: "Jette mon livre" (Throw away my book); then he can follow the final precept: "Crée de toi . . . le plus irremplaçable des êtres" (Create from yourself . . . the most irreplaceable of beings).

Gide then turned to drama. He viewed the theater as "le lieu de caractères" (the place of characters), where individual truths are pretexts for generalization. In his view, Christianity discouraged characters—strong individual personalities—and no entirely Christian theater could exist. His dramatic corpus relies on Greek and biblical material, both treated freely. Critic Paul Surer asserted in his *Cinquante ans de théâtre* (1969, Fifty Years of Theater) that Gide was "le premier à deviner le parti qu'un dramaturge pouvait tirer des légendes bibliques ou des fictions antiques pour exprimer son éthique personnelle ou des préoccupations toutes modernes" (the first to perceive the advantage that a playwright could draw from biblical legends or ancient tales to express his personal ethic or quite modern concerns). Gide's plays illustrate especially well the rich potential of mythology for modern applications. But for decades he barely had a theatrical public.

Saül (translated, 1952) was finished in 1898, published in 1903, then produced by Jacques Copeau (who had the title role) at the Vieux-Colombier in 1922. According to Martin du Gard, it was one of Gide's best works. Based on material from I Samuel 17, 18, and 28, the five-act drama depicts King Saul's undoing, politically and personally. It was a warning, said Gide, against the hedonism and self-indulgence to which *Les Nourritures terrestres* invited readers. Such swings between renunciation and self-gratification are characteristic of Gide's works and often his behavior. The premier was, in Gide's own words, "un four" (a flop). Attendance was good throughout the run, but reviews less so. As a psychological drama involving an unknown self, the play is modern, despite the biblical basis. (Gide had encountered writings by Friedrich Nietzsche in the 1890s and was drawn to, or had developed independently, elements of their ethics.) Saül exclaims: "Je deviens très étonnant!—Ma valeur est dans ma complication" (I am becoming very astonishing!—My value lies in my complexity).

Saül is a deranged personality struggling for self-knowledge and self-control, torn between strength and weakness. He is beset by demons—actual actors—representing his temptations and weaknesses. "Tout ce qui t'est charmant t'est hostile" (Everything that is charming to you is hostile to you), says the pythoness of Endor. He tries to cultivate his will; instead, it disintegrates. His self-ignorance makes him vulnerable: "Ils veulent savoir mon secret et je ne le sais pas moi-même!" (They want to know my secret and I don't know it myself!). As the Philistines besiege the kingdom, Saül, having exterminated the soothsayers, has attempted vainly to read the stars. The queen and others try to manipulate him by introducing as their spy the handsome shepherd David, who shortly kills Goliath. When David befriends Jonathan, the king's weak son, the king feels jealousy. Saül is obviously fascinated with David, and the love between David and Jonathan, while never explicitly sexual, does suggest homoerotic attraction. The homosexual suggestions have often been noted; according to Martin du Gard's *Journal* (1992–1993), his friend Pierre Margaritis wrote that despite his admiration, he was bothered by the "côté pédéraste" (pederastic side). Demons, having assumed attractive forms, settle in Saül's tent. He asks: "Avec quoi l'homme se consolera-t-il d'une déchéance? sinon avec ce qui l'a déchu" (With what will a man be consoled after a downfall? if not with what brought him down). The political solution comes when David replaces Saül as king; the personal solution is Saül's death at the hands of a treacherous courtier.

Philoctète (1899; translated as *Philoctetes*, 1952), a subject treated also by Sophocles, was, according to Gide's prefatory note, a moral treatise, not intended for presentation. It has been staged, however. With its elevated tone, long speeches, simple plot involving a moral dilemma, and few actors, this short five-act work resembles French classical dramas inspired by Greek models. The play includes themes typical of Gide's work: competing rights and duties; the individual; and, chiefly, self-discipline and self-sacrifice. Philoctète, bitten by a serpent and suffering a stinking wound, has been abandoned on a frozen, deserted island by his compatriots, armed only with his bow and arrows (a legacy from Heracles). The gods having decreed that those weapons alone can prevail against the Trojans, Ulysse and young Néoptolème, Achilles' son, have been sent to wrest them from Philoctète by ruse. Néoptolème protests against the use of treachery toward his father's friend; Ulysse argues that reasons of state outweigh and must prevail over individual rights and ethics, following divine will. But Philoctète observes: "Au-dessus des dieux . . . il y a quelque chose" (Above the gods . . . there is something else). The problem is identifying the higher good. In the end, trickery is not necessary: Philoctète surrenders the bow and arrows willingly, through devotion to something he cannot name—an internal rather than external imperative. "Ce que l'on entreprend au-dessus de ses forces . . . voilà ce qu'on appelle vertu" (What one undertakes beyond one's strength . . . that's what is called virtue).

The second of the farcical narratives that Gide later labeled *soties* appeared in 1899 under the title *Le Prométhée mal enchaîné*. Though short, it is important as well as original. While it includes the story of Prometheus, the myth is just a kernel of the story. Like *Paludes*, it is characterized by what the author called *le saugrenu*—a type of absurdity involving incongruity and bizarre humor. Like all of Gide's *saugrenu* and irony, it is pointed. Prométhée kills the eagle who ate his liver—a clear rejection of the idea of punishment, and thus of morality. The work is connected intertextually to *Paludes* by its character Tityre, who appears in both works in a story-within-the-story. Moreover, it similarly calls attention to itself as fiction when, at the end, Prométhée, having eaten his dead eagle, announces he used one of its feathers to write the book that the reader has just finished, thereby confusing diegetic and extradiegetic planes. A brief epilogue reinforces this element of metafiction by denying authorial omnipotence: "Pour tâcher de faire croire au lecteur que si ce livre est tel ce n'est pas la faute de l'auteur" (To try to make the reader believe that if this book is such as it is, it isn't the author's fault). Just as important, the work is the first introduction into Gide's work of the important concept and plot resource he called *l'acte gratuit*, or gratuitous act—an arbitrary deed that sets in motion an unpredictable chain of consequences. Gide treats it as an illustration of human freedom, which allows man to go beyond the needed, the predictable, and to invent behavior.

Le Roi Candaule (translated as *King Candaules*, 1952), published in 1901, was first produced that year by Aurélien Lugné-Poe, who resisted realist modes in favor of poetic drama. The play, in three acts and free verse, closed after its first performance; the few laudatory reviews were offset by several attacks. Greatly disappointed, Gide indicted his contemporaries by observing that drama can flourish only in the absence of public hypocrisy. The story of *Le Roi Candaule* has a basis in both fact and fable. Sources include the *Clio* of Herodotus and Plato's *Republic*. In Gide's version, the emphasis is on character and motivation, not the marvelous. The historical character Gyges was king of Lydia in the seventh century B.C. According to Plato, Gyges, a humble shepherd in the royal service, discovered a ring with the power to make its wearer invisible. Armed with the ring, he slipped into the palace of King Candaules, seduced the queen and murdered Candaules, then acceded to the throne and married the queen. Herodotus, in contrast, presents Gyges as a trusted member of the king's bodyguard. The king, having often praised his wife's beauty to Gyges, finally had him observe her in her bedchamber; for this betrayal, she compelled Gyges to kill Candaules and take the throne. His assumption of power was justified after the fact by the Delphic oracle.

Like *Saül, Le Roi Candaule* illustrates self-destruction. Candaule's excessive and misplaced generosity amounts to manipulating and experimenting with others. He seeks to dazzle those around him, including Gygès, a poor fisherman, with his wealth and happiness, then to impose them, on the pretext that privileges are not complete unless shared. (The theme of voluntary divestiture, intended to create greater freedom and enjoyment, appears also in *Les Nourritures terrestres* and *L'Immoraliste*. Gide himself displayed contradictory impulses with respect to wealth, oscillating between acquisition and divestiture, thrift and expenditure.) Such imposition is a means of controlling others; the king's annoyance when his gifts are not thoroughly appreciated shows that his generosity is really directed toward himself.

His scheme to have Gygès observe Queen Nyssia's beauty by becoming invisible succeeds: Gygès observes her, unseen, then shares her bed without disclosing his identity. When Nyssia tells Candaule that it was their greatest night of love, he is shaken; his gift has turned back on him. Gide is less interested, however, in Candaule's sexual discomfiture than in questions of power and conduct. Learning how her husband betrayed her, Nyssia, as in the legend, compels Gygès to kill him. He then assumes the throne and obliges the queen, who has removed her veils, since modesty was mocked, to replace them. Power under his reign will be exercised directly, not through mediation. Contemporary and later readings of the play as a socialist manifesto conflict with Gide's aesthetics.

In 1902 Gide published his *récit* or short novel *L'Immoraliste,* one of his best narrative works, admired for its style, composition, narrative technique, and psychology, including absence of self-knowledge, or obtuseness. Gide's genius for pithy observations and *litotes* (condensed sayings or understatements) is well illustrated throughout: for example, "Envier le bonheur d'autrui, c'est folie: on ne saurait pas s'en servir" (To envy others' happiness is folly; one wouldn't know what to do with it). Michel, the protagonist-narrator, an early example of the modern unreliable narrator, tells his story, without commentary, to three friends he has summoned (an echo of Job's listeners). This narrative is framed within an outer one, consisting of a letter written by one of the listeners and including Michel's account so that the addressee, a high government official, may take his case under consideration. The outer narrator's voice is heard again at the close of Michel's account. It may be assumed that the protagonist's retrospective version is self-serving, although not crudely so; he can be self-critical. But what is not said plays a role along with what is expressed. The listeners, and readers, must draw their own conclusions.

Largely based on Gide's own experiences, the story nevertheless departs from them significantly. It may be viewed as an example of the *bourgeon* or "bud" theory and an occasion for catharsis, since, as the author later noted, Michel errs by carrying too far the hedonism and emancipation praised in *Les Nourritures terrestres*. While Michel's demons are entirely psychological, unlike the projected demons in *Saül,* the resulting self-destruction is identical. The novel is an early-twentieth-century lesson in the dangers of freedom: "Savoir se libérer n'est rien; l'ardu, c'est savoir être libre" (To be able to liberate oneself is nothing; the difficult part is to know how to be free).

In part 1, Michel, a bookish young Protestant scholar, marries at his father's wish. He and his wife, Marceline, travel to Algeria for their honeymoon. He falls ill of pulmonary disease; she helps nurse him back to health. As his strength increases, he ventures out alone and meets Arab boys, whom he befriends. Their health, rawness, and amorality appeal to him; when he observes one stealing Marceline's scissors, he is strangely fascinated. He abandons his ethics of high culture, work, and traditional beliefs, all directed either to past or future, for values he does not quite fathom, based in the present, presupposing freedom and involving pleasure and self-cultivation. The couple returns to Europe via Italy. After a struggle with a disorderly and presumably drunken coachman, Michel makes love to his wife for the first time.

Part 2 takes place in Normandy, on La Morinière, an estate modeled on Gide's property La Roque-Baignard, which he sold in 1900. Michel has embarked on a program of self-development and scientific exploitation of his property, following a new ethic of economy, directed toward maximizing resources. Marceline is pregnant. Michel is fascinated by a young man, the son of his overseer. He spends some time in Paris also, lecturing and visiting salons, where he runs into Ménalque. The latter is no longer the underdeveloped Virgilian figure of *Les Nourritures terrestres,* expressing himself lyrically, but a semiplausible modern character, based in part on Wilde. Ménalque does not seek disciples; rather, he listens, asks questions, and lets his interlocutors make discoveries in themselves. He draws Michel's attention to his desire to go beyond ordinary ethics to identify a "new man." (Gide makes use of the biblical distinction between the "old man" of the law, before grace, and the "new man" of salvation.) Ménalque suggests that his friend's lectures, property, and wife conflict with unfettered self-exploration. One night, while Michel is with Ménalque, Marceline has a miscarriage. Back in Normandy, Michel, greatly changed, takes up with the coarsest of his neighbors. He listens to tales of incest; learns with indifference, even curiosity, that his own staff robs him; and even poaches on his own property while paying his overseer to discover poachers' traps. In a fit of exasperation, or desire to divest himself of impediments to a new life, he sells La Morinière.

In part 3, the couple leaves again for Italy and Algeria. Marceline is ill; Michel must care for her. He professes the deepest love for her, but his actions belie his concern: he makes her move frequently, prowls around the port in Syracuse seeking adventure, and shows impatience with her: "J'ai cherché, j'ai trouvé ce qui fait ma valeur: une espèce d'entêtement dans le pire" (I have sought, I have found the source of my value: a kind of persistence in the worst). She becomes so fragile that the scent of almond flowers makes her ill. After her death he summons his friends, admitting that "je ne sais plus le dieu ténébreux que je sers" (I no longer know what dark god I serve). He asks his friends to tear him away: "Je souffre de cette liberté sans emploi" (I suffer from this freedom without use). What he needs, he says, is something to prove he has not gone beyond his right. The ending illustrates a major twentieth-century problem, that of individual freedom and its use. No solution is offered. There is also a final suggestion of pederastic desire. Albert Guerard is one critic among many who have seen in Michel an unaware homosexual; Gide admitted the validity of the interpretation. But the *récit* is less concerned with any sexual problem than with the existential questions of freedom and the foundation of values.

Gide's acquaintance with Claudel dated from the 1890s, when they met in Paris. The two began corresponding in 1899, while Claudel was in China. In 1905 Claudel returned to France on leave; Gide read his ode "Les Muses" (The Muses) and met with him. Gide was, at the time, in low spirits. *Les Nourritures terrestres, Saül,* and *Le Roi Candaule* had been popular failures; *L'Immoraliste* had sold few copies. He was respected in the most discriminating literary circles, but he had not achieved significant success. His inspiration may have fallen; apart from a collection of critical articles and a few other pages, he wrote nothing new for five years. His sixth journey to North Africa (Algeria and Tunisia) in 1903 did not break his writer's paralysis. In 1904 he wrote in his journal: "Depuis le 25 octobre 1901, jour où j'achevais *L'Immoraliste,* je n'ai plus sérieusement travaillé. . . . Un morne engourdissement de l'esprit me fait végéter depuis trois ans" (For three years, since 25 October 1901, the day when I finished *L'Immoraliste,* I have not worked seriously. . . . A gloomy deadening of the mind has made me vegetate).

Moreover, his personal life was not calm. The pursuit of boys, in which he engaged with his friend Henri Ghéon, a physician and writer whom he had met in 1897, made dissimulation with Madeleine Gide and others necessary and brought frustration as well as satisfaction. The liaison in which the two engaged in 1905 with Maurice Schlumberger, the younger brother of novelist Jean Schlumberger, brought further drama into Gide's life. Claudel, sensing a disturbed man, seized upon the opportunity to attempt to convert Gide to Roman Catholicism. Gide's ability to share others' feelings–which he called sympathy in its full sense–made him receptive to Claudel's initiatives. Shortly, however, he realized that he had ventured too far: though he had listened and even appeared ripe for conversion, in fact he could not seriously entertain the possibility.

A short work of 1907, *Le Retour de l'enfant prodigue* (translated as *The Return of the Prodigal,* 1953), was, by the author's admission, a reply to Claudel's conversion attempts. It consists almost entirely of dialogue but was not conceived as drama, though occasionally it has been brought to the stage. It treats the biblical material freely and idiosyncratically, but with respect, and is another statement of Gide's predilection for a free-thinking, rather vagabond Christ figure. Following Gide's conviction that institutions have distorted Christ's message, the parable becomes an indictment of the Roman Catholic Church, the "house" to which the prodigal son, weakened by hardship, returns. While the mother receives him with love and forgiveness, and the father with understanding, the elder brother, with his pretension to exclusive truth, speaks harshly. "Hors la Maison, point de salut pour toi" (Outside the house, there is no salvation for you) is his formula. Gide develops the parable further by adding a younger brother, who idolizes the prodigal and will imitate him. While others denounce the ethic of freedom, discovery, self-development, and what Gide called vagabondage, the boy's imminent departure signals their validity. As the boy leaves, the prodigal holds the lamp–his legacy of illumination. Despite this transparent statement, Claudel continued well into 1914 to urge Gide to convert.

In 1909 Gide helped found the preeminent literary monthly in twentieth-century France, *La Nouvelle Revue Française (NRF),* where for decades he was an important behind-the-scenes figure. In that year he published *La Porte étroite* (translated as *Strait Is the Gate,* 1924), another autobiographical narrative. The title refers to the narrow gate through which one must pass to be saved and thus underlines the difficulty of salvation. Claudel, writing to Gide, called it a very Protestant book. Gide stated that, like *L'Immoraliste,* it illustrated the dangers of extreme behavior–in this case, asceticism; the two works are antidotes to each other. Its structure and tone have been greatly admired, although some readers have found the protagonist's character irritating. The story is told by Jérôme, a passive young man, in love with his cousin, Alissa. It includes long passages from her letters and fragments of her diary.

The two share tastes in literature and music and are similarly pious, but there is no passion. Both fear intimate contacts, even hand-holding. Alissa, who calls sanctity an "obligation," places obstacles in the way of their marriage, though without refusing Jérôme's suit explicitly, and places before him what amount to tests of character and endurance. She denies the validity of happiness, foreign to the human soul; "nous ne sommes pas nés pour le bonheur" (we are not born for happiness). For herself, she makes "une vertu de la résistance" (a virtue out of resistance), and imposes this ethic upon him by what he calls a "piège de la vertu" (trap of virtue). By a bargain she imposes, he must cease seeing her and leave without protest on the evening when she will no longer wear the amethyst cross he has given her. He respects the agreement. On a subsequent visit, he finds that, pushing her renunciation ever farther, she has given up what she likes the most and also become a shadow of herself. When Jérôme protests, she accuses him of loving only an image of the past; she even blames him for having made her dream of love so lofty it could not be satisfied in this world. After Alissa's death, alone in a hospice, he reads some of her diary, and learns both of her wavering faith and her tardy (and questionable) admission to herself that he would have had to make only a gesture to overcome her denial of the flesh. The use of diary excerpts to offer correcting viewpoints on another's version of events later became an important technique for Gide.

In 1911 Gide published anonymously and clandestinely, in twelve copies and under the title *C.R.D.N.*, an apology for homosexuality, which in 1920 appeared under its full title, *Corydon*. Mass circulation and indication of authorship were out of the question in the moral climate prior to World War I. Gide was concerned, furthermore, about his wife; though she generally read his manuscripts, and he shared with her much of his intellectual and personal life, he wished for his darker side to remain concealed. The arguments by which he attempted to justify homosexual practice were drawn from both nature and history. That same year his *récit* called *Isabelle* was published. It is a frame narrative in which a first narrator, speaking as Gide, listens, with his friend the poet Francis Jammes, to an account given by a second narrator. The story, somewhat melodramatic, is more removed from Gide's life than the two previous *récits* and other earlier work; in that respect it constitutes progress toward less outwardly personal writing. It involves elements of mystery and romantic idealization, which is deflated by reality and mocked by the narrative devices; its critical dimension is thus integral to the structure.

Gide then embarked on his second longest narrative, titled *Les Caves du Vatican* (1914; translated as *The Vatican Swindle*, 1925). It reintroduced into early twentieth-century French fiction, which was excessively psychological, elements of what Jacques Rivière called the adventure novel, and it occupies an important place as a kind of rehearsal for *Les Faux-Monnayeurs*. The label *sotie*, which it bore (and which Gide then applied retrospectively to earlier works), is particularly apt because the medieval farce by that name mocked religious ceremonies. The work was originally conceived in 1893, the year in which the action takes place. Gide had chosen originally as an epigraph a quotation from Claudel's *L'Annonce faite à Marie* (1912; translated as *The Tidings Brought to Mary*, 1916). When, in 1913, Claudel discovered the title of the forthcoming work, he asked Gide to remove the epigraph; Gide complied. When Claudel read an excerpt in the *NRF*, he was shocked by a slightly scabrous passage and asked Gide not only to delete the offending lines but to repent of his sins. Gide refused to alter his text. The entire work was highly offensive to pious Catholics. Like earlier writings, it did not find its audience immediately; but in the 1920s its young hero and apparent amorality began to appeal to restless, rebellious youth, primed by Dada and Surrealism.

This five-part work has a complex structure, large cast of characters, and multiple plots and themes. It belies accusations that Gide had weak inventive powers. The tone ranges from the humorous, farcical, and burlesque to the mock-serious and, occasionally, the serious, grave, or tender. Unlike Gide's earlier narratives, it has no first-person narrator, though there are ironic authorial interventions that create distance between author and work, yet invite confusion between diegetic and extradiegetic planes. The following phrase illustrates the technique: "Lafcadio, mon ami, vous donnez dans un fait divers et ma plume vous abandonne" (Lafcadio, my friend, you're getting into the anecdotal and my pen is abandoning you). Elsewhere, the authorial voice denies its omniscience: "Je ne sais trop que penser de Carola Venitequa" (I don't quite know what to think of Carola Venitequa). The characters are often caricatures, befitting the burlesque tone and mockery of the book. Among the themes are belief and superstition; the Church as an institution; scientific knowledge and its reductionism; pompous, academic literature; social classes and manners; the individual versus society; illegitimacy (already appearing in *Isabelle* and an important theme later); sincerity; morality and responsibility; human potentiality; and the gratuitous act. Some are connected to the larger theme of being versus appearances, true versus false, or to that of freedom, or what the young hero, Lafcadio Wluiki, calls "la libre disposition de soi-même" (the free disposition of oneself).

The principal plotline, to which others are connected—Lafcadio uses the word "un carrefour" (an intersection)—concerns a swindle by which pious and wealthy Catholics, duped into believing that the pope has been kidnapped from his throne, imprisoned in the Vatican cellars, and replaced by an impostor, pay large sums to obtain his release. (The "caves" of the title are the cellars, but the word is also slang for "dupes.") A subplot involves a crusade to Rome undertaken by Amédée Fleurissoire, a naive provincial, in the hope of freeing the Holy Father. His good faith is repeatedly tried and mocked, and his absurd quest is undermined as he is tormented by bedbugs, lice, and mosquitoes. He falls into the clutches of Carola, a prostitute of the "heart of gold" variety, and finally dies absurdly when Lafcadio, a fellow-passenger in a moving train, pushes him out as a sort of game with fate—the best-known example of Gide's gratuitous act. Another plotline turns on the recognition by Lafcadio that he is the illegitimate son of old Juste-Agénor de Baraglioul and thus the brother of an eminent writer.

The theme of responsibility is carried out in multiple ways. "Si seulement on pouvait être certain que cela ne tire pas à conséquence" (If only one could be certain that it would be of no consequence), says the disguised Protos, an agent of "Mille-pattes" (Millipede), the gang of swindlers. No freedom is limitless or unconditional; even criminals operate by rules. The brief liaison of Juste-Agénor with Lafcadio's mother produced Lafcadio; his gratuitous act has unseen consequences that could be disastrous, were it not for Protos, who for his own reasons touches up the crime. In a trick of fate, Protos is misidentified as Amédée's killer after he strangles Carola and is captured. Lafcadio, who makes demands on himself, like Stendhal's hero Julien Sorel (a model) in *Le Rouge et le noir* (1830; translated as *Red and Black*, 1898), thinks of turning himself in, but the book ends on a question mark—an open ending, suiting the theme of freedom.

Gide wrote little during World War I. For some months, he worked for a charitable organization, the Foyer Franco-Belge, which cared for refugees. In 1916 he underwent a crisis, reflected in diary pages published as *Numquid et tu . . .?* (1922; translated in *The Journals of André Gide*, 1947-1951). The somber atmosphere of the war played a role in his despondency, but it was inspired mainly by deep moral distress, concern over his excessive sexual desires, rereading of Scripture, and spiritual anguish. His distress was so great that he expressed the fear of being possessed by the devil. His position was that, whether the demon was merely a metaphor for his own weakness or a real presence, his power was real. This interlude was his last period of profound religious feeling; his position thenceforth evolved toward a serene atheism. He continued, however, to honor the figure of Christ. In 1917 Gide became sentimentally and sexually involved with Marc Allégret, the son of a longtime family friend, pastor Elie Allégret. His outlook changed dramatically. In summer 1918 he left to spend three months in England with his young protégé and lover. The long-suffering Madeleine Gide realized what this trip signified. During his absence she burned, in an act of revenge and finality, Gide's lengthy correspondence with her, which he later described as the best of his writing.

The event wounded Gide deeply and led to an open estrangement between them that lasted for many years. The separation gave him new freedom. He established a close (though nonsexual) relationship with Maria (Madame Théo) van Rysselberghe, a friend of long standing; their daily lives were closely intertwined, and for nearly a quarter century they resided in adjoining flats in Paris. From 1918 on she kept a detailed diary (published as *Les Cahiers de la Petite Dame,* 1973-1977, The Notebooks of the "Little Lady") recording his conversations and activities. It is an invaluable source of information on him and his friends, including Martin du Gard and André Malraux.

As early as 1893 Gide had planned to write about a blind girl. Long delayed, the project came to fruition as *La Symphonie pastorale* (1919; translated as *The Pastoral Symphony,* 1931). Close in structure and narrative technique to the earlier *récits,* it is admired for its style. The narrator is a Protestant pastor; the pastoral motif is carried out also by the biblical parable of the lost sheep, mentions of Ludwig van Beethoven's Sixth Symphony, and the setting—a Swiss village and surrounding countryside. The other principal character is Gertrude, a blind girl whom the pastor has rescued and with whom he falls in love, thereby wounding his wife deeply. The entire text consists of the pastor's diary, first retrospective, then approximating by time of composition the events related, finally virtually simultaneous with events. Gide skillfully uses the diary in such a way that the pastor, another unreliable or "blind" narrator, both deceives himself and yet relates what readers must know to not only follow the story but also understand its implications before the pastor does. It is less a question of hypocrisy than of deep and skillful self-deception. Discussions between the pastor and his son Jacques about the epistles of St. Paul set forth Gide's own ideas; the pastor accuses St. Paul of distorting the Christian message, whereas Jacques sees how his father's free-thinking interpretations of Scripture have led him into error. Like *L'Immoraliste* and *La Porte étroite,* the short novel ends in the heroine's death; moral blindness leads to tragedy.

The original two volumes of *Si le grain ne meurt* appeared in 1920 and 1921. While its style, composition, and portraits are masterly, its frank statement of Gide's homosexuality, along with the trade edition of *Corydon,* made him notorious. But by 1921 he occupied such an important position on the literary landscape that he could not be ignored. The difference in reception of his works and perception of his importance between the years around 1900 and the 1920s reflects changes in French mores but, even more, demonstrates how his work had, finally, "invented" his public, both admirers and a broad circle of enemies. His acknowledged importance was such that in 1921 Gallimard published, with the epigraph "Les extrêmes me touchent" (Extremes touch me), his *Morceaux choisis* (Selected Pieces), a small-format anthology of pages he deemed among his best or most important; another publisher brought out that year a selection of excerpts called simply *André Gide* (sometimes referred to as *Pages choisies*). A 1923 book on Fyodor Dostoevsky, whose novels Gide admired greatly, and a 1924 collection of critical pieces called *Incidences,* added to Gide's stature. In 1924 critic André Rouveyre called him "le contemporain capital" (the crucial contemporary). The same year critic Henri Béraud made Gide his chief target in his *La Croisade des longues figures* (The Crusade of the Long Faces), attacking him for the so-called unhealthiness of his work and his domination of the writers associated with the *NRF*.

In 1923 Maria van Rysselberghe's daughter, Elisabeth, gave birth to Gide's child, named Catherine. The child was chiefly a pedagogical and feminist experiment; there was friendship between Gide and the emancipated Elisabeth but no passion. Madeleine Gide was told of the birth but not the parentage; it seems likely that she divined he was the father. Gide now had, even more clearly than before, two homes and families, as it were, one with Madeleine and their many nieces and nephews in Normandy, the other in the freethinking van Rysselberghe circle in Paris or at their property in the south of France. The irony of this arrangement on the part of someone who had written "Familles, je vous hais" has not gone unobserved. His tendency toward contradiction, opposition, and self-dialogue was well illustrated, and well served, in this divided private life.

Les Faux-Monnayeurs, which Gide called his only novel (contrasted with the *récits* and *soties*), begun in 1919 and finished in 1925, was, he said, the first work that was not, in some way, written for Madeleine Gide. A complex, vivid, multithemed work with several subplots, it is Gide's most developed illustration of *la composition en abyme* and other features of metafiction. Again, he demonstrated his inventiveness. Originally, its young hero Bernard, a bastard, was named Lafcadio, making clear the organic connection with the 1914 *sotie*. Gide consulted on the novel with Martin du Gard, to whom it is dedicated. Concurrently to its composition, he kept a "diary" of the novel, *Journal des Faux-Monnayeurs* (1926; translated as *Logbook of the Coiners,* 1952), in which he introduced characters and possible plot elements and expressed the wish that the work be a "carrefour de problèmes" (intersection of problems), a broad panorama of life; composition of the novel is reflected also in his regular diary. Moreover, Gide's character Edouard, who resembles his creator, is at work on a novel to be called "Les Faux-Monnayeurs." The narrative focus often switches among characters; different viewpoints on identical matters establish an inner perspectival reality, enriched by texts outside the novel. This perspectival quality is a principal modernist feature of the work.

The book is in three parts, the outer two of eighteen chapters each, the inner one of seven chapters. While there is a third-person narrator who says *I*–an authorial persona–his narration is supplemented by first-person voices: Edouard's lengthy diary excerpts, which constitute whole chapters, and various letters by other characters. Omniscience is eschewed; the authorial voice mentions limitations to his knowledge about his characters or his concern for their actions. At the end of part 2, the author judges his characters and their potentialities for the future. The diegetic and extradiegetic planes are thereby joined momentarily. No portion of Edouard's novel-in-progress is finished, but notes for the work become part of his journal, and he also discusses his theory of fiction. He rejects as unsuitable for his work certain events that belong to Gide's plot. Despite this variance and other qualifications brought by the text to Edouard's ideas, critics often take Edouard's statements as standing for Gide's, not without some justification. The structure is not circular, but, suggesting Gide's forward-looking temperament, the ending opens onto the future when Edouard writes in the final sentence (alluding to a boy of whom he has only heard): "Je suis bien curieux de connaître Caloub" (I am very curious to meet Caloub).

The work is a novel of ideas as well as a novel of manners. Cleverness and insight abound. The title refers to producers of counterfeit coins; but more broadly it stands for those who practice hypocrisy, insincerity, cheating, mendacity, and posing of all sorts. Both Bernard, who leaves home when he discovers that he is not the son of the man he called father, and Edouard, who denounces inauthenticity and mendacity in literature, help carry out the theme, but it is omnipresent, contrasted with what Bernard calls probity. Other themes and topics include youth, self-development and self-indulgence, illegitimacy, fiction, psychiatry, moral responsibility, education, love and sexuality, religion (Protestant), and evil. Overlapping social circles (mostly bourgeois) and other connections establish a web in which acts have unpredictable consequences. Evil appears in various guises, among them the devil, a shadowy, circulating figure. His status is not that of other characters—he is invisible except to the authorial voice, and unheard—but he listens in the shadows and intervenes just enough to produce an effect. He may also be personified in a strange character named Strouvilhou, who manipulates others, and in Vincent, who ends up believing he is possessed by the devil or rather is the devil. Fittingly, the novel has at times a somber tone. Evil seems to triumph at the close, as a schoolboy, Boris, shoots himself with his grandfather's pistol to carry out his part of a childish suicide pact, into which he has been led through Strouvilhou's sadistic manipulations. The grandfather says he cannot pardon God: "Il s'amuse avec nous, comme un chat avec la souris qu'il tourmente . . . La cruauté, voilà le premier des attributs de Dieu" (He plays with us, like a cat with the mouse he torments . . . The first attribute of God is cruelty). Offsetting such evil, partially at least, is an angel who appears to Bernard. Additionally, genuine sentiments are disclosed: Bernard's, at the close, for his adoptive father; and Edouard's for young Olivier, his half-sister's son, with whom he falls in love. Similarly, Rachel, a self-sacrificing young woman, the daughter of a Protestant pastor with whom Edouard has connections, devotes herself genuinely to her family, doing even menial tasks when there is no money for a housemaid.

The reception given to *Les Faux-Monnayeurs* varied: some critics saluted it as a modernist masterpiece; others dwelt on its presumed weaknesses (for instance, the rather narrow social spectrum), proclaimed it a failure, or denounced it for godlessness. It has been translated into at least fourteen languages, and the critical literature on it is enormous. Time has demonstrated its durability, and it continues to compare favorably with other major novels of the modernist period.

In 1925, after finishing his novel, Gide was invited by the French government to inspect timber-growing concessions in French colonies, and he left with Allégret for an eleven-month journey to Africa. Allégret filmed their travels. The human misery and injustices Gide observed led him to publish two documentary works relating the journey and exposing abuses of the colonial administration. He also became interested in communism. Never a party member, however, and with scant interest in political theory, he said it was Christ, not Marx, who drew him to Soviet-style socialism.

In 1928 the Editions du Capitole in Paris published an homage volume of 330 pages titled simply *André Gide*. It was composed of adulatory assessments of his work (along with a few essays expressing reservations) by dozens of renowned authors and critics. Among the contributors were many friends of Gide, such as Jacques Copeau, Martin du Gard, and Valéry, but also figures from outside his circle of acquaintance. The following year, Gide was excoriated in a series of essays by Henri Massis titled "André Gide ou l'immoralisme" (André Gide or Immoralism), included in his *Jugements*.

Gide had long shown little interest in women's social situations and concerns; his feminine figures had been, generally, either almost saintly women—Alissa in *La Porte étroite* and Rachel in *Les Faux-Monnayeurs,* for whom resignation was the mode of being—or fanciful or dangerous creatures. (He has even been accused of misogyny.) During the 1920s he developed greater sensitivity to women's practical and sentimental lives. His 1929 narrative *L'Ecole des femmes* (translated as *The School for Wives,* 1929) reflects this new concern for women's situations and psychology. Yet, the composition was long and laborious. In the form of a confession, it relates the story of Eveline, who falls in love with Robert and marries him against her parents' advice, then discovers that he is the mediocre man they had recognized, a hypocrite and an opportunist. The work was followed by *Robert* (1930; translated, 1950), in which Robert tells his side of the story—another instance when Gide provided correcting perspectives on events. *Geneviève* (1936; translated as *Geneviève, or The Unfinished Confidence,* 1950) is the story of their daughter, who becomes emancipated and proposes having an illegitimate child with an older, respected family friend, Dr. Marchand. (The parallel with Gide's life is obvious.) While feminist critics have ascribed great importance to these three narratives and especially to Geneviève's example, they are far less impressive than the earlier *récits*. Social criticism came easily to Gide, but his attempts at such *littérature engagée* (committed literature) concerning social themes produced inferior work.

Gide's major dramatic work from the interwar period, *Œdipe* (composed in 1930, published in 1931; translated as *Oedipus,* 1950), in three acts and prose, was staged first in 1931 by Georges Pitoëff, who played the title role. Contemporary diction, anachronisms (such as reference to Freudian repression), and wit give a modern flavor to the text. The reception was mixed, with several unfavorable assessments. Gide believed that later critics would recognize the play as excellent. Gide's Oedipus is a hero, but flawed by early hubris: pride in his accomplishments, happiness, and independent thinking. The hero's individualism offset by fatality fulfilled Gide's notion of a pagan theater. His version also expresses his social concerns of the 1930s and the enduring humanism of his maturity: anticlericalism, belief in progress, and God as a human concept. Humanity's goal is ahead; it is not the fulfillment of some preordained model but a process of self-discovery and improvement for the entire species.

The answer to the Sphinx's riddle (in Sophocles' tragedy), wrote Gide, was *man,* because the answer is always man:

> Persuadez-vous qu'à chacune de ses questions la réponse reste pareille; oui, qu'il n'y a qu'une seule et même réponse à de si diverses questions; et que cette réponse unique, c'est: l'Homme; et que cet homme unique, pour un chacun de nous, c'est: Soi.
>
> (Convince yourself that for each of its questions the answer remains the same; yes, that there is only a single, identical reply to such diverse questions; and that this unique answer, is: Man; and that this unique man, for each of us, is: Himself.)

For Œdipe, there can be no divine answer and no universal model: "Je me sentais une réponse à je ne savais encore quelle question" (I felt I was an answer to a question yet unknown). God is man projected: "Dieu, c'est tout simplement ce que tu mets au bout de cet élan de ta pensée" (God is simply what you place at the end of that thrust of your thought). Popular credulity and priestly manipulation are mocked repeatedly, although priest and gods have the last word.

Self-development is counterbalanced, however, by the impulse toward self-discipline. After Jocasta is found hanged, Œdipe blinds himself. The deed expresses not self-blame but paradoxically clear-sighted acknowledgment of his previous blindness and desire to go beyond it ("passer outre," in a phrase repeated in Gide's work): "C'est volontiers que je m'immole. J'étais parvenu à ce point que je ne pouvais plus dépasser qu'en prenant élan contre moi-même" (I immolate myself willingly. I had reached the point where I go farther only in taking impetus against myself). He desires, he says, only what is difficult.

With other high-profile fellow travelers, Gide participated in many left-wing activities during the 1930s; he and Malraux traveled in 1934 to Berlin to intervene in favor of political prisoners incarcerated by Adolf Hitler's regime. In 1930 and again in 1935 public debates were held concerning Gide's work and ideas, the proceedings of which were published; in the second, *André Gide et notre temps* (André Gide and Our Time), Catholic and conservative intellectuals challenged Gide's political positions. Far from disturbing or silencing him, these challenges, like the attacks of the 1920s, served him by increasing his notoriety and helping him affirm his thought and, particularly, his willingness to express it. In 1936, upon invitation, he visited the Soviet Union. This visit led to disappointment; the reality was far from what he imagined. He was particularly incensed by policies restricting sexual freedom; it became clear also that his visit had been arranged to produce the effects the Soviet authorities wished. Two short works published after his return denounced Soviet errors and led to his estrangement from the left wing. He gradually abandoned his socialist views.

Madeleine Gide died in 1938. Gide appears to have felt genuine grief along with guilt; she had been an essential pole of his moral life. After the defeat of France in 1940, he contributed to the *NRF* until it became clear that the editorship was politically compromised as pro-collaborationist. During the remainder of World War II, he resided in the south with friends, then in Tunisia, Morocco, and Algeria (until summer 1945), where he kept his diary, helped found a literary magazine, and pursued other projects. Though many considered him too controversial for the conservative Académie Française, Georges Duhamel, its secretary, was sent after the war to sound him out concerning his willingness to stand as a candidate; Gide declined the invitation. His Oxford honorary doctorate and the Nobel Prize in Literature in 1947 confirmed his stature in the international literary community.

Gide's Nobel Prize was given, according to the citation, "for his comprehensive and artistically significant writings, in which human problems and conditions have been presented with a fearless love of truth and keen psychological insight." The award evoked widespread and loud outcries from many of those who considered Gide a poisoner of youth and a scandal for France. Even before the official announcement of the selection, French newspapers had intimated it might be made but specified that discussion was heated. Gide's friend Martin du Gard, noting privately that "l'élection a été très disputée" (the choice was very controversial), suggested in a letter to Gide that the committee's marked emphasis on "love of truth," the spirit that gave rise to *Corydon,* was not calculated to discourage opposition. Martin du Gard expressed his delight at the award but admitted to a certain embarrassment that it had come so long after his own (1937). Gide replied publicly in *Le Figaro* (21 November 1947) to the Nobel announcement, acknowledging his emotion upon receiving the prize, while stressing that he had never sought honors, even though he had striven after fame, which he had expected to be posthumous; what surprised him was that it had arrived before his death. He surmised that the Nobel jury had taken into account less his writings themselves than the spirit that animated them—the spirit of free inquiry, independence, even insubordination, the "sel de la terre, qui peut encore sauver le monde" (salt of the earth, which can still save the world). According to Gide's *Journal* (volume 2), he told a Swedish interviewer, who asked whether he regretted publishing any of his books (having in mind, Gide surmised, *Corydon* or *Retour de l'URSS*), that not only did he not disavow any of them but also that if, in order to obtain the prize, he had been obliged to denounce some of his writings, "j'aurais certainement tiré ma révérence" (I would have bowed out). He noted in his *Journal* in early 1948 that, because of the Nobel Prize, there was considerable demand for his books, and many were out of print.

As Anders Österling said in presenting the award, Gide was "among the first literary names of France," despite being "in the first rank of sowers of anxiety." Perspicaciously, Österling noted that an important period in the spiritual history of Europe was outlined in Gide's work; yet, it gained recognition only slowly because its evaluation required a long perspective and space adequate for its development.

Gide was not well enough to attend the ceremony in Stockholm. However, he traveled within Europe on other occasions and continued to publish until nearly the end of his life. His last major work was *Thésée* (1946; translated as *Theseus*, 1948). Though it can be grouped with his earlier *récits* because it is a first-person narrative, it is not a modern psychological novel but rather a witty, original recounting of the Theseus legend, full of themes and insights characteristic of the author, who clearly speaks through his hero. It is thus closer thematically to *Œdipe;* Gide even has Oedipus and Theseus meet. There is a vein of misogyny, along with an anti-egalitarian note. The contemporary social problems that drew Gide's attention from the late 1920s well into the 1930s have disappeared; *Thésée* is concerned with timeless questions of ethics and self-development. Thésée's account of his life is also his testament, which may be viewed as Gide's. Two principal themes are interwoven: the individual (with the admonition to know oneself); and the connection of this self to others, especially to the heritage of the past (biological and cultural). But this past must not be an impediment to self-development, which is obtained through discipline and effort and which serves society: "L'humanité, pensais-je sans cesse, peut plus et vaut mieux" (Humanity, I kept thinking, can do more and is worth more). The atheism of Thésée is opposed to the mysticism of Dédale (Daedalus): "Les premières et les plus importantes victoires que devait remporter l'homme, c'est sur les dieux" (The first and most important victories that man had to win were over the gods). The narrative closes with a valediction: "Derrière moi, je laisse la cité d'Athènes.... Pour le bien de l'humanité future, j'ai fait mon oeuvre. J'ai vécu" (Behind me, I leave the city of Athens.... For the good of future humanity, I have done my work. I have lived).

Gide's translation (1930) of William Shakespeare's *Hamlet* was staged in Paris in October 1946. In December 1950, a stage version of *Les Caves du Vatican* was produced at the Comédie-Française; it was favorably received. André Gide died on 19 February 1951 and was buried at Cuverville. The religious rite at his grave was the object of vigorous protest by Martin du Gard and other friends. In 1952 Gide's works were placed on the Roman Catholic Index of Prohibited Books. Abundant scholarship, colloquia in America and Europe, readership in Africa, Asia, and Australia as well as the Occident, critical editions, inexpensive reprints, a vast published correspondence, and the presence of Gide's works on school syllabi now testify to his lasting importance as a stylist and a bold, far-seeing, thought-provoking master.

Letters:

Lettres (Liège: A la Lampe d'Aladdin, 1930);

Correspondance Francis Jammes–André Gide 1893–1938, edited by Robert Mallet (Paris: Gallimard, 1948);

Marcel Proust, *Lettres à André Gide;* includes letters by Gide (Neuchâtel & Paris: Ides et Calendes, 1949);

Correspondance, 1899–1926, Paul Claudel–André Gide, edited by Mallet (Paris: Gallimard, 1949); translated by John Russell as *The Correspondence, 1899–1926, between Paul Claudel and André Gide* (New York: Pantheon, 1952);

Correspondance, 1909–1926, Rainer Maria Rilke–André Gide, edited by Renée Lang (Paris: Corrêa, 1952);

Correspondance Paul Valéry–André Gide 1890–1942, edited by Mallet (Paris: Gallimard, 1955); abridged and translated by June Guicharnaud as *Self-Portraits: The Gide-Valéry Letters, 1890–1942* (Chicago: University of Chicago Press, 1966);

Rilke, Gide et Verhaeren: correspondance inédite, edited by Carlo Bronne (Paris: Messein, 1955);

Correspondance André Gide–Charles Péguy 1905–1912, edited by Alfred Saffrey (Persan: Imprimerie de Persan-Beaumont, 1958);

The Correspondence of André Gide and Edmund Gosse, 1904–1928, edited by Linette F. Brugmans (New York: New York University Press, 1959; London: Owen, 1960);

Correspondance André Gide–Arnold Bennett 1911–1931: Vingt ans d'amitié littéraire, edited by Brugmans (Geneva & Paris: Droz & Minard, 1964);

Correspondance André Gide–Roger Martin du Gard 1913–1951, edited by Jean Delay, 2 volumes (Paris: Gallimard, 1968);

Jean Cocteau, *Lettres à André Gide,* edited by J.-J. Kihm; includes letters by Gide (Paris: Table Ronde, 1970);

Correspondance André Gide–François Mauriac, 1912–1950, edited by Jacqueline Morton (Paris: Gallimard, 1971);

Correspondance d'André Gide et Georges Simenon, edited by Francis Lacassin and Gilbert Sigaux (Paris: Plon, 1973);

Charles Brunard, *Correspondance avec André Gide et souvenirs* (Paris: La Pensée Universelle, 1974);

Gide and Albert Mockel, *Correspondance (1891–1938),* edited by Gustave Vanwelkenhuyzen (Geneva: Droz, 1975);

Henri Ghéon and Gide, *Correspondance,* edited by Jean Tipi and Anne-Marie Moulènes, 2 volumes (Paris: Gallimard, 1976);

Correspondance André Gide–Jules Romains, edited by Claude Martin (Paris: Flammarion, 1976);

Gide and Jacques-Emile Blanche, *Correspondance: 1892–1939,* edited by Georges-Paul Collet (Paris: Gallimard, 1979);

André Gide–Justin O'Brien, Correspondance 1937–1951, edited by Morton (Lyons: Centre d'Etudes Gidiennes, 1979);

Correspondance André Gide–Dorothy Bussy, 1918–1951, edited by Jean Lambert, notes by Richard Tedeschi, 3 volumes (Paris: Gallimard, 1979, 1981, 1982); translated by Tedeschi as *Selected Letters of André Gide and Dorothy Bussy* (London: Oxford University Press, 1983);

Deutsch-französische Gespräche 1920–1950: La Correspondance de Ernst Robert Curtius avec André Gide, Charles Du Bos et Valery Larbaud, edited by Herbert and Jane M. Dieckmann (Frankfurt: Klostermann, 1980);

Gabrielle Vulliez, *La Tristesse d'un automne sans été: Correspondance de Gabrielle Vulliez avec André Gide et Paul Claudel (1923–1931)* (Bron: Centre d'Etudes Gidiennes, Université Lyon II, 1981);

Gide and François-Paul Alibert, *Correspondance: 1907–1950,* edited by Martin (Lyons: Presses Universitaires de Lyon, 1982);

André Gide–Jean Giono, Correspondance 1929–1940, edited by Roland Bourneuf and Jacques Cotnam (Lyons: Centre d'Etudes Gidiennes, 1984);

D'un monde à l'autre. La Correspondance André Gide–Harry Kessler (1903–1933), edited by Claude Foucart (Lyons: Centre d'Etudes Gidiennes, Université Lyon II, 1985);

Gide, *Correspondance avec Jef Last (1934–1950),* edited by C. J. Greshoff (Lyons: Presses Universitaires de Lyon, 1985);

Anna de Noailles and Gide, *Correspondance (1902–1928),* edited by Claude Mignot-Ogliastri (Lyons: Centre d'Etudes Gidiennes, Université Lyon II, 1986);

Gide and Thea Sternheim, *Correspondance (1927–1950),* edited by Foucart (Lyons: Centre d'Etudes Gidiennes, Université Lyon II, 1986);

Gide, *Correspondance avec Francis Vielé-Griffin (1891–1931),* edited by Henry de Paysac (Lyons: Presses Universitaires de Lyon, 1986);

Gide and Jacques Copeau, *Correspondance,* edited by Jean Claude, 2 volumes (Paris: Gallimard, 1987);

Gide, *Correspondance avec André Ruyters (1895–1950),* edited by Martin and Victor Martin-Schmets (Lyons: Presses Universitaires de Lyon, 1987);

Gide, *Correspondance avec sa mère, 1880–1895,* edited by Martin (Paris: Gallimard, 1988);

Gide and Jean Schlumberger, *Correspondance 1901–1950,* edited by Pascal Mercier and Peter Fawcett (Paris: Gallimard, 1993);

Gide and Henri de Régnier, *Correspondance (1891–1911),* edited by David J. Niederauer and Heather Franklyn (Lyons: Presses Universitaires de Lyon, 1997);

Franz Blei and Gide, *Briefwechsel* (Darmstadt: Wissenschaftliche Buchgesellschaft, 1997);

Gide and Jacques Rivière, *Correspondance 1909–1925,* edited by Pierre de Gaulmyn and Alain Rivière, with the collaboration of Kevin O'Neill and Stuart Barr (Paris: Gallimard, 1998);

L'Enfance de l'art: Correspondances avec Elie Allégret, 1886–1896, edited by Daniel Durosay (Paris: Gallimard, 1998);

Georges Simenon–André Gide: Sans trop de pudeur: Correspondance 1938–1950, edited by Benoît Denis (Paris: Omnibus, 1999);

Gide and Jean Malaquais, *Correspondance 1935–1950, précédée de Historique de ma rencontre avec André Gide . . . ,* edited by Pierre Masson and Geneviève Millot-Nakach (Paris: Phébus, 2000);

Gide and Pierre de Massot, *Correspondance 1923–1950,* edited by Jacques Cotnam (Nantes: Centre d'Etudes Gidiennes, 2001);

Gide and Edouard Ducôté, *Correspondance 1895–1921,* edited by Pierre Lachasse (Nantes: Centre d'Etudes Gidiennes, 2002);

Gide, "Cher vieux. Lettres à Marcel Drouin (1895–1925)," *La Nouvelle Revue Française,* nos. 560, 561, 562 (January, April, June 2002): 1–29, 332–352, 338–360;

Gide and Aline Mayrisch, *Correspondance 1903–1946,* edited by Masson and Cornel Meder (Paris: Gallimard, 2003);

Gide, Pierre Louÿs, and Valéry, *Correspondances à trois voix, 1888-1920,* edited by Fawcett and Mercier (Paris: Gallimard, 2004);

Gide and Marc Allégret, *Correspondance 1917-1949,* edited by Claude and Masson (Paris: Gallimard, 2005).

Interviews:

Entretiens avec Jean Amrouche (Paris: Gallimard, 1949); 2 CDs (Paris: INA/Radio France, 1996);

Eric Marty, *André Gide, qui êtes-vous? Avec les entretiens André Gide–Jean Amrouche* (Paris: La Manufacture, 1987).

Bibliographies:

Arnold Naville, *Bibliographie des écrits d'André Gide 1891-1952* (Paris: Guy le Prat, 1949);

Jacques Cotnam, *Bibliographie chronologique de l'oeuvre d'André Gide 1889-1973* (Boston: G. K. Hall, 1974);

Cotnam, *Inventaire bibliographique et index analytique de la correspondance d'André Gide, publiée de 1897 à 1971* (Boston: G. K. Hall, 1975);

"Inventaire des traductions des oeuvres d'André Gide," *Bulletin des Amis d'André Gide,* nos. 28, 29, 30, 31, 35, 42, 46, 58 (1975-1983);

Claude Martin and others, *La Correspondance générale d'André Gide,* fascs. 1-8, 1879-1951 (Lyons: Centre d'Etudes Gidiennes, Université Lyon II, 1985);

Catharine Savage Brosman, *An Annotated Bibliography of Criticism on André Gide 1973-1988* (New York & London: Garland, 1990).

Biographies:

Justin O'Brien, *Portrait of André Gide: A Critical Biography* (London: Secker & Warburg, 1953);

Jean Schlumberger, *Madeleine et André Gide* (Paris: Gallimard, 1956); translated by Richard H. Akeroyd as *Madeleine and André Gide* (Tuscaloosa, Ala.: Portals Press, 1980);

Jean Delay, *La Jeunesse d'André Gide,* 2 volumes (Paris: Gallimard, 1956-1957); abridged and translated by June Guicharnaud as *The Youth of André Gide* (Chicago: University of Chicago Press, 1963);

Claude Martin, *André Gide par lui-même* (Paris: Seuil, 1963);

George D. Painter, *André Gide, A Critical Biography* (New York: Atheneum, 1968);

Pierre de Boisdeffre, *Vie d'André Gide 1869-1951: Essai de biographie critique* (Paris: Hachette, 1970);

Maria van Rysselberghe, *Les Cahiers de la Petite Dame,* 4 volumes, Cahiers André Gide (Paris: Gallimard, 1973-1977);

Martin, *La Maturité d'André Gide: De "Paludes" à "l'Immoraliste" 1895-1902* (Paris: Klincksieck, 1977);

Auguste Anglès, *André Gide et le premier groupe de "La Nouvelle Revue Française,"* 3 volumes (Paris: 1978, 1986, 1986);

Pierre Lepape, *André Gide le messager: Biographie* (Paris: Seuil, 1997);

Martin, *André Gide ou la vocation du bonheur* (Paris: Fayard, 1998);

Alan Sheridan, *André Gide: A Life in the Present* (Cambridge, Mass.: Harvard University Press / Oxford: Oxford University Press, 1999);

André Gide, homme solaire (Le Lavandou: Réseau Lalan, 2001);

Alain Goulet, *André Gide: écrire pour vivre* (Paris: Corti, 2002).

References:

André Gide, nos. 1-11, special issues of *Revue des Lettres Modernes* (1970-);

Emily Apter, *André Gide and the Codes of Homotextuality* (Saratoga, Calif.: Anma Libri, 1987);

Archives André Gide, nos. 1-5, Archives des Lettres Modernes (Paris: Minard, 1964-);

Arthur E. Babcock, *Portraits of Artists: Reflexivity in Gidean Fiction, 1902-1946* (York, S.C.: French Literature Publications, 1982);

Christopher D. Bettinson, *Gide: "Les Caves du Vatican"* (London: Edward Arnold, 1972);

Bettinson, *Gide: a Study* (Totowa, N.J.: Rowman & Littlefield, 1977);

Georges Brachfeld, *André Gide and the Communist Temptation* (Geneva: Droz, 1959);

Germaine Brée, *André Gide, l'insaisissable Protée* (Paris: Les Belles Lettres, 1953); revised and enlarged in English as *André Gide* (New Brunswick, N.J.: Rutgers University Press, 1963); French version revised and enlarged (Paris: Les Belles Lettres, 1970);

Catharine Savage Brosman, *Existential Fiction* (Detroit: Gale Group, 2000);

Bulletin des Amis d'André Gide, 34 volumes to date, with index in number 135/136 (Lyons: Centre d'Etudes Gidiennes, Université de Lyon II, 1968-April 1985; Montpellier: Centre d'Etudes Littéraires du XXe Siècle, Université de Montpellier III, July 1985-1988; Paris X-Nanterre: Centre d'Etudes des Sciences de la Littérature, 1989-1990; Paris X-Nanterre: Centre de Sémiotique/ Recherches Interdisicplinaires sur les textes modernes, 1991; Lyons: Centre d'Etudes Gidiennes, 1992-April 1994; Nantes: Centre d'Etudes Gidiennes, July-October 1994-);

Cahiers André Gide (Paris: Gallimard, 1969-);

Tom Conner, *André Gide's Politics: Rebellion and Ambivalence* (New York: Palgrave, 2000);

Thomas Cordle, *André Gide* (New York: Twayne, 1969);

J. C. Davies, *Gide: "L' Immoraliste" and "La Porte étroite"* (London: Edward Arnold, 1968);

Eugene H. Falk, *Types of Thematic Structure: The Nature and Function of Motifs in Gide, Camus, and Sartre* (Chicago & London: University of Chicago Press, 1967);

Gérard Genette, *Figures III* (Paris: Seuil, 1972), partly translated by Jane E. Lewin as *Narrative Discourses: An Essay in Method* (Ithaca, N.Y.: Cornell University Press, 1908);

Pamela Antonia Genova, *André Gide dans le labyrinthe de la mythotextualité* (West Lafayette, Ind.: Purdue University Press, 1995);

Albert Guerard, *André Gide* (Cambridge, Mass.: Harvard University Press, 1951);

W. W. Holdheim, *Theory and Practice of the Novel: A Study on André Gide* (Geneva: Droz, 1968);

Jean Hytier, *André Gide* (Algiers: Charlot, 1938, 1945); translated by Richard Howard (New York: Ungar, 1967);

G. W. Ireland, *Gide* (Edinburgh: Oliver & Boyd, 1963);

Ireland, *Gide, A Study of His Creative Writings* (London: Oxford University Press, 1970);

David Littlejohn, ed., *Gide: A Collection of Critical Essays* (Englewood Cliffs, N.J.: Prentice-Hall, 1970);

Klaus Mann, *André Gide and the Crisis of Modern Thought* (New York: Creative Age Press, 1943);

Harold March, *Gide and the Hound of Heaven* (Philadelphia: University of Pennsylvania Press, 1952);

Roger Martin du Gard, *Notes sur André Gide 1913–1951* (Paris: Gallimard, 1951); republished in Martin du Gard, *Œuvres complètes,* volume 2 (Paris: Gallimard, 1955); translated by John Russell as *Notes on André Gide* (London: Deutsch, 1953);

Pierre Masson and Claude Martin, eds., *André Gide et l'écriture de soi* (Lyons: Presses Universitaires de Lyon, 2002);

James H. McLaren, *The Theatre of André Gide: Evolution of a Moral Philosopher* (Baltimore: Johns Hopkins University Press, 1953);

H. J. Nersoyan, *André Gide: The Theism of an Atheist* (Syracuse, N.Y.: Syracuse University Press, 1969);

Kevin O'Neill, *André Gide and the Roman d'aventure* (Sydney: Sydney University Press, 1969);

Allan H. Pasco, "Subversive Structure in Gide's *L'Immoraliste*," in his *Novel Configurations,* second edition (Birmingham, Ala.: Summa Publications, 1994);

Kenneth I. Perry, *The Religious Symbolism of André Gide* (The Hague: Mouton, 1969);

Patrick Pollard, *André Gide, Homosexual Moralist* (New Haven: Yale University Press, 1991);

Vinio Rossi, *André Gide: The Evolution of an Aesthetic* (New Brunswick, N.J.: Rutgers University Press, 1967);

Ben Stoltzfus, *Gide's Eagles* (Carbondale & Edwardsville: Southern Illinois University Press / London & Amsterdam: Feffer & Simons, 1969);

Michael Tilby, *Gide: "Les Faux-Monnayeurs"* (London: Grant & Cutler, 1981);

C. D. E. Tolton, *André Gide and the Art of Autobiography* (Toronto: Macmillan, 1975);

David H. Walker, *André Gide* (New York: St. Martin's Press, 1990);

Walker, *Gide: "Les Nourritures terrestres" and "La Symphonie pastorale"* (London: Grant & Cutler, 1990);

Walker, ed., *André Gide* (London & New York: Longman, 1996);

Walker and Brosman, eds., *Retour aux "Nourritures terrestres"* (Amsterdam & Atlanta: Rodopi, 1997);

Helen Watson-Williams, *André Gide and the Greek Myth: A Critical Study* (Oxford: Clarendon Press, 1967);

W. D. Wilson, *André Gide: "La Symphonie pastorale"* (London: Macmillan, 1971).

Papers:

Fifty of André Gide's manuscripts and about twelve thousand letters are deposited at the Bibliothèque Littéraire Jacques Doucet, Paris. These manuscripts are listed in the *Catalogue de Fonds Spéciaux de la Bibliothèque Littéraire Jacques Doucet* (Boston: G. K. Hall, 1972). Among them are the manuscripts of almost all of Gide's novels, in addition to plays such as *Œdipe;* one notable exception is that of *Les Faux-Monnayeurs,* which was purchased from a private collection at auction in 2001 by the Bibliothèque Nationale de France. Some manuscripts are located in the Harry Ransom Humanities Research Center at the University of Texas, Austin. Many others remain in private hands.

1947 Nobel Prize in Literature Presentation Speech

by Anders Österling, Permanent Secretary of the Swedish Academy

On the first page of the remarkable journal kept by André Gide for half a century, the author, then twenty years old, finds himself on the sixth floor of a building in the Latin Quarter, looking for a meeting place for "The Symbolists," the group of youths to which he belonged. From the window he looked at the Seine and Notre Dame during the sunset of an autumn day and felt like the hero of a Balzac novel, a Rastignac ready to conquer the city lying at his feet: "And now, we two!" However,

Gide's ambition was to find long and twisting paths ahead; nor was it to be contented with easy victories.

The seventy-eight-year-old writer who this day is being honoured with the award of the Nobel Prize has always been a controversial figure. From the beginning of his career he put himself in the first rank of the sowers of spiritual anxiety, but this does not keep him today from being counted almost everywhere among the first literary names of France, or from enjoying an influence that has persisted unabatedly through several generations. His first works appeared in the 1890's; his last one dates from the spring of 1947. A very important period in the spiritual history of Europe is outlined in his work, constituting a kind of dramatic foundation to his long life. One may ask why the importance of this work has only so recently been appreciated at its true value: the reason is that André Gide belongs unquestionably to that class of writers whose real evaluation requires a long perspective and a space adequate for the three stages of the dialectic process. More than any of his contemporaries, Gide has been a man of contrasts, a veritable Proteus of perpetually changing attitudes, working tirelessly at opposite poles in order to strike flashing sparks. This is why his work gives the appearance of an uninterrupted dialogue in which faith constantly struggles against doubt, asceticism against the love of life, discipline against the need for freedom. Even his external life has been mobile and changing, and his famous voyages to the Congo in 1927 and to Soviet Russia in 1935—to cite only those—are proof enough that he did not want to be ranked among the peaceful stay-at-homes of literature.

Gide comes from a Protestant family whose social position permitted him to follow his vocation freely and to devote greater attention than most others can afford to the cultivation of his personality and to his inner development. He described this family milieu in his famous autobiography whose title *Si le grain ne meurt* (1924) [*If It Die . . .*] is taken from St. John's words about the grain of wheat that must die before its fruition. Although he has strongly reacted against his Puritan education, he has nonetheless all his life dwelled on the fundamental problems of morality and religion, and at times he has defined with rare purity the message of Christian love, particularly in his short novel, *La Porte étroite* (1909) [*Strait Is the Gate*], which deserves to be compared with the tragedies of Racine.

On the other hand, one finds in André Gide still stronger manifestations of that famous "immoralism"—a conception which his adversaries have often misinterpreted. In reality it designates the free act, the "gratuitous" act, the liberation from all repressions of conscience, something analogous to what the American recluse Thoreau expressed, "The worst thing is being the slave dealer of one's soul." One should always keep in mind that Gide found some difficulty in presenting as virtue that which is composed of the absence of generally recognized virtues. *Les Nourritures terrestres* (1897) [*Fruits of the Earth*] was a youthful attempt from which he later turned away, and the diverse delights he enthusiastically sings of evoke for us those beautiful fruits of southern lands which do not bear keeping. The exhortation which he addresses to his disciple and reader, "And now, throw away my book. Leave me!", has been followed first of all by himself in his later works. But what leaves the strongest impression, in *Nourritures* as elsewhere, is the intense poetry of separation, of return, captured by him in so masterly a fashion in the flute-song of his prose. One rediscovers it often, for example in this brief journal entry, written later, near a mosque at Brusa on one May morning: "Ah! begin anew and on again afresh! Feel with rapture this exquisite tenderness of the cells in which emotion filters like milk. . . . Bush of the dense gardens, rose of purity, indolent rose in the shade of plane trees, can it be that thou hast not known my youth? Before? Is it a memory I dwell in? Is it indeed I who am seated in this little corner of the mosque, I who breathe and I who love thee? or do I only dream of loving thee? . . . If I were indeed real, would this swallow have stolen so close to me?"

Behind the strange and incessant shift in perspective that Gide's work offers to us, in the novels as well as in the essays, in the travel diaries, or in the analyses of contemporary events, we always find the same supple intelligence, the same incorruptible psychology, expressed in a language which, by the most sober means, attains a wholly classic limpidity and the most delicate variety. Without going into the details of the work, let us mention in this connection the celebrated *Les Faux-Monnayeurs* (1926) [*The Counterfeiters*], with its bold and penetrating analysis of a group of young French people. Through the novelty of its technique, this novel has inspired a whole new orientation in the contemporary art of the narrative. Next to it, put the volume of memoirs already mentioned, in which the author intended to recount his life truthfully without adding anything that could be to his advantage or hiding what would be unpleasant. Rousseau had had the same intention, with this difference, that Rousseau exhibits his faults in the conviction that all men being as evil as he, none will dare to judge or condemn him. Gide, however, quite simply refuses to admit to his fellows the right to pass any judgment on him; he calls on a higher tribunal, a vaster perspective, in which he will present himself before the sovereign eye of God. The significance of these memoirs thus is indicated in the mysterious Biblical quotation of the grain of wheat which here represents the personality:

as long as the latter is sentient, deliberate, and egocentric, it dwells alone and without germinating power; it is only at the price of its death and its transmutation that it will acquire life and be able to bear fruit. "I do not think," Gide writes, "that there is a way of looking at the moral and religious question or of acting in the face of it that I have not known and made my own at some moment in my life. In truth, I have wished to reconcile them all, the most diverse points of view, by excluding nothing and by being ready to entrust to Christ the solution of the contest between Dionysus and Apollo."

Such a statement throws light on the intellectual versatility for which Gide is often blamed and misunderstood, but which has never led him to betray himself. His philosophy has a tendency toward regeneration at any price and does not fail to evoke the miraculous phoenix which out of its nest of flames hurls itself to a new flight.

In circumstances like those of today, in which, filled with admiring gratitude, we linger before the rich motifs and the essential themes of this work, it is natural that we pass over the critical reservations which the author himself seems to enjoy provoking. For even in his ripe age, Gide has never argued in favor of a full and complete acceptance of his experiences and his conclusions. What he wishes above all is to stir up and present the problems. Even in the future, his influence will doubtless be noted less in a total acceptance than in a lively controversy about his work. And in this lies the foundation of his true greatness.

His work contains pages which provoke like a defiance through the almost unequalled audacity of the confession. He wishes to combat the Pharisees, but it is difficult, in the struggle, to avoid shocking certain rather delicate norms of human character. One must always remember that this manner of acting is a form of the impassioned love of truth which, since Montaigne and Rousseau, has been an axiom of French literature. Through all the phases of his evolution, Gide has appeared as a true defender of literary integrity, founded on the personality's right and duty to present all its problems resolutely and honestly. From this point of view, his long and varied activity, stimulated in so many ways, unquestionably represents an idealistic value.

Since Mr. André Gide, who has declared with great gratitude his acceptance of the distinction offered him, has unfortunately been prevented from coming here by reasons of health, his Prize will now be handed to His Excellency the French Ambassador.

[© The Nobel Foundation, 1947.]

Gide: Banquet Speech

As Gide was unable to be present at the Nobel Banquet at the City Hall in Stockholm, 10 December 1947, the speech was read by Gabriel Puaux, French Ambassador (Translation):

It would no doubt be of little purpose to dwell on my regrets at not being able to be present on this solemn occasion nor to have my own voice bear witness to my gratitude, compelled as I am to forgo a trip that promised to be both pleasant and instructive.

I have, as you know, always declined honours, at least those which as a Frenchman I could expect from France. I confess, gentlemen, that it is with a sense of giddiness that I suddenly receive from you the highest honour to which a writer can aspire. For many years I thought that I was crying in the wilderness, later that I was speaking only to a very small number, but you have proved to me today that I was right to believe in the virtue of the small number and that sooner or later it would prevail.

It seems to me, gentlemen, that your votes were cast not so much for my work as for the independent spirit that animates it, that spirit which in our time faces attacks from all possible quarters. That you have recognized it in me, that you have felt the need to approve and support it, fills me with confidence and an intimate satisfaction. I cannot help thinking, however, that only recently another man in France represented this spirit even better than I do. I am thinking of Paul Valéry, for whom my admiration has steadily grown during a friendship of half a century and whose death alone prevents you from electing him in my place. I have often said with what friendly deference I have constantly and without weakness bowed to his genius, before which I have always felt "human, only too human." May his memory be present at this ceremony, which in my eyes takes on all the more brilliance as the darkness deepens. You invite the free spirit to triumph and through this signal award, given without regard for frontiers or the momentary dissensions of factions, you offer to this spirit the unexpected chance of extraordinary radiance.

Prior to the speech, Arne Tiselius, Deputy Chairman of the Nobel Foundation, made the following comment: "Unfortunately, Mr. André Gide, due to ill health, has had to give up his original intention to attend the ceremonies. We regret this, indeed, and would like to extend our reverence and our sympathy to the venerable master of French literature whose genius has so profoundly influenced our time."

[© The Nobel Foundation, 1947. André Gide is the sole author of his speech.]

Karl Gjellerup

(2 June 1857 – 11 October 1919)

Poul Houe
University of Minnesota

This entry was expanded by Houe from his Gjellerup entry in *DLB 300: Danish Writers from the Reformation to Decadence, 1550–1900*.

BOOKS: *En Idealist: Skildring*, as Epigonos (Copenhagen: C. A. Reitzel, 1878);
"Det unge Danmark": En Fortælling fra vore Dage (Copenhagen: C. A. Reitzel, 1879);
Antigonos: En Fortælling fra det andet Aarhundrede (Copenhagen: Schou, 1880);
Rødtjørn: Sange og Fantasier (Copenhagen: Schou, 1881);
Arvelighed og Moral: En Undersøgelse tilkjendt Universitetets Guldmedaille (Copenhagen: Schou, 1881);
Aander og Tider: Et Rekviem over Charles Darwin (Copenhagen: Schou, 1882);
Germanernes Lærling: Et Livsafsnit fra vore Dage (Copenhagen: Schou, 1882);
Romulus: En Novelle (Copenhagen: Schou, 1883; revised, 1889);
G-Dur: En Kammer-Novelle (Copenhagen: Schou, 1883);
Brynhild: En Tragedie (Copenhagen: Schou, 1884; revised edition, Copenhagen: Lybecker, 1910);
En klassisk Maaned: Billeder og Stemninger fra en Grækenlandsrejse (Copenhagen: Schou, 1884);
Vandreaaret: Skildringer og Betragtninger (Copenhagen: Schou, 1885);
Saint-Just: Historisk Sørgespil i fem Handlinger (Copenhagen: Schou, 1886);
En arkadisk Legende (Copenhagen: Schou, 1887);
Kampen med Muserne: Dramatisk Digt (Thamyris 1) (Copenhagen: Schou, 1887);
Helikon: Et dramatisk Digt (Thamyris 2) (Copenhagen: Schou, 1887);
Hagbard og Signe: En erotisk Tragedie i fem Handlinger (Copenhagen: P. G. Philipsen, 1888);
Bryllupsgaven: Rococo-Komedie fra det galante Sachsen i fem Handlinger (Copenhagen: Schou, 1888);
Min Kjærligheds Bog (Copenhagen: P. G. Philipsen, 1889);
Minna (Copenhagen: P. G. Philipsen, 1889); translated by C. L. Nielsen as *Minna: A Novel from the Danish*

Karl Gjellerup, circa 1910 (Danish Royal Library, Copenhagen)

(London: Heinemann, 1913); revised German edition, *"Seit ich zuerst sie sah"* (Leipzig: Quelle & Meyer, 1918);
Richard Wagner i hans Hovedværk "Niebelungens Ring" (Copenhagen: P. G. Philipsen, 1890); enlarged as *Richard Wagner i hans Hovedværker* (Copenhagen: Gyldendal, 1915);
Herman Vandel: Sørgespil i tre Handlinger (Copenhagen: P. G. Philipsen, 1891);
Ti Kroner og andre Fortællinger (Copenhagen: Gyldendal, 1893);
Kong Hjarne Skjald: Tragedie i fem Handlinger (Copenhagen: Gyldendal, 1893);

Wuthhorn: Sørgespil i fem Handlinger (Copenhagen: Schou, 1893);

Pastor Mors: Eine seltsame Geschichte (Dresden: Minden, 1894); republished in Danish as *Pastor Mors: En underlig Historie* (Copenhagen: Gyldendal, 1894);

Eine Million: Schauspiel, by Gjellerup and Wilhelm Wolters (Dresden: E. Pierson, 1894); translated into Danish by Gjellerup as *En Million: Skuespil i tre Handlinger. Efter Nikolaus Pawlows Novelle* (Copenhagen: Gyldendal, 1894);

Hans Excellence: Skuespil indledet ved en Efterskrift til mine Dramer (Copenhagen: Gyldendal, 1895);

Møllen: Roman i fem Bøger (Copenhagen: Gyldendal, 1896; revised, 1911);

Mit formentlige Højforræderi mod det danske Folk: En Redegjørelse i Anledning af Denunciationerne i Flensborg Avis (Copenhagen: Gyldendal, 1897);

Konvolutten: En graphologisk Studie (Copenhagen: Schubothe, 1897);

Ved Grændsen: Roman (Copenhagen: Gyldendal, 1897);

Fabler (Copenhagen: Gyldendal, 1898);

Gift og Modgift: Komedie i fem Akter og paa Vers (Copenhagen: Gyldendal, 1898);

Tankelæserinden: Sjællandsk Præstegaardsidyl (Copenhagen: Gyldendal, 1901);

Die Opferfeuer: Ein Legenden-Stück, illustrated by Walther Witting (Leipzig: Hermann Seemann, 1903); translated into Danish by Gjellerup as *Offerildene: Et Legendestykke,* illustrated by Witting (Copenhagen: Schubothe, 1903);

Elskovsprøven: En Borgscene i Niebelungenvers (Copenhagen: Gyldendal, 1906);

Pilgrimen Kamanita (Copenhagen: Gyldendal, 1906); translated by John E. Logie as *The Pilgrim Kamanita: A Legendary Romance* (London: Heinemann, 1911; New York: Dutton, 1912);

Den fuldendtes Hustru: Et Legendedrama (Copenhagen: Gyldendal, 1907);

Verdensvandrerne: Romandigtning i tre Bøger (Copenhagen: Gyldendal, 1910);

Fra Vaar til Høst, illustrated by Hans Tegner (Copenhagen: Gyldendal, 1910);

Villaen ved Havet/Judas: To Fragmenter (Copenhagen: Gyldendal, 1910);

Rudolph Stens Landpraksis, 2 volumes (Copenhagen: Gyldendal, 1913);

Guds Venner (Copenhagen: Gyldendal, 1916);

Den gyldne Gren (Copenhagen: Gyldendal, 1917);

Das heiligste Tier: Ein Elysisches Fabelbuch, illustrated by Paul Hartmann (Leipzig: Quelle & Meyer, 1919);

Madonna della laguna: Eine venezianische Künstlergeschichte, illustrated by Hartmann (Leipzig: Quelle & Meyer, 1920).

Editions and Collections: *Karl Gjellerup, der Dichter und Denker: Sein Leben in Selbsterzeugnissen und Briefen,* 2 volumes, with an introduction by P. A. Rosenberg (Leipzig: Quelle & Meyer, 1921, 1922);

Romulus, with an introduction by Svend Erichsen (Copenhagen: Westermann, 1942).

PLAY PRODUCTIONS: *Herman Vandel: Sørgespil i tre Handlinger,* Copenhagen, Folketeatret (Studentersamfundets fri Teater), 14 May 1892;

Wuthhorn: Sørgespil i fem Handlinger, Copenhagen, Dagmarteatret, 2 March 1893;

Kong Hjarne Skjald: Tragedie i fem Handlinger, Copenhagen, Dagmarteatret, 1 December 1893;

En Million: Skuespil i 3 Handlinger, by Gjellerup and Wilhelm Wolters, Copenhagen, Dagmarteatret, 20 February 1894;

Hans Excellence: Skuespil, Copenhagen, Folketeatret (Studentersamfundets fri Teater), 27 April 1895;

Gift og Modgift: Komedie i fem Akter og paa Vers, Copenhagen, Dagmarteatret, 1 September 1898;

Møllen, Copenhagen, Casino, 12 April 1901;

Offerildene: Et Legendestykke, Copenhagen, Kongelige Teater, 3 September 1904;

Kampen med Muserne (Thamyris, 1–2): Dramatisk Digt, Copenhagen, Kongelige Teater, 9 February 1908.

OTHER: *Nyere dansk Lyrik,* edited by contributing authors, contributions by Gjellerup (Copenhagen: Stochholm, 1883), pp. 353–370;

Tusindfryd: Udvalgte Digte af nyere Forfattere, contributions by Gjellerup (Copenhagen: Schou, 1893), pp. 37–50;

Den ældre Eddas Gudesange, introduced, translated, and explained by Gjellerup (Copenhagen: P. G. Philipsen, 1895);

Johannes Fibiger, *Mit Liv og Levned, som jeg selv har forstaaet det,* edited by Gjellerup (Copenhagen: Gyldendal, 1898);

Nutids-Lyrik: En Samling danske Digte fra Aarhundredets Slutning—1872–1900, edited by Aage Matthison-Hansen, contributions by Gjellerup (Copenhagen: Bergmann, 1899), pp. 71–76;

Danske Kærlighedsdigte, edited by Kai Hoffmann, contributions by Gjellerup (Copenhagen: Gyldendal, 1916), pp. 167–169; (Copenhagen, 1923), pp. 162–164;

Dansk Poesi 1880–1920, edited by Dansk Forfatterforening, contributions by Gjellerup (Copenhagen, Christiania, London & Berlin: Gyldendal, 1922), pp. 8–13;

Digternes Danmark, edited by Frederik Nygaard, contribution by Gjellerup (Copenhagen: Schultz, 1941), pp. 41–42;

Danske lyriske Digte, edited by Mogens Brøndsted and Marie-Louise Paludan, contributions by Gjellerup (Copenhagen: Politiken, 1953), pp. 130–131.

TRANSLATIONS: Richard Wagner, *Valkyrjen, Første Dag af Trilogien "Niebelungens Ring"* (Copenhagen: P. G. Philipsen, 1891);

Otto Weininger, *Kjøn og Character: En principiel Undersøgelse* (Copenhagen: Christiansen, 1905);

Wagner, *Tristan og Isolde* (Copenhagen: Gyldendal, 1912).

While the Nobel Prize in Literature in most instances confirms the career of an author already prominent, in the case of Karl Gjellerup it marked the end of a lifelong struggle for artistic recognition. In spite of his prolific output in many genres and on many subjects, Gjellerup was both an anachronistic and a disharmonious writer, whose high-flown style, passionate abstractions, and indirect language failed to reconcile him with most audiences. He was an erudite freethinker in most of his poetry, drama, and fiction, and his peculiar versatility betrays a moral and religious claim to core convictions that he never found within the confines of Danish culture. Gjellerup's irrepressible idealistic drive led him into various uneasy relations with modern forms of realism.

While his collected work may never achieve classical status, its formal and artistic incoherence—in part acknowledged by the author himself, in part established by leading scholars and critics—is sufficiently interesting to qualify Gjellerup as an intermediary between the modern and the traditional. His remarkably cultured background and upbringing, and his voluntary residence in Dresden during the last half of his life, contribute to a "cross-cultural" literary production that illuminates the intersections between Danish and German traditions.

Karl Adolph Gjellerup was born in Roholte in Zealand on 2 June 1857 to a clergyman, Carl Adolph Gjellerup, and his second wife, Anna Johanne Elisabeth Gjellerup, née Fibiger. Karl had two sisters, Margrethe and Elisabeth, and seven half siblings from his father's first marriage, one of whom was historian Sophus Gjellerup. When Karl's father, who had moved from Roholte to the vicarage of Landet-Lyde in Lolland in 1858, died in 1860, Karl was sent to be raised by another clergyman, his mother's cousin Johannes Fibiger, who was perpetual curate of the Copenhagen Garrison Church, and his wife, Amalie.

While keeping in touch with his mother and sisters, Gjellerup found in the home of his foster parents both emotional devotion and intellectual inspiration. Fibiger was a high-strung and able theologian with deep philological and aesthetic interests, whose own literary ambitions never met with general approval but whose linguistic aptitude and spiritual influence did not leave young Karl untouched. Among the visitors to the Fibiger home were Mathilde Fibiger, his mother's sister and his foster father's cousin, who founded the modern women's movement in Denmark and was a writer in her own right, and historian Edvard Holm, who was married to Amalie Fibiger's sister, Gjellerup's beloved "aunt" Edle.

Gjellerup favored the traditional values of his uncle Edvard over his aunt Mathilde's novelties, and despite his own later ventures into secular modernism and freethinking, his emotional ties to the Fibigers and their old-world universe were never severed. Initially, they secured him good preparatory schooling in Copenhagen, where he was taught by émigré teachers from the formerly Danish duchy in South Jutland. After Fibiger's appointment to the provincial vicarages of Vallensved by Næstved and later Ønslev-Eskildstrup in Falster, the Fibigers gave Gjellerup a hospitable foothold in the pleasurable parsonage culture and nature of Denmark's southern island kingdom, to which he repeatedly returned in later years.

On a superficial level, his departure from home to study theology, with aesthetics and moral philosophy on the side, at the University of Copenhagen seemed to be a pursuit of the same intellectual course that his foster father had followed. Gjellerup, however, had no intention to prepare himself for the ministry. Both the German Bible criticism that attracted his attention and his dissertation on Darwinian evolution and morals, for which he won a gold medal at the university, make evident that the impulses of his upbringing were far from uncontested.

In his many early attempts at poetry, drama, and fiction, Gjellerup had essentially sought to process the cultural stimuli he had absorbed in his home. Its staples were heroic ideals composed of ingredients from Percy Bysshe Shelley, A. C. Swinburne, and German Romantic music and literature, interspersed with the elements of free spirit known from Greek antiquity, Johann Wolfgang von Goethe, and Friedrich Schiller, and a variety of clichés picked up from slightly younger Danish Romantics. Between graduation in 1878 and the prize-winning dissertation of 1880, Gjellerup became a published writer with a stridently modern agenda implanted into a body of immaturely received idealistic norms and values.

As Poul Houe has argued, the way Gjellerup's career began presaged the outcome. Chronologically, Gjellerup debuted with *En Idealist: Skildring* (1878, An Idealist: A Depiction) under the pen name Epigonos, while the first title under his own name was *"Det unge*

Danmark": *En Fortælling fra vore Dage* (1879, The Young Denmark: A Contemporary Narrative). While Epigonos was meant to suggest the author's belonging to the classical tradition, it has been misconstrued to mean an inappropriate imitator. Critics from Herman Bang to Houe, however, have pointed out that idealistic tradition and empirical modernity were conflated from the outset and have remained the mixed blessing of Gjellerup's artistic legacy. His early radicalism was strained and tendentious, and he never managed to silence a different and deeper-seated idealism.

Gjellerup himself later admitted as much in an exchange with poet Holger Drachmann, who had welcomed Epigonos as a young disciple of critic Georg Brandes. In his memorial preface to an anniversary edition of *En Idealist* in 1903, Gjellerup justifiably took issue with Drachmann's verdict. While the protagonist of the novel, an idealistic young aesthete with the German name Max Stauff, insists he is a realist, his more realistic counterpart in *"Det unge Danmark,"* the sequel to *En Idealist,* is an unsuccessful young poetic writer with the unmistakably Danish name Knud Vinge, who has reason to consider himself an idealist. In the final analysis, Max and Knud are characters of a kind—fragmented Romantic heroes (in the tradition of heroes in the works of George Gordon, Lord Byron), yet deprived of romantic fortunes in real life.

For his depictions of such idealistic characters, Gjellerup found inspiration in the realism of Ivan Turgenev's Russian novels. The Danish German Max Stauff is his version of Turgenev's prototype Rudin, and the tragic destiny Max shares with Knud Vinge typifies Gjellerup's reception of his Russian artistic role model. Johan Fjord Jensen has argued that Turgenev's poetic realism was a revelation to Gjellerup and that, while Schiller satisfied Gjellerup's bent for high poetry and grand style, Turgenev influenced his realistic fiction without compromising his virtuous idealism. Throughout the initial phase of his work, Gjellerup found in Turgenev's characters, dramatic compositions, and descriptive impressionism a spiritual alternative to the virtual monopoly of French naturalism on the realistic doctrine of the "Modern Breakthrough" in Nordic literature.

Even more characteristic of Turgenev's influence are the virtuous female characters and the homey situations that frame and subdue them. Turgenev's Helena, the principal character of his novel *On the Eve* (1860) and one of his prototypal women, is related to Helene of *En Idealist,* whose philosophy of love further anticipates Arthur Schopenhauer's philosophy of death, which becomes noticeable in Gjellerup's later work. In like manner, the motif of lost love in the early novels, connoted by the tragic beauty of a setting sun, is at once a reflection of Turgenev and a possible premonition of the total dissolution of individual personality that most scholars find prevalent in the later, Indian phase of Gjellerup's work. As Georg Buchreitz states, Gjellerup's "sympathies for the far East date far back."

During the same period, Gjellerup continued to be involved in more immediate concerns. *Antigonos: En Fortælling fra det andet Aarhundrede* (1880, Antigonos: A Tale from the Second Century) is a narrative, dedicated to radical intellectual Edvard Brandes, about a second-century Christian convert who ends up reverting to the gods of antiquity. Gjellerup appears still to be waging theological war on his own heritage, thinly and abstractly veiling his radical heresies as tributes to classical paganism.

Even less veiled is the cultural radicalism in *Rødtjørn: Sange og Fantasier* (1881, Red Hawthorn: Songs and Fantasies), a collection of lyrical poetry dedicated to Georg Brandes, who gave the work its title and under whose supervision it was composed. Brandes and his brother Edvard had earlier served as mentors to the young writer, correcting his manuscripts and reviewing his books, and in *Rødtjørn* the Brandesian spirit was credited in explicitly sacred terms. In a 7 August 1880 letter to J. P. Jacobsen, Edvard Brandes openly concedes that he and his brother were united in deliberate efforts to prepare "the little Gjellerup" for service in their army of true radicals. But apart from achieving status as the enfant terrible of this camp and frequently attracting the ire of staunch conservatives, little came of Gjellerup's radicalism.

Swedish playwright August Strindberg, in a 26 June 1882 letter to Edvard Brandes, wrote of his delight in *Rødtjørn,* but such prominent modern novelists as Jacobsen were unconvinced of Gjellerup's literary talent, and eventually both Edvard and Georg Brandes gave up on Gjellerup's abstractions and anti-Semitic slurs. Gjellerup's absence in Georg Brandes's *Det moderne Gjennembruds Mænd* (1883, The Men of the Modern Breakthrough) is no less conspicuous than his presence in Bang's *Realisme og Realister* (1879, Realism and Realists) with its less partisan and more artistically inclined view of modern realism.

The uneven mix of classical poetic forms in *Rødtjørn* was but one object of Jacobsen's harsh critique; in addition, its author's thematic exercises in anti-Christian freethinking were pronounced more stridently than Jacobsen could tolerate. Niels Møller, as paraphrased by Claus Jensen, opines that Gjellerup's idealistic search for meaning attracted him to such radicals as Brandes, with whom he had in common only the rejection of conventional Christendom. In the end, says P. A. Rosenberg, Gjellerup's "anti-religious radicalism proved merely a point of transition on his way to an absolute Arian and religious idealism." An ideological gap was opening at this point in his life between his adopted radical view and his own intellectual history, and as the chasm widened, his search for personal balance suggests why he later was inclined toward Buddhist thinking.

In his prizewinning dissertation, *Arvelighed og Moral: En Undersøgelse tilkjendt Universitetets Guldmedaille* (1881, Heredity and Morality: An Investigation Awarded the Gold Medal of the University), Gjellerup's detailed history of Darwinism foreshadowed his own naturalism, and he made a particularly radical turn by adding a section on the moral right to suicide, a move that provoked a reprimand from the university. Nevertheless, as Fjord Jensen points out, Gjellerup's dissertation did not initiate any systematic appropriation of naturalism; instead, Gjellerup turned to the art of Turgenev and the thoughts of Schopenhauer. What appealed to Gjellerup in Charles Darwin's theory of heredity was its transindividual implications, which set it apart from earlier theories of individualism.

Gjellerup's position was not scientific, and in his next book, *Aander og Tider: Et Rekviem over Charles Darwin* (1882, Spirits and Times: A Requiem over Charles Darwin), the title alone professes that positivistic naturalism was a lesser priority than spirituality and musicality. In *Germanernes Lærling: Et Livsafsnit fra vore Dage* (1882, The Teutons' Apprentice: A Period of Life from Our Own Time) the author's radical period was nearing its conclusion. As the narrator battles—on Gjellerup's behalf—with both theology and an actual theologian in fictional disguise, he exposes the tumultuous history of his radicalism. Influenced by the anti-German sentiments of his southern Jutland relatives, the narrator is still attracted to the spirits of Gotthold Ephraim Lessing, Goethe, and Schiller and even fails his divinity-school exam for voicing tenets of German Bible criticism in which he barely believes.

In many respects this Teutons' apprentice is his author's alter ego and so portrays Gjellerup's personal and authorial leanings toward German culture, at least as the alternative to French culture. Danish critic Hakon Stangerup mentions how the social dimension supplants the poetic in this literary work, and his German colleague Heinrich Anz adds that the epochal clash between radical realism and classical idealism, which dominated the cultural scene in Denmark, was transposed by Gjellerup to a strife between undesirable Danish modernity and desirable German classicism. In the same vein, the preferential treatment in the novel of the German woman Johanna foreshadows not only protagonists such as the title figure in *Minna* (1889) but also Eugenia Anna Caroline Heusinger Bendix, a woman Gjellerup had recently met.

Bendix was married to Fritz Bendix, a musician and Brandes's cousin. Gjellerup found her a liberating soul mate and kindred spirit of his other chosen affinities of German origin. Awaiting the outcome of a lengthy divorce procedure, Bendix, who suffered from both the physical and the spiritual climate in Denmark, relocated temporarily to Dresden; Gjellerup joined her there intermittently between 1885 and 24 October 1887, when the couple married. After five years' residence in suburban Copenhagen, they and Bendix's young daughter, Margrethe, moved to Dresden, where they appear to have led a modest and reclusive life.

Preceding his German self-exile, Gjellerup in 1883 went abroad on his principal *Bildungsreise* (journey of spiritual education) to Germany, Switzerland, Italy, Greece, and Russia. In Venice he proofread his novel *Romulus: En Novelle* (1883, Romulus: A Novel) and wrote defensive letters home (for example, on 14 March 1883, in response to Otto Borchsenius, who had reviewed the book) about his use of factual material behind the dramatic story. A psychological treatment of a horse subjected to military abuse, the novel extends its humaneness to the human experience of love. Its female protagonist comes to self-realization as she learns to reach beyond the protective barrier of her social class by identifying with the suffering animal, and her reticent male counterpart comes to her defense as she stands up to the creature's tormentor. Her practical ethics becomes his source of inspiration, and in siding with her, he comes to realize how to reclaim an innocent past as part of a dual responsibility. Meanwhile, as the suffering horse finally succumbs to its mortal destiny, the modern world barely takes notice.

The uplifting dimension of this novel is its compelling plea for community—between individuals and between their community and the larger world. It defies the more radical Brandesian notion of social responsibility, and Georg Brandes, who otherwise constructively suggested condensation of the narrative (adopted in its subsequent editions), failed to appreciate its venture into a social realism that is both formal and thematic, both tragic and poetic. When the images of virtuous womanhood modeled on Eugenia Gjellerup and the import of Turgenev on Gjellerup's style and characterization are added to this mix, the allegiance of the book to the modern movement is ambiguous. Its literal juxtaposition of Darwin the scientific naturalist and Richard Wagner the musical monumentalist further suggests that Gjellerup is both ahead of and behind the times.

In his subsequent novel, *G-Dur: En Kammer-Novelle* (1883, G-Major: A Chamber Story), the musical title and looser atmospheric composition point to an attenuated Russian influence. The tragedy *Brynhild* (1884), finally, shows the departure from Brandes's artistic prescriptions to be nearly complete. While *Brynhild* may seem a drama about problems debated in the 1870s, it is rather, by Paul V. Rubow's account, a problematic case of superhumans battling society in the mode of Wagner's theatrical aesthetics. Hans Brix calls *Brynhild* a post-Romantic drama of ideals, for which Drachmann had paved the way, and Brix claims that its complexity encompasses characterization, pictorial language, dialogue, the role of the choir, and many other technical and substantive elements. While its composition tends to defy logic, the central struggle between Brynhild and Gudrun—to the detriment of their male counterparts Gunnar and Sigurd—is powerful and revealing of a love so uncompromisingly ideal that only death can see it through. Compared to the heroic sternness of the Norse source material, Gjellerup's version, according to C. E. Jensen, emphasizes romantic passion; but it also brings the philosophical state of Nirvana to the fore. Ultimately, the will to live succumbs to nothingness, and the individual personality ceases to exist, as Schopenhauer envisioned.

Brynhild is dedicated to Eugenia Gjellerup, and critics agree that it celebrates both the author's struggle to win her hand in marriage and the virtuous and monogamous sanctification of holy matrimony to which she (like so many of his female characters) bears witness. The embracement of eternal values and rejection of instant gratification in *Brynhild* made it "the most significant dramatic work in the grand style by century's end," according to Vilhelm Andersen, and Gjellerup never achieved anything else similar to it. The critical reception, by such critics as Carl Behrens, Julius Clausen, and later Rubow, was favorable, although no theatrical performance ever ensued.

While his break with naturalistic realism was now complete, Gjellerup's formal denouncement of his former associates came upon his return from his 1883 European journey. In *En klassisk Maaned: Billeder og Stemninger fra en Grækenlandsrejse* (1884, A Classical Month: Images and Poetic Descriptions from a Journey to Greece) he deals rather straightforwardly with the Grecian leg of the trip, whereas in *Vandreaaret: Skildringer og Betragtninger* (1885, The Year of Wandering: Depictions and Reflections), in which he treats the remaining sites of his tour, he admits to having lacked a personal center of gravity and a natural sense of balance between conflicting attractions in his intellectual environment. His formal resolution confirms his earlier experience—that his future lies with stylistic monumentality and with actual reality only insofar as it informs a style of this nature. The artistic goal is not an aesthetic affirmation of the momentary, but an ethical-religious striving to move beyond this world and its partisan bickering. Accordingly, he is less enthusiastic about the Italian Renaissance than about idyllic scenes in Switzerland, not to mention the tastes of a pessimism he enjoys in Russia and the near Orient.

In *Saint-Just: Historisk Sørgespil i fem Handlinger* (1886, Saint-Just: Historical Tragedy in Five Acts), a play about Louis Saint-Just, Maximilien Robespierre's incorrigible match in revolutionary zeal, Gjellerup attempted to dress his supreme idealism in historical costume. His failure to do so to the satisfaction of any theater director caused him deeper distress than any of his many other aborted bids for a career as playwright. A similar fate befell his dramatic poem *Thamyris* (1887). Like its precursor, it obstructed the alleged purpose in *Vandreaaret* to serve art before (cultural) politics. It, too, was art of a second order—literature about literature—and with an incoherent fusion of Nordic Germanic and classical idioms underneath its high and learned style.

Rosenberg sees the hero's blindness as signifying a denial of this world and insight into one beyond finitude. Buddhist-like elusiveness attached itself to Greek particulars. The sequel to the poem, called *Helikon: Et dramatisk Digt* (1887, Helikon: A Dramatic Poem), with ingredients of Friedrich Nietzsche and Goethe, and mythological figures Marsyas and Midas as parts of its erudition, affords an even more imaginative confrontation of idealism and realism. No less ambitious than *Thamyris*, *Helikon* met with authorial disappointment, as documented by Georg Nørregård, although an abbreviated version was eventually performed at the Kongelige Teater (Royal Theater) in Copenhagen in 1908.

Gjellerup's next work, *En arkadisk Legende* (1887, A Legend from Arcadia), is a prose narrative situated in the same Greek antiquity as *Thamyris*. In *Hagbard og Signe: En erotisk Tragedie i fem Handlinger* (1888, Hagbard and Signe: An Erotic Tragedy in Five Acts), written after his marriage to Eugenia Gjellerup and dedicated to her, Gjellerup returns to drama and to the kind of Nordic source material that inspired *Brynhild*. But his effort to incorporate literary impulses from a "non-historical early Medieval" into difficult ancient and medieval meters failed. And in *Bryllupsgaven: Rococo-Komedie fra det galante Sachsen i fem Handlinger* (1888, The Wedding Gift: A Rococo Comedy from Gallant Saxony in Five Acts), set in Dresden, he fails to make the rococo elegant and the comedy humorous.

The novel *Minna*, on the other hand, marks one of Gjellerup's few popular successes. It, too, takes place in the Dresden area, and its title character is cast in the same mold as Eugenia Gjellerup and the fictive females in her wake. In a conflict between her physical desire for one man and an ethical affinity to the narrator of the novel, Minna's weakness for the former leads to insanity and death, albeit with the empathy of both narrator and author. Minna may be an anachronism, but the world in which she is doomed is a contemporary one. The work includes clear references to Goethe and Schiller, though the poetic side of the text is not mired in cliché.

In 1889 Gjellerup wrote an essay titled "Schiller, Flaubert, Schandorph, Rudolf Schmidt," a harsh polemic in defense of Schiller against charges by critic Rudolf Schmidt that Schiller's later dramas sacrifice quotidian realism for an indistinct idealism. Gjellerup retorted that Schiller always sought to express the general in the individual, but then he went on to say that in Schiller's work the individual at its best is the typical—or the most deeply humane. The claim to realism is precisely what makes a text by Schiller a valid idealistic construction, according to Gjellerup, who views a text by himself in the same light.

In *Min Kjærligheds Bog* (1889, My Love Book), a Danish version of Heinrich Heine's *Buch der Lieder* (1827, The Book of the Songs), Gjellerup gathered older and new poems around his recurrent love motif. Critic C. E. Jensen compares the collection, with its intended classicism, to "a bouquet of wilted violets." Most of Gjellerup's anthologized poems are from this volume, including four lines titled "Et Par" (A Couple). Bordering on the chaotic, love in this poem remains part of a conflicted harmony that gives nightly birth to an ever-recurrent world. The unity of real and ideal, eternal and dynamic is consistent with Gjellerup's growing interest in Indian philosophy. "Et Par" also alludes to the ideas and feelings associated with music that he explored in 1889 in the leitmotivs of Wagner's principal work, *Der Ring Des Niebelungen* (1874, The Ring of the Niebelung). His extensive work on Wagner, which was honored by his being extended an invitation to the Wagner festival in Bayreuth in 1914, includes translations of the Valkyrie parts of *Der Ring Des Niebelungen* and later of *Tristan and Isolde* (1912). It is a work related to Gjellerup's general interest in Norse lore, as demonstrated later in his 1895 translations from *Den ældre Eddas Gudesange*.

Herman Vandel: Sørgespil i tre Handlinger (1891, Herman Vandel: Tragedy in Three Acts; first performed, 1892), like *Minna*, is about the catastrophic consequences of love gone astray. Herman's commitment to marry the girl he has seduced at the expense of the choice of his heart is considered immoral and is paid for with suicide. C. E. Jensen compares Gjellerup's charges against conventional marriage to Søren Kierkegaard's assault upon the state church. One betrays the absolute idea of marriage; the other, the idea of self-sacrificing Christianity. In *Wuthhorn: Sørgespil i fem Handlinger* (1893, Wuthhorn: A Tragedy in Five Acts; first performed, 1893) another triangular love drama unfolds on a Swiss mountaintop, whereas *Kong Hjarne Skjald: Tragedie i fem Handlinger* (1893, King Hjarne Skald: Tragedy in Five Acts; first performed, 1893) is a play about love and war in the mythic past of Denmark; its skaldic rhetoric in iambic verse is both powerful and cumbersome. In *En Million: Skuespil i tre Handlinger. Efter Nikolaus Pawlows Novelle* (1894, A Million: A Play in Three Acts. Based on Nikolaus Pawlow's Short Story; first performed in Danish as *En Million: Skuespil i 3 Handlinger,* 1894), initially written in German by Gjellerup with Wilhelm Wolters to earn money and premiered in Berlin, the theme is love and money, while the novel *Pastor Mors: En underlig Historie* (Pastor Mors: A Strange Story, 1894) is a peculiar tale about young love resurrected in the imagination of an old divinity professor. Unlike the Christian resurrection of the flesh, the professor's love story is reborn in an incorporeal sphere above and beyond the mundane world of human vanity. An allegorical dissolution of individual mortality, Gjellerup's learned theological and philosophical text is written on the border between neo-Danish and neo-German spiritual life with an unmistakable leaning away from Lutheran doctrine toward the Buddhistic teachings about Nirvana.

The love triangle in *Hans Excellence: Skuespil indledet ved en Efterskrift til mine Dramer* (1895, His Excellency: A Play Introduced by a Postscript to My Dramas; first performed, 1895) includes a prominent politician who bestows marital sentiments upon his wife and erotic passion upon his mistress in accordance with Nietzsche's moral code for the superhuman. Human affairs are once again depicted in high style, yet with realistic settings, and the experimental text is prefaced by a "postscript to my dramas," in which Gjellerup praises Schopenhauer, whose thinking led him to the Indian and Buddhist teachings for final clarification of his innermost spiritual needs. Moral superiority is not individualism but religious self-abrogation, as illustrated by Wagner's musical dramas. C. E. Jensen finds Gjellerup's moral code religious in spite of all his rebellion and calls it Buddhism interspersed with Christian redemption. Self-assertion and self-denial become one—above the heads of common crowds. And, as Rosenberg writes, with the guidance of Schopenhauer's philosophy of will as the core principle of life, of suffering as the common state of life, of compassion as the foundation of ethics, and of self-annihilation as liberation, Gjellerup definitively found his way out of the spheres of influence of radical Copenhagen and out of the shadows of Darwin and his philosophical counterpart, Herbert Spencer.

In 1896 Gjellerup published another dramatic love story in prose, *Møllen: Roman i fem Bøger* (The Mill: A Novel in Five Books; first performed, 1901), written in Dresden but set in the Danish island environment of his youth. The newly widowed miller contemplates marriage to the sister of a religious forester; yet, both the miller and his journeyman are infatuated with the maid of the mill. Suddenly the miller proposes to the maid, but while he is in town to secure royal permission to marry the girl, she enters the mill to flirt and conspire against him with the journeyman. Later he catches them unaware and is able, unnoticed, to arrange for the machinery of the mill to crush them. He then marries the forester's sister, but, tormented by guilt, he confesses to his crime and dies in prison.

Gjellerup's combination of Christian and Indian thought is here extended with elements of superstition. Yet, the author still endeavors to reconcile the metaphysical aspects of the novel with its realistic environment, specifically verisimilitude in mill design. The psychological analysis is intimate; the composition is clear and atmospheric; and the mix of natural and supernatural is both mythical and symbolic. While Edvard Brandes rejected the irrational features, Andersen valued that even domestic animals function within the mythological universe in place of gods and demons. *Møllen* is one of Gjellerup's memorable accomplishments; it was adapted for both stage and screen productions.

Gjellerup's many years in Dresden were marked by solitude and health problems, vacations in the surrounding areas and abroad, and occasional professional visits to Denmark. A few Danish friends and family members dropped by now and then, but the unremarkable daily routines prevailed. Musical events were his preferred entertainment, and he continued with mixed results to pursue the theatrical career he felt he had been denied in Denmark. Yet, his output as a German writer was limited chiefly to newspaper articles and German versions of his books, and the kudos he received came from a few critics and academics. Meanwhile, his personal ties to Denmark remained vivid even as his professional and intellectual attachments gradually vanished or soured. An occasional recipient of the Ancherske Travel Stipend, he was awarded a Civil List Pension in 1889. All the same, he was never wealthy.

Mit formentlige Højforræderi mod det danske Folk (1897, My Alleged High Treason against the Danish People) is an indication of his ambiguous feelings for Denmark; it is a booklet in which he rejects charges leveled against him that he has betrayed his Danish language and culture. While gladly conceding an admiration for such Germans as Otto von Bismarck, he holds the Danish national-liberals responsible for loss of the southern provinces of Denmark and for alienating her German roots.

After the well-crafted story *Konvolutten: En graphologisk Studie* (1897, The Envelope: A Study in Graphology) came the novel *Ved Grændsen* (1897, At the Border), which refers in its title not to the contested southern frontier but to the sea border farther east, south of the island of Falster, where *Møllen* was also set. Idyllic provincial towns and landscapes, viewed through the exilic writer's nostalgic lens, constitute ties otherwise severed by the contested political border. A drama performed in Copenhagen and called *Gift og Modgift: Komedie i fem Akter og paa Vers* (1898, Poison and Antidote: A Comedy in Five Acts and in Verse; first performed, 1898) continues Gjellerup's depictions of love as both confusing and tragic, and a collection of *Fabler* (1898, Fables) includes a versified story told by Buddha. In *Tankelæserinden: Sjællandsk Præstegaardsidyl* (1901, The Female Thought-Reader: A Zealand Vicarage Idyll), the author returns to his foster father's idyllic vicarage of Vallensved for yet another love intrigue and yet another exilic reflection on the land of his youth.

With the exception of the short *Elskovsprøven: En Borgscene i Niebelungenvers* (1906, The Love Trial: A Castle Scene in Niebelungen Verse), a play in one act and medieval meter set in a castle on the Rhine, the first decade of the 1900s is dominated by Gjellerup's major Indian works, of which *Fabler* gave but a simple taste. *Offerildene: Et Legendestykke* (1903, The Sacrificial Pyres: A Play of Legend; first performed, 1904), based on passages from the Upanishads (treatises that deal with Brahma knowledge), was performed by the Kongelige Teater in Copenhagen and at different locations in Germany. Its lead character is a Vedic-Age Brahman who is summoned by his king in northern India to join a speech competition, which he wins; meanwhile, one of his apprentices, left behind in the master's house, has won the love of the Brahman's daughter and eventually obtains the returning Brahman's position and prize of one thousand white cows as well. Rosenberg mentions how the confrontation of self-worship and worship of the world god in the play maps the only way to redemption, while Rubow more specifically notes that the play remains at the stage of the Upanishads, where it develops the pessimism of late Brahmanism and reminds one of Schopenhauer's thought, to which Gjellerup had been guided by his German friend Paul Deussen.

In *Pilgrimen Kamanita* (1906; translated as *The Pilgrim Kamanita: A Legendary Romance*, 1911), in particular, Gjellerup articulates his Buddhist subject matter in the style of late Jugend or art nouveau, the flowery ornamental style typical of the fin-de-siècle period and its search for artistic freedom. Fritz Paul has demonstrated how this decorative, precious, and heavily symbolic style and esoteric arrangement is in perfect concert with the content of the novel and its combined spirit of

Schopenhauer, Nietzsche, and Wagner. In the first part, Kamanita, in his search for the Buddha, meets the elevated one himself but fails to recognize him. Yet, in the process of telling his unfulfilled life story to the goldsmith's lovable daughter Vasithi, he experiences Buddha's philosophy. This exuberant and exotic narrative is then deciphered in the pseudophilosophical appendix to the second part in the manner of Nietzsche's Zarathustra. Here the reader learns of Kamanita's cosmic existence after death; his reencounter on the beaches of the divine Ganges with Vasithi, from whose affection circumstances of life had estranged him; and finally his disappearance into the endless Brahma world of night and grayness.

As opposed to Rubow, who saw Gjellerup's Indian phase as a self-absorbed abstraction immune to outside influences, Paul points to a process of transformation in which Nietzsche is turned into a Buddhist with a bent for neo-Romantic biology. Incompatible stylistic elements are brought together to render rationally comprehensible a universe composed of esoteric mythology and idioms of decadence. On the one hand, many of these influences are subject to Gjellerup's biases about the Orient; on the other hand, his appropriations do foreshadow fin-de-siècle and later stylistic movements. His pseudoscientific Jugend style and various exotic forms lend themselves to kitsch but also to modernistic constructs and radical revisions. The reality they elicit lies in the power of an imaginative will whose verbal expression is suggestive rather than referential.

While Gjellerup's biographer Nørregård deems the Danish version of *Kamanita* "exceptionally well-written," Paul considers the German version less disruptive of the aesthetic illusion. But linguistics aside, the core of the story is indisputably the creative nihilism included in the narrator's dictum that comprehending the downfall of creation enables comprehension of the uncreated. In *Den fuldendtes Hustru: Et Legendedrama* (1907, The Perfect One's Wife: A Legend Drama) and the cognate novel *Verdensvandrerne: Romandigtning i tre Bøger* (1910, The World Wanderers: Novelistic Fiction in Three Books), the soul continues its wanderings toward Nirvana through mystical stages and levels. Rubow finds this drama life-denying in the extreme, like "the idea of life as smoke from a fire that has never burnt," a nihilism less creative than pure. Rosenberg, by contrast, stresses Gjellerup's ability to evoke such exotic Indian environs solely on the basis of his imagination.

Subsequent to the Indian decade, Gjellerup returned with new insights to cultural settings closer to home. A small selection of his poetry, *Fra Vaar til Høst* (From Spring to Autumn), and two epic fragments, *Villaen ved Havet/Judas: To Fragmenter* (The Villa by the Sea/Judas: Two Fragments), are both from 1910, but his first major attempt to integrate the Nirvana-thought into a familiar milieu is the novel *Rudolph Stens Landpraksis* (1913, Rudolph Sten's Country Practice), another intricate love story endowed with an atmosphere of the country culture the author knew from his youth and laden with the philosophizing his readers had come to expect from his later years. Eventually, realism gives way to an impersonal escape from time and space. In the allegedly historical novel *Guds Venner* (1916, God's Friends), the Buddhist trend has yielded to Christian sentiments. Finally, in his last book in Danish, *Den gyldne Gren* (1917, The Golden Bough), Gjellerup, following in the footsteps of James Frazer's work with the same title, depicts characters and events in classical Rome.

According to Nørregård, Gjellerup's desire for the Nobel Prize was driven not by claims to honor and fame; rather, he primarily coveted the award as recognition for his artistic form, and only secondly as relief from dire financial need. This depiction is debatable. What is not in dispute is that Gjellerup, years before he actually received the prize, repeatedly bombarded influential authors, critics, and literary scholars (including his cousin, the philosopher Harald Høffding, a Nobel candidate himself) with letters soliciting both their support of his candidacy and various actions on his behalf. To the best of his ability he even sought to promote himself for consideration and did not mince words about those who stood in his way, be they other potential candidates, members of the Swedish Academy and Nobel committee, or people who failed to act in his favor the way he expected. Arguments concerning his literary worthiness do surface in these letters, but a disillusioned craving for monetary rescue was the foremost propellant behind the indigent author's appeal to his recipients.

Besides Nørregård, both Ahnlund and Claus Jensen have outlined the long road leading from Gjellerup's first nomination for the prize in 1911 to his receiving it in 1917. In 1911 he and Ernst von der Recke were nominated by professors at Copenhagen University for sharing the prize, which, incidentally, was not the solution Gjellerup (who was also backed by several learned German men of letters) preferred. But again, his financial dearth compelled him to swallow his pride, especially if he were to receive the lion's share of the total amount in exchange for agreeing to a split prize.

Responding sarcastically to this failed nomination was Georg Brandes, who himself was already considered an important Danish contender for the Nobel Prize in Literature (and who also, behind a mask of indifference, pined for the award). But the idealism that seemed to unite von der Recke with Gjellerup, and both of them with a core stipulation in Alfred Nobel's will, was conspicuous by its absence in Brandes's realist and modernist writings as they were understood by the governing bodies behind the prize.

A significant minority nevertheless disagreed with this narrow interpretation of "idealism," and the Brandes candidacy remained a possibility for years. At the same time the apparent weakness of Gjellerup's artistic work put his candidacy in jeopardy. At an exilic distance from Danish life and language, yet not entirely adapted to German culture either, Gjellerup, moreover, was in a precarious no-man's-land position, especially considering the anti-German sentiments in Denmark during World War I. Under the caption: "Danish author Karl Gjellerup travels to Denmark as a German tourist on Swedish money," a 1917 cartoon caricature depicted a minuscule and bewildered Gjellerup in a *Wandervogel* outfit, arriving in Denmark and timidly asking a policeman for directions: "Could somevun please show me ze way to ze Dänisch authors' association?"

Still, for all his bloodless abstractions and stylistic exaggerations, often bordering on the ridiculous, Gjellerup's work remained unquestionably "idealistic," even in the Christian sense of the word, after the author had recently revisited Christian positions he had earlier abandoned for excursions into Indian thought and mysticism. Given the insufficient support for Brandes, the proposal of a shared Nobel Prize for Denmark with Gjellerup as one of the recipients picked up momentum, if not immediately. The prizes between 1912 and 1916 (there was no prize in 1914) went to no Danes but to other nationals such as the Swedish author Verner von Heidenstam in 1916.

Both Heidenstam and the 1890s in Swedish literature, which he espoused, were deeply beholden to influences from Gjellerup's fin-de-siècle style—more deeply beholden than were any Danish writers—and so the elevation of Heidenstam to the Swedish Academy greatly enhanced his Danish role model's chances for securing the Nobel award.

The problem was Henrik Pontoppidan, the author who had emerged as Gjellerup's major competition for the prize. Born the same year, these two writers could well have been from different planets. A powerful presence in Danish letters, firmly rooted in its national traditions, and producing the most merciless, yet classical, realism of the age, Pontoppidan was by Danish standards an author head and shoulders above Gjellerup, for whom he, incidentally, harbored tacit but utter contempt.

Yet, Pontoppidan too failed the test of "idealism" as it was implemented by the conservative Swedish Academy members and the Nobel committee. It took a recommendation of Gjellerup and Pontoppidan (in the event Georg Brandes proved unacceptable to the Swedes) by the foremost historian of Danish literature, Professor Vilhelm Andersen, to sway the historian Harald Hjärne, the leading member of the Swedish opposition to Pontoppidan, to revise his position, which he did only partially, and chiefly under the influence of Andersen's recent monograph on Pontoppidan. In those days a single work by a contending author was usually the basis for the Nobel award, and Pontoppidan's latest opus, the novel sequence *De Dødes Rige* (1912–1916, The Realm of the Dead), was the only one that Hjärne would narrowly grant his idealistic approval (Gjellerup's counterpart, by his own account, being most likely the tragedy *Brynhild*).

Eventually, the compromise, or shared award to Pontoppidan and Gjellerup, was hammered out, not least because it also showed some consideration for Brandes, who would now receive the signal that while he himself might not pass idealistic muster, he could at least take comfort in the fact that it took two authors to counterbalance him. It was, altogether, an emergency solution and a tricky balancing act that left Gjellerup with half of the 1917 Nobel Prize in Literature. In fact, his belated luck probably also rested upon the death in 1917 of Jakob Knudsen, a more profound conservative idealist than Gjellerup, and one with strong support at least in the Nobel committee.

Not only did the prize come too late to buttress Gjellerup's artistic ego or his finances, but also the reactions to his award were mostly critical reminders of his strained artistic grappling with a versatility of philosophical outlooks and symbolic endeavors. Unlike his corecipient Pontoppidan, he did not fare well in his own times, nor has he since. Hence, his final status as Nobel laureate came to symbolize his troubled and defiant life and work.

In 1919 and 1920 two more books by Gjellerup appeared in Germany. *Das heiligste Tier: Ein Elysisches Fabelbuch* (1919, The Holiest Animal: An Elysian Book of Fables) is built on animal legends and myths with tributes to Buddha, and the posthumous *Madonna della laguna: Eine venezianische Künstlergeschichte* (1920, Madonna of the Lagoon: The Story of a Venetian Artist) is a narrative with traits of comedy and Venetian atmosphere. These late works of fiction were followed by another posthumous publication in German, *Karl Gjellerup, der Dichter und Denker: Sein Leben in Selbsterzeugnissen und Briefen* (1921, 1922), Gjellerup's autobiography as artist and thinker, supplemented with a selection of his letters and an introduction by his Danish friend Rosenberg.

This finale is indicative of Gjellerup's development. He always relished strains of German culture, but after moving to Dresden his immersion approached identification. Most of his books were written in both languages, often in German first, if not in German only. During World War I he even wrote the bulk of his large correspondence in German in order to accommodate his censors. Meanwhile, the war broke his spirit. By the end of his life, his defiance had merged with despair, and he often wrote home to Denmark that his authorial ambitions had come to naught. The thought of death became increasingly comforting to his pride, and he died on 11 October 1919, about a year after the armistice. His grave is in Dresden.

In a letter from 1880, pastor Fibiger predicted that his adopted son would return to Christianity after his radical experiments. The pastor was proven both right and wrong. Religious fervor did fill his son's personality, but with thoughts and sentiments that tended toward eliminating the notion of personhood as an integral whole. Karl Gjellerup's artistic gifts and priorities have been debated by critics, as have his political attitudes; yet, there is no denying that as a writer he crossed cultural borders and served as an intermediary between the traditional and the modern. From his position at the margins of modern letters in both Denmark and Germany, he made his mark on a few notable Scandinavians at center stage—for example, Swedish Nobel laureate Heidenstam and Danish Nobel nominee Valdemar Rørdam.

Letters:

"Karl Gjellerup: Nogle Breve [to William Behrend]," *Tilskueren*, 2, no. 36 (1919): 407–420.

Biography:

Georg Nørregård, *Karl Gjellerup—en biografi* (Copenhagen: C. A. Reitzel, 1988).

References:

Claes Ahlund, "Karl Gjellerup: *Germanernes Lærling* (1882)," in *Den skandinaviska universitetsromanen 1877–1890* (Stockholm: Almqvist & Wiksell International, 1990), pp. 74–85;

Knut Ahnlund, "Ett delat Nobelpris," in *Diktarliv i Norden: Litterära essäer* (Stockholm: Brombergs, 1981), pp. 248–279;

Vilhelm Andersen, "Firsernes Folk," in *Illustreret dansk Litteraturhistorie*, 4, no. 2 (Copenhagen: Gyldendal, 1925), pp. 376–393;

Heinrich Anz, "Ein Literarischer Grenzgänger im Fin de siècle: Karl Gjellerup zwischen dänischer und deutscher Literatur," in *Kulturelle Identitäten in der deutschen Literatur des 20. Jahrhunderts*, edited by Heinrich Detering and Herbert Krämer (Frankfurt am Main: Peter Lang, 1998), pp. 21–33;

Anz, "'Rastloses Schaffen in zwei Sprachen': Karl Gjellerup (1857–1919) im interkulturellen Kontext," in *Blickwinkel: Kulturelle Optik und interkulturelle Gegenstandskonstitution*, edited by Alois Wierlacher and Georg Stötzel (Munich: Ludicium, 1996), pp. 489–502;

Herman Bang, "Karl Gjellerup," in his *Realisme og Realister* (Copenhagen: Schubothe, 1879), pp. 97–113;

Edvard Brandes and Georg Brandes, *Brevveksling med nordiske Forfattere og Videnskabsmænd*, volumes 1–6, 8, edited by Morten Borup, with the assistance of Francis Bull and John Landquist (Copenhagen: Gyldendal, 1939–1942);

Hans Brix, "Karl Gjellerup," in his *Danmarks Digtere* (Copenhagen: Aschehoug, 1951), pp. 441–445;

Georg Buchreitz, "Europæiske paavirkninger paa Karl Gjellerups forfatterskab til 1900," *Edda*, 30 (1930): 400–433;

Kjell Espmark, *Det litterära Nobel priset: Principer och värderingar bakom besluten* (Stockholm: Norstedts, 1986); translated as *The Nobel Prize in Literature: A Study of the Criteria behind the Choices* (Boston: G. K. Hall, 1991);

Johan Fjord Jensen, "Karl Gjellerup—poetisk realisme," in his *Turgenjev i dansk åndsliv* (Copenhagen: Gyldendal, 1961), pp. 222–223, 235–252;

Vridhagiri Ganeshan, *Das Indienbild deutscher Dichter um 1900: Dauthendey, Bonsels, Mauthner, Gjellerup, Hermann Keyserling und Stefan Zweig: Ein Kapitel deutschindischer Geistesbeziehungen im frühen 20. Jahrhundert* (Bonn: Bouvier Verlag Herbert Grundmann, 1975), pp. 188–233;

Constantin Grossman, "Karl Gjellerup: Ein Gedankenblatt," *Dreiundzwanzigstes Jahrbuch der Schopenhauer-Gesellschaft*, 23 (1936): 249–268;

Poul Houe, "Begyndelsen på enden: Karl Gjellerups debutroman(er)," in *On the Threshold: New Studies in Nordic Literature*, edited by Janet Garton and Michael Robinson (Norwich, U.K.: Norvik Press, 2002), pp. 144–151;

Houe, "Det epokaltypiske grænsetilfælde [Review of Olaf C. Nybo, *Karl Gjellerup*]," *Nordica*, 20 (2003): 344–350;

C. E. Jensen, "Karl Gjellerup," in *Vore Dages Digtere: Karakteristiker* (Copenhagen: Det nordiske Forlag, 1898), pp. 1–16;

Claus Jensen, "Karl Gjellerup and Henrik Pontoppidan (Literature 1917): An Odd Couple," in *Neighbouring Nobel: The History of the Nobel Prizes*, edited by Henry Nielsen and Keld Nielsen (Aarhus: Aarhus University Press, 2001), pp. 147–206;

Marius Kristensen, "Karl Gjellerup," in *Hovedtræk af nordisk Digtning i Nutiden*, edited by Ejnar Skovrup (Copenhagen: Aschehoug, 1920), pp. 103–109;

Sven Møller Kristensen, *Impressionismen i dansk prosa 1870–1900* (Copenhagen: Gyldendal, 1965);

Olaf C. Nybo, *Karl Gjellerup–ein literarischer Grenzgänger des Fin-de-siècle* (Hamburg: Verlag Dr. Kovac, 2002);

Fritz Paul, "Gjellerup und die Aufwertung des Jugendstils," *Danske Studier,* 66 (1971): 81–90;

P. A. Rosenberg, "Karl Gjellerup," *Ord och Bild,* 27 (1918): 218–226;

Paul V. Rubow, "Herman Bangs Samtidige: Karl Gjellerup," in his *Herman Bang og flere kritiske Studier* (Copenhagen: Gyldendal, 1958), pp. 79–86;

Rudolf Schmidt, "Et Gjensyn," *Literatur og Kritik,* 1 (1889): 288–296;

Kalle Sorainen, "Gjellerup och Höffding," *Orbis Litterarum,* 6 (1948): 115–132;

Hakon Stangerup, "Karl Gjellerup," in *Danmarks store Digtere,* volume 2, edited by Stangerup (Odense: Skandinavisk Bogforlag, 1944), pp. 73–82;

Stangerup, *Kulturkampen,* 2 volumes (Copenhagen: Gyldendal, 1946);

Nicolae Zberae, "K. Gjellerup: A Master of Expression of Indian Thought," *Indo-Asian Culture,* 19, no. 1 (1970): 30–33.

Papers:

The major collections of Karl Gjellerup's letters and manuscripts are at the Danish Royal Library in Copenhagen and at the *Sächsischen Landesbibliothek* in Dresden.

1917 Nobel Prize in Literature Presentation

Karl Gjellerup received the Nobel Prize in Literature on 8 November 1917. There was no award ceremony, presentation, or lecture that year. This account of the works of Gjellerup and fellow winner Henrik Pontoppidan was written by Sven Söderman, Swedish critic, sometime after the awarding of the prize.

Karl Gjellerup was born in 1857 and died on October 11, 1919. Like Henrik Pontoppidan, he came from a family of ministers. He chose a career in the clergy although he felt no special calling for it; rather his inclinations drew him strongly toward literature, and alongside his "bread and butter studies" he devoted himself to reading the Greek, English, and especially the German classics. In the course of his theological studies, he came gradually to take a purely negative attitude toward theology and became attracted by the literary radicalism led by Georg Brandes. In 1878 he made his literary début under the pseudonym of "Epigonos" with a short novel entitled *En idealist* [An Idealist]. He published next, in quick succession, a series of tales and poems in which he posed as a fanatic enemy of all theology and as a sworn partisan of Darwin and the doctrine of evolution.

After this first period of anti-theological battles, not marked by a profound originality, Gjellerup undertook a trip abroad during which he collected his thoughts and found his intellectual equilibrium. At the same time his literary talent took on more distinct outlines: the description of an era, *Romulus* (1883); the beautiful short story "G-Dur" (1883) [G-Major], a portrait of intimacy; and especially the great drama *Brynhild* (1884), which marks the peak of his talent during this period. The theme of this drama is the episode of the Volsunga Saga in which Sigurd and Brunhilde, finding themselves on the same mountain, are separated by their destiny but dream of and desire one another. This waiting, full of torment, this quiet desire, imbues with sentiment the tragedy which is presented with strength and with great poetic and pictorial richness. The verse, especially in the choruses composed in the ancient fashion, attains great lyric beauty. The scope of the work is due to its depth and form; through its idealism and moral elevation it contrasts absolutely with the other productions of the naturalistic period during which it was written. In spite of his freedom of thought, Gjellerup had at bottom only a few common bonds with the naturalistic school. He had, on the contrary, many more addresses with German classicism, with the literature of antiquity, and with the wealth of sentiments of Wagner, and when he realized this fact, he broke sharply and publicly with the school of Brandes in his travel book, *Vandreaaret* (1885) [Wander Year]. His literary production (plays, lyric poems, stories) was henceforth oriented toward idealism, but at the beginning it only barely succeeded from the artistic point of view, even though the richness of his poetic gifts was always visible in it. The best of the books he published during the last years of this period was the charming novel *Minna* (1889), a truly beautiful love story and a delicate study of feminine psychology which must be classed in the highest rank of Scandinavian novels. Let us cite also that novel with the broadest foundations and a solid construction, *Møllen* (1896) [The Mill], a curious analysis of the state of mind of a murderer who becomes remorseful and denounces himself; it is a work of tragic grandeur. Less remarkable as works of art, but expressive of Gjellerup's high moral ideas about marriage and the relationship between the sexes, are his modern bourgeois dramas *Herman Vandel* (1891), *Wuthhorn* (1893), and *Hans Excellence* (1895). These dramas are not a plea for marriage. Indeed, the author puts the idea of marriage above banal conventions, and precisely because he puts it so high, he does not find it realized in ordinary marriages. He proposes as a purer model the free union, even though it would not have the consecration of church or state, provided that this union is the only one in a human life.

These dramas, whose tendency is religious despite their individualistic revolts, form a transition between the first ideas of the author and those which characterize the last and most significant period of his literary life. It was without doubt the enthusiasm for the musical drama of Wagner, to which he devoted a masterly work, which led him to the study of Buddhist wisdom with its annihilation of the personality in the universal world of Nirvana. Among the works written by Gjellerup in the twentieth century, the best ones are inspired precisely by these speculations on India and place on stage Hindu subjects which he has treated so poetically and idealistically that they have aroused general admiration. This period of his work began with a musical play, *Offerildene* (1903) [The Sacrificial Fires], the legend of a young disciple of Brahma who in the simplicity of his pious soul discovers wisdom beneath the literal sense of the law, and who wishes to preserve in the world the three sacrificial fires: the fire of the soul, the flame of love, and the fire of the funeral pyre which consumes the body. Philosophical thought is here allied freely and harmoniously with the creative imagination of a poet. In the great mythic novel, *Pilgrimen Kamanita* (1906), which contains a history of Buddha's era, Gjellerup has elucidated the essential characteristics of the Buddhist conception of the world, its doctrine of renunciation, its effort toward perfection, and its dreams of paradise, of Nirvana, and of universal destruction. Kamanita is the man in search of earthly satisfactions who, after seeing the fragility of all things, desires instead eternal treasures. We follow him not only during his earthly life but also during the different transformations he undergoes in the "Western Paradise," in which the tropical sumptuousness of India is rediscovered. Those who have destroyed themselves awaken here and leave their lotus buds to participate in the dance of the blessed and to undergo new incarnations, following which their souls begin a new existence in the empire of the Buddha of the hundred thousand cycles. In spite of its uninterrupted speculations on Hindu philosophy, this poem exercises a singular fascination. Quite intuitively the poet seems to have penetrated into the spiritual life of a far-off people and to have expressed their dreams of it with the visionary's gift. In certain passages of this poem one finds the spirit of the Arabian Nights, and certain parts of the Western Paradise present a penetrating picture of the sumptuous magnificence of the life of the blessed. In the same way the drama *Den fuldendtes hustru* (1907) [The Wife of the Perfect One], which deals with the purifications that Buddha's wife must undergo to attain perfection, is a masterpiece. The author has succeeded in permitting his own nature and genius to shine through these dogmatic and philosophical revelations of a millennial philosophy. Gjellerup's last great work, *Verdens vandrerne* (1910) [World Wanderers], with its half-Oriental, half-western moral, does not attain the same artistic beauty, but it contains beautiful details and holds our interest through a mysticism full of imagination as much as through the development of the action.

Karl Gjellerup was that strange combination, a scholar as well as a poet. His inventive imagination and his gifts of visionary poetry were often difficult to harmonize with his specific knowledge and his lively intelligence. His earlier works are characterized by very broad but sometimes clumsy descriptions, philosophical rather than spontaneous. They occasionally neglect artistic form, but they are always rich in ideas and full of promises of originality. Among them are such remarkable works as *Brynhild* and *Minna*. A poet who gathers all the flowers; a spirit that seeks tirelessly until it reaches its true domain in the world of Hindu mysticism, in which his profound thought and his ideal effort to clarify the enigmas of truth and life are combined with his artistic instinct: such is the Gjellerup of the second period. Thought charged with emotion, a great knowledge of the soul, a great desire for beauty, and a poetic art have given birth to works of enduring value. The author of *Pilgrimen Kamanita* and *Den fuldendtes hustru* has justifiably been called the "classic poet of Buddhism."

* * *

Henrik Pontoppidan belongs to the generation of writers who followed closely the "modern renaissance" of Danish literature after 1870, which had as its principal representatives Georg Brandes, Holger Drachmann, and J. P. Jacobsen. As a writer, his particular province is the novella. As an observer of human nature, as historian of the moral life of his time, he assuredly ranks first among contemporary Danish novelists. Born in Jutland in 1857, he was the son of a Protestant minister whose ideas were tinged with the doctrine of Grundtvig. He was educated at a polytechnic college. Later he taught school, but soon he gave up all professions to follow only his vocation as a writer. His first book, *Staekkede vinger* [Clipped Wings], appeared in 1881; since then he has published a great number of books, among them works of great and lasting value. During his youth he had bitter experiences of the Danish character and life which must have been a determining influence on his career as a writer. All his work is a struggle against what seemed to him deceptive and perfidious illusions, false authority, romanticism, superstitious belief in beautiful phrases, and the intoxication of lofty words, exalted sentiments, and moral fear. In a word, it is "the process of lyric putrefaction" by which the society of the Old World, in his judgment, is heading toward its ruin.

Thus in *Sandinge menighed* (1883) [The Parish of Sandinge], he finds fault with the falsities in the higher educational system; in *Skyer* (1890) [Clouds], he criticizes the leftist Danish politician of sonorous but empty phrases under the provisory laws of Estrup; in *Den gamle Adam* (1894) [The Old Adam] and *Højsang* (1896) [Song of Songs], he exposes the ravings of the amorous imagination and lofty sentiments; and in *Natur* (1890), he exercises his irony on the exaltation of nature. *Mimoser* (1886) [Mimosas] supports a theory completely opposed to the idea which had been dominant since Bjørnson defended it in *En hanske* [A Gauntlet], the idea which demanded man's purity and fidelity in sexual relations. *Det ideale hjem* (1900) [The Ideal Home] is a defence of matriarchy against marriage. *Nattevagt* (1894) [Night Watch] and the play *Asgaardsrejen* (1906) [The Wild Chase] contain attacks against modern art and lyric poetry which are only objects of luxury. To anaemic culture, the enemy of life, Pontoppidan opposes nature as it is developed in freedom. He shows an ardent sympathy especially for the social and revolutionary struggle and for the ideas of rational positivism. However, he never speaks in his own name; the characters whom he puts on stage speak for themselves, but the spirit of his books is revolutionary. What is curious, however, is that he himself was nourished on the "stale milk of romanticism" and that he is a lyricist in spite of his realistic spirit—a deep-seated contradiction which has permitted him to clothe reality in romantic veils and at the same time to undermine romanticism by means of irony.

Pontoppidan's masterpieces are the three-volume novel *Det forjaettede land* (1891–1895) [The Promised Land] and the novel *Lykke-Per* [Lucky Peter], originally published in eight volumes (1898–1904) but later condensed (1905)—two monumental works which give a tableau of the spiritual life of Denmark after 1860. The first of these novels, a vast picture of rustic life, portrays the opposition between the peasants and the inhabitants of the cities. It shows that even the most enthusiastic attempts to restore these classes to unity are doomed to certain failure. The principal character, an idealistic priest from Copenhagen, motivated by a strong feeling of duty, wishes to live with the peasants in order to lift them out of their condition; but he finds himself deceived in his faith in the people, as well as in his mission as a priest and the possibility of adapting it to everyday life and actions. He ends as an unbalanced visionary. Lykke-Per, on the contrary, is a young provincial, an engineer, who has firmly decided to achieve happiness in the capital. Contrary to the priest of *Det forjaettede land,* he is a man who is interested only in positive reality; he dislikes everything religious, metaphysical, or aesthetic. He behaves like a man of energy whom nothing can stop in the realization of his bold plans. But he also lacks that strength of domination over himself which is the necessary condition for a free soul, and he falls victim to that Christian romanticism which he has in his blood and which is precisely what he scorned. What is remarkable in this book is the masterly exposition of the essential differences between Jewish and Germanic ideas. A third cycle of novels, *De dødes rige* (1912–1916) [The Kingdom of the Dead], whose last parts were completed during the World War, also gives a whole series of images of Denmark at the end of the nineteenth and beginning of the twentieth century. Its subject is the unfortunate attempt of a radical politician to awaken a "people who are sleeping." It contains interesting social descriptions and vivid portraits (based on living models), but on the whole this work cannot be compared with the key works of the preceding period.

Henrik Pontoppidan has been called the classicist of the new Danish realism. He writes in a nervous and supple prose which has the peaceful, regular rhythm of healthy breathing. He narrates simply and easily without vain search for artistic words, but he has the rare gift of expressing reality clearly and in a lively manner. One finds the whole of Denmark in his writings: Jutland, the islands, and the capital; the commercial city and the country with its manors, its parsonages, its schools, and its taverns. One feels that the author has lived what he writes about. Moreover, the countryside is not described for itself but for the men who live there; it has value only because it conditions men. The essential object of Pontoppidan is man and his destiny, and in the objective description of human destiny he reveals himself as an incomparable artist. He has knowledge of the different classes of Danish people; he really knows their language, their manners, their habits, and their disposition. He is skilled in making out of his characters portraits in prominent relief, but he knows also how to endow them with an intense interior life which expresses their personalities. When one has read his work, one remembers a great number of distinctly individualized characters and the conditions of their existence. It is a broad avenue traced across Danish life during several decades. In the two central works, especially, there are admirable descriptions and characters whose emotional lives are portrayed in changing psychological situations and in scenes of great beauty. All the details appear, but the different parts of each novel and its details are put together effortlessly to give a generally unified work. Henrik Pontoppidan is an epic author of great range who, in an imposing endeavour, seeks to realize a work of monumental dimensions.

[© The Nobel Foundation, 1917.]

Gjellerup: Autobiographical Statement

(Written at the time of the awarding of the Nobel Prize)

I was born on June 2, 1857, in the Roholte vicarage at Praestö. My father was Pastor Carl Adolph Gjellerup, my mother, Anna Fibiger. After my father's death in 1860, in Landet vicarage on Lolland (from which I still have a number of memories), I went in November of the same year to the home of my mother's cousin, Pastor Johannes Fibiger, parish minister of the garrison church in Copenhagen, and author of *Johannes den Døber* (1857) [John the Baptist], *Nogle sagn* (1865) [Some Stories], *Kors og kjælighed* (1858) [Cross and Love], *Den evige strid* (1878) [The Eternal Strife], and *Mit liv og levned* (1898) [My Life]. I was graduated summa cum laude from Haerslevs Grammar School in 1874. Before this I had made several attempts at writing; immediately after graduation I wrote a tragedy, *Scipio Africanus,* and a drama, *Arminius,* both of which were shown to my uncle, Professor Edvard Holm, who encouraged me and showed the latter to Christian Molbech. Nevertheless, I studied theology and lived much in the country (in Vallensved on South Sjaelland, where Fibiger was the minister, and after 1881 in Ønslev on Falster), a country life which made an indelible impression on my mind and has left its mark in all of my novels. I earned my B.D. (summa cum laude) in June of 1878. I immediately began writing *En idealist* (1878) [An Idealist], which was published in November on the same day as *Den evige strid,* both under a pseudonym. Because both books created something of a sensation, I then came into contact with Høffding, Drachmann, Schandorph, Borchsenius, the brothers Brandes, J. P. Jacobsen, and many artists. Ceaseless production followed, temporarily taking a scientific direction in *Arvelighed og moral* (1881) [Heredity and Morals], a book with an evolutionary viewpoint, which was awarded the University Gold Medal. The novel *Germanernes laerling* (1882) [The Apprentice of the Teutons] (in its very title a program for existence), a collection of poems entitled *Rødtjørn* (1881) [Hawthorne], and *Aander og tider* (1882) [Spirits and Times], a requiem on Darwin, are the most noteworthy works from this time. A small inheritance made it possible for me to undertake a longer trip abroad in 1883. During a three-month stay in Rome, I pursued studies in water colour with Kronberg; later I studied pastel and oil painting. My return trip went through Switzerland, Greece, and Russia, and via Stockholm I arrived home at Christmastime. In the meantime two short stories, *Romulus* (1883) and *G-Dur* (1883) [G-Major], had come out. The travel impressions, *En klassisk maaned* (1884) [A Classical Month] and *Vandreaaret* (1885) [Wander Year], followed. In the latter of these two I broke off from the followers of Georg Brandes. Then appeared the first work of mine which was received with excitement, the lyrical tragedy *Brynhild* (1884), which had already been sketched during my student years, and which was dedicated to Eugenia. From the summer of 1885 to the fall of 1887 I lived in Dresden, where I wrote the scenes from the revolution, *Saint-Just* (1886) (reworked for the stage in German in 1913 and still not published), and the dramatic-lyrical poem "Thamyris" (1887). The latter along with *Brynhild* was responsible for my receiving a state pension for life. In October of 1887 I married Eugenia Bendix, née Heusinger, and settled in Hellerup. The lyrical tragedy *Hagbard og Signe* (1888) [Hagbard and Signe], the novel *Minna* (1889), the poetry collection *Min kjærligheds bog* (1889) [The Book of My Love], and the plays *Herman Vandel* (1891) and *Wuthhorn* (1893) (performed at the Dagmar Theatre over 100 times) were written in Hellerup. I also wrote an essay about Wagner's Nibelungenring and translated the songs of the gods in the *Edda*.

In March of 1892 I settled in Dresden. The tragedy *Kong Hjarne* (1893) [King Hjarne] and the verse comedy *Gift og Modgift* (1898) [Toxin and Antitoxin] were performed at the Dagmar Theatre. After *Fabler* [Fables], *Fra vaar til høst* [From Spring to Autumn], and *To fragmenter* [Two Fragments] I bade farewell to Danish poetry. The novels *Møllen* (1896) [The Mill], *Ved Grændsen* (1897) [At the Border], *Tankelæserinden* (1901) [The Soothsayer], and *Rudolf Stens Landpraxis* or *Reif für das Leben* (1913) [Ripe for Life] were written in German, and this language, in which I had made my debut with *Pastor Mors* (1894), now became my true artistic medium. The dramas *Die Opferfeuer* (1903) [The Sacrificial Fires] (produced at the court theatres in Dresden and Dessau) and *Das Weib des Vollendeten* (1907) [The Wife of the Perfect One] (produced at the court theatre in Stuttgart) and the poetic novels *Der Pilger Kamanita* (1906) [The Pilgrim Kamanita], *Die Weltwanderer* (1910) [The World Travellers], *Der goldene Zweig* (1917) [The Golden Bough], and *Die Gottesfreunde* (1916) [The Friends of God] belong chiefly to German literature and–like *Reif für das Leben*–have found their true understanding and appreciation almost exclusively in Germany. When my first book appeared forty years earlier, it had been influenced by German idealism. Just three years later (in the thesis awarded the gold medal) I was a follower of English naturalism, after which I returned to a position under those elevated signs of the zodiac which constitute my rightful habitat, only this time the guiding star was not Hegel as in *En idealist,* but Kant and Schopenhauer.

[© The Nobel Foundation, 1917. Karl Gjellerup is the sole author of the text.]

William Golding
(19 September 1911 – 19 June 1993)

Michael C. Prusse
Pädagogische Hochschule Zürich
Zurich University of Applied Sciences, School of Education

See also the Golding entries in *DLB 15: British Novelists, 1930–1959*; *DLB 100: Modern British Essayists, Second Series*; *DLB 255: British Fantasy and Science-Fiction Writers, 1918–1960*; *DLB 326: Booker Prize Novels: 1969–2005*; and *DLB Yearbook: 1983*.

BOOKS: *Poems* (London: Macmillan, 1934; New York: Macmillan, 1935);

Lord of the Flies (London: Faber & Faber, 1954; New York: Coward-McCann, 1955);

The Inheritors (London: Faber & Faber, 1955; New York: Harcourt, Brace & World, 1962);

Pincher Martin (London: Faber & Faber, 1956; New York: Capricorn, 1956); republished as *The Two Deaths of Christopher Martin* (New York: Harcourt, Brace, 1957);

The Brass Butterfly: A Play in Three Acts (London: Faber & Faber, 1958); republished with introduction by Golding (London: Faber & Faber, 1963);

Free Fall (London: Faber & Faber, 1959; New York: Harcourt, Brace & World, 1960);

The Spire (London: Faber & Faber, 1964; New York: Harcourt, Brace & World, 1964);

The Hot Gates and Other Occasional Pieces (London: Faber & Faber, 1965; New York: Harcourt, Brace & World, 1966);

The Pyramid (London: Faber & Faber, 1967; New York: Harcourt, Brace & World, 1967);

The Scorpion God: Three Short Novels (London: Faber & Faber, 1971; New York: Harcourt Brace Jovanovich, 1972);

Darkness Visible (London: Faber & Faber, 1979; New York: Farrar, Straus & Giroux, 1979);

Rites of Passage (London: Faber & Faber, 1980; New York: Farrar, Straus & Giroux, 1980);

A Moving Target (London: Faber & Faber, 1982; New York: Farrar, Straus & Giroux, 1982; revised, 1984);

Nobel Lecture, 7 December 1983 (Leamington Spa, U.K.: Sixth Chamber, 1984);

William Golding at the 1983 Nobel Prize ceremony in Stockholm (Hulton Archive/Getty Images)

The Paper Men (London: Faber & Faber, 1984; New York: Farrar, Straus & Giroux, 1984);

An Egyptian Journal (London & Boston: Faber & Faber, 1985);

Close Quarters (London: Faber & Faber, 1987; New York: Farrar, Straus & Giroux, 1987);

Fire Down Below (London: Faber & Faber, 1989; New York: Farrar, Straus & Giroux, 1989);

To the Ends of the Earth (London: Faber & Faber, 1991)—comprises *Rites of Passage, Close Quarters,* and *Fire Down Below;*

The Double Tongue (London: Faber & Faber, 1995; New York: Farrar, Straus & Giroux, 1995).

PLAY PRODUCTIONS: *The Brass Butterfly,* Oxford, New Theatre, 24 February 1958; London, Strand Theatre, April 1958; New York, Lincoln Square Theatre, West Side YMCA, 11 December 1965.

PRODUCED SCRIPTS: "Our Way of Life," radio, *Third Programme,* BBC, 15 December 1956;

"Miss Pulkinhorn," radio, *Third Programme,* BBC, 20 April 1960;

"Break My Heart," radio, *Third Programme,* BBC, 19 March 1961.

OTHER: "Envoy Extraordinary," in *Sometime, Never: Three Tales of Imagination,* by Golding, John Wyndham, and Mervyn Peake (London: Eyre & Spottiswoode, 1956; New York: Ballantine, 1957), pp. 3–60;

"Miss Pulkinhorn," in *The Penguin Book of Modern British Short Stories,* edited by Malcolm Bradbury (Harmondsworth: Penguin, 1988), pp. 99–107;

"Foreword," in *William Golding: A Bibliography 1934–1993,* edited by R. A. Gekoski and P. A. Grogan (London: Deutsch, 1994).

SELECTED PERIODICAL PUBLICATIONS—UNCOLLECTED: "The Writer in His Age," *London Magazine,* 4 (May 1957): 45–46;

"Pincher Martin," *Radio Times,* 38 (21 March 1958): 8;

"The Anglo-Saxon," *Queen,* 215 (22 December 1959): 27–30;

"Androids All," review of *New Maps of Hell,* by Kingsley Amis, *Spectator,* 206 (24 February 1961): 263–264;

"Before the Beginning," review of *World Prehistory,* by Grahame Clark, *Spectator,* 206 (26 May 1961): 768;

"It's a Long Way to Oxrhynchus," *Spectator,* 207 (7 July 1961): 9;

"The Condition of the Novel," *New Left Review* (January–February 1965): 34–35;

"Egypt and I," *Holiday,* 34 (April 1966): 32, 46–49;

"Delphi: The Oracle Revealed," *Holiday,* 43 (August 1967): 60–61, 87–88, 90, 150.

The novels of William Golding can be characterized as depicting individuals or isolated groups of human beings in archetypal circumstances, confronted with their humanity and experiencing the limits of civilization. By focusing on man's capacity for both good and evil, Golding's fiction frequently displays the quality of fable or approximates myth—the latter is the taxonomy that the novelist himself preferred. Stephen Medcalf, in *The Times Literary Supplement* (2 September 2005), called Golding "the celebrator of the height, depth and greatness of the human character." Peter O. Stummer just as aptly classifies Golding's narratives as accounts of "man's beastliness to man," whereas David Lodge asserts that Golding created his own particular genre, "the fable of spiritual crisis." Elucidating on his own narrative strategies in his essay "Fable" (included in *The Hot Gates and Other Occasional Pieces,* 1965), Golding writes that "the fabulist is didactic, desires to inculcate a moral lesson." However, it would be wrong to brand Golding as a simple moral fabulist, since his stories, as the English critic Frank Kermode once put it, do not "yield themselves at one reading." Virginia Tiger even maintains that the more time one devotes to the study of Golding's work, "the more one is struck by its increasing complexity, ambiguity, and equivocation."

Even if Golding's narratives with their mythological qualities are understood as complex representations of reality, which enable readers to recognize existential contradictions that his protagonists fail to perceive, his assumption of authority is problematic. In "Fable," Golding argues that, in order to succeed in having his story read, the storyteller has to sugarcoat the pill, and even then he will meet with hostility because he "has made an unforgivable assumption; namely that he knows better than his reader; nor does good intention save him." Golding's explicit claim to "authorial" power in an era in which critical theory questioned this authority has divided his readers into two camps: the first group view him as one of the greatest British writers of the twentieth century, with a reputation reaching far beyond his native land, while the second group perceive him as clinging to a single determinist notion—human sinfulness—which he analyzes in several variations.

William Gerald Golding was born in St. Columb Minor (near Newquay) in Cornwall on 19 September 1911. His father, Alec Golding, was a schoolteacher, while his mother, Mildred (née Curnoe), was a keen supporter of the suffragettes. Golding had one older brother, Jose, and a younger adopted sister, Eileen (actually his first cousin). Golding's father taught at Marlborough Grammar School in Wiltshire, and like his older brother, Golding went to school there before going on to Brasenose College Oxford in 1930, where he studied natural sciences for two years. Feeling dissatisfied with his subject, he opted for English literature instead and graduated in 1935. During his time at

Oxford the future novelist published his first book, a slim volume of poems. Before and after studying for a Diploma in Education he held a series of odd jobs as a teacher, part-time actor, stage manager, and producer. On 30 September 1939, just after the outbreak of World War II, he married Ann Brookfield and became a teacher at Bishop Wordsworth's School in Salisbury.

Golding joined the Royal Navy in December 1940 and served on various ships until the end of the war, except for some time in New York and a period spent on a weapons-development program. He was involved in the pursuit of the *Bismarck* and was deeply affected by the deaths and injuries he witnessed. His service on minesweepers, destroyers, cruisers, and a rocket launcher—which he commanded at the rank of lieutenant—left a lasting impression on Golding and acutely influenced his early novels. According to Golding's friend the British historian and writer Andrew Sinclair (in a 1996 BBC documentary on Golding), the writer's decision to take his rocket ship—a "flying time-bomb"—across a minefield in order to be in time for the D-Day operations, had a profound effect since Golding had to weigh the moral choice of risking the lives of his men against being late for the assault on the beaches of Normandy. Later, he discovered that the minefield did not exist—it had been put on the map to deter the Germans—and this incident provided the author with an example of how questions about life and death can be conjured up and lead to passionate involvement when, in reality, there is no foundation for them.

After the war, Golding returned to teaching English, philosophy, and the classics in Salisbury and wrote several novels. Publishers rejected all of them, and even his best-known book, *Lord of the Flies* (1954), collected twenty-one rejection slips until publisher Charles Monteith picked the manuscript up from a pile of rejects and noticed the comment of the professional reader. As Monteith recalled in "Strangers from Within" (1986), the reader's verdict began with the words "Absurd and uninteresting fantasy" and ended with "Rubbish and dull. Pointless." Nevertheless, Monteith read the manuscript and was intrigued by it, a fascination that led to the subsequent publication of the novel by Faber and Faber in 1954.

Lord of the Flies—the title is a literal translation of *Beelzebub* from Hebrew—is an allegorical dystopia that relates the fate of a group of schoolboys who are evacuated during a future nuclear war and whose plane crashes on a desert island in the tropics. Since there are no adult survivors, the boys at first attempt to act sensibly to ensure their survival: "We've got to have rules and obey them. After all, we're not savages. We're English; and the English are best at everything. So we've got to do the right things." Ralph is elected as their leader, whereas Jack, "chapter chorister and head boy," becomes his chief rival. Jack's choirboys turn into hunters who chase and kill the feral pigs on the island, while Ralph's chief supporters—Piggy, a fat, bespectacled intellectual, and Simon, who suffers from epilepsy and later becomes a Cassandra-like prophet figure—build shelters.

The first dispute results from the signal fire that the group keeps going on the mountain and which the hunters fail to sustain because they are all involved in chasing a pig, and thus a ship passing by fails to rescue them. Furthermore, the boys are frightened by "the beast"—a product of their imagination that seems to become real when they mistake a dead parachutist hanging between the trees for physical evidence of the beast. When Simon rushes out of the jungle to inform them that the beast is in fact just a corpse, the panicked boys assume he is the beast and kill him. Simon is the only one to be illuminated about the residence of evil within themselves when the "Lord of the Flies"—in fact a pig's skull on a stake beset by flies—tells him that he is not a beast that can be hunted and killed: "I'm part of you." Though he perceives that the true beast resides within the boys themselves, he cannot communicate this insight.

When Jack loses another leadership contest against Ralph, there is a rift between them that results in the former founding a tribal society. Gradually all the boys drift into Jack's camp, and when Ralph leads his last three supporters to negotiate, Piggy is killed and the others are taken prisoner. Ralph is chased like a pig across the island and eventually, in despair, stumbles onto the beach, where he encounters a British officer and is saved. The basic idea of this novel is, according to Carmen Callil and Colm Tóibín, "that within us all, eagerly waiting to be let out, lie savages."

In his essay "Fable," Golding confirms what the words of the officer ("Jolly good show. Like the Coral Island") already spelled out: that he consciously rewrote Robert Ballantyne's Victorian adventure novel *The Coral Island* (1857) with a view to challenge its simplistic message of English supremacy. Golding even kept the names of two of Ballantyne's main characters, Ralph and Jack. Instead of the third one, Peterkin, Golding uses an almost biblical figure, Simon, who, like the man from Cyrene, is "compelled to bear his cross" (Matthew 27:32). The novelist also compares the boys' urge to conquer the island to British imperial sway, encouraging critics such as Kevin McCarron to maintain that Golding was writing about colonialism in the tradition of Rudyard Kipling, George Orwell, Winifred Holtby, Joyce Cary, and Paul Scott. William Shakespeare's *The Tempest* might be added to the list since it also deals with the subduing and domination of wild and aboriginal forces in the figure of Caliban.

The main theme of Golding's fiction—the truth about human nature, the capacity for both good and evil—permeates his first novel. In "Fable" he documents the various thoughts that led to the conception of the narrative. He freely admits that *Lord of the Flies* is an adventure story that carries a moral message: the purpose of the adventure is to serve as sugar coating, which is necessary to entice readers into learning their moral lesson. The novelist was moved by his experiences of World War II to think that mankind was incorrigible in its habits: "man produces evil as a bee produces honey." He was struck by Ballantyne's notion in *The Coral Island* that evil resides outside its three protagonists and is present only in the savages and pirates that visit the islands. *Lord of the Flies,* according to Golding, describes the boys' attempt at constructing a civilization on the island, which "breaks down in blood and terror because the boys are suffering from the terrible disease of being human." Apart from the movie versions—Peter Brook filmed the first version in 1963, and another debuted in 1990—there exists one dramatized version that Golding approved of, by the British novelist and playwright Nigel Williams (first performed by students in 1991 and professionally in 1995).

In this productive phase of his life, which kept Golding writing in addition to his teaching duties, he published two more novels, *The Inheritors* in 1955 and *Pincher Martin* in 1956. *The Inheritors* relates the fate of a small group of Neanderthals who struggle for survival in the harsh environmental circumstances of the Stone Age and of their lethal encounter with the ancestors of mankind, *Homo sapiens*. The setting of the narrative in the distant past was inspired by "The Grisly Folk," a short story by H. G. Wells, which was first published in *Storyteller Magazine* in 1921. The theme of one race waning and another ascending must have appealed to the novelist. As much as *The Coral Island* influenced *Lord of the Flies,* Wells's short story must have provoked Golding by means of presumptions such as the "queer inhuman fashion" of the Neanderthals' appearance or their supposed cannibalism: "The Neandertalers thought the little children of men fair game and pleasant eating."

At the outset of Golding's narrative the small band loses its leader, and the other members are gradually killed off by the new men. Once again there is a chase in which the protagonist has to run for his life. Lok takes flight from the race of new arrivals, to whom he is curiously attracted and whom he completely fails to understand. His desperate flight is probably even more terrifying than Ralph's, since the Neanderthal man (after his wife, Fa, has been felled by an arrow) is dimly aware of the fact that he might be the last of his race. The novel is generally perceived as difficult, although it relates a rather simple story. The difficulty arises from the fact that the author writes from the perspective of a Neanderthal man, who is incapable of sophisticated thought. Once the reader has learned to read Lok's impressionist perception of his surroundings, the story can easily be grasped. An example of Golding's technique is a scene in which an arrow is shot at Lok; since he is not familiar with the concept of bow and arrow, he simply relays the information his senses procure:

> The stick began to grow shorter at both ends. Then it shot out to full length again.
>
> "Clop!"
>
> The dead tree by Lok's ear acquired a voice.
>
> His ears twitched and he turned to the tree. By his face there had grown a twig that smelt of other, and of goose, and of the bitter berries that Lok's stomach told him he must not eat.

The last chapter of the novel, like that of *Lord of the Flies,* is written from a different perspective, namely that of a Cro-Magnon man. More refined in their language and thinking, and also as producers of art, the newcomers are not innocent like the Neanderthals. Rather, they think pragmatically, logically, and are capable of both good and evil, and the artist-protagonist is aware of this fact.

Many critics claim that *The Inheritors* is Golding's greatest achievement. The writer Arthur Koestler (quoted by Medcalf) called it "an earthquake in the petrified forest of the English novel." Monteith believed it to be "the best book he ever wrote" and asserted (in the BBC documentary) that Golding himself thought so too. S. J. Boyd compares the narrative to William Blake's *Songs of Innocence and Experience* (1795) because the innocents, the Neanderthals, are destroyed by contact with the new people, who even leave gifts for those they call "the devils," namely their rotten honey—an alcoholic drink that has an overwhelming effect on Fa and Lok. Moreover, their similarity to Adam and Eve has been noted by Lawrence S. Friedman, who declares that the two Neanderthals "partake of the knowledge of evil" when they witness how the new people ritually sacrifice and eat Liku, a young Neanderthal. Kermode comments on the problematic nature of the fall: "Not to know evil is, in a sense, to know nothing." According to Boyd, by relating how a group of people that live in harmony with nature are cast as devils by men and ruthlessly pursued and exterminated, Golding explains how mankind gained its position: "The world of the new people is essentially *our* world. We are their inheritors." The notion that human beings are the pinnacle of evolution is severely challenged by this outside contemplation of man's behavior. According to Kermode, "Golding believes in human guilt and the human sense of paradise lost."

Golding's third novel, *Pincher Martin,* concentrates on one individual, namely Christopher Hadley Martin, who saves himself from a destroyer that was torpedoed by a German submarine by swimming to a rock in the middle of the Atlantic. On this rock Martin, by means of flashbacks, is confronted with his rather unpleasant personality: "I am who I was." One particularly shocking memory evokes the coldness with which Martin raped his best friend's fiancée. His nickname, Pincher, refers both to the greed that makes him such an unattractive person and to the intense tenacity with which he clings to life. The protagonist attempts to create his reality—his life—by creating this rock in the middle of the Atlantic, by naming its different parts and by continuously asserting his belief that rescue is imminent. The novel refers to certain philosophical positions assumed by Jean-Paul Sartre and Albert Camus, the two leading French exponents of existentialism, and also directly alludes to myth when Martin declares: "I am Atlas. I am Prometheus." Martin is clearly a Sisyphus figure, indebted to Camus and his essay *Le Mythe de Sisyphe* (1942; translated as *The Myth of Sisyphus,* 1955). Like the French existentialists, Golding is concerned with the question of choice: "You gave me the power to choose and all my life you led me carefully to this suffering because the choice was my own." Eventually, Martin's tale of endurance on the rock is exposed as no more than the hallucinations of a drowning man, a mirage that echoes the miraculous but illusory escape of the protagonist who is hanged in Ambrose Bierce's "An Occurrence at Owl Creek Bridge" (1892).

Several critics, including McCarron and Tiger, have noted that Golding's first three novels, although describing vastly different characters in distinct settings, feature a certain structural similarity. All of them end with a shift in perspective that permits the reader to step outside the densely woven fictional world and perceive matters from an alternative point of view. In *Lord of the Flies* it is the officer who arrives on the island and, misapprehending the situation, congratulates the boys on their "jolly good show." At the end of *The Inheritors* readers are given the thoughts of one of the new race who hunted and exterminated the Neanderthals. Last but not least, the ending of *Pincher Martin* reveals, to all those who failed to identify the clues provided by Golding, that the protagonist was imagining his quest for survival during his death struggles in the sea. The irony of the statement by Davidson, the officer who steps on the Scottish shore to identify the body, is only evident to the reader; Davidson believes that Martin died instantly: "He didn't even have time to kick off his seaboots." Tiger has provided a name for this technique of narrative structuring "whereby two points of view are turned on one situation"; she calls it "the ideographic structure." Its purpose is, as Tiger asserts, to make Golding's "readers embrace paradoxes of existence which his own characters cannot recognize."

Golding's growing reputation drew him into the London literary scene and permitted him to supplement his income by writing essays, reviews, and travel reports. In 1955 he was made a fellow of the Royal Society of Literature. Golding's novella "Envoy Extraordinary" was published in a collective volume of three narratives in 1956; the other contributions were by John Wyndham and Mervyn Peake. Two years later, in 1958, he transformed this story into a play, *The Brass Butterfly,* which was first performed in Oxford and toured the provinces before appearing in London. In the following year he published his fourth novel, *Free Fall* (1959), as well as many reviews and travel pieces.

Free Fall is the quest into the past of the artist Sammy Mountjoy, who wants to find "the point where I began," to discover at what point in his life he lost his "innocence" and chose to become "evil." Looking back at his childhood, he describes himself as "wandering in paradise. I can only guess our innocence, not experience it." Apart from the obvious allusion to Blake's *Songs of Innocence and Experience,* Golding refers to one of his favorite themes—namely, the notion of a fall from paradise that inevitably occurs in the course of human lives. Sammy's surname has frequently been read as a variation on the theme of paradise, but it is also the name of a well-known prison in Dublin—a metaphor that fittingly describes Sammy's condition: trapped in choices.

Sammy, whose confessional notes are presented in a gesture of atonement, is clearly related to the protagonists of French existentialism, who also probe into the freedom of the will and into human choices, as typified by the writings of Sartre and Camus. Sammy's notion of people being other people's hell—"We are forced here and now to torture each other"—is most certainly indebted to Sartre's play *Huis Clos* (1945; translated as *In Camera,* 1946). The tormenting of his Dante-inspired lover, Beatrice Ifor, whom Sammy possibly drives to madness, is one such instance; the agonies that Sammy suffers at the orders of Dr. Halde in a German prison camp during World War II provide another. The fact that the protagonist of *Free Fall* opts for sin of his own free will suggests parallels to the protagonist of *La Chute* (1956; translated as *The Fall,* 1957) by Camus—a narrative that also proclaims the fall in its title.

The novel furthermore carries an autobiographical touch, illuminating Golding's wandering between the world of science and the spiritual: Nick, the science master, is based upon Golding's father, as the author admitted in an interview with John Carey. Miss Pringle, who teaches religion, perceives that Sammy has talents in the realm of the spiritual and attempts to expose him as a fake. Eventually, Sammy recognizes that everything is to be had at a price, and, since he is willing to sacrifice everything to get Beatrice, this realization is probably the decisive moment where the protagonist overstepped the limit.

Golding's short story "Miss Pulkinhorn" (1960) is a variation on faith, fanaticism, and "goodness," describing through the eyes of the cathedral organist, Sir Edward, how Miss Pulkinhorn, a religious zealot and "God's own chicken," is responsible for the death of a saintly and rather odd vicar. The narrative gives the reader, according to Medcalf, insights into "the vulnerability of the more innocent, the totality of self-deception in the less innocent." The novelist spent the academic year of 1961 in the United States since he had been appointed writer-in-residence at Hollins, a women's liberal arts college in Virginia. Realizing that his writing interfered with his teaching and vice versa, Golding resigned from his post at Bishop Wordsworth's School in 1962 and became a full-time writer.

The Spire, the novel that was inspired by his residence in Salisbury and the impressive town cathedral, was published in 1964. Golding wrote, in *A Moving Target* (1982), that he was prompted to write about this building because of the curious absence of it in Anthony Trollope's Barsetshire novels. In *The Spire*, set in the fourteenth century, Dean Jocelin acts on his vision that God has selected him to erect a tower rising to four hundred feet above Barchester Cathedral, and he pursues this goal ruthlessly and persistently, regardless of costs, particularly of human lives. The workmen murder a crippled employee of the cathedral, possibly as a heathen sacrifice for the impossible task, and the dean is aware of this incident and other unchristian proceedings. The builder, aptly named Roger Mason, who has an illicit relationship with the wife of the murdered man, sets his technological knowledge against Jocelin's fanatic faith: according to the builder, the foundations cannot support the weight of such a construction. Against all expectations the spire rises triumphantly, while those involved in its construction are either dead or dying.

As McCarron puts it, the novel accounts for the appalling costs that result from Jocelin's hubris. Jocelin soon becomes aware of what he has to sacrifice to his vision when friendships are lost, and he reveals his fierce determination: "I didn't know how much you would cost up there, the four hundred feet of you. I thought you would cost no more than money. But still, cost what you like." With Jocelin the reader learns about the gradual rise in cost, until the narrative assumes the dimensions of a Greek tragedy: "I never guessed in my folly that there would be a new lesson at every level, and a new power." Ultimately, some uneasy questions remain: does the spire remain standing because of the human sacrifice or despite it? Do good intentions condone evil acts? *The Spire* is a complex investigation into what life entails. Mark Kinkead-Weekes and Ian Gregor sum up their interpretation: "The Spire is built in heavy stone, in faith, in sin: all three things are true, and contradictory." According to English novelist and critic Victoria Glendinning, writing in the *Observer* (20 June 1993), the building of the spire "may stand for many kinds of aspiration yet the toil and sweat of the artisans, and the materials with which they are working, are utterly real."

In 1965 Golding published *The Hot Gates and Other Occasional Pieces,* a collection of his essays, followed in 1967 by *The Pyramid,* a narrative with several autobiographical elements; the title alludes to Golding's lifelong fascination with Egyptology. The collection of essays also includes two autobiographical pieces, "Billy the Kid" and "The Ladder and the Tree," in which the roots of Golding's love of books are traced back to his childhood. *The Pyramid,* apart from focusing on growing up in an English country town with the telling name of Stilbourne (a village nearby is just as tellingly called Bumstead), presents a harsh analysis of the British class system. It is told from the point of view of Oliver, its lower-middle-class protagonist, and allows glances into other spheres, mainly because of his relationships with working-class Evie Babbacombe and with the upper-middle-class doctor's son, Robert Ewan. At the beginning of *The Pyramid,* Robert announces that Oliver is his slave. When Oliver doubts this statement, his opponent reasons: "Yes you are. My father's a doctor and yours is only his dispenser." Class plays a role in all of Oliver's decisions: what friendships to form, what course of studies to pursue: "Nobody mentioned the line, but everybody knew it was there."

Golding, who was a keen amateur pianist, conceived a narrative that abounds with music and musical allusions. Although music has primarily positive attributes, a life dedicated to music can also be "hell," as Friedman writes—the example is Miss Dawlish, Oliver's piano teacher, who eventually burns her sheet music and metronome and smashes her bust of Ludwig von Beethoven. In the course of the novel Oliver forsakes his musical ambitions and talent and becomes an industrial chemist who is involved in the production of poison gas—his worldly success is, like the erection of the spire in Golding's previous novel, only to be had at a price. Oliver, who lusted after Evie in the first part of the novel, later only considers her from the point of class and thus treats her like a sex object, not a human being. There are further scenes of chances missed: the town itself rejects the modern age and hence becomes even more provincial, a theme that is highlighted in the disastrous production of an opera by the appropriately named Stilbourne Operatic Society (SOS), and by the rise of Henry Williams, a mechanic, who owns most of the town by the end of the novel. The sonata form of the story was, as Golding commented in an interview with Mary Lynn Scott, not conceived from the beginning; but once he became aware of this slant, the novelist decided to adopt this structure: "I more precisely shaped it in that direction so that the last story about the old music teacher is really an air and variations: it comes back in different forms." The middle part is clearly a scherzo, and although Golding is frequently described as a novelist lacking in humor, *The Pyramid* shows traces of farce and is, on the whole, quite funny.

Despite these features, *The Pyramid* did not fare well with the critics, who diagnosed deteriorating creative faculties. The same fate met the novelist's next publication, *The Scorpion God* (1971), a volume consisting of three long stories or novellas, namely "The Scorpion God," "Clonk, Clonk," and "Envoy Extraordinary." The first of these is set in Egypt at the time of the pharaohs and deals with incest, rituals, and a court jester, called the Liar, who brings to bear a different perspective on the sterile, death-oriented Egyptian culture. However, since he is not in harmony with his environment (as the Egyptians are), the step forward in human evolution that the Liar's rational thinking will produce is inevitably linked to the loss of this harmonious existence. "Clonk, Clonk" is an optimistic narrative that is set a hundred thousand years ago somewhere in Africa and describes the lives of an ancient matriarchal tribe of hunters and planters. The women look after the camp and the crops and brew beer, while the men are mostly out hunting. When one of the hunters, who suffers from a weak ankle that goes "clonk" at a decisive moment during the hunt, creeps back to the camp and sleeps with Palm Woman, the leader of that society, the complementary nature of women and men becomes evident.

The last novella in the volume, "Envoy Extraordinary," describes events in Capri during the third century A.D. as the Roman emperor encounters the inventor Phanocles, who wants to convince the leader to adopt three of his best inventions: a steam barge, gunpowder, and the printing press. While the emperor enjoys the culinary results of a variation of the first invention, a pressure steam cooker, the others result in revolt among the slaves (who are worried that steam will make them redundant) and by the military leader Posthumus, who attempts to usurp the throne because he perceives the steamship as a military threat. While the coup fails, the steam barge is destroyed, and the emperor makes Phanocles an "envoy extraordinary" and sends him with the gunpowder and the printing press to China. Like the other two narratives, "Envoy Extraordinary" deals with a crucial moment in history that is characterized by a shift in consciousness. While Phanocles clings to the idealistic beliefs that his inventions will make the world a better place, the cost of progress is recognized by the emperor: "There will always be slaves though the name may change. What is slavery but the domination of the weak by the strong? How can you make them equal? Or are you fool enough to think that men are born equal?"

The late 1960s and the early 1970s were an arid period in Golding's writing career; apart from writer's block, he suffered from depression and struggled with alcohol. While wrestling with these difficulties he wrote two novels: *Darkness Visible* (1979), which won the James Tait Black Memorial Prize, and *Rites of Passage* (1980), which was declared winner of the Booker Prize. In the period leading up to the genesis of these narratives the novelist had terrible dreams that he noted in his diary, and out of these nightmares the hellish visions of *Darkness Visible* arose. The opening scene, which Monteith (in the BBC documentary) called "the most powerful piece of prose he ever wrote," describes how a severely burned child, later named Matty (Matthew) Septimus Windrove, miraculously appears in the aftermath of an air raid on London in World War II. The fire, compared to a burning bush and by implication to the scene in Moses, establishes a context of biblical allusions. Saved by a group of firemen, tended by doctors and nurses, and named by an official, Matty grows up in a school for orphans. There a pedophile teacher, Sebastian Pedigree, is assigned by the headmaster to give private lessons to Matty rather than to his current favorite, Henderson, in order to assuage any suspicion of his particular inclinations. When Henderson, feeling thwarted, commits suicide and Pedigree is fired, Matty becomes a tragic hero since he believes himself guilty of having caused both Henderson's death and Pedigree's dismissal, although he is, in fact, also a victim. He is sent off to work in an ironmonger's shop and later migrates to Australia, where he has several odd jobs and eventually wanders through the outback. Hideously scarred by the fire, Matty is on a quest for his identity and is haunted by questions about his existence and purpose. When he returns to Britain, to the Celtic influences of Golding's native Cornwall, he finds himself addressed by spirits who give him a task that he does not understand but unquestioningly accepts: he goes back to Greenfield, near London, and obtains employment as an odd-job man at Wandicott, a boarding school for boys from the ruling classes.

The second part of the novel introduces the twins Sophy and Toni Stanhope. Sophy is characterized by a disturbing scene in which she, as a child, kills a dabchick quite brutally with a stone, simply because she can. Sophy's powerful attraction to evil forces is strongly reminiscent of Roger in *Lord of the Flies,* who first playfully flicks stones at one of the smaller boys, Henry, and later is the one to murder Piggy. Sophy and her twin sister are abandoned by their father after his wife has run off with another man. While Sophy discovers her ability to manipulate others, especially men—except for the orgasms, sex does not mean much to her—Toni leaves for Afghanistan and learns about postcolonial politics and becomes a terrorist. Sophy allies herself with Gerry, a former officer in the army, and his friend, Bill, a private who enjoys killing (a soulmate for Sophy, who relishes similar "pleasures"). Gerry and Bill are petty criminals who are led by Sophy into contemplating more daring schemes: they plan a raid on Wandicott in order to kidnap an Arabian prince and demand a huge ransom.

The third part focuses mostly on two witnesses in Greenfield, Edwin Bell and Sim Goodchild, the owner of a bookshop. They are selected by Matty to help him in his task of protecting the Arabian prince, who, according to his spiritual advisers, is destined to play a significant role in the future. Eventually, the raid takes place and fails: although Matty has been knocked down, he succeeds in manipulating the diversionary fire in such a fashion that Bill drops the Saudi prince. Matty, however, is killed in the fire that the raiders have started. Thus, Matty, who was the innocent cause of the death of a boy at the beginning, now dies saving another boy.

The title, *Darkness Visible,* is an allusion to John Milton's *Paradise Lost* (1667), specifically to the moment when Lucifer surveys his new abode and notices the horrible lightless dungeon, where, by means of "darkness visible," he perceives nothing but "sights of woe." Matty's name clearly hints at Matthew 7:1, which begins with the words "Judge not, that ye be not judged." Again, the thematic focus is on the human capacity for good and evil, but matters are complicated by Matty's unattractive appearance and his fanatic and unquestioning faith, which is reminiscent of earlier characters in Golding's fiction, such as Jocelin in *The Spire.* Medcalf perhaps characterizes the two antagonists in *Darkness Visible* best when writing of Sophy that "in her heart she is diabolically mad where Matty is, perhaps, angelically sane." Henri Petter points out that Matty and Sophy are contrastive figures: one mutilated, the other stunningly attractive; one of limited intelligence, the other a prodigy. According to Petter, Matty tries to find his role and considers the afterlife, while Sophy's hubris consists in her belief that she can master fate, and she is utterly focused on the here and now. There are, however, some similarities between them: he is an orphan, and she a semi-orphan; he renounces love, while she loses her father's love.

Most critics were surprised at the comparatively lighthearted tone of *Rites of Passage,* which followed *Darkness Visible.* However, the narrative is not without its grave moments, since it relates the fate of a clergyman who shames himself in public and consequently wills himself to die. The story is told by Edmund Talbot, a young man of neoclassical tastes, who is extremely conceited and destined to become a member of the governor's entourage in New South Wales. He travels aboard an unnamed old ship of the line—her name is presumably *Britannia*—to the Antipodes, and in the course of the passage, he undergoes several rites that nudge him toward maturity. The ship features a microcosm of British society: apart from the tyrannical captain, Anderson, who tolerates Talbot because he writes a journal for his godfather, who is a rich and influential politician, the vessel carries several emigrants of various classes as well as the officers and crew.

When the ship crosses the equator, the clergyman, Robert James Colley, is selected as a victim for the seamen's entertainment, during which he is baptized in a container of foul fluids, including urine. Indignant at what he perceives as an attack on his office, Colley in vain asks for the support of the captain. Eventually, he ventures to the forecastle to berate the seamen, but instead he gets drunk and ends up performing fellatio on a young sailor he particularly admires and submitting to sodomy. This shaming experience eventually results in his death. In contrast to Talbot, Colley is a romantic, and his fervor is not just for God but also for nature; the admiration of nature and natural phenomena is effusively expressed in letters addressed to his sister, which Talbot discovers after the clergyman's death.

Summers, the ship's first lieutenant, makes Talbot recognize the unfavorable role he has played in the Colley affair (Talbot's defiance of Anderson's authority had provoked Colley to act in a similar fashion, but since Colley did not have Talbot's powerful connections to protect him, the captain retaliated harshly). When the young man finds the clergyman's letters, he realizes how much he is to blame for his hauteur and pomposity and for relying on his privileges, and he understands how events look completely different from another point of view. One of the modern themes of *Rites of Passage* is Golding's insistence on proving the unreliability of narrative. Luke Strongman interprets the novel as the author's attempt at "metafictional play."

In his foreword for *To the Ends of the Earth* (1991), which collects *Rites of Passage* and its two sequels, *Close Quarters* (1987) and *Fire Down Below* (1989), Golding asserts that apart from the language of the seamen and the sea, it is class or "rank" that pervades his book: "This is a difficult subject since we British are still so dunked from childhood in that hierarchy we become unaware of it." As Paul Crawford points out, by juxtaposing "issues of textuality and constructedness with 'constructions' of class," Golding makes the reader aware of class as a construct by means of language and communication.

In 1982 the author published *A Moving Target*, a collection of essays, reviews, and travel accounts. The title essay, his "Address to Les Anglicistes" at a congress in Rouen in 1976, illustrates some of Golding's notions concerning the state and the future of the novel. In an obvious admonition to this audience of academics and professional critics, the author censures the tendency of critics to entomb living writers in theoretical pigeonholes, which do not account for the writer's potential for development. He clearly refers to an aspect discerned by Tiger, namely that "the assessment must be balanced against the fact that the whole creative body of work shifts with the publication of each new novel." Advising a student looking for a subject for her thesis, the novelist agrees with her professor that preferably she ought to focus on a dead author: "She could guarantee filling him with a shower of critical small-shot at any time she wanted. But as for me, I am a moving target." It is no coincidence that the ending of his next novel, *The Paper Men* (1984), features an author being shot at his desk like a sitting duck.

In 1983 Golding was awarded the Nobel Prize in Literature, an announcement that caused some controversy. The London newspapers of 7 October 1983 carried headlines such as "Row over Golding's Nobel Prize" *(Times)* or "Uproar as Golding Takes Nobel Prize" *(Daily Telegraph)*. The Academy secretary, Lars Gyllensten, had originally informed reporters that the choice of Golding was the result of a smooth and almost unanimous selection process. Julian Isherwood, relying on sources from within the Nobel committee, noted in the *Daily Telegraph* (7 October 1983) that two voting sessions had been required to give Golding the award—the French author Claude Simon (who eventually won the prize in 1985) coming in a close second. In any case, Gyllensten's announcement was contested by the Swedish poet Artur Lundkvist, a fierce opponent of an award to Golding, who claimed in a *Guardian* article by Paul Keel and W. L. Webb (7 October 1983) that the second vote took place in his absence and that the decision of the committee amounted to a coup against him. Furthermore, as Michael Specter records, Lundkvist dismissed Golding as "a little English phenomenon of no special interest." A further dissenting voice belonged to *Time* critic Paul Gray, who agreed with Lundkvist that Golding "was decent but hardly in the Nobel Prize class." According to Gray, Golding "should have been spared both the Nobel Prize and the controversy surrounding its unexpected arrival."

Despite this harsh criticism, the majority of the commentators applauded the Swedish Academy's decision. In an article in *Newsweek* (17 October 1983), Peter S. Prescott even showed surprise at the "rift in the secrecy that traditionally attends the Academy's proceedings" because he qualified Golding's selection as sensible. Fellow writers also reacted in a positive fashion: as Keel and Webb reported, Doris Lessing stated that she was "absolutely delighted" with the decision, while John Fowles, best known for his novel *The French Lieutenant's Woman* (1969), expressed his conviction that Golding was "the best British novelist of his generation."

In their laudation the Nobel Foundation commended Golding on his status of being "a writer for the learned and the unlearned" and compared him to Jonathan Swift and Herman Melville. The novelist was characterized as "a writer of myth," and there was praise for his "novels which, with the perspicuity of realistic narrative art and the diversity and universality of myth, illuminate the human condition in the world of today."

The author's own reactions at being awarded the prize are revealed in the entry in his diary for 6 October 1983, reproduced on his website (<http://www.william-golding.co.uk/p_honours.html>). Apparently, he had received a phone call at ten o'clock in the morning by a reporter called Ingmar from Stockholm—the novelist did not catch the surname—who insinuated that the odds were at fifty percent that Golding would be awarded the Nobel Prize. Golding was indignant with the journalist for trying to stir up excitement and probably just striving for the scoop of being the first to get his reaction. Golding deliberately attempted to dismiss the thought and to remain calm. However, in the early afternoon it was official, and he began to experience the harassment of journalists in earnest. In order to absorb the news, he went horseback riding. His official reaction was, on the one hand, patriotic, since in the *Guardian* (7 October 1983) he expressed his delight "not just for myself but because the prize has been won after 30 years by an Englishman." On the other hand, the novelist declared in the *Times* (7 October 1983) that the award was for most writers "a kind of supposing, a kind of daydream." He also admitted to feeling "stunned, overwhelmed, incredulous," but added that these adjectives could not really describe his true state.

In December 1983 the Goldings traveled to Stockholm for the award ceremony. Monteith, who had first printed *Lord of the Flies,* accompanied the couple. In "Strangers from Within," Monteith relates what passed between the novelist and the king of Sweden at the great ball on the evening of the presentation: Carl XVI Gustaf informed Golding that it was "a great pleasure to meet" him, since the king had "had to do *Lord of the Flies* at school." In his Nobel lecture, Golding described how he had once thoughtlessly accepted the label of "pessimist" and declared that he was, in fact, "a universal pessimist but a cosmic optimist." He thus addressed an issue regularly debated in books and articles about him. It is interesting to note that in this respect the author already contradicts himself in his early essays: the regularly quoted statement of his pessimistic outlook can be found in his essay on education, "On the Crest of the Wave," included in *The Hot Gates and Other Occasional Pieces.* In the same volume, namely in "Fable," the author states quite clearly that he is a European "and an optimist." Later in his career, in the foreword for *To the Ends of the Earth,* he even expressed strong disagreement with the common opinion that diagnosed him as pessimist. Glendinning confirmed this assessment in her *Observer* article, writing that Golding "was more hopeful about man's condition than his books might suggest."

A further point that the author referred to in his address at the Nobel award ceremony was the fact that the English language was possibly suffering "from too wide a use rather than too narrow a one." Stressing the significance of stories, Golding also expressed his concern with the state of the planet and raised the question of environmental issues. He then focused on the writer's craft, saying that words "may through the luck of writers prove to be the most powerful thing in the world." Ending on a wry note, he related how a police officer had explained to him how to pay a parking ticket, only to add as an afterthought: "And may we congratulate you on winning the Nobel Prize for Literature."

The honor brought certain side effects with it, as Judy Carver, Golding's daughter, recalls in a 2004 essay about her parents' lives: "My father became a quarry—for journalists, zealous readers, academics," even sightseers. Golding consequently left the proximity of London in 1985 and moved to an elegant Georgian house near Truro in Cornwall. Golding, who remarked in the 1986 interview with Carey that there "is nothing to a writer but his books," resented the intrusions into his private life, and his apparently vitriolic reaction to literary paparazzi is evident in his first post-Nobel novel, *The Paper Men.*

Glendinning, in her *Observer* article, called *The Paper Men* Golding's "tragicomic cautionary tale for all literary biographers." In fact, *The Paper Men* not only comments on certain vulture-like excesses observable in some academics when focusing on the papers of a specific author but also presents a deeply disturbing portrait of a writer. Ultimately, the novel unveils the symbiotic relationship between author and critic and, as McCarron explains, addresses the issue raised by Roland Barthes and later hotly debated in academic circles, namely, the literary theory that postulates "the death of the author."

The novel begins on a farcical note when Wilf Barclay, a famous English novelist, shoots Rick L. Tucker, a pertinacious American literary biographer, with an air gun because he mistakes him for a badger plundering the rubbish bins. In reality, Tucker is researching scraps for his biography, and since he discovers a reference to a former lover, his research causes the breakup of Barclay's frail marriage. The writer attempts to escape Tucker's clutches and begins to travel on the highways and byways of Europe, his mind fogged by enormous quantities of alcohol. When Tucker appears to save Barclay's life in a mountaineering accident in Switzerland, the writer feels indebted but nevertheless takes to the road again. A coincidental meeting at a conference gives Golding the opportunity to vent his feelings about academic proceedings: "A sleepy bunch of professors, lecturers, postgraduate students were all trying their hardest to stay awake and Professor Tucker was making it difficult for them."

As the narrative progresses, it becomes evident that Barclay and Tucker are the paper men of the title, both in the metonymic sense since they "live off and by paper" and "in the metaphorical sense of being two-dimensional, incomplete human beings," as Lodge observes in "Life Between Covers" (1984) and as Barclay himself recognizes: "Neither of us, critic and author, we knew nothing about people or not enough." Both are in a spiritual crisis, willing to sacrifice everything to their success, either as author or critic. Barclay baits, tortures, and humiliates Tucker because, although he is reluctant to have his biography written, worried about what the critic might detect, he also feels flattered that he should be subject to such interest. Their mutual dependence ultimately leads to the death of the author at the hands of the critic.

Those readers who understand *The Paper Men* simply as a determined attack on academic literary criticism are misled: the novelist was clearly aware of his public role. As he had already stated in "Fable," he no longer believed "that the author has a sort of patria potestas over his brainchildren. Once they are printed they have reached their majority and the author has no more authority over them, knows no more about them, perhaps knows less about them than the critic who comes fresh to them, and sees them not as the author hoped they would be, but as what they are."

In the course of his career the novelist was awarded many honorary doctorates by universities; his country also recognized his stature and, having been made a Commander of the Order of the British Empire (CBE) in 1966, Golding was knighted by the queen in 1988. The year before, he had published *Close Quarters,* a sequel to *Rites of Passage,* and in 1989 *Fire Down Below* completed the sea trilogy. Two years later, in a rare case of editing his work, Golding revised the three books and Faber and Faber released them in a single volume titled *To the Ends of the Earth.* In his foreword to the trilogy Golding admits that he "did not foresee volumes two and three" when he wrote *Rites of Passage.*

Close Quarters resumes the narrative of Edmund Talbot. When the *Britannia* loses her topmasts and damages her foremast as a result of a negligent omission by Lieutenant Deverel, the frigate *Alcyone* can catch up with her. Apart from the news about the end of the war with France, she carries two ladies, the captain's wife and a dependent relative. Talbot, who has severely injured his head in the excitement preceding the arrival of the possible enemy ship, instantly falls in love with the second lady, Miss Chumley. To celebrate the news that Napoleon Bonaparte has been vanquished (he is to become king of Elba) and the announcement of peace, a ball and other festivities take place on the high seas. A surprise member of the *Alcyone* crew is Talbot's steward, Wheeler, who mysteriously disappeared from the ship in *Rites of Passage.* He fell into the sea—actually, he was most likely pushed, since he had informed on sailor Billy Rogers's involvement in the abusing of Colley—and had been picked up by the frigate when drifting in the Atlantic. As a result of Talbot's infatuation with Miss Chumley, who sails off to India on the *Alcyone,* the next phase in his education begins.

The *Britannia* has been severely slowed down by a carpet of plants that settled on the ship in the doldrums, and Lieutenant Bénet—who swapped places with Deverel—devises a method to rid the hull of these obstacles. When the operation appears to remove part of the keel and threatens crew and passengers with drowning, Wheeler, who cannot bear the idea of another turn in the ocean, shoots himself in Talbot's cabin.

While Talbot stands "halfway between the classic and the romantic" in *Rites of Passage,* as Golding himself asserted in his foreword to the collected edition of his sea trilogy, there are many signals in *Close Quarters* that also point at the watershed between the waning of the Romantic and the arrival of the Victorian era. The description of the *Alcyone* being dragged out of Plymouth Sound by a steam tug carries distinct echoes of William Turner's famous painting *The Fighting Temeraire tugged to her last berth to be broken up* (1838)—which portrays an old ship of the line being towed by steam tug against a colorful sunset—and thus of the ascendancy of steam and steel and concurrently the decline of sail and wood. The narrative is also characterized by several metafictional instances: unlike in *Rites of Passage,* where Talbot had a task, namely, to report events to his godfather, he now is faced with writing for himself—a project that daunts him and makes him frequently compare his meager talents in this respect with the effusive style of Colley's letters. In his "postscriptum" Talbot even proclaims the eventual title for the sea trilogy, which he envisages with "gusto" in "three splendid volumes" as "*Talbot's Voyage* or *The Ends of the Earth!*"

With *Fire Down Below,* Golding concludes Talbot's voyage to Sydney Cove. The microcosm of the ship is still governed by changes among the relationships between the different individuals. Talbot is steadfast in his friendship to Lieutenant Summers but also befriends fellow passengers the Prettimans (a revolutionary philosopher and a governess who were married aboard the ship) and is tempted but ultimately not convinced by their visions of socialist utopias. His education, already furthered by his *coup de foudre* (intense love at first sight) in *Close Quarters,* progresses as a result of the discussions with the Prettimans. *Fire Down Below* also reveals one of the purposes of Talbot's journey, namely to spy on Aloysius Prettiman and to keep an eye on the printing press, which the latter transports in the hull to the colonies.

The foremast of the ship is mended by means of an ingenious device proposed by Lieutenant Bénet—a process involving fire that ultimately spells doom for the *Britannia*. However, the fixing of the mast allows the vessel to survive in one of the central scenes of the narrative, namely, an enormous storm that threatens the crew and the passengers and bears a strong resemblance to other "literary" storms such as in Joseph Conrad's *The Nigger of the Narcissus* (1897) and *Typhoon* (1903), and Richard Hughes's *In Hazard* (1938). The repaired mast also allows the ship to escape the ice cliffs of Antarctica, on which the voyage almost comes to an end.

When Talbot arrives in Sydney, he receives the news that his godfather has died and his prospects are shattered; but his misfortune is tempered when he later learns that he has been elected to Parliament. A further disaster is the fire on the *Britannia* that destroys the ship and kills Lieutenant Summers. The happy end is the result of the arrival of Miss Chumley, who accepts Talbot's suit. Nevertheless, the novel ends on a melancholy note: although Talbot has risen to power in British government and reveals himself to be an utter colonialist—a prime example is his outrage at an Aborigine gazing at Sydney's harbor "as if he owned the place!"—there is an awareness of the price he had to pay by not giving in to his idealistic notions and by not following Prettiman, whose bones—as Talbot's journal implies—probably bleach somewhere in the Australian outback.

The two sequels suffer from those structural defects that frequently arise when a narrative is continued beyond its original end. Thus, Boyd is accurate in his assessment of *Close Quarters* and *Fire Down Below* as "soap-operatic," even if it is soap opera of a high standard. He discerns the "lack of allegorical or symbolical density" that marked *Rites of Passage*. The brief excerpt from a letter by a friend of Talbot inserted in *Fire Down Below*—its author is an eminent geographer who has not traveled much himself and who disputes the existence of Antarctica—is too slight to orchestrate a similar impact as Colley's letters in the first volume of the trilogy and to succeed in introducing a different point of view. As if to confirm the potential for soap opera, *To the Ends of the Earth* was filmed for television and broadcast by the British Broadcasting Corporation (BBC 2) on 6, 13, and 20 July 2005.

When Golding died in his Cornwall home on 19 June 1993, he was in the process of revising another completed novel, *The Double Tongue*—the title was the one that the novelist had written on the manuscript. The book, posthumously published by Faber and Faber in 1995, resumes the novelist's fascination with the Greeks. Set in Delphi in the first century B.C., it traces the careers of Arieka, the Pythia at the famous oracle of Delphi (she is the first-person narrator of events), and of her mentor, Ionides Peisistrades, the homosexual priest of Apollo. The notion of one age waning—here, the Greek—and another one ascending, namely, the Roman Empire, is one of the author's favorite topics and is once again employed to describe the human condition. Despite "its unpolished state," Medcalf writes, "*The Double Tongue* is as intransigent, as fresh as any of Golding's greatest novels."

The novelist's death was widely regretted: Glendinning, for instance, in her *Observer* article, described the author as the "Grand Old Man" of the British literary scene. She also noted that Golding "believed in a god, but rejected organised religion." The lack of an official biography—Carey has been commissioned to write it—makes it difficult to assess the accuracy of such statements. It appears, however, that the novelist, raised as an atheist and set for a career as a scientist, was brought to a halt by some sort of spiritual crisis, and, as Medcalf writes, "Golding's sense of his own creativity was deeply bound up with his belief in God."

In an interview included in the 1996 BBC documentary, William Golding declared that he was first and foremost a storyteller: "What matters to me is that there should be a story with a beginning, a middle, and an end." This approach is too modest for an author who could be characterized in the words that Talbot uses for Prettiman in *Fire Down Below:* "his mind ranged vastly through the universe of space and time as it did through the other universe of books!"

Interviews:

Victoria Glendinning, "William Golding: The Old Man and the Sea," *Sunday Times,* 19 October 1980: 39;

John Carey, "William Golding Talks to John Carey," in *William Golding. The Man and His Books: A Tribute on His 75th Birthday,* edited by Carey (London: Faber & Faber, 1986), pp. 171–189;

Mary Lynn Scott, "Universal Pessimist, Cosmic Optimist: William Golding," *Aurora Online,* <http://aurora.icaap.org/archive/golding.html>.

Bibliography:

R. A. Gekoski and P. A. Grogan, *William Golding: A Bibliography 1934–1993* (London: André Deutsch, 1994).

References:

Anonymous, "Golding: Moralist Exploring Evil Through Parable," *Times,* 7 October 1983: 3;

Anonymous, "Row Over Golding's Nobel Prize," *Times,* 7 October 1983: 1;

S. J. Boyd, *The Novels of William Golding,* revised edition (New York: Harvester Wheatsheaf, 1990);

Carmen Callil and Colm Tóibín, "1954: Lord of the Flies," in *The Modern Library: The Two Hundred Best Novels in English Since 1950* (London: Picador, 1999), p. 66;

John Carey, "The Man Who Died of Shame," *Sunday Times,* 19 October 1980: 42;

Judy Carver, "Harbour and Voyage: The Marriage of Ann and Bill Golding," in *Living With a Writer,* edited by Dale Salwak (Basingstoke: Palgrave Macmillan, 2004), pp. 44–55;

Paul Crawford, *Politics and History in William Golding: The World Turned Upside Down* (Columbia: University of Missouri Press, 2002);

L. L. Dickson, *The Modern Allegories of William Golding* (Tampa: University of South Florida Press, 1990);

John Fowles, "Golding and 'Golding,'" in *William Golding. The Man and His Books: A Tribute on His 75th Birthday,* edited by John Carey (London: Faber & Faber, 1986), pp. 146–156;

Lawrence S. Friedman, *William Golding* (New York: Continuum, 1993);

James Gindin, *William Golding* (London: Macmillan, 1988);

Victoria Glendinning, "Golding's Voyage Ends Without Landfall," *Observer,* 20 June 1993;

Paul Gray, "A Prize as Good as Golding," *Time* (17 October 1983): 97;

Great Writers of the Twentieth Century: William Golding, BBC, 1996;

David Holloway, "Multi-layered Work of Golding is an Academic's Dream," *Daily Telegraph,* 7 October 1983: 11;

Philip Howard, "Fiction Prize for William Golding," *Times,* 22 October 1980: 1;

Julian Isherwood, "Uproar as Golding Takes Nobel Prize," *Daily Telegraph,* 7 October 1983: 1;

Paul Keel and W. L. Webb, "Patriotic Golding Claims Nobel Prize for England," *Guardian,* 7 October 1983: 1;

Frank Kermode, "On William Golding" [1962], in *The English Novel: Developments in Criticism since Henry James,* edited by Stephen Hazell (Basingstoke: Macmillan, 1978), pp. 151–162;

Mark Kinkead-Weekes and Ian Gregor, eds., *William Golding: A Critical Study of the Novels,* third revised edition (London: Faber & Faber, 2002);

David Lodge, "Life Between Covers" [1984], in his *Write On: Occasional Essays 1965–1985* (London: Penguin, 1988), pp. 174–179;

Kevin McCarron, *The Coincidence of Opposites: William Golding's Later Fiction* (Sheffield: Sheffield Academic Press, 1995);

McCarron, *William Golding* (Plymouth: Northcote, 1994);

Stephen Medcalf, "Island Skies–William Golding Reappraised," *Times Literary Supplement,* 2 September 2005: 12–13;

Charles Monteith, "Strangers from Within," in *William Golding. The Man and His Books: A Tribute on His 75th Birthday,* edited by John Carey (London: Faber & Faber, 1986);

Henri Petter, "Golding's *Darkness Visible,*" in *Modes of Interpretation: Essays Presented to Ernst Leisi,* edited by Richard J. Watts and Urs Weidmann (Tübingen: Narr, 1984), pp. 159–166;

Peter S. Prescott and Edward Behr, "A Nobel Prize for Britain," *Newsweek* (17 October 1983): 97;

Michael Specter, "Letter from Stockholm: The Nobel Syndrome," *New Yorker,* 5 October 1998 <http://www.michaelspecter.com/ny/1998/1998_10_05_nobel.html>;

Robin Stringer, "Golding Wins £10,000 Booker Prize," *Daily Telegraph,* 22 October 1980: 17;

Peter O. Stummer, "Man's Beastliness to Man: The Novels of William Golding," in *Essays on the Contemporary British Novel,* edited by Hedwig Bock and Albert Wertheim (Munich: Max Hueber, 1986), pp. 79–100;

Luke Strongman, *The Booker Prize and the Legacy of Empire* (Amsterdam: Rodopi, 2002);

V. V. Subbarao, *William Golding: A Study* (London: Oriental University Press, 1987);

Virginia Tiger, "William Golding's 'Wooden World': Religious Rites in *Rites of Passage,*" in *Critical Essays on William Golding,* edited by James R. Baker (Boston: G. K. Hall, 1988), pp. 135–149;

W. L. Webb, "Lord of the Prize," *Guardian,* 7 October 1983: 12.

Papers:

Most of William Golding's papers are still in the possession of his family. His daughter, Judy Carver, is editing his journals and letters for future publication.

1983 Nobel Prize in Literature Presentation Speech

by Professor Lars Gyllensten, of the Swedish Academy
(Translation from the Swedish)

Your Majesties, Your Royal Highnesses, Ladies and Gentlemen,

William Golding's first novel–*Lord of the Flies,* 1954–rapidly became a world success and has so remained. It has reached readers who can be numbered in tens of millions. In other words, the book was a bestseller, in a way that is usually granted only to adventure stories, light reading and children's books. The same goes for several of his later novels.

The reason is simple. These books are very entertaining and exciting. They can be read with pleasure and profit without the need to make much effort with learning or acumen. But they have also aroused an unusually great interest in scholars, writers and other interpreters, who have sought and found deep strata of ambiguity and complication in Golding's work. In those who use the tools of narration and linguistic art they have incited to thinking, discovery and creation of their own, in order to explore the world we live in and to settle down in it. In this respect William Golding can perhaps be compared to the American Herman Melville, whose works are full of equivocal profundity as well as fascinating adventure. In fact the resemblance extends farther than that. Golding has a very keen sight and sharp pen when it comes to the power of evil and baseness in human beings. He often chooses his themes and the framework for his stories from the world of the sea or from other challenging situations in which odd people are tempted to reach beyond their limits, thereby being bared to the very marrow. His stories usually have a fairly schematic drama, almost an anecdote, as skeleton. He then covers this with a richly varied and spicy flesh of colourful characters and surprising events.

It is the pattern of myth that we find in his manner of writing.

A very few basic experiences and basic conflicts of a deeply general nature underlie all his work as motive power. In one of his essays he describes how as a young man he took an optimistic view of existence. He believed that man would be able to perfect himself by improving society and eventually doing away with all social evil. His optimism was akin to that of other utopians, for instance H. G. Wells. The Second World War changed his outlook. He discovered what one human being is really able to do to another. And it was not a question of headhunters in New Guinea or primitive tribes in the Amazon region—he writes. They were atrocities committed with cold professional skill by well-educated and cultured people—doctors, lawyers and those with a long tradition of high civilization behind them. They carried out their crimes against their own equals. He writes:

"I must say that anyone who moved through those years without understanding that man produces evil as a bee produces honey, must have been blind or wrong in the head."

Golding inveighs against those who think that it is the political or other systems that create evil. Evil springs from the depths of man himself—it is the wickedness in human beings that creates the evil systems or that changes what from the beginning is, or could be, good into something iniquitous and destructive.

There is a mighty religious dimension in William Golding's conception of the world, though hardly Christian in the ordinary sense. He seems to believe in a kind of Fall. Perhaps rather one should say that he works with the myth of a Fall. In some of his stories, chiefly the novel *The Inheritors*, 1955, we find a dream of an original state of innocence in the history of mankind. The Fall came with the motive power of a new species. The aggressive intelligence, the power-hungry self-assertion and the overweening individualism are the source of evil and violence—individual as well as social violence. But these qualities and incentives are also innate in man as a created being. They are therefore inseparably a part of his character and make themselves felt when he gives full expression to himself and forms his societies and his private destiny.

We come across this tragic drama in many different ways in William Golding's novels. In *Lord of the Flies* a group of young boys are isolated on a desert island. Soon a kind of primitive society takes shape and is split into warring factions, one marked by decency and willingness to co-operate, the other by worship of force, lust for power and violence. The novel *Pincher Martin,* 1956, depicts how the main character, the narrator, is drowning. In his passionate absorption in himself he seems for a time to get the better of death. He does so by recounting his life, a life full of ruthless egoism and cruelty to others, a miserable life yet it was his and on no account does he want to lose it. He, the dead man, tries to make the rock to which he is clinging into a picture of himself. It is a weird ghost story, a fable of a will to live without shame or moderation.

In the novel *Rites of Passage,* 1980, the drama is enacted in the microcosm that the author arranges on a ship of the line at the beginning of the 19th Century. The book gives a cruel and drastic description of social barriers and aggressions on this ship, with an underlying black comedy and a masterly command of the characters' various linguistic roles. The scapegoat—one of many in Golding's works—is a priest who, naively trusting in the authority of his office, tries to assert his own dignity. He is subjected to outrages, each worse than the last, himself taking part in them, and ends up in such a desperate situation that he dies of shame.

All is not evil in the world of mankind, however, and all is not black in William Golding's imagined world. According to him, man has two characteristics—the ability to murder is one, belief in God the other. Innocence is not entirely lost. There is a striving away from evil. This striving often goes astray in self-assertion and illusionism. But it is there nevertheless and is allied with something that is not merely human. In the novel *The Spire,* 1964, this striving is embodied in a story about the building of a medieval cathedral. The builder is a priest who believes he has been ordered by God to build a spire that defies all reasonable calculations and measurements. His striving is both good and bad, containing the most complex reasons—humility and conviction but also arrogance, wilfulness and furtive sexual motives.

William Golding's novels and stories are not only sombre moralities and dark myths about evil and about treacherous, destructive forces. As already mentioned they are also colourful tales of adventure which can be read as such, full of narrative joy, inventiveness and excitement. In addition there are plentiful streaks of humour, biting irony, comedy and drastic jesting. There is a vitality which breaks through what is tragic and misanthropic, frightening in fact. A vitality, a vigour, which is infectious owing to its strength and intractability and to the paradoxical freedom it possesses as against what is related. His fabled world is tragic and pathetic, yet not overwhelming and depressing. There is a life which is mightier than life's conditions.

Dear Mr. Golding,

In interviews and essays you have sometimes made fun of commentators who have tried to summarize what you have written in a formula and fit your outlook on life into some pattern or other. That is impossible–simply because if it were possible there would be no reason for you to write your books and–as I hope–to continue to write. So I have not tried anything like that. I have only given a few reflexions, a few reactions to some of your novels–in the hope of conveying to those who might not yet be familiar with your works a glimpse of the fascination and stimulation which they afford. My second task is to express the warm congratulations of the Swedish Academy and to ask you to receive from the hands of His Majesty the King this year's Nobel Prize for Literature.

[© The Nobel Foundation, 1983.]

Golding: Banquet Speech

Golding's speech at the Nobel Banquet, 10 December 1983:

Your Majesties, your Royal Highnesses, your Excellencies, Fellow Laureates, Ladies and Gentlemen,

I came to Sweden characterized as a pessimist, though I am an optimist. Now something–perhaps the wonderful warmth of your hospitality–has changed me into a comic. That is a hard position to sustain. It reminds me of days long ago when as a poor teacher I would take turn about during the night with my wife, getting our infant daughter to sleep. I remember once, how at three o'clock in the morning when I began to creep away from the cradle with its sleeping child, she opened her eyes and remarked: "Daddy, say something funny."

However, the moment has come for me to put off the jester's cap and bells.

I do thank Sweden for its wonderfully warm hospitality and I do thank the Nobel Foundation and the Swedish Academy for the welcome and unexpected way in which they have, so to speak, struck me with lightning. I only wish all borders were as easy to cross and all international exchanges as friendly.

I have been in many countries and I have found there people examining their own love of life, sense of peril, their own common sense. The one thing they cannot understand is why that same love of life, sense of peril and above all common sense, is not invariably shared among their leaders and rulers.

Then let me use what I suppose is my last minute of worldwide attention to speak not as one of a nation but as one of mankind. I use it to reach all men and women of power. Go back. Step back now. Agreement between you does not need cleverness, elaboration, manoeuvres. It needs common sense, and above all, a daring generosity. Give, give, give!

It would succeed because it would meet with worldwide relief, acclaim and rejoicing: and unborn generations will bless your name.

[© The Nobel Foundation, 1983. William Golding is the sole author of his speech.]

Golding: Nobel Lecture, 7 December 1983

Those of you who have some knowledge of your present speaker as revealed by the loftier-minded section of the British Press will be resigning yourselves to a half hour of unrelieved gloom. Indeed, your first view of me, white bearded and ancient, may have turned that gloom into profound dark; dark, dark, dark, amid the blaze of noon, irrecoverably dark, total eclipse. But the case is not as hard as that. I am among the older of the Nobel Laureates and therefore might well be excused a touch of—let me whisper the word—frivolity. Pray do not misunderstand me. I have no dancing girls, alas. I shall not sing to you or juggle or clown—or shall I juggle? I wonder! How can a man who has been defined as a pessimist indulge in anything as frivolous as juggling?

You see it is hard enough at any age to address so learned a gathering as this. The very thought induces a certain solemnity. Then again, what about the dignity of age? There is, they say, no fool like an old fool.

Well, there is no fool like a middle-aged fool either. Twenty-five years ago I accepted the label "pessimist" thoughtlessly without realising that it was going to be tied to my tail, as it were, in something the way that, to take an example from another art, Rachmaninoff's famous Prelude in C sharp minor was tied to him. No audience would allow him off the concert platform until he played it. Similarly critics have dug into my books until they could come up with something that looked hopeless. I can't think why. I don't feel hopeless myself. Indeed I tried to reverse the process by explaining myself. Under some critical interrogation I named myself a universal pessimist but a cosmic optimist. I should have thought that anyone with an ear for language would understand that I was allowing more connotation than denotation to the word "cosmic" though in derivation universal and cosmic mean the same thing. I meant, of course, that when I consider a universe which the scientist constructs by a set of rules which stipulate that this construct must be repeatable and identical, then I am a pessimist and bow down before the great god Entropy. I am optimistic when I consider the spiritual dimension which the scientist's discipline forces him to ignore. So worldwide is the fame of the Nobel Prize that people have taken to quoting from my works and I do not see why I should not join in this fashionable pastime. Twenty years ago I tried to put the difference between the two kinds of experience in the mind of one of my characters, and made a mess of it. He was in prison.

"All day long the trains run on rails. Eclipses are predictable. Penicillin cures pneumonia and the atom splits to order. All day long year in year out the daylight explanation drives back the mystery and reveals a reality usable, understandable and detached. The scalpel and the microscope fail. The oscilloscope moves closer to behaviour.

"But then, all day long action is weighed in the balance and found not opportune nor fortunate nor ill-advised but good or evil. For this mode which we call the spirit breathes through the universe and does not touch it: touches only the dark things held prisoner, incommunicado, touches, judges, sentences and passes on. Both worlds are real. There is no bridge."

What amuses me is the thought that of course there is a bridge and that if anything it has been thrust out from the side which least expected it, and thrust out since those words were written. For we know now, that the universe had a beginning. (Indeed, as an aside I might say we always did know. I offer you a simple proof and forbid you to examine it. If there was no beginning then infinite time has already passed and we could never have got to the moment where we are.) We also know or it is at least scientifically respectable to postulate that at the centre of a black hole the laws of nature no longer apply. Since most scientists are just a bit religious and most religious are seldom wholly unscientific we find humanity in a comical position. His scientific intellect believes in the possibility of miracles inside a black hole while his religious intellect believes in them outside it. Both, in fact, now believe in miracles, credimus quia absurdum est. Glory be to God in the highest. You will get no reductive pessimism from me.

A greater danger facing you is that an ancient schoolmaster may be carried away and forget he is not addressing a class of pupils. A man in his seventies may be tempted to think he has seen it all and knows it all. He may think that mere length of years is a guarantee of wisdom and a permit for the issuing of admonition and advice. Poor young Shakespeare and Beethoven, he thinks, dead in their youth at a mere fifty-two or three! What could young fellows such as that know about anything? But at midnight perhaps, when the clock strikes and another year has passed he may occasionally brood on the disadvantages of age rather than the advantages. He may regard more thoughtfully a sentence which has been called the poetry of the fact, a sentence that one of those young fellows stumbled across accidentally, as it were, since he was never old enough to have worked the thing out through living. "Men," he wrote, "must endure their going hence, even as their coming hither." Such a consideration may modify the essential jollity of an old man's nature. Is the old man right to be happy? Is there not something unbecoming in his cheerful view of his own end? The words of another English poet seem to rebuke him.

> King David and King Solomon
> Led merry, merry lives,
> With many, many lady friends
> And many, many wives;
> But when old age crept over them,
> With many, many qualms,
> King Solomon wrote the Proverbs
> And King David wrote the Psalms.

Powerful stuff that, there's no doubt about it. But there are two views of the matter; and since I have quoted to you some of my prose which are generally regarded as poetic I will now quote to you some of my Goon or McGonagall poetry which may well be regarded as prosaic.

> Sophocles the eminent Athenian
> Gave as his final opinion
> That death of love in the breast
> Was like escape from a wild beast.
> What better word could you get?
> He was eighty when he said that.
> But Ninon de L'Enclos
> When asked the same question said, no
> She was uncommonly matey
> At eighty.

Evidently age need not wither us nor custom stale our infinite variety. Let us be, for a while, not serious but considerate. I myself face another danger. I do not speak in a small tribal language as it might be one of the six hundred languages of Nigeria. Of course the value of any language is incalculable. Your Laureate of 1979, the Greek poet Elytis, made quite clear that the relative value of works of literature is not to be decided by counting heads. It is, I think, the greatest tribute one can pay your committees that they have consistently sought for value in a work without heeding how many people can or cannot read it. The young John Keats spoke of Greek poets who "died content on pleasant sward, leaving great verse unto a little clan." Indeed and indeed, small can be beautiful. To quote yet another poet-prose writer though I am you will have begun to realise where my heart is—Ben Jonson said:

> It is not growing like a tree
> In bulk, doth make man better be,
> Or standing long an oak, three hundred year,
> To fall a log at last, dry, bald and sere:
> A lily of a day,
> Is fairer far in May,
> Although it fall and die that night;
> It was the plant and flower of light.
> In small proportions we just beauties see,
> And in short measures, life may perfect be.

My own language, English, I believe to have a store of poets, of writers that need not fear comparison with those of any other language, ancient or modern. But today that language may suffer from too wide a use rather than too narrow a one—may be an oak rather than a lily. It spreads right round the world as the medium of advertisement, navigation, science, negotiation, conference. A hundred political parties have it daily in their mouths. Perhaps a language subjected to such strains as that may become, here and there, just a little thin. In English a man may think he is addressing a small, distinguished audience, or his family or his friends, perhaps; he is brooding aloud or talking in his sleep. Later he finds that without meaning to he has been addressing a large segment of the world. That is a daunting thought. It is true that this year, surrounded and outnumbered as I am by American laureates, I take a quiet pleasure in the consideration that though variants of my mother tongue may be spoken by a greater number of people than are to be found in an island off the West coast of Europe nevertheless they are speaking dialects of what is still centrally English. Personally I cannot tell whether those many dialects are being rendered mutually incomprehensible by distance faster than they are being unified by television and satellites; but at the moment the English writer faces immediate comprehension or partial comprehension by a good part of a billion people. His critics are limited in number only by the number of the people who can read his work. Nor can he escape from knowing the worst. No matter how obscure the publication that has disembowelled him, some kind correspondent—let us call him "X"—will send the article along together with an indignant assurance that he, "X," does not agree with a word of it. I think apprehensively of the mark I present, once *A Moving Target* but now, surely a fixed one, before the serried ranks of those who can shoot at me if they choose. Even my most famous and distinguished fellow laureate and fellow countryman, Winston Churchill, did not escape. A critic remarked with acid wit of his getting the award, "Was it for his poetry or his prose?" Indeed it was considerations such as these which have given me, I suppose, more difficulty in conceiving, let alone writing this lecture than any piece of comparable length since those distant days when I wrote set essays on set subjects at school. The only difference I can find is that today I write at a larger desk and the marks I shall get for my performance will be more widely reported.

Now when, you may say, is the man going to say something about the subject which is alleged to be his own? He should be talking about the novel! Well, I will for a while, but only for a while, and as it were, tangentially. The truth is that though each of the subjects for which the prizes are awarded has its own and unique importance, none can exist wholly to itself. Even the novel, if it climbs into an ivory tower, will find no audience except those with ivory towers of their own. I used to think that the outlook for the novel was poor. Let me quote myself again. I speak of boys growing up—not exceptional boy, but average boy.

> Boys do not evaluate a book. They divide books into categories. There are sexy books, war books, westerns, travel books, science fiction. A boy will accept anything from a section he knows rather than risk another sort. He has to have the label on the bottle to know it is the mixture as before. You must put his detective story in a green paperback or he may suffer the hardship of reading a book in which nobody is murdered at all;—I am thinking of the plodders, the amiable majority of us, not particularly intelligent or gifted; well-disposed, but left high and dry among a mass of undigested facts with their scraps of saleable technology. What chance has literature of competing with the defined categories of entertainment which are laid on for them at every hour of the day? I do not see how literature is to be for them anything but simple, repetitive and a stop-gap for when there are no westerns on the telly. They will have a far less brutish life than their Nineteenth-Century ancestors, no doubt. They will believe less and fear less. But just as bad money drives out good, so inferior culture drives out superior. With any capacity to make value judgements vitiated or undeveloped, what mass future is there, then, for poetry, for belles-lettres, for real fearlessness in the theatre, for the novel which tries to look at life anew—in a word, for intransigence?

I wrote that some twenty years ago I believe and the process as far as the novel is concerned has developed but not improved. The categories are more and more defined. Competition from other media is fiercer still. Well, after all the novel has no build—it claims on immortality.

"Story" of course is a different matter. We like to hear of succession of events and as an inspection of our press will demonstrate have only a marginal interest in whether the succession of events is minutely true or not. Like the late Mr. Sam Goldwyn who wanted a story which began with an earthquake and worked up to a climax, we like a good lead in but have most pleasure in a succession of events with a satisfactory endpoint. Most simply and directly—when children holler and yell because of some infant tragedy or tedium, at once when we take them on our knee and begin shouting if necessary—"once upon a time" they fall silent and attentive. Story will always be with us. But story in a physical book, in a sentence what the West means by "a novel"—what of that? Certainly, if the form fails let it go. We have enough complications in life, in art, in literature without preserving dead forms fossilised, without cluttering ourselves with Byzantine sterilities. Yes, in that case, let the novel go. But what goes with it? Surely something of profound importance to the human spirit! A novel ensures that we can look before and after, take action at whatever pace we choose, read again and again, skip and go back. The story in a book is humble and serviceable, available, friendly, is not switched on and off but taken up and put down, lasts a lifetime.

Put simply the novel stands between us and the hardening concept of statistical man. There is no other medium in which we can live for so long and so intimately with a character. That is the service a novel renders. It performs no less an act than the rescue and the preservation of the individuality and dignity of the single being, be it man, woman or child. No other art, I claim, can so thread in and out of a single mind and body, so live another life. It does ensure that at the very least a human being shall be seen to be more than just one billionth of one billion.

I spoke of the ivory tower and the unique importance of each of our studies. Now I must add, having said my bit about the novel—that those studies converge, literature with the rest. Put bluntly, we face two problems—either we blow ourselves off the face of the earth or we degrade the fertility of the earth bit by bit until we have ruined it. Does it take a writer of fiction to bring you the cold comfort of pointing out that the problems are mutually exclusive? The one problem, the instant catastrophe, is not to be dealt with here. It would be irresponsible of me to turn this platform into a stage for acting out some antiatomic harangue and equally irresponsible at this juncture in history for me to ignore our perils. You know them as well as I do. As so often, when the unspeakable is to be spoken, the unthinkable thought, it is Shakespeare we must turn to; and I can only quote Hamlet with the skull:

> Not one now, to mock your own grinning? Quite chop-fallen? Now get you to my lady's chamber and tell her, let her paint an inch thick, to this favour she must come; make her laugh at that.

I am being rather unfair to the lady, perhaps, for there will be skulls of all shapes and sizes and sexes. I speak tangentially. No other quotation gives the dirt of it all, another kind of poetry of the fact. I must say something of this danger and I have said it for I could do no less. Now as far as this matter is concerned, I have done.

The other danger is more difficult to combat. To quote another laureate, our race may end not with a bang but a whimper. It must be nearer seventy years ago than sixty that I first discovered and engaged myself to a magic place. This was on the west coast of our country. It was on the seashore among rocks. I early became acquainted with the wonderful interplay of earth and moon and sun, enjoying them at the same time as I was assured that scientifically you could not have action influenced at a distance. There was a particular phase of the moon at which the tide sank more than usually far down and revealed to me a small recess which I remember as a cavern. There was plenty of life of one sort or another round all the rocks and in the pools among them. But this pool, farthest down and revealed, it seemed, by an influence from the sky only once or twice during the times when I had the holiday privilege of living near it—this last recess before the even more mysterious deep sea had strange inhabitants which I had found nowhere else. I can now remember and even feel but alas not describe the peculiar engagement, excitement and, no, not sympathy or empathy, but passionate recognition of a living thing in all its secrecy and strangeness. It was or rather they were real as I was. It was as if the centre of our universe was there for my eyes to reach at like hands, to seize on by sight. Only a hand's breadth away in the last few inches of still water they flowered, grey, green and purple, palpably alive, a discovery, a meeting, more than an interest or pleasure. They were life, we together were delight itself; until the first ripples of returning water blurred and hid them. When the summer holidays were over and I went back again about as far from the sea as you can get in England I carried with me like a private treasure the memory of that cave—no, in some strange way I took the cave with me and its creatures that flowered so strangely. In nights of sleeplessness and fear of the supernatural I would work out the phase of the moon, returning in thought to the slither and clamber among the weeds of the rocks. There were times when, though I was far away, I found myself before the cavern watching the moon-dazzle as the water sank and was comforted somehow by the magical beauty of our common world.

I have been back, since. The recess—for now it seems no more than that—is still there, and at low water springs if you can bend down far enough you can still look inside. Nothing lives there any more. It is all very clean now, ironically so, clean sand, clean water, clean rock. Where the living creatures once clung they have worn two holes like the orbits of eyes, so that you might well sentimentalize yourself into the fancy that you are looking at a skull. No life.

Was it a natural process? Was it fuel oil? Was it sewage or chemicals more deadly that killed my childhood's bit of magic and mystery? I cannot tell and it does not matter. What matters is that this is only one tiny example among millions of how we are impoverishing the only planet we have to live on.

Well now, what has literature to say to that? We have computers and satellites, we have ingenuities of craft that can land a complex machine on a distant planet and get reports back. And so on. You know it all as well and better than I. Literature has words only, surely a tool as primitive as the flint axe or even the soft copper chisel with which man first carved his own likeness in stone. That tool makes a poor showing one would think among the products of the silicon chip. But remember Churchill. For despite the cynical critic, he got the Nobel Prize neither for poetry nor prose. He got it for about a single page of simple sentences which are neither poetry nor prose but for what, I repeat, has been called finely the poetry of the fact. He got it for those passionate utterances which were the very stuff of human courage and defiance. Those of us who lived through those times know that Churchill's poetry of the fact changed history.

Perhaps then the soft copper chisel is not so poor a tool after all. Words may, through the devotion, the skill, the passion, and the luck of writers prove to be the most powerful thing in the world. They may move men to speak to each other because some of those words somewhere express not just what the writer is thinking but what a huge segment of the world is thinking. They may allow man to speak to man, the man in the street to speak to his fellow until a ripple becomes a tide running through every nation—of commonsense, of simple healthy caution, a tide that rulers and negotiators cannot ignore so that nation does truly speak unto nation. Then there is hope that we may learn to be temperate, provident, taking no more from nature's treasury than is our due. It may be by books, stories, poetry, lectures we who have the ear of mankind can move man a little nearer the perilous safety of a warless and provident world. It cannot be done by the mechanical constructs of overt propaganda. I cannot do it myself, cannot now create stories which would help to make man aware of what he is doing; but there are others who can, many others. There always have been. We need more humanity, more care, more love. There are those who expect a political system to produce that; and others who expect the love to produce the system. My own faith is that the truth of the future lies between the two and we shall behave humanly and a bit humanely, stumbling along, haphazardly generous and gallant, foolishly and meanly wise until the rape of our planet is seen to be the preposterous folly that it is.

For we are a marvel of creation. I think in particular of one of the most extraordinary women, dead now these five hundred years, Juliana of Norwich. She was caught up in the spirit and shown a thing that might lie in the palm of her hand and in the bigness of a nut. She was told it was the world. She was told of the strange and wonderful and awful things that would happen there. At the last, a voice told her that all things should be well and all manner of things should be well and all things should be very well.

Now we, if not in the spirit, have been caught up to see our earth, our mother, Gaia Mater, set like a jewel in space. We have no excuse now for supposing her riches inexhaustible nor the area we have to live on limitless because unbounded. We are the children of that great blue white jewel. Through our mother we are part of the solar system and part through that of the whole universe. In the blazing poetry of the fact we are children of the stars.

I had better come down, I think. Churchill, Juliana of Norwich, let alone Ben Jonson and Shakespeare—Lord, what company we keep! Reputations grow and dwindle and the brightest of laurels fade. That very practical man, Julius Caesar—whom I always think of for a reason you may guess at, as Field Marshal Lord Caesar—Julius Caesar is said to have worn a laurel wreath to conceal his baldness. While it may be proper to praise the idea of a laureate the man himself may very well remember what his laurels will hide and that not only baldness. In a sentence he must remember not to take himself with unbecoming seriousness. Fortunately some spirit or other—I do not presume to put a name to it—ensured that I should remember my smallness in the scheme of things. The very day after I learned that I was the laureate for literature for 1983 I drove into a country town and parked my car where I should not. I only left the car for a few minutes but when I came back there was a ticket taped to the window. A traffic warden, a lady of a minatory aspect, stood by the car. She pointed to a notice on the wall. "Can't you read?" she said. Sheepishly I got into my car and drove very slowly round the corner. There on the pavement I saw two county policemen.

I stopped opposite them and took my parking ticket out of its plastic envelope. They crossed to me. I asked if, as I had pressing business, I could go straight to the Town Hall and pay my fine on the spot. "No, sir," said the senior policeman, "I'm afraid you can't do that." He smiled the fond smile that such policemen reserve for those people who are clearly harmless if a bit silly. He indicated a rectangle on the ticket that had the words "name and address of sender" printed above it. "You should write your name and address in that place," he said. "You make out a cheque for ten pounds, making it payable to the Clerk to the Justices at *this* address written here. Then you write the same address on the outside of the envelope, stick a sixteen penny stamp in the top right hand corner of the envelope, then post it. And may we congratulate you on winning the Nobel Prize for Literature."

[© The Nobel Foundation, 1983. William Golding is the sole author of the text.]

Nadine Gordimer

(20 November 1923 –   )

Rowland Smith
University of Calgary

This entry has been expanded by Smith from his Gordimer entry in *DLB 225: South African Writers*. See also the Gordimer entry in *DLB Yearbook: 1991*.

BOOKS: *Face to Face: Short Stories* (Johannesburg: Silver Leaf, 1949);

The Soft Voice of the Serpent and Other Stories (New York: Simon & Schuster, 1952; London: Gollancz, 1953);

The Lying Days (London: Gollancz, 1953; New York: Simon & Schuster, 1953);

Six Feet of the Country (London: Gollancz, 1956; New York: Simon & Schuster, 1956);

A World of Strangers (London: Gollancz, 1958; New York: Simon & Schuster, 1958);

Friday's Footprint and Other Stories (London: Gollancz, 1960; New York: Viking, 1960);

Occasion for Loving (London: Gollancz, 1963; New York: Viking, 1963);

Not For Publication and Other Stories (London: Gollancz, 1965; New York: Viking, 1965);

The Late Bourgeois World (London: Gollancz, 1966; New York: Viking, 1966);

A Guest of Honour (New York: Viking, 1970; London: Cape, 1971);

Livingstone's Companions (New York: Viking, 1971; London: Cape, 1972);

African Literature: The Lectures Given on this Theme at the University of Cape Town's Public Summer School, February, 1972 (Cape Town: Board of Extramural Studies, University of Cape Town, 1972);

The Black Interpreters: Notes on African Writing (Johannesburg: Spro-Cas/Ravan, 1973);

The Conservationist (London: Cape, 1974; New York: Viking, 1975);

Selected Stories (London: Cape, 1975; New York: Viking, 1976); republished as *Some Monday for Sure: Selected Short Stories* (London: Heinemann Educational, 1976); republished as *No Place Like: Selected Stories* (Harmondsworth, U.K.: Penguin, 1978);

Nadine Gordimer (Time & Life Pictures/Getty Images)

Burger's Daughter (London: Cape, 1979; New York: Viking, 1979);

A Soldier's Embrace: Stories (London: Cape, 1980; New York: Viking, 1980);

What Happened to Burger's Daughter, Or How South African Censorship Works, by Gordimer and others (Johannesburg: Taurus, 1980);

Town and Country Lovers (Los Angeles: Sylvester & Orphanos, 1980);

July's People (London: Cape, 1981; New York: Viking, 1981; Braamfontein, South Africa: Ravan / Emmarentia, South Africa: Taurus, 1981);

Something Out There (London: Cape, 1984; New York: Viking, 1984; Braamfontein, South Africa: Ravan / Emmarentia, South Africa: Taurus, 1984); abridged edition (London: Bloomsbury, 1994);

A Sport of Nature (London: Cape, 1987; New York: Knopf, 1987; Cape Town: David Philip, 1987);

The Essential Gesture: Writing, Politics and Places, edited by Stephen Clingman (London: Cape, 1988; New York: Knopf, 1988; Johannesburg: Taurus, 1988);

My Son's Story (London: Bloomsbury, 1990; New York: Farrar, Straus & Giroux, 1990; Cape Town: David Philip, 1990);

Jump and Other Stories (London: Bloomsbury, 1991; New York: Farrar, Straus & Giroux, 1991; Cape Town: David Philip, 1991);

Three in a Bed: Fiction, Morals, and Politics, Ben Belitt Lectureship Series, no. 13 (Bennington, Vt.: Bennington College, 1991);

Crimes of Conscience: Selected Short Stories (Oxford & Portsmouth, N.H.: Heinemann, 1991);

Why Haven't You Written?: Selected Stories, 1950–1972 (New York: Penguin, 1993);

None To Accompany Me (London: Bloomsbury, 1994; New York: Farrar, Straus & Giroux, 1994; Cape Town: David Philip, 1994);

Writing and Being (Cambridge, Mass. & London: Harvard University Press, 1995);

Harald, Claudia, and Their Son Duncan [excerpt from *The House Gun*] (London: Bloomsbury, 1996);

The House Gun (New York: Viking, 1998; London: Bloomsbury, 1998; Cape Town: David Philip, 1998);

Living in Hope and History: Notes from Our Century, edited by Liz Calder (London: Bloomsbury, 1999; New York: Farrar, Straus & Giroux, 1999; Cape Town: David Philip, 2000);

Selected Stories (London: Bloomsbury, 2000);

The Pickup (New York: Farrar, Straus & Giroux, 2001; London: Bloomsbury, 2001; Cape Town: David Philip, 2001);

The Ultimate Safari (Johannesburg: Artist's Press, 2001);

Loot and Other Stories (New York: Farrar, Straus & Giroux, 2003; London: Bloomsbury, 2003; Glosderry, South Africa: David Philip, 2003);

Get a Life (New York: Farrar, Straus & Giroux, 2005; London: Bloomsbury, 2005; Claremont, South Africa: David Philip, 2005).

PRODUCED SCRIPTS: *Praise*, video, Profile Productions, 1981;

Country Lovers, video, Profile Productions, 1982;

Choosing for Justice: Allan Boesak, video, script by Gordimer and Hugo Cassirer, 1983;

Oral History, video, Profile Productions, 1983;

"The Ingot and the Gun, Mozambique–South Africa," television, *Frontiers*, BBC 1, June 1990;

A Chip of Glass Ruby, video, Films for the Humanities & Sciences/Profile Productions, 1995;

Berlin & Johannesburg: The Wall & The Colour Bar, video, script by Gordimer and Cassirer, 1998.

RECORDING: *Nadine Gordimer Reads: A City of the Dead, A City of the Living and The Termitary*, read by Gordimer, N.p., Spoken Arts, 1986.

OTHER: *The First Circle*, in *Six One-act Plays by South African Authors* (Pretoria, South Africa: Van Schaik, 1949);

South African Writing Today, edited by Gordimer and Lionel Abrahams (Harmondsworth, U.K.: Penguin, 1967);

"Being a Product of Your Dwelling Place," in *The Writing Life: Writers on How They Think and Work*, edited by Marie Arana (New York: Public Affairs, 2003).

A Nobel Prize winner, an outspoken critic of apartheid, a frequently controversial public figure in her native South Africa, and one of the leading novelists of her age, Nadine Gordimer has been writing since her teens. Her first short story (for children) was published in 1937, when she was thirteen; her first story for adults appeared two years later. Known at first as a writer of fiction, with many early critics believing that she was more successful in the compressed short-story format than in novels, she has become progressively important as a commentator on South African affairs in nonfiction published throughout the English-speaking world. Her political writing and her criticism are often cited in the world of international letters, but she has stated time and again that her fiction is a truth about her society as her nonfiction (which she considers secondary) can never be. Her fiction chronicles the changes in South African society since the late 1940s and offers a remarkable account of the corrosive effects of life in the apartheid state, presented with compassion, irony, and evocative accuracy. In her later fiction she uses the truths learned in the South African situation to examine contemporary issues in the world at large, especially those related to the exercise of privilege and the attempts of the unprivileged to gain access to a better existence. Throughout her career, Gordimer has had to steer a middle path between the conflicting claims of conservative white readers who resented her relentless analyses of white privilege, and of "committed" readers—both white and black—who regarded as trivial or indulgent her insistence that art should not become propaganda.

Nadine Gordimer was born in Springs, a small mining town outside Johannesburg in Transvaal, South Africa, on 20 November 1923. Her father, Isidore Gordimer, was an immigrant Jewish watchmaker from Lithuania who had arrived in South Africa at the age of thirteen; her mother, Nan Myers, had been born in England. A shop-owning family, the Gordimers were part of the white, English-speaking middle class, and Nadine, an only child, was introduced at an early age to the social conformism of that group. Her first novel, *The Lying Days* (1953), is a bildungsroman that describes in vivid detail the sheltered life of its protagonist, growing up on a mine property in a small town east of Johannesburg.

The central event in Gordimer's childhood was revealed in an interview with Jannika Hurwitt, published in the *Paris Review* in 1983 and included in *Conversations with Nadine Gordimer* (1990). Gordimer's mother had died in 1976, and it was only after her death that the writer was able to talk publicly about her childhood. In the interview Gordimer describes the loneliness that resulted from her mother's decision to take her out of school on the pretext of a heart ailment; from the ages of eleven to sixteen, she was educated privately at home. Not only did she have to give up her dancing, which she loved, but also she lived a life cut off from others of her age. She regards access to the local municipal library as her real education, and notes that if she had been a black child, membership would have been barred to her; she says perhaps she would never have become a writer. Reading and then writing took the place of companionship with other children, while the status of alien observer further prepared her for her writing career. The accuracy of Gordimer's observations and her ear for dialogue have always been noteworthy features of her art.

Before being taken out of school, Gordimer had attended the Convent of Our Lady of Mercy in Springs. She had no further formal education except for a year in a general studies program at the University of the Witwatersrand in Johannesburg in 1945.

Early short stories first published separately in the 1940s illustrate both Gordimer's sharp eye for detail and her indirect, ironic manner of commenting on the intractability of the injustices entrenched by racial separation. Three of the best-known stories illustrating this theme were published in 1947, before the victory of the National Party—the party that systematized and codified white hegemony in the practice of apartheid—in the general election of 1948. They were republished in her first collection, *Face to Face,* which appeared in Johannesburg in 1949, and in *The Soft Voice of the Serpent and Other Stories,* which was published in New York in 1952 and in London the following year and included many of the stories in the earlier volume.

As in so many of her early works, these short stories deal with relations between white overlords and black underlings. The belittling nature of official racial privilege is shown to affect the white characters just as much as the black. The inappropriateness of a bland response to anguish, the soiling effect of a struggle to hang onto possessions, the selfishness of an assertion of control, all these traits are implied in fictional closures that highlight unfulfillment and disconnection.

The protagonist in "Ah, Woe Is Me" is a white woman, visited regularly by her former maid's daughter, who comes to receive family castoffs and handouts after her mother has ceased to work because of illness. On one visit the daughter is overcome with sobs because of the severity of her mother's condition. The white woman, not knowing what else to do, merely offers a handkerchief. The puniness of this response provides the ironic power of the story. Even when the protagonist is not obtuse, however, a similar sense of powerlessness and contamination is created from the perspective of the white observer through whose eyes the narrative unfolds.

In "Is There Nowhere Else Where We Can Meet?" the viewpoint is that of a young white woman who is attacked by a ragged black man as she walks alone in the arid winter landscape of the Transvaal. Terrified by his dirt and tattered otherness, she struggles with him until her handbag and parcel fall, and the assailant turns to them, allowing her to run off. She comes to a road with houses and calms down as she approaches safety and order:

> She thought of the woman coming to the door, of the explanations, of the woman's face, and the police. Why did I fight, she thought suddenly. What did I fight for? Why didn't I give him the money and let him go? His red eyes, and the smell and those cracks in his feet, fissures, erosion. She shuddered. The cold of the morning flowed into her.
>
> She turned away from the gate and went down the road slowly, like an invalid, beginning to pick the blackjacks from her stockings.

Although both attacker and attacked are diminished by the event, it is the black man who is portrayed as the ultimate victim, and this knowledge leaves the protagonist a kind of invalid. The invalid status attendant on the enjoyment of constant privilege is one of the main themes of Gordimer's fiction during the apartheid period.

In "The Train From Rhodesia" the protagonist is a young woman returning from honeymooning with her husband. At a stop in the middle of nowhere the callow young man haggles with an African carver selling his wares alongside the stationary train. Carelessly he forces a bargain as the train pulls away, and gives his wife the carved lion head she has eyed; but the meanness of his treatment of the artist overwhelms her, making her feel ashamed.

Gordimer married Gerald Gavron in 1949; their daughter, Oriane, was born in 1950. Gordimer and Gavron were divorced in 1952. The following year the firms of Victor Gollancz and Simon and Schuster published *The Lying Days*. This book, Gordimer's first published novel (she had abandoned at least two earlier attempts), shows all the evocative skill of the stories but is not as tightly narrated or plotted. It is nevertheless a powerful depiction of both the ethos of Gordimer's childhood Springs and of the concerns facing someone of her generation, a young adult in South Africa just after World War II. Despite the autobiographical elements, this novel shows Gordimer's gift for using her imagination to create individual truths that reflect more general, public truths.

The protagonist of *The Lying Days*, Helen Shaw, experiences personally the crises typical of her era. As an adolescent she is absorbed into the blinkered provincialism of the mine community and her mother's world. That community manifests not only classic colonial traits but also the more specifically white South African characteristic of living in a world quite separate—physically, imaginatively, and morally—from the raw, teeming humanity of the black mine laborers. Aware of the narrowness of her home life, Helen goes to university in Johannesburg and then moves in a bohemian world in which black people exist as individuals and in which the issues of racial politics are insistently discussed. Helen's attempts to befriend a black fellow student are both difficult in themselves and viewed with predictably dismissive prejudice by her family. Growing up into such political awareness is accompanied by an increasing maturity in personal relations.

One of the major problems facing Helen and her friends is the spreading nastiness of racial politics in Johannesburg and the corresponding desire to escape from intractable South African society. "South Africa's a battleground; you can't belong on a battleground," says Helen to her old friend Joel as he is about to leave the country. But on the last page of the book, in a moment of epiphany, she takes comfort from the thought that she will return to South Africa: "I'm not running away. Whatever it was I was running away from—the risk of love? the guilt of being white? the danger of putting ideals into practice?—I'm not running away from now because I know I'm coming back here."

The option of flight—both from commitment to political action itself and from the personal restrictions of South African life—becomes a recurrent element in Gordimer's fiction. The necessity of staying on—and staying on committed—is investigated insistently in the middle and later fiction.

In 1954 Gordimer married Reinhold Cassirer, a German Jewish refugee from the Nazi regime who had a distinguished career with British Intelligence during World War II and later became an art dealer. Their son, Hugo, was born in 1955. Since her marriage (which lasted until Cassirer's death in 2001) Gordimer has lived in Johannesburg, with extended travels abroad in many countries.

Gordimer's second novel, *A World of Strangers*, was published in 1958 at the height of the liberal movement in South Africa—though the book was banned in that country for twelve years. The late 1950s were years in which intellectuals and artists of all colors strove to live personal lives disregarding the increasingly restrictive codes of official apartheid. Their belief was that ignoring the rules and ethos of separation would ensure its ultimate failure—that good will would triumph over regulations. Much of Gordimer's fiction from the 1950s on was concerned with analyzing just how mistaken and privileged was this belief, mainly held by well-meaning whites.

That heady aura of unofficial racial mixing in an officially segregated world is vividly captured in *A World of Strangers*. The late 1950s was the era of a surge of black writing from those who worked on *Drum* magazine; the articulation, in a not-yet-muzzled press, of the absurdity of government policies; and the pre–Black Consciousness cooperation of student leaders in a nonracial national student union. It was the age of illegal racially mixed parties and the heyday of black "shebeens"—speakeasies patronized by black workers, criminals, and intellectuals, as well as by white intellectuals and activists.

This background forms the setting of *A World of Strangers*, a title ominously at odds with the intended camaraderie in the "liberal" racial mixing depicted. The protagonist, Toby, is a young Englishman sent to South Africa to work for a publishing house. He finds himself taken up by a group of affluent whites and accepted by a group of bohemian, fast-living blacks. Moving between the lavish bourgeois entertainment of the white social set and the exciting and dangerous shadow-world of his black friends, he has a shallow relationship with a white woman and a searing friendship with a black man. In addition, he meets a genuine political activist, a white labor organizer ultimately arrested for her activities. Her form of quiet commitment contrasts strongly with the pleasure-seeking he encounters in his social adventures on either side of the racial chasm. The death of his black friend in a car accident forces him to recognize the intractability of white suzerainty and the privilege that has enabled him to move "freely" among the two otherwise divided groups. His visitor status has been an additional protection against real involvement in that separated society. He begins to understand not only the falsity of his attempt to remain free of political commitment but also the reality of difference created by systematized racism.

The liberalism of the 1950s ended violently with the Sharpeville massacre in 1960, when white police shot down blacks protesting laws that forbade nonwhites from traveling freely in South Africa. The violence resulted in the declaration of a state of emergency and the subsequent arrest and detention without trial of many political figures. From that point, increasingly repressive legislation was introduced, establishing the police state that silenced organized political opposition and drove into exile most of the black intellectuals associated with the liberal renaissance of the 1950s.

In her early work Gordimer depicts the ambiguity and compromises of white liberalism; in her writing published between 1960 and 1994 she analyzes its failure. *Occasion for Loving* (1963) evokes the period leading up to Sharpeville and investigates the one-sidedness of racial mingling in the Johannesburg of that era. The nonfulfillment at the closing of the novel and the splintering of relationships that it depicts point the way to the aridity of post–1950s life in authoritarian, apartheid South Africa.

Occasion for Loving deals with an aspect of life in mid-century South Africa that featured as the stock-in-trade of some political fiction. Sex across the color line, which was unlawful in that period, resulted in many human indignities, publicly recorded in the press, as law enforcers spied their way into the bedrooms and trysting places of those who were involved with sexual partners of a different race. Both the absurdity of morality squad antics and the human waste involved in "immorality act" prosecutions are treated in some fiction of the period as sensational evidence of the inhumanity of apartheid.

The plot of *Occasion for Loving* deals with a relationship between a young white woman, educated in England, and a black artist. It is typical of Gordimer's subtlety that her investigation of illicit love in racially segregated Johannesburg focuses on the commitment or betrayal of the partners themselves—within the context of apartheid corrosion—rather than on the dehumanizing effect of the law itself or the inhumanity of the law-enforcers.

In *Occasion for Loving* the traumatic interracial love affair is observed by a benign, considerate white woman, Jessie Stilwell, in whose house a visiting white couple have come to stay. Jessie's husband is a university historian concerned with presenting the overlooked experience of Africans. The young visiting couple, Boaz and Ann, epitomize prejudice-free attitudes of the time; Boaz is involved with black music and musicology. Gideon Shibalo, with whom Ann has her torrid affair, is a black artist, living the high-voltage artistic life of the last moments of racially mixed liberal-bohemian Johannesburg.

The liberal dream of impartiality or freedom from political constraint is presented ironically; even fair-mindedness can be one of the doomed illusions of the privileged white middle class. When Ann becomes embroiled in her love affair with Gideon, Boaz tries to behave decently and not force her to return to him. The delicacy with which those around the lovers allow them the freedom to pursue their dangerously illegal liaison is another example of consideration based on privilege. When Ann abandons her black artist lover and returns to Boaz, she has the freedom to make that choice and pick up a fulfilling life. Gideon has no such privileges, and his shattered reaction to her leaving him is as much a consequence of the politics of his unprivileged status as of the personal pain of losing his lover. To Ann, her love affair with Gideon is part of the exoticism of Africa; to Gideon, his relationship with Ann is an entree to a richer world.

The poisonous effect of this disparity in freedom is wide-ranging. At the end of the book Jessie comes across drunken Gideon at a party. His furious rejection of her encapsulates the pain (for all parties) of entrenched racial privilege and the folly of assuming that liberal attitudes alone can transcend the horrors of apartheid law and practice.

The scene is much darker in Gordimer's next novel, and the sense of confinement much more marked. *The Late Bourgeois World* appeared in 1966 when the police and state controls instituted after Sharpeville had taken hold. This novel was also banned by the South African censors. The setting is no longer the world of interracial partying and well-meaning gestures in opposition to apartheid codes and customs but rather the much narrower world of high-risk underground political activity (financed and planned from outside the country), occasional and dangerous meetings of old political acquaintances from another racial group, and violent (if often futile) opposition to the state.

The Late Bourgeois World investigates this strange world of middle-class liberal intellectuals turned saboteurs as part of Gordimer's continuing analysis of the failure of liberalism in the South African context. The protagonist is Liz, a young, white Johannesburg divorced woman, and the action is confined to the day following her receiving an early-morning telegram informing her that her former husband, Max, has killed himself by driving into Cape Town harbor. She remembers their early life together and reflects on his mixed motives in becoming a "liberal" saboteur. Son of a wealthy and powerful family, he had first thrown himself into nonviolent political opposition and then had made and planted a bomb. Sentenced to five years in prison, he had appeared as a state witness in the trials of others in his group.

The feeling of impasse in the book is not confined to the unraveling of Max's hopelessly compromised need to find respect through a kind of politics that would be totally opposed to the values of his established family. His position is doomed from the start: "He wanted to come close; and in this country the people—with all the huddled warmth of the phrase—are black. Set aside with whites, even his own chosen kind, he was still left out, he experienced the isolation of his childhood become the isolation of his colour."

The way Gordimer creates a sense of dead end in this society provides a constant unease and tension in *The Late Bourgeois World*. For all the posturing of Max's ineffectual acts, they do involve deadly danger. The presence of both real risk and self-centered display gives an underlying stress to all Liz's actions. Visited unexpectedly by Luke, an old black acquaintance now underground in the service of a militant black resistance, Liz comes face to face with the possibility of terrifyingly viable political action. He asks her to act as a banker for the movement by allowing money from overseas to be deposited to an account of hers. This activity is useful but would involve her in serious criminal charges if caught. The crisis is not resolved by the end of the book, but the fear and inflexibility in her choice are the chilling factors left dominating her world as she lies awake at the end of the day that opened with the telegram about Max's death: "the slow, even beats of my heart repeat to me, like a clock; afraid, alive, afraid, alive, afraid, alive."

The bleak mood of *The Late Bourgeois World,* and the stasis it depicts, left many readers wondering in what direction Gordimer's fiction could move. She had argued consistently that she set out to present public and social truths through her representation of private or personal truths, and the public truths of her normal subject matter—life in Johannesburg—seemed fixed in the iron grip of the Afrikaner police state.

The intransigence of the local scene did not inform her next novel, which is set outside South Africa. In *A Guest of Honour* (1970) she was able to pursue her investigation of both the white person's role in Africa and the emotional effects of commitment to action, especially political action, without revisiting the dead end revealed in *The Late Bourgeois World*.

A Guest of Honour is set in an imaginary African state that has recently gained its independence. The protagonist, James Bray, had been a colonial administrator there, sympathetic to the aspirations of the independence movement, and sent home at the insistence of enraged white settlers ten years earlier. As the novel opens, he has been invited to return from retirement in England as a guest of his old friend, the new president, to join the independence celebrations.

The non–South African setting offers Gordimer an opportunity to explore both the politics of African independence with its neocolonial undertow and the personal effect on Bray of the demands of political action. She uses her narrative and descriptive skill to evoke the new African state, capturing its sights, sounds, and smells; in this respect the novel is literally on new ground for her. The dilemma facing Bray, however, is the perennial one in Gordimer's work: what can a white person do in the context of African politics? How legitimate is white intervention in black affairs, and what are the personal consequences of either inaction or commitment? These themes are implicit in her early fiction and become explicit in the later work. Coupled with the issue of what the consequences are for Bray if he chooses political commitment while officially a "guest" is an involved analysis of sexual potency, sexual jealousy, and the link between invigorating political action—however dangerous—and sexual action (or adventure), however dangerous.

The political situation in the new state soon reveals a bitter tension between the president, Mweta, and a formidable former ally in the struggle for independence, the popular, middle-aged Shinza. Mweta's attempt to preserve links with international capital force him to take increasingly restrictive actions to silence opposition to his rule, including emergency measures and a Preventive Detention Bill.

Bray finds himself increasingly distressed by Mweta's position. When asked to stay and produce a report on education, Bray is delighted to commit himself to postretirement action. Not only does he begin to experience the sights and sounds of Africa more vividly as he takes on a new, active role, but also the memory of his retired life in Wiltshire, and the ordered house he has left there, becomes increasingly associated in his imagination with death-like stasis.

The sexual theme manifests itself in this connection between the stimulation of his senses and his invigorating role as someone with a public purpose. The aura of sexual potency surrounding the middle-aged Shinza fascinates Bray when they first meet again after years of absence. Shinza's confident physicality is of a piece with his unbowed opposition to the repression of the new regime. Bray feels "a queer alarm," "a restlessness" that "stirred resentfully," and he sees Shinza as a heroic figure.

When Bray returns to the capital, he makes love to Rebecca Edwards, a young white woman who has been an unobtrusive part of the independence celebrations. While he is making love to her, however, the image of Shinza preoccupies him: "extraordinarily, he was thinking of Shinza. Shinza's confident smile, Shinza's strong bare feet. Shinza smoking cigars in the room that smelled of baby. Shinza. Shinza."

As Bray becomes more deeply involved in the affairs of the new country—and inevitably more closely aligned with Shinza—his love affair with Rebecca deepens. Being alive in every way, then, is associated in *A Guest of Honour* with Bray's newfound political purpose and his sexual commitment to Rebecca. Although contained within the narrative of a novel set outside South Africa, this personal flowering once the risks of action have been accepted can be seen as Gordimer's wrestling with the problems of commitment by whites in South Africa. She returned to that theme in later texts.

The tension between the local rivals grows, and Bray finally agrees to align himself formally with Shinza by going to Europe on his behalf. Before he can leave the country, he is attacked and killed by a rampaging mob, who have no knowledge of his role or allegiances. The random nature of his violent death does not nullify his decision to become involved in the affairs of Mweta's state but rather underscores the complexity of political action and its outcome. Although in a superficial sense Bray's political intervention comes to nought, the personal transformation that he has achieved underscores the rightness of his decision to act.

The message of the text is encapsulated in Rebecca's observations at the end of the novel: "He [Bray] had made his life in accordance with some conscious choice. . . . It didn't have much to do with being what her father would have called a nigger-lover. But it had something to do with life itself. . . . Bray lived not as an adversary but a participant." The existential validation of Bray's choice has been implicit throughout the text, and this judgment of Rebecca's reinforces it. *A Guest of Honour* won the James Tait Black Memorial Prize in the United Kingdom and the Central News Agency (CNA) Prize in South Africa.

After *A Guest of Honour*, Gordimer returned to South African topics with one of her best-known works, *The Conservationist*, in 1974. This novel displays both a new confidence in the inevitable "return" to the land by its autochthonous, albeit currently displaced, inhabitants and a new complexity in her narrative method. In *The Conservationist*, Gordimer uses a constantly changing point of view, which is usually reflective and part of the ruminative consciousness of its characters. Central to the streams of consciousness in the novel is its protagonist, Mehring, a pig-iron industrialist who has bought a "weekend farm" just outside Johannesburg. His fears, prejudices, and relived personal history are at the core of the text, and not only do his reveries and memories reflect on one another to form a complex pattern of evasions and truths, but also the often indifferent points of view of those of all races existing on the fringes of his domain further illuminate both the context of his thoughts and the gaps in that thinking.

To Mehring, the farm is an escape from the pressing concerns of his successful Johannesburg life, a place to bring a woman, and part of a sentimental belief that he is "attached" to "his" land when enjoying the privacy and slow pace of the weekend estate. The text investigates the folly of this belief and the superficiality of his claim to belong. Parallel to his musings runs a series of descriptions of the events and concerns of the motley band of black laborers and their hangers-on who live on his land and about whom he knows next to nothing. The indestructible reality of their unprivileged and yet intimate link to the place, owned but not lived-on by the absentee Mehring, is suggested in the record of their actions and the faint but nonetheless important connection those actions have to ancient indigenous custom. To Mehring, the activities of his black laborers are incomprehensible and, like the proximity of a black "location" just off his land, part of the cross he has to bear while maintaining his privacy and his property.

The major worries that confront Mehring in his relentless internal debate over the circumstances of his life are provoked by the discovery of a black corpse, never identified, on his land. The local white police callously bury the body in a shallow grave and depart, leaving Mehring unnerved by both their brutish unconcern and by the alien presence in rather than on his land. The crisis in Mehring's imagination grows when the corpse is washed up in a flood. He experiences a vicarious sensuous identification with the corpse in his unguarded moments of reverie, and he smells or feels the earth and mud and reeds in his imagination as if he were indeed as possessed by the land as is the black body.

This sabotage by his sensory imagination is one element in Mehring's unease. Another is his dislike of the self-righteousness of his liberal former mistress, Antonia, and the half-baked political orthodoxies of his teenage son, Luke. As he remembers and relives encounters with these two intimates, all three are shown to be self-righteous in different ways, and the sterility of the debate between "liberalism" and "realism" in their interchanges is of a piece with the aridity of Mehring's daily world of possessions and things. In contrast to these unsettling and inconclusive discussions, the landscape is constantly evoked, as is the earthbound life of the black farm-dwellers.

At the end of the novel, when Mehring takes flight—abroad—from his growing paranoia, the blacks on the farm ceremoniously rebury the nameless corpse in a closing passage that celebrates the enduring certainty of their claim to be there, in contrast with

Mehring's indulgent and temporary ownership of the land:

> The one whom the farm received had no name. He had no family but their women wept a little for him. There was no child of his present but their children were there to live after him. They had put him away to rest, at last; he had come back. He took possession of this earth, theirs; one of them.

The apartheid regime appeared to be immutably established in 1974 when *The Conservationist* appeared. Gordimer's joint focus in that text on the intellectual and emotional underpinnings of white occupation in South Africa as well as on the abiding nature of the black presence was courageously optimistic, almost utopian, at that time. Although the novel is best known for the subtlety with which Mehring's culture is examined, it is the first South African novel by Gordimer to show a positive hint of an ultimate black return to the land. That closing mainly serves to highlight the puniness of the involuted claims to ownership made by Mehring and those like him, but the image of black repossession of the land was a new element in Gordimer's work. *The Conservationist* won both the Booker Prize in the United Kingdom and the CNA Prize in South Africa.

In her later work, written during the tumultuous period of social upheaval and change after the apartheid state was dismantled, the optimistic element is more pronounced; however flawed the attempts to achieve revolutionary change in these texts, Gordimer never doubts the ultimate certainty of change. Once change has occurred and is entrenched, she does investigate the shabby accommodations made by both sides of the former racial divide to preserve—or gain access to—privilege and wealth.

In Gordimer's next novel, *Burger's Daughter* (1979), the failures on the road to change are examined at the same time as the "sanctity" of political commitment. In its examination of the connections between personal and public obligation, and in its treatment of the nature of political engagement, *Burger's Daughter* returns to the issues first raised in *A Guest of Honour*. The mood of the later text is much more intense, however, and its context more intractable. *Burger's Daughter* became her third novel to be banned in South Africa.

Again, Gordimer's narrative in *Burger's Daughter* is complex. It includes direct narration, sections addressed to an imagined listener or reader by the protagonist herself, and passages of inner reflection. The result is a multilayered weaving of revelation and comment in which the dialogic nature of the "truth" of any situation is presented in different voices and from different vantage points.

The protagonist, Rosa Burger, is the daughter of a renowned, white South African communist who dies in prison serving a life sentence for his political activities. Born into a family in which political commitment and action in the face of an oppressive regime are taken to be natural and inevitable obligations, Rosa grows up immersed in political activity and sacrifice. After her father's death, Rosa seeks an identity of her own, other than that of "Lionel's daughter," with all the automatic assumptions of political allegiance that go along with that name. In reaction to the constant suffering of her past, she finds her "silence hammered sullen, hysterical, repetitive without words: sick, sick of the maimed, the endangered, the fugitive, the stoic; sick of courts, sick of prisons, sick of institutions scrubbed bare for the regulation endurance of dread and pain."

The ethos of her family house, with its logical application of Marxist theory to daily events and its easy acceptance of comradeship in the struggle, regardless of race, is established throughout the text, both in Rosa's memories and in the contacts she has with those of the political faithful still alive and out of jail. The weirdness of that life and the extreme nature of its demands are pointed out to her constantly by the individualistic young man, Conrad, with whom she shares a cottage. His existential concerns are entirely personal and private. Conrad's irony reinforces Rosa's own uneasiness with the automatic obligations she is expected, as her father's daughter, to shoulder. The emptiness of Conrad's self-centered worldview also emerges quite clearly, and his inability even to understand the transcendent, ultimately liberating nature of the Burger ethos tips the balance of their debate.

When faced with both the routine expectations from the tight circle of the faithful and the compromises of her white status in the static world of apartheid-triumphant South Africa, Rosa decides that she can no longer live in Lionel's country. She obtains a passport and travels to the South of France to visit her father's first wife.

Here the tone of the book alters, as does its pace. Rosa tries to learn—as an adult—how to live a private life without public obligations. She enters a world of slow time, totally different from the steely and hurried ethos of courts, prisons, political meetings, and police surveillance of Johannesburg. In the lush scenery and leisured atmosphere of the Côte d'Azur, she moves in a circle of charming and comparatively aimless people to whom political freedoms and civil rights are topics for discussion in an established democracy that is home to political refugees like Rosa.

Rosa begins a "civilised" relationship with a married French schoolteacher as part of her adaptation to a new, private life. Her plans to remain in this unpressured milieu—and lapse into the timeless French role of mistress—are overturned after a searing encounter in London. At a meeting of South African exiles and activists she meets the now adult black man who had been her childhood friend in her father's house. Son of a black activist close to Lionel, the black child and Rosa had shared all normal childhood experiences in the nonracial atmosphere of "that house." As an embittered adult, he resents Rosa's easy acceptance of their past relationship and the celebrated status she enjoys as her father's daughter. His father, too, was a victim of the struggle, and is now forgotten. Rosa's condescension—he argues—entails her thinking that she can share an intimacy with him. The unsurmountable nature of their difference is epitomized by Rosa's addressing him as "Baasie," the name by which she knew him in childhood. He points out to her the inappropriateness now of this "white" nickname used in the Burger household when his real name is "Zwelinzima"—meaning "suffering land."

Infuriated by his attack on her personally and on her memories of childhood, Rosa hits back with insults of her own, and is horrified to find herself using the weapons of whiteness and feeling the guilt of whiteness—both activities scorned in the rational mode of the Burger house in its prime. Rosa accuses Zwelinzima of making brave statements when he is safely out of the country, and even asks him if it is money he wants. Those sneers are part of her retrospective humiliation: "In one night we succeeded in manoeuvring ourselves into the position their history books back home have had ready for us—him bitter; me guilty."

There is no other option for Rosa but to return to South Africa and take up the responsibility from which she has attempted to flee. In the section of the text addressed to her dead father, Rosa acknowledges that "No one can defect"; that she has joined the inevitable struggle against suffering: "Yes, it's strange to live in a country where there are still heroes. Like anyone else, I do what I can." The novel ends with her in prison on a political charge.

The issues raised in *Burger's Daughter* are debated with great subtlety. The novel offers both a tribute to old-guard South African communists and an analysis of their strengths and weaknesses. To date, it is the last of Gordimer's novels to treat political and personal issues within the critical realist mode. After *Burger's Daughter* she stopped using the technique of allowing a close examination of personal truths to reveal general, public truths. She began to incorporate speculation into her texts and to predict imagined events. Those events have a paradigmatic quality and, like the personal sagas in her earlier fiction, reveal an emblematic truth. Often, their verisimilitude (a Gordimer trademark since her earliest writing) is coupled to a clearly "unrealistic"—because imagined—narrative located in the future.

Her next novel, *July's People,* which appeared in 1981, is set in the future and shows Gordimer's skill at the re-creation of the texture of local setting and scenery. The combination of speculation about future events and minutely accurate depictions of the locales in which they occur is Gordimer's way of analyzing not so much the path of events to come but elements in the reality of the present that could lead to such events.

July's People is set in a period of increasing anarchy as revolutionary civil war grips South Africa. The white protagonists, Bam and Maureen Smales, flee from their suburban Johannesburg home as urban guerilla fighting reaches the Witwatersrand. With their children and household servant, July, they take refuge in the small black village from which July comes. There, anonymously part of the peasant population, they are safe from the fighting but have to cope with the loss of their old identities and existence.

While the children accommodate themselves comparatively easily to their rudimentary new lives, the white adults have more difficulty. Bam tries desperately to hold onto the symbols of his white male authority, his shotgun and his van. But in the limited circumstances of the village, even these are "shared," or taken from him. Maureen, who has had the closest relation to July, has most difficulty adjusting her "liberal" views on race relations to her new dependency on her servant.

Gordimer offers a relentless analysis of the tainted nature of the entwined relations between mistress (or master) and servant. Even Maureen's "liberal" scruples—in the Johannesburg days—about the way July should be treated are shown to have been indulgent attempts by her to set the terms of the relationship. In a crucial final confrontation with July, Maureen at last "understands everything" when he angrily speaks back at her in his own language, which—linguistically—she cannot understand at all. *July's People* presupposes the collapse of white South African military power at some point in the future, but it is the collapse of white moral authority in the present that the novel analyzes.

Something Out There (1984), in which Gordimer continued her emblematic approach to the present with an imaginative investigation of events that could take place, is a collection of short stories and the title novella, *Something Out There,* which was republished separately under the same title in 1994. The collection reveals Gordimer's interest in forms of betrayal, a theme that suits the turbulent, violent mood of South Africa in the 1980s, when the post-Soweto era combined massive police repression and an increasingly confident amount of organized, violent resistance to the regime. The mood was no longer static, as it had been from the mid

1960s to the mid 1970s, and the short fiction reflects this period of "interregnum."

The novella *Something Out There* vividly captures the moods and modes of a cross-section of white South Africans from the Johannesburg area who are disturbed and confused by the antics of an escaped ape that appears and disappears at inconvenient moments. The quirkish and insular reactions of the "besieged" whites to the inexplicable forays of the ape are counterpoised against their ignorance of the real threat in their midst. Parallel to the ape subplot runs the narrative of a racially mixed group of saboteurs who rent a small farm outside Johannesburg (the black saboteurs pose as the whites' servants or laborers) in order to prepare for an attack on a power station. The anonymity of the group is both "official"—the police have to deduce who they were after the attack—and embodied in the text. The reader knows them only superficially, as they concentrate totally on their task, and the obtuse locals have no idea of their true motives. The novella concludes with a passage similar to that at the end of *The Conservationist*, predicting the inevitable "rightness" of a return to autochthonous ownership.

Gordimer has written short stories throughout her career, and her collections have appeared at regular intervals. *Friday's Footprint and Other Stories* (1960) won the W. H. Smith Literary Award, and other collections have been enthusiastically received. Her *Selected Stories*, which first appeared in 1975, is a much-read collection of her best short fiction published up to that date.

The themes and styles of her stories follow the same general development as the novels: from those early evocations of the compromised positions of whites under apartheid to more complex presentations of the "colonial" world in both South Africa and the Africa beyond its borders. Interspersed with stories that reflect Gordimer's perennial political concerns are apolitical tales that reveal aspects of human relationships—and the failure of those relationships—brought into sudden focus by a chance word or deed or moment of understanding. The title novella illustrates the path Gordimer's fiction took at this point of her career; an imaginative re-creation of how things could be. Her later fiction frequently has this conditional impulse as its starting point.

A Sport of Nature (1987) developed the speculative, conditional mood. Its plot involves typically realistic evocations of the Johannesburg liberal/left world from the 1960s on, with fictional re-creation of historical events, the inclusion of real persons into the overarching historical narrative, cameo appearances by characters such as Rosa Burger from Gordimer's other works, and the imagined course of events in the future, such as the successful conclusion to the liberation struggle in South Africa.

At the heart of the novel is its protagonist, Hillela, the white "sport" (or freak) of nature who breaks through the impasse created in so much of Gordimer's fiction. Hillela's vision of a transcending, nonracial partnership is embodied in a recurring image of clasped hands and enacted in her physical union with two black political figures. Her first husband, an exiled African National Congress (ANC) official, is assassinated by South African agents. Her second husband, an African general, regains military control over his state and plays a Pan-African role as its leader. She produces a "rainbow family" with the birth of her decidedly nonwhite daughter, acts effectively in many capacities for the ANC, and is there with her second husband at the final independence celebrations in Cape Town.

Her mixture of personal unscrupulousness and unerringly accurate public moves is treated wryly in the text. "Trust Hillela" is a comment made by many who know her, and it is made with all imaginable nuances of tone, from approval or admiration to exasperated understanding of her inevitably self-centered behavior. In much of the work of Gordimer's middle period the folly of asserting liberal values in the brutal apartheid state was the focus of her irony. In *A Sport of Nature* a life lived without liberal sensibility is shown to be disconcertingly self-assured, even though Hillela's freakish directness enables her to achieve what no other white character does in Gordimer's fiction. In order to create a white character successfully integrated into the liberation struggle, Gordimer has to produce a "sport of nature" and postulate a utopian ending to the liberation wars.

A Sport of Nature is a complex book, and its tone is difficult to pin down. What it does show is the tendency of Gordimer's later fiction to align itself closely with the necessity and value of radical political action itself. Her focus of interest has changed. In her earlier work she investigates what individuals do in demanding situations, and implicit in the truth of these personal actions is a general truth. In her later work she sets out to represent how certain kinds of political action or commitment could occur.

Gordimer's change of focus is particularly evident in *My Son's Story* (1990) and in many of the short stories collected in *Jump and Other Stories* (1991). Some of the stories are fable-like tales about the South African situation; others take incidents (such as a mob attack on a rival black figure) typical of the daily news, using reports of violence and horror as the starting point for investigations of what it would be like to be involved in those incidents. *My Son's Story* is an extended depiction of the nature of determined opposition to apartheid and of risk-taking to overcome it. For the first time, the protagonists in a Gordimer novel are mainly nonwhite.

The protagonist of *My Son's Story* appears at first to be Sonny, a mixed-race schoolteacher dedicated to resistance to apartheid and service to the liberation movement. Part of the narrative comes directly from his son, Will, who struggles with his father's marital infidelity and the effect it has on the family. At the end of the novel, Will records his own emergence as a writer—the trauma of political and personal strain has driven him to writing—and the whole account of the family saga is presented as his. Much of the preceding third-person narrative entails approving, impassioned comment on the nature of resistance by downtrodden political figures like Sonny. That celebration of the phoenix-like quality of nonwhite determination to acquire its due share of the country is typical of the tone of Gordimer's later work, even if offered as that of the sensitive, easily bruised, young novelist Will.

Just as Will emerges as a protagonist equally important as his at-first dominant father, Sonny, so do the actions of the women in the family become progressively more significant. Aila, the wife and mother of the family, has much to put up with. Sonny's political career means that he is constantly under surveillance and serves time in prison. He becomes infatuated with a young white political ally and is obsessed by his relationship with her. Seen at first as merely the dutiful wife who endures both the political stresses of life with Sonny and the shame of his infidelity, Aila emerges as a secret activist at the end of the novel, and one who has chosen a far more violent path than that taken by her husband, whose resistance activities are those of the old guard. The apparently vacant, pleasure-seeking younger daughter is also shown to have a secret, committed life, and she flees the country before the police catch up with her. Her father and brother are until then unaware of her links with the violent underground.

The tone of commitment to such action in Gordimer's works in the 1980s reflects a change from the neutral and ironic mode of her early and middle works. As the scene in South Africa became more violent and volatile, her celebration of those single-minded activists—and her certainty that their cause would prevail—became an insistent feature of her writing.

When Gordimer was awarded the Nobel Prize in Literature in 1991, there was widespread approval. The prize was seen as appropriate recognition of her lifelong commitment to both the art of fiction and to opposing the horrors of apartheid in her writing. This significant act of public recognition came at a time when South Africa itself was in the process of change, and Gordimer's role as critic was turning into that of an internationally recognized commentator on the complexities of political change. She had been an international figure for more than twenty years before the Nobel Prize, and that latest honor did not change her lifelong commitment to clear-sighted analysis—whatever the political or personal consequences. She spent the prize money on her family, and in part on the Congress of South African Writers.

Once political change became really possible in South Africa, Gordimer's manner itself changed. Nelson Mandela was released in 1990 after many years of imprisonment, and negotiations began among the still-ruling Afrikaner National Government and all interested parties, including previously banned groups such as the ANC, to produce a new constitution that would lead to general elections open to all in 1994. That same year, Gordimer's novel *None To Accompany Me* appeared. In it she attempts to explain both the courage of members of "The Movement," negotiating the first democratic state under threat of assassination from a shadowy Third Force, and their vulnerability to disclosure for past actions (regarded by some as crimes) in the old underground resistance. In this uneasy period, beset with distrust and disbelief that the old regime will keep its word, the characters are shown to live out their public lives. There is a major change in Gordimer's approach: the public truth is more important than the personal. Near the end of the novel the protagonist muses, "The evidence of personal life was around her, but her sense was of the personal life as transitory, it is the political life that is transcendent."

In *None To Accompany Me* sexual attitudes are discussed openly in the same way as political positions are analyzed. The two are fused in the contrast between Didymus, an old-time activist in The Movement, and his wife, Sibongile, a newcomer to politics and a powerful personality in the period of negotiation for a new state. But the new confidence of the female politician vis-à-vis the traditional caution of the male member of the old political guard is not as central to the texture of the novel as the ongoing discussion between the protagonist, Vera Stark, and her lesbian daughter. Vera is a white lawyer, working for the Legal Foundation committed to representing black interests in cases involving apartheid-era "resettlement" (segregation) of communities and the current claim of blacks to return to the areas from which they had been removed. Vera's sexual past is one of the features of her life that she has to reassess in the light of her daughter's declared sexual preference. Vera sees her own infidelities (with her current husband) during her first marriage as a feature in her daughter's own sexual makeup. This realization, together with her growing sense of quiescence as the struggle to end apartheid is taken over by newcomers like Sibongile, leads her to leave her former home and live as a tenant with her black colleague, Zeph Rapulana.

.246.

four feet deep, his head would stick out like an unwary rabbit's. But there are some for whom it would be large enough; those tribes who bury in the kneeling foetal position.

They have dug one good hole and it remains to make sure they don't think they've done enough hard work for the day and slack off on the next one. The rhythmical grunts with which their picks are flying up, over there, and hooking into the ground with a thud, doesn't mean they won't try to get away with going down only three feet instead of four. They've stopped. Jacobus is making a show of heaving at something; it's a rock they've struck. On the desk at the office in town there is a grey-brown chunk of stone that bears marks of having been shaped, a kind of petrified whittling, that he once picked up when they were ploughing. But this is nothing but a boulder that has come to light.

The chestnut trees are buried up to the bole in a mixture of bone-meal, manure, well-dried manure and the soil the digging displaced. All the colours of the layers are mixed up, now, there will be a fault, negligible, on the natural scale—where now stand the two small trees like branches children have stuck in sand to make a "garden" that will wither in an hour.

There are a number of other positions he could have chosen them. He sees that, walking over the farm with his trees in mind, superimposing two large chestnuts in flower (pink or white?—he forgot to ask the nurseryman, but perhaps one doesn't know until the first blooming) at various points in his landscape.

Page from a corrected typescript of Gordimer's 1974 novel, The Conservationist *(The Lilly Library/Nadine Gordimer)*

The use of a word such as "tenant" is typical of the emblematic element in Gordimer's writing after 1990. Just as her own stark emotional condition at the end of the novel mirrors her name, so Vera moves into an almost elegiac mode as the book ends and she accepts her white tenant status in the about-to-be-born homeland of the previously dispossessed.

None To Accompany Me is set in a specific period and deals predominantly with the issues of that moment of negotiation when the old regime had not departed and the new era had not yet arrived. The problems of those negotiating the change and returning from exile or underground are her focus. This closely focused historical impulse leaves the novel somewhat dated now that those concerns are past.

Gordimer's next novel, *The House Gun* (1998), is set in the new South Africa after Mandela and the ANC had clearly won the first democratic election in 1994. The new regime, unquestionably in power, is nevertheless beset with the chronic problem of random violence and crime in a society throwing off a recognition of civil authority together with the authoritarian trappings of the former era. Gordimer's interest in *The House Gun* is not so much on the present but on the legacy of the past and how that has produced the violent contemporary climate.

The plot hinges on the catastrophic change wrought in the lives of a white professional Johannesburg couple and their son when the latter shoots dead a homosexual former lover who has seduced his current heterosexual partner. Suddenly, the mother-protagonist, Claudia, finds herself in the same situation as that of the many black mothers of sons awaiting trial for murder; her son, Duncan, finds a new identity with the nameless mass of common criminals, mainly black, in prison. The title of the novel offers an emblematic pointing to the past causes of the violent present. The murder is committed spontaneously with the house gun, which lies around the dwelling shared by Duncan, his lover, and others. Its casual presence is a symbol of the omnipresence of violence in the new state. The text investigates the cause of this reliance on violence after years of rule based on force rather than legitimacy.

Duncan's parents, Claudia and Harald, have to adjust not only to a world in which they are suddenly linked emotionally and physically (in jail and court) with the masses, but also to their client status with a black lawyer, newly returned from exile, who defends their son. His manner, both professional and domestic, is alien to their middle-class white conventions, and both his otherness and their dependence on him entail a realization of their ingrained prejudices as well as their need to suppress them.

Gordimer has often used personal crises as a means of examining public or political values. The difference between her treatment of the interaction of the public and the private in classic works such as *The Conservationist* and *Burger's Daughter* and the themes in *The House Gun* is that in the late work she abandons the layered, dialogic method of the middle-period texts and resorts to a much more explicit, didactic tone.

A need to explain both the suppressed evidence of the apartheid era and–through "testimony" of what is unknown or unexamined in that period–to recognize a common identity with all South Africans in the new state is one of the issues Gordimer discusses in *Writing and Being* (1995), which consists of the Charles Eliot Norton lectures that she delivered at Harvard in 1994. In three of those lectures Gordimer focuses on the legacy of the years under apartheid and points to the possibility of reconstructing an understanding of the apartheid era as an essential part of understanding the present and the nature of a common national identity: "testimony in my country today is not only provision against forgetting what we knew; it is also the provision of what we never knew." The easy use of the possessive "my" in "my country" and the equally natural use of "we" form a feature of the new South Africa that Gordimer celebrates in *Writing and Being*. South Africans need no longer, in her view, be distinguished either by color or by political views.

Even after the official demise of apartheid and the emergence of the new state, Gordimer is still analyzing the present in terms of the effects of the authoritarian racism that formed the subject of almost all her fiction. The accompanying theme is the present dilemma of the flood of refugees from conflict, poverty, and oppression worldwide. In *The Pickup* (2001) the legacy of apartheid-era privilege informs the text from the outset. The protagonist, Julie Summers, is white and independent. She lives an ostentatiously "liberated" life among a group of like-minded, young, middle-class South Africans of all colors who meet in the would-be trendy L. A. Café and discuss their world in a rather determinedly open-minded way. There, Julie is in her defining milieu, "a bazaar of all that the city had not been allowed to be by the laws and traditions of her parents' generation." But the confident assertion of this sense of liberation is undercut–in Gordimer's external descriptions–by a sense of its smugness. That externality is a constant feature in *The Pickup*.

Julie's life changes when she meets Abdu, an illegal Arab immigrant who fixes her broken-down car. She takes him from the grungy garage in which he works to the L.A. Café to meet her circle, begins a relationship with him, and takes him to her father's bourgeois Sunday lunch in the prosperous suburb that she believes she has forever rejected. The guests at the Sunday ritual are not all white. The new power elite is there in force, and all share a confident acceptance of influence and prestige. Julie is mortified at her inherited privilege being revealed to her impoverished lover, and she watches him as he "listens to this intimate language of money. . . . She is overcome by embarrassment—what is he thinking of these people—she is responsible for whatever that may be. She is responsible for *them*." Abdu's reaction is, however, quite different from what she imagines. Back in the room they share as a love nest, Julie is bewildered by his realistic appraisal of the usefulness of the background she rejects: "Interesting people there. They make a success."

Julie marries Abdu; when he is deported from South Africa, she returns with him to his home village on the fringes of the desert. As his "accompanying wife" she is likely to be influential in securing him an entry visa in his relentless pursuit of immigration to the industrialized West and escape from the confines of his home and its customs in the Islamic village. Yet, in that village Julie begins to experience an authenticity that she sees as superior to Abdu's incessant search for immigrant status in the West. Her divorced mother in California does eventually prove useful, and Abdu receives immigration clearance for the United States.

At this point of apparent triumph—and a kind of vindication of her marriage and support—Julie decides that life in the genuineness of the village is preferable to the constant humiliation of life as a third-world immigrant in the West:

> Living in a dirty hovel, a high-rise one or a shed behind a garage, what's the difference, with Christ knows what others of the wrong colours, poor devils like himself (as he used to say), cleaning American shit . . . doing the jobs that *real people,* white Americans, won't do themselves.

Abdu is infuriated by her decision to remain in the village rather than accompany him. When he asks where she got the idea, an authorial voice gives the answer: "And while his anguish batters them both she now knows where. The desert."

Gordimer has used non–South African settings frequently in her fiction. In some texts her South African characters spend periods abroad as part of their means of coping with South Africa. In others the setting is entirely outside South Africa. *The Pickup* is distinct, however, in that the South African baggage that Julie carries with her abroad is intricately connected to her reaction to life in the world at large and the issues that affect far more than her native land.

In *Loot and Other Stories* (2003) there is a familiar mixture of stories set entirely outside South Africa and those dealing with life in the "new" South Africa. In "Visiting George," the memory of an old antiapartheid fighter living in London during the apartheid era is delicately created in the description of an imagined meeting. The aura of his life and surroundings and values is seen as part of a vanished era.

A distinctive piece in this volume is "Karma," in which the possibilities of reincarnation or "transmigration" are examined; varied narrative voices and personae recount incidents that occur at different periods but have overlapping elements. Explicit depiction of the corruption and cronyism in the new South Africa appears for the first time in "Karma," and the deadpan mode with which Gordimer allows the facts of her story to emerge is reminiscent of the most effective moments of her middle career. One of the protagonists, living an idyllic life in a desirable house with her successful husband and children, is found guilty of accepting bribes as an important player in the new state. Norma is white and was active in the resistance movement under apartheid. Her reward in the new state has been to become influential first in public works and then in an ostensibly private contracting company. Her lawyer explains the situation to her husband, Arthur; he has "obtained the best that could be expected: a heavy fine and suspended sentence. . . . Her background as a white who had suffered to bring about a just society, and the fact that she was female, the lawyer lectured, were the only mitigating factors in her favour." The innocent and naive Arthur finds himself bewildered: "And even if this had saved Norma, Arthur felt angry at the insult to her intelligence, all she had been and was. And there was bewilderment in him, at his anger: would he rather accept that his Norma was deviously dishonest?" The suspension of explicit judgment in the writing, and the clarity in the presentation of the complexity of the situation itself, are reminiscent of Gordimer's best works.

In *Get a Life* (2005) the multiracial reality of the new South Africa is a given. Not only do members of all racial groups mix constantly, but also the public concerns raised by the novel are not directly related to the racial issues of the fiction written during the apartheid era or that written as the new state emerged. Protection of the environment in the face of international "development" projects emerges as a crucial concern in this South Africa.

The novel falls into two parts. In the first, personal health threatened by radioactivity is an issue for all those connected to protagonist Paul, who is living in relative isolation in his parents' house while recuperating from surgery for thyroid cancer and subsequent radiation treatment. In the second, environmental health—with a threat of nuclear-reactor development—becomes the dominant concern as Paul, now totally recovered, returns to the outside world and his career as an ecologist. In both parts he reflects on the values of his mother, a successful lawyer, and his wife, a prominent advertising executive; both are creatures of the public world "out there."

In the second part of the novel the "health" of the environment, threatened by development projects of all kinds (dams, nuclear reactors, and drainage of natural swamp lands) becomes the central focus of both Paul's own thoughts and the conversations he has with others and in particular with his effervescent black colleague, Thapelo. A proposed "pebble-bed reactor" to be placed in an environmentally unique—and sensitive—area takes over the choric threat of Paul's personal radioactivity in the earlier parts of the novel.

The style of *Get a Life* is different from that of Gordimer's previous work. Just as the juxtaposition of a personal, medical threat in the first part with an overriding environmental threat in the second is strained, so too Gordimer's prose is often clotted. She uses authorial commentary throughout. Terse, choric sentences—often difficult to read—frequently break up whatever action there is as the author reflects on the issues being presented. "So, what is this kind of stuff, thinking. . . . Heresy, how can it come to one who when asked, And what is your line, answers, What am I, I'm a conservationist, I'm one of the new missionaries here not to save souls but to save the earth." This stylistic approach is decidedly different from that in her major mid-career work on a "conservationist." What *Get a Life* illustrates is Gordimer's continual focus on the changing realities of the world she depicts and her concern for the "health"—however broadly defined—of that world.

Nadine Gordimer's career is remarkable for the range of work she has produced and for the consistently penetrating analyses of her society that she offers. The changes of emphasis in those analyses have been remarkably constant indicators of the changes in the society itself. The style of her latest fiction shows that she is still developing new approaches in her lifelong attempt to understand the human condition in her strife-torn native land and in the current world at large.

Interviews:

Nancy Topping Bazin and Marilyn Dallman Seymour, eds., *Conversations with Nadine Gordimer* (Jackson & London: University Press of Mississippi, 1990).

References:

Ariel, special Gordimer issue, 19 (October 1988);
Stephen Clingman, *The Novels of Nadine Gordimer: History from the Inside* (London: Allen & Unwin, 1985);
John Cooke, *The Novels of Nadine Gordimer: Private Lives/Public Landscapes* (Baton Rouge: Louisiana State University Press, 1985);
Bruce King, ed., *The Later Fiction of Nadine Gordimer* (London: Macmillan, 1993);
Judie Newman, *Nadine Gordimer* (London & New York: Routledge, 1988);
Salmagundi, special Gordimer issue, 62 (Winter 1984);
Rowland Smith, ed., *Critical Essays on Nadine Gordimer* (Boston: G. K. Hall, 1990).

Papers:

The Nadine Gordimer Papers, in The Lilly Library, Indiana University, Bloomington, Indiana, is the most significant holding of Gordimer's papers. This collection includes approximately 6,700 items covering the years 1934 to 1991 and consists of correspondence with colleagues, literary agents, and publishers; manuscripts, typescripts, and corrected proofs of short stories, novels, articles, lectures, and speeches; a childhood diary, notebooks, and research materials. The Nadine Gordimer Collection of the Harry Ransom Humanities Research Center, University of Texas at Austin, consists of thirteen corrected typescripts for short stories published in *Friday's Footprint and Other Stories* (1960) and *Not for Publication and Other Stories* (1965), and the corrected typescript for the novel *A World of Strangers* (1958).

1991 Nobel Prize in Literature Presentation Speech

by Professor Sture Allén, Permanent Secretary of the Swedish Academy (Translation from the Swedish)

Your Majesties, Your Royal Highnesses, Ladies and Gentlemen,

Art is on the side of the oppressed, Nadine Gordimer says in one of her essays, urging us to think before we dismiss this heretical idea about the freedom of art. If art is freedom, she asks, how could it exist within the oppressors?

Nadine Gordimer agrees with last year's Laureate, Octavio Paz, in asserting the importance of regaining the meanings of words, as a first step in the critical process. She has had the courage to write as if censorship did not exist, and so has seen her books banned, time after time.

Above all, it is people, individual men and women, that have captured her and been captured by her. It is their lives, their heaven and hell, that absorb her. The outer reality is ever present, but it is through her characters that the whole historical process is crystallized.

Conveying to the reader a powerful sense of authenticity, and with wide human relevance, she makes visible the extremely complicated and utterly inhuman living conditions in the world of racial segregation. She feels political responsibility, and does not shy away from its consequences, but will not allow it to affect her as a writer: her texts are not agitatorial, not propagandistic. Still, her works and the deep insights she offers contribute to shaping reality.

In one of her great novels we meet Maureen, the stronger of husband and wife in a family who, with the help of their boy, have fled the fighting, taking refuge in a hut in his native village. Here, gradually, the strains on their mode of life, language and everyday relations become unbearable. One day Maureen notices a helicopter landing. She does not know whether it brings friends or enemies but, stricken with unspeakable horror, she instinctively leaves the hut and starts running towards the sound. She runs ever faster and more frantically. She runs with all the suppressed trust of a lifetime. She runs for her survival, the enemy of all responsibility.

This is the closing scene of the novel. Were there still possibilities ahead of her? Or was this the very end? To Maureen and what she stands for, the future appears to hold out the opposite of utopia, a dystopia. This is not Nadine Gordimer's only vision, but it is one which she has found it necessary to give expression to.

In this way, artistry and morality fuse.

People are more important than principles.

A truly living human being cannot remain neutral.

No one is in possession of all goodness, and no one has a monopoly of evil.

Irony does not need any prompting.

Children who meet, gladly meet halfway.

The power of love makes the mountain tremble.

Thoughts and impressions such as these are called forth by novels like *A Guest of Honour, The Conservationist, Burger's Daughter, July's People,* and *My Son's Story.* However, in a manner as absorbing as in her novels, Nadine Gordimer develops her penetrating depiction of character, her compassion and her powers of precise wording in her short stories, in collections like *Six Feet of the Country* and, as yet untranslated, *A Soldier's Embrace* and *Something Out There.*

Your Majesties, Your Royal Highnesses, Ladies and Gentlemen, it is remarkable how often Nadine Gordimer succeeds in her artistic intent—to burn a hole through the page.

Dear Miss Gordimer,

Ninety years ago, the prize citation mentioned "the qualities of both heart and intellect." Indeed, these words apply no less today when the Swedish Academy points to the Nobelian concept of outstanding literary achievement as an important means of conferring benefit on mankind, in terms of human value and freedom of speech. It is my privilege and pleasure, on behalf of the Swedish Academy, to convey to you the warmest congratulations on the Nobel Prize in Literature 1991 and to invite you to receive the Prize from the hands of His Majesty the King.

[© The Nobel Foundation, 1991.]

Gordimer: Banquet Speech

Gordimer's speech at the Nobel Banquet, 10 December 1991:

Your Majesties, Your Royal Highnesses, Your Excellencies, Fellow Laureates, Ladies and Gentlemen,

When the six-year-old daughter of a friend of mine overheard her father telling someone that I had been awarded the Nobel Prize, she asked whether I had ever received it before. He replied that the Prize was something you could get only once. Whereupon the small girl thought a moment: "Oh" she said, "so it's like chicken-pox."

Well, Flaubert said that "honours dishonour" the writer, and Jean-Paul Sartre declined this particular honour, but whether as malediction or malady one cannot say. I certainly find being the recipient at this celebratory dinner more pleasurable and rewarding than chicken-pox, having now in my life experienced both.

But the small girl was not entirely wrong. Writing is indeed, some kind of affliction in its demands as the most solitary and introspective of occupations. We writers do not have the encouragement and mateyness I imagine, and even observe, among people whose work is a group activity. We are not orchestrated; poets sing unaccompanied, and prose writers have no cue on which to come in, each with an individual instrument of expression to make the harmony or dissonance complete. We must live fully in order to secrete the substance of our work, but we have to work alone. From this paradoxical inner solitude our writing is what Roland Barthes called "the essential gesture" towards the people among whom we live, and to the world; it is the hand held out with the best we have to give.

When I began to write as a very young person in a rigidly racist and inhibited colonial society, I felt, as many others did, that I existed marginally on the edge of the world of ideas, of imagination and beauty. These, taking shape in poetry and fiction, drama, painting and sculpture, were exclusive to that distant realm known as "overseas." It was the dream of my contemporaries, white and black, to venture there as the only way to enter the world of artists. It took the realization that the colour bar—I use that old, concrete image of racism—was like the gate of the law in Kafka's parable, which was closed to the supplicant throughout his life because he didn't understand that only he could open it. It took this to make us realize that what we had to do to find the world was to enter our own world fully, first. We had to enter through the tragedy of our own particular place.

If the Nobel awards have a special meaning, it is that they carry this concept further. In their global eclecticism they recognize that no single society, no country or continent can presume to create a truly human culture for the world. To be among laureates, past and present, is at least to belong to some sort of one world.

[© The Nobel Foundation, 1991. Nadine Gordimer is the sole author of her speech.]

Press Release: The Nobel Prize in Literature 1991

from the Office of the Permanent Secretary of the Swedish Academy, 3 October 1991

The Swedish Academy has decided to award the Nobel Prize for Literature for 1991 to Nadine Gordimer. She is a South African, her mother English, her father Lithuanian. Her work comprises novels and short stories in which the consequences of apartheid form the central theme. She was born in 1923.

Gordimer writes with intense immediacy about the extremely complicated personal and social relationships in her environment. At the same time as she feels a political involvement—and takes action on that basis—she does not permit this to encroach on her writings. Nevertheless, her literary works, in giving profound insights into the historical process, help to shape this process.

A landmark in the first half of her career is the novel *A Guest of Honour* (1970). This is a close-textured and pregnant novel, classical in style. With great intensity she succeeds in conveying the complexity of events as a nation comes into existence. The returning former colonial administrator becomes involved in the conflicts and is torn by loyalties in several directions. The course of events is reflected in the parallel love affair of the protagonist. His adventitious, totally unheroic death gives rise to reflection on the role of the individual in the great game for the future.

Since the middle of the 70s Gordimer has developed a more complex technique in her novels. This phase of her writing has produced three masterpieces: *The Conservationist* (1974), *Burger's Daughter* (1979) and *July's People* (1981). Each in its own way illustrates conceivable personal standpoints in the complicated spiritual and material environment of an Africa in which black consciousness is growing. Gordimer takes the question of the justification of the privileges of white people—even benevolent white people—to its extreme.

Among these powerful novels *July's People* deserves particular mention. The events in Soweto form the background against which the novel is set. Confronted by armed rebellion, the Smales, a white family, flee with the help of July, their boy, to his own village, where they have to survive in a primitive, evacuated hut. As time goes by, the master-servant relationship is turned upside down by the family's increasing reliance on July. The ambiguity of the novel's title etches itself fast—July's people are the white family he still serves but also the members of his tribe. The description of the cultural and physical coarsening which the circumstances evoke is masterly. Communication between husband and wife dries up. He tries to articulate the new situation without the old phraseology, "but the words would not come." To refer to his wife, a pronoun is used: "Her." Not "Maureen." Not "His wife." The ones who find it easiest to adapt, both linguistically and socially, are the children. The author has her reasons for using the children's relationships to cast light on those of the adults in the novel.

Gordimer's latest book *My Son's Story* was published in 1990. Its subject is love in an insupportable society, the complications and obstacles inherent in the path to change. The relationship of the lovers is described with great tenderness. At the same time the unyielding political reality constantly intrudes. The twofold narrative perspective makes richly faceted description of the characters possible, its most surprising element being the heroism finally exhibited by the wife. The novel is ingenious and revealing and at the same time enthralling because of its poetic values.

The powerful novels should not make us forget the shorter works. Compact and dense, they are extremely telling and show Gordimer at the height of her creative powers. *Selected Stories* (1975) provides a survey. The fundamental themes are reworked successfully, as the title story in the collection *A Soldier's Embrace* (1980). Gordimer's specifically feminine experiences, her compassion and her outstanding literary style characterise her short stories as well.

[© The Nobel Foundation, 1991.]

Gordimer: Nobel Lecture, 7 December 1991

Writing and Being

In the beginning was the Word.

The Word was with God, signified God's Word, the word that was Creation. But over the centuries of human culture the word has taken on other meanings, secular as well as religious. To have the word has come to be synonymous with ultimate authority, with prestige, with awesome, sometimes dangerous persuasion, to have Prime Time, a TV talk show, to have the gift of the gab as well as that of speaking in tongues. The word flies through space, it is bounced from satellites, now nearer than it has ever been to the heaven from which it was believed to have come. But its most significant transformation occurred for me and my kind long ago, when it was first scratched on a stone tablet or traced on papyrus, when it materialized from sound to spectacle, from being heard to being read as a series of signs, and then a script; and travelled through time from parchment to Gutenberg. For this is the genesis story of the writer. It is the story that wrote her or him into being.

It was, strangely, a double process, creating at the same time both the writer and the very purpose of the writer as a mutation in the agency of human culture. It was both ontogenesis as the origin and development of an individual being, and the adaptation, in the nature of that individual, specifically to the exploration of ontogenesis, the origin and development of the individual being. For we writers are evolved for that task. Like the prisoner incarcerated with the jaguar in Borges' story,[1] "The God's Script," who was trying to read, in a ray of light which fell only once a day, the meaning of being from the marking on the creature's pelt, we spend our lives attempting to interpret through the word the readings we take in the societies, the world of which we are part. It is in this sense, this inextricable, ineffable participation, that writing is always and at once an exploration of self and of the world; of individual and collective being.

Being here.

Humans, the only self-regarding animals, blessed or cursed with this torturing higher faculty, have always wanted to know why. And this is not just the great ontological question of why we are here at all, for which religions and philosophies have tried to answer conclusively for various peoples at various times, and science tentatively attempts dazzling bits of explanation we are perhaps going to die out in our millenia, like dinosaurs, without having developed the necessary comprehension to understand as a whole. Since humans became self-regarding they have sought, as well, explanations for the common phenomena of procreation, death, the cycle of seasons, the earth, sea, wind and stars, sun and moon, plenty and disaster. With myth, the writer's ancestors, the oral story-tellers, began to feel out and formulate these mysteries, using the elements of daily life—observable reality—and the faculty of the imagination—the power of projection into the hidden—to make stories.

Roland Barthes[2] asks, "What is characteristic of myth?" And answers: "To transform a meaning into form." Myths are stories that mediate in this way between the known and unknown. Claude Levi-Strauss[3] wittily de-mythologizes myth as a genre between a fairy tale and a detective story. Being here; we don't know who-dun-it. But something satisfying, if not the answer, can be invented. Myth was the mystery plus the fantasy—gods, anthropomorphized animals and birds, chimera, phantasmagorical creatures—that posits out of the imagination some sort of explanation for the mystery. Humans and their fellow creatures were the materiality of the story, but as Nikos Kazantzakis[4] once wrote, "Art is the representation not of the body but of the forces which created the body."

There are many proven explanations for natural phenomena now; and there are new questions of being arising out of some of the answers. For this reason, the genre of myth has never been entirely abandoned, although we are inclined to think of it as archaic. If it dwindled to the children's bedtime tale in some societies, in parts of the world protected by forests or deserts from international megaculture it has continued, alive, to offer art as a system of mediation between the individual and being. And it has made a whirling comeback out of Space, an Icarus in the avatar of Batman and his kind, who never fall into the ocean of failure to deal with the gravity forces of life. These new myths, however, do not seek so much to enlighten and provide some sort of answers as to distract, to provide a fantasy escape route for people who no longer want to face even the hazard of answers to the terrors of their existence. (Perhaps it is the positive knowledge that humans now possess the means to destroy their whole planet, the fear that they have in this way themselves become the gods, dreadfully charged with their own continued existence, that has made comic-book and movie myth escapist.) The forces of being remain. They are what the writer, as distinct from the contemporary popular mythmaker, still engage today, as myth in its ancient form attempted to do.

How writers have approached this engagement and continue to experiment with it has been and is, perhaps more than ever, the study of literary scholars. The writer in relation to the nature of perceivable reality and what is beyond—imperceivable reality—is the basis for all these studies, no matter what resulting concepts are labelled, and no matter in what categorized microfiles writers are stowed away for the annals of literary historiography. Reality is constructed out of many elements and entities, seen and unseen, expressed, and left unexpressed for breathing-space in the mind. Yet from what is regarded as old-hat psychological analysis to modernism and post-modernism, structuralism and poststructuralism, all literary studies are aimed at the same end: to pin down to a consistency (and what is consistency if not the principle hidden within the riddle?); to make definitive through methodology the writer's grasp at the forces of being. But life is aleatory in itself; being is constantly pulled and shaped this way and that by circumstances and different levels of consciousness. There is no pure state of being, and it follows that there is no pure text, "real" text, totally incorporating the aleatory. It surely cannot be reached by any critical methodology, however interesting the attempt. To deconstruct a text is in a way a contradiction, since to deconstruct it is to make another construction out of the pieces, as Roland Barthes[5] does so fascinatingly, and admits to, in his linguistic and semantical dissection of Balzac's story, "Sarrasine." So the literary scholars end up being some kind of storyteller, too.

Perhaps there is no other way of reaching some understanding of being than through art? Writers themselves don't analyze what they do; to analyze would be to look down while crossing a canyon on a tightrope. To say this is not to mystify the process of writing but to make an image out of the intense inner concentration the writer must have to cross the chasms of the aleatory and make them the word's own, as an explorer plants a flag. Yeats' inner "lonely impulse of delight" in the pilot's solitary flight, and his "terrible beauty" born of mass uprising, both opposed and conjoined; E. M. Forster's modest "only connect"; Joyce's chosen, wily "silence, cunning and exile"; more contemporary, Gabriel García Márquez's labyrinth in which power over others, in the person of Simon Bolivar, is led to the thrall of the only unassailable power, death—these are some examples of the writer's endlessly varied ways of approaching the state of being through the word. Any writer of any worth at all hopes to play only a pocket-torch of light—and rarely, through genius, a sudden flambeau—into the bloody yet beautiful labyrinth of human experience, of being.

Anthony Burgess[6] once gave a summary definition of literature as "the aesthetic exploration of the world." I would say that writing only begins there, for the exploration of much beyond, which nevertheless only aesthetic means can express.

How does the writer become one, having been given the word? I do not know if my own beginnings have any particular interest. No doubt they have much in common with those of others, have been described too often before as a result of this yearly assembly before which a writer stands. For myself, I have said that nothing factual that I write or say will be as truthful as my fiction. The life, the opinions, are not the work, for it is in the tension between standing apart and being involved that the imagination transforms both. Let me give some minimal account of myself. I am what I suppose would be called a natural writer. I did not make any decision to become one. I did not, at the beginning, expect to earn a living by being read. I wrote as a child out of the joy of apprehending life through my senses—the look and scent and feel of things; and soon out of the emotions that puzzled me or raged within me and which took form, found some enlightenment, solace and delight, shaped in the written word. There is a little Kafka[7] parable that goes like this; "I have three dogs: Hold-him, Seize-him, and Nevermore. Hold-him and Seize-him are ordinary little Schipperkes and nobody would notice them if they were alone. But there is Nevermore, too. Nevermore is a mongrel Great Dane and has an appearance that centuries of the most careful breeding could never have produced. Nevermore is a gypsy." In the small South African gold-mining town where I was growing up I was Nevermore the mongrel (although I could scarcely have been described as a Great Dane . . .) in whom the accepted characteristics of the townspeople could not be traced. I was the Gypsy, tinkering with words second-hand, mending my own efforts at writing by learning from what I read. For my school was the local library. Proust, Chekhov and Dostoevsky, to name only a few to whom I owe my existence as a writer, were my professors. In that period of my life, yes, I was evidence of the theory that books are made out of other books . . . But I did not remain so for long, nor do I believe any potential writer could.

With adolescence comes the first reaching out to otherness through the drive of sexuality. For most children, from then on the faculty of the imagination, manifest in play, is lost in the focus on day dreams of desire and love, but for those who are going to be artists of one kind or another the first life-crisis after that of birth does something else in addition: the imagination gains range and extends by the subjective flex of new and turbulent emotions. There are new perceptions. The writer begins to be able to enter into other lives. The process of standing apart and being involved has come.

Unknowingly, I had been addressing myself on the subject of being, whether, as in my first stories, there was a child's contemplation of death and murder in the necessity to finish off, with a death blow, a dove mauled by a cat, or whether there was wondering dismay and early consciousness of racism that came of my walk to school, when on the way I passed storekeepers, themselves East European immigrants kept lowest in the ranks of the Anglo-Colonial social scale for whites in the mining town, roughly those whom colonial society ranked lowest of all, discounted as less than human—the black miners who were the stores' customers. Only many years later was I to realize that if I had been a child in that category—black—I might not have become a writer at all, since the library that made this possible for me was not open to any black child. For my formal schooling was sketchy, at best.

To address oneself to others begins a writer's next stage of development. To publish to anyone who would read what I wrote. That was my natural, innocent assumption of what publication meant, and it has not changed, that is what it means to me today, in spite of my awareness that most people refuse to believe that a writer does not have a particular audience in mind; and my other awareness: of the temptations, conscious and unconscious, which lure the writer into keeping a corner of the eye on who will take offense, who will approve what is on the page—a temptation that, like Eurydice's straying glance, will lead the writer back into the Shades of a destroyed talent.

The alternative is not the malediction of the ivory tower, another destroyer of creativity. Borges once said he wrote for his friends and to pass the time. I think this was an irritated flippant response to the crass question—often an accusation—"For whom do you write?", just as Sartre's admonition that there are times when a writer should cease to write, and act upon being only in another way, was given in the frustration of an unresolved conflict between distress at injustice in the world and the knowledge that what he knew how to do best was write. Both Borges and Sartre, from their totally different extremes of denying literature a social purpose, were certainly perfectly aware that it has its implicit and unalterable social role in exploring the state of being, from which all other roles, personal among friends, public at the protest demonstration, derive. Borges was not writing for his friends, for he published and we all have received the bounty of his work. Sartre did not stop writing, although he stood at the barricades in 1968.

The question of for whom do we write nevertheless plagues the writer, a tin can attached to the tail of every work published. Principally it jangles the inference of tendentiousness as praise or denigration. In this context, Camus[8] dealt with the question best. He said that he liked individuals who take sides more than literatures that do. "One either serves the whole of man or does not serve him at all. And if man needs bread and justice, and if what has to be done must be done to serve this need, he also needs pure beauty which is the bread of his heart." So Camus called for "Courage in and talent in one's work." And Márquez[9] redefined tender fiction thus: The best way a writer can serve a revolution is to write as well as he can.

I believe that these two statements might be the credo for all of us who write. They do not resolve the conflicts that have come, and will continue to come, to contemporary writers. But they state plainly an honest possibility of doing so, they turn the face of the writer squarely to her and his existence, the reason to be, as a writer, and the reason to be, as a responsible human, acting, like any other, within a social context.

Being here: in a particular time and place. That is the existential position with particular implications for literature. Czesław Miłosz[10] once wrote the cry: "What is poetry which does not serve nations or people?" and Brecht[11] wrote of a time when "to speak of trees is almost a crime." Many of us have had such despairing thoughts while living and writing through such times, in such places, and Sartre's solution makes no sense in a world where writers were—and still are—censored and forbidden to write, where, far from abandoning the word, lives were and are at risk in smuggling it, on scraps of paper, out of prisons. The state of being whose ontogenesis we explore has overwhelmingly included such experiences. Our approaches, in Nikos Kazantzakis'[12] words, have to "make the decision which harmonizes with the fearsome rhythm of our time."

Some of us have seen our books lie for years unread in our own countries, banned, and we have gone on writing. Many writers have been imprisoned. Looking at Africa alone—Soyinka, Ngugi wa Thiong'o, Jack Mapanje, in their countries, and in my own country, South Africa, Jeremy Cronin, Mongane Wally

Serote, Breyten Breytenbach, Dennis Brutus, Jaki Seroke: all these went to prison for the courage shown in their lives, and have continued to take the right, as poets, to speak of trees. Many of the greats, from Thomas Mann to Chinua Achebe, cast out by political conflict and oppression in different countries, have endured the trauma of exile, from which some never recover as writers, and some do not survive at all. I think of the South Africans, Can Themba, Alex la Guma, Nat Nakasa, Todd Matshikiza. And some writers, over half a century from Joseph Roth to Milan Kundera, have had to publish new works first in the word that is not their own, a foreign language.

Then in 1988 the fearsome rhythm of our time quickened in an unprecedented frenzy to which the writer was summoned to submit the word. In the broad span of modern times since the Enlightenment writers have suffered opprobrium, bannings and even exile for other than political reasons. Flaubert dragged into court for indecency, over *Madame Bovary,* Strindberg arraigned for blasphemy, over *Marrying,* Lawrence's *Lady Chatterley's Lover* banned—there have been many examples of so-called offense against hypocritical bourgeois mores, just as there have been of treason against political dictatorships. But in a period when it would be unheard of for countries such as France, Sweden and Britain to bring such charges against freedom of expression, there has risen a force that takes its appalling authority from something far more widespread than social mores, and far more powerful than the power of any single political regime. The edict of a world religion has sentenced a writer to death.

For more than three years, now, wherever he is hidden, wherever he might go, Salman Rushdie has existed under the Muslim pronouncement upon him of the fatwa. There is no asylum for him anywhere. Every morning when this writer sits down to write, he does not know if he will live through the day; he does not know whether the page will ever be filled. Salman Rushdie happens to be a brilliant writer, and the novel for which he is being pilloried, *The Satanic Verses,* is an innovative exploration of one of the most intense experiences of being in our era, the individual personality in transition between two cultures brought together in a postcolonial world. All is re-examined through the refraction of the imagination; the meaning of sexual and filial love, the rituals of social acceptance, the meaning of a formative religious faith for individuals removed from its subjectivity by circumstance opposing different systems of belief, religious and secular, in a different context of living. His novel is a true mythology. But although he has done for the postcolonial consciousness in Europe what Günter Grass did for the post-Nazi one with *The Tin Drum* and *Dog Years,* perhaps even has tried to approach what Beckett did for our existential anguish in *Waiting For Godot,* the level of his achievement should not matter. Even if he were a mediocre writer, his situation is the terrible concern of every fellow writer for, apart from his personal plight, what implications, what new threat against the carrier of the word does it bring? It should be the concern of individuals and above all, of governments and human rights organizations all over the world. With dictatorships apparently vanquished, this murderous new dictate invoking the power of international terrorism in the name of a great and respected religion should and can be dealt with only by democratic governments and the United Nations as an offense against humanity.

I return from the horrific singular threat to those that have been general for writers of this century now in its final, summing-up decade. In repressive regimes anywhere—whether in what was the Soviet bloc, Latin America, Africa, China—most imprisoned writers have been shut away for their activities as citizens striving for liberation against the oppression of the general society to which they belong. Others have been condemned by repressive regimes for serving society by writing as well as they can; for this aesthetic venture of ours becomes subversive when the shameful secrets of our times are explored deeply, with the artist's rebellious integrity to the state of being manifest in life around her or him; then the writer's themes and characters inevitably are formed by the pressures and distortions of that society as the life of the fisherman is determined by the power of the sea.

There is a paradox. In retaining this integrity, the writer sometimes must risk both the state's indictment of treason, and the liberation forces' complaint of lack of blind commitment. As a human being, no writer can stoop to the lie of Manichean "balance." The devil always has lead in his shoes, when placed on his side of the scale. Yet, to paraphrase coarsely Márquez's dictum given by him both as a writer and a fighter for justice, the writer must take the right to explore, warts and all, both the enemy and the beloved comrade in arms, since only a try for the truth makes sense of being, only a try for the truth edges towards justice just ahead of Yeats's beast slouching to be born. In literature, from life,

> we page through each other's faces
> we read each looking eye
> ... It has taken lives to be able to do so.

These are the words of the South African poet and fighter for justice and peace in our country, Mongane Serote.[13]

The writer is of service to humankind only insofar as the writer uses the word even against his or her own loyalties, trusts the state of being, as it is revealed, to hold somewhere in its complexity filaments of the cord of truth, able to be bound together, here and there, in art: trusts the state of being to yield somewhere fragmentary phrases of truth, which is the final word of words, never changed by our stumbling efforts to spell it out and write it down, never changed by lies, by semantic sophistry, by the dirtying of the word for the purposes of racism, sexism, prejudice, domination, the glorification of destruction, the curses and the praise-songs.

1. "The God's Script" from *Labyrinths & Other Writings* by Jorge Luis Borges. Translator unknown. Edited by Donald H. Yates & James E. Kirby. Penguin Modern Classics, page 71.
2. *Mythologies* by Roland Barthes. Translated by Annette Lavers. Hill & Wang, page 131.
3. *Historie de Lynx* by Claude Lévi-Strauss. ". . . je les situais à mi-chemin entre le conte de fées et le roman policier." Plon, page 13.
4. *Report to Greco* by Nikos Kazantzakis. Faber & Faber, page 150.
5. *S/Z* by Roland Barthes. Translated by Richard Miller. Jonathan Cape.
6. London *Observer* review. 19/4/81. Anthony Burgess.
7. The Third Octavo Notebook from *Wedding Preparations in the Country* by Franz Kafka. Definitive Edition. Secker & Warburg.
8. *Carnets* 1942–5 by Albert Camus.
9. Gabriel García Márquez. In an interview; my notes do not give the journal or date.
10. "Dedication" from *Selected Poems* by Czesław Miłosz. The Ecco Press.
11. "To Posterity" from *Selected Poems* by Bertolt Brecht. Translated by H. R. Hays. Grove Press, page 173.
12. *Report to Greco* by Nikos Kazantzakis. Faber & Faber.
13. *A Tough Tale* by Mongane Wally Serote. Kliptown Books.

[© The Nobel Foundation, 1991. Nadine Gordimer is the sole author of the text.]

Günter Grass

(16 October 1927 -   )

Sigrid Mayer
University of Wyoming

This entry has been expanded by Mayer from her Grass entry in *DLB Yearbook 1999*. See also the Grass entries in *DLB 75: Contemporary German Fiction Writers, Second Series;* and *DLB 124: Twentieth-Century German Dramatists, 1919–1992*.

BOOKS: *Die Vorzüge der Windhühner* (Berlin & Neuwied: Luchterhand, 1956);

Die Blechtrommel: Roman (Darmstadt, Berlin & Neuwied: Luchterhand, 1959); translated by Ralph Manheim as *The Tin Drum* (London: Secker & Warburg, 1962; New York: Pantheon, 1963); excerpts from the German version published as *Der Kampf um die polnische Post* (Göttingen: Steidl, 2000);

O Susanna; ein Jazzbilderbuch: Blues, Balladen, Spirituals, Jazz, German text by Grass, pictures by Horst Geldmacher, music by Hermann Wilson (Cologne & Berlin: Kiepenheuer & Witsch, 1959);

Gleisdreieck (Darmstadt, Berlin & Neuwied: Luchterhand, 1960);

Stoffreste: Ballett in einem Akt, music by Aribert Reimann (Berlin: Bote & Bock, 1960);

Katz und Maus: Eine Novelle (Neuwied & Berlin: Luchterhand, 1961); translated by Manheim as *Cat and Mouse* (New York: Harcourt, Brace & World, 1963; London: Secker & Warburg, 1963); German version, edited by Edgar Lohner (Waltham, Mass.: Blaisdell, 1969); German version, edited by H. F. Brookes and C. E. Fraenkel (London: Heinemann Educational, 1971);

Die bösen Köche: Stück (Berlin: Kiepenheuer, 1961); translated by A. Leslie Willson as *The Wicked Cooks* in Grass, *Four Plays* (New York: Harcourt, Brace & World, 1967; London: Secker & Warburg, 1968); original German expanded as *Die bösen Köche: Ein Drama in 5 Akten. Mit 5 Reproduktionen nach Radierungen des Autors* (Stuttgart: Reclam, 1978);

Hundejahre: Roman (Neuwied: Luchterhand, 1963): translated by Manheim as *Dog Years* (New York: Harcourt, Brace & World, 1965; London: Secker & Warburg, 1965);

Hochwasser: Ein Stück in zwei Akten (Frankfurt am Main: Suhrkamp, 1963); translated by Manheim as *Flood* in *Four Plays;*

Die Ballerina (Berlin: Wolff's Bücherei, 1963);

Onkel, Onkel! Ein Spiel in vier Akten. Mit neun Zeichnungen des Autors (Berlin: Wagenbach, 1965); translated by Manheim as *Mister, Mister* (*Onkel, Onkel* in British edition) in *Four Plays;*

Rede über das Selbstverständliche (Neuwied & Berlin: Luchterhand, 1965);

Dich singe ich, Demokratie (Neuwied & Berlin: Luchterhand, 1965);

Die Plebejer proben den Aufstand: Ein deutsches Trauerspiel (Neuwied & Berlin: Luchterhand, 1966); translated by Manheim as *The Plebeians Rehearse the Uprising: A German Tragedy* (New York: Harcourt, Brace & World, 1966; London: Secker & Warburg, 1967);

Ausgefragt: Gedichte und Zeichnungen (Neuwied & Berlin: Luchterhand, 1967);

Der Fall Axel C. Springer am Beispiel Arnold Zweig: Eine Rede, ihr Anlaß und die Folgen (Berlin: Voltaire, 1967);

Über meinen Lehrer Döblin und andere Vorträge (Berlin: Literarisches Colloquium, 1968);

Über das Selbstverständliche: Reden, Aufsätze, offene Briefe, Kommentare (Neuwied: Luchterhand, 1968);

Briefe über die Grenze: Versuch eines Ost-West-Dialogs, by Grass and Pavel Kohout (Hamburg: Wegner, 1968);

Geschichten, as Artur Knoff (Berlin: Literarisches Colloquium, 1968);

Davor: Ein Stück in 13 Szenen (Berlin: Kiepenheuer, 1969); translated by Willson and Manheim as *Max: A Play* (New York: Harcourt Brace Jovanovich, 1972); revised German edition, edited by Victor Lange and Frances Lange (New York: Harcourt Brace Jovanovich, 1973);

Günter Grass (left) receiving the 1999 Nobel Prize in Literature from King Carl XVI Gustaf of Sweden (AP Photo/Tobias Rostlund, Pool)

örtlich betäubt: Roman (Neuwied: Luchterhand, 1969); translated by Manheim as *Local Anaesthetic* (New York: Harcourt, Brace & World, 1970; London: Secker & Warburg, 1970);

Die Schweinekopfsülze (Hamburg: Merlin, 1969);

Freiheit: Ein Wort wie Löffelstiel [by Grass]; *Gegen Gewalt und Unmenschlichkeit* [by Paul Schallück]: *Zwei Reden zur Woche der Brüderlichkeit* (Cologne: Schäuble, 1969);

Theaterspiele (Neuwied: Luchterhand, 1970)—comprises *Hochwasser; Onkel, Onkel!; Noch zehn Minuten bis Buffalo; Die bösen Köche; Die Plebejer proben den Aufstand;* and *Davor; Noch zehn Minuten bis Buffalo* translated by Manheim as *Only Ten Minutes to Buffalo* in *Four Plays*;

Demokratie und Sozialismus 1971, by Grass, H. P. Tschudi, and A. Schmid (Bern: SPS, 1971);

Gesammelte Gedichte (Neuwied: Luchterhand, 1971);

Aus dem Tagebuch einer Schnecke (Neuwied: Luchterhand, 1972); translated by Manheim as *From the Diary of a Snail* (New York: Harcourt Brace Jovanovich, 1973; London: Secker & Warburg, 1974);

Der Schrifsteller als Bürger—Eine Siebenjahresbilanz (Vienna: Dr. Karl Renner-Institut, 1973);

Mariazuehren; Hommageàmarie; Inmarypraise (Munich: Bruckmann, 1973); *Inmarypraise* translated by Christopher Middleton (New York: Harcourt Brace Jovanovich, 1973);

Liebe geprüft: Sieben Gedichte mit sieben Radierungen (Bremen: Schünemann, 1974); translated by Michael Hamburger as *Love Tested: Seven Poems with Seven Etchings* (New York: Harcourt Brace Jovanovich, 1975);

Der lesende Arbeiter; Bildungsurlaub: Zwei Reden vor Gewerkschaften, Schriftenreihe der Industriegewerkschaft Druck und Papier, no. 23 (Bonlanden: Weinmann, 1974);

Der Bürger und seine Stimme: Reden, Aufsätze, Kommentare (Darmstadt & Neuwied: Luchterhand, 1974);

Radierungen 1972–1974 (Berlin: Galerie Andre, Anselm Dreher, 1974);

Mit Sophie in die Pilze gegangen: Gedichte und Lithographien (Mailand: Grafica Uno, 1976; Göttingen: Steidl, 1987);

Der Butt: Roman (Darmstadt & Neuwied: Luchterhand, 1977); translated by Manheim as *The Flounder* (New York: Harcourt Brace Jovanovich, 1978; London: Secker & Warburg, 1978); excerpt from the German version published as *Vatertag* (Göttingen: Steidl, 1999);

Denkzettel: Politische Reden und Aufsätze (Darmstadt & Neuwied: Luchterhand, 1978);

Das Treffen in Telgte: Eine Erzählung (Darmstadt & Neuwied: Luchterhand, 1979); translated by Manheim as *The Meeting at Telgte* (New York: Harcourt Brace Jovanovich, 1981; London: Secker & Warburg, 1981);

Die Blechtrommel als Film, by Grass and Volker Schlöndorff (Frankfurt am Main: Zweitausendeins, 1979);

Werkverzeichnis der Radierungen (Berlin: Galerie Andre, Anselm Dreher, 1979);

Kopfgeburten oder Die Deutschen sterben aus (Darmstadt & Neuwied: Luchterhand, 1980); translated by Manheim as *Headbirths; or, The Germans Are Dying Out* (New York: Harcourt Brace Jovanovich, 1982);

Aufsätze zur Literatur (Darmstadt & Neuwied: Luchterhand, 1980);

Danziger Trilogie (Darmstadt & Neuwied: Luchterhand, 1980)—comprises *Die Blechtrommel, Katz und Maus, Hundejahre;* translated by Manheim as *The Danzig Trilogy* (San Diego: Harcourt Brace Jovanovich / New York: Pantheon, 1987);

Nachruf auf einen Handschuh: Sieben Radierungen und ein Gedicht (Berlin: Galerie Andre, Anselm Dreher, 1982);

Zeichnen und Schreiben I: Zeichnungen und Texte 1954–1977 (Darmstadt & Neuwied: Luchterhand, 1982); translated by Hamburger and Manheim as *Graphics and Writing I: Drawings and Words 1954–1977* (San Diego: Harcourt Brace Jovanovich, 1983);

Bin ich nun Zeichner oder Schreiber? (Regensburg: Schürer, 1982);

Kinderlied: Poems and Etchings (Northridge, Cal.: Lord John Press, 1982);

Ach Butt, dein Märchen geht böse aus: Gedichte und Radierungen (Darmstadt & Neuwied: Luchterhand, 1983);

Die Vernichtung der Menschheit hat begonnen: Rede anläßlich der Verleihung des Feltrinelli-Preises am 25. November 1982 (Hauzenberg: Pongratz, 1983);

Widerstand lernen: Politische Gegenreden 1980–1983 (Darmstadt & Neuwied: Luchterhand, 1984);

Zeichnen und Schreiben II: Radierungen und Texte 1972–1982 (Darmstadt & Neuwied: Luchterhand, 1984); translated by Hamburger, Manheim, and others as *Graphics and Writing II: Etchings and Words 1972–1982* (San Diego: Harcourt Brace Jovanovich, 1985);

Nachdenken über Deutschland: Stefan Heym und Günter Grass diskutierten am 21. November 1984 in Brüssel (Berlin & Brussels: Goethe-Institut Brüssel, 1984);

Geschenkte Freiheit: Rede zum 8. Mai 1945 (Berlin: Akademie der Künste, 1985);

Die Rättin: 3 Radierungen und 1 Gedicht (Homburg: Beck, 1985);

In Kupfer, auf Stein. Das grafische Werk (Göttingen: Steidl, 1986; enlarged, 1994);

Die Rättin (Darmstadt & Neuwied: Luchterhand, 1986); translated by Manheim as *The Rat* (San Diego: Harcourt Brace Jovanovich, 1987);

Ausstellung anläßlich des 60. Geburtstags von Günter Grass: Hundert Zeichnungen 1955–1987, edited by Jens Christian Jensen (Kiel: Kunsthalle und Schleswig-Holsteinischer Kunstverein, 1987);

Radierungen, Lithographien, Zeichnungen, Plastiken, Gedichte (Berlin: Kunstamt, 1987);

Werkausgabe in zehn Bänden, edited by Volker Neuhaus (Darmstadt: Luchterhand, 1987)—comprises volume 1, *Gedichte und Kurzprosa;* volume 2, *Die Blechtrommel;* volume 3, *Katz und Maus; Hundejahre;* volume 4, *örtlich betäubt; Aus dem Tagebuch einer Schnecke;* volume 5, *Der Butt;* volume 6, *Das Treffen in Telgte; Kopfgeburten oder Die Deutschen sterben aus;* volume 7, *Die Rättin;* volume 8, *Theaterspiele—*includes *Beritten hin und zurück: Vorspiele auf dem Theater,* translated by Michael Benedikt and Joseph Goradza as *Rocking Back and Forth,* in *Postwar German Theatre,* edited by Benedikt and George E. Wellwarth (New York: Dutton, 1967), pp. 261–275; volume 9, *Essays, Reden, Briefe, Kommentare;* and volume 10, *Gespräche;*

Calcutta: Zeichnungen (Bremen: Kunsthalle Bremen, 1988);

Die Gedichte 1955–1986 (Darmstadt: Luchterhand, 1988);

Zunge zeigen (Darmstadt: Luchterhand, 1988); translated by John E. Woods as *Show Your Tongue* (San Diego: Harcourt Brace Jovanovich, 1989; London: Secker & Warburg, 1989);

Ecoutez-moi—: Paris-Berlin, aller, retour, by Grass and François Giroud, edited by René Wintzen (Paris: Sell, 1988); translated into German by Sabine Mann and Ilse Strasmann as *Wenn wir von Europa sprechen: Ein Dialog* (Frankfurt am Main: Luchterhand, 1989);

Alptraum und Hoffnung: Zwei Reden vor dem Club of Rome (Göttingen: Steidl, 1989)—comprises "Globale Industrialisierung–Entdeckungen und Verluste des Geistes," by Tschingis Aitmatow; and "Zum Beispiel Calcutta," by Grass;

Meine grüne Wiese: Kurzprosa (Zurich: Manesse, 1989);

Skizzenbuch (Göttingen: Steidl, 1989);

Deutscher Lastenausgleich: Wider das dumpfe Einheitsgebot: Reden und Gespräche (Frankfurt am Main: Luchterhand, 1990);

Deutschland, einig Vaterland? Ein Streitgespräch, by Grass and Rudolf Augstein (Göttingen: Steidl, 1990);

Kahlschlag in unseren Köpfen (Berlin: Kunstamt Reinickendorf, 1990);

Ein Schnäppchen namens DDR: Letzte Reden vorm Glockengeläut (Frankfurt am Main: Luchterhand, 1990);

Tierschutz: Gedichte (Ravensburg: Maier, 1990);

Schreiben nach Auschwitz: Frankfurter Poetik-Vorlesung (Frankfurt am Main: Luchterhand, 1990);

Totes Holz: Ein Nachruf (Göttingen: Steidl, 1990);

Brief aus Altdöbern (Remagen: Rommerskirchen, 1991);

Gegen die verstreichende Zeit: Reden, Aufsätze und Gespräche 1989–1991 (Hamburg & Zürich: Luchterhand, 1991);

Vier Jahrzehnte: Ein Werkstattbericht, edited by G. Fritze Margull (Göttingen: Steidl, 1991); enlarged as *Ein Werkstattbericht 1951–1992* (Göttingen: Steidl und Staatliche Kunsthalle Berlin, 1992); revised as *Fünf Jahrzehnte: Ein Werkstattbericht* (Göttingen: Steidl, 2001);

Unkenrufe. Eine Erzählung (Göttingen: Steidl, 1992); translated by Manheim as *The Call of the Toad* (New York: Harcourt Brace Jovanovich, 1992; London: Secker & Warburg, 1992);

Rede vom Verlust: Über den Niedergang der politischen Kultur im geeinten Deutschland (Göttingen: Steidl, 1992); translated as "Essay on Loss," in *The Future of German Democracy, with an Essay on Loss,* edited by Robert Gerald Livingston and Volkmar Sander (New York: Continuum, 1993);

Novemberland: 13 Sonette (Göttingen: Steidl, 1993);

Studienausgabe, 12 volumes (Göttingen: Steidl, 1993–1994);

Angestiftet, Partei zu ergreifen, edited by Daniela Hermes (Munich: Deutscher Taschenbuch, 1994);

Die Deutschen und ihre Dichter, edited by Hermes (Munich: Deutscher Taschenbuch, 1995);

Ein weites Feld: Roman (Göttingen: Steidl, 1995); translated by Winston as *Too Far Afield* (New York: Harcourt Brace, 2000; London: Faber & Faber, 2000);

Gestern, vor 50 Jahren: Ein deutsch-japanischer Briefwechsel, by Grass and Kenzaburo Oe (Göttingen: Steidl, 1995); translated by John Barrett as *Just Yesterday, Fifty Years Ago: A Critical Dialogue on the Anniversary of the End of the Second World War* (Paris: Alyscamps Press, 1999);

Der Schriftsteller als Zeitgenosse, edited by Hermes (Munich: Deutscher Taschenbuch, 1996);

Fundsachen für Nichtleser (Göttingen: Steidl, 1997);

Ohne die Feder zu wechseln: Zeichnungen, Druckgraphiken, Aquarelle, Skulpturen (Göttingen: Steidl, 1997);

Rede über den Standort (Göttingen: Steidl, 1997);

Werkausgabe, 16 volumes, edited by Neuhaus and Hermes (Göttingen: Steidl, 1997);

Auf einem anderen Blatt: Zeichnungen (Göttingen: Steidl, 1999);

Mein Jahrhundert, with watercolors by Grass (Göttingen: Steidl, 1999; text-only edition, Göttingen: Steidl, 1999); translated by Michael Henry Heim as *My Century* (New York: Harcourt Brace, 1999; London: Faber & Faber, 1999);

Fortsetzung folgt– [Rede anlässlich der Verleihung des Nobelpreises für Literatur]; Literatur und Geschichte [Rede anlässlich der Verleihung des "Prinz von Asturien"-Preises] (Göttingen: Steidl, 1999);

Vom Abenteuer der Aufklärung: Werkstattgespräche, by Grass and Harro Zimmermann (Göttingen: Steidl, 1999);

Für- und Widerworte (Göttingen: Steidl, 1999);

Ohne Stimme: Reden zugunsten des Volkes der Roma und Sinti (Göttingen: Steidl, 2000);

Marthas Hochzeit (Göttingen: Steidl, 2000);

Stockholm: Der Literaturnobelpreis für Günter Grass: Ein Tagebuch mit Fotos von Gerhard Steidl (Göttingen: Steidl, 2000);

Mit Wasserfarben: Aquarelle (Göttingen: Steidl, 2001);

Im Krebsgang: Eine Novelle (Göttingen: Steidl, 2002); translated by Winston as *Crabwalk* (Orlando: Harcourt Brace, 2002; London: Faber & Faber, 2003);

Fundsachen für Grass-Leser, 7 volumes, edited by Karin Kiwus and Wolfgang Trautwein (Göttingen: Steidl, 2002);

"Fortsetzung folgt . . ." / " To Be Continued . . ." / "Leanfar de . . .": The Nobel Lecture, Trilingual Edition, edited by Hans-Christian Oeser and Marco Sonzogni (Dublin: Irish Translators' and Interpreters' Association, 2002);

Gebrannte Erde: Plastiken aus eigener Werkstatt (Göttingen: Steidl, 2002);

Wörter auf Abruf: 77 Gedichte (Berlin: Wagenbach, 2002);

Letzte Tänze. Aquarelle und Zeichnungen (Göttingen: Steidl, 2003);

Der Schatten: Hans Christian Andersens Märchen–gesehen von Günter Grass, artwork by Grass, text by Hans Christian Andersen (Göttingen: Steidl, 2004);

Lyrische Beute: Gedichte und Zeichnungen aus fünfzig Jahren (Göttingen: Steidl, 2004);

Freiheit nach Börsenmass; Geschenkte Freiheit: Zwei Reden zum 8. Mai 1945 (Göttingen: Steidl, 2005);

"Wir leben im Ei": Geschichten aus fünf Jahrzehnten, edited by Dieter Stolz (Frankfurt am Main: Suhrkamp, 2005);

Beim Häuten der Zwiebel (Göttingen: Steidl, 2006).

Editions in English: *Selected Poems,* translated by Michael Hamburger and Christopher Middleton (London: Secker & Warburg, 1966; New York: Harcourt, Brace & World, 1966);

New Poems, translated by Hamburger (New York: Harcourt, Brace & World, 1968);

Speak Out! Speeches, Open Letters, Commentaries, translated by Manheim and others (New York: Harcourt, Brace & World, 1969; London: Secker & Warburg, 1969);

Poems of Günter Grass, translated by Hamburger and Middleton (Harmondsworth, U.K.: Penguin, 1969);

In the Egg and Other Poems, translated by Hamburger and Middleton (New York: Harcourt Brace Jovanovich, 1977; London: Secker & Warburg, 1978);

The Flounder: Written and Illustrated by Günter Grass, 3 volumes, translated by Manheim (New York: Limited Editions Club, 1985);

On Writing and Politics 1967–1983, translated by Manheim (San Diego: Harcourt Brace Jovanovich, 1985; London: Secker & Warburg, 1985);

Two States—One Nation? translated by Krishna Winston and A. S. Wensinger (San Diego: Harcourt Brace Jovanovich, 1990);

Cat and Mouse and Other Writings, edited by A. Leslie Willson (New York: Continuum, 1994);

Novemberland: Selected Poems 1956–1993, translated by Hamburger (New York: Harcourt Brace, 1996);

The Günter Grass Reader, edited by Helmut Frielinghaus (Orlando: Harcourt Brace, 2004); German version published as *Wenn ich Pilze und Federn sammle: Ein Lesebuch,* edited by Frielinghaus (Göttingen: Steidl, 2005).

PLAY PRODUCTIONS: *Hochwasser,* Frankfurt am Main, Neue Bühne, 19 January 1957;

Onkel, Onkel! Cologne, Bühnen der Stadt Köln, 3 March 1958;

Beritten hin und zurück: Vorspiel auf dem Theater, Frankfurt am Main, Neue Bühne, 16 January 1959;

Noch zehn Minuten bis Buffalo, Bochum, Schauspielhaus, 19 February 1959;

Stoffreste, music by Aribert Reimann, Essen, Stadt-theater, February 1961;

Die bösen Köche, Berlin, Schiller-Theater, 16 February 1961; translated as *The Wicked Cooks,* New York, Orpheum Theater, 21 January 1967;

Mystisch–barbarisch–gelangweilt, Düsseldorf, Kammerspiele, 1963;

Goldmäulchen, Munich, Werkraumtheater, July 1964;

Die Plebejer proben den Aufstand, Berlin, Schiller-Theater, 15 January 1966; translated as *The Plebeians Rehearse the Uprising,* Rhode Island, Theatre Company of Boston, 7 September 1967;

Davor, Berlin, Schiller-Theater, 14 February 1969; translated as *Uptight,* Washington, D.C., Kreeger Theatre, 22 March 1972;

Die Vogelscheuchen, music by Reimann, Berlin, 1970.

On 30 September 1999 the early-morning Internet readers of *The New York Times* were among the first to learn that the 1999 Nobel Prize in Literature had been awarded to Günter Grass, German author whose best-known works include *Die Blechtrommel* (1959; translated as *The Tin Drum,* 1962). The Associated Press reported the reaction of the seventy-one-year-old writer: "I'm happy." Although Grass had been a possible candidate for the Nobel Prize for the last forty years (1959–1999), critics felt the timing of the award in the last year of the century was appropriate. Grass's keen sense of history, both past and present, had just been confirmed by his latest book, *Mein Jahrhundert,* published in July 1999 and translated as *My Century* in November 1999. The cover of the first German edition—with a design, as usual, by the author-artist—shows a flaming bonfire of historical dates topped by combinations of the 1900s and 1990s.

The decision had been an easy one for the eighteen members of the Swedish Academy. They had required only two sessions to agree on Grass as an especially deserving laureate. German chancellor Gerhard Schröder sent Grass a congratulatory telegram in which he expressed his hope that this international recognition might provide some satisfaction after the political vituperations Grass had to endure in his own country. He mentioned Grass's contributions to German cultural heritage and identity and maintained that, thanks to Grass, the dialogue between politics and culture has again become possible in Germany.

The prize was awarded for Grass's complete body of work. This consideration is an important one, for it includes the writer's novels, plays, poetry, essays, and speeches as well as his work in the fine arts that has been, especially since the 1970s, an intrinsic part of his literary work.

Günter Wilhelm Grass was born on 16 October 1927 to Kashubian-German parents, Willy and Helena Knoff Grass, in the then "Free City of Danzig." At the age of seventeen, in 1944, he was drafted from high school to serve (as he claimed for many years) as an aide with an air force antiaircraft battery. Wounded at Cottbus in 1945, he was hospitalized at Marienbad in Czechoslovakia and processed through an American prisoner-of-war camp in Bavaria in 1946. This processing included a tour of the Dachau concentration camp, which left a profound and lasting impression on the teenager. His parents and sister had fled to the West in 1945 when Danzig became Polish Gdansk, and Grass worked in a potash mine to maintain financial independence before he decided to study at the Academy of Fine Arts in Düsseldorf. There he worked as an apprentice stonecutter for a gravestone manufacturer and played in a jazz trio until the war-damaged academy reopened in the fall of 1948.

Grass pursued studies in sculpture, first in Düsseldorf and then at the Berlin Academy of Fine Arts until 1956. At the same time he experimented with poetry. He won third prize in a lyric contest in 1955, and in that year he was also invited to read his poetry at a meeting of Gruppe 47 (Group 47), an informal workshop that had been initiated by Hans Werner Richter in 1947. Since Nazi abuse had poisoned the German language, these writers had to find their own voice, new starting points, and different values in order to write about their experiences of pain, accusation, and guilt. The members of Gruppe 47 felt strongly that they, as writers, were responsible for shaping a new postwar society. During group meetings they read from their manuscripts and received constructive criticism from their fellow writers.

In 1956 Grass published *Die Vorzüge der Windhühner* (The Advantages of Windfowl), his first volume of poetry and drawings. The surrealistic images of the poems and the fine-lined drawings of stylized birds and oversized insects hold keys to much of Grass's subsequent work. The poem "Hochwasser" (Flood), for example, sets the stage for a play first performed in 1957 with that title. Of several other Grass plays that originated in the 1950s, only two ballets and *Onkel, Onkel!* (1965; translated as *Mister, Mister*, 1967) were first performed before the publication of *Die Blechtrommel* in 1959.

In 1956 Grass and his Swiss-born wife, dancer Anna Schwarz, whom he had married in Berlin in 1954, moved to Paris. There she continued her ballet training while Grass was working as a stoker in the basement room of their apartment house, where he was writing versions of his first novel. In 1957 he became the father of twin boys, Franz and Raoul, and the following year his reading from the manuscript of *Die Blechtrommel* won the Gruppe 47 Prize. He also visited his former hometown in Poland to check on some historic sites for his novel. Following the publication of *Die Blechtrommel*, his fame was established.

In this novel of 3 books, 46 chapters, and 750 pages, Grass presents an unabashed insider's view of society in the Third Reich, from an unusual visual perspective. His protagonist, Oskar Matzerath, possesses an adult intelligence in the body of a three-year-old; his stunted growth is a consequence of his decision not to grow up like the adults around him. Oskar's toy drum—harking back, perhaps, to Grass's experience in a jazz trio and also corresponding to the author's strong sense of rhythm in language—becomes his powerful instrument of self-expression, speech, and protest.

As Oskar tells his story from the hospital bed of an institution for the criminally insane, drumming enables him to conjure up the events and emotions from the past. By observing society literally and figuratively from the ground up, Oskar obtains the demonic license to ignore all social taboos. His transgression of these taboos initially caused some moral outrage about the novel: amid accusations of blasphemy and pornography, the City Senate of Bremen refused to award Grass the Bremen literature prize that a jury had agreed to confer on him. But as Hans Magnus Enzensberger wrote in an 18 November 1959 review for *Süddeutscher Rundfunk*, "What legitimates Grass's brusque invasions and turns them into artistic deeds is the perfect naturalness and impartiality with which he carries them out; he does not chase after the taboo . . . he simply doesn't notice it."

After the American publication of *The Tin Drum*, Frederic Morton wrote in *The New York Times Book Review* (10 April 1963): "Grass brings off what no German has managed or even dared to attempt–to show that the Nazis were not a black breed apart, imposing their exotic evil on the good little people. The Nazis were the good little people themselves." Morton observed that "the book often lapses into a jungle of symbols," and the search for symbolic meanings in the book, which remained on the best-seller list of *The New York Times* for three months, has continued to characterize American readings of the novel. Oskar has mistakenly been identified with the Nazi spirit, with the drumbeat of its propaganda, and even with Adolf Hitler himself. Yet, the diverse interpretations, especially of the protagonist, demonstrate the rich potential of the novel, which led the Swedish Academy to remark in a 30 September 1999 press release that "*The Tin Drum* will become one of the enduring literary works of the 20th century."

After the success of *Die Blechtrommel*, Grass and his family moved back to Berlin, where in 1960 he published *Gleisdreieck* (Rail Triangle), his second volume of poetry and drawings, which he named after an East-West Berlin railroad station. Larger in format than the 1956 collection and dominated by drawings in charcoal and India ink, this volume offers several motifs and statements about aesthetics that recur throughout Grass's works. The author's plays written in the 1950s were now in demand for first performances. In 1961 his daughter Laura was born. That same year, *Die bösen Köche* (translated as *The Wicked Cooks*, 1967) was successfully performed at the Schiller-Theater in Berlin, and he published *Katz und Maus* (translated as *Cat and Mouse*,

1963), a novella with the harbor waters of Danzig as its background.

The cat-and-mouse game that the narrator, Pilenz, plays with the Adam's apple of Mahlke, his friend, apparently triggers Mahlke's ultimately destructive obsession with hiding it. Pilenz later feels compelled to tell the story in writing, "denn was mit Katz und Maus begann, quält mich heute" (for what began with cat and mouse, torments me now). Mahlke's desire to hide his Adam's apple eventually becomes an obsession to obtain the Knight's Cross in order to cover up his "mouse." Once he has earned this prized object by destroying a record number of Russian tanks, Mahlke finds that it fails to procure for him what he really wants: recognition by his former teachers and classmates as "the great Mahlke." Outstaying his furlough, he dives, in the presence of his friend Pilenz, to the sunken Polish minesweeper in the harbor as he had done so often in the past to the amazement of his peers. In those high-school years he had dived with a screwdriver hanging from his neck, which he used to gain access to a dry space in the sunken vessel. This time, however, he dives without a screwdriver or anything else around his neck. Pilenz counts the seconds and waits in vain for a signal; but Mahlke fails to resurface anywhere. For Pilenz, the despair and ultimate death of his friend, including his own presumed role in that death, remain unfathomed. Critical approval for this novella both in Germany and abroad prevailed over some attempts in Germany to ban it for young readers because its frank language broke some sexual taboos of the time.

When *Die Blechtrommel* won the prestigious French Prix du Meilleur Livre Etranger in 1962, Grass was working on the third part of what came to be known as his "Danzig Trilogy." The voluminous novel *Hundejahre* (1963; translated as *Dog Years*, 1965) was published in the same year that Ralph Manheim's translation of *Die Blechtrommel* appeared in the United States.

Although *Hundejahre* covers the same period (from the 1920s to the 1950s) that had been scrutinized in *Die Blechtrommel* and, like that first novel, begins at the mouth of the Vistula River and ends in the postwar West, *Hundejahre* differs from that novel in every other respect. Instead of employing a single narrator, it uses a "collective" of three narrators to report on the childhood years, the war years, and the postwar years of the two main protagonists. Yet, the reports of these narrators intertwine, and, to bridge any disparities, a dog is central. The dog, Prince, whose genealogy goes back to Danzig, becomes Hitler's personal property. He escapes from the government headquarters just before the collapse of the Reich, swims across the Elbe River, and winds up in the West.

The first narrator—Amsel, alias Brauxel, son of a Jewish business family—and the third narrator, Matern, son of a miller's family, are childhood friends. Their adventures along the shores of the Vistula are narrated in a lyrical language that suggests a suspended early-morning harmony among all creations of men and nature. Amsel, whose birth and name are related to blackbirds, absorbs the world with the eyes of an artist. He constructs scarecrows in the image of man. During their school years Matern sees himself as Amsel's guardian, protecting him from the teasing of schoolmates. Later, disguised among a gang of Sturmabteilung troopers, Matern betrays and almost kills his friend. Amsel loses all his teeth and becomes transfigured into another person named Brauxel. During the same night another gang, led by Tulla Pokriefke, rolls plump little Jenny into a snowman, and she emerges from this experience as a frail ballerina.

Tulla's cousin Harry relates the war years in love letters to Tulla, who first appeared in *Katz und Maus*. These letters recount Harry's family life in a carpentry in Danzig Langfuhr, where the shepherd dog Harras (Prince's father) holds center stage. Among Tulla's uncontrollable, often malicious, sometimes emotionally charged deeds and misdeeds, Harry records her discovery of mountains of skeletal remains and a proliferation of rats near the Stutthof concentration camp. When, after the war, Brauxel and Matern, the latter accompanied by Prince the Führer-dog, meet again in the West, they descend to the subterranean showrooms of Brauxel's scarecrows, which are now exported all over the world. They leave Prince, alias Pluto (the hellhound), behind as they return to daylight.

Such a summary fails to take into account Grass's new language in this novel about an artist by an artist. Critics as well as translators had a hard time adapting to his style, which they described as Joycean, Rabelaisian, expressionistic, or lyrical. A reviewer for *Time* (13 April 1970), in an inset on the "Trials of a Translator," mentions "those long inventories of physical objects" as part of Grass's *Dingmagie* (thing magic). German critics were arguing how far Grass could take this object-syntax without verbs. They also argued about Grass's parodies of Martin Heidegger's philosophical language in *Sein und Zeit* (1927; translated as *Being and Time*, 1962), while *Time* enjoyed Grass's spoofing of Hitler's military jargon in German headquarters' commands to recapture the dog Prince: "On the Jüterbog-Torgau line, projected antitank trenches are replaced by Führerdogtraptrenches." Grass describes the shepherd dog who fathered Prince as having hair that glistened "black, umbrella-black, priest-black, widow-black, SS-black, blackboard-black, Falange-black, blackbird-black,

Othello-black, dysentery-black, violet-black, tomato-black, lemon-black, flour-black, milk-black, snow-black."

In the wake of the Danzig Trilogy and the attention he won with it, Grass went on the stump for the Social Democrats (SPD). He had assisted Willy Brandt, then mayor of West Berlin, with speech writing since 1961; and when the Berlin Wall went up in that year, he requested a public statement from Anna Seghers, the renowned writer from the German Democratic Republic (GDR). It was not forthcoming. After 1963 he campaigned for Brandt and the Social Democrats, and when the SPD lost in the 1965 elections, Grass continued to advocate political change in his acceptance speech for the Büchner Prize that year. His new play, *Die Plebejer proben den Aufstand: Ein deutsches Trauerspiel* (1966; translated as *The Plebeians Rehearse the Uprising: A German Tragedy*, 1966) caused a scandal when it was performed in Berlin in 1966.

The play recalls a workers' uprising that was cruelly put down by Soviet tanks in Berlin on 17 June 1953. Grass combines the historical event with the fact that socialist playwright Bertolt Brecht was working in Berlin at the time. Although Grass never refers to Brecht by name, the "boss" who rehearses the *Plebeians' Uprising* in this play refuses to support the actual workers' rebellion against higher quotas and other injustices. While Grass wanted to show a gap between theory and practice in German history, Berlin audiences saw him challenging Brecht's image. Later performances of *Die Plebejer proben den Aufstand* in the United States and eventually in Calcutta (1986) more successfully conveyed Grass's message.

In 1966 Grass also took part in the meeting of Gruppe 47 at Princeton University, just before the demise of that organization the following year. His address, "On Writers as Court Jesters and on Non-Existent Courts," included as its closing statement this remark on the relationship between writers (and their work) and politics: "A poem knows no compromise, but men live by compromise. The individual who can stand up under this contradiction and act is a fool and will change the world."

In the 1967 volume of poetry and drawings, *Ausgefragt* (Questioned), Grass tried unsuccessfully to engage the protest movement of the New Left in constructive election activity. *Ausgefragt*, like his previous volumes of poetry, includes statements on his poetic and/or aesthetic principles. Grass published *Über das Selbstverständliche* (On the Self-Evident), a volume of collected speeches, essays, and open letters, in 1968. The English translation *Speak Out! Speeches, Open Letters, Commentaries* (1969) includes most but not all of these pieces. Several more volumes of his political speeches and writings followed over the next decades. Grass received the Berlin Fontane Prize and addressed the general assembly of the Social Democratic Party in 1968. By the time the Social Democrats under Brandt came to power in 1969, Grass had contributed nearly a hundred election speeches toward this goal.

Aus dem Tagebuch einer Schnecke (1972; translated as *From the Diary of a Snail*, 1973) recounts for his children the fate of the Jewish community in Danzig during World War II and also the events of election campaigns from March to September 1969. Before publishing *Aus dem Tagebuch einer Schnecke*, Grass had completed a new novel, *örtlich betäubt* (1969; translated as *Local Anaesthetic*, 1970), and shaped from it a new play, *Davor* (1969; translated as *Max*, 1972). This novel, Grass's first fictional departure from his Danzig origins, is set for the most part in Berlin and deals with the protest movement against the Vietnam War. A television screen attached within sight of a dentist's chair allows for a complex structure of flashbacks in *örtlich betäubt*, and its protagonists confront each other more directly in the play *Davor*.

Starusch, a high-school teacher who is receiving dental treatment (and for whom the television screen provides a distracting "local anaesthetic"), discusses with the dentist a student's plan to set fire to his dog on the showy Kurfürstendamm Street in West Berlin. Scherbaum, the student, will not be dissuaded from this act, which he hopes will arouse people to the realities of war. In the end, no dog is burned, but "there is always new pain," as the last sentence of *örtlich betäubt* points out. The novel was considered a failure in Germany because it seemed to belittle the problems at hand. In the United States, however, it earned Grass a cover story in *Time* (13 April 1970) in which he was characterized as a "Novelist between the Generations—A Man Who Can Speak to the Young." Even though the young at that time did not listen to Grass, whom *Time* had dubbed "a fanatic for moderation," *örtlich betäubt* demonstrates his continuing involvement with contemporary issues of historic significance.

While he was working on *Aus dem Tagebuch einer Schnecke*, Grass had several other projects on his mind in addition to the ongoing election campaigns. He had been asked to give a speech for the five-hundredth-anniversary celebration of the birth of Albrecht Dürer and was carrying with him a picture postcard of Dürer's famous engraving "Melencolia I." This challenging print from the year 1514 (reproduced in the English edition of *From the Diary of a Snail*) inspired his choice of topic. Grass's speech, "Vom Stillstand im Fortschritt" (translated as "On Stasis in Progress"), is appended to *Aus dem Tagebuch einer Schnecke*. The title of the speech alludes to the image of the snail that Grass had rediscovered while writing this "diary." When his children asked, "What do you mean by the snail?" he answered, "The snail is progress."

Grass was also taking up Dürer's medium when he began to etch his visions of the snail in copperplates. In conjunction with the American publication of *From the Diary of a Snail*, prints of Grass's etchings were exhibited in galleries in the United States. Most of the etchings combined the snail with various subjects, such as the author's self-portrait, or with objects such as his fountain pen. The etchings also included snail races, double-headed snails, and snails in Israel—to which, in 1972, Grass accompanied Brandt on a visit. The history of the Jewish community in Danzig and the fate of some of its members as refugees from the Nazis form one of the narrative strands of *Aus dem Tagebuch einer Schnecke,* with "Doubt" as the protagonist. All these motifs—progress, the snail, and Melencolia and her counterpart Utopia—are woven into Grass's account of campaign travels for the SPD. In *Aus dem Tagebuch einer Schnecke* he combines his first self-portrait in an etching—showing the snail in his eye—with what is also the closest to being a literary self-portrait in his works.

In 1976 Grass published *Mit Sophie in die Pilze gegangen* (Mushrooming with Sophie), a limited edition of lithographs and poems, and several poems from this collection were included among the forty-six poems in his 1977 novel *Der Butt* (translated as *The Flounder,* 1978). The comprehensive design of this novel evolved progressively from the etchings through the concise language of poetry. Not until the second year of Grass's work on the novel did he integrate the talking fish, the *Butt* (Flounder) from the fairy tale by Jakob and Wilhelm Grimm, "The Fisherman and His Wife." It is the mythical fish who from the beginning of time has whispered ideas into the fisherman's (and author's) ear, as illustrated on the dust jacket of the book. In Grass's version of the tale, the narrator's wife, Ilsebill, becomes pregnant, and the nine sections of the book correspond to the months of her pregnancy. Each section also presents a major era of history, from mythical and prehistoric times to the present. The parallels between historic eras, represented by female cooks, and the nine months of the human gestation period correspond to timelines of the past and present. This structure allows the first-person narrator to be present at all times and in all male roles. On the present timeline, a women's tribunal of eleven feminists sits in council over the Flounder, the male element they have caught, isolated, and indicted.

Cooks, for Grass, have always signified more than ordinary cooking; they are figures endowed with creative and magical power. The "wicked cooks" in *Die bösen Köche* appear to be in a political power struggle. The historical female cooks in *Der Butt,* limited as they are by the natural resources available to them, become great through their personal resourcefulness as providers of nourishment. The Flounder, representing the male component of human nature, subverts the cooks' work to ensure survival, by instigating wars and by inventing new means of human destruction.

It took Grass five years to finish this epic in time for his fiftieth birthday. It was dedicated to his daughter Helena, born in 1974. While the book was extremely popular in Germany, it required some time to sink in with readers abroad. In 1978 Grass and his wife divorced. The following year, he married Ute Ehrhardt, a Berlin organist.

Grass's next novel, *Das Treffen in Telgte* (1979; translated as *The Meeting at Telgte,* 1981), depicts some twenty poets from all parts of Germany converging on the little town of Telgte in 1647, just before the end of the Thirty Years' War, to contribute to the negotiations leading up to the 1648 Peace of Westfalia. The story was Grass's birthday present for seventy-year-old Richter, who had founded Gruppe 47 three hundred years after the fictitious meeting at Telgte and whose convocation of poets had been concerned about the peace after World War II. The implied correspondence of historical events accounts for Grass's remarkable opening sentence in *Das Treffen in Telgte:* "Gestern wird sein, was morgen gewesen ist" (The thing that hath been tomorrow is that which shall be yesterday). It also explains the dust-jacket etching of a hand holding a quill raised above rubble.

In *Das Treffen in Telgte,* well-known poets from the baroque period who lived to see the end of the Thirty Years' War are shown reading and discussing their works, exchanging opinions about poetry and politics, and hoping to influence the terms of the humiliating peace through a manifesto signed by all. Yet, the manifesto is destroyed when the inn where they stay burns down, and the writers part in disarray. Grass succeeds in portraying each poet through that poet's particular style and diction, combined with Grass's own tongue-in-cheek humor. The wildest portrayal is that of the young "Gelnhausen" (Hans Jakob Christoffel von Grimmelshausen, author of *Simplizissimus* [1668], a novel about the Thirty Years' War). Some parallels between Gelnhausen's character and Grass's role within Gruppe 47—such as his grotesque humor and baroque style (for example, in *Die Blechtrommel*) and his love for women—are unmistakable, and it is tempting to look for further correlations between the baroque poets and those of Gruppe 47.

The 1980s were approaching as Grass finished his first draft for *Kopfgeburten oder Die Deutschen sterben aus* (1980; translated as *Headbirths; or, The Germans are Dying Out,* 1982). The beginning of that decade was coinciding with new elections in Germany, with Helmut

Schmidt running against Franz Josef Strauss, the candidate of the conservative Bavarian Christian Democrats, who warned that the Germans might be dying out under the rule of the Social Democrats. Grass saw this approach as "fear-mongering" used to provide a political program, and he used Strauss's picturesque reference to writers as "rats and blowflies" as inspiration for a self-portrait with blowfly.

The term "headbirths" recalls the birth of Athena, the Greek goddess of wisdom, from the head of Zeus—"a paradox," Grass writes, "that has impregnated male minds to this day." The book is written in the style of a movie script for Volker Schlöndorff, who had just directed the prize-winning movie version of *Die Blechtrommel* (1979). Later in 1979 the Schlöndorffs and the Grasses took a tour of East Asia sponsored by the Goethe Institute, and in Grass's novel Harm and Dörte Peters, a couple of politically active young teachers, go on a similar tour sponsored by the Travel Agency Sisyphus. Harm and Dörte wish to educate themselves about Third World realities in order to decide whether or not to have a child in an overpopulated world. Grass refers to *Headbirths* within the text as "title of the film or book, or both" and frequently designs specific scenarios for the "Headbirths movie."

The movie-script concept allows the author to flash backward and forward in time. Recalling how critics have preferred his writings about the past to those of "undistanced involvement with the present," Grass anticipated the criticism awaiting this book. In the novel, he admits:

> We've learned in school that the present comes after the past and is followed by the future. But I work with a fourth tense, the paspresenture. That's why my form gets untidy. On my paper more is possible. Here only chaos foments order. Here even holes are contents. And loose threads are threads that have been left radically untied. Here everything doesn't have to come out even.

In German literary circles, Grass's new coinage "Vergegenkunft," translated by Manheim as "paspresenture," has become a frequently cited term.

In the first two years of the 1980s Grass deliberately refrained from writing, concentrating his creative energies on new etchings, lithographs, and some clay sculptures. When he found a man's glove washed ashore by the sea, the discovery inspired a cycle of seven etchings, *Nachruf auf einen Handschuh* (1982, Obituary on a Glove). The six prints, following a self-portrait titled *Thoughtfully With Glove*, all bespeak "was bleiben wird" (what will remain) after the demise of humankind. Part of it, like "the sailor's glove," will be "our garbage." On receiving the Antonio Feltrinelli Prize in Rome in 1982, Grass questioned in his acceptance speech whether the book he was planning to write could assume a future, since a future had become questionable at present. In 1983 he wrote the first fragments of this book, *Die Rättin* (1986; translated as *The Rat*, 1987), on clay pages; in retrospect, Grass remarked in his *Ein Werkstattbericht 1951–1992* (A Studio Report 1951–1992) that he should have written all five hundred pages of the novel in this form, one copy only.

To appreciate the apocalyptic visions, or rather the travesty of the apocalypse that takes place in *Die Rättin*, it helps to recall the doomsday mood that prevailed in central Europe during the 1980s. The escalating arms race between the superpowers, the real possibility of destroying the world, had provoked a genuine fear that such a disaster would happen, accidentally or otherwise. Grass's book was a relative latecomer in a wave of "Endgame" literature (named after Samuel Beckett's 1957 play). The narrator of *Die Rättin*, who has received a she-rat for Christmas, is subjected in his dreams to the rat's teachings about the inevitability of the second "big bang" that will lead to the demise of mankind. The rat—an animal with historical significance ever since the days of Noah's Ark, which refused to shelter it—has much survival experience and can become the creature that ultimately outlasts all.

When the big bang takes place, it affects diverse figures in the novel at the same time. The sixty-year-old Oskar Matzerath, who has anticipated events, hides under the skirts of his grandmother at the party for her 107th birthday, where the explosion of the neutron bomb transforms him into a shriveled, leathery object. Famous fairy-tale characters, who try to rescue what remains of their forest by promoting the Brothers Grimm to higher posts in the government, and a ship with female crew members who have just located the sunken utopian realm of Vineta, are also affected by the disaster.

D. J. Enright (*The New York Review of Books*, 24 September 1987) identified four main narrative strands in *Die Rättin*, one of which includes the story of an artist, Lothar Malskat, who forged copies of Gothic paintings that had miraculously reappeared in a Lübeck cathedral. Enright interprets this thread as a parable about the "double forgery" by the East and West German politicians Walter Ulbricht and Konrad Adenauer. Writing for *The New York Times Book Review* (5 July 1987), Janette Turner Hospital discussed the fear and panic felt by the readers of *Die Rättin* because of the switching back and forth between "all six story lines." As Hospital saw it, "In the age of logorrhea, Grass's novels (mutating in form and syntax along with his hominoid protagonists, writhing like indomitable victims of some linguistic

Chernobyl) are passionate attempts 'to put off the end with words' even as words themselves must be scraped free of the counterfeiter's muck."

Before *Die Rättin* was published in Germany in February 1986, Manheim's English translation of selected Grass essays and speeches, *On Writing and Politics, 1967–1983,* had been published, and it was later reviewed in *The New York Times* (17 June 1985). The reviewer, Christopher Lehmann-Haupt, had maintained that it was "boring to read Mr. Grass on technology, industrial waste, missile arms and the imminent arrival of the end of time . . . because what he has to say has been said so many times before." Lehmann-Haupt continued, "If what he says is true, as it well may be, then we ought to be awakened to the threats instead of numbed by their repetition." *Die Rättin* attempts to sound just such a wake-up call.

In the summer of 1986 Grass and his wife left Europe for a prolonged stay in Calcutta. It was his second visit to this city, the first one since 1975 when, as a guest of the Indian government, he had resolved to return. In *Zunge zeigen* (1988; translated as *Show Your Tongue,* 1989) Grass writes:

> Wovon ich wegfliege: von Wiederholungen, die sich als Neuigkeiten ausgeben; von Deutschland und Deutschland, wie schwerbewaffnete Todfeinde einander immer ähnlicher werden; von Einsichten, aus zu naher Distanz gewonnen; von meiner nur halblaut eingestandenen Ratlosigkeit, die mitfliegt.
>
> (What I am flying away from: from repetition that claims to be news; from Germany and Germany, the way two deadly foes, armed to the teeth, grow ever more alike; from insights achieved from too close up; from my own perplexity, admitted only sotto voce, flying with me.)

The couple lived in the Calcutta suburbs through January 1987.

In *Zunge zeigen,* Grass records his experience of Calcutta by synthesizing three forms. The first, a prose report, is based in part on diary entries, including small drawings. In its final form, the report contains both fact and reflection—the latter inspired by memories held fast in drawings and by the books the couple had brought along. The second part of *Zunge zeigen* presents fifty-six expressionistic drawings integrating pictures and words. These drawings were developed in part from Grass's *Skizzenbuch* (1989, Sketchbook) but mostly from a collection of three hundred drawings he produced while experimenting with different graphic techniques. They feature garbage squares, garbage mountains being combed through by human figures, cows, crows, pavement dwellers, sleepers, squatters, and empty coconut shells reminiscent of decapitated heads—over which hovers the black goddess Kali showing her tongue in shame. Also recurring are scenes from public transportation, public crematoriums, and nightly floods and feasts.

Kali, the goddess of destruction, dominates the third section, a twelve-part poem titled "Zunge zeigen." On her festival, Kali Puja, she unleashes the final flood: "I show my tongue, I cross banks, I abolish borders, I make / an end." Each part of this book evolves from the preceding part, the poem combining narration and images in reflection upon each other. Clark Blaise (*The New York Times Book Review,* 21 May 1989) described it as a "one-man-show of a book" and found it to be "despite its virtuosity, a modest, very personal book. It charts Mr. Grass's inner journey to a kind of fundamental, uncomplicated political esthetic." Blaise is referring to Grass's enthusiasm over the slum dwellers' ingenious ways of surviving in rows of hovels composed of industrial waste materials: "Sacks, straw mats weighed down with stones and sticks, tin rusting on tin, tires on top, flabby hoses, a car hood rolled flat. And jammed together: baskets, sieves, crates. Tied up in wire, sisal ropes. Layer on layer of chance, items found by chance—wretchedness, or wealth of a different sort." For readers who remember the "items found by chance" from which young Amsel built his scarecrows in *Hundejahre,* the aesthetic Grass discovers in the slum hovels of Calcutta is familiar.

Six collections of Grass's speeches, essays, and discussions were published in 1990, and *Gegen die verstreichende Zeit* (1991, Against the Passing Time) collected additional writings he had published from 1989 through 1991. A selection of these speeches and discussions was published in English translation as *Two States–One Nation?* (1990). The title of this collection is based on Grass's speech "Deutschland–zwei Staaten–eine Nation?" in the 1990 collection *Deutscher Lastenausgleich: Wider das dumpfe Einheitsgebot.* In February 1990 Grass debated with Rudolf Augstein, editor of *Der Spiegel* magazine. This discussion and other television and radio debates concerning the question of German unity were collected in *Deutschland, einig Vaterland?* (1990). Augstein countered Grass's objections with the statement: "The train has left, nothing can stop it." Grass asked in an open letter: "The train has left, but where is it going?"

In August 1990 Grass published *Totes Holz: Ein Nachruf* (Dead Wood: An Obituary), a volume of fifty charcoal and ink drawings of dying forests in Denmark and in East and West Germany. On foot with his dog and his graphics equipment he had spent three years collecting the sad evidence of massive forest death.

Pointed observations and brief citations, in part from government statistics, provide captions for the drawings—a passionate, graphic record documenting the decline of nature in a world oriented predominantly toward industrial growth.

In the spring of 1992 Grass published another of his fables about contemporary and, possibly, some future history. *Unkenrufe* (translated as *The Call of the Toad*, 1992) became the last of his books translated by Manheim, who died in September of that year. In *Unkenrufe*, which Herbert Mitgang (*The New York Times*, 18 November 1992) called Grass's "most linear and readable novel in recent years," the voice of an animal that folk legend associates with gloom and death expresses a subtle but unmistakable warning. This warning comes amid an appealing, heartwarming love story between Alexander Reschke, a widowed art professor from Germany, and Alexandra Piatkowska, a widowed art restorer from Poland. These two characters meet by chance on All Souls' Day, November 1989, in a market in Gdansk. Together they buy rust-red asters and late wild mushrooms and then visit a Gdansk cemetery. When Alexandra recalls how her parents, refugees from Lithuania, had wished to be buried in Wilna, Alexander ponders his parents' desire to return in death to Danzig. At this point, an idea for founding a Polish-German-Lithuanian Cemetery Association (PGLCA) in Gdansk is born to the couple. Their plan materializes, now that the borders are open not only for travel by the living but also for transport of the dead. The new "Cemetery of Reconciliation" is dedicated on the day the Polish-German border is ratified.

On a picnic, while listening to the late day call of a toad, Alexandra realizes that it is time to terminate the project, because wealthy Westerners are investing in it so eagerly that their capital threatens to retake Poland from its people. But Alexander explains that it is already too late to stop the project—that the business of selling gravesites, homesites for the aged, and golf courses and other facilities for people to enjoy even before they die will continue and can no longer be stopped. At a later stage Alexandra says, in thinking about the administrators of the company that has taken over the project planning and made merely honorary members of her and Alexander, "Now they sell us piece by piece." When the lovers die together on their honeymoon in a traffic accident near Naples, they are buried in the unmarked graves of a local cemetery.

On 14 December 1992 Grass's reading from *Unkenrufe* at the Ninety-second Street YMCA in New York was the occasion of one of his last visits, to date, in the United States. John Irving gave the introductory presentation, calling Grass "the world's greatest living writer." After Grass's reading in German, Irving read from the English translation of the novel and conducted the question-and-answer session that followed.

Following his first visit in 1964 Grass has returned to the United States for at least eleven visits. In 1965 and 1976 he received honorary doctorates from Kenyon College and Harvard University, respectively. Etchings and lithographs by Grass were exhibited in nineteen countries during the 1970s and 1980s. Grass's books have been translated into thirty-four languages. Concerned about the difficulties facing his translators, Grass arranged with his publishers to hold regular conferences with translators of his major works.

Poetry is perhaps Grass's favorite literary genre, and several volumes of his selected poems have been published in English translation. Michael Hamburger has been the most frequent translator of Grass's poetry, and *Novemberland: Selected Poems 1956–1993* (1996) takes its title from a collection of thirteen sonnets Grass published in March 1993. Grass wrote these sonnets, each accompanied by a sepia drawing, in November 1992, when he also wrote his speech *Rede vom Verlust* (1992; translated as "Essay on Loss," 1993). The speech, delivered in Munich on 18 November 1992 following several murderous attacks on asylum seekers and foreigners, presents one of the author's most outspoken critiques of what he describes as the "declining democratic process in the united Germany." The poems, by contrast, mourn the losses within the strictly prescribed limitations of the sonnet form. Following early baroque tradition, each sonnet consists of two quartets and one sestet in the iambic rhythm of the alexandrine, mostly in alternating rhymes.

The first-person speaker of the poems prefers the plural form "we" and "us" but on occasion refers pointedly to the burden of guilt, "for which I am accountable." The motifs characterizing his "Novemberland" include the beauty of the hills widely spread "as if in travel leaflets," the November dead, Poland, All Souls' Day with open graves, storm warnings, influenza epidemic, anticipation of the first advent, newspapers drifting under wind and hail showers alluding to the journalists' hour zero: unification. The lyrical images within the confines of the narrow sonnet form let readers stumble all the harder over tough conclusions such as this one: "Auf Siegers Seite lebten wir, behütet und getrennt, / bis uns die Einheit schlug, die keine Gnade kennt" (On the victor's side we lived, divided, safe from stress, / till unity struck us and proved merciless).

In 1997 Grass presented quite a different affirmation of his love for poetry and pictures. *Fundsachen für Nichtleser* (Found Objects for Nonreaders) is dedicated to "meine Enkelkinder in wachsender Zahl" (my grandchildren in growing number). It includes 131 short poems with 116 watercolors. These works clearly represent another version of Grass's "items found by chance" such as the materials Amsel used for his scarecrows, or the articles that compose the slum hovels in Calcutta.

Fundsachen für Nichtleser remains untranslated—not because the short poems, sometimes reminiscent of haiku, could not be translated, but because they are inscribed in the watercolors and are intrinsic parts of the pictures. Grass names the images "Aquadichte" (from *Aquarell* and *Gedichte*) or "aqua-poems," thus expressing their inseparable nature. A sample illustrates the effect of this poetry: "Moist in Moist / until the hard objects, / the hammer, the pliers / the nail are melting down, / and quickly, / before the color dries, / few words made to flow . . . / aqua-poems—listen to me, please, / do not look away." It is one thing to read the words in print but quite another to see them happen in colors.

Grass's *Fundsachen* are no surrealistic objets trouvés but rather ordinary things one uses or sees every day, at home or at work, inside or outside. Yet, these familiar items presented in quick-drying brush strokes of saturated watercolor acquire new impact and dynamism. Some objects, such as a collection of buttons from the sewing basket, speak with each other—"speaking all for themselves, at once." Though written for "nonreaders" and dedicated to grandchildren, *Fundsachen für Nichtleser* requires the ability to read and listen.

Publication of Grass's major novel of the 1990s, *Ein weites Feld* (1995; translated as *Too Far Afield,* 2000) preceded *Fundsachen für Nichtleser* by two years. In late 1992 Grass had begun work on what was to be a panorama of German history from the failed March revolution of 1848 to the present. The actual narrated time extends from the fall of the Berlin Wall (November 1989) to the reunification of Germany. The action is set for the most part in Berlin, particularly in the *Haus der Ministerien*—the site of government administration for the former GDR, the former Third Reich aviation center under Hermann Göring, and finally the seat of the Bonn *Treuhand* institution for "unwinding" all state property in the GDR—which serves as a focus of political change.

Ever since *Zunge zeigen* it was apparent that Grass had become fascinated with the life and career of the writer Theodor Fontane, who as a journalist had taken part in military campaigns until the "unification" of Germany under Bismarck in 1871. Fontane's gifts as a writer of socially critical novels and as a contemporary theater critic did not surface until the last two decades of his life. The title of *Ein weites Feld* alludes to the dictum "that is too wide a field," spoken by the aristocrat father of Fontane's tragic character Effi Briest in the 1895 novel by that name.

The main character of Grass's novel, Theo Wuttke, nicknamed "Fonty," reincarnates Fontane by recalling nineteenth-century events from his lifetime and writings in the context of life in twentieth-century Berlin. Fonty, a former cultural attaché, runs document errands in the "House of Ministries" guarded by a professional government spy. Hoftaller (modeled on the spy Tallhover, created by Grass's colleague Hans Joachim Schädlich) becomes Fonty's "day-and-night shadow." Fonty, his wife, and Hoftaller (an unavoidable yet sometimes useful evil) experience events from the viewpoint of former GDR citizens after the borders have been opened. With his sons having left for careers in the West, Fonty's beloved daughter marries a Western entrepreneur. His own moves, including an attempt to flee the country, are effectively controlled by Hoftaller's blackmail strategies, as the spy threatens to make revelations about Fonty's past.

One of these revelations is the existence of Madeleine, Fonty's granddaughter from a wartime affair during his service in France. Thanks to the maneuverings of Hoftaller, Fonty's granddaughter is united with him in Berlin. "La petite," as she is called, not only speaks fluent and charming German but also is familiar with all the writings of Fonty's nineteenth-century past. When Fonty's wife and daughter move permanently to the West to take over the business left behind by a son-in-law, Fonty suddenly disappears after having delivered a public speech. All searches of his colleagues in the archives of the *Treuhand* are fruitless—until Hoftaller finds Fonty riding the Ferris wheels with Madeleine on the Berlin fairground. The two men part, going in different directions. A postcard informs the archivists about the contented existence of Fonty and his granddaughter in a French region devoid of humans, but with an end of "the field" in sight.

The eight-hundred-page novel outraged some critics in Germany. Even before people had a chance to buy or read it, devastating reviews appeared in major newspapers. *Der Spiegel* (21 August 1995) featured a cover showing the literary critic Marcel Reich-Ranicki tearing up the book. In a six-page open letter to Grass, Reich-Ranicki maintained, among other reasons for his objections to the book, that it is unclear which letters and documents ascribed to Fonty are actually Fontane's and which are Grass's inventions. Generally, the novel was criticized as boring, one-sided, and an imposition on the reader. Reviewers considered Fonty a hopelessly confused character who has understood nothing about the historical developments during the last decade of the twentieth century. The judgment of the newspaper critics, however, ended up sparking the curiosity of readers. Despite (and in part because of) the initial outrage of critics, analysis of this fable about German history is continuing. Kjell Espmark, in his 2001 study of the history of the Nobel Prize in Literature, points out that the announcement of the 1999 prize for Grass, while calling special attention to *Die Blechtrommel*, "refused to share the politically biased German view of *Ein weites Feld*."

The American edition of Grass's retrospective *Mein Jahrhundert* is missing the author's watercolors that accompany the first German edition of 1999. Although not vital to the one hundred stories in the book (one for each year of the century), these watercolors provide structures that let the reader pause and think. For instance, portions of the centennial bonfire on the cover, which is burning up the 1900s, occur at intervals throughout the book: between 1961 (the year the Berlin Wall was erected) and 1962 (the year the Adolf Eichmann trials were held), or between 1945 (the year World War II ended) and 1946.

First reviews of the book were not enthusiastic. Peter Gay (*The New York Times Book Review*, 19 December 1999), referring to the book as a novel, found it to be a "collection of fragments that fail to cohere." Yet, much as readers might want to see *Mein Jahrhundert* as a novel–preferably with a happy outcome–reality, especially in a multifarious retrospective, does not cohere. The annals in *Mein Jahrhundert* consist of memories by different witnesses, stories or "black fables," strung together on a timeline. They offer a selection from the historical raw materials that–as Grass has shown in his work ever since the 1950s–can occasionally be shaped into novels.

The art of storytelling corresponds to the human need to make historical raw material cohere, to fill with meaning the mechanical passage of time–and, in Grass's words, "to write against the current of time." According to one of his translated poems from *Ausgefragt*, writing presents "Chaos / more skillfully executed." But this attempt to create order from the chaos necessarily includes revealing its logical rifts, gaps, and grotesque inconsistencies. Grass accentuates those gaps and inconsistencies by letting witnesses speak in retrospect, a technique that often polarizes their impressions. Erich Maria Remarque, author of *Im Westen nichts Neues* (1929; translated as *All Quiet on the Western Front*, 1929), a pacifist novel about World War I, and Ernst Jünger, author of *In Stahlgewittern* (1920; translated as *The Storm of Steel*, 1929), a novel filled with approval for World War I, both recall their different impressions in their fictitious meeting during the mid 1960s. Other polarized, imagined retrospectives include those of Brecht and Gottfried Benn in 1956, the year they both died; or the poet Paul Celan, known for his "Todesfuge" (1944, Fugue of Death) about the concentration camps of the Holocaust, in an encounter with the "silent" philosopher Heidegger, who did not speak out against the Nazi regime.

Presenting different speakers reminiscing about the same events in *Mein Jahrhundert* also raises the question of why the same facts would hold such different values in the memories of individuals. The disparities in values explain why the future of the world is so uncertain. When Grass resurrects his mother for her 103rd birthday in the year 1999 to allow her to look back at her century and forward to the new one, she draws the one conclusion that the century suggested to her: "Wenn nur nicht Krieg ist wieder . . . Erst da unten und dann überall. . . ." (If only there won't be war again . . . first down there [among the young ones] and then everywhere. . . .). This last sentence of *Mein Jahrhundert* is missing in the 1999 American edition.

In his Nobel Prize acceptance speech Grass envisioned what chances the future may hold for the literary arts "To Be Continued. . . ." This formula generated by the rise of the serialized novel in the nineteenth century holds both a promise and a command at the beginning of the twenty-first century: "Our common novel must be continued."

After the prize ceremonies in Stockholm, documented by Gerhard Steidl in a journal with photographs (2000), Grass's own work continued. In 2002 he published *Im Krebsgang: Eine Novelle* (translated as *Crabwalk*, 2002). The title and the first sentence of the work–"'Why only now?' he says, this person not to be confused with me"–indicate that Grass's choice of narrative technique and narrator are integral parts of his story. Grass applies the nonlinear spatial progression of the crab to the narrative movement in historical time, "seeming to go backward but actually scuttling sideways, and thereby working my way forward fairly rapidly." This "crabwalk" approach to time reveals a surprising coincidence of historical dates: "on 30 January 1945, fifty years to the day after the martyr's [Wilhelm Gustloff's] birth, the ship named after him began to sink, signaling the downfall of the Thousand-Year Reich, twelve years–again to the day–since the Nazis' seizure of power." This observation is the turning point of the novella, and all other "side-steps" revolve around it. Grass also chooses this fatal date for the birth of his narrator, Paul Pokriefke, thus linking Paul's life directly to the 1945 disaster when the *Wilhelm Gustloff*, with some ten thousand refugees and wounded German soldiers on board, went down in the Baltic Sea after being torpedoed by a Soviet submarine.

Paul is the son of Tulla Pokriefke, the controversial character who had featured as a spindly child among the teenage boys in *Katz und Maus* and who, in *Hundejahre*, had been unable to carry to term her first pregnancy. But Paul was born on a rescue boat during the night when the *Wilhelm Gustloff* sank. Coming ashore with her baby, the eighteen-year-old mother, whose hair had turned white within the course of a single night, tried to head west but got stuck behind Russian lines in the town of Schwerin. As Paul grew up, Tulla sent him to West Berlin to study journalism and to lodge with "aunt Jenny," the former ballerina from *Hundejahre*. Tulla hopes that her son, a journalist, will write her version of the *Wilhelm Gustloff* story. J. M. Coetzee, in a review essay for *The New York Review of Books* (12 June 2003), considered Tulla one of the most interesting characters in Grass's work, suggesting that on the societal level she represents an ethnic populism that has its own slanted, but deeply felt account of what happened in Germany in the twentieth century, an account that resents being repressed and will not go away.

The first, expository chapter of the book presents three historical protagonists in a tightening plotline: Wilhelm Gustloff, a Nazi Party leader working in Switzerland; David Frankfurter, the young Jewish medical student who assassinated Gustloff in 1936; and Aleksander Marinesko, captain of the submarine that sank the *Wilhelm Gustloff*. The events surrounding these figures are interwoven with Paul's life and those of his mother and his son, Konrad.

At the outset of each of the nine chapters of his report the narrator refers to an anonymous person, "a certain someone, who is about Mother's age" (both Tulla and Grass were born in 1927), "the old boy" or "boss" who has written himself dry, a shadowy kind of father figure, who seems to have engaged the unwilling journalist as a ghost writer and keeps prodding him along for his own purposes. Grass's self-portrait looking over the shoulder of the narrator is as recognizable and ironic as some of his graphic self-depictions. Some of the work sessions between the two even suggest that the older man may be Paul's father.

At another meeting with Paul, the elderly writer confesses that writing the story of the *Wilhelm Gustloff* should have been his task a long time ago: "Soon after the publication of that mighty tome, *Dog Years*," he should have dug through the material at his disposal, including the fate of Tulla and the Pokriefkes. He had failed to do so because, owing to the demands of the present in the mid 1960s, "he'd had it with the past," and now it was too late for him. But he had discovered the narrator among the survivors, after a long search, "like a piece of lost property." Although this relationship sounds like a metalepsis—the author meeting the character he created—saturated with irony, it can also be taken at face value, especially in conjunction with a more far-reaching self-accusation. At the outset of the fifth chapter, the "old boy" describes the hardships the refugees from East Prussia had to endure: "Never, he said, should his generation have kept silent about such misery, merely because its own sense of guilt was so overwhelming."

Paul's Internet research leads him to a website run by his own son, Konrad, who (under the influence of Tulla) glorifies the "martyrdom" not only of the people on the ship but also of Gustloff himself. A chatroom debate between Konrad, acting as Gustloff's advocate, and another young man who identifies himself with Frankfurter, leads to a meeting in which Konrad fatally shoots the other teen. After he is sentenced to seven years in juvenile detention for manslaughter, his father finds a new website dedicated to the unrepentant Konrad: "We believe in you, we will wait for you, we will follow you." The despairing narrator concludes: "It doesn't end. Never will it end."

The author, by contrast, is trying to find a measure of closure by his historically accurate, albeit novelistic account of the events surrounding the *Wilhelm Gustloff* tragedy. Moreover, the dedication of the book "in memoriam" encompasses the victims of the Holocaust as well as those of World War II and the three generations for whom the trauma of these events will not end within living memory.

In 2004 Grass dedicated another large-format volume to his children and grandchildren: *Der Schatten: Hans Christian Andersens Märchen–gesehen von Günter Grass* (The Shadow: Hans Christian Andersen's Tales–As Seen by Günter Grass). The book combines a selection of thirty tales by Andersen (in their German translation) with prints from more than a hundred lithographs done by Grass to accompany the stories. The volume received an enthusiastic welcome in Denmark.

In August 2006, weeks before the scheduled publication of his autobiographical volume *Beim Häuten der Zwiebel* (By Peeling the Onion), Grass confessed in an interview for the German newspaper *Frankfurter Allgemeine Zeitung* that he had been a member of the Waffen SS, a combat branch that fought alongside regular military units. He was a seventeen-year-old conscript at the time, and his enlistment lasted only a few months until he was captured by American forces; but the revelation sparked much controversy. Some critics were less upset that the teenaged Grass was influenced by Nazi propaganda than by the fact that he was silent about the truth for sixty years afterward, even misleading his biographers. Other commentators even viewed the admission as a publicity stunt for the book (fueled by the fact that the publisher moved up the release date and ordered additional copies printed after the news broke).

Some critics felt that Grass's Nobel Prize should be revoked, but an article in *The New York Times* (16 August 2006) quoted Michael Sohlman, executive director of the Nobel Foundation in Stockholm, as having replied: "The decisions are absolute, and it has never happened that a prize has been revoked." Lech Walesa, Nobel Peace laureate and former president of Poland, initially called for Grass to give up his honorary citizenship in Gdansk but was later satisfied by a letter of explanation that Grass wrote to Pawel Adamowicz, mayor of Gdansk, on 20 August; in the letter, Grass said that the episode of his SS service "weighed on me heavily. . . .Only now, with age, I have found the right formula to talk about it in a wider perspective." In the *Frankfurter Allgemeine Zeitung* interview, he said: "My silence during all these years is one reason that led me to write this book. It had to come out."

It is still too early to arrive at summary conclusions about Günter Grass's place in German and world literature. Horace Engdahl, in his presentation speech for Grass's Nobel Prize, aptly formulated the merits of Grass's literary work: "You have shown that as long as literature remembers what people hasten to forget, it remains a power to be reckoned with."

Letters:
Briefe 1959–1994, by Grass and Helen Wolff, edited by Daniela Hermes (Göttingen: Steidl, 2003).

Bibliographies:
Jean M. Woods, "Günter Grass Bibliography," *West Coast Review,* 5, no. 3 (1971): 52–56; 6, no. 1 (1971): 31–40;

George A. Everett, *A Select Bibliography of Günter Grass* (New York: Burt Franklin, 1974);

Patrick O'Neill, *Günter Grass: A Bibliography 1955–1975* (Toronto: University of Toronto Press, 1976).

References:
Scott H. Abbott, "Günter Grass' *Hundejahre:* A Realistic Novel about Myth," *German Quarterly,* 55 (1982): 212–220;

Susan C. Anderson, *Grass and Grimmelshausen: Günter Grass's "Das Treffen in Telgte" and Rezeptionstheorie* (Columbia, S.C.: Camden House, 1987);

Peter Arnds, *Representation, Subversion, and Eugenics in Günter Grass's* The Tin Drum (Rochester, N.Y.: Camden House, 2004);

H. E. Beyersdorf, "The Narrator as Artful Deceiver: Aspects of Narrative Perspective in *Die Blechtrommel,*" *Germanic Review,* 55 (1980): 129–138;

Wesley V. Blomster, "The Documentation of a Novel: Otto Weininger and *Hundejahre* by Günter Grass," *Monatshefte,* 61 (1969): 122–138;

Philip Brady, Timothy McFarland, and John J. White, eds., *Günter Grass's "Der Butt": Sexual Politics and the Male Myth of History* (Oxford: Clarendon Press, 1990);

James C. Bruce, "The Motif of Failure and the Act of Narrating in Günter Grass's *Örtlich Betäubt,*" *Modern Fiction Studies,* 17, no. 1 (1971): 45–60;

Lester Caltvedt, "Oskar's Account of Himself: Narrative 'Guilt' and the Relationship of Fiction to History in *Die Blechtrommel,*" *Seminar,* 14 (1978): 284–294;

Mark E. Cory, "Sisyphus and the Snail: Metaphors for the Political Process in Günter Grass' *Aus dem Tagebuch einer Schnecke* and *Kopfgeburten oder Die Deutschen sterben aus,*" *German Studies Review,* 6 (1983): 519–533;

W. G. Cunliffe, "Aspects of the Absurd in Günter Grass," *Wisconsin Studies,* 7, no. 3 (1966): 311–327;

Cunliffe, *Günter Grass* (New York: Twayne, 1969);

Subhoranjan Dasgupta, *The Tin Drummer's Odyssey: Essays on Günter Grass* (Calcutta: Dasgupta, 2002);

Antoinette T. Delaney, *Metaphors in Grass' Die Blechtrommel* (New York: Peter Lang, 2004);

Edward Diller, *A Mythic Journey: Günter Grass's "Tin Drum"* (Lexington: University Press of Kentucky, 1974);

Thomas Di Napoli, "Guilt and Absolution: The Contrary World of Günter Grass," *Cross Currents* (Winter 1977): 435–446;

Manfred Durzak, "Günter Grass," in *West German Poets on Society and Politics,* edited by Karl H. Van D'Elden (Detroit: Wayne State University Press, 1979), pp. 162–179;

Kjell Espmark, *Litteraturpriset: Hundra år med Nobels uppdrag* (Stockholm: Norstedt, 2001);

Martin Esslin, "Günter Grass the Dramatist," in his *Reflections: Essays on Modern Theatre* (New York: Doubleday, 1969), pp. 143–150;

"Germany's Günter Grass," *Time* (13 April 1970): 69–78;

Michael Hamburger, "Moralist and Jester: The Poetry of Günter Grass," in his *Art as Second Nature: Occasional Pieces, 1950–1974* (Cheadle: Carcanet New Press, 1975), pp. 134–149;

Ronald Hayman, *Günter Grass* (London & New York: Methuen, 1985);

Michael Hollington, *Günter Grass: The Writer in a Pluralist Society* (London & New York: Marion Boyars, 1980);

John Irving, "Günter Grass: King of the Toy Merchants," in his *Trying To Save Piggy Sneed* (New York: Arcade, 1996), pp. 397–432;

Martin Kämpchen, ed., *My Broken Love: Günter Grass in India and Bangladesh* (New Delhi & New York: Viking, 2001);

Alan Frank Keele, *Understanding Günter Grass* (Columbia: University of South Carolina Press, 1988);

Stephen Kinzer, "Günter Grass: Germany's Last Heretic," *New York Times Book Review,* 22 October 1995, p. 47;

Richard H. Lawson, *Günter Grass* (New York: Ungar, 1985);

Irène Leonard, *Günter Grass* (New York: Barnes & Noble, 1974);

Ann L. Mason, *The Skeptical Muse: A Study of Günter Grass' Conception of the Artist* (Bern: Herbert Lang, 1974);

Sigrid Mayer, "Günter Grass in Calcutta and the Aesthetics of Poverty," in *Intertextuality: German Literature and Visual Art from the Renaissance to the Twentieth Century,* edited by Ingeborg Hoesterey and Ulrich Weisstein (Columbia, S.C.: Camden House, 1993), pp. 142–158;

Siegfried Mews, "Grass' *Kopfgeburten:* The Writer in Orwell's Decade," *German Studies Review,* 6 (1983): 501–517;

Mews, ed., *"The Fisherman and His Wife": Günter Grass's "The Flounder" in Critical Perspective* (New York: AMS Press, 1983);

Keith Miles, *Günter Grass* (London: Vision / New York: Barnes & Noble, 1975);

Janice Mouton, "Gnomes, Fairy-Tale Heroes, and Oskar Matzerath," *Germanic Review,* 56 (1981): 28–33;

"Nobel Prize Winner Explains Nazi Service," CNN.com, 22 August 2006 <http://www.cnn.com/2006/SHOWBIZ/books/08/22/poland.guentergrass.ap/index.html?section=cnn_topstorie>;

Patrick O'Neill, *Günter Grass Revisited* (New York: Twayne, 1999);

O'Neill, ed., *Critical Essays on Günter Grass* (Boston: G. K. Hall, 1987);

Heinz D. Osterle, "An Orwellian Decade? Günter Grass Between Despair and Hope (with a Campaign Speech of 1983)," *German Studies Review,* 8 (1985): 481–507;

Gertrud Bauer Pickar, "*Silberpappeln* and *Saatkartoffeln:* The Interaction of Art and Reality in Grass' *Die Plebejer proben den Aufstand,*" in *Theatrum Mundi: Essays on German Drama and German Literature,* edited by Edward R. Haymes (Munich: Fink, 1980), pp. 198–220;

Pickar, ed., *Adventures of a Flounder: Critical Essays on Günter Grass' "Der Butt"* (Munich: Fink, 1982);

Julian Preece, *The Life and Work of Günter Grass: Literature, History, Politics* (Houndmills, Basingstoke & New York: Palgrave, 2001);

John Reddick, "Action and Impotence: Günter Grass's *örtlich betäubt,*" *Modern Language Review,* 67 (1972): 563–578;

Reddick, *The "Danzig Trilogy" of Günter Grass* (London: Secker & Warburg / New York: Harcourt Brace Jovanovich, 1975);

Alan Riding, "Nobelist is Bedeviled by SS Past," *New York Times,* 17 August 2006: B1, B8;

David Roberts, "The Historikerstreit, the Self-Understanding of the Federal Republic and the Self-Understanding of a Generation: Jürgen Habermas and Günter Grass," *Thesis Eleven,* 28 (1991): 33–55;

Salman Rushdie, "On Günter Grass," *Granta,* 15 (1985): 180–185;

Peter Russell, "Floundering in Feminism: The Meaning of Günter Grass's *Der Butt,*" *German Life and Letters,* 33 (April 1980): 245–256;

Richard Erich Schade, "Poet and Artist: Iconography in Grass' *Treffen in Telgte,*" *German Quarterly,* 55 (1982): 200–211;

M. K. Sosnoski, "Oskar's Hungry Witch," *Modern Fiction Studies,* 17, no. 1 (1971): 61–77;

George Steiner, "A Note on Günter Grass," in his *Language and Silence* (New York: Atheneum, 1967), pp. 110–117;

Kurt Lothar Tank, *Günter Grass,* translated by John Conway (New York: Ungar, 1969);

Noel Thomas, *The Narrative Works of Günter Grass* (Amsterdam & Philadelphia: John Benjamins, 1982);

William Underhill, "Murky Conscience," *Newsweek,* 18 August 2006 <http://www.msnbc.msn.com/id/14417128/site/newsweek>;

John Updike, "Snail on the Stump," *New Yorker* (15 October 1973): 182–185;

Alexander Weber, *Günter Grass's Use of Baroque Literature* (Leeds: W. S. University of London, 1995);

Ray Lewis White, *Günter Grass in America: The Early Years* (Hildesheim & New York: Olms, 1981);

A. Leslie Willson, ed., *A Günter Grass Symposium* (Austin: University of Texas Press, 1971).

Papers:
The Günter Grass Archive is in the Deutsches Literaturarchiv (German Literature Archives), Marbach am Neckar, Germany.

1999 Nobel Prize in Literature Presentation Speech

by Dr. Horace Engdahl, Member of the Swedish Academy, Secretary of its Nobel Committee

Your Majesties, Your Royal Highness, Ladies and Gentlemen,

These days, we often hear talk of the diminishing importance of literature. We are told that it has been reduced to entertainment or to a hobby for an isolated elite. But just as a philosopher in ancient Greece, wishing to reject the Eleatic theory that motion is impossible, simply walked about in front of the Eleatics meeting place in the hall of pillars, so having Günter Grass present is enough to make us realize that literature will not easily be pushed to the margin.

Publication of *The Tin Drum* meant a second birth for the German novel of the twentieth century. Not since Thomas Mann's *Buddenbrooks* had a first book caused such a stir. This kind of attention has its price. Just like Mann, Grass later met with the reproach that, after being so loved by readers and critics, he had the audacity to write . . . differently. In Thomas Mann's case, this reproach turned up even in the Swedish Academy's citation for his Nobel Prize in 1929. The 1999 citation contains no such reservation.

To the merits of Günter Grass belong not only his creation of a narrative carnival like *The Tin Drum,* but also the fact that he hasn't spent his life trying to repeat this feat. Time and again, he has left behind the established critical measures of his greatness and ventured with astonishing liberty into new undertakings. He has set himself above prohibitions and expectations, esthetical as well as political. He continues to do so in the newest texts that have come from his workshop.

It's often said that, with *The Tin Drum,* Grass saved a vanished world from oblivion—the town of Danzig as it existed before the Nazis and the war. But readers intent on a magical time tour should perhaps rather read *Cat and Mouse,* the short story in which the friendships of boyhood are recalled with the keenness of loss and guilt. *The Tin Drum,* however, is something else. It seems to stage the very march of history with a formidable array of characters and tall stories. But everything is viewed from an unusually low position a yard above the ground. *The Tin Drum* has its temper from a first person narrator who resembles nothing in literature or on earth. Regardless of all the tricksters of folklore, regardless of mythical infants equipped with the wisdom of old men, regardless of Shakespeare's Puck and Hoffmann's Kleinzach, Oskar Matzerath is a completely original creation: an infernal intelligence in the body of a three-year old, a monster who victoriously approaches mankind with the aid of a tin drum, an intellectual with infantility as his critical method. If, as one voice in the novel suggests, our time could wear the motto "Mysticism, barbarism, gloom," then Oskar is its sworn enemy. From Dadaism and other cheerfully destructive avant-garde groups of the beginning of our century, he has inherited the creative irreverence, but, unlike them, hasn't jettisoned reason.

Other German writers—I'm thinking of Arno Schmidt and Heinrich Böll—portrayed the collapse of human values as apocalypse or tragedy. Grass preferred a literary method more akin to the one adopted by the anonymous parodist who, sometime after Homer, depicted martial heroism as the battle between the frogs and the mice. Grass broke the spell that lay over the German past and sabotaged the German sublime, the taste for the somberly blazing magnificence of foredoomed destruction. This was an achievement far more radical than all the ideological criticism directed against Nazism. Grass's novels strip their characters of grand words and emphasize the solidity of the flesh by bringing human forms close to the animal world. We all have a place in his menagerie of cat and mouse, dog, snail, flounder, frog and scarecrow.

The different books that followed—the feverish *Dog Years,* the patiently arguing diary novels from the period when the author was engaged in party politics, the great fables of the seventies and eighties and so on—taught us to read in a new way, with our ears and stomachs just as much as with our eyes and brains. Günter Grass in his expansive phrases brings together not only the high and the low but also the subject and its distorted representation in general opinion, that spiteful mutter for which no one is responsible and of which no one is innocent. His text displays not the homophony of letters but the polyphony of orality, like a noisy inn where a voice is raised without necessarily silencing friends and opponents. His irony has as many shades as his graphic prints.

The major codes of his work—animals and food—meet in *The Flounder,* a great novel of the formation and malformation of civilization. The author musters the courage to engage in a dialogue with feminism, and attempts a new version of the history of progress, here told as the story of how eminent female cooks taught the people to feed on appetizing and wholesome dishes. With the serious motto that you mustn't cook without historical consciousness, Grass develops a mode of thinking one would like to call *gastrosophy.*

In his much-debated *Ein weites Feld*—Grass takes the daring step of giving an undramatic view of the relationship between the henchmen of totalitarianism and its victims. He plays off the eternal humanist against the eternal police informer, sympathetic understanding against the endless inquisition that keeps prying into old mistakes even beyond the grave. Of the two main characters he says: "Seen from the front, they looked very ill-matched, from behind however, as fitting to each other as two pieces of a jigsaw puzzle." There is something so hilariously insolent, independent and relativistic in Grass's rendering of life in Berlin around the Fall of the Wall, that he was bound to infuriate many readers of his home country.

Günter Grass! Your sense of proportion has done mankind a genuine service. Your new book has the title *Mein Jahrhundert*—My Century. The fact that you are receiving the twentieth century's last Nobel Literature Prize is confirmation of the reasonableness of such a title. In your cavalcade of the past hundred years, you give ample proof of your uncanny ability to impersonate the voices of the thoughtless: all those bewitched by the hopes of politics and technology, rendered stupid by the great perspectives. The core of thoughtlessness is enthusiasm. I read *Mein Jahrhundert* as a critique of enthusiasm and a celebration of its opposite, a good memory. Your style, with its repetitions and specifications and stratification of different voices, tells us that we shall not be in a hurry either when dealing with the past or when dealing with the future. You have shown that as long as literature remembers what people hasten to forget, it remains a power to be reckoned with.

I would like to express the warm congratulations of the Swedish Academy as I now request you to receive the Nobel Prize for Literature from the hands of His Majesty the King.

[© The Nobel Foundation, 1999.]

Grass: Banquet Speech

Grass's speech at the Nobel Banquet, 10 December 1999:

Eure Majestäten und Ihre Königliche Hoheit, hocherfreute Preistäger, werte Gäste,

Lange ist's her. Mitte September 1964 traf sich in der Nähe Stockholms, nämlich in Sigtuna, die "Gruppe 47," eine Vereinigung deutschsprachiger Schriftsteller, die sich nach Ende des Zweiten Weltkrieges gefunden hatte; oder besser: die der Einladung des Schriftstellers Hans Werner Richter gefolgt waren. Fortan lud er immer wieder junge Autoren zu den alljährlichen Treffen ein. So kam auch ich Mitte der fünfziger Jahre dazu. So war auch ich in Schweden dabei, als uns Gustav Korlén im Namen der Stockholmer Universität eingeladen hatte. Es war eine bewegte, literarisch streitbare Tagung. Wir lasen uns aus Manuskripten vor. Auch schwedische Schriftsteller waren dabei. Es sah so aus, als könne das zerrissene Band zwischen zwei Literaturen wieder geknüpft werden.

Deshalb möchte ich nun–in Erinnerung an die Tagung in Sigtuna–meines literarischen Mentors, Hans Werner Richter, der 1993 hochbetagt gestorben ist, dankbar gedenken. Er hat mir, dem jungen, ganz auf sich bedachten Autor, Toleranz beigebracht; ich lernte von ihm das aufmerksame Zuhören; dem Einzelgänger, der ich war, wurde durch ihn Kollegialität vermittelt. Auch ermunterte er mich, den Bürger im Schriftsteller zu Wort kommen zu lassen, und das nicht nur in Wahlkampfzeiten.

Damals, in Sigtuna, las ich den Kollegen aus dem Manuskript meines deutschen Trauerspiels "Die Plebejer proben den Aufstand" vor. Noch heute hallt in mir die Debatte nach, die meine streitbaren Dialoge ausgelöst hatten.

Das alles geschah in einem gastlichen Land, umgeben von schwedischen Freunden, die dem Wortgefecht der deutschsprachigen Gäste mit einigem Erstaunen zugehört haben mögen. Und weil ich mir gewiss bin, dass die mir heute erwiesene Ehre auch meinem literarischen Mentor und der deutschsprachigen Literatur gilt, erhebe ich mein Glas im Gedenken an Hans Werner Richter und mit freundschaftlichem Gruss an Gustav Korlén. –Übrigens fand ich in Sigtuna, während Pausen im literarischen Streit, herrliche Pilze, unter ihnen Steinpilze, die auf Schwedisch "Karl Johanssvamp" heissen.

[© The Nobel Foundation, 1999. Günter Grass is the sole author of his speech.]

Translation by Rebecca Hughes

Your Majesty and Your Highness, elated laureates, worthy guests,

It's been a long time. In mid-September of 1964 I was near Stockholm, namely in Sigtuna, part of Gruppe 47, a consortium of German-speaking writers founded after the end of World War II; or better still: writers acting on the invitation of author Hans Werner Richter. Henceforth he invited young authors to join this union of writers of all ages. So I, too, found myself there in the middle of the 1950s. As a result, I was also in Sweden when Gustav Korlén, in the name of Stockholm University, extended an invitation. It was eventful: a literary, disputatious conference. We read our manuscripts. Swedish writers were also in attendance. It appeared that the severed tether between two literatures could be repaired.

Because of that–in remembrance of the conference in Sigtuna–I would now like to celebrate with thanks my literary mentor, the late Hans Werner Richter, who passed with much esteem in 1993. He guided me, the young, self-absorbed author, to tolerance; from him I learned to listen attentively; the loner in me was able to learn teamwork because of him.

He also encouraged me to let the commoner speak through the author's words, and not only in times of campaigning. At that time in Sigtuna I read to my colleagues from the manuscript of my German tragedy "The Plebeians Rehearse the Uprising." The debate triggered by my controversial dialogues still resonates within me today.

All of this happened in a convivial nation, surrounded by Swedish friends, who probably listened to the bickering of their German guests with at least a bit of astonishment. And because I myself am certain that the honor given to me today also belongs to my literary mentor as well as German literature, I raise my glass to the memory of Hans Werner Richter and with friendly greetings to Gustav Korlén. —By the way, in Sigtuna, during the breaks in our literary battle, I discovered some exquisite mushrooms, among them porcini, which are called "Karl Johannssvamp" in Swedish.

Press Release: The Nobel Prize in Literature 1999

from the Office of the Permanent Secretary of the Swedish Academy, 30 September 1999

Günter Grass

"Whose frolicsome black fables portray the forgotten face of history"

When Günter Grass published *The Tin Drum* in 1959 it was as if German literature had been granted a new beginning after decades of linguistic and moral destruction. Within the pages of this, his first novel, Grass recreated the lost world from which his creativity sprang, Danzig, his home town, as he remembered it from the years of his infancy before the catastrophe of war. Here he comes to grips with the enormous task of reviewing contemporary history by recalling the disavowed and the forgotten: the victims, losers and lies that people wanted to forget because they had once believed in them. At the same time the novel breaks the bounds of realism by having as its protagonist and narrator an infernal intelligence in the body of a three-year-old, a monster who overpowers the fellow human beings he approaches with the help of a toy drum. The unforgettable Oskar Matzerath is an intellectual whose critical approach is childishness, a one-man carnival, dadaism in action in everyday German provincial life just when this small world becomes involved in the insanity of the great world surrounding it. It is not too audacious to assume that *The Tin Drum* will become one of the enduring literary works of the 20th century.

Günter Grass has described himself as a "Spätaufklärer," a belated apostle of enlightenment in an era that has grown tired of reason. He is a fabulist and a scholarly lecturer, recorder of voices and presumptuous monologist, pasticheur and at the same time creator of an ironic idiom that he alone commands. In his mastery of German syntax and his readiness to exploit its labyrinthine subtleties he recalls Thomas Mann. His writing constitutes a dialogue with the great traditions of German culture, conducted with punctilious affection.

After *The Tin Drum,* Grass returned to the theme of Danzig in two very different works. *Cat and Mouse* is an austere narrative that shows how the magical friendship of boyhood comes to grief when war games encounter the reality of combat. *Dog Years* is Grass's most modernist work, a text with no determinable centre, an arena for voices and a meeting place for fevered dreams that turn out to coincide with life.

In other novels Grass adopted a discursive approach, pleading for doubt and the will to do good. In public debate in Germany he is a source of strength and of irritation, but for major literary figures in the world at large such as García Márquez, Rushdie, Gordimer, Lobo Antunes and Kenzaburo Oe he is an admired predecessor.

His novel *The Flounder* involves a return to the grand style in his writing, taking the form of a global history crammed with truthful yarns and hot-tempered ideological discussions. Grass portrays the development of civilisation as a struggle between men's destructive dreams of grandeur and female accomplishment. The outcome is uncertain. As the counsellor of the women, the talking flounder, recruited from the Grimm brothers, constitutes an Absolute Idea that would have been inconceivable to Hegel. The narrator himself, on the other hand, remains a notoriously unreliable male individual, preserving the margin of mischief without which art dies.

Both of the protagonists in *Ein weites Feld,* the eternal humanist and the eternal informer, enact the relationship of artistic imagination to political power against the background of Wilhelmine Germany and today's Federal Republic. The novel has been a source of contention for German literary critics, but it confirms the author's position as the great prober of the history of this century. His most recent work, *My Century,* is a running commentary on the 20th century with a particularly keen eye for stupefying enthusiasms. In his excavation of the past Günter Grass goes deeper than most and he unearths the intertwined roots of good and evil. As *Dog Years* puts it: "While God was still at school, in the heavenly playground he came up with the idea of creating the world, together with his schoolmate, the talented little Devil."

[© The Nobel Foundation, 1999.]

Grass: Nobel Lecture, 7 December 1999

"To Be Continued . . ."
(Translated from German by Michael Henry Heim)

Honoured Members of the Swedish Academy, Ladies and Gentlemen:

Having made this announcement, nineteenth-century works of fiction would go on and on. Magazines and newspapers gave them all the space they wished: the serialized novel was in its heyday. While the early chapters appeared in quick succession, the core of the work was being written out by hand, and its conclusion was yet to be conceived. Nor was it only trivial horror stories or tearjerkers that thus held the reader in thrall. Many of Dickens' novels came out in serial form, in instalments. Tolstoy's *Anna Karenina* was a serialized novel. Balzac's time, a tireless provider of mass-produced serializations, gave the still anonymous writer lessons in the technique of suspense, of building to a climax at the end of a column. And nearly all Fontane's novels appeared first in newspapers and magazines as serializations. Witness the publisher of the *Vossische Zeitung*, where *Trials and Tribulations* first saw print, who exclaimed in a rage, "Will this sluttish story never end!"

But before I go on spinning these strands of my talk or move on to others, I wish to point out that from a purely literary point of view this hall and the Swedish Academy that invited me here are far from alien to me. My novel *The Rat*, which came out almost fourteen years ago and whose catastrophic course along various oblique levels of narration one or two of my readers may recall, features a eulogy delivered before just such an audience as you, an encomium to the rat or, to be more precise, the laboratory rat.

The rat has been awarded a Nobel Prize. At last, one might say. She's been on the list for years, even the short list. Representative of millions of experimental animals—from guinea pig to rhesus monkey—the white-haired, red-eyed laboratory rat is finally getting her due. For she more than anyone—or so claims the narrator of my novel—has made possible all the Nobelified research and discoveries in the field of medicine and, as far as Nobel Laureates Watson and Crick are concerned, on the virtually boundless turf of gene manipulation. Since then maize and other vegetables—to say nothing of all sorts of animals—can be cloned more or less legally, which is why the rat-men, who increasingly take over as the novel comes to a close, that is, during the post-human era, are called Watsoncricks. They combine the best of both genera. Humans have much of the rat in them and vice versa. The world seems to use the synthesis to regain its health. After the Big Bang, when only rats, cockroaches, flies, and the remains of fish and frog eggs survive and it is time to make order out of the chaos, the Watsoncricks, who miraculously escape, do more than their share.

But since this strand of the narrative could as easily have ended with "To Be Continued . . ." and the Nobel Prize speech in praise of the laboratory rat is certainly not meant to give the novel a happy end, I can now—as what might be called a matter of principle— turn to narration as a form of survival as well as a form of art.

People have always told tales. Long before humanity learned to write and gradually became literate, everybody told tales to everybody else and everybody listened to everybody else's tales. Before long it became clear that some of the still illiterate storytellers told more and better tales than others, that is, they could make more people believe their lies. And there were those among them who found artful ways of stemming the peaceful flow of their tales and diverting it into a tributary, that, far from drying up, turned suddenly and amazingly into a broad bed, though now full of flotsam and jetsam, the stuff of subplots. And because these primordial storytellers—who were not dependent upon day or lamp light and could carry on perfectly well in the dark, who were in fact adept at exploiting dusk or darkness to add to the suspense—because they stopped at nothing, neither dry stretches nor thundering waterfalls, except perhaps to interrupt the course of action with a "To Be Continued . . ." if they sensed their audience's attention flagging, many of their listeners felt moved to start telling tales of their own.

What tales were told when no one could yet write and therefore no one wrote them down? From the days of Cain and Abel there were tales of murder and manslaughter. Feuds—blood feuds, in particular—were always good for a story. Genocide entered the picture quite early along with floods and droughts, fat years and lean years. Lengthy lists of cattle and slaves were perfectly acceptable, and no tale could be believable without detailed genealogies of who came before whom and who came after, heroic tales especially. Love triangles, popular even now, and tales of monsters—half man, half beast—who made their way through labyrinths or lay in wait in the bulrushes attracted mass audiences from the outset, to say nothing of legends of gods and idols and accounts of sea journeys, which were then handed down, polished, enlarged upon, modified, transmogrified into their opposites, and finally written down by a storyteller whose name was supposedly Homer or, in the case of the Bible, by a collective of storytellers. In China and Persia, in India and the Peruvian highlands, wherever writing flourished, storytellers—whether as groups or individuals, anonymously or by name—turned into literati.

Writing-fixated as we are, we nonetheless retain the memory of oral storytelling, the spoken origins of literature. And a good thing too, because if we were to forget that all storytelling comes through the lips—now inarticulate, hesitant, now swift, as if driven by fear, now in whisper, to keep the secrets revealed from reaching the wrong ears, now loudly and clearly, all the way from self-serving bluster to sniffing out the very essence of life—if our faith in writing were to make us forget all that, our storytelling would be bookish, dry as dust.

Yet how good too that we have so many books available to us and that whether we read them aloud or to ourselves they are permanent. They have been my inspiration. When I was young and malleable, masters like Melville and Döblin or Luther with his Biblical German prompted me to read aloud as I wrote, to mix ink with spit. Nor have things changed much since. Well into my fifth decade of enduring, no, relishing the moil and toil called writing, I chew tough, stringy clauses into manageable mush, babble to myself in blissful isolation, and put pen to paper only when I hear the proper tone and pitch, resonance and reverberation.

Yes, I love my calling. It keeps me company, a company whose polyphonic chatter calls for literal transcription into my manuscripts. And there is nothing I like more than to meet books of mine—books that have long since flown the coop and been expropriated by readers—when I read out loud to an audience what now lies peacefully on the page. For both the young, weaned early from language, and the old, grizzled yet still rapacious, the written word becomes spoken, and the magic works again and again. It is the shaman in the author earning a bit on the side, writing against the current of time, lying his way to tenable truths. And everyone believes his tacit promise: To Be Continued . . . .

But how did I become a writer, poet, and artist—all at once and all on frightening white paper? What homemade hubris put a child up to such craziness? After all, I was only twelve when I realized I wanted to be an artist. It coincided with the outbreak of the Second World War, when I was living on the outskirts of Danzig. But my first opportunity for professional development had to wait until the following year, when I found a tempting offer in the Hitler Youth magazine *Hilf mit!* (Lend a Hand). It was a story contest. With prizes. I immediately set to writing my first novel. Influenced by my mother's background, it bore the title *The Kashubians,* but the action did not take place in the painful present of that small and dwindling people; it took place in the thirteenth century during a period of interregnum, a grim period when brigands and robber barons ruled the highways and the only recourse a peasant had to justice was a kind of kangaroo court.

All I can remember of it is that after a brief outline of the economic conditions in the Kashubian hinterland I started in on pillages and massacres with a vengeance. There was so much throttling, stabbing, and skewering, so many kangaroo-court hangings and executions that by the end of the first chapter all the protagonists and a goodly number of the minor characters were dead and either buried or left to the crows. Since my sense of style did not allow me to turn corpses into spirits and the novel into a ghost story, I had to admit defeat with an abrupt end and no "To Be Continued . . . ." Not for good, of course, but the neophyte had learned his lesson: next time he would have to be a bit more gentle with his characters.

But first I read and read some more. I had my own way of reading: with my fingers in my ears. Let me say by way of explanation that my younger sister and I grew up in straitened circumstances, that is, in a two-room flat and hence without rooms of our own or even so much as a corner to ourselves. In the long run it turned out to be an advantage, though: I learned at an early age to concentrate in the midst of people or surrounded by noise. When I read I might have been under a bell jar; I was so involved in the world of the book that my mother, who liked a practical joke, once demonstrated her son's complete and utter absorption to a neighbour by replacing a roll I had been taking an occasional bite from with a bar of soap—Palmolive, I believe—whereupon the two women—my mother not without a certain pride—watched me reach blindly for the soap, sink my teeth into it, and chew it for a good minute before it tore me away from my adventure on the page.

To this day I can concentrate as I did in my early years, but I have never read more obsessively. Our books were kept in a bookcase behind blue-curtained panes of glass. My mother belonged to a book club, and the novels of Dostoevsky and Tolstoy stood side by side and mixed in with novels by Hamsun, Raabe, and Vicky Baum. Selma Lagerlöf's *Gösta Berling* was within easy reach. I later moved on to the Municipal Library, but my mother's collection provided the initial impulse. A punctilious businesswoman forced to sell her wares to unreliable customers on credit, she was also a great lover of beauty: she listened to opera and operetta, melodies on her primitive radio, enjoyed hearing my promising stories, and frequently went to the Municipal Theatre, even taking me along from time to time.

The only reason I rehearse here these anecdotes of a petty bourgeois childhood after painting them with epic strokes decades ago in works peopled by fictitious characters is to help me answer the question "What made you become a writer?" The ability to daydream at length, the job of punning and playing with language in general, the addiction to lying for its own sake rather than for mine because sticking to the truth would have been a bore—in short, what is loosely known as talent was certainly a factor, but it was the abrupt intrusion of politics into the family idyll that turned the all too flighty category of talent into a ballast with a certain permanence and depth.

My mother's favourite cousin, like her a Kashubian by birth, worked at the Polish post office of the Free City of Danzig. He was a regular at our house and always welcome. When the War broke out the Hevelius Square post office building held out for a time against the SS-Heimwehr, and my uncle was rounded up with those who finally surrendered. They were tried summarily and put before a firing squad. Suddenly he was no more. Suddenly and permanently his name was no longer mentioned. He became a non-person. Yet he must have lived on in me through the years when at fifteen I donned a uniform, at sixteen I learned what fear was, at seventeen I landed in an American POW camp, at eighteen I worked in the black market, studied to be a stone-mason and started sculpting in stone, prepared for admission to art school and wrote and drew, drew and wrote, fleet-footed verse, quizzical one-acts, and on it went until I found the material unwieldy—I seem to have an inborn need for aesthetic pleasure. And beneath the detritus of it all lay my mother's favourite cousin, the Polish postal clerk, shot and buried, only to be found by me (who else?) and exhumed and resuscitated by literary artificial respiration under other names and guises, though this time in a novel whose major and minor characters, full of life and beans as they are, make it through a number of chapters, some even holding out till the end and thus enabling the writer to keep his recurrent promise: To Be Continued . . . .

And so on and so forth. The publication of my first two novels, *The Tin Drum* and *Dog Years,* and the novella I stuck between them, *Cat and Mouse,* taught me early on, as a relatively young writer, that books can cause offence, stir up fury, even hatred, that what is undertaken out of love for one's country can be taken as soiling one's nest. From then on I have been controversial.

Which means that like writers banished to Siberia or suchlike places I am in good company. So I have no grounds to complain; on the contrary, writers should consider the condition of permanent controversiality to be invigorating, part of the risk involved in choosing the profession. It is a fact of life that writers have always and with due consideration and great pleasure spit in the soup of the high and mighty. That is what makes the history of literature analogous to the development and refinement of censorship.

The ill humour of the powers-that-be forced Socrates to drain the cup of hemlock to the dregs, sent Ovid into exile, made Seneca open his veins. For centuries and to the present day the finest fruits of the western garden of literature have graced the index of the Catholic church. How much equivocation did the European Enlightenment learn from the censorship practised by princes with absolute power? How many German, Italian, Spanish, and Portuguese writers did fascism drive from their lands and languages? How many writers fell victim to the Leninist-Stalinist reign of terror? And what constraints are writers under today in countries like China, Kenya, or Croatia?

I come from the land of book-burning. We know that the desire to destroy a hated book is still (or once more) part of the spirit of our times and that when necessary it finds appropriate telegenic expression and therefore a mass audience. What is much worse, however, is that the persecution of writers, including the threat of murder and murder itself, is on the rise throughout the world, so much so that the world has grown accustomed to the terror of it. True, the part of the world that calls itself free raises a hue and cry when, as in 1995 in Nigeria, a writer like Ken Saro-Wiwa and his supporters are sentenced to death and killed for taking a stand against the contamination of their country, but things immediately go back to normal, because ecological considerations might affect the profits of the world's number one oil colossus Shell.

What makes books—and with them writers—so dangerous that church and state, politburos and the mass media feel the need to oppose them? Silencing and worse are seldom the result of direct attacks on the reigning ideology. Often all it takes is a literary allusion to the idea that truth exists only in the plural—that there is no such thing as a single truth but only a multitude of truths—to make the defenders of one or another truth sense danger, mortal danger. Then there is the problem that writers are by definition unable to leave the past in peace: they are quick to open closed wounds, peer behind closed doors, find skeletons in the cupboard, consume sacred cows or, as in the case of Jonathan Swift, offer up Irish children, "stewed, roasted, baked, or boiled," to the kitchens of the English nobility. In other words, nothing is sacred to them, not even capitalism, and that makes them offensive, even criminal. But worst of all they refuse to make common cause with the victors of history: they take pleasure milling about the fringes of the historical process with the losers, who have plenty to say but no platform to say it on. By giving them a voice, they call the victory into question, by associating with them, they join ranks with them.

Of course the powers-that-be, no matter what period costume they may be wearing, have nothing against literature as such. They enjoy it as an ornament and even promote it. At present its role is to entertain, to serve the fun culture, to de-emphasize the negative side of things and give people hope, a light in the darkness. What is basically called for, though not quite so explicitly as during the Communist years, is a "positive hero." In the jungle of the free market economy he is likely to pave his way to success Rambo-like with corpses and a smile; he is an adventurer who is always up for a quick fuck between battles, a winner who leaves a trail of losers behind him, in short, the perfect role model for our globalized world. And the demand for the hard-boiled he-man who always lands on his feet is unfailingly met by the media: James Bond has spawned any number of Dolly-like children. Good will continue to prevail over evil as long as it assumes his cool-guy pose.

Does that make his opposite or enemy a negative hero? Not necessarily. I have my roots, as you will have noticed from your reading, in the Spanish or Moorish school of the picaresque novel. Tilting at windmills has remained a model for that school down through the ages, and the picaro's very existence derives from the comic nature of defeat. He pees on the pillars of power and saws away at the throne knowing full well he will make no dent in either: once he moves on, the exalted temple may look a bit shabby, the throne may wobble slightly, but that is all. His humour is part and parcel of his despair. While *Die Götterdämmerung* drones on before an elegant Bayreuth audience, he sits sniggering in the back row, because in his theatre comedy and tragedy go hand in hand. He scorns the fateful march of the victors and sticks his foot out to trip them, yet much as his failure makes us laugh the laughter sticks in our throat: even his wittiest cynicisms have a tragic cast to them. Besides, from the point of view of the philistine, rightist or leftist, he is a formalist—even a mannerist—of the first order: he holds the spyglass the wrong way; he sees time as a train on a siding: he puts mirrors everywhere; you can never tell whose ventriloquist he is; given his perspective, he can even accept dwarfs and giants into his entourage.

The reason Rabelais was constantly on the run from the secular police and the Holy Inquisition is that his larger-than-life Gargantua and Pantagruel had turned the world according to scholasticism on its head. The laughter they unleashed was positively infernal. When Gargantua stooped bare-arsed on the towers of Notre-Dame and pissed the length and breadth of Paris under water, everyone who did not drown guffawed. Or to go back to Swift: his modest culinary proposal for relieving the hunger in Ireland could be brought up to date if at the next economic summit the board set for the heads of state were groaning with lusciously prepared street children from Brazil or southern Sudan. Satire is the name of the art form I have in mind, and in satire everything is permitted, even tickling the funny bone with the grotesque.

When Heinrich Böll gave his Nobel Lecture here on 2 May 1973, he brought the seemingly opposing positions of reason and poetry into closer and closer proximity and bemoaned the lack of time to go into another aspect of the issue: "I have had to pass over humour, which, though no class privilege, is ignored in his poetry as a hiding place for resistance." Now Böll knew that Jean Paul, the poet in question, had a place in the German Culture Hall of Fame, little read though he is nowadays; he knew to what extent Thomas Mann's literary oeuvre was suspected—by both the right and the left—of irony at the time (and still is, I might add). Clearly what Böll had in mind was not belly-laugh humour but rather inaudible, between-the-lines humour, the chronic susceptibility to melancholy of his clown, the desperate wit of the man who collected silence, an activity, by the way, that has become quite the thing in the media and—under the guise of "voluntary self-control" on the part of the free West—a benign disguise for censorship.

By the early fifties, when I had started writing consciously, Heinrich Böll was a well-known if not always well-received author. With Wolfgang Koeppen, Günter Eich, and Arno Schmidt he stood apart from the culture industry. Post-war German literature, still young, was having a hard time with German, which had been corrupted by the Nazi regime. In addition, Böll's generation—but also the younger writers like myself—were stymied to a certain extent by a prohibition that came from Theodor Adorno: "It is barbaric to write a poem after Auschwitz, and that is why it has become impossible to write poetry today . . ."

In other words, no more "To Be Continued . . . ." Though write we did. We wrote by bearing in mind, like Adorno in his *Minima Moralia: Reflections from Damaged Life* (1951), that Auschwitz marks a rift, an unbridgeable gap in the history of civilization. It was the only way we could get round the prohibition. Even so, Adorno's writing on the wall has retained its power to this day. All the writers of my generation did public battle with it. No one had the desire or ability to keep silent. It was our duty to take the goose step out of German, to lure it out of its idylls and fogged inwardness. We, the children who had had our fingers burned, we were the ones to repudiate the absolutes, the ideological black or white. Doubt and scepticism were our godparents and the multitude of gray values their present to us. In any case, such was the asceticism I imposed on myself before discovering the richness of a language I had all too sweepingly pronounced guilty: its seducible softness, its tendency to plumb the depths, its utterly supple hardness, not to mention the sheen of its dialects, its artlessness and artfulness, its eccentricities, and beauty blossoming from its subjunctives. Having won back this capital, we invested it to make more. Despite Adorno's verdict or spurred on by it. The only way writing after Auschwitz, poetry or prose, could proceed was by becoming memory and preventing the past from coming to an end. Only then could post-war literature in German justify applying the generally valid "To Be Continued . . . " to itself and its descendants; only then could the wound be kept open and the much desired and prescribed forgetting be reversed with a steadfast "Once upon a time."

How many times when one or another interest group calls for considering what happened a closed chapter—we need to return to normalcy and put our shameful past behind us—how many times has literature resisted. And rightly so! Because it is a position as foolish as it is understandable; because every time the end of the postwar period is proclaimed in Germany—as it was ten years ago, with the Wall down and unity in the offing—the past catches up with us.

At that time, in February 1990, I gave a talk to students in Frankfurt entitled "Writing After Auschwitz." I wanted to take stock of my works book by book. In *The Diary of a Snail*, which came out in 1972 and in which past and present crisscross, but also run parallel or occasionally collide, I am asked by my sons how I define my profession, and I answer, "A writer, children, is someone who writes against the current of time." What I said to the students was: "Such a view presumes that writers are not encapsulated in isolation or the sempiternal, that they see themselves as living in the here and now, and, even more, that they expose themselves to the vicissitudes of time, that they jump in and take sides. The dangers of jumping in and taking sides are well known: The distance a writer is supposed to keep is threatened; his language must live from hand to mouth; the narrowness of current events can make him narrow and curb the imagination he has trained to run free; he runs the danger of running out of breath."

The risk I referred to then has remained with me throughout the years. But what would the profession of writer be like without risk? Granted, the writer would have the security of, say, a cultural bureaucrat, but he would be the prisoner of his fears of dirtying his hands with the present. Out of fear of losing his distance he would lose himself in realms where myths reside and lofty thoughts are all. But the present, which the past is constantly turning into, would catch up to him in the end and put him through the third degree. Because every writer is of his time, no matter how he protests being born too early or late. He does not autonomously choose what he will write about, that choice is made for him. At least I was not free to choose. Left to my own devices, I would have followed the laws of aesthetics and been perfectly happy to seek my place in texts droll and harmless.

But that was not to be. There were extenuating circumstances: mountains of rubble and cadavers, fruit of the womb of German history. The more I shovelled, the more it grew. It simply could not be ignored. Besides, I come from a family of refugees, which means that in addition to everything that drives a writer from book to book—common ambition, the fear of boredom, the mechanisms of egocentricity—I had the irreparable loss of my birthplace. If by telling tales I could not recapture a city both lost and destroyed, I could at least re-conjure it. And this obsession kept me going. I wanted to make it clear to myself and my readers, not without a bit of a chip on my shoulder, that what was lost did not need to sink into oblivion, that it could be resuscitated by the art of literature in all its grandeur and pettiness: the churches and cemeteries, the sounds of the shipyards and smells of the faintly lapping Baltic, a language on its way out yet still stable-warm and grumble-rich, sins in need of confession, and crimes tolerated if never exonerated.

A similar loss has provided other writers with a hotbed of obsessive topics. In a conversation dating back many years Salman Rushdie and I concurred that my lost Danzig was for me—like his lost Bombay for him—both resource and refuse pit, point of departure and navel of the world. This arrogance, this overkill lies at the very heart of literature. It is the condition for a story that can pull out all the stops. Painstaking detail, sensitive psychologizing, slice-of-life realism—no such techniques can handle our monstrous raw materials. As indebted as we are to the Enlightenment tradition of reason, the absurd course of history spurns all exclusively reasonable explanations.

Just as the Nobel Prize—once we divest it of its ceremonial garb—has its roots in the invention of dynamite, which like such other human headbirths as the splitting of the atom and the likewise Nobelified classification of the gene has wrought both weal and woe in the world, so literature has an explosive quality at its root, though the explosions literature releases have a delayed-action effect and change the world only in the magnifying glass of time, so to speak, it too wreaking cause for both joy and lamentation here below. How long did it take the European Enlightenment from Montaigne to Voltaire, Diderot, Kant, Lessing, and Lichtenberg to introduce a flicker of reason into the dark corners of scholasticism? And even that flicker often died in the process, a process censorship went a long way towards inhibiting. But when the light finally did brighten things up, it turned out to be the light of cold reason, limited to the technically doable, to economic and social progress, a reason that claimed to be enlightened but that merely drummed a reason-based jargon (which amounted to instructions for making progress at all costs) into its offspring, capitalism and socialism (which were at each other's throats from the word go).

Today we can see what those brilliant failures who were the Enlightenment's offspring have wrought. We can see what a dangerous position its delayed-action, word-detonated explosion has hurled us into. And if we are trying to repair the damage with Enlightenment tools, it is only because we have no others. We look on in horror as capitalism—now that his brother, socialism, has been declared dead—rages unimpeded, megalomaniacally replaying the errors of the supposedly extinct brother. It has turned the free market into dogma, the only truth, and intoxicated by its all but limitless power, plays the wildest of games, making merger after merger with no goal than to maximize profits. No wonder capitalism is proving as impervious to reform as the communism that managed to strangle itself. Globalization is its motto, a motto it proclaims with the arrogance of infallibility: there is no alternative.

Accordingly, history has come to an end. No more "To Be Continued . . . ," no more suspense. Though perhaps there is hope that if not politics, which has abdicated its decision-making power to economics, then at least literature may come up with something to cause the "new dogmatism" to falter.

How can subversive writing be both dynamite and of literary quality? Is there time enough to wait for the delayed action? Is any book capable of supplying a commodity in so short supply as the future? Is it not rather the case that literature is currently retreating from public life and that young writers are using the internet as a playground? A standstill, to which the suspicious word "communication" lends a certain aura, is making headway. Every scrap of time is planned down to the last nervous breakdown. A cultural industry vale of tears is taking over the world. What is to be done?

My godlessness notwithstanding, all I can do is bend my knee to a saint who has never failed me and cracked some of the hardest nuts. "O Holy and (through the grace of Camus) Nobelified Sisyphus! May thy stone not remain at the top of the hill, may we roll it down again and like thee continue to rejoice in it, and may the story told of the drudgery of our existence have no end. Amen."

But will my prayer be heard? Or are the rumours true? Is the new breed of cloned creature destined to assure the continuation of human history?

Which brings me back to the beginning of my talk. Once more I open *The Rat* to the fifth chapter, in which the laboratory rat, representing millions of other laboratory animals in the cause of research, wins the Nobel Prize, and I am reminded how few prizes have been awarded to projects that would rid the world of the scourge of mankind: hunger. Anyone who can pay the price can get a new pair of kidneys. Hearts can be transplanted. We can phone anywhere in the world wire-free. Satellites and space stations orbit us solicitously. The latest weapon systems, conceived and developed, they too, on the basis of award-winning research, can help their masters to keep death at bay. Anything the human mind comes up with finds astonishing applications. Only hunger seems to resist. It is even increasing. Poverty deeply rooted shades into misery. Refugees are flocking all over the world accompanied by hunger. It takes political will paired with scientific know-how to root out misery of such magnitude, and no one seems resolved to undertake it.

In 1973, just when terror—with the active support of the United States—was beginning to strike in Chile, Willy Brandt spoke before the United Nations General Assembly, the first German chancellor to do so. He brought up the issue of worldwide poverty. The applause following his exclamation "Hunger too is war!" was stunning.

I was present when he gave the speech. I was working on my novel *The Flounder* at the time. It deals with the very foundations of human existence including food, the lack and superabundance thereof, great gluttons and untold starvelings, the joys of the palate and crusts from the rich man's table.

The issue is still with us. The poor counter growing riches with growing birth rates. The affluent north and west can try to screen themselves off in security-mad fortresses, but the flocks of refugees will catch up with them: no gate can withstand the crush of the hungry.

The future will have something to say about all this. Our common novel must be continued. And even if one day people stop or are forced to stop writing and publishing, if books are no longer available, there will still be storytellers giving us mouth-to-ear artificial respiration, spinning old stories in new ways: loud and soft, heckling and halting, now close to laughter, now on the brink of tears.

[© The Nobel Foundation, 1999. Günter Grass is the sole author of the text.]

Knut Hamsun
(4 August 1859 - 19 February 1952)

Harald Næss
University of Wisconsin–Madison

This entry was expanded by Næss from his Hamsun entry in *DLB 297: Twentieth-Century Norwegian Writers.*

BOOKS: *Den Gaadefulde: En Kjærlighedshistorie fra Nordland,* as Kn. Pedersen (Tromsø: Urdal, 1877);

Bjørger: Fortælling, as Knud Pedersen Hamsund (Bodø: A. F. Knudsen, 1878; Brooklyn, N.Y.: Knudsen Printing and Publishing, 1925);

Fra det moderne Amerikas Aandsliv (Copenhagen: Philipsen, 1889); edited and translated by Barbara Morgridge as *The Cultural Life of Modern America* (Cambridge, Mass.: Harvard University Press, 1969);

Lars Oftedal: Udkast (Bergen: Mons Litlere, 1889);

Sult (Copenhagen: Philipsen, 1890); translated by George Egerton (pseudonym of Mary Chavelita Dunne) as *Hunger* (London: Smithers, 1899; New York: Knopf, 1920);

Mysterier: Roman (Copenhagen: Philipsen, 1892); translated by Arthur G. Chater as *Mysteries* (New York: Knopf, 1927);

Redaktør Lynge: Roman (Copenhagen: Philipsen, 1893);

Ny Jord: Roman (Copenhagen: Philipsen, 1893); translated by Carl Christian Hyllested as *Shallow Soil* (New York: Scribners, 1914);

Pan: Af Løjtnant Thomas Glahns Papirer (Copenhagen: Philipsen, 1894); translated by W. W. Worster as *Pan* (London: Gyldendal, 1920; New York: Knopf, 1921);

Ved Rigets Port: Forspil (Copenhagen: Philipsen, 1895);

Livets Spil (Copenhagen: Det Nordiske Forlag, 1896);

Siesta: Skitser (Copenhagen: Gyldendal, 1897)—includes "Ringen," translated by Hanna Astrup Larsen as "The Ring," in *Told in Norway,* edited by Larsen (New York: American-Scandinavian Foundation, 1927), pp. 133–134; and "En ganske almindelig Flue," translated by Hallberg Hallmundsson as "Just an Ordinary Fly of Average Size," in his *An Anthology of Scandinavian Literature: From the Viking Age to the Twentieth Century* (New York: Collier-Macmillan, 1965), pp. 144–148;

Aftenrøde: Slutningsspil (Copenhagen: Gyldendal, 1898);

Knut Hamsun (Hulton Archive/Getty Images)

Victoria: En Kærligheds Historie (Christiania: Cammermeyer, 1898); translated by Chater as *Victoria: A Love Story* (London: Gyldendal, 1923);

Munken Vendt: Brigantinens Saga, 1 (Copenhagen: Gyldendal, 1902);

I Æventyrland: Oplevet og drømt i Kaukasien (Copenhagen: Gyldendal, 1903); translated by Sverre Lyngstad as *In Wonderland* (Brooklyn, N.Y.: IG, 2004);

Dronning Tamara: Skuespil i tre Akter (Copenhagen: Gyldendal, 1903);

Kratskog: Historier og Skitser (Copenhagen: Gyldendal, 1903)–includes "Kærlighedens Slaver," translated by James W. McFarlane as "Slaves of Love," in *Slaves of Love and Other Stories*, edited by McFarlane and Janet Garton (New York: Oxford University Press, 1982), pp. 30–36; "Sachæus," translated by Sverre Arestad as "Zachaeus," in *Short Stories from Norway 1850–1900*, edited by Henning K. Sehmsdorf, WITS: Wisconsin Introductions to Scandinavia II, no. 3 (Madison: Department of Scandinavian Studies, University of Wisconsin–Madison, 1986), pp. 89–99; and "Rædsel" and "Paa Prærien," translated by Arestad as "Fear" and "On the Praerie," *Norwegian-American Studies*, 24 (1970): 166–179;

Det vilde Kor: Digte (Copenhagen: Gyldendal, 1904)–includes "Skjærgaardsø," translated by Martin S. Allwood as "Island off the Coast," in *20th Century Scandinavian Poetry*, edited by Allwood (Mullsjö, Sweden: Marston Hill, 1950), pp. 119–120;

Sværmere: Roman (Copenhagen & Christiania: Gyldendal, 1904); translated by Worster as *Dreamers* (New York: Knopf, 1921); translation republished as *Mothwise* (London: Gyldendal, 1921);

Stridende Liv: Skildringer fra Vesten og Østen (Copenhagen & Christiana: Gyldendal, 1905)–includes "Paa Blaamandsø," translated by Worster as "On the Island," *Dial*, 75 (1923): 209–224; and "Vagabonds Dager" and "Kvindeseir," translated by Arestad as "Vagabond Days" and "Feminine Victory," *Norwegian-American Studies*, 24 (1970): 155–166;

Under Høststjærnen: En Vandrers Fortælling (Christiania: Gyldendal, 1906); translated by Worster as "Under the Autumn Star," in *Wanderers* (New York: Knopf, 1922; London: Gyldendal, 1922);

Benoni: Roman (Christiania: Gyldendal, 1908); translated by Chater (New York: Knopf, 1925);

Rosa: Af Student Parelius' Papirer (Christiania: Gyldendal, 1908); translated by Chater as *Rosa* (New York: Knopf, 1926);

En Vandrer spiller med Sordin (Christiania: Gyldendal, 1909); translated by Worster as "A Wanderer Plays on Muted Strings," in *Wanderers*;

Livet ivold: Skuespil i fire Akter (Christiania & Copenhagen: Gyldendal, 1910); translated by Graham Rawson and Tristan Rawson as *In the Grip of Life* (New York: Knopf, 1924; London: Gyldendal, 1924);

Den sidste Glæde: Skildringer (Christiania: Gyldendal, 1912); translated by Paula Wiking as *Look Back on Happiness* (New York: Coward-McCann, 1940);

Børn av Tiden: Roman (Christiania: Gyldendal, 1913); translated by J. S. Scott as *Children of the Age* (New York: Knopf, 1924; London: Gyldendal, 1924);

Segelfoss By, 2 volumes (Copenhagen: Gyldendal, 1915); translated by Scott as *Segelfoss Town* (New York: Knopf, 1925);

Markens Grøde: Roman, 2 volumes (Copenhagen: Gyldendal, 1917); translated by Worster as *Growth of the Soil* (London: Gyldendal, 1920; New York: Knopf, 1921);

Konerne ved Vandposten: Roman, 2 volumes (Copenhagen: Gyldendal, 1920); translated by Chater as *The Women at the Pump*, 1 volume (New York: Knopf, 1928);

Siste Kapitel: Roman, 2 volumes (Christiania: Gyldendal, 1923); translated by Chater as *Chapter the Last*, 1 volume (New York: Knopf, 1929; London: Knopf, 1930);

Landstrykere: Roman, 2 volumes (Oslo: Gyldendal, 1927); translated by Eugene Gay-Tifft as *Vagabonds*, 1 volume (New York: Coward-McCann, 1930);

August: Roman, 2 volumes (Oslo: Gyldendal, 1930); translated by Gay-Tifft as *August*, 1 volume (New York: Grosset & Dunlap, 1931);

Men Livet lever: Roman, 2 volumes (Oslo: Gyldendal, 1933); translated by Gay-Tifft as *The Road Leads On*, 1 volume (New York: Coward-McCann, 1934);

Ringen sluttet: Roman, 2 volumes (Oslo: Gyldendal, 1936); translated by Gay-Tifft as *The Ring Is Closed*, 1 volume (New York: Coward-McCann, 1937);

Artikler, edited by Francis Bull (Oslo: Gyldendal, 1939)–includes "Festina lente," originally published in English as "What Is Progress?" *St. Louis Post-Dispatch*, 30 December 1928;

Paa gjengrodde Stier (Oslo: Gyldendal, 1949); translated by Carl L. Anderson as *On Over-grown Paths* (New York: Paul S. Eriksson, 1967); translation republished as *On Overgrown Paths* (London: MacGibbon & Kee, 1968);

Paa Turné: Tre foredrag om litteratur, edited by Tore Hamsun (Oslo: Gyldendal, 1960);

Livsfragmenter: Ni noveller, edited by Lars Frode Larsen (Oslo: Gyldendal, 1988); translated by Tiina Nunnally as *Night Roamers and Other Stories* (Seattle: Fjord Press, 1992)–comprises "Night Roamers," "My Traveling Companion," "Small Town Life," "On Tour," "Sin," "Around Christmas," "Bad Days," "At the Clinic," and "A Fragment of Life";

Over havet: Artikler, reisebrev, edited by Larsen (Oslo: Gyldendal, 1990);

Hamsuns polemiske skrifter, edited by Gunvald Hermundstad (Oslo: Gyldendal, 1998);

En Fløite lød i mit Blod: Nye dikt, edited by Larsen (Oslo: Gyldendal, 2003);

Livets røst: Noveller i utvalg, edited by Larsen and Ingar Sletten Kolloen (Oslo: Gyldendal, 2003).

Collection: *Samlede verker,* 15 volumes (Oslo: Gyldendal, 1954–1956).

Editions in English: *Pan,* translated by James W. McFarlane (London: Artemis Press, 1955; New York: Noonday Press, 1956);

Hunger, translated by Robert Bly, introduction by Isaac Bashevis Singer (New York: Farrar, Straus & Giroux, 1967);

Victoria: A Love Story, translated by Oliver Stallybrass (New York: Farrar, Straus & Giroux, 1969; London: Souvenir Press, 1974);

Mysteries, translated by Jerry Bothmer (New York: Farrar, Straus & Giroux, 1971; London: Souvenir Press, 1973);

The Wanderer, translated by Oliver Stallybrass and Gunnvor Stallybrass (New York: Farrar, Straus & Giroux, 1975);

The Women at the Pump, translated by Oliver Stallybrass and Gunnvor Stallybrass (New York: Farrar, Straus & Giroux, 1978);

Wayfarers, translated by McFarlane (New York: Farrar, Straus & Giroux, 1980);

Dreamers, translated by Tom Geddes (New York: New Directions, 1996);

Hunger, translated by Sverre Lyngstad (Edinburgh: Rebel Inc, 1996);

Rosa, translated by Lyngstad (Los Angeles: Sun & Moon Press, 1997);

Tales of Love and Loss, translated by Robert Ferguson (London: Souvenir Press, E & A, 1997);

Pan: From the Papers of Lieutenant Thomas Glahn, translated and edited by Lyngstad (New York: Penguin, 1998);

On Overgrown Paths, translated by Lyngstad (Copenhagen & Los Angeles: Green Integer, 1999);

Mysteries, translated by Lyngstad (New York: Penguin, 2001);

Knut Hamsun Remembers America: Essays and Stories, 1885–1949, translated and edited by Richard Nelson Current (Columbia: University of Missouri Press, 2003);

The Last Joy, translated by Lyngstad (Copenhagen & Los Angeles: Green Integer, 2003);

Victoria, translated by Lyngstad (New York: Penguin, 2005).

Knut Hamsun is Norway's best-known novelist and one of the major world writers of modern times. He is commonly ranked immediately below the four great names of Scandinavian literature: Hans Christian Andersen, Søren Kierkegaard, Henrik Ibsen, and August Strindberg. His works are available in more than thirty languages, and he has won many admirers among European and American men of letters. Germany's Thomas Mann saw in Hamsun a direct descendant of Fyodor Dostoevsky and Friedrich Nietzsche; the Russians celebrated him for his dramatic works; Arthur Koestler praised his tender love stories; and H. G. Wells lauded his powerful prose epic, *Markens Grøde* (1917; translated as *Growth of the Soil,* 1920), for which he won the Nobel Prize in Literature in 1920. Isaac Bashevis Singer spoke with admiration of Hamsun's modern subjectivism, his fragmentariness, his use of flashbacks, and his lyricism, and Hamsun has been recognized as a precursor of European modernism whose literary techniques anticipate Marcel Proust, James Joyce, and Virginia Woolf. Despite its often sordid details and tragic tone, the typical Hamsun novel has humor, charm, love of life, and, above all, a joy in nature that can be appreciated by readers everywhere.

The fourth of seven children, Hamsun was born Knut Pedersen on 4 August 1859 in Gudbrandsdalen; scholars disagree as to whether Lom or the neighboring community of Vågå was his actual birthplace. The valley is the heart of Norway, known both for its scenic beauty and for its acclaimed artists and cultural achievements; two of Norway's best twentieth-century poets, Olav Aukrust and Tor Jonsson, came from Lom. His father, Peder Pedersen, was an itinerant tailor from Vågå; his mother, Tora Olsdatter Garmotraedet Pedersen, came from an old and respected Lom family, although her immediate relatives had recently come down in the world. When Knut was four, the family moved six hundred miles north to the island of Hamarøy in Nordland, where Knut's maternal uncle Hans Olsen, a shopkeeper, librarian, and postmaster, had acquired a farm called "Hamsund," from which Knut Pedersen later took his pseudonym; Peder Pedersen took over the management of the farm. Northern Norway, with its midnight summer sun and its snow-clad peaks rising out of the ocean, is even more a fairyland than Gudbrandsdalen. At that time it was mostly populated by poor fishermen and smallholders; in a few large estates along the coast wealthy merchants plied their trade, imitating the life of the bourgeoisie of Christiania (which became Oslo in 1925) and enjoying the privileges of nobility elsewhere. Although Knut Pedersen never became a genuine Nordlander, he studied the mannerisms and language of his northern neighbors and used this material in his later work.

To repay a debt Olsen claimed they owed him, Knut's parents had him work for his uncle, a hard taskmaster with no understanding of children. These years with his uncle have been explored by psychoanalysts and by critics trying to explain Hamsun's hatred of England: they claim that Hamsun associated his uncle with "the old colonial power, England," while seeing himself as "young Germany, asking for *Lebensraum* [living space]." Pedersen received no education beyond grade school, and after his confirmation he spent five years working variously as a peddler, a shoemaker's apprentice, a bailiff's assistant, and a schoolteacher. These experiences served him well in his writing career, which began with the publication of a novella, *Den Gaadefulde: En Kjærlighedshistorie fra Nordland* (1877, The Enigmatic Man: A Love Story from Northern Norway).

Pedersen's next book, the novel *Bjørger* (1878), published under the pseudonym Knud Pedersen Hamsund, was written in imitation of the style of Bjørnstjerne Bjørnson, who had tried to revive the old Icelandic saga narrative in his rustic novels. This melodramatic story of the young poet Bjørger's love of a woman named Laura is significant mainly as a study for Hamsun's later novel *Victoria: En Kærligheds Historie* (1898; translated as *Victoria: A Love Story*, 1923).

With the help of a loan from the Nordland merchant Erasmus B. K. Zahl, Pedersen spent the summer of 1879 in southern Norway, where he completed the novel "Frida"; it was rejected by Frederik Hegel, the director and owner of the Gyldendal publishing firm in Copenhagen, and the manuscript was lost. After a brief attempt to become an actor in 1880, Pedersen worked as a member of a road construction crew north of Christiania. There he made the acquaintance of people who were willing to pay for his transportation to the United States, where he hoped to establish himself as a poet in the Norwegian immigrant community. Before leaving for the United States, Pedersen sought the advice of Bjørnson, who had made a lecture tour of the Midwest in 1880–1881 at the invitation of Rasmus Anderson, a professor at the University of Wisconsin in Madison. Unlike many Scandinavian visitors to the New World, Bjørnson was enthusiastic about the democratic experiment being conducted there, and he suggested that Hamsun contact Anderson. When he arrived in Madison in February 1882, however, Pedersen did not receive the help for which he had hoped. In the following months he worked on farms around Elroy, Wisconsin, where his older brother Peter had settled, and at a store in town. He also gave lectures on literary topics. In December 1882 he inscribed what has come to be known as his "Elroy Manifesto" in a friend's autograph book: "My life is a peaceless flight through all the land, my religion is the moral of the wildest naturalism but my world is the aesthetical literatur *[sic]*."

In early 1884 Pedersen moved to Madelia, Minnesota, where he met and became the secretary of the Norwegian poet and Unitarian minister Kristofer Janson. In Janson's home in Minneapolis he found a good library and a stimulating literary milieu; Janson's wife, Drude, a frustrated artist, fell in love with the young writer. In the late spring of 1884 he was diagnosed with terminal tuberculosis. He wanted to return to Norway to die, and friends again paid for his passage. In August he arrived in Christiania, where his disease was rediagnosed as bronchitis. He was advised to move inland, where he could benefit from the mountain air.

Pedersen spent the next year and a half working as a postal clerk in Valdres, in the mountains midway between Christiania and Bergen. He acquired the final version of his name when a printer accidentally left the *d* off of *Hamsund* in the byline of an article he wrote on Mark Twain that appeared in the *Ny illustreret Tidende* on 22 and 29 March and 4 April 1885. Hamsun praises Twain's ability to "bruse op med Latter og Larm–og slaa" (to work up the audience with laughter and noise–and then suddenly to strike). A lecture tour to the small towns of eastern Norway ended in disappointment when he realized that more profitable work would be needed to keep him alive. He was often without food and sometimes had to spend the night in a shack or at the police station; he used the experiences in his first great novel, *Sult* (1890; translated as *Hunger,* 1899). In July 1886 he fled from his creditors and returned to the United States. He was determined to make enough money to pay his debts so that he could return to Norway and live on his writing.

Hamsun worked on the construction of a cable-car line in Chicago; in the fall he was employed as a conductor on the Halsted Line and later on the Cottage Line. He was unable to save any money, however, and in the end he appealed to the meatpacking magnate Philip Armour. Touched by the helpless tone of Hamsun's letter, Armour paid for him to join his friends in Minneapolis. During the summer of 1887 Hamsun worked on one of the bonanza farms in North Dakota (bonanza farms were farms of three thousand or more acres that were built on land granted by the federal government for the construction of the Northern Pacific Railroad and sold off after the railroad company went bankrupt in 1872). In the fall he returned to Minneapolis.

In the winter of 1887–1888 Hamsun presented a series of lectures at Dania Hall in Minneapolis on the French writers Honoré de Balzac, Gustave Flaubert, and Emile Zola and the new Scandinavian realist writers Bjørnson, Ibsen, Jonas Lie, Janson, Alexander L. Kielland, and Strindberg. His final lecture, "Estetiske Tanker–Livet i Minneapolis" (Aesthetic Reflections–Life in Minneapolis), delivered in March, was an amusing assessment of American cultural life.

Hamsun left the United States in the summer of 1888. On the way to New York he sold an article, "August Strindberg," to the Chicago weekly *America;* said to be the first ever published in English on the Swedish writer, it appeared on 20 December. Hamsun praises the dramatist for "his rude force" and elaborates on Strindberg's notion of a new kind of hero: split and complex, both good and bad, subtly differentiated in his nature, and ever changing in his actions.

When Hamsun's ship docked in Christiania, the memory of the miserable time he had spent in the city two years earlier was so painful that he did not go ashore but traveled on to Copenhagen. In Denmark he once more lived in poverty; yet, he wrote to a friend in the United States, "How I find this country agreeable! I assure you, the whole existence–way of life–here is in deep harmony with my temperament, my nature. Here is Europe, and I am a European, thank God!"

In the fall of 1888 Hamsun published in the Danish periodical *Ny Jord* (New Earth) an article on Janson and a chapter of what became *Sult;* the latter made him famous almost overnight. He was invited to the homes of well-known literati and lectured at the Student Union of the University of Copenhagen on his experiences in America; the lectures were published in April 1889 as *Fra det moderne Amerikas Aandsliv* (translated as *The Cultural Life of Modern America,* 1969). Hamsun attacks the American obsession with profit, growth, and speed and denounces democracy because it leads to isolationism and provincialism and does not further the arts. In his treatment of American literature Hamsun omits Twain and calls Walt Whitman a barbarian and Ralph Waldo Emerson a poor philosopher. Reviewing the book in the Minneapolis newspaper *Budstikken* for 17 June 1889, Janson wrote of Hamsun: "jeg har aldrig truffet paa noget Menneske som har havt den sygelige Lidenskab for æstetisk Skjønhed som ham, hvis hele Aandsretning har været saa behersket af denne Lidenskab som ham" (I have never met anyone who has had as morbid a passion for aesthetic beauty as he and whose whole way of thinking has been to such an extent dominated by that passion).

Although Hamsun, after his second return from the United States, used every opportunity to ridicule the Americans, his colleagues in Scandinavia looked on him as an American–an epithet often applied to him during the early 1890s was "Yankee." His need to be in the news and his compulsion to attack the old and clear ground for the young, for instance, were seen as American characteristics. Georg Brandes, in his 28 April 1889 review of *Fra det moderne Amerikas Aandsliv* in the newspaper *Verdens Gang,* found that Hamsun's constant hunting for effect was an American feature of his style.

In his article "Fra det ubevidste Sjæleliv" (From the Unconscious Life of the Mind), published in the journal *Samtiden* in 1890, Hamsun launched his idea of a new literature:

Hvad nu om Literaturen i det hele taget begyndte at beskæftige sig lidt mer med sjælelige Tilstande, end med Forlovelser og Baller og Landture og Ulykkeshændelser som saadan? Man maatte da ganske vist give Afkald paa at skrive "Typer,"–som allesammen er skrevne før,–"Karakterer,"–som man træffer hver Dag paa Fisketorvet. Men . . . til Gengæld . . . fik vi erfare lidt om de hemmelige Bevægelser, som bedrives upaaagtet paa de afsides Steder i Sjælen, den Fornemmelsernes uberegnelige Uorden, det delikate Fantasiliv holdt under Luppen, disse Tankens og Følelsernes Vandringer i det blaa, skridtløse, sporløse Rejser med Hjærnen og Hjærtet, sælsomme Nervevirksomheder, Blodets Hvisken, Benpibernes Bøn, hele det ubevidste Sjæleliv.

(Now what if literature on the whole began to deal a little more with mental states than with engagements and balls and hikes and accidents as such? Then one would, to be sure, have to relinquish creating "types," as all have been created before, "characters" whom one meets every day in the fishmarket. . . . But in return . . . we would experience a little more of the secret movements which are unnoticed in the remote places of the soul, the capricious disorder of perception, the wandering of these thoughts and feelings out of the blue; motionless, trackless journeys with the brain and the heart, strange activities of the nerves, the whispering of the blood, the pleading of the bone, the entire unconscious life.)

For those who wondered what he meant by "the whispering of the blood," Hamsun provided an answer six months later with the appearance of *Sult,* one of his two most widely known novels–*Markens Grøde* being the other–and, some critics have argued, his best.

Sult includes the central elements of the author's later fiction–a tragic love story, poetic rendering of natural scenery, shockingly realistic detail–and is related in a manner that reveals the fluctuations of a youthful temperament; but the book also features a combination of humor, exuberance, hope, and despair that was never fully repeated by the mature Hamsun. It is also more directly autobiographical than anything Hamsun wrote before his memoir, *Paa gjengrodde Stier* (1949; translated as *On Over-grown Paths,* 1967): the unnamed hero's address, Tomtegaten no. 11, was Hamsun's during his stay in Christiania in 1880; like the protagonist, Hamsun lived in a shack in Møllergaten and spent a night at the police station; and the hero's final escape on a Russian ship bound for Leith, Scotland, resembles Hamsun's flight to the United States in 1886. The use of a first-person narrator is unusual in a novel of the naturalistic period.

Hamsun claimed in an 1890 letter to the Swedish writer Gustaf af Geijerstam that with regard to the plot of *Sult* he was playing on one string: the four parts that make up the novel are much alike in mood and content. A young man searches unsuccessfully for food, lodging, and part-time work in a big, unfriendly city where he wishes to try his luck as a writer; in parts 1, 2, and 4 he is saved from catastrophe–by a newspaper editor who buys an article, by an old friend who has some money to spare, and, at the end, by taking a job on a ship and sailing away from the city. The novel describes an experiment in living on the most elemental level: how to support the body–with food, rest, and sex–so that it, in turn, can support an exceptional mind. The experiment is unsuccessful, and the protagonist's body and mind are finally at the point of breaking down. The reader, however, follows his course with undivided attention, fascinated alternately by the interplay of crass realism in the description of his physical decline and the astounding turns of his vivid imagination.

Even within the continuous flow of scenes in the novel it is possible to discern a certain structuring of events. The first part offers the general pattern: the search for food, money, and work. Part 2, describing a night spent in a cell at the city jail, marks the first low point in the protagonist's misery and shows how easily hunger pains are overshadowed by the fear of death when he has an intense attack of claustrophobia after the lights are shut off and he is left in total darkness. Part 3 includes the climax, the expectation and excitement of two meetings with a woman he fantastically refers to as Ylajali. In part 4 he loses Ylajali, destroys his manuscript, and gives up the experiment.

The novel develops on a single course of steady decline. This development is reinforced by the change of season from fall to winter; the protagonist's move from the upscale west to the poor east side of Christiania; his drop in social status from being in the company of the intellectual elite of the city when Ylajali first sees him at the theater to having even servants laugh at him; and, finally, his moral fall when he accepts unearned money. Although in part 4 the protagonist does not suffer from a lack of food, as he does in the earlier sections, the reader has learned by now that there are worse pains than hunger. The ugliness of his surroundings, and particularly his own inability to produce beauty in any form, finally leave the hero without hope.

Ibsen's statement that "at dikte er at se" (to be a poet is to see) applies to the hero to an extraordinary degree: under the influence of hunger, in mental states that today might be called psychedelic, he registers objects and events with the fidelity of the most sensitive camera: "Intet undgik min opmærksomhet, jeg var klar og åndsnærværende, alle ting strømmet ind på mig med en skinnende tydelighet som om det plutselig var blit et stærkt lys omkring mig" (Nothing escaped my eyes. I was sharp and my brain was very much alive, everything poured in toward me with a staggering distinctness as if a strong light had fallen on everything around me). But he is not always a mere medium: by creating special conditions, he can make his mental "camera" yield impressions that are dream-like or grotesque.

The protagonist is an aesthete: the sight of an invalid, a toothless woman, or an old man strikes him with a revulsion that he tries unsuccessfully to counteract with his daydreams of beauty: Ylajali, elevated to a princess reclining on a bed of yellow roses. In his desperate fight to preserve his life he cannot avoid reminders of death: they are fearful in the prison scene, grotesque in the newspaper advertisement for shrouds, and peaceful in the many graveyard scenes in the book. He continually playacts: he simulates to confuse his enemy, the Christiania bourgeoisie; he pretends to be experiencing life, whereas he is, in fact, a voyeur, deriving vicarious pleasures and pains–except for his hunger pangs–from observing others.

The hero's real antagonist is Christiania, "denne forunderlige by som ingen forlater før han har fåt mærker av den" (that strange city no one escapes from until it has left its mark on him), and in *Sult* it assumes a personality as in few other Norwegian novels. Actually, there is little description of the city–only glimpses from the hero's endless walks in the streets, one or two drab interiors, an occasional view from a window, and a lyrical snapshot in the harbor quarter, where the sea shines like mother-of-pearl. This highly accomplished impressionism gives way, when hunger affects the protagonist, to expressionism: inanimate objects assume personalities; people become animals; and incidents become symbols. He experiences his shoes as old friends, as a soft, whispering sound coming toward him; the fall roses seem to take on a fever, their petals a strange and unnatural flush; silent couples and noisy groups on Karl Johan Street remind him of mating times, of a warm swamp, and of cats copulating with high-pitched shrieks.

Sult can be read as an example of Scandinavian naturalism of the 1880s; for stark realism, some of its scenes were long unsurpassed in Norwegian literature. But the book also marks the end of the naturalistic period. The hero is finally felled by inner and outer circumstances; but in his attempt to overcome the weakness of his body, he scores a victory for the free human spirit. Even more than its hero, however, the style of *Sult* brought something new to Nordic literature. The old Romantic rhetoric, with its emphasis on color and rhythm, comes to life as it had not done previously: the sentence "jeg . . . frisket op de døde punkter med et farvefuldt ord hist og her" (I . . . tried to liven up the dead points with a colorful word) applies not only to the hero of *Sult* but also to Hamsun's composition of the novel, as does the newspaper editor's comment on the hero's writing: "Der er altid for megen feber" (There's always too much fever).

What makes *Sult* different from Hamsun's other "rhetorical" books, such as *Pan: Af Løjtnant Thomas Glahns Papirer* (1894, Pan: From the Papers of Lieutenant Thomas Glahn; translated as *Pan,* 1920), however, is its humor, which gives a special irony to scenes that would otherwise be merely pathetic or theatrical. The "Russian" quality of *Sult*–the gray, ultimately resigned despair that appears in Dostoevsky's work–has often been pointed out, but equally important is a sense of absurdity in the style of Twain. Hamsun never again quite achieved this balance of naturalism and Romanticism, of humor and despair.

In the summer of 1890 Hamsun settled in the tiny town of Lillesand on the south coast of Norway to work on his next book, planned to be a collection of weird stories. In the article "Smaabyliv" (Small-Town Life), published in the newspaper *Bergens Tidende* on 9 August and collected in his *Kratskog: Historier og Skitser* (1903, Brushwood: Stories and Sketches), he ridicules the town, although from his letters one can see that he was attracted by its young ladies and intrigued by his housemate, Grøgaard, a destitute creature of good family background. After a few weeks in Lillesand, Hamsun abandoned his plans for a volume of stories and began writing the novel *Mysterier* (1892; translated as *Mysteries,* 1927). Johan Nilsen Nagel, a disillusioned young agronomist traveling along the south coast of Norway on a steamer, is struck by the idyllic appearance of a small town and decides to try life there. He falls in love with Dagny Kielland, a woman of exceptional charm and beauty. Like all of the inhabitants of the town, who are puzzled by his curious dress–he wears a bright yellow suit–and odd behavior, she finds him interesting; but she is engaged to a naval officer who is away at sea. He then proposes to a spinster, Martha Gude, with whom he hopes to live a simple cotter's life. But Dagny prevents the union, and he drowns himself. At the end Dagny and Martha walk arm in arm and comment on the unusual qualities of the departed protagonist.

Nagel is, indeed, an enigmatic man; he exemplifies Hamsun's own desire to become a myth, a subject for storytellers. In a letter dated 10 October 1890 to the Bergen critic Bolette Pavels Larsen, Hamsun describes his ambition "at kunne dukke op anonymt, uventet, med pludselig Virkning, Gang paa Gang, ved hver Bog med pludselig Virkning, og saa dukke under igen–til næste Gang" (to pop up anonymously, unexpectedly, with sudden effect, time after time, each book having its own sudden effect, and then to dive down again–until the next time). The theme is central in Hamsun's first novella, *Den Gaadefulde,* as well as in *Mysterier.*

Although the point of view in *Mysterier* is consistently that of the protagonist, it achieves the greater distance of a third-person narrative. It is also more of a social novel in that Nagel, unlike the isolated protagonist of *Sult,* acquires friends and acquaintances with whom he discusses politics and poetry. Finally, *Mysterier* differs from *Sult* in the many tales told by Nagel; they are fully incorporated into the text, although they may have originated as some of the stories Hamsun had planned to publish after *Sult.*

In *Sult* the hero is plagued by a sort of double: a crippled man who walks in front of him and stops when he stops. In *Mysterier* this motif is developed into a central theme, with the character Grøgård reflecting certain qualities of the protagonist, Nagel. Grøgård, also known as Minutten (the Midget), is the village idiot; he will dance in the market square for anyone who gives him a penny. Nagel befriends the man and pays him to keep him from debasing himself by his ridiculous performance but at the same time watches him carefully as if he were a criminal. Minutten seems to be a good and humble man; as a disciple of Nietzsche, Nagel takes this appearance to mean that he is covering up some secret crime. Nagel never catches Minutten red-handed, but in the end he is proven right: Minutten, the reader learns, is, in fact, guilty of a secret crime against Martha. More significant is the way in which Minutten represents another side of the hero–not the proud elitist Nagel/Hamsun but the provocative humbug Nagel/Hamsun, who will do anything to be in the news. Nagel speaks of his dream of "en gjærning på jorden, noget som kunde 'tælle,' nogen bedrifter som kjøtæterne kunde korse sig over" (accomplishing something in this world–something meaningful that would make the carnivores all sit up and take notice). This mission may have been to create a new nobility, as proposed by Nietzsche, or, on a lower level, to instill pride in people such as Minutten. In the latter regard, his defeat becomes total when, toward the end of the novel, he sees Minutten once more playing the buffoon in the market square.

In a 20 October 1918 interview in *Verdens Gang* Hamsun criticized *Mysterier:*

> Nei, nei. Det er ingen god bok. Der er altfor meget snak og ikke nok liv. Og alle de meninger som jeg lar mine personer uttale i "Mysterier," om Ibsen og Bjørnson og Tolstoj og de franske forfattere, alt det er bare ord.

(No, no, that's not a good book. There is too much talk and not enough life. And then all the opinions I allow my characters to pronounce in *Mysteries,* on Ibsen, Bjørnson and Tolstoy and the French authors, all that's only words.)

Nevertheless, though it is not one of Hamsun's popular novels, it has always been a favorite among discriminating readers, probably because it includes so much of what they admire in his works: a love story, beautifully wrought language, and, particularly, the odd tales and actions of its quintessential Hamsun hero, Johan Nilsen Nagel.

Hamsun spent the years 1893 to 1896 in Paris, associating with Strindberg and other writers and working on two plays. He did not learn French, as he had hoped to do, and the stay had no apparent influence on his work. He had chosen the city as the stronghold of culture and intellectuality, but, like Jean-Jacques Rousseau, he decided that human beings are not meant to be crowded together in anthills: "Jeg hører skogene og ensomheten til" (I belong to the forests and the solitude), he wrote in *Pan,* which he began in Paris and completed in Norway's southernmost city, Christiansand. The novel, however, is mostly set in northern Norway, the region of his childhood.

Pan is the diary of retired army lieutenant Thomas Glahn, who in 1857 receives a letter from a woman named Edvarda; it contains two green feathers he had presented to her when he spent the summer in northern Norway two years previously. Glahn goes on to recount the events of that time in his diary.

A city dweller of good family background and education, Glahn is driven by a melancholy weariness of the world to travel to Sirilund in northern Norway, where he seeks unspoiled nature. He rents a forest hut from the ruler of the district, Ferdinand Mack, a rich and powerful merchant. Mack's twenty-year-old daughter, Edvarda, despises her father, although she is willing to consider the suitors he brings to their home, including a lame doctor and an old Finnish baron who is also a pedantic natural scientist. Glahn and Edvarda fall in love: during a picnic on an island Edvarda exclaims, quite unabashedly, "Det er løitnant Glahn jeg vil ha. Jeg gider ikke løpe efter nogen anden" (I want Lieutenant Glahn. I don't care to run after anyone else).

As so often in Hamsun's novels, the climax of the romance is reached fairly soon—only a third of the way through the novel—as Glahn and Edvarda's intense happiness dissolves in misunderstanding and acrimony followed by painful and prolonged scenes of love-hate. Glahn comforts himself with the blacksmith's wife, Eva, "en ung pike med et hvitt uldtørklæ om hodet, hun hadde meget mørkt hår" (a young girl with a white woolen scarf, she had very dark hair). Later he learns that she is Mack's mistress. Age—he is forty-six—has not reduced Mack's sexual prowess or his inclination to jealousy and hatred. When Eva gives him up for Glahn, he burns down Glahn's hut in the woods. Mack's style, including his poise and sharp intelligence, is reminiscent of an Eastern potentate's, and Glahn respects him as a worthy antagonist.

Edvarda, meanwhile, is seen more and more in the company of the Finnish baron. At a ball Glahn, pretending to whisper something to the baron, spits in his ear. When Edvarda hears of Glahn's meetings with Eva, her love is reawakened by jealousy; she comes back to him wearing a white scarf like that of her rival. But it is too late: Glahn's cruel treatment by the fickle Edvarda has made him deaf to her confession of love.

As in *Sult,* the development of the love story is accompanied by a seasonal movement, but here the progression of the seasons, and in particular the arrival of the fall, with its first killing frost—the so-called *jernnetter* (iron nights)—pushes the pitch of Hamsun's prose to heights it never reached before or after. Glahn is always aroused by nature, and his language assumes its rhythms. The long, involved periods of a discursive style, with its many subordinate clauses, are replaced by short sentences, either completely without conjunctions or else studded with them.

When the baron sets out to return to Finland, Glahn gives him a good-riddance salute by blasting a cliff and sending boulders crashing into the sea as his ship passes by. Mack, knowing of the plan, has set Eva to work tarring a boat on the beach below. Glahn, who is becoming mentally unbalanced, knows that Mack has spied on his blasting project, and he has seen Eva at the foot of the mountain; yet, although he was formerly astute in reading all manner of signs, he takes no heed, and Eva is killed by the falling rocks.

When Glahn is about to leave in the autumn, Edvarda asks to keep his dog, Aesop, in memory of him. Fearing that she will mistreat the animal—and out of spite—he shoots it and sends her the body. Edvarda later marries the baron.

In the midst of all this melodrama, with the faithful maiden brutally killed, the proud heroine married off to a wizened scientist, and the hero slowly losing his mind, Hamsun's joy in life is still manifest. *Pan* owes its Norwegian popularity less to its tale of passion than to Glahn's eloquent declarations of his love of nature: "En skål for den miskundelige stilhet på jorderik, for stjærnene og for halvmånen, ja for dem og den!" (A toast to the merciful stillness over the earth, to the stars and the crescent moon, yes to it and to them!).

Pan ends with an epilogue, "Glahns Død" (Glahn's Death), which Hamsun first published in

Samtiden a year before the novel appeared. The epilogue is purported to have been written in 1859 by a hunting companion of Glahn's in India. Glahn receives another letter from Edvarda, saying that she is now a widow and is free to marry him. Glahn dresses as if for a wedding, then provokes the narrator into shooting him to death.

Hamsun's next novel, *Victoria,* published in 1898, was advertised by its English publisher as "one of the great love stories of world literature." The sweetest of Hamsun's books, it was once considered a suitable confirmation present in Norway. The atmosphere is relatively harmonious, reflecting Hamsun's happiness after his marriage to the twenty-five-year-old divorcée Bergljot Beck in May 1898 and their honeymoon with old friends in Valdres. Johannes and Victoria are childhood lovers; but she is the daughter of an estate owner whose home is referred to as "Slottet" (The Palace), while he is the son of a neighboring tenant farmer and miller. When they grow up, Victoria's father needs a rich son-in-law to save his estate, and Victoria sacrifices her happiness and becomes engaged to the wealthy but unattractive Otto. Johannes, meanwhile, becomes a writer. Otto dies, leaving Victoria free to marry Johannes, but he has become engaged to Camilla. After their engagement Johannes has less time for Camilla than for the books he is writing, and she leaves him for another man. Meanwhile, Victoria has died of tuberculosis. At the end of the novel Johannes reads a long letter from Victoria that explains that she always loved only him but had to give him up when her father implored her to save the family honor. As in the epilogue to *Pan,* then, the point of view changes at the end of the novel; but here it is striking that Hamsun—known for his sexist attitudes—lets a woman have the last word. Like *Mysterier, Victoria* includes several stories that are woven into the text. Furthermore, it describes Johannes's methods of writing, which presumably were Hamsun's own.

After the scrupulous realism of *Sult,* a reduction of detail has clearly taken place in *Victoria:* the reader is not told Johannes's, Victoria's, or Otto's last name (Camilla's last name—Seier—is mentioned once); their parents are referred to simply as the miller and the castle master, respectively; other characters are known only as the tutor, the mother in blue, the mother in black, the lord, the lady, and similar designations. The subtle psychology Hamsun used in "Fra det ubevidste Sjæleliv" has given way to tale, allegory, mood, color, and ornament—a lighter and more sentimental kind of literature that Hamsun himself, in a 24 December 1898 letter to Brandes, called "intet andet end lit Lyrik" (nothing but a little poetry); and at the time he wrote the novel, he described poetry in a 23 August 1898 letter to Gerda Welhaven as "den eneste Digtning, som ikke er baade pretentiøs og intetsigende, men bare intetsigende" (the only form of writing that is not both pretentious and inconsequential but merely inconsequential). *Victoria* lacks the power of Hamsun's other great novels of the 1890s, but it is still the quintessential Hamsun love story: with nothing really new to say, the author has stated his case more simply, clearly, and economically than in his earlier works. In the words of Johannes: "Og kjærligheten blev verdens ophav og verdens hersker; men alle dens veier er fulde av blomster og blod, blomster og blod" (Love is creation's source, creation's ruler; but all love's ways are strewn with blossoms and blood, blossoms and blood).

In 1899 Hamsun traveled in Finland, Russia, and the Near East. After his return he spent most of his wife's fortune at a casino in Ostende; later he was known for his wild parties at Bernina, a restaurant in Copenhagen. Hamsun, who contributed the poem "Bjørnson på hans 70 års fødselsdag" (Bjørnson on his 70th Birthday) to a festschrift honoring the older writer in 1902, slowly came to realize that Bjørnson had drawn strength from his family life and his country home. He tried to salvage his marriage by designing and building a home for his wife and their daughter, Victoria, born on 15 August 1902, near Christiania; but it was too late, and they were divorced in 1906. In 1909 he married a twenty-eight-year-old actress, Marie Andersen, who had grown up on a farm; two years later they bought and moved to the farm Skogheim at Hamarøy in northern Norway. Tore, Arild, and Ellinor, the first three of their four children, were born there on 6 March 1912, 3 May 1914, and 23 October 1915, respectively. The fourth child, Cecilia, was born on 13 May 1917 in Larvik, where the family lived from May 1917 until October 1918, when they moved to Nørholm, a farm near Grimstad.

During these years Hamsun published the plays *Munken Vendt: Brigantinens Saga, 1* (1902, The Monk Vendt: Saga of the Brigantine), *Dronning Tamara: Skuespil i tre Akter* (1903, Queen Tamara), and *Livet ivold* (1910; translated as *In the Grip of Life,* 1924); the travel book *I Æventyrland: Oplevet og drømt i Kaukasien* (1903, In a Wondrous Land: My Life and Dreams in Caucasia; translated as *In Wonderland,* 2004); two collections of short stories, *Kratskog* in 1903 and *Stridende Liv: Skildringer fra Vesten og Østen* (1905, Struggling Life: Tales from the East and the West); a book of verse, *Det vilde Kor* (1904, The Wild Chorus); and six novels. Although Hamsun's plays—he ultimately wrote six—were well received in Russia, where they supplied him with a steady income for years, they have never had lasting success elsewhere. His book of verse combines unusual rhythms and a pleasing singability but is otherwise unremarkable.

Hamsun's fame rests on his novels, of which he wrote two series during these years. Both series are different from anything he had done earlier. *Sværmere* (1904; translated as *Dreamers*, 1921, and as *Mothwise*, 1921), *Benoni* (1908; translated, 1925), and *Rosa: Af Student Parelius' Papirer* (1908; translated, 1926) have the same setting as *Pan*–northern Norway and the house of Mack–but the heroes are upstart businessmen or inventors who win the "princess." In these novels tragedy gives way to humor, and psychology to the simple typology and plot development of the fairy tale; the emphasis is on local color, including dialect. In the Wanderer trilogy–*Under Høststjærnen: En Vandrers Fortælling* (1906; translated as "Under the Autumn Star," 1922), *En Vandrer spiller med Sordin* (1909; translated as "A Wanderer Plays on Muted Strings," 1922), and *Den sidste Glæde: Skildringer* (1912; translated as *Look Back on Happiness*, 1940)–the enigmatic-man theme of *Mysterier* is repeated in a new manner: this time the hero is not an agronomist in a striking yellow suit, like Nagel, but a middle-aged writer dressed as a tramp. He is looking for work as a jack-of-all-trades but does not really need the money: he is a refugee from the wasting café life of big cities hoping to find new inspiration in the country. Furthermore, his name is not an aristocratic Nagel or Glahn but the prosaic Pedersen, Hamsun's own birth name. A humorous low style replaces the high melodrama of *Mysterier* and *Pan*: Pedersen digs ditches, cuts cordwood, and makes love to the minister's wife in the barn. Nevertheless, the Wanderer books differ from the folksy Benoni novels in their sentimentality. During a church service Pedersen is overcome with emotion, and he loves the wife of his employer, Captain Falkenberg, with a hopeless, never-ending passion. Finally, he acts as a god in disguise, helping the farmers with good advice and serving as a matchmaker for a neurotic city girl, whom he marries off to a healthy farm boy.

Volumes one and two of the Wanderer trilogy are minor masterworks, mixing realism and romanticism in their prose. The final novel is more didactic, although its prose sometimes breaks into poetry. In the last chapter Hamsun addresses gainfully employed women with his typically sexist attitudes. The chapter reads like a reprimanding letter to his wife, who, Hamsun thought, missed the city and deplored the fact that, as a farmer's wife, her liberal-arts education was being wasted. Actually, she was the farmer of the two; he was the footloose, neurotic artist taking on the guise of Rousseau and seeing humanity's only salvation in a return to nature and the soil. Despite the years he had spent in cities–Christiania, Chicago, Minneapolis, Copenhagen, Paris, and Helsinki–Hamsun's urban experience was superficial. He was drawn reluctantly to cities by their cultural attractions, but he had no understanding of their importance as places for emigrants from the countryside to find work and security. Rather, cities were like anthills, as he writes in the novel *Konerne ved Vandposten* (1920; translated as *The Women at the Pump*, 1928): "Alle mennesker er optat med sit, de krysser hverandres veier, de puffer hverandre tilside, stundom går de over hverandre. Det kan ikke være anderledes, stundom går de over hverandre" (Everyone busy with his own affairs, crossing each other's path, elbowing each other aside, sometimes even trampling on each other. That's the way it is, sometimes they even trample on each other).

The novels *Børn av Tiden* (1913; translated as *Children of the Age*, 1924) and *Segelfoss By* (1915; translated as *Segelfoss Town*, 1925) chronicle the industrialization of the Segelfoss estate, a former feudal community in northern Norway owned by the generous but arrogant Lieutenant Willatz Holmsen III. The enterprising Tobias Holmengrå, who has worked himself up from nothing, returns to the area, buys up most of Holmsen's land little by little, harnesses the waterfall, and builds a mill. After selling or mortgaging most of his property, Holmsen finds an old family treasure, pays his debts, and dies a proud and honest man–the closest thing to a conventional hero in all of Hamsun's work. In the second novel the urban development is completed. A lawyer and a doctor move in; a newspaper is established; traveling salesmen begin to visit the town; and at the end a touring theater group arrives. Both novels feature dozens of characters, multiple plotlines, much local color, and humorous dialogue. Hamsun has little sympathy for his city dwellers, particularly the university-trained emigrants from southern Norway, but the satire is good-humored rather than bitter.

On 16 January 1915 Hamsun took a harsh stand in a discussion in the Christiania newspaper *Morgenbladet* of unwed parents who kill their newborns out of shame: "En slik Mor og en slik Barnefar er haapløse, hæng dem!" (Such a mother and such a father are hopeless, hang them!). But two years later, in *Markens Grøde*, his sympathy with two women who commit infanticide is striking. Isak Sellanraa, "en født bærer, en pram gjennom skogene" (a lumbering barge of a man), establishes a homestead in northern Norway. He tells passersby that he needs a woman to help him, and soon Inger arrives from the next parish. She has a harelip but is a hard worker, and, even more important, she owns a cow. Isak and Inger have two sons: Eleseus and Sivert; when their third child is a girl with a harelip, Inger, recalling what she has suffered because of her disfigurement, kills the baby. The grave is discovered, and Inger goes to prison for six years.

She returns a different person: she has learned reading, writing, and dressmaking; she likes to have people around and even dances with some newly arrived telegraph workers; and she urges Eleseus to accept an engineer's offer of an office job in town. This decision turns out to be costly for the parents: corrupted by town life, Eleseus spends his time and their money on useless pursuits, grows restless, and finally immigrates to America and is never heard from again.

A subplot in the novel concerns another settler, Axel, and his housekeeper, Barbro, in a darker and more realistic variation on Isak and Inger's story. Axel is less generous and good-humored than Isak, and Barbro is a less remorseful child murderer than Inger. Yet, even for Barbro there is hope: a life in the countryside, close to nature, can heal all wounds.

Geissler, the bailiff, is a curious character. He is a benefactor to Isak, helping with the latter's homesteading and discovering and buying a copper lode on Isak's property; but by bringing miners and industry to the area he ultimately destroys the rural community. He tells Sivert: "Vær tilfreds! dere har alt å leve av, alt å leve for, alt å tro på, dere fødes og frembringer, dere er de nødvendige på jorden.... Fra slægt til slægt er dere til i lutter avl, og når dere dør tar den nye avl til. Det er det som menes med det evige liv" (You be content! You've everything to live on, everything to live for, everything to believe in, being born and bringing forth, you are the needful on earth.... Generation to generation, breeding ever anew; and when you die, the new stock goes on. That's the meaning of eternal life).

Hamsun had no real understanding of peasants, but in the years before World War I he had come to look on farming as the only workable compromise between the dangers of untamed nature and the corruptions of the city, and he wanted to make his new message simple, beautiful, and free from doubt. Hence, despite its many dark scenes and seemingly worthless characters, *Markens Grøde* has the outline structure and the optimism of myth and fairy tale, rather than the close-up perspective and resignation of true realism. Wells wrote of *Markens Grøde:* "I am not usually lavish with my praise, but indeed the book impresses me as among the very greatest novels I have ever read. It is wholly beautiful; it is saturated with wisdom and humor and tenderness."

The 1920 Nobel Prize in Literature was awarded to Hamsun for this novel. Hamsun's name had been suggested by his friend, Norwegian art historian Harry Fett, in 1918; but not until 1920 did a majority of the Swedish Academy's members, led by its secretary, the poet Erik Axel Karlfeldt, select Hamsun. His name was well known in Germany and the Mediterranean countries, and his candidacy was well received at home and abroad. The prize led to increased recognition, particularly in England and America, where most of Hamsun's work had not yet been available in translation. Hamsun spent the prize money on his new farm, Nørholm, and on the education of his children. However, he was also a generous donor, in particular supporting young artists.

Readers who had expected a permanent change in Hamsun's writing after *Markens Grøde* were surprised by the pessimism and openly anti-English tone of his next novel: *Konerne ved Vandposten* was published in 1920, after Hamsun's favorite country–Germany– had been defeated. In the novel one character declares, "Engelskmanden har sin egen religion her i verden og retfærdiggjør den på fuldt engelsk måte. Han undertvinger folk efter folk, tar selvstændigheten fra dem, kastrerer dem og gjør dem tykke og stille. Så en dag sier engelskmanden: Lat os nu ifølge Skriften være retfærdige! Og så gir han kastraterne noget som han kalder selvstyre" (The Englishman enslaves one people after another, takes their independence from them, castrates them, makes them fat and placid. Then one day the Englishman says: Let us now be righteous according to the Scriptures. And so he gives the eunuchs something he calls self-government). Hamsun's next novel, *Siste Kapitel* (1923; translated as *Chapter the Last,* 1929), is similar to his *Den sidste Glæde:* the earlier work takes place at a mountain resort, the later one at a mountain sanatorium, and both novels concern the slow transformation of a neurotic city woman into a happy farmwife and mother. *Siste Kapitel* is, however, almost totally free of the didacticism that mars the earlier book.

Suffering from writer's block, in 1926 Hamsun became one of the first Norwegians to undergo psychoanalysis. Toward the end of the following year he completed his longest novel, *Landstrykere* (1927; translated as *Vagabonds,* 1930), the first part of a trilogy that also includes *August* (1930; translated, 1931) and *Men Livet lever* (1933; translated as *The Road Leads On,* 1934). In *Landstrykere,* Edevart Andersen is born in the 1850s in Polden in northern Norway and grows up to be a big, strong farm boy. He meets the sailor August, two years older than he, and the two begin a vagabond existence that involves enterprises ranging from modest peddling in the countryside to daring and imaginative business projects that sometimes reap handsome rewards. Edevart falls in love with a married woman, Lovise Magrete; the description of their first meeting at her farm is one of the most touching scenes in all of Hamsun's works. She asks Edevart for money so that she can go to America with her family; she later returns without her husband, but the once happy and industrious Lovise Magrete has acquired the restlessness of the New World. Edevart marries her, and they spend several years on small farms in the United States. In the second part of the trilogy, *August,* they return to Polden; but Lovise Magrete misses her children in the United States. Edevart decides to follow her but perishes in a storm while sailing out to catch the ship and board it at sea. In the meantime, August has carried on with his enterprises, including a tobacco plantation and a herring-meal factory. In part 3 of the trilogy, *Men Livet lever,* he begins raising sheep in the grand style he knows from his days on the Argentine pampas. One day, in a tight spot on his newly constructed mountain road, his thousand sheep are frightened by an automobile and plunge off a nine-hundred-foot precipice, bearing August along in their midst. The novel ends: "Et hav av sau blev sjømandens grav" (An ocean of sheep was the sailor's death). On 14 March 1930 Hamsun wrote to his wife about *August:* "Det hele er et Angrep paa Industrien. *Det* er jo all right nok, men om jeg har greid det rent dikterisk, det er det det spørst om" (It is an attack on industry. Now, that is all right, but whether I have managed it from a literary point of view is another matter).

In 1934 Carl von Ossietzky, a German pacifist whom the Nazis had placed in a concentration camp, was proposed by some Norwegians as a candidate for the Nobel Peace Prize. Hamsun attacked the proposal as an insult to Germany; in response, the Norwegian Authors Union issued a statement deploring the fact that "den mest berømte blant nålevende norske forfattere, fri, velhavende, og i enhver henseende betrygget, går til angrep på en mann som sitter i tysk konsentrasjonsleir ene og alene fordi han har sine meningers ubetingede mot, og med sitt liv går inn for dem" (the most famous among living Norwegian authors, free, prosperous, and in every respect secure, attacks a man imprisoned in a German concentration camp only because he has the courage of his convictions and defends them with his life).

In his old age Hamsun became increasingly reactionary and authoritarian; but he was able to side with the young in their struggles against the older generation in his last novel, the unfinished *Ringen sluttet* (1936; translated as *The Ring Is Closed,* 1937). Abel Brodersen lives at the lighthouse near a small southern Norwegian coastal town; his father is a niggardly old former sea captain turned lighthouse keeper, and his mother is an alcoholic. Rejected by Olga, the pharmacist's daughter, he goes to sea. Returning after his parents' deaths, he exhausts his inheritance and then lives in a shack with little to eat. He is, however, quick-witted, skillful, and courageous: he is the only person in town willing to risk his life to save a fellow citizen, and the reader is told that "i al hans ringhet var han ikke uten karakter. Det var noget. Han hadde en Guds likegyldighet for hvordan det gik. Det var noget . . . en suverænitet hos ham" (in the depths of his obscurity, he was not lacking in character. He possessed a sublime indifference toward all conditions he encountered. It rendered him independent—a sovereign in his own way). The reader gradually learns that during Abel's absence he had married an American woman with a French-sounding name, Angèle, with whom he had lived in Green Ridge, Kentucky, until he shot her after finding her with Lawrence, his best friend; Lawrence had been convicted of the crime and sent to the electric chair. The novel ends with Abel leaving again for the United States. Hamsun's son Tore says in his 1959 biography that his father had intended to have Abel confess his crime.

Abel's defeatist attitude was not accepted by Norwegians in the optimistic and enterprising 1930s; they regarded him as something close to an animal. The hero of Hamsun's last novel is what today would be called a hippie; such a character would be just as out of place in the oil-rich Norway of the early twenty-first century as he would have been at the time the novel was published.

Hamsun's novels had been discovered by the Germans in the 1890s, and from Germany their fame had spread to the Mediterranean countries and to the Middle and Far East. After receiving the Nobel Prize, he won a name for himself in the English-speaking world. By 1939 his works had appeared in more than thirty languages. If he had not survived his eightieth birthday that year, he would have died as the most popular of Norway's great writers. But during the German occupation of Norway from 1940 until 1945 Hamsun produced propaganda for the Nazis. He also, however, tried to help Norwegians who had been imprisoned by the occupation forces. In January 1941 he met with Joseph Terboven, the Reichskommissar for Norway, and pleaded successfully for the release of one of the writers, Ronald Fangen. In an article published in the newspaper *Fritt Folk* (Free People) on 20 February 1943 titled "Nu igjen–!" (Now Once More–!) Hamsun described letters he had received from people whose sons had been sentenced to death for resisting the Nazis; he deplored not only the fact that the men had sided with England but that they were young and had to die. In June 1943 Hamsun met Adolf Hitler at Berchtesgaden in Germany. According to Thorkild Hansen's *Prosessen mot Hamsun* (1959, The Hamsun Trial), Hamsun criticized Terboven: "Reichskommissars metoder passer ikke hos oss, hans Preusseri er uantakelig hos oss, og så henrettelsene–vi gider ikke mer!" (The methods of the Reichskommissar are not appropriate in our country. His Prussian manner is not acceptable to us, and then these executions—it's enough!). Hamsun began to weep; Hitler asked the interpreter to calm the old novelist and left the meeting.

On 7 May 1945 Hamsun published an obituary of Hitler in the newspaper *Aftenposten* in which he described the German dictator as "en Kriger for Menneskeheden og en Forkynder av Evangeliet om Ret for alle Nasjoner" (a warrior for mankind and a preacher of the gospel of rights for all nations). He explained the eulogy to his son Tore as an example of his wish to be consistent to the end. Three weeks after the obituary appeared, Hamsun and his wife were interned at Nørholm. After another three weeks Hamsun was transferred to the Grimstad hospital, where he was interrogated by the magistrate on two occasions. Hamsun did not deny his sympathy for Germany, but he said that he did not consider himself guilty of treason, because his conscience told him that he had worked for his country. After three months at Grimstad, he was sent to an old-age home near Landvik. As a result of the hearings before the magistrate Hamsun was indicted under a new law that made membership in the Nasjonal Samling (Norwegian Nazi Party) punishable with imprisonment or fines up to one million Norwegian crowns. Though it was never proved that Hamsun had been a member of Nasjonal Samling, Nørholm was confiscated, and Hamsun was arrested.

In October 1945 Hamsun was moved to a psychiatric clinic in Oslo, where he was examined by Gabriel Langfeldt and Ørnulv Ødegård. In February 1946, after what Hamsun later described as four terrible months in the psychiatric clinic, he was returned to the old-age home at Landvik. Langfeldt and Ødegård signed a report declaring that they did not believe Hamsun to be insane then or to have been insane at the time of his offensive actions; but they considered him "en person med varig svekkede sjelsevner" (a person with permanently impaired mental faculties). Two weeks later, the attorney general announced that although Hamsun must be considered responsible for his actions since he was not insane, the government did not wish to bring a criminal case against him because of his mental impairment and because he was practically deaf. The Directorate for Reparations, however, was pursuing a civil case against him.

Hamsun's case was finally heard in December 1947. In a speech to the court he contended that he had written his wartime articles to save Norwegian lives; he had also, he said, sent many telegrams to Terboven and to Hitler asking for clemency. The judges, however, found that although Hamsun had not technically been a member of the Nasjonal Samling, he had supported the enemy throughout the war—a transgression that was all the more serious because of the novelist's prestige in Norway. He was sentenced to pay a fine of 425,000 crowns, 85 percent of what the court determined to be his net worth.

Two years later Hamsun published a brilliant and moving account of his trial, *Paa gjengrodde Stier,* which was well received by critics and made readers wonder what Langfeldt and Ødegård had meant by "permanently impaired mental faculties." A 175-page chronicle of contemporary events and impressions without chapter divisions, *Paa gjengrodde Stier* lacks the intensity and artistic form of Hamsun's earlier work; but the chief compositional device of *Sult*—the protagonist's gradual displacement from the pleasures of the Palace Gardens to the slums behind the East Station—is repeated in Hamsun's depiction of the various places in which he was confined. What seems at first to be a day-to-day account of trivial events suddenly reveals the great novelist's sense of scene and dialogue, of humor and pathos, as he forces the reader to confront the question of whether he deserved this treatment.

Paa gjengrodde Stier also shows Hamsun's Renaissance mind at work as he inspects new and old buildings, criticizes carpentry and vocabulary, and deplores the new spelling of Norwegian—the country had had three spelling reforms in Hamsun's lifetime—as well as the lack of old-fashioned respect in modern forms of greeting. And there are scenes that show some of Hamsun's former ecstasy over the mysteries of nature, as when he looks at the Nørholm inlet and sees the moon "klavre op fra havet som en maneter våt av guld" (coming up from the sea like a jellyfish dripping with gold). Although written by an old man living in isolation, *Paa gjengrodde Stier* exudes a warmth that reminded Norwegian readers of what they owed this once beloved writer and led many of them to ask whether the old sinner could not have been treated more leniently.

In 1950 Hamsun broke down and cried at the news that the Gyldendal publishing house would begin republishing his books: his worst punishment had been his total neglect by readers and scholars during the first years after the war. Since Hamsun's death on 19 February 1952, an increasing number of books and articles on his life and works have appeared in many countries. A useful guide is Arvid Østby's bibliography (1972), though it is now somewhat dated. Of critical approaches to Hamsun's early work, James W. McFarlane's article in *PMLA* (1956) is a pioneering essay, followed several years later by Rolf Nyboe Nettum's dissertation from 1970. Interesting and important are also Olaf Øyslebø's examination of Knut Hamsun's literary style (1964) and Atle Kittang's analysis of Hamsun's "novels of disillusion" (1984).

Hamsun's early life and career is the subject of Lars Frode Larsen's impressive three-volume history (1998–2002), while Hamsun's wartime support of Germany and his postwar trial for aiding the enemy is treated in Hansen's massive and well-written account. Hamsun's political views and his wartime articles were also examined by Sten Sparre Nilson (1960).

After the war, Marie Hamsun published two interesting volumes (1953, 1959) on her more than forty years as Hamsun's wife, while her oldest son, Tore, published a biography of his father—the first to cover Hamsun's life from birth to death—in 1952. More objective is Robert Ferguson's *Enigma: The Life of Knut Hamsun,* originally published in English in 1987. So far, the most detailed account of Hamsun's life from cradle to grave is Ingar Sletten Kolloen's two-volume biography (2003–2004), volume one covering the first sixty-seven years of the writer's life and volume two the remaining twenty-six.

Knut Hamsun's reputation derives from two main sources. For critics it is his position in the forefront of literary modernism. His manic-depressive heroes, his elitism, his emphasis on the unconscious life of the mind, and his stream-of-consciousness techniques make him a pioneer in the development of twentieth-century European writing. His popular appeal, on the other hand, results from the melodrama of his love stories and, above all—and particularly for Norwegian readers—from the central place of nature in his work: his idealization of the simple life, his emphasis on *trivsel* (a pan-Scandinavian word denoting well-being and peace of mind), and his insistence that industry and materialism do not hold promise for the future. Ultimately, however, Hamsun's appeal is universal. He is the only Norwegian writer besides Ibsen and Sigrid Undset who belongs to world literature.

Letters:
Selected Letters, 2 volumes, edited by Harald Næss and James W. McFarlane (Norwich, U.K.: Norvik Press, 1990, 1998);

Knut Hamsuns brev, 7 volumes, edited by Næss (Oslo: Gyldendal, 1994–2001).

Bibliography:
Arvid Østby, *Knut Hamsun: En bibliografi* (Oslo: Gyldendal, 1972).

Biographies:
Einar Skavlan, *Knut Hamsun* (Oslo: Gyldendal, 1929);

Tore Hamsun, *Knut Hamsun: Min far* (Oslo: Gyldendal, 1952); revised as *Knut Hamsun* (Oslo: Gyldendal, 1959);

Marie Hamsun, *Regnbuen* (Oslo: Aschehoug, 1953);

Marie Hamsun, *Under gullregnen* (Oslo: Aschehoug, 1959);

Thorkild Hansen, *Prosessen mot Hamsun* (Oslo: Gyldendal, 1959);

Harald Næss, *Knut Hamsun og Amerika* (Oslo: Gyldendal, 1969);

Sigrid Stray, *Min klient Knut Hamsun* (Oslo: Aschehoug, 1979);

Robert Ferguson, *Enigma: The Life of Knut Hamsun* (New York: Farrar, Straus & Giroux, 1987);

Øystein Rottem, *Hamsuns liv i bilder* (Oslo: Gyldendal, 1996);

Lars Frode Larsen, *Den unge Hamsun: 1859–1888* (Oslo: Schibsted, 1998);

Larsen, *Radikaleren Hamsun ved gjennombruddet: 1888–1891* (Oslo: Schibsted, 2001);

Larsen, *Tilværelsens udlænding: Hamsun ved gjennombruddet (1891–1893)* (Oslo: Schibsted, 2002);

Ingar Sletten Kolloen, *Hamsun: Svermeren* (Oslo: Gyldendal, 2003);

Kolloen, *Hamsun: Erobreren* (Oslo: Gyldendal, 2004);

Jørgen Haugan, *Solgudens fall: Knut Hamsun—en litterær biografi* (Oslo: Aschehoug, 2004).

References:
Walter Baumgartner, *Knut Hamsun* (Reinbek bei Hamburg: Rowohlt, 1997);

Walter Berendsohn, *Knut Hamsun* (Munich: Albert Langen, 1929);

Trygve Braatøy, *Livets cirkel* (Oslo: Cappelen, 1929);

Knut Brynhildsvoll, *Sult, sprell og Altmulig: Alte und neue Studien zu Knut Hamsuns antipsychologischer Romankunst* (Frankfurt am Main: Peter Lang, 1998);

Aasmund Brynildsen, *Svermeren og hans demon* (Oslo: Dreyer, 1973);

Ståle Dingstad, *Hamsuns strategier: Realisme, humor, kynisme* (Oslo: Gyldendal, 2003);

Alrik Gustafson, *Six Scandinavian Novelists* (New York: American-Scandinavian Foundation, 1940);

Martin Humpál, *The Roots of Modernist Narrative: Knut Hamsun's Novels* Hunger, Mysteries *and* Pan (Oslo: Solum, 1999);

Peter Kierkegaard, *Knut Hamsun som modernist* (Copenhagen: Medusa, 1975);

Atle Kittang, *Luft, vind, ingenting* (Oslo: Gyldendal, 1984);

Nils Magne Knutsen, *Makt–avmakt: En studie av Hamsuns* Benoni *og* Rosa (Oslo: Gyldendal, 1975);

John Landquist, *Knut Hamsun* (Tübingen: Fischer, 1927);

Leo Lowenthal, *Literature and the Image of Man* (Boston: Beacon, 1957);

Sverre Lyngstad, *Knut Hamsun, Novelist: A Critical Assessment* (New York & Oxford: Peter Lang, 2005);

Jan F. Marstrander, *Det ensomme menneske i Knut Hamsuns diktning* (Oslo: Det norske studentersamfunds kulturutvalg, 1959);

Marstrander, *Livskamp og virkelighetsoppfatning: Knut Hamsuns forfatterskap frem mot gjennombruddet (1877–1887)*, edited by Lars Frode Larsen (Oslo: ProArk, 1993);

James W. McFarlane, "The Whisper of the Blood," *PMLA*, 71 (1956): 563–594;

Martin Nag, *Geniet Knut Hamsun—en norsk Dostojewskij* (Oslo: Solum, 1998);

Rolf Nyboe Nettum, *Konflikt og visjon* (Oslo: Gyldendal, 1970);

Sten Sparre Nilson, *En ørn i uvær: Knut Hamsun og politikken* (Oslo: Gyldendal, 1960);

Gregory Nybø, *Knut Hamsuns* Mysterier (Oslo: Gyldendal, 1969);

Harald Næss, *Knut Hamsun* (Boston: Twayne, 1984);

Ronald Popperwell, "Critical Attitudes to Knut Hamsun," *Scandinavica*, 9 (1970): 1–23;

Alan Powers, *Front Cover: Great Book Jackets and Cover Design* (London: Mitchell Beazley, 2001);

Øystein Rottem, *Guddommelig galskap* (Oslo: Gyldendal, 1998);

Rottem, *Hamsun og fantasiens triumf* (Oslo: Gyldendal, 2002);

Rottem, *Knut Hamsuns* Landstrykere: *en ideologikritisk analyse* (Oslo: Gyldendal, 1978);

Henning Sehmsdorf, "Knut Hamsun's *Pan*," *Edda* (1974): 345–393;

James Allen Simpson, *Knut Hamsuns* Landstrykere, translated by Jan F. Marstrander (Oslo: Gyldendal, 1973);

Jørgen Tiemroth, *Illusionens vej* (Copenhagen: Gyldendal, 1974);

Rolf Vige, *Knut Hamsuns* Pan (Oslo: Universitetsforlaget, 1963);

H. G. Wells, *The Salvaging of Civilization* (London: Cassell, 1921), p. 124;

Joseph Wiehr, "Knut Hamsun: His Personality and His Outlook upon Life," *Smith College Studies in Modern Languages*, 3, nos. 1–2 (1921–1922): 1–129;

Olaf Øyslebø, *Knut Hamsun gjennom stilen* (Oslo: Gyldendal, 1964).

Papers:

Most of Knut Hamsun's manuscripts and other papers are in the Nasjonalbiblioteket (National Library) in Oslo. Other large collections are at the University Library in Bergen, Det Kongelige Bibliotek (The Royal Library) in Copenhagen, and the Puskinskij Dom (Pushkin House) in St. Petersburg, Russia.

1920 Nobel Prize in Literature Presentation Speech

by Harald Hjärne, Chairman of the Nobel Committee of the Swedish Academy, 10 December 1920

In accordance with the statutes of the Nobel Foundation, the Swedish Academy has awarded the literary Prize for 1920 to the Norwegian novelist Knut Hamsun for his work, *Markens Grøde* (1917) [*Growth of the Soil*].

It would be superfluous to give a detailed account of a book that in a short time has spread everywhere in its original form or in translation. Through the originality of its plot and style, it has aroused the liveliest interest in many countries and has found favourable reception with the most diverse groups of readers. Only recently a leading and distinctly conservative English reviewer wrote that this book, which had appeared in England only this year, was universally acclaimed as a masterpiece. The reasons for this incontestable success will no doubt hold the attention of literary critics for a long time, but even now, under the impact of first impressions, they deserve to be pointed out at least in their broad features.

In spite of current opinions of our time, those who want to find in literature above all a faithful reproduction of reality, will recognize in *Markens Grøde* the representation of a life that forms the basis of existence and of the development of societies wherever men live and build. These descriptions are not distorted by any memories of a long, highly civilized past; their immediate effect is due to the evocation of the harsh struggle all active men must in the beginning endure (in varying external conditions, of course) against an indomitable and rebellious nature. It would be difficult to conceive of a more striking contrast with works usually called "classic."

Nonetheless, this work may rightly be called classic, but in a deeper and more profound sense than usual if this epithet is to express something other and more than vague praise. The classic, in the culture we have inherited from antiquity, is less the perfect which calls for imitation than the significant which is taken directly from life and which is rendered in a form of enduring value even for future ages. The insignificant, that which in itself is of no consequence, cannot be comprehended in this notion any more than that which is formally provisional or defective. But apart from that, whatever is precious in human life, although it may appear common, can be placed in the same category as the extraordinary and the brilliant, with a significance and a form of equal value, once it is presented for the first time in its proper light. In this sense it is no exaggeration to maintain that in *Markens Grøde* Hamsun has given to our times a classic that can be measured against the best we already have. Antiquity does not possess in this respect a monopoly inaccessible to future generations; for life is always new and inexhaustible and as such can always be presented in new forms created by new geniuses.

Hamsun's work is an epic of labour to which the author has given monumental lines. It is not a question of disparate labour which divides men within and among themselves; it is a question of the concentrated toil which in its purest form shapes men entirely, which mollifies and brings together divided spirits, which protects and increases their fruits with a regular and uninterrupted progress. The labour of the pioneer and the first farmer with all its difficulties, under the poet's pen, thus takes on the character of a heroic struggle that yields nothing to the grandeur of the manly sacrifice for one's country and companions in arms. Just as the peasant poet Hesiod described the labours of the field, so Hamsun has put in the foreground of his work the ideal labourer who dedicates his whole life and all his powers to clearing the land and to triumphing over the obstacles with which men and the forces of nature confront him. If Hamsun has cast behind him all the weighty memories of civilization, he has by his own work contributed to a precise understanding of the new culture that our era expects to arise from the progress of physical labour as a continuation of ancient civilization.

Hamsun does not present so-called types on his stage. His heroes and heroines are all very much alive, all in quite modest circumstances. Certain among them, and the best, are unimaginative in their goals and thoughts, the principal example being the tireless and silent farmer himself. Others are drifting, troubled, and often even bewildered by egoistic aspirations and follies. They all carry the mark of their Norwegian origin; they are all conditioned in some manner by "the fruits of the earth." It is one of the characteristics of our sister languages that often the same words express very different nuances of meaning by the images they evoke. When we Swedes speak of the "fruits of the earth," we think immediately of something fertile, abundant, succulent, preferably in an agricultural region that has been cultivated for a long time. The thought of Hamsun's book is not oriented in this direction. "The earth" here is the rugged and forbidding fallow soil. Its fruits do not fall from a cornucopia of abundance; they comprise all that can germinate and grow in this ungrateful soil, the good and the bad, the beautiful and the ugly, among men and animals as well as in the forest and the fields. Such are the kinds of fruits Hamsun's work offers for our harvest.

However, we Swedes, or at least many Swedes, do not feel strange in the regions and circumstances described to us here. We rediscover the atmosphere of the North with all that is a part of its natural and social milieu, and with many parallels on both sides of the frontier. Moreover, Hamsun also presents Swedish characters who are drawn to the newly cultivated land, most of them no doubt attracted by the mirage of brilliant economic success, as the cities on the Norwegian coasts appear on the horizon like snares of the great worldly life enticing defenceless hearts from the heavy toil of the land.

These and other quite human projections, far from weakening, reinforce the impression produced by the classic content of the story. They dissipate the apprehension one could feel in seeing the light of the ideal at the expense of truth; they guarantee the sincerity of the design, the truth of the images and the characters. Their common humanity escapes no one. The proof is in the welcome this work has found among peoples of different mentalities, languages, and customs. Furthermore, through the light touch of smiling humour with which the author treats even the saddest things he relates, he has proved his own compassion for human destiny and human nature. But in the story, he never departs from the most complete artistic serenity. The style, stripped of vain ornaments, renders the reality of things with certainty and clarity, and one rediscovers in it, under a personal and powerful form, all the richness of nuance of the writer's mother tongue.

Mr. Knut Hamsun–In facing the rigours of the season as well as the fatigues of a long trip particularly arduous at this time in order to come to receive the Prize awarded you, you have given great joy to the Swedish Academy, which will certainly be shared by all the persons present at this ceremony. In the name of the Academy, I have tried as well as possible in the short time accorded me to express at least some of the major reasons for which we appreciate so highly your work which has just been crowned. Thus, in addressing myself now to you personally, I do not wish to repeat what I have said. It remains for me only to congratulate you in the name of the Academy and to express the hope that the memories you will keep of your visit with us will be ties that will link you to us also in the future.

[© The Nobel Foundation, 1920.]

Hamsun: Banquet Speech

Hamsun's speech at the Nobel Banquet at Grand Hôtel, Stockholm, 10 December 1920 (Translation):

What am I to do in the presence of such gracious, such overwhelming generosity? I no longer have my feet planted on the ground, I am walking on air, my head is spinning. It is not easy to be myself right now. I have had honours and riches heaped on me this day. I myself am what I am, but I have been swept off my feet by the tribute that has been paid to my country, by the strains of her national anthem which resounded in this hall a minute ago.

It is as well perhaps that this is not the first time I have been swept off my feet. In the days of my blessed youth there were such occasions; in what young person's life do they not occur? No, the only young people to whom this feeling is strange are those young conservatives who were born old, who do not know the meaning of being carried away. No worse fate can befall a young man or woman than becoming prematurely entrenched in prudence and negation. Heaven knows that there are plenty of opportunities in later life, too, for being carried away. What of it? We remain what we are and, no doubt, it is all very good for us!

However, I must not indulge in homespun wisdom here before so distinguished an assembly, especially as I am to be followed by a representative of science. I will soon sit down again, but this is my great day. I have been singled out by your benevolence, chosen amongst thousands of others, and crowned with laurels! On behalf of my country I thank the Swedish Academy and all Sweden for the honour they have bestowed on me. Personally, I bow my head under the weight of such great distinctions, but I am also proud that your Academy should have judged my shoulders strong enough to bear them.

A distinguished speaker said earlier tonight that I have my own way of writing, and this much I may perhaps claim and no more. I have, however, learned something from everyone and what man is there who has not learned a little from all? I have had much to learn from Sweden's poetry and, more especially, from her lyrics of the last generation. Were I more conversant with literature and its great names, I could go on quoting them *ad infinitum* and acknowledge my debt for the merit you have been generous enough to find in my work. However, coming from a person like me, this would be mere name-dropping, shallow sound effects without a single bass note to support them. I am no longer young enough for this; I have not the strength.

No, what I should really like to do right now, in the full blaze of lights, before this illustrious assembly, is to shower every one of you with gifts, with flowers, with offerings of poetry—to be young once more, to ride on the crest of the wave. That is what I should wish to do on this great occasion, this last opportunity for me. I dare not do it, for I would not be able to escape ridicule. Today riches and honours have been lavished on me, but one gift has been lacking, the most important one of all, the only one that matters, the gift of youth. None of us is too old to remember it. It is proper that we who have grown old should take a step back and do so with dignity and grace.

I know not what I should do—I know not what is the right thing to do, but I raise my glass to the youth of Sweden, to young people everywhere, to all that is young in life.

Prior to the speech, Professor Oscar Montelius remarked to Hamsun: "I know that you prefer to be talked about as little as possible; but I cannot refrain from assuring you that all of us who admire your Growth of the Soil *rejoice in having made your personal acquaintance."*

[© The Nobel Foundation, 1920. Knut Hamsun is the sole author of his speech.]

Gerhart Hauptmann

(15 November 1862 - 6 June 1946)

Roy C. Cowen
University of Michigan

This entry has been expanded by Cowen from his Hauptmann entry in *DLB 118: Twentieth-Century German Dramatists, 1889–1918*. See also the Hauptmann entry in *DLB 66: German Fiction Writers, 1885–1913*.

BOOKS: *Liebesfrühling: Ein lyrisches Gedicht* (Salzbrunn: Privately printed, 1881);

Promethidenloos: Eine Dichtung (Berlin: Ißeib, 1885);

Das bunte Buch: Gedichte, Sagen & Märchen (Leipzig & Stuttgart: Meinhard, 1888);

Vor Sonnenaufgang (Berlin: Conrad, 1889); translated by Leonard Bloomfield as *Before Dawn* (Boston: Badger, 1909);

Das Friedensfest: Eine Familienkatastrophe. Bühnendichtung (Berlin: Fischer, 1890); translated by Janet Achurch and C. E. Wheeler as *The Coming of Peace: A Family Catastrophe* (Chicago: Sergel, 1900);

Einsame Menschen (Berlin: Fischer, 1891); translated by Mary Morison as *Lonely Lives* (New York: De Witt, 1898);

Der Apostel; Bahnwärter Thiel: Novellistische Studien (Berlin: Fischer, 1892); *Bahnwärter Thiel* translated by Adele S. Seltzer as "Flagman Thiel," in *Great German Short Novels and Stories,* edited by Bennett A. Cerf (New York: Modern Library, 1933);

College Crampton: Komödie (Berlin: Fischer, 1892); translated by Roy Temple House and Ludwig Lewisohn as *Colleague Crampton*, in *The Dramatic Works of Gerhart Hauptmann*, edited by Lewisohn, volume 3 (New York: Huebsch, 1914);

Die Weber: Schauspiel aus den vierziger Jahren (Berlin: Fischer, 1892); translated by Morison as *The Weavers* (New York: Russell, 1899); translated by F. Marcus as *The Weavers* (London: Methuen, 1980);

Der Biberpelz: Eine Diebskomödie (Berlin: Fischer, 1893); translated by Lewisohn as *The Beaver Coat*, in *The Dramatic Works of Gerhart Hauptmann*, edited by Lewisohn, volume 1 (New York: Huebsch, 1912);

Hannele Matterns Himmelfahrt (Berlin: Fischer, 1893); republished as *Hannele: Traumdichtung in zwei Teilen*

Gerhart Hauptmann

(Berlin: Fischer, 1894); translated by William Archer as *Hannele* (London: Heinemann, 1894); translated by Charles Henry Meltzer as *Hannele* (New York: Doubleday, Page, 1908); original republished as *Hanneles Himmelfahrt: Traumdichtung* (Berlin: Fischer, 1896);

Florian Geyer (Berlin: Fischer, 1896); translated by Bayard Quincy Morgan as *Florian Geyer*, in *The Dramatic Works of Gerhart Hauptmann*, edited by Lewisohn, volume 9 (New York: Viking, 1929);

Die versunkene Glocke: Ein deutsches Märchendrama (Berlin: Fischer, 1897); translated by Mary Harned as *The Sunken Bell* (Boston: Badger, 1898);

Fuhrmann Henschel: Schauspiel (Berlin: Fischer, 1899); translated by Marion A. Redlich as *Drayman Henschel* (Chicago: Dramatic Publishing Co., 1910);

Helios: Fragment eines Dramas (N.p., 1899); translated by Lewisohn as *Helios (Fragment)*, in *The Dramatic Works of Gerhart Hauptmann*, edited by Lewisohn, volume 7 (New York: Huebsch, 1917);

Michael Kramer: Drama in vier Akten (Berlin: Fischer, 1900); translated by Lewisohn as *Michael Kramer*, in *The Dramatic Works of Gerhart Hauptmann*, edited by Lewisohn, volume 3 (New York: Huebsch, 1914);

Schluck und Jau: Spiel zu Scherz und Schimpf (Berlin: Fischer, 1900); translated by Lewisohn as *Schluck and Jau*, in *The Dramatic Works of Gerhart Hauptmann*, edited by Lewisohn, volume 5 (New York: Huebsch, 1916);

Der rote Hahn: Tragikomödie in vier Akten (Berlin: Fischer, 1901); translated by Lewisohn as *The Conflagration*, in *The Dramatic Works of Gerhart Hauptmann*, edited by Lewisohn, volume 1 (New York: Huebsch, 1912);

Der arme Heinrich: Eine deutsche Sage (Berlin: Fischer, 1902); translated by Lewisohn as *Henry of Auë*, in *The Dramatic Works of Gerhart Hauptmann*, edited by Lewisohn, volume 4 (New York: Huebsch, 1915);

Rose Bernd: Schauspiel in fünf Akten (Berlin: Fischer, 1903); translated by Lewisohn as *Rose Bernd*, in *The Dramatic Works of Gerhart Hauptmann*, edited by Lewisohn, volume 2 (New York: Huebsch, 1913);

Elga (Berlin: Fischer, 1905); translated by Harned as *Elga* (Boston: Badger, 1909);

Und Pippa tanzt! Ein Glashüttenmärchen in vier Akten (Berlin: Fischer, 1906); translated by Harned as *And Pippa Dances* (Boston: Badger, 1909);

Gesammelte Werke, 6 volumes (Berlin: Fischer, 1906);

Die Jungfern von Bischofsberg: Lustspiel (Berlin: Fischer, 1907); translated by Lewisohn as *The Maidens of the Mount*, in *The Dramatic Works of Gerhart Hauptmann*, edited by Lewisohn, volume 6 (New York: Huebsch, 1916);

Griechischer Frühling (Berlin: Fischer, 1908);

Kaiser Karls Geisel: Legendenspiel (Berlin: Fischer, 1908); translated by Lewisohn as *Charlemagne's Hostage*, in *The Dramatic Works of Gerhart Hauptmann*, edited by Lewisohn, volume 5 (New York: Huebsch, 1916);

Griselda (Berlin: Fischer, 1909); translated by Alice Kauser as *Griselda* (Binghampton, N.Y.: Binghampton Book Manufacturing Co., 1909);

Der Narr in Christo Emanuel Quint (Berlin: Fischer, 1910); translated by Thomas Seltzer as *The Fool In Christ Emanuel Quint* (New York: Huebsch, 1911);

Die Ratten: Berliner Tragikomödie (Berlin: Fischer, 1911): translated by Lewisohn as *The Rats*, in *The Dramatic Works of Gerhart Hauptmann*, edited by Lewisohn, volume 2 (New York: Huebsch, 1913);

Atlantis: Roman (Berlin: Fischer, 1912); translated by Adele S. Seltzer and Thomas Seltzer as *Atlantis* (New York: Huebsch, 1912);

Gabriel Schillings Flucht: Drama (Berlin: Fischer, 1912); translated by Lewisohn as *Gabriel Schilling's Flight*, in *The Dramatic Works of Gerhart Hauptmann*, edited by Lewisohn, volume 6 (New York: Huebsch, 1916);

Gesammelte Werke: Volksausgabe in 6 Bänden, 6 volumes (Berlin: Fischer, 1912);

Festspiel in deutschen Reimen (Berlin: Fischer, 1913); translated by Morgan as *Commemoration Masque*, in *The Dramatic Works of Gerhart Hauptmann*, edited by Lewisohn, volume 7 (New York: Huebsch, 1917);

Lohengrin (Berlin: Ullstein, 1913);

Der Bogen des Odysseus (Berlin: Fischer, 1914); translated by Lewisohn as *The Bow of Odysseus*, in *The Dramatic Works of Gerhart Hauptmann*, edited by Lewisohn, volume 7 (New York: Huebsch, 1917);

Parsival (Berlin: Ullstein, 1914); translated by Oakley Williams as *Parsifal* (New York: Macmilan, 1915);

Winterballade: Eine dramatische Dichtung (Berlin: Fischer, 1917); translated by Willa and Edwin Muir as *A Winter Ballad*, in *The Dramatic Works of Gerhart Hauptmann*, edited by Lewisohn, volume 8 (New York: Huebsch, 1924);

Der Ketzer von Soana (Berlin: Fischer, 1918); translated by Morgan as *The Heretic of Soana* (New York: Huebsch, 1923; London: Secker, 1923);

Der weiße Heiland: Dramatische Phantasie (Berlin: Fischer, 1920); translated by Willa and Edwin Muir as *The White Saviour*, in *The Dramatic Works of Gerhart Hauptmann*, edited by Lewisohn, volume 8 (New York: Huebsch, 1924);

Indipohdi: Dramatisches Gedicht (Berlin: Fischer, 1920); translated by Willa and Edwin Muir as *Indipohdi*, in *The Dramatic Works of Gerhart Hauptmann*, edited by Lewisohn, volume 8 (New York: Huebsch, 1924);

Anna: Ein ländliches Liebesgedicht (Berlin: Fischer, 1921);

Peter Brauer: Tragikomödie (Berlin: Fischer, 1921);

Das Hirtenlied: Ein Fragment (Berlin: Holten, 1921); translated by Lewisohn as *Pastoral (Fragment)*, in *The*

Dramatic Works of Gerhart Hauptmann, edited by Lewisohn, volume 7 (New York: Huebsch, 1917);

Für ein ungeteiltes deutsches Oberschlesien: Öffentliche Protestversammlung zu Berlin (Berlin: Zentralverlag, 1921);

Sonette (Berlin: Voegel, 1921);

Deutsche Wiedergeburt: Vortrag (Vienna: Heller, 1921);

Gesammelte Werke: Große Ausgabe, 12 volumes (Berlin: Fischer, 1922);

Rußland und die Welt, by Hauptmann, Fridtjof Nansen, and Maksim Gorki (Berlin: Verlag für Politik und Wirtschaft, 1922);

Phantom: Aufzeichnungen eines ehemaligen Sträflings (Berlin: Fischer, 1923); translated by Morgan as *Phantom* (New York: Huebsch, 1922; London: Secker, 1923);

Fasching (Berlin: Holten, 1923);

Ausblicke (Berlin: Fischer, 1924);

Festaktus zur Eröffnung des Deutschen Museums, text by Hauptmann, music by H. Zilcher (Munich: Knorr & Hirth, 1925);

Die Insel der Großen Mutter oder Das Wunder von I'le des Dames (Berlin: Fischer, 1925); translated by Willa and Edwin Muir as *The Island of the Great Mother; or, The Miracle of I'le des Dames* (New York: Huebsch, 1925);

Veland: Tragödie (Berlin: Fischer, 1925); translated by Edwin Muir as *Veland,* in *The Dramatic Works of Gerhart Hauptmann,* edited by Lewisohn, volume 9 (New York: Viking, 1929);

Dorothea Angermann: Schauspiel (Berlin: Fischer, 1926);

Die blaue Blume (Berlin: Fischer, 1927);

Till Eulenspiegel: Ein dramatischer Versuch (Leipzig: Klinkhardt, 1927);

Des großen Kampffliegers, Landfahrers, Gauklers und Magiers Till Eulenspiegel Abenteuer, Streiche, Gaukeleien, Gesichte und Träume (Berlin: Fischer, 1928);

Gedanken an Walther Rathenau, by Hauptmann, Wilhelm Marx, Arnold Brecht, and Edwin Redslob (Dresden: Reinßner, 1928);

Ansprache bei der Eröffnung der internationalen Buchkunst-Ausstellung Leipzig (Leipzig, 1928);

Wanda (Der Dämon): Roman (Berlin: Fischer, 1928);

Der Baum von Gallowayshire (Heidelberg: Kampmann, 1929);

Spuk: Die schwarze Maske, Schauspiel; Hexenritt: Ein Satyrspiel (Berlin: Fischer, 1929);

Buch der Leidenschaft, 2 volumes (Berlin: Fischer, 1930);

Drei deutsche Reden (Leipzig: Gesellschaft der Freunde der Deutschen Bücherei, 1930);

Die Spitzhacke: Ein phantastisches Erlebnis (Berlin: Fischer, 1931);

Die Hochzeit auf Buchenhorst: Erzählung (Berlin: Fischer, 1932);

Vor Sonnenuntergang: Schauspiel (Berlin: Fischer, 1932);

Um Volk und Geist: Ansprachen (Berlin: Fischer, 1932);

Das dramatische Werk: Gesamtausgabe zum siebzigsten Geburtstag des Dichters, 2 volumes (Berlin: Fischer, 1932);

Die goldene Harfe: Schauspiel (Berlin: Fischer, 1933);

Das Meerwunder: Eine unwahrscheinliche Geschichte (Berlin: Fischer, 1934);

Hamlet in Wittenberg: Schauspiel (Berlin: Fischer, 1935);

Das epische Werk, 2 volumes (Berlin: Fischer, 1935);

Im Wirbel der Berufung: Roman (Berlin: Fischer, 1936);

Das Abenteuer meiner Jugend, 2 volumes (Berlin: Fischer, 1937);

Ährenlese: Kleinere Dichtungen (Berlin: Fischer, 1939);

Die Tochter der Kathedrale: Schauspiel (Berlin: Fischer, 1939);

Ulrich von Lichtenstein: Komödie (Berlin: Fischer, 1939);

Iphigenie in Delphi: Tragödie (Berlin: Suhrkamp, 1941);

Der Schuß im Park: Novelle (Berlin: Fischer, 1941);

Der Dom (Dramenfragment) (Chemnitz: Gesellschaft der Bücherfreunde, 1942);

Magnus Garbe: Tragödie (Berlin: Fischer, 1942);

Der große Traum: Dichtung (Leipzig: Insel, 1942); enlarged edition, edited by Hans Reisiger (Gütersloh: Bertelsmann, 1956);

Das gesammelte Werk: Ausgabe letzter Hand zum achtzigsten Geburtstag des Dichters, 17 volumes (Berlin: Fischer, 1942);

Der neue Christophorus: Ein Fragment (Weimar: Gesellschaft der Bibliophilen, 1943); enlarged, edited by H.-E. Hass (Berlin: Propyläen, 1965);

Iphigenie in Aulis: Tragödie (Berlin: Suhrkamp, 1944);

Neue Gedichte (Berlin: Aufbau, 1946);

Die Finsternisse: Ein Requiem, introduction by Walter A. Reichart (Aurora, N.Y.: Hammer, 1947);

Mignon: Novelle (Berlin: Suhrkamp, 1947);

Agamemnons Tod; Elektra: Tragödien (Berlin: Suhrkamp, 1948);

Galahad oder Die Gaukelfuhre: Dramatische Fragmente, edited by C. F. W. Behl (Lichtenfels: Fränkische Bibliophilengesellschaft, 1948);

Die Atriden-Tetralogie: Tragödie (Berlin: Suhrkamp, 1949);

Herbert Engelmann: Drama in vier Akten, Aus dem Nachlaße, completed by Carl Zuckmayer (Munich: Beck, 1952);

Winckelmann: Das Verhängnis. Roman, edited and completed by Frank Thiess (Gütersloh: Bertelsmann, 1954);

Der große Traum, edited by Reisiger (Gütersloh: Bertelsmann, 1956);

Sämtliche Werke: Centenar-Ausgabe zum hundertsten Geburtstag des Dichters 15. November 1962, edited by Hass, Martin Machatzke, and W. Bungies, 11 volumes (Frankfurt am Main & Berlin: Propyläen, 1962–1974);

Italienische Reise: Tagebuchaufzeichnungen, edited by Machatzke (Berlin: Propyläen, 1976);

Diarium 1917 bis 1933, edited by Machatzke (Berlin: Propyläen, 1980);

Notiz-Kalender 1889 bis 1891, edited by Machatzke (Frankfurt am Main, Berlin & Vienna: Propyläen, 1982);

Tagebuch 1892 bis 1894, edited by Machatzke (Frankfurt am Main, Berlin & Vienna: Propyläen, 1985);

Tagebucher 1897–1905, edited by Machatzke (Frankfurt am Main: Propyläen, 1987).

Edition in English: *Before Daybreak,* translated by Peter Bauland (Chapel Hill: University of North Carolina Press, 1978).

PLAY PRODUCTIONS: *Vor Sonnenaufgang,* Berlin, Lessingtheater, 20 October 1889;

Das Friedensfest, Berlin, Ostendtheater, 1 June 1890;

Einsame Menschen, Berlin, Residenztheater, 11 January 1891;

Kollege Crampton, Berlin, Deutsches Theater, 16 January 1892;

Die Weber, Berlin, Neues Theater, 26 February 1893;

Hanneles Himmelfahrt, Berlin, Königliches Schauspielhaus, 14 September 1893;

Der Biberpelz, Berlin, Deutsches Theater, 21 September 1893;

Florian Geyer, Berlin, Deutsches Theater, 4 January 1896;

Die versunkene Glocke, Berlin, Deutsches Theater, 2 December 1896;

Fuhrmann Henschel, Berlin, Deutsches Theater, 5 November 1898;

Schluck und Jau, Berlin, Deutsches Theater, 3 February 1900;

Michael Kramer, Berlin, Deutsches Theater, 21 December 1900;

Der rote Hahn, Berlin, Deutsches Theater, 27 November 1901;

Der arme Heinrich, Vienna, Hofburgtheater, 29 November 1902;

Rose Bernd, Berlin, Deutsches Theater, 31 October 1903;

Elga, Berlin, Lessingtheater, 4 March 1905;

Und Pippa tanzt! Berlin, Lessingtheater, 19 January 1906;

Die Jungfern von Bischofsberg, Berlin, Lessingtheater, 2 February 1907;

Kaiser Karls Geisel, Berlin, Lessingtheater, 11 January 1908;

Griselda, Berlin, Lessingtheater, and Vienna, Hofburgtheater, 6 March 1909;

Die Ratten, Berlin, Lessingtheater, 13 January 1911;

Gabriel Schillings Flucht, Bad Lauchstedt, Goethes Theater, 14 June 1912;

Festspiel in deutschen Reimen, Breslau, Jahrhunderthalle, 31 May 1913;

Der Bogen des Odysseus, Berlin, Deutsches Künstlertheater, 17 January 1914;

Winterballade, Berlin, Deutsches Theater, 17 October 1917;

Der weiße Heiland, Berlin, Großes Schauspielhaus, 28 March 1920;

Peter Brauer, Berlin, Lustspielhaus, 1 November 1921;

Indipohdi, Dresden, Staatliches Schauspielhaus, 23 February 1922;

Festaktus zur Eröffnung des Deutschen Museums in München, Munich, Deutsches Museum, 7 May 1925;

Veland, Hamburg, Deutsches Schauspielhaus, 19 September 1925;

Dorothea Angermann, Vienna, Theater in der Josefstadt; Munich, Kammerspiele; Leipzig, Schauspielhaus; Brunswick, Landestheater; and thirteen other theaters, 20 November 1926;

Shakespeare: Hamlet, adapted by Hauptmann, Dresden, Staatliches Schauspielhaus, 8 December 1927;

Spuk: Die schwarze Maske and *Hexenritt,* Vienna, Burgtheater, 3 December 1929;

Vor Sonnenuntergang, Berlin, Deutsches Theater, 16 February 1932;

Die goldene Harfe, Munich, Kammerspiele, 15 October 1933;

Hamlet in Wittenberg, Leipzig, Altes Theater; Altona, Stadttheater; and Osnabrück, Deutsches Nationaltheater, 19 November 1935;

Die Tochter der Kathedrale, Berlin, Staatliches Schauspielhaus, 3 October 1939;

Ulrich von Lichtenstein, Vienna, Burgtheater, 11 November 1939;

Iphigenie in Delphi, Berlin, Staatliches Schauspielhaus, 15 November 1941;

Iphigenie in Aulis, Vienna, Burgtheater, 15 November 1943;

Agamemnons Tod and *Elektra,* Berlin, Deutsches Theater, 10 September 1947;

Herbert Engelmann, adapted by Carl Zuckmayer, Vienna, Akademietheater, 8 March 1952;

Die Finsternisse, Göttingen, Studio, 5 July 1952;

Magnus Garbe, Düsseldorf, Schauspielhaus, 4 February 1956;

Herbert Engelmann (original version), Putbus/Rügen, Theater, 12 November 1962.

OTHER: Herman Georg Fiedler, ed., *The Oxford Book of German Verse,* foreword by Hauptmann (London: Oxford University Press, 1911);

William Shakespeare, *Die tragische Geschichte von Hamlet Prinzen von Dänemark in deutscher Sprache,* translated and adapted by Hauptmann (Weimar: Cranach-presse, 1929);

Johann Wolfgang von Goethe, *Werke*, 2 volumes, introduction by Hauptmann (Berlin: Knaur, 1931).

SELECTED PERIODICAL PUBLICATIONS–UNCOLLECTED: "Deutschland und Shakespeare," *Jahrbuch der deutschen Shakespeare-Gesellschaft*, 51 (1915): vii–xii;

"Hamlet: Einige Worte zu meinem Ergänzungsversuche," *Sächsische Stadttheater: Schauspielhaus Dresden 1927* (1927);

"Goethe," *Germanic Review*, 7 (1932): 101–122;

"Die Wiedertäufer: Romanfragment," *Gerhart Hauptmann-Jahrbuch*, 1 (1936): 12–37;

"Über Tintoretto," *Die neue Rundschau*, 49 (1938): 209–226;

"Johann Winckelmanns letzte Jahre: Novelle (Fragment)," *Das XX. Jahrhundert*, 2 (1940): 331–334, 337;

"Das Märchen," *Die neue Rundschau*, 52 (1941): 686–694;

"Die Wiedertäufer," *Die neue Rundschau*, 53 (1942): 488–494.

When dramatist Gerhart Hauptmann became the thirteenth recipient of the Nobel Prize in Literature, in 1912, only two of his predecessors (Rudyard Kipling in 1907 and Maurice Maeterlinck in 1911) had received this recognition at an earlier age. Yet, as deserving as Hauptmann's achievements and reputation had already made him, his success cannot be attributed to an unusually early or even exclusive interest in literature. Hauptmann had first attempted to express himself artistically as a sculptor. But once he had discovered his literary talents, he explored all possible literary forms: novellas, novels, epics and lyrical poetry, and drama. While he had artistic and popular success with his novellas and novels, Hauptmann achieved his broadest recognition as a playwright. He rapidly became the most prolific and most imitated dramatist since Friedrich Schiller, whose plays dominated German thinking about this genre up to the advent of naturalism. Without its success on the stages in Berlin, naturalism would probably have remained only a mildly disruptive occurrence on the German literary scene; and this success would have been impossible without Hauptmann's plays. On the other hand, without the emergence of naturalism, Hauptmann might never have found the proper vehicle for his talents, let alone gained such prominence and influence.

Hauptmann remains for most theatergoers and literary historians alike the outstanding representative of strongly realistic, character-oriented, socially critical plays. Not only did he achieve his first triumphs with them, but he continued to succeed in writing such dramas—interspersed with works in other genres and modes—long after radical realism had ceased to be in fashion. He gradually expanded the potential of realistic drama far beyond that recognized by his contemporaries during and after the period of naturalism. He accommodated it to his own changing views of human existence and incorporated into it elements of such subsequent developments as neo-Romanticism, symbolism, *Jugendstil* (art nouveau), and expressionism.

His parents, Robert and Marie Straehler Hauptmann, who already had three other children–Georg, Johanna (Lotte), and Carl–have never been viewed as being directly influential on the later artistic success of their youngest child, who was born on 15 November 1862 and was baptized Gerhard *[sic]* Johann Robert Hauptmann in 1863. Nor did his formal education contribute much to his achievements. Hauptmann's elementary schooling, which began in his birthplace, Ober-Salzbrunn (now Szczawno, Poland), and continued in Breslau (now Wrocław, Poland), ended abruptly in 1878 as a consequence of his father's loss of the resort hotel he owned.

Nonetheless, the indirect influence of these early years proved to be lasting. Hauptmann gained literary immortality through his depiction of flesh-and-blood characters from all classes and environments. In his diary he wrote on 29 November 1898: "Erst Menschen, hernach das Drama. An ein Drama von Puppen kann niemand glauben" (First the people, then the drama. No one can believe a drama of puppets). Hauptmann was convinced that realistically portrayed characters would necessarily evoke a plot, and he always made his characters as heterogeneous as possible. At his father's hotel he was exposed as a child to just such a mixed bag of social classes, the wealthy bourgeoisie and members of the German, Polish, and Russian nobility. Ober-Salzbrunn, situated in a rural area, provided Hauptmann's first contact with simpler people and farmers, which was augmented in 1878 and 1879 by his work as an agricultural trainee on the estates of his uncle Gustav Schubert in Lohning and Lederose. During his formative years Hauptmann made the acquaintance of many people who later provided models for literary characters, such as Alfred Ploetz, who was a close friend for many years and served as the model for Loth in *Vor Sonnenaufgang* (1889; translated as *Before Dawn*, 1909), Alf in *Helios* (1899; translated, 1917), and Schmidt in *Atlantis* (1912; translated, 1912). Since these characters, albeit based on one real person, are so different, it is obvious that Hauptmann, when drawing on people he had known, utilized only those traits he needed or could show within the confines of a given work.

In 1880 Hauptmann resumed his formal education at the Royal Art and Trade School in Breslau. He also tried his hand at writing; his products—poems, an alliterative epic, and several dramatic fragments—all betray the then-fashionable obsession with the Germanic and the influence of the very writers against whom the naturalists soon took up arms. His efforts in art school resulted in failure and expulsion. He then began private instruction with the sculptor Robert Haertel, who first helped him to reenter the art school and then assisted him in enrolling at the University of Jena, where Hauptmann heard lectures by such eminent scholars as Rudolf Eucken and Ernst Haeckel. His studies remained unsystematic and ended after a year.

In 1883 his fiancée, Marie Thienemann, whose sisters married his brothers Georg and Carl, financed Hauptmann's trip to the Mediterranean; among the cities he visited were Málaga, Barcelona, Marseilles, Naples, Pompeii, Rome, and Florence. He went back to Germany only to return soon afterward to Rome, where he took up residence as a sculptor. But his efforts ended in failure in 1884, and six weeks of study at the Dresden Academy of Arts in the summer of that year likewise produced nothing. Two semesters at the University of Berlin in 1884 and 1885 provided no academic inspiration; thereafter, Hauptmann turned once and for all to creative writing.

In retrospect one can recognize that academic success would have had little direct effect on his eventual achievement, for Hauptmann's most salient asset proved to be his ability to observe and listen to the persons around him as human beings, not as representatives of ideas. In his greatest plays Hauptmann does let his characters express ideas and principles that transcend their immediate situations; nonetheless, these ideas are not necessarily Hauptmann's own beliefs. Instead, they are means of portraying a character with a definite personality and sometimes quite distinct views. Moreover, Hauptmann never produced any theoretical writings of significance on his own or other writers' works. Art as life, not as art or as a vehicle for his own philosophical notions, remained his strength. Yet, the lack of a formal education left its mark on Hauptmann, who developed typically autodidactic strengths and weaknesses: great learning and many allusions in his works to both well-known and obscure subjects that serve primarily intuitive associations, not a systematic, logical approach.

On 5 May 1885 Hauptmann married Thienemann and moved with her to Berlin. In September they moved to Erkner, a suburb of Berlin, where Hauptmann met many of the people who reappeared in his plays. He also encountered young writers such as Max Kretzer (later called the "Berlin Zola"); Wilhelm Bölsche, whose *Die naturwissenschaftlichen Grundlagen der Poesie* (1887, The Scientific Foundations of Literature) became one of the most important manifestos of German naturalism; and Bruno Wille, a strong advocate of the Social Democratic Party. Since 1884 Hauptmann had been taking acting lessons from Alexander Heßler, who provided the model for the politically and artistically conservative theater director Hassenreuter in *Die Ratten* (1911; translated as *The Rats,* 1913). This instruction, which lasted until 1886, offered Hauptmann insights into conventional modes of acting and the practical demands of the theater, but also, as *Die Ratten* reveals, into those artificial aspects of traditional theater against which his own first plays were directed. In his mature years Hauptmann directed many of his own and other playwrights' works, and he always demonstrated a concern for the practicalities of the stage.

In 1887 Hauptmann visited the new literary club "Durch" (Through), where he met more representatives of what later became known as naturalism. Although the theoretical discussions of this club—like those of the others springing up all over Berlin at that time—achieved little more than to keep alive the younger generation's demand for a new, modern, realistic literature, Hauptmann made an outstanding contribution befitting his own nontheoretical, practice-oriented thinking: he read to the members from the little-known works of Georg Büchner, one of the most important precursors of naturalism and subsequent literary movements such as expressionism and the theater of the absurd. Also in 1887 Hauptmann wrote his first two successful novellas. *Fasching* (Carnival) was based on a newspaper account and appeared in 1887 in *Siegfried,* an obscure magazine (it was published in book form in 1923). *Bahnwärter Thiel* (1892; translated as "Flagman Thiel," 1933) appeared in 1888 in the first important journal of naturalism, *Die Gesellschaft* (Society), founded in 1885 in Munich. *Bahnwärter Thiel,* strongly influenced by Büchner, proved to be a masterpiece and is still read in schools.

Always interested less in the rational side of humanity than in its irrational side—emotions, psychological problems, and mystical leanings—Hauptmann spent several weeks in 1888 studying under Auguste Forel, a prominent psychiatrist and director of a clinic in Zurich. There Hauptmann also associated with the playwright Frank Wedekind, who later accused Hauptmann of using in *Das Friedensfest: Eine Familienkatastrophe* (1890; translated as *The Coming of Peace: A Family Catastrophe,* 1900) intimate details he had recounted from his own life. Wedekind sought revenge in his comedy *Die junge Welt* (1898, The Young World), in which he satirized Hauptmann's "notebook" technique and naturalism in general.

The year 1889 was a turning point in the development of naturalism and also in Hauptmann's career. Until then, Munich had been the most important city for German naturalism. From then on, however, Berlin played this role. This change was not caused by a lack or waning of enthusiasm in the Bavarian capital. Instead, the shift in influence has to be attributed to the inability of the writers there to develop the truly new and revolutionary approach to literature for which they had themselves been clamoring. For his part, Hauptmann, although living elsewhere, also seemed to lack direction. He had tried several genres, and not totally without success. Still, along with the relative achievements of *Fasching* and *Bahnwärter Thiel,* he had also published in 1885 the formally unremarkable epic poem *Promethidenloos,* about a disillusioned, Byronic character, and in 1888 *Das bunte Buch,* a collection of poems dating back to the previous decade.

For most people, Hauptmann's name is synonymous with German naturalism. The twenty-first-century reading public encounters him first and perhaps solely as the author of *Bahnwärter Thiel,* a brilliant psychological study of the conflict leading to the tragic end of Thiel, a solitary, withdrawn, and socially insignificant switchman. Arguably, this novella already incorporates many motifs, values, and goals that recur not only in several of Hauptmann's plays but also, albeit in varying forms, in much of subsequent naturalist literature. There is, for example, the eternal conflict between the spiritual and the earthy: Thiel cannot free himself from the sexual attraction exercised by his second wife, while he constantly tortures himself with memories of his first wife as an ethereal vision. Yet, despite all that is unquestionably new and led to *Bahnwärter Thiel* being published by a journal devoted to "modern" literature and life, much in the style of this novella is still indebted to the works of the so-called realists of the previous generation. Hauptmann, like the entire naturalist movement in Germany, was destined by what was happening in Berlin to shift attention almost exclusively to drama. To be sure, Hauptmann continued showing confidence as a writer of verse by using it after 1889 in several plays. But he published only one other nondramatic work for almost two decades: the novella *Der Apostel* (The Apostle), which appeared in the periodical *Moderne Dichtung* in 1890 and as a book in 1892. It draws heavily on experiences acquired during his visit to Zurich in 1888 and, like *Bahnwärter Thiel,* has its roots in Büchner's novella *Lenz* (1839).

The first of the crucial events of 1889 was the publication of one of the most radically "realistic" prose works thus far seen in Germany: the short-story collection *Papa Hamlet,* by Arno Holz and Johannes Schlaf. Until then, Hauptmann had been reading the works of foreign models for the new "realists" (the German naturalists seldom called themselves "naturalists"): Leo Tolstoy, Emile Zola, Ivan Turgenev, Fyodor Dostoevsky, and Walt Whitman. Admittedly, Hauptmann never went to the same stylistic extremes. But what was revolutionary in Holz's and Schlaf's stories, which they called "studies," was also what propelled the naturalists in general toward the stage. As far as possible, these two writers tried to eliminate all traces of the subjective, personal narrator implicit even in realistic storytelling by reducing the texts to stream of consciousness, direct dialogue, and onomatopoeia, that is, the replication of sounds made by inanimate objects such as dripping water and a ringing doorbell. In short, these "studies," by recounting "second for second," became miniature, one-act dramas.

The second significant event was the founding of the "Freie Bühne" (Free Stage), a club devoted to the performance of "modern" (naturalist) drama (a year later a periodical by the same name was founded, which later became *Die neue Rundschau* [The New Review]; one member of the board was Samuel Fischer, whose publishing house brought out many plays of the young naturalists and published Hauptmann's works for many years). Its first chairman was Otto Brahm, who developed the naturalist style of stage direction and production that dominated German theater until the end of the century. Since the Freie Bühne was a private club, it could stage plays forbidden by the censor. With an eye for a proven theatrical success, Brahm began on 15 September 1889 with a production of *Ghosts* (1881), by Henrik Ibsen, whose *A Doll's House* (1879) had already become a rallying point for advocates of women's emancipation. In August 1889 Hauptmann's first mature, modern play, the social drama *Vor Sonnenaufgang,* had been published in Berlin and had caught the attention of many literary figures there. Needing a German playwright to make his undertaking a success, Brahm premiered Hauptmann's play on 20 October 1889. The work launched not only a series of imitations but also a frenzied conflict between conservative forces and the naturalists.

In some respects *Vor Sonnenaufgang* incorporates the innovations of Ibsen that characterize much of subsequent German naturalist drama; in other respects, however, Hauptmann goes far beyond Ibsen both in subject and in style. Ibsen's influence can be seen in the structure, which uses "analytic exposition"—the practice of beginning with a situation and gradually exposing what has led to it. A second technique, closely allied with the first and likewise perfected by Ibsen, is the use of a "messenger from the outside," a stranger who serves as a catalyst for the analytic exposition, sometimes without intending to do so. Alfred Loth, a journalist with an education in sociology and economics and an impassioned believer in social justice, abstinence, and the power of heredity, arrives at the farm of the Krause family, which has suddenly become wealthy through the discovery of coal and the exploitation of the other residents of the area. Loth looks up his old friend from his university days, the engineer Hoffmann. This reunion provides a "realistic" setting for revelations regarding their respective activities and changes in character since they last met: Loth's abortive attempt to establish a utopian community in the New World resulted in his imprisonment for supposedly collecting money for the socialists; Hoffmann, who now denies ever sharing Loth's idealism, has by devious means married into the Krause family and has been the driving force behind the manipulation and exploitation of the farmers and workers.

Loth falls in love with Helene, Hoffmann's sister-in-law, who is apparently the sole uncorrupted member of the household. She falls in love with him, seeing in him the opportunity to escape her situation. But through Dr. Schimmelpfennig, another former friend from the university, Loth learns that Helene's sister and father are alcoholics. Believing first in his social mission, which includes not only the emancipation of women but also the responsibility of handing down healthy genes to future generations, Loth writes a note to Helene and leaves. True to naturalist principles, Hauptmann strives for the greatest possible realism, which does not allow him to reveal any more about a character's thoughts and motives than a real person would reveal under the given circumstances. Thus, the characters are trapped in a closed, almost suffocating atmosphere, and the audience must watch for subtle gestures or chance words to gain insights into their various motives and intentions. Personalities, not principles, evoke most of the conflicts. Loth's fanaticism, coupled with his inability to effect any social reform, removes him from the conventional role of the playwright's spokesman. The play has remained a subject of lively critical debate mainly because of the questionable motives of the characters. In fact, Hauptmann scarcely ever created a "hero" or "heroine" who might be interpreted as his spokesperson; at the same time, as he himself said, he never created a true "villain."

What distinguishes *Vor Sonnenaufgang* from Ibsen's plays is, first, the frankness and crassness with which sexuality and other manifestations of decadence and moral corruption are presented, as when Helene's drunken father grasps her in a lustful manner. Many contemporary naturalists in Germany had been calling for "truth" rather than beauty, and Hauptmann's play seems to respond to this demand. Second, Hauptmann incorporates working-class and rural characters and lets them speak in dialect, a device he also uses with the Krause family to reveal how thin the veneer of culture acquired through wealth is. Hauptmann reveals his models for these innovations in his autobiography, *Das Abenteuer meiner Jugend* (1937, The Adventure of My Youth): "Dieses Drama würde ohne *Thérèse Raquin* von Zola, ohne die *Macht der Finsternis* von Tolstoi und die Vehemenz des *Buches der Zeit* und seines Dichters wohl kaum entstanden sein" (This play would probably never have come about without *Thérèse Raquin* by Zola, *The Power of Darkness* by Tolstoy and the vehemence of the *Book of Time* and its author [Arno Holz]). Tolstoy's play, which was later performed by the Freie Bühne, particularly inspired Hauptmann to expand his realistic social drama to include not only the bourgeois hypocrisy that had been the subject of Ibsen's dramas but also the lot of farmers and laborers. Until then the general public had gleaned its literary images of country life from the *Dorfnovellen* and *Dorfromane* (village novellas and novels) that had flourished since the 1830s. In selecting locales for his works Hauptmann returns frequently to rural life in Silesia, but he does not idealize it.

During his lifetime Hauptmann had forty-one plays published, and five more appeared posthumously. His plays can be divided into three categories: at least seven have remained uncontested as literary masterpieces; twenty-two have evoked some degree of favorable critical and popular response or maintain interest because of their historical importance; and seventeen have had relatively little popular or critical impact. While one might dispute the numbers in each category, one would certainly confer masterpiece status on *Die Weber* (published 1892; performed, 1893; translated as *The Weavers*, 1899), *Der Biberpelz* (1893; translated as *The Beaver Coat*, 1912), *Hannele Matterns Himmelfahrt* (Hannele Mattern's Ascension; published, 1893; performed as *Hanneles Himmelfahrt*, 1893; translated as *Hannele*, 1894), *Fuhrmann Henschel* (1899; translated as *Drayman Henschel*, 1910), *Rose Bernd* (1903; translated, 1913), *Die Ratten*, and *Vor Sonnenuntergang* (1932, Before Sundown). Five of these works appeared before 1906, the year Hauptmann's seventeenth play, *Und Pippa tanzt!* (1906; translated as *And Pippa Dances*, 1909), was published. By this time Hauptmann had averaged one drama per year since his first appearance as a playwright. While he completed another twenty-nine stage works, every one of the plays through 1906 falls into one of the first two categories. Given Hauptmann's succession of controversial or aesthetically interesting plays, the theater-going public awaited with enthusiasm every new drama he wrote. Only infrequently did his audience leave the theater totally disappointed. Nonetheless, Hauptmann's enduring fame depends primarily on the plays written by 1906. When Oxford University awarded him an honorary doctorate in 1905, it confirmed that Hauptmann's fame had become an international phenomenon.

Hauptmann's first six plays conform to the general goal of naturalism: to show people as products of their heredity and milieu. Yet, *Die Weber* is both the extreme example of a supposedly strict adherence to such principles and also theatrically distinctive. In his lifetime Hauptmann was known not only as the foremost realist but also, more specifically, as the author of *Die Weber*. The naturalists had, from the beginning, denounced historical drama, a genre that dominated the serious stage following Schiller's death in 1805. *Die Weber* portrays the life of Silesian weavers in the days leading up to their revolt on 3 June 1844, but it was considered by its first audiences a dramatization of almost contemporary events. The weavers' revolt had been crushed by government troops after only a few days, and their situation had not changed by 1891, when Hauptmann completed the first version of his play. Various literary works had kept alive the memory of the revolt, and newspapers throughout Germany were still publishing articles on the misery of the weavers. True to the naturalist tendency toward ascertaining and reproducing all the sociopolitical details of a situation, Hauptmann traveled to the site of the revolt, where he spoke with survivors. He later recorded in "Zweites Vierteljahrhundert" (Second Quarter-Century), the unpublished continuation of *Das Abenteuer meiner Jugend,* his impressions of what he saw on these visits:

> Der Menschheit ganzer Jammer, wie man sagt, faßte mich nicht zum ersten Male an. Ich hatte in dieser Beziehung, wie das Buch meiner Jugend beweist, schon in Salzbrunn vieles gesehen. Grimmiger Treffendes dann in Zürich unter den Kranken des Burghölzli, der Kantonalirrenanstalt. Was sich in diesen Weberhütten enthüllte, war, ich möchte sagen: das Elend in seiner klassischen Form.
>
> (The entire suffering of humanity, as one says, did not seize me for the first time. In this connection I had, as the book of my youth proves, already seen much in Salzbrunn. More horribly moving things then in Zurich among the patients of Burghölzli, the Canton Insane Asylum. What was revealed in these huts of the weavers was, I would like to say, misery in its classical form.)

After recounting many details, he admits that he could never show the true depths of this misery in his play.

The censor, aware that the plight of the weavers was a live political issue, banned Hauptmann's play as dangerous—first in its almost incomprehensible original version in the Silesian dialect, then in the second version, which, as a concession to the Berliners, was written according to Hauptmann in a dialect "dem Hochdeutschen angenähert" (approaching High German). The second version was performed by the Freie Bühne on 26 February 1893 and, after a court trial, elsewhere. A ban by the censor was not in itself remarkable; bans were often deliberately sought by the naturalists, who were intent on shocking contemporary audiences. What made—and still makes—*Die Weber* less political propaganda than a work of art is its aesthetic quality and its dramaturgical daring. There is no traditional "hero"; only one relatively minor character, who serves as a barometer for the rising emotional pressure among the weavers, appears in all five acts. The acts take place without any regard for the temporal and spatial limitations typical of most naturalist drama. At first glance, the play seems to consist of five individual one-act dramas, each with a different locale and with only occasionally recurring characters. Yet, there is more than thematic unity, for the play does have a hero: the weavers themselves as a collective. As in classical drama, the climax comes at the end of the third act, when one of the weavers says, "A jeder Mensch hat halt 'ne Sehnsucht" (Everyone has something he yearns for). Almost every character, even those speaking only a few lines, comes across as an individual. Despite its subtle, underlying adherence to traditional dramaturgical principles, *Die Weber,* unlike classical drama, ends on a note of ambiguity befitting the naturalist commitment to a "slice of life" having neither a real beginning nor a true conclusion. *Die Weber* is probably the greatest mass drama in German literature and influenced all subsequent writers of such dramas, including the expressionists.

Hauptmann concludes his play on an ironic note that leaves the impression that the weavers will triumph, but everyone in his audience knew that the real weavers were quickly defeated and forced back into their former life. While Hauptmann portrays the revolt as unavoidable, the play cannot be interpreted as a call for another revolt—unless deeper changes occur first in the people themselves.

Nonetheless, *Die Weber* was considered by many to be virtually seditious. When it was publicly performed for the first time, Kaiser Wilhelm II canceled his loge at the Deutsches Theater. And when Hauptmann was suggested for the prestigious Schiller Prize in 1896 and again in 1899, Wilhelm personally rejected him both times. But Hauptmann had already exacted his revenge against the intolerance and stupidity of Wilhelminian officialdom with his masterful comedy *Der Biberpelz,* which uses as its heroine a washerwoman, Frau Wolff. Hauptmann changed his model, an honest worker, into a petty thief who first poaches, then takes home carelessly stored firewood, and finally steals and sells a beaver coat—progressively greater crimes that, because the victim is both wealthy and ludicrous, do not transgress the limits of a comedy. She commits these acts under the eyes of a local official, who is more concerned with the supposed danger of socialists, especially with one patently harmless character modeled after Hauptmann himself. The role of the thieving washerwoman is one of the most famous, and this comedy one of the most frequently performed, in German theatrical history.

The initial reaction to *Der Biberpelz* was far from auspicious. The censor's office, substantiating Hauptmann's low opinion of public officials, allowed the play to be presented only because it was considered too boring to have a long run. The first audience remained seated after the last curtain because they expected a fifth act in which Frau Wolff would be discovered and punished. But the comedy ends with the official's reiteration of his belief in her innocence and good character and his reassertion of the danger of the suspected "socialist."

Der Biberpelz was Hauptmann's second comedy; the first was *Kollege Crampton* (performed 1892; published as *College Crampton,* 1892; translated as *Colleague Crampton,* 1914), a study of a drunken painter and teacher whose real-life counterpart Hauptmann had met in 1880 at the Breslau Art Academy. But the focus in the first comedy remained relatively narrow, and at the end the audience questions only the protagonist's ability to fulfill his good resolutions, not the social and political background. In his second comedy Hauptmann expands the comic potential of naturalism beyond the depiction of individual characters. While Crampton is an outsider or even a victim, Frau Wolff asserts her mastery over her environment. Always one step ahead of other characters and able to manipulate them, Frau Wolff appears as the rogue figure of many traditional comedies. At the same time she is always a realistically portrayed individual with a specific background and discernible limitations.

It was not popular morality, with its desire to see this "thief" punished, but the dictates of realism that led Hauptmann to write a sequel, *Der rote Hahn* (1901; translated as *The Conflagration,* 1912)—but as a tragicomedy, not a comedy. In the sequel Hauptmann shows that Frau Wolff's seemingly harmless, victimless crimes were motivated by capitalistic avarice; in the time since the end of the first play she has committed arson for profit. An innocent man is punished for her crime, but she refuses to confess. She dies at the end with the words: "Ma langt . . . Ma langt nach was" (One reaches . . . One reaches for something). Here is the culmination of Hauptmann's vision of his characters as individuals obeying their own instincts, drives, and emotions to the end, for the final, truly criminal acts of Frau Wolff were already implied by her personality in *Der Biberpelz.* The sequel enjoyed neither the favorable critical reception nor the popularity of the original; but the consistency of thought and character connecting the two plays was noted by Bertolt Brecht, who tried to mold them into a single drama in his stage production *Biberpelz und Roter Hahn* (1951).

To many, *Hanneles Himmelfahrt* seemed to initiate Hauptmann's break with naturalism. After *Die Weber* and *Der Biberpelz,* the lesser exponents of naturalism assumed that little else remained to be done technically and that subsequent works would distinguish themselves solely through new subjects and issues. *Hanneles Himmelfahrt,* however, reveals that Hauptmann had not abandoned the fundamental goals of naturalism but had expanded its artistic means.

The initial reception of *Hanneles Himmelfahrt* was not favorable. Paul Schlenther, one of the cofounders of the Freie Bühne and a close friend as well as first biographer of Hauptmann, commented that the overly pious members of the audience wanted to ascribe the play to the Social Democrats, while the Social Democrats found it too religious. The first of the two acts depicts in thoroughly naturalistic manner a poorhouse whose inhabitants take in the freezing girl Hannele; a victim of poverty and maltreatment by her drunken stepfather, she has attempted to drown herself. In the second act the audience shares in Hannele's dream, in which Christ appears looking like her schoolteacher, and Hannele is prepared by angels for her wedding with him. At the end of the play the action returns to the real world, and the audience learns that Hannele has died.

Hauptmann incorporates in this play many aspects of the same literary tendencies—neo-Romanticism and *Jugendstil*—that were developing as reactions against the naturalists' exclusion of everything not recognized by science and their emphasis on the banal and ugly side of life. Hauptmann's intention was to dramatize the creation of a work of art. In an April 1894 letter replying to one of his critics, Hauptmann asserted:

> Wie das Märchen ist, suchte ich mir ein Aschenbrödel, um es, wiederum wie das Märchen tut, aus tiefstem Elend zu höchstem Glück zu führen. Gleich dem Märchen, welches nach Möglichkeit real zu sein versucht, suchte ich nun aber innerhalb des Märchenrahmens ebenfalls so viel mir möglich, real zu sein. . . . Das Kind stellte für mich gleichsam ein Stückchen des Urbodens dar, aus dem alle Religion und alle Poesie entkeimt ist.
>
> (As in a fairy tale, I looked for a Cinderella in order to lead her, as a fairy tale does, out of the deepest misery to the highest happiness. Like the fairy tale, which tries as far as possible to be real, I now, however, likewise sought to be as real as possible within the framework of a fairy tale. . . . That child represented for me more or less a small piece of the mother earth from which all religions and all poetry have sprung.)

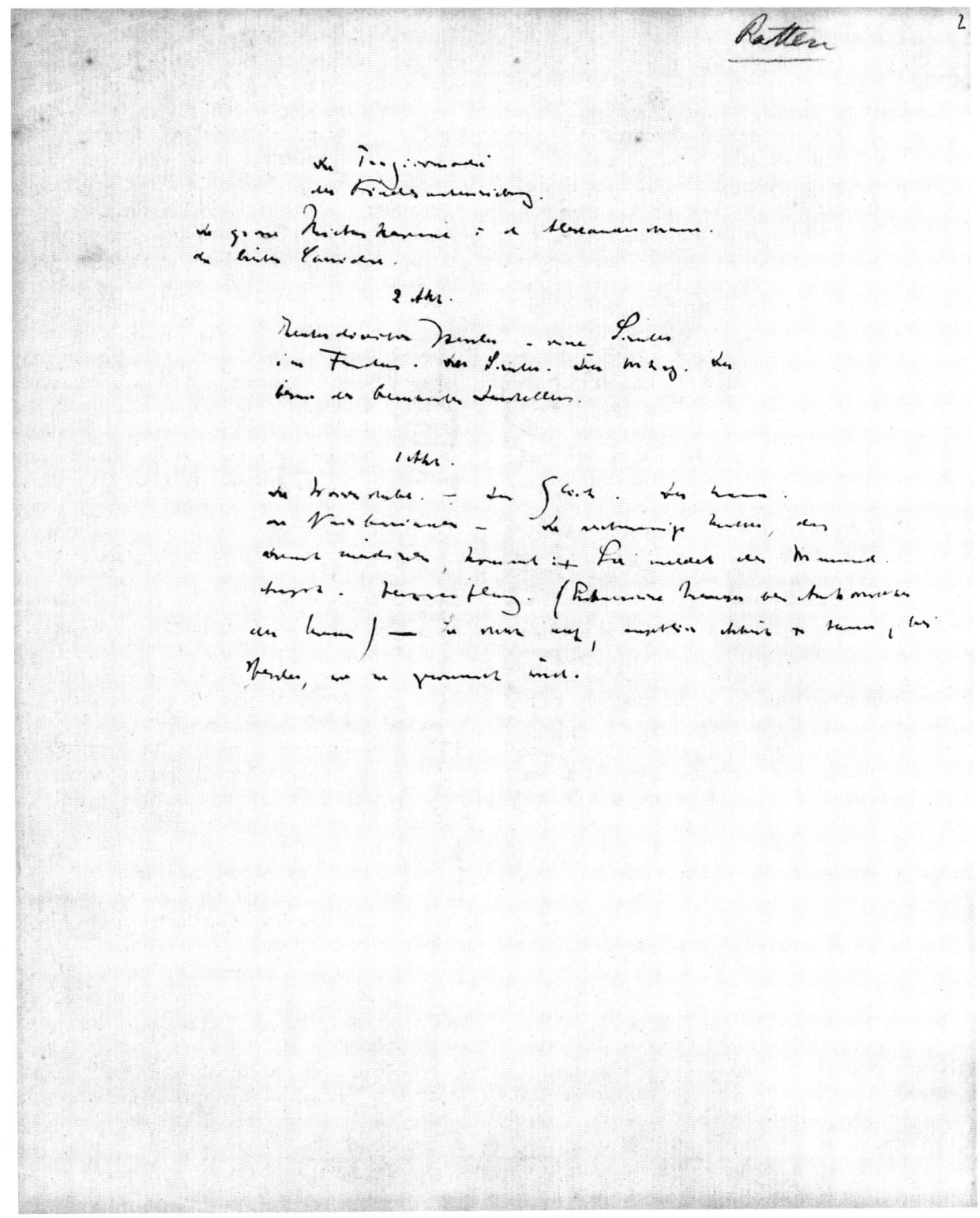

Manuscript notes from April 1909 for Hauptmann's 1911 play Die Ratten, translated as The Rats, 1913
(Bildarchiv Preussischer Kulturbesitz/Art Resource, New York)

Hannele's dream, to be sure, represents the extreme example of personal escapism; but a similar desire to manipulate and transcend reality motivates all poetic expression.

Hauptmann's next attempt to dramatize such a line of thought, *Die versunkene Glocke* (performed, 1896; published, 1897; translated as *The Sunken Bell,* 1898), was more accessible to contemporary audiences. One of his most popular plays and the first one to earn a substantial amount of money for Hauptmann, *Die versunkene Glocke,* which bears the subtitle *Ein deutsches Märchendrama* (a German Fairy-Tale Drama) and is presented in verse, was its author's concession to bourgeois taste and to the fashion set by Maeterlinck; it is considered today to be a weak work. Of far greater scope and of more lasting critical interest, however, is the still frequently puzzling *Und Pippa tanzt!,* which begins almost as naturalistically as *Hanneles Himmelfahrt* but allows its nonrealistic elements even more autonomy. In fact, its almost allegorical tendencies mark it as a forerunner of expressionist drama.

After moving in 1889 to Charlottenburg, another suburb of Berlin, Hauptmann made a trip in 1890 to Zurich, Italy, and Monaco; in 1891 he traveled to Silesia for studies for *Die Weber*. By this time he and his wife had three sons—Ivo, born in 1886; Eckart, born in 1887; and Klaus, born in 1889—and she had inherited enough money to make the family financially secure. In 1891 the Hauptmanns moved to Schreiberhau (now Szklarska Poreba, Poland) in Silesia. Hauptmann soon fell in love with the sister of Max Marschalk, the composer of the music for *Hanneles Himmelfahrt* and later for more of Hauptmann's works. Hauptmann had met Margarete Marschalk in 1889, when she was fourteen. She had later studied violin under Joseph Joachim but for health reasons had had to give up a musical career. Hauptmann, who knew Gustav Mahler, Richard Strauss, and other prominent musical figures, was undoubtedly drawn to Marschalk in part because of her musical talent. She reentered his life as a guest at the dinner Hauptmann gave after the premiere of *Hanneles Himmelfahrt* in September 1893. After spending the following days with her in Berlin, he returned to his wife and children, who had remained in Silesia. Hauptmann confessed his new love to his wife. He returned shortly thereafter to Berlin, where he saw Marschalk again. When he went to Paris for the opening of *Hanneles Himmelfahrt* there, Marie Hauptmann left for America, where she stayed with Ploetz in Meriden, Connecticut. Hauptmann hurried after her, and they reconciled. Hauptmann gained mostly unfavorable impressions of the United States. Shortly after the failure of *Hanneles Himmelfahrt* in New York on 1 May 1894, he returned with his family to Germany.

The reconciliation did not last long; but Marie Hauptmann refused to give the playwright a divorce, even though Marschalk gave birth to Hauptmann's son Benvenuto on 1 June 1900. In the fall of that year Marie Hauptmann and the children moved into a house in Dresden that Hauptmann had built for them, and he moved with Marschalk into Wiesenstein, a house he had constructed for himself and his new family in Agnetendorf. Finally, in 1904, his wife divorced him, and in September of that year he married Marschalk.

In September 1905 he met a sixteen-year-old girl, Ida Orloff, who became a threat to the new marriage. Hauptmann broke off this affair in 1906 or 1907. But while there are few figures in his works reminiscent of Margarete Hauptmann, Orloff recurs frequently in his plays and fiction—sometimes in a positive, sometimes in a negative light—even long after he had stopped seeing her. One should not, however, ascribe such figures to her alone, for their occurrence in Hauptmann's works coincides with the obsession of many *Jugendstil* and symbolist poets for the *femme-enfant* and femme fatale.

During these years Hauptmann suffered some artistic disappointments. The most notable came with the premiere of *Florian Geyer* (published, 1896; translated, 1929) on 4 January 1896. Although it has a "hero," this play about the Peasant Wars of 1524–1525 has much in common with *Die Weber;* it represents one of the best attempts to write a thoroughly naturalistic drama on an historical subject remote in time. Hauptmann had begun his preliminary studies in 1891, while he was working on *Die Weber;* as in the case of *Die Weber* he went to the areas concerned, this time southern Germany. As a naturalist, Hauptmann always strove for a rigorously accurate phonetic reproduction of linguistic peculiarities and dialects, which allowed his audience to pinpoint the educational and social level and regional background of a character. Opinions vary on Hauptmann's success in reproducing the language of the sixteenth century, but if he had not tried to reproduce it—including differentiations among the various characters and classes—then *Florian Geyer* would have been merely another costume piece, the type that the naturalists consciously rejected.

Moreover, the naturalist seeks the "complete" truth, not a "higher" or more poetic one. Hauptmann gathered an enormous amount of material on Geyer, his friends and enemies, and the times in general. Nonetheless, the play, admittedly not well staged or acted, was rejected by critics and public alike at its premiere. But in 1904 it was successfully performed with Rudolf Rittner in the title role, and thereafter it served as a vehicle for several other actors of stature.

Before 1906 Hauptmann created two more masterpieces, *Fuhrmann Henschel* and *Rose Bernd*. Both represent a refinement of naturalist technique rather than an expansion of it to previously untried subjects. At the same time, in both plays Hauptmann lets his audience feel that more than the forces of biological and sociological determinism produces the tragic outcome.

Fuhrmann Henschel portrays, against the background of the industrial and economic changes of the contemporary world, the unhappy marriage of a man to his former maid, a sexually active, domineering woman, after he promises his dying first wife that he will not marry the maid. Many contemporaries heard echoes in the play of the so-called fate tragedies of the early nineteenth century. But Hauptmann avoids the crudity of the emphasis in those plays on a vague concept of fate: his protagonist commits suicide only after the audience has seen him destroyed by his guilt, the changes in the socioeconomic world, and his unfaithful second wife. The tragedy, which premiered on 5 November 1898 in Berlin, was an immediate success there and in Paris, where André Antoine, founder of the "théâtre libre," the model for the Freie Bühne, praised not only the presentation of the milieu but also the "clarity and sobriety" of the play. Many critics have subsequently likened it to Attic tragedy.

In 1897 and again in 1898 Hauptmann traveled to Italy, where he began several works on exotic subjects that, with the exception of material that was later integrated into *Der arme Heinrich* (1902, Poor Henry; translated as *Henry of Auë,* 1915) and *Und Pippa tanzt!,* never appeared on the stage. Another drama in a realistic manner, if not a great one, followed: *Michael Kramer* (1900; translated, 1914) was rejected at its premiere on 21 December 1900, although the fourth act, with Kramer's almost lyrical comments on death, found admirers in Rainer Maria Rilke and Thomas Mann.

Then another masterpiece, *Rose Bernd,* premiered on 31 October 1903 in Berlin. Although the theme of an unmarried mother killing her child had been a favorite of the Sturm und Drang writers of the 1770s and had been given its most famous treatment by Johann Wolfgang von Goethe in *Faust I* (1808), Hauptmann's direct inspiration can be found neither in the past nor in the contemporary naturalist concern for fallen or victimized women. Instead, it came from his participation as a juror from 15 to 17 April 1903 at the trial of a waitress accused of murdering her child.

A criticism made of virtually all of Hauptmann's strongly realistic character dramas surfaced again in the case of *Rose Bernd:* that the play is too epic, that is, not "dramatic" enough. By 1903 the naturalist style of acting had dominated the stages of Germany for several years, and *Rose Bernd* seemed to many critics an anachronism. Moreover, despite the artistic liberties introduced by naturalism since 1889, the subject of *Rose Bernd* was still considered controversial enough for the play to be removed by royal order from the repertoire in Vienna.

Nevertheless, the tragedy gained in popularity and in 1919 became the first of Hauptmann's plays to be filmed. Adaptations of many of his plays followed, but none of them contribute much toward an assessment of Hauptmann as a playwright. Almost without exception they take great liberties with his texts. Unlike Carl Zuckmayer, Brecht, and other playwrights, Hauptmann never wrote an original screenplay.

In 1907 Hauptmann traveled to Greece. The most immediate result of his sojourn there was his diary, *Griechischer Frühling* (1908, Grecian Spring). In later years many critics saw this work as a turning point in Hauptmann's career, and one not in the right direction. Yet, what Hauptmann says in *Griechischer Frühling* about Greek tragedy obviously stems from seeing it through the eyes of a dramatist schooled in the perspective and expectations of naturalism: "Tragödie heißt: Freundschaft, Verfolgung, Haß und Liebe als Lebenswut! Tragödie heißt: Angst, Not, Gefahr, Pein, Qual, Marter, heißt Tücke, Verbrechen, Niedertracht, heißt Mord, Blutgier, Blutschande, Schlächterei" (Tragedy means: friendship, persecution, hate and love as existential passion! Tragedy means: fear, misery, danger, anguish, torment, torture; means deception, crime, depravity; means murder, bloodthirstiness, incest, butchery). Hauptmann's works reflecting the forms and themes of antiquity remained for a long time mainly nondramatic ones; his only play on a classical source to appear before his old age was *Der Bogen des Odysseus* (1914; translated as *The Bow of Odysseus,* 1917), which he began during this trip but completed only after much work. The long genesis produced a play that relies more on characterization and the bucolic than on Homer, from whom Hauptmann takes only the plot. Despite its originality, the play enjoyed only moderate success.

By 1907 Hauptmann had become financially successful, although, as his correspondence reveals, he spent all his income. Public honors became more frequent: after an honorary doctorate from Oxford in 1905, he received another from the University of Leipzig in 1909. The number and types of honors accorded to Hauptmann during the year of his fiftieth birthday attest to the continuing worldwide respect for his achievements as a playwright. All of these displays of international renown took place despite the diminishing favor that the plays premiered after 1903 had found among theatergoers and critics.

This lack of public success might well have prompted Hauptmann to write and publish his first two novels. *Der Narr in Christo Emanuel Quint* (1910; translated as *The Fool in Christ Emanuel Quint,* 1911) immediately found some detractors but also some equally engaged admirers, including George Bernard Shaw, Hugo von Hofmannsthal, and the expressionist artist Franz Marc. Yet, sales remained modest until the appearance of a less expensive popular edition in 1916. Thereafter, its sales rose rapidly and remained high for many years. Any negative reception of the novel was not the result of Hauptmann's artistic handling of the material, which was, in fact, generally praised. Instead, the depiction of a simpleminded man who tries to imitate Christ and who achieves a mystical union with the Savior in a dream was too religious for some readers, too scientific for others. Modern critics tend toward viewing the novel as a study in pathology. Still, Hauptmann gives the supernatural and spiritual an almost independent existence in some of his works. In his early years, Hauptmann began writing "Jesus-Studien" and left fragments of dramas about Christ. In the novel about the naive Quint, he shows his fidelity to the foundation of naturalism: its intention to limit representations of the world to what is scientifically verifiable. Yet, at the same time he shows himself capable of providing binding insights into an individual reality like the one in which a Thiel, Hannele, or Quint lives.

Hauptmann completed his second novel, *Atlantis,* in the winter of 1911–1912, and it appeared soon afterward in serial form in the newspaper *Berliner Tageblatt.* He made only minor corrections when it was published as a book in 1912. For his first novel, Hauptmann had historical models that provided him with experiences he could recount with detachment and empathy simultaneously. But in *Atlantis* he draws exclusively on scarcely disguised, painfully remembered events and persons in his own life (friends, as well as later works, revealed that his personal difficulties with his first wife had left Hauptmann with feelings of guilt that lasted for the rest of his life). It is therefore not surprising that the objectivity of the first novel is missing when he chronicles the story of Dr. Friedrich von Kammacher, who leaves his wife because of a sixteen-year-old dancer. When he sails with her on the ship *Roland* to America, he discovers how shallow the dancer is. The news of his wife's suicide causes him to suffer a breakdown; but he regains his health with the help of the sculptress Eva Burns, who subsequently accompanies him back to Germany. The knowledgeable reader might try to ignore the embarrassing autobiographical details, but no one can ignore the flaws that this novel shares with so many that appeared in serialized installments: careless, hasty writing and structural looseness. Whatever popularity this weak novel enjoyed stemmed largely from the "prophetic" parallel between the sinking of the *Roland* and the collision of the *Titanic* with an iceberg in April 1912.

Hauptmann was frequently admired by and developed friendships with younger writers representing new literary movements, such as Hofmannsthal, Rilke, Mann, and Georg Kaiser; James Joyce is said to have learned German just to read Hauptmann. Invitations to lecture in major cities came frequently, and in 1912 Hauptmann received the Nobel Prize in Literature.

Hauptmann's receipt of the Nobel Prize could not have surprised anyone in Germany. More often than any other German writer since Goethe, he had already been praised, honored, and imitated by his contemporaries, a fact substantiated by the widespread celebrations of his fiftieth birthday, the most notable one taking place in November in Berlin and attended by many prominent literary figures. Still, after being asked in 1933 by the Copenhagen newspaper *Ekstra Bladet* for an article on the Nobel Prize, Hauptmann wrote in his response (found in his estate) that when the prizes were first established, he could not envision himself ever being among the recipients of one. He goes on to say that the award provided him with an inestimable motivation that stemmed not only from its material benefits but also from the people who had suggested him and those who had conferred it on him. His life, he continues, acquired a new *Widerstandskraft* (power of resistance) that he would subsequently need in Italy, which his newly acquired freedom opened up to him for all times. He mentions, however, no political transformation brought about by the award. In his banquet speech in Stockholm, his mention of world peace as a shared goal could be dismissed as a strictly formulaic acknowledgment of Alfred Nobel's ideals. But Hauptmann's next stage of work was in undeniable harmony with such ideals as well as with his own convictions.

During this time his published works were mainly in fiction, and up to the advent of the Nazi dictatorship his stage triumphs became increasingly rare and never duplicated those before 1906. He could, nevertheless, still create controversy. For example, he was commissioned to write a festival play to commemorate the centenary of the Wars of Liberation in 1813. The result, *Festspiel in deutschen Reimen* (1913, Festival Performance in German Rhymes; translated as *Commemoration Masque,* 1917), applied not the expected blind reverence but a note of irony toward the revered figures of German history and caused a scandal. Nonetheless, at the outbreak of World War I in 1914, Hauptmann joined other writers in composing patriotic poems. While Hauptmann's attitudes and statements frequently contradict each other, on balance he is usually patriotic but not nationalistic or sycophantic toward the rulers.

In the years between *Rose Bernd* and World War I, Hauptmann wrote another truly great work for the stage, a tragicomedy that perhaps remains his most "modern" play. *Die Ratten* is the most complex and subtle play in Hauptmann's canon. Its main plot is strongly naturalistic: Frau John, a cleaning woman who lives in a rat-infested former barracks, adopts the illegitimate child of a Polish maid but convinces her husband, a bricklayer, that she has given birth to it. She is discovered despite her brother's murder of the true mother and commits suicide. The time of the play is 1884–1885–that is, before the theatrical breakthrough of naturalism with *Vor Sonnenaufgang*–and a second plot revolves around the acting school of Hassenreuter, which is housed in the same building. It provides an ironic, largely comic foil to the plot about Frau John. Hassenreuter, who is something of a philanderer, provides a sharp contrast to the cleaning woman, who tries to attain middle-class stability and happiness in her marriage but is driven to suicide by her husband's inflexible attitude toward her "crime." Hassenreuter is an exponent of Schiller's classical, declamatory style of acting. His opponent in a series of arguments is his student Spitta, who advocates more reality–the naturalism that soon put such people as Frau John on the stage as tragic heroes and heroines. Neither Hassenreuter nor Spitta notices that Frau John's plight has all the qualities of a tragedy in both the naturalistic and the classical senses, and they remain as ludicrous in their theoretical arguments as Frau John remains tragic in her real life. *Die Ratten* represents a reckoning both with the forces that made naturalism necessary and with the ultimate impotence of the naturalist as a reformer.

Few plays are recognized immediately as having the qualities of lasting greatness, and *Die Ratten* was no exception. After Hauptmann gained a court decision against a petty objection by the censor, the premiere took place on 13 January 1911 in Berlin. The reaction was subdued. Even Alfred Kerr, one of the most perceptive theater critics, an exponent of naturalism, and an enthusiastic supporter of Hauptmann, had little to say about *Die Ratten* that was good. But five years later, when the play was performed again, another critic, Siegfried Jacobsohn, wrote in the periodical *Die Schaubühne*: "Kritik ist Selbstkritik. Weswegen bin ich 1911 vor diesen Ratten durchgefallen?" (Criticism is self-criticism. Why did I flop in 1911 when confronted by *Die Ratten?*). In retrospect, it can be seen that the cause of the rejection in 1911 is the very "modernity" and relevance of *Die Ratten*: its complex intertwining of the tragic and comic and its ironic, disquieting view of human existence and social values.

During World War I Hauptmann wrote little of note for the stage. When peace came in 1918, Hauptmann welcomed it; the following year he also welcomed the Weimar Republic, which, in turn, lionized him to an extent previously unknown in Germany or elsewhere. His sixtieth and seventieth birthdays became events of national importance. Honorary doctorates from the German University in Prague in 1921 and Columbia University in 1932 show that his fame grew in foreign countries as well.

During these years, Hauptmann devoted much of his energy to nondramatic genres. At the end of World War I he published *Der Ketzer von Soana* (1918; translated as *The Heretic of Soana,* 1923), which some critics consider his best prose work. More than 300,000 copies were sold by the end of the 1950s. Such success, though not repeated by the subsequent novels, must have provided Hauptmann with some measure of consolation for the unfavorable receptions of his dramas being premiered during this period.

The "heretic" in this novel is the young Catholic priest Francesco Velda, who succumbs to the beauty of Agata and to the pagan lifestyle of her family living in isolation from society. He comes to recognize that the power of nature, Eros, and the Dionysian pleasures are greater than religious dogma. His action is intended to be seen as an affirmation of life in all of its fullness. Many critics view the effect of Hauptmann's experience in Greece as the driving force in his unconcealed extolling of paganism in this work, which, begun in 1911, could also be interpreted as establishing an antipode to the values underlying *Der Narr in Christo Emanuel Quint.*

A relatively large amount of narrative prose followed, but, with the exception of a couple of novellas, it did little to enhance or even sustain Hauptmann's reputation, which nonetheless remained that of Germany's greatest writer. At best, his prose output broadened understanding of how wide-ranging his talent was; even among the less distinguished novels there is great diversity. In *Phantom* (published as a book in 1923, after serial publication in the *Berliner Illustrierte*) Lorentz Labota, who has served a prison sentence, relates how he became a criminal. Public interest proved to be moderate, and despite praise for the author's handling of Labota's personality and even occasional comparisons of Hauptmann's protagonist with Mann's Felix Krull, this novel has awakened relatively little critical interest. Some of the late novellas, however, have retained a readership.

Of the published novels, one more is noteworthy because it bridges Hauptmann's prose and drama. Between 1925 and 1936 Hauptmann was intensely preoccupied with William Shakespeare's *Hamlet.* He wrote an original play, *Hamlet in Wittenberg* (1935), which portrays the years before the beginning of Shakespeare's play. He also wrote an adaptation of the Shakespeare play (performed, 1927; published, 1929) and a novel, *Im Wirbel der Berufung* (1936, Following My Calling), about staging the play. The purpose of all of these works was to show that Hamlet could not have been as passive and indecisive as he seems to be in Shakespeare's play. Critical reception of the Hamlet works was unfavorable.

During the 1920s, when—if not verifiably because—his new dramas were encountering little popular enthusiasm, Hauptmann returned to the verse epic. The majority of these poems—*Anna: Ein ländliches Liebesgedicht* (1921, Anna: A Rural Love Poem), *Die blaue Blume* (1927, The Blue Flower), *Mary* (which appeared in its final version in the verse collection *Ährenlese* [1939, The Gleaning]), and *Der große Traum* (1942, The Great Dream), which Hauptmann called his "Vermächtnis" (bequest)—have few readers today, and then mainly among scholars. Yet, the lengthiest of the verse epics, *Des großen Kampffliegers, Landfahrers, Gauklers und Magiers Till Eulenspiegel Abenteuer, Streiche, Gaukelein, Gesichte und Träume* (1928, The Adventures, Pranks, Tricks, Visions and Dreams of the Great Combat Pilot, Vagabond, Trickster, and Magician Till Eulenspiegel) deserves mention, if only because its content is so timely but its form so remarkable. The voluminous title resembles those of novels in the Baroque period, from which its Alexandrine verse has been lifted. Yet, Hauptmann's epic has nothing to do with either the Baroque period or with the "pranks" and time of the legendary Till Eulenspiegel, who supposedly died around 1350 and became the subject of chapbooks in 1515 and 1519. In Hauptmann's own time, this character had already been immortalized in the music of Strauss in 1890. Like Christian Dietrich Grabbe in the early nineteenth century, Hauptmann originally wanted to write a drama about this "rascal" but never got beyond fragments. The protagonist of his epic poem is a modern flier from World War I who experiences much of the turmoil of the years immediately thereafter, and, as the "eternal German" who can be seen simultaneously as a fool and a Faust, eventually commits suicide. Always in need of money, Hauptmann sought and received an enormous advance for this epic, but despite great efforts by his publisher, not even the rather modest first edition was sold out. To this day the three questions raised by the initial critics are still being contested: How good and appropriate is the verse? How successfully does this work capture the "modern" world that it obviously wants to interpret? And what is the meaning of the mythological and legendary allusions? While the work was a financial catastrophe, its artistic merits have yet to be established.

Hauptmann's last unquestionably great and popular play, *Vor Sonnenuntergang,* which premiered in the midst of his Hamlet studies on 16 February 1932, grew out of an interest in another Shakespearean play. Hauptmann had set out to write a new *King Lear,* but soon the play embraced a multitude of other influences and stimuli. *Vor Sonnenuntergang* portrays the family conflicts that arise when Matthias Clausen, a dignified, cultured, and sensitive man of seventy, falls in love with his gardener's niece, Inken Peters, fifty years his junior. The main parallels to *King Lear* stem from the opposition of Clausen's sons and daughters to this union, which they oppose for financial reasons. In the printed version there is a fifth act in which Clausen commits suicide, but in the premiere and in many subsequent performances he dies of a heart attack in the fourth act.

The model for Matthias Clausen was Max Pinkus, a bibliophile and longtime friend of the author. Clausen quotes Goethe, has named his children after Goethe or Goethe's characters or friends, and is celebrating his seventieth birthday on the hundredth anniversary of Goethe's death. Moreover, everyone in the audience at the premiere probably remembered that the seventy-three-year-old Goethe had fallen in love with an eighteen-year-old girl. These parallels and allusions to Goethe are intended to reinforce the impression of Clausen as the last representative of a bygone concept of culture and humanism.

Vor Sonnenuntergang had its premiere the year before Adolf Hitler became chancellor. The more perceptive writers did not have to wait until the Nazis had actually assumed power to predict the manner and consequences of their rule. For example, in Mann's *Mario und der Zauberer* (1930; translated as *Mario and the Magician,* 1930) the stage technique of the demonic magician Cipolla shows great similarity to Hitler's observations on political rallies in *Mein Kampf* (1925–1926, My Struggle). Also in 1932 Brecht was already working on his anti-Nazi play *Die Rundköpfe und die Spitzköpfe* (1957; translated as *Roundheads and Peakheads,* 1966). In his novella Mann proves himself to be especially adept in evoking the atmosphere that breeds a Cipolla and allows him to succeed. In the same way, Hauptmann's minor figures in *Vor Sonnenuntergang* represent an entire society's role in bringing about the "sundown" of traditional forms of family relationships and cultural values.

The "sundown" in the title of the play obviously alludes to Hauptmann's first success, which came just before a "dawn." On 20 July 1933, not quite five months after the burning of the Reichstag and less than a week after the creation of a one-party state in Germany, Hauptmann said to C. F. W. Behl: "Meine Epoche beginnt mit 1870 und endigt mit dem Reichstagsbrand" (My epoch begins with 1870 [the establishment of the Second Reich] and ends with the burning of the Reichstag). In other words, his time, the time that understood and revered culture, was over. Even if its prophetic implications had not been fulfilled through the dictatorship of the Nazis, *Vor Sonnenuntergang* would still capture the atmosphere of an era that bred radical opponents of traditional cultural values.

Many Jews and intellectuals left Germany in 1933 and the following years. But Hauptmann, who had turned seventy in 1932, felt himself too old to follow their lead. His remaining in Germany, his "inner emigration," subjected him to attacks from exiles such as his old friend Kerr. Even today this issue is occasionally raised as a stigma on his reputation. Hauptmann's attitude toward the new rulers can, however, be inferred from their policy toward him: he and his works were relegated to the status of museum pieces. Hauptmann did not publish a single artistic work that could be called an homage to the new masters.

Hauptmann and his wife were the only Gentiles at the funeral of his Jewish friend Pinkus in 1934. Although Pinkus had been the model for the protagonist of *Vor Sonnenuntergang,* Hauptmann had ignored Pinkus's Jewishness in the play—even though Hauptmann had long wanted to write a drama about the mysteries of Judaism. In 1937 he finally accomplished this goal with *Die Finsternisse* (The Darknesses), which was inspired by Pinkus's funeral. In the last year of the war Hauptmann, fearing a police search, had the manuscript burned. But a copy found its way to the United States, where it was published in 1947 by Walter A. Reichart; it was first performed in 1952. Dramatically, this work leaves much to be desired; but it is an eloquent statement of Hauptmann's humanity. This play about a Jewish funeral documents not only Hauptmann's lifelong preoccupation with the "Magie des Todes" (magic of death) but also his increasing tendency toward religious mysticism and interest in a "Zwischenreich" (middle kingdom between the real and mythical worlds).

During the Nazi years Hauptmann wrote a couple of minor stage works and some fiction. Then, almost eighty years old, he made one last great effort as a dramatist. This last creative surge began with *Iphigenie in Delphi* (1941). His inspiration was a passage in Goethe's *Italienische Reise* (1816–1817; translated as *Travels in Italy,* 1846) describing how Goethe would have written a sequel to his *Iphigenie auf Tauris* (1800; translated as *Iphigenia on Tauris,* 1851). But Hauptmann's Iphigenia, although she sacrifices herself to atone for the crimes committed by the house of Atreus, bears little resemblance to the Goethean personification of the all-too-human. Goethe adhered to J. J. Winckelmann's concept of Greek culture and art as representative of "edle Einfalt und stille Größe" (noble simplicity and quiet grandeur). Hauptmann, on the other hand, remains true to what he said about Greek tragedy in *Griechischer Frühling*: that regardless of how it might be disguised, a human sacrifice is "die blutige Wurzel der Tragödie" (the bloody root of tragedy). Nonetheless, *Iphigenie in Delphi* ends on a conciliatory note, with the crimes of Agamemnon, Orestes, Klytemnestra, and Electra expiated. This outcome seems to be consistent with Goethe's view that in his *Iphigenie auf Tauris* pure humanity atones for all human feelings.

Once he had completed his play, Hauptmann felt compelled to portray the events for which Iphigenia atones. He completed *Iphigenie in Aulis* (performed, 1943; published, 1944) in 1943, *Agamemnons Tod* (Agamemnon's Death; performed, 1947; published, 1948) in 1944, and *Elektra* (performed, 1947; published, 1948) in 1945 as the first three parts of a tetralogy. Of all the plays in the tetralogy, *Iphigenie in Aulis,* the second to be written but first in terms of the chronology of the plot, proved the most difficult for Hauptmann to complete and exists in the greatest number of manuscript versions; the two one-act dramas that fill out the intervening action of the tetralogy followed rather quickly. Hauptmann needed so long to finish *Iphigenie in Aulis* because he was freeing himself of Goethe's influence and rethinking the implications of the legend within the framework of his own conception of Greek tragedy.

No critic has denied that the tetralogy represents a remarkable accomplishment for any playwright, especially for one in his eighties. But this observation has been the sole point of general agreement. Critics have condemned the language, the lack of dramatic qualities, and the naturalistic approach to the characters. The most damning criticism concerns the obvious differences in tone and in underlying attitude toward the human condition between *Iphigenie in Delphi,* which is usually interpreted as optimistic, and the three subsequently written parts, which take an essentially pessimistic view of the human ability to avert or rectify disaster.

Many critics see in the tetralogy Hauptmann's reckoning with the Nazi dictatorship and the war it brought about; in 1962 the director Erwin Piscator tried to stage the tetralogy (in much shortened form) as a symbolic representation of Nazi rule. But the texts themselves refute any direct equations of individual characters with contemporary historical personages. One can also demonstrate that Hauptmann was most interested in the Greek legend in itself, not as a vehicle for expressing essentially modern views.

When World War II ended, Gerhart Hauptmann was a broken, tired man, although the Russians occupying Silesia treated the author of *Die Weber* with respect. He died on 6 June 1946 and was buried on the island of Hiddensee, where he had spent some of the most enjoyable times of his life and had, in 1930, bought the house "Seedorn" in Kloster. There are now Hauptmann museums in Kloster and Erkner maintained by the German government.

Letters:

Gerhart Hauptmann und Ida Orloff: Dokumentation einer dichterischen Leidenschaft (Berlin: Propyläen, 1969);

Walter A. Reichart, "Gerhart Hauptmann and His British Friends: Documented in Some of Their Correspondence," *German Quarterly,* 50 (November 1977): 424-451;

Klaus Bohnen, "Briefwechsel zwischen Gerhart Hauptmann und Georg Brandes," *Jahrbuch der deutschen Schiller-Gesellschaft,* 23 (1979): 55-68;

Klaus W. Jonas, "Gerhart Hauptmann und Hans von Seeckt: Erinnerungen eines Sammlers und Bibliographen. Mit unveröffentlichten Briefen," *Imprimatur,* 9 (1980): 216-239;

Gerhart Hauptmann–Ludwig von Hofmann: Briefwechsel 1894-1944, edited by Herta Hesse-Frielinghaus (Bonn: Bouvier, 1983);

Otto Brahm–Gerhart Hauptmann: Briefwechsel 1889-1912, edited by Peter Sprengel (Tübingen: Narr, 1985).

Interviews:

H. D. Tschörtner, ed., *Gespräche und Interviews mit Gerhart Hauptmann (1894-1946)* (Berlin: Schmidt, 1984).

Bibliographies:

Max Pinkus and Viktor Ludwig, *Gerhart Hauptmann: Werke von ihm und über ihn* (Neustadt: Schlesien, 1922; revised by Ludwig, 1932);

Walter Requardt, *Gerhart Hauptmann Bibliographie,* 3 volumes (Berlin: Selbstverlag, 1931);

C. F. W. Behl, "Gerhart Hauptmann-Bibliographie," *Gerhart Hauptmann-Jahrbuch,* 1 (1936): 147-162; 2 (1937): 150-160;

Walter A. Reichart, "Fifty Years of Hauptmann Study in America (1894-1944): A Bibliography," *Monatshefte,* 37 (1945): 1-31; 54 (1962): 297-310;

Reichart, "Bibliographie der gedruckten und ungedruckten Dissertationen über Gerhart Hauptmann und sein Werk," *Philobiblon,* 11 (June 1967): 121-134;

Reichart, *Gerhart-Hauptmann-Bibliographie* (Bad Homburg: Gehlen, 1969);

Klaus W. Jonas, "Gerhart Hauptmanns Manuskripte in Europa," *Börsenblatt für den deutschen Buchhandel,* 26 (28 July 1970): A121-A139;

Jonas, "Gerhart Hauptmann Collections in America and England," *Stechert-Hafner Book News,* 26 (February 1971): 77-82;

H. D. Tschörtner, *Gerhart-Hauptmann-Bibliographie* (Berlin: Deutsche Staatsbibliothek, 1971);

Rudolf Ziesche, *Der Manuskriptnachlaß Gerhart Hauptmanns* (Wiesbaden: Harrassowitz, 1977);

Sigfrid Hoefert, *Internationale Bibliographie zum Werk Gerhart Hauptmann,* 2 volumes (Berlin: Schmidt, 1986-1989);

Hoefert, "Gerhart Hauptmann: Nachträge zur Internationalen Bibliographie (III)," *Schlesien,* 4 (1994): 234-244.

Biographies:

Paul Schlenther, *Gerhart Hauptmann: Sein Lebensgang und seine Dichtung* (Berlin: Fischer, 1898; revised, 1912; revised by A. Eloesser, 1922);

C. F. W. Behl and F. A. Voigt, *Chronik von Gerhart Hauptmanns Leben und Schaffen* (Munich: Korn, 1957);

Wolfgang Leppmann, *Gerhart Hauptmann: Leben, Werk und Zeit* (Munich: Scherz, 1986).

References:

E. Bialek, E. Tomiczek, and M. Zybura, eds., *Leben–Werk–Lebenswerk: Ein Gerhart Hauptmann–Gedenkband* (Liegnitz: Orbis Linguarum, 1997);

Roy C. Cowen, *Hauptmann-Kommentar zum dramatischen Werk* (Munich: Winkler, 1980);

Cowen, *Hauptmann-Kommentar zum nichtdramatischen Werk* (Munich: Winkler, 1981);

Cowen, *Der Naturalismus: Kommentar zu einer Epoche* (Munich: Winkler, 1973);

Peter Delvaux, *Leid soll lehren: Historische Zusammenhänge in Gerhart Hauptmanns Atriden–Tetralogie* (Amsterdam & Atlanta: Rodopi, 1994);

C. T. Dussère, *The Image of the Primitive Giant in the Work of Gerhart Hauptmann* (Stuttgart: Heinz, 1979);

Gustav Erdmann, *Der bekannte und unbekannte Gerhart Hauptmann: Ausgewählte Aufsätze* (Schwerin: Helms, 2000);

Erdmann, ed., *Gerhart Hauptmann: Neue Akzente–neue Aspekte* (Berlin: Stapp, 1992);

Ullrich Erdmann, *Vom Naturalismus zum Nationalsozialismus? Zeitgeschichtlich–biographische Studien zu Max Halbe, Gerhart Hauptmann, Johannes Schlaf und Hermann Stehr* (Frankfurt: Lang, 1997);

Hugo F. Garten, "Formen des Eros im Werk Gerhart Hauptmanns," *Zeitschrift für deutsche Philologie,* 90 (1971): 242-258;

Garten, *Gerhart Hauptmann* (Cambridge: Bowes & Bowes, 1954);

Charles F. Good, *Domination, Dependence, Denial and Despair: Father–Daughter Relationships in Grillparzer, Hebbel and Hauptmann* (New York: Peter Lang, 1993);

Karl S. Guthke, *Gerhart Hauptmann: Weltbild im Werk* (Göttingen: Vandenhoeck & Ruprecht, 1980);

Klaus Hildebrandt, *Naturalistische Dramen Gerhart Hauptmanns* (Munich: Oldenbourg, 1983);

Hildebrandt and Krzystof A. Kuczynski, eds., *Weggefährten Gerhart Hauptmanns* (Würzburg: Korn, 2002);

Eberhard Hilscher, *Gerhart Hauptmann* (Berlin: Verlag der Nation, 1988);

Sigfrid Hoefert, *Gerhart Hauptmann* (Stuttgart: Metzler, 1982);

Hoefert, *Gerhart Hauptmann und der Film* (Berlin: Schmidt, 1996);

K. G. Knight and F. Norman, eds., *Hauptmann Centenary Lectures* (London: University of London Institute of Germanic Studies, 1964);

Krzystof A. Kuczynski and Peter Sprengel, eds., *Gerhart Hauptmann—Autor des Jahrhunderts* (Würzburg: Königshausen & Neumann, 1991);

Ward B. Lewis, "O'Neill and Hauptmann: A Study in Mutual Admiration," *Comparative Literature Studies*, 22 (Summer 1985): 231–243;

Thomas Mann, *Gerhart Hauptmann* (Gütersloh: Bertelsmann, 1953);

Alan Marshall, *The German Naturalists and Gerhart Hauptmann* (Frankfurt am Main & Bern: Peter Lang, 1982);

Friedhelm Marx, *Gerhart Hauptmann* (Stuttgart: Reclam, 1998);

Peter Mast, ed., *"Es steckt Ungehobenes in meinem Werk . . .": Zur Bedeutung Gerhart Hauptmanns für unsere Zeit* (Bonn: Kulturstiftung der deutschen Vertriebenen, 1993);

Warren R. Maurer, *Gerhart Hauptmann* (Boston: Twayne, 1982);

Hans Mayer, *Gerhart Hauptmann* (Velber bei Hannover: Friedrich, 1972);

Edward McInnes, *German Social Drama 1840–1900: From Hebbel to Hauptmann* (Stuttgart: Heinz, 1976);

Philip Mellen, *Gerhart Hauptmann and Utopia* (Stuttgart: Heinz, 1976);

Mellen, *Gerhart Hauptmann: Religious Syncretism and Eastern Religions* (Bern, Frankfurt am Main & New York: Peter Lang, 1984);

Gerdt Oberembt, *Gerhart Hauptmann: Der Biberpelz* (Paderborn, Munich, Vienna & Zurich: Schöningh, 1987);

Oberembt, *Großstadt, Landschaft, Augenblick: Über die Tradition von Motiven im Werk Gerhart Hauptmanns* (Berlin: Schmidt, 1999);

John Osborne, *The Naturalist Drama in Germany* (Manchester: Manchester University Press / Totowa, N.J.: Rowman & Littlefield, 1971);

Jill Perkins, *Joyce and Hauptmann: Before Sunrise* (San Marino, Cal.: Huntington Library Press, 1978);

Jörg Platiel, *Mythos und Mysterium: Die Rezeption des Mittelalters im Werke Gerhart Hauptmanns* (Frankfurt: Peter Lang, 1993);

Walter A. Reichart, *Ein Leben für Gerhart Hauptmann: Aufsätze aus den Jahren 1929–1990* (Berlin: Schmidt, 1991);

Ilse H. Reis, *Gerhart Hauptmanns Hamlet-Interpretationen in der Nachfolge Goethes* (Bonn: Bouvier, 1969);

Walter Requardt and Martin Machatzke, *Gerhart Hauptmann und Erkner* (Berlin: Schmidt, 1980);

Yeong-Don Roh, *Gerhart Hauptmann und die Frauen: Studien zum naturalistischen Werk* (Siegen: Böschen, 1998);

Daria Santini, *Gerhart Hauptmann zwischen Modernität und Tradition: Neue Perspektiven zur Atriden–Tetralogie* (Berlin: Schmidt, 1998);

Barbara Schmidt-Krayer, *Kontinuum der Reflexion: Der arme Heinrich: Mittelalterliches Epos Hartmanns von Aue und modernes Drama Gerhart Hauptmanns* (Göppingen: Kümmerle, 1994);

Peter Sprengel, *Gerhart Hauptmann: Epoche-Werk-Wirkung* (Munich: Beck, 1984);

Sprengel, *Von Luther zu Bismarck: Kulturkampf und nationale Identität bei Theodor Fontane, Conrad Ferdinand Meyer und Gerhart Hauptmann* (Bielefeld: Aisthesis, 1999);

Sprengel, *Die Wirklichkeit der Mythen: Untersuchungen zum Werk Gerhart Hauptmanns aufgrund des handschriftlichen Nachlasses* (Berlin: Schmidt, 1982);

Sprengel and Philip Mellen, eds., *Hauptmann-Forschung: Neue Beiträge—Hauptmann Research: New Directions* (Bern, Frankfurt am Main & New York: Peter Lang, 1986);

TEXT + KRITIK, special Hauptmann issue, edited by Arnold Heinz Ludwig, 142 (April 1999);

H. D. Tschörtner, "Bertolt Brecht und Hauptmann," *Weimarer Beiträge*, 32, no. 3 (1986): 386–403;

Tschörtner, *Ungeheures erhofft: Zu Gerhart Hauptmann—Werk und Wirkung* (Berlin: Der Morgen, 1986);

Felix A. Voigt, *Gerhart-Hauptmann-Studien 1934–1958* (Berlin: Schmidt, 1999);

Voigt and Reichart, *Hauptmann und Shakespeare* (Breslau: Maruschke & Berendt, 1938; revised, Goslar: Deutsche Volksbücherei, 1947);

Bernhard Zeller, ed., *Gerhart Hauptmann: Leben und Werk: Eine Gedächtnisausstellung des Deutschen Literaturarchivs zum 100. Geburtstag des Dichters* (Stuttgart: Turmhaus-Druckerei, 1962).

Papers:
Manuscript materials of Gerhart Hauptmann are at the Staatsbibliothek Preußischer Kulturbesitz, Berlin.

1912 Nobel Prize in Literature Presentation Speech

by Hans Hildebrand, Acting Secretary of the Swedish Academy, 10 December 1912

There is an old saying that times change and men change with them. If we look back on past ages we discover its truth. We, who are no longer young, have had the opportunity in our bustling lives to experience the truth of the saying, and every day confirms it anew. As far back as history extends we find that new things emerged, but were not at first recognized although they were to be important in the future. A seed came alive and grew to magnificent size. Certain names in contemporary science illustrate the discrepancy between modest beginnings and later developments.

The same is true of dramatic poetry. This is not the place to trace its development through twenty-five centuries. There is a tremendous difference, however, between the satyr choruses of the Dionysiac festivals, called tragedies because of the goat skins worn by the chorus, and the demands the modern age makes on dramatic poetry, and this difference indicates considerable progress.

In our time Gerhart Hauptmann has been a great name in the field of drama. He turned fifty recently; he is thus in his prime of life and can look back on an exceptionally rich career as an artist. He submitted his first work to the stage at the age of twenty-seven. At the age of thirty he proved himself a mature artist with his play *Die Weber* (1892) *[The Weavers]*. This work was followed by others which confirmed his reputation. In most of his plays he deals with conditions of the lowclass life which he had numerous occasions to study, especially in his native Silesia. His descriptions are based on keen observations of man and his milieu. Each of his characters is a fully developed personality—there is not a trace of types or clichés. Nobody even for a moment could doubt the truthfulness of his observations; they have established Hauptmann as a great realist. But he nowhere praises the life of these so-called low characters. On the contrary, when one has seen or read these plays and identified himself deeply with the conditions they represent, he feels the need for fresh air and asks how such misery can be abolished in the future. The realism in Hauptmann's plays leads necessarily to brighter dreams of new and better conditions and to the wish for their fulfilment.

Hauptmann has also written dramas of a totally different nature: he calls them "Märchendramen." Among them is the delightful *Hanneles Himmelfahrt* (1893) *[The Assumption of Hannele]*, in which the misery of life and the bliss of heaven emerge with such striking contrast. Among these plays is also *Die versunkene Glocke* (1897) *[The Sunken Bell]*, the most popular of his plays in his own country. The copy used by the Nobel Committee of the Swedish Academy bore the stamp of the sixtieth impression.

Hauptmann has also distinguished himself in the genres of historical drama and comedy. He has not published a collection of his lyrical poems, but incidental poems in his plays bear witness to his talent in this field.

In his early years he had published a few short stories, but in 1910 he brought out his novel *Der Narr in Christo Emanuel Quint [The Fool in Christ: Emanuel Quint]*, the result of many years of work. The story "Der Apostel" of 1892 is a sketch of the final work in which we learn about the inner life of a poor man who, without any education other than that acquired from the Bible and without any critical judgment of what he has read, finally reaches the conclusion that he is the reincarnation of Christ. It is not easy to give a correct account of the development of a human soul that can be considered normal, in view of all the forces and circumstances that affect its development. But it is even more difficult to attain the truth if one describes the inner development of a soul that is in certain respects abnormal. The attempt is bold; its execution took decades of creative work. Judgment of the work has differed widely. I am happy to join the many who consider *Emanuel Quint* a masterly solution of a difficult problem.

Hauptmann's particular virtue is his penetrating and critical insight into the human soul. It is this gift that enabled him in his plays and in his novels to create truly living individuals rather than types representing some particular outlook or opinion. All the characters we meet, even the minor ones, have a full life. In his novels one admires the descriptions of the setting, as well as the sketches of the people that come in more or less close contact with the protagonist of the story. The plays reveal his great art by their powerful concentration which holds the reader or spectator from beginning to end. Whatever subject he treats, even when he deals with life's seamy side, his is always a noble personality. That nobility and his refined art give his works their wonderful power.

The preceding remarks were intended to sketch the reasons why the Swedish Academy has awarded this year's Nobel Prize to Gerhart Hauptmann.

Dr. Hauptmann—In your significant and controversial book *Der Narr in Christo Emanuel Quint* you say: "It is impossible to uncover the necessary course of a human life in all its stages, if only because every human being is something unique from beginning to end and because the observer can comprehend his object only within the limits of his own nature."

That is indeed true. But there are many kinds of observers. The everyday man in the midst of his bustling life has neither the opportunity nor the will to study his fellow men in greater depth. We see the outside but do not care to see beneath it unless we happen to have a special interest in learning another's motives. Even those who are not drawn into the turmoil of present life, who limit their intercourse with the outside world and are on intimate terms with their immediate surroundings, do not generally go very far in their study of the human soul. We are attracted or repelled; we love or hate, if we are not indifferent. We praise or blame.

The poet, however, is not an everyday man. He is able to extend the scope of his imagination much further. For he has the divine gift of intuition. And you, Dr. Hauptmann, possess this wonderful gift to the highest degree. In your many works you have created innumerable characters. But they do not exist merely as so many types of such and such a nature. To the reader and spectator of your plays, each of your characters is a fully developed individual, living and acting together with others, but different from all of them. That is the reason for much of the magic of your work.

It has been said that at least in some of your works you have been a marked realist. You have had rich opportunities to use your gift of observation and become acquainted with the misery of whole classes of people, and you have described it faithfully. If after seeing or reading such a play one is deeply moved by it, he cannot help thinking, "These conditions must be improved." One cannot deny the existence of the seamy side of life, and it must have its place in literature in order to teach wisdom to the living.

Your manifold activities as a writer have given us other marvellous works. I shall mention only two here, *Hanneles Himmelfahrt* and *Die versunkene Glocke*. The latter seems to enjoy great popularity in your country.

Through the mouth of the ambitious and unfortunate Michael Kramer you say:

> *If someone has the effrontery to paint the man with the crown of thorns—it will take him a lifetime to do it. No pleasures for him: lonely hours, lonely days, lonely years. He must be alone with himself and with his God. He must consecrate himself daily. Nothing common must be about him or in him. And then when he struggles and toils in his solitude the Holy Ghost comes. Then he can sometimes catch a glimpse. It swells, he can feel it. Then he rests in the eternal and he has it before him in quiet and beauty. He has it without wanting it. He sees the Saviour. He feels him.*

Although in your work you have not represented the Saviour with the crown of thorns, you have represented a poor man ultimately driven to the delusion that he is the second Christ. But Kramer's words reflect your own attitude. Your novel *Der Narr in Christo Emanuel Quint* appeared in 1910, but the story "Der Apostel" of 1892 shows that the plan for writing the novel had occurred to you twenty years earlier.

True art does not consist in writing down and handing to the public the thoughts of the moment, but rather in subjecting potentially useful ideas to close scrutiny, to the conflict of different opinions and the apprehensive consideration of their eventual effect. This process will gradually lead the true artist to the precious conviction, "I have finally reached the truth." You have attained the highest rank of art by painstaking but never pedantic preparatory research, by the consistency of your feelings, thoughts, and actions, and by the strict form of your plays.

The Swedish Academy has found the great artist Gerhart Hauptmann worthy of receiving this year's Nobel Prize, which his Majesty the King will now present to him.

[© The Nobel Foundation, 1912.]

Hauptmann: Banquet Speech

Hauptmann's speech at the Nobel Banquet in Stockholm, 10 December 1912:

Als Empfänger des diesjährigen litterarischen Nobelpreises danke ich Ihnen für die warmen und freundlichen Worte, die auch an mich gerichtet worden sind. Sie dürfen überzeugt sein, daß ich und mit mir meine Nation die Ehre völlig verstehen und schätzen, die mir widerfahren ist. Der Nobeltag ist zu einer Kulturangelegenheit des ganzen Erdballs geworden, und der großartige Stifter hat auf unübersehbare Zeiten hin seinen Namen mit dem Kulturleben aller Nationen verknüpft. Hervorragende Männer aus allen Himmelsstrichen werden wie heute noch in späten Zeiten den Namen Nobel mit ähnlichen Gefühlen aussprechen, wie Menschen in früheren Zeiten ihren Schutzpatron nannten, dessen hilfreiche Kraft nicht bezweifelt werden konnte. Und seine Denkmünze wird in Familien unter allen Völkern von Geschlecht zu Geschlecht vererbt und in Ehren gehalten werden.

Es ziemt sich daher, daß ich diesem grossen Donator den Tribut von Ehrfurcht zolle, der sich ständig erneut, und nach ihm der ganzen schwedischen Nation, die diesen Mann hervorgebracht hat, und die so getreu sein humanitäres Testament verwaltet. Und dabei habe ich auch den Männern zu danken, deren aufopfernde Lynkeusarbeit dazu ausersehen ist, über die Kulturarbeit der ganzen Erde zu wachen, auf daß gute Keime aufsprießen mögen und das Unkraut vermindert werde.

Ich danke Ihnen und wünsche, daß Sie nie in der segensreichsten aller Tätigkeit ermüden und nie wirklich reiche Ernten vermissen mögen.

Und nun trinke ich darauf, daß das Ideal, das der Stiftung zugrunde liegt, seiner Verwirklichung immer näher geführt werden möge, ich meine das Ideal des Weltfriedens, das ja das höchste Ideal der Wissenschaft und der Kunst in sich schließt. Die Kunst und die Wissenschaft, die dem Kriege dient, ist nicht die höchste und echte, die ist es, die der Friede erzeugt und die den Frieden erzeugt. Und ich trinke auf den grossen letzten und rein idealen Nobelpreis, den die Menschheit dann sich wird zuerkennen dürfen, wenn die rohe Kraft unter den Völkern ebenso verhaßt geworden ist, wie die rohe Kraft es bereits unter den menschlichen Individuen der zivilisierten Gesellschaft ist.

[© The Nobel Foundation, 1912. Gerhart Hauptmann is the sole author of his speech.]

Translation by Rebecca Hughes

As recipient of this year's Nobel Prize in Literature, I thank you for the kind words that have been directed at me. Rest assured that I, along with my country, completely understand and appreciate the magnitude of the honor which has been bestowed. Nobel Day has become a global cultural affair and the outstanding founder bound his name with the cultural being of all nations. Today, and also in the future, distinguished men from all walks of life will speak the name Nobel with similar feelings to those felt by people from times past as they called upon their patron saints, whose power to aid could never be doubted. And his medallion will be esteemed and handed down in families all over the world from generation to generation.

It is fitting that I should pay tribute out of reverence to this tremendous donor, whose memory is constantly renewed, and also to the entire Swedish nation, which produced this man and which has faithfully continued his testament for humanity. Additionally, I thank the men whose self-sacrificing watchfulness is destined to oversee the cultural efforts of the whole world, encouraging its flowers to blossom and holding the weeds at bay.

I thank you all and I hope that you never tire of the most serving tasks nor suffer a poor harvest.

And now I drink to the ideal which lies at the foundation of this establishment, always nearer to being realized: the ideal of world peace, comprising the highest notion of scholarship and art. Art and scholarship are not in their highest and most real forms when serving war, but rather when they are being created by peace and creating peace. I drink also to that great, final, and absolutely perfect Nobel prize, which mankind will one day be able to award, when the crude agency of humanity has become as abhorred as the raw energy already disguised under human individuals in civilized society.

Hauptmann: Autobiographical Statement

(Written at the time of the awarding of the Nobel Prize)

I was born on November 15, 1862. The place of my birth is Bad Obersalzbrunn, a spa famous for its medicinal springs. The house of my birth is the inn "Zur Preussischen Krone." My father was Robert Hauptmann, my mother Marie Hauptmann, née Straehler. I am the youngest of four children. I remember growing up in an educated and lively middle-class house.

I attended the village school, learned some Latin from a tutor, and had violin lessons. Later I went to Breslau, the capital of our province, where I lived in boardinghouses and attended a Gymnasium. Fortunately, my Breslau school period did not crush me, but it left scars from which I only slowly recovered.

I should have perished if there had not been a way out. I went to the country and began to study agriculture. The tortures of school, begun in 1874, ended in 1878. But agriculture remained an episode. Once in solitude I dreamed to stand on my own feet and have my own thoughts. I grew conscious of myself, my value, and my rights. In this way I gained independence, firmness, and a freedom of intellect that I still enjoy today.

Hungry for culture, I resumed to Breslau where I spent a second, happier period. I attended the art academy, did sculpturing, learned what youth, hope, and beauty are, the value of friends, masters, and teachers.

I drew, sculptured, drank, wrote poems, made plans, and built castles in Spain. In this mood I exchanged the art academy of Breslau for the University of Jena in Thuringia. In this mood I exchanged Jena for Rome, and later Rome for Berlin.

Although I still worked as a sculptor in Rome, it was here that I finally decided upon literature. A play *Vor Sonnenaufgang [Before Dawn]* made me publicly known in 1889.

My later works I wrote partly in Berlin, partly in Schreiberhau in the Riesengebirge, partly in Agnetendorf, partly in Italy: they are the condensation of outward and inward fortunes.

[© The Nobel Foundation, 1912. Gerhart Hauptmann is the sole author of the text.]

Seamus Heaney
(13 April 1939 -   )

Brendan Corcoran
Indiana State University

See also the Heaney entries in *DLB 40: Poets of Great Britain and Ireland Since 1960* and *DLB Yearbook 1995*.

BOOKS: *Eleven Poems* (Belfast: Festival Publications, Queen's University, 1965);

Death of a Naturalist (London: Faber & Faber, 1966; New York: Oxford University Press, 1966);

Room to Rhyme, by Heaney, David Hammond, and Michael Longley (Belfast: Arts Council of Northern Ireland, 1968);

A Lough Neagh Sequence, edited by Harry Chambers and Eric J. Morten (Manchester, U.K.: Phoenix Pamphlets Poets Press, 1969);

Door into the Dark (London: Faber & Faber, 1969; New York: Oxford University Press, 1969);

Wintering Out (London: Faber & Faber, 1972; New York: Oxford University Press, 1973);

The Fire i' the Flint: Reflections on the Poetry of Gerard Manley Hopkins (London: Oxford University Press, 1975);

Stations (Belfast: Ulsterman, 1975);

North (London: Faber & Faber, 1975; New York: Oxford University Press, 1976);

Bog Poems (London: Rainbow Press, 1975);

Glanmore Sonnets (Hamburg, Germany: Editions Monika Beck, 1977);

In Their Element: A Selection of Poems, by Heaney and Derek Mahon (Belfast: Arts Council of Northern Ireland, 1977);

Robert Lowell: A Memorial Address and Elegy (Boston & London: Faber & Faber, 1978);

Field Work (London: Faber & Faber, 1979; New York: Farrar, Straus & Giroux, 1979);

Gravities: A Collection of Poems and Drawings, by Heaney and Noel Connor (Newcastle upon Tyne, U.K.: Charlotte Press, 1979);

Hedge School: Sonnets from Glanmore (Salem, Ore.: Charles Seluzicki, 1979);

Selected Poems 1965–1975 (Boston & London: Faber & Faber, 1980); republished as *Poems: 1965–1975* (New York: Farrar, Straus & Giroux, 1980);

Preoccupations: Selected Prose 1968–1978 (London: Faber & Faber, 1980; New York: Farrar, Straus & Giroux, 1980);

Poems and a Memoir, edited by Henry Pearson (New York: Limited Editions Club, 1982);

A Personal Selection: August 20 – October 24, 1982 (Belfast: Ulster Museum, 1982);

Among Schoolchildren: A Lecture Dedicated to the Memory of John Malone (Belfast: John Malone Memorial Committee, 1983);

An Open Letter (Derry: Field Day Theatre Company, 1983);

Hailstones (Dublin: Gallery Press, 1984);

Station Island (London: Faber & Faber, 1984; Farrar, Straus & Giroux, 1985);

Place and Displacement: Recent Poetry of Northern Ireland (Grasmere, U.K.: Trustees of Dove Cottage, 1985);

The Haw Lantern (London: Faber & Faber, 1987; New York: Farrar, Straus & Giroux, 1987);

The Government of the Tongue: The 1986 T. S. Eliot Memorial Lectures and Other Critical Writings (London: Faber & Faber, 1988); republished as *The Government of the Tongue: Selected Prose 1978–1987* (New York: Farrar, Straus & Giroux, 1988);

The Place of Writing (Atlanta: Scholars Press, 1989);

New Selected Poems, 1966–1987 (London & Boston: Faber & Faber, 1990);

Seeing Things (London: Faber & Faber, 1991; New York: Farrar, Straus & Giroux, 1991); excerpt published as *Squarings: A Sequence of Forty-Eight Poems* (San Francisco: Arion, 2003);

Joy or Night: Last Things in the Poetry of W. B. Yeats and Philip Larkin, W. D. Thomas Memorial Lecture (Swansea, U.K.: University College of Swansea, 1993);

The Redress of Poetry: Oxford Lectures (London: Faber & Faber, 1995; New York: Farrar, Straus and Giroux, 1995);

Crediting Poetry (Loughcrew, Ireland: Gallery Press, 1995; New York: Farrar, Straus & Giroux, 1996);

Seamus Heaney (left) receiving the 1995 Nobel Prize in Literature from King Carl XVI Gustaf of Sweden (photograph by Eric Roxfelt, Associated Press, AP)

The Spirit Level (London: Faber & Faber, 1996; New York: Farrar, Straus & Giroux, 1996);

Homage to Robert Frost, by Heaney, Joseph Brodsky, and Derek Walcott (New York: Farrar, Straus & Giroux, 1996; London: Faber & Faber, 1997);

Audenesque (Paris: Maeght Editeur, 1998);

Opened Ground: Selected Poems, 1966–1996 (London: Faber & Faber, 1998; New York: Farrar, Straus & Giroux, 1998);

Electric Light (London: Faber & Faber, 2001; New York: Farrar, Straus & Giroux, 2001);

Finders Keepers: Selected Prose 1971–2001 (London: Faber & Faber, 2002; New York: Farrar, Straus & Giroux, 2002);

"Room to Rhyme": "Greatest Minds Lecture" Delivered at the Celebration of Graduation at the University of Dundee, July 2003 (Dundee, U.K.: University of Dundee, 2004);

Anything Can Happen: A Poem and Essay (Dublin: TownHouse, 2004);

The Testament of Cresseid: A Retelling of Robert Henryson's Poem (London: Enithermon, 2004);

District & Circle (London: Faber & Faber, 2006; New York: Farrar, Straus & Giroux, 2006).

SELECTED BROADSIDES: *Boy Driving His Father to Confession* (Farnham, U.K.: Sceptre Press, 1970);

Night Drive (Crediton, U.K.: Richard Gilbertson, 1970);

Servant Boy (Detroit: Red Hanrahan Press, 1971);

After Summer (Old Deerfield, Mass.: Deerfield Press / Dublin: Gallery Press, 1978);

Toome (Dublin: National College of Art and Design, 1980);

Sweeney Praises the Trees (New York: Henry Pearson, 1981);

From the Republic of Conscience (Dublin: Amnesty International, 1985);

The Tree Clock (Belfast: Linen Hall Library, 1990);

Keeping Going (Concord, N.H.: Bow and Arrow Press, 1993).

PLAY PRODUCTIONS: *The Cure at Troy: A Version of Sophocles' Philoctetes,* Derry, U.K., Guildhall Derry, 1 October 1990; New York: Unterberg Poetry Center, 15 March 1993;

The Burial at Thebes: Sophocles' Antigone, Dublin, Abbey Theatre, 31 March 2004.

RECORDINGS: *The Northern Muse,* by Heaney and John Montague, Dublin, Claddagh Records, 1968;

The Rough Field, by Heaney, Montague, Benedict Kiely, Tom MacGurk, and Patrick Magee, Dublin, Claddagh Records, 1973;

Seamus Heaney and Tom Paulin, introduced by Craig Raine, London, Faber & Faber, 1983;

Stepping Stones: Selected Poems, New York, Penguin Audiobooks, 1995;

The Spirit Level, New York, Farrar, Straus & Giroux, 1996;

Station Island, London, Faber & Faber/Penguin Audiobooks, 1997;

The Inferno of Dante: A New Verse Translation, by Heaney, Frank Bidart, Louise Glück, and Robert Pinsky, New York, Penguin Audiobooks, 1998;

Beowulf, London, Penguin, 1999; St. Paul, Minn., HighBridge, 2000;

Electric Light, London, Penguin, 2000.

OTHER: *New Poems, 1970–1971,* edited by Heaney, Alan Brownjohn, and Jon Stallworthy (London: Hutchinson, 1971);

Soundings: An Annual Anthology of New Irish Poetry, edited by Heaney (Belfast: Blackstaff Press, 1972);

Soundings II, edited by Heaney (Belfast: Blackstaff Press, 1974);

"A Tale of Two Islands: Reflections on the Irish Literary Revival," in *Irish Studies I,* edited by P. J. D. Drury (Cambridge: Cambridge University Press, 1980), pp. 1–20;

The Rattle Bag: An Anthology of Poetry, edited by Heaney and Ted Hughes (London: Faber & Faber, 1982; New York: Oxford University Press, 1982);

The Essential Wordsworth, edited by Heaney (New York: Ecco Press, 1988);

"Correspondences: Emigrants and Inner Exiles," in *Migration: The Irish at Home and Abroad,* edited by Richard Kearney (Dublin: Wolfhound Press, 1989), pp. 21–31;

"William Butler Yeats (1865–1939)," in *Field Day Anthology of Irish Writing,* volume 2, edited by Seamus Deane (Derry, U.K.: Field Day, 1991), pp. 783–790;

"For Liberation: Brian Friel and the Use of Memory," in *The Achievement of Brian Friel,* edited by Alan J. Peacock (Buckinghamshire, U.K.: C. Smythe, 1993), pp. 229–240;

The School Bag, edited by Heaney and Hughes (London: Faber & Faber, 1997);

W. B. Yeats: Poems, edited by Heaney (London: Faber & Faber, 2000);

William Wordsworth: Poems, edited by Heaney (London: Faber & Faber, 2001).

TRANSLATIONS: *Ugolino,* from Dante's *Inferno* (Dublin: Andrew Carpenter, 1979);

Sweeney Astray: A Version from the Irish (Derry, U.K.: Field Day Theatre Company, 1983; London: Faber & Faber, 1984; New York: Farrar, Straus & Giroux, 1984); revised, with photographs by Rachel Giese, as *Sweeney's Flight* (London: Faber & Faber, 1992; New York: Farrar, Straus & Giroux, 1992);

Sophocles, *The Cure at Troy: A Version of Sophocles' Philoctetes* (Derry, U.K.: Field Day, 1990; London: Faber & Faber, 1990; New York: Farrar, Straus & Giroux, 1991);

The Midnight Verdict, based on translations of Ovid's *Metamorphoses* and Brian Merriman's *Cúirt an Mheán Oíche* (Loughcrew, Ireland: Gallery Press, 1993);

Jan Kochanowski, *Laments,* translated by Heaney and Stanislaw Baranczak (London: Faber & Faber, 1995; New York: Farrar, Straus & Giroux, 1995);

Leos Janácek and Ozef Kalda, *Diary of One Who Vanished: A Song Cycle* (London: Faber & Faber, 1999; New York: Farrar, Straus & Giroux, 2000);

Beowulf (London: Faber & Faber, 1999; New York: Farrar, Straus & Giroux, 1999);

Sophocles, *The Burial at Thebes: Sophocles' Antigone* (London: Faber & Faber, 2004; New York: Farrar, Straus & Giroux, 2004).

SELECTED PERIODICAL PUBLICATIONS–UNCOLLECTED: "Out of London: Ulster's Troubles," *New Statesman,* 1 July 1966, pp. 23–24;

"Old Derry's Walls," *Listener,* 24 October 1968, pp. 521–523;

"The Poetry of John Hewitt," *Threshold,* no. 22 (Summer 1969);

"A Poet's Childhood," *Listener,* 11 November 1971, pp. 660–661;

"The Trade of an Irish Poet," *Guardian,* 25 May 1972;

"Deep as England," *Hibernia,* 1 December 1972, p. 13;

"Seamus Heaney Recalls When Li'l Abner Breezed in from Castledawson," *Education Times,* 20 December 1973;

"John Bull's Other Island," *Listener,* 29 September 1977;

"The Interesting Case of John Alphonsus Mulrennan," *Planet,* 41 (1978): 34–37;

"Treely and Rurally," *Quarto*, 9 (August 1980): 14;

"English and Irish," *TLS: The Times Literary Supplement*, 24 October 1980, p. 1199;

"Above the Brim: On Robert Frost," *Salmagundi*, 88–89 (Fall 1990–Winter 1991): 275–294;

"The Sense of the Past," *History Ireland*, 1 (Winter 1993): 33–37;

"Time and Time Again: Poetry and the Millennium," *European English Messenger*, 10 (Autumn 2001): 19–23;

"The Trance and the Translation," *Guardian*, 30 November 2002, pp. 4, 6;

"A Story that Sings Down the Centuries," *London Sunday Times*, 21 March 2004, p. 41.

In October 1995 the Swedish Academy announced that it had awarded Seamus Heaney the Nobel Prize in Literature, "for works of lyrical beauty and ethical depth, which exalt everyday miracles and the living past." The poet, who was vacationing in Greece, was unaware of this honor until the following day when he received word from family in Ireland. The Swedish Academy's announcement emphasized two interconnected aspects of Heaney's work as a poet, essayist, and translator: his profound connection to the people, language, and place of his upbringing in rural Ulster, and his persistent "analysis of violence in Northern Ireland." Many of his poems reflect the violent times in which he has lived or explicitly address world and Irish history, including, notably, the so-called Troubles in Northern Ireland. That said, Heaney's work also attests to the fact that he is far more than the "laureate of violence," a title given to him by Ciaran Carson in an *Honest Ulsterman* (Winter 1975) review of Heaney's 1975 volume *North*. One of the most respected aspects of Heaney's writing in poetry and prose is his lifelong struggle to discern the necessary relationship of art to life.

Heaney is widely acknowledged as one of the most popular and important poets of the late twentieth century. For decades, his work has validated the local, whether in terms of language, place, customs, characters, history, or mythology—and in doing so it has dealt with what Counties poet Patrick Kavanagh calls "the fundamentals." Heaney's worldwide readership has come to know his home ground, whether in Counties Derry or Wicklow, as not just the locus of wells, bogs, and the implements, rhythms, and characters of rural Ireland, but as a place where the literary imagination responds to fundamental challenges afflicting individuals and societies.

Much of his early poetry through *Door into the Dark* (1969) revisits Heaney's native ground through recollections of childhood in Mossbawn, the farm he grew up on and a place he sees as suspended "between the archaic and the modern," as he wrote in *Crediting Poetry*, his 1995 Nobel Prize in Literature acceptance speech. As a locus for Heaney's early poetic imagination, Mossbawn was situated between a timeless, idyllic past and current social turmoil; yet, it is precisely this status as a place in between contradictory forces that relates to one of Heaney's core concerns: namely, as he wrote in the essay "Something" (included in *Finders Keepers: Selected Prose 1971–2001*, 2002), "the subject of boundaries and borders and frontiers and divisions."

Seamus Justin Heaney was born on 13 April 1939 on a fifty-acre farm near the shores of Lough Neagh in County Derry. He was the oldest of nine children born to Patrick and Margaret Heaney, who were Catholic. In discussing the etymology of Mossbawn in his 1972 essay "Belfast," Heaney says that "in the syllables of my home I see a metaphor of the split culture of Ulster. . . . I was symbolically placed between the marks of English influence and the lure of the native experience, between 'the desmesne' and 'the bog.'"

After attending the local Anahorish School from 1944 to 1951, Heaney left Mossbawn to study from 1951 to 1957 at St. Columb's College in Derry city. Growing up reading the stories of Celtic heroes and studying the Irish language for six years at school, Heaney was disposed from an early age to develop a markedly Irish identity in a state where the majority saw themselves as British. His attendance at the Catholic boarding school, where he studied both Irish and Latin, solidified his cultural and religious affiliations. Along with other illustrious late-1950s graduates of St. Columb's—including the scholar Seamus Deane, the politician John Hume, and the political activist Eamonn McCann—Heaney benefited from the 1947 Northern Ireland Education Act, which opened up quality secondary and university education to rural, urban, and often Catholic working classes. After graduating with honors from St. Columb's, Heaney earned a prestigious scholarship to attend Queens University, Belfast, from 1957 to 1961. There he studied Anglo-Saxon and developed a taste for the linguistic intensity of writers such as Geoffrey Chaucer, John Webster, John Keats, and especially Gerard Manley Hopkins, even as he maintained close connections to his family and parish life back home. At this time, Heaney began to write poetry and try his hand at publication. Under the pen name "Incertus," some of his earliest poems were published in the student literary magazines *Gorgon* and *Q*.

Though he graduated from Queens with first-class honors in English language and literature, a literary and scholarly life was in no way certain for Heaney. Despite encouragement to continue graduate work at Oxford—he had always assumed he would become a secondary-school teacher—Heaney opted to continue his studies for a teacher's diploma at St. Joseph's College of Education in Andersontown, Belfast. During this year, he also encountered the work of several contemporary Irish poets, notably John Hewitt, Thomas Kinsella, John Montague, and Richard Murphy. In autumn 1962 Heaney began teaching at St. Thomas's Intermediate School in Ballymurphy, Belfast, where the headmaster, the short-story writer Michael McLaverty, lent Heaney a complete volume of Kavanagh's poetry. In a 1977 interview with Deane, Heaney said that from Kavanagh he learned "that my local County Derry experience, which I had considered archaic and irrelevant to 'the modern world,' was to be trusted."

The other poet who gave Heaney confidence in the poetic validity of his own experiences was Ted Hughes. In a 1979 interview with James Randall, Heaney recalled his November 1962 encounter with Hughes's *Lupercal* (1960) in the Belfast Public Library. Having grown up on a farm where pigs were slaughtered, Heaney said that he read Hughes's "View of a Pig" and "suddenly, the matter of contemporary poetry was the material of my own life." He added, "I had had some notion that modern poetry was far beyond the likes of me—there was Eliot and so on—so I got this thrill out of trusting my own background, and I started [writing poetry in earnest] about a year later." This affection for Hughes's work led to a close friendship with the English poet in the early 1970s, a relationship that continued until Hughes's death in 1998. The same month he discovered Hughes's work, Heaney placed his poem "Tractors" in his first nonuniversity publication, the *Belfast Telegraph*. Other poems, including "Midterm Break," were published shortly thereafter in various Irish periodicals.

In autumn 1963 Heaney began teaching English literature at St. Joseph's College. At this time he came to know Philip Hobsbaum, a new lecturer at Queens University and a poet who also took a great interest in Hughes's poetry. Hobsbaum, who had organized from 1955 to 1962 a writing workshop known as the Group in Cambridge and London, was forming a similar gathering of writers in Belfast. The Belfast Group brought together such soon-to-be prominent figures as Michael Longley, Derek Mahon, James Simmons, and Stewart Parker. Hobsbaum's Belfast Group sessions continued until 1966, when Heaney took over organizational responsibilities. Though Group meetings ceased entirely in 1972, at a time of profound political turmoil and violence, Heaney's sessions similarly offered encouragement to such younger writers as Carson, Paul Muldoon, and Frank Ormsby. In addition to providing the poets with opportunities to read and critique each other's work, these meetings fostered many significant personal and literary friendships that have sustained a community of poets in Northern Ireland.

Heaney's first volume, *Death of a Naturalist* (1966), consists of many poems, including "Digging," "Blackberry Picking," and "Personal Helicon," that were first publicly presented at Group sessions. Hobsbaum not only nurtured poetic talent, he promoted it. In 1964 he ensured that various London editors received a selection of Heaney's poetry. "Digging" was immediately accepted by the *New Statesman* and published in December 1964. Having himself submitted a book manuscript titled "Advancements of Learning" to the Dolmen Press in Ireland in late 1964, Heaney was astounded to receive a letter of solicitation from Faber and Faber in January 1965. As a result of this offer, he withdrew "Advancements of Learning" from Dolmen, and an enlarged and revised version of the manuscript (now titled *Death of a Naturalist*) was accepted in late summer, around the time of his marriage to teacher and journalist Marie Devlin on 5 August 1965. The volume was published by Faber and Faber in May 1966.

The volume was well received both in Ireland and in Britain, with many reviewers noting an originality and poise that bespoke genuine literary promise. Along with the critical praise for *Death of a Naturalist*, Heaney received the Gregory Award for young writers, the Somerset Maugham Award, and the Geoffrey Faber Memorial Prize. *Death of a Naturalist* launched not only Heaney's poetic career but his lifelong affiliation with the academy: he began teaching at Queens University, Belfast, in autumn 1966. This involvement with institutions of higher learning, including St. Joseph's, Queens, Carysfort, Harvard, Oxford, and Emory Universities, exemplifies not only Heaney's early vocational commitment to teaching but his professional interest in literary scholarship.

In *Death of a Naturalist*, most notably in the first and last poems ("Digging" and "Personal Helicon"), Heaney voices many of the images, themes, and stylistic maneuvers that have come to define his poetry. According to Rand Brandes, "Digging" is "a synecdoche of sorts for the poet's entire oeuvre." A poem about the poetic vocation, it imagines the poet apart from, yet umbilically attached to, his source, be it the ancestors, the home, or the earth itself. Above all, this poem introduces the image of digging as a protean figure for the procedures of poetry: "Between my finger and my thumb / The squat pen rests. / I'll dig with it." The idea of digging to some degree governs Heaney's first five books of poetry. In a 1981 interview with John Haffenden, Heaney said: "I'm certain that up to *North*, that that was one book; in a way it grows together and goes together."

"Personal Helicon" shows the poet not digging but descending into the literal earth he knows and into the self or personal memory. At the outset of the poem, Heaney exposes the child's sense of wonder at not only the human contrivances, the "old pumps with buckets and windlasses," used for drawing fresh water out of the earth, but also the more mysterious qualities of a well, its "dark drop, the trapped sky, the smells / Of waterweed, fungus and dank moss." The title refers to the home of the Greek poet Hesiod, to whom the Muses appeared on Mount Helicon; the poem establishes the well as a literal site of Heaney's poetic inspiration and a larger figure for the processes of poetry that delve into the common stuff of the world and human lives so as to draw out something meaningful.

Shortly after the publication of *Death of a Naturalist*, the Heaneys' first son, Michael, was born. A second son, Christopher, arrived in 1968, and their daughter, Catherine Ann, was born in 1973. As his family grew, Heaney continued work as a lecturer at Queens and increasingly contributed literary journalism to various periodicals. He also made frequent public appearances on BBC radio and television. The poetry collected in his second volume, *Door into the Dark,* continued many of the same images and themes of his first book. In poems such as "Thatcher" or the mysterious and tentatively political "Lough Neagh Sequence," dedicated to the local eel fishermen, Heaney not only continues the self-examination apparent in "Personal Helicon" but confirms one of the chief assets of his poetry: the extraordinary attention to precise description of rural life.

One of the most important developments of *Door into the Dark* involves Heaney's identification of the bog as both "a genuine obsession," as he commented in the interview with Randall, and another landscape crucial to his poetry. "Bogland," the final poem of the volume, presents what Heaney (in a 2000 interview with Mike Murphy) called "a 'going through' experience." He said the poem is "about equating Irish experience to some extent with the bogs," adding, "It was not autobiographical. It was beyond me in a good way, and that was a terrific confirmation. It was a second growth-ring for me." This poem begins with the "encroaching horizon" of the Irish landscape that coalesces in the bogs' liquefaction of solid ground and the human endeavor to excavate the incompletely defined strata for turf and whatever else the bog as natural time capsule might yield up.

Included in *Door into the Dark* is "Requiem for the Croppies," a poem written for the fiftieth anniversary commemorations of the 1916 Easter Rising. Heaney's poem roots the 1916 rebellion in the United Irishmen's uprising against the British in 1798. This poem displays both Heaney's nationalist leanings and his abiding concern for how poetry addresses historical circumstance. The proper intersection of art and life became increasingly difficult to ascertain as the Catholic Civil Rights movement of the late 1960s was opposed violently by Protestant Loyalists in 1968, setting off the sectarian violence of the Troubles. Speaking to his friend Deane in 1979, Heaney explained that growing up in a "mixed" area, where "Protestants and Catholics lived in proximity to and in harmony with one another," he acquired "a kind of double awareness of division and, at the same time, of a courtesy that wasn't quite a duplicity." This intimate awareness of divisions between people is conveyed in "The Other Side" from *Wintering Out* (1972), a poem that also expresses the mutual desire of Catholic and Protestant neighbors to transcend perceived cultural differences.

Yet, the sectarian violence in late-1960s Northern Ireland confirmed and intensified the old distrust between Protestants and Catholics, Unionists and Nationalists. The British Army's introduction into Northern Ireland and the establishment of the Provisional Irish Republican Army in 1969 exacerbated tensions. In Belfast until late summer 1970, when he left Queens University for a year as a visiting professor at the University of California at Berkeley, Heaney lived in the midst of Ulster's violence. Conditioned by an early awareness of borders and divisions as well as the opportunities and risks of occupying in-between positions, Heaney's "Catholic and nationalist" identification nonetheless posed a challenge to the artist's equanimity, as he told Deane. Though criticized in some quarters for not vociferously confronting the political crisis, *Wintering Out,* in Neil Corcoran's view, addresses "if not the conflict itself, then the context out of which that conflict sprang." According to Michael Parker, the volume depicts "the origins and hinterland of the conflict . . . through elegiac poems celebrating the identity, history, territory and tongue of his people, the Northern Catholic Irish."

The dedication of *Wintering Out* is addressed to Heaney's friends, the musician David Hammond and the poet Longley. Acknowledging the contemporary reality of killings and the August 1971 imposition of extrajudicial internment—the British Army policy of arresting and imprisoning suspected IRA sympathizers—this dedication introduces a subtly political volume that marks a watershed in the relation of Heaney's poetry to the contemporary situation. The volume remains haunted by memory, what Heaney calls in a poem of the same name, "the backward look." Other poems throughout the dominant first section similarly evoke a strong sense of the artifactual and the linguistic past. Poems such as "Traditions," "A New Song," and the sequence "Gifts of Rain" delve into the powerful unity of "locale" and "utterance" that links the deep past with the present.

In "Feeling into Words," a 1974 essay included in *Preoccupations: Selected Prose 1968–1978* (1980), Heaney states that as the violence took off in 1969, "the problems of poetry moved from being simply a matter of achieving the satisfactory verbal icon to being a search for images and symbols adequate to our predicament." He explains how he discovered "some of these emblems . . . in a book that was published in English translation, appositely, the year the killing started, in 1969." This book was P. V. Glob's *The Bog People,* a study of ritualized killing in Iron Age Jutland based upon the remarkably well-preserved evidence of corpses unearthed in bogs. The detailed and graphic photographs of these bodies offered Heaney images that became not just corollaries for the contemporary violence but figures embodying the human need to seek meaning from meaningless death. Parker points out that Glob's text raises key issues, such as "landscape, religion, sexuality, violence, history, myth," that dominate both *Wintering Out* and *North*. Though Heaney's interest in *The Bog People* shadows the entire period during which he wrote *Wintering Out*, "The Tollund Man" is the only poem in the volume that addresses Glob's images. The poem ends with an imaginative identification with the Tollund Man just before his murder. Ever attentive to place names, Heaney envisions "Saying the names // Tollund, Grabaulle, Nebelgard," and experiencing in the imagined present "something" of that unimaginable yet universally human instant when mortality is consummated.

Though the rural Ulster phrase "to winter out" means "to see through and survive a crisis," during the period from 1972 until the publication of *North* in 1975 the violence in Northern Ireland intensified. In the bloodiest year of the Troubles, 1972, all sides entrenched hard-line positions and resigned themselves to the intractability of the political crisis. Thus, in the title poem from *North*, Heaney concludes by harkening to the sibylline voice of the Viking "longship's swimming tongue" warning of the terrible momentum of revenge. This voice reminds the poet that simply waiting out the crisis will not do; he must somehow respond.

In order to "put the practice of poetry more deliberately at the centre of my life" and avoid being cast as a "spokesman for the Catholic minority" in a time of crisis, as he recalls in *Preoccupations,* Heaney chose to resign from Queens in spring 1972 and accept the offer of renting an inexpensive house in County Wicklow, Republic of Ireland. For a poet who had already achieved substantial notoriety in the North, this move was viewed by many as a political gesture emphasizing Heaney's Irish cultural identity over his officially British nationality. Heaney's uprooting move to the South in the months before the publication of *Wintering Out* defines not only the writing of *North* but the critical response to this volume, Heaney's most popular and frequently taught. In the Murphy interview, Heaney said: "You can't get away from answerability, either to your time or your calling, but it's the way you answer that's the important thing. . . . *North* is a very oblique and intense book. It was fused at a very high pressure and had to do with all of my past, really, up until that stage."

Beginning the volume with "Mossbawn: Two Poems in Dedication for Mary Heaney" (a beloved aunt), the poet casts an affectionate and nostalgic gaze back to his place of origin, where love and warmth are nonetheless tinctured by what he calls "a sunlit absence." This more personal retrospection is further wrenched into the present crisis when Heaney says in "Funeral Rites" that: "Now as news comes in / of each neighbourly murder / we pine for ceremony, / customary rhythms." Heaney's desire to find a way not merely to represent but to mourn and memorialize the bloodshed in the North is fulfilled in the sequence of bog body poems that, in following from the earlier experiment with "The Tollund Man," dominate the first section of the book. "Come to the Bower," "Bog Queen," "The Grauballe Man," "Punishment," and "Strange Fruit" each explore the ability of poetry to encompass both the individuality and the generic anonymity of the deaths figured by the bog bodies.

In "Punishment," Heaney begins by empathetically identifying with a young murdered woman whose corpse had been preserved in a Jutland bog. The poet recognizes this figure as a "scapegoat" akin to the contemporary images of young Catholic women who were publicly humiliated and tortured for consorting with British soldiers in Northern Ireland. Yet, in a self-indicting gesture that is replicated at various times in his career, Heaney admits to being "an artful voyeur," who "would have cast . . . the stones of silence." He goes on to indict not only his own silence before contemporary atrocity but his own capacity to comprehend "the exact / and tribal, intimate revenge."

Heaney's efforts to express how Glob's images might be "hung in the scales / with beauty and atrocity" has led to both effusive praise and charges that these poems aestheticize and potentially demean the brutal actuality "of each hooded victim, / slashed and dumped," whether in the Iron Age or the late twentieth century. Despite the attention *North* received in Ireland, Britain, and the United States, Heaney recalled in the Randall interview that in a letter to Brian Friel shortly after publication of the book, he declared that he "no longer wanted a door into the dark—I wanted a door into the light" that would free him "to be able to use the first person singular" in reference to his personal life and time. Such a yearning for release is reflected in "Exposure," the concluding poem in *North*. This poem examines Heaney's notion of the poet as hero, "His gift like a slingstone / Whirled for the desperate," but it then bluntly asks: "How did I end up like this?" Though ensconced in the tranquility of Wicklow, Heaney suspected that the cost of sustained political engagement is a loss of appreciation for what he later termed the "marvelous."

While *North* ends with a note of self-doubt and wistful regret, *Field Work* (1979), despite a more overtly elegiac air, opens out into a more freewheeling appreciation of poetry as personal expression: "I ate the day / Deliberately, that its tang / Might quicken me all into verb, pure verb." Heaney demonstrates his dual sense of poetry as not only "self-delighting" and "inventive" linguistic expression but "a representation of things in the world." The dual role of poetry in the world has fascinated Heaney across his entire career; in his first Oxford lecture in 1989 (published in 1995), he finally defines this antithetical aspect as the "redress of poetry."

Early in *Field Work* Heaney continues to confront the ongoing Troubles in various poems including "Triptych," "The Toome Road," and the major elegies "The Strand at Lough Beg," "A Postcard from North Antrim," and "Casualty." This last elegy, written in memory of Louis O'Neill, a Catholic fisherman and acquaintance of Heaney, movingly catalogues the poet's admiring observations of this solitary drinker whose "deadpan sidling tact . . . fisherman's quick eye / And turned observant back" were "blown to bits" by an IRA bomb detonated as a reprisal for the Bloody Sunday murders of thirteen civil-rights demonstrators in Derry. Heaney uses this eel fisherman's individuality to at once mourn his death and indict the vulgar pointlessness of such violence. This elegy also points to the manner in which Heaney's later poetry, most notably in *Station Island* (1984), presents lyric encounters with the dead who instruct, critique, and provoke the living poet. "The Strand at Lough Beg" creates a similarly Dantesque encounter with the dead, this time Heaney's cousin Colum McCartney, a victim of random sectarian assassination.

Though "Singing School" in *North* opens with epigraphs from William Butler Yeats and William Wordsworth, and "Exposure" alludes to the Russian "inner émigré" Osip Mandelstam, the more archeological and even documentary rhetoric of *North* is not as infused with the voices of other poets as might be expected given that Heaney intensely studied Dante, Yeats, Mandelstam, and Robert Lowell while in Glanmore (1972–1975). Dante's importance to Heaney is underscored by the decision to close *Field Work* with "Ugolino," Heaney's translation of Cantos 32 and 33 of the *Inferno* (also published separately in 1979). Written in May 1978, "Ugolino" presents a scene of cannibalistic loathing and despair that suits the larger mood of building crisis after IRA prisoners began the late 1976 "blanket protest," which led to the hunger strikes of 1980 and 1981. "The Strand at Lough Beg" also makes direct reference to the mythogical Irish king Sweeney. Upon arriving in Wicklow, Heaney had begun to translate the medieval *Buile Suibhne,* an Irish long poem about the peregrinations of the mad, bird-like king haunted and cursed by his experiences of war. Fearing that the first effort at translation incorporated too much contemporary reference, Heaney stopped work on the project until 1979. It was eventually published as *Sweeney Astray: A Version from the Irish* in 1983. Both "Ugolino" and *Sweeney Astray* point to the central role of translation in general and, in particular, the presence of other poets' voices in Heaney's work from the mid 1970s onward.

By 1975 Heaney decided to return to teaching. When he accepted a job in the English Department at Carysfort Teachers' Training College, where he served as department chairman from 1976 to 1981, the family left Glanmore and purchased a house in Sandymount, Dublin. Heaney's sequence "Glanmore Sonnets," positioned at the center of *Field Work,* commemorates this crucial time during which Heaney confirmed his vocation as a poet and further deepened his relationship to the Irish, English, American, and European poetic traditions. The first of ten sonnets celebrates not only the intrinsic connection of art to the earth but also the poet's satisfaction, even satiation, with a time well spent: "My lea is deeply tilled." The second sonnet ends at the point where the mechanisms of language meet the world the poet knows: "Vowels ploughed into other, opened ground, / Each verse returning like the plough turned round." Here Heaney's philological interests combine with rural verities at the site of an archetypal definition of poetry.

As he produced the poems that constitute *Station Island,* during the late 1970s and early 1980s, the chaos in the North continued, and Heaney's poetic stature, especially in America, increased significantly. For a semester in 1979 Heaney succeeded Robert Lowell as director of Harvard's poetry workshops for undergraduates. Then, in 1980, the year he published his first volume of selected poems, Harvard's English Department offered him a job teaching one semester each year. Leaving Carysfort in 1981, Heaney began at Harvard in the spring of 1982. This appointment led to his being honored with the Boylston Chair of Rhetoric and Oratory in 1984, a position he held until spring 1996.

Also in late 1980 Heaney joined Deane, Hammond, and Tom Paulin to became a director of the Field Day Theatre Company. Founded in Derry earlier in 1980 by the playwright Friel and the actor Stephen Rea to promote theatrical and literary projects, the company explored, albeit from a nationalist perspective, the relationship of identity, politics, and culture in Ulster's fractured civil society. Under Field Day's auspices, Heaney published both *Sweeney Astray* and *An Open Letter* in 1983. Having grown up "in sight of some of Sweeney's places and in earshot of others," Heaney was familiar with the mythological bird-king's domain; he also identified with Sweeney's peripatetic flights across Ireland and even over the Irish Sea. *Sweeney Astray* was especially suitable for Field Day because the project retained some of the political intensity of 1972, the year it was begun. But for Heaney, as he wrote in the introduction, Sweeney also offered "a figure of the artist, displaced, guilty, assuaging himself by his utterance" and engaging in "the quarrel between free creative imagination and the constraints of religious, political, and domestic obligation." In a similar vein of political engagement, Heaney wrote the Field Day pamphlet *An Open Letter* as a piquant corrective to his inclusion as a "British" poet in a recently published anthology edited by Blake Morrison and Andrew Motion. *An Open Letter* poetically affirms Heaney's overarching sense of his national Irish identity: "My passport's green. / No glass of ours was ever raised / To toast *The Queen*."

Station Island also affirms Heaney's personal connection to an Irish Catholic and nationalist community even as it demonstrates the catholicity of his artistic affiliations with other poets, living and dead. He dedicates poems to longtime friends and fellow poets Mahon, Muldoon, and Montague. "The Birthplace" records a pilgrimage to Thomas Hardy's first home and admires Hardy's ability to connect the actual world and the elsewhere of writing. Speaking as much of this vital exemplar as of himself, Heaney acknowledges "the unperturbed, reliable / ghost life . . . carried" within both poets. The first of three sections in the volume opens with "The Underground," a poem that combines a couple's hurry through the London Tube with Ovid's accounts of Apollo's pursuit of Daphne and Orpheus's failed rescue of Eurydice. "Sandstone Keepsake" makes further direct and politicized references to Dante's *Inferno*, while "Chekhov on Sakhalin" re-creates the Dantesque scene of the writer Anton Chekhov as historical witness to the horrors of the Russian penal colony, where "He who thought to squeeze / His slave's blood out and waken the free man / Shadowed a convict guide through Sakhalin."

Dante's influence is most pronounced in "Station Island," the title sequence that constitutes the second section of the volume. In this sequence the poet, participating in a Catholic pilgrimage to St. Patrick's Purgatory, a small island in Lough Derg, County Donegal, meets the instructive and challenging ghosts of dead writers, family members, friends, and acquaintances. For instance, in the eighth poem, Heaney again encounters his murdered cousin McCartney; however, this time, the ghost refuses the poet's naively consolatory ablutions. Instead, the murder victim indicts the poet for blithely eliding the brutality and terror suffered by Heaney's own relative: "You confused evasion with artistic tact." As Heaney ultimately accuses himself of having "whitewashed ugliness," he revises not only the earlier "The Strand at Lough Beg" but his sense of what poetry can and should do in the face of violence and death. Poetry, Heaney reminds himself, must continually remain "equidistant from self-justification and self-obliteration," abdicating neither its role as witness to the "catastrophe of history" nor its ultimately "redemptive" possibility. The final poem of the sequence presents, in Dante's terza rima, an equally stirring confrontation with James Joyce, who dismisses any fealty to narrow political positions and affirms instead the primacy of art for the artist:

You lose more of yourself than you redeem
doing the decent thing. Keep at a tangent.
When they make the circle wide, it's time to swim

out on your own and fill the element
with signatures on your own frequency,
echo soundings, searches, probes, allurements,

elver-gleams in the dark of the whole sea.

With the third section of the volume, "Sweeney Redivivus," presenting Heaney's meditations on the figure and significance of Sweeney, this "book of changes" shows the poet consciously using encounters with history and literature to foster his own voice and lyric vision.

In 1988 Heaney published *The Government of the Tongue: Selected Prose 1978–1987,* a book that established him as one of the major poet-critics of his generation. Though published almost as a companion volume to the poems of *The Haw Lantern* (1987), this second essay collection charts Heaney's evolution from a writer who uses poetry to address history to a poet whose use of historical circumstance is part of a larger sense of the integral relationship of art to the human condition. While all of these essays explore Heaney's understanding of his art, two essays may be read as "defenses of poetry" that explicitly articulate Heaney's own poetics. The first of these, "The Interesting Case of Nero, Chekhov's Cognac and a Knocker," doubles as the introduction to the volume and moves to square the artful and pleasurable properties of poetry with its role as historical witness. The title essay, originally presented in 1986 as the first of Heaney's T. S. Eliot Memorial Lectures at Eliot College, University of Kent, moves from Eliot to Zbigniew Herbert to Elizabeth Bishop in its examination of these poets' "fidelity . . . to the demands and promise of the artistic event" and their simultaneous "desire to witness exactly."

Heaney inaugurated the Richard Ellmann Lectures at Emory University in April 1998 and published these three public lectures as *The Place of Writing* (1989). These essays confirm the movement of Heaney's thinking about poetry toward what Ron Schuchard, in an introduction, calls a "poetic transcendence" that "is not an evasion of sympathy with national conditions but rather a transposition of that sympathy into symbol." Though Heaney's interest in symbol stretches back most notably to the bog bodies, this shift in emphasis accelerated especially with the 1987 publication of *The Haw Lantern*.

While *Station Island* portrays the middle-aged poet as a beneficiary of Dantesque literary and historical influences impelling him to "strike my own note," *The Haw Lantern*, which won the Whitbread Award, seeks access to the ghostly, the imaginary, the strange in the actual. According to Helen Vendler, this book attempts to make the invisible visible, the imaginary real, and the strange ordinary. Above all, *The Haw Lantern* dwells upon absence. The volume is governed overwhelmingly by the deaths of Heaney's mother in October 1984 and his father in October 1986. Other influences include Heaney's engaged reading and personal contacts with Eastern European poets such as Herbert, Czesław Miłosz, Miroslav Holub, and Joseph Brodsky. Heaney's dedicatory verse is instructive, for it demonstrates the shift in the poet's gaze: "The riverbed, dried-up, half-full of leaves. / Us, listening to a river in the trees." The old sources of inspiration have their limits; new and more imaginative sources of poetic sustenance must be found.

One of the most important poems of *The Haw Lantern* is "Terminus," which shows the poet understanding himself in terms of self-criticism and self-revision: "Is it any wonder when I thought / I would have second thoughts?" This poem, like the volume, projects Heaney's "capacity to be," as he says in "Something to Write Home About" (1998, included in *Finders Keepers*), "attracted at one and the same time to the security of what is intimately known and the challenges and entrancements of what is beyond us—it is this double capacity that poetry both springs from and addresses." Claiming the territory of the in-between, Heaney avows in a 1993 essay called "Frontiers of Writing" that "within our individual selves we can reconcile two orders of knowledge which we might call the practical and the poetic," where "each form of knowledge redresses the other and [affirms] that the frontier between them is there for the crossing." Reversing his earlier aesthetic practice of using poetry to examine politics and history, he now uses social realities for the aesthetic purpose of describing a larger experience of containment and release, endurance and respite.

The deaths of Heaney's parents are more specifically registered in several elegies. In "The Stone Verdict," a poem written just before the death of his mother, Heaney actually anticipates his father's death and uses the cattleman's "speechlessness" to define this imagined absence. At the center of *The Haw Lantern* lies the elegiac sonnet sequence "Clearances," written in memory of Heaney's mother. This series of eight poems opens with a symbolic lesson in splitting coal blocks and calls on Heaney's mother to continue as a spirit of poetic instruction and inspiration: "Teach me now to listen, / To strike it rich behind the linear black." The poems of "Clearances" memorialize the dead by bringing the poet and his mother into an exquisite communion, whether in the sanctuary of the tidy kitchen or by way of shared chores such as peeling potatoes or folding sheets.

In 1988 Heaney was elected to a five-year term as the Oxford University Professor of Poetry. This appointment, from 1989 to 1994, required Heaney to present three public lectures each year; collected and published in 1995 as *The Redress of Poetry*, these essays further consolidated Heaney's stature as a teacher of poetry. Yet, just as Heaney's critical prose from the late 1960s onward parallels in illustrative ways his poetry, various small and large translation projects simultaneously reflect his scholarly interests and feed his lyric poetry.

After *Sweeney Astray*, Heaney continued to further his interest in Irish-language poetry. While regularly translating works by Irish writers from the fifteenth to the twentieth centuries, he has also translated from Homer's Greek, Virgil's and Ovid's Latin, Dante's Italian, J. C. Bloem's Dutch, Marin Sorescu's Romanian, Leos Janacek's Czech, and Jan Kochanowski's Polish. Though his first attempts to translate the *Buile Suibhne* stalled in the early 1970s, this project lingered until Heaney's own poetic development yielded a fuller purchase on the original. This same pattern has held true for *Beowulf*, begun in 1985 but not published until 1999.

One substantial work that does not follow this pattern is the *The Cure at Troy*. Begun in early 1990 as a commission for Field Day, the work explores political ideas more prominently rendered in "The Government of the Tongue" than in *The Haw Lantern* or his next poetry volume, *Seeing Things* (1991). Nevertheless, late in the play, Neoptolemus upbraids Philoctetes by saying: "Stop licking your wounds. Start seeing things." The play is about the physical and mental wounds of war and the Herculean efforts to transcend the given and heal both individuals and societies. Examining various strategies for achieving reconciliation, the play establishes poetry as the medium through which the inexorable symbiosis of the "murderous" and the "marvelous" (as he describes in *Crediting Poetry*) may be grasped.

Another translation opens *Seeing Things*, the loose first section of which consists of several lyrics referencing the death of Heaney's father. As a prefatory lyric, "The Golden Bough," a translation of a passage from Virgil's *Aeneid*, suggests that the volume as a whole is a descent into the Underworld. This poem describes Aeneas' encounter with the Cumaean Sibyl before whom the hero prays "for one look, one face-to-face meeting with my dear father." Part 1 of the book then begins with another reference to the Underworld in "The Journey Back." Here, the journey into hell apparently accomplished, nothing remains but the exit back into the known world of the quotidian, where poetry itself constitutes that sought-after alternate universe where the unimaginable might be revealed and a living son might reunite with his dead father.

Vendler suggests that "the airiness of *Seeing Things* occurs because Heaney is contemplating the physical through the scrim of extinction." But these poems, despite their palpable sense of emptiness, frequently endeavor to comprehend this alternative, lyric reality: "He felt at one with space, // unroofed and obvious— / surprised in his empty arms / like some fabulous high-catcher / coming down with the ball." Though "Fosterling" expresses the midlife epiphany in which Heaney admits to "waiting until I was nearly fifty / To credit marvels," this poet's visionary trust in an alternative understanding of an obviously violent world—a way of seeing and understanding the world through poetry—has been a crucial part of Heaney's poetics since the late 1970s.

All of these developments are put into practice in the second section of *Seeing Things*, an extended sequence of twelve-line poems called "Squarings." Heaney commented in a 2003 interview with Dennis O'Driscoll that he found the "shifting brilliancies" of the first of these poems to be "marvelous stuff . . . strange and unexpected," and so he enthusiastically pursued the possibilities of his new form. He most frequently recites "Lightenings viii," the eighth of his "Squarings," a poem from the Annals of Clonmacnoise. With the monks at prayer, a visionary ship "appeared above them in the air," and its deep-set anchor snags on the altar rails. To free the ship, a sailor slides down the rope and struggles to release the anchor. The abbot then says: "This man can't bear our life here and will drown . . . unless we help him." And so they help; "the freed ship sailed, and the man climbed back / Out of the marvelous as he had known it."

In 1995 Heaney published ten of his fifteen Oxford lectures as *The Redress of Poetry*. In addition to pieces on various key poets, the essays "The Redress of Poetry" and "Frontiers of Writing" stand alongside "The Government of the Tongue" as defenses of poetry in the tradition of Philip Sidney, Percy Bysshe Shelley, and Matthew Arnold. "The Redress of Poetry" once again attempts to ascertain the right relationship of art to history. This essay considers the responsibility of poetry to be "of present use" and to confront the world's injustices. Heaney begins with Wallace Stevens's idea of the "nobility" of poetry, recognized as "the imagination pressing back against the pressure of reality." This "activity of poetry" involves what he calls "redress," a "tilt of the scales of reality towards some transcendent equilibrium." However, because redress involves a continuous recalibration of the right relationship between poetry and its world, Heaney is adamant about protecting the aesthetic aspect of poetry from overemphasis on its political nature. This statement is a crucial summation of Heaney's views regarding the rights and responsibilities of not only his own work but poetry as an art form in the world.

Also in 1995 Heaney received the Nobel Prize in Literature. Critics of this prize frequently suspect that the Swedish Academy awards particular writers at particular times based on relevant contemporary political developments. It is also true that thirteen months before Heaney's laureateship was announced, the Irish Republican Army declared a unilateral cease-fire, which created the first opportunity in many years for Northern Ireland to approach a political resolution of its sectarian violence. Though tempting, it has always been a mistake to associate too closely Heaney's work—or the Swedish Academy's decision—with Northern Ireland's civil strife. Scholars, critics, journalists, and readers around the world greeted with enthusiasm the Swedish Academy's judgment in the case of Heaney.

Although his life was full of public engagements before the Swedish Academy bestowed the Nobel, Heaney told Tom Adair in 1996 that despite counting other recent laureates including Brodsky, Miłosz, and Derek Walcott as friends or mentors, he "was panicked by the intensity" of the global fame and the new pressures not just on his public life but on his writing life. However, in the years after what he calls "the Stockholm intervention," Heaney has continued his peregrinations around the globe while maintaining a steady

MAKING RETURNS

~~THE RECORDS~~
His bicycle stood at the window-sill,
~~It was standing up to the sill,~~
the rubber cowl of a mud-splasher
skirting the front mudguard,
its ~~the~~ fat black handlegrips

heating in sunlight
~~like cushes~~, the "spud"
of the dynamo gleaming and cocked back,
the pedal treads ~~hanging~~ hanging relieved
of the boot of the law.

His cap was upside down
on the floor, next his chair.
The line of its pressure ran
like a bevel in his slightly sweating hair.

He had unstrapped
the heavy ledger, and my father
concocted ~~made stabs at exact mensuration~~ tillage returns
in acres, roods and perches.

Arithmetics (of dread) and fear.
I sat staring at the polished holster
with its buttoned flap, the braid cord
looped into the revolver butt.

"
     As
"~~What about~~ other ~~crops~~ root-crops?
Mangolds? Marrowstems? ~~Turnips?~~ Anything like that?"
"No." But was there not a line
Of turnips where the seed ran out

Working draft of the poem published as "A Constable Calls" in Heaney's 1975 collection North *(courtesy of the author)*

in the potato field? I assumed
small guilts ~~like that.~~ and sat   the black hole in
~~The barracks had a black hole.~~ eying   the books.
He stood up, shifted the baton-case

further round on his belt,
closed the domesday book, ~~fitted~~
fitted ~~His~~ cap back with ~~his~~ two hands
and looked at me as he said good-bye.

A shadow bobbed in the window.
He was snapping the carrier-spring
Over the ledger. His boot pusehd off
and the bicycle ticked, ~~into memory.~~ ticked, ~~ticked.~~

ticked at the back of my mind
until now, ~~self~~ letting me off
with a cautioning this time
and this time

production of poems, articles, and essays. One respite occurred in July 1997, when Harvard appointed Heaney the Ralph Waldo Emerson Poet in Residence at Harvard. This position, which he still holds, allowed him to maintain his affiliation with the university while reducing substantially the teaching responsibilities that had been associated with the Boylston Chair, which he then relinquished in 1998.

His first book after the Nobel Prize, *The Spirit Level* (1996), winner of the Whitbread Book of the Year Award, departs from the visionary and spectral *Seeing Things*. Heaney says that he associates *The Spirit Level* "with dungarees, the long pocket, the solidity of work, and of being eye to eye with your democratic life." But, like his preceding books, *The Spirit Level* responds to the deaths of his parents and confronts historical atrocity as it taps visionary resources contained in the most quotidian of things. This volume begins with an invocatory poem, "The Rain Stick," which captures the unstable simplicity of a cactus stalk filled with grit or dry seeds. When revolved, this object becomes not only a musical instrument but a simulacrum for the climate of Ireland. The poem declares: "Upend the rain stick and what happens next / Is a music that you never would have known / To listen for." The poem then acknowledges central truths about poetry:

Upend the stick again. What happens next

Is undiminished for having happened once,
Twice, ten, a thousand times before.
Who cares if all the music that transpires

Is the fall of grit or dry seeds through a cactus?
You are like a rich man entering heaven
Through the ear of a raindrop. Listen now again.

The Spirit Level aspires to create bridges to the domain of the marvelous, especially in other poems about vocation, such as "Whitby-sur-Moyola," "The Thimble," or "Mint." But the political situation in the North once again receives attention in poems such as "Keeping Going," "Two Lorries," and "The Flight Path." The latter recalls a May 1979 encounter with a hard-core Republican on the train to Belfast. It captures the dilemma Heaney as a public figure has faced for years: this man "enters and sits down / Opposite and goes for me head on. / 'When, for fuck's sake, are you going to write / Something for us?'" Answering all the critics, the poet says: "If I do write something, / Whatever it is, I'll be writing for myself."

On 9 February 1996 the IRA withdrew from its cease-fire just before a massive car bomb exploded in the Canary Wharf district of London. Though sectarian bombings and murders continued through 19 July 1997, when the IRA restored its 1994 cease-fire, Heaney reflected a widespread if guarded optimism when he said in 1996 that "I am hopeful we've moved away from the atrocious into the messy." Indeed, the 1997 renewal of the IRA's cease-fire allowed all-party talks to continue after Sinn Féin, the IRA's political wing, rejoined negotiations. These deliberations finally yielded the Belfast (or Good Friday) Agreement on 10 April 1998. A province-wide referendum on 22 May 1998 overwhelmingly approved the complicated power-sharing deal. In autumn 1998 John Hume and David Trimble, representatives for the majority Catholic and Protestant political parties, respectively, won the Nobel Peace Prize.

Against this backdrop, Heaney finished his translation of *Beowulf* and prepared the poems in *Electric Light* (2001). Commissioned by the American publishing house W. W. Norton, the translation, which also won the Whitbread Book of the Year Award, quickly became a best-seller in both Britain and the United States, with hundreds of thousands of copies sold.

Heaney's conscious effort to occasionally use distinctly Hiberno-English words reflects both the originality of Heaney's work and the fact that the translation was being produced against the backdrop of nearly twenty years of violent conflict in Northern Ireland. A prime example of this translation strategy is Heaney's description of Hrothgar's Hall using the Elizabethan English word "bawn." Like the overall translation project, this word, which stems from the Irish word *bó-dhún*, meaning a fortified shelter for cattle, points to the "complex history of conquest and colony, absorption and resistance, integrity and antagonism" that defines the relationship between Ireland and England, as Heaney states in the introduction. While initially attracted by the "sounds and shapes of the lines," Heaney admitted in a 2000 interview with Karl Miller to remaining confident of "the adequacy of the poetry [in *Beowulf*] to the present time."

With the violence of history understood as a continuous "horizon of dread," Heaney's *Beowulf* puts special emphasis on the various funerary passages and laments comprising "moments of lyric intensity" that unite metrical and sensory elements with a more visionary scope. As he explains in the introduction, it was a single word—the Old English *polian*, meaning "to suffer"—that accessed his "right-of-way" into the text. This Old English word, Heaney realized, "was not strange at all, for it was the word that older and less educated people would have used in the country where I grew up." Heard in the Hiberno-English speech of Heaney's family, *polian* became an "enabling note," justifying the project and prompting a particular, familiar tone of voice. A triumph of Heaney's career-long endeavor to bridge the most local with the universal, Heaney's *Beowulf* perhaps most poignantly communicates to the present world with the anonymous Geat woman's lament before Beowulf's funeral pyre. In the introduction, Heaney writes:

> The Geat woman who cries out in dread as the flames consume the body of her dead lord could come straight from a late-twentieth-century news report, from Rwanda or Kosovo; her keen is a nightmare glimpse into the minds of people who have survived traumatic, even monstrous events and who are now being exposed to a comfortless future. We immediately recognize her predicament and the pitch of her grief and find ourselves the better for having them expressed with such adequacy and dignity and unforgiving truth.

In the wake of *Beowulf,* Heaney published *Electric Light,* an intense, burnished volume of poems. *Electric Light* confirms the ability of poetry to bridge past and present, self and other, and shows how such seeming opposites symbiotically coexist. The first section of the volume is dominated by Virgilian eclogues and other pastoral lyrics deriving power from the "earthed lightning" of natural beauty found in such places as Greece, Spain, or Ireland. The second section–elegies for poets, friends, and family members–mourns these dead, yet listens for what remains despite death's obdurate silence. Heaney's elegy for Hughes likens his friend's poetry to "a single span . . . Over the railway lines at Anahorish." Standing under the "cranial acoustic of the stone" bridge, Heaney memorializes Hughes's life and poetry by demonstrating its lasting and confirming effect on his own verse.

In "Known World," Heaney confronts the hardly unfamiliar internecine violence in the former Yugoslavia, where the displacements and massacres of Bosnian Muslims and Serbs prompt more questions than answers. Murders in Ireland–that of Michael Collins in 1922 and Sean Brown in 1997–intrude into the "The Loose Box" and "The Augean Stables," respectively. Like "At Toomebridge," which also memorializes a political killing from 1798, these poems are attentive to but not preoccupied with historical reference.

After the terrorist attacks in America on 11 September 2001, Heaney turned to Horace and *Beowulf* to address this question of what remains after catastrophe while putting terrible spectacle into perspective. Heaney says that his poem "Horace and the Thunder," first published in *The Irish Times* on 17 November 2001, describes "poetry's covenant with the irrational . . . thunder in the clear, blue sky." The poem begins by declaring: "Anything can happen." It repeats: "Anything can happen, the tallest things // Be overturned, those in high places daunted, / Those overlooked regarded."

The poem is akin to Yeats's apocalyptic "The Second Coming" in its timeless vision of human vulnerability, as "stropped-beaked Fortune / Swoops, making the air gasp, tearing the crest / Off one, setting it down bleeding on the next." Going beyond 11 September, the poem, Heaney says, "expresses the sudden casual desolations of the opening years of our new millennium." It attests to the ability of poetry to decry, yet understand, that atrocity of all types is an inexorable part of human history. "Horace and the Thunder" and Heaney's other "September 11" poem, "The Helmet" (included in *District & Circle,* 2006), offer no panacea beyond the trust that something (like a voice) will survive.

In 2004 Heaney retitled "Horace and the Thunder" as "Anything Can Happen" and republished it in a small book to support the work of Amnesty International. *Anything Can Happen* includes Heaney's poem and translations of the poem into twenty-three "languages of conflict," displayed on facing pages. The languages include English and Irish, Xhosa and Afrikaans, Hebrew and Arabic, Serbian and Bosnian, Chinese and Tibetan, Spanish and Basque, Hindu and Urdu, and Turkish and Greek.

After several years of discussions with various universities in the United States, Heaney announced on 23 September 2003 that Emory University had acquired a substantial collection of his personal and literary papers dating from 1964 to the present and including thousands of letters and other printed materials, as well as photographs and recordings. The collection does not include manuscripts of his poems, translations, or prose works. In 2002 Heaney published *Finders Keepers: Selected Prose 1971–2001,* which won the Truman Capote Award for literary criticism. This volume brings together key essays from Heaney's four previously published books of criticism in addition to many other uncollected essays and reviews. The volume, like *Opened Ground: Selected Poems, 1966–1996* (1998) and the placement of his papers, represents a stocktaking as he enters the fifth decade of his writing life.

A related stocktaking occurs in *The Burial at Thebes,* Heaney's translation of Sophocles' *Antigone,* commissioned to honor the centenary of Dublin's Abbey Theatre. In a review for the *Irish Times* (4 April 2004) Thomas Kilroy emphasized that *The Burial at Thebes* "is a companion piece" to Heaney's other Sophocles translation, *The Cure at Troy.* Kilroy pointed out the importance, in both plays, of Heaney's title changes that focus on "the healing, restorative product of tragedy rather than the dark journey itself."

Heaney's translation, laced with the prosaic verbiage of contemporary American and British politicians, addresses the international conflicts of the new millennium. In "A Story that Sings Down the Centuries"

(2004) Heaney wrote that he found his own "poetic go-ahead" in his recollection of the note of grief in the eighteenth-century Irish-language poem known as "The Lament for Art O'Leary," by Eibhlin Dhubh Ní Chonaill. The "three-beat line" of Ní Chonaill's voice in mourning satisfied Heaney's sense of Antigone's first "speedy, haunted" utterances. Heaney said he found it "easy enough to play variations" on this metrical foundation, "making the chorus, for example, speak a version of the four-beat, alliterating, Old English line." The Anglo-Saxon connection is not only metrical but thematic: from "The Lament for Art O'Leary," it is an easy jump to the Geat woman's lament in *Beowulf* and then to Antigone's outcries against Creon's injustice. Another impetus for this play is rooted in the 2003 American and British invasion of Iraq. Heaney says that "Creon puts it to the chorus in these terms: either you are a patriot, a loyal citizen and regard Antigone as an enemy of the state because she does honour to her traitor brother, or else you yourselves are traitorous because you stand up for a woman who has broken the law and defied my authority." In a review of the Abbey Theatre production for *Dublin* (6 April 2004) Harvey O'Brien commented: "Though Heaney makes claims for a contemporary context to this production through reference to George W. Bush's division of the world based on unconditional loyalty to his foreign policy, such a reading is not necessarily invited or exclusive." O'Brien also noted that "Heaney has been careful not to be too rigorous with domestic applicability even given the presentation of the production as part of the Abbey Centenary," but he added, "This is not to say that there is any 'fuzziness' in Heaney's script . . . the richness and power of this classic piece of theatre have been respected while the needs and the ear of a contemporary audience have also been addressed."

Seamus Heaney once said in an essay on Yeats, another Irish poet who spoke from the Nobel Laureate's podium in Stockholm, "The poet who would be most the poet has to attempt an act of writing that outstrips the conditions even as it observes them . . . it is essential that the vision of reality which poetry offers should be transformative, more than just a print-out of the given circumstances of its time and place." Heaney's statement holds true for his own work as well.

Interviews:

Seamus Deane, "Unhappy and at Home," *Crane Bag*, 1, no. 1 (1977): 61–67;

Robert Druce, "A Raindrop on a Thorn," *Dutch Quarterly Review*, 9, no. 1 (1978): 24–37;

James Randall, "An Interview with Seamus Heaney," *Ploughshares*, 5, no. 3 (1979): 7–22;

Deane, "Talk with Seamus Heaney," *New York Times*, 2 December 1979, p. 47;

John Haffenden, "Meeting Seamus Heaney: An Interview," in his *Viewpoints: Poets in Conversation with John Haffenden* (London: Faber & Faber, 1981; Boston: Faber & Faber, 1981), pp. 57–75;

Frank Kinahan, "An Interview with Seamus Heaney," *Critical Inquiry*, 8 (Spring 1982): 405–414;

June Beisch, "An Interview with Seamus Heaney," *Literary Review*, 29 (Winter 1986): 31–42;

Rand Brandes, "Seamus Heaney: An Interview," *Salmagundi*, 80 (Fall 1988): 4–21;

Tom Adair, "Calling the Tune," *Linen Hall Review*, 6 (Fall 1989): 5–8;

Henri Cole, "The Art of Poetry, LXXV," *Paris Review*, 144 (Fall 1997): 88–138;

George Morgan, "Interview with Seamus Heaney," *Cycnos*, 15, no. 2 (1998): 227–235;

Luigi Amara, David Huerta, and Julio Trujillo, "Conversación con Seamus Heaney: La conciencia poética," *Letras Libres*, 1 (April 1999): 36–40;

Heaney and Robert Hass, *Sounding Lines: The Art of Translating Poetry* (Berkeley, Cal.: Doreen B. Townsend Center for the Humanities, 2000);

Karl Miller, *Seamus Heaney in Conversation with Karl Miller* (London: Between the Lines, 2000);

Mike Murphy, "Seamus Heaney," in *Reading the Future: Irish Writers in Conversation with Mike Murphy*, edited by Cliodhna Ni Anluain (Dublin: Lilliput, 2000), pp. 81–97;

John Brown, "Seamus Heaney," in his *In the Chair: Interviews with Poets from the North of Ireland* (Cliffs of Moher, Ireland: Salmon, 2002);

Dennis O'Driscoll, "The Lannan Foundation: Readings and Conversations: Seamus Heaney with Dennis O'Driscoll," 1 October 2003 <http://www.lannan.org/docs/semus-heaney-031001-trans-conv.pdf>.

Bibliographies:

Michael J. Durkan and Rand Brandes, *Seamus Heaney: A Reference Guide* (New York: G. K. Hall, 1996; London: Prentice Hall International, 1996);

Jonathan Allison, "Seamus Heaney: A Reference Guide," *ANQ*, 13, no. 1 (2000): 44–46.

References:

Tom Adair, "Caught Inside a Raindrop," *Scotsman*, 28 April 1996, p. 13;

Agenda, special Heaney issue, edited by William Cookson and Peter Dale, 27 (Spring 1989);

Michael Allen, ed., *Seamus Heaney* (New York: St. Martin's Press, 1997);

Elmer Andrews, *The Poetry of Seamus Heaney: All the Realms of Whisper* (New York: St. Martin's Press, 1988);

Andrews, ed., *Seamus Heaney: A Collection of Critical Essays* (London: Macmillan, 1992);

Calvin Bedient, "The Music of What Happens," *Parnassus*, 8 (Fall/Winter 1979): 109–122;

Harold Bloom, ed., *Seamus Heaney* (New York: Chelsea House, 1986);

Rand Brandes, "The Dismembering Muse: Seamus Heaney, Ciaran Carson, and Kenneth Burke's 'Four Master Tropes,'" *Bucknell Review*, 38, no. 1 (1994): 177–194;

Edward Broadbridge, ed., *Seamus Heaney* (Copenhagen: Danmarks Radio, 1977);

Terence Brown, "Four New Voices: Poets of the Present," in *Northern Voices: Poets from Ulster* (Totowa, N.J.: Rowman & Littlefield, 1975; Dublin: Gill & Macmillan, 1975), pp. 171–213;

Sidney Burris, *The Poetry of Resistance: Seamus Heaney and the Pastoral Tradition* (Athens: Ohio University Press, 1990);

Robert Buttel, *Seamus Heaney* (Lewisburg, Pa.: Bucknell University Press, 1975);

Colby Quarterly, special Heaney issue, 30 (March 1994);

Neil Corcoran, *The Poetry of Seamus Heaney: A Critical Study* (London & Boston: Faber & Faber, 1998);

Patricia Coughlan, "'Bog Queens': The Representation of Women in the Poetry of John Montague and Seamus Heaney," in *Gender in Irish Writing*, edited by Toni O'Brien Johnson and David Cairns (Philadelphia: Open University Press, 1991);

Tony Curtis, ed., *The Art of Seamus Heaney*, third edition (Bridgend, Mid Glamorgan: Poetry Wales Press, 1994);

Seamus Deane, "Seamus Heaney: The Timorous and the Bold," in his *Celtic Revivals: Essays in Modern Irish Literature 1880–1980* (London: Faber & Faber, 1985);

Desmond Fennell, "Whatever You Say, Say Nothing," *Stand*, 32 (Fall 1991): 38–65;

Field Day Theatre Company, *Ireland's Field Day* (London: Hutchinson, 1985);

John Wilson Foster, *The Achievement of Seamus Heaney* (Dublin: Lilliput, 1995);

Thomas C. Foster, *Seamus Heaney* (Boston: Twayne, 1989);

Adrian Frazier, "Anger and Nostalgia: Seamus Heaney and the Ghost of the Father," *Éire-Ireland: A Journal of Irish Studies*, 36 (Fall–Winter 2001): 7–38;

Robert F. Garratt, ed., *Critical Essays on Seamus Heaney* (New York: G. K. Hall / London: Prentice Hall International, 1995);

Henry Hart, *Seamus Heaney: Poet of Contrary Progressions* (Syracuse, N.Y.: Syracuse University Press, 1992);

Jonathan Hufstader, *Tongue of Water, Teeth of Stones: Northern Irish Poetry and Social Violence* (Lexington: University of Kentucky Press, 1999);

Elmer Kennedy-Andrews, *The Poetry of Seamus Heaney: All the Realms of Whisper* (London: Macmillan, 1988);

John Kerrigan, "Earth Writing: Seamus Heaney and Ciaran Carson," *Essays in Criticism*, 48 (April 1998): 144–168;

Benedict Kiely, "A Raid into Dark Corners: The Poems of Seamus Heaney," *Hollins Critic*, 7 (October 1970): 1–12;

David Lloyd, "'Pap for the Dispossessed': Seamus Heaney and the Poetics of Identity," *Boundary*, 2 (Winter–Spring 1985): 319–342;

Edna Longley, "Poetry and Politics in Northern Ireland," in her *Poetry in the Wars* (Newcastle upon Tyne: Bloodaxe, 1986);

Longley, "Stars and Horses, Pigs and Trees," *Crane Bag*, 3, no. 2 (1979);

Michael Longley, "Poetry," in *Causeway: The Arts in Ulster*, edited by Longley (Belfast: Arts Council of Northern Ireland, 1971), pp. 95–109;

Catharine Malloy and Phyllis Carey, eds., *Seamus Heaney: The Shaping Spirit* (Newark, Del.: University of Delaware Press / London: Associated University Presses, 1996);

Arthur E. McGuinness, "The Craft of Diction: Revision in Seamus Heaney's Poems," in *Image and Illusion: Anglo-Irish Literature and its Contexts*, edited by Maurice Harmon (Dublin: Wolfhound Press, 1979), pp. 62–91;

McGuinness, *Seamus Heaney: Poet and Critic* (New York: Peter Lang, 1994);

Michael R. Molino, *Questioning Tradition, Language, and Myth: The Poetry of Seamus Heaney* (Washington, D.C.: Catholic University of America Press, 1994);

Blake Morrison, *Seamus Heaney* (New York & London: Methuen, 1982);

Sean O'Brien, "Seamus Heaney: *The Space Made by Poetry*," in his *The Deregulated Muse* (Newcastle upon Tyne: Bloodaxe, 1998), pp. 89–96;

Bernard O'Donoghue, *Seamus Heaney and the Language of Poetry* (New York & London: Harvester Wheatsheaf, 1994);

Jay Parini, "Seamus Heaney: The Ground Possessed," *Southern Review*, 16 (Winter 1979): 100–123;

Michael Parker, *Seamus Heaney: The Making of the Poet* (Iowa City: University of Iowa Press, 1993);

Marjorie Perloff, "Seamus Heaney: Peat, Politics and Poetry," *Washington Post Book World*, 25 January 1981: 5, 11;

Peter Sacks, "Unleashing the Lyric: Seamus Heaney," *Antioch Review*, 48 (Summer 1990): 381–389;

Salmagundi, special Heaney issue, 80 (Fall 1988);

Robert Tracy, "Into an Irish Free State: Heaney, Sweeney and Clearing Away," in *Poetry in Contemporary Irish Literature*, edited by Michael Kenneally (Gerrards Cross, U.K.: Colin Smythe, 1995), pp. 238–262;

Helen Vendler, *The Breaking of Style: Hopkins, Heaney, Graham* (Cambridge, Mass.: Harvard University Press, 1995);

Vendler, *Seamus Heaney* (Cambridge, Mass.: Harvard University Press, 1998);

Stephen Wade, *More on the Word-Hoard: The Work of Seamus Heaney* (Nottingham, U.K.: Paupers' Press, 1993).

Papers:

A collection of Seamus Heaney's papers is housed at the Manuscript, Archives, and Rare Book Library of Emory University in Atlanta, Georgia.

1995 Nobel Prize in Literature Presentation Speech

by Mr. Östen Sjöstrand, Member of the Swedish Academy (Translation from the Swedish)

Your Majesties, Your Royal Highnesses, Ladies and Gentlemen,

The Irish poet Seamus Heaney was born in County Derry in Northern Ireland. The thatched farmhouse he grew up in was called Mossbawn—a name that has become mythical in Heaney's poetry. It is a place that occurs and re-occurs in concrete nearness in Heaney's poetry, from his debut in 1966 with *Death of a Naturalist* until *Seeing Things*, the most recent, published in 1991. As an example of his choice of subject matter and his style, one can choose the opening lines of "A Drink of Water," from *Field Work*, published in 1979: "She came every morning to draw water / Like an old bat staggering up the field: / The pump's whooping cough, the bucket's clatter / And slow diminuendo as it filled, / Announced her."

It is no pastoral idyll that Seamus Heaney conjures up, but rather the toilsome, lethargic greyness of the diurnal. Like Wordsworth, Seamus Heaney can well describe each human being as "a Child of Earth." For Seamus Heaney, poetry, like the soil, is evidently something to be ploughed and turned over.

The poet has little time for the Emerald Isle of the tourist brochures. For him Ireland is first and foremost *The Bogland*.

Heaney sees Ireland's peat bogs as a symbol of its identity, just as the potato is—with all that this recalls of the suffering during The Great Hunger in the middle of the 19th century.

The peat bogs also evoke, in their special way, the feeling of the past. One of Seamus Heaney's most expressive poems accounts for his experience of the Iron Age Tollund Man, whose body was preserved in a peat bog in Jutland. In his figure Heaney conjures forth, brutally and movingly, a culture that is both alien and familiar, a distinctive subject of ritual sacrifice, human voices silenced by the boggy landscape.

The water in the peat bogs, indeed all water, is something Seamus Heaney associates with the feminine, the Gaelic, the Catholic, the creative element in his nature. All this is deeply grounded in the poet's very being, a childhood preserved—as it were—which has not been overshadowed by his secularised British upbringing or the bitter experiences of The Troubles, the conflict in Ulster. In this context it must be said that Seamus Heaney never reduces reality to a matter of political slogans, he writes about the fates of individuals, of personal friends who have been afflicted by the heedless violence—in the background somewhere there is Dante, who could yoke the political to the transcendental.

Heaney also has links with the academic world. He has taught in Belfast and Dublin, he has been Professor of Poetry at Oxford, and since 1982 he has been teaching rhetoric and oratory at Harvard in the United States.

Seamus Heaney comes from a humble, farming community, but at the same time we meet in him a learned poet who in the very microcosm of language cultivates and reveals the Celtic, pre-Christian and Catholic literary heritage. He does this in his poetry, and in five collections of eminently readable essays, including *The Government of the Tongue* (1968), *The Place of Writing* (1989) and *The Redress of Poetry*—the volume published this year that contains the lectures he gave at Oxford.

In his essays and meditations, Heaney also specifies the poetic turning points which arose from confrontation with some remarkable poets—British, Irish, American and European—not infrequently in the spirit of his compatriot and great predecessor Patrick Kavanagh's principle: the local can articulate the universal . . . God is in the bits and pieces of the Everyday.

Dear Seamus Heaney,

I have just given the audience some "bits and pieces" about reality and symbol in your poems. Let me now remind you of your own Declaration of Independence–Poetry can never be reduced to a political, historical or moral issue. In the final resort poetry is its own reality. Ever since *Death of a Naturalist* I have admired the way in which you turn your back on the systematisers, to defend instead poetic creativity as a free, natural, biological process. We all admire your revealing and compelling images and rhythms, we are gladdened by your quest for sacred wells and the sudden eruption of Beauty. I am happy to convey to you, on behalf of the Swedish Academy, our warmest congratulations on the Nobel Prize in Literature for 1995 and to invite you to receive the Prize from the hands of His Majesty the King.

[© The Nobel Foundation, 1995.]

Heaney: Banquet Speech

Heaney's speech at the Nobel Banquet, 10 December 1995:

Your Majesties, Your Royal Highnesses, Ladies and Gentlemen,

Today's ceremonies and tonight's banquet have been mighty and memorable events. Nobody who has shared in them will ever forget them, but for the laureates these celebrations have had a unique importance. Each of us has participated in a ritual, a rite of passage, a public drama which has been commensurate with the inner experience of winning a Nobel Prize. The slightly incredible condition we have lived in since the news of the prizes was announced a couple of weeks ago has now been rendered credible. The mysterious powers represented by the words Nobel Foundation and Swedish Academy have manifested themselves in friendly human form. For me, it has been a great joy and a great reassurance to come to Stockholm and to meet at every turn people of such grace, such intelligence and such good will. Which is another way of saying that the whole week has not only been ceremonially impressive: it has also felt emotionally true, and it is that sense of something personally trustworthy at the centre of the great event that I finally value most, and cherish and give you thanks for. It has helped more than anything else to bring home to me the reality of the great honour I have received. Oscar Wilde once said that the only way to survive temptation was to yield to it. So here and now, I happily and gratefully yield to the temptation to believe that I am indeed the winner of a Nobel Prize. Thank you very much.

[© The Nobel Foundation, 1995. Seamus Heaney is the sole author of his speech.]

Press Release: The Nobel Prize for Literature 1995

from the Office of the Permanent Secretary of the Swedish Academy, 5 October 1995

Seamus Heaney

"for works of lyrical beauty and ethical depth, which exalt everyday miracles and the living past"

Seamus Heaney was born on a farm some distance west of Belfast in Northern Ireland 56 years ago. After studies and marriage he moved to the Irish Republic and has been living in Dublin since 1976. He has held a post as visiting professor in rhetoric at Harvard since 1982, and from 1989 to 1994 he was Professor of Poetry at Oxford. Heaney is a poet, essayist and translator.

One point of departure for Heaney is what he calls, in one of the poems in his collection *North* (1975), northern reticence. He sympathises with this stance but is of course at the same time aware of the risks it involves for a writer. In an interview, he acknowledges that he feels a form of guilt when he writes. He assumes that generations of rural ancestors–who while not illiterate were not literary either–are asserting themselves within him. He speaks with warmth of the rich experience his parents have communicated, but can also express some impatience with their reticence. It is against this background that one can read the poem "Alphabets" (in *The Haw Lantern*, 1987) with the lines "The poet's dream stole over him like sunlight / And passed into the tenebrous thickets."

As an Irish Catholic he has concerned himself with analysis of the violence in Northern Ireland–with the express reservation that he wants to avoid the conventional terms. In his opinion, the fact that there has been unwillingness on both sides to speak out–even about manifest injustices–has been of great importance in the explosive development. But he also opposes the defeatism of the Catholics, as in the poem "From the canton of expectation" (in *The Haw Lantern*) which begins: "We lived deep in a land of optative moods, / under high, banked clouds of resignation."

In collections of essays such as *The Government of the Tongue* (1988) and *The Place of Writing* (1989) Heaney discusses the role of poetry and the poet, a theme he often returns to. Experiences from the lives of Osip Mandelstam and other 20th century writers lead him to the conclusion that the task of the poet is to ensure the survival of beauty, especially in times when tyrannical regimes threaten to destroy it.

In 1990 Heaney published *The Cure at Troy,* a translation of Sophocles' *Philoctetes,* from the point of view of composition the most modern of the classical dramas. The play was staged by the Field Day Theatre in the same year and received a positive reception although no direct link was made to his poetry. It can, however, be seen as one element of Heaney's continual endeavour to find poetic expression for complex ethical issues. The translation points forward to his next collection of poems.

Seeing Things (1991) includes the very interesting section "Squarings." Here the poems consist of twelve lines, their fixed, restrained form matching only superficially the content of the poems with their breadth of variation. A poem like "Lightenings viii," on the miracle at Clonmacnoise, is a crystallisation of much of Heaney's imaginative world: history and sensuality, myths and the day-to-day—all articulated in Heaney's rich language.

[© The Nobel Foundation, 1995.]

Heaney: Nobel Lecture, 7 December 1995

Crediting Poetry

When I first encountered the name of the city of Stockholm, I little thought that I would ever visit it, never mind end up being welcomed to it as a guest of the Swedish Academy and the Nobel Foundation. At the time I am thinking of, such an outcome was not just beyond expectation: it was simply beyond conception. In the nineteen forties, when I was the eldest child of an ever-growing family in rural Co. Derry, we crowded together in the three rooms of a traditional thatched farmstead and lived a kind of den-life which was more or less emotionally and intellectually proofed against the outside world. It was an intimate, physical, creaturely existence in which the night sounds of the horse in the stable beyond one bedroom wall mingled with the sounds of adult conversation from the kitchen beyond the other. We took in everything that was going on, of course—rain in the trees, mice on the ceiling, a steam train rumbling along the railway line one field back from the house—but we took it in as if we were in the doze of hibernation. Ahistorical, pre-sexual, in suspension between the archaic and the modern, we were as susceptible and impressionable as the drinking water that stood in a bucket in our scullery: every time a passing train made the earth shake, the surface of that water used to ripple delicately, concentrically, and in utter silence.

But it was not only the earth that shook for us: the air around and above us was alive and signalling too. When a wind stirred in the beeches, it also stirred an aerial wire attached to the topmost branch of the chestnut tree. Down it swept, in through a hole bored in the corner of the kitchen window, right on into the innards of our wireless set where a little pandemonium of burbles and squeaks would suddenly give way to the voice of a BBC newsreader speaking out of the unexpected like a *deus ex machina*. And that voice too we could hear in our bedroom, transmitting from beyond and behind the voices of the adults in the kitchen; just as we could often hear, behind and beyond every voice, the frantic, piercing signalling of morse code.

We could pick up the names of neighbours being spoken in the local accents of our parents, and in the resonant English tones of the newsreader the names of bombers and of cities bombed, of war fronts and army divisions, the numbers of planes lost and of prisoners taken, of casualties suffered and advances made; and always, of course, we would pick up too those other, solemn and oddly bracing words, "the enemy" and "the allies." But even so, none of the news of these world-spasms entered me as terror. If there was something ominous in the newscaster's tones, there was something torpid about our understanding of what was at stake; and if there was something culpable about such political ignorance in that time and place, there was something positive about the security I inhabited as a result of it.

The wartime, in other words, was pre-reflective time for me. Pre-literate too. Pre-historical in its way. Then as the years went on and my listening became more deliberate, I would climb up on an arm of our big sofa to get my ear closer to the wireless speaker. But it was still not the news that interested me; what I was after was the thrill of story, such as a detective serial about a British special agent called Dick Barton or perhaps a radio adaptation of one of Capt. W. E. Johns's adventure tales about an RAF flying ace called Biggles. Now that the other children were older and there was so much going on in the kitchen, I had to get close to the actual radio set in order to concentrate my hearing, and in that intent proximity to the dial I grew familiar with the names of foreign stations, with Leipzig and Oslo and Stuttgart and Warsaw and, of course, with Stockholm.

I also got used to hearing short bursts of foreign languages as the dial hand swept round from BBC to Radio Eireann, from the intonations of London to those of Dublin, and even though I did not understand what was being said in those first encounters with the gutturals and sibilants of European speech, I had already begun a journey into the wideness of the world beyond. This in turn became a journey into the wideness of language, a journey where each point of arrival—whether in one's poetry or one's life—turned out to be a stepping stone rather than a destination, and it is that journey which has brought me now to this honoured spot. And yet the platform here feels more like a space station than a stepping stone, so that is why, for once in my life, I am permitting myself the luxury of walking on air.

*

I credit poetry for making this space-walk possible. I credit it immediately because of a line I wrote fairly recently instructing myself (and whoever else might be listening) to "walk on air against your better judgement." But I credit it ultimately because poetry can make an order as true to the impact of external reality and as sensitive to the inner laws of the poet's being as the ripples that rippled in and rippled out across the water in that scullery bucket fifty years ago. An order where we can at last grow up to that which we stored up as we grew. An order which satisfies all that is appetitive in the intelligence and prehensile in the affections. I credit poetry, in other words, both for being itself and for being a help, for making possible a fluid and restorative relationship between the mind's centre and its circumference, between the child gazing at the word "Stockholm" on the face of the radio dial and the man facing the faces that he meets in Stockholm at this most privileged moment. I credit it because credit is due to it, in our time and in all time, for its truth to life, in every sense of that phrase.

*

To begin with, I wanted that truth to life to possess a concrete reliability, and rejoiced most when the poem seemed most direct, an upfront representation of the world it stood in for or stood up for or stood its ground against. Even as a schoolboy, I loved John Keats's ode "To Autumn" for being an ark of the covenant between language and sensation; as an adolescent, I loved Gerard Manley Hopkins for the intensity of his exclamations which were also equations for a rapture and an ache I didn't fully know I knew until I read him; I loved Robert Frost for his farmer's accuracy and his wily down-to-earthness; and Chaucer too for much the same reasons. Later on I would find a different kind of accuracy, a moral down-to-earthness to which I responded deeply and always will, in the war poetry of Wilfred Owen, a poetry where a New Testament sensibility suffers and absorbs the shock of the new century's barbarism. Then later again, in the pure consequence of Elizabeth Bishop's style, in the sheer obduracy of Robert Lowell's and in the barefaced confrontation of Patrick Kavanagh's, I encountered further reasons for believing in poetry's ability—and responsibility—to say what happens, to "pity the planet," to be "not concerned with Poetry."

This temperamental disposition towards an art that was earnest and devoted to things as they are was corroborated by the experience of having been born and brought up in Northern Ireland and of having lived with that place even though I have lived out of it for the past quarter of a century. No place in the world prides itself more on its vigilance and realism, no place considers itself more qualified to censure any flourish of rhetoric or extravagance of aspiration. So, partly as a result of having internalized these attitudes through growing up with them, and partly as a result of growing a skin to protect myself against them, I went for years half-avoiding and half-resisting the opulence and extensiveness of poets as different as Wallace Stevens and Rainer Maria Rilke; crediting insufficiently the crystalline inwardness of Emily Dickinson, all those forked lightnings and fissures of association; and missing the visionary strangeness of Eliot. And these more or less costive attitudes were fortified by a refusal to grant the poet any more license than any other citizen; and they were further induced by having to conduct oneself as a poet in a situation of ongoing political violence and public expectation. A public expectation, it has to be said, not of poetry as such but of political positions variously approvable by mutually disapproving groups.

In such circumstances, the mind still longs to repose in what Samuel Johnson once called with superb confidence "the stability of truth," even as it recognizes the destabilizing nature of its own operations and enquiries. Without needing to be theoretically instructed, consciousness quickly realizes that it is the site of variously contending discourses. The child in the bedroom, listening simultaneously to the domestic idiom of his Irish home and the official idioms of the British broadcaster while picking up from behind both the signals of some other distress, that child was already being schooled for the complexities of his adult predicament, a future where he would have to adjudicate among promptings variously ethical, aesthetical, moral, political, metrical, sceptical, cultural, topical, typical, post-colonial and, taken all together, simply impossible. So it was that I found myself in the mid-nineteen seventies in another small house, this time in Co. Wicklow south of Dublin, with a young family of my own and a slightly less imposing radio set, listening to the rain in the trees and to the news of bombings closer to home—not only those by the Provisional IRA in Belfast but equally atrocious assaults in Dublin by loyalist paramilitaries from the north. Feeling puny in my predicaments as I read about the tragic logic of Osip Mandelstam's fate in the 1930s, feeling challenged yet steadfast in my noncombatant status when I heard, for example, that one particularly sweetnatured school friend had been interned without trial because he was suspected of having been involved in a political killing. What I was longing for was not quite stability but an active escape from the quicksand of relativism, a way of crediting poetry without anxiety or apology. In a poem called "Exposure" I wrote then:

> If I could come on meteorite!
> Instead, I walk through damp leaves,
> Husks, the spent flukes of autumn,
>
> Imagining a hero
> On some muddy compound,
> His gift like a slingstone
> Whirled for the desperate.
>
> How did I end up like this?
> I often think of my friends'
> Beautiful prismatic counselling
> And the anvil brains of some who hate me
>
> As I sit weighing and weighing
> My responsible *tristia*.
> For what? For the ear? For the people?
> For what is said behind-backs?
>
> Rain comes down through the alders,
> Its low conducive voices
> Mutter about let-downs and erosions
> And yet each drop recalls
>
> The diamond absolutes.
> I am neither internee nor informer;
> An inner émigré, grown long-haired
> And thoughtful; a wood-kerne
>
> Escaped from the massacre,
> Taking protective colouring
> From bole and bark, feeling
> Every wind that blows;
>
> Who, blowing up these sparks
> For their meagre heat, have missed
> The once in a lifetime portent,
> The comet's pulsing rose.
> (from *North*)

In one of the poems best known to students in my generation, a poem which could be said to have taken the nutrients of the symbolist movement and made them available in capsule form, the American poet Archibald MacLeish affirmed that "A poem should be equal to / not true." As a defiant statement of poetry's gift for telling truth but telling it slant, this is both cogent and corrective. Yet there are times when a deeper need enters, when we want the poem to be not only pleasurably right but compellingly wise, not only a surprising variation played upon the world, but a re-tuning of the world itself. We want the surprise to be transitive like the impatient thump which unexpectedly restores the picture to the television set, or the electric shock which sets the fibrillating heart back to its proper rhythm. We want what the woman wanted in the prison queue in Leningrad, standing there blue with cold and whispering for fear, enduring the terror of Stalin's regime and asking the poet Anna Akhmatova if she could describe it all, if her art could be equal to it. And this is the want I too was experiencing in those far more protected circumstances in Co. Wicklow when I wrote the lines I have just quoted, a need for poetry that would merit the definition of it I gave a few moments ago, as an order "true to the impact of external reality and . . . sensitive to the inner laws of the poet's being."

*

The external reality and inner dynamic of happenings in Northern Ireland between 1968 and 1974 were symptomatic of change, violent change admittedly, but change nevertheless, and for the minority living there, change had been long overdue. It should have come early, as the result of the ferment of protest on the streets in the late sixties, but that was not to be and the eggs of danger which were always incubating got hatched out very quickly. While the Christian moralist in oneself was impelled to deplore the atrocious nature of the IRA's campaign of bombings and killings, and the "mere Irish" in oneself was appalled by the ruthlessness of the British Army on occasions like Bloody Sunday in Derry in 1972, the minority citizen in oneself, the one who had grown up conscious that his group was distrusted and discriminated against in all kinds of official and unofficial ways, this citizen's perception was at one with the poetic truth of the situation in recognizing that if life in Northern Ireland were ever really to flourish, change had to take place. But that citizen's perception was also at one with the truth in recognizing that the very brutality of the means by which the IRA were pursuing change was destructive of the trust upon which new possibilities would have to be based.

Nevertheless, until the British government caved in to the strong-arm tactics of the Ulster loyalist workers after the Sunningdale Conference in 1974, a well-disposed mind could still hope to make sense of the circumstances, to balance what was promising with what was destructive and do what W. B. Yeats had tried to do half a century before, namely, "to hold in a single thought reality and justice." After 1974, however, for the twenty long years between then and the ceasefires of August 1994, such a hope proved impossible. The violence from below was then productive of nothing but a retaliatory violence from above, the dream of justice became subsumed into the callousness of reality, and people settled in to a quarter century of life-waste and spirit-waste, of hardening attitudes and narrowing possibilities that were the natural result of political solidarity, traumatic suffering and sheer emotional self-protectiveness.

*

One of the most harrowing moments in the whole history of the harrowing of the heart in Northern Ireland came when a minibus full of workers being driven home one January evening in 1976 was held up by armed and masked men and the occupants of the van ordered at gunpoint to line up at the side of the road. Then one of the masked executioners said to them, "Any Catholics among you, step out here." As it happened, this particular group, with one exception, were all Protestants, so the presumption must have been that the masked men were Protestant paramilitaries about to carry out a tit-for-tat sectarian killing of the Catholic as the odd man out, the one who would have been presumed to be in sympathy with the IRA and all its actions. It was a terrible moment for him, caught between dread and witness, but he did make a motion to step forward. Then, the story goes, in that split second of decision, and in the relative cover of the winter evening darkness, he felt the hand of the Protestant worker next to him take his hand and squeeze it in a signal that said no, don't move, we'll not betray you, nobody need know what faith or party you belong to. All in vain, however, for the man stepped out of the line; but instead of finding a gun at his temple, he was thrown backward and away as the gunmen opened fire on those remaining in the line, for these were not Protestant terrorists, but members, presumably, of the Provisional IRA.

*

It is difficult at times to repress the thought that history is about as instructive as an abattoir; that Tacitus was right and that peace is merely the desolation left behind after the decisive operations of merciless power. I remember, for example, shocking myself with a thought I had about that friend who was imprisoned in the seventies upon suspicion of having been involved with a political murder: I shocked myself by thinking that even if he were guilty, he might still perhaps be helping the future to be born, breaking the repressive forms and liberating new potential in the only way that worked, that is to say the violent way— which therefore became, by extension, the right way. It was like a moment of exposure to interstellar cold, a reminder of the scary element, both inner and outer, in which human beings must envisage and conduct their lives. But it was only a moment. The birth of the future we desire is surely in the contraction which that terrified Catholic felt on the roadside when another hand gripped his hand, not in the gunfire that followed, so absolute and so desolate, if also so much a part of the music of what happens.

As writers and readers, as sinners and citizens, our realism and our aesthetic sense make us wary of crediting the positive note. The very gunfire braces us and the atrocious confers a worth upon the effort which it calls forth to confront it. We are rightly in awe of the torsions in the poetry of Paul Celan and rightly enamoured of the suspiring voice in Samuel Beckett because these are evidence that art can rise to the occasion and somehow be the corollary of Celan's stricken destiny as Holocaust survivor and Beckett's demure heroism as a member of the French Resistance. Likewise, we are rightly suspicious of that which gives too much consolation in these circumstances; the very extremity of our late twentieth century knowledge puts much of our cultural heritage to an extreme test. Only the very stupid or the very deprived can any longer help knowing that the documents of civilization have been written in blood and tears, blood and tears no less real for being very remote. And when this intellectual predisposition co-exists with the actualities of Ulster and Israel and Bosnia and Rwanda and a host of other wounded spots on the face of the earth, the inclination is not only not to credit human nature with much constructive potential but not to credit anything too positive in the work of art.

Which is why for years I was bowed to the desk like some monk bowed over his prie-dieu, some dutiful contemplative pivoting his understanding in an attempt to bear his portion of the weight of the world, knowing himself incapable of heroic virtue or redemptive effect, but constrained by his obedience to his rule to repeat the effort and the posture. Blowing up sparks for meagre heat. Forgetting faith, straining towards good works. Attending insufficiently to the diamond absolutes, among which must be counted the sufficiency of that which is absolutely imagined. Then finally and happily, and not in obedience to the dolorous circumstances of my native place but in despite of them, I straightened up. I began a few years ago to try to make space in my reckoning and imagining for the marvellous as well as for the murderous. And once again I shall try to represent the import of that changed orientation with a story out of Ireland.

This is a story about another monk holding himself up valiantly in the posture of endurance. It is said that once upon a time St. Kevin was kneeling with his arms stretched out in the form of a cross in Glendalough, a monastic site not too far from where we lived in Co. Wicklow, a place which to this day is one of the most wooded and watery retreats in the whole of the country. Anyhow, as Kevin knelt and prayed, a blackbird mistook his outstretched hand for some kind of roost and swooped down upon it, laid a clutch of eggs in it and proceeded to nest in it as if it were the branch of a tree. Then, overcome with pity and constrained by his faith to love the life in all creatures great and small, Kevin stayed immobile for hours and days and nights and weeks, holding out his hand until the eggs hatched and the fledglings grew wings, true to life if subversive of common sense, at the intersection of natural process and the glimpsed ideal, at one and the same time a signpost and a reminder. Manifesting that order of poetry where we can at last grow up to that which we stored up as we grew.

*

St. Kevin's story is, as I say, a story out of Ireland. But it strikes me that it could equally well come out of India or Africa or the Arctic or the Americas. By which I do not mean merely to consign it to a typology of folktales, or to dispute its value by questioning its culture-bound status within a multi-cultural context. On the contrary, its trustworthiness and its travel-worthiness have to do with its local setting. I can, of course, imagine it being deconstructed nowadays as a paradigm of colonialism, with Kevin figuring as the benign imperialist (or the missionary in the wake of the imperialist), the one who intervenes and appropriates the indigenous life and interferes with its pristine ecology. And I have to admit that there is indeed an irony that it was such a one who recorded and preserved this instance of the true beauty of the Irish heritage: Kevin's story, after all, appears in the writings of Giraldus Cambrensis, one of the Normans who invaded Ireland in the twelfth century, one whom the Irish-language annalist Geoffrey Keating would call, five hundred years later, "the bull of the herd of those who wrote the false history of Ireland." But even so, I still cannot persuade myself that this manifestation of early Christian civilization should be construed all that simply as a way into whatever is exploitative or barbaric in our history, past and present. The whole conception strikes me rather as being another example of the kind of work I saw a few weeks ago in the small museum in Sparta, on the morning before the news of this year's Nobel Prize in literature was announced.

This was art which sprang from a cult very different from the faith espoused by St. Kevin. Yet in it there was a representation of a roosted bird and an entranced beast and a self-enrapturing man, except that this time the man was Orpheus and the rapture came from music rather than prayer. The work itself was a small carved relief and I could not help making a sketch of it; but neither could I help copying out the information typed on the card which accompanied and identified the exhibit. The image moved me because of its antiquity and durability, but the description on the card moved me also because it gave a name and credence to that which I see myself as having been engaged upon for the past three decades: "Votive panel," the identification card said, "possibly set up to Orpheus by local poet. Local work of the Hellenistic period."

*

Once again, I hope I am not being sentimental or simply fetishizing—as we have learnt to say—the local. I wish instead to suggest that images and stories of the kind I am invoking here do function as bearers of value. The century has witnessed the defeat of Nazism by force of arms; but the erosion of the Soviet regimes was caused, among other things, by the sheer persistence, beneath the imposed ideological conformity, of cultural values and psychic resistances of a kind that these stories and images enshrine. Even if we have learned to be rightly and deeply fearful of elevating the cultural forms and conservatisms of any nation into normative and exclusivist systems, even if we have terrible proof that pride in an ethnic and religious heritage can quickly degrade into the fascistic, our vigilance on that score should not displace our love and trust in the good of the indigenous per se. On the contrary, a trust in the staying power and travel-worthiness of such good should encourage us to credit the possibility of a world where respect for the validity of every tradition will issue in the creation and maintenance of a salubrious political space. In spite of devastating and repeated acts of massacre, assassination and extirpation, the huge acts of faith which have marked the new relations between Palestinians and Israelis, Africans and Afrikaners, and the way in which walls have come down in Europe and iron curtains have opened, all this inspires a hope that new possibility can still open up in Ireland as well. The crux of that problem involves an ongoing partition of the island between British and Irish jurisdictions, and an equally persistent partition of the affections in Northern Ireland between the British and Irish heritages; but surely every dweller in the country must hope that the governments involved in its governance can devise institutions which will allow that partition to become a bit more like the net on a tennis court, a demarcation allowing for agile give-and-take, for encounter and contending, prefiguring a future where the vitality that flowed in the beginning from those bracing words "enemy" and "allies" might finally derive from a less binary and altogether less binding vocabulary.

*

When the poet W. B. Yeats stood on this platform more than seventy years ago, Ireland was emerging from the throes of a traumatic civil war that had followed fast on the heels of a war of independence fought against the British. The struggle that ensued had been brief enough; it was over by May, 1923, some seven months before Yeats sailed to Stockholm, but it was bloody, savage and intimate, and for generations to come it would dictate the terms of politics within the twenty-six independent counties of Ireland, that part of the island known first of all as the Irish Free State and then subsequently as the Republic of Ireland.

Yeats barely alluded to the civil war or the war of independence in his Nobel speech. Nobody understood better than he the connection between the construction or destruction of state institutions and the founding or foundering of cultural life, but on this occasion he chose to talk instead about the Irish Dramatic Movement. His story was about the creative purpose of that movement and its historic good fortune in having not only his own genius to sponsor it, but also the genius of his friends John Millington Synge and Lady Augusta Gregory. He came to Sweden to tell the world that the local work of poets and dramatists had been as important to the transformation of his native place and times as the ambushes of guerrilla armies; and his boast in that elevated prose was essentially the same as the one he would make in verse more than a decade later in his poem "The Municipal Gallery Revisited." There Yeats presents himself amongst the portraits and heroic narrative paintings which celebrate the events and personalities of recent history and all of a sudden realizes that something truly epoch-making has occurred: "'This is not,' I say, / 'The dead Ireland of my youth, but an Ireland / The poets have imagined, terrible and gay.'" And the poem concludes with two of the most quoted lines of his entire oeuvre:

> Think where man's glory most begins and ends,
> And say my glory was I had such friends.

And yet, expansive and thrilling as these lines are, they are an instance of poetry flourishing itself rather than proving itself, they are the poet's lap of honour, and in this respect if in no other they resemble what I am doing in this lecture. In fact, I should quote here on my own behalf some other words from the poem: "You that would judge me, do not judge alone / This book or that." Instead, I ask you to do what Yeats asked his audience to do and think of the achievement of Irish poets and dramatists and novelists over the past forty years, among whom I am proud to count great friends. In literary matters, Ezra Pound advised against accepting the opinion of those "who haven't themselves produced notable work," and it is advice I have been privileged to follow, since it is the good opinion of notable workers—and not just those in my own country—that has fortified my endeavour since I began to write in Belfast more than thirty years ago. The Ireland I now inhabit is one that these Irish contemporaries have helped to imagine.

Yeats, however, was by no means all flourish. To the credit of poetry in our century there must surely be entered in any reckoning his two great sequences of poems entitled "Nineteen Hundred and Nineteen" and "Meditations in Time of Civil War," the latter of which contains the famous lyric about the bird's nest at his window, where a starling or stare had built in a crevice of the old wall. The poet was living then in a Norman tower which had been very much a part of the military history of the country in earlier and equally troubled times, and as his thoughts turned upon the irony of civilizations being consolidated by violent and powerful conquerors who end up commissioning the artists and the architects, he began to associate the sight of a mother bird feeding its young with the image of the honey bee, an image deeply lodged in poetic tradition and always suggestive of the ideal of an industrious, harmonious, nurturing commonwealth:

> The bees build in the crevices
> Of loosening masonry, and there
> The mother birds bring grubs and flies.
> My wall is loosening; honey-bees,
> Come build in the empty house of the stare.
>
> We are closed in, and the key is turned
> On our uncertainty; somewhere
> A man is killed, or a house burned,
> Yet no clear fact to be discerned:
> Come build in the empty house of the stare.
>
> A barricade of stone or of wood;
> Some fourteen days of civil war;
> Last night they trundled down the road
> That dead young soldier in his blood:
> Come build in the empty house of the stare.
>
> We had fed the heart on fantasies,
> The heart's grown brutal from the fare;
> More substance in our enmities
> Than in our love; O honey-bees,
> Come build in the empty house of the stare.

I have heard this poem repeated often, in whole and in part, by people in Ireland over the past twenty-five years, and no wonder, for it is as tender-minded towards life itself as St. Kevin was and as tough-minded about what happens in and to life as Homer. It knows that the massacre will happen again on the roadside, that the workers in the minibus are going to be lined up and shot down just after quitting time; but it also credits as a reality the squeeze of the hand, the actuality of sympathy and protectiveness between living creatures. It satisfies the contradictory needs which consciousness experiences at times of extreme crisis, the need on the one hand for a truth telling that will be hard and retributive, and on the other hand, the need not to harden the mind to a point where it denies its own yearnings for sweetness and trust.

It is a proof that poetry can be equal to and true at the same time, an example of that completely adequate poetry which the Russian woman sought from Anna Akhmatova and which William Wordsworth produced at a corresponding moment of historical crisis and personal dismay almost exactly two hundred years ago.

*

When the bard Demodocus sings of the fall of Troy and of the slaughter that accompanied it, Odysseus weeps and Homer says that his tears were like the tears of a wife on a battlefield weeping for the death of a fallen husband. His epic simile continues:

> At the sight of the man panting and dying there,
> she slips down to enfold him, crying out;
> then feels the spears, prodding her back and shoulders,
> and goes bound into slavery and grief.
> Piteous weeping wears away her cheeks:
> but no more piteous than Odysseus' tears,
> cloaked as they were, now, from the company.

Even to-day, three thousand years later, as we channel-surf over so much live coverage of contemporary savagery, highly informed but nevertheless in danger of growing immune, familiar to the point of overfamiliarity with old newsreels of the concentration camp and the gulag, Homer's image can still bring us to our senses. The callousness of those spear shafts on the woman's back and shoulders survives time and translation. The image has that documentary adequacy which answers all that we know about the intolerable.

But there is another kind of adequacy which is specific to lyric poetry. This has to do with the "temple inside our hearing" which the passage of the poem calls into being. It is an adequacy deriving from what Mandelstam called "the steadfastness of speech articulation," from the resolution and independence which the entirely realized poem sponsors. It has as much to do with the energy released by linguistic fission and fusion, with the buoyancy generated by cadence and tone and rhyme and stanza, as it has to do with the poem's concerns or the poet's truthfulness. In fact, in lyric poetry, truthfulness becomes recognizable as a ring of truth within the medium itself. And it is the unappeasable pursuit of this note, a note tuned to its most extreme in Emily Dickinson and Paul Celan and orchestrated to its most opulent in John Keats, it is this which keeps the poet's ear straining to hear the totally persuasive voice behind all the other informing voices.

Which is a way of saying that I have never quite climbed down from the arm of that sofa. I may have grown more attentive to the news and more alive to the world history and world-sorrow behind it. But the thing uttered by the speaker I strain towards is still not quite the story of what is going on; it is more reflexive than that, because as a poet I am in fact straining towards a strain, seeking repose in the stability conferred by a musically satisfying order of sounds. As if the ripple at its widest desired to be verified by a reformation of itself, to be drawn in and drawn out through its point of origin.

I also strain towards this in the poetry I read. And I find it, for example, in the repetition of that refrain of Yeats's, "Come build in the empty house of the stare," with its tone of supplication, its pivots of strength in the words "build" and "house" and its acknowledgment of dissolution in the word "empty." I find it also in the triangle of forces held in equilibrium by the triple rhyme of "fantasies" and "enmities" and "honey-bees," and in the sheer in-placeness of the whole poem as a given form within the language. Poetic form is both the ship and the anchor. It is at once a buoyancy and a steadying, allowing for the simultaneous gratification of whatever is centrifugal and whatever is centripetal in mind and body. And it is by such means that Yeats's work does what the necessary poetry always does, which is to touch the base of our sympathetic nature while taking in at the same time the unsympathetic nature of the world to which that nature is constantly exposed. The form of the poem, in other words, is crucial to poetry's power to do the thing which always is and always will be to poetry's credit: the power to persuade that vulnerable part of our consciousness of its rightness in spite of the evidence of wrongness all around it, the power to remind us that we are hunters and gatherers of values, that our very solitudes and distresses are creditable, in so far as they, too, are an earnest of our veritable human being.

[© The Nobel Foundation, 1995. Seamus Heaney is the sole author of the text.]

Verner von Heidenstam
(6 July 1859 – 20 May 1940)

Ann-Charlotte Gavel Adams
University of Washington

BOOKS: *Vallfart och vandringsår: Dikter* (Stockholm: Bonnier, 1888);
Från Col di Tenda till Blocksberg: Reseskizzer (Stockholm: Bonnier, 1888);
Endymion (Stockholm: Bonnier, 1889);
Renässans: Några ord om en annalkande ny brytningstid inom litteraturen (Stockholm: Bonnier, 1889);
Pepitas bröllop: En literaturanmälan, by Heidenstam and Oscar Levertin (Stockholm: Bonnier, 1890);
Hans Alienus (Stockholm: Bonnier, 1892);
Modern Barbarism: Några ord mot restaurerandet af historiska byggnader (Stockholm: Bonnier, 1894);
Dikter (Stockholm: Bonnier, 1895);
Om svenskarnes lynne (Stockholm: Wahlström & Widstrand, 1897);
Karolinerna: Berättelser, 2 volumes (Stockholm: Bonnier, 1897, 1898); translated by Axel Tegnier as *A King and His Campaigners* (London: Duckworth, 1902); translated by Charles Wharton Stork as *The Charles Men,* 2 volumes (New York: American-Scandinavian Foundation, 1920; London: Cape, 1933); selections translated by Agnes A. Allnutt in a bilingual edition as *Five Stories Selected from The Karolines / Fem berättelser hämtade från "Karolinerna"* (London: Harrap / New York: Brentano's, 1922);
Klassicitet och germanism: Några ord om världsstriden (Stockholm: Bonnier, 1898);
Tankar och teckningar (Stockholm: Bonnier, 1899);
Sankt Göran och draken: Berättelser (Stockholm: Bonnier, 1900)—comprises "Sankt Göran och draken," "Bröderna," "Spåmannen," and "Guds födelse"; "Spåmannen" translated by Karoline M. Knudsen as *The Soothsayer* (Boston: Four Seas, 1919); "Guds födelse" translated by Knudsen as *The Birth of God* (Boston: Four Seas, 1920);
Heliga Birgittas pilgrimsfärd: Berättelse (Stockholm: Bonnier, 1901);
Ett folk (Stockholm: Bonnier, 1902);
Skogen susar: Berättelser och sagor (Stockholm: Bonnier, 1904);

Verner von Heidenstam

Folkungaträdet: Folke Filbyter (Stockholm: Bonnier, 1905); translated by Arthur Chater as *The Tree of the Folkungs I: Folke Filbyter* (London: Gyldendal, 1925; New York: Knopf, 1925);
Folkungaträdet: Bjälboarfvet (Stockholm: Bonnier, 1907); translated by Chater as *The Tree of the Folkungs II: The Bellbo Heritage* (London: Gyldendal, 1925; New York: Knopf, 1925);

Svenskarna och deras hövdingar: Berättelser för unga och gamla, 2 volumes (Stockholm: Bonnier, 1908, 1910); translated by Stork as *The Swedes and Their Chieftains* (New York: American-Scandinavian Foundation, 1925);

Dagar och händelser: Tal, inlägg och fantasier (Stockholm, 1909); republished as *Uppsatser, tal och fatasier* (Stockholm: Bonnier, 1929);

Samlade skrifter, 14 volumes in 4 (Stockholm: Bonnier, 1909–1912);

Proletärfilosofiens upplösning och fall: Några ord vid det nya århundradets tröskel (Stockholm: Bonnier, 1911);

Drottning Omma (Stockholm: Åhlen & Åkerlund, 1914);

Nya dikter (Stockholm: Bonnier, 1915);

Skissbok: Reseminnen 1876–1877 (Stockholm: Bonnier, 1939);

När kastanjerna blommade: Minnen från Olshammar, edited by Kate Bang and Fredrik Böök (Stockholm: Bonnier, 1941);

Tankar och utkast, edited by Bang and Böök (Stockholm: Bonnier, 1941);

Sista dikter, edited by Bang and Böök (Stockholm: Bonnier, 1940).

Editions and Collections: *Samlade Verk,* 23 volumes in 11, edited by Kate Bang and Fredrik Böök (Stockholm: Bonnier, 1943–1944);

Verner von Heidenstam: Poesi och prosa i urval, edited by Carl Olof Josephson (Hedemora: Gidlunds, Alla Tiders Klassiker, 1996).

Editions in English: "The Spark," "The Crucifix," "The Heart's Secret," and "The Home," in *Under the Swedish Colours: A Short Anthology of Modern Swedish Poets,* translated by Francis Arthur Judd (London: Elkin Mathews, 1911);

"The Little Sister," English edition of *Julstämning* (Chicago & Göteborg, 1912);

"The Shadow," *British Review,* 4 (1913): 429–431;

"Midsummer Play," translated by Jacob Wittmer Hartmann, *American-Scandinavian Review,* 2 (1914): 26–27;

"A Clean White Shirt," translated by N. Tourneur, *American-Scandinavian Review,* no. 3 (1915): 339–341;

"The Boundary Stone," translated by Anna E. B. Fries, *American-Scandinavian Review,* no. 4 (1916): 212–215;

"Home Land," "Fellow Citizens," "My Life," "Starting on the Journey," "A Man's Last Word to a Woman," "Sweden," "The Dove of Thought," "Grant that We Die Young," "Moonlight," "Invocation and Promise," "A Day," "The Burial of Gustaf Fröding," "At the End of the Way," "Nameless and Immortal," "Alone by the Lake," "Home," and "How easily men's cheeks are hot with wrath," in *Anthology of Swedish Lyrics from 1750 to 1915,* translated by Charles Wharton Stork (New York: American-Scandinavian Foundation / London: Oxford University Press, 1917);

Sweden's Laureate: Selected Poems of Verner von Heidenstam, translated by Charles Wharton Stork (New Haven: Yale University Press, 1919; London: Milford, 1919);

"When the Bells Ring," "The Fortified House," "The Queen of the Marauders," and "Captured," in *Modern Swedish Masterpieces,* translated by Stork (New York: Dutton, 1923);

"Sigrid the Haughty and Her Wooers," translated by Stork, *American-Scandinavian Review,* no. 12 (1924);

"A Statue of the Virgin at Heda," translated by Stork, *American-Scandinavian Review,* no. 13 (1925);

"The Shield-Maiden" and "A Clean White Shirt," translated by Stork, in *Sweden's Best Stories: An Introduction to Swedish Fiction,* edited by Hanna Astrup Larsen (New York: American-Scandinavian Foundation / Norton, 1928);

"Nameless and Immortal," "What place on earth shall I fairest call?" "At the End of the Road," "After a Thousand Years," "Kindling of Stars," "The Hour of Paradise," and "A Friendly Farm," translated by C. D. Locock, in *A Selection from Modern Swedish Poetry* (New York: Macmillan, 1929);

"The Tenant of Brasse," translated by E. Sprigge and C. Napier, in *Modern Swedish Short Stories* (London: Cape, 1934);

"A Wish," "Night," and "The Cloud," translated by Locock, in *Modern Swedish Poetry: Part II* (London: H. & W. Brown, 1936);

Christmas Eve at Finnstad, translated by Margaret Sperry (Stockholm: Published by arrangement with the Heidenstam Foundation by B. Russak, 1950);

"The Haunted Room at Ingvaldboda: A Short Story," translated by Signild V. Gustafson, *American-Scandinavian Review,* no. 41 (1953);

"Gunnel the Stewardess," translated by Stork, in *An Anthology of Scandinavian Literature,* selected and edited by Hallberg Hallmundsson (New York: Collier, 1965).

Swedish writer Verner von Heidenstam was awarded the Nobel Prize in Literature in 1916. The citation from the Swedish Academy read: "in recognition of his significance as the leading representative of a new era in our literature." No one contests Heidenstam's importance as the most influential poet and introducer of the neo-Romantic, nationalistic movement of the 1890s in Sweden. He was much honored in his lifetime, but since his death in 1940, the literary worth of his works has been debated. Pär Lagerkvist, his successor in chair number 8 in the Swedish Academy and winner of the Nobel Prize in Literature in 1951, characterized him as a "fantast, en högt spänd människa, problematisk och ytterlig" (dreamer, a high-strung man, problematic, and extreme) in his introductory speech at the Swedish Academy. Today, his name is primarily kept alive through the prestigious Övralid Prize, named after the estate where he lived during the last twenty-five years of his life. The prize, substantially funded by the Nobel Prize money, is awarded every year on Heidenstam's birthday, 6 July, to a prominent Swedish author.

Heidenstam is no longer a widely read author, except among literary scholars and students of literature, although a few poems have become classics in Swedish literature. His name is most often associated with patriotic poems, such as "Sverige" (Sweden), which is played on Swedish National Radio every New Year's Eve, set to music by composer Wilhelm Stenhammar, or his two-volume historical epos, *Karolinerna* (1897, 1898; translated as *A King and His Campaigners*, 1902, and as *The Charles Men*, 1920), which was on the required-reading list in public schools in Sweden during the first part of the twentieth century. Most Swedes can recognize Heidenstam's aristocratic facial profile in photos or paintings, perhaps mainly because of the two well-known and often-reproduced portraits by painter Hanna Hirsch Pauli, one from 1896 and another from the last year of the author's life. Many of his poems and novels, however, seem dated and forced to modern readers.

Carl Gustaf Verner von Heidenstam was born on 6 July 1859 at his maternal grandmother's summer estate, Olshammar, by Lake Vättern. He was the only child of Nils Gustaf von Heidenstam and his wife, Magdalena Charlotta Rütterskiöld, both belonging to families of old Swedish nobility. His childhood home was in Stockholm, where he attended the prestigious private school Beskowska skolan from 1869 to 1875. The most influential periods of his childhood were the summers, spent at the Olshammar estate with his mother, grandmother, and two elderly unmarried aunts, who did their best to spoil the boy. His father was an enterprising man, stoic in nature and financially successful. Nils Gustaf von Heidenstam had the title of colonel in a government department, corresponding to the Army Corps of Engineers, and was much respected for his constructions of lighthouses along the Swedish coast. The colonel was dissatisfied with his son's upbringing and education, and he rarely joined the family at Olshammar. Father and son were not close.

The alley leading up to the Olshammar manor house was lined with chestnut trees. Heidenstam's posthumously published memoir of his childhood was given the title *När kastanjerna blommade: Minnen från Olshammar* (1941, When the Chestnut Trees Bloomed: Memories from Olshammar), an allusion to his grandmother's standing invitation: "Welcome to Olshammar when the chestnuts bloom." He enjoyed playing fantasy games, like most children, and dreamed of being king of the imaginary country of Lajsputta, perhaps an allusion to the island Laputta in Jonathan Swift's *Gulliver's Travels* (1726); the doting women around him played along with his games.

Young Verner's health was poor, and he had little interest in school, so he was allowed to quit at the age of sixteen. The family was well-to-do and could afford to send their son abroad to complete his education. On his first trip, to Italy, Greece, and the Middle East (1876–1877), Verner was accompanied by his cousin Ernst von Heidenstam. On his second trip, to Athens, Beirut, Jerusalem, and Cairo (1877–1878), he traveled with the linguist and orientalist Carlo Landberg, who later was elevated to count in Italy. Landberg called his young charge "Hopeful" and wrote to his father: "Allow Hopeful to be educated in freedom, then he can become something great, otherwise not. He has sufficient character to resist the temptations of the world." The exoticism of the Middle East made a deep impression on young Verner, and the Orient became an important motif in his first literary works. During these early travels, he drew, painted, and kept a diary. He spent much of 1879 and 1880 in Rome, for the purpose of learning painting.

On 20 October 1880 Heidenstam married Emilie Uggla. She also belonged to a family of Swedish nobility. Both families objected initially to the marriage; Heidenstam was only twenty-one years old, had no income of his own, and had no clear ambitions or plans for the future. The newlyweds traveled to Rome for the winter, where Heidenstam planned to pursue art studies under Swedish painter Julius Kronberg. The young couple, financially supported by Heidenstam's father, spent more time being tourists than studying. Established Scandinavian painters in Rome viewed Heidenstam with irony and amusement, considering him somewhat pompous, rather naive, and secretive regarding his own paintings. Nobody was allowed to see the grand paintings that he supposedly was creating. In July 1881 Heidenstam and his wife moved to Paris, where his wealth and noble family background had gained him acceptance into Ecole des Beaux-Arts as a student of the famous painter and sculptor Gérôme. The discipline at the school did not suit him, and he soon gave up the idea of painting. After some encouragement from Finnish-Swedish author Zacharias Topelius, Heidenstam decided to try his hand at writing instead.

In July 1882 Heidenstam and his wife returned to Scandinavia to see his mother. The most urgent reason for the trip was to assure continued financial support, now that he had abandoned painting. He had no intention of visiting his father, who—he was sure—would disapprove of his plans. In October 1882 the young couple returned to France with new funds in their pockets, first to Paris and then to the French Riviera. For the next four and a half years, until spring 1887, they lived a rather ambulatory life in Europe.

In 1884 Heidenstam met the radical Swedish author August Strindberg. The ensuing friendship with Strindberg stimulated his thinking and writing and expanded his intellectual horizons. It was the first time that Heidenstam had entered into a close artistic friendship with an older, recognized author, with whom he could debate both social and creative ideas. At this time, Strindberg and Heidenstam had similar sympathies and antipathies: they boasted about their liberated ideas and competed in making shocking statements. They proclaimed themselves freethinkers and reveled in cynical ideas of atheism, polygamy, and egotism, in formulations that today sound embarrassingly juvenile. In a letter to Strindberg (5 September 1885) Heidenstam writes that he intends to "stryka skorna af fötterna och pådra de polygama österländska tofflorna" (take off his shoes and put on his oriental, polygamous slippers). He signed this letter as many others: "Verner Hundhedning" (Verner Heathen Dog). Their correspondence often took on a puerile tone, something both writers later abandoned. On 1 May 1886 the Heidenstams rented the castle Schloss Brunegg in Switzerland, and Strindberg settled with his family in the nearby Otmarsingen. They often got together, and Heidenstam later described their meetings and discussions in his collection of travel essays *Från Col di Tenda till Blocksberg* (1888, From Col di Tenda to Blocksberg), as Strindberg had done in his autobiography *Tjänstekvinnans son* (1886; translated as *The Son of a Servant*, 1913).

During the summer of 1886 Heidenstam became ill with typhoid, resulting in chronic stomach problems. The doctors advised him to move to the milder climate of the French Riviera. In spring 1887 Heidenstam was called back to his parents' home in Sweden. His father was seriously ill with kidney disease and suffered constant, severe pain. Father and son had not seen each other for seven years. His father had even refused to read Heidenstam's letters home. Although father and son had had a chilly relationship, they seem to have reconnected during the last part of the father's illness. However, on 2 June 1887, his sixty-fifth birthday, the colonel committed suicide by shooting himself in the temple.

In the spring of 1888 Heidenstam's first collection of poetry, *Vallfart och vandringsår* (Pilgrimages and Wander Years), was published. It created quite a stir in literary circles in Sweden but was initially met with more surprise than admiration. The form was new: a mixture of verse and prose with predominantly oriental motifs and colorful visual imagery. The motifs and images seemed highly exotic and somewhat peculiar at a time when realism and naturalism were the styles of writing in vogue in Scandinavia. However, the Orient of Heidenstam's poetic world had little relationship to the real Middle East of the time; it was a kind of sensual and wishful dream, more a symbol for imagination, joy of life, and personal freedom. Examples of this depiction are evident in the poems "Muhails aftonbön" (Muchail's Evening Prayer), "Djufars visa" (Djufar's Song), and "Isissystrarna's bröllop" (The Wedding of the Sisters of Isis). In "Ensamhetens tankar" (Thoughts in Solitude), another series of short personal poems in the collection, Heidenstam presents himself as more introspective and humble. He also reveals a deep love for the natural Swedish environment around his childhood summer home, Olshammar. In one often-quoted—but also often-ridiculed (by critics and fellow writers, including Strindberg)—poem, he writes:

> Jag längtar hem sen åtta långa år.
> I själva sömnen har jag längtan känt.
> Jag längtar var jag går
> —men ej till människor! Jag längtar marken,
> jag längtar stenarna där barn jag lekt.
>
> (I've longed for home for eight long years.
> In sleep as well as through the day, I long.
> I long for home wherever I go—
> But not for people! I long for the fields where I would stray,
> And for the stones where as a child I used to play.)

The same year that *Vallfart och vandringsår* appeared, Heidenstam also brought forth *Från Col di Tenda till Blocksberg*. In a letter to Strindberg (3 August 1888) he characterized his new book as "unimportant, partly already published travel prose." It became a critical and popular success, however, and with that success came all kinds of other attentions.

Heidenstam was a stately man, aristocratic, and a good conversationalist. Women were charmed by him, something he took advantage of as the opportunities presented themselves. In May 1888, while still married to Uggla, he started sending love poems to another young woman of the nobility, Ellen Belfrage, daughter of the lord chancellor of King Oscar II. The love poems led to a relationship, which resulted in a pregnancy. This situation did not seem to concern Heidenstam. In November 1888 he decided to travel to Davos, Switzerland, for reasons of health, accompanied by his wife. He wrote a goodbye letter/poem to Belfrage. In March

1889 Belfrage gave birth in Rouen, France, to a son, Nils Oluf, the only surviving child Heidenstam ever had. However, claiming bad health and his deteriorating financial position, Heidenstam told Belfrage that a divorce from his wife was out of the question and that he could not afford to support two women at the same time. Surprisingly, Belfrage seems to have accepted his response. She never wrote anything critical either to or about Heidenstam, and she brought up her son alone, with love and pride. Heidenstam never took an interest in Nils Oluf and even refused to meet him. Heidenstam did write a series of five poems, called "Gullebarns vaggsånger" (Cradle Songs of Goldilocks), as a reflection on his son's birth. They were included as part of his second important book of poems, *Dikter* (1895, Poems). In 1893 Heidenstam and his wife divorced, though she, like Belfrage, remained devoted to Heidenstam for the rest of her life.

Heidenstam followed his first two books with a novel, *Endymion* (1889), which takes place in Damascus, Syria. It is Heidenstam's most detailed and in-depth description of oriental culture. Critics and scholars differ in their opinions: some call it a trivial work, and others consider it the most underestimated novel in Heidenstam's production. The main theme of the novel is the clash/contrast between Western civilization and oriental culture. The main characters are an American writer, Mr. Harven, a Mark Twain of sorts, and his daughter Nelly. Father and daughter have traveled to Damascus to collect material for Harven's humorous stories. Nelly accompanies her father because of a general cultural interest. Harven and Nelly represent the Western lifestyle and civilization. Another character, Dr. von Blumenbach, represents the materialistic/capitalistic interests of the West. His main ambition is to earn money and gain a position of power. Two themes are woven together in the novel, a love story and a political/religious conflict. Nelly falls in love with a young, romantic Arab nationalist, Emin, and their love represents an attempt to bridge the gap between the two cultures. Heidenstam's affair with Belfrage is said to be the inspiration for the relationship between Emin and Nelly. Emin becomes the leader of an uprising against the Western/Christian influence in the Middle East; but when the uprising is crushed, Emin is sentenced to death, and Nelly is forced to accept the Western way of life. In the end, Dr. von Blumenbach's materialistic way of life wins. Harven gets the final words: "An unyielding conviction is in my eyes equal to a hardened heart, one that is not receptive to arguments of people of other persuasions." He urges his daughter to try to live an oriental lifestyle in the West.

On 21 September 1889 Heidenstam finished the manuscript to *Renässans: Några ord om en annalkande ny brytningstid inom litteraturen* (Renaissance: Some Words about the Approaching New Breakthrough in Literature), and he was eager to get the pamphlet published as soon as possible. The essay was short (forty-five pages), but he insisted on having it published as a book because it included his entire aesthetic program, as he wrote to his publisher, Albert Bonnier. He called for a rejection of the pedantic "shoemaker realism" and naturalism and advocated a return to the joy of life and beauty. Another important point of his program was the return to nationalism and focus on things Swedish. The pamphlet was met with criticism by many of his contemporaries, and polemics broke out in the newspapers. The following year, he developed his aesthetic program further in collaboration with poet and critic Oscar Levertin, when they published *Pepitas bröllop: En literaturanmälan* (1890, Pepita's Wedding: A Literary Review), a fictitious review of a Spanish novel. These two essays caused the first rift in the friendship with Strindberg. From a twenty-first-century perspective, *Renässans* and *Pepitas bröllop* did indeed usher in a new era, because they were the first to break with naturalism and to introduce neo-Romanticism—the cult of beauty, the joy of life—and nationalism into Swedish literature.

Hans Alienus (1892) is an ambitious, but uneven, autobiographical-ideological work in verse and prose in three parts and amost seven hundred pages. It was Heidenstam's largest work to date and an attempt to explain his aesthetic program and view of life. A hedonistic lifestyle is pitted against a more reflective, melancholy way of life. Hans Alienus (Hans the Alienated) is Heidenstam's alter ego. Part 1, "Löftet" (The Promise), takes place in Rome. Hans, a young papal librarian at the Vatican, and his friends take an oath to pursue a full year of pleasure, promiscuity, and instant gratification. The point seems to be a glorification of a Dionysian lifestyle and a critique of the modern, industrialized, materialistic Europe. The ideal seems to have been that man should pursue all kinds of erotic pleasures, without concern for other people's happiness or suffering, and selfishly follow his own instincts and cravings.

In Part 2, titled "Hades," the Pope has sent Hans Alienus as nuncio to King Sardanapal of Assyria. This part is more of a fantasy or a dream than a realistic narrative. At first, Hans marries simultaneously the three daughters of a weaver and gets their mother in the bargain. In his meeting with Sardanapal, the emptiness of the self-centered, pleasure-seeking life is revealed, in spite of all the luxury and opulence. Critics generally agree that "Hades" is particularly uneven as a literary composition. The allegories seem forced, and it is difficult to decipher what the symbols might stand for. The first two parts of this massive novel reveal that Heidenstam was not only uninformed about life in the Vatican, but he also lacked an understanding of the Muslim world he wrote about.

Part 3, "Hemkomsten" (The Return Home), is the strongest of the three parts. Hans Alienus returns to an estate by Lake Vättern and is reunited with his father, gaining his trust and friendship. As in Heidenstam's own life, Hans's father commits suicide. "Hemkomsten" is introduced by a poem, "Pilgrimens julsång" (The Pilgrim's Yule Song), expressing melancholy and loneliness. The pursuit of pleasure and beauty as the meaning of life has proven false:

> Kedjad vid livet min stav jag bär
> Rolös kring världen jag ledes.
> Längtar dit där jag icke är
> Främmande allestädes.
>
> (Fettered to life I roam the earth,
> Driven without cessation,
> Seeking, but finding only dearth,
> Stranger/alienated in every nation.)

With his 1895 volume, *Dikter,* Heidenstam wrote what several critics consider to be his most important poetic work. Fredrik Böök has called it "drömmens och inbillningens uppror mot den nyktra och gråa verkligheten" (the rebellion of dreams and imagination against the sober, gray reality). The imagery is concrete and striking. Several poems, such as "Malatestas morgonsång" (The Morning Song of Malatesta), reveal a romantic disdain for life, which is reminiscent of George Gordon, Lord Byron. There are also poems in a more classic style, such as "Hur lätt bli människornas kinder heta" (How easily men's cheeks are hot with wrath). In this collection, Heidenstam's poetry has gained in both power and clarity. This development may in part have to do with the fact that he has abandoned the oriental motifs from earlier works and picked up motifs from Swedish nature and nostalgia for home, as in "Ett Hem" (A Home):

> Ett hem! Det är det fästet,
> Vi rest med murar trygga
> —vår egen värld—den enda
> vi mitt i världen bygga.
>
> (A home! How firm its base is
> By walls securely shielded
> —our world—the only one
> we in this world can build.)

In addition to the longing for a home, love of the natural beauty of his home province, and respect for memories and old traditions, themes of patriotism and nationalism also take on more importance in this collection. Sweden is described as "Den sovande systern" (A Slumbering Sister) who must be awakened. This national awakening became Heidenstam's most fervent goal for the rest of the 1890s. In *Om svenskarnes lynne* (1897, On the Swedish Temperament) he preached against what he saw as his countrymen's exaggerated enthusiasm and unwarranted respect for everything that came from abroad. In *Klassicitet och germanism: Några ord om världsstriden* (1898, Classicism and Germanism: Some Words about the World Struggle), Heidenstam places Swedish culture on a pedestal between the rivaling Eastern and Western civilizations. The poetry collection *Ett folk* (One People) was the culmination of Heidenstam's patriotic ambitions, and it established him as the national poet of Sweden. *Ett folk* was first published in the daily newspaper *Svenska Dagbladet* on 22 September 1899 and later appeared as a booklet of fourteen pages in 1902. This collection includes the important poems "Sverige," which he submitted unsuccessfully to a competition for a new national anthem, and "Medborgarsången" (Fellow Citizens), in which he argued for universal suffrage—some twenty years before it became a reality in Sweden.

In 1896, three years after his divorce from Uggla, Heidenstam married a twenty-four-year-old woman named Olga Matilda Wiberg. The wedding took place on an island, Blå Jungfrun in the Baltic, and was turned into quite a spectacle, with groom and groomsmen draped in Greek togas. This marriage lasted for five years. The couple separated in 1901, and the divorce became final on 18 April 1903.

Heidenstam's best-known epic work is *Karolinerna.* It is a series of short stories about King Charles XII of Sweden and his men during his unsuccessful campaign to defend Sweden's position as a great empire at a time when Denmark, Poland, and Russia had entered an alliance to attack Sweden in 1700. The motifs for the stories are mainly taken from the last years of national humiliation, after the defeat at the battle of Poltava in Russia on 28 June 1709. In the first part of the book, the portrayal of King Charles XII is rather critical. He is described as a man who has caused suffering and deprivation for his people and constantly demands too many sacrifices from his men. In the second part, patriotism and nationalistic exaltations take on a more prominent role. The stories are tableau-like, rather different in style and content, but one motif unites them: the honorable common man and woman, who are ennobled by their sacrifice and suffering and through their faithful service to the king. The prominent position in Swedish literature of *Karolinerna* is partly because of the fact that it was on the required-reading lists in most public schools during the first part of the twentieth century.

In 1900 Heidenstam published a less important prose work, *Sankt Göran och draken* (1900, Saint George and the Dragon), consisting of several shorter pieces such as "Spåmannen" and "Guds födelse," which have been translated into English as *The Soothsayer* (1919) and *The Birth of God* (1920) respectively. His next historical novel of rank is *Heliga Birgittas pilgrimsfärd* (1901, St. Birgitta's Pilgrimage), which focuses on Birgitta Birgersdotter, Swedish visionary and religious writer, canonized as a saint in 1391. Heidenstam was quite familiar with the life and reputation of Birgitta, since she was born and raised in Östergötland, the same province as he. In Heidenstam's family there were also legends that she had lived at Olshammar and that she had mounted her horse from a big stone by the manor house before setting out on one of her pilgrimages. Heidenstam was not religious, but he had a certain respect for Birgitta. What seemed to fascinate him most of all was her personality: strong, lonely, and tragic. In some respects, he created Birgitta to his own likeness and drew on some of his own personality traits, however unflattering. His intentions were not to create an historically accurate portrait of the saint. He presents her as a rather ruthless person, a fanatic, most of all interested in achieving glory. But Birgitta is as merciless to herself as she is to others. Her own daughter, Karin, is forced to leave her husband, who is ill in Sweden, and accompany Birgitta to Rome. When Karin's husband dies, Karin exclaims bitterly: "Övergivna hem och nyskottade gravar ropa efter henne, hur långt hon än vallfärdar" (Deserted homes and newly-dug graves call after her, however far she travels on her pilgrimages).

On 12 October 1903, six months after his divorce from Wiberg, Heidenstam married Anna Margaretha (Greta) Sjöberg. She was seventeen years old, and he was forty-four. Heidenstam was an acquaintance of Greta's father and had been a frequent guest in her home since she was fifteen. In her eyes, Heidenstam appeared as an exciting and romantic figure: a famous poet, rich, twice married, and a real ladies' man. Their affair began after he seduced the sixteen-year-old Greta on a bearskin rug by the fireplace in his home in Djursholm, a suburb of Stockholm. With the girl's mother as an accomplice, Heidenstam and Greta set out on a trip through Germany, Switzerland, Italy, and France, under the pretext that Greta was attending a finishing school in Switzerland. Greta's father eventually found out what was going on and demanded that Heidenstam marry his daughter. The couple settled on the estate of Naddö by Lake Vättern. Heidenstam had bought the estate earlier in the year and was having it remodeled. Greta was addressed by servants, neighbors, and family as "Lilla hennes nåd" (Her little Ladyship). In September 1904 Greta gave birth to a son, Dag, who was stillborn. The couple separated two years later, in 1906, after it was discovered that Greta had had an extramarital encounter with an old boyfriend. She continued to live at Naddö until the formal divorce on 6 June 1916, after which she married Anders Österling, another poet and later a member of the Swedish Academy.

During his third marriage, Heidenstam worked on what became his masterpiece of historical fiction: *Folkungaträdet,* volume one, titled *Folke Filbyter* (1905; translated as *The Tree of the Folkungs I: Folke Filbyter,* 1925), and volume two, titled *Bjälboarfvet* (1907; translated as *The Tree of the Folkungs II: The Bellbo Heritage,* 1925). These two works are considered by some Swedish critics to be the most important historical novels ever written in Swedish.

Folkungaträdet is a medieval chronicle, set in Heidenstam's home province of Östergötland. It is a work in which Heidenstam merges myth with history. Part 1 focuses on Folke Filbyter, a heathen, brutal, greedy Viking chieftain, who lives only for increasing his wealth and the size of his farm, Folketuna. Folke's only redeeming quality is his great love for his grandson. When the grandson is kidnapped by a Christian priest, Folke sets out to find him. Year after year, Folke rides on his horse from place to place, searching for his grandson. In his determination to find the boy, Folke achieves a kind of tragic greatness. After many years, he finds his sons and grandson—at the court of the Christian king Inge. There is no happy reunion, however; his sons and grandson neither want to recognize him nor admit that they are related to him. Folke Filbyter is rejected as an uncouth heathen. He bequeaths all his accumulated riches to his sons and grandson, but the one thing he had come to value most—his children's love—he is denied.

In Part 2, *Bjälboarfvet,* Heidenstam continues the family saga of the Folkung dynasty, which ruled Sweden from 1250 to 1364. This volume required more historical research, and Heidenstam often had to travel up to Stockholm to consult historical works and sources at the Royal Library. The central focus of *Bjälboarfvet* is on Birger Jarl's sons Valdemar (king 1266–1275) and Magnus (king 1275–1290). A main substory is that of young Jutta, who has come up from Denmark to visit her sister, the queen, and ends up becoming the lifelong lover and mistress of King Valdemar. As in his earlier works, Heidenstam let his personal affairs and experiences color the love story between Valdemar and Jutta. Heidenstam had probably intended to continue the chronicle up to the last king of the dynasty, Magnus Eriksson (1332–1364), and tie it together with Saint Birgitta and her eventual curse on the Folkung dynasty for their immorality. However, other projects got in the way, and Heidenstam never continued the chronicle.

Soon after finishing *Bjälboarfvet,* Heidenstam received a commission from Bonnier and a prominent educator, Alfred Dalin, to write a history reader to be used in public schools. The two-volume result, *Svenskarna och deras hövdingar: Berättelser för unga och gamla* (1908, 1910, translated as *The Swedes and Their Chieftains*, 1925), is a series of short stories that critics agree do not live up to the inspired and colorful scenes in *Folkungaträdet*.

At his fiftieth birthday, in 1909, Heidenstam was at the top of his career. He was celebrated as a national poet and the foremost writer of Sweden. He received an honorary doctorate from Stockholm University on 7 December 1909. In 1912 he was elected into the Swedish Academy.

In 1910 the so-called Strindberg Feud broke out, which was the beginning of the questioning of Heidenstam's importance as a national monument. It began with an article by Strindberg called "Faraon-dyrkan" (Pharaoh Worship), published in the leftist liberal newspaper *Afton-Tidningen* on 29 April 1910. The article was an attack on what he considered to be the cult of King Charles XII, with an obvious address to Heidenstam. This article started a fierce public debate in the newspapers that lasted until 1912. The debate, dealing with topics from the religious and the political to the literary and aesthetic, divided the country into two camps. Strindberg came to represent the liberal-socialist side, while Heidenstam stood for the conservative side. Heidenstam kept quiet at first but felt eventually compelled to respond. He did so with the pamphlet *Proletärfilosofiens upplösning och fall* (1911, The Decline of the Proletarian Philosophy), which includes a rather sharp attack on Strindberg's barbarism, his lack of morals, and his artistic faults. This interchange put an end to the friendship between the two authors.

Heidenstam published only one additional collection of poetry in his lifetime after the Strindberg Feud: *Nya dikter* (1915, New Poems). This collection is counted among his best. *Nya dikter* was not so "new," in spite of its title. It includes poems he had written during the past twenty-year period, ever since 1895. In these poems, he no longer revels in the colorful, the pompous, and the exotic motifs of the earlier *Dikter* and focuses more on short, reflective, still, and simple poems, articulated in a quiet tone, similar to the "Ensamhetens tankar" from 1895. This volume was a main reason that Heidenstam was awarded the Nobel Prize in Literature in 1916. The turmoil of World War I made 1916 a difficult year to award the Nobel Prize in Literature. Although Heidenstam was a member of the Swedish Academy, which might have posed a conflict, he was already showing signs of mental deterioration, and his conservative and admiring friends in the Academy decided to honor him for having ushered in neo-Romanticism and nationalism in Swedish literature. (Österling, who had married Heidenstam's former wife Greta Sjöberg, was not yet a member of the Academy.) Because of the war, the 1916 award ceremonies did not have the usual pomp and circumstance.

Shortly after the publication of *Nya dikter*, Heidenstam met a Danish woman, Kate Bang, thirty-three years his junior. She became his confidante, secretary, and companion for the rest of his life. After some years of traveling, they settled in 1925 at Övralid, an estate that Heidenstam himself had designed. In a letter to Bang at the end of March 1925, he described the house:

> Om du tänker dig ett strängt gammalt biskopshus, som vandrat upp till en säter bland skogar och små stugor och där i en dröm om en italiensk villa avlat barn med en svensk herrgård, då får du ett enkelt rätlinjigt hus, ett trähus, men ett förnämt, som ser ut som ett slott både utan och innan.
>
> (Imagine an old austere-looking bishop's residence, which has moved up on a meadow among forested areas and small cottages, and there, in a dream of an Italian villa, conceived a Swedish manor house, then you can imagine this manor house, with clean lines and straight angles, but very distinguished looking, like a castle both inside and out.)

Bang wrote two books on her life with Heidenstam during his last decades: *Vägen till Övralid* (1945, The Road to Övralid) and *Övralid: Drömmens verklighet* (1946, Övralid: The Dream Becomes Reality). These books are the most important sources of information about his later years, when he withdrew from public life. The man who in his earlier years had enjoyed flamboyance and spectacle now found peace his greatest wish: in *Övralid*, Bang quotes him as saying, "Att i tyst hus i ett tyst landskap föra ett tyst och kontemplativt liv, det är för mig den största tänkbara lycka" (To live a quiet and contemplative life in a silent house in silent landscape/nature, that is for me the greatest imaginable happiness).

During the last twenty-five years of his life, Heidenstam was able to complete only a handful of poems, which were published posthumously as *Sista dikter* (Last Poems) in 1942. Writing became increasingly difficult for Heidenstam, as early signs of senility or dementia started showing. Bang wrote:

> When he was thinking or forming his ideas, he paced back and forth on the floor. Almost always, he held a book in his hand, usually the Concise Dictionary of Swedish Academy (Svenska Akademiens Ordlista). It was not a coincidence that it was precisely that book. He was very unsure when it came to spelling and he looked up even the most common words. The dictio-

nary was so worn by the end of the year, that I always gave him a new copy as my annual Christmas present.

Scholars have debated the cause of Heidenstam's problems with spelling, which were evident as early as the 1880s in his letters to Strindberg, in which he apologized for his errors. Editors and printers frequently helped him, as did Bang later in his career. Some scholars have argued that he was dyslexic; others have suggested that his six years of schooling were too short for him to learn Swedish orthography, and that this deficiency showed up in his later writings. Later scholars, who have examined his letters, doubt both diagnoses. They think that Heidenstam suffered from early stages of senility or Alzheimer's disease during his last twenty-five years, and that the disease made him forget the spelling of even the most common words.

Visitors to Övralid (now a museum) are surprised when they learn that the books in the library are arranged according to color rather than according to author or genre. Heidenstam wanted the afternoon sun to illuminate the gold lettering on the backs of the books on the east wall of the library. Bang wrote that the books were arranged by an artist rather than a bibliophile or librarian. Heidenstam and Bang read aloud to each other, taking turns, starting before dinner and continuing after dinner. Eventually, Bang had to take over all the reading. When Heidenstam turned seventy-three years old in 1932, it became increasingly difficult for him to pay attention and follow along, even when Bang read, and he would fall asleep.

From 1928 to 1935 Heidenstam tried to work on an autobiography. After writing the first longer pieces of text on his childhood at Olshammar, he lost his inspiration. He did agree that the book could be edited and published even if he did not have time to complete it himself. By 1935 his mental capacity was exhausted, and the hope that he might finish the book had to be abandoned. In 1941 *När kastanjerna blommade* was published, edited by Bang and literary historian Böök. This book remains one of Heidenstam's best works and perhaps the easiest for present-day readers to enjoy.

Verner von Heidenstam died on 20 May 1940 at the age of eighty-one from complications of the flu, followed by pneumonia. The epitaph on his tombstone, which he had composed himself, includes the lines: "Mig förunnades det ofattbara / Att som människa / Få leva några år på jorden" (I was granted the unfathomable experience / To live a couple of years on this earth / as a human being).

Letters:
Brev: I urval och med förklaringar, edited by Kate Bang and Fredrik Böök (Stockholm: Bonnier, 1949);

Heidenstam and August Strindberg, *Brev: 1884–1890,* edited by Gudmund Fröberg (Stockholm: Wahlström & Widstrand, 1999).

Bibliography:
Allan Ranius, *Verner von Heidenstam: En bibliografi* (Linköping: A. Ranius, 2002).

Biographies:
Kate Bang, *Vägen till Övralid* (Stockholm: Bonnier, 1945);

Fredrik Böök, *Verner von Heidenstam,* 2 volumes (Stockholm: Bonnier, 1945–1946);

Bang, *Övralid: Drömmens verklighet* (Stockholm: Bonnier, 1946);

Staffan Björk, *Verner von Heidenstam* (Stockholm: Natur och Kultur, 1959);

Sven Stolpe, *Verner von Heidenstam* (Stockholm: Askild & Kärnekull, 1980);

Karin Österling, *Älskade Verner! En romantisk biografi on Heidenstam* (Stockholm: Bonnier, 1989).

References:
Ingmar Algulin, "Poetry at the Turn of the Century: Heidenstam, Fröding, Karlfeldt, Ekelund," in *A History of Swedish Literature,* translated by John Weinstock (Stockholm: Swedish Institute, 1989), pp. 138–143;

Gunnar Axberger, *Diktaren och elden: Den Heidenstamstudie* (Stockholm: Bonnier, 1959);

Staffan Björk, *Heidenstam och sekelskiftets Sverige: Studier I hans nationella och sociala författarskap* (Stockholm: Natur och Kultur, 1946);

Susan Brantley, "Heidenstam's *Karolinerna* and the Fin de Siècle," in *Fin(s) de Siècle in Scandinavian Perspective: Studies in Honor of Harald S. Naess,* edited by Faith Ingwersen, Mary Kay Norseng, and others (Columbia, S.C.: Camden House, 1993);

Brantley, "Into the Twentieth Century: 1890–1950," in *A History of Swedish Literature,* edited by Lars G. Warme (Lincoln & London: University of Nebraska Press, 1996), pp. 277–279;

Ulla Callmander, "Verner von Heidenstam," in *Aspects of Modern Swedish Literature,* edited by Irene Scobbie (Norwich: Norvik Press, 1988), pp. 57–63;

Gudmund Fröberg, *"Inifrån det svenska": Studier i Heidenstams roman* Folke Filbyter (Stockholm: Carlssons 1994);

Fröberg, ed., *Kring Verner von Heidenstam* (Stockholm: Carlssons, 1993);

Helge Gullberg, *Gullebarns levnadssaga: Verner von Heidenstams och Ellen Belfrages son, föräldrarna och gudmodern in samtida dokument* (Göteborg: Rundqvist, 1983);

Magnus Halldin, "Några tankar kring Heidenstams Renässans," *Parnass*, no. 4 (1999): 8–11;

Hugo Kamras, *Den unge Heidenstam: Personlighet och idéutveckling* (Stockholm: Gebers, 1942);

Martin Kylhammar, *Maskin och idyll: Teknik och pastorala ideal hos Strindberg och Heidenstam* (Stockholm: Liber, 1985);

Bo Ollén, *Heidenstam som barnboksförfattare: Om Svenskarna och deras hövdingar* (Hedemora: Svenska barnboksinstitutet, 1992);

Parnass, special Heidenstam issue, no. 4 (2000);

Magnus von Platen, *Verner von Heidenstam och Emilia Uggla: Ett äktenskap* (Stockholm: Fischer, 1994).

Papers:
Verner von Heidenstam's papers and literary remains, the "Övralidsarkivet" (Övralid Archives), are located at Stifts-och Landsbiblioteket in Linköping, Sweden.

1916 Nobel Prize in Literature Presentation

by Sven Söderman

In the constellation of original artists who regenerated Swedish poetry at the end of the last century, Verner von Heidenstam was the most brilliant star. He was the leader of the generation of poets of 1890; he was the first to set forth in theory and also to realize in his works the ideal of new Swedish generations. Even in his first poems he opened new paths for imagination and form; and his later collections are in large part pure masterpieces of the lyric art. Not less significant—but more impressive because of its great dimensions—is his work in prose. Inspired by national subjects from the very beginning, it succeeds in capturing the most genuine characteristics of national life; it depicts the destinies of the Swedish people in epic poems, which by the richness of their imagination, the sharpness of their contours, and their composition, are works of the highest order in Scandinavian literature. No competent and impartial judge has ever questioned the rare originality of his genius, and Heidenstam has long been ranked among the masters of Swedish national literature.

Born in 1859 into an old family of the Swedish nobility, he first wanted to be a painter, but he abandoned the study of painting to devote himself to his vocation as a poet. His first collection of poems, *Vallfart och vandringsår* (1888) [Pilgrimage: The Wander Years], which contains predominantly Oriental themes, marked an epoch in the modern literature of Sweden. In truth it gave the final blow to the realistic school, enemy of all imagination, which was then dominant in Sweden and which since 1880 had darkened literature with its sadness and its gloom. This was the first manifestation of a new poetry in which free individuals, led only by the logic of their imagination, worshipped beauty for its own sake. This "renaissance," which a small polemical work (*Renässans*, 1889) announced a little later, was already completely realized in these poems, rich in colours and bold in form. They reaffirmed the right of man to the naive pleasure of living and surprised with their new rhythms and their poetic accents.

The Oriental poems which played so charmingly with colours and forms had inaugurated a new era and had made the renewal of Swedish poetry apparent to the eyes and to the imagination. In the great prose-poem intermixed with verse, *Hans Alienus* (1892), the tragic Odyssey of an uprooted worshipper of beauty, and especially in his *Dikter* (1895) [Poems] Heidenstam opens perspectives to an inner life. The time of hymns to voluptuousness is past; gravity and sadness are now persistent moods. Sentiment and duty are appreciated at their just value and what is firmly rooted in the depths of the human personality finds itself intuitively explained. What is characteristic in this conception of life, born of noble and unhappy experiences, is a proud and tolerant virility which constitutes the very essence of the suffering, the hope, and the intoxication of the poet, and a newly acquired capacity to reach the spiritual world by renunciation. An ample and profound imagination, genial sentiment, and pure humanity fill these poems—which are also admirable in the sense of form—and make Heidenstam a manly poet and a master of the lyric genre.

A new aspect of Heidenstam's development appeared in his patriotic poetry. He had discovered early that love for the ancestral hearth and for the home of one's birth is what most strongly links man to life. To this love he gave an intense expression even in the poems of his youth; this love henceforth linked him more closely to his country and to his people and oriented his poetic genius toward the historic tales and memories of Sweden. Compelled by such love, he summarized, in a cycle of poems, *Ett folk* (1902) [One People], all that is Swedish into a unity with the same rights and obligations for those who enter therein; and his love finally suggested a patriotic dream of grandeur and called forth this passionate demand: "No people may be greater than you; that is the goal, no matter what the cost." A whole series of great prose-poems bears witness to his patriotism. In *Karolinerna* (1897–98) [The Charles Men] he describes, in the form of separate narratives, the inevitable ruin of Swedish greatness through the act of Charles XII; with a few quick strokes he sketches the tragic character of this national hero and shows that in the end he was only the echo of an ancient saga. In *Heliga Birgittas pilgrimsfärd* (1901) [Saint Bridget's Pilgrimage] he gives a penetrating explanation of this remarkable woman, suggesting that she quite consciously sought sainthood but that she attained it unconsciously when of her own will she divested herself of her pride. Truly monumental are the two volumes of *Folkungaträdet* (1905–07) [The Tree of the Folkungs], *Folke Filbyter and Bjälboarfvet* [The Bjälbo Inheritance], which constitute the trunk and lower branches of "the genealogical tree of the Folkungs," a great historical prose epic in which he retraces the character of a clan of chieftains and the destinies of the Swedes during a period of the Middle Ages. Here the historical imagination of the author, sustained by an inspiration forever fresh, follows all threads in weaving the fates of his characters. His imagination, with its symbolic visions, glistens before the eye.

While Heidenstam was working on this epic about the life and character of the Swedes, his cult for man was taking shape, and one finds traces of it in the work. This cult often includes the necessity to renew life through sacrifice and to aspire to a more elevated earthly existence, an idea which is opposed to love and the cult of woman and results logically in the exaltations of stories *Sankt Göran och draken* (1900) [St. George and the Dragon] and *Skogen susar* (1904) [The Forest Whispers]. This collection contains, in particular, the great prose-poem "Herakles."

Beside these works, Heidenstam has published, among other things, stories and memories of a trip, *Från Col di Tenda till Blocksberg* (1888) [From Col di Tenda to Blocksberg]; the novel *Endymion* (1889), Oriental to the core; the book of historical lectures *Svenskarna och deras hövdingar* (1908–10) [The Swedes and Their Chieftains]; and the collections *Tankar och teckningar* (1899) [Thoughts and Notes] and *Dagar och händelser* (1909) [Days and Occurrences]. In this last book he has notably treated subjects of aesthetics and general culture.

The final aspect of Heidenstam's concept of life is offered us through his *Nya dikter* (1915) [New Poems], a collection mainly of philosophical poems of an elevated humanity, of a mellow wisdom, of a beauty of images strangely serene. In loneliness men come to understand themselves; love is the bond which should unite them, and creative humility is the great force which builds the world and which raises statues of the gods.

"O Man, you will become wise only when you reach the summit of the evening-cool heights where all the earth is beheld."

[© The Nobel Foundation, 1916.]

Ernest Hemingway
(21 July 1899 – 2 July 1961)

John C. Unrue

See also the Hemingway entries in *DLB 4: American Writers in Paris, 1920–1939; DLB 9: American Novelists, 1910–1945; DLB 102: American Short-Story Writers, 1910–1945, Second Series; DLB 210: Ernest Hemingway: A Documentary Volume; DLB 316: American Prose Writers of World War I: A Documentary Volume; DLB Yearbook 1981; DLB Yearbook 1987; DLB Yearbook 1999; DLB Documentary Series 1: Sherwood Anderson, Willa Cather, John Dos Passos, Theodore Dreiser, F. Scott Fitzgerald, Ernest Hemingway, Sinclair Lewis; DLB Documentary Series 15: American Expatriate Writers: Paris in the Twenties;* and *DLB Documentary Series 16: The House of Scribner, 1905–1930.*

BOOKS: *Three Stories & Ten Poems* (Paris: Contact Editions, 1923);
in our time (Paris: Three Mountains Press, 1924; London: Jackson, 1924);
In Our Time (New York: Boni & Liveright, 1925; London: Cape, 1926; revised edition, New York: Scribners, 1930);
The Torrents of Spring (New York: Scribners, 1926; London: Cape, 1933);
The Sun Also Rises (New York: Scribners, 1926); republished as *Fiesta* (London: Cape, 1927);
Men Without Women (New York: Scribners, 1927; London: Cape, 1928);
A Farewell to Arms (New York: Scribners, 1929; London: Cape, 1929);
Death in the Afternoon (New York: Scribners, 1932; London: Cape, 1932);
God Rest You Merry Gentlemen (New York: House of Books, 1933);
Winner Take Nothing (New York: Scribners, 1933; London: Cape, 1934);
Green Hills of Africa (New York: Scribners, 1935; London: Cape, 1936);
To Have and Have Not (New York: Scribners, 1937; London: Cape, 1937);
The Spanish Earth (Cleveland: J. B. Savage, 1938);
The Fifth Column and the First Forty-Nine Stories (New York: Scribners, 1938; London: Cape, 1939); repub-

Ernest Hemingway after being informed he had won the 1954 Nobel Prize in Literature (Time & Life Pictures/Getty Images)

lished as *The Short Stories of Ernest Hemingway* (New York: Scribners, 1954);
The Fifth Column: A Play in Three Acts (New York: Scribners, 1940; London: Cape, 1968);
For Whom the Bell Tolls (New York: Scribners, 1940; London: Cape, 1941);
Across the River and Into the Trees (New York: Scribners, 1950; London: Cape, 1950);
The Old Man and the Sea (New York: Scribners, 1952; London: Cape, 1952);
The Collected Poems, unauthorized edition (San Francisco, 1960);

Hemingway: The Wild Years, edited by Gene Z. Hanrahan (New York: Dell, 1962);

A Moveable Feast (New York: Scribners, 1964; London: Cape, 1964);

By-Line, Ernest Hemingway: Selected Articles and Dispatches of Four Decades, edited by William White (New York: Scribners, 1967; London: Collins, 1968);

The Fifth Column and Four Stories of the Spanish Civil War (New York: Scribners, 1969);

Ernest Hemingway, Cub Reporter: Kansas City Star Stories, edited by Matthew J. Bruccoli (Pittsburgh: University of Pittsburgh Press, 1970);

Islands in the Stream (New York: Scribners, 1970; London: Collins, 1970);

Ernest Hemingway's Apprenticeship: Oak Park, 1916–1917, edited by Bruccoli (Washington, D.C.: Bruccoli Clark/NCR Microcard Editions, 1971);

The Nick Adams Stories, edited by Philip Young (New York: Scribners, 1972);

88 Poems, edited by Nicholas Gerogiannis (New York & London: Harcourt Brace Jovanovich/Bruccoli Clark, 1979); enlarged as *Complete Poems* (Lincoln & London: University of Nebraska Press, 1983);

Ernest Hemingway on Writing, edited by Larry W. Phillips (New York: Scribners, 1984; London: Granada, 1985);

The Dangerous Summer (New York: Scribners, 1985; London: Hamilton, 1985);

Dateline, Toronto: The Complete Toronto Star Dispatches, 1920–1924, edited by William White (New York: Scribners, 1985);

The Garden of Eden (New York: Scribners, 1986; London: Hamilton, 1987);

The Complete Short Stories of Ernest Hemingway (New York: Scribners, 1987);

True at First Light, edited by Patrick Hemingway (New York: Scribners, 1999); reedited and republished as *Under Kilimanjaro*, edited by Robert W. Lewis and Robert E. Fleming (Kent, Ohio: Kent State University Press, 2005);

Hemingway and the Mechanism of Fame: Statements, Public Letters, Introductions, Forewords, Prefaces, Blurbs, Reviews, and Endorsements, edited by Bruccoli and Judith S. Baughman (Columbia: University of South Carolina Press, 2005).

Editions and Collections: *The Enduring Hemingway*, edited by Charles Scribner Jr. (New York: Scribners, 1974);

The Sun Also Rises: A Facsimile Edition, 2 volumes, edited by Matthew J. Bruccoli (Detroit: Manly/Omnigraphics, 1990);

Hemingway on Fishing, edited by Nick Lyons (New York: Lyons Press, 2000);

Hemingway on Hunting, edited by Seán Hemingway (New York: Scribners, 2003);

Hemingway on War, edited by Seán Hemingway (New York: Scribners, 2003).

OTHER: "The Spanish War," *Fact*, no. 16 (15 July 1938): 7–72;

Men at War, edited, with an introduction, by Hemingway (New York: Crown, 1942; London & Glasgow: Collins, 1946).

By the time he was thirty years old, Ernest Hemingway was considered a stylistic master, and his stories and novels influenced a generation of writers. From the beginning of his writing career Hemingway created a persona and legend, causing many to conclude that Ernest Hemingway's greatest character was himself. Yet, he was not one character but several, underscoring F. Scott Fitzgerald's observation about the difficulty of writing a good biography of a novelist because "he is too many people if he is any good."

Hemingway translated his life into art in a series of stages during which he moved himself into his fictional world, first in his letters and his newspaper articles, becoming the character later developed in the conventional and disciplined stages of his composition. It was a process by which he became a part of a fiction from which he did not always extricate himself. Consequently, he is so closely bound to his fictional characters that it is difficult to separate him from them.

Hemingway was fiercely competitive. As a sportsman he wanted to be the best fisherman or hunter, but his greatest goal was to be the best writer. He told his father in 1925 that in his writing he wanted "to get the feeling of actual life across—not just to depict life or criticize it—but to actually make it alive." Hemingway was a complicated man, proving himself capable of brutality and betrayal as well as kindness and compassion. When he published *The Old Man and the Sea* (1952), he said that he "tried to make a real old man, a real boy, a real sea and real sharks," and that if he "made them true enough they would mean many things." He was speaking not only of his novella, but also of his life and art.

Ernest Miller Hemingway was born in Oak Park, Illinois, an affluent and conservative suburb of Chicago, on 21 July 1899. He was the second of six children and the first son of Clarence Edmunds Hemingway, a physician, and Grace Hall Hemingway. In childhood and adolescence Hemingway spent summers with his family at Windemere, their house at Lake Walloon in northern Michigan in the area of Petoskey. His hunting and fishing adventures and his contact with the Ojibway Indians, as well as his observations of the troubled relationship between his parents, became the material for stories such as "Indian Camp" (1925), "Ten Indians" (1927), "The Doctor and the Doctor's Wife" (1924), "The End of Something" (1925), "The Three-Day Blow" (1925), and "Fathers and Sons" (1933), all featuring Nick Adams, a recurrent Hemingway autobiographical protagonist.

Hemingway also derived from his parents positive and enduring values that shaped his career and guided his conduct. His mother introduced him to the arts and made books available. His father instilled in him a respect for and knowledge of nature.

Despite its religious fundamentalism, political conservatism, and adherence to what it saw as moral certainties, the village of Oak Park was progressive; it had a good library and a high school that provided Hemingway with a sound education, especially in composition, language, literature, and history. He read Geoffrey Chaucer, William Shakespeare, John Milton, Alexander Pope, and Matthew Arnold, and he gained valuable experience writing for the school newspaper, *The Trapeze,* and its literary magazine, *Tabula,* to which he contributed three stories during his junior year that reveal his early interest in violent death and suicide. Hemingway's competitive spirit drove him to box, play football, and run track, but he was never an outstanding athlete.

Between November 1916 and May 1917 Hemingway wrote twenty-four articles for *The Trapeze.* Although the quality of his work was unexceptional, his experience helped prepare him for his first job following high school, as a cub reporter with the *Kansas City Star,* considered one of the best newspapers in America. In addition to having the advice of first-rate journalistic professionals, Hemingway had to make his writing comply with the 110 rules of the *Kansas City Star* style sheet, requiring him to avoid adjectives and to use short sentences, brief paragraphs, vigorous English, and fresh phrases. Later, Hemingway remarked that these rules, which influenced his style as a fiction writer, were the best he had ever learned.

Determined to get to Europe and participate in World War I, which the United States had entered in the spring of 1917, Hemingway left the *Kansas City Star* at the end of April 1918 and joined an American Red Cross ambulance unit that assisted the Italian Army. On 8 July at Fossalta he was hit by shrapnel from an Austrian trench mortar and suffered severe leg wounds. He was sent to an American Red Cross hospital in Milan.

When Hemingway arrived home in January 1919, he exaggerated his war service, creating a heroic persona for himself that he embellished throughout most of his life. He pursued a writing career ever more diligently, imitating Rudyard Kipling, O. Henry, and Ring Lardner, optimistic that he could follow a formula that would enable him to sell his stories to *The Saturday Evening Post* and other mass-market magazines. But he had yet to find his own narrative voice or his own material, and his work, predictably amateurish, was rejected.

Hemingway left home in January 1920 for Toronto, where he became a freelancer for the *Toronto Star.* He returned to Chicago in May and worked for *The Cooperative Commonwealth,* a monthly magazine. He met and became engaged to twenty-eight-year-old Hadley Richardson, whom he married on 3 September 1921 in Horton Bay, Michigan. In Chicago he also met Sherwood Anderson, whose *Winesburg, Ohio* (1919) had gained wide acclaim. Anderson befriended Hemingway, encouraged his writing efforts, and convinced him that Paris was the place for a serious writer. Supported by Hadley Hemingway's trust fund, which yielded approximately $3,000 annually, Hemingway and his wife left for Paris at the end of the year. He carried letters of introduction from Anderson to Gertrude Stein, Sylvia Beach (owner of the bookstore and lending library Shakespeare and Company), and Ezra Pound.

In February 1922 Hemingway met Pound, who became one of his most important literary friends and helped him get his early work published. Pound also oversaw Hemingway's literary education and recommended that he read works by T. S. Eliot and James Joyce. The major figure in the imagist movement during the period from 1909 to 1918, Pound encouraged Hemingway to focus upon natural objects, to delete unnecessary words, and to permit images to give meaning. With Pound's advice Hemingway developed what he called the "true" sentence and "true" paragraph.

Hemingway met Stein on 8 March 1922. Stein had derived her own ideas about the possible uses of language from William James's psychological theories and had gained recognition for her experimental prose that showed the influence of painters from whose planes of color she had begun to model sentences. At her apartment at 27 rue de Fleurus, Hemingway studied paintings by Henri Matisse, Georges Braque, Juan Gris, Pablo Picasso, and especially Paul Cézanne, whose ability to capture landscape he admired. In the original ending to "Big Two-Hearted River" Nick Adams says that he wants to write the way Cézanne painted. Hemingway also observed Stein's repetition of key words and phrases and her attempt to convey a continuous present. Hemingway credited Stein with helping him understand prose rhythms.

Continuing to work as a stringer for the *Toronto Star,* Hemingway went to Lausanne, Switzerland, in November 1922 to cover a peace conference on a territorial dispute between Greece and Turkey. He had asked Hadley Hemingway to join him, and in the Paris Gare de Lyon on the evening of 2 December a thief stole her valise, which contained all of Hemingway's unpublished work except "My Old Man," "Up in Michigan," six poems that had been sent to magazines, and one chapter of a fishing story about Nick Adams. Hemingway was by then writing finely honed miniatures or vignettes, illustrating the imagist technique championed by Pound. The papers were never recovered.

In June 1923 Hemingway made his first trip to Spain, accompanied by Robert McAlmon, a writer and publisher, and William Bird, a newsman and publisher. Hemingway immersed himself in the culture of bullfighting, or as McAlmon observed, making everything about bullfighting "into a literary or artistic experience." The following month Hemingway made a second trip to Spain, this time with Hadley Hemingway, to see their first Fiesta of San Fermín and the bullfights and to gather material.

In August 1923 McAlmon published Hemingway's first book, *Three Stories & Ten Poems*. Although the poems in the volume merited little acclaim, the stories—"My Old Man," an initiation story about horse racing with a narrative voice bearing a resemblance to that in Anderson's "I Want to Know Why"; "Up in Michigan," a seduction story Stein thought too sexually explicit to be publishable; and "Out of Season," about tension and conflict in a marriage during a fishing trip in Italy—received praise. Hemingway and his wife left Paris for Toronto, where he was on salary as a full-time reporter with the *Toronto Star*. There they awaited the birth of their child and news of Hemingway's second book, *in our time*, which William Bird published in 1924. John Hadley Nicanor (Bumby) Hemingway was born in Toronto on 10 October 1923.

Among the articles Hemingway wrote for the *Toronto Star Weekly* during this period was one that provided his most extensive early comment about the Nobel Prize. In "'Nobelman' Yeats" (24 November 1923) he praised the awarding of the prize that year to William Butler Yeats, saying that Yeats had written, "with the exception of a few poems by Ezra Pound, the very finest poetry of our time." By giving the prize to Yeats, Hemingway said, "the Nobel Prize-givers had made up for a lot of things." He criticized the Nobel Committee for many of its previous awards. He thought the works of recipients Maurice Maeterlinck (1911), Rabindranath Tagore (1913), Verner von Heidenstam (1916), and Karl Adolph Gjellerup and Henrik Pontoppidan (1917) were greatly inferior to those of Thomas Hardy or Joseph Conrad and would not endure. Hemingway also chided the Nobel Committee for waiting so long to give an award to Anatole France (1921).

After Christmas, Hemingway resigned his position at the *Toronto Star* and returned to France in 1924. He was soon serving as an unpaid assistant editor for the *transatlantic review,* a journal founded by Ford Madox Ford that published experimental fiction. The first issue included Hemingway's story "Indian Camp." "The Doctor and the Doctor's Wife" and "Cross Country Snow" were published in the December 1924 and January 1925 issues respectively. Hemingway also used the *transatlantic review* as a forum to attack writing contemporaries, including most memorably Eliot. After the death of Conrad, Hemingway wrote in the October 1924 issue that if he could bring the Polish-born novelist back to life "by grinding Mr. Eliot into fine dry powder and sprinkling that powder over Mr. Conrad's grave," he "would leave for London tomorrow with a sausage grinder."

By April 1924 Hemingway's *in our time,* a thirty-two-page volume consisting of eighteen vignettes, was on sale in Paris at Shakespeare and Company. It was limited to 170 copies. Brief paragraphs depict executions, bullfights, festivals, gorings, refugees in Adrianople, and war scenes. Hemingway found another outlet for his fiction when Ernest Walsh and Ethel Moorhead started a little magazine called *This Quarter*. One of his best stories, "Big Two-Hearted River," was published in the first issue, May 1925, and another excellent story, "The Undefeated," appeared in the second issue, Autumn–Winter 1925.

In late April 1925, in the Dingo Bar in Montparnasse, Hemingway met Fitzgerald. Despite Fitzgerald's being the established and successful writer, with two collections of short stories and three novels, including *The Great Gatsby* (1925), while Hemingway had published two slim volumes totaling eighty-eight pages and 470 copies, Fitzgerald was in awe of Hemingway, impressed by his talent and intimidated by him. Their meeting was the beginning of one of the most complex friendships in American literary history.

In March, Hemingway had signed a contract with Boni and Liveright for his first trade publication, a collection of stories called *In Our Time*. The new book consisted of fifteen stories and reprinted vignettes from *in our time;* it included seven Nick Adams stories, showing Nick as a child and young man experiencing initiation as he confronts death, insanity, loss, disillusionment, consequences of matrimony and fatherhood, and in the best story, "Big Two-Hearted River," healing and revitalization on a trout stream. *In Our Time* was published on 5 October 1925. Although the collection includes some excellent stories and reveals Hemingway's talent, it did not sell well.

Nevertheless, reviewers praised *In Our Time* and saw in Hemingway's vignettes and stories what critic

Edmund Wilson had called earlier in a review for *Dial* (October 1924) of *Three Stories & Ten Poems* and *in our time* "a distinctively American development in prose" that was "strikingly original." Hemingway's short declarative sentences captured the essence of an object or subject. Fitzgerald's review for *The Bookman* (May 1926) noted that Hemingway conveyed emotion "without the aid of comment" or "recourse to exposition." Others agreed; Paul Rosenfeld in the *New Republic* (25 November 1925) found "little analysis in this narrative art" and welcomed the freshness of Hemingway's prose with its absence of "psychologizings." Louis Kronenberger, writing for *The Saturday Review of Literature* (13 February 1926) saw the young author's work as "experimental and very modern." Most critics pointed to the effectiveness of Hemingway's style and diction and agreed that a promising new American writer's career was being launched.

In July 1925 Hemingway and Hadley Hemingway returned to the Fiesta of San Fermín with humorist Donald Ogden Stewart; Bill Smith, Hemingway's old fishing friend from northern Michigan; novelist Harold Loeb; Lady Duff Twysden, an alcoholic Englishwoman and Montparnasse fixture; and her alcoholic Scottish fiancé, Pat Guthrie. Hemingway experienced the excitement of the fiesta and observed the tension, jealousy, resentment, and bad behavior in the group. When the fiesta concluded, Hemingway began writing a new novel. Paris, Spain, his friends, the fiesta, and the brilliant young bullfighter Niño de la Palma provided the material. He finished the first draft on 21 September.

Confident that he had written a good novel, Hemingway had begun to see that Fitzgerald was right when he said that Hemingway would fare better at Scribners than at Boni and Liveright. Before revising his new novel, Hemingway wrote a parody of Anderson's *Dark Laughter* (1925), a book he found disappointing and fake, and submitted it to Boni and Liveright, also Anderson's publisher, knowing that his contract with its three-book option would be invalidated if Boni and Liveright refused to publish his parody, called *The Torrents of Spring*. By 30 December 1925, Horace Liveright rejected *The Torrents of Spring*, calling it "a vicious caricature of Sherwood Anderson."

Although Hemingway claimed that he did not intend for *The Torrents of Spring* to be a contract breaker, it was; and with Fitzgerald's encouragement Hemingway turned to editor Maxwell Perkins at Scribners, Fitzgerald having notified Perkins that he could get Hemingway and his new novel, *The Sun Also Rises*, if Scribners published *The Torrents of Spring*. Perkins agreed to the arrangement, and *The Torrents of Spring* was published on 28 May 1926.

In addition to brokering the agreement between Hemingway and Scribners, Fitzgerald provided editorial advice concerning Hemingway's new novel. He read a carbon copy of the novel before 5 June while proofs were being set and advised Hemingway to cut the opening of the novel substantially. Hemingway acted upon Fitzgerald's recommendations, strengthening the book, but throughout his lifetime Hemingway denied that Fitzgerald had helped. The Hemingways returned to Pamplona in July, taking along other friends, including Pauline Pfeiffer, a wealthy American who worked for the Paris edition of *Vogue* and who had accompanied the Hemingways on skiing trips to Austria. By the end of the festival Hadley Hemingway knew that her husband was having an affair with Pfeiffer. The Hemingways returned to Paris and set up separate residences.

The Sun Also Rises was published on 22 October 1926. It advanced Hemingway's literary career, introducing him to an American audience and expanding his reputation beyond Paris. The first printing of five thousand copies sold quickly, and it was reprinted in November, December, and January 1927, and twice in February. The epigraphs of *The Sun Also Rises* were taken from a quotation by Stein referring to those who survived World War I as "a lost generation" and from a passage in Ecclesiastes that provided the title of the novel and acknowledged that the earth "abideth forever." Hemingway was skeptical about Stein's "lost-generation" label, and he sarcastically referred to it as the "so-called (but not by me) lost generation." He used the Ecclesiastes passage to balance Stein's quotation, which he found presumptuous for attempting to judge his generation.

With distinctively spare, idiomatic language, Jake Barnes, the first-person narrator, an American newspaperman made impotent by a war wound, recounts the experiences of a postwar generation who have become members of a disillusioned and self-destructive expatriate community. Rejecting the traditional values and moral remedies of a world left behind, most of Barnes's friends avoid consequences and responsibilities while steadily anesthetizing themselves with alcohol. In July, Barnes leads four friends from Paris to the Fiesta of San Fermín in Pamplona, where they join in the revelry of a bacchanalian week fueled by drunkenness, jealousies, self-destruction, corruption, and betrayal.

The reviewer for *The New York Times* (31 October 1926) thought *The Sun Also Rises* fulfilled the promise of Hemingway's earlier work and that the novel was "unquestionably one of the events of an unusually rich year in literature." Conrad Aiken said in the *New York Herald Tribune Books* (31 October 1926) that "in many respects" Hemingway was "the most exciting of contemporary writers of fiction." Wilson reportedly thought it the best novel written by anyone in Hemingway's generation, and in his *Exile's Return* (1951) Malcolm Cowley observed Hemingway's influence upon young men and women who were acting out roles suggested by Jake Barnes and Brett Ashley. Looking back at *The Sun Also Rises* in 1953, biographer/critic Carlos Baker underscored qualities noted by contemporary reviewers of the novel that caused it to endure and contribute to Hemingway's literary reputation. Baker cited the purity of Hemingway's language and denotative power of dialogue; his devotion to fact and personal knowledge; his skill in evoking and controlling emotional states; and his use of symbolic landscape.

Explaining that all the stories lacked "the softening feminine influence" resulting from "training, discipline, death, or other causes," Hemingway titled his second short-story collection *Men Without Women* (1927). Reviews were mixed. Dorothy Parker praised the collection, and Virginia Woolf was critical, calling Hemingway "self-consciously virile" with a "contracted" talent (*New York Herald Tribune Books*, 9 October 1927). Although general admiration was expressed for "The Killers," "Hills Like White Elephants," and "In Another Country," the collection was considered uneven.

Hemingway's divorce from Hadley Hemingway became final in mid April 1927, and Hemingway and Pfeiffer were married in May. By March 1928 Hemingway had begun a novel inspired by some of the stories in *Men Without Women:* "In Another Country," "Now I Lay Me," and "Italy, 1927," later called "Chi Ti Dice La Patria," all concerned with scenes and sentiments associated with his war experiences. The novel was *A Farewell to Arms* (1929).

Hemingway had wanted to return to the United States for several years, and he and Pauline Hemingway, who was pregnant, sailed on 17 March 1928 for Key West from France. Their son Patrick was born on 28 June 1928. Hemingway received a telegram on 6 December informing him of the death of his father. Having suffered depression for many years, Clarence Hemingway had shot himself. Following the funeral, Hemingway finished *A Farewell to Arms*. In April 1929 Hemingway and his family returned to France, where he revised the page proofs for serial publication of *A Farewell to Arms* in *Scribner's Magazine* and rewrote the ending.

A Farewell to Arms was published on 27 September 1929. It was praised from the outset, and the first printing of 31,050 copies sold rapidly, with additional printings in September, October, and November. By February 1930 Hemingway had earned more than $30,000 in royalties.

In *The Sun Also Rises* Hemingway had shown the effects of World War I upon the generation whose lives it touched. In his second novel he focused upon the war itself, tracing the events that took a toll on the young people who participated in it. Severely wounded on the Austrian front while serving as a Red Cross ambulance driver, Frederic Henry is sent to a hospital in Milan, where he falls in love with his English nurse, Catherine Barkley, who becomes pregnant with his child. He returns to the front, where he sees incompetence, chaos, and destruction and is nearly executed by Italian battle police who epitomize the madness the war has become. Frederic searches for meaning in a world in which he can find no meaning and no reason for his pain or for Catherine's eventual death during delivery of their stillborn baby. He concludes that there is no one or no force to whom he can turn for help or whom he can blame. Ultimately, he is a man alone confronting his fate.

Frederic Henry's discovery was one Hemingway had made earlier when he observed bullfighters in the bullring confronting their fate. Manuel in "The Undefeated" stands "very much alone in the ring." In *The Sun Also Rises* as the three matadors Belmonte, Romero, and Lalanda enter the bullring, Jake Barnes observes, "They were all alone." And when Romero fights his bull, he is "out in the center of the ring, all alone." It was the aloneness with which Hemingway identified and that he saw inherent in the life of the artist. Hemingway concluded *A Farewell to Arms* with one of his most admired understated sentences: "After a while I went out and left the hospital and walked back to the hotel in the rain."

The novel was widely reviewed, and critical response was predominantly favorable, affirming that Hemingway had become a major writer who exerted strong influence upon American literature. Henry Hazlitt of *The New York Sun* (28 September 1929) thought the novel Hemingway's "finest," called him "the young master," and observed that it was Hemingway whom young and older writers were imitating. There was evolving not only a "Hemingway school" but also a "Hemingway cult," strengthened by convincing dialogue and a distinctive style. In *The Nation* (30 October 1929) Clifton Fadiman acknowledged Hemingway as "one of the best craftsmen alive" and concluded, "There seems no reason why *A Farewell to Arms* should not secure the Pulitzer Prize." Although the book did not win a Pulitzer, the high regard for Hemingway's work was so commonplace that Henry Seidel Canby said in *The Saturday Review of Literature* (12 October 1929) that among things "not permitted in contemporary criticism" was "to attack Ernest Hemingway." By 1930 Hemingway's high critical reputation was established, and as Cowley had observed in the *New York Herald Tribune Books* (6 October 1929), Hemingway had gained the respect "one normally accords to a legendary figure."

Hemingway's influence upon fiction of the 1930s was profound. Writers who came after him were influenced by his style and his "cult of violence." He was, said Alfred Kazin in his *On Native Ground* (1942), "the greatest single influence on the hard-boiled novel of the thirties," and "no one . . . had anything like Hemingway's dominance over American fiction." Among the writers Hemingway influenced were James T. Farrell, John O'Hara, Nelson Algren, James Jones, and Norman Mailer. Ralph Ellison, in "The World and the Jug" (included in *Shadow and Act,* 1964), called Hemingway "the true father-as-artist of so many of us who came to writing during the late thirties."

Hemingway had been considering a big book on bullfighting even before he began writing *The Sun Also Rises*. He wanted to re-create the experience of the bullfight rather than explain it for an English-speaking public ignorant of the spectacle. He began working on this project soon after his return to Key West from Paris in February 1930. In November, when he learned that Sinclair Lewis had won the 1930 Nobel Prize in Literature, he was angry and wrote in a letter to Archibald MacLeish that the news was "a hell of a blow." That the committee gave the prize to Lewis, whom he had long disliked and resented, rather than Pound or Joyce was "a filthy business." He declared that "the only difference between the Nobel Prize and other prizes" was that it was worth more money.

On 12 November 1931 Pauline Hemingway gave birth to son Gregory, and the following month Hemingway finished *Death in the Afternoon*. It was published on 23 September 1932. Although the book revealed Hemingway's considerable research and knowledge about bullfighting, as well as his most extensive public presentation of his writing philosophy, *Death in the Afternoon* was not embraced by Americans during the Depression. Some reviewers attacked Hemingway personally, faulting his remarks about other writers.

Five months before the publication of *Death in the Afternoon* Hemingway reported that he had written six stories for a new collection. He called it *Winner Take Nothing,* explaining in the epigraph that unlike other "forms of lutte [struggle] or combat conditions," the winner would take nothing, not ease or pleasure, nor ideas of glory, and "if he win far enough," there would be "no reward within himself." The collection was published on 27 October 1933, and the reviews were mixed. Some critics regarded Hemingway's lower-class characters as intellectually limited and uninteresting. Although the collection includes "A Clean, Well-Lighted Place," *Winner Take Nothing* was thought the weakest of Hemingway's three story collections. Nevertheless, it sold 12,000 copies by mid December in the third year of the Depression.

While many scoffed at Hemingway's sporting activities, he added to his considerable fame and greater celebrity by capitalizing upon his game-fishing and hunting adventures. He agreed to contribute hunting and fishing articles to Arnold Gingrich's new men's magazine, *Esquire,* promoting his sportsman image and the growing Hemingway persona. Hemingway also published in *Esquire* twenty-five "letters" and six short stories between 1933 and 1939.

As 1933 ended, the Hemingways went to Africa for a two-month safari. After he returned to Key West in April 1934, Hemingway began writing *Green Hills of Africa,* an experimental book in which he attempted, he said in the foreword, "to see whether the shape of a country and the pattern of a month's action can, if truly presented, compete with a work of the imagination." After appearing serially in *Scribner's Magazine,* the book was published on 25 October 1935.

In addition to writing about his hunting adventures Hemingway provided an assessment of literary history and dangers to which writers are vulnerable. "All American literature," he said, "comes from one book by Mark Twain called *Huckleberry Finn*. . . . All American writing comes from that. There was nothing before. There has been nothing as good since." He attacked other writers who had politicized art by acquiescing to the directives of critics such as Granville Hicks, who had argued in 1932 that literature in a "period of transition . . . must be used as a weapon" and lamented that Hemingway had not written a novel about a strike or looked "squarely at the contemporary American scene." Hemingway stated his commitment to art, observing:

> A country finally erodes and the dust blows away, the people all die and none of them were of any importance permanently, except those who practiced the arts, and these now wish to cease their work because it is too lonely, too hard to do, and it is not fashionable. A thousand years makes economics silly and a work of art endures forever, but it is very difficult to do and now it is not fashionable.

Hemingway indicated that his position was also dangerous for writers in the 1930s. Both "politics" and "a lack of politics" could put an author at risk with critics as could "women, drink, money and ambition," dangers that appear frequently in his later stories and novels. Although *Green Hills of Africa* is not fiction, it does have the structure of a fictional work, and its form illustrates Hemingway's aesthetic goal: to take the reader where the author has been and to involve the reader in the emotion of place and time.

Most critics thought *Green Hills of Africa* a failed experiment. Leftist reviewers found Hemingway's subject inappropriate for the times and again chided him for ignoring the ills of society and for attacking political dogma and the Marxist school of writing. Many others were offended by his judgments about contemporary rival writers and thought his literary discussions self-aggrandizing and superficial. Hemingway had also attacked the critics themselves, calling them "the lice who crawl on literature."

Hemingway had begun writing a long story in February 1933 about Harry Morgan, the owner of a charter fishing boat in Key West who had become a smuggler in order to support his family during the Depression. It was titled "One Trip Across" and was published in *Cosmopolitan* in April 1934. A second Harry Morgan story, "The Tradesman's Return," in which Harry has lost an arm and his boat is confiscated, was published in *Esquire* in 1936. Rather than include these stories in a collection, Hemingway decided to use them as a major portion of a new novel, to which he added a third Harry Morgan story as well as another story contrasting Harry's strength to the weaknesses of the yacht-club "haves" and of a writer named Richard Gordon, who has become "fashionable" by writing about a strike. Hemingway told Perkins that his plan for *To Have and Have Not* (1937) was to show "the mechanics of revolution" and its effects upon those involved in it and to show also "the decline of the individual." Harry Morgan's dying words are, "One man alone ain't got . . . no bloody fucking chance."

Hemingway became involved in the Loyalist cause in the Spanish Civil War and covered the conflict for the North American Newspaper Alliance (NANA). His personal life had also become complicated, as he had begun an affair with Martha Gellhorn, a young writer he met in Key West and who also went to Spain as a correspondent for *Collier's*. *To Have and Have Not* was published on 15 October 1937. Although a reviewer for *New Masses,* a radical magazine, thought this work better than Hemingway's previous novels, *To Have and Have Not* was generally regarded as structurally flawed and unsuccessful. Yet, it was a Hemingway book, and it sold 38,000 copies in five months.

In the summer of 1937 Hemingway assisted in the production of *The Spanish Earth,* a documentary movie about the Spanish Civil War, and recorded the narration he had written. He also wrote a play, *The Fifth Column* (1938), focusing upon the activities of two counterespionage men in Madrid who capture members of a fifth-column group supporting the Fascists. (It was not produced at the time but was adapted by Benjamin Glazer for performance at the Alvin Theater in New York in March 1940.) Philip Rawlings, the protagonist, appears to be indifferent, but he in fact is committed to the Loyalist cause and even more emphatically committed to saving mankind and democracy. Rawlings proves himself focused, disciplined, and prepared to sacrifice all for the cause, including Dorothy Bridges, an American writer in Spain with whom he has had an affair. He will not go with Dorothy to places he has loved and remembers vividly; he has "left them all behind." Duty and responsibility take precedence in Rawlings's life over Dorothy and all other temptations or destructive forces. "Where I go now I go alone," Rawlings says, "or with others who go there for the same reason." Hemingway contended that the play was not an endorsement of the "Reds," a declaration his next novel affirmed.

Hemingway's collection *The Fifth Column and the First Forty-Nine Stories* was published on 14 October 1938 and included two of his best stories, both set in Africa. "The Short Happy Life of Francis Macomber" (first published in *Cosmopolitan,* September 1936) portrays a husband's initial cowardice during a safari and a triangle involving himself, his wife, and their white hunter. The story ends with the husband's experiencing euphoria as he regains his courage, bravely facing a charging buffalo before his wife shoots him, intentionally or unintentionally, ending his short happy moment and her dominance. "The Snows of Kilimanjaro" (first published in *Esquire,* August 1936) concerns a dying writer who is corrupted by a rich wife and who regrets wasting his writing talent. Seldom able to resist the opportunity to attack fellow writers, Hemingway included a comment about "poor Scott Fitzgerald" (later changed to Julian) and a mocking and distorted reference to the line "The rich are very different from you and me" from Fitzgerald's story "The Rich Boy" (1926). Autobiographical, the story reflected loss and dangers to which Hemingway felt vulnerable.

Most critics praised the collected stories but found *The Fifth Column* unsatisfactory. Elmer Davis said in *The Saturday Review of Literature* (15 October 1938), "Nobody else now living could show forty-nine stories that good." Those who had not liked Hemingway's work since the publication of *A Farewell to Arms* found even less to like in a play they regarded as "propaganda" and "melodrama," a self-conscious indulgence on the part of the author. Critic Lionel Trilling, writing for the *Partisan Review* (Winter 1939), saw *The Fifth Column* as evidence that Hemingway had felt the pressures of leftist critics, that the 1930s cultural environment had led to "the recent falling off" of Hemingway's work. Leftist critic Edwin Berry Burgum (*New Masses,* 22 November 1938) welcomed the play, praising Heming-

> Having no faculty for speech making and no command of oratory nor any domination of rhetoric I wish to thank the administrators of the generosity of Alfred Nobel for this prize.
>
> No writer who knows the great writers who did not receive the prize can receive it other than with humility. There is no need to list these writers. Everyone here may make his own list according to his knowlege and his conscience.
>
> It would be impossible for me to ask the Ambassador of my country to read a speech in which I said all of the things which are in my heart. But I will try to write them.

Page from a manuscript draft of Hemingway's speech read at the Nobel Banquet (10 December 1954) by U.S. Ambassador John C. Cabot, as the author was unable to attend (Ernest Hemingway Collection, John F. Kennedy Library) way for having continued to recognize "that art must have its roots in social events" and asserting that "the whole of Hemingway's development" is "implicit in the character of Philip Rawlings."

In February 1939 Hemingway went to Cuba to begin writing his much-anticipated big book on the Spanish Civil War. Following him there in April, Gellhorn rented the Finca Vigía, near Havana. By summer 1940 he had finished his novel, and Pauline Hemingway had filed for divorce. *For Whom the Bell Tolls*, dedicated to Gellhorn, was published on 21 October 1940.

For Whom the Bell Tolls is the story of Robert Jordan, a college Spanish teacher from Montana who joins the Loyalist forces in Spain during the Spanish Civil War and is assigned to blow a bridge behind Fascist lines in order to prevent Fascist troops from crossing the bridge during a Loyalist attack. Jordan is another Hemingway character who accepts his "orders" and performs his duty heroically. Like *A Farewell to Arms*, this novel is a story of love and war, or love and death, but unlike *A Farewell to Arms* or *The Sun Also Rises*, *For Whom the Bell Tolls* has a more compressed time frame, sixty-eight hours, requiring extensive use of flashbacks and recollections by characters in order to show the scope and complex history of the conflict. Hemingway used also a third-person, omniscient narrator rather than the first-person narrator of his first two major novels, broadening the dimensions of character consciousness, moving from the spare language of early stories and novels to more rhetorical and lyrical passages, appropriate for the romantic and heroic character he had created in Robert Jordan. After completing the novel, Hemingway took its title from John Donne's "Meditation 17" (1624) with its "No Man is an Island" theme. Hemingway had shown that while participants in the war were bound by their common humanity, they were also bound by a common capacity for murderous action, Communists and Fascists alike. Robert Jordan discovers that "to get a full picture of what is happening you cannot read only the party organ." Hemingway had told an American Writers' Congress in 1937, "It is very dangerous to write the truth in war, and the truth is also very dangerous to come by." He demonstrated this fact in *For Whom the Bell Tolls*.

Although reviewers in the leftist journals condemned the novel that attacked Communists and the Communist leaders in the Spanish Civil War, *For Whom the Bell Tolls* received positive reviews in major American newspapers and in leading magazines. It was hailed by many as the best book Hemingway had written, showing continued growth of Hemingway's novelistic talent since *The Sun Also Rises* and *A Farewell to Arms*. Howard Mumford Jones wrote in *The Saturday Review of Literature* (26 October 1940) that it was "one of the finest and richest novels of the decade." An unnamed reviewer for *Time* (21 October 1940) who had feared that Hemingway had declined "past the point of recovery" said that with the appearance of *For Whom the Bell Tolls* Hemingway had again "emerged as a sensitive artist." The reviews were consistent with the public reception. The Book-of-the-Month Club selected it, and Paramount Pictures paid $100,000 for movie rights. The novel sold 491,000 copies within six months of its publication. Hemingway's critical reputation, which had declined throughout the 1930s, had once again been restored, and his fame and fortune had never been greater. His divorce from Pauline Hemingway became final on 4 November 1940, and he and Gellhorn were married at Sun Valley, Idaho, on 21 November.

As biographer Michael Reynolds observed, Hemingway's continuing insistence that prizes were not important to him was not accurate. When the Pulitzer Prize Committee announced that there would be no award for fiction for 1940, when *For Whom the Bell Tolls* would have been the probable winner, Hemingway was disappointed but responded characteristically in an interview for the *St. Louis Star-Times* (23 May 1941): "If I'd won that prize . . . I'd think I was slipping. I've been writing for twenty years and never have won a prize. I've gotten along alright." Although the Nobel Prize was not awarded during the years 1940 to 1943, Hemingway had begun to think of himself as a serious contender for it following the success of *For Whom the Bell Tolls*.

After the publication of *For Whom the Bell Tolls*, Hemingway's literary productivity waned. At the end of 1940 he bought the Finca Vigía, and he and Gellhorn left at the beginning of the new year to cover the war in China, Gellhorn for *Collier's* and Hemingway for *PM*, a liberal New York tabloid. In his dispatches for *PM* he often appeared prophetic, predicting that the United States would be forced into war when Japan attacked American bases in the Pacific. Yet, he produced just eight articles during his Far East assignment, "only enough," he said, "to keep from being sent home." In the spring of 1942 he edited and wrote an introduction for the anthology *Men at War*, which was published in October.

With an influx of Nazi agents into Cuba and U-boats steadily sinking ships in the Caribbean, Hemingway proposed to officials at the American Embassy and to the U.S. ambassador to Cuba that he set up a private counterintelligence agency. The Cuban prime minister granted him permission, and Hemingway organized a group he called the Crook Factory and outfitted his fishing boat the *Pilar* for U-boat surveillance. During this time Hemingway's drinking increased, and his marriage deteriorated as Gellhorn spent more time away from Cuba on journalistic assignments.

At the end of October 1943 Gellhorn left Cuba again to cover the war in Europe for *Collier's*. Early in 1944 Hemingway usurped her position with the magazine, agreeing to go to Europe for *Collier's* as their front-line correspondent, a role women were not permitted to fill. Hemingway began an affair with Mary Welsh, an American journalist in London whose marriage to Australian reporter Noel Monks also had become fragile. On D-Day, 6 June 1944, Hemingway was on a landing craft taking soldiers ashore at Omaha Beach. Biographer Michael Reynolds records that after taking German machine-gun fire trained on the boat, the lieutenant in charge put back out to sea and rejoined the attack transport *Dorothea M. Dix* that Hemingway reboarded, losing his opportunity to go ashore on D-Day (though Gellhorn did go ashore from a hospital ship on 7 June). Ten other landing craft were destroyed attempting to land. Reporting on the confusion, fear, death, and destruction, Hemingway observed, "Real war is never like paper war, nor do accounts of it read much the way it looks."

After a brief assignment as a correspondent with General George Patton's Third Army, Hemingway was assigned to the Twenty-second Infantry Regiment, where he acted as an irregular soldier, often violating his noncombatant status. Recalling his feelings about Paris as he looked down on the city with American forces of liberation, he wrote, "I couldn't say anything more then, because I had a funny choke in my throat and I had to clean my glasses because there now, below us, gray and always beautiful, was spread the city I love best in all the world." On 25 August 1944 Hemingway entered Paris with the American and French armies.

He contributed only six articles to *Collier's* recounting his observations as a correspondent during the war. However, he wrote to Welsh from Belgium that he had material for four short stories that would provide funds while he wrote a novel. In March 1945 Hemingway returned to Cuba, and Welsh arrived shortly afterward. On 14 March 1946, their respective divorces final, Hemingway and Welsh were married in Havana.

Hemingway began an ambitious writing project in 1945, a trilogy that would encompass the land, sea, and air from the mid 1930s to the mid 1940s. He had not published any fiction for five years. He returned to a Bimini fragment he had begun before going to London in 1944 that became *Islands in the Stream* (1970). By 1946 he was also writing a novel he called *The Garden of Eden* (1986). Both novels were published posthumously. News stories and magazine articles about him increased; Hollywood bought more of his work; and the Hemingway legend grew. In 1947 he was awarded the Bronze Star for his war service during 1944.

In September 1948 the Hemingways went to Italy. In Venice he met Adriana Ivancich, an attractive eighteen-year-old girl who became Hemingway's fantasy and regenerative muse. By March 1949 he had begun a new novel, *Across the River and Into the Trees*, about the dying fifty-year-old Colonel Cantwell, who while duck hunting east of Venice during the final weekend of his life recalls to himself a past in which he was wounded and scarred, but undefeated. All is set in bold relief by the presence of a young woman with whom the colonel has found love. The hunt itself serves as a metaphor for one last example of the pattern of conduct by which the colonel has lived his life and by which he faces his impending death, aware that "the shooting is over" but that he has "shot well." The novel was published on 7 September 1950.

Reviewers were highly polarized in their assessments of *Across the River and Into the Trees*. Many were hostile and vitriolic. Cyril Connolly called Cantwell "a drink-sodden and maundering old bore," and Morton Zabel thought the "new novel the poorest thing its author has ever done." Yet, a *Newsweek* reviewer called *Across the River and Into the Trees* Hemingway's "best and most carefully thought out book," and although he was not referring to *Across the River and Into the Trees*, O'Hara called Hemingway "the most important author living today, the outstanding author since the death of Shakespeare" (*The New York Times Book Review*, 10 September 1950).

Hemingway's response to the bad reviews suggests that he was aware of his vulnerability as he looked forward to a better era of criticism "when books are read and criticized, rather than personalities attacked" (*The New York Times Book Review*, 3 December 1950). As often had been the case, negative reviews had little effect upon the sales of the novel. The first printing of 75,000 copies sold out rapidly, and by the end of the year 125,000 copies had been sold. On Christmas Eve 1950 Hemingway finished a draft of *Islands in the Stream*.

On 10 November 1950 it was announced that William Faulkner had won the Nobel Prize in Literature for 1949. Two other American writers had been under consideration for the award: John Steinbeck and Hemingway. The selection of Faulkner was more disappointing to Hemingway than that of any other previous recipient. Hemingway saw it as the most prestigious affirmation of Faulkner's superiority over him.

Hemingway began writing what he considered a final section of the sea portion of his planned land, sea, and air trilogy: the story of an old Cuban fisherman who had gone eighty-four days without catching a fish and who had taken his small boat far out to sea where he hooked and fought a giant marlin for three days. After lashing the great fish to his boat, he must fight sharks that devour the fish. Hemingway clearly identified with the circumstances of the old man, who had not had a big fish for a long time, but who was "born" to fish. The conditions under which Hemingway was pursuing his art by 1951 were the most difficult he had faced. Although he was only fifty-one years old, his physical condition had deteriorated during the last decade as a result of serious head injuries, infections, and alcohol abuse, all of which exacerbated his depression.

Hemingway worked rapidly to complete *The Old Man and the Sea,* which was published in its entirety in *Life* magazine on 1 September 1952 with a printing of more than 5 million copies. The following week Scribners published it, and 50,000 copies sold out in ten days; the Book-of-the-Month Club distributed 153,000 copies. Most reviewers were effusive in their praise of the novella, saying that Hemingway had written a masterpiece and that he had returned to his true form. Canby thought Hemingway had "no superiors in the art of writing about the sea in any language" (*Book of the Month Club News,* August 1952). W. M. Frohock said in *Southwest Review* (Winter 1953), "We had been waiting for something of such quality" from Hemingway since 1940 and thought *The Old Man and the Sea* gave "clear evidence that he has all his powers." Unlike *Across the River and Into the Trees* with its "garrulous colonel" (*Harper's,* October 1952), the new Hemingway book was a "stripped, lean, objective narrative" (*Atlantic,* September 1952) without "self-indulgence" (*New Republic,* 6 October 1952). Paul Pickerel reported in *The Yale Review* (Autumn 1952) that "the critical keening" for Hemingway "was premature." Faulkner began his brief review of the novella with the words "His best," and he added that the book might prove to be "the best single piece of any of us" (*Shenandoah,* Autumn 1952). *The Old Man and the Sea* remained twenty-six weeks on *The New York Times* best-seller list and was rushed into translations throughout the world.

Responding to speculation that he might receive the Nobel Prize, Hemingway said in a 27 June 1952 letter to Harvey Breit that it meant nothing to him because he had "no respect for that institution." But when he considered that *The Old Man and the Sea* might be read by as many as five million readers, that, he said, was a greater honor than winning the Nobel Prize. In May 1953 Hemingway was awarded the Pulitzer Prize.

By the end of August the Hemingways had gone to Africa for a safari. At the conclusion of the safari, an airplane sight-seeing trip on 23 January 1954 proved nearly fatal when their pilot crash-landed, leaving Mary Hemingway with broken ribs and Hemingway with back, shoulder, and arm injuries. A second plane crashed while attempting takeoff the following day, causing Hemingway serious internal injuries and a concussion. When an air search found the wreckage with no one nearby, newspapers throughout the world carried obituaries for Hemingway and his wife. Hemingway reported in "The Christmas Gift" (*Look,* 20 April and 4 May 1954) that he had been unable to resist reading his obituaries, referring to them as his "new and attractive vice" as he observed the inaccuracies of reporters. He said that a German newspaper reported that he had attempted to land one of the airplanes himself on the summit of Mount Kilimanjaro, and an Italian paper carried comments by people who called themselves his "only true and intimate friends . . . who knew the innermost contents of my heart." Nearly all obituaries, he said, "emphasized that I had sought death all my life," an observation he rejected.

After Hemingway's near-fatal crashes, several members of the Swedish Academy expressed regret that they had not awarded him a Nobel Prize in previous years. He had been passed over for the Nobel Prize for 1953, although he had been rumored as the probable recipient, when the committee awarded it to Sir Winston Churchill.

For Hemingway 1954 became a year of prizes. In March he accepted the Award of Merit Medal from the American Academy of Arts and Letters, and upon his return to Cuba he accepted on his fifty-fifth birthday Cuba's highest award: the Order of Carlos Manuel de Cespedes.

On 28 October 1954 it was announced that Ernest Hemingway was the winner of the Nobel Prize in Literature "for his powerful, style-forming mastery of the art of modern narration, as most recently evinced in *The Old Man and the Sea.*" He was the fifth American writer to win the prize. Charles Poore wrote in *The New York Times* (29 October 1954) that "Hemingway more than any other writer of his time in America, has given new directions to the course of story telling, new cadences in prose, particularly in dialogue." Anders Österling, the Permanent Secretary of the Swedish Academy, observed in his presentation speech that Hemingway's work demonstrates "an artistic self-discipline of uncommon strength." He noted also Hemingway's central theme—"the bearing of one who is put to the test and who steels himself to meet the cold cruelty of existence, without, by doing so, repudiating the great and generous moments" and who shows that "a man can be destroyed but not defeated." Hemingway was also praised because he had written not "to illustrate theses and principles of one kind or another." Österling declared that the 1954 prize "has therefore been awarded to one of the great authors of our time, one of those who, honestly and undauntedly, reproduces genuine features in the hard countenance of the age."

Biographer Reynolds concurred with the observations of the Nobel Committee, pointing out that Hemingway remained an experimental writer throughout his life and that, although he was not always successful, Hemingway consistently attempted innovative structure, challenging conventions in each new novel. Hemingway was in the vanguard of his craft, testing the genres, including stories within stories, writing about fiction within fiction, and laying the groundwork for many of those postmodernists who followed him.

Hemingway accepted the Nobel Prize in Literature graciously, expressing pleasure and pride, wishing that Twain and Henry James could have received the award, too (*The New York Times*, 29 October and 7 November 1954). During a *Time* magazine interview (13 December 1954) he took the opportunity to make a plea for Pound, "a great poet," who had been committed to an insane asylum to spare him from trial and possible execution for actions judged treasonable during World War II. It was time, Hemingway said, that Pound be free to write poems again.

Hemingway did not attend the Nobel award ceremony, excusing himself because of his recent injuries. He returned to work, writing steadily on a new African book and assisting in the filming of *The Old Man and the Sea* until illnesses, including hepatitis, put him in bed from November 1955 to January 1956. By fall Hemingway was well enough to travel to Europe, and he and Mary Hemingway stayed in Paris until January 1957. Hemingway suffered from deteriorating health during much of the trip, and by the time he sailed for the United States he had high blood pressure and an enlarged liver.

Back in Cuba, despite his poor health and constant interruptions, Hemingway returned to his work: an African book (*True at First Light*, 1999), *The Garden of Eden* (1986), and a new project, *A Moveable Feast* (1964), a memoir about Paris in the 1920s. As revolutionary activity increased in Cuba, Hemingway feared he would be a target during the overthrow of the Batista government, and he and his wife left Cuba for Ketchum, Idaho. They departed for Spain in 1959 after Hemingway agreed to write about the bullfight season for *Life* magazine. During the Spanish trip he displayed erratic behavior and hostility.

Hemingway went back to Spain in August 1960 to gather more material but returned to Ketchum in October. His depression and insomnia growing, his paranoia more obvious, and his nerves uncontrollable, he entered the Mayo Clinic in Rochester, Minnesota, at the end of November and underwent a series of electroshock therapy treatments. He was released on 22 January 1961. By March, Hemingway's depression had returned, and he had to be restrained because of suicide attempts. He returned to the Mayo Clinic for additional electroshock therapy on 25 April and was released on 26 June, his psychiatrist confident of Hemingway's improvement. Back in Idaho, in the early morning of 2 July 1961, Hemingway killed himself with one of his favorite shotguns.

Five Hemingway books have been published posthumously. *A Moveable Feast*, edited by Mary Hemingway, includes twenty sketches of persons Hemingway knew in Paris in the 1920s, many of whom were important to his career–Fitzgerald, Stein, Pound, and Ford–and his recollections of his experiences during his apprentice years. Although critics praised the craft and artistry of the memoir and the opportunity to read Hemingway's recollections, they found many of his portraits, especially that of Fitzgerald, nasty and mean.

Islands in the Stream was a novel Hemingway intended to be part of the sea portion of the planned trilogy. It is the story of painter Thomas Hudson. The novel is divided into three sections. The first, "Bimini," takes place during the summer of 1934 or 1935 when Hudson is visited by his three sons, with whom he fishes and swims and shares memories of his early life in Paris. The second, "Cuba," is set in Havana in February 1944 when Hudson chases German U-boats and drinks heavily as he learns that his three sons have been killed. The third, "At Sea," occurs during May 1944 as Hudson searches for the crew of a sunk German submarine, finds them, kills them, and is probably mortally wounded following the battle. *Islands in the Stream* is of uneven quality; nevertheless, readers found good writing and powerful scenes in individual sections while acknowledging that the novel was a work in progress, lacking Hemingway's finishing touch.

Originally cut for publication in *Life* magazine in 1960, *The Dangerous Summer* (1985) is a nonfiction book, edited by others, about the bullfight competition in Spain in 1959 between Antonio Ordóñez and Luis Miguel Domínguín, two of Spain's best matadors. In addition to its focus upon the bullfights, the book includes descriptions of the Spanish landscape, comments about food and wine, strategies in the art of bullfighting, and interpretations of the complex psychology Hemingway associated with the matadors. The writing sometimes unclear and confusing, *The Dangerous Summer* was not well received by critics, who saw it as inferior work, written at the low point of Hemingway's deterioration.

Considered his most complex and provocative posthumously published book, *The Garden of Eden* is set primarily in the south of France during the spring and fall of 1923. It is the story of writer David Bourne and his new wife, Catherine, a bisexual who insists upon sexual role reversals with her husband and bringing another woman into their lives and bed. The novel depicts Catherine's resentment of David's career and her increasing mental instability. She finally burns his manuscripts and destroys their marriage. In his fullest treatment of the theme of androgyny, Hemingway demonstrates in *The Garden of Eden* the primacy of art in the life of the artist, the artist's resiliency, and the essential solitariness of the creative process. Many critics disapproved of Scribners' editing of the manuscript, which was reduced to one-third of its original content, but they were cautiously receptive to the novel, recognizing what they regarded as a new direction for a major writer who had continued to develop.

On 21 July 1999, in honor of Hemingway's centennial anniversary, Scribners published *True at First Light,* edited by Hemingway's son Patrick. It is based upon Hemingway's experiences during his African safari in 1953. The text recalls his service as a temporary game warden when he claimed to protect a village against hostile attacks while immersing himself in African culture that enabled him to adopt a new persona other than that of "literary character." It was republished uncut as *Under Kilimanjaro* (2005).

Following Ernest Hemingway's death, authors, critics, and literary historians throughout the world spoke of his reputation and legacy. *The New York Times* (3 July 1961) carried several responses: Trilling said, "There is no one in the whole range of literature of the modern world who has a better claim than he to be acknowledged as a master." Van Wyck Brooks saw Hemingway as "the inventor of a style that has influenced other writers more than any other in our time." C. P. Snow said, "No novelist in the world has produced such a direct effect on other people's writing." Robert Frost observed, "His style dominated our story-telling long and short." And Faulkner proclaimed, "He is not dead. Generations not yet born of young men and women who want to write will refute that word as applied to him."

Letters:

Ernest Hemingway: Selected Letters, 1917–1961, edited by Carlos Baker (New York: Scribners, 1981);

Hemingway in Love and War: The Lost Diary of Agnes von Kurowsky, Her Letters and Correspondence of Ernest Hemingway, edited by Henry Serrano Villard and James Nagel (Boston: Northeastern University Press, 1989);

The Only Thing That Counts: The Ernest Hemingway/Maxwell Perkins Correspondence, 1927–1947, edited by Matthew J. Bruccoli (New York: Scribners, 1996);

At the Hemingways: With Fifty Years of Correspondence Between Ernest and Marcelline Hemingway (Moscow, Idaho: University of Idaho Press, 1999);

Dear Papa, Dear Hotch: The Correspondence of Ernest Hemingway and A. E. Hotchner, edited by Albert J. DeFazio III (Columbia: University of Missouri Press, 2005).

Interviews:

Conversations with Ernest Hemingway, edited by Matthew J. Bruccoli (Jackson: University Press of Mississippi, 1986).

Bibliographies:

Audre Hanneman, *Ernest Hemingway: A Comprehensive Bibliography* (Princeton: Princeton University Press, 1967);

Philip Young and Charles W. Mann, *The Hemingway Manuscripts: An Inventory* (University Park & London: Pennsylvania State University Press, 1969);

Jackson J. Benson, "A Comprehensive Checklist of Hemingway Short Fiction Criticism, Explication and Commentary," in *The Short Stories of Ernest Hemingway: Critical Essays,* edited by Benson (Durham, N.C.: Duke University Press, 1975), pp. 312–375;

Hanneman, *Supplement to Ernest Hemingway: A Comprehensive Bibliography* (Princeton: Princeton University Press, 1975);

Linda Welshimer Wagner, *Ernest Hemingway: A Reference Guide* (Boston: G. K. Hall, 1977);

Jo August, *Catalog of the Ernest Hemingway Collection at the John F. Kennedy Library,* 2 volumes (Boston: G. K. Hall, 1982).

Biographies:

Carlos Baker, *Ernest Hemingway: A Life Story* (New York: Scribners, 1969);

Mary Welsh Hemingway, *How It Was* (New York: Knopf, 1976);

Peter Griffin, *Along With Youth: Hemingway: The Early Years* (New York: Oxford University Press, 1985);

Jeffrey Meyers, *Hemingway: A Biography* (New York: Harper & Row, 1985);

Michael Reynolds, *The Young Hemingway* (Oxford: Blackwell, 1986);

Reynolds, *Hemingway: The Paris Years* (Oxford: Blackwell, 1989);

Griffin, *Less Than a Treason: Hemingway in Paris* (New York: Oxford University Press, 1990);

James R. Mellow, *Hemingway: A Life without Consequences* (Boston: Houghton Mifflin, 1992);

Reynolds, *Hemingway: The American Homecoming* (Oxford: Blackwell, 1992);

Matthew J. Bruccoli, *Fitzgerald and Hemingway: A Dangerous Friendship* (New York: Carroll & Graf, 1994; London: André Deutsch, 1995);

William Burrill, *Hemingway: The Toronto Years* (Toronto: Doubleday Canada, 1994);

Reynolds, *Hemingway: The 1930s* (New York: Norton, 1997);

Reynolds, *Hemingway: The Final Years* (New York: Norton, 1999).

References:

Carlos Baker, *Hemingway: The Writer as Artist,* fourth edition (Princeton: Princeton University Press, 1972);

Susan F. Beegel, *Hemingway's Craft of Omission: Four Manuscript Examples* (Ann Arbor: UMI Research Press, 1988);

Matthew J. Bruccoli and C. E. Frazer Clark Jr., comps., *Hemingway at Auction, 1930-1973* (Detroit: Gale, 1973);

Morley Callaghan, *That Summer in Paris* (New York: Coward-McCann, 1963);

Scott Donaldson, *The Cambridge Companion to Hemingway* (Cambridge & New York: Cambridge University Press, 1996);

Charles A. Fenton, *The Apprenticeship of Ernest Hemingway* (New York: Farrar, Straus & Young, 1954);

Fitzgerald/Hemingway Annual (Washington, D.C.: Microcard Editions, 1969-1976; Detroit: Bruccoli Clark/Gale, 1977-1979);

Hemingway Notes (1971-1974, 1979-1981);

Hemingway Review (1981-);

Nicholas Joost, *Ernest Hemingway and the Little Magazines: The Paris Years* (Barre, Mass.: Barre Publishers, 1968);

Bernice Kert, *The Hemingway Women* (New York: Norton, 1983);

Harold Loeb, *The Way It Was* (New York: Criterion, 1959);

George Monteiro, ed., *Critical Essays on Ernest Hemingway's A Farewell to Arms* (New York: G. K. Hall, 1994);

James Nagel, ed., *Critical Essays on Ernest Hemingway's The Sun Also Rises* (New York: G. K. Hall, 1995);

Michael Reynolds, *Hemingway: An Annotated Chronology* (Detroit: Manly/Omnigraphics, 1991);

Reynolds, *Hemingway's First War: The Making of A Farewell to Arms* (Princeton: Princeton University Press, 1976);

Reynolds, *Hemingway's Reading, 1910-1940* (Princeton: Princeton University Press, 1981);

Bertram D. Sarason, *Hemingway and the Sun Set* (Washington, D.C.: Bruccoli Clark/NCR Microcard Editions, 1972).

Papers:

Ernest Hemingway's papers are located at the John F. Kennedy Library in Boston, Massachusetts. Other major collections are found at the Princeton University Library; the Harry Ransom Humanities Research Center, University of Texas at Austin; the University of Virginia Library; The Lilly Library, Indiana University; the University of Delaware Library; and the University of South Carolina.

1954 Nobel Prize in Literature Presentation Speech

by Anders Österling, Permanent Secretary of the Swedish Academy

In our modern age, American authors have set their stamp more and more strongly on the general physiognomy of literature. Our generation in particular has, during the last few decades, seen a reorientation of literary interest which implies not only a temporary change in the market but, indeed, a shifting of the mental horizon, with far-reaching consequences. All these swiftly rising new authors from the United States, whose names we now recognize as stimulating signals, had one thing in common: they took full advantage of the Americanism to which they were born. And the European public greeted them with enthusiasm; it was the general wish that Americans should write as Americans, thereby making their own contribution to the contest in the international arena.

One of these pioneers is the author who is now the focus of attention. It is hardly an exaggeration to say that Ernest Hemingway, more than any of his American colleagues, makes us feel we are confronted by a still young nation which seeks and finds its exact form of expression. A dramatic tempo and sharp curves have also characterized Hemingway's own existence, in many ways so unlike that of the average literary man. With him, this vital energy goes its own way, independent of the pessimism and the disillusionment so typical of the age. Hemingway evolved his style in the herd school of journalistic reporting. In the editorial office of the Kansas City newspaper where he served his apprenticeship, there was a kind of pressman's catechism, the first dictum of which was: "Use short sentences. Use short paragraphs." Hemingway's purely technical training clearly led to an artistic self-discipline of uncommon strength. Rhetoric, he has said, is merely the blue sparks from the dynamo. His master in older American literature was Mark Twain in *Huckleberry Finn,* with its rhythmical stream of direct and unconventional narrative prose.

The young journalist from Illinois was flung headlong into the First World War when he volunteered to serve as an ambulance driver in Italy, where he received his baptism of fire at the Piave front and was severely wounded by shell splinters. The nineteen-year-old's first violent experience of war is an essential factor in Hemingway's biography. Not that he was daunted by it; on the contrary, he found that it was a priceless asset for a writer to see war at first hand—like Tolstoy at Sevastopol—and to be able to depict it truthfully. Several years were to elapse, however, before he could bring himself to give an artistically complete account of his painfully confused impressions from the Piave front in 1918: the result was the novel *A Farewell to Arms* in 1929, with which he really made his name, even if two very talented books with a European post-war setting, *In Our Time* (1925) and *The Sun Also Rises* (1926), had already given proof of his individuality as a storyteller. In the following years, his instinctive predilection for harrowing scenes of action and grim spectacle drew him to Africa with its big-game hunting and to Spain with its bullfighting. When the latter country was transformed into a theatre of war, he found inspiration there for his second significant novel, *For Whom the Bell Tolls* (1940), in which an American champion of liberty fights for "man's dignity"—a book in which the writer's personal feelings seem more deeply involved than anywhere else.

When mentioning these principal elements in his production, one should not forget that his narrative skill often attains its highest point when cast in a smaller mould, in the laconic, drastically pruned short story, which, with a unique combination of simplicity and precision, nails its theme into our consciousness so that every blow tells. Such a masterpiece, more than any other, is *The Old Man and the Sea* (1952), the unforgettable story of an old Cuban fisherman's duel with a huge swordfish in the Atlantic. Within the frame of a sporting tale, a moving perspective of man's destiny is opened up; the story is a tribute to the fighting spirit, which does not give in even if the material gain is nil, a tribute to the moral victory in the midst of defeat. The drama is enacted before our eyes, hour by hour, allowing the robust details to accumulate and take on momentous significance. "But man is not made for defeat," the book says. "A man can be destroyed but not defeated."

It may be true that Hemingway's earlier writings display brutal, cynical, and callous sides which may be considered at variance with the Nobel Prize's requirement for a work of an ideal tendency. But on the other hand, he also possesses a heroic pathos which forms the basic element in his awareness of life, a manly love of danger and adventure with a natural admiration for every individual who fights the good fight in a world of reality overshadowed by violence and death. In any event, this is the positive side of his cult of manliness, which otherwise is apt to become demonstrative, thereby defeating its own ends. It should be remembered, however, that courage is Hemingway's central theme—the bearing of one who is put to the test and who steels himself to meet the cold cruelty of existence, without, by so doing, repudiating the great and generous moments.

On the other hand, Hemingway is not one of those authors who write to illustrate theses and principles of one kind or another. A descriptive writer must be objective and not try to play God the Father—this he learned while still in the editorial office in Kansas City. That is why he can conceive of war as a tragic fate having a decisive effect on the whole of his generation; but he views it with a calm realism, void of illusion, which disdains all emotional comment, a disciplined objectivity, stronger because it is hard-won.

Hemingway's significance as one of this epoch's great moulders of style is apparent in both American and European narrative art over the past twenty-five years, chiefly in the vivid dialogue and the verbal thrust and parry, in which he has set a standard as easy to imitate as it is difficult to attain. With masterly skill he reproduces all the nuances of the spoken word, as well as those pauses in which thought stands still and the nervous mechanism is thrown out of gear. It may sometimes sound like small talk, but it is not trivial when one gets to know his method. He prefers to leave the work of psychological reflection to his readers, and this freedom is of great benefit to him in spontaneous observation.

When one surveys Hemingway's production, definite scenes flare up in the memory—Lieutenant Henry's flight in the rain and mud after the panic at Caporetto, the desperate blowing up of the bridge in the Spanish mountains when Jordan sacrifices his life, or the old fisherman's solitary fight with the sharks in the nocturnal glow of lights from Havana.

Moreover, one may trace a distinctive linking thread—let us say a symbolic warp reaching back a hundred years in the loom of time—between Hemingway's latest work, *The Old Man and The Sea,* and one of the classic creations of American literature, Herman Melville's novel *Moby Dick,* the white whale who is pursued in blind rage by his enemy, the monomaniac sea captain. Neither Melville nor Hemingway wanted to create an allegory; the salt ocean depths with all their monsters are sufficiently rewarding as a poetic element. But with different means, those of romanticism and of realism, they both attain the same theme—a man's capacity of endurance and, if need be, of at least daring the impossible. "A man can be destroyed but not defeated."

This year's Nobel Prize in Literature has therefore been awarded to one of the great authors of our time, one of those who, honestly and undauntedly, reproduces genuine features in the hard countenance of the age. Hemingway, now fifty-six years old, is the fifth American author so far to be honoured in this way. As the Prize winner himself is unfortunately unable to be present for reasons of health, the Prize will now be handed to the United States Ambassador.

[© The Nobel Foundation, 1954.]

Hemingway: Banquet Speech

Introductory remarks by H. S. Nyberg, Member of the Swedish Academy, at the Nobel Banquet at the City Hall in Stockholm, 10 December 1954:

Another deep regret is that the winner of this year's Nobel Prize in Literature, Mr. Ernest Hemingway, on account of ill health has to be absent from our celebration. We wish to express our admiration for the eagle eye with which he has observed, and for the accuracy with which he has interpreted the human existence of our turbulent times; also for the admirable restraint with which he has described their naked struggle. The human problems which he has treated are relevant to all of us, living as we do in the confused conditions of modern life; and few authors have exercised such a wide influence on contemporary literature in all countries. It is our sincere hope that he will soon recover health and strength in pursuit of his life-work.

As Hemingway was unable to be present, the speech was read by John C. Cabot, United States Ambassador

Having no facility for speech-making and no command of oratory nor any domination of rhetoric, I wish to thank the administrators of the generosity of Alfred Nobel for this Prize.

No writer who knows the great writers who did not receive the Prize can accept it other than with humility. There is no need to list these writers. Everyone here may make his own list according to his knowledge and his conscience.

It would be impossible for me to ask the Ambassador of my country to read a speech in which a writer said all of the things which are in his heart. Things may not be immediately discernible in what a man writes, and in this sometimes he is fortunate; but eventually they are quite clear and by these and the degree of alchemy that he possesses he will endure or be forgotten.

Writing, at its best, is a lonely life. Organizations for writers palliate the writer's loneliness but I doubt if they improve his writing. He grows in public stature as he sheds his loneliness and often his work deteriorates. For he does his work alone and if he is a good enough writer he must face eternity, or the lack of it, each day.

For a true writer each book should be a new beginning where he tries again for something that is beyond attainment. He should always try for something that has never been done or that others have tried and failed. Then sometimes, with great luck, he will succeed.

How simple the writing of literature would be if it were only necessary to write in another way what has been well written. It is because we have had such great writers in the past that a writer is driven far out past where he can go, out to where no one can help him.

I have spoken too long for a writer. A writer should write what he has to say and not speak it. Again I thank you.

[© The Nobel Foundation, 1954. Ernest Hemingway is the sole author of his speech.]

Hermann Hesse
(2 July 1877 – 9 August 1962)

Joseph Mileck
University of California, Berkeley

This entry was expanded by Mileck from his Hesse entry in *DLB 66: German Fiction Writers, 1885–1913*.

SELECTED BOOKS: *Romantische Lieder* (Dresden & Leipzig: Pierson, 1899);

Eine Stunde hinter Mitternacht (Leipzig: Diederichs, 1899);

Hinterlassene Schriften und Gedichte von Hermann Lauscher: Herausgegeben von Hermann Hesse (Basel: Reich, 1901);

Gedichte (Berlin: Grote, 1902); republished as *Jugendgedichte* (Hamm: Grote, 1950);

Boccaccio (Berlin & Leipzig: Schuster & Loeffler, 1904);

Franz von Assisi (Berlin & Leipzig: Schuster & Loeffler, 1904);

Peter Camenzind (Berlin: Fischer, 1904); translated by W. J. Strachan (London: Owen, 1961); translated by Michael Roloff (New York: Farrar, Straus & Giroux, 1969);

Unterm Rad (Berlin: Fischer, 1906); translated by Strachan as *The Prodigy* (London: Owen, Vision, 1957); translated by Roloff as *Beneath the Wheel* (New York: Farrar, Straus & Giroux, 1968);

Diesseits: Erzählungen (Berlin: Fischer, 1907; enlarged edition, 1930);

Selma Lagerlöf (Munich: Langen, 1907);

Nachbarn: Erzählungen (Berlin: Fischer, 1908);

Gertrud: Roman (Munich: Langen, 1910); translated by Adèle Lewisohn as *Gertrud and I* (New York: International Monthly, 1915); translated by Hilde Rosner as *Gertrude* (London: Owen, 1955);

Unterwegs: Gedichte (Munich: Müller, 1911; enlarged edition, 1915);

Umwege: Erzählungen (Berlin: Fischer, 1912);

Aus Indien: Aufzeichnungen von einer indischen Reise (Berlin: Fischer, 1913);

Die Heimkehr (Wiesbaden: Volksbildungsverein, 1914);

In der alten Sonne (Berlin: Fischer, 1914);

Roßhalde (Berlin: Fischer, 1914); translated by Ralph Manheim as *Rosshalde* (New York: Farrar, Straus & Giroux, 1970);

Hermann Hesse, 1926 (Associated Press, Musée Suisse, Gret Widmann)

Der Lateinschüler (Hamburg: Verlag der Deutschen Dichter-Gedächtnis-Stiftung, 1914);

Am Weg (Konstanz: Reuss & Itta, 1915);

Musik des Einsamen: Neue Gedichte (Heilbronn: Salzer, 1915);

Knulp: Drei Geschichten aus dem Leben Knulps (Berlin: Fischer, 1915); translated by Manheim as *Knulp: Three Tales from the Life of Knulp* (New York: Farrar, Straus & Giroux, 1971);

Brief ins Feld (Munich-Pasing: Lang, 1916);

Zum Gedächtnis: Nachruf auf seinen Vater (Zurich: Polygraphisches Institut, 1916);

Hans Dierlamms Lehrzeit: Vorfrühling (Berlin: Künstlerdank-Gesellschaft, 1916);

Schön ist die Jugend: Zwei Erzählungen (Berlin: Fischer, 1916);

Alte Geschichten: Zwei Erzählungen (Bern: Bücherzentrale für deutsche Kriegsgefangene, 1918);

Zwei Märchen (Bern: Bücherzentrale für deutsche Kriegsgefangene, 1918);

Demian: Die Geschichte einer Jugend von Emil Sinclair (Berlin: Fischer, 1919); translated by N. H. Priday as *Demian* (New York: Boni & Liveright, 1923);

Kleiner Garten: Erlebnisse und Dichtungen (Vienna: Tal, 1919);

Märchen (Berlin: Fischer, 1919);

Zarathustras Wiederkehr: Ein Wort an die deutsche Jugend. Von einem Deutschen (Bern: Stämpfli, 1919);

Gedichte des Malers: Zehn Gedichte (Bern: Seldwyla, 1920);

Blick ins Chaos: Drei Aufsätze (Bern: Seldwyla, 1920);

Klingsors letzter Sommer: Erzählungen (Berlin: Fischer, 1920); "Klingsors letzter Sommer" translated by Richard Winston and Clara Winston as *Klingsor's Last Summer* (New York: Farrar, Straus & Giroux, 1970);

Wanderung: Aufzeichnungen (Berlin: Fischer, 1920); translated by James Wright as *Wandering: Notes and Sketches* (New York: Farrar, Straus & Giroux, 1972);

Elf Aquarelle aus dem Tessin (Munich: Recht, 1921);

Ausgewählte Gedichte (Berlin: Fischer, 1921);

Siddhartha: Eine indische Dichtung (Berlin: Fischer, 1922); translated by Rosner as *Siddhartha* (New York: New Directions, 1951; London: Owen, 1956);

Die Offizina Bodoni in Montagnola (Hellerau: Hegner, 1923);

Im Pressel'schen Gartenhaus: Eine Zeichnung aus dem alten Tübingen (Stettin, 1923);

Italien: Verse (Berlin: Euphorion, 1923);

Sinclairs Notizbuch (Zurich: Rascher, 1923);

Psychologia Balnearia oder Glossen eines Badener Kurgastes (Montagnola: Privately printed, 1924); republished as *Kurgast: Aufzeichnungen von einer Badener Kur* (Berlin: Fischer, 1925);

Aufzeichnungen eines Herrn im Sanatorium: Fragment aus einem nicht ausgeführten Roman (Vienna: Phaidon, 1925);

Erinnerung an Lektüre (Vienna: Braumüller, 1925);

Piktors Verwandlungen: Ein Märchen (Chemnitz: Gesellschaft der Bücherfreunde, 1925);

Bilderbuch: Schilderungen (Berlin: Fischer, 1926);

Die Nürnberger Reise (Berlin: Fischer, 1927);

Der schwere Weg (Leipzig: Wolf, 1927);

Der Steppenwolf (Berlin: Fischer, 1927); translated by Basil Creighton as *Steppenwolf* (New York: Holt, 1929; translation revised by Joseph Mileck, New York: Holt, Rinehart & Winston, 1963);

Verse im Krankenbett (Bern: Stämpfli, 1927);

Krisis: Ein Stück Tagebuch (Berlin: Fischer, 1928); translated by Manheim as *Crisis: Pages from a Diary* (New York: Farrar, Straus & Giroux, 1975);

Betrachtungen (Berlin: Fischer, 1928);

Eine Bibliothek der Weltliteratur (Leipzig: Reclam, 1929);

Trost der Nacht: Neue Gedichte (Berlin: Fischer, 1929);

Der Zyklon und andere Erzählungen (Berlin: Fischer, 1929);

Zum Gedächtnis unseres Vaters, by Hesse and A. Hesse (Tübingen: Wunderlich, 1930);

Narziss und Goldmund: Erzählung (Berlin: Fischer, 1930); translated by Geoffrey Dunlop as *Death and the Lover* (New York: Dodd, 1932); translated by Ursule Molinaro as *Narcissus and Goldmund* (New York: Farrar, Straus & Giroux, 1968);

Kinderseele und Ladidel: Zwei Erzählungen, edited by W. M. Dutton (Boston: D. C. Heath, 1930; London: Harrap, 1948);

Jahreszeiten: Zehn Gedichte (Zurich: Fretz, 1931);

Weg nach Innen: Vier Erzählungen (Berlin: Fischer, 1931);

Die Morgenlandfahrt: Eine Erzählung (Berlin: Fischer, 1932); translated by Rosner as *The Journey to the East* (London: Owen, Vision, 1956; New York: Noonday, 1957);

Kleine Welt: Erzählungen (Berlin: Fischer, 1933);

Schön ist die Jugend (Darmstadt: Winklers, 1933);

Vom Baum des Lebens: Ausgewählte Gedichte (Leipzig: Insel, 1934);

Fünf Gedichte (Zurich: Fretz, 1934);

Magie des Buches (Berlin: Privately printed, 1934);

Fabulierbuch: Erzählungen (Berlin: Fischer, 1935);

Das Haus der Träume: Eine unvollendete Dichtung (Olten: Vereinigung Oltner Bücherfreunde, 1936);

Stunden im Garten: Eine Idylle (Vienna: Bermann-Fischer, 1936);

Tragisch: Eine Erzählung (Vienna: Reichner, 1936);

Der Brunnen im Maulbronner Kreuzgang (Leipzig: Poeschel & Trepte, 1937);

Gedenkblätter (Berlin: Fischer, 1937; expanded edition, Zurich: Fretz & Wasmuth, 1947; expanded again, Frankfurt am Main: Suhrkamp, 1984);

Neue Gedichte (Berlin: Fischer, 1937);

Der lahme Knabe: Eine Erinnerung aus der Kindheit (Zurich: Fretz, 1937);

Ein Traum Josef Knechts: Zum 2. Juli 1937 (Montagnola: Privately printed, 1937);

Zehn Gedichte (Bern: Stämpfli, 1939);

Der Novalis: Aus den Papieren eines Altmodischen (Olten: Vereinigung Oltner Bücherfreunde, 1940);

Kleine Betrachtungen: Sechs Aufsätze (Bern: Stämpfli, 1941);

Die Gedichte (Zurich: Fretz & Wasmuth, 1942);

Das Glasperlenspiel: Versuch einer Lebensbeschreibung des Magister Ludi Josef Knecht samt Knechts hinterlassene Schriften, 2 volumes (Zurich: Fretz & Wasmuth, 1943); translated by Mervyn Savill as *Magister Ludi* (New York: Holt, 1949); translated by Clara Winston and Richard Winston as *The Glass Bead Game* (New York: Farrar, Straus & Giroux, 1969);

Zwei Aufsätze (Zurich: Fretz, 1945);

Berthold: Ein Romanfragment (Zurich: Fretz & Wasmuth, 1945);

Der Blütenzweig: Eine Auswahl aus den Gedichten (Zurich: Fretz & Wasmuth, 1945);

Zwei Briefe, by Hesse and Thomas Mann (St. Gallen: Tschudy, 1945);

Der Pfirsichbaum und andere Erzählungen: Werbegabe (Zurich: Büchergilde Gutenberg, 1945);

Rigi-Tagebuch 1945 (Bern: Stämpfli, 1945);

Traumfährte: Neue Erzählungen und Märchen (Zurich: Fretz & Wasmuth, 1945);

Eine Bibliothek der Weltliteratur: Mit den Aufsätzen "Magie des Buches" und "Lieblingslektüre" (Zurich: Classen, 1946);

Statt eines Briefes (Montagnola: Privately printed, 1946);

Dank an Goethe (Zurich: Classen, 1946);

Der Europäer (Berlin: Suhrkamp, 1946);

Feuerwerk: Aufsatz aus dem Jahre 1930 (Olten: Vereinigung Oltner Bücherfreunde, 1946);

Gedichte (Stuttgart & Bad Cannstatt: Cantz, 1946);

Späte Gedichte (St. Gallen: Tschudy, 1946);

Krieg und Frieden: Betrachtungen zu Krieg und Politik (Zurich: Fretz & Wasmuth, 1946);

Haus Zum Frieden: Aufzeichnungen eines Herrn im Sanatorium (Zurich: Johannes-Presse, 1947);

Heumond: Aus Kinderzeiten (Basel: Verein gute Schriften, 1947);

Stufen der Menschwerdung (Olten: Vereinigung Oltner Bücherfreunde, 1947);

Berg und See: Zwei Landschaftsstudien (Zurich: Büchergilde Gutenberg, 1948);

Blätter vom Tage (Zurich: Fretz, 1948);

Legende vom indischen König (Burgdorf: Jenzer, Berner Handpresse, 1948);

Frühe Prosa (Zurich: Fretz & Wasmuth, 1948);

Musikalische Notizen (N.p., 1948);

Notizen aus diesen Sommertagen (Basel: National-Zeitung, 1948);

Preziosität (N.p., 1948);

Die Stimmen und der Heilige: Ein Stück Tagebuch (N.p., 1948);

Zwei Erzählungen: Der Novalis, Der Zwerg, edited by Anna Jacobson and Anita Ascher (New York: Appleton-Century-Crofts, 1948);

Gerbersau (Tübingen: Wunderlich, 1949);

Glück (St. Gallen: Tschudy, 1949);

Aus vielen Jahren: Gedichte, Erzählungen und Bilder (Bern: Stämpfli, 1949);

Brief an einen schwäbischen Dichter, edited by W. Matheson (Olten: Vereinigung Oltner Bücherfreunde, 1950);

Zwei Briefe: An einen jungen Künstler; Das junge Genie (St. Gallen: Tschudy, 1950);

Gartenfreuden: Eine Bilderfolge, edited by K. Jud (Zurich: Die Arche, 1950);

Eine Auswahl, edited by R. Buchwald (Bielefeld, Hannover & Berlin: Velhagen & Klasing, 1951);

Bericht aus Normalien: Ein Fragment aus dem Jahre 1948 (Gelterkinden: Lustig, 1951);

Erinnerung an André Gide (St. Gallen: Tschudy, 1951);

Zwei Gedichte (St. Gallen: Tschudy, 1951);

Aus einem Notizbuch (St. Gallen: Tschudy, 1951);

Späte Prosa (Berlin: Suhrkamp, 1951);

Die Verlobung und andere Erzählungen (Berlin & Darmstadt: Deutsche Buchgemeinschaft, 1951);

Gesammelte Dichtungen, 6 volumes (Berlin & Frankfurt am Main: Suhrkamp, 1952); enlarged as *Gesammelte Schriften,* 7 volumes (Frankfurt am Main: Suhrkamp, 1957); enlarged again as *Gesammelte Werke in Zwölf Bänden,* 12 volumes (Frankfurt am Main: Suhrkamp, 1970);

Herbstliche Erlebnisse: Gedenkblatt für Otto Hartmann (St. Gallen: Tschudy, 1952);

Geburtstag: Ein Rundbrief. Juli 1952 (Montagnola: Privately printed, 1952);

Großväterliches (St. Gallen: Tschudy, 1952);

Hermann Hesse als Badener Kurgast, by Hesse, Robert Mächler, and Uli Münzel (St. Gallen: Tschudy, 1952);

Lektüre für Minuten: Ein paar Gedanken aus meinen Büchern und Briefen. Zu Ehren des fünfundsiebzigsten Geburtstages von Hermann Hesse (Bern: Stämpfli, 1952);

Rückblick: Ein Fragment aus der Zeit um 1937 (Zurich: Fretz, 1952);

Engadiner Erlebnisse: Ein Rundbrief (Zurich: Fretz, 1953);

Kaminfegerchen (St. Gallen: Tschudy, 1953);

Nachruf für Marulla: 1880–1953 (St. Gallen: Tschudy, 1953);

Über das Alter (Olten: Vereinigung Oltner Bücherfreunde, 1954);

Beschwörungen: Rundbrief im Februar 1954 (St. Gallen: Tschudy, 1954);

Die Nikobaren (Basel: National-Zeitung, 1954);

Notizblätter um Ostern (Montagnola: Privately printed, 1954);

Rundbrief aus Sils-Maria (St. Gallen: Tschudy, 1954);

Aquarelle aus dem Tessin (Baden-Baden: Klein, 1955);

Beschwörungen: Späte Prosa, neue Folge (Berlin: Suhrkamp, 1955);

Knopf-Annähen (Basel: National-Zeitung, 1955);

Abendwolken: Zwei Aufsätze; Abendwolken: Bei den Massageten (St. Gallen: Tschudy, 1956);

Weltanschauliche Briefe politischer Richtung (N.p., 1956);

Zwei jugendliche Erzählungen (Olten: Vereinigung Oltner Bücherfreunde, 1956);

Weihnachtsgaben und anderes (Montagnola: Privately printed, 1956);

Freunde: Erzählung (Olten: Vereinigung Oltner Bücherfreunde, 1957);

Malfreude, Malsorgen (N.p., 1957);

Tessin (Zurich: Verlag der Arche, 1957);

Der Trauermarsch: Gedenkblatt für einen Jugendkameraden (St. Gallen: Tschudy, 1957);

Wenkenhof: Eine romantische Jugenddichtung (Basel: National-Zeitung, 1957);

Antworten (St. Gallen: Tschudy, 1958);

Klein und Wagner: Erzählung (Berlin: Suhrkamp, 1958);

Vier späte Gedichte (St. Gallen: Tschudy, 1959);

Chinesische Legende (St. Gallen: Tschudy, 1959);

Freund Peter (Zurich: Fretz, 1959);

Sommerbrief (St. Gallen: Tschudy, 1959);

Ein paar Aufzeichnungen und Briefe (St. Gallen: Tschudy, 1960);

Bericht an die Freunde: Letzte Gedichte (Olten: Vereinigung Oltner Bücherfreunde, 1960);

An einen Musiker (Olten: Vereinigung Oltner Bücherfreunde, 1960);

Rückgriff (St. Gallen: Tschudy, 1960);

Aus einem Tagebuch des Jahres 1920 (Zurich: Arche, 1960);

Stufen: Alte und neue Gedichte in Auswahl (Frankfurt am Main: Suhrkamp, 1961);

Tractat vom Steppenwolf (Frankfurt am Main: Suhrkamp, 1961); translated by B. Creighton as *Treatise on the Steppenwolf*, with paintings by Jaroslav Bradac (Cremorne: Angus & Robertson / London: Wildwood House / New York: Paddington Press, 1975);

Aerzte: Ein paar Erinnerungen (Olten: Vereinigung Oltner Bücherfreunde, 1963);

Die späten Gedichte (Frankfurt am Main: Insel, 1963);

Geheimnisse: Letzte Erzählungen (Frankfurt am Main: Suhrkamp, 1964);

Erwin (Olten: Vereinigung von Freunden der Oltner Liebhaberdrucke, 1965);

Der vierte Lebenslauf Josef Knechts: Zwei Fassungen, edited by Ninon Hesse (Frankfurt am Main: Suhrkamp, 1966);

Aus Kinderzeiten und andere Erzählungen (Frankfurt am Main: Suhrkamp, 1968);

Politische Betrachtungen (Frankfurt am Main: Suhrkamp, 1970);

Lektüre für Minuten: Gedanken aus seinen Büchern und Briefen, edited by Volker Michels (Frankfurt am Main: Suhrkamp, 1971); revised as *Lektüre für Minuten: Gedanken aus seinen Büchern und Briefen: Neue Folge* (Frankfurt am Main: Suhrkamp, 1975);

Mein Glaube (Frankfurt am Main: Suhrkamp, 1971);

Eigensinn: Autobiographische Schriften, edited by Siegfried Unseld (Frankfurt am Main: Suhrkamp, 1972);

Die Erzählungen, 2 volumes (Frankfurt am Main: Suhrkamp, 1973);

Glück: Späte Erzählungen, Betrachtungen (Frankfurt am Main: Suhrkamp, 1973);

Iris: Ausgewählte Märchen (Frankfurt am Main: Suhrkamp, 1973);

Die Kunst des Müßiggangs: Kurze Prosa aus dem Nachlaß, edited by Michels (Frankfurt am Main: Suhrkamp, 1973);

Meistererzählungen (Frankfurt am Main: Suhrkamp, 1973);

Kindheit des Zauberers: Ein autobiographisches Märchen (Frankfurt am Main: Insel, 1974);

Das erste Abenteuer: Erzählungen, edited by Michels (Frankfurt am Main: Suhrkamp, 1975);

Die Fremdenstadt im Süden (Frankfurt am Main: Suhrkamp, 1975);

Legenden, edited by Michels (Frankfurt am Main: Suhrkamp, 1975);

Eine Literaturgeschichte in Rezensionen und Aufsätzen (Frankfurt am Main: Suhrkamp, 1975);

Musik: Betrachtungen, Gedichte, Rezensionen und Briefe, edited by Michels (Frankfurt am Main: Suhrkamp, 1976);

Stunden im Garten; Der lahme Knabe: Zwei Idyllen, edited by Gunter Böhmer (Frankfurt am Main: Suhrkamp, 1976);

Die Gedichte, 2 volumes (Frankfurt am Main: Suhrkamp, 1977);

Die Welt der Bücher: Betrachtungen und Aufsätze zur Literatur, edited by Michels (Frankfurt am Main: Suhrkamp, 1977);

Kleine Freuden: Prosa aus dem Nachlaß, edited by Michels (Frankfurt am Main: Suhrkamp, 1977);

Magie des Buches: Betrachtungen (Frankfurt am Main: Suhrkamp, 1977);

Politik des Gewissens: die Politischen Schriften 1914–1962, edited by Michels, 2 volumes (Frankfurt am Main: Suhrkamp, 1977);

Von Wesen und Herkunft des Glasperlenspiels: Die vier Fassungen der Einleitung zum Glasperlenspiel, edited by Michels (Frankfurt am Main: Suhrkamp, 1977);

Der Lateinschüler: Geschichten und Erinnerungen aus Kindheit und Schulzait (Berlin: Aufbau, 1977);

Der verbannte Ehemann oder Anton Schievelbeyn's ohnfreywillige Reisse (Frankfurt am Main: Insel, 1977);

Die Romane und die Grossen Erzählungen, 8 volumes (Frankfurt am Main: Suhrkamp, 1977);

Die Stadt: Ein Märchen (Frankfurt am Main: Insel, 1977);

Hermann Hesse als Maler: 44 Aquarelle (Frankfurt am Main: Suhrkamp, 1977);

Der Zauberer: Faksimile der Handschrift, edited by Bernhard Zeller (Marbach am Neckar: Deutsches Literaturarchiv / Stuttgart: Klett, 1977);

Gesammelte Erzählungen, edited by Michels, 6 volumes (Frankfurt am Main: Suhrkamp, 1977–1982);

Aus Indien: Aufzeichnungen, Tagebücher, Gedichte, Betrachtungen und Erzählungen (Frankfurt am Main: Suhrkamp, 1980);

Hesse as Painter: Painting for Pleasure, translated by Ralph Manheim (Frankfurt am Main: Suhrkamp, 1980);

Magie der Farben: Aquarelle aus dem Tessin (Frankfurt am Main: Insel, 1980);

Ein Jahr voll Freude, text by Hesse, photographs by Sepp Hofer (Frankfurt am Main: Unschau, 1983);

Italien: Schilderungen, Tagebücher, Gedichte, Aufsätze, Buchbesprechungen und Erzählungen, edited by Michels (Frankfurt am Main: Suhrkamp, 1983);

Bäume: Betrachtungen und Gedichte (Frankfurt am Main: Insel, 1984);

Casanovas Bekehrung; und Pater Matthias: Zwei Erzählungen (Frankfurt am Main: Suhrkamp, 1985);

Der Weltverbesserer; und Dr. Knölges Ende: Zwei Erzählungen (Frankfurt am Main: Suhrkamp, 1985);

Emil Kolb: Erzählung (Frankfurt am Main: Suhrkamp, 1985);

Bilderbuch der Erinnerungen, edited by Fritz Hofmann (Berlin: Aufbau, 1986);

Die Einheit hinter den Gegensätzen: Religion und Mythen, edited by Michels (Frankfurt am Main: Suhrkamp, 1986);

Die Hölle ist überwindbar: Krisis und Wandlung, edited by Michels (Frankfurt am Main: Suhrkamp, 1986);

Eigensinn macht Spaß: Individuation und Anpassung, edited by Michels (Frankfurt am Main: Suhrkamp, 1986);

Jedem Anfang wohnt ein Zauber inne: Lebensstufen, edited by Michels (Frankfurt am Main: Suhrkamp, 1986);

Wer lieben kann, ist glücklich: Über die Liebe, edited by Michels (Frankfurt am Main: Suhrkamp, 1986);

Bericht aus Normalien: Humoristische Erzählungen, Gedichte und Anekdoten, edited by Michels (Frankfurt am Main: Suhrkamp, 1986);

Bodensee: Betrachtungen, Erzählungen, Gedichte, edited by Michels (Frankfurt am Main: Suhrkamp, 1986);

Der Bettler; und Unterbrochene Stunden: Zwei Erzählungen (Frankfurt am Main: Suhrkamp, 1988);

Die Marmorsäge; Taedium vitae: Zwei Erzählungen (Frankfurt am Main: Suhrkamp, 1988);

Die Welt im Buch: Leseerfahrungen I: Rezensionen und Aufsätze aus den Jahren 1900–1910, edited by Michels (Frankfurt am Main: Suhrkamp, 1988);

Mit Hermann Hesse durch Italien: Ein Reisebegleiter durch Oberitalien, edited by Michels (Frankfurt am Main: Insel, 1988);

Robert Aghion: Erzählung (Frankfurt am Main: Suhrkamp, 1988);

Die blaue Ferne: Reisebilder und Naturbetrachtungen, edited by Hofmann (Berlin: Aufbau, 1989);

Beschreibung einer Landschaft: Schweizer Miniaturen, edited by Unseld (Frankfurt am Main: Suhrkamp, 1990);

Mit Hermann Hesse reisen: Betrachtungen und Gedichte, edited by Michels (Frankfurt am Main: Insel, 1990);

Mit der Reife wird man immer jünger: Betrachtungen und Gedichte über das Alter (Frankfurt am Main: Insel, 1990);

Tessin: Betrachtungen, Gedichte und Aquarelle, edited by Michels (Frankfurt am Main: Suhrkamp, 1990);

Im Garten: Betrachtungen, Gedichte und Bilder, edited by Michels (Frankfurt am Main: Insel, 1992);

Lesebuch: Erzählungen, Betrachtungen und Gedichte (Frankfurt am Main: Suhrkamp, 1992);

Jahreszeiten: Betrachtungen, Gedichte und Aquarelle (Frankfurt am Main: Insel, 1993);

Luftreisen, edited by Michels (Leipzig: Reclam, 1993; expanded edition, Frankfurt am Main: Insel, 1994);

Ausgewählte Werke, 6 volumes (Frankfurt am Main: Suhrkamp, 1994);

Lebenszeiten, edited by Unseld (Frankfurt am Main: Insel, 1994);

Liebesgeschichten, edited by Michels (Frankfurt am Main: Suhrkamp, 1995);

Freude am Garten: Betrachtungen, Gedichte und Fotografien mit farbigen Aquarellen des Dichters, edited by Michels (Frankfurt am Main: Insel, 1996);

Traumgeschenk: Betrachtungen, Tagebücher, Erzählungen und Gedichte über das Träumen, edited by Michels (Frankfurt am Main: Suhrkamp, 1996);

Farbe ist Leben: Eine Auswahl seiner schönsten Aquarelle, edited by Michels (Frankfurt am Main: Insel, 1997);

Die Welt im Buch: Leseerfahrungen II: Rezensionen und Aufsätze aus den Jahren 1911–1916, edited by Michels (Frankfurt am Main: Suhrkamp, 1998);

Wunder der Liebe: Liebesgedichte, edited by Michels (Frankfurt am Main: Insel, 1998);

Wolken: Betrachtungen und Gedichte, edited by Michels (Frankfurt am Main: Insel, 1999);

Vogel: Ein Märchen, edited by Michels (Frankfurt am Main: Insel, 2000);

Wege nach Innen: 25 Gedichte, edited by Unseld (Frankfurt am Main: Insel, 2000);

Der Zauberer: Fragmente zu einem Roman, edited by Michels (Frankfurt am Main: Suhrkamp, 2001);

In Weihnachtszeiten: Betrachtungen, Gedichte und Aquarelle des Verfassers, edited by Michels (Frankfurt am Main: Insel, 2001);

Blick nach dem fernen Osten: Erzählungen, Legenden, Gedichte und Betrachtungen, edited by Michels (Frankfurt am Main: Suhrkamp, 2001);

Über das Glück: Betrachtungen und Gedichte, edited by Michels (Frankfurt am Main: Suhrkamp, 2001);

Sämtliche Werke, 20 volumes, edited by Michels (Frankfurt am Main: Suhrkamp, 2001–2005);

Das Leben bestehen: Krisis und Wandlung, edited by Michels (Frankfurt am Main: Insel, 2002);

Das Lied des Lebens: Die schönsten Gedichte, edited by Michels (Frankfurt am Main: Insel, 2002);

Die schönsten Erzählungen, edited by Michels (Frankfurt am Main: Suhrkamp, 2002);

Liebesgedichte, edited by Michels (Frankfurt am Main: Insel, 2002);

Mit dem Erstaunen fängt es an: Herkunft und Heimat; Natur und Kunst (Frankfurt am Main: Suhrkamp, 2002);

Tessiner Bilderbuch (Frankfurt am Main: Insel, 2002);

Nur wer liebt lebendig: Frühe Liebesgeschichten, edited by Michels (Frankfurt am Main: Insel, 2003);

"Verliebt in die verrückte Welt": Betrachtungen, Gedichte, Erzählungen, Briefe, edited by Ursula Michels-Wenz (Frankfurt am Main & Leipzig: Insel, 2003).

Only a few German writers of the twentieth century have enjoyed worldwide acclaim. Undisputably numbered among these are Thomas Mann, Franz Kafka, Bertolt Brecht, and Hermann Hesse. Hesse's major works have been translated into some forty languages. Of all foreign countries, the United States, followed closely by Japan, has been most taken with Hesse. The fifteen million or so books that had been published in the United States by 1987 equaled the number that had been sold in Germany, and exceeded the fourteen million or more that readers had bought in Japan. Only Romain Rolland has attracted more attention in Japan than Hesse. While interest in Hesse in both India and China has been little more than mild, he had by the mid 1970s become the most popular of all foreign writers in South Korea. In the West, Hesse has, since the 1950s, enjoyed his most widespread popularity in the English- and Spanish-speaking countries.

Hesse's father, Johannes Hesse, was born in Weissenstein, Estonia; his mother, Marie Gundert, daughter of the missionary and Indologist Hermann Gundert, was born in Talatscheri, India. Both branches of the family were given to a severe form of Pietism. Following his studies at the Basler Missionsanstalt (Mission Society of Basel), Johannes Hesse served as a missionary in India. Brought back to Europe by ill health, he settled in Calw, a little town at the edge of the Black Forest, to assist Gundert, then director of the Calwer Verlagsverein, a Pietist publishing house. There he met and married Marie Gundert, and there Hermann Hesse was born on 2 July 1877, the second of six children.

A hypersensitive, imaginative, lively, and extremely headstrong child, Hesse was long a source of annoyance and anxiety. He tyrannized his parents, and school held little attraction for him. In January 1890 Hesse was sent off to the Latin School in nearby Göppingen; in September 1891 he began his studies at the exclusive Protestant church school in Maulbronn, ostensibly in preparation for the pulpit. His stay was unexpectedly brief: the deeply disturbed youngster left abruptly and unannounced in March 1892 and was withdrawn in May, much to the relief of the school authorities, who had begun to doubt his sanity. He fared no better at schools for retarded and emotionally disturbed children in Bad Boll and Stetten or at a secondary school in Bad Cannstatt. Hesse's parents finally permitted him to return home in the autumn of 1893. He spent the next six months gardening, assisting his father in the publishing house, and reading avidly in his grandfather's library. In early June 1894, after his father had denied him permission to leave home to prepare himself for a literary career, Hesse became an apprentice machinist in Calw. He believed that this trade would afford him a livelihood that he could someday ply abroad and that would permit him ample time for his literary interests. Fifteen months of grimy labor disabused him of this romantic notion. In October 1895 he began a more appropriate apprenticeship in a bookshop in Tübingen.

Hesse's four years in Tübingen were relatively tranquil. He continued to be a lonely outsider, applying himself diligently in the bookshop and otherwise preoccupied with his writing and self-education. During his preceding two years in Calw he had steeped himself in the German literature of the eighteenth and nineteenth centuries; in Tübingen he continued his prodigious reading but narrowed its scope drastically. For a time he devoted himself almost exclusively to Johann Wolfgang von Goethe. Then he fell under the spell of the German Romantics, Novalis in particular. Under their influence and that of the late-nineteenth-century aestheticism, he created his own beauty-worshipping realm of the imagination, a retreat from and substitute for the crass outer world in which he was an unappreciated misfit. Hesse was tolerably content; he had found a niche and a way of life.

According to his mother's letters and diaries, Hesse had begun to compose ditties before he could even wield a pencil, and at the age of thirteen he had decided to become a poet or nothing at all. In Tübingen, no longer in the shadow of home or school, Hesse was finally able to pursue his literary interests as he pleased. His poems began to appear in a Viennese periodical in 1896; *Romantische Lieder* (Romantic Songs), his first book of poetry, was published at the beginning of 1899; and *Eine Stunde hinter Mitternacht* (An Hour After Midnight), his first book of prose, followed in mid 1899. These early poetry and prose tales, reveries, and monologues display the sweetly scented atmosphere, the muted sounds, and the brilliant colors of an uncontained Romanticism. A lonely and aristocratic outsider indulges in melodramatic fantasies and melodic lament, is morbidly preoccupied with love and death, seeks his retreat in temples and castles, communes with his muse, consorts with ethereal maidens, and burns incense at the altar of beauty far from the profane world. Neither book attracted more than a modicum of attention.

In September 1899 Hesse left Tübingen for more cosmopolitan Basel, where he made a determined effort to escape the loneliness that had begun to plague him. He soon found his way into Basel's intellectual and art circles and became a frequent guest of some of the most culturally prominent families. Even so, Hesse remained essentially an outsider, distinctly uncomfortable at social gatherings, a loner who preferred the company of nature to that of people. In the spring of 1900—while writing "Lulu," his fairy-tale paean to Julie Hellmann, whom he had courted hesitantly and vainly while vacationing in Kirchheim unter Teck the previous August—Hesse fell in love with Elisabeth La Roche, the "Elisabeth" of his poems and prose of the time. When the hopelessness of his shyly pursued love became apparent, he began a more successful courtship of Maria Bernoulli, of Basel's mathematically celebrated Bernoulli family.

Long hours in a bookshop and few holidays left Hesse with neither time nor energy for his literary career and little opportunity for travel. With enough money to tide him over for some months, he quit his job in February 1901, returned to Calw, wrote the first four of his many brief recollections of his childhood, left for northern Italy at the end of March, returned to Calw in mid May, and went back to Basel later in the summer. Hesse's diary notes, rewritten soon after his return from Italy and published in the *Basler Anzeiger* that autumn, were the first of his many travel journals.

Aestheticism peaked and began to ebb in the poeticized recollections and ruminations, the diary excerpts, and the poems of *Hinterlassene Schriften und Gedichte von Hermann Lauscher: Herausgegeben von Hermann Hesse* (1901, Posthumous Writings and Poems of Hermann Lauscher: Edited by Hermann Hesse), which Hesse called "Dokumente der eigentümlichen Seele eines modernen Aestheten und Sonderlings" (documents of the peculiar soul of a modern aesthete and eccentric). Three of these "documents" look to the past in both their sentiment and manner, and three are telling intimations of things to come in Hesse's life and art. "Meine Kindheit" (My Childhood), a recollection of childhood in Bern, anticipates the more realistic narrative style that Hesse soon cultivated, and it is the beginning of what became—and, until *Demian* (1919; translated, 1923), remained—an obsessive preoccupation with childhood and youth. "Lulu," a fictionalized recollection of his vacation in Kirchheim unter Teck, foreshadows Hesse's fairy tales and his novels *Demian*, *Der Steppenwolf* (1927; translated as *Steppenwolf*, 1929), and *Die Morgenlandfahrt* (1932; translated as *The Journey to the East*, 1956) in both their blending of the magic realm of the imagination and the commonplace world, and their focus upon the pendulousness between isolation and contact, spirituality and sensuality, and the ideal and the real—the fluctuation that remained the characteristic rhythm of Hesse's life and the lives of his protagonists. An embryonic Harry Haller (protagonist of *Der Steppenwolf*), just discernible in the allegory of "Lulu," assumes a clear outline in "Tagebuch 1900" (Diary 1900), another of the "documents." Lauscher emerges a potential Steppenwolf, like Haller a sensitive misfit, an observer of life and not a participant, an extreme individualist dedicated to the ideal and disdainful of the real.

Gedichte (Poems), a second volume of romantic poetry, appeared in 1902. Hesse made another trip to northern Italy in April 1903; following his return on 24 April, he gave the finishing touches to his first novel. Hesse had begun *Peter Camenzind* (translated 1961) in November 1901 but had progressed slowly until the end of 1902. With the novel scheduled to be published in January 1904, Hesse decided in September 1903 to quit the bookselling trade and become a full-time author.

Peter Camenzind marks the beginning of the second stage in the evolution of Hesse's writings. His preceding shorter prose characteristically reflects the author-protagonist's inner self almost to the exclusion of any interaction with the physical world, and his prevailing aesthetic concerns find appropriate expression in an ornate narrative manner. *Peter Camenzind*, in contrast, mirrors both inner and outer circumstances, and Hesse's incipient cultivation in Bern of the art of life and of love finds expression in the blending of Romanticism and realism. The shades and airy worlds of the earlier works yield to living people involved in real events. Emotive adjectives and adverbs become less profuse, abstractions less common, imagery less choice, and narrative less punctured by rhetorical questions and exclamatory outbursts. But Hesse's characters and settings continue to be felt rather than seen, and nature continues to be for Camenzind the mirror for moods and the setting for protracted reflection that it has always been for Romantics. Nor did a writer of vignettes suddenly emerge a full-fledged storyteller. Camenzind's spotty memory, unevenly developed recollections, and propensity for rumination make his story less a smooth continuum of evolving action firmly anchored in space and time than a series of loosely juxtaposed reminiscences with liberally interspersed self-contemplation, nature description, and social comment.

Camenzind, an embittered loner, frustrated writer, misanthropist, and caustic sociocultural critic, seeks solace in wine and a refuge in nature. He finds a new ideal in the love and service exemplified by St. Francis of Assisi, then returns to his native Alpine peasant village prepared, though still in his prime, to turn his back upon life, to shelve his writing, and to become a simple innkeeper. Relenting enough to resume what had for him become a "miserable métier," Camenzind tells his narratively frail story. In his unhurried musing, he recalls his idyllic childhood, dwells sentimentally and at length on his love of nature, alludes to his early interest in books and writing, skims his formative years in high school, then turns his attention to his errant ambling through life and his disenchanting exposure to the cultural world. This story is Hesse's own veiled literary self-disclosure, prompted by his psychological need to dwell on his attempted new adjustment to life in Basel, to account for its failure, and to lend approbation to his decision to forgo any further efforts to socialize. The gauche and inhibited misfit Camenzind is what Hesse was in the years 1901 to 1903; his affable, happy, and carefree friend Richard is the man of the world Hesse aspired to become. Richard's death is Hesse's symbolic realization of the hopelessness of this aspiration. Except for his successful courtship of Maria Bernoulli (to whom he became engaged in the spring of 1903), Hesse might indeed, like his protagonist, have sought his comfort in solitary withdrawal.

While Hesse spent the autumn of 1903 and the winter and spring of 1904 in Calw writing the novel *Unterm Rad* (1906, Beneath the Wheel; translated as *The Prodigy*, 1957) and monographs on Giovanni Boccaccio and St. Francis of Assisi, his fiancée scoured the countryside around the Bodensee for an appealing rural retreat. Both had had their fill of sophisticated city life. She found an old farmhouse for rent in the secluded and picturesque village of Gaienhofen on the German side of the Untersee. They were married on 2 August 1904, moved immediately to Gaienhofen, and began a Rousseauesque experiment in simple living.

Hesse continued to cultivate the poetic-realistic narrative manner of *Peter Camenzind* in his three remaining pre–World War I novels. *Unterm Rad* is more realistic than poetic; *Gertrud* (1910; translated as *Gertrud and I*, 1915) is as realistic as it is poetic; and *Roßhalde* (1914; translated as *Rosshalde*, 1970) is again more realistic than poetic; and all three, like *Peter Camenzind*, remain more study than story. Autobiography continues to be the matrix of Hesse's narration; psychological need is still the creative thrust; and protagonists remain reflections of the discontented loner Hesse had become.

Unterm Rad was Hesse's contribution to the tendentious literature fashionable in German letters at the turn of the century. Like most of these school novels and dramas, it is a severe indictment of the adult world. Parents, teachers, and pastors are upbraided for their lack of understanding, neglect, and victimization of their wards, and for their smugness, incompetence, and hypocrisy. Only the thick-skinned children escape relatively unscathed by their mistreatment; the sensitive and gifted are brushed aside or ground under. Hesse's acrid social satire is an overstatement less intent on exposing and reforming social institutions than on purging painful memories and venting latent anger.

Hesse's first son, Bruno, was born in December 1905. In the autumn of 1907 the family moved into a larger and more comfortable home on a knoll overlooking Gaienhofen and the lake. A second son, Heiner, was born in March 1909.

Gaienhofen marked a new chapter in Hesse's life, a new period in his career, and a new phase in his writing. With the publication of *Peter Camenzind* in 1904, an unknown aspirant suddenly became a celebrity. That same year his maiden novel was awarded the Bauernfeld Prize of Vienna, the first of many literary awards. Before Gaienhofen, Hesse's poetry and prose were intimately personal and highly lyrical. With his marriage and increased concern with everyday life, he became less obviously personal and more prose conscious, and he began to cultivate a more down-to-earth literary style. The novella became his favorite medium of expression.

The writing of *Unterm Rad* not only purged Hesse of painful school recollections but also evoked treasured memories of Calw. His birthplace, which he renamed Gerbersau in his work, became a persistent preoccupation that gave his art fresh impetus and new direction. This little provincial community was his wonderful world of childhood, where he had been part of a social complex and not yet the lonely outsider. In Gaienhofen, this *Heimat* (home) transfigured in Hesse's memory became the setting of his art: a mythicized community reminiscent of Gottfried Keller's Seldwyla. Together with *Unterm Rad*, Hesse's three volumes of Gerbersau tales—*Diesseits* (1907, In This World), *Nachbarn* (1908, Neighbors) and *Umwege* (1912, Byways)—represent the

Swabian period of his career, when he chose to look to the past and tell traditional stories.

Hesse's traditional stories were not confined to his Swabian tales. While still in Basel, fascinated by both Boccaccio and St. Francis of Assisi, he had begun to write stories in the manner of the Italian novella and legends in the manner of traditional hagiography. He continued this practice in Gaienhofen. Many of these Italianate tales and legends were republished in *Fabulierbuch* (1935, Book of Fables). His literary essays, personal ruminations, nature sketches, diary-like recollections, and travel reports were published in newspapers and magazines and republished in such miscellanies as *Aus Indien* (1913, From India), *Bilderbuch* (1926, Book of Pictures), and *Betrachtungen* (1928, Observations). In Gaienhofen, Hesse also continued to write his romantic poems, but in drastically reduced number. Some of these appeared in *Unterwegs* (1911, Under Way) and *Musik des Einsamen* (1915, Music of the Lonely One).

Hesse's third novel, *Gertrud,* written in the winter of 1908–1909, was as much a self-appraisal as *Peter Camenzind* had been. In Camenzind's story Hesse was primarily intent upon accounting for his brief asocial withdrawal after his futile efforts in Basel to become sociable; in *Gertrud* he was eager to account for his passive adjustment to life in Gaienhofen. The inner world of the violinist-composer Kuhn, like that of Camenzind, remains intimately autobiographical; and Kuhn's outer world, albeit decidedly more fictive than Camenzind's, draws freely upon the personal for its filler detail. Kuhn starts out as the person Hesse had been in Basel, the lonely misfit-observer, and he becomes Hesse the disenchanted artist-bourgeois of Gaienhofen, desperately intent upon making self-acceptance possible and life palatable. To this end, Kuhn embraces a fatalistic philosophy, evolves a Nietzschean theory of art, argues a Schopenhauerian conception of love, and advocates, as had Camenzind, a St. Francis of Assisi adjustment: fate is responsible for the unalterable circumstances of life; loneliness and suffering are the sine qua non for creativity; love between man and woman is essentially a flighty, brutal, and painfully demeaning passion; and social love, with its commitment to service, is man's ultimate solace. That Hesse himself was as little convinced by Kuhn's assessment of, and adjustment to, life as he had been by Camenzind's is clearly reflected in the last of his prewar novels, *Roßhalde.*

As the novelty of marriage and his new way of life wore off, Hesse became convinced that he had given up too much for too little. He and his wife, who was not only nine years his senior but just as strong willed and self-preoccupied as he, began to drift apart. Hesse's growing discontent became chronic wanderlust, which culminated in September 1911 in a trip to the East.

Accompanied by the Swiss painter Hans Sturzenegger, Hesse visited Ceylon, Malaya, and Sumatra. He vaguely expected to find the wisdom of India, a more innocent community, and answers to his personal problems, but found only appalling poverty and depressingly commercialized Buddhism. Disenchanted, suffering from dysentery, and exhausted by the oppressive heat, Hesse left for home in December without visiting India proper. Nine months later the Hesses settled in a spacious and elegant seventeenth-century country house on the outskirts of Bern. Remote Gaienhofen had lost its attraction and was no place for schoolchildren, and Hesse and his wife hoped that a return to Switzerland would be salutary for their crumbling marriage.

Roßhalde, written between July 1912 and January 1913, is a depiction of the climactic stage of an infelicitous marriage, and it drew as heavily on Hesse's life as had each of his preceding major works. Veraguth, a painter, is the temperamental, lonely romantic who lives in dreamy anticipation, is quickly sated by realization, and carefully nurtures his chronic disillusionment. His wife, Adele, staid and humorless, possessive mother and unresponsive wife, is patterned after Maria Hesse. Veraguth's decision to terminate his marriage and to begin life anew, on a different basis, and alone, anticipates Hesse's separation from his wife and children; and his planned interim trip to India with his carefree friend Burkhardt recalls Hesse's own flight. *Roßhalde* is Hesse's frank confession not only of the failure but even more of the folly of his attempt in marriage to achieve an intimate relationship with life and to find a place for himself in society. Hesse had become convinced that the artist was essentially an observer and a creator, and that to try to be a participant in life was to play a role and not to live as oneself. For the artist, therefore, marriage was a mistake. Like Hesse, Veraguth had only compounded his error by long resigning himself to it. Unlike Lauscher, who had settled for aestheticism, Camenzind, who had settled for nature, and Kuhn, who had settled for resigned retirement, an embittered Veraguth decides belatedly to settle for nothing less than the self.

This resolve is supported by a new concept of fate. Until *Roßhalde,* Hesse's protagonists characteristically assume that everything happens or does not happen to them; adjustment to circumstances is their primary concern, and minimal involvement is their ideal. Until his decision to leave family, home, and false identity behind him, Veraguth belongs to these timorous bystanders. Convinced finally that fate is not intrusive but inherent, he becomes determined to seek his own medium and to try only to be himself. He now recognizes that he is by nature an outsider and an observer, that art is his destiny and not just his consolation, and that loneliness is his element and not something to be feared. Reluctant acceptance of circumstances yields to joyous self-acceptance, and bitter renunciation will become self-realization. On this note Veraguth's story, like Camenzind's and Kuhn's, ends abruptly and inconclusively. A new and more meaningful way of life is proposed but left untested. Hesse again took his protagonist no farther than the point he himself had reached.

Hesse's move to Bern in the hope of resolving his personal and family problems proved to be as abortive as his trip to the East. Unable to cope with their extremely irritable youngest son, Martin, following his severe illness in the spring of 1914, Hesse and his wife put the boy into a foster home. The outbreak of World War I left an already unsettled Hesse badly shaken. His initial ambiguous political stance—he was nationalistic enough to sympathize with Germany and to hope for German victory, but he also argued for internationalism and abhorred war—at first attracted only scattered suspicion, but by the autumn of 1915 it elicited not only denunciation by militarists but also rebuke by pacifists. That Hesse had volunteered his services to the German embassy in Bern and was collecting books and coediting two weeklies for German prisoners of war did little to dissuade his detractors. The death of Hesse's father in March 1916 added an acute sense of guilt to his growing despair. Exhausted, Hesse sought help in psychoanalysis. From the end of April 1916 to November 1917, he had some seventy-two sessions with Dr. J. B. Lang, who had become one of Carl Gustav Jung's students. This encounter with psychoanalysis provided Hesse with the incentive to appraise himself and his adjustment to life and afforded him the insights necessary to begin his long *Weg nach Innen* (inward path), that tortuous road that he hoped would lead to self-knowledge and ultimately to greater self-realization.

By the beginning of 1916 Hesse was so distressed by the criticism of militarists and pacifists and by the futility of his own protests that he stopped writing about the war. The lull that followed was a period of reconsideration and incubation, the beginning of what Hesse later called his *Erwachen* (awakening) and his *Wandlung* (transformation). In the middle of 1917 Hesse began again to address himself publicly to politics, excoriating proponents of war and pleading for immediate peace. He continued his berating and exhorting in the immediate postwar period, shifting gradually from international and national politics to the individual and from the outer to the inner world. Hesse's words were primarily directed to youth: a challenge to emulate Friedrich Nietzsche in an acceptance of the self and of life's inherent loneliness and suffering, and an invitation to undertake the self-scrutiny and self-realization he himself had just embarked upon.

Hesse concluded that to "live the self" would involve emancipation from traditional religion and morality and the cultivation of a personal ethos. Heeding his *Eigensinn* (self-will) and not the *Herdensinn* (herd-will), Hesse was determined to follow Nietzsche's path of individuation, prepared not only to accept but to extol loneliness and suffering in the manner of the Nietzschean elect. This world was of and for the *Herdenmensch* (herd man), a dated society. A better world could be ushered in by an enlightened few girded for a Nietzschean transvaluation of values. Christianity became the focal point of this transvaluation for Hesse, just as it had for Nietzsche. Because of Christianity, the here and the beyond had become an unnecessary and trying duality of incompatibles. A religion with a deity who was both God and Satan and a morality beyond absolutist good and evil, a credo appreciative of wholesome self-love and tolerant of self-expression and self-realization, would be more in accord with the nature of things. The old would give way to the new: a new God, a new morality, a new man, and a new world.

This Nietzschean sentiment found its immediate expression in *Demian*, written in September and October 1917. The novel depicts emancipation from traditional belief and thought and the crystallization of his own ethos, ascribed to precocious Emil Sinclair in his passage from youth to young manhood. The ten-year-old Sinclair is the sensitive and unruly youngster Hesse had been; his home and family are modeled on Hesse's; his *helle Welt* (light world) is Hesse's cloistered world of childhood; and this childhood paradise ends for Sinclair, as it had for Hesse, with a growing awareness of and painful involvement with seductive and profane life at large, *die dunkle Welt* (the dark world). Sinclair's first encounter with evil in the person of the young blackmailer Kromer, his own first lies and theft, his awareness of sin and torment by guilt, his unhappy and dissolute school years, his despair and thoughts of suicide, his distant worship of an older girl, his disenchantment with academia, and his attraction to Nietzsche had all been Hesse's early experiences. The mystagogic Pistorius's tutoring of Sinclair in gnosticism and the interpretation of dreams reflects Hesse's indebtedness to his psychiatrist. Sinclair's belief that war is the birth pangs of a new and better age had also been Hesse's.

Nevertheless, *Demian*, like all of Hesse's preceding tales, is not strictly autobiography. Hesse's past and present were only the matrix of his art; his recollection was always selective, and his imagination remained vivid. Max Demian, Sinclair's mentor, and Demian's mother, Eva—the two most important figures except the protagonist—were products of this imagination: pivotal points around which Hesse structured a tale in which psychic experiences are rendered visible and actuality is conceptualized. Demian and Frau Eva are multidimensional symbols. Demian is Sinclair's Socratic *daimon,* his admonishing inner self, but he is also a Jungian imago, Sinclair's mental image of the ideal self, and is also the reflective, culturally unconditioned alter ego Sinclair must become before he can begin to "live himself." Frau Eva is Sinclair's Jungian anima, the soul, the unconscious with which his conscious mind must establish rapport in the process of individuation, and also life in all its fullness, heaven and earth, an actualized *Magna Mater,* mankind's origin and destiny. Demian's and Frau Eva's actions and Sinclair's interactions with them are primarily psychic experience externalized. Hesse was awarded the Theodore Fontane Prize of Berlin for *Demian* in 1919.

Hesse's six and a half years in Bern were quite productive. His essays on war and politics, sundry recollections, literary studies, travel reports, congratulatory articles, and general observations on the human condition written during the period were collected in *Kleiner Garten* (1919, Small Garden), *Wanderung* (1920; translated as *Wandering,* 1972), *Sinclairs Notizbuch* (1923, Sinclair's Notebook), *Bilderbuch,* and *Betrachtungen.* He edited thirty-nine books and two weeklies and maintained a continuous flow of book reviews. He also added considerably to his fiction: besides *Roßhalde* and *Demian,* he published *Knulp: Drei Geschichten aus dem Leben Knulps* (translated as *Knulp: Three Tales from the Life of Knulp,* 1971) in 1915, and *Märchen* (Fairy Tales), seven stories written between 1913 and 1917, in 1919. Many of the poems written in Bern became part of the second edition of *Unterwegs* (1915), of *Musik des Einsamen,* and of *Ausgewählte Gedichte* (1921, Selected Poems).

After Maria Hesse became psychotic in October 1918, Hesse put Bruno and Heiner into a boarding school. When he was released from his wartime job in March 1919 he immediately left for the canton of Ticino in southern Switzerland. Domesticity had not agreed with Hesse: his Rousseauesque adventure in Gaienhofen had ended in tedium and frustration, and his life in Bern had become a nightmare. Neither his early aestheticism nor his rise into the bourgeoisie had served Hesse well. In Ticino he was determined just to be himself, come what may.

By the beginning of May, Hesse had settled in a Spartan apartment in the Casa Camuzzi, a baroque country house in Montagnola, a village on the outskirts of Lugano, where he lived until August 1931. From 1919 to 1923 Hesse emerged rarely and only reluctantly from his retreat. Since his postwar royalties from Germany had little monetary value in Switzerland, he was compelled to give sporadic public readings of his works. While in Zurich for this purpose in May 1921 he had a few analytic sessions with Jung. After 1923 his lecture tours were extended to Germany and continued until the late 1920s. The generosity of Fritz Leuthold, a wealthy friend, enabled Hesse to spend his winters from 1925 to 1931 in a small apartment in Zurich.

Hesse first turned to painting in the summer of 1916, when writing became distasteful to him and music unbearable. A modest beginning in Bern became a passion in Montagnola. He painted hundreds of little watercolors in the summer of 1919 and hundreds more during the following summers. In Hesse's writing he explored life's shadows, but in his painting he exposed its lively colors. The paintings are for the most part pastoral scenes: peacefully cluttered houses either graphically detailed or skimpily outlined, mountain landscapes, scattered dwellings surrealistic in their distortions, and placid lakes, gardens, trees, and wayside chapels, all depicted in a disarmingly naive manner. Rural Ticino was transfigured by poetic license. Hesse's new, therapeutic pastime remained a lifetime pursuit. Many of these watercolors have been internationally exhibited, and many have been made public in pamphlet publications and postcard reproductions.

Hesse had hardly settled in Montagnola before he became acquainted with twenty-two-year-old Ruth Wenger, daughter of the Swiss writer Lisa Wenger, who lived in nearby Carona. Hesse terminated his marriage in July 1923 and married Ruth Wenger on 11 January 1924. His second marital misadventure was short-lived: distraught and ill, Wenger returned to her parents in April 1924. Hesse's efforts to achieve a reconciliation were futile, and Wenger was granted a divorce in April 1927. A shy outsider, most at home in his study, in the concert hall, and in nature, Hesse became a desperate frequenter of Zurich's bars and dance halls. By late 1926 this sensual eruption had run its course. Early that year, while in Zurich, Hesse had met Ninon Dolbin, née Ausländer, a longtime devotee of his writing and a native of Czernowitz, Rumania. She joined him in the Casa Camuzzi in June 1927, although she remained married until September 1931.

Politically, the period from 1919 to 1931 was no less discouraging for Hesse than the preceding years in Bern. Persuaded that a disenchanted postwar Germany would be susceptible to changes for the better, he helped to found and edit *Vivos Voco,* a periodical devoted to social reform, pacifism, and internationalism. Quickly disabused of his hopes by resurgent nationalism and spreading communism, Hesse terminated his association with the monthly in the autumn of 1921,

Manuscript page with drawing by Hesse for his 1928 volume Krisis: Ein Stück Tagebuch *(translated as* Crisis: Pages from a Diary, *1975), which included his poetry (Suhrkamp Verlag, Frankfurt am Main)*

only two years after its first issue. By then he had again become a favorite target of invective, and public self-defense was again futile. Continued indignities and waning faith in Germany's political future persuaded Hesse to become a citizen of Switzerland in November 1924 and to resign from the Prussian Academy of Art in November 1930.

Hesse's twelve years in the Casa Camuzzi were the most exciting chapter of his life and the most productive period in his art. In his relentless quest for himself, his writing received fresh impetus and assumed new directions. A traditionalist before the war, he emerged an innovator. Hesse's fictive documentation of his self-quest started with "Klein und Wagner" (Klein and Wagner), begun immediately after he arrived in Montagnola and completed by mid July 1919; it was serialized in *Vivos Voco* from October to December 1919. "Klingsors letzter Sommer" (translated as *Klingsor's Last Summer*, 1970) was ready for publication by the beginning of September. It was published together with "Klein und Wagner" as *Klingsors letzter Sommer: Erzählungen* (1920). The first eight chapters of *Siddhartha* (1922; translated, 1951) were written from December 1919 to the end of July 1920, the last four from March to May 1922. *Kurgast: Aufzeichnungen von einer Badener Kur* (1925, Guest at a Spa: Notes of a Water Cure in Baden), the ironic psychologizing and philosophizing of an embittered rheumatic, was written in October 1923, and *Die Nürnberger Reise* (1927, The Journey to Nuremberg), acerbic memoirs of a reading tour, in the late autumn of 1925. *Der Steppenwolf*, a surrealistic self-exposure that began to preoccupy Hesse in November 1924, was finished at the end of 1926. *Narziss und Goldmund* (1930; translated as *Death and the Lover*, 1932), begun in mid 1927, was completed by the end of 1928, and *Die Morgenlandfahrt*, started during the latter half of 1929, was finished by April 1931. These major works were accompanied by Hesse's usual stream of poetry, most of which was included in *Krisis* (1928; translated as *Crisis*, 1975) and *Trost der Nacht* (1929, The Solace of the Night), and by his continued output of shorter tales, literary essays, and recollections, many of which were brought together in his miscellanies. During these years Hesse also managed to edit sixteen books and to continue his prolific reviewing.

Roßhalde boldly proclaims a new way of life: the protagonist will be what he is and live as he was meant to live. *Demian* depicts the emancipation from traditional religion and morality necessary for this new style of life. "Klein und Wagner" proceeds from the brash manifesto of *Roßhalde* and the optimistic celebrations of *Demian* to an actual venture, one that is a faithful rendition of Hesse's separation from his family in the spring of 1919, his trip, and the mental and emotional anguish of his first few weeks in Ticino. Klein is a respectable member of society, a conscientious employee, a faithful husband, a good father, and a reliable provider. He is also a man who has never taken the trouble to find himself. Disillusionment, frustration, and resultant murderous impulses compel him to bolt. He embezzles, forges documents, procures a revolver, and flees. Distraught, he tries desperately to assess himself and his actions, to ponder life and morality, and to become an authentic human being. His belated efforts to establish his own identity, to fashion his own values, and to "live himself" are futile. Long hours of excruciating thought, a bout of gambling, and a whirl of sex only add to his agitation. The blissful moments when he is at peace with himself and with life are too few and too elusive to sustain him. Guilt and anxiety plague him; his new way of life leaves him wallowing in self-contempt, and destructive impulses once more become urgent. Klein begins to falter, and flight again becomes imperative. Since life no longer holds any attraction for him and since his own inner resources are depleted, just one week after his flight he succumbs to his long-nurtured passion for suicide.

Klein's attempt to emancipate himself from the Christian-bourgeois ethos as Sinclair does, and to "live himself" as Veraguth proposes to do, fails. Whereas actual experience had almost persuaded Hesse—as it does persuade Klein—that this new ideal was more pipe dream than possibility, a surge of faith in the essential oneness, eternity, and meaningfulness of life convinced Hesse to the contrary. This faith finds its expression in the epiphanic concluding moments of Klein's life. Given this faith, the individual has only to "sich fallen lassen" (let himself fall), to surrender himself to himself and to life, fully and with no regard for consequences. Of Hesse's major tales, Klein's encompasses the shortest span of time, involves the smallest cast, and presents the most concentrated treatment of theme.

Autobiography was mythicized in *Demian* and dramatized in "Klein und Wagner"; it is fantasized in "Klingsors letzter Sommer." Klingsor's story, decidedly more portrait than narrative, is a memorial to the summer of 1919, Hesse's first in Ticino. Klingsor, born on 2 July, forty-two years old and unattached, painter, poet, philosopher, and hypochondriac troubled by the thought of death, possessed by a passion for life and art, and given to revelry and depression, is obviously Hesse. The setting is clearly Lugano and its vicinity; actual place-names are only playfully distorted. Klingsor's July excursion to Kareno with his coterie of friends to meet the Queen of the Mountains is Hesse's fantasized depiction of his first visit to Carona to meet Ruth Wenger. A night with Jup der Magier, a night given to revelry and morbid preoccupation with cultural decline and death, is based on Hesse's frequent night bouts of alcohol and argument with his astrologer friend Josef Englert.

The splintered structure of the tale and its lack of homogeneity mirror and highlight Klingsor's inner discord and the chaotic structure of his lifestyle. The hectic flow and rhythm of the sentences reflect Klingsor's alternately frantic and ecstatic inner state. Nature, evocatively depicted and excitingly animated by garish color and brilliant sound, becomes an accentuating mirror for frenzied thoughts. Hesse's language assumes a vitality that lends Klingsor's story gripping immediacy. This work represents Hesse's intuitively controlled artistry at its best.

Klingsor's emancipation, unlike Klein's, is complete. He has left society and his socialized self behind without any moral compunctions. But he has not come to terms with death: he tries to blot out the reality of death by rushing headlong into an oblivion of intoxicating experience. But sex, alcohol, and painting prove to be ineffectual weapons against death. He is not capable of letting himself "fall into life" until he is finally able to come to terms fully with both life and death. Klingsor's painting of his self-portrait symbolizes his confrontation with—and his resultant affirmation of—the self, life, and death. He is now in accord with all, no longer suffers from anxiety, and is finally able to let himself fall into life. At this critical juncture, Hesse's narration terminates in its usual abrupt manner: Klingsor dies mysteriously soon after putting the finishing touches on his self-portrait.

What had become a passionate ideal for Hesse finally received its full expression in *Siddhartha*. Just as for Klein and Klingsor, life for Hesse's new standard-bearer consists primarily of two areas of experience: *Geist*, the world of the mind and thought, and *Natur*, the world of the body and physical action. Klein is at home in neither realm; Klingsor lives in the intoxication of each; Siddhartha exhausts both possibilities and, in their exhaustion, transcends them and finds himself miraculously in a third realm: that of the soul, the ultimate stage of being in which the individual lives in complete accord with himself and life, when he is finally able, fully and not just for chance moments, to experience the essential oneness and meaningfulness of everything. After his encounter with the Buddha, and with his subsequent awakening to the realization that the incidental "I" of his senses is no less he than the incidental "I" of his thoughts, Siddhartha, the Brahmin once dedicated to ritual and speculation and the *Samana* (ascetic) once given to self-denial, leaves the realm of the mind behind. Through his affair with Kamala the courtesan; his partnership with Kamaswami the businessman; his reveling in wealth, power, and sloth; his constant self-disgust; and his attempt to commit suicide, he leaves the realm of the flesh behind. And after his return to the river and Vasudeva the ferryman, his encounter with his son, and his last bout with anxious love and fearful concern, Siddhartha emerges transfigured, a wise, saintly figure given to his fellow humans in love and service; paradoxically, he has achieved self-transcendence through self-realization.

Hesse's ideal is an exemplary Western approach to life, opposed to the exemplary Eastern approach advocated by the Gautama Buddha. To accord his literary credo something of timeless, mythic validity, Hesse locates his tale in remote India of a time long past. To enhance the gospel quality of the tale, Hesse cultivates an antiquated, liturgical mode of expression reminiscent of both Pali scriptures and the Bible. And to stress his equal concern with, and approbation of, each of the three areas of human experience, Hesse carefully adjusts manner to matter. Structurally, the tale is a balanced tripartite, in keeping with Siddhartha's balanced progression from the realm of the mind, through that of the body, to that of the soul. This triadic structure is extended to the very mechanics of expression: to sentences, clauses, phrases, words, and paragraphs. And in keeping with this three-beat pattern, Hesse even extends his customary projection of the actual self and one alternative to the actual self and three possibilities. Siddhartha is Hesse's fictionalized self, and Govinda, Buddha, and Vasudeva are the possibilities: Govinda is the self-effacing, institution-oriented person Siddhartha should not become; Buddha represents a laudable but undesirable life-denying model; and Vasudeva is an exemplary life-affirming ideal. And when Siddhartha becomes this ideal, Vasudeva leaves the scene, just as Demian vanished when Sinclair became his ideal self. Just as "Klingsors letzter Sommer" is intuitively controlled artistry, *Siddhartha* is conscious craftsmanship.

The third major crisis in Hesse's life began when he and Wenger separated at the end of March 1924. Withdrawal, bitter self-hatred, a lusting for both death and raw life, and an experiencing of the bars and dance halls of Zurich in early 1926 were followed in mid 1926 by a return to Montagnola, his art, his ideals, and his solitude. During this crisis, the most radical of Hesse's characteristic swings from spirituality to sensuality and back, *Der Steppenwolf* was created. Harry Haller's story and *Krisis*, its poetic counterpart, are also the most painfully honest of Hesse's literary renditions of these sporadic ordeals. *Krisis*, in particular, is a brutally sincere reflection of Hesse's attempted drowning of the self in sex, jazz, and alcohol, and of his agonizing recognition that he would always be an outsider. Hesse has his prose counterpart recount his experience in less strident detail and buffered by a touch of fantasy.

In *Der Steppenwolf,* Haller—intellectual, writer, and uncompromising idealist, too long ascetically devoted to mental pursuits—becomes emotionally unhinged. His aloneness has become a torment, his freedom repugnant, and all his interests and ideals questionable. He is unable to continue in his estrangement, is tempted but not prepared to commit suicide, and will not compromise and join the throng. He has no choice but to relax, to emerge from his isolation, and to seek relief in the world of the senses. Late one night, Haller meets Hermine, a well-groomed prostitute who responds sympathetically to his plight. At the outset of their involvement she informs him that she will make him fall in love with her, then will order him to kill her and will expect him to comply. In the interim she teaches Haller to dance, laugh, and live. She introduces him to handsome young Pablo, a jazz-band saxophonist, and arranges a bedroom friendship for him with the sensual Maria.

At a masked ball only four weeks after their first meeting, Haller and Hermine dance a passionate wedding dance and then accept Pablo's invitation to his quarters for a climactic drug party, an introduction to his Magic Theater. Awakening slightly from his drug-induced fantasizing and finding Pablo and Hermine side by side, exhausted from their sexual intercourse, Haller hallucinates that he plunges a knife into Hermine's heart. Slipping back into a deep daze, he imagines a conversation with Wolfgang Amadeus Mozart, then a trial in which he is sentenced to eternal life for his imagined murder of an imaginary figure. Sober again, Haller is prepared to resume the game of life, to suffer its agonies and senselessness once more, hopeful that he will someday be able to distinguish between ideas and appearance and to rise above it all and laugh. Thus, like every major Hesse tale before it, *Der Steppenwolf* ends abruptly and on a note of optimism. And like each of the tales beginning with Sinclair's, Haller's is yet another of Hesse's experiments in narrative possibility, a surrealistic admixture of psychological realism and symbolism, fantasy, and hallucination.

By the beginning of 1927 Hesse's crisis had run its course, and in the relative tranquility that followed he looked to the past and reviewed his thoughts. The embittered Haller was forgotten, and the dramatic tempo of *Der Steppenwolf* yielded to the more epic flow of *Narziss und Goldmund.* Just as in Siddhartha's exotic tale, also written during a period of relative equanimity following considerable agitation, there is little in the outer detail of Goldmund's medieval world that is discernibly autobiographical. Goldmund's schooling, friendships, experiences in the Mariabronn monastery, and eventual stealthy departure from the monastery are a colorful reflection of Hesse's sojourn in and flight from the monastery in Maulbronn. All that follows—Goldmund's restless peregrinations from forest to forest and village to village; parade of brief sexual encounters; restrictive years of sculpturing under the tutelage of Master Niklaus; happy return to the open road; exposure to the horrors of the plague; last dangerous dalliance; apprehension; rescue from death by his boyhood friend and mentor Narziss, now abbot of Mariabronn; return to the monastery; dedication to his art; last worldly sally; and self- but not life-affirming death—was born of Hesse's imagination. On the other hand, Goldmund's thoughts, feelings, basic problems, and aspirations, like Siddhartha's, are no less self-projections than those of all of Hesse's other protagonists. Like most of Hesse's tales, *Narziss und Goldmund* juxtaposes and scrutinizes two human possibilities, the ideal possible and the dubious actual: Goldmund is the possible and Narziss the actual.

In December 1928, while putting the finishing touches on *Narziss und Goldmund,* Hesse began again to experience sharp qualms about himself, life, and art. This new attack of doubt and Hesse's usual determination to find order and meaning in apparent chaos provided the impetus and matter for *Die Morgenlandfahrt.* Protagonist H.H.'s acceptance into the Order of the Eastern Wayfarers, his year of probation, his initiation, his participation in the order's Journey to the East, his defection after a few months, his ten-year period of lonely suffering and suicidal despair, his months of grueling effort to recall and record his association with the order, and his culminating readmission into its ranks extend over some twelve years. This time frame represents Hesse's twelve years of quest, despair, and new hope following his departure from Bern in the spring of 1919. H.H. is what Hesse was during the years from 1919 to 1931, undisguised even in name. His background, friends, interests, aspirations, and conflicts reflect Hesse's own life; however, H.H.'s relationship with the supreme head of the Eastern Wayfarers and his ceremonious admission and readmission into the order are not fictionalized actuality but psychic process externalized in pure fantasy and playful mystification. H.H. and Leo are another of Hesse's double self-projections: the distraught individualist he actually was, and the confident master-servant he hoped he might become. Like Demian and Hermine, Leo is both the admonishing and enlightening *daimon* and the more ideal alter ego, rendered visible. Hesse's focus of interest had shifted from his characteristic self-concern and adjustment to oneself to self-justification and adjustment to a community, a transcendent world. With this shift Hesse's renascent aestheticism, a blending of Lauscher's Romanticism and Haller's Platonism, was complete.

In the summer of 1931, after four years together in their inadequate quarters in the Casa Camuzzi, Hesse and Dolbin moved into a house built nearby for their lifelong use by Hans C. Bodmer, a wealthy patron. They were married on 14 November 1931. Hesse's third marriage afforded him the comfort and contentment that neither of his previous marriages had. His life began to revolve almost ritually around his writing, reading, extensive correspondence, music, painting, and gardening. With Adolf Hitler's rise to power in 1933, Hesse quickly became host and benefactor to a steady flow of German and Austrian refugee artists and intellectuals.

Hesse had permitted World War I to divert him from his conviction that an artist should divorce himself from politics, tend to his art, and nurture his humanitarian ideals; but his political activism had been of no advantage to himself, his art, or Germany. He remained more mindful of his better judgment during the political mayhem of the 1930s and World War II. Because of his public silence, Hesse's works continued to be published freely in Germany until he began to feature Jews, as well as Catholic and Protestant writers in bad standing, in his reviews. Newspapers and periodicals throughout Germany suddenly lost interest in his literary comments. In 1935, when he began to publish (in Sweden's *Bonniers Litterära Magasin*) surveys of contemporary German literature in which he continued to feature writers who had become silenced undesirables in Germany, he was assailed by the thoroughly Nazified journal *Die Neue Literatur* as a Jew-loving traitor. A letter written to the journal in self-defense only attracted more invective. While Nazis in Germany maligned Hesse for promoting the cause of Jewry in literature, émigré German Jews in Paris took him to task for abetting National Socialism by allegedly writing for the *Frankfurter Zeitung*. Hesse's public statement that he had stopped contributing to the paper when Hitler came to power was ineffectual, and he again lapsed into silence. As a result of this silence, some of his older and politically innocuous works continued to be published throughout the war; but after the war broke out in 1939, rationed paper was suddenly no longer available for his new books.

What had been novelty and abundance in the Casa Camuzzi became primarily recollection and collection in the Casa Bodmer. Hesse's production of tales, poetry, essays, and reviews slowed. From 1931 to 1945 new books appeared at regular intervals but consisted largely of earlier prose and poetry: *Vom Baum des Lebens* (1934, From the Tree of Life), *Fabulierbuch* (1935), *Gedenkblätter* (1937, Commemorations), *Neue Gedichte* (1937, New Poems), and *Die Gedichte* (1942, The Poems). During these fourteen years Hesse added to his fiction only a fairy tale, "Vogel" (1932, Bird), and the last of his novels, *Das Glasperlenspiel* (1943, The Glass Bead Game; translated as *Magister Ludi*, 1949). He received the Gottfried Keller Prize of Zurich in 1936.

In 1927 it had first occurred to Hesse that a narrative in which a protagonist experiences the great epochs of history in several reincarnations, a biography both individual and archetypal, might give apt expression to the stability in life's flux, to the continuity of man's spiritual-intellectual tradition. *Die Morgenlandfahrt* expressed Hesse's unqualified extolment of and commitment to this timeless realm of the soul and the mind. Returning to his originally envisaged series of biographies soon after completion of *Die Morgenlandfahrt* in the spring of 1931, and almost immediately questioning and modifying his unconditional homage and dedication of 1931, Hesse proceeded slowly and tenaciously through the most challenging of his many literary ventures: *Das Glasperlenspiel,* which was completed in 1942. The book, purportedly written in the year 2400, comprises an introductory history of the Glass Bead Game; a biography of Josef Knecht, the celebrated Master of the Game in the educational province of Castalia circa 2200; a cluster of his poems; and three of his conjectural autobiographies, official assignments preceding his admission to the Order of the Glass Bead Game.

Hesse's life and personal problems, interests, and convictions never ceased to be the stuff of his art. In *Das Glasperlenspiel,* the final installment of his serial projection of the self, autobiography furnished the matter for a world of tomorrow. *Das Glasperlenspiel* not only highlights a particular period of Hesse's life but also draws heavily upon all of the preceding years. Young Knecht at the Latin School in Berolfingen, then at Castalia's elite school in Escholz, receives Hesse's schooling at Göppingen's Latin School and at Maulbronn's exclusive church school. The little town of Waldzell owes its physical profile to Maulbronn; the Benedictine abbey Mariafels is indebted for its history and structural detail to Maulbronn's former Cistercian monastery; and Castalia and its order are derived from Hesse's impressions of Maulbronn and its monasticism. Knecht's ten years of independent study and preparation for admission into the order equate with Hesse's journeyman years as a writer, from *Peter Camenzind* to *Roßhalde*. Knecht treasures seclusion during this period in his career as much as had Hesse; the game becomes the passion for him that writing became for Hesse, and he achieves the fame that Hesse gained before World War I. The three to four years after Knecht's admission to the order and before his elevation to Castalia's most exalted magistery correspond to World War I in Hesse's career. This interim is for Knecht the hiatus of sociopolitical involvement it had been for Hesse: Knecht commits himself to a reconciliation of Castalia and the Catholic Church, just as Hesse had committed himself to the cause of peace. The eight years between Knecht's investiture and his resignation and departure from Castalia correspond to the period in Hesse's life from the end of the war to the mid 1930s. These are for Knecht the years of dedicated application, major achievements, severe conflict, and drastic decision, as they had been for Hesse. Knecht now dedicates himself wholeheartedly to the bead game as Hesse had devoted himself to his writing: his seven grand annual games are counterparts to the seven major tales published by Hesse from *Demian* to *Die Morgenlandfahrt*.

Success notwithstanding, the polar possibilities of life gradually became for Knecht the crucial and disturbing concern they had become for Hesse. He is caught between isolation and contact, reflection and involvement, and the mind and the body, just as Hesse had been. He, like Hesse, is left convinced that he has become an artist but not a human among humans. He also becomes convinced that Castalia is less than the impeccable ideal he had believed it to be, just as Hesse had lost his unqualified faith in the timeless realm of art and thought courted in *Der Steppenwolf* and extolled in *Die Morgenlandfahrt*. The novel is one more of Hesse's appraisals of the self and life, the last stage of his preoccupation with self-realization, and the climax of his serial quarrel with the real world.

With their protagonists located in widely dispersed times and places, but similarly engrossed in thought and moved by ideals, the novels from *Demian* to *Die Morgenlandfahrt* were an unwitting expression of a growing interest and deepening belief in a universal spiritual-intellectual continuum. What is only intimated by this series of separate works and symbolically expressed by the timeless and widespread membership of Haller's Immortalia and H.H.'s Order of Eastern Wayfarers, is clearly illustrated and deliberately argued by Hesse's organized cluster of concluding tales with their common protagonist, Knecht, who in several reincarnations experiences some of the major epochs of human history from the Stone Age to a distant future, and who in each reincarnation partakes of an appropriately different but analogous spiritual-intellectual tradition. In *Das Glasperlenspiel*, Hesse adds a philosophy of history to the psychology of history that he had proposed in the essays in *Blick ins Chaos* (1920, A Glance into Chaos) to account for what he believed to be the inevitable and imminent cultural collapse of Western Europe.

The final seventeen years of Hesse's life were relatively uneventful and tranquil. He gave his mornings and afternoons to gardening, painting, and his enormous correspondence, and his evenings to books, music, and writing. He left Montagnola as infrequently as he had in the 1930s; and then only briefly, and never for places beyond Switzerland, not even when awarded the Goethe Prize of Frankfurt am Main and the Nobel Prize in Literature in 1946. The citation for the Nobel Prize read: "for his inspired writings which, while growing in boldness and penetration, exemplify the classical humanitarian ideals and high qualities of style."

With the collapse of National Socialism in 1945 and Hesse's Nobel Prize in 1946, German scholars and Germany's reading public suddenly rediscovered Hesse. For the next decade he enjoyed both political and literary approval as never before. His works could not be printed fast enough, and the swell of books, pamphlets, dissertations, articles, and reviews surpassed by far, in both quality and quantity, all the secondary literature of the preceding four decades. An undesirable German of questionable literary merits had become a man of insight, foresight, and humanity, an heir to the noblest heritage of the German people, a guide and inspiration for his fellow humans, and a worthy addition to Germany's pantheon of illustrious authors. Contrary views were almost as rare and muted as those of Hesse's defenders had been during the preceding twelve years.

This reverential acclaim peaked in the mid 1950s, then declined rapidly. By the early 1960s, Hesse was again relegated to the limbo of spent writers. Only a relatively small following of enthusiasts continued to read him, and there was just as sudden and sharp a decrease in scholarly attention. Yet, another wave of interest in Hesse began to spread in Germany in the early 1970s, occasioned in part by America's Hesse boom of the 1960s. His books again became best-sellers, and he again received intense and appreciative scholarship and was publicly celebrated throughout Germany. But by the early 1980s, despite the vigorous promotion of his publisher, this wave of popularity had receded.

By 1946 only three of Hesse's major works had been translated into English. Reviews had been politely condescending or by and large superciliously negative, and none of the books found a reading public. When *Demian* appeared in 1923, it was brushed aside in the *Boston Transcript* of 14 April as "a nightmare of abnormality, a crazed dream of a paranoiac." In *Bookman* (October 1929), *Steppenwolf* was dismissed as "a peculiarly unappetizing conglomeration of fantasy, philosophy, and moist eroticism." *Death and the Lover (Narziss und Goldmund)* elicited polite praise in 1932 but, like the other two books, for decades did little more than gather dust in a few bookshops and warehouses. Little wonder that the English-speaking world raised its eyebrows when Hesse was awarded the Nobel Prize. Few knew who Hesse was, and to most of these few he was just another odd and suspect German writer. For the next fifteen years the critics were generally unimpressed, and the reading public apparently had better things to do than to read Hesse, Nobel Prize winner though he was.

Publishers, however, alerted to a potential market by the prize, began to scramble for translations. *Magister Ludi (Das Glasperlenspiel)* appeared in 1949, *Siddhartha* in 1951, *Gertrude* in 1955, *The Journey to the East* in 1956, *The Prodigy (Unterm Rad)* in 1957, and *Peter Camenzind* in 1961. Despite this commercial priming of Hesse's pump, his works continued to sell relatively poorly until the beginning of the Hesse boom in America during the mid 1960s, when, suddenly, what had long been inconsequential became acutely relevant. Book after book became best-sellers, and their author was a sensation, by far the most popular of foreign writers.

Unprepared for this sudden swell of interest in Hesse, with no backlog of unpublished translations, publishers had to make do with the nine novels available in English by 1961. Hesse's remaining novels, as well as many short stories, essays, poetry, and letters, did not appear in English translation until the 1970s; fourteen volumes of this material were published from 1970 to 1976. By 1976 the tide that had begun to sweep across America in the mid 1960s and that had peaked in 1970 had spent itself. The deluge was over, but not before almost fifteen million copies of Hesse's works had been sold within a single decade—a literary phenomenon without precedent in America.

American Hesse scholarship followed in the wake of the general public's attraction to and the publishers' financial interest in Hesse after the Nobel Prize. Before 1946 the scholarly field was oblivious to Hesse; in the years following, it gradually picked up momentum with the appearance of half a dozen books and pamphlets, twenty-seven dissertations, and some sixty articles. Scholarly activity accelerated in the mid 1960s and crested in the mid 1970s, a few years after the reading community had already begun to lose interest in Hesse. As many dissertations, more articles, and four times as many books and pamphlets were written from the mid 1970s as in the preceding two decades. This activity then tapered off to become a slow but steady flow. By the turn of the century, American Hesse scholarship was second in quantity only to its German counterpart and had in quality surpassed it.

With the national and international recognition that accompanied the Nobel Prize, Hesse became the dean of German letters, a celebrity feted in Germany, Switzerland, and Austria upon the occasion of his seventieth birthday and on every fifth anniversary thereafter. He was awarded the Wilhelm Raabe Prize of Braunschweig in 1950 and was appointed a member of the Friedensklasse des Ordens *Pour le Mérite* in 1955. That same year, he received the Peace Prize of the German Book Trade. But Hesse was far less elated by this official and popular acclaim than he was troubled by gradually declining health. Though quite fragile by the late 1950s, he continued to paint and to write.

For the septuagenarian Hesse, the world of memory gradually became the fascination and consolation that the world of the imagination had been at the beginning of his career. Remembrance of things past produced a steady flow of memorials, congratulatory articles, reminiscences, ruminations, and circular letters. Many of these were brought together in such miscellanies as *Krieg und Frieden* (1946, War and Peace), *Späte Prosa* (1951, Late Prose), and *Beschwörungen* (1954, Conjurations). No fiction was written during these final years, and only some fifty poems, some of which appear in *Stufen* (1961, Stages) and *Die späten Gedichte* (1963, The Late Poems). The last period of Hesse's life was also one of literary entrenchment. A lifetime of work was sifted (and occasionally, but not often, revised) and made more readily available in many reprints, in new editions, and particularly in such collections as *Traumfährte* (1945, Dream Trail), *Frühe Prosa* (1948, Early Prose), and the *Gesammelte Dichtungen* (1952, Collected Writings).

This lively publication of old and new material became even livelier following Hesse's death from leukemia on 9 August 1962. A new edition of his collected works appeared in 1970, another in 1977, other collections in 1982 and 1994; and *Sämtliche Werke,* the most comprehensive and most scholarly edition of collected works, was published from 2001 to 2005 (twenty volumes). These publications were complemented by more than a dozen volumes of letters and dozens of volumes of miscellanies in the series Suhrkamp Taschenbuch, Insel Taschenbuch, and Bibliothek Suhrkamp.

The Nobel Prize briefly reawakened an earlier interest in Hesse in Denmark, France, Holland, and Sweden; America's Hesse boom had brief cultish reverberations in Denmark, Holland, Sweden, and Finland as well as Germany in the early 1970s; and in the late 1970s the international celebration of the hundredth anniversary of Hesse's birth occasioned a broad and again brief Hesse renaissance. Worldwide interest in Hesse continued to simmer up to and beyond the turn of the century. The success of the biennial Internationales-Hermann-Hesse-Kolloquium in Calw (1977–) is reflective of this continued interest. The eleventh meeting of the colloquium in May 2002 attracted the usual crowd of committed laymen and scholars. This continued active interest in Hesse was confirmed in 2002 by an impressive spurt of republications and new publications by and about Hesse and by the plethora of varied worldwide celebrations upon the occasion of the 125th anniversary of his birth.

Hermann Hesse excelled in the depiction of personal crisis and private agony; such literature seems to be particularly popular during periods of cultural crisis, which accounts by and large for Hesse's idolization in Germany immediately after two devastating wars no less than for his similar idolization in America during the politically and socially chaotic 1960s and 1970s. Similar swells of popularity at future times are not unthinkable. Hesse's fortunes will probably continue to rise and fall with the times, and this ebb and flow is likely to secure his place in both German and world literature.

Letters:

Briefe (Berlin & Frankfurt am Main: Suhrkamp, 1951; expanded editions, 1959, 1964); expanded further as *Ausgewählte Briefe* (Suhrkamp Taschenbuch, 1974);

Ein Handvoll Briefe (Zurich: Büchergilde Gutenberg, 1951);

Hermann Hesse/Romain Roland: Briefe (Zurich: Fretz & Wasmuth, 1954);

Kindheit und Jugend vor Neunzehnhundert: Hermann Hesse in Briefen und Lebenszeugnissen, 2 volumes, edited by Ninon Hesse and Gerhard Kirchhoff (Frankfurt am Main: Suhrkamp, 1966, 1978);

Hermann Hesse/Thomas Mann: Briefwechsel, edited by Anni Carlsson (Frankfurt am Main: Suhrkamp, 1968; expanded edition, 1999);

Hermann Hesse/Peter Suhrkamp: Briefwechsel, edited by Siegfried Unseld (Frankfurt am Main: Suhrkamp, 1969);

Hermann Hesse/Helene Voigt-Diederichs: Zwei Autorenporträts in Briefen, edited by Bernhard Zeller (Düsseldorf & Cologne: Diederichs, 1971);

Hermann Hesse/Karl Kerényi: Briefwechsel aus der Nähe, edited by Magda Kerényi (Munich & Vienna: Langen-Müller, 1972);

Gesammelte Briefe, 4 volumes, edited by Volker Michels (Frankfurt am Main: Suhrkamp, 1973, 1979, 1982, 1986);

Briefe an Freunde: Rundbriefe 1946-1962, edited by Michels (Frankfurt am Main: Suhrkamp, 1977);

Hermann Hesse/R. J. Humm: Briefwechsel, edited by Michels and Ursula Michels (Frankfurt am Main: Suhrkamp, 1977);

Christian Wagner/Hermann Hesse: Ein Briefwechsel, edited by Friedrich Pfäfflin (Stuttgart-Bad Cannstatt: Dr. Cantz'sche Druckerei, 1977);

Herman Hesse/Heinrich Wiegand: Briefwechsel, edited by Klaus Pezold (Berlin & Weimar: Aufbau, 1978);

Der kuriose Dichter Hans Morgenthaler: Briefwechsel mit Ernst Morgenthaler und Hermann Hesse, edited by Roger Perret (Basel: Lenos, 1983);

Hermann Hesse/Hans Sturzenegger: Briefwechsel, edited by Kurt Bächtold (Schaffhausen: Meili, 1984);

Die Antwort bist du selbst: Briefe an junge Menschen, edited by Michels (Frankfurt am Main: Insel, 2000);

Ninon Hesse: Lieber, lieber Vogel: Briefe an Hermann Hesse, edited by Gisela Kleine (Frankfurt am Main: Suhrkamp, 2000);

Stufen des Lebens: Briefe, edited by Unseld (Frankfurt am Main: Insel, 2002);

Hermann Hesse: In Calw daheim: Briefwechsel und Begegnungen mit Calwer Bürgern und Freunden der Schwarzwald Stadt, edited by Siegfried Greiner (Frankfurt am Main: R. G. Fischer, 2002);

Hermann Hesse: Briefwechsel 1921–1927 mit Hugo Bell und Emmy Bell-Hennings, edited by Bärbel Reetz (Frankfurt am Main: Suhrkamp, 2003).

Bibliographies:

Horst Kliemann and Karl H. Silomon, *Hermann Hesse: Eine Bibliographische Studie* (Frankfurt am Main: Bauersche Giesserei, 1947);

Martin Pfeifer, *Hermann Hesse: Bibliographie der im Gebiet der DDR seit 1945 erschienenen Schriften* (Leipzig: VEB, 1955);

Joseph Mileck, *Hermann Hesse and His Critics: The Criticism and Bibliography of Half a Century* (Chapel Hill: University of North Carolina Press, 1958);

Helmut Waibler, *Hermann Hesse: Eine Bibliographie* (Bern & Munich: Francke, 1962);

Hermann Hesse: Ein Gesamtverzeichnis seines Werkes im Suhrkamp Verlag (Frankfurt am Main: Suhrkamp, 1962);

Otto Bareiss, *Hermann Hesse: Eine Bibliographie der Werke über Hermann Hesse,* 2 volumes (Basel: Maier-Bader, 1962–1964);

Hans W. Bentz, *Hermann Hesse in Übersetzungen* (Frankfurt am Main: H. W. Bentz, 1965);

Pfeifer, *Hermann-Hesse-Bibliographie: Primär- und Sekundärschriftum in Auswahl* (Berlin: Schmidt, 1973);

Mileck, *Hermann Hesse: Biography and Bibliography,* 2 volumes (Berkeley: University of California Press, 1977);

Hesse-Magazin: Bücher, Termine, Ausstellungen, Veranstaltungen im Hesse-Jahr 2002 (Frankfurt am Main: Suhrkamp Insel, 2002);

Michael Limberg, *Hermann-Hesse-Literatur, 9. Jahrgang 2002* (Stuttgart: Staatsanzeiger Verlag, 2002).

Biographies:

Hugo Ball, *Hermann Hesse: Sein Leben und sein Werk* (Berlin: Fischer, 1927; revised edition, Zurich: Fretz & Wasmuth, 1947);

Edmund Gnefkow, *Hermann Hesse, Biographie* (Freiburg im Breisgau: G. Kirchhoff, 1952);

Bernhart Zeller, ed., *Hermann Hesse: Eine Chronik in Bildern* (Frankfurt am Main: Suhrkamp, 1960);

Zeller, *Hermann Hesse in Selbstzeugnissen und Bilddokumenten* (Reinbek bei Hamburg: Rowohlt, 1963); translated by Mark Hallebone as *Portrait of Hesse: An Illustrated Biography* (New York: Herder & Herder, 1971);

Volker Michels, ed., *Hermann Hesse: A Pictorial Biography* (New York: Farrar, Straus & Giroux, 1975);

W. Staudenmeyer, *Hermann Hesse und Calw* (Calw: Kreissparkasse Calw, 1977);

Michels, ed., *Hermann Hesse: Sein Leben in Bildern und Texten* (Frankfurt am Main: Suhrkamp, 1979);

Gisela Kleine, *Ninon und Hermann Hesse: Leben als Dialog* (Sigmaringen: Thorbecke, 1982);

Herbert Schnierle-Lutz, *Literaturreisen auf den Spuren Hermann Hesses von Calw nach Montagnola* (Stuttgart & Dresden: Klett, 1991);

Uli Rothfuss, *Hermann Hesse privat: In Texten, Bildern und Dokumenten* (Berlin: edition q, 1992);

Thomas Feitknecht, *Hermann Hesse in Bern* (Bern: Hans Huber, 1997);

Schnierle-Lutz, ed., *Hermann Hesse: Schauplätze sienes Lebens* (Frankfurt am Main: Insel, 1997);

Alois Prinz, *"Und jedem Anfang wohnt ein Zauber inne": Die Lebensgeschichte Hermann Hesses* (Weinberg & Basel: Belz, 2000);

Wilfried Setzler, *Hesse in Tübingen* (Tübingen: Silberberg, 2002);

Michael Limberg, *Hermann Hesse: Leben Werk Wirkung* (Frankfurt am Main: Suhrkamp, 2005).

References:

Ursula Apel, ed., *Hermann Hesse: Personen und Schlüsselfiguren in seinem Leben,* 2 volumes (Munich & London: Saur, 1989, supplement, 1993);

Winifred Babcock. *Jung, Hesse, Harold* (New York: Dodd, Mead, 1983);

Jan Badewien and Hans-George Schmidt, eds., *Hermann Hesse: Dichter der Suchenden* (Karlsruhe: Herrenalber Forum, Band 36, 2003);

Günter Baumann, *Der archetypische Heilsweg: Hermann Hesse, C. G. Jung und die Weltreligionen* (Rheinfelden: Schäuble, 1990);

Baumann, *Hermann Hesse: Dichter und Weiser* (Berlin: Schäuble, 1997);

Mark Boulby, *Hermann Hesse: His Mind and Art* (Ithaca, N.Y.: Cornell University Press, 1967);

Friedrich Bran and Martin Pfeifer, eds., *Begegnungen mit Hermann Hesse* (Bad Liebenzell: Gengenbach, 1984);

Bran and Pfeifer, eds., *Hermann Hesse und die Religion* (Bad Liebenzell: Gengenbach, 1990);

Bran and Pfeifer, eds., *Hermann Hesses Glasperlenspiel* (Bad Liebenzell: Gegenbach, 1987);

Bran and Pfeifer, eds., *Wege zu Hermann Hesse: Dichtung, Musik, Malerei, Film* (Bad Liebenzell: Gengenbach, 1989);

Kyung Yang Cheong, *Mystische Elemente aus West und Ost im Werk Hermann Hesses* (Frankfurt am Main & Bern: Lang, 1991);

Ingo Cornils and Osman Durrani, eds., *Hermann Hesse Today / Hermann Hesse Heute* (Amsterdam & New York: Amsterdam Beiträge zur Neueren Germanistik, 2005);

Eugen Drewermann, *Das Individuelle gegen des Normierte verteidigen. Zwei Aufsätze zu Hermann Hesse* (Frankfurt am Main: Suhrkamp, 1995);

Helga Esselborn-Krumbiegel, *Hermann Hesse: "Der Steppenwolf"* (Munich: Oldenbourg, 1985);

Robert Farquharson, *An Outline of the Works of Hermann Hesse* (Toronto: Forum House, 1973);

Kurt J. Fickert, *Hermann Hesse's Quest: The Evolution of the "Dichter" Figure in His Work* (Fredericton, N.B.: York Press, 1978);

G. W. Field, *Hermann Hesse* (New York: Twayne, 1970);

Ralph Freedman, *Hermann Hesse: Pilgrim of Crisis* (London: Cap, 1979);

Güntner Gottschalk, *Hesse-Lyrik-Konkordanz: Mit Wortindex und Wortfrequenzlisten* (Munich, London & New York: K. G. Saur, 1987);

Siegfried Greiner, *Hermann Hesse: Jugend in Calw* (Sigmaringen: Thorbecke, 1981);

Richard C. Helt, *A Poet or Nothing at All: The Tübingen and Basel Years of Hermann Hesse* (Providence, R.I. & Oxford: Berghahn, 1996);

Adrian Hsia, *Hermann Hesse und China* (Frankfurt am Main: Suhrkamp, 1974);

Walter Jahnke, *Hermann Hesse: Demian: Ein Erlesener Roman* (Paderborn: Schöningh, 1984);

Walter Jens and Hans Küng, eds. *Anwälte der Humanität: Thomas Mann, Hermann Hesse, Heinrich Böll* (Munich: Kindler, 1989);

Claudia Karstedt, *Die Entwicklung des Frauenbildes bei Hermann Hesse* (Bern & Frankfurt am Main: Lang, 1983);

Andreas Kiryakakis, *The Idea of Heimat in the Works of Hermann Hesse* (New York & Bern: Lang, 1988);

Beate Kory, *Hermann Hesses Beziehung zur Tiefenpsychologie: Traumliterarische Projekte* (Hamburg: Kovac, 2003);

Annette Kym, *Hermann Hesses Rolle als Kritiker: Eine Analyse seiner Buchbesprechungen in März, Vivos Voco, und Bonniers Litterära Magasin* (Bern & Frankfurt am Main: Lang, 1984);

Birgit Lahann, *Hermann Hesse: Dichter für die Jugend der Welt: Ein Lebensbild* (Frankfurt am Main: Suhrkamp, 2002);

Judith Lieberman, ed., *Hermann Hesse: A Collection of Criticism* (New York: McGraw-Hill, 1977);

Michael Limberg, ed., *Hermann Hesse in seinen Briefen* (Bad Liebenzell: Gengenbach, 1994);

Limberg, ed., *Kunst als Therapie: Hermann Hesse und die Psychoanalyse* (Bad Liebenzell: Gengenbach, 1997);

Limberg, ed., *Zwischen Eigen-Sinn und Anpassung* (Bad Liebenzell: Gengenbach, 1999);

Hans Jürg Lüthi, *Hermann Hesse: Natur und Geist* (Stuttgart: Kohlhammer, 1970);

Carlee Marrer-Tising, *The Reception of Hermann Hesse by the Youth in the United States* (Bern & Frankfurt am Main: Lang, 1982);

Volker Michels, ed., *Materialen zu Hermann Hesses "Demian,"* 2 volumes (Frankfurt am Main: Suhrkamp, 1996, 1997);

Michels, ed., *Materialen zu Hermann Hesses "Siddhartha",* 2 volumes (Frankfurt am Main: Suhrkamp, 1975, 1976);

Michels, ed., *Materialen zu Hermann Hesses "Das Glasperlenspiel,"* 2 volumes (Frankfurt am Main: Suhrkamp, 1973, 1974);

Michels, ed., *Materialen zu Hermann Hesses "Der Steppenwolf"* (Frankfurt am Main: Suhrkamp, 1972);

Michels, ed., *Über Hermann Hesse,* 2 volumes (Frankfurt am Main: Suhrkamp, 1976–1977);

Joseph Mileck, *Hermann Hesse: Between the Perils of Politics and the Allure of the Orient* (New York: Peter Lang, 2003);

Mileck, *Hermann Hesse: Life and Art* (Berkeley: University of California Press, 1978);

Mileck, *Herman Hesse: Life, Work, and Criticism* (Fredericton, N.B.: York Press, 1984);

Anna Otten, ed., *Hesse Companion* (Frankfurt am Main: Suhrkamp, 1970; Albuquerque: University of New Mexico Press, 1977);

Georg Patzer, *Hermann Hesse: Unterm Rad* (Stuttgart: Reclam, 2004);

Martin Pfeifer, ed., *Hermann Hesse und die Politik* (Bad Liebenzell: Gengenbach, 1992);

Pfeifer, ed., *Hermann Hesses weltweite Wirkung: Internationale Rezeptionsgeschichte,* 3 volumes (Frankfurt am Main: Suhrkamp, 1977–1991);

Pfeifer, ed., *Hesse Kommentar zu samtlichen Werken* (Munich: Winkler, 1980; revised and expanded edition, Frankfurt am Main: Suhrkamp, 1990);

Herbert W. Reinchert, *The Impact of Nietzsche on Hermann Hesse* (Mount Pleasant, Mich.: Enigma Press, 1972);

Edmund Remys, *Hermann Hesse's Das Glasperlenspiel: A Concealed Defence of the Mother World* (Bern & Frankfurt am Main: Lang, 1983);

David G. Richards, *Exploring the Divided Self: Hermann Hesse's "Steppenwolf" and Its Critics* (Columbia, S.C.: Camden House, 1996);

Richards, *The Hero's Quest for the Self: An Archetypal Approach to Hesse's "Demian" and Other Novels* (Lanham, Md.: University Press of America, 1987);

Ernest Rose, *Faith from the Abyss: Hermann Hesse's Way from Romanticism to Modernity* (New York: New York University Press, 1965);

Hans Jürgen Schmelzer, *Auf der Fährte des Steppenwolfs: Hermann Hesses Herkunft, Leben und Werk* (Stuttgart: Hohenheim, 2002);

Klaus von Seckendorff, *Hermann Hesses propagandische Prosa: Selbstzerstörerische Entfaltung als Botschaft in seinen Romanen vom Demian bis zum Steppenwolf* (Bonn: Bouvier, 1982);

Eugene L. Steltzig, *Hermann Hesse's Fictions of the Self* (Princeton: Princeton University Press, 1988);

Lewis W. Tusken, *Understanding Hermann Hesse: The Man, His Myth, His Metaphor* (Columbia: University of South Carolina Press, 1998);

Siegfried Unseld, *Begegnungen mit Hermann Hesse* (Frankfurt am Main: Suhrkamp, 1975);

Unseld, *Hermann Hesse: Werk und Wirkungsgeschichte* (Frankfurt am Main: Suhrkamp, 1985);

Klaus Walter, *Hermann Hesse* (München: Deutscher Taschenbuch, 2002);

Kurt Weibel, *Hermann Hesse und die deutsche Romantik* (Winterthur: Keller, 1954);

Uwe Wolff, *Hermann Hesse: Demian–Die Botschaft vom Selbst* (Bonn: Bouvier, 1979);

Helmut W. Ziefle, *Hermann Hesse und das Christentum* (Wuppertal & Zurich: Brockhaus, 1994);

Theodore Ziolkowski, *The Novels of Hermann Hesse: A Study in Theme and Structure* (Princeton: Princeton University Press, 1965);

Ziolkowski, *Der Schriftsteller Hermann Hesse* (Frankfurt am Main: Suhrkamp, 1979);

Ziolkowski, ed., *Hesse: A Collection of Critical Essays* (Englewood Cliffs, N.J.: Prentice-Hall, 1973).

Papers:

Hermann Hesse's extensive *Nachlaß* (literary remains) is housed in the Hermann-Hesse-Archiv of the Schiller-Nationalmuseum, Marbach am Neckar, Germany. Significant additional Hesseana is housed in the Hermann-Hesse-Museum in Calw and in the Hermann-Hesse-Höri-Museum in Gaienhofen, Germany. Some seventeen thousand letters and postcards sent to Hesse are located in the Hermann-Hesse-Briefarchiv in the Schweizerische Landesbibliothek, Bern, Switzerland.

1946 Nobel Prize in Literature Presentation Speech

by Anders Österling, Permanent Secretary of the Swedish Academy

This year's Nobel Prize in literature has been awarded to a writer of German origin who has had wide critical acclaim and who has created his work regardless of public favour. The sixty-nine-year-old Hermann Hesse can look back on a considerable achievement consisting of novels, short stories, and poems, partly available in Swedish translation.

He escaped from political pressure earlier than other German writers and, during the First World War, settled in Switzerland where he acquired citizenship in 1923. It should not be overlooked, however, that his extraction as well as his personal connections had always justified Hesse in considering himself as much Swiss as German. His asylum in a country that was neutral during the war allowed him to continue his important literary work in relative quiet, and at present Hesse, together with Mann, is the best representative of the German cultural heritage in contemporary literature.

With Hesse, more than with most writers, one has to know his personal background to understand the rather surprising components that make up his personality. He comes from a strictly pietist Swabian family. His father was a well-known church historian, his mother the daughter of a missionary. She was of French descent and was educated in India. It was taken for granted that Hermann would become a minister, and he was sent to the seminary at the cloister of Maulbronn. He ran away, became an apprentice to a watchmaker, and later worked in bookshops in Tübingen and Basle.

The youthful rebellion against the inherited piety that nonetheless always remained in the depth of his being, was repeated in a painful inner crisis, when in 1914 as a mature man and an acknowledged master of regional literature he went new ways which were far removed from his previous idyllic paths. There are, briefly, two factors that caused this profound change in Hesse's writings.

The first was, of course, the World War. When at its beginning he wanted to speak some words of peace and contemplation to his agitated colleagues and in his pamphlet used Beethoven's motto, "O Freunde, nicht diese Töne," he aroused a storm of protest. He was savagely attacked by the German press and was apparently deeply shocked by this experience. He took it as evidence that the entire civilization of Europe in which he had so long believed was sick and decaying. Redemption had to come from beyond the accepted norms, perhaps from the light of the East, perhaps from the core hidden in anarchic theories of the resolution of good and evil in a higher unity. Sick and doubt-ridden, he sought a cure in the psychoanalysis of Freud, eagerly preached and practised at that time, which left lasting traces in Hesse's increasingly bold books of this period.

This personal crisis found its magnificent expression in the fantastical novel *Der Steppenwolf* (1927) *[Steppenwolf]*, an inspired account of the split in human nature, the tension between desire and reason in an individual who is outside the social and moral notions of everyday life. In this bizarre fable of a man without a home, hunted like a wolf, plagued by neuroses, Hesse created an incomparable and explosive book, dangerous and fateful perhaps, but at the same time liberating by its mixture of sardonic humour and poetry in the treatment of the theme. Despite the prominence of modern problems Hesse even here preserves a continuity with the best German traditions; the writer whom this extremely suggestive story recalls most is E. T. A. Hoffmann, the master of the *Elixiere des Teufels*.

Hesse's maternal grandfather was the famous Indologist Gundert. Thus even in his childhood the writer felt drawn to Indian wisdom. When as a mature man he travelled to the country of his desire he did not, indeed, solve the riddle of life; but the influence of Buddhism soon entered his thought, an influence by no means restricted to *Siddhartha* (1922), the beautiful story of a young Brahman's search for the meaning of life on earth.

Hesse's work combines so many influences from Buddha and St. Francis to Nietzsche and Dostoevsky that one might suspect that he is primarily an eclectic experimenter with different philosophies. But this opinion would be quite wrong. His sincerity and his seriousness are the foundations of his work and remain in control even in his treatment of the most extravagant subjects.

In his most accomplished novellas we are confronted both directly and indirectly with his personality. His style, always admirable, is as perfect in rebellion and demonic ecstasy as in calm philosophical speculation. The story of the desperate embezzler Klein, who flees to Italy to seek there his last chance, and the marvellously calm description of his late brother Hans in the *Gedenkblätter* (1937) *[Reminiscences]* are masterly examples from different fields of creativity.

In Hesse's more recent work the vast novel *Das Glasperlenspiel* (1943) *[Magister Ludi]* occupies a special position. It is a fantasy about a mysterious intellectual order, on the same heroic and ascetic level as that of the Jesuits, based on the exercise of meditation as a kind of therapy. The novel has an imperious structure in which the concept of the game and its role in civilization has surprising parallels with the ingenious study *Homo ludens* by the Dutch scholar Huizinga. Hesse's attitude is ambiguous. In a period of collapse it is a precious task to preserve the cultural tradition. But civilization cannot be permanently kept alive by turning it into a cult for the few. If it is possible to reduce the variety of knowledge to an abstract system of formulas, we have on the one hand proof that civilization rests on an organic system; on the other, this high knowledge cannot be considered permanent. It is as fragile and destructible as the glass pearls themselves, and the child that finds the glittering pearls in the rubble no longer knows their meaning. A philosophical novel of this kind easily runs the risk of being called recondite, but Hesse defended his with a few gentle lines in the motto of the book, ". . . then in certain cases and for irresponsible men it may be that non-existent things can be described more easily and with less responsibility in words than the existent, and therefore the reverse applies for pious and scholarly historians; for nothing destroys description so much as words, and yet there is nothing more necessary than to place before the eyes of men certain things the existence of which is neither provable nor probable, but which, for this very reason, pious and scholarly men treat to a certain extent as existent in order that they may be led a step further toward their being and their becoming."

If Hesse's reputation as a prose writer varies, there has never been any doubt about his stature as a poet. Since the deaths of Rilke and George he has been the foremost German poet of our time. He combines exquisite purity of style with moving emotional warmth, and his musical form is unsurpassed in our time. He continues the tradition of Goethe, Eichendorff, and Mörike and renews its poetic magic by a colour peculiar to himself. His collection of poems, *Trost der Nacht* (1929) [The Solace of Night], mirrors with unusual clarity not only his inner drama, his healthy and sick hours, and his intense self-examination, but also his devotion to life, his pleasure in painting, and his worship of nature. A later collection, *Neue Gedichte* (1937) [New Poems], is full of autumnal wisdom and melancholy experience, and it shows a heightened sensibility in image, mood, and melody.

In a summary introduction it is impossible to do justice to the many changing qualities which make this writer particularly attractive to us and which have justly given him a faithful following. He is a problematic and a confessional poet with the wealth of the South German mind, which he expresses in a very individual mixture of freedom and piety. If one overlooked the passionate tendency to protest, the ever-burning fire that makes the dreamer a fighter as soon as the matters at stake are sacred to him, one might call him a romantic poet. In one passage Hesse says that one must never be content with reality, that one should neither adore nor worship it, for this low, always disappointing, and desolate reality cannot be changed except by denying it through proving our superior strength.

Hesse's award is more than the confirmation of his fame. It honours a poetic achievement which presents throughout the image of a good man in his struggle, following his calling with rare faithfulness, who in a tragic epoch succeeded in bearing the arms of true humanism.

Unfortunately, reasons of health have prevented the poet from making the journey to Stockholm. In his stead the envoy of the Swiss Federal Republic will accept the Prize.

Your Excellency, I ask you now to receive from the hands of His Majesty the King the Prize awarded by the Swedish Academy to your countryman, Hermann Hesse.

[© The Nobel Foundation, 1946.]

Hesse: Banquet Speech

Introductory remarks by Sigurd Curman, President of the Royal Academy of Sciences, at the Nobel Banquet at the City Hall in Stockholm, 10 December 1946:

Hermann Hesse has carried on his battle against these microbes of the soul in the field of literature. He has endeavoured, in his stylistically exquisite poems and stories, to show us the way to rise out of this slough. He shouts to all of us the motto of young Joseph Knecht in *Das Glasperlenspiel*: "Transzendieren!" Advance, mount higher, conquer yourself! For to be human is to suffer an incurable duality, to be drawn toward both good and evil. And we can achieve harmony and peace only when we have killed the selfishness within us. This is Hesse's message to the people of a ravaged age, resounding with screams of self-vindication from East and West. It is principally as a profound philosopher and bold critic of the contemporary period in his stories that Hesse deserves the Nobel Prize.

As Hesse was unable to be present, the speech was read by Henry Vallotton, Swiss Minister (Translation):

We deeply regret that illness keeps Hermann Hesse in Switzerland. But his thoughts are with us, and his gratitude speaks through this message which he asked me to read to you:

In sending cordial and respectful greetings to your festive gathering, I should like above all to express my regrets at not being able to be your guest in person, to greet and to thank you. My health has always been delicate, and I have been left a permanent invalid by the afflictions of the years since 1933 that have destroyed my life's work and have again and again burdened me with heavy duties. But my mind has not been broken, and I feel akin to you and to the idea that inspired the Nobel Foundation, the idea that the mind is international and supra-national, that it ought to serve not war and annihilation, but peace and reconciliation.

My ideal, however, is not the blurring of national characteristics, such as would lead to an intellectually uniform humanity. On the contrary, may diversity in all shapes and colours live long on this dear earth of ours. What a wonderful thing is the existence of many races, many peoples, many languages, and many varieties of attitude and outlook! If I feel hatred and irreconcilable enmity toward wars, conquests, and annexations, I do so for many reasons, but also because so many organically grown, highly individual, and richly differentiated achievements of human civilization have fallen victim to these dark powers. I hate the *grands simplificateurs,* and I love the sense of quality, of inimitable craftsmanship and uniqueness. As your grateful guest and colleague I therefore extend my greetings to Sweden, your country, to her language and civilization, her rich and proud history, and her perseverance in maintaining and shaping her individual nature. I have never been to Sweden, but for decades many a good and kind thing has come to me from your country since that first present which I received from it: it is now forty years ago and it was a Swedish book, a copy of the first edition of *Christ Legends* with a personal dedication by Selma Lagerlöf. In the course of years there has been many a valuable exchange with your country until you have now surprised me with the final great present. Let me express to you my profound gratitude.

[© The Nobel Foundation, 1946. Hermann Hesse is the sole author of his speech.]

Hesse: Autobiographical Statement

(Written at the time of the awarding of the Nobel Prize)

I was born in Calw in the Black Forest on July 2, 1877. My father, a Baltic German, came from Estonia; my mother was the daughter of a Swabian and a French Swiss. My father's father was a doctor, my mother's father a missionary and Indologist. My father, too, had been a missionary in India for a short while, and my mother had spent several years of her youth in India and had done missionary work there.

My childhood in Calw was interrupted by several years of living in Basle (1880–86). My family had been composed of different nationalities; to this was now added the experience of growing up among two different peoples, in two countries with their different dialects.

I spent most of my school years in boarding schools in Wuerttemberg and some time in the theological seminary of the monastery at Maulbronn. I was a good learner, good at Latin though only fair at Greek, but I was not a very manageable boy, and it was only with difficulty that I fitted into the framework of a pietist education that aimed at subduing and breaking the individual personality. From the age of twelve I wanted to be a poet, and since there was no normal or official road, I had a hard time deciding what to do after leaving school. I left the seminary and grammar school, became an apprentice to a mechanic, and at the age of nineteen I worked in book and antique shops in Tübingen and Basle. Late in 1899 a tiny volume of my poems appeared in print, followed by other small publications that remained equally unnoticed, until in 1904 the novel *Peter Camenzind*, written in Basle and set in Switzerland, had a quick success. I gave up selling books, married a woman from Basle, the mother of my sons, and moved to the country. At that time a rural life, far from the cities and civilization, was my aim. Since then I have always lived in the country, first, until 1912, in Gaienhofen on Lake Constance, later near Bern, and finally in Montagnola near Lugano, where I am still living.

Soon after I settled in Switzerland in 1912, the First World War broke out, and each year brought me more and more into conflict with German nationalism; ever since my first shy protests against mass suggestion and violence I have been exposed to continuous attacks and floods of abusive letters from Germany. The hatred of the official Germany, culminating under Hitler, was compensated for by the following I won among the young generation that thought in international and pacifist terms, by the friendship of Romain Rolland, which lasted until his death, as well as by the sympathy of men who thought like me even in countries as remote as India and Japan. In Germany I have been acknowledged again since the fall of Hitler, but my works, partly suppressed by the Nazis and partly destroyed by the war; have not yet been republished there.

In 1923, I resigned German and acquired Swiss citizenship. After the dissolution of my first marriage I lived alone for many years, then I married again.

Faithful friends have put a house in Montagnola at my disposal.

Until 1914 I loved to travel; I often went to Italy and once spent a few months in India. Since then I have almost entirely abandoned travelling, and I have not been outside of Switzerland for over ten years.

I survived the years of the Hitler regime and the Second World War through the eleven years of work that I spent on the *Glasperlenspiel* (1943) *[Magister Ludi]*, a novel in two volumes. Since the completion of that long book, an eye disease and increasing sicknesses of old age have prevented me from engaging in larger projects.

Of the Western philosophers, I have been influenced most by Plato, Spinoza, Schopenhauer, and Nietzsche as well as the historian Jacob Burckhardt. But they did not influence me as much as Indian and, later, Chinese philosophy. I have always been on familiar and friendly terms with the fine arts, but my relationship to music has been more intimate and fruitful. It is found in most of my writings. My most characteristic books in my view are the poems (collected edition, Zürich, 1942), the stories *Knulp* (1915), *Demian* (1919), *Siddhartha* (1922), *Der Steppenwolf* (1927) *[Steppenwolf]*, *Narziss und Goldmund* (1930), *Die Morgenlandfahrt* (1932) *[The Journey to the East]*, and *Das Glasperlenspiel* (1943) *[Magister Ludi]*. The volume *Gedenkblätter* (1937, enlarged ed. 1962) [Reminiscences] contains a good many autobiographical things. My essays on political topics have recently been published in Zürich under the title *Krieg und Frieden* (1946) *[War and Peace]*.

I ask you, gentlemen, to be contented with this very sketchy outline; the state of my health does not permit me to be more comprehensive.

[© The Nobel Foundation, 1946. Hermann Hesse is the sole author of the text.]

Paul Heyse
(15 March 1830 - 2 April 1914)

Charles H. Helmetag
Villanova University

This entry has been expanded by Helmetag from his Heyse entry in *DLB 129: Nineteenth-Century German Writers, 1841–1900*.

BOOKS: *Frühlingsanfang 1848* (Berlin: Schade, 1848);

Der Jungbrunnen: Neue Märchen von einem fahrenden Schüler, anonymous (Berlin: Duncker, 1850)–comprises "Das Märchen von der guten Seele," "Glückspilzchen," "Das Märchen von Musje Morgenroth und jungfer Abendbrod," "Veilchenprinz," "Das Märchen von Blindekuh," and "Fedelint und Funzifudelchen"; revised edition (Berlin: Paetel, 1878);

Francesca von Rimini: Tragödie in fünf Akten (Berlin: Hertz, 1850);

Die Brüder: Eine chinesische Geschichte in Versen (Berlin: Hertz, 1852);

Studia romanensia: Particula I. Dissertatio inauguralis (Berlin: Schade, 1852);

Urica: Novelle in Versen (Berlin: Hertz, 1852);

Hermen: Dichtungen (Berlin: Hertz, 1854)–comprises "Margherita Spoletina," "Urica," "Idyllen von Sorrent," "Die Furie," "Die Brüder," "Michelangelo Buonarotti," and "Perseus: Eine Puppentragödie";

Meleager: Eine Tragödie (Berlin: Hertz, 1854);

Novellen (Berlin: Hertz, 1855)–comprises "Die Blinden," "Marion," "L'Arrabbiata," and "Am Tiberufer";

Die Braut von Cypern: Novelle in Versen. Mit einem lyrischen Anhang (Stuttgart & Augsburg: Cotta, 1856);

Thekla: Ein Gedicht in neun Gesängen (Stuttgart: Cotta, 1858);

Neue Novellen: 2. Sammlung (Stuttgart: Cotta, 1858)–comprises "Erkenne dich selbst"; "Das Mädchen von Treppi," translated by A. W. Hinton as *The Maiden of Treppi; or, Love's Victory* (New York: Hinton, 1874); "Der Kreisrichter"; and "Helene Morten";

Vier neue Novellen: 3. Sammlung (Berlin: Hertz, 1859)–comprises "Die Einsamen," translated anonymously as "The Lonely Ones," in Eugenie Marlitt, *Magdalena*; Paul Heyse, *The Lonely Ones* (Philadel-

Paul Heyse, circa 1870–1880 (Library of Congress Prints and Photographs Division)

phia: Lippincott, 1869); "Anfang und Ende"; "Maria Franziska"; and "Das Bild der Mutter";

Die Sabinerinnen: Tragödie in fünf Akten (Berlin: Hertz, 1859);

Die Grafen von der Esche: Schauspiel in fünf Akten (Munich: Deschler, 1861);

Neue Novellen: 4. Sammlung (Berlin: Hertz, 1862)–comprises "Annina"; "Im Grafenschloß"; "Andrea

Delfin," translated anonymously as *Andrea Delfin* (Boston: Burnham, 1864); and "Auf der Alm";

Ludwig der Bayer: Schauspiel in fünf Akten (Berlin: Hertz, 1862);

Rafael: Eine Novelle in Versen (Stuttgart: Kröner, 1863);

Elisabeth Charlotte: Schauspiel in fünf Akten (Berlin: Hertz, 1864);

Gesammelte Novellen in Versen (Berlin: Hertz, 1864)—comprises "Die Braut von Cypern," "Die Brüder," "König und Magier," "Margherita Spoletina," "Urica," "Die Furie," "Rafael," "Michelangelo Buonarotti," and "Die Hochzeitsreise an den Walchensee"; enlarged edition (1870)—includes "Thekla," "Syritha," "Der Salamander," "Schlechte Gesellschaft," and "Das Feenkind";

Meraner Novellen: 5. Sammlung (Berlin: Hertz, 1864)—comprises "Unheilbar," translated by Mrs. H. W. Eve as *Incurable* (London: Nutt, 1890); "Der Kinder Sünde der Väter Fluch"; and "Der Weinhüter";

Maria Moroni: Trauerspiel in fünf Akten (Berlin: Hertz, 1865);

Hadrian: Tragödie in fünf Akten (Berlin: Hertz, 1865);

Hans Lange: Schauspiel in fünf Akten (Berlin: Hertz, 1866);

Fünf neue Novellen: 6. Sammlung (Berlin: Hertz, 1866)—comprises "Franz Alzeyer," "Die Reise nach dem Glück," "Die kleine Mama," "Kleopatra," and "Die Witwe von Pisa";

Die glücklichen Bettler: Morgenländisches Märchen in drei Akten, frei nach Carlo Gozzi (Berlin: Hertz, 1867);

Novellen und Terzinen: 7. Sammlung der Novellen (Berlin: Hertz, 1867)—comprises "Syritha: Novelle in Versen," "Mutter und Kind: Novelle," "Auferstanden: Novelle," "Der Salamander: Novelle in Versen," and "Beatrice: Novelle";

Colberg: Historisches Schauspiel in fünf Akten (Berlin: Hertz, 1868);

Der Rothmantel: Komische Oper in drei Aufzügen nach Musäus' Volksmärchen (Munich: Wolf, 1868);

Moralische Novellen: 8. Sammlung (Berlin: Hertz, 1869)—comprises "Die beiden Schwestern," "Lorenz und Lore," "Vetter Gabriel," "Am toten See," and "Der Thurm von Nonza";

Die Göttin der Vernunft: Trauerspiel in fünf Akten (Berlin: Hertz, 1870);

Adam und Eva: Operette in 1. Aufzuge, music by Robert von Hornstein (Munich: Straub, 1870);

Ein neues Novellenbuch: 9. Sammlung (Berlin: Hertz, 1871)—comprises "Barbarossa," "Die Stickerin von Treviso," "Lottka," "Der letzte Zentaur," "Der verlorene Sohn," "Das schöne Käthchen," "Geoffroy und Garcinde," and "Die Pfadfinderin";

Die Franzosenbraut: Volksschauspiel in fünf Akten (Munich: Straub, 1871);

Der Friede: Ein Festspiel für das Münchener Hof- und National-Theater, music by Baron von Perfall (Munich: Oldenbourg, 1871);

Gesammelte Werke, 38 volumes (volumes 1–29, Berlin: Hertz / volumes 30–38, Stuttgart & Berlin: Cotta, 1872–1914)—includes *Die Pfälzer in Irland: Trauerspiel in fünf Akten,* volume 9 (1872),

Kinder der Welt: Roman in sechs Büchern, 3 volumes (Berlin: Hertz, 1873); translated anonymously as *Children of the World: A Novel* (London: Chapman & Hall, 1882; New York: Munro, 1883);

Neue Novellen: Der Novellen 10. Sammlung (Berlin: Hertz, 1875)—comprises "Er soll dein Herr sein," "Die ungarische Gräfin," "Ein Märtyrer der Phantasie," "Judith Stern," and "Nerina";

Ehre um Ehre: Schauspiel in fünf Akten (Berlin: Hertz, 1875);

Im Paradiese: Roman in sieben Büchern, 3 volumes (Berlin: Hertz, 1875); translated anonymously as *In Paradise,* 2 volumes (New York: Appleton, 1878);

Skizzenbuch: Lieder und Bilder (Berlin: Hertz, 1877);

Graf Königsmark: Trauerspiel in fünf Akten (Berlin: Hertz, 1877);

Elfride: Trauerspiel in fünf Akten (Berlin: Hertz, 1877);

Neue moralische Novellen: 11. Sammlung der Novellen (Berlin: Hertz, 1878)—comprises "Jorinde," "Getreu bis in den Tod," "Die Kaiserin von Spinetta," "Das Seeweib," and "Die Frau Marchesa";

Zwei Gefangene: Novelle (Leipzig: Reclam, 1878); translated anonymously as *Two Prisoners* (London: Simpkin, 1893);

Das Ding an sich und andere Novellen: 12. Sammlung der Novellen (Berlin: Hertz, 1879)—comprises "Das Ding an sich," "Zwei Gefangene," "Die Tochter der Excellenz," and "Beppe der Sternseher";

Die Madonna im Oelwald: Novelle in Versen (Berlin: Hertz, 1879);

Verse aus Italien: Skizzen, Briefe und Tagebuchblätter (Berlin: Hertz, 1880);

Die Weiber von Schorndorf: Historisches Schauspiel in vier Akten (Berlin: Hertz, 1880);

Frau von F. und römische Novellen: 13. Sammlung der Novellen (Berlin: Hertz, 1881)—comprises "Frau von F."; "Die talentvolle Mutter"; "Romulusenkel"; and "Die Hexe vom Korso," translated by George W. Ingraham as *The Witch of the Corso* (New York: Munro, 1882);

Das Glück von Rothenburg: Novelle (Augsburg: Reichel, 1881); translated by C. L. Townsend as "The Spell of Rothenburg," in *The German Classics of the Nineteenth and Twentieth Centuries,* volume 13, edited by Kuno Francke and William Guild Howard (New York: German Publication Society, 1914), pp. 105–152;

Troubadour-Novellen: 14. Sammlung der Novellen (Berlin: Hertz, 1882; New York: Munro, 1883)—comprises "Der lahme Engel," "Die Rache der Vizgräfin," "Die Dichterin von Carcassonne," "Der Mönch von Montaudon," "Ehre über alles," and "Der verkaufte Gesang";

Alkibiades: Tragödie in drei Akten (Berlin: Hertz, 1883);

Das Recht des Stärkeren: Schauspiel in drei Akten (Berlin: Hertz, 1883);

Don Juan's Ende: Trauerspiel in fünf Akten (Berlin: Hertz, 1883); translated anonymously as *The Last Days of Don Juan* (London, n.d.);

Unvergeßbare Worte und andere Novellen: 15. Sammlung der Novellen (Berlin: Hertz, 1883)—comprises "Unvergeßbare Worte," "Die Eselin," "Das Glück von Rothenburg," and "Geteiltes Herz";

Buch der Freundschaft: Novellen. 16. Sammlung der Novellen (Berlin: Hertz, 1883)—comprises "David und Jonathan"; "Grenzen der Menschheit"; and "Nino und Maso," translated by Alfred Remy as "Nino and Maso: A Tale Drawn from a Sienese Chronicle," in *The German Classics of the Nineteenth and Twentieth Centuries*, volume 13 (1914), pp. 74-104;

Siechentrost: Novelle (Augsburg: Reichel, 1883);

Buch der Freundschaft: Neue Folge. 17. Sammlung der Novellen (Berlin: Hertz, 1884)—comprises "Siechentrost," "Die schwarze Jakobe," "Gute Kameraden," and "Im Bunde der Dritte";

Drei einaktige Trauerspiele und ein Lustspiel (Berlin: Hertz, 1884)—comprises *Ehrenschulden, Frau Lukrezia, Simson,* and *Unter Brüdern: Lustspiel in einem Akt;*

Spruchbüchlein (Berlin: Hertz, 1885);

Gedichte (Berlin: Hertz, 1885; enlarged, 1889);

Himmlische und irdische Liebe–F.V.R.I.A.–Auf Tod und Leben: Novellen. 18. Sammlung der Novellen (Berlin: Hertz, 1886; New York: Munro, 1886);

Getrennte Welten: Schauspiel in vier Akten (Berlin: Hertz, 1886);

Die Hochzeit auf dem Aventin: Trauerspiel in fünf Akten (Berlin: Hertz, 1886);

Die Weisheit Salomo's: Schauspiel in fünf Akten (Berlin: Hertz, 1887);

Der Roman der Stiftsdame: Eine Lebensgeschichte (Berlin: Hertz, 1887); translated by J. M. Percival [Mary Joanna Safford] as *The Romance of the Canoness: A Life-History* (New York: Appleton, 1887);

Villa Falconieri und andere Novellen: 19. Sammlung der Novellen (Berlin: Hertz, 1888)—comprises "Villa Falconieri," "Doris Sengeberg," "Emerenz," and "Die Märtyrerin der Phantasie";

Gott schütze mich vor meinen Freunden: Lustspiel in drei Akten (Berlin: Hertz, 1888);

Prinzessin Sascha: Schauspiel in vier Akten (Berlin: Hertz, 1888);

Weltuntergang: Volksschauspiel in fünf Akten (Berlin: Hertz, 1889);

Kleine Dramen: Erste Folge (Berlin: Hertz, 1889)—comprises *Im Bunde der Dritte, Der Venusdurchgang, Nur keinen Eifer,* and *In sittlicher Entrüstung;*

Kleine Dramen: Zweite Folge (Berlin: Hertz, 1889)—comprises *Eine erste Liebe, Eine Dante-Lektüre, Zwischen Lipp und Bechersrand,* and *Die schwerste Pflicht;*

Liebeszauber: Orientalische Dichtung (Munich: Hanfstaengl, 1889);

Novellen: Auswahl fürs Haus, 3 volumes (Berlin: Hertz, 1890)—comprises "L'Arrabbiata," "Anfang und Ende," "Andrea Delfin," "Unheilbar," "Vetter Gabriel," "Die beiden Schwestern," "Er soll dein Herr sein," "Der verlorene Sohn," "Nerina," "Unvergeßbare Worte," "Die Dichterin von Carcassonne," "Das Glück von Rothenburg," and "Siechentrost";

Ein überflüssiger Mensch: Schauspiel in vier Akten (Berlin: Hertz, 1890);

Die schlimmen Brüder: Schauspiel in vier Akten und einem Vorspiel (Berlin: Hertz, 1891);

Weihnachtsgeschichten (Berlin: Hertz, 1891)—comprises "Eine Weihnachtsbescherung," "Das Freifräulein," "Die Geschichte von Herrn Wilibald und dem Frosinchen," and "Die Dryas";

Merlin: Roman in sieben Büchern, 3 volumes (Berlin: Hertz, 1892);

Marienkind (Stuttgart: Engelhorn, 1892);

Wahrheit?: Schauspiel in drei Akten (Berlin: Hertz, 1892);

Ein unbeschriebenes Blatt: Lustspiel in vier Akten (Berlin: Hertz, 1893);

Jungfer Justine: Schauspiel in vier Akten (Berlin: Hertz, 1893);

Aus den Vorbergen: Novellen (Berlin: Hertz, 1893)—comprises "Vroni," "Marienkind," "Xaverl," and "Dorfromantik";

In der Geisterstunde und andere Spukgeschichten (Berlin: Hertz, 1894)—comprises "In der Geisterstunde: Die schöne Abigail," translated by Frances A. Van Santford as *At the Ghost Hour: The Fair Abigail* (New York: Dodd, Mead, 1894); "In der Geisterstunde: Mittagszauber," translated by Van Santford as "Mid-Day Magic," in *At the Ghost Hour: Mid-Day Magic* (New York: Dodd, Mead, 1894); "In der Geisterstunde: Lisabethle," translated by Van Santford as "Little Lisbeth," in *At the Ghost Hour: Mid-Day Magic;* "In der Geisterstunde: Das Waldlachen," translated by Van Santford as *At the Ghost Hour: The Forest Laugh* (New York: Dodd, Mead, 1894); "Martin der Streber"; and "Das Haus 'Zum unglaubigen Thomas' oder des Spirits

Rache," translated by Van Santford as *At the Ghost Hour: The House of the Unbelieving Thomas* (New York: Dodd, Mead, 1894);

Wolfram von Eschenbach: Ein Festspiel (Munich: Knorr & Hirth, 1894);

Melusine und andere Novellen (Berlin: Hertz, 1895)—comprises "Hochzeit auf Capri," translated anonymously as "The Wedding at Capri," *Cosmopolitan*, 16 (January 1894): 318–331; "Fedja"; "Donna Lionarda"; "Die Rächerin"; and "Melusine";

Über allen Gipfeln: Roman (Berlin: Hertz, 1895);

Roland's Schildknappen oder Die Komödie vom Glück: Volksmärchen in drei Akten und einem Vorspiel (Berlin: Hertz, 1896);

Vanina Vanini: Trauerspiel in vier Akten (Berlin: Hertz, 1896);

Die Fornarina: Trauerspiel in fünf Akten (Leipzig: Naumann, 1896);

Das Goethe-Haus in Weimar (Berlin: Hera, 1896);

Verrathenes Glück; Emerenz: Zwei Geschichten (Stuttgart: Krabbe, 1896);

Einer von Hunderten und Hochzeit auf Capri (Stuttgart: Franckh, 1896);

Abenteuer eines Blaustrümpfchens (Stuttgart: Krabbe, 1897); translated anonymously as "Adventures of a Little Blue-Stocking," *International*, 1 (1896): 329–338;

Das Räthsel des Lebens und andere Charakterbilder (Berlin: Hertz, 1897)—comprises "Der Dichter und sein Kind," "Der Siebengescheite," "Ehrliche Leute," "Einer von Hunderten," "Ein Mädchenschicksal," "Das Steinchen im Schuh," and "Das Räthsel des Lebens";

Männertreu; Der Sohn seines Vaters: Zwei Novellen (Stuttgart: Krabbe, 1897);

Drei neue Einakter (Berlin: Hertz, 1897)—comprises *Der Stegreiftrunk: Drama in einem Akt*; *Schwester Lotte: Lustspiel in einem Akt*; and *Auf den Dächern: Dramatischer Scherz in einem Akt*;

Neue Gedichte und Jugendlieder (Berlin: Hertz, 1897);

Der Sohn seines Vaters und andere Novellen (Berlin: Hertz, 1898)—comprises "Der Sohn seines Vaters," "Verratenes Glück," "Medea," "Männertreu," and "Abenteuer eines Blaustrümpfchens";

Der Bucklige von Schiras: Komödie in vier Akten (Berlin: Hertz, 1898);

Martha's Briefe an Maria: Ein Beitrag zur Frauenbewegung (Stuttgart: Cotta, 1898);

Neue Märchen (Berlin: Hertz, 1899)—comprises "Holdrio, oder Das Märchen vom wohlerzogenen Königssohn," "Das Märchen vom Herzblut," "Die vier Geschwister," "Der Jungbrunnen," "Lilith," "Die gute Frau," "Die Nixe," "Das Märchen von Niels mit der offenen Hand," "Johannisnacht," and "Die Dryas";

Das literarische München: 25 Porträtskizzen (Munich: Bruckmann, 1899);

Die Macht der Stunde; Vroni: Zwei Novellen (Stuttgart: Krabbe, 1899); "Die Macht der Stunde" translated anonymously as "The Power of the Hour," *English Illustrated Magazine*, 31 (May 1904): 155–183;

Maria von Magdala: Drama in fünf Akten (Berlin: Hertz, 1899); translated by A. I. Coleman as *Mary of Magdala* (New York: Lederer, 1900);

Fräulein Johanne; Auf der Alm: Zwei Novellen (Stuttgart: Krabbe, 1900);

Der Schutzengel: Novelle (Leipzig: Keil, 1900);

Jugenderinnerungen und Bekenntnisse (Berlin: Hertz, 1900; revised and enlarged, 2 volumes, Stuttgart: Cotta, 1912);

Das verschleierte Bild zu Sais: Drama in drei Akten (Stuttgart & Berlin: Cotta, 1901; New York: Lederer, 1901);

Tantalus; Mutter und Kind: Zwei Novellen (Stuttgart: Krabbe, 1901);

Ninon und andere Novellen (Stuttgart & Berlin: Cotta, 1902)—comprises "Ninon," "Zwei Seelen," "Der Blinde von Dausenau," "Fräulein Johanne," "Tantalus," and "Ein Mutterschicksal";

Der Heilige: Trauerspiel in fünf Akten (Berlin & Stuttgart: Cotta, 1902);

Novellen vom Gardasee (Stuttgart & Berlin: Cotta, 1902)—comprises "Gefangene Singvögel," "Die Macht der Stunde," "San Vigilio," "Entsagende Liebe," "Eine venezianische Nacht," and "Antiquarische Briefe";

Romane und Novellen, 42 volumes (Stuttgart: Cotta, 1902–1912);

Moralische Unmöglichkeiten und andere Novellen (Stuttgart & Berlin: Cotta, 1903)—comprises "Moralische Unmöglichkeiten," "Er selbst," "Zwei Wittwen," and "Ein Idealist";

Ein Wintertagebuch (Gardone 1901–1902) (Stuttgart: Cotta, 1903);

Mythen und Mysterien (Stuttgart: Cotta, 1904)—comprises "Lilith: Ein Mysterium," "Kain: Ein Mysterium," "Perseus: Puppentragödie in vier Akten," "Am Thor der Unterwelt," "Der Waldpriester: Ein Satyrspiel," and "Gespräche im Himmel";

Crone Stäudlin: Roman (Stuttgart: Cotta, 1905);

Die thörichten Jungfrauen: Lustspiel in drei Akten (Stuttgart & Berlin: Cotta, 1905);

Ein Canadier: Drama in drei Akten (Stuttgart & Berlin: Cotta, 1905);

Sechs kleine Dramen (Stuttgart & Berlin: Cotta, 1905)—comprises *Eine alte Geschichte: Familienszene in einem Akt*; *Die Zaubergeige: Drama in einem Akt*; *Zu treu: Genrebild in einem Akt*; *Horaz und Lydia*; *Der Stern von*

Mantua: Schauspiel in zwei Akten; and *Die Tochter der Semiramis: Tragödie in einem Akt*;

Victoria Regia und andere Novellen (Stuttgart & Berlin: Cotta, 1906)—comprises "Victoria Regia," "Lucile," "Tante Lene," "Die Ärztin," "Der Hausgeist," and "Ein Ring";

Gegen den Strom: Eine weltliche Klostergeschichte (Stuttgart: Cotta, 1907);

Menschen und Schicksale: Charakterbilder (Stuttgart: Cotta, 1908)—comprises "Das Karussell," "Das Unglück, Verstand zu haben," "Lottchen Täppe," "Verfehlter Beruf," "Die gute Tochter," "Ein Luftschiffer," "Mei Bübche," "Fromme Lüge," "Florian," "Iwan Kalugin," "Ein Christuskopf," "Ein Menschenfeind," and "Ein literarischer Vehmrichter";

Helldunkles Leben: Novellen (Stuttgart: Cotta, 1909)—comprises "Unüberwindliche Mächte," "Rita," "Ein unpersönlicher Mensch," "Eine Collegin," and "Clelia";

Die Geburt der Venus: Roman (Stuttgart & Berlin: Cotta, 1909);

König Saul: Biblische Historie in fünf Akten (Leipzig: Reclam, 1909);

Mutter und Tochter: Drama in fünf Akten (Leipzig: Reclam, 1909);

Das Ewigmenschliche: Erinnerungen aus einem Alltagsleben von ***; Ein Familienhaus: Novelle (Stuttgart: Cotta, 1910);

Plaudereien eines alten Freundespaares (Stuttgart: Cotta, 1912)—comprises "Faustrecht," "Das schwächere Geschlecht," "Altruismus," "Don Juan," "Erste Liebe," "Oliva von Planta," "Vendetta," and "Der Jubilar";

Letzte Novellen (Stuttgart: Cotta, 1914)—comprises "Die bessere Welt," "Fanchette," and "Unwiederbringlich."

Editions and Collections: *Ausgewählte Gedichte*, edited by Erich Petzet (Stuttgart & Berlin: Cotta, 1920);

Gesammelte Novellen, 5 volumes, edited by Erich Petzet (Stuttgart & Berlin: Cotta, 1921);

Italienische Novellen, 2 volumes (Stuttgart: Cotta, 1924);

Gesammelte Werke, 15 volumes (Stuttgart: Cotta, 1924); new edition (Hildesheim, Zurich & New York: Olms, 1984-2002);

Die Reise nach dem Glück: Eine Auswahl aus dem Werk, selected by Gerhard Mauz (Stuttgart: Cotta, 1959);

Das Mädchen von Treppi: Italienische Liebesgeschichten (Berlin: Der Morgen, 1965);

Andrea Delfin und andere Novellen (Berlin & Weimar: Aufbau, 1966);

Die Hexe vom Corso und andere Novellen mit der Novellentheorie (Munich: Goldmann, 1969);

L'Arrabbiata; Das Mädchen von Treppi, edited by Karl Pörnbacher (Stuttgart: Reclam, 1969);

Novellen, introduction by Manfred Schunicht (New York & London: Johnson Reprint, 1970)—comprises "L'Arrabbiata," "Andrea Delfin," "Kleopatra," "Beatrice," "Der letzte Zentaur," "Der lahme Engel," "Das Glück von Rothenburg," "Die Kaiserin von Spinetta," "Siechentrost," "Einleitung zu Deutscher Novellenschatz"; and "Meine Novellistik";

Werke, mit einem Essay von Theodor Fontane, 2 volumes, edited by Bernhard Knick, Johanna Knick, and Hildegard Korth (Frankfurt am Main: Insel, 1980);

Novellen, Die Große Erzähler-Bibliothek der Weltliteratur, volume 54 (Dortmund: Harenberg, 1986)—comprises "L'Arrabbiata," "Helene Morten," "Andrea Delfin," "Der letzte Zentaur," "Judith Stern," and "Victoria Regia";

Novellen, edited by Rainer Hillenbrand (Zurich: Manesse, 1998).

Editions in English: *Four Phases of Love*, translated by G. H. Kingsley (London: Routledge, 1857)—comprises "Eye-Blindness and Soul-Blindness," "Marion," "La Rabbiata," and "By the Banks of the Tiber";

L'Arrabiata and Other Tales, translated by Mary Wilson (Leipzig: Tauchnitz / New York: Leypoldt & Holt, 1867)—comprises "L'Arrabiata," "Count Ernest's Home," "Blind," and "Walter's Little Mother";

The Dead Lake and Other Tales, translated by Wilson (Leipzig: Tauchnitz / New York: Low, Marston, Searle & Rivington, 1870)—comprises "A Fortnight at the Dead Lake," "Doomed," "Beatrice," and "Beginning and End";

Barbarossa and Other Tales, translated by L. C. S. (Leipzig: Tauchnitz / London: Low, Marston, Low & Searle, 1874)—comprises "Barbarossa," "The Embroideress of Treviso," "Lottka," "The Lost Son," "The Fair Kate," and "Geoffroy and Garcinde";

Tales from the German of Paul Heyse (New York: Appleton, 1879)—comprises "Count Ernest's Home," "The Dead Lake," "The Fury (L'Arrabiata)," and "Judith Stern";

Selected Stories, from the German of Paul Heyse (Chicago: Schick, 1886)—comprises "L'Arrabiata," "Beppe, the Star-Gazer," and "Maria Francisca";

La Marchesa, a Tale of the Riviera and Other Tales, translated by John Philips (London: Stock, 1887)—comprises "La Marchesa," "Her Excellency's Daughter," and "A Divided Heart";

Words Never to Be Forgotten and The Donkey: Two Novellettes from the German of Paul Heyse, translated by A. E. Fordyce (Union Springs, N.Y.: Hoff, 1888);

A Divided Heart, and Other Stories, translated by Constance Stewart Copeland (New York: Brentano's, 1894)—comprises "A Divided Heart," "Minka," and "Rothenburg on the Tauber."

TRANSLATIONS: *Spanisches Liederbuch* [anthology], translated and edited and with contributions by Heyse and Emanuel Geibel (Berlin: Hertz, 1852);

José Caveda, *Geschichte der Baukunst in Spanien,* edited by Franz Kugler (Stuttgart: Ebner & Seubert, 1858);

Italienisches Liederbuch [anthology], edited and translated by Heyse (Berlin: Hertz, 1860);

William Shakespeare, *Antonius und Kleopatra* (Leipzig: Brockhaus, 1867);

Shakespeare, *Timon von Athen* (Leipzig: Brockhaus, 1868);

Giuseppe Guisti, *Gedichte,* edited and translated by Heyse (Berlin: Hofmann, 1875);

Giacomo Leopardi, *Werke* (Berlin: Hertz, 1878);

Italienische Dichter seit der Mitte des 18. Jahrhunderts: Übersetzungen und Studien [anthology], 5 volumes (volumes 1–4, Berlin: Hertz; volume 5, Stuttgart & Berlin: Cotta, 1889–1905);

Italienische Volksmärchen [anthology] (Munich: Lehmann, 1914);

Drei italienische Lustspiele aus der Zeit der Renaissance, translated by Heyse (Jena: Diederichs, 1914)—comprises *Die Cassaria,* by Ludovico Ariosto; *Die Aridosia,* by Lorenzo de' Medici; and *Mandragola,* by Niccolò Machiavelli.

OTHER: "Frohe Botschaft," "Freischarenlied," "Hurrah!," "Unser Wahlspruch," "An die deutschen Frauen," "Morgenandacht," "Hurrah!," "Einen Mann!" in *Fünfzehn neue deutsche Lieder zu alten Singweisen: Den deutschen Männern Ernst Moritz Arndt und Ludwig Uhland gewidmet,* edited by Franz Kugler (Berlin, 1848), pp. 5–6, 13–14, 22–25, 27–30;

Romanische inedita auf ltaliänischen Bibliotheken gesammelt, edited by Heyse (Berlin: Hertz, 1856);

Antologia dei moderni poeti italiani, edited by Heyse (Stuttgart: Hallberger, 1869);

Deutscher Novellenschatz, 24 volumes, edited by Heyse and Hermann Kurz (Munich: Oldenbourg, 1871–1876);

Novellenschatz des Auslandes, 14 volumes, edited by Heyse and Kurz (Munich: Oldenbourg, 1872–1875);

Kurz, *Gesammelte Werke: Mit einer Biographie des Dichters,* 10 volumes, edited by Heyse (Stuttgart: Kröner, 1874);

Italienische Novellisten, 6 volumes, edited by Heyse (Leipzig: Grunow, 1877–1878);

Lodovico Ariosto, *Rasender Roland,* 2 volumes, translated by Kurz, edited by Heyse (Breslau: Schottlaender, 1880–1881);

Neues Münchener Dichterbuch, edited, with contributions, by Heyse (Stuttgart: Kröner, 1882);

Neuer deutscher Novellenschatz, 24 volumes, edited by Heyse and Ludwig Laistner (Munich: Oldenbourg, 1884–1887);

"Meine Erstlingswerke," in *Die Geschichte des Erstlingswerkes,* edited by Karl Emil Franzos (Leipzig: Titze, 1894), pp. 53–63;

Lodovico Ariostos Satiren, translated by Otto Gildemeister, edited by Heyse (Berlin: Behr, 1904);

Hermann Lingg, *Ausgewählte Gedichte,* edited by Heyse (Stuttgart & Berlin: Cotta, 1905).

SELECTED PERIODICAL PUBLICATIONS–UNCOLLECTED: "Die Geister des Rheins: Ein Märchenschwank," *Süddeutsche Monatshefte,* 7 (1910): 417–441;

"Luco de Grimaud: Eine ungedruckte Versnovelle von Paul Heyse," *Euphorion,* 29 (1928): 471–479.

Paul Heyse, editor, translator, essayist, and author of novellas, novels, poetry, and dramas, was revered by the German middle class throughout much of his life as the successor to Johann Wolfgang von Goethe. He was such a prominent and prolific author that some of his contemporaries maintained that the second half of the nineteenth century would be remembered as the "Age of Heyse." Others accused him of endangering morality through the glorification of the nonconformist in his works, although twentieth-century critics tended to regard his novellas as compromising tributes to the very social order they seem to attack.

Many of Heyse's works were first published in literary periodicals and were sought after by German and foreign editors—even prestigious periodicals such as the *Deutsche Rundschau*—because of their immense popularity. He played a leading role in the cultural and social life of Munich and was also a proponent of education for young women. He never hesitated to take a stand against any form of censorship or prejudice. Heyse also was known for his kindness toward writers who were trying to get established. Because of his reputation, his great contemporaries Gottfried Keller, Theodor Storm, and Theodor Fontane and younger authors such as Frank Wedekind sought his opinion and support of their works. He translated William Shakespeare and Spanish poetry, but his primary interest in translation was Italian literature, and he became the most important mediator of Italian literature in Germany. When he was awarded the Nobel Prize in Literature in 1910, his reputation as a major author had already begun to wane. Since the 1980s, however, his collected works have been republished, and there has been renewed scholarly interest in his life and works, especially the novellas and translations, for their significance as a reflection of the popular taste of the German middle class in the nineteenth century.

Paul Johann Ludwig Heyse was born in Berlin on 15 March 1830, the second of two sons of Karl Wilhelm Ludwig and Julie Saaling Heyse. Both his father and his grandfather Johann Christian August Heyse were well-known philologists. Prior to his appointment to the faculty at the University of Berlin, Karl Heyse had been a tutor to Felix Mendelssohn-Bartholdy. There was a connection to Mendelssohn on Heyse's mother's side, as well: her mother and Mendelssohn's mother were cousins. Julie Heyse came from a prominent banking family, was fluent in French and English, and was a member of Rahel Varnhagen von Ense's literary salon. In imitation of Goethe, Paul Heyse attributed his own balanced personality to the contrasting natures of his conscientious Germanic father and his witty, irrepressible "Oriental" mother.

Heyse excelled as a pupil at the Friedrich Wilhelms-Gymnasium, especially in classical languages and French. While still in school he helped proofread the dictionary his father was preparing; wrote his first play, a tragedy titled "Don Juan de Pedillo" that was never published or performed; and began writing nature and love poems. In 1845 he established a poets' society, the "Club," with his classmates Bernhard Endrulat, Richard Göhde, and Felix von Stein, the great-grandson of Goethe's friend Charlotte von Stein. In poems written between 1845 and 1847 he described his feelings for Stein's sister Anna, a love thwarted by class differences. Heyse's early poems were clearly influenced by Heinrich Heine and Joseph Freiherr von Eichendorff, two of the favorite models of the Club's young poets. Except for Endrulat, Göhde, and Stein, Heyse had little rapport with his classmates; eventually, he realized that he would have to compromise with the values of his peers. Some critics have regarded this attitude as the basis for the immense popularity of his stories—he gave his readers what they wanted—and, at the same time, the reason for the disturbing lack of realism in his works.

In 1846 the poet Emanuel Geibel saw some poems Heyse had written in school and arranged a meeting with him. Under Geibel's influence Heyse's inclination toward an emphasis on form over content was further cultivated. In March 1847 Heyse matriculated at the University of Berlin to study classical philology. As a student he wrote political poetry in support of the revolution of 1848, including his first published poem, *Frühlingsanfang 1848* (1848, The Beginning of Spring 1848) and the seven poems he contributed to Franz Kugler's *Fünfzehn neue deutsche Lieder zu alten Singweisen* (1848, Fifteen New German Songs for Old Singing Styles). The events of 1848 made a great impact on the eighteen-year-old Heyse. Seeing his contemporaries die in the streets probably helped inspire the central theme in his works: the conflict between the individual and the inflexible forces of society. The events he witnessed may also be responsible for the nonrevolutionary tendency in his works.

In cultured Berlin homes and salons the young Heyse came in contact with artists, musicians, and writers such as Fontane, Mendelssohn, Wilhelm Hensel, Peter Cornelius, and Franz Liszt. Especially important for Heyse's development were the associations formed in the home of the art historian Franz Kugler. There he met his future wife—Kugler's daughter Margarethe—as well as Fontane and the historian Jakob Burckhardt, who inspired his love for Italy and the Renaissance. Fontane, well known at the time for his ballads, inspired Heyse's competitive spirit. Heyse regarded the older poet as a worthy opponent, and, despite some friction at first, they became lifelong friends and carried on a correspondence until Fontane's death in 1898.

In the spring of 1849, at Burckhardt's suggestion, Heyse transferred to the University of Bonn. During his summer vacation in 1849 he visited Burckhardt in Basel and began a correspondence with him that continued until 1890. Burckhardt encouraged and cultivated Heyse's veneration of harmonious beauty, a veneration that colored Heyse's works and his perception of reality. Before returning to Bonn he went hiking in the Swiss Alps, where a chambermaid in his hotel fell in love with him. She was possibly the earliest inspiration for a character type that appears in many of his stories: a girl of classical Roman beauty and elemental passion. In January 1850 Heyse changed his major to Romance languages and literatures, a field that complemented his literary talents. His first published play, *Francesca von Rimini,* and the fairy-tale collection *Der Jungbrunnen* (The Fountain of Youth) were published the same year. The inspiration for *Francesca von Rimini* was Heyse's love affair with Sophie Ritschl, the young wife of a Bonn professor. The tragic situation of lovers who go against conventional morality was repeated often in his works. Heyse returned to Berlin in 1851 to complete his doctoral dissertation on the poetry of the troubadours. His preoccupation with Italian, Spanish, and French literature resulted in many translations, several of which were set to music. It also left its mark on his literary works, which frequently have southern European settings, characters, flavor, and form.

While writing his dissertation, Heyse immersed himself again in the social life of the Berlin artists and writers. He had joined the literary group "Der Tunnel über der Spree" (The Tunnel over the River Spree) in January 1849. Most of the group's members were would-be writers from the Prussian military and bureaucracy, but Kugler, Fontane, and Geibel were also members. Everyone in the group had a special Tunnel name; Heyse's was "Hölty II," after the eighteenth-century author of love and nature poetry Ludwig Heinrich Christoph Hölty. Each member's literary endeavors were subject to the others' criticism, which made the Tunnel a valuable apprenticeship for a young writer. Heyse became a celebrity in the Tunnel as well as in its offshoot, "Rütli" (named for a place on Lake Luzerne), to which Geibel, Fontane, Kugler, and Storm also belonged. He wrote his verse novella *Die Brüder* (1852, The Brothers) during this period. In Berlin literary circles a Heyse cult developed that compared his form-conscious works to those of the young Goethe.

In June 1852 Heyse was awarded a doctorate in Romance philology. The same year brought the publication of his and Geibel's *Spanisches Liederbuch* (Book of Spanish Songs), a collection of translations of Spanish poems and folk songs, many of which were later set to music and remain popular today. The *Spanisches Liederbuch* also includes original poems by Heyse and Geibel under Spanish pseudonyms. Heyse continued his activity as a translator and editor throughout his life.

In the fall of 1852 Heyse received a grant from the Prussian Ministry of Culture to study unpublished Provençal manuscripts in Italy. He traveled with Otto Ribbeck, a former classmate in Bonn, who was consulting manuscripts in Italian libraries for an edition of the works of Virgil. In Rome, Heyse stayed with his uncle Theodor Heyse, who had translated the works of Catullus. There was a sizable German colony in Rome, and Heyse became acquainted with Arnold Böcklin and many other artists and sculptors. He found ample opportunity to make sketches of dark-haired, dark-eyed Italian girls who epitomized his idea of classical Mediterranean beauty. The high point of his Italian journey was the spring of 1853, which he spent in Naples and Sorrento, enthusiastically observing the life of the people. He eventually did publish a volume of old manuscripts, *Romanische inedita* (1856), but the main product of the trip was a series of poems and stories with Italian settings and passionate female characters, works that became associated with Heyse in the minds of the German middle-class reading public for the rest of his life.

Heyse spent two weeks of his stay in the Rosa Magra, an inn in Sorrento frequented by artists, with Josef Viktor von Scheffel, the author of historical novels such as *Der Trompeter von Säckingen* (1854; translated as *The Trumpeter of Säkkingen*, 1877). Nearly twenty-five years later he sent a poem to Scheffel in which he recalled an incident with a servant girl at the inn who inspired his first published novella, "L'Arrabbiata" (translated as "La Rabbiata," 1857). He portrayed her in these lines as a tan, uninhibited fifteen-year-old who scurried about the dining room and nearly bit him with her sharp, white cat's teeth when he grabbed her by the hair. In 1854 the novella appeared in *Argo*, the literary yearbook edited by Fontane, and established Heyse's reputation. It went through fourteen editions between 1857 and 1914, in addition to ten editions in the first collection of Heyse's novellas (1855) and many textbook editions for American students (as recently as 2003 in *An Anthology of German Novellas*, edited by Siegfried Weing).

"L'Arrabbiata" opens with Sorrento fishermen casting off at dawn in the Bay of Naples. In one of the boats sit the young fisherman Antonio and the local priest, Father Curato, who is taking Holy Communion to a wealthy patroness in Capri. The two men are joined by a striking young woman named Laurella, barely eighteen, who has a habit of tossing her head in a wild and somewhat imperious manner. Externally she is the typical Heyse Italian female, with her brown face, black hair, full lips, fine nose, and flashing black eyes. Laurella's coyness and reserve result from her father's abusive treatment of his wife. Laurella is wary of suitors, since she fears that they might treat her the same way, but she accepts Antonio's invitation to return to Sorrento with him in the afternoon while the priest remains on the island. The young fisherman declares his love for her; when she rejects him, he tries to drown her and himself. She bites his hand, jumps overboard, and starts swimming for shore. When Antonio rows after her and apologizes, she climbs back on board. That evening she brings him herbs to stop the bleeding and reveals that she has been in love with him for a long time but was afraid to trust her emotions. When Father Curato hears her confession, he is secretly delighted that Laurella's stubbornness has been overcome by true love. Laurella's encounter with Antonio makes her realize that she cannot act contrary to her inmost nature. The theme of self-realization through love is repeated throughout Heyse's stories.

Heyse returned to Berlin in September 1853. During the following months his lifelong friendship with Storm began. Heyse corresponded with most of the major German literary figures of the second half of the nineteenth century, but his correspondence with Storm reveals the closest personal relationship. In 1853 Heyse also began writing for Friedrich Eggers's *Literaturblatt des deutschen Kunstblattes* (Literary Journal of the German Art Journal). He contributed perceptive essays on Storm and Eduard Mörike to the journal and served as its editor in 1858. In March 1854, at Geibel's recommendation, Heyse received an invitation to live in Munich on a stipend from King Maximilian II of Bavaria with no obligation except to write and participate in the symposia of authors and artists sponsored by the court. The appointment also gave Heyse the right to lecture at the University of Munich, but he preferred to devote his time and energy to writing. Storm, with a tinge of envy, compared Heyse's position to that of Goethe at the court at Weimar. Heyse enjoyed and encouraged the comparison to Goethe.

On 15 May 1854 Heyse married Margarethe Kugler. They settled in Munich and had two sons, one of whom died at the age of twelve, and two daughters. The Berliner Heyse quickly adjusted to Munich, where the lifestyle reminded him of Italy, and he resisted repeated invitations from Grand Duke Carl Alexander of Saxony to move to Weimar.

Maximilian wanted to make Munich a cultural and scientific capital, and Heyse and Geibel quickly became the nucleus of the literary branch of this endeavor. In 1856 Heyse and the Thuringian poet Julius Grosse founded the literary group "Der heilige Teich der Krokodile" (The Holy Pond of the Crocodiles), generally known as "Krokodil," in an attempt to reconcile the native Bavarian authors with the predominantly North German writers whom Maximilian had brought in for his symposia. The founding members included Geibel; the Munich poet Hermann Lingg, from whose poem "Das Krokodil zu Singapur" (1854, The Crocodile of Singapore) the group's name was derived; Friedrich Bodenstedt; Felix Dahn; Heinrich Leuthold; the journalist Adolf Wilbrandt, who later became director of the Vienna Burgtheater; and the medievalist and translator Wilhelm Hertz. Scheffel was an honorary member. Unlike the Tunnel membership, most of the Crocodiles, who also became known as the "Münchner Dichterkreis" (Munich Poets' Circle), were professional writers or academics who wrote on the side. Heyse was the president of the group, Geibel the spiritual leader. The Crocodiles met weekly in various coffeehouses for twenty-seven years.

Heyse wrote more than forty plays, including historical dramas and plays dealing with classical antiquity and biblical themes. His plays enjoyed a respectable number of performances. The tragedy *Hadrian* (1865), considered by some to be Heyse's best play, deals with the relationship between the first-century Roman emperor Hadrian and the Greek youth Antinous, representatives respectively of the insufficiency of wealth and power and the contentment to be found in a life of simplicity and freedom. *Hans Lange* (1866), a theatrically effective Prussian patriotic play, was performed on every major German stage. *Colberg* (1868), an historical drama commemorating the defense of the Prussian harbor town Colberg against superior French forces in 1807, was performed in Berlin more than 139 times through the end of World War I and sold 180,000 copies during Heyse's lifetime, assisted by the patriotic fervor of 1870–1871 and 1914.

Heyse's wife had died on 30 September 1862; in 1867 he married Anna Schubart, a beautiful, dark-haired seventeen-year-old from Munich society. Near the Glyptothek Museum he built a splendid villa, which became a center of Munich cultural life; he and his wife spent the winters in a second home in Gardone on Italy's Lake Garda. The son and daughter from Heyse's second marriage both died in childhood. In the 1860s Heyse openly supported the struggles for freedom in Italy and Schleswig-Holstein; in 1868 he gave up his stipend from Ludwig II, who had succeeded Maximilian in 1864, to preserve his political independence.

The collection *Novellen und Terzinen* (Novellas and Terza Rimas) appeared in 1867. The narrator in one of these stories, "Beatrice," introduces the concept of the tragic conflict between the norms of society and the instinctive desires of those nonconformists whom Heyse refers to elsewhere as "Ausnahmemenschen" (exceptional individuals). He calls this phenomenon "der Streit der Pflichten" (the conflict of duties). His most extensive statement of the concept is found in the introduction to his *Moralische Novellen* (1869, Moral Novellas), an essay titled "Brief an Frau Toutlemonde in Berlin" (Letter to Mrs. Everybody in Berlin) and written in response to the criticism provoked by the *Novellen und Terzinen*. ("Frau Toutlemonde" is generally considered to refer to Fontane's wife, Emilie, a devoted admirer of Heyse's works.) Heyse regards conventional morality as a universal code of conduct, which, in attempting to guarantee the general welfare, sometimes infringes on the rights of the exceptional individual. The latter is justified in acting in harmony with his or her instinctive personal morality, although such action inevitably leads to conflict with the forces of society and convention and frequently to the death or lifelong unhappiness of the exceptional individual. The conflict of duties provided Heyse, by his own account, with many of his most interesting and challenging themes.

"Die Stickerin von Treviso" (1871, The Embroideress of Treviso) was one of Heyse's favorite stories. In fourteenth-century Italy the knight Attilio Buonfigh helps his fellow townsmen regain the city of Treviso from the soldiers of Vicenza. Recovering from a neck wound at the home of Emilia Scarpa, a citizen of Vicenza, he agrees to marry her in an attempt to end the feud that has separated their cities for years. When he returns to Treviso, however, he falls in love with the embroideress Gianna. As so often is the case in Heyse's works, true love is accompanied by self-realization.

Attilio asks why his eyes were opened too late, why he did not come to know himself until after he had made a vow to Emilia. He and Gianna resolve to spend each night together until his wedding and then never to see each other again. When he is mortally wounded in a tournament held in honor of his fiancée's arrival in Treviso, however, Gianna sacrifices her reputation by claiming the right to be at her lover's side during his last moments alive. For the Ausnahmemensch, the supreme obligation is fidelity to oneself.

The novella "Himmlische und irdische Liebe" (1886, Heavenly and Earthly Love), another of Heyse's favorites, justifies adultery when one partner is unworthy or inimical to the personal development of the other. Professor Chlodwig commits suicide when, for the sake of public opinion, his poetess wife refuses to let him leave her for the simple and emotionally honest seamstress Traud. Before he met Traud, Chlodwig had defended German bourgeois morality, even philistinism, as potentially beneficial; afterward he rejects convention as restrictive and destructive. Heyse implies that it is each partner's duty to promote the other's potential; where there is no mutual support, the individual has the right to be unfaithful to a spouse rather than deny his or her own inner voice. In a letter to Fontane of 2 January 1879, Heyse said that he preferred a tragic resolution to such conflicts rather than a life founded on halfhearted relationships and wretched compromises.

Occasionally, Heyse lets the conflict with society end in resignation rather than tragedy. In the novella "Der letzte Zentaur" (1871, The Last Centaur) he selected his friend Bonaventura Genelli, who was known for his paintings of centaurs and who had died in 1868, to represent the strong personality in conflict with the conservative society around him. In an elaborate story-within-a-story-within-a-story Genelli relates his encounter with the mythical creature, which suddenly appeared in the philistine milieu of a Bavarian village. The artists to whom he tells the story are lonely outsiders like himself who would have admired the classical beauty of the centaur.

One August, Genelli relates, he went to a mountain village outside Munich to escape the heat of the city. As he sat at an inn drinking Tirolean wine, the giant centaur approached, followed by a crowd of curious children and old people. The creature grabbed two bottles of wine from the pretty waitress Nanni, drank the contents, and asked Genelli—in Greek, of course—where he was. He explained that he had been making his rounds as a country doctor to shepherds and bear hunters, had become intoxicated from the homemade concoctions with which they paid for his services, and had gone into an ice grotto to sleep it off. When he awakened, he had found the forests thinner, the wine more sour, and the women (except for Nanni) less graceful and shapely than before. On the outskirts of the village he had been moved by the sight of a crucifix and had offered to help the man on the cross. Attracted by the sounds emanating from a church, he had been struck by the beauty of a statue of a blue-eyed, blonde Virgin Mary. The village priest had dissuaded the curious villagers from associating with the creature, who surely had never been baptized and was probably immoral; only Genelli was friendly to the centaur.

Genelli, the centaur, and Nanni left the inn together. At a church carnival the centaur partook of more Tirolean wine and stole customers from the concession where a two-headed calf was on display. When the musicians began to play, he set the voluptuous Nanni on his bare back and enthusiastically joined the townsfolk in a dance. The festivities were interrupted, however, by the concessionaire and the village police, who had been called by Nanni's fiancé. Genelli explained to the centaur that these men were hunters who wanted to lock him in a stall to reflect on the benefits of the law and the progress of civilization. The creature jumped over the heads of the crowd, Nanni still on his back, and ran away. High on a mountainside he released the girl to return to her fiancé and jumped into a gorge, never to be seen again. The story implies that Genelli and his artist friends cannot be at home in the bourgeois Catholic society of nineteenth-century Bavaria, since their ideals and appetites are those of classical antiquity. Genelli has accepted ostracism as the price of his creativity.

In an age that paralleled the Victorian era in England, Heyse was considered by many a dangerously immoral writer, a reputation that contributed to his immense popularity during his lifetime. Most of Heyse's novellas either portray Italy—or young Italian women—as an idealized model of natural beauty or depict the psychological problems of characters living in nineteenth-century Germany. Heyse tended to portray exceptional cases rather than timeless human conflicts and problems; nevertheless, some of his novellas still make for diverting reading because of their cosmopolitan style and exotic subject matter, especially those set in pre-nineteenth-century Italy or France such as "Die Stickerin von Treviso"; "Andrea Delfin" (1862; translated, 1864), a story of failed revenge in eighteenth-century Venice; and "Geoffroy und Garcinde" (1871), a troubadour novella dealing with conflict between filial piety and personal happiness in medieval Provence. Of those set in Germany, "Der letzte Zentaur" offers a contrast of nineteenth-century Bavaria with the naturalness of classical antiquity.

Heyse co-edited two important collections of German novellas, the twenty-four-volume *Deutscher Novellen-*

schatz (1871–1876, Treasury of German Novellas) and *Neuer deutscher Novellenschatz* (1884–1887, New Treasury of German Novellas), likewise in twenty-four volumes. He also edited an anthology of works of modern Italian poets, *Antologia dei moderni poeti italiani* (1869); the fourteen-volume *Novellenschatz des Auslandes* (1872–1875, Treasury of Foreign Novellas); and the six-volume *Italienische Novellisten* (1877–1878, Italian Short-Story Writers). He edited and translated two collections of Italian poetry: *Italienisches Liederbuch* (1860, Book of Italian Songs) and *Italienische Dichter seit der Mitte des 18. Jahrhunderts: Übersetzungen und Studien* (1889–1905, Italian Poets since the Middle of the Eighteenth Century: Translations and Studies), as well as selected works of Giuseppe Guisti (1875) and Giacomo Leopardi (1878). He also translated William Shakespeare's *Antony and Cleopatra* (1867) and *Timon of Athens* (1868) and a collection of comedies by Ludovico Ariosto, Niccolò Machiavelli, and Lorenzo de' Medici (1914). His five-volume *Italienische Dichter seit der Mitte des 18. Jahrhunderts* made the works of Leopardi and D'Annunzio available to the German-speaking public for the first time. Heyse was the most important mediator of Italian literature in Germany in the nineteenth century.

Heyse's statements on the German novella in his introduction to *Deutscher Novellenschatz* were embraced by his and later generations as one of the most important theories of the genre. Each of the stories in the collection, Heyse maintained, possesses a "Grundmotif" (basic motif) that can be summarized in a few lines. He compares the basic motif to a "starke Silhouette" (strong silhouette) in painting and cites as an example the story from Giovanni Boccaccio's *Decamerone* (1351–1353) of the impoverished nobleman who prepares his prized falcon as a meal for his lady. Heyse suggests that a storyteller ask himself at the outset "wo 'der Falke' sei, das Spezifische, das diese Geschichte von tausend anderen unterscheidet" (where "the falcon" is, the specific thing that distinguishes this story from a thousand others). Heyse's idea soon became known as the "falcon theory," a designation he himself eventually adopted. Many scholars have misinterpreted the demand for a "falcon" as a requirement that every "true" novella include a symbol, a requirement that Heyse never mentions in his comments on the novella.

As the novel became the dominant form of fiction in Germany, Heyse turned to the genre. Between 1873 and 1906 he produced seven novels. The best known are *Kinder der Welt* (1873; translated as *Children of the World*, 1882) and *Im Paradiese* (1875; translated as *In Paradise*, 1878). Although both were best-sellers, Heyse never attained the level of technical skill in the novel that he had in the more concentrated form of the novella.

Kinder der Welt deals with artists and academics in Berlin during the forming of the Second German Empire. Heyse divides the characters into the children of God and the children of the world. The former group includes the artist König; his daughter, the young artist Lea; and the theology student Lorinser. The children of the world are the young philosopher and freethinker Edwin; his sickly brother Balder; Toinette Marchand, the mistress of a count; the music teacher Christiane Falk; and the poet Heinrich Mohr. Edwin is attracted to Toinette, who marries the count although she does not love him. After Balder's death Edwin suffers from a severe fever and is consoled by reading the diary of his former pupil Lea, which was entrusted to him by her father, König. He falls in love with her. They get married and move to a city in Thuringia, where he works as a mathematics teacher. Several years later Edwin visits his friend Mohr and learns that Toinette has become estranged from her husband after bearing him a child and that she is mentally ill. At Mohr's urging, Edwin visits Toinette and tries to help her. She declares her love for him, but now it is he who cannot return her affection, because he loves Lea. Soon thereafter, Toinette dies as a result of a fall from a horse. A few years later Edwin, who is now a contented husband and father, takes his family back to Berlin, where he visits his old haunts and the friends of his youth.

Both *Kinder der Welt* and *Im Paradiese*, which deals with the artists' world in Munich, aroused controversy for advocating free love. In Heyse's conception of love and marriage, which owes much to German romanticism, a relationship derives its sanctity not from the external bonds of marriage but from a balance of physical and spiritual attraction. Even so, Edwin marries and remains faithful to Lea, and the lovers in *Im Paradiese* feel required to have their union sanctified by church and state once they have children.

Beginning with *Die Weisheit Salomo's* (1887, The Wisdom of Solomon), Heyse wrote several plays based on biblical themes. *Maria von Magdala* (1899; translated as *Mary of Magdala*, 1900), which was later adapted by Maurice Maeterlinck, provoked scandals both in Germany and in New York for its portrayal of Judas as a Hebrew patriot, disillusioned follower of Jesus, and lover of Mary Magdalene. Next to "L'Arrabbiata," it appears to be the work of Heyse most frequently translated into English. Its banning by the Prussian censors in 1903 created so much interest in the play that it went through twenty-eight editions in that year alone.

Heyse's works seldom deviate from the theme of the exceptional individual in conflict with the forces of society. He has been placed among such representatives of the Gründerzeit (the years of reckless financial speculation following the Franco-Prussian War) as Conrad

Ferdinand Meyer, Friedrich Nietzsche, and the mature Storm, portrayers of larger-than-life figures who live according to their own rules. During the 1880s and 1890s Heyse was the object of severe personal attacks from critics who considered his works immoral and from the naturalists, for whom his work represented everything that was artificial and untrue in the works of the older generation. Heyse responded with the novel *Merlin* (1892), about an idealistic young dramatist who stages his last play in an insane asylum and then commits suicide.

On his eightieth birthday Heyse was elevated to the nobility, was made an honorary citizen of Munich, and had a street in the city named after him. In an article in the Munich *Allgemeine Zeitung*, the Munich professor Franz Muncker argued that Stefan George's efforts on behalf of artistic form would not have been possible without the influence of Heyse's accomplishments in poetry and prose. The same year he turned eighty, Heyse was awarded the Nobel Prize in Literature, the first German literary author to be so honored. (The first German to receive the Nobel Prize in Literature was the historian Theodor Mommsen in 1902, followed in 1908 by the philosopher Rudolf Eucken.) Illness prevented Heyse from traveling to Stockholm for the award ceremonies.

In establishing the prize for literature, Alfred Nobel indicated that recipients should be recognized for "the most outstanding work in an ideal direction." Carl David af Wirsén, the permanent secretary of the Swedish Academy from 1901 until 1912, interpreted Nobel's adjective as "idealistic." Heyse was awarded the Nobel Prize near the end of his life and career in recognition of his entire body of work and his idealism. Early in 1910 Muncker nominated Heyse for the prize and acquired the signatures of eighty-two academics in Germany and Austria. It was the first time Heyse's name had been put forward as a candidate. Twenty-five candidates were proposed that year, including Anatole France, Georg Brandes, and Maurice Maeterlinck. In the nomination, Muncker called Heyse "the most venerable living German author" and cited his accomplishments in the novella, the novel, drama, poetry, and translation and his dedication to beauty. He stressed Heyse's stand against the naturalists in defense of idealism in literature.

The Swedish literary historian Karl Warburg also prepared a report in support of Heyse's candidacy for the Nobel Prize. Like Muncker, he blamed the opposition of the naturalists for the fact that "the old admirer of beauty" had not been nominated earlier. He praised Heyse for his "passionate battle against that which is ugly." He gave particular significance to Heyse's novellas and his translations from the Italian and said that he deserved the award because he had striven his entire life "for the ideal in art."

In his presentation speech Wirsén called Heyse "the most important lyrical poet of contemporary Germany" and praised him as a master of the novella and "the creator of the modern psychological novella." Wirsén observed that the naturalists had attacked Heyse in the 1890s, but "Now a miracle seems to have changed everything. The honorable veteran . . . has been flooded with honors." The prize, Wirsén stated, should serve "as a tribute to the consummate artistry, permeated with idealism, which he has demonstrated during his long productive career." He mentioned in particular Heyse's early novellas that the members of the awards committee had enjoyed in their youth. The award seems clearly to be a recognition of Heyse's prolific career and his veneration of beauty.

By 1910, however, Heyse had outlived his reputation. The younger generation of naturalistic authors was highly critical of the Swedish Academy for awarding the prize to him. For more than twenty years they had been criticizing him as out of touch, a "salon poet," an author of unrealistic novels and novellas who put form and beauty above truth. Despite such attacks, the German middle class continued reading his works; the Nobel Prize probably made little difference to the average reader. Heyse died on 2 April 1914 and was buried, with no religious ceremony, in the Waldfriedhof Cemetery in Munich. Soon after his death and the outbreak of World War I, Heyse was largely forgotten.

The naturalists' opinion of Heyse prevailed throughout much of the twentieth century. Then in 1984 Georg Olms Verlag began publishing a reprint of his collected works, and since the 1980s there has been a renaissance of interest in Heyse: his significance as a prose author, his works as a reflection of the literary taste of his time, his correspondence with the major authors of the nineteenth century, his role as a mediator of Italian and Spanish literature, and his intriguing status as the representative German author of the nineteenth century.

Most studies of the history of the novella still acknowledge Heyse as one of the major theoreticians of the genre and compilers of collections of novellas, German and foreign. A few of his own novellas can still be enjoyed today. In the twenty-first century, however, it is primarily his translations that are remembered. His translations of Italian and Spanish poetry, set to music by Hugo Wolf, Johannes Brahms, and others, are part of the standard vocal repertoire.

Letters:
"Paul Heyse und Heinrich Leuthold: Aus unveröffentlichten Briefen Heyses," edited by Georg J.

Plotke, *Das literarische Echo,* 16 (1 May 1914): columns 1034–1036;

"Briefe von Paul Heyse und seinen Angehörigen an die Hahnsche Buchhandlung, Hannover," edited by G. Schmidt, *Börsenblatt für den Deutschen Buchhandel,* 81 (1914): 793–797;

Der Briefwechsel von Jakob Burckhardt und Paul Heyse, edited by Erich Petzet (Munich: Lehmann, 1916);

Der Briefwechsel zwischen Paul Heyse und Theodor Storm, 2 volumes, edited by Plotke (Munich: Lehmann, 1917–1918);

Paul Heyse und Gottfried Keller im Briefwechsel, edited by Max Kalbeck (Braunschweig: Westermann, 1919);

"Aus dem Briefwechsel zwischen Paul Heyse und Hermann Kurz," edited by Hugo Falkenheim, *Der schwäbische Bund,* 1 (November 1919): 218–229; (December 1919): 346–352;

"Der Briefwechsel von Paul Heyse und Fanny Lewald," edited by Rudolf Göhler, *Deutsche Rundschau,* 183 (May 1920): 274–285; (June 1920): 410–441;

Der Briefwechsel von Emanuel Geibel und Paul Heyse, edited by Petzet (Munich: Lehmann, 1922);

"Freundesbriefe an Richard Voß," edited by Paul Weiglin, *Velhagen & Klasings Monatshefte,* 38 (September 1923): 89–94;

"Briefe von Paul Heyse und Otto und Emma Ribbeck," edited by Petzet, *Euphorion,* 27 (1926): 424–462;

"Aus dem Briefwechsel Paul Heyse–Ernst Wichert, 1900–1902," edited by Paul Wichert, *Deutsche Rundschau,* 207 (April/June 1926): 35–44;

Der Briefwechsel von Theodor Fontane und Paul Heyse, 1850–1897, edited by Petzet (Berlin: Weltgeist-Bücher Verlags-Gesellschaft, 1929);

"Der Briefwechsel zwischen Albert Dulk und Paul Heyse," edited by Ernst Rose, *Germanic Review,* 4 (January 1929): 1–32; (April 1929): 131–152;

Briefwechsel zwischen Joseph Victor von Scheffel und Paul Heyse, edited by Conrad Höfer (Karlsruhe: Gräff, 1932);

"Briefwechsel von Paul Heyse und Marie von Ebner-Eschenbach," in *Die Lebens- und Weltanschauung der Freifrau Marie von Ebner-Eschenbach,* by Mechtild Alkemade, Deutsche Quellen, and Studien, volume 15 (Würzburg & Graz: Wächter, 1935), pp. 257–398;

"Sieben Briefe von Paul Heyse und Feodor Löwe, 1859–1862," edited by Claire Strube Schradieck, *PMLA,* 52 (March 1937): 261–271;

Monika Walkhoff, *Der Briefwechsel zwischen Paul Heyse und Hermann Kurz in den Jahren 1869–1873 aus Anlaß der Herausgabe des "Deutschen Novellenschatzes"* (Munich: Foto-Druck Frank, 1967);

Theodor Storm–Paul Heyse: Briefwechsel. Kritische Ausgabe, 3 volumes, edited by Clifford Albrecht Bernd (Berlin: Schmidt, 1969–1974);

Der Briefwechsel zwischen Theodor Fontane und Paul Heyse, edited by Gotthard Erler (Berlin & Weimar: Aufbau, 1972);

"Emilie Fontane und Paul Heyse: Brief um Fontane," edited by Joachim Krueger, *Fontane Blätter,* 5, no. 3 (1983): 280–286;

"Du hast alles, was mir fehlt . . .": Gottfried Keller im Briefwechsel mit Paul Heyse, edited by Fridolin Stähli (Stafa: Gut, 1990);

Ein Buch der Freundschaft über getrennte Welten hinweg: Die Korrespondenz zwischen Wilhelm Bolin und Paul Heyse, edited by Susanne Frejborg (Frankfurt am Main & New York: Peter Lang, 1992);

Ein Gefühl der Verwandtschaft: Paul Heyses Briefwechsel mit Eduard Mörike, edited by Rainer Hillenbrand (Frankfurt & New York: Peter Lang, 1997);

Paul Heyses Briefe an Wilhelm Petersen: Mit Heyses Briefen an Anna Petersen, Vier Briefen Petersens an Heyse und einigen ergänzenden Schreiben aus dem Familienkreise, edited by Hillenbrand (Frankfurt & New York: Peter Lang, 1998).

Bibliographies:

Charles H. Helmetag, "Paul Heyse-Bibliographie (Sekundärliteratur)," *Börsenblatt für den Deutschen Buchhandel,* 25 (14 October 1969): 2557–2564;

Werner Martin, *Paul Heyse: Eine Bibliographie seiner Werke* (Hildesheim: Olms, 1978);

Helmetag, "Paul Heyse-Bibliographie: Sekundärliteratur 1968–1978," *Börsenblatt für den Deutschen Buchhandel,* 26 (28 March 1980): A116–A120;

Rainer Hillenbrand, "Heyse-Bibliographie 1974–1995," in his *Heyses Novellen: Ein literarischer Führer* (Frankfurt am Main & New York: Peter Lang, 1998), pp. 963–973.

Biographies:

Helene Raff, *Paul Heyse* (Stuttgart: Cotta, 1910);

Michail Krausnick, *Paul Heyse und der Münchener Dichterkreis* (Bonn: Bouvier, 1974).

References:

E. K. Bennett, "The Novelle as a Literary Genre" and "The Psychological Novelle," in his *A History of the German Novelle,* revised and continued by H. M. Waidson (Cambridge: Cambridge University Press, 1961), pp. 1–19, 206–240;

Georg Brandes, "Paul Heyse," in his *Creative Spirits of the Nineteenth Century,* translated by Rasmus R. Anderson (New York: Crowell, 1923), pp. 54–105;

Gerhard Friedrich, "Theodor Fontanes Kritik an Paul Heyse und seinen Dramen," in *Fontane aus heutiger Sicht,* edited by Hugo Aust (Munich: Nymphenburger, 1980), pp. 81–117;

Hans Norbert Fügen, "Geibel und Heyse: Elemente und Strukturen des literarischen Systems im 19. Jahrhundert. Dokumentation und Analyse," in his *Dichtung in der bürgerlichen Gesellschaft: Sechs literatursoziologische Studien* (Bonn: Bouvier, 1972), pp. 28–50;

Véronique de la Giroday, *Die Übersetzertätigkeit des Münchener Dichterkreises* (Wiesbaden: Athenaion, 1978);

Charles Hugh Helmetag, "Love and the Social Morality in the Novellen of Paul Heyse," dissertation, Princeton University, 1968;

Jost Hermand, "Zur Literatur der Gründerzeit" and "Hauke Haien: Kritik oder Ideal des gründerzeitlichen Übermenschen?" in his *Von Mainz nach Weimar (1793–1919): Studien zur deutschen Literatur* (Stuttgart: Metzler, 1969), pp. 211–249, 250–268;

Rainer Hillenbrand, *Heyses Novellen: Ein literarischer Führer* (Frankfurt am Main & New York: Peter Lang, 1998);

Annemarie von Ian, "Die zeitgenössische Kritik an Paul Heyse 1850–1914," dissertation, University of Munich, 1965;

Gabriele Kroes-Tillman, *Paul Heyse Italianissimo: Über seine Dichtungen und Nachdichtungen* (Würzburg: Königshausen & Neumann, 1993);

Donald LoCicero, "Paul Heyse: 'Falkentheorie,'" in his *Novellentheorie: The Practicality of the Theoretical* (The Hague: Mouton, 1970), pp. 66–83;

Warren R. Maurer, *The Naturalist Image of German Literature* (Munich: Fink, 1972);

J. A. Michielsen, "Paul Heyse and Three of His Critics: Theodor Fontane, Gottfried Keller and Theodor Storm," dissertation, University of Toronto, 1970;

Robert McBurney Mitchell, *Heyse and His Predecessors in the Theory of the Novelle* (Frankfurt am Main: Baer, 1915);

Sigrid von Moisy, ed., *Paul Heyse, Münchner Dichterfürst im bürgerlichen Zeitalter: Ausstellung in der Bayerischen Staatsbibliothek, 23. Januar bis 11. April 1981* (Munich: Beck, 1981);

Boyd Mullan, "From Bavaria to Berlin: Stations in Paul Heyse's Career as a Patriotic Dramatist," *Euphorion*, 95 (2001): 129–165;

Kenneth Negus, "Paul Heyse's *Novellentheorie*: A Revaluation," *Germanic Review*, 40 (May 1965): 173–191;

Brigitte Schader, "Paul Heyse: 'Unheilbar,'" in her *Schwindsucht—Zur Darstellung einer tödlichen Krankheit in der deutschen Literatur vom poetischen Realismus bis zur Moderne* (Frankfurt am Main & Bern: Peter Lang, 1987), pp. 8–45;

Manfred Schunicht, "Der 'Falke' am 'Wendepunkt': Zu den Novellentheorien Tiecks und Heyses," *Germanisch-romanische Monatsschrift*, new series 10 (1960): 44–56;

Margaret G. Sleeman, "Variations on Spanish Themes: The *Spanisches Liederbuch* of Emanuel Geibel and Paul Heyse and Its Reflection in the Songs of Hugo Wolf," *Proceedings of the Leeds Philosophical and Literary Society,* 18, part 2 (1982): 159–274;

Bernhard Spies, "Ein bürgerlicher Großschriftsteller: Paul Heyses Briefweschel," in *Briefkultur im 19. Jahrhundert,* edited by Rainer Baasner (Tubingen: Niemeyer, 1999), pp. 207–238;

Martin Swales, *The German Novelle* (Princeton: Princeton University Press, 1977);

Christiane Ullmann, "Form and Content of Paul Heyse's Novelle *Andrea Delfin*," *Seminar*, 12 (May 1976): 109–120;

Roland A. Wolff, "Der *Falke* am *Wendepunkt* Revisited: Some Thoughts on Schunicht's Theory and on the German *Novelle* in General," *New German Studies,* 5 (1977): 157–168.

Papers:

The Heyse Archive of the Bayerische Staatsbibliothek (Bavarian State Library) includes unpublished early works and fragments, letters, diaries, newspaper reviews, school and university records, works of German and Italian literature from Paul Heyse's personal library, and a considerable amount of material on his dramas. The Schiller National Museum in Marbach has an extensive collection of letters, poems, drama manuscripts, and other materials.

1910 Nobel Prize in Literature Presentation Speech

by C. D. af Wirsén, Permanent Secretary of the Swedish Academy, 10 December 1910

Many famous writers from several countries have been proposed for this year's Nobel Prize in Literature. The Swedish Academy has awarded it to a writer whose nomination has been supported by more than sixty German experts on art, literature, and philosophy. His name is Paul Heyse. The name revives the memory of our youth and manhood; we still remember the literary pleasure that his novellas, in particular, gave to us. Now an old but still active man, he is a figure that the jury could not pass over if it was to express its admiration by awarding the high distinction to the most significant literary work. Nor was the jury to be swayed by considerations of age or, indeed, anything other than true merit.

Paul Heyse was born in Berlin in 1830. His father was the philologist Karl Wilhelm Heyse, a gentle but determined scholar. From his Jewish mother, Julie Saaling, Heyse perhaps inherited his warm and lively temperament. Heyse, who was nature's favourite in so many ways, had the good fortune of growing up in a carefree home. His school years passed quickly. He was an easy learner. For a while he was a student in Berlin and later he studied Romance philology under Friedrich Diez at Bonn University. In 1852 he received his doctorate in Berlin *multa cum laude*. Subsequently Heyse was awarded a scholarship that enabled him to travel in Italy, with whose art and literature he was to become so familiar. He soon became engaged to Margarete Kugler, the daughter of the art historian to whose house he had been introduced by his patron, the poet Emanuel Geibel. Not sure where to look for a position, he was freed from all material worries by Geibel, who once more helped him. At Geibel's recommendation Maximilian II offered him a titular professorship at Munich. His only duty consisted in taking part in the literary soirees of the King. On May 15, 1854, he was married to Margarete and the happy young couple settled in Munich, where Heyse has lived ever since, with the exception of occasional sojourns in his beloved Italy. Soon he became the central figure of a thriving cultural life. Since this is not the place for a detailed biography of Heyse, suffice it to say that several years after the death of Margarete he married again, this time the charming Anna Schubart.

Between 1855 and 1862 Heyse wrote the first four volumes of his prose novellas, a genre in which he became a master. Among Heyse's many novellas we may mention here *L'Arrabbiata* (1853); *Andrea Delfin* (1859), rich in Venetian colours; the deeply felt *Nerina* (1875), an episode from Leopardi's life; the profoundly moral *Bild der Mutter* (1859) [Portrait of a Mother]; and the marvellous troubadour novella *Marion* (1855). In his novellas Heyse observes strict rules of composition without doing violence to the charm and freedom of the story. He developed his own theory of the novella. "A novella of literary value," he wrote, "should represent an important human destiny. It must not be an everyday occurrence but should reveal to us a new side of human nature. The narrow scope of the tale calls for strict concentration."

It has rightly been said that Heyse is the creator of the modern psychological novella. He is rarely tendentious in his novellas, and that is probably the reason we prefer their Goethean objectivity to his longer narratives *Kinder der Welt* (1872) [*The Children of the World*] and *Im Paradiese* (1875) [*In Paradise*], which deal with moral problems, the former with the independence of morality from narrow dogmas, the latter with a defence of art against an austere puritanism. Both works unmistakably show the humanism of their creator. In *Im Paradiese* there is in addition a vivid description of the artists' world in Munich. In *Gegen den Strom* (1904) [Against the Stream] Heyse courageously challenged engrained prejudices by turning against the practice of duelling. A curiously youthful power is evident in the book *Geburt der Venus* (1909) [Birth of Venus], which appeared last year and in which he consistently and emphatically develops his lifelong aesthetic convictions both by defending the freedom of art from a one-sided asceticism and by polemizing against the naturalistic technique of copying the low, the common, and the simple-minded.

Heyse, however, is not only a writer of novels and novellas; he is the most important lyrical poet of contemporary Germany. He has written delightful novellas in verse, of which the admirable *Salamander* (1879) in terza rime is especially memorable. Although drama was not his natural medium, he has nonetheless written excellent plays, among them–to select two from a total of over fifty–the patriotic play *Kolberg* (1865) and the interesting drama *Hadrian* (1865), in which the wisdom and sadness of Hadrian are combined and represented in a most moving manner.

Heyse's taste is very independent. While he had great admiration for *The Pretenders and Vikings at Helgeland* by his friend Ibsen, he liked neither *Ghosts* nor the following symbolic plays. He is deeply musical, but not so much moved by Wagner as by Beethoven, Mozart, Schubert, Chopin, and Brahms.

In all critical situations of life Heyse has maintained the same independence. When his friend Geibel lost his salary as a poet at the Bavarian court because of a poem to King William in which he expressed his hope for a united Germany under Prussia, Heyse, too, in a respectful letter offered to resign his position, since he agreed with Geibel on every point and therefore wished to share his fate as well.

Heyse is almost as popular in Italy as in Germany. His numerous brilliant translations have made Italian literature known in Germany. It is due to him that Leopardi, Manzoni, Foscolo, Monti, Parini, and Giusti are now widely read and admired there.

But it would be wrong to assume that the brilliant Heyse, so often called the laurel-crowned favourite of fortune, was always free from cares or was always acknowledged in the leading circles of his country. As a father he was deeply afflicted by the loss of several of his beloved children. He expressed his grief in deeply poetic songs which despite their gloom radiate an unending beauty. . . .

As for literary opinion, it is true that the Apollonian and charming poet enjoyed early popularity, but it is equally true that there was a time when the situation changed. Naturalism, which burst forth in the eighties and dominated the scene for the next decade, directed its iconoclastic attack especially against Heyse, its most powerful opponent. He was too harmonious, too fond of beauty, too Hellenic and lofty for those who, slandering him at any price, demanded sensation, effect, bizarre licentiousness, and crass reproductions of ugly realities. Heyse did not yield. His sense of form was offended by their uncouth behaviour; he demanded that literature should see life in an ideal light that would transfigure reality. In his detailed and sensitive story *Merlin* (1892) he expressed his sense of injury in a manly way. Now the tide has turned again, and Heyse would probably have been proposed earlier by his country for the world prize had it not been for the partisan dislike of the naturalists. Now a miracle seems to have changed everything. The honourable veteran has been the object of admiration everywhere; he is an honorary citizen of Munich where a street has been named after him; he has been flooded with honours. To the manifold distinctions, the Swedish Academy, acting at the recommendation of many critics, has now added its token of admiration by presenting to the old poet the rare homage of the Nobel Prize.

Heyse has gone his own ways. Aesthetically he has been faithful to truth, but in such a manner that he mirrored inner in external reality. Schiller's well-known words, "Life is serious, art serene," properly understood, express a profound truth which can be found in the life and work of Heyse. Beauty should liberate and recreate: it should neither imitate reality slavishly nor drag it into the dust. It should have a noble simplicity. Heyse reveals beauty in this aspect. He does not teach morals, which would deprive beauty of its immediacy, but there is much wisdom and nobility in his works. He does not teach religion, but one would look in vain for anything that would seriously hurt religious feelings. Although he puts greater emphasis on the ethical than on the dogmatic side of religion, he has expressed his deep respect for every serious opinion. He is tolerant but not indifferent. He has praised love, but it was its heavenly and not its earthly aspect that he glorified. He likes men who are faithful to their nature, but the individuals to whom Heyse is most sympathetic adhere to their higher rather than their lower nature.

On this festive occasion, which Heyse has not been able to attend because of illness, we thank him for the joy that his works have given to thousands, and we send our regards to the house in the Louisenstrasse in Munich, which has been for so many years the home of the Muses: "Glaubt mir, es ist kein Märchen, die Quelle der Jugend sie rinnet / wirklich und immer. Ihr fraget, wo? 'In der dichtenden Kunst.'"

At the banquet, Professor Oscar Montelius made the following comments: "I regret that we do not have the pleasure to see among us the great poet to whom this year's Nobel Prize in Literature has been awarded. But he is being worthily represented by the German Minister, Count von Pückler—and I ask you, Count, to assure him that, when toasts were proposed to the laureates, we did not forget him."

The Minister, Count von Pückler, speaking in behalf of Paul Heyse, recalled that two years ago the Nobel Prize in Literature had been given to a German philosopher, this time to a popular poet. He attested to the lively exchange between Swedish and German literature, which had increased ever since the Swedish Academy became the Areopagus in charge of following closely the literary production of the entire world and of distributing the Nobel Prizes among the great masters of letters. He ended by paying his respect to the first of the international Areopaguses, the Swedish Academy.

[© The Nobel Foundation, 1910.]

Heyse: Autobiographical Statement

(Written at the time of the awarding of the Nobel Prize)

I was born in Berlin on March 15, 1830, the second son of the royal university professor K. W. L. Heyse and his wife Julie, née Saaling, who came from a Jewish family. After attending the Gymnasium between my eighth and seventeenth years, I studied classical philology at Berlin University for two years under Boeckh and Lachmann, and with the friendly support of Emanuel Geibel and Franz Kugler I dabbled in all sorts of poetry. In Bonn, where I studied for a year, I changed from classical to Romance philology, taught there by its great founder, F. Diez, and at the beginning of 1852 I received the doctorate for a dissertation on the refrain in Provençal poetry. In the autumn of the same year I went to Rome on a grant by the Prussian Ministry of Culture. For a year I stayed at various Southern places, continuing my Romance studies at Italian libraries. The findings were published by W. Hertz in 1856 under the title *Romanische Inedita*.

The year 1853 yielded even greater results in creative writing. In the spring of 1854 some of my publications persuaded King Maximilian II of Bavaria to offer me, at the suggestion of Emanuel Geibel, a position in Munich with an annual salary of 1000 guilders, to take part in his so-called symposia, weekly soirées at which scholars and poets were gathered. Before I moved I was married to Kugler's daughter Margarete, whom death took away from me in the autumn of 1862 after she had borne me four children. Five years later I married a young woman from Munich, Anna Schubart, with whom for forty-four years I have lived happily, except for the premature deaths of two children and a son from my first marriage. I have given a detailed account of the first four decades of my life until the death of my dear royal patron in my *Jugenderinnerungen und Bekenntnisse* (Berlin, 1900) [Memories of my Youth and Confessions]. From that time on outward events receded; my life has passed without particular events or adventures and has been devoted entirely to writing. Here is a list of books published by the Cotta Publishing House:

Gesammelte Werke (1871–1910) [Collected Works], 36 vols.; *Dramatische Dichtungen* (1864–1905) [Dramatic Works], 36 vols.; *Romane, Novellen, lyrische und epische Gedichte* (1902–1912) [Novels, Novellas, Lyrical and Epic Poems], series I, 12 vols.; series II, 40 vols.; *Italienische Dichter seit der Mitte des 18. Jahrhunderts: Übersetzungen und Studien* (1889–1905) [Italian Poets since the Middle of the 18th Century: Translations and Studies], 5 vols. Published by other publishers: *Deutscher Novellenschatz* (1871–76) [Treasury of German Novellas], 24 vols.; *Novellenschatz des Auslands* (1872–76) [Treasury of Foreign Novellas], 14 vols.; *Neuer Deutscher Novellenschatz* (1884–88) [New Treasury of German Novellas], 24 vols. Also, a translation of José Caveda y Nava's history of Spanish architecture, *Geschichte der Spanischen Baukunst* (1858).

[© The Nobel Foundation, 1910. Paul Heyse is the sole author of the text.]

Elfriede Jelinek

(20 October 1946 –)

Steve Dowden
Brandeis University

See also the Jelinek entry in *DLB 85: Austrian Fiction Writers After 1914*.

BOOKS: *Lisas Schatten: Gedichte* (Munich: Relief-Verlag-Eilers, 1967);

wir sind lockvögel baby! (Reinbek: Rowohlt, 1970);

Michael: Ein Jugendbuch für die Infantilgesellschaft (Reinbek: Rowohlt, 1972);

Materialien zu Musiksoziologie, by Jelinek, Ferdinand Zellwecker, and Wilhelm Zobl (Vienna & Munich: Jugend & Volk, 1972);

Die Liebhaberinnen: Roman (Reinbek: Rowohlt, 1975); translated by Jorn K. Bramann as *Brassiere Factory* (New York: Adler, 1988); translated by Martin Chalmers as *Women as Lovers* (London & New York: Serpent's Tail, 1994);

bukolit: Hörroman (Vienna: Rhombus, 1979);

Die Ausgesperrten: Roman (Reinbek: Rowohlt, 1980); translated by Michael Hulse as *Wonderful, Wonderful Times* (London: Serpent's Tail, 1990);

Die endlose Unschuldigkeit: Prosa, Hörspiel, Essay (Schwifting: Schwiftinger Galerie-Verlag, 1980);

ende: Gedichte von 1966–1968 (Schwifting: Schwiftinger Galerie-Verlag, 1980);

Was geschah, nachdem Nora ihren Mann verlassen hatte, oder, Stützen der Gesellschaften (Vienna: Sessler, 1980); translated by Tinch Minter as *What Happened After Nora Left Her Husband, or, Pillars of Society,* in *Plays by Women,* volume 10, edited by Annie Castledine (London: Methuen Drama, 1994), pp. 23–65;

Die Klavierspielerin: Roman (Reinbek: Rowohlt, 1983); translated by Joachim Neugroschel as *The Piano Teacher* (New York: Weidenfeld & Nicolson, 1988; London: Serpent's Tail, 1989);

Theaterstücke, edited by Ute Nyssen (Cologne: Prometh, 1984)—includes *Was geschah, nachdem Nora ihren Mann verlassen hatte, oder, Stützen der Gesellschaften; Clara S.: Musikalische Tragödie;* and *Burgtheater: Posse mit Gesang;* expanded edition (Reinbek: Rowohlt, 1992)—includes *Krankheit, oder, Moderne Frauen,* edited by Regine Friedrich; *Clara S.* translated by Anthony Vivis as *Clara S.: Three Parts* (Cologne: Theaterverlag Ute Nyssen & J. Bansemer, 1997);

Oh Wildnis, oh Schutz vor ihr: Prosa (Reinbek: Rowohlt, 1985);

Krankheit, oder, Moderne Frauen, edited by Friedrich (Cologne: Prometh, 1987);

Lust (Reinbek: Rowohlt, 1989); translated by Hulse (London & New York: Serpent's Tail, 1992);

Wolken.Heim. (Göttingen: Steidl, 1990);

Isabelle Huppert in Malina: Ein Filmbuch, based on Ingeborg Bachmann's novel (Frankfurt am Main: Suhrkamp, 1991);

Totenauberg: Ein Stück (Reinbek: Rowohlt, 1991);

Sturm und Zwang: Schreiben als Geschlechterkampf, by Jelinek, Jutta Heinrich, and Adolf-Ernst Meyer (Hamburg: Klein, 1995);

Die Kinder der Toten: Roman (Reinbek: Rowohlt, 1995);

Stecken, Stab und Stangl; Raststätte, oder, Sie machens alle; Wolken.Heim.: Neue Theaterstücke (Reinbek: Rowohlt, 1997)—includes "Sinn egal: Körper zwecklos"; *Raststätte, oder, Sie machens alle* translated by Nick Grindell as *Services, or, They All Do It,* published with *Cat and Mouse (Sheep)* by Gregory Motton, *Gate Biennale* (London: Methuen Drama in association with the Gate Theatre, 1996);

Ein Sportstück (Reinbek: Rowohlt, 1998);

Jelineks Wahl: Literarische Verwandtschaften, edited by Brigitte Landes (Munich: Btb, 1998);

er nicht als er (zu, mit Robert Walser): Ein Stück (Frankfurt am Main: Suhrkamp, 1998);

Macht nichts: Eine kleine Trilogie des Todes (Reinbek: Rowohlt, 1999)—comprises *Erlkönigin; Der Tod und das Mädchen; Der Wanderer;* and *Nachbemerkung;*

Gier: Ein Unterhaltungsroman (Reinbek: Rowohlt, 2000); translated by Chalmers as *Greed* (London: Serpent's Tail, 2006);

Das Lebewohl: 3 kleine Dramen (Berlin: Berlin Verlag, 2000)—comprises *Das Lebewohl; Das Schweigen;* and *Der Tod und das Mädchen II;*

Elfriede Jelinek receiving the 2004 Nobel Prize in Literature from Horace Engdahl, permanent secretary of the Swedish Academy, at the Swedish ambassador's residence in Vienna, Austria (photograph by Robert Jaeger, Pool, Associated Press, APA Pool)

In den Alpen: Drei Dramen (Berlin: Berlin Verlag, 2002)— comprises *In den Alpen, Der Tod und das Mädchen III (Rosamunde),* and *Das Werk;*

Der Tod und das Mädchen I–V: Prinzessinnendramen (Berlin: Berliner Taschenbuch Verlag, 2003)—comprises *Schneewittchen; Dornröschen; Rosamunde; Jackie;* and *Die Wand;*

Bambiland; Babel: Zwei Theatertexte (Reinbek: Rowohlt, 2004);

Ungebärdige Wege, zu spätes Beghen; Die Zeit flieht (Salzburg: Tartin Editionen, 2005);

Einar, translated by P. J. Blumenthal (Sausalito, Cal.: Post-Apollo Press, 2006).

PLAY PRODUCTIONS: *Was geschah, nachdem Nora ihren Mann verlassen hatte, oder, Stützen der Gesellschaften,* Graz, Vereinigte Bühnen/steirischer herbst, 6 October 1979;

Clara S.: Musikalische Tragödie, Bonn, Bühnen der Stadt, 24 September 1982;

Burgtheater: Posse mit Gesang, Bonn, Bühnen der Stadt, 10 November 1985;

Begierde und Fahrerlaubnis (eine Pornographie), Graz, steirischer herbst, 20 September 1986;

Krankheit, oder, Moderne Frauen: Wie ein Stück, Bonn, Schauspiel, 12 February 1987;

Wolken.Heim. Bonn, Schauspiel, 21 September 1988;

Der Wald: Ein tönendes Fastfoodgericht, libretto by Jelinek, music by Olga Neuwirth, Vienna, Theater im Künstlerhaus, in conjunction with Wiener Festwochen and Staatsoper Stuttgart, 18 May 1991;

Unruhiges Wohnen: Ballettlibretto, libretto by Jelinek, composition by Roman Haubenstock-Ramati, Linz, ars electronica, in conjunction with Zürich, Opernhaus, 12 September 1991;

Totenauberg, Vienna, Burgtheater (Akademietheater), 18 September 1992;

Präsident Abendwind: Ein Dramolett, sehr frei nach Johann Nestroy, Innsbruck, Tiroler Landestheater, 20 November 1992;

Raststätte, oder, Sie machens alle: Eine Komödie, Vienna, Burgtheater, 5 November 1994;

Stecken, Stab und Stangl: Eine Handarbeit, Hamburg, Deutsches Schauspielhaus, 12 April 1996;

Ein Sportstück, Vienna, Burgtheater, 23 January 1998;

er nicht als er (zu, mit Robert Walser), Salzburger Festspiele, in conjunction with Hamburg, Deutsches Schauspielhaus, 1 August 1998;

Bählamms Fest: Musiktheater in 13 Bildern nach Leonora Carrington, libretto by Jelinek, music by Neuwirth, based on Leonora Carrington's *The Feast of the Lambs,* Vienna, Sofiensäle, in conjunction with Wiener Festwochen and Opéra National du Rhine, Strasbourg/Mulhouse/Colmar, 19 June 1999;

Das Schweigen, Hamburg, Deutsches Schauspielhaus, 27 May 2000;

Der Tod und das Mädchen II, text by Jelinek, music by Neuwirth, Hanover, EXPO 2000, in conjunction with Saarländisches Staatstheater Saarbrücken and ZKM Karlsruhe, 30 September 2000;

Das Lebewohl (Les Adieux), Berlin, Berliner Ensemble, 9 December 2000;

MACHT NICHTS–Eine kleine Trilogie des Todes, Zürich, Schauspielhaus, 11 April 2001;

In den Alpen, Munich, Münchner Kammerspiele, in conjunction with Zürich, Schauspielhaus, 5 October 2002;

Prinzessinnendramen: Der Tod und das Mädchen, parts I–III: Hamburg, Deutsches Schauspielhaus, 22 October 2002; parts IV–V: Berlin, Deutsches Theater, 24 November 2002;

Das Werk, Vienna, Burgtheater (Akademietheater), 11 April 2003;

Bambiland, Vienna, Burgtheater, 12 December 2003;

Babel (Irm – Margit – Peter), Vienna, Burgtheater (Akademietheater), 18 March 2005;

Sportchor [radio version], Berlin, Deutsches Theater, October 2006;

ULRIKE MARIA STUART: Königinnendrama, Hamburg, Thalia Theater, 28 October 2006.

OTHER: "Die Bienenkönige," in *Die siebente Reise: 14 utopische Erzählungen,* edited by Roman Ritter and H. P. Piwitt (Munich: Autoren Edition, 1978), pp. 141–158;

"wenn die sonne sinkt, ist für manche auch noch büroschluß," in *Und wenn du dann noch schreist: Deutsche Hörspiele der 70er Jahre,* edited by Klaus Klöckner (Munich: Goldmann, 1980), pp. 151–176;

"Die Ausgesperrten," in *Das Wunder von Vienna: 16 österreichische Hörspiele,* edited by Bernd Schirmer (Leipzig: Reclam, 1987), pp. 225–261;

"Präsident Abendwind: Ein Dramolett," in *Anthropophagen im Abendwind,* edited by Herbert Wiesner (Berlin: Literaturhaus Berlin, 1988).

SELECTED PERIODICAL PUBLICATIONS–UNCOLLECTED: "Für den Funk dramatisierte Ballade von drei wichtigen Männern sowie dem Personenkreis um sie herum: Hörspiel," *Protokolle,* no. 2 (1974): 133–152;

"Der Krieg mit anderen Mitteln: Über Ingeborg Bachmann," *Die schwarze Botin,* 21 (1983): 149–153;

"Ich möchte seicht sein," *Theater heute* (1983 Jahrbuch);

"Ich schlage sozusagen mit der Axt drein," *Theater Zeitschrift,* no. 7 (1984): 4–16;

"In der Mitte bebt und zuckt die Lüge: Büchner-Preisrede," *Frankfurter Allgemeine Zeitung,* 19 October 1998;

"Schleef oder mit der Natur zu streiten: Dankesrede zum Berliner Theaterpreis," *Theater der Zeit,* no. 6 (2002): 4–5;

"Die Kunst geht sich nie aus: Dankesrede zur Verleihung des Mülheimer Dramatikerpreises," *Theater heute,* no. 7 (2002): 1–2;

"Österreich, ein deutsches Märchen: Festrede zur Entgegennahme des Heine-Preises 2002 der Landeshauptstadt Düsseldorf," *Theater der Zeit,* no. 2 (2003): 8–14.

When the Swedish Academy awarded Elfriede Jelinek the Nobel Prize in Literature in 2004, surprise and even irritation were widespread. As an Austrian novelist, poet, librettist, and playwright little known outside the German world, she did not fit the popular image of a Nobel winner. Conventional expectations incline toward writers who have already achieved worldwide fame: Samuel Beckett, Günter Grass, Saul Bellow, Nadine Gordimer, Gabriel García Márquez, Toni Morrison, or V. S. Naipaul. And in her native Austria, where she has long been a figure of controversy (often acrimonious), many felt that her work does not typify the best literary writing Austria has to offer—meaning that her books and plays are often difficult, formally daring, and spilling over with lurid sex and violence. Jelinek presents Austrian life in a bleak, unflattering, unforgiving light. Certainly she is not a typical Austrian writer. But writers who earn Nobel recognition are by definition atypical, those who distinguish themselves from the common run of other good writers.

Perhaps Thomas Mann, who accepted the prize in 1929, four years before Adolf Hitler's seizure of power, embodies the received idea of the "great writer" as Nobel winner more than any other. Elegant, cosmopolitan, and surveying life as if from a lofty height, Mann in his own time seemed on intimate terms with other great writers of the past. He spoke with collegial self-assurance of Johann Wolfgang von Goethe, Leo Tolstoy, and Fyodor Dostoevsky. Moreover, he perceived himself as belonging to their tradition, if only to the end of it.

In his own Nobel banquet speech, Mann celebrated the redemptive power of literature to reconcile terrible experience. He was referring especially to the horrors of World War I and its aftermath, expressing himself in terms that even by 1929 had become dubious. "Through her poetry," he assured his Swedish benefactors and the world, "Germany has exhibited grace in suffering. She has preserved her honour, politically by not yielding to the anarchy of sorrow, yet keeping her unity; spiritually by uniting the Eastern principle of suffering with the Western principle of form—by creating beauty out of suffering."

The creation of beauty from the crude raw material of human suffering: this alchemy belonged to the Romantic era into which Mann had been born. By 1933 at the latest, though, he was moving into a new, darker, and unexplored time and world. The consoling view of art as an unmixed blessing could not survive the unfolding events of the twentieth century. After World War II few German and Austrian writers—including Mann—could still harbor the illusion that art might redeem German honor or convert what he had referred to as "the Eastern principle of suffering" into beauty. The disenchanted postwar Austria in which Jelinek grew up during the 1950s was one of toxic silence around the stain of National Socialist atrocity, faux amnesia about the Austrian role in it, and disillusionment over the power of art to vindicate, redeem, or otherwise ennoble human suffering.

In an essay of 1951 that still provokes discussion, "Kulturkritik und Gesellschaft" (Cultural Criticism and Society), Theodor Adorno observed that Auschwitz has undone the traditional idea that art and literature hold the moral high ground in civilized culture: no more poetry after Auschwitz, he wrote. And though his phrase has often been misleadingly cited and abused as a slogan, its meaning should be plain. High culture—from its historical guarantors such as Wolfgang Amadeus Mozart, Ludwig von Beethoven, and Richard Wagner to Nazi-era Nobel laureates such as Knut Hamsun and Gerhart Hauptmann (both of whom endorsed Hitler's vision)—had served as the window dressing to camouflage Nazi barbarism. Not only had the much-vaunted civilizing force of Western literature and music done nothing to prevent the European catastrophe, but their cultural prestige had even helped to legitimate a monstrous regime. Consequently, what Mann had once celebrated as the saving power he attributes to the "Western principle of form" had proven false. More concretely, art cannot in good conscience overlook, nor can it use, the suffering inflicted on Jews and other targeted groups (tellingly perceived by Nazis as "Eastern") to create beauty. The passage of time has reinforced the truth of Adorno's hyperbole. The idea that literature might transform the "Eastern principle of suffering" in Cambodian or Bosnian or Rwandan experience into poetic beauty can only strike postwar generations as a grotesquely tactless expression of romantic self-indulgence. Yet, it would also be indecent to fall silent.

This impasse is Jelinek's aesthetic terrain. Human decency in the Austria of the postwar world order is her subject, and the theme to which she most often returns in expressing it is the savage indecency of human relations, especially between the sexes. Though she is not a writer with a political message, her works are informed by Marxism and socialism; though she does not write about World War II, the way it insinuates itself into domestic Austrian life figures everywhere in her works; though she has shown some reluctance to endorse the label most often applied to her—"feminist writer"—feminists have always been among her most outspoken admirers; though Mann's redemptive notion of the dignity of European form means nothing to Jelinek, both human suffering and aesthetic form are her most elemental concerns.

Elfriede Jelinek was born on 20 October 1946 in Mürzzuschlag, a medium-sized town in the mountains of Styria, about halfway between Vienna and Graz. She spent her childhood and youth in Vienna's eighth district, not far from the musically and historically rich inner ring of the city, and she has lived in Vienna ever since, apart from stays in Munich with Gottfried Hüngsberg, her husband since 1974. Jelinek's father, Friedrich Jelinek, was a Czech Jew who survived the war because the Nazis found his skill as a chemist useful; however, his mental health broke down in the early 1950s, and he eventually died in a Viennese psychiatric clinic in 1969. In interviews Jelinek has often stressed the importance to her of her Eastern, Jewish, Slavic roots. Jelinek's mother, Olga Ilona Buchner Jelinek, was an ethnically German Austrian of Catholic background, and as a child Jelinek attended Catholic schools. Her mother raised the talented girl (an only child) ambitiously, with an eye toward the arts, especially music.

At the age of eighteen, while recuperating from a breakdown of her own (from the combined stress of rigorous schoolwork, musical studies, and her parents' difficulties), Jelinek began to experiment with writing. At about the same time she began studies at the University of Vienna (in theater, art history, and languages) but did not finish her degree because she suffered another nervous breakdown. She also studied piano, organ, and composition at the celebrated Vienna Conservatory, from which she graduated in 1971. She was active in the student movement and joined the Austrian Communist Party in 1974. (In 1991 she left the party.) The outward events of her life are not exciting, unusual, or revealing—indeed, Jelinek energetically resists emphasis on an explanatory link between her works and her life. The excitement lies in the relationship of her works to the world: their verbal creativity, ethical engagement with reality, and originality.

The world of Jelinek's youth was one of slow national recovery from the many catastrophic devastations of World War II. Postwar Austria, a neutral and autonomous state beginning in 1955, found itself with an identity crisis. The end of the Habsburg empire in 1918 was followed by two more debacles: the end of the First Republic in 1938 and the end of the Third Reich in 1945. The general answer to the question "what does it mean to be Austrian?" (a question often posed to Jelinek and other Austrian writers) found a generalized answer not in the variously discredited political pasts but in the realm of culture. Austrians were the German-speaking multicultural descendants of a transnational empire, heirs to a rich and varied cultural tradition that includes above all music (Mozart, Joseph Haydn, Beethoven, and Anton Bruckner on the one hand, Arnold Schoenberg, Anton Webern, and Alban Berg on the other) and theater, above all the Burgtheater and State Opera in Vienna and the Salzburg Festival every August, which combines music and theater.

The Salzburg Festival was founded by Hugo von Hofmannsthal and other postimperial luminaries as a way of celebrating and holding fast to the way of life that had vanished when the empire died in 1918. The political authorities after World War II followed the same general tack, representing Austria to its citizens and to the outside world as an apolitical (neutral) nation with not much history apart from that of its lasting cultural accomplishments. The complicity of Austrians in implementing Hitler's policies, above all the monstrous cruelty that Austrians inflicted on Austrian and other Jews—whose own legitimate claim to Austrian identity reaches deep into Habsburg history—seemed to evaporate. But the celebrated cultural ascendency in question was mostly historical: Beethoven and the various Strausses, not Schoenberg or György Ligeti; Arthur Schnitzler and Hofmannsthal, not Hermann Broch or Thomas Bernhard; museums of art, not contemporary artists. In many ways the working artists of the 1960s, 1970s, and 1980s felt Austria was a mausoleum of high culture. However, the avant-garde art scene was also intensely lively in Austria, and often intensely adversarial. Consequently, Jelinek and many of her fellow artists stridently challenged and still challenge the supremacy of official high culture, what Mann had referred to as the dignity of form and its supposed power to redeem. In Austrian cultural life, high culture is a cog in the machinery of forgetting.

One of the most shocking responses to this culture, but in many ways most telling and most characteristic, was the Viennese Actionism movement of the early 1960s. It was a variety of performance art that featured blood, excrement, and disemboweled animal carcasses, sometimes with nude people in action. What may be characteristic of the Austrian scene here is the extremity and the focus on horror and violence. Actionism is perhaps best understood as a return of the repressed, an expression of a national unconscious that finds manifestation only along the margins, for, needless to say, the movement did not find a wide audience. Together with Bernhard and many other writers, Jelinek has been criticized for her rhetoric of excess, for the brutality, crudity, and violence of her writings. The grotesquerie, the satirical extremity, and the exhaustion of high culture are central features of Jelinek's imaginative world. Naturally this rejection of traditional art is not total; Jelinek is also an organist trained and accredited by the Vienna Conservatory. But as a writer, she seeks a path into the future via the avant-garde. She wants to disrupt the language of media, of high culture, and of everyday life. Her means are puns, unconventional use of verb tense, satirically pointed quotation, and verbal horseplay of all sorts. Speaking to interviewer Gitta Honegger in 1994, Jelinek described her aim, with characteristically vivid force, as a desire "to smash language, to strip it to the bone, to tear the last bits of truth out of it, to rip open its chest."

This attitude is not so unusual in Austria. Jelinek's crucial association in the 1960s was with the circle of writers in the Wiener Gruppe (Vienna Group) and in Graz, where various cliques found an outlet in the journal *manuskripte*. Both avant-garde groups take the verbal dimension of literature—the importance and flexibility of words and their texture, of sound, syntax, orthography, grammar, and appearance—as decisive. The avant-gardists of Vienna and Graz largely abandoned the conventional forms of poetry, drama, and fiction to see where a more open and playful but also adversarial approach to words and performance might lead. It did not lead to popular forms. The general mistrust of official culture in this first phase of Jelinek's life as a writer registered first as a literary exploration and demolition of the pop culture that enveloped her generation and still does. The distrust of high culture did not entail enthusiasm for the media of popular culture, much of which was imported from the United States.

In *wir sind lockvögel baby!* (1970, We're Decoys Baby!) and *Michael: Ein Jugendbuch für die Infantilgesellschaft* (1972, Michael: Juvenile Literature for the Infantile Society)—her first two "novels," if that word fits the nonlinear structure of the works—Jelinek mounts a critique of a world in which the commodification of just about anything seems not only possible but likely. Both works present people not as flourishing individuals but as puppet-like consumers awash in the desires imposed on them by advertising, radio, sports, movies, television, and the other forces of conformity at work in the postwar recovery.

In *Die Liebhaberinnen* (1975; translated as *Brassiere Factory*, 1988; as *Women as Lovers*, 1994) Jelinek takes up the question of domestic life in rural Austria. The extraordinary natural beauty of the Austrian mountains forms the setting for this parable of modern life. Two young women, Brigitte and Paula, are ground down by circumstances mostly beyond their control, working in a ladies' undergarment factory and being married to worthless, cruelly thoughtless men. The main protagonist is teenaged Paula, a country girl, who marries a handsome but dull-witted woodcutter, a moped enthusiast who soon becomes a drunkard and then an enthusiastic wife-beater. Brigitte, the grasping town girl, sexually hooks and reels in a fellow whom she foolishly imagines to have good prospects in life, but she is deceived. Obese, fatuous, and spoiled by his doting parents, her husband will not serve her as a means of attaining the good life. Brigitte will have to make do with the household appliances her husband's standard of living makes available to her. A third protagonist, Susi, is the complacently pretty middle-class girl angling for a university-educated husband and a better life than working-class Paula and Brigitte. She presents herself as a prancing thoroughbred alongside two plodding workhorses and offers Jelinek a means of exploring small-town class resentments. Each of the three—brainwashed by magazines, television, and movies—thinks of love as a universal solvent that will melt away the loneliness, isolation, and sadness that imprisons them. Jelinek's basic theme is the concentric circles of entrapment from which none of them can ever escape: entrapment in self, in family, in marriage, in sex, in class, in work, in consumer culture, and in their own shabby, stunted imaginations.

In outline *Die Liebhaberinnen* sounds like a dreary morality play. What makes it work as a novel, though, is the form of Jelinek's prose. It has some of the incidental trappings of her avant-garde background: the absence of capital letters, for instance, an affectation that Jelinek soon abandoned. More important is her mode of storytelling. It is basically satirical parody, modeled on forms of popular narrative, in this instance the romance novel—a genre that Jelinek turns upside down. Most broken of all is erotic love, which is presented as an illusion dear to girls and women. They believe that sex gives them power over men, and so also over their own lives. Jelinek's protagonists become slaves to cherished illusions, and she is harshly critical of their willing complicity in their fates. Aware of the danger that readers will identify with them as victims and engage in moral sentimentalizing, Jelinek uses a narrative ploy resembling Bertolt Brecht's classic alienation effect in theater. She systematically holds readers' empathy at bay, constantly reminding them that the story is a fiction, that the characters are types and not individuals. Her narrator is archly detached from the story, commenting freely in apostrophes to the reader and keeping the reader distant from the unfolding events. Moreover, the crude and lurid sexual language presents eros in its most sordid aspect. Jelinek intends neither to titillate (as in the obligatory eroticism of conventional movies and fiction) nor even to shock (as in the avant-garde's traditional antibourgeois gesture of self-congratulation) but rather to arouse disgust and so force her readers into a defensively critical and reflective posture. Certainly many readers are put off by this tactic: "shrill" and "strident" are the usual terms of censure directed at her. Still, a majority of the Nobel panel accepted her visceral approach as a legitimate artistic mode of expression.

In 1980 Jelinek continued her exploration of postwar Austrian life in the novel *Die Ausgesperrten,* which literally means "the outsiders" or "those locked out." It appeared in English as *Wonderful, Wonderful Times* (1990). The motivating force of her art is perhaps clearest in this work. The setting is Vienna of the 1950s; the story unfolds at the historical moment when Austria is still reeling under the impact of the war, and the economic boom is making the war easy to forget. Thus, it is also a time of blithe hedonism that masks a deeper, pent-up violence. Her protagonists are four teenagers who embody both the outer forms and the inner impulses of postwar Austrian culture. Anna Witkowski is a budding pianist, and her twin brother, Rainer Maria (named for poet Rainer Maria Rilke), writes poetry. Vienna is the city of high culture, but the twins live in low, impoverished circumstances. The father is a bitter, resentful, and sexually depraved former SS officer with a modest pension, and their cow-like mother is more or less his slave. The father's service revolver hangs in the family home, and as Anton Chekhov famously observed of such props, it will have to be fired by the end of the story. Sophie Pachofen, in a reprise of the Susi-type from *Die Liebhaberinnen,* is a rich girl, pretty and spoiled. Hans Sepp is working class, an electrician's apprentice, and like Rainer he is in love with Sophie, which is to say they are in love with upward mobility. The novel begins as the four friends ferociously attack and brutalize a lone man walking in a public park.

The Austrian novelist Ingeborg Bachmann once remarked that fascist brutality in Austria did not end when the war ended; instead, it simply migrated into family and private life. Much of Jelinek's writing, and perhaps the beginning of *Die Ausgesperrten* in particular, appears to be predicated on this thought. The rage that drives Anna, Rainer, Sophie, and Hans cannot easily be accounted for psychologically. Jelinek does not write psychological fiction. It is more a matter of ethical, historical, and political allegory. In this case the urge to destroy arises from a sense of imprisonment that links *Die Ausges-*

perrten to *Die Liebhaberinnen*. Where Paula and Brigitte hoped that sex might provide them with relief, these teens seek the pleasure of violence and inflicting pain as a way of relieving the nausea and hatred they feel. Their sadism and nihilism are directed at the Austrian world but also at their families. In the end Rainer turns his father's SS service pistol on his parents and his sister.

Anna's last thoughts are of Schoenberg's opus 33a, a piece she was trying to master. As a pianist, she had sometimes entertained thoughts of immigrating to the United States and starting over–a rare ray of optimism in Jelinek's fictional world. Her art seemed to hold some promise as a way out. This aspect of *Die Ausgesperrten* is also developed in Jelinek's next novel, *Die Klavierspielerin* (1983; translated as *The Piano Teacher*, 1988). Erika Kohut, the eponymous pianist, is a sort of grown-up version of Anna Witkowski. Like Anna's mother, Erika's mother has invested great hopes (and money) in the daughter's talent. In Vienna, world capital of Western music, art promises transcendence. However, Erika has already failed as the novel begins. She has not reached the level of achievement that her mother had envisioned for her, which means that their dreams of wealth and power, measured in terms of property and household appliances, have come to nothing. The father is absent (a victim of mental illness, though presumably his awful wife literally drove him crazy), so Erika lives alone with her petulant, tyrannical mother in their small apartment (images of cramped space abound in Jelinek's fiction). Erika is a piano teacher instead of a concert pianist. She is middle-aged, sexually frustrated, and embittered. Erika bullies her music students at the conservatory much as her mother bullies her, so that a complete cycle of misery is formed. Her only outlet is voyeurism, which she pursues with the same kind of iron discipline with which she pursues her music. Basically, though, Erika is numb both to erotic pleasure and to music. Her characteristic lack of feeling is expressed in her pathology: she secretly cuts herself with razor blades. Even pain is better than no feeling at all.

In *Die Klavierspielerin* Jelinek deftly weaves together her themes of art, sex, and violence. A young man, Walter Klemmer, is attracted to Erika's icy, forbidding manner. The erotic attraction is a matter of the power relationship rather than affection: he is the student, and she is the teacher. He works to break down the reserve and seduce her. Klemmer, a good-looking, athletic fellow, sees in her a challenge to his virility. He intends to master Erika, who accepts the challenge in the spirit he offers it, at first leading him on and sexually teasing him. Filled with self-loathing, Erika makes unseemly demands of him, requesting–in writing–sadistic acts to satisfy her masochistic desires but at the same time hoping that love will prevent him from harming her. Like Paula and Brigitte, Erika nurses a deep wish for redemptive male love. And like them Erika has virtually no experience of life and consequently has become entrapped in private fantasies. She has been both driven and sheltered by her tyrannical mother. Her dedication to art has been a cloister from which she can only guess at and glimpse (as if at a peep show) what living might be like.

Confused, Klemmer refuses her demands in disgust, less from love or compassion than because Erika is still giving the orders. Even in abjection she is the master, he the servant of her will. Eventually Klemmer reaches his breaking point. He beats her savagely, rapes her, and goes his own way, gloating over his manly victory. The next day Erika leaves the house with a knife in her purse, but with no clear purpose in mind. She looks for Klemmer, evidently thinking of stabbing him. Still numb even after all the abuse she has taken–perhaps the more so because of it–she stabs herself in an effort to recover some kind of feeling.

Erika Kohut is Jelinek's most vivid, most striking creation. As a novelistic character, Erika belongs to a tradition of negative protagonists that includes figures such as Franz Kafka's Josef K. and Robert Walser's Jakob von Gunten. In fact, there is a perhaps excessive allusion to Josef K.'s quasi-suicide on the last page of *Die Klavierspielerin*. Like K. and Jakob, Erika is locked out of life and exploring the dark margins of what it means to be incapable of participating in the world, hence the theme of her numbness. She is betrayed by sex and by art. In trying to use them as means to an end–to dominate Klemmer and to take high art as a means of clawing her way into what she thinks of as life (that is, commercial success)–Erika has mistaken the very nature of sex and music, which are ends in themselves. Both are closed to her because she takes them not as features of lived experience but as mere instruments to be exploited for ulterior gain.

In 1989 Jelinek returned to the milieu of small-town Austria with *Lust* (translated, 1992), this time setting the action in a ski resort rather than a brassiere factory. The thematics are familiar–brutal sex and gratuitous violence that send up the genre of pornographic novel–but in this work she is more firmly in control of the rhetorical means she has been developing. The material is dreadful; yet, the tone is breezy. Jelinek's narrator has the air of a television voice-over, rather like a sports-show announcer describing a man catching fish or hunting pheasant. This voice has the same sort of voluble, disinterested enthusiasm as it describes how the bear-like Direktor of the resort treats his wife in bed:

Seine Flinte will der Direktor heute noch einmal abschießen, um sich seiner Frau wieder sicher zu sein, wenn sie blutend daliegt, da sie ihm zur Unzeit in den

Weg gelaufen ist. Sie atmet and würgt. Der Schlaf weht ihr aus den Augen. Fast würde sie erbrechen vor dem, der da in ihr sausendes, brausendes Haus einbricht.

(The Direktor wants to fire his gun again today. To be sure of his wife–lying there bleeding, breathing, retching. Sleep heavy in her eyes. Bile rising in her gorge as this intruder rises in her gorge.)

The puns, the heartlessly sportive language, and the cheery tone all serve to keep the reader off balance. There is not much reading pleasure of the ordinary sort to be had in the prose; Jelinek uses every means at her disposal to push readers away from the story. The pleasure has more to do with catching onto the satire than becoming involved with the lives of the characters.

This narrative mode is characteristic for Jelinek. For example, in *Gier: Ein Unterhaltungsroman* (2000, Greed: A Trashy Novel; translated, 2006) she takes pulp trashiness over the top. The greed in question is mainly that of Kurt Janish, a psychotic highway patrolman in rural Styria. He uses his position of authority to seduce women and girls, and then he murders them for their property, or just for the fun of it. Catching on to the satire here entails understanding that the form of Jelinek's book mimics the classic American dime-store paperbacks from the mid twentieth century, the hardboiled crime stories of the sort popularized by James M. Cain, Jim Thompson, and David Goodis. Thompson's novel *The Killer Inside Me* (1952) bears an especially close resemblance to the contours of *Gier*, except that Jelinek inverts the genre and turns it against itself. The male reading pleasures of noir fiction–domination, voyeurism, and vicarious sexual exploits–are deflated rather than celebrated.

Jelinek's novels have been widely translated into other languages, and her international prestige rests largely on her accomplishments as a fiction writer. Over the years, the Nobel Prize in Literature has gone to fiction writers much more often than to playwrights, perhaps because drama and theater often do not travel well. Before Jelinek's Nobel Prize drew global attention to her and her work, productions of her stage works were somewhat rare outside the German world (though they have been staged in Sweden, Denmark, France, Hungary, and the Czech Republic). However, this scarcity is not to suggest that her works for the theater are somehow inferior to her novels. In fact, the spoken word may well be Jelinek's most powerful mode. The speech act is central to her concept of art; the written word approximates it at second hand. Her stage works are powerful, demanding, and confrontational. Still, Jelinek's dramas remain largely confined to the German stage, where they often meet with both praise and hostile criticism.

In the same sense that Jelinek mounts a frontal assault on genre works and lazy assumptions in fiction and fiction-reading, she also refuses to take theater conventions for granted, and she refuses to accept the conventional wisdom about the relation of theater to moral life. In her first play, *Was geschah, nachdem Nora ihren Mann verlassen hatte, oder, Stützen der Gesellschaften* (1977; translated as *What Happened After Nora Left Her Husband, or, Pillars of Society*, 1994), Jelinek questions conventional feminist ideology by turning one of its cherished representatives, the heroine of Henrik Ibsen's play *A Doll's House* (1879), into a factory worker. This Nora does not escape at all; instead, she becomes a pawn in male games of sex and power. Moreover, the language of the drama is not naturalistic dialogue. The characters are more like wooden puppets than the theatrical approximations of living, feeling people.

Her next play, *Clara S.: Musikalische Tragödie* (1984, Clara S.: Musical Tragedy; translated as *Clara S.: Three Parts*, 1997), hews close to the thematics of *Die Klavierspielerin*. Outlandishly, she brings together Robert Schumann, his gifted concert-pianist wife, Clara, and their young daughter Marie with the great novelist of decadence, Gabriele D'Annunzio, at his villa in fascist Italy. Her theme is the abject support that even the most gifted girls and women provide to enable the mad fantasies of male genius, which is identified with fascist authoritarianism. Little Marie embodies this female submission as she fellates D'Annunzio while he pontificates, a shocking scene that anticipates similar scenes and relationships in later works, above all in *Die Klavierspielerin*.

The central theater of the German world has long been Vienna's Burgtheater. It is a cultural institution of supreme importance and therefore also an important target for Jelinek's critique. In her play *Burgtheater: Posse mit Gesang* (1984, Burgtheater: Farce with Choral Music), written in 1982, Jelinek sends up its compromised status during the era of Austria's romance with National Socialism. Many cultural celebrities were supporters of Hitler and actively used their prestige to promote his agenda. After the war, they were able to continue their careers as if nothing had happened. Jelinek's play focuses attention on a family of Burgtheater celebrities, transparently modeled on the Burg actors Paula Wessely and her husband, Attila Hörbiger, and their daughters. These people are caught up in acting out roles on the stage and in life that are not only phony but also morally corrupt. With language itself at the center, Jelinek carefully works out a false-sounding idiom that contains admixtures of Viennese patois, stage German, and Nazi jargon. This violence to natural language goes hand in glove with the characteristic physical violence of the play. As the Russians arrive in 1945, these voices comically seek to divest themselves of Nazi chatter and once again become the innocent speakers of a self-consciously un-German Austrian dialect. Verbally, they have become the hapless victims of a foreign invasion rather than its willing sympathizers.

The Heideggerian thought that humans are more that which is spoken than they are speakers opens into *Wolken.Heim.* (1990, Clouds.Home.), which consists largely of a montage of citations from classic writers and thinkers including Martin Heidegger, Heinrich von Kleist, Friedrich Hölderlin, and Georg Wilhelm Friedrich Hegel. Heidegger is also at the center of Jelinek's *Totenauberg* (1991). The title refers to Heidegger's mountain retreat, actually Todtnauberg, a cabin he liked to think of as a wholesome refuge from modern technology and urban life. Heidegger, the central philosopher of language and nature in the German tradition, was also a member of the Nazi party and liked to wear lederhosen and other folkloristic garb in moments of repose. Such predilections and habitual patterns of verbal expression cannot easily be separated from nationalist and fascist habits of mind. In this theater piece Jelinek links the jargon of the contemporary ecology movement to the kind of language that Heidegger cultivated, a way of speaking and writing that was perniciously implicated in a Nazi rhetoric that traded on cliches of nature, race, sex, blood, and soil.

This problematic entwinement of language and life is a well-established international theme. George Orwell famously dealt with some of its ramifications for the Anglophone world in his essay "Politics and the English Language" (1946). Language not only expresses what people think and believe, but it also shapes thought, belief, and action. Modern German is in many ways a broken, polluted, and abused resource. It is not unique in this way, but German—because of its conspicuously fraught ideological history—is a particularly clear case of the more general problem that makes Elfriede Jelinek's writing of more than local Austrian or German importance.

Jelinek's response to her 2004 Nobel Prize was unusual. She refused to attend the award ceremony (citing her anxiety disorders as the reason) and delivered her inaugural address in absentia by video. Since it cannot be entirely secret whose names the Nobel committee may be weighing at any given moment, Jelinek must have known that she was being considered. Yet, she has repeatedly professed her surprise at being chosen. In interviews she has more than once offered the view that, among Austrian writers, Peter Handke would have been the more likely choice than she.

Surprise at her selection was general, and Handke would indeed have been the more conventional choice—though perhaps his public support of the Serbian cause since the 1990s has knocked him out of the running for good. Left or at least liberal political sensibilities appear to be a consistent feature of contemporary Nobel laureates in literature. Jelinek fits this pattern. She has been and remains a blunt, outspoken, and fearless critic of the reactionary status quo in Austria and elsewhere since the end of World War II.

However, now that the Nobel Prize has gained her international recognition, she has become rather more than an Austrian writer. As far as her own writing goes, she seems to have been encouraged to turn her critique to world affairs rather than her more narrowly focused attention on Austrian and German life. In her next works for the theater, *Bambiland* (performed in 2003, published in 2004) and *Babel* (published in 2004, performed in 2005) she turned her satire on the United States, its invasion of Iraq, and the media coverage of the war. It would also be fair to say, however, that few critics or readers in the United States have noticed the attack.

It appears unlikely that Jelinek, even with a Nobel Prize to her credit, will reach a much wider audience outside of Germany, Austria, and Switzerland. First, the style of her prose—rich in complex allusion, wordplay, and elaborate turns of wit—does not lend itself readily to translation. She is the opposite of Samuel Beckett: where he pares language down, struggles against allusion and polysemy, and explores the realm of lessness, Jelinek writes in the vein of a satirical moreness and every manner of excess: intensely provocative themes, wildly luxuriant and verbally promiscuous language, and an archness that leaves many readers feeling acutely uncomfortable. Even since the Nobel award in 2004, several of her novels remain untranslated.

Second, genre also plays a role in Jelinek's modest reception outside her native language. In Austria and Germany, the theater remains an important cultural venue—especially in Vienna—and one that is supported extensively by the state as a matter of course. Jelinek's challenges to the theater as a cultural and political institution are moot outside of her own milieu. They do not translate into matters of pressing importance in many countries. Harold Pinter's 2005 Nobel Prize in Literature notwithstanding, few of the awards have gone to playwrights since the end of World War II. This decline presumably represents the waning importance of the stage in most countries, saturated as they are by electronic media venues. The theater remains prestigious, certainly, but its status is coming to resemble that of ballet or opera. In Germany, Austria, and Switzerland, however, theater remains a central form of artistic expression. But for the rest of the world, Jelinek the novelist may be of more importance.

In his presentation of Jelinek's work to the Swedish Academy at the Nobel ceremony, Horace Engdahl emphasized Jelinek's achievement: "Elfriede Jelinek deliberately opens her work to the clichés that flood the news media, advertising and popular culture—the collective subconscious of our time. She manipulates the codes of pulp literature, comics, soap operas, pornography and folkloristic novels *(Heimatsroman),* so that the inherent madness in these ostensibly harmless consumer phenomena shines through. She mimics the prejudices we would never admit to, and captures, hidden behind common sense, a poisonous mumble of no origin or address: the voice of the masses."

Interviews:

Gitta Honegger, "The German Language . . . An Interview with Elfriede Jelinek," *Theater,* 25, no. 1 (1994): 14–22;

Brenda L. Bethman, "My Characters Live Only Insofar as They Speak: Interview with Elfriede Jelinek," *Women in German Yearbook: Feminist Studies in German Literature and Culture,* 16 (2000): 61–72.

References:

Katherine Arens and Jorun B. Johns, eds., *Elfriede Jelinek: Framed by Language* (Riverside, Cal.: Ariadne, 1994);

Daniela Bartens and Paul Pechmann, eds., *Elfriede Jelinek–Die internationale Rezeption* (Graz: Droschl, 1999);

Maria E. Brunner, *Die Mythenzertrümmerung der Elfriede Jelinek* (Neuried: ars una, 1997);

Oliver Claes, *Fremde, Vampire: Sexualität, Tod und Kunst bei Elfriede Jelinek und Adolf Muschg* (Bielefeld: Aisthesis, 1994);

Annette Doll, *Mythos, Natur und Geschichte bei Elfriede Jelinek: Eine Untersuchung ihrer literarischen Intentionen* (Stuttgart: M&P Verlag für Wissenschaft und Forschung, 1994);

du: Zeitschrift für Kultur [Zurich], special Jelinek issue, 700 (October 1999);

Allyson Fiddler, *Rewriting Reality: An Introduction to Elfriede Jelinek* (Oxford: Berg, 1994);

Fiddler, "Staging Jorg Haider: Protest and Resignation in Elfriede Jelinek's *Das Lebewohl* and Other Recent Texts for the Theater," *Modern Language Review,* 97, no. 2 (2002): 253–265;

Gail Finney, "Komödie und Obszönität: Der sexuelle Witz bei Jelinek und Freud," *German Quarterly,* 70, no. 1 (1997): 27–38;

Finney, "Performing Vienna: Theatricality in Jelinek's *Burgtheater*," *German Politics and Society,* 23, no. 1 (2005): 24–38;

Konstanze Fliedl, "Natur und Kunst: Zu neueren Texten Elfriede Jelineks," in *Das Schreiben der Frauen in Österreich seit 1950,* edited by the Walter-Buchebner-Gesellschaft (Vienna: Böhlau, 1991), pp. 95–104;

Brigid Haines, "Beyond Patriarchy: Marxism, Feminism, and Elfriede Jelinek's *Die Liebhaberinnen,*" *Modern Language Review,* 92, no. 3 (1997): 643–656;

Beatrice Hanssen, "Elfriede Jelinek's Language of Violence," *New German Critique,* 68 (1996): 79–105;

Petra Heyer, *Von Verklärern und Spielverderbern: Eine vergleichende Untersuchung neuerer Theaterstücke Peter Handkes und Elfriede Jelineks* (Frankfurt am Main: Peter Lang, 2001);

Pia Janke and others, *Werkverzeichnis Elfriede Jelinek* (Vienna: Edition Praesens, 2004);

Janke, ed., *Die Nestbeschmutzerin: Jelinek & Österreich* (Salzburg: Jung & Jung, 2003);

Marlies Janz, *Elfriede Jelinek* (Stuttgart: Metzler, 1995);

Janz, "Das Verschwinden des Autors: Die Celan-Zitate in Elfriede Jelineks Stück *Stecken, Stab und Stangl,*" *Celan-Jahrbuch,* 7 (1997/98): 279–292;

Britta Kallin, "In Brecht's Footsteps or Way beyond Brecht? Brechtian Techniques in Feminist Plays by Elfriede Jelinek and Marlene Streeruwitz," *Communications from the International Brecht Society,* 29 (2000): 62–66;

Joanna Kavenna, "The Untranslatables," *Daily Telegraph,* 27 November 2004, Books pp. 1–2;

Matthias Konzett, *The Rhetoric of National Dissent in Thomas Bernhard, Peter Handke, and Elfriede Jelinek* (Rochester, N.Y.: Camden House, 2000);

Barbara Kosta, "Murderous Boundaries: Nation, Memory and Austria's Fascist Past in Elfriede Jelinek's *Stecken, Stab und Stangl,*" in *Writing Against Boundaries: Nationality, Ethnicity and Gender in the German-Speaking Context,* edited by Kosta and Helga Kraft (Amsterdam: Rodopi, 2003), pp. 81–98;

John Pizer, "Modern vs. Postmodern Satire: Karl Kraus and Elfriede Jelinek," *Monatshefte,* 86, no. 4 (1994): 500–513;

Jay Rosellini, "Jelineks Haider: Anmerkungen zur literarischen Populismus-Kritik," *Text & Kontext* (2003): 125–138;

Erika Swales, "Pathography as Metaphor," *Modern Language Review,* 95, no. 2 (2000): 437–449;

text + kritik, special Jelinek issue, edited by Heinz Ludwig Arnold, expanded edition, no. 117 (1999);

Sabine Treude, "Vom Übersetzen zum Verschwiegenen: Einige Überlegungen zum Übersetzungsverfahren in den Texten von Elfriede Jelinek und Martin Heidegger," *Sprache im technischen Zeitalter,* 153 (2000): 75–87;

Treude and Günther Hopfgartner, "'Ich meine alles ironisch': Ein Gespräch," *Sprache im technischen Zeitalter,* 153 (2000): 21–31;

Sabine Wilke, "The Body Politic of Peformance, Literature, and Film: Mimesis and Citation in Valie Export, Elfriede Jelinek, and Monika Treut," *Paragraph,* 22, no. 3 (1999): 228–248.

2004 Nobel Prize in Literature Presentation Speech

by Professor Horace Engdahl of the Swedish Academy,
10 December 2004

Your Majesties, Your Royal Highnesses, Ladies and Gentlemen,

What first perplexes when reading Elfriede Jelinek is the strange, mixed voice that speaks from her writing. The author is everywhere and nowhere, never quite standing behind her words, nor ever ceding to her literary figures in order to allow the illusion that they should exist outside her language. There is nothing but a stream of saturated sentences, seemingly welded together under high pressure and leaving no room for moments of relaxation.

Elfriede Jelinek deliberately opens her work to the clichés that flood the news media, advertising and popular culture—the collective subconscious of our time. She manipulates the codes of pulp literature, comics, soap operas, pornography and folkloristic novels (*Heimatsroman*), so that the inherent madness in these ostensibly harmless consumer phenomena shines through. She mimics the prejudices we would never admit to, and captures, hidden behind common sense, a poisonous mumble of no origin or address: the voice of the masses. She has said that she taps at language to hear its hidden ideologies, much as a doctor will tap on a patient's chest. Aghast, we discover how class oppression, sexism, chauvinism and the distortion of history echo through everyday conversation. Sport is immediately suspect: its militaristic drills, the uniforms, the cult of the strong and the victorious. Nature: a political trap. Austria's alpine landscape has been the perfect backdrop for her destruction of the idyllic.

When our normal ideals and daydreams are rendered with Elfriede Jelinek's instrumentation of heartless word-plays, macabre metaphors and infernally twisted quotations from the classics, they are never again the same. Her insinuating tone, like infrared light, elucidates the hidden writing of civilisation. Where we saw normal society, we now see a locked-down system of male/female, assault and submission, hunter and prey. Indeed, we are forced to accept that we find the hunter's language sexier than the prey's. Elfriede Jelinek's social criticism is formed not from the safe distance of superior knowledge but from the depths of an unqualified contamination. In her works, the dead return not to comfort but to bear witness. Ghosts are as ubiquitous as the living, and there is no clear distinction between them. The woman's being is like the vampire's, at once alive and dead, since her full expression is forbidden. Some of Elfriede Jelinek's heroines seem to have stepped out of male fantasies of blood-sucking she-monsters from the turn of the 20th century. As heir to a long line of linguistically critical Austrian writers, from Johann Nepomuk Nestroy to Ingeborg Bachmann and Thomas Bernhard, she also knows the importance of deflating the pathos of disaster. Her parade of luckless princesses from fairytales and real life in the drama suite *Der Tod und das Mädchen* is condensed into the picture of Marilyn Monroe's blonde hair billowing out from under the lid when they close the coffin at her funeral. Swiftly comes the deprecating simile: "like foam seeping from a fire extinguisher."

Literary genres pale to disappearance under Jelinek's hand. Her plays are not theatre, rather "texts to be spoken," liberated from the tyranny of dramatical roles. Astonished directors find she has delivered into their hands material to revolutionise theatre.

Her novels—the sweet girls as losers in *Women as Lovers*, the murderous logic of youth revolt in *Wonderful, Wonderful Times*, the aesthetic of self-mutilation in *The Pianist*, the endless repetition of the simple fact of penetration in *Lust*, the ABC of the violation of women in *Gier*—cheerfully break the laws of classic narrative art. The author does not cede the floor, observing her characters almost as insects under a glass cover. Her phrasing is itself the action. Through the musical interchange of voices and counter-voices, a world comes into being, illuminated by her life-giving fury.

What is a hero in a literary work? Other differences aside, it is *someone who is right when the world is wrong*. In male modernism, it has often been the author himself, disguised as the solitary voice of the outcast ego. This invites empathy and identification, thereby producing literature's eternal karaoke-effect, where the reader joins in on the chorus. The difficulty in reading Elfriede Jelinek is that there is no sympathetic narrator in whom the reader can rest and with whom the reader can identify. It is an awakening from the narcissism of reading.

Her writings perhaps give us a dark picture of life, but she is no pessimist, since in pessimism there is generally a whiff of self-pity and a tacit plea. Rather, grinding through her imprecations is a scandalous joviality without hope, rays from a black sun.

Most honoured Elfriede Jelinek!

In the words of Hegel, woman is society's irony. Through your writing, you have given new currency to an heretical feminine tradition and have expanded the art of literature. You negotiate with neither society nor your time, nor do you adapt to your readers. If literature by definition is a force that bends to nothing, you are in our day one of its truest representatives.

[© The Nobel Foundation, 2004.]

Jelinek: Nobel Lecture, 7 December 2004

Sidelined
(Translation from German by Martin Chalmers)

Is writing the gift of curling up, of curling up with reality? One would so love to curl up, of course, but what happens to me then? What happens to those, who don't really know reality at all? It's so very dishevelled. No comb, that could smooth it down. The writers run through it and despairingly gather together their hair into a style, which promptly haunts them at night. Something's wrong with the way one looks. The beautifully piled up hair can be chased out of its home of dreams again, but can anyway no longer be tamed. Or hangs limp once more, a veil before a face, no sooner than it could finally be subdued. Or stands involuntarily on end in horror at what is constantly happening. It simply won't be tidied up. It doesn't want to. No matter how often one runs the comb with the couple of broken off teeth through it–it just doesn't. Something is even less right than before. The writing, that deals with what happens, runs through one's fingers like the time, and not only the time, during which it was written, during which life stopped. No one has missed anything, if life stopped. Not the one living and not dead time, and the one who is dead not at all. When one was still writing, time found its way into the work of other writers. Since it is time, it can do everything at once: find its way into one's own work and simultaneously into the work of others, blow into the tousled hairstyles of others like a fresh, even if malign wind, which has risen suddenly and unexpectedly from the direction of reality. Once something has risen, then perhaps it doesn't lie down again so quickly. The angry wind blows and sweeps everything with it. And it sweeps everything away, no matter where, but never back to this reality, which is supposed to be represented. Everywhere, except there. Reality is what gets under the hair, under the skirts and just that: sweeps them away and into something else. How can the writer know reality, if it is that which gets into him and sweeps him away, forever onto the sidelines. From there, on the one hand, he can see better, on the other he himself cannot remain on the way of reality. There is no place for him there. His place is always outside. Only what he says from the outside can be taken up inside, and that because he speaks ambiguities. And then there are already two who fit, two whose faces are right, who warn, that nothing is happening, two who construe it in different directions, reach out to the inadequate grounds, which have long ago broken off like the fangs of the comb. Either or. True or false. It had to happen sooner or later, since the ground as building ground was quite inadequate. And how could one build on a bottomless pit anyway? But the inadequacy that enters the writers' field of vision, is still adequate enough for something, that they could also take or leave. They could take or leave it, and they do leave it. They don't kill it. They merely look at it with their bleary eyes, but it does not become arbitrary because of this bleary gaze. The gaze is well aimed. Whatever is struck by this gaze says, even as it sinks down, although it has hardly been looked at, although it has not even been exposed to the sharp gaze of the public, whatever has been struck never says, that it could also have been something else, before it fell victim to this one description. It says exactly what had been better left unsaid (because it could have been better said?), what always had to remain unclear and groundless. Too many have already sunk into it up to their stomachs. It's quicksand, but it doesn't quicken anything. It is groundless, but not without grounds. It is as you like, but it is not liked.

The sidelines are at the service of the life, that precisely does not take place there, otherwise we would not all be in the thick of it, in the fullness, the fullness of human life, and it is at the service of the observation of the life, which is always taking place somewhere else. Where one is not. Why insult someone, because he cannot find his way back to the path of journeying, of life, of life's journey, if he has borne it–and this bearing is no bearing someone, but nor is it any kind of bearing on–has simply fortuitously borne it, like the dust on a pair of shoes, which is pitilessly hunted down by the housewife, if a little less pitilessly than the stranger is hunted down by the locals. What kind of dust is it? Is it radioactive or active by itself, just like that, I'm only asking, because it leaves this strange trail of light on the way? Is what is running alongside and never meeting up with the writer again, the way, or is the writer the one who is running alongside, onto the sidelines? He has not yet passed away, but he's already passed the line nevertheless. From there he sees those who have parted from him, but from one another too, in all their variety, in order to represent them in all their credulity, in order to get them on form, because form is the most important thing, anyway he sees them better from there. But that, too, is chalked up against him, so are those chalk marks and not particles of luminous matter, which mark the way of writing? At any rate it's a marking out, which simultaneously shows and obscures and afterwards carefully covers up again the trail he himself laid. One was never there at all. But nevertheless one knows what's up. The words have come down from a screen, from blood-smeared faces distorted with pain, from laughing, made-up faces, with lips pumped up beforehand just for the make-up or from others, who gave the right answer to a question in a quiz, or born mouthers, women, who have nothing for and nothing against, who stood up and took off a jacket to point their freshly hardened breasts, which were once steeled and belonged to men, at the camera. In addition any amount of throats, out of which singing comes like bad breath, only louder. That is what could be seen on the way, if one were still on it. One goes out of the way of the way. Perhaps one sees it from a distance, where one remains alone, and how gladly, because one wants to see the way, but not walk it. Did this path make a noise just now? Does it want to draw attention to itself with noises now and not just with lights, loud people, loud lights? Is the way, which one cannot walk, afraid of not being walked at all, when so many sins are being constantly committed after all, torture, outrages, theft, threatening behaviour, necessary threat in the manufacture of significant world fates? It makes no difference to the way. It bears everything, firmly, even if groundlessly. Without ground. On lost ground. My hair, as already mentioned, is standing on end, and no setting lotion there, which could force it to firm up again. No firmness in myself either. Not on me, not in me. When one's on the sidelines, one always has to be ready to jump a bit and then another bit to the side, into the empty space, which is right next to the sidelines. And the sidelines have brought their sideline pitfall along with them, it's ready at any time, it gapes wide, to lure one even further out. Luring out is luring in. Please, I don't want to lose sight now of the way, which I'm not on. I would so like to describe it honestly and above all truly and accurately. If I'm actually looking at it, it should also do something for me. But this way spares me nothing. It leaves me nothing. What else is there left for me? I am prevented from being on my way, I can hardly make my way at all. I am out, while not going out. And there, too, I should certainly like to have protection against my own uncertainty, but also against the uncertainty of the ground, on which I'm standing. It runs to make certain, not only to protect me, my language right beside me, and checks, whether I am doing it properly, describing reality properly wrongly, because it always has to be described wrongly, there's no other way, but so wrongly, that anyone who reads or hears it, notices the falseness immediately. Those are lies! And this dog, language, which is supposed to protect me, that's why I have him, after all, is now snapping at my heels. My protector wants to bite me. My only protector against being described, language, which, conversely, exists to describe something else, that I am not—that is why I cover so much paper—my only protector is turning against me. Perhaps I only keep him at all, so that he, while pretending to protect me, pounces on me. Because I sought protection in writing, this being on my way, language, which in motion, in speaking, appeared to be a safe shelter, turns against me. No wonder. I mistrusted it immediately, after all. What kind of camouflage is that, which exists, not to make one invisible, but ever more distinct?

Sometimes language finds itself on the way by mistake, but it doesn't go out of the way. It is no arbitrary process, speaking with language, it is one that is involuntarily arbitrary, whether one likes it or not. Language knows what it wants. Good for it, because I don't know, no not at all. Talk, talking in general keeps on talking over there now, because there's always talking, talking, without beginning or end, but there's no speaking. So there's talking over there, wherever the others are staying, because they don't want to linger, they're very occupied. Only them over there. Not me. Only the language, which sometimes moves away from me, to the people, not the other people, but moves away over to the real, genuine, on the well-signposted way (who can go astray here?), following their every movement like a camera, so that it at least, the language, finds out, how and what life is, because then it is precisely not that, and afterwards all of it must be described, even in what it precisely is not. Let's talk about the fact, that we are supposed to go for a medical check-up once again. Yet all at once we suddenly speak, with due rigour, like someone who has a choice, whether or not to speak. Whatever happens, only the language goes away from me, I myself, I stay away. The language goes. I stay, but away. Not on the way. And I'm speechless.

No, it's still there. Has it perhaps been there all the time, did it weigh up, whom it could weigh down? It has noticed me now and immediately snaps at me, this language. It dares to adopt this tone of command to me, it raises its hand against me, it doesn't like me. It would gladly like the nice people on the way, alongside whom it runs, like the dog it is, feigning obedience. In reality it not only disobeys me, but everyone else, too. It is for no-one but itself. It cries out through the night, because no-one has remembered to put up lights beside this way, which are supplied by nothing but the sun and no longer need any current at all from the socket, or to find the path a proper path name. But it has so many names, that it would be impossible to keep up with all the naming, if one tried. I shout across, in my loneliness, stamping across these graves of the departed, because since I am already running alongside, I cannot pay attention as well to what I'm treading on, whom I'm treading down, I would only somehow like to get to the place where my language already is, and where it smirks mockingly across at me. Because it knows, that, if I ever tried to live, it would soon trip me up, then rub salt in my wounds. Good. So I will scatter salt on the way of the others, I throw it down, so that their ice melts, coarse salt, so that their language loses its firm ground. And yet it has long been groundless. What bottomless cheek on its part! If I do not have solid ground under my feet, then my language can't either. Serve it right! Why did it not stay with me, on the sidelines, why did it part from me? It wanted to see more than me? On the highway over there, where there are more people, above all more likeable ones, chatting nicely to each other? It wanted to know more than me? It has always known more than me, it's true, but it has to know even more than that. It will end up killing itself by eating into itself, my language. It will overindulge on reality. Serve it right! I spat it out, but it spits nothing out, it's good at keeping it down. My language calls over to me, over on the sidelines, it likes best of all to call over to the sidelines, it doesn't have to take such careful aim, but it doesn't have to, because it always hits the target, not by saying something or other, but by speaking with the "austerity of letting be," as Heidegger says about Trakl. It calls me, language does, today anyone can do it, because everyone always carries their language around with them in a small gadget, so that they can speak, why would they have learned it?, so it calls me where I am caught in the trap and cry out and thrash about, but no, it's not true, my language isn't calling, it's gone, too, my language has gone from me, that's why it has to call, it shouts in my ear, no matter out of which gadget, a computer or a mobile phone, a phone booth, from where it roars in my ear, that there's no point in saying something out loud, it already does that anyway, I should simply say what it tells me; because there would be even less point in for once speaking what was on one's mind to a dear person, who has fallen down on the case and whom one can trust, because he has fallen and won't get up again so quickly, in order to pursue one and, yes, to chat a little. There's no point. The words of my language over there on the pleasant way (I know it's more pleasant than mine, which is actually no way at all, but I can't see it clearly, but I know, that I too would like to be there), the words of my language have, therefore, in parting from me, immediately become a speaking out. No, no talking it out with someone. A speaking out. It listens to itself speaking out, my language, it corrects itself, because speaking can still be improved at any time; yes, it can always be improved, it is even entirely there to be improved and then to make a new linguistic ruling, but then only to be able immediately to overturn the rules again. That will then be the new way to salvation, of course I mean solution. A quick fix. Please, dear language, don't you for once want to listen first? So that you learn something, so that you at last learn the rules of speaking. . . . What are you shouting and grumbling about over there? Are you doing it, language, so that I graciously take you in you again? I thought, you didn't want to come back to me at all! There was no sign, that you wanted to come back to me, it would have been pointless anyway, I wouldn't have understood the sign. You only became language to get away from me and to ensure that I got on? But nothing is ensured. And by you not at all, as well as I know you. I don't even recognise you again. You want to come back to me of your own accord? I won't take you in any more, what do you say to that? Away is away. Away is no way. So if my loneliness, if my constant absence, my uninterrupted existence on the sidelines came in person to fetch back language, so that it, well-looked-after by me, at last came home, to a beautiful sound, which it could utter, then it would only happen, so that with this sound, this penetrating, piercing howling of a siren, blown by the wind, it could drive me further, ever further back from the sidelines. Because of the recoil of this language, which I myself produced and which has run away from me (or did I produce it for that purpose? So that it immediately runs away from me, because I have not managed to run away from myself in time?), I am chased ever deeper into this space beyond the sidelines. My language is already wallowing blissfully in its muddy pool, the little provisional grave on the way, and it looks up at the grave in the air, it wallows on its back, a friendly creature, which would like to please human beings like any respectable language, it wallows, opens its legs, presumably to let itself be stroked, why else. It's greedy for caresses, after all. That stops it from gazing after the dead, so that I must gaze after them instead, and of course in the end it's down to me. So I had no time to curb my language, which now shamelessly rolls around under the hands of the caressers. There are simply too many dead, whom I have to see to, that's an Austrian technical term for: whom I have to look after, whom I have to treat well, but then we're famous for that, for always treating everyone well. The world is looking to us, no need to worry. We don't have to take care of that. Yet the more clearly this demand, to gaze at the dead, sounds in me, the less am I able to pay attention to my words. I must gaze at the dead, while meanwhile the strollers are stroking the good old language and chucking it under the chin, which doesn't make the dead any more alive. No one is to blame. Even I, dishevelled as I and my hair are, am not to blame for the dead staying dead. I want the language over there to finally stop making itself the slave of strangers' hands, no matter how good it feels, I want it to begin by stopping making demands, but itself become a demand, to finally face up to, not the caresses, but a demand to come back to me, because language always has to face up, only doesn't always know it and doesn't listen to me. It has to face up, because the people who want to adopt it instead of a child, it's so lovable, if one loves it, people therefore never face up, they decide, they don't answer calls, many of them even immediately destroyed, tore up, burnt their call-up order to sociability, and the flag along with it. So the more people who take up the invitation of my language to scratch its stomach, to ruffle something, to affectionately accept its friendliness, the further I stumble away, I have finally lost my language to those who treat it better, I'm almost flying, where on earth was this way, that I need in order to hurry down? How do I get where to do what? How do I get to the place, where I can unpack my tools, but in reality can right away pack them up again? Over there something bright is gleaming under the branches, is that the place, where my language first of all flatters the others, rocks them into a sense of security, only in order for itself to be lovingly rocked in the end for once? Or does it want to snap again? It always wants to do nothing but bite, only the others don't know it yet, but I know it very well, it was with me for a long time. Beforehand there's first of all cuddles and whispering sweet nothings to this seemingly tame creature, which everyone has at home anyway, why should they bring a strange animal into the house? So why should this language be any different from what they already know? And if it were different, then perhaps it might be dangerous to take it in. Perhaps it won't get on with the one they already have. The more friendly strangers there are, who know how to live, but are nevertheless very far from knowing their life, since they pursue their caressing intents, because they always have to pursue something, the more my seeing no longer clearly sees the way through to the language any more. Miles and more. Who else should be able to see through things, if not seeing? Speaking wants to take over seeing as well? It wants to speak, before it has even seen? It wallows there, is groped by hands, buffeted by winds, caressed by storms, insulted by listening, until it stops listening altogether. Well, then: all listen here for once! Whoever doesn't want to listen, must speak without being listened to. Almost everyone is not listened to, although they speak. I am listened to, although my language does not belong to me, although I can hardly see it any more. Much is said against it. So it no longer has much to say for itself, that's fine. It's listened to, as it slowly repeats, while somewhere a red button is pressed, which sets off a terrible explosion. There's nothing left to say except: Our Father, which art. It cannot mean me, although after all I am father, that is: mother, of my language. I am the father of my mother tongue. The mother tongue was there from the beginning, it was in me, but no father was there, who might have belonged to it. My language was often unbecoming, that was often made clear enough to me, but I didn't want to take the hint. My fault. The father left this nuclear family along with the mother tongue. Right he was. In his place I would not have stayed either. My mother tongue has followed my father now, it's gone. It is, as already mentioned, over there. It listens to the people on the way. On the father's way, who went too soon. Now the language knows something, that you don't know, that he didn't know. But the more it knows, the less it says. Of course, it's constantly saying something, but it's saying nothing. And already the loneliness is taking its leave. It's no longer needed. No one sees, that I am still inside, in the loneliness. I am not heeded. Perhaps I am honoured, but I am not heeded. How do I ensure that all these words of mine say something, that could say something to us? I cannot do it by speaking. In fact I cannot even speak, because my language is unfortunately not at home just now. Over there it says something else, which I didn't ask it to either, but it has already forgotten my command from the start. It doesn't tell me, although it belongs to me, after all. My language doesn't tell me anything, how should it then tell others something? But nor is it saying nothing, you must admit that! It says all the more, the further away from me it is, indeed, only then does it dare say something, that it wants to say itself, then it dares to disobey me, to resist me. When one looks, one moves further away from the object, the longer one looks at it. When one speaks, one catches hold of it again, but one cannot hold onto it. It tears itself away and hurries after its own naming, the many words I have made and I have lost. Words have been exchanged often enough, the exchange rate is incredibly bad, and then it's no more than: incredible. I say something, and then it's already been forgotten from the start. That's what it strove for, it wanted to get away from me. The unspeakable is spoken every day, but what I say, that isn't to be allowed. That's mean of what has been spoken. That is incredibly mean. The spoken doesn't even want to belong to me. It wants to be done, so that one can say: said and done. I would even be satisfied, if it denied belonging to me, my language, but it should belong to me nevertheless. How can I ensure, that it is at least a little attached to me? Nothing sticks to the others after all, so I offer myself to it. Come back! Come back, please! But no. Over there on the path it's listening to secrets, that I'm not supposed to know, my language, and it passes them on, these secrets, to others who don't want to hear them. I would want to, it would be my right, indeed, it would go down well, if you like, but it doesn't stand still, and speak to me, it doesn't do that either. It is in the empty space which is distinguished and differentiates itself from me, in that there are very many there. Emptiness is the way. I am even on the sidelines of emptiness. I have left the way. I have only said things after another. Much has been said about me, but hardly any of it is true. I myself have only said what others have said, and I say: that is now what is really said. As I said—simply incredible! It's a long time since so much has been said. One's listening can't keep up any more, although one must listen, in order to be able to do something. In this respect, which in reality is a looking away, even a looking away from myself, there's nothing to be said about me, there's nothing to be said, nothing more to be said. I'm always only gazing after life, my language turns its back on me, so that it can present its stomach to strangers to caress, shameless, to me it only shows its back, if anything at all. Too often it doesn't give me a sign and doesn't say anything either. Sometimes I don't even see it over there any more, and now I can't even say "as has already been said," because while I've already said it often enough, I cannot say it any more, I'm lost for words. Sometimes I see the back or the soles of the feet, on which they can't really walk, the words, but faster than I have been able to for a long time and even now. What am I doing there? Is that why my dear language has lain down some distance away from me? That way it will, of course, always be faster than me, jump up and run away, when I go across to it from my place of work, to fetch it. I don't know, why I should fetch it. So that it doesn't fetch me? Perhaps it, who ran away from me, knows? Who doesn't follow me? Who now follows the looking and speaking of others, and really can't mix up them with me. They are other, because they are the others. For no other reason, except that they are the others. That's good enough for my speaking. The main thing is, I don't do it: speaking. The others, always the others, so that it's not me, who belongs to it, sweet language. I would so much like to stroke it, like the others over there, if I could only catch hold of it. But then it's over there, so that I can't catch hold of it.

When will it silently make off? When will something make off, so there's silence? The more the language over there makes off, the louder it can be heard. It's on everyone's lips, only not on my lips. My mind is clouded. I have not passed out, but my mind is clouded. I am worn out from gazing after my language like a lighthouse by the sea, which is supposed to light someone home and so has itself been lit up, and which as it revolves always reveals something else from the darkness, but is there anyway, whether it is lit up or not, it's a lighthouse, which doesn't help anyone, no matter how hard that man wishes it would, so as not to have to die in the water. The harder I try to make it out, the more obstinately it doesn't go out, language. I now put out this language light mechanically, I switch to the pilot light, but the more I try to clap myself over it, a snuffer on the end of a long pole, with which in my childhood the candles in the church were extinguished, the more I try to snuff out this flame, the more air it seems to have. And all the more loudly it cries out, rolling around under thousands of hands, which do it good, which unfortunately I have never done, I don't know myself, what would do me good, so it's crying out now, so it can keep away from me. It shouts at the others, so that they too join in and cry out like it, so that the noise grows louder. It shouts, that I shouldn't come too close. No one should come too close to anyone at all. And what has been said should also not come too close to what one wants to say. One shouldn't get too close to one's own language, that is an insult, it is quite capable of repeating something after itself, piercingly loud, so that no one hears, that what it says, was earlier recited to it. It even makes me promises, so that I will stay away from it. It promises me everything, if I just don't come close to it. Millions are allowed to get close to it, except me! Yet it's mine! What do you think of that? I just can't tell you, what I think of that. This language must have forgotten its beginnings, I've got no other explanation. With me it started small. No, how big it's grown, I can't tell you! Like this I don't even recognise it. I knew it, when it was just so high. When it was so quiet, when the language was still my child. Now it has all at once become gigantic. That's not my child any more. The child has not grown up, only big, it doesn't know that it has not yet outgrown me, but it's wide awake nevertheless. It is so wide awake, that it drowns itself out with its crying, and anyone else who cries louder than it. Then it spirals up to an incredible pitch. Believe me, you really don't want to hear it! Also, please don't believe that I'm proud of this child! At its beginning I wanted it to remain as quiet as when it was still speechless. Even now, I don't want it to sweep over something like a storm, causing others to roar even louder and to raise their arms and throw hard objects, which my language can no longer even grasp and catch, it has, my fault, too, always been so unathletic. It doesn't catch. It can throw, but it can't catch. I remain imprisoned in it, even when it's away. I am the prisoner of my language, which is my prison warder. Funny—it's not even keeping an eye on me! Because it is so certain of me? Because it is so certain, that I won't run away, is that why it believes, it can leave me? Here comes someone, who has already died, and he talks to me, although that is not planned for him. He's allowed to, many dead are speaking now in their choked voices, now they dare to, because my own language is not keeping any eye on me. Because it knows, it isn't necessary. Even if it runs away from me, I won't slip through its hands. I am at hand for it, but it has slipped through my hands. But I remain. But what remains, the writers do not make. What remains is gone. The flight of fancy was cut. Nothing and no one has come. And if nevertheless, against all reason, something that has not come at all, a little would like to remain, then what does remain, language, the most fleeting of all, has disappeared. It has replied to a new situations vacant advert. What should remain, is always gone. It is at any rate not there. So what is left to one.

[© The Nobel Foundation, 2004. Elfriede Jelinek is the sole author of the text.]

Johannes V. Jensen
(20 January 1873 - 25 November 1950)

Sven Hakon Rossel
University of Vienna

This entry was expanded by Rossel from his Jensen entry in *DLB 214: Twentieth-Century Danish Writers*.

BOOKS: *Danskere* (Copenhagen: Det Nordiske, 1896);
Einar Elkær: Roman (Copenhagen: Det Nordiske, 1898);
Himmerlandsfolk: Historier (Copenhagen: Det Nordiske, 1898);
Intermezzo: Dolores, Forsvundne Skove, Louison (Copenhagen: Det Nordiske, 1899);
Foraarets Død (Copenhagen: Det Nordiske, 1900);
Den store Sommer (Copenhagen: Det Nordiske, 1900);
Den gotiske Renaissance (Copenhagen: Det Nordiske, 1901);
Vinteren (Copenhagen: Det Nordiske, 1901);
Kongens Fald (Copenhagen: Det Nordiske, 1901)—comprises *Foraarets Død, Den store Sommer,* and *Vinteren;* translated by P. T. Federspiel and Patrick Kirwan as *The Fall of the King* (London: Grayson & Grayson, 1933; New York: Holt, 1933);
Kirken i Farsø: Skitse (Minneapolis & Chicago: C. Rasmussen, 1903);
Madame D'Ora (Copenhagen: Gyldendal, 1904);
Nye Himmerlandshistorier (Copenhagen: Gyldendal, 1904)—includes "Kirstens sidste Rejse," translated by Lee Marshall as "Kirsten's Last Journey," in *Anthology of Danish Literature: Bilingual Edition,* edited by F. J. Billeskov Jansen and P. M. Mitchell (Carbondale: Southern Illinois University Press, 1971), pp. 300–379;
Skovene (Copenhagen: Gyldendal, 1904);
Hjulet (Copenhagen: Gyldendal, 1905);
Digte (Copenhagen: Gyldendal, 1906); revised and enlarged as *Digte: Anden Udgave,* 1917; revised and enlarged as *Digte: Tredie Udgave,* 1921; revised and enlarged as *Digte: 1901–1941,* 1943; revised and enlarged as *Digte,* 1948—includes "Ved Frokosten" and "Paa Memphis Station," translated by Alexander Taylor as "At Lunch" and "At Memphis Station," in *Contemporary Danish Poetry,* edited by Line Jensen and others (Copenhagen: Gyldendal, 1958), pp. 91–92;

Johannes V. Jensen (photograph © Bettman/Corbis)

Myter og Jagter (Copenhagen: Gyldendal, 1907)—includes "Fusijama," translated by Elias Bredsdorff as "Fujiyama," in his *Contemporary Danish Prose: An Anthology* (Copenhagen: Gyldendal, 1958), pp. 85–90;
Den ny Verden: Til international Belysning af nordisk Bondekultur (Copenhagen: Gyldendal, 1907);
Singapore Noveller (Copenhagen: Gyldendal, 1907);

Nye Myter (Copenhagen: Gyldendal, 1908);

Bræen: Myter om Istiden og det første Menneske (Copenhagen: Gyldendal, 1908); translated by Arthur G. Chater in *Fire and Ice,* volume 1 of *The Long Journey* (London: Gyldendal, 1922; New York: Knopf, 1923);

Lille Ahasverus (Copenhagen: Gyldendal, 1909);

Myter: Ny Samling (Copenhagen: Gyldendal, 1910);

Himmerlandshistorier: Tredie Samling (Copenhagen: Gyldendal, 1910);

Nordisk Aand: Kroniker og Karakteristiker (Copenhagen: Gyldendal, 1911);

Skibet (Copenhagen: Gyldendal, 1912);

Myter: Fjerde Samling (Copenhagen: Gyldendal, 1912);

Rudyard Kipling (Copenhagen: Gyldendal, 1912);

Olivia Marianne (Copenhagen: Gyldendal, 1915);

Introduktion til vor Tidsalder (Copenhagen: Gyldendal, 1915);

Aarbog 1916 (Copenhagen: Gyldendal, 1916);

Eksotiske Noveller (Copenhagen: Gyldendal, 1916)—comprises *Singapore Noveller, Lille Ahasverus,* and *Olivia Marianne;*

Aarbog 1917 (Copenhagen: Gyldendal, 1917);

Norne-Gæst (Copenhagen: Gyldendal, 1919); translated by Chater in *The Cimbrians,* volume 2 of *The Long Journey* (London: Gyldendal, 1923; New York: Knopf, 1923);

Det tabte Land: Mennesket før Istiden (Copenhagen: Gyldendal, 1919); translated by Chater in *Fire and Ice,* volume 1 of *The Long Journey* (London: Gyldendal, 1922; New York: Knopf, 1923);

Johannes Larsen og hans Billeder (Copenhagen: Gyldendal, 1920);

Christofer Columbus (Copenhagen: Gyldendal, 1921); translated by Chater as *Christopher Columbus,* volume 3 of *The Long Journey* (London: Gyldendal, 1924; New York: Knopf, 1924);

Sangerinden (Madame d'Ora): Drama i fem Akter (Copenhagen: Gyldendal, 1921);

Cimbrernes Tog (Copenhagen: Gyldendal, 1922); translated by Chater in *The Cimbrians,* volume 2 of *The Long Journey* (London: Gyldendal, 1923; New York: Knopf, 1923);

Æstetik og Udvikling: Efterskrift til Den lange Rejse (Copenhagen: Gyldendal, 1923);

Aarstiderne, illustrated by Johannes Larsen (Copenhagen: Gyldendal, 1923);

Myter: Tredie Bind, 1914–1924 (Copenhagen: Gyldendal, 1924);

Hamlet: Til Forklaring af Hamletskikkselen (Copenhagen: Gyldendal, 1924);

Evolution og Moral (Copenhagen: Gyldendal, 1925);

Aarets Højtider (Copenhagen: Gyldendal, 1925);

Verdens Lys: Nye Digte (Copenhagen: Gyldendal, 1926);

Jørgine (Copenhagen: Hage & Clausens Forlag, 1926);

Dyrenes Forvandling: Til Udviklingens Plastik (Copenhagen: Gyldendal, 1927);

Ved Livets Bred og andre Myter (Copenhagen: Gyldendal, 1928);

Aandens Stadier (Copenhagen: Gyldendal, 1928);

Retninger i Tiden: Artikler 1925–30 (Copenhagen: Gyldendal, 1930);

Den jydske Blæst: Digte 1926–1930 (Copenhagen: Gyldendal, 1931);

Form og Sjæl: Portræter og Personligheder (Copenhagen: Gyldendal, 1931);

Paa danske Veje, illustrated by Larsen (Copenhagen: Gyldendal, 1931);

Pisangen (Copenhagen: Gyldendal, 1932);

Kornmarken (Copenhagen: Gyldendal, 1932);

Sælernes Ø (Copenhagen: Gyldendal, 1934);

Det Blivende: Tankens Revolutionering i det 19de Aarhundrede og Tilbagefaldet i det 20de (Copenhagen: Gyldendal, 1934);

Dr. Renaults Fristelser (Copenhagen: Gyldendal, 1935);

Gudrun (Copenhagen: Gyldendal, 1936);

Darduse, Bryllupet i Peking: Eventyrkomedie i fire Akter (Copenhagen: Gyldendal, 1937);

Paaskebadet: Digte 1931–1937 (Copenhagen: Gyldendal, 1937);

Jydske Folkelivsmalere: Dalsgaard, Michael Ancher, Hans Smidth (Copenhagen: Arthur Jensen, 1937);

Den lange Rejse, 2 volumes (Copenhagen: Gyldendal, 1938)—comprises volume 1, *Det tabte Land, Bræen,* and *Norne-Gæst;* and volume 2, *Cimbrernes Tog, Skibet,* and *Christofer Columbus;*

Thorvaldsen: Haandværkeren og Manden (Copenhagen: Arthur Jensen, 1938);

Nordvejen: Indtryk af norsk Natur (Copenhagen: Gyldendal, 1939);

Fra Fristaterne: Rejsebreve, med et Tilbageblik (Copenhagen: Gyldendal, 1939);

Gutenberg: Til Bogtrykkerkunstens Historie, by Jensen and Aage Marcus (Copenhagen: Bianco Lunos Bogtrykkeri, 1939);

Mariehønen (Copenhagen: Gyldendal, 1940);

Udvalgte Prosastykker, edited by Morten Borup and Peter Ilsøe (Copenhagen: Gyldendal, 1940);

Mindets Tavle: Portræter og Personligheder (Copenhagen: Gyldendal, 1941);

Vor Oprindelse (Copenhagen: Gyldendal, 1941);

Om Sproget og Undervisningen (Copenhagen: Gyldendal, 1942);

Kvinden i Sagatiden (Copenhagen: Gyldendal, 1942);

Folkeslagene i Østen (Copenhagen: Gyldendal, 1943);

Møllen (Copenhagen: Gyldendal, 1944);

Myter, 2 volumes (Copenhagen: Gyldendal, 1946);

Bogbinderen (Copenhagen: Printed by J. H. Schultz, 1947);

Afrika: Opdagelsesrejserne (Copenhagen: Gyldendal, 1949);

Danske Køretøjer (Copenhagen: Thaning & Appel, 1949);

Swift og Oehlenschläger (Copenhagen: Gyldendal, 1950);

Tilblivelsen (Copenhagen: Gyldendal, 1951);

Mytens ring: Efterladte myter og beskrivelser (Copenhagen: Gyldendal, 1957);

Ungt er endnu Ordet: Portræter og Personligheder, edited by Carl Bergstrøm-Nielsen (Copenhagen: Gyldendal, 1958);

Trods, edited by Sven Hakon Rossel (Copenhagen: Museum Tusculanum, 2002).

Editions and Collections: *Den jydske blæst og andre digte,* selected by Ole Wivel (Copenhagen: Gyldendal, 1957);

Bræen, edited by Martin Larsen (Copenhagen: Gyldendal, 1963);

Himmerlandshistorier, edited, with an afterword, by Jørgen Elbek, Gyldendals Bibliotek, no. 24 (Copenhagen: Gyldendal, 1963);

Johannes Larsen og Aarstiderne, edited, with a foreword, by Aage Marcus, Gyldendals Uglebøger, no. 56 (Copenhagen: Gyldendal, 1963);

Jordens Kreds, selected by Marcus, introduction by Niels Birger Wamberg (Copenhagen: Gyldendal, 1967);

Myter i Digte i Udvalg, selected by Leif Nedergaard (Copenhagen: Gyldendal, 1969);

Himmerlandshistorier, edited by Povl Marstal (Copenhagen: Gyldendal, 1970);

Mørkets frodighed; Tidlige myter, selected by Wamberg (Copenhagen: Gyldendal, 1973);

12 Himmerlandshistorier, edited by Sven Moller Kristensen (Copenhagen: Gyldendal, 1979);

Tretten Myter: Johannes V. Jensen, selected and illustrated by Jens Jensen (Copenhagen: Gyldendal, 1982);

Himmerlandshistorier: Et udvalg, selected by Sonja Carlberg (Copenhagen: Gyldendal, 1984);

Kender du Johannes V. Jensen, selected by Margit Mørk (Copenhagen: Grafisk, 1986);

Christofer Columbus, foreword by Ib Michael (Copenhagen: Gyldendal, 1992);

Madame D'Ora; Hjulet, edited by Sven Hakon Rossel (Copenhagen: Det Danske Sproge-og Litteraturselskab/Borgen, 1997);

Digte: Johannes V. Jensen, edited by Frits Johansen (Copenhagen: Gyldendal, 1998).

Editions in English: "Ane og Koen," translated by Victor Folke Nelson as "Ann and the Cow"; "Forsvundne Skove," translated by Henry Commager as "Lost Forests," in *Denmark's Best Stories,* edited by Hanna Astrup Larsen (New York: American-Scandinavian Foundation/Norton, 1928), pp. 327–340;

Garden Colonies in Denmark, translated by F. Aubrey Rush (Copenhagen: Danske selskab, 1949);

Denmark's Johannes V. Jensen, translated by Marion L. Nielsen (Logan: Utah State Agricultural College, 1955);

The Waving Rye, selected by C. A. Bodelsen, translated by Ronald Bathgate and others (Copenhagen: Gyldendal, 1958; New York: American-Scandinavian Foundation, 1959);

The Fall of the King, translated by Alan Bower and edited by Sven Hakon Rossel (Seattle: Mermaid Press, 1992; revised edition, Traverse City: Stonehill, 1995).

PLAY PRODUCTIONS: *Trods,* Chicago, Scandia Hall, 1 February 1903;

Sangerinden, Odense, Odense Teater, 16 November 1923;

Darduse, Bryllupet i Peking: Eventyrkomedie i fire akter, Copenhagen, Royal Theater, 22 January 1937;

Hamlet, translation of William Shakespeare's play, Copenhagen, Royal Theater, 24 April 1937.

OTHER: Jack London, *Naar Naturen kalder,* translated by Aslaug Mikkelsen, foreword by Jensen (Copenhagen: Peter Hansen, 1907);

Ditleff von Zeppelin, *Fugletræk,* edited by Jensen and Otto Gelsted (Copenhagen: Gyldendal, 1916);

Thorvaldsens Portrætbuster, introduction by Jensen, biographical notes by Aage Marcus (Copenhagen: Gyldendal, 1926).

TRANSLATIONS: Frank Norris, *Af Hvedens Saga: Polypen, en Bog om Kalifornien* (Copenhagen: Gyldendal, 1907);

Rudyard Kipling and Wolcott Balestier, *Nauhlaka: Fortælling fra Vesten og Østen,* translated by Jensen and Aslaug Mikkelsen (Copenhagen: V. Pio, 1911);

Kipling, *Fribytterbreve; De rædselsfulde Nætters By og andre Skizzer,* translated by Jensen and Mikkelsen (Copenhagen: V. Pio, 1912);

Kipling, *Fra Hav til Hav,* translated by Jensen and Mikkelsen (Copenhagen: V. Pio, 1913);

Kipling, *Liv og Drøm,* translated by Jensen and Mikkelsen (Copenhagen: V. Pio, 1913);

Kipling, *Med Natexpressen Aar 2000 og andre Fortællinger,* translated by Jensen and Mikkelsen (Copenhagen: V. Pio, 1914);

Rudolf Requadt, *Krigsflyveren* (Copenhagen: Fr. Ravn, 1916);

Adelbert von Chamisso, *Peter Schlemihls vidunderlige Historie* (Copenhagen: Høst & Søn, 1918);

Walt Whitman, *Digte,* translated by Jensen and Otto Gelsted (Copenhagen: Nyt Nordisk, 1919);

De islandske Sagaer, 3 volumes, translated by Jensen, Knud Hjortø, and Hans Kyrre (Copenhagen: Gyldendal, 1930–1932);

William Shakespeare, *Hamlet* (Copenhagen: Gyldendal, 1937);

Egil Skallagrimssons Saga (Copenhagen: Gyldendal, 1943);

Snorre Sturlason, *Heimskringla: Norges Kongesagaer,* translated and edited by Jensen and Kyrre (Copenhagen: Gyldendal, 1948).

SELECTED PERIODICAL PUBLICATIONS–UNCOLLECTED: *Skatten paa Korsøgaard: Fortælling fra Aarhundredets Begyndelse,* as Ivar Lykke, *Revuen* (2 January–21 July 1895);

Dødssejleren: Fortælling, as Lykke, *Revuen* (24 July 1895–26 January 1896);

Blodfesterne i Arizona: Mexikansk, historisk Fortælling, as Lykke, *Revuen* (26 January–31 May 1896);

Jim Blacksools Revolver: Roman fra det fjerne Vesten, as Lykke, *Revuen* (31 May–30 September 1896);

Falskmønterbandens blodige Bog: Kriminal-Roman, as Lykke, *Revuen* (1 July–13 December 1896);

Nihilistens Ed: En Nutidsroman, as Lykke, *Revuen* (19 July–23 September 1896);

Taterkongens ni Sønner og deres Blodhævn: Roman fra Dronning Margrethes Tid, as Lykke, *Revuen* (9 December 1896 – 5 May 1897);

Milliontyvenes Høvding eller den røde Tiger: Original illustreret New Yorkerroman, as Lykke, *Revuen* (9 May–22 September 1897);

Hakon Blodøxes Bedrifter: Roman fra Vikingetiden, as Lykke, *Revuen* (26 September 1897 – 9 March 1898);

Ridder Tages Dødsridt eller de blodige Sporer: Original historisk Roman fra Valdemar den Stores Tid, as Lykke, *Revuen* (13 March–20 July 1898).

By revolting against the introspection of Danish turn-of-the-century literature and the psychological and social naturalism of the nineteenth century, Johannes V. Jensen became one of the most prolific, innovative spirits in Danish cultural life. His worship of modern science and technology, the bustling life in the international metropolis, and pragmatic materialism and capitalism made him instrumental in the reorientation of Danish literature away from continental French and German models toward Anglo-American cultural life. His enthusiasm for American literature resulted in the introduction and promotion in Denmark of the works of many American writers.

Charles Darwin's theories were an important source of inspiration for Jensen's depictions of nature scenes and animals but had a disastrous impact on his questionable evolutionary and anthropological ideas. Despite his scientific and anti-idealistic orientation, Jensen was never able to let go of his deep-rooted dependence on the Jutland peasant traditions of his childhood and an equally deep-rooted fascination with Christian metaphysics. This contradiction or split resulted in an existential insecurity that manifests itself in a fragmentation both with regard to content and form, which gives Jensen's fictional work continuing relevance. It places him in the modernist tradition of the twentieth century, adding to some of his texts a vibrant and eclectic, almost postmodern, quality. However, when Jensen was able to bridge this split in his myths and poetry, he created pieces of timeless art in which observation and vision, present time and eternity, reality and dream are seamlessly merged.

Johannes Vilhelm Jensen was born on 20 January 1873 in Farsø in the northern Jutland province of Himmerland. His parents were both of peasant stock. His mother, Marie Kirstine Jensen, had a prosaic and practical view of life, but she also possessed a vivid imagination and a hot temper; his father, Hans Jensen, was the district veterinarian and was an expert in botany and zoology. He inspired Jensen's later studies of nature and discovery of Darwin's evolutionary theories. Although the family was strongly antireligious, in the late 1880s Jensen's father became interested in spiritualism, an interest that became lifelong for Jensen's sister, the writer Thit Jensen. Johannes V. Jensen later criticized this occult interest, although it was undoubtedly one of the causative factors for the longing for eternity and spiritual expansion that became an essential feature in his writing. Jensen also had one younger brother, who became a painter under the name Hans Deuvs.

In the autobiographical sketch *Kirken i Farsø: Skitse* (1903, The Church in Farsø: Sketch), Jensen described his boyhood with his siblings and friends from the small town and the neighborhood farms, emphasizing his boldness and extroversion. A somewhat different description comes from one of Jensen's friends, Peder Bach, quoted in Oluf Friis's 1974 biography of Jensen: "Han var en besynderlig Dreng, ikke som de andre, men for det meste tavs og indesluttet, og han gik gerne og saa ned i Jorden i sine egne dybe Tanker; men til Tider kunde han vaagne op, og da husker jeg at hans Snebolde blev temmelig haarde" (He was a strange boy, not like the others, but mostly silent and reticent, and he usually walked around looking down deep in his thoughts; but at times he could wake up, and then I remember that his snowballs became rather hard). A characteristic trait was his joy in reading. Jensen himself, in *Mytens ring: Efterladte myter og beskrivelser* (1957, The Ring of the Myth: Posthumous Myths and Descriptions), recalled his first books: children's readers; accounts by Captain James Cook, Henry Morton Stanley, and David Livingstone of their expeditions; a history of Denmark; and Hans Christian Andersen's tales—all works that he found on his father's bookshelves.

After two years at Farsø School, followed by private tutoring, Jensen went in 1890 to Viborg Katedralskole (cathedral school) for three years, where he became familiar with the humanistic, bourgeois educational tradition that for hundreds of years had formed the basis for spiritual life in Denmark. Jensen's years in Viborg, depicted in the first two chapters of his first novel, *Danskere* (1896, Danes), were not harmonious, and his opposition was nourished in particular by reading the German poet Heinrich Heine, whom Jensen called, in his monograph *Rudyard Kipling* (1912), "denne Dynamitsjæl" (this explosive spirit), and the British author Rudyard Kipling, in whose works Jensen experienced a new world of activity and international settings. Although classes in Viborg did not include modern literature, Jensen read works by contemporary writers in private. Both the neo-Romantic Danish poet Johannes Jørgensen and the Norwegian Knut Hamsun, whom Jensen regarded as the first to break with the older realism and naturalism—what Jensen called "den galliske knirkende Fornuftspoesi" (the Gallic, creaking literature of reason)—became additional models for the future writer.

Jensen passed his university entrance exams in 1893 and began the study of medicine at the University of Copenhagen in the fall. In January 1894 he published four poems, basically derivative of neo-Romantic literature, that include motifs foreshadowing his later settlement with the introverted and spiritual attitude that was prevalent in Danish literature at the time of his debut and remained part of Jensen's own personality. Likewise without artistic quality are ten serial novels written under the pseudonym Ivar Lykke and published in the Copenhagen journal *Revuen* between 1895 and 1898. In *Mytens ring,* Jensen hints at the main ingredients of these serial novels, remarking that "Hvert Kapitel havde sit horrible Mord" (Each chapter contained a horrible murder). The novels hold no trace of his later mastery of style but are not without importance, as in them Jensen introduces motifs that he took up again later.

Jensen had his true literary debut in 1896 with the novel *Danskere*. After he abandoned his medical studies in 1898, he published *Einar Elkær: Roman* (1898, Einar Elkær: Novel). Between the publication of the two novels he took a brief trip to New York City in 1896, the first of many travels that, altogether, brought Jensen to the United States six times. Both the character Buris in the first novel and Einar Elkær in the second are students from the provinces who are confronted with the modern metropolis, Copenhagen. They are obsessed by paralyzing self-absorption that prevents them from establishing a spontaneous rapport with other people, in particular with women. Whereas Jensen hints at the possibility that the disintegration of Buris's personality may stop, Einar constantly lapses into his ravings and dreams and dies at a mental hospital, where "Sektionen viste blød Hjærne" (the autopsy showed a soft brain). Even though the two novels are strongly dependent on literary models—their melancholy atmosphere, big-city sceneries, and self-reflective protagonists can be found in the early works of Jørgensen and Hamsun—their rebellion against both the fin-de-siècle spirit of the 1890s and literary and philosophical authority in general has a genuine ring. Jensen later excluded his first two books from lists of his works, perhaps because he recognized too much of his own introverted personality in his two protagonists. They are desperate outsiders, whose longing for happiness finds no fulfillment. This longing, which in so many of Jensen's characters manifests itself as a longing to travel, is in reality a longing for the expansion of the soul.

Introspection remains a major issue in the two travelogues, *Intermezzo: Dolores, Forsvundne Skove, Louison* (1899, Intermezzo: Dolores, Lost Forests, Louison) and *Skovene* (1904, The Woods), both written under the influence of Heine's capricious, ironic style. The first was based on Jensen's two visits as a reporter for the liberal newspaper *Politiken* to Spain, Germany, and France in 1898 and also includes the first of his many attacks on the works of Friedrich Nietzsche, whose theories of the superman constituted the "bad Darwinism" that Jensen later saw as the indirect cause of the two world wars. The second book was inspired by Jensen's five-week stay in Singapore and on the Malay Peninsula during his first trip around the world in 1902 and 1903, which also took him to China, Japan, and the United States. In his description of a tiger hunt Jensen incorporates lyrical and satirical passages, witticisms, and brilliantly executed, precise but poetic descriptions of animals and nature. The strong stylistic contrasts in the volume reflect the self-ironic and didactic approach Jensen takes toward his own glorification of the primitive, against which he sets his homesickness and longing.

The reworked travel letters from his visit to Spain in 1898 and another to the World's Exhibition in Paris in 1900, which Jensen incorporated into his *Den gotiske Renaissance* (1901, The Gothic Renaissance), on the other hand, include an enthusiastic endorsement of progress and reality: "Det tyvende Aarhundrede suser over Hovedet. Jeg bekender mig til Virkeligheden, jeg bekender" (The twentieth century roars above our heads. I profess to reality, I profess). This work glorifies the expansive spirit of the Gothic, that is, Anglo-Saxon, race, the fullest expression of which Jensen found in the American pragmatic and progressive view of life as it brought liberation from the decadence of the previous century. The volume climaxes in Walt Whitman–inspired prose hymns to progress and technology. Jensen's theory was that the Gothic race had its origin in his home region, Himmerland. Its nature and people are portrayed in the realistic short stories in *Himmerlandsfolk: Historier* (1898, Himmerland People: Stories), which constitute a counterbalance to Jensen's introspective writings from the same period, and in the two collections *Nye Himmerlandshistorier* (1904, New Himmerland Stories) and *Himmerlandshistorier: Tredie Samling* (1910, Himmerland Stories: Third Collection). The early texts are marked by Jensen's preoccupation with the meaninglessness of day-to-day existence and death. Later stories include masterful character studies of grotesque, roaming eccentrics, heroic accounts of man's stubborn fight against either sordid surroundings or the callous forces of nature, and comic or satiric exposures of human folly. Jensen's intimate knowledge of the flaws and meanness of his characters is balanced by a profound veneration for the old peasant traditions they also represent. In such texts Jensen has distanced himself from the uncritical glorification of technology and progress in *Den gotiske Renaissance,* and these stories are far above traditional regional literature.

In 1900 and 1901 Jensen published an historical novel in three parts: *Foraarets Død* (1900, Spring's Death), *Den store Sommer* (1900, The Full Summer), and *Vinteren* (1901, Winter). Jensen combined the works into a single volume under the title of *Kongens Fald* (1901; translated as *The Fall of the King,* 1933). With *Kongens Fald,* Jensen successfully merged the extrovert/naturalistic and introvert/spiritual elements in his writing into a splendid mythic composition. In Jensen's works there are many attempts at defining "the mythic." In his 1932 article on Jensen, Aage Marcus reports Jensen as saying: "Leave out the plot, concentrate on those short flashes of the essence of things that illumine man and time, and you have the myth." As Jensen writes in his *Aarbog 1916* (Yearbook 1916), his point of departure is generally a concrete observation from which an expansion in time and space takes place, a technique that entails a revelation, "ingen lang møjsommelig Opregning men et Spring ind i et Billede" (rather a leap into an image than a long painstaking account). Crucial components of the myth are the tensions between the close and the distant, the tangible and the transcendental, and the concrete and the inexplicable, frequently establishing a perspective of time in which present, past, and future are bound together.

Kongens Fald can be read as a purely historical novel, attacking the passivity and indecisiveness that Jensen perceived as a major component of Danish mentality. These negative qualities are embodied in the Renaissance king Christian II and his companion, the mercenary Mikkel Thøgersen. However, Jensen ignores both historical accuracy and a structured psychological character delineation. Instead, by mingling dream-like passages of poetic beauty with harsh, naturalistic scenes of violence and destruction, he creates magnificent, deeply pessimistic visions of man's inability to reach happiness. Like Buris in *Danskere,* the introverted outsider Mikkel completely lacks the ability to devote himself to enjoying the present: he can only act when his anguish turns into hatred and blind destructiveness. He rapes Ane Mette, the fiancée of his rival Otte Iversen, and many years later he kills Otte's son, the carefree and spontaneous Axel, whose success with women stirs Mikkel's feelings of alienation, envy, and hatred. He assaults the unarmed Axel, who later, without any bitterness, dies of blood poisoning, fever-stricken and dreaming that he is sailing into "den store Sommers Land, Dødens Land" (the land of full summer, the land of death). Axel's "fall," one of the lyrical highlights of the novel, corresponds on the historical level to the king's "fall" during the fateful night in 1523 when Christian II, accompanied by Mikkel, irresolutely sails back and forth between two regions of Denmark wondering whether or not to take up the fight against the rebellious nobility—a dramatic highlight and at the same time a penetrating analysis of the paralysis of action by doubt. However, of crucial importance is not the outward fall as demonstrated in the king's destiny. Jensen's masterpiece must be read as a book about the inner fall, about man's impermanence, and about death as his inexorable destiny in the midst of burgeoning life, illustrated in Axel's fate. *Kongens Fald* is a book about the total absurdity of life and love, illustrated in Mikkel's person. All of humanity is subject to the law of the fall, and only death brings the desired peace.

On his first trip around the world Jensen crossed the Pacific Ocean from Japan, stopping in the Hawaiian Islands and disembarking in San Francisco on 26 October 1902. His stay in the United States, primarily in Chicago and New York during the winter and spring of 1902–1903, provided him with the scenery for the two novels *Madame D'Ora* (1904) and *Hjulet* (1905, The Wheel), with which Jensen—only in part successfully—intended to continue the antimetaphysical trend in his authorship. Intentionally he disregards the rules of the traditional, naturalistic novel as he sets out to portray not individuals but various stages in man's evolution within the framework of a fierce Darwinian struggle for the "survival of the fittest." In *Madame D'Ora* this struggle takes place between "the missing link"–the cynical lay preacher, charlatan, and murderer Evanston–and the scientist Edmund Hall, a Faustian character fascinated with the transcendental, a neurasthenic dreamer who not only fails to reciprocate the passionate and unconditional feelings of the opera singer Leontine D'Ora but also falls an easy prey to Evanston because of his preoccupation with spiritual experiences.

In the sequel, *Hjulet,* the young poet Lee, Jensen's alter ego, kills Evanston, who has now changed his name to the symbolic Cancer and has become an even clearer example of the Nietzschean vulgarization of Darwinism that Jensen had earlier attacked in *Intermezzo*. Through his struggle Lee overcomes his earlier passivity and turns into a man of action who condemns all aesthetics as nothing but "en Sygdom i Sansen for Virkeligheden" (a disease in the perception of reality). Passages parodying the detective novels of Sir Arthur Conan Doyle alternate with lengthy monologues (in particular by the constantly talking Cancer), congenial translations of poems by Whitman, and Lee's sweeping visions, ranging from prehistoric, evolutionary stages in man's development to his view of Christopher Columbus as a man of Nordic descent and a bridge builder between Europe's past and America's present. These visions–indeed prose poems of compelling poetic force–as well as the totally negative portrayal of the representative of pure materialism, Evanston/Cancer, prove that Jensen could not let go of the aesthetics that he lets Lee reject. The enthusiasm for the United States expressed in these two novels foreshadows later works of fiction and nonfiction, as Jensen returned to both theories of Columbus and Faustian motifs.

After Jensen returned to Copenhagen from New York City in the summer of 1903, he published a series of newspaper articles. In these articles his violent criticism of Danish superficiality and provincialism demonstrates how difficult it was for him to resign himself to staying home. He was particularly irritated by Danish literary life, partly because of his own aggressive nature, which isolated him among colleagues, and partly because he rejected both the neo-Romantics and the radical circle around the influential critic Georg Brandes, whom he had earlier admired. He was also unhappy because his books received mostly negative reviews and sold poorly.

Nevertheless, the period from 1904 to 1906 was characterized by a hectic productivity: two novels, a travelogue, a new volume of stories from Himmerland, and finally an epoch-making collection of poetry. All these publications were projects that Jensen felt he wanted to finish and move on. *Digte* (1906, Poems; revised and enlarged, 1917, 1921, 1943, 1948) includes almost all of his youthful poetry, except for those poems that he had published during his first year at the university, which have never been collected. Two of Jensen's earliest prose poems from 1901, "Interferens" (Interference) and "Ved Bordet" (At the Table), published in a newspaper, were revised and incorporated in *Digte*. Prose poetry came to dominate this volume, especially with the inclusion of the Whitman translations, first published in the novel *Hjulet*. This preponderance of free verse has contributed to the popular but erroneous view that Jensen's poetry consists mostly of prose poetry, with Whitman as the predominant model. The truth is rather that Jensen's prose poems, modeled after the free verse of Johann Wolfgang von Goethe and Heine, belong to the period of 1901 to 1906, after which he increasingly devoted himself to poems in regular meters with either Old Norse alliterative verse or the classical rhymed stanza as models.

Digte is a milestone in the development of Danish lyric poetry. Its highly developed, bold imagery is filled with contrasts and tension both in content and in style, a style that veers from cynical statement to ecstatic exclamation to heart-rending simplicity and tenderness–the heritage of the 1890s. This metaphoric language is based on a sharp sensory perception that often takes the shape of a merciless self-analysis at the same time as it incorporates images from modern technology and everyday life.

At the center of the volume are three texts, the two prose poems "Interferens" and "Paa Memphis Station" (At Memphis Station), and the ballad-like "Christofer Columbus." In "Interferens," Jensen seeks, as he does in several of the poems, to reconcile the clash between extroversion and introversion, optimism and pessimism, belief in progress and wish for death–the two poles in his writing. When they intersect or rather become fused in one single state of mind, the myth emerges, as in "Christofer Columbus," originally published in *Madame D'Ora,* where it was a warning to Hall to abandon his insatiable ambitions to transgress the boundaries of empirical science. It can, however, also be read as an anticipation of the novel *Christofer Columbus* (1921; translated as *Christopher Columbus,* 1924), as a portrait of Jensen's tragic alter ego, Columbus, who is invoked in the poem "Afsked" (Departure). Here, another crucial theme from Jensen's novels, the longing to travel, is introduced in an attack on humdrum everyday life in provincial Denmark. The poem was written in 1902 just before Jensen's voyage around the world. Inspired by the voyage itself is "Paa Memphis Station," a commitment to a reality that must encompass even the experience of death. This realization ignites the poet's zest for a life that must be conquered through travel. Thus Columbus must move on, but the outcome of his travel turns out to be tragic, as Jensen points out in the succeeding poem, "Hverdagene" (Everyday Life). Its concluding request to "gaa frygtløst ind i Hverdagene" (enter into everyday life fearlessly) is preceded by lines about the merciless passage of time and unavoidable death:

> Somren slaar sine Kister i.
> Unge er vi saa ikke mere.
> Men har Haabet ikke beskæmmet os tilstrækkeligt?
> Nu kommer vor rige Dødstid, Broder.
>
> (Summer is closing its chests.
> So we are young no longer.
> But has hope not shamed us sufficiently?
> Now comes a plentiful dying time, brother.)

Such lines point ahead to perhaps the most difficult of all lyrical genres, the memorial poem, a genre that Jensen mastered to a degree not reached by any other Danish writer. In the second edition of Jensen's collected poems, *Digte: Anden Udgave* (1917, Poems: Second Edition), there are two such poems, "Leonora Christine" and "Bjørnstjerne Bjørnson," written in traditional iambic meter. The first is a portrait of Leonora Christine, a Danish Renaissance princess who spent twenty-two years in prison and whose tragic destiny Jensen perceives in a mythic perspective. The second poem is a glorification of the active and extroverted Norwegian writer, written on the occasion of Bjørnson's death in 1910. The poem is pervaded with pantheism; however, Jensen concludes with lines negating that pantheism: "O Solopgang paa Bjergets Sne – / ham skal du aldrig mere se" (Oh sunrise on the mountain's snow – / you shall never see him again). The last poem in the volume is "Envoi," which Jensen kept revising until it received its final form in the third edition of his collected poems. This poem is noteworthy for its haiku-like simplicity, with a perfect form embracing time and space, a myth concentrated around the eternity of love placed in the cycle of nature.

Jensen's productivity after his return from his journey around the world in 1902 and 1903 was also caused by the need to make a living for his family. On 15 April 1904 he married twenty-six-year-old Else Marie Ulrik, with whom he had three sons, Jens, Villum, and Emmerick. On 2 July 1906 Jensen began his own newspaper, *Pressen* (The Press), with John Martin. Modeled on contemporary American tabloids, *Pressen* was filled with sensational news, cartoons, and many advertisements. As Jensen did not have any political or cultural program for the newspaper, he did not find any readers, and *Pressen* lasted only until 31 July. This project was preceded by several trips to Himmerland and Berlin, and at the same time Jensen began translating Frank Norris's novel *The Octopus* (1901), eventually published as *Af Hvedens Saga: Polypen, en Bog om Kalifornien* (1907, From the Wheat's Saga: The Octopus, a Book about California). By writing the foreword to *Naar Naturen kalder,* a translation in 1907 of Jack London's *The Call of the Wild* (1903), Jensen called attention in Denmark to another American writer; he introduced a third American writer, Ernest Hemingway, to the Danish public with an essay in *Politiken* (30 May 1930).

As a result of a 1905 trip to New York City, Jensen began writing a series of articles in March 1906 for *Politiken* about journalism, literature, and social issues in the United States. These essays were republished in the collection *Den ny Verden: Til international Belysning af nordisk Bondekultur* (1907, The New World: For an International Illustration of Nordic Peasant Culture). The heroes of the book are the American reporter Norris, who successfully portrayed the hectic pioneer spirit during the growth of the United States, and Theodore Roosevelt, who is seen as the epitome of American civilization because of his dynamic and extroverted nature. From the fall of 1906 to the summer of 1907 Jensen was preoccupied with polemical exchanges with various Danish writers and critics. For this reason the collection of prose *Myter og Jagter* (Myths and Hunts), from 1907, includes primarily texts that had previously been published. *Singapore Noveller* (Singapore Stories), also from 1907, was likewise based on older material. Together with the texts in *Lille Ahasverus* (1909, Little Ahasuerus) and *Olivia Marianne* (1915), the stories in *Singapore Noveller* were collected in *Eksotiske Noveller* (1916, Exotic Stories). They form an exotic counterpart to the stories about Himmerland. The United States provides the setting for some of the stories, but most of them are set in Java and China, inspired by Jensen's Far East trip in the summer and fall of 1902, and owe their quality mainly to the exquisitely drawn scenery and linguistic virtuosity. In their somewhat simplistic view of the life of Europeans among the natives, the stories are an example of the strong influence Kipling had on Jensen's early writings.

In the summer of 1907 Jensen, tired of literary disputes—although he had provoked them himself—made a trip to Norway, and in the following winter he went to Sweden. These visits resulted in several realistic hunting descriptions for *Politiken,* later included in the volume *Nye Myter* (1908, New Myths), which also includes one of Jensen's best prose texts, "Darwin og Fuglen" (Darwin and the Bird). It opens with a magnificent spring scene, then is extended into a portrait of Darwin, the man whose evolutionary theories influenced Jensen's writing for the remaining forty-three years of his life. With this volume and *Myter og Jagter*, Jensen had begun to create a series of brief, somewhat uneven prose texts, so-called *myter* or myths, which usually were first printed in newspapers; from 1910 to 1944 nine additional volumes were published. In essays and sketches based on reading and traveling, Jensen incorporates

> Øjebliksbilleder fra Gaden, indre dæmrende Erindringer omspændende alle fem Verdensdele, Historien, Urtiden og en fjern Barndom . . . mellem hinanden, men *sandt* til Hobe forsaa vidt som det hænger sammen og har Tone og Farve.
>
> (snapshots from the street, inner dawning memories encompassing all five continents, history, the earliest times and a distant childhood . . . intermingled, but every bit of it *true* in so far as it has coherence and resonance and color.)

Jensen presents his basic ideas in a symbolic, concentrated form: a full acceptance of present reality as the source and final goal of all longing as in "Fusijama" (1907; translated as "Fujiyama," 1958) and a belief in eternity as it is found in the cyclic reappearance of the seasons as in "Nordisk Foraar" (1912, Nordic Spring). Jensen's myths are based on his belief in the necessity of placing oneself in a meaningful context with nature as in "Haren" (1908, The Hare) and creating links to the most distant memories from history and prehistory as in "Dansk Natur" (1910, Danish Nature). This myth gives a superb description of Denmark seen in the light of the country's past, incarnated in ancient monuments and in visions of the life of Stone Age people. It is actually one of several myths exemplifying the impossibility of seizing and preserving the present moment in isolation and thus—characteristic of the split in Jensen between materialism and spirituality—partially contradicting the "Fusijama" myth. Directly dealing with man's quest for the indefinite and eternal are the myths "Moderen og Barnet" (1917, Mother and Child) and "Den store Kristoffer" (1917, The Great Christopher). "Moderen og Barnet," which in his *Æstetik og Udvikling: Efterskrift til Den lange Rejse* (1923, Aesthetics and Evolution: Postscript to The Long Journey) Jensen called "nok det gyldigste jeg har gjort" (probably the most valid thing I have ever written), is based on the Roman Catholic concept of the Madonna and child, "Livets skønneste Symbol, Slægten i et Afbillede, som var Slægten selv, det højeste Under, og samtidigt den højeste Moral" (life's most beautiful symbol, the family in a single image that is the family itself, the highest miracle and at the same time the highest ethics). In his retelling of the legend of St. Christopher, Jensen makes a Northerner of him. His staff, which changed into a palm, is interpreted mythically as the Northerner's longing for the South, which is finally satisfied when the South comes to him in the person of the infant Jesus, whom Christopher carries across the river and into the North, an achievement that is duplicated when his namesake, Columbus, brings Christianity to the New World.

These two myths, as well as several others, were reworked and incorporated into the six books that became *Den lange Rejse* (1938; translated as *The Long Journey*, 3 volumes, 1922–1924). This multivolume novel comprises an evolutionary history or rather a fantasy of mankind. It was intended as a scientific counterpart to the biblical legends but turned out to be a collection of legends itself. Jensen sees the challenge of nature as the driving force of progress that brings about evolution. *Bræen: Myter om Istiden og det første Menneske* (1908, The Glacier: Myths of the Ice Age and of the First Man; translated in *Fire and Ice*, 1922) is the first written in the series and also its most popular. Here the Glacial Age has forced the humans to migrate southward; only Dreng (Boy) turns in defiance to the north and founds, together with the woman Moa (Mother), a large family. In a memorable scene Dreng rediscovers fire by striking sparks from flint, while Moa collects seeds and begins to till the soil.

Det tabte Land: Mennesket før Istiden (1919, The Lost Land: Man Before the Ice Age; translated in *Fire and Ice*) is a Darwinian myth of creation about the transition from animal to Homo sapiens in the preglacial rain forests of Jutland. The major character of the volume is Fyr (Fire), who climbs a volcano and, like Prometheus, steals the fire. Up on the mountain he sees the ocean in the distance, and the feeling of longing is stirred in him for the first time.

In *Norne-Gæst* (1919; translated in *The Cimbrians*, 1923), Jensen follows the lives of the Northerners from the Glacial Age to the Great Migration. The opening lines describe the newborn title character's first glimpse of the blue sky between the leaves. This vision is to become crucial for his insatiable longing to travel that will drive Norne-Gæst around the world, encountering, for instance, Greek and Roman civilization, and up through the Bronze and Iron Ages. *Cimbrernes Tog* (1922, The Raids of the Cimbri; translated in *The Cimbrians*), the last volume of the series to be published, is also mainly set abroad. It opens with Norne-Gæst wandering up through Jutland in order to attend the spring festivals in Himmerland, home of the Cimbrians. Suddenly climatic deterioration sets in with floods and famine, and the Cimbrians set off under the command of Bojerik, a name modeled after a Boiorix mentioned in one of Jensen's sources, Plutarch's *Parallel Lives*. The narrative then follows the everyday life of the Cimbrians as they raid down through Europe, with intervening mythic scenes as observed and commented upon by the omnipresent Norne-Gæst. Other tribes join the Cimbrians, and together they win their first battles against the Romans. Here the Northerner and the Southerner, separated in *Bræen,* meet again. Eventually, the Cimbrians, having acquired the decadence of the foreign lands, are defeated in a bloody battle; yet, the volume concludes on a conciliatory note in which the spirits of antiquity and of the North merge harmoniously.

In *Skibet* (1912, The Ship) the Nordic longing to travel is embodied in the Vikings and their raids to the Mediterranean. In the North, Christianity is introduced through a monk, Brother Parvus. Jensen's description of Parvus's works of charity belongs among his best passages, forming an essential correlation to his frequently stressed anti-Christian attitude. The first church is erected by turning the Viking ship upside down. In the deepest sense the forest itself becomes a cathedral, while the longing to go abroad takes on a religious dimension.

Longing as the basic trait of the Nordic people becomes personified by the title character of the 1921 novel *Christofer Columbus*—whom Jensen had previously described as a reddish-blond Northerner in *Hjulet*—and his voyages of discovery. Jensen's view of the defiant and struggling individual as the creator of culture, fundamental to *Den lange Rejse,* is paralleled by his concept of the basic trait of the Nordic people—"the Gothic race"—as being the dream about warmth and sun. This dream, which is Jensen's explanation of the religious sentiment, is expressed through a longing for distant places, in the final account a longing for paradise that becomes embodied in the structures of the ship and the upward-reaching Gothic cathedral. The Viking migrations, the "raids of the Cimbri," were a result of this longing, as was the voyage of the Goth, Columbus. His attempt at finding legendary lands resulted, however, in the discovery of America, of reality; and yet, at the conclusion of his life, Columbus realizes that his new discovery has brought him nothing but homelessness and loneliness. Now the initial optimism turns into tragic resignation, as Columbus subsequently chooses not a metaphysical solution but a return to his memories of the past. He does not realize that he must let his journey continue toward the eternal as it is depicted in the myth, "Ave Stella," that concludes the volume.

Den lange Rejse is not a novel with a traditional plot centered around the adventures of a hero, nor should the work be read as a scientifically correct depiction of various cultural stages. The fact that so many of its theories are contrary to modern history, anthropology, and archeology is irrelevant and cannot weaken the work as literature. Rather, *Den lange Rejse* is a vision written by an artist with a formidable ability to identify with other periods and conditions. The outcome proves the impossibility of creating a meaningful coherence based on evolution alone, and Jensen's project defies any organizing structure; however, the six volumes form a grandiose and gripping artistic work that is outstanding as a depiction of the ages of history and of mankind.

Jensen gradually turned away from the writing of fiction in favor of a growing involvement in current cultural and scientific issues; this reorientation was accompanied by a focusing on the feature article and the essay with the purpose of popularizing the theories of evolution. In Jensen's collection of essays *Nordisk Aand: Kroniker og Karakteristiker* (1911, Nordic Spirit: Chronicles and Characteristics), the American society that he had glorified in *Den ny Verden* was analyzed further and seen as an implementation of the program in *Den gotiske Renaissance,* indeed as the true expression of the Nordic character; the Scandinavian prototype of this character is Bjørnson, who is portrayed with several other Danish and Norwegian writers. The volume concludes with a fierce attack on contemporary Danish literary critics for not appreciating Jensen's work.

In April 1911 Jensen traveled with his wife to Paris and London via Berlin and Cologne. His fascination with the cathedral in Cologne found powerful expression in his next essay collection; and in a 10 May 1911 travel letter to *Politiken* from Normandy, where he looked for traces of the ancient Nordic population, can be seen the first impulses for the novel *Skibet,* which is set during the Viking Age. In 1912 Jensen also published a monograph, *Rudyard Kipling,* written in connection with several translations of various Kipling stories that he and Aslaug Mikkelsen had begun in 1911. Although Jensen was strongly influenced by the English writer during the composition of *Singapore Noveller* and the two additional volumes of short stories from 1909 and 1915, he is strongly critical of Kipling's imperialistic attitude and deprecation of women.

In the fall of 1912 Jensen began his second great journey to Asia, from which he returned the following year. His reflections en route were later included in the philosophical travelogue *Introduktion til vor Tidsalder* (1915, Introduction to Our Epoch). "I det indiske Hav" (In the Indian Ocean) displays pure poetry in some passages, where Jensen describes the voyage until the vessel sails into the Ceylonese port of Colombo in December. Singapore is revisited, and the homesickness that Jensen had experienced a decade earlier overtook him again. In China he found the theme for a lyrical short story, "Darduses Myndlinge" (Darduse's Wards), which was later adapted for the stage as the comedy *Darduse, Bryllupet i Peking: Eventyrkomedie i fire akter* (1937,

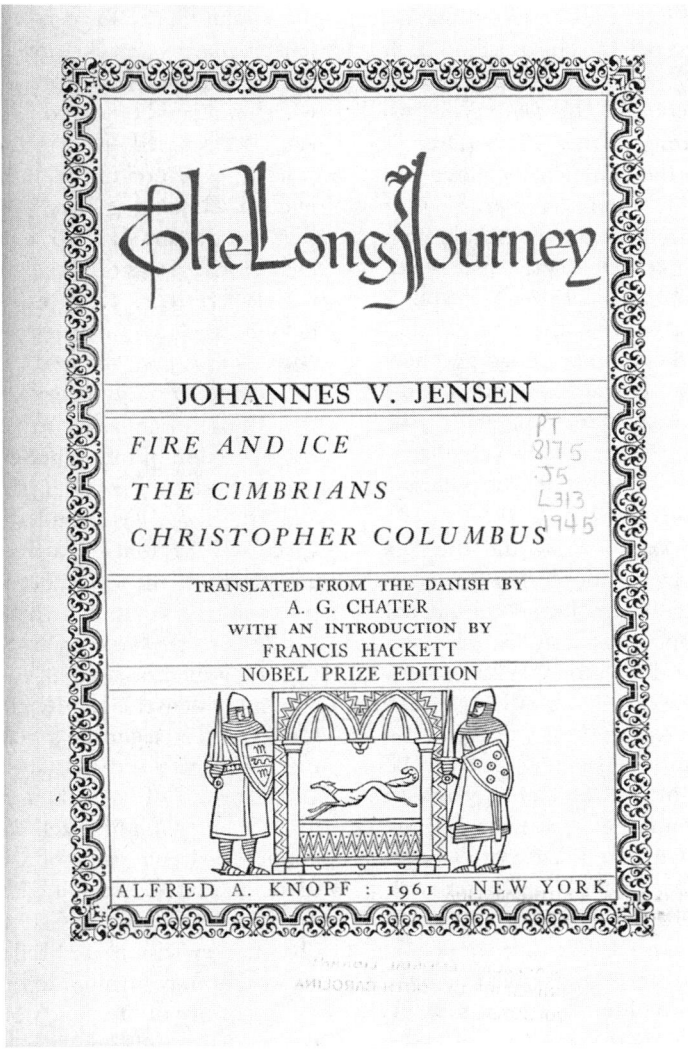

Title page for a special edition of the 1945 translation of Jensen's multivolume historical work published in 1938 as Den lange Rejse (Thomas Cooper Library, University of South Carolina)

Darduse, Wedding in Peking: Fairy Tale Comedy in Four Acts). From Manchuria, Jensen continued on his trip, describing in the chapter "fra Østen til Evropa" (from the East toward Europe) his experiences traveling on the Trans-Siberian Railroad, seeing again with joy the European peasant culture, and describing jubilantly his return to Scandinavia. In its analysis of the Northerner's longing, the book forms a striking link between *Den gotiske Renaissance* and *Christofer Columbus*. At the same time, Jensen's attempt to give religious feelings a purely physiological explanation is one more bit of evidence that the question of immortality kept troubling him.

Jensen planned to make still another journey to Asia, by way of the United States, the following summer, but did not complete his trip. In March 1914 he embarked for New York City, but the joy of rediscovery was moderate. Even though Jensen still admired the American press and the hectic and progressive atmosphere in the country, he sharply attacked what he saw as the childishness and bigotry of the Americans. In mid April, Jensen decided to return to Copenhagen, and a few months later World War I broke out. Since Denmark remained neutral, Jensen could leave for Berlin in August in order to negotiate with his German publisher, Samuel Fischer. During his visit he became strongly critical of the bellicosity that was shared by all of the German political parties, and he bitterly regretted the clash between Germany and Britain, since both nations had the same Gothic origin.

During the war Jensen was mainly occupied with writing the last volumes of *Den lange Rejse*. He also prepared a greatly enlarged edition of his collected poems, *Digte: Tredie Udgave* (1921, Poems: Third Edition). It includes—in addition to several memorial poems and other portraits—nine poems from *Den lange Rejse*. Of these, the alliterative "Drengs Gravsang" (Dreng's Elegy) from *Bræen* binds up the experience of love and boundless longing in a mythic vision. "Vor Frue" (Our Lady), structured on the prosody of the medieval hymn "Dies irae," and the ballad-like "Den sørgeligste Vise" (The Saddest Song) from *Christofer Columbus* treat other recurrent themes in Jensen's writing: the first glorifies woman as a saving force and culminates in an apotheosis of the Madonna, while the second is one of the most overwhelming interpretations in Danish poetry of the futility of life. Disillusion and resignation also characterize the majority of remaining poems in the volume, many of which are in alliterative form.

Negative reviews of *Cimbrernes Tog* and the *Den lange Rejse* project as a whole by a critic for *Politiken* led to another of Jensen's many literary feuds and culminated in a break with the newspaper that lasted until 1926. Shortly after the break, in December 1922, Jensen began the publication of his own periodical, *Forum: Tidsskrift for Litteratur, Biologi og Samfundsspørgsmål* (Forum: Periodical of Literature, Biology, and Social Issues), which survived for only one and a half years. In the first issue of *Forum* he published his most succinct and best-written settlement with the misuse of Darwinism, "Den daarlige Darwinisme" (The Bad Darwinism). In addition, *Forum* included a few insignificant poems about birds that, together with other animal poems illustrated by Jensen's close friend the painter Johannes Larsen, were collected in the volume *Aarstiderne* (1923, The Seasons). Jensen's interest in this painter and in the visual arts in general—he was himself a painter and was also an accomplished sculptor—resulted in several art books, two of which deal with the renowned Danish sculptor Bertel Thorvaldsen. Related to these works is the collection of newspaper articles about art, *Form og Sjæl: Portræter af Personligheder* (1931, Form and Soul: Portraits of Personalities), one more expression of Jensen's love for classicism and of sculpture.

Essential for an understanding of Jensen's fiction is his 1923 work *Æstetik og Udvikling*. The book is a sort of afterword to *Den lange Rejse*, in which Jensen also launches his "gradus" theory, a conception designating the gliding steps of evolution that he wanted to stress rather than the static species—further developed in later volumes, such as *Aandens Stadier* (1928, Stages of the Mind). In *Æstetik og Udvikling*, Jensen writes: "*Den lange Rejse* handler ikke eksklusivt om en Race, den handler om Udviklingstrin. Den ene Race er Udviklingstrinet af den anden" (*Den lange Rejse* does not deal exclusively with a race, it deals with stages of evolution. One race is the evolutionary stage of another). At the same time Jensen sharply attacks novels that focus exclusively on individuals as being pre-Darwinian and thus hero-worshiping and outdated. The concept of "bad Darwinism" is discussed again in the obscure and insignificant collection of previously published articles about Darwinism, *Evolution og Moral* (1925, Evolution and Ethics).

At the end of 1925, Jensen once again set out on a long journey; this time the goal was the Egyptian health resort of Helwan. From Egypt and later from Palestine, he sent several travel letters home to the newspaper *Social-Demokraten*, revised versions of which were included in *Aandens Stadier*.

Jensen continued to write memorial poems, and his perfection of this genre can be seen in the undervalued collection *Verdens Lys* (1926, The Light of the World). *Verdens Lys* includes six alliterative poems from *Cimbrernes Tog* that—in a mythic perspective—juxtapose and celebrate the union between North and South. Distinct among Jensen's works in its focus on artistic expression is "Graven i Sne" (The Snow-Covered Grave), a memorial poem to the Danish Romantic poet Adam Oehlenschläger. It is both an idealized portrait of Oehlenschläger, Jensen's beloved model as both a harmonious artist and human being—"To Gange gav han Livet Form, / i Livet selv, i ædel Norm" (Twice he gave to life a form, / in life itself, in noble norm)—and a poem about the eternal value of art in spite of the inevitability of death. It becomes a glorification of Jensen's own poetic art, as it is expressed in a structure that combines observation, vision, and reflection into a perfect artistic entity that may turn out to be the only way to overcome the absurdity of life. The poems in memory of Jensen's father offer an affectionate portrait of a man who lived in close intimacy with the miracles of life in nature, a closeness to nature inherited by the poet although not without discord. A much more somber tone is heard in the obituary for Jensen's mother, the concluding poem of the volume, "Ved min Moders Død" (At My Mother's Death), as well as in the hymn-like "Kirken i Hardanger" (The Church in Hardanger), in which the reader can perceive, behind the stoic resignation that results from placing oneself in the hands of the cycle of nature, the author's fear of annihilation, which is so powerful that it threatens to break up the poetic form.

In 1927 *Dyrenes Forvandling: Til Udviklingens Plastik* (The Transformation of Animals: A Contribution to the Plasticity of Evolution) was published; it was another presentation of evolutionary theories but without the fierce attacks on Christianity that characterize some of his earlier writings. Jensen attempts—and the task appears scientifically absurd—to describe the animal soul and ethics as they change through all stages of evolution. Trips to Madeira and Rome followed in

1928, and impressions from both trips were likewise included in the anthropological study of human origin and development, *Aandens Stadier*.

In May 1929 Jensen received an honorary doctorate from the University of Lund. At the same time Jensen began to focus again on Nordic issues and started his translation of *Egil's Saga* for a planned edition of *De islandske Sagaer* (The Icelandic Sagas), which was published in three volumes from 1930 to 1932. At the same time he returned to his preoccupation with Nordic archaeology in a series of articles subsequently published in the volume *Paa danske Veje* (1931, On Danish Roads) with his own photos and drawings by Larsen. With this work Jensen got involved in a fierce public debate about the preservation of the ancient burial mounds and stirred up so much political attention that stringent conservation laws were put into effect in 1937. His introduction to *De islandske Sagaer*, in which he discusses the sagas as products of a genuine Nordic mentality untouched by the traditions of antiquity and Christianity, points ahead to his book about women in the Viking Age, *Kvinden i Sagatiden* (1942, The Woman in the Saga Period), which also includes retellings of selected saga texts. For a new edition of Snorre Sturlason's *Heimskringla*, published in 1948, Jensen took upon himself the difficult task of translating all 539 stanzas.

The transcendental aspect in his earlier poetry is not found in *Den jydske Blæst: Digte 1926-1930* (1931, The Jutland Wind: Poems 1926-1930), Jensen's last important poetry collection. Whereas death in, for instance, the memorial poem "Knut Hamsun" is still accepted as a pantheistic amalgamation into nature, most of the texts are structured on the tragic contrast between active life and the corruption of death, as in the memorial poem "Otto Benzon," and now nature brings no consolation: "I Kammerdøren peb Vindens Røst, / en ensom Jammer, ingen Trøst" (The voice of the wind whistled in the chamber door / a lonesome lamentation, no comfort). When the memorial poem over others becomes a poem about Jensen himself, as in the concluding title poem, one finds the same death motif, the portrayal of death as man's tragic but only certain verity. Jensen's writing has this motif in common with Baroque literature, albeit without Heaven as the final destination.

On his sixtieth birthday, 20 January 1933, Jensen had reached such an esteemed position that a torchlight procession was held in his honor in Copenhagen and a festschrift published, *Unge Digteres Hyldest til Johannes V. Jensen* (Young Writers' Homage to Johannes V. Jensen). In response to virulent public criticism of his lack of political commitment, Jensen, in an article published in *Politiken* on his birthday, emphasized—as he had done throughout his career—his independence as a freelance writer outside the political parties. Nevertheless, in a review of Hartvig Frisch's *Pest over Europa* (1933, Plague over Europe) in the same newspaper on 3 December, he once again attacked Nietzsche's philosophy and its consequences in the Germany of the early 1930s. Here Jensen strongly dissociated himself from contemporary political developments in Europe toward dictatorship, and, in the 1938 article "Hagekorset" (The Swastika), he publicly expressed his disgust with anti-Semitism.

In 1930 Jensen published the collection of essays and articles *Retninger i Tiden: Artikler 1925-30* (Trends of the Times: Articles 1925-30); however, during the first part of the 1930s Jensen turned away from the essay form, with the exception of his short history of ideas, *Det Blivende: Tankens Revolutionering i det 19de Aarhundrede og Tilbagefaldet i det 20de* (1934, The Permanent: The Revolution of Thought in the 19th Century and the Backslide in the 20th), written in a more concise and concentrated style than his other philosophical works. With the underrated novel *Dr. Renaults Fristelser* (1935, The Temptations of Dr. Renault) he again took up fiction, reworking the Faust motif into a plot that, in contrast to the version presented by Goethe, lets the title character win over Mephistopheles because he is ready to fully accept the present. As in *Hjulet*, aestheticism is regarded as a barrier between man and reality, and in a significant scene Dr. Renault throws a valuable statue of Aphrodite into the sea, so that nothing will stand between him and life.

In October 1936 Jensen went on a short trip to the United States in order to collect material for a sequel to *Dr. Renaults Fristelser*, in spite of the negative reception that the book had received. The continuation never materialized. Instead, Jensen published the novel *Gudrun* (1936), a realization of a much older project: a contemporary novel of the Copenhagen woman, and thus also a novel about the city of Copenhagen, but completely different from Jensen's first two novels. The city is no longer seen through the eyes of a student from the provinces. Now a citizen of Copenhagen for many years—and a matured artist—Jensen delivers a deeply intimate tribute to this city as a swarming, animated organism. Most of Jensen's poems written in the 1930s were collected in 1937 as *Paaskebadet: Digte 1931-1937* (The Easter Bath: Poems 1931-1937).

That same year, Jensen's play adaptation of *Darduse, Bryllupet i Peking*, a "Fairy Tale Comedy in Four Acts," had its premiere on 22 January at the Royal Theater in Copenhagen and was performed sixteen times. It was a weak play, carried by excellent acting and Knudåge Riisager's rousing music. Jensen's relationship with the theater was, on the whole, marked by a lack of success. During his stay in Chicago in the winter of

1902–1903 he had his own dramatization of some of his Himmerland stories performed by Danish-American amateurs with the title *Trods* (2002, Defiance). The one and only performance was a resounding fiasco. A dramatization of *Madame D'Ora,* titled *Sangerinden* (The Singer) and published as *Sangerinden (Madame d'Ora): Drama i fem Akter* (1921, The Singer [Madame d'Ora]: Drama in Five Acts), was performed unsuccessfully in 1923, premiering at the Odense Teater on 16 November; and when, on 24 April 1937, Jensen's translation of William Shakespeare's *Hamlet* was performed at the Royal Theater, it provoked such fierce criticism that the production had to be canceled.

Shortly before the outbreak of World War II, Jensen managed to visit Norway, described in the travelogue *Nordvejen: Indtryk af norsk Natur* (1939, The Way North: Impressions of Norwegian Nature), and then the United States; in March 1939 he left Denmark for his sixth journey to the New World. His travel letters were first printed in *Politiken* and subsequently as a book, titled *Fra Fristaterne: Rejsebreve, med et Tilbageblik* (1939, From the Free States: Travel Letters with a Retrospect). This time Jensen's encounter with the United States was marked by ambivalence. In the chapter "Fra Stillehavet til Atlanten" (From the Pacific Ocean to the Atlantic), which is among the best sections of the book, the impressions from the trip are summed up. Although his overall impressions were still positive, Jensen was disappointed by what he saw as the increasing vulgarity and materialism of American society, where technology had become an end in itself, not an expression of man's inventiveness and ingenuity. After having arrived on the East Coast, Jensen became ill and had to return home earlier than planned. Back in Copenhagen in May 1939 he added a concluding chapter on Thomas Jefferson, meant as a counterweight to the current antidemocratic trends in Europe.

Jensen had planned a tour to France for September 1939 in order to visit the regions where traces of prehistoric man had been discovered, but this plan was thwarted by the outbreak of World War II and had to be postponed until spring 1948. When the Germans occupied Denmark in April 1940, Jensen, apparently fearing arrest, took the precaution of burning his diaries from the previous thirty years, together with all personal letters written to him. In this way much data related to the writing of his books and—most important—notes from his many travels were lost for posterity. Nevertheless, he continued to write throughout the occupation from 1940 to 1945. In 1941 came *Mindets Tavle: Portræter og Personligheder* (Plaque of Commemoration: Portraits and Personalities) with portraits of Nordic and British explorers, scientists, writers—and Darwin once again—and in 1943 the collection of some unimportant ethnographic articles, *Folkeslagene i Østen* (The People of the Orient). Of greater quality is the study *Vor Oprindelse* (1941, Our Origin), describing humanity's gradual acquisition of civilization. Again Jensen's myth-creating fantasy bloomed in a visionary description of cultural progress. At the same time he offers a subtle analysis of his authorship, clearly drawing up a balance sheet and expressing his feeling that he was at the end of the road, a feeling that is also expressed in the essay "Tak til Sproget" (Thanks to Language), Jensen's farewell to literature; this essay was included, together with some linguistic studies, in a small book, *Om Sproget og Undervisningen* (1942, About Language and Teaching).

After having been nominated several times for the Nobel Prize in Literature, Jensen finally received it on 9 November 1944. The Nobel Committee announced that the prize was awarded in recognition of "the remarkable force and richness of his poetic imagination, combined with a wide-ranging intellectualism and bold, innovative sense of style," and *Den lange Rejse* appeared to be a decisive factor for the committee. In his speech of thanks at the City Hall of Stockholm on 10 December 1945, the writer once again paid tribute to Darwin and identified himself with the scientist: "To him [Darwin], evolution was not only the subject of a life's study but the very essence of life, proof of the inexhaustible richness and wonder of nature, revealed each day and taken to heart."

Since 1925 a large number of Danish, Norwegian, and Swedish intellectuals, literary scholars, and scientists had been proposing Jensen for the prize. Initially, the proponents pointed to his earlier works, in particular his myths, and his distinctive handling of style and language as well as his depictions of the Danish mind and Danish nature as qualifying him for the prize. Judged negatively, however, were Jensen's anthropological essays for their lack of speculative content as well as their polemical tone.

The publication in 1938 of the two-volume edition of *Den lange Rejse* once again drew attention to Jensen's major series of novels, and the positive attitude was strengthened further in 1943 with the publication of his poetry collection *Digte: 1901–1941*. Also, the German occupation of Denmark during World War II probably had an impact on the decision to award Jensen the prize in 1944.

In Denmark the Nobel Prize was welcomed by the entire press, which published large articles on Jensen on their front pages and had his friends and colleagues comment on the significance of the award as well as on Jensen's authorship in general. The underground press also noticed the prize, even though Jensen was not an active member of the resistance. Because of the war, however, the event did not attract much attention abroad.

Jensen definitely appreciated having been awarded the Nobel Prize and expressed a certain amount of pride and self-esteem in his banquet speech in Stockholm; but he was not dependent on the money, and the award did not have any visible impact on his personal life or his writing. Neither did it contribute to increase his reputation abroad, which had reached its zenith in the interwar years, particularly in Germany and the Scandinavian countries; he never became a popular writer in the Anglo-American countries.

During the last years of Jensen's life his productivity decreased significantly. After an operation in September 1948 he managed to finish a book about the great explorers, *Afrika: Opdagelsesrejserne* (1949, Africa: Journeys of Discovery), demonstrating that one of the favorite topics of his childhood reading was still inspiring him. Otherwise, Jensen was primarily occupied with the preparation of a combined, revised edition of the three books *Dyrenes Forvandling, Aandens Stadier,* and *Vor Oprindelse,* but he managed to complete only the first volume, published posthumously in 1951 in the volume *Tilblivelsen* (Genesis). Troubled by an ear disease, he also suffered from shingles during the summer of 1949 and was hospitalized. He still managed to write a few more articles; the most valuable of these, "Adam Oehlenschläger 1779–1850," published in the book *Swift og Oehlenschläger* (1950, Swift and Oehlenschläger), is a finely drawn portrait of his artistic model as a man of simple nature, without stiltedness, who calmly accepted death as Jensen had described in the poem "Graven i Sne." On 31 January 1950 Jensen commented on his second great model, Darwin, in a short article, "Træk fra vor Oprindelse" (Traits from Our Origin). These two personalities, the poet Oehlenschläger and the scientist Darwin, perfectly symbolize the two facets of Jensen's authorship. In his later years natural science came to dominate, but the first element stands as the most valuable, the one that will survive.

Johannes V. Jensen died on 25 November 1950. Brandes once claimed that as a thinker and preacher Jensen could not be taken seriously. Brandes had a point: the content of Jensen's many collections of essays and articles dealing with natural science, archaeology, and anthropology are often based on dubious scientific theories and deductions. In addition, in these volumes Jensen linguistically turns from lyrical expressiveness to a terse, matter-of-fact diction. But one must not fail to notice that in spite of the scientific topic, his stylistic mastery often breaks forth in evocative passages that can be read as sublime prose poetry. Jensen's critics have also frequently overlooked that he was brilliant as a journalistic writer. He was unusually well-informed about current trends, and his knowledge of American society and literature was unique for a Dane of his time. Neither should his contributions as a translator be overlooked. Besides his accomplished translations from Old Norse, his outstanding rendering of Whitman's poetry in Danish must be acknowledged.

Jensen reached perfection as a lyrical poet and a creator of myth, both in his collections of poetry and myths and when he succeeded in combining the two genres, as in *Kongens Fald, Skovene, Den lange Rejse,* and several of his stories of Himmerland. With his debut collection of poems, Jensen introduced modernism in Danish poetry, and he became the writer who, arguably, has had the strongest impact on twentieth-century Danish literature.

Bibliographies:

Frits Johansen and Aage Marcus, *Johannes V. Jensen: En Bibliografi,* 2 volumes (Copenhagen: Gyldendal, 1933–1951);

Aage Jørgensen, *Litteratur om Johannes V. Jensen En bibliografi* (Odense: Odense University Press, 1998).

Biographies:

K. K. Nicolaisen, *Johannes V. Jensen: Bidrag til hans Biografi og Karakteristik* (Aalborg: Viggo Madsens Boghandel, 1914);

Oluf Friis, *Den unge Johannes V. Jensen 1873–1902,* 2 volumes (Copenhagen: Gad, 1974);

Villum Jensen, *Min fars hus: Erindringer om Johannes V. Jensen og hans miljø* (Copenhagen: Gyldendal, 1976);

Leif Nedergaard, *Johannes V. Jensen,* third edition (Copenhagen: C. A. Reitzel, 1993);

Lars Handesten, *Johannes V. Jensen: Liv og Værk* (Copenhagen: Gyldendal, 2000).

References:

Harry Andersen, *Afhandlinger om Johannes V. Jensen* (Rødovre: Rolv, 1982);

Andersen, *Studier i Johannes V. Jensens Lyrik: Verseteknik, Sprog og Stil* (Copenhagen: Levin & Munksgaard, 1936);

Jørgen Elbek, *Johannes V. Jensen* (Copenhagen: Gyldendal, 1966);

Otto Gelsted, *Johannes V. Jensen: Kurven i hans Udvikling* (Copenhagen: Arthur Jensen, 1938);

Alf Henriques, *Johannes V. Jensen* (Copenhagen: H. Hirschsprung, 1938);

Iben Holk, *Jærtegn: Et essay om Johannes V. Jensens myter* (Copenhagen: C. A. Reitzel, 2000);

Poul Houe, *Johannes V. Jensens lange rejse: En postmoderne myte* (Copenhagen: Museum Tusculanum, 1996);

Niels Ingwersen, "America as Setting and Symbol in Johannes V. Jensen's Early Works," *American Norvegica*, 3 (1971): 272–293;

Bent Haugaard Jeppesen, *Johannes V. Jensen og den hvide mands byrde: Eksotisme og imperialisme* (Copenhagen: Rhodos, 1984);

Aage Jørgensen, "Johannes V. Jensen (Literature): '. . . a good enough poet and; nowadays, a good enough human being. . . .'" in *Neighbouring Nobel: The History of Thirteen Danish Nobel Prizes*, edited by Henry Nielsen and Keld Nielsen (Aarhus: Aarhus University Press, 2001), pp. 207–243;

Jørgensen and Helene Kragh-Jacobsen, eds., *Columbus fra Himmerland* (Farsø: Farsø Bibliotek, 1994);

Jørgensen and Anders Thyrring Andersen, eds., *Et spring ind i et billede: Johannes V. Jensens mytedigtning* (Odense: Odense Universitetsforlag, 2000);

Aage Marcus, "Johannes V. Jensen," *American-Scandinavian Review*, 20 (1932): 339–347;

Felix Nørgaard and Aage Marcus, eds., *Johannes V. Jensen. 1873–20. Januar–1943* (Copenhagen: Gyldendal, 1943);

Sven Hakon Rossel, "Andersen og Jensen–Eventyret og myten," in *Hvad Fatter gjør . . . Boghistoriske, litterære og musikalske essays tilegnet Erik Dal*, edited by Henrik Glahn and others (Herning: Poul Kristensen, 1982), pp. 392–402;

Rossel, *Johannes V. Jensen* (Boston: Twayne, 1984);

Aage Schiøttz-Christensen, *Om sammenhængen i Johannes V. Jensens forfatterskab* (Copenhagen: Borgen, 1956);

Henrik Wivel, *Den titaniske eros: Drifts- og karakterfortolkning i Johannes V. Jensens forfatterskab* (Copenhagen: Gyldendal, 1982).

Papers:
The major collection of correspondence and manuscripts is in the Johannes V. Jensen Archives at Det kongelige Bibliotek (The Royal Library), Copenhagen. Additional material is located at Statsbiblioteket, Århus, and the Farsø Bibliotek. Forty-three letters from Jensen to various Norwegian writers and friends are located at the University Library, Oslo.

1944 Nobel Prize in Literature Broadcast Presentation

On 10 December 1944 a luncheon was held under the auspices of the American-Scandinavian Foundation at the Waldorf-Astoria Hotel in New York to take the place of the customary ceremonies in Stockholm. Jensen was not present at the gathering, although he did participate in the official ceremonies of the Nobel Foundation in Stockholm in 1945, when he received his diploma and the gold medal. This lecture by Per Hallström, Chairman of the Nobel Committee of the Swedish Academy, was presented at the New York luncheon and was broadcast in Stockholm on the same date.

Among Johannes V. Jensen's prose works *Den lange Rejse* (1908–22) [The Long Journey] stands foremost in popular estimation. The theme of this immense epic is man's development from the soulless and inarticulate herd-life when more than any other creature he was a prey to the forces of nature–to a state of primitive and gradually progressive civilization. The six long stories are full of adventures actuated, Jensen thinks, by obscure but profound nostalgia for the tropical world that was man's first home.

The first saga takes place somewhere in the primeval forests of Europe near a huge volcano. Fire glows on its summit and sometimes burning lava pours down the slopes, destroying everything in its path. For countless ages, primitive man has worshipped the fire-god in dumb terror. But at last comes the first great moment in the history of mankind: the emergence from the herd of a man with a mind and a will, a Prometheus.

Fearlessly confronting the unknown, he solves the riddle of fire and brings it down on a torch to serve man. With it he lights campfires to keep off wild beasts. But he does much more. Observing the movements of the stars he infers the notion of time, the first abstract idea won from the darkness of chaos. He also takes the first step toward civilized intercourse between individuals, discovering tenderness in sexual relations, the inaugural burgeoning of what we know as love. In the end he dies a prophet's death at the hands of the obtuse masses, but he bequeaths a rich legacy to posterity.

Thus ends the first saga. The next, with a second prehistoric patriarch, begins after another measureless lapse of time. The world has changed now, the volcano is extinct, the climate cooling. There is a general migration to the south. But one man sets off in the opposite direction to grapple with hardship. He is a sort of Cain, a slayer avoided by his fellow men, whom he holds in such contempt that he does not even condescend to take their god, fire, with him to the icy lands of the North. Defying the cold, he grows hardy and strong. With a woman who has somehow found her way up there he becomes the father of the Nordic race which is so dear to Jensen, who follows its destiny.

He rediscovers fire, not simply borrowing it as before but by a stroke of genius striking it out of two minerals. And thus he founds a new civilization.

The theme is repeated in a third saga with another genius who invents means of locomotion: wagons and boats driven by oar or sail. The men of the North, ready now to listen to the old call to the summer lands, begin the long journey proper.

The later sagas describing the journey take us down to historical times: we see the Cimbrians marching on Rome and the Vikings' raids. But the story does not end until Columbus realizes that dream of a tropical paradise which is the leading idea of the book.

Jensen's imaginative resources are rich and inexhaustible, his power of vivid presentation unfailing.

The whole book is like a series of huge decorative paintings in which characterization is less important than the range of composition and the incomparable skill of the brush strokes.

Characters of much greater psychological interest will be found in Jensen's tales from life in his native Himmerland, *Himmerlandshistorier* (1909–1910). Its inhabitants, descendants of the Cimbrians, have kept much of their ancestors' primitive savage energy, forced as they are to struggle hard for meagre reward in a country of heath and sand. They are men of action, rugged, swayed by strong passions. On intimate terms with tragedy, they bear it staunchly. They have their own mordant humour, too, and Jensen renders the tragic and the comic in the most congenial way. The art of these peasant tales is so consummate that they already rank as Danish classics.

The master hand is even more apparent in a later Himmerland story of very different flavour, a short novel called *Jørgine* (1926). This book shows us another facet of Jensen's remarkably versatile talent. It is a simple, quiet story: a deceived peasant girl saves herself from disaster and shame by an unromantic marriage and becomes a dutiful, hard-working wife and self-sacrificing mother. *Jørgine* is an excellent piece of work, deep in feeling, penetrating in its knowledge of life, wonderfully fresh and alert, and written with that virtuosity of style which is always at Jensen's command. Since *Jørgine* he has more than once turned his attention to similar placid lives, creating from them minor works of classic art.

For many years Jensen has collected very heterogeneous pieces of writing in volumes entitled *Myter* (1907–45) [Myths]. The whole series of these is so well known that the word "myth" has acquired in Danish the additional sense of a new literary genre. That sense is not easy to define. Sometimes it means that Jensen has left the everyday world to explore that realm of fantasy which is the domain he masters. This can happen even when he is telling his own experiences in the first person. Just as often he tells in a "myth," events and experiences which must be taken as factual, or he expounds, with utmost sincerity, his ideas and theories. His presentation then is of unique graphic clarity and verisimilitude.

Sometimes natural phenomena are described with such profound intuition and imaginative insight that the word "myth" can be understood in its ordinary sense. The common factor in all these diverse works is indeed only their brilliant and direct style. This same style in Jensen's innumerable studies and manifestoes in popular science allows us to classify them as belles-lettres.

The exigencies of space prevent me from mentioning more than one of these works here. I choose *Vor Oprindelse* (1941) [Our Origin] since it constitutes a sort of parallel and complement to the sagas in *Den lange Rejse*. The book opens at the point in time when man himself, ceasing to be merely passive, begins to influence the forces of evolution.

In the introduction Jensen says important things about the blessings of work–a subject on which he is undoubtedly an authority, for he has been an indefatigable worker all his life.

This becomes evident in more ways than one in *Vor Oprindelse*. He has re-enacted every one of the advances made by man in that long history he so brilliantly relates–from the mastery of fire and the making of the first weapons to the slowly perfected mastery of the crafts. It is a most impressive book, one of his best.

The Danes think as highly of his verse as of his prose. As a poet his major characteristic is an ever-deepening devotion to his native soil, expressed in quite varying tones. Sometimes he uses a revived old alliterative measure; sometimes modern "free verse"–but with the great improvement that rhythm is retained and syntax respected. Some of his poems are in regular verse, their pure melodies recalling the golden age of Danish poetry. In them Jensen rises to the zenith of his powers and reveals yet another aspect, new and surprising, of his art and his personality.

Primarily he directed all his love to the machine age. He seemed spellbound by the astonishing and ever more rapid march of science. The faster the pace, the greater his enchantment. Such an outlook has no use for old values. It flies high over the nations, has no thought for them. Its Utopia needs no flowering meadows to walk in, no infinite space for dreams.

Fortunately, Johannes V. Jensen's richly creative mind has taken frequent holidays from the marvels of the future to dwell instead on those inherited aesthetic and emotional values which are fundamental to the spirit of man.

[© The Nobel Foundation, 1944.]

1944 Nobel Prize in Literature Presentation Speech

by Anders Österling, Permanent Secretary of the Swedish Academy, 10 December 1945

Today Johannes V. Jensen will receive in person the Nobel Prize in Literature for 1944, and we are happy to salute the great Danish writer who since the beginning of the century has been in the front rank, always active, for a long time controversial, but universally admired for his vitality. This child of the dry and windy moors of Jutland has, almost out of spite, astonished his contemporaries by a remarkably prolific production. He could well be considered one of the most fertile Scandinavian writers. He has constructed a vast and imposing literary œuvre, comprising the most diverse genres: epic and lyric, imaginative and realistic works, as well as historical and philosophical essays, not to mention his scientific excursions in all directions.

This bold iconoclast and stylistic innovator has increasingly become a patriarchal classic, and in his heart he feels close to the poetry of the golden age and hopes that one day he will be counted among the life-giving tutelary spirits of his nation.

Johannes V. Jensen has been such a passionate student of biological and philosophical evolution that he should be amazed at the singular course of his own development. A conquering instinct forms the basis of his being. He was a native of Himmerland, a relatively dry region in western Jutland, and his impressions of men and things were engraved indelibly on his consciousness. Later he was to remember those resources that were hidden beneath the sensations of childhood, the ancient treasure of family memories. His father, the veterinarian of Farsø, came from that area, and through his paternal grandfather, the old weaver of Guldager, Jensen is directly descended from peasants. Characteristically enough, his first book dealt with the province of his origin. His incomparable *Himmerlandshistorier* offer an original portrait gallery of primitive and half-savage creatures who are still subject to ancient fears. The promised land of his childhood, powerful and alive with the past, is found again in his mature poetry.

The first books of Johannes V. Jensen reveal him as a young man from the provinces; a student of opposition, living in Copenhagen; an arduous and agitated youth, fighting passionately against intellectual banality and narrow-mindedness. This native of Jutland, self-conscious, difficult to approach, but sensitive, was soon to find his country too narrow. Stifled by the familiar climate of the Danish isles, he threw himself into exotic romanticism with the cool passion of a gambler. His travels across foreign continents for the first time opened to him the space needed by his restless, unchained imagination. During that period of his life he sang the praise of technology and mechanization. Just as his compatriot H. C. Andersen was perhaps the first to describe the charms of railway travel, Johannes V. Jensen was the prophet of the marvels of our age, of skyscrapers, motor cars, and cinemas, which he never tires of praising in his American novels, *Madame D'Ora* (1904) and *Hjulet* (1905) [The Wheel]. But soon he entered into a new stage of his development; at the risk of simplifying matters we might say that, having satisfied his passion for distant travel, he began to look in time for what he had pursued in space. The same man who had sung the modern life, with its rapid pace and noisy machines, has become the spectator of ancient epochs and has devoted himself to the study of the long, slow periods during which man first sought adventure.

Thus we come to perhaps his most important creation, the six volumes combined under the title *Den lange Rejse*, which leads us from the ice age to Christopher Columbus. The central theme or one of the central themes of this work is the universal mission of the Scandinavian people, from the great migrations and the Norman invasion to the discovery of America. Jensen considers Christopher Columbus a descendant of the Lombards, in short a Nordic man, if not a Jutlander like himself. In this monumental series appears a legendary figure, Nornagestr. He is not at all the same person who appears at the court of King Olaf Tryggvason to tell his stories and die there. According to the Icelandic saga he was three hundred years old; but Jensen makes him even older and turns him into a kind of Ahasverus, ubiquitous, always behind his time, a stranger among the new generations, but nevertheless younger than they because he lived at a time when existence itself was young and mankind closer to its origins. The writer has followed tradition only as far as it was useful to him. Three prophetesses came to Nornagestr's mother to see the child and one of them predicted that he would die as soon as the candle could no longer burn. Gro, the mother, immediately extinguished the candle and gave it to the child as an amulet. In the work of Johannes V. Jensen, Nornagestr sometimes lights it in foreign lands and whenever he does so a deep abyss of time opens before him. When he comes to again, seized by the love of life, he is transported to his country, the fresh and green Zealand.

All legends exist because reason alone cannot clarify experience. What then is Nornagestr, who plays such an important role in the epic of the Danish master? Perhaps it is the spirit of the Nordic people rising from the night like a phantom or like an atavistic creature. One suspects that this unique globetrotter with his harp is closely related to the author himself, who has given him many ideas about life and death, and about the close relation between the present and eternity—the precious fruits of experiences gathered from the lands and seas of the globe.

For Johannes V. Jensen, who grew up on a Jutland moor where the horizon is often indented by a line of tumuli, it was natural to divide his interests between facts and myths and to seek his way between the shadows of the past and the realities of the present. His example reveals to us both the attraction of the primitive for a sensitive man and the necessity of transforming brute force into tenderness. He has attained the summit of his art by means of these violent contrasts. A fresh, salty breeze blows through his work, which unfolds with vivid language, powerful expression, and singular energy. Precisely in the poets most deeply rooted in their country do we find this poetic genius for words. Jensen is the voice of Jutland and of Denmark. With his talents he deserves the title of the most eminent narrator of the victorious struggle of the Nordic people against nature, and of the continuity of the Nordic spirit throughout the ages.

Mr. Jensen—If you have listened to what I have just said you will certainly think that the few moments I had were much too short to accomplish the long voyage through your work, and that I have neglected important aspects of it. It is fortunate for us as well as for you that a proper presentation is hardly necessary at all in your case. You are a well-known member of our great family and as such you are now asked to receive from the hands of our King the distinction which the Swedish Academy has awarded you.

At the banquet, Professor A. H. T. Theorell, Director of the Department of Biochemistry at the Nobel Institute of Medicine, called Mr. Jensen "the splendid representative of the proud literary tradition of our dear sister country, Denmark."

[© The Nobel Foundation, 1944.]

Jensen: Banquet Speech

Jensen's speech at the Nobel Banquet at the City Hall in Stockholm, 10 December 1945 (Translation):

I thank the venerable Swedish Academy and the Swedish nation for the honour they have bestowed upon me in awarding me the Nobel Prize in Literature. Present in all our thoughts today is the founder, Alfred Nobel, whose generosity has done so much good for science, literature, and peace throughout the world. This great Swedish scientist and humanist linked the name of Sweden with a broad vision that stretches far beyond the frontiers of one nation and serves to bring all nations closer to one another.

When one thinks of great Swedish minds of international fame, our thoughts turn to Alfred Nobel's forerunner, that great genius of natural science, Linné, who gave animals their proper names and, long before anyone had ever dreamt of evolution, classified monkeys, apes, and man under the name of primates. Passion for nature, for all that stirred and breathed, was the driving force in Linné's genius. Whenever one reads of the determination of the species, or opens a book on natural science and history, in whatever language, one inevitably comes across the name of Linné. There is something of the freshness of mind, of the lightness of spirit in Linné which for centuries has been linked in people's minds with the mountains of Sweden and Swedish joy in nature.

I cannot talk of Linné without being reminded of Charles Darwin, remembering him not only as a man of science who has drawn a line between two epochs, but also as the most lovable, the kindest of human beings, the best of fathers; his distinguished name is now carried by the third and fourth generation of his descendants. To him, evolution was not only the subject of a life's study but the very essence of life, proof of the inexhaustible richness and wonder of nature, revealed each day and taken to heart.

Were one to determine the degree of maturity of each nation according to its capacity for reasoning and comprehension, England would come out on top for her sense of realism, and the man who put forward these basically English ideas in a simple, unaffected manner was Charles Darwin.

Linné's designation of species was the foundation which subsequently enabled Darwin to form his conclusions on their origin. This Anglo-Swedish sense of reality, derived from our common Nordic background, has established for all time the place of mankind in nature.

I should like to mention on this occasion another name in Danish literature which is linked with Swedish tradition, that of Adam Oehlenschläger. You will remember that when he met Sweden's national poet, Esaias Tegnér, at Lund in 1829, he was hailed by him as the great poet and simple man that he was. A hundred years later, in 1929, it was my lot to receive in the same town a degree from the University of Lund. I am not Oehlenschläger's successor, but I do count myself among his followers and admirers.

It is with a feeling of Scandinavian fellowship that I now wish to thank the great and free Swedish nation which once crowned my countryman Adam Oehlenschläger with laurels, and has on two occasions judged my literary efforts worthy of distinction.

[© The Nobel Foundation, 1944. Johannes V. Jensen is the sole author of his speech.]

Jensen: Autobiographical Statement

(Written at the time of the awarding of the Nobel Prize)

I was born on the 20th of January, 1873, in a village in North Jutland, the second son of the district veterinary surgeon, H. Jensen, a descendant on both sides of farmers and craftsmen. In 1893, at the age of twenty, I graduated from the Cathedral School of Viborg, and subsequently studied medicine for three years at the University of Copenhagen. I earned my living by my pen until it became necessary for me to choose between further studies and literature. The grounding in natural sciences which I obtained in the course of my medical studies, including preliminary examinations in botany, zoology, physics, and chemistry, was to become decisive in determining the trend of my literary work.

My literary career began near the turn of the century with the publication of *Himmerlandshistorier* (1898–1910 [Himmerland Stories]), comprising a series of tales set in that part of Denmark where I was born. This was followed in the years up to 1944 by "legends" and "myths" representing literary forms I have particularly liked, and of which nine volumes have appeared (*Myter,* 1907–45 [Myths]). I have also written poetry, a few plays, and many essays, chiefly on anthropology and the philosophy of evolution.

For many years I was engaged in journalism, writing articles and chronicles for the daily press without ever joining the staff of any newspaper. Nor have I ever belonged to any political party. After extensive journeys to the East, to Malaya and China, and several visits to the United States, I inspired a change in the Danish literature and press by introducing English and American vigour, which was to replace the then dominant trend of decadent Gallicism. The essence of my literary work is to be found in my collection of poems, which may be regarded as a reaction against the fastidious style of the day bearing Baudelaire's poisonous hall-mark. My poems represented a turn to simple style and sound subject matter (*Digte, 1904–41,* 1943 [Poems]).

A probing analysis of the problems of evolution forms the basis of my prose. During half a century of literary work, I have endeavoured to introduce the philosophy of evolution into the sphere of literature, and to inspire my readers to think in evolutionary terms. I was prompted to do this because of the misinterpretation and distortion of Darwinism at the end of the 19th century. The concept of the *Übermensch* had disastrous consequences in that it led to two world wars, and was destroyed only with the collapse of Germany in 1945. In the course of opposing this fallacious doctrine, I have arrived at a new interpretation of the theory of evolution and its moral implications.

[© The Nobel Foundation, 1944. Johannes V. Jensen is the sole author of the text.]

Juan Ramón Jiménez
(24 December 1881 – 29 May 1958)

Howard T. Young
Pomona College

This entry was expanded by Young from his Jiménez entry in *DLB 134: Twentieth-Century Spanish Poets, Second Series.*

SELECTED BOOKS: *Almas de violeta* (Madrid: Moderna, 1900);
Ninfeas (Madrid: Moderna, 1900);
Rimas (Madrid: Fernando Fé, 1902);
Arias tristes: Arias otoñales, Nocturnos, Recuerdos sentimentales (Madrid: Fernando Fé, 1903);
Jardines lejanos (Madrid: Fernando Fé, 1904);
Elegías puras (Madrid: Revista de Archivos, 1908);
Elegías intermedias (Madrid, 1909);
Olvidanzas I: Las hojas verdes (Madrid: Revista de Archivos, 1909); enlarged as *Olvidanzas* (Madrid: Revista de Archivos, 1909);
Elegías lamentables (Madrid, 1910);
Baladas de primavera (Madrid: Revista de Archivos, 1910);
Poemas mágicos y dolientes (Madrid: Revista de Archivos, 1911);
La soledad sonora (Madrid: Revista de Archivos, 1911);
Pastorales (Madrid: Renacimiento, 1911);
Melancolía (Madrid: Revista de Archivos, 1912);
Laberinto (Madrid: Renacimiento, 1913);
Platero y yo: Elegía andaluza (Madrid: La Lectura, 1914; enlarged edition, Madrid: Calleja, 1917); translated by William and Mary Roberts as *Platero and I: An Andalusian Elegy* (Oxford: Dolphin, 1956; New York: Duschnes, 1956);
Estío (Madrid: Calleja, 1916);
Sonetos espirituales (Madrid: Calleja, 1917); translated by Carl W. Cobb as *Spiritual Sonnets* (Lewiston, N.Y.: Edwin Mellen Press, 1996);
Diario de un poeta recién casado (Madrid: Calleja, 1917); republished as *Diario de poeta y mar* (Buenos Aires: Losada, 1948; revised and expanded edition, Madrid: Afrodisio Aguado, 1955); translated by Hugh A. Harter as *Diary of a Newlywed Poet,* bilingual edition (Selinsgrove, Pa.: Susquehanna University Press, 2004);

Juan Ramón Jiménez, 1956 (Associated Press)

Poesías escojidas (1899–1917) (New York: Hispanic Society of America, 1917);
Eternidades (Madrid: Angel de Alcoy, 1918);
Piedra y cielo (Madrid: Fortanet, 1919); translated as *Sky and Rock* (Van Nuys, Cal.: C'est moi meme, 1989);
Antolojía poetica (Buenos Aires: Losada, 1922);
Segunda antolojía poética (1898–1918) (Madrid: Espasa-Calpe, 1922);
Poesía (Madrid: Talleres Poligráficos, 1923);

Belleza (Madrid: Talleres Poligráficos, 1923);

La realidad invisible: Libro inédito (Madrid, 1924); expanded as *La realidad invisible (1917–1920, 1924)*, edited by Antonio Sánchez Romeralo (London: Tamesis, 1983); translated by Antonio T. de Nicolás as *Invisible Reality: (1917–1920, 1924)* (New York: Paragon House, 1987);

Poesía en prosa y verso (1902–1932) de Juan Ramón Jiménez, edited by Zenobia Camprubí Aymar (Madrid: Signo, 1932);

Sucesión (Madrid: Signo, 1932);

Canción (Madrid: Signo, 1936);

Política poética (Madrid: Ministerio de Instrucción Pública y Bellas Artes, Instituto del Libro Español, 1936);

Ciego ante ciegos (Havana: Secretaría de Educación, Dirección de Cultura, 1938);

Españoles de tres mundos (Buenos Aires: Losada, 1942);

Voces de mi copla (Mexico City: Stylo, 1945);

El zaratán (Mexico City: Antigua Librería Robredo, 1946);

La estación total con las Canciones de la nueva luz (Buenos Aires: Losada, 1946);

Romances de Coral Gables (Mexico City: Stylo, 1948);

Animal de fondo (Buenos Aires: Pleamar, 1949);

Antología para niños y adolescentes, selected by Norah Borges and Guillermo de Torres (Buenos Aires: Losada, 1951 [i.e., 1950]);

Tercera antolojía poética (1898–1953) (Madrid: Biblioteca Nueva, 1957);

Moguer (Madrid: Dirección General de Archivos y Bibliotecas, 1958; expanded edition, Moguer: Ediciones de la Fundación Juan Ramón Jiménez, 1996);

Primeros libros de poesía, edited by Francisco Garfias (Madrid: Aguilar, 1959);

El romance, rio de la lengua española (San Juan: University of Puerto Rico, 1959);

Olvidos de Granada, 1924–1928 (Río Piedras: University of Puerto Rico, 1960);

Cuadernos, edited by Garfias (Madrid: Taurus, 1960);

La corriente infinita: Crítica y evocación, edited by Garfias (Madrid: Aguilar, 1961);

Por el cristal amarillo, edited by Garfias (Madrid: Aguilar, 1961);

El trabajo gustoso: Conferencias, edited by Garfias (Mexico City & Madrid: Aguilar, 1961);

El modernismo: Notas de un curso (1953), edited by Ricardo Gullón and Eugenio Fernández Méndez (Mexico City: Aguilar, 1962);

Primeras prosas, edited by Garfias (Madrid: Aguilar, 1962);

La colina de los chopos (Barcelona: Vergara, 1963);

Sevilla, edited by Garfias (Seville: Ixbiliah, 1963);

Poemas revividos del tiempo de Moguer (Barcelona: Chapultepec, 1963);

Dios deseado y deseante, edited by Antonio Sánchez-Barbudo (Madrid: Aguilar, 1964); translated by Nicolás as *God Desired and Desiring* (New York: Paragon House, 1987);

Libros inéditos de poesía, 2 volumes, edited by Garfias (Madrid: Aguilar, 1964, 1967);

Retratos líricos (Madrid: R. Díaz-Casariego, 1965);

Estética y ética estética: Crítica y complemento, edited by Garfias (Madrid: Aguilar, 1967);

Fuego y sentimiento (Madrid: Artes Gráficas L. Pérez, 1969);

Juan Ramón y yo; Rios se que van, by Jiménez and Zenobia Camprubí de Jiménez (Madrid: Luis Pérez, 1971);

Con el carbón del sol: Antología de prosa lírica, edited by Garfias (Madrid: EMESA, 1973);

El andarín de su órbita: Selección de prosa crítica, edited by Garfias (Madrid: EMESA, 1974);

En el otro costado, edited by Aurora de Albornoz (Madrid: Júcar, 1974);

Crítica paralela, edited by Arturo del Villar (Madrid: Nárcea, 1975);

La obra desnuda, edited by Villar (Seville: Aldebarán, 1976);

Leyenda, 1896–1956, edited by Antonio Sánchez Romeralo (Madrid: Cupsa, 1978);

Historias y cuentos, edited by Villar (Barcelona: Bruguera, 1979); translated by Nicolás as *Stories of Life and Death* (New York: Paragon House, 1986 [i.e., 1985]);

Autobiografía y artes poéticas, edited by Villar (Madrid: Libros de Fausto, 1981);

Canta pájaro lejano: Antología juvenil (Madrid: Espasa-Calpe, 1981);

Espacio, edited by Albornoz (Madrid: Nacional, 1982); translated by Nicolás in *Time and Space: A Poetic Autobiography* (New York: Paragon House, 1988);

Alerta, edited by Francisco J. Blasco Pascual (Salamanca: Universidad de Salamanca, 1983);

Autobiografía y autocrítica, edited by Villar (Madrid: Libros de Fausto, 1985);

Guerra en España, 1936–1953, edited by Angel Crespo (Barcelona: Seix Barral, 1985);

Hijo de la alegría (Madrid: El Observatorio, 1986);

Luz de la atención: 1918–1923: Libro inédito (Madrid: El Observatorio, 1986);

Poemas y cartas de amor, by Jiménez and Camprubí de Jiménez, edited by Gullón (Santander: Sur, 1986);

Tiempo (un parrafo) y Espacio (3 estrofas), edited by Villar (Madrid: EDAF, 1986); translated by Nicolás in *Time and Space: A Poetic Autobiography* (New York: Paragon House, 1988);

Cuadernos de Zenobia y Juan Ramón, by Jiménez and Camprubí de Jiménez, 10 volumes, edited by Villar (Madrid: Los Libros de Fausto, 1987–1994);

Metamórfosis, edited by Romeralo (Barcelona: Anthropos, 1990);

Mi Rubén Darío, edited by Romeralo (Moguer: J. R. Jiménez, 1990);

Poemas inéditos (Seville: Cuadernos D. Roldán, 1991);

Lluvia de junio: Seis nuevos poemas inéditos de Laberinto (1910–1911), edited by José Luis Puerto (Salamanca: Amarú, 1992).

Editions and Collections: *Libros de poesía,* edited by Agustín Caballero (Madrid: Aguilar, 1957)—comprises *Sonetos espirituales, Estío, Diario de un poeta recien casado, Eternidades, Piedra y cielo, Belleza, Poesía, La estacíon total,* and *Animal de fondo;*

Páginas escojidas: Prosa, edited by Ricardo Gullón (Madrid: Gredos, 1958);

Páginas escojidas: Verso, edited by Gullón (Madrid: Gredos, 1958);

Y para recordar por qué he venido, edited by Francisco J. Blasco Pascual (Valencia: Pre-Textos, 1990);

Primeros poemas, edited by Jorge Urrutia (Seville: Editorial Point de Lunettes, 2003).

Editions in English: *Fifty Spanish Poems,* translated by J. B. Trend (Oxford: Dolphin, 1950; Berkeley: University of California Press, 1951);

Platero and I, translated by Eloïse Roach (Austin: University of Texas Press, 1957; London: Thomas Nelson, 1958);

Selected Writings, translated by H. R. Hays, edited by Eugenio Florit (New York: Farrar, Straus & Cudahy, 1957);

Three Hundred Poems, 1903–1953, translated by Roach (Austin: University of Texas Press, 1962);

Forty Poems, translated by Robert Bly (Madison, Wis.: Sixties, 1967);

Platero and I: An Andalusian Elegy, 1907–1916, translated by Antonio T. de Nicolás (Boulder, Colo. & London: Shambhala, 1978);

Light and Shadows: Selected Poems and Prose, translated by Bly and others, edited by Dennis Maloney (Fredonia, N.Y.: White Pine Press, 1987);

The Complete Perfectionist: A Poetics of Work, edited and translated by Christopher Maurer (New York: Doubleday, 1997).

PLAY PRODUCTION: *Jinetes hacia el mar,* translated by Jiménez and Zenobia Camprubí Aymar from John Millington Synge's *Riders to the Sea,* Madrid, Teatro Ritz, 1920.

TRANSLATIONS: Romain Rolland, *Vida de Beethoven* (Madrid: Residencia de Estudiantes, 1915);

John Millington Synge, *Jinetes hacia el mar,* translated by Jiménez and Zenobia Camprubí Aymar (Madrid: Fortanet, 1920);

Rabindranath Tagore, *Obra escojida,* translated by Jiménez and Camprubí Aymar (Madrid: Aguilar, 1955).

Juan Ramón Jiménez, known simply as Juan Ramón in the Hispanic world, dominated Spanish poetry for the first three decades of the twentieth century, and at the outbreak of the Spanish Civil War in 1936 he was still a figure of influence and importance. Later, in exile in the United States and Puerto Rico, he expanded his already considerable influence, made the acquaintance of Robert Frost and Ezra Pound, and was greeted with enthusiasm on a trip to Buenos Aires in 1948. The unabashed and imperfectly assimilated modernism of Jiménez's first books yielded in *Rimas* (1902, Rhymes) and *Arias tristes* (1903, Sad Airs) to a delicate, sensitive, and sentimental tone that drew much from Spanish Romanticism. After 1916 he entered a new phase, for which he is well known: stripping anecdote and obvious sentiment from his lines, he made heavy use of symbols in a self-referential poetry surprising for its sheerness and its difficulty. Its major themes are the relation of the poet to poetry; of poetry to the world; and love, memory, and death. This phase gradually gave way just before the civil war and afterward to a period in which moments of epiphany become longer and deeper, and the poet experiences a serene union with nature. His final works apotheosize the creative spirit and carry forward the Romantic, symbolist tradition of the poet as a divine seer. *Platero y yo* (1914, expanded 1917; translated as *Platero and I,* 1956) is a series of vignettes of small-town life and rural scenes in and around his birthplace, Moguer. The combination of Platero and Moguer may be, after that of Don Quixote and La Mancha, one of the most universally known in literature. Jiménez's Andalusian roots were, like William Butler Yeats's Irishness, a source of inspiration and pride. As the Spaniard's fame grew, he never ceased to remind his public of his heritage, calling himself "El andaluz universal" (The Universal Andalusian). Jiménez said he wanted to bring Moguer to the world, and so he did via *Platero y yo,* one of the most often translated books in Spanish literature.

The Jiménez family operated a comfortable business as wine and tobacco merchants, with their own vineyards, ships, warehouses, and a tobacco monopoly granted by the state. Their products became known in Gibraltar, southern Spain, and around Bordeaux at the time of the phylloxera (1883–1893), when a small insect contaminated French grapes; Spanish vineyards escaped, and the Jiménez family flourished. Such commerce enabled the young Juan Ramón Jiménez Mantecón, born on 24 December 1881, to enjoy the upbringing of a typical Andalusian *señorito* (well-to-do young gentleman). His parents were Victor Jiménez and Purificacíon Mantecón y Lopez Parejo. There were six children born to the poet's father: three from his first marriage, and three from his second. Juan Ramón was the youngest and undoubtedly the most pampered of the lot. He remembered pleasant visits to his father's ships and warehouses and rides in the country astride his colt, Almirante. But Juan Ramón was also an introspective, solitary boy who spent long hours playing with a kaleidoscope and developing his imagination.

In October 1893, after finishing primary school in Huelva, he and his brother Eustaquio entered the Jesuit Colegio de San Luis Gonzaga in Puerto de Santa María near Jerez de la Frontera. Except for the view from his dormitory window that looked out on the ocean with Cádiz in the distance, Juan Ramón found school gloomy and disturbing. A delicate and docile nature made him the easy butt of his classmates' pranks. At the onset of puberty his natural sensitivity grew more marked, and his character began to show a strong narcissistic trend, a development abetted by his mother's love and indulgence.

At the *colegio*, Jiménez filled the margins and blank pages of his textbooks with drawings. His favorite subject was French, and selections that he read in this school made an indelible impression on his mind, for one finds references to them among the hundreds of notes that he left as an adult poet. He also enjoyed texts on rhetoric, as well as an 1882 edition of Thomas à Kempis's fourteenth-century work *The Imitation of Christ,* in which Jiménez underlined passages that confirmed his penchant for reticence and solitude; one such passage is "Show not thy heart to every man." In 1896 he concluded his studies for the *bachillerato* (high-school diploma).

Two aspects of Jiménez's life between the ages of thirteen and sixteen are especially revealing for a deeper understanding of the man and his poetry. The adolescent Juan Ramón had, he admitted, a tyrannical nature; he argued endlessly with his uncles and insisted on having the last word on all matters pertaining to literature and art; he verbally attacked one of his cousins whenever she came to dinner, because of a nervous tic she had. He would go storming to his room after these scenes, refusing to apologize and leaving his mother in tears, a reaction on her part that increased his guilt and consequently his fury. Guns fascinated him, he recalls in *Por el cristal amarillo* (1961, Through the Yellow Glass), a collection of prose pieces about Moguer, and he hunted everything that was fair game and much that was not, including his turtle and his cousin's pet eaglet. The adult Jiménez's fondness for birds, symbols for him of the natural divine music that poetry should emulate, stands in startling contrast to the image of this youth, in critic Donald F. Fogelquist's phrase, "cannonading the countryside." Although this aspect of Jiménez's character might come as a surprise, assiduous readers have long recognized his darker side, the sinister alter ego mentioned in a few of his poems—the individual dressed in black peering at him through his bedroom window. Such instability of character plagued Jiménez throughout his life.

This tyrannous adolescent fell in love with Blanca Hernández-Pinzón, the daughter of Moguer's judge; she was descended from the Pinzón family who at the request of Queen Isabel had donated two caravels for Christopher Columbus's expedition and helped recruit some of the crew. Blanca and Juan Ramón met through her brother José, who was courting Juan Ramón's sister Victoria. Blanca and Juan Ramón exchanged furtive kisses while her mother dozed, but Blanca's family, fearful of the impetuous Moguer marksman, discouraged the association. Biographer Graciela Palau de Nemes believes that this young love planted in Jiménez's mind the ideal of the white *(blanca)*, chaste, beautiful, and unattainable woman, one of the guiding symbols for his verse. She was the first of his many sweethearts, real and fanciful. Like Percy Bysshe Shelley, he was in love with love.

Victor Jiménez wanted Juan Ramón to be a lawyer, but the young man believed he had talent as an artist and cherished the thought of becoming a painter. It was finally decided that he would begin the course of studies for prelaw at the University of Seville and at the same time take instruction in studio art. In autumn 1896 he enrolled in the university and began his art apprenticeship in the studio of Salvador Clemente, a genre painter from Cádiz, whose many scenes of vineyards and flamenco dancers sold well to tourists. Under the tutelage of the capricious Clemente, Jiménez drew the obligatory still lifes and landscapes and showed himself an apt pupil in the impressionist style. His paintings reveal a more-than-ordinary talent and a preference for a blend of subdued blues, grays, whites, and greens that coincides exactly with the hues in his poetry. While his chromatic sense was exceptional and became especially notable in his verse, his drawings betray an eye still struggling with perspective. He continued to paint busily until 1900. In the exhibition of his paintings and drawings arranged in Moguer on the occasion of the centennial of his birth, the gentle impressionistic landscapes and the portraits of gypsy girls were the best indication of the plastic skills that yielded to the art of painting with words.

Jiménez once remarked that of the three great loves of his life—painting, poetry, and music—painting beckoned first when he was fifteen and then gave way a year or two later to poetry. (His devotion to music began when he was twenty.) The reasons for his decision not to continue as a painter are unclear. Certainly the bohemian lifestyle of Clemente and his friends did not appeal to the correct young man, who was compulsive about neatness and order. Ruminating on the situation afterward, Jiménez said that if he had had a different master, he might have gone on to become a painter of note.

During his year at the University of Seville, his ambition to be a poet crystallized. He immersed himself in lyrical verse, read through the night, and composed his own lines as he walked along the banks of the Guadalquivir, which glides through Seville out into the Atlantic. In the city that much of Europe viewed as the quintessence of Romanticism, Jiménez spent his money and most of the energy and time he was not devoting to art lessons to reading and declaiming the poetry of Alphonse Lamartine; George Gordon, Lord Byron; and Heinrich Heine. These initial encounters installed in his temperament a need for the insistent expression of personal feelings and confirmed his tendency toward sentimentality and melancholy. He did not, however, neglect the poets of his native language. Poetry by José de Espronceda, the "Spanish Byron," made an impression, as did, most notably, Gustavo Adolfo Bécquer, whose *Rimas* (1860, 1861), published two decades before Jiménez's birth, resembled works by Heine and Shelley and foreshadowed the suggestive musicality of the French symbolists. (It was no accident that Jiménez's first important book is also titled *Rimas*.) At this early stage he also became acquainted with the poetry of Rosalía de Castro, a Galician who, like Bécquer, signaled the way to a more finely tuned expression of self-consciousness than that of Espronceda, and who also, like Emily Dickinson, made of her solitude and subjective eye for nature a topic for poetry.

Early in 1897 the *Programa,* a Seville newspaper, accepted one of Jiménez's poems, and, thus encouraged, he joined a literary group in Seville called the Ateneo and began to send poems to provincial magazines and newspapers. Soon he enjoyed a good reputation in the city and started work on a book of poetry to be called "Nubes" (Clouds). The demands of poetry and painting left him no time for studies, and, upon failing Spanish history, he withdrew from the university at the end of the spring term to devote himself full-time, with the blessing of an indulgent family, to painting and writing. He collaborated on the reviews *Hojas Sueltas* and *Quincena,* the latter under the guidance of Timoteo Orbe, a novelist and playwright. Orbe was a product of *krausismo,* a form of German idealism introduced into Spain by Julián Sanz del Río that had a decided effect on an intellectual minority with liberal tendencies. At a time when an air of pessimism hung heavy over Europe, this small cadre believed that in the powers of art and the highly selective spirit of the artist lay a way of lifting from humankind the weight imposed by the ideas of Friedrich Nietzsche and Charles Darwin.

In the small library maintained by the *Quincena,* Jiménez ran across the verses of Rubén Darío, the great poet from Nicaragua. Blending French Romanticism, Parnassianism, and symbolism, Darío had managed to inject new life into Hispanic poetry at the turn of the century. Jiménez long remembered the exhilaration produced by his first contact with Darío's works.

In 1899 *Vida Nueva,* a Madrid review, accepted a poem by Jiménez that was inspired by a humanitarian concern for the lower classes. "Las amantes del miserable" (The Beggar's Lovers) has some compassionate, if overwrought, lines about a beggar on a cold winter night in Madrid; his only friends are the prostitutes Loneliness and Death. *Vida Nueva* published this piece on 3 December 1899 with a photo of the broodingly handsome young author and sent him, on the basis of his apparent concern with social problems, five pieces by Henrik Ibsen, already translated into Spanish, which Jiménez polished into poetic prose. Thus began a lifelong interest in the art of translation. *Vida Nueva* published his Ibsen translations on 7 January 1900, and the stage was set for Jiménez to go to Madrid.

A postcard signed by Darío and Francisco Villaespesa, a young poet who was an avid reader of *Vida Nueva,* was Jiménez's invitation to come to Madrid and assist in the task of revitalizing Spanish poetry. Needing no urging, he arrived in Madrid on Good Friday of 1900, to be swept up into the bohemian life of the *modernistas.*

Darío, fresh from the triumph in 1896 of his *Prosas profanas* (Profane Prose), was sent by *La Nación* of Buenos Aires to report on conditions in Spain after its devastating defeat at the hands of the United States in 1898. He arrived in early 1899 at the age of thirty-two, preceded by the reputation gained from the success of his *Azul* (1888, Blue) and *Prosas profanas,* and he found what he thought was an old, tired country, with a middle class indifferent to the disaster of 1898 and most of the writers past their prime. Charles-Pierre Baudelaire, Paul Verlaine, the decadents, and the Parnassians were not unknown in Spain when Darío arrived (Jiménez having read works by Verlaine before meeting Darío), but Darío's masterful synthesis of these currents, plus traces of the influence of such classic Spanish writers as St. Teresa of Ávila and Luis de Góngora, pointed the way toward a successful renovation of poetic language. Darío's themes were limited, but his skill was unquestionable, and his lines have an elegance and sensuality about them that stand in vivid contrast to the lyrics of Ramón de Campoamor, Gaspar Núñez de Arce, and Juan Zorrilla, the reigning poets at that time. Thus, Darío, a mestizo from Central America, became the leader of the reform movement in Spanish poetry.

Spanish political stagnation was on a par with that of its poetry. The restoration of the Bourbon monarchy in 1874 and the suppression of Carlist opposition in 1876 had established a solidly reactionary basis of government, and during the last decades of the nineteenth century the political system seemed to be devised to keep anyone from rocking the boat: liberals and conservatives rotated in power, and debates in the *Cortes* (parliament) were either vapid or baroque. No one tackled the large social problems.

Nevertheless, while Darío's assessment of poetry may have been accurate, Spanish literature was far from moribund. Miguel de Unamuno's trenchant style and erudition, after a flirtation with Marxism, took the lead in the development of a multifaceted body of essays, novels, and philosophical works that, if only for its lack of frivolity and suppression of sensuality, contrasted sharply with the *modernistas*. Azorín (José Martínez Ruiz), moving away from his early anarchistic sympathies, was, along with Pío Baroja, about to reinvigorate the Spanish novel, and Ramón del Valle-Inclán, who intellectually absorbed the decadent trends from France and England more thoroughly than some of his cohorts, soon introduced to readers his infamous alter ego, the Marqués de Bradomín, an old, ugly, sentimental, and Catholic Don Juan (in the *Sonata* novels, 1902–1905).

Into this atmosphere the idealistic, somewhat affected, and highly proper Andalusian poet Jiménez appeared in the middle of April 1900. He formed a lasting friendship with Darío, saw Valle-Inclán often, met Azorín and the playwright Jacinto Benavente (who, like Jiménez, went on to win a Nobel Prize), and became good friends with Gregorio Martínez Sierra, a dramatist who was later an influence on him. His companions pointed out that the large amount of material he had tentatively titled "Nubes" could easily be divided into two books, and he set about to follow their advice. The disorderliness, to say nothing of the debauchery, of bohemian life did not suit Jiménez, and six weeks after his arrival in Madrid he was back in Moguer, busy separating and regrouping the poetry of "Nubes."

Almas de violeta (Violet Souls) and *Ninfeas* (Water Lilies), printed respectively in violet and green ink, were published in September 1900. *Almas de violeta*, the title of which was suggested by Darío, includes a passionate prologue by Villaespesa; Valle-Inclán introduced *Ninfeas*; and Darío wrote from Paris to bless Jiménez and welcome him into the ranks of the guardians of beauty. The older Jiménez took a violent dislike to these early effusive books of his poetry and destroyed every copy he could get his hands on, thus assuring their rarity. The critical reception was almost equally negative and violent, but, like most juvenilia, these poems are of interest for the glimpses they provide of a nascent talent, and they are valuable historical records of the tastes, themes, and spasms of early Spanish modernism. Although Jiménez eventually remedied most of the faults, some of the themes were too imbedded in his life ever to disappear.

Villaespesa's combative prologue to *Almas de violeta* underscores the schism between the modern, cosmopolitan, generous young writers and their critics, whom he characterizes as eunuchs. He emphasizes that his cohorts are immoral and pagan by nature and that "Art for Art's Sake" is inscribed on their banner.

But Jiménez was not by nature immoral and certainly not pagan: he drank with moderation and intensely disliked brothels. His inability to live up to decadent standards of conduct may, along with the callowness of his years, account for the sense of contrivance and superficiality that many readers have found in his first two books. He once remarked that the sadness that encrusted his work was attributable in large part to a sense of not belonging, of being apart from the crowd. The encounter with the *modernistas*, invigorating and beneficial as it was, did little to alleviate this underlying notion of separateness, probably connected with Jiménez's narcissism, which, in conjunction with other aspects of his character, clouds his poetry with such heavy melancholy.

Almas de violeta shows this sentimental sadness. The loss of a young and tender loved one seems to lie behind such sorrow: "¡Ya murió la virgen que me consolaba!" (The virgin who consoled me is now dead!) is repeatedly announced in various ways throughout both *Almas de violeta* and *Ninfeas*. Edgar Allan Poe postulated that the death of a beautiful woman is the quintessential subject for poetry, and Dante Gabriel Rossetti, whom Jiménez came to admire, exploited the same theme.

One aspect of Jiménez's abiding neurosis was his abnormal fear of death. In *Almas de violeta* he sublimates this necrophobia by dwelling on innocent faces in white coffins. At times he leans dangerously toward an unhealthy attraction to a dead little body: "Elegíaca" (Elegiac) focuses on the work of worms as they eat away the small white face and burrow into the heart once inflamed by passion.

One or two poems give glimpses into Jiménez's sense of himself. In "Negra" (Black) he manages to achieve a certain ironic distance from his gloomy nature: his pains, he writes, are so fatigued at the end of the day from fighting him that they fall asleep exhausted, only to awake next day, refreshed and ready to do battle once again.

A natural and delicate voice occasionally breaks through in the book, as in the rendition of Andalusian popular songs. "Remembranzas" (Remembrances) is a poem so good that Jiménez incorporated it without change in his next book and eventually rewrote it toward the close of his life in a masterful summary of the prolongation of childhood and its memories. This deftly poignant poem describes the way in which the magical dimensions that are open to the senses of childhood disappear with age.

The clumsier aspects of *Almas de violeta* are continued and exacerbated in the longer *Ninfeas*. The highly mannered vocabulary (one does not "kiss"; one "osculates") carries the same themes, with less morbidity perhaps, but certainly not lacking in overwrought passion. There is still the claim, rooted in Romanticism, that the poet will never encounter the pure innocence he so ardently seeks, and there are moments that foreshadow the mature Jiménez voice, such as in "Recuerdos" (Memories), with its suggestion of Verlaine's style. Obverse to the topic of unrequited love is a scene that is repeated often in Jiménez's later books: the poet tenderly takes leave of a beautiful girl, presumably in search of the ideal. *Ninfeas,* in terms of metrics, registers seven attempts by Jiménez to re-create the remarkable rhythm of the Colombian poet José Asunción Silva's *Nocturnos,* which had been published in Spain in 1900.

Jiménez had been back in Moguer six weeks when, on 3 July 1900, his father died suddenly. The shock aggravated the morbidity noticeable in his first books and further activated his abnormal fear of death, the symptoms of which he never completely overcame. He believed that he, too, would die suddenly like his father, and, in order to prevent this occurrence, he insisted on always being near a doctor, or knowing where one was immediately available. This compelling need ordered all living arrangements for the rest of his life. Although examinations continually proved the contrary, he was convinced that he had a defective heart. During periods when his neurosis worsened, he required a doctor at his side. The most dreaded aspect of his illness, and the one that made life difficult for his associates, came in the recurring bouts of heavy depression. Long fallow stretches appeared in his creative life; in his last years in the United States he often entered a hospital for treatment of this emotional state. Between these bouts Jiménez could be active, cheerful, assiduously warm, elaborately courteous, full of Andalusian wit, and remarkably fecund. He was truly, as he himself noted, a man whose life was presided over by fierce Manichaean contrasts, such as light and darkness, sanity and madness.

During the year following his father's death, Jiménez's symptoms mounted, and his family, via contacts in southern France through their wine business, sent him to the sanatorium of Castel d'Andorte, near Bordeaux, to be placed under the care of Jean Gaston Lalanne, a noted authority on persecution complexes. The poet arrived at the sanatorium in the first part of May 1901. An investigation by biographer Ignacio Prat has shed much light on this period. In between fits of despondency Jiménez was reasonably active, making short trips into the Pyrenees and delighting in the company of Lalanne's children. In a letter of 18 July 1901 to the poet's mother, Lalanne described what became the common pattern of Jiménez's life: he would begin to feel a bit better and give himself up to poetry, his ruling passion; then the intellectual effort would reawaken the neurasthenia, causing a kind of vicious circle. Jiménez had other passions besides poetry. Internal evidence in the poems he wrote at the sanatorium and the studies of Prat indicate that he proved irresistible to the women he encountered in France, including Lalanne's wife and the children's governess. By the end of August, Jiménez was gone from France, and soon he settled down in a rest home in Madrid and formed a lasting friendship with the neurologist Luis Simarro.

In later life Jiménez said that it was during his stay at Castel d'Andorte that he first read Baudelaire and made the acquaintance of such French poets as Albert-Victor Samain, Jean Moréas, Jules Laforgue, Stéphane Mallarmé, Henri Frédéric Amiel, and Verlaine. However, Jiménez's poetry written during that time, under the tentative title "Rimas de sombra" (Shadow Rhymes), published as *Rimas,* registers no significant traces of these authors. Instead, *Rimas* reflects the continuing influences of the *modernistas* he had met at the beginning of 1900, notably that of Villaespesa, plus touches of Darío, and surprising notes from the sonorous Spanish romantic Zorrilla. Bécquer's is, however, the presiding spirit, from the title to many of the images, as well as some of the metrical combinations. *Rimas* met with critical success and is an improvement over Jiménez's first two books, for he has toned down the excesses of modernism and allowed more latitude to the lyrical voice buried under the earlier sentimentality and melancholy.

Although an epigraph from Augusto Ferrán, Bécquer's contemporary, stresses that death is possible every day, there is much that is not morbid in *Rimas*. The scenario of lovers taking leave of each other is deftly handled, and the first of many hauntingly beautiful garden scenes makes an appearance in Jiménez's poetry. Children's voices, which echo in much of European poetry in the late nineteenth and early twentieth centuries (in that of Verlaine, T. S. Eliot, and Antonio Machado, for example), sound among these early Jiménez gardens, and there is also a vision of a delicate white-robed virgin. Eventually, she is changed into a rose so that the values attached to her may have a wider symbolic radius. One poem records an early instance of Jiménez's urge to transcend, an urge that dominates his late poetry: by running to the horizon he hopes to lose himself in the stars. In *Rimas,* as Angel González notes, Jiménez introduces the poet as narrator and subject of much of the poetry for the first time. The discovery of this persona enabled Jiménez to channel his subjectivity into an alter ego that would help him control his emotions and advance toward what would eventually be a major topic: the relation of poetry and the poet to the world.

The Sanatorio del Rosario, located in what was then a semirural part of Madrid, provided Jiménez with two of the happiest years of his life (1902 and 1903). Close to doctors and ministered to by the sisters of the Sanatorio, he felt suitably protected and cared for and was able to give full vent to his creative interests. The individuals who visited him turned his rooms into a kind of literary salon: Valle-Inclán, Benavente, Manuel Reina, Salvador Rueda, Martínez Sierra, Pérez de Ayala, and the Machado brothers. With the exception of Unamuno, the key writers of the time came to the Sanatorio to talk literature. *Modernismo,* still vilified by older authors and bourgeois critics, had nevertheless taken hold in Spain. In Jiménez's room these literati hatched the plans for a *modernista* review to be called *Helios.* One of the most coherent and successful platforms for Spanish modernism, *Helios* (April 1903–May 1904) was carefully edited by Jiménez, who contributed translations of Verlaine as well as many unsigned pieces. Notably international in outlook and hospitable not only to French but also to Anglo-American literature, *Helios* was impressive also for its idealistic and restrained tone. The absence of decadent frissons may be partially attributed to the changing times, but the influence of Jiménez, who had come to see the errors of *Almas de violeta* and *Ninfeas,* cannot be denied.

Arias tristes, published in 1903, includes the poetry he wrote at the Sanatorio. It is Jiménez's first well-balanced and cohesive book, one in which his natural lyric voice, expressed in the traditional ballad meter of eight syllables to the line, receives full range. Critics from José Ortega y Gasset to Darío praised it, and its success established Jiménez as a poet of undeniable talent.

The structure of *Arias tristes* reveals his deep love of music. Each of the three sections is preceded by the score of a lied by Franz Schubert. This striking conjunction of notes and words suggests the profound relationship between poetry and music that informed Jiménez's life. (In America, Arturo Toscanini was his great cultural hero.) The sentimental beauty of Schubert's songs finds its counterpart in the poetry. In a small introduction to the nocturnes of part 2, Jiménez acclaims Heine, Bécquer, Verlaine, and Alfred de Musset as the poets in whom he encounters like sentiments. The emotional inspiration, then, of *Arias tristes* is essentially a throwback to Romanticism. Between these two camps–Romanticism and *modernismo*–Jiménez wrote, with varying effect but increasing frustration, until 1913, when he began to sense a new pathway.

Fogelquist aptly describes the many landscapes of *Arias tristes* with their subdued light, mist-shrouded valleys, quiet rivers, and a lonely star. Jiménez resorts frequently to a device first labeled by the Romantics: the pathetic fallacy. Alongside nature and the poet, one finds the nearly continuous presence of a woman, represented only by the pronoun *ella* (her), for which the referents are both specific and general. Soon Jiménez expanded the pronoun to include the concepts of beauty, music, and poetry, all nouns of feminine gender in the Spanish language.

Simarro, the neurologist Jiménez had met on the way to Bordeaux, began taking on boarders after the death of his wife in 1903. Jiménez, delighted to have a doctor available on a daily basis, stayed with him. The experience of living with Simarro broadened Jiménez's intellectual horizons as well. In Simarro's well-stocked library, Jiménez read the works of William Shakespeare, Johann Wolfgang von Goethe, and Shelley, and Nietzsche's aphorisms particularly impressed him. One of the other boarders was the gifted biologist Nicolás Achúcarro, who was later in charge of the mental hospital in Washington, D.C., where Pound was interned.

Through Simarro, Jiménez came to know the work of the Institución Libre de Enseñanza. An offspring of the idealism of the *krausistas,* the Institución members believed that the reform of Spain must begin in its educational institutions. Founded in 1876 by Francisco Giner de los Ríos as a lay school at a time when all education was under the aegis of the Catholic church, the Institución deeply affected the life of a liberal intellectual minority. Jiménez accompanied Simarro to its lectures and noted that they always came away with many new ideas. The religiosity of the Institución, unattached to dogma and the church, provided Jiménez with a broad and liberal religious impulse that he, too, pointedly kept free of entanglement with any specific form of Christianity. Jiménez's friendship with Ortega y Gasset also dates from this period. Through these contacts the sensitive and talented author of *Arias tristes* gradually broadened his outlook and increased his intellectual concerns.

Jardines lejanos (Faraway Gardens), published in February 1904, is the last part of a trilogy that begins with *Rimas* and includes *Arias tristes. Jardines lejanos* continues the practice of introducing each section with a musical score: this time the composers honored are Christoph Willibald Gluck, Robert Schumann, and Felix Mendelssohn-Bartholdy. Dedicated to the "Divine memory of Enrique Heine," *Jardines lejanos* essentially continues the themes of *Arias tristes.* A more pronounced sensuality, an occasional flash of humor, and persistent memories of Francina–the Lalanne children's governess, with whom Jiménez had a brief affair—set *Jardines lejanos* apart from its predecessors. The garden scenes in particular pulsate with underlying sexuality. In one poem, as he peers into a fountain in expectation of seeing a rosebush reflected, the speaker instead is startled by the image of a naked woman (which is likely the first appearance of this key Jiménez icon); he senses a stirring of unsaintly feelings and, in a moment of synesthesia, says "Todo era aroma de senos" (All was the odor of breasts).

One of the most compelling poems begins with a question: "¿Soy yo quien anda esta noche / por mi cuarto, o el mendigo / que rondaba mi jardín / al caer la tarde?" (Is it I who wanders / about my room tonight, or is it the beggar / who patrolled my garden / at dusk?). Jiménez has allowed his apprehension of a dual personality within himself to enter into his poetry, and from this point on it appears intermittently in his work, always raising important questions about identity.

Giner de los Ríos was an avid nature lover, and he persuaded Jiménez to accompany him on excursions to the Guadarrama Mountains, which border Madrid to the north. These hikes accounted for the poetry of *Pastorales* (written in 1904 but not published until 1911). After writing these pleasant and gentle songs of nature, Jiménez temporarily retired the ballad meter he had introduced in *Rimas* and began to experiment with longer lines and different stanza forms that clothe a troubled and monotonous content.

In view of the illness of Simarro and the absence of several close friends (among them Martínez Sierra, who had gone to Brussels, and Achúcarro, who was studying in Germany), Jiménez in the fall of 1905 decided to return to Moguer. There he stayed until 29 December 1912, when he left to go back for good to Madrid. Thus, for nearly seven years the poet lived with his family in the semiseclusion of their Andalusian village. He renewed his idyll with Hernández-Pinzón and became infatuated with María Almonte, the wife of the local doctor. Jiménez's struggle with his morbid obsession drained a good deal of his psychic energy. Adding to his woes, the family's financial plight—economic problems that in 1911 resulted in bankruptcy—began to be apparent. On the whole, however, little is known about his life during this period, which he later referred to as a time of "soledad literaria" (literary solitude).

Seven years of provincial exile in Moguer, interrupted by an occasional trip, turned out to be, except for bouts of depression, incredibly productive. Jiménez wrote enough to fill several collections of poetry and one book of prose that were published beginning in 1908, and sufficient material remained to fill seven posthumous volumes.

Aside from the obvious technical virtuosity of this poetry, its main interest lies in offering an example of how a hypersensitive and repressed poet handled the fin de siècle decadent themes in a provincial environment. Recurring topics are anecdotal love scenes (real or imaginary), disguised in flower symbolism; pervasive and at times seemingly self-indulgent sadness bordering on despair and ennui; sensitivity to nature and music; and predominant gardens. Good individual poems tend to be blanketed by the surrounding repetition. The persona of the poet, introduced in *Rimas*, fades into the background. Eroticism in itself was insufficient to meet the needs of Jiménez's psyche. Yearning for the ideal woman (also the dream of Shelley, Espronceda, and Bécquer) nourished his spiritual life and proved once more how firmly rooted he was in this aspect of the Romantic tradition.

Olvidanzas I: Las hojas verdes (Forgettings I: Green Leaves), written in 1906 and published in 1909, and *Baladas de primavera* (Spring Ballads), composed in 1907 and published in 1910, represent a transition from *Pastorales* into the more lugubrious work that follows. Memories of the sanatorium at Castel d'Andorte and readings of French poetry (by Verlaine, Samain, and Laforgue) crowd the sorrowful pages of *Olvidanzas I*. In contrast, *Baladas de primavera* celebrates nature in a lighter tone: the perfection of the day finds expression in a phrase, apt for the Andalusian sky and resonant of works by Victor Hugo and Mallarmé: "Dios está azul" (God is blue). Three volumes of *Elegías* (Elegies, written in 1908 and 1909 and published respectively in 1908, 1909, and 1910) crowd out any sense of buoyancy and introduce low spirits and mournfulness: "Días sin emoción, sin novia y sin correo / desesperanza en tiempo de fríos y de niebla" (Days without feelings, women or mail / desperation in cold foggy weather).

Another sheaf of poems, written in 1908, was printed three years later under the title *La soledad sonora* (Sonorous Silence), a phrase from San Juan de la Cruz. Descriptions of abandoned palaces and old towns relieve the usual panorama of dulcet gardens and amorous longings. Jiménez, nearing thirty years of age, dedicated this book to Luisa Grimm de Muriedas, an American woman he had met in 1905. Estranged from her Spanish husband, Grimm, a native of Philadelphia, left Spain to live in England, Switzerland, and France, but she kept in touch with Jiménez. In their lengthy correspondence, which began in 1907, Grimm set herself up as his guide to the pleasures of English verse, urging him to read Yeats and Francis Thompson and constantly quoting her beloved Byron. Echoes of these writers can be found throughout Jiménez's subsequent writings. The rapport between the poet and Grimm strengthened his growing conviction about the high value of Anglo-American poetry. Grimm also embodied for him the ideal woman, beautiful and cultivated.

In the often lusterless Moguer period of Jiménez's writing, *Platero y yo,* his most universally acclaimed book, stands out. Nothing he wrote before or after gained such a wide readership. Read with pleasure by both schoolchildren and adults, these descriptions of life in a small Andalusian town, as seen through the sensitive eyes of the poet/narrator and his inseparable companion, the woolly white donkey Platero, have reached, after Miguel de Cervantes's *Don Quixote* (1605, 1615), perhaps the widest audience of any work in Spanish literature.

Jiménez began to write *Platero y yo* in 1906, shortly after he returned to Moguer, and in tone and style it resembles *Baladas de primavera,* of which it was originally intended to be a part. He took the manuscript when he went back to Madrid. The first edition of *Platero y yo* was published in 1914, followed by a considerably enlarged final edition in 1917. Assigned reading for schoolchildren in many countries, *Platero y yo* has been associated with children's literature but does not exclusively belong to that category any more than does Mark Twain's *Tom Sawyer* (1876). In a prologue that has too often been omitted from the hundreds of editions of *Platero y yo,* Jiménez took pains to point out that he had never written directly for children because he believed, with certain obvious exceptions, that adults and children could read with profit the same books.

The 138 vignettes of *Platero y yo,* written in poetic prose, register a Franciscan love of animals and nature; an idealism not far removed from the Institución Libre de Enseñanza and its founder, Giner de los Ríos; and an almost biblical acceptance of solitude and separateness as a means of achieving the good life. The poet/narrator, wearing a long Nazarene beard and a wide-brimmed black hat, is taunted by the village ragamuffins as he rides off into the countryside astride his little burro to contemplate the spectacle of a sunset, while the rest of the townsfolk, redolent with cigars and brandy, head for a bullfight. In a benevolent monologue the poet/narrator comments gently and sometimes sadly on the passing scene. The use of the burro as an alter ego, perhaps suggested by certain poems by Francis Jammes, provided Jiménez with the foil that he needed to keep free of the philosophical labyrinths of his *Elegías.*

Platero y yo presents a gallery of village portraits, ranging from dirty, unkempt gypsy children to the kindly village doctor, and shows a decided sympathy for the downtrodden and unfortunate. The book consists of equal doses of Blakean innocence and experience and of happiness and grief, emotions paired, says Jiménez, like Platero's ears. Against the backdrop of cobalt blue skies, bougainvillea, bees, butterflies, and bird songs, there are rabid dogs, cockfights, fear, superstition, idiocy, and poverty. The ingredients of life in a poor Mediterranean village in the second decade of the twentieth century combine with a delicate and balanced poetic tone to account for the accomplishment of *Platero y yo.*

In 1911 the Banco de España impounded the vineyards and other goods of the financially struggling Jiménez family. Jiménez took this situation as a warning that he might need to earn money, and since there were more economic opportunities in Madrid than in Moguer, he took the step he had long been considering: a return to the Spanish capital. By the end of 1912, the people of Moguer saw him as an occasional visitor, but he had finally loosened the ties with his native village. He struck up a friendship with the avant-garde writer Ramón Gómez de la Serna and entered into the literary and intellectual life of the capital.

Given his innate liberalism and his contact with Simarro and the Institución in 1903, Jiménez found himself quickly attracted to an offshoot of the Institución–the Residencia de Estudiantes, a dormitory set up in 1910 along the lines of a university college at Oxford or Cambridge. By 1912 it had been enlarged by three new buildings and was well on its way to becoming an important intellectual center in Spain and, to a certain extent, a cultural haven in Europe during World War I. All the great Spanish writers of the 1920s and 1930s (such as Jiménez, Unamuno, Ortega y Gasset, and Machado) were associated with it in some way; Federico García Lorca, Luis Buñuel, and Salvador Dalí lived there as students; and its doors were open to such distinguished foreigners as John Maynard Keynes, Albert Einstein, and Paul Valéry.

Jiménez attended a lecture at the Residencia in the summer of 1913. In the audience was a pert, blonde woman, twenty-six years old, named Zenobia Camprubí Aymar. She spoke Spanish with a slight accent because, although born in Barcelona, she had been educated in the United States. She had a strong interest in children's literature, knew Charles Lamb's *Tales from Shakespeare* (1807), and was translating into Spanish Rabindranath Tagore's vignettes about children in *The Crescent Moon* (1913). Camprubí Aymar was descended on her mother's side from Benjamín Aymar, a highly successful New York merchant; her father was a Catalan engineer who met and married Isabel Aymar in Puerto Rico. Jiménez fell in love at once with Camprubí Aymar, and a long and volatile courtship ensued. They were married in New York City on 2 March 1916. It would be difficult to exaggerate her impact on his life. Vivacious, optimistic, and outgoing, her temperament was a perfect foil for his moody, withdrawn, and doleful nature. Bilingual in Spanish and English, she was a cultivated woman (like Grimm) who further acquainted him with the world of Anglo-American poetry, which after 1916 replaced French verse as the chief influence on his work. His deep and abiding love for Camprubí Aymar played a large part in reordering his poetry, leading him partially out of his narcissistic snare and allowing him the rare privilege of encountering in his private life a situation in which for considerable periods the ideal and reality were contiguous.

Much of what Jiménez had written in Moguer held little appeal for Camprubí Aymar (she particularly disliked *Laberinto* [Labyrinth], published the year they met), but she was sensitive to his stature as a poet. Her own interest in writing was fully developed, and by 1912 she had contributed articles to *Vogue, St. Nicholas,* and the *Craftsman.* Jiménez exploited their common love of literature and used it as a bond to hold them together during their difficult courtship. He helped Camprubí Aymar prepare her translation of Tagore's *The Crescent Moon* in the summer of 1914. It was published as *La luna nueva* (1915), and its immediate success led them to continue their collaboration; eventually they translated and published twenty books by the prolific Tagore, all of which sold well in Spain and Latin America. During their courtship, they began a translation of Lamb's *Tales from Shakespeare* and some poems by Shelley. After their marriage they translated John Millington Synge's 1903 play *Riders to the Sea* as *Jinetes hacia el mar* (1920) and saw it produced in Madrid the same year it was published in Spanish. Scenes from this translation influenced Lorca's *Bodas de sangre* (performed, 1933; published, 1936; translated as *Blood Wedding,* 1939).

Translation continually played an essential role in the Jiménezes' life together. They had begun work on a selection of Yeats's poetry as well as his plays *The Countess Cathleen* (1892) and *The Land of Heart's Desire* (1894), but, when an argument over royalties could not be resolved, Yeats refused publication permission. With the help of Camprubí Aymar, Jiménez prepared and published translations of works by Dickinson, Frost, William Blake, Thompson, and Eliot.

The years 1913 to 1916 marked a time of transition. The sentimental and mournful voice began to give way to brief hermetic poems; compression, in the manner of Dickinson, whom he read for the first time in 1916, supplanted ambulatory alexandrines. At the same time, under the influence of Shakespeare's sonnets, which he had undertaken to translate with his wife, he tackled a classical meter. Glimpses of the new manner and tone first appear in *Estío* (1916, Summer) and *Sonetos espirituales* (translated as *Spiritual Sonnets,* 1996), which he began writing in 1914 and published in 1917. His use of the Italian sonnet form produced a successful book. From background readings of Shakespeare and Garcilaso de la Vega, he derived a series of love sonnets loosely modeled on the Renaissance tradition and directed to Camprubí Aymar. Other themes take on importance as well, for in this book he begins to demonstrate that identification of his mind with nature can provide an escape from the labyrinth of the self. Perhaps the most significant event in the *Sonetos espirituales* is the rediscovery of the poet persona. Sonnet 40, "A mi alma" (To My Soul), foreshadows one of the great themes of Jiménez's mature period: the relationship between the creative intelligence and its ambience (the poet and the world). By 1914 he was beginning to see that poetic intelligence could place an indelible signature on reality, that through his sensitivity he could re-create the world, and that uppermost among his responsibilities was the need to be alert and prepared for this task.

Even more significant in these months of transition is *Estío,* written in the summer of 1915 and published at the end of the following year. Shelley's "Mutability," which the Jiménezes were translating into Spanish, is the epigraph for *Estío.* Camprubí Aymar's changing moods, her indecision about their future together, and her whims and caprices could be summed up by the title of Shelley's poem. How to describe the mingling in the encounter of love is a challenge Jiménez meets with a delicate touch: the lovers are portrayed as blending together unwittingly as do the sea and the sky. Sentient variations find more meaningful metaphors than in his past poetry: "Yo no sé cómo saltar / desde la orilla de hoy" (I know not how to leap / from the edge of today).

When Camprubí Aymar stipulated that their marriage take place in New York City, she unwittingly supplied the context for one of the most unusual books in modern Spanish poetry. *Diario de un poeta recién casado* (1917, translated as *Diary of a Newlywed Poet,* 2004) is a record in poetry of Jiménez's feelings and thoughts about his journey from Cádiz to New York and his stay in the United States. He describes his first encounter with the sea and goes on to register experiences of bewilderment, frustration, and amazement in the milieu of New York City, as well as a reaction to American poetry. *Diario de un poeta recién casado* had considerable influence on the poetry written in Spain during the next decade.

In terms of form, *Diario de un poeta recién casado* introduces what Jiménez christened "poesía desnuda" (naked poetry) or "verso desnudo" (naked verse). After writing *Sonetos espirituales* he began to experiment with free verse in *Estío,* and for *Diario de un poeta recién casado* he perfected a short stanza, usually of no greater length than a dozen lines, in which rhyme is excluded and the measure of the lines themselves varies, according to no set pattern, from three to eleven syllables. Internal rhyme, delicate diction, and a conscious but restrained use of repetition provide the musical substance for "verso desnudo." The form pleased Jiménez and suited the temperament of his new style. (It was used to varying degrees in the early poetry of, among others, Pedro Salinas and Lorca.) The sections of *Diario de un poeta recién casado* dealing with New York City and Boston and with American poetry societies are written in prose poetry. Using phrases from advertisements and brochures, snatches of newspaper headlines, translations of Dickinson, quotations from Thompson and Amy Lowell, and the sensitivity of observation typical of *Platero y yo,* Jiménez created a noteworthy experiment along the lines of a collage.

In its subject matter *Diario de un poeta recién casado* is self-referential, but the anecdotal quality diminishes; emotions, instead of being baldly stated, begin to be implied; and the symbolic value of words comes to be realized. Emotions are set out in pellucid verse, and the continuity of experience is fragmented into intensely idealized moments. Fourteen poems directly concerning his love for Camprubí Aymar are less effective than the ones that speak of wonderment in the face of the ocean. When the book was republished in 1948, Jiménez retitled it *Diario de poeta y mar* (Diary of Poet and Sea). It is a dramatic encounter between the creative mind and a vast, imposing presence that seems as if it should have a consciousness worthy of its size but is also a slate-gray *nada* (nothingness). In a key metaphor Jiménez compares the movement of the waves and their relation to each other to his own thoughts: an eternal series of meetings and partings, of knowing and not knowing. He thus laid the groundwork for the fusion of subject and object that he carried out in the coming years. In this attractively varied book he presents several Saussurian musings on the linguistic experience inherent in being plunged forcibly into a foreign-language environment. Struck by the arbitrary relationship between the signifier and the signified, he wondered, for example, at the gap of feeling, and perhaps meaning, between the English word *sky* and the Spanish word *cielo,* which can also mean "heavens" or "canopy."

With a new direction for his poetry firmly in mind and a steamer trunk full of volumes of Anglo-American verse to be read and translated, Jiménez returned to Spain in July 1916 to begin the most significant period of his life. Several books and chapbooks of his new poetry, seventeen of his translations of works by Tagore, an influential anthology of his lengthy canon, and several journalistic collaborations made these years the most important and fruitful ones of his life. His dominance of the poetic scene in Spain was unchallenged. In *Indice,* a review he edited in 1921, he gave space to young poets such as Lorca, Salinas, Gerardo Diego, Jorge Guillén, and Dámaso Alonso. This so-called Generation of 1927 took its first steps with Jiménez's encouragement and support. As the group developed its own tone and voice, Jiménez, displaying the temperament of the adolescent who refused to be gainsaid in discussions of arts and letters, became offended with the natural reactions between generations, and his relationships with the new poets—to whom he had been, at the outset, the soul of generosity and who, in turn, learned a great deal from his diction, his high standards, and his unwavering devotion to the art of poetry—grew acrimonious.

The style hinted at in *Estío* attained full development in *Diario de un poeta recién casado.* "Naked poetry" offers short lines, free verse, suppression of anecdote, and recurring nouns charged with multiple meanings (*rose, tree, woman*). Four books exemplify the kind of poetry he sought to produce: *Eternidades* (1918, Eternities), *Piedra y cielo* (1919, Stone and Sky; translated as *Sky and Rock,* 1989), *Poesía* (1923, Poetry), and *Belleza* (1923, Beauty). These volumes represent the height of his achievement in Spanish poetry and put him in the ranks of Valéry, Yeats, Rainer Maria Rilke, and Eliot, all of whom wrote poetry about poetry—so-called metapoetry, a topic that fascinated Jiménez. *Eternidades* opens with a statement that his ultimate word is not yet made, and, in a poem that follows, he pleads with intelligence itself to give him the exact word, knowing that inspiration must be controlled by intellect and also that the exact name for him is multileveled, involving intelligence, himself, and the world. Recognition that words operate with a plurality of meaning and that language possesses magic qualities that lead to a special way of knowing makes this poem the first clear statement of symbolist doctrine in the Spanish language.

Pursuing his favorite symbol, he writes in *Eternidades* a celebrated statement of his poetics, which can also be read as a capsule history of his verse. Poetry, he says, first appeared to him in the form of an innocent and pure woman, and he loved her with the simplicity and naturalness of a child, until she began to dress ostentatiously and to hide her purity. Gradually, however, the pompous gowns slipped off, and the lovely lady appeared in her original tunic, which in the last stanza she removes to stand before him as the passion of his life. Both Yeats and Tagore wrote about the necessity of stripping adornment from their songs, and for Yeats there was great value in figuratively walking naked. Jiménez's poem is a sketch of various stages in his poetry: the early Romanticism, the modernist paraphernalia, the erotic labyrinths of Moguer, and finally the "poesía desnuda" of 1916. Naked poetry implies sheerness, lucidity, and pellucidness. However, its generic vocabulary as used by Jiménez—rose, stone, woman, and so on—ranges through various levels of meaning that, coupled with its self-referential base, makes "poesía desnuda" not as simple or as accessible as it seems at first glance. The dedication of many of his books to "La inmensa minoría" (the immense minority), with its echoes of Ortega y Gasset and Eliot, implies that his hermetic verse, like much modernist writing, demands a special effort in order to be appreciated.

A heightened awareness of his methods and goals caused Jiménez to begin speaking of "la Obra" (the Work). The capital *O* adds dignity and force to the word as he muses about the nature of what he is writing; it also implies a Platonic ideal of which the work on the written page may be, at times, only a dim reflection. He longs for his Obra to be like the sky on a starry night: a sense of the presence of truth free of history (as in *Piedra y cielo*). He wonders about the relationship of his Obra to the future, to readers, and to himself.

A nascent need in *Rimas* and *Pastorales* to identify affectively with nature has attained full force and foreshadows the unusual mysticism of his final writings. His four books of 1918, 1919, and 1923 include many epiphanies. Elements of nature meld together under his gaze—does the light sustain the leaf, or the leaf the light? *(Poesía)*—and eventually the contemplator fuses with the object: it is not sweet russet branches swaying in the afternoon wind, it is his soul *(Belleza)*. He feels himself to be the trunk of a universal tree, enmeshed with birds and stars, and should a woodsman swing his axe, the firmament will come crashing down *(Eternidades)*. Each day the poetic consciousness (soul) carries out the role first discovered in the sonnet "A mi alma" of *Sonetos espirituales:* it will remake the world.

One of Jiménez's greatest triumphs in this period is to broach the ultimate theme of death and, in spite of his pathological morbidity, present it in humanistic and noble terms. In an existentialist insight he saw that life cannot be meaningfully lived without the persistent awareness of death. The cord, he says in *Poesía*, that links one's life to life in general should, when need be, bind one to death. Death depends on life, Jiménez avers in one of his most moving poems; therefore, one should have no fear, for death is blind without life *(Poesía)*.

Also during this period, perhaps influenced by George Bernard Shaw, Jiménez decided to simplify Spanish spelling and make it more phonetic. Accordingly, with the publication of *Eternidades,* he introduced some orthographic variations from standard Spanish. These are slight—including the substitution of *j* for *ge* and *gi,* and *s* for *x* before certain consonants—and represent, at best, a quixotic endeavor, for Spanish orthography was already highly phonetic. In any event, the concern and care he brought to all aspects of his books became legendary. His insistence on the use of Elzevir type, set on quality paper with wide margins, produced volumes that in appearance contrast sharply with many of the shoddy publishing efforts in Spain at that time.

After *Belleza* and *La realidad invisible* (1924; translated as *Invisible Reality: (1917–1920, 1924)* (1987), many years passed before Jiménez published another book of original verse. He participated heavily in newspapers and journals; undertook the task of editing his "complete" works, a project that involved an enormous amount of revision, for he, like Yeats, developed an antagonism toward his juvenilia; and continued sporadically his translations of works by Anglo-American poets such as Blake, Frost, and Eliot.

Political events soon forced a radical change in his life. His lecture *Política poética* (Poetic Politics), prepared in May 1936 for the annual Spanish book fair, struck what seemed to many an impossibly idealistic note in view of the turbulence of the Spanish scene. Ascribing to poetry, as did Shelley, a moral force and an inclination toward social justice, Jiménez proposed that poets should become legislators. The admonition must have fallen on unbelieving ears, yet sometime later in the United States, when he met Henry A. Wallace, he saw that a creative and sensitive person could also be a politician.

Jiménez and his wife had often talked of returning to America. The outbreak of the Spanish Civil War gave them the motive to do so, and on 26 August 1936, carrying the title of honorary cultural attaché of the Spanish Republican government, Jiménez sailed with his wife from Cherbourg to New York. It was the last they saw of Europe. In New York and Washington, D.C., he tried with limited success to drum up support for the Republican cause. He visited the editorial offices of the *New Republic* and talked with Malcolm Cowley. Jiménez toured Puerto Rico and Cuba amid the adulation of poets young and old, and he returned to settle down in Coral Gables, Florida, where the climate and lowlands reminded him of his beloved Moguer. In his new environment, his reticence and aloofness became less marked, and, for a time, he was a more outgoing figure who could be occasionally persuaded to give special lectures. At the University of Miami, where he and his wife taught, he presented two lectures in 1940 that are keys to understanding his ideas about poetry and society. "Poesía y literatura" (Poetry and Literature) begins with the distinction made by Verlaine between the two and goes on to develop it in more explicitly Platonic terms: the poet is a medium possessed by a god, and what he writes is original; literature is merely a translation of these divine seizures. "Aristocracia y democracia" (Aristocracy and Democracy), influenced by Giner de los Ríos and the idealism of the Institución, says that true aristocracy resides in a cultivated and naturally sincere individual and that there are many examples among the Spanish common people. *Política poética* underwent a title change to become "El trabajo gustoso" (Pleasant Work) and was presented in Puerto Rico, Cuba, and Miami. These and other lectures were collected for publication in 1961 under the title *El trabajo gustoso.*

Ten days after Pearl Harbor was attacked by the Japanese, Jiménez wrote to Richard Pattee in the State Department to offer whatever services a fifty-nine-year-old poet could provide to the country that had treated him with such hospitality. The response was slow, but in July 1943 the Office of the Coordinator of Inter-American Affairs requested him to prepare ninety fifteen-minute programs to be broadcast to Latin America. The lectures were to treat two topics: modernism in Spain and Latin America, and contemporary poetry in the United States. Jiménez prepared more than a dozen of these lectures and had notes for several others, but in October he withdrew from the project for reasons partially involved with the question of censorship. The lectures already written were subsequently published in Colombia, Argentina, and Puerto Rico. Jiménez continued to be an important antifascist Hispanic voice for the State Department, and on 21 June 1944 he was invited to Savannah, Georgia, to participate in the launching of the liberty ship *Rubén Darío*.

Restlessness marked the lives of Jiménez and his wife during the 1940s in the United States as they sought work teaching and writing and battled his sieges of depression. After teaching at Duke University in 1942, they moved to Washington, D.C. In 1944 they began their association with the University of Maryland, where today the Juan Ramón Jiménez Hall of Languages commemorates that relationship. In 1946 he was hospitalized for eight months in Takoma Park, Maryland. Two years later he accepted an invitation to give a series of lectures in Buenos Aires. The press trumpeted his arrival; crowds pressed to see the author of *Platero y yo;* and in Montevideo the senate went into special session to hear him speak.

After *Platero y yo,* Jiménez's greatest prose work is *Españoles de tres mundos* (1942, Spaniards of Three Worlds), a series of lyrical caricatures written between 1914 and 1940. The Spaniards of three worlds (Europe, America, and the "other world") range from close friends, to well-known acquaintances, to dead authors whose works had special meaning for Jiménez. The caricatures balance skillfully the mordant and the lyrical. Nowhere in his lengthy work are the baroque exuberance and the nervous tension that exist as the obverse of his controlled pure style better displayed than in these portraits.

Many of the poems in *La estación total con las Canciones de la nueva luz* (1946, The Total Season with the Songs of New Light), which includes material composed between 1932 and 1936, describe transcendent experiences. Evidently, the moments of epiphany limned in *Eternidades* and *Belleza* have expanded and deepened. Nature closes in and envelops the speaker with a feeling of unity so that his spirit identifies with a sublime sense of the landscape. Woman, poetry, love, music, and roses—all these symbols are drawn into the center of a divine circle. Harbingers of this transcendence are often birds, and two poems, "Criatura afortunada" (Fortunate Creature) and "Mirlo fiel" (Faithful Blackbird), are moving evocations of the pantheistic effect of bird song; these poems are comparable with the best of Blake and William Wordsworth. The poems that open and close *La estación total con las Canciones de la nueva luz* show the importance of the perceiver: the poet's senses provide infinite resources. That glory arises from within is Jiménez's Blakean message, tinged with the idealism of the *institucionalistas*.

As the title announces, *Romances de Coral Gables* (1948, Ballads of Coral Gables) signals a return to the eight-syllable line of the traditional Spanish ballad, and these lyrics, composed in the Miami suburb that reminded Jiménez of Andalusia, recall the delicate musical voice in his early poetry and his "poesía desnuda." Once again, the sea represents a sense of infinity. Childhood is evoked as the common state from which people never truly exit—"el niño soy yo de viejo" (the boy I am as an old man).

Contact with the sea inevitably freed Jiménez's spirit. The voyage on the steamship *Río Juramento* that preceded his welcome to Buenos Aires in 1948 was no exception. Twenty-nine poems in free verse were published in 1949 as *Animal de fondo* (Animal of Depth). Despite the vocabulary common to the classical Spanish mystics *(fire, flame, torch, love)*, Jiménez's poetry does not accord in a doctrinaire manner with this tradition. The initial poem points out that the god to be celebrated is not a redeemer, brother, son, or father—in other words, not the Christian God—and the poet insists also that, unlike the mystics, he has nothing to purge. *Animal de fondo* extols the discovery of a "dios deseado y deseante" (a desired and desiring god). This dynamic god, identified explicitly as "conciencia" (consciousness), is desired by the poet as an expanded creative existence that at the same time is desirous of the poet, a relationship best described metaphorically as that of air and flame: mutual need in rapidly shifting contours. All former symbols were seen by Jiménez as mere surrogates for this final divinity.

Pound, whom the Jiménezes had been visiting at Saint Elizabeth's Hospital in the first half of 1948, wrote in a note to Jiménez that *Animal de fondo* was a fine book, much needed in the "post-Hegelian squalor." The collection is the culmination of the Romantic-symbolist tradition of the poet as a divine seer who through the use of words can unlock universal secrets, and, like Blake, *Animal de fondo* praises the divinity that resides within the human being.

Spurred on by the opinion of Octavio Paz, late-twentieth-century critics and poets have acclaimed Jiménez's long prose poem *Espacio* (Space, translated in *Time and Space: A Poetic Autobiography,* 1988), first published in the periodical *Poesía Española* in April 1954 and as a book in 1982. For a writer who had maintained since 1918 that good poetry is inevitably brief and that inspiration must always be subject to the control of intelligence, *Espacio* seems revolutionary, for its length is inordinate and its content the result of a pell-mell association of ideas that, in places, bears a resemblance to automatic writing.

In *Espacio,* Jiménez ruminates on all his usual themes and employs all the tried-and-true symbols to recap his career. The large, flat, lowland space of the Florida Everglades is no more infinite than the space in his mind, and the homesick poet allows images of the past to blend into the present. The sound of a barking dog is the same in Madrid, New York City, or Miami. Again the creative mind becomes the locus for meaning; identification and memory, out of the past, take shape only in the present. External space is internalized and expressed in the flow of time. The lines relentlessly move onward, impelled by the technique of association: the poet is not only the present but also a torrent of flight, an eternal succession of impressions and memories.

If there is a link between the first two fragments of *Espacio,* it is the theme of love, which is the single constant. The third fragment, concluded in Puerto Rico in 1954, well after *Animal de fondo,* opens with a series of recondite personal allusions, goes on to equate destiny with life and death, recounts how the poet demolished a crab on the beach, and concludes with a humanistic cry asking how a soul can leave a body that has loved it. Repeating the opening line of the first fragment, he proclaims once more the insight of *Animal de fondo:* "Los dioses no tuvieron mas sustancia de la que tengo yo" (The gods had no more substance than I).

The Jiménezes moved to Puerto Rico in 1951 and remained there until their deaths. Its benign climate, associations with Camprubí Aymar's past, and above all the return to a Spanish-speaking environment influenced the poet in the last few active years of his life. He donated his papers and books to the University of Puerto Rico at Río Piedras, taught a course on modernism there in 1953, and continued to write and publish poetry along the lines of *Animal de fondo.* The latter he intended to incorporate into a larger book to be called *Dios deseado y deseante* (published posthumously in 1964; translated as *God Desired and Dying,* 1987). But he was about to lose his loyal and devoted helpmate: Camprubí Aymar, who had undergone an operation for cancer in 1951, worsened after a period of remission. On 28 October 1956, just three days after the Swedish Academy voted to award Jiménez the Nobel Prize in Literature, she died. Jaime Benítez, the president of the University of Puerto Rico, attended the Nobel award ceremonies on behalf of Jiménez and read a short acceptance speech in which the poet expressed his debt to his wife. With her death, he became increasingly withdrawn and more or less ceased to write, so the Nobel Prize had no effect on his career. The prize was, however, celebrated by the Latin American community, which felt that the award also represented the achievements of Antonio Machado and Federico García Lorca and encouraged the reception of such writers as Gabriel García Márquez and Pablo Neruda. In his last years, Jiménez occasionally visited the room at the university that housed his papers, stared at his wife's photos, and awaited his own death. It came finally on 29 May 1958.

Letters:

The Literary Collaboration and the Personal Correspondence of Rubén Darío and Juan Ramón Jiménez, edited by Donald F. Fogelquist (Coral Gables, Fla.: University of Miami Press, 1956);

Monumento de amor: Cartas de Zenobia Camprubí y Juan Ramón Jiménez, edited by Ricardo Gullón (San Juan, P.R.: Ediciones de la Torre, 1959);

Cartas, primera selección, edited by Francisco Garfias (Madrid: Aguilar, 1962);

Selección de cartas (Barcelona: Picazo, 1973);

Cartas literarias, edited by Garfias (Barcelona: Bruguera, 1977);

Cartas de Juan Ramón Jiménez al poeta malagueño José Sánchez Rodríguez: Relaciones literarias entre dos jóvenes poetas, edited by Antonio Sánchez Trigueros (Granada: Don Quijote, 1984);

Cartas: Antología, edited by Garfias (Madrid: Espasa-Calpe, 1992).

Interviews:

Ricardo Gullón, *Conversaciones con Juan Ramón Jiménez* (Madrid: Taurus, 1958).

Bibliography:

Antonio Campoamor González, *Bibliografía general de Juan Ramón Jiménez* (Madrid: Taurus, 1982; revised and expanded edition, Moguer: Fundación Juan Ramón Jiménez, 1999).

Biographies:

Francisco Garfias, *Juan Ramón Jiménez* (Madrid: Taurus, 1958);

Ricardo Gullón, *El último Juan Ramón* (Madrid: Alfaguara, 1968);

Graciela Palau de Nemes, *Vida y obra de Juan Ramón Jiménez: La poesía desnuda,* 2 volumes (Madrid: Gredos, 1975);

Antonio González Campoamor, *Vida y poesía de Juan Ramón Jiménez* (Madrid: Sedmay, 1976);

Palau de Nemes, *Inicios de Zenobia y Juan Ramón Jiménez en América* (Madrid: Fundación Universitaria Española, 1982);

Ignacio Prat, *El muchacho despatriado: Juan Ramón Jiménez en Francia (1901)* (Madrid: Taurus, 1986);

Juan Guerrero Ruiz, *Juan Ramón de viva voz*, 2 volumes (Valencia: Pre-Textos, 1998–1999);

Enrique González Duro, *Biografía interior de Juan Ramón Jiménez* (Madrid: Ediciones Libertarias, 2002);

Rafael Alarcón Sierra, *Juan Ramón Jiménez: Pasión perfecta* (Madrid: Espasa-Calpe, 2003).

References:

Aurora de Albornoz, ed., *Juan Ramón Jiménez* (Madrid: Taurus, 1980);

Zenobia Camprubí de Jiménez, *Diario*, 2 volumes, edited by Graciela Palau de Nemes (Madrid: Alianza / Río Piedras: Universidad de Puerto Rico, 1991, 1995);

Camprubí de Jiménez, *Vivir con Juan Ramón*, edited by Arturo del Villar (Madrid: Los Libros de Fausto, 1986);

Richard A. Cardwell, *Juan R. Jiménez: The Modernist Apprenticeship, 1895–1900* (Berlin: Colloquium, 1977);

Melvyn Coke-Enguídanos, *Word and Work in the Poetry of Juan Ramón Jiménez* (London: Tamesis, 1982);

Leo R. Cole, *The Religious Instinct in the Poetry of Juan Ramón Jiménez* (Oxford: Dolphin, 1967);

Angel Crespo, *Juan Ramón Jiménez y la pintura* (Río Piedras: University of Puerto Rico, 1974);

Estudios sobre Juan Ramón Jiménez (Mayagüez: University of Puerto Rico, 1981);

Donald F. Fogelquist, *Juan Ramón Jiménez* (Boston: Twayne, 1976);

María Teresa Font, *"Espacio": Autobiografía lírica de Juan Ramón Jiménez* (Madrid: Insula, 1972);

Bernardo Gicovate, *La poesía de Juan Ramón Jiménez: Obra en marcha* (Barcelona: Ariel, 1973);

Angel González, *Juan Ramón Jiménez* (Madrid: Júcar, 1974);

Ricardo Gullón, *Estudios sobre Juan Ramón Jiménez* (Buenos Aires: Losada, 1960);

William Kluback, *Encounters with Juan Ramón Jiménez* (New York: Peter Lang, 1995);

Paul R. Olson, *Circle of Paradox: Time and Essence in the Poetry of Juan Ramón Jiménez* (Baltimore: Johns Hopkins University Press, 1967);

Michael P. Predmore, *La obra en prosa de Juan Ramón Jiménez* (Madrid: Gredos, 1966);

Predmore, *La poesía hermética de Juan Ramón Jiménez: El "Diario" como centro de su mundo poético* (Madrid: Gredos, 1973);

Antonio Sánchez-Barbudo, *La segunda época de Juan Ramón Jiménez (1916–1953)* (Madrid: Gredos, 1962);

Ceferino Santos-Escudero, *Símbolos y dios en el último Juan Ramón Jiménez: El influjo oriental en "Dios deseado y deseante"* (Madrid: Gredos, 1975);

Carlos del Saz-Orozco, *Dios en Juan Ramón* (Madrid: Razón & Fe, 1966);

John C. Wilcox, *Self and Image in Juan Ramón Jiménez* (Urbana: University of Illinois Press, 1987);

Howard T. Young, "La fina y dulce Luisa," *Unidad* [Moguer] (February 2000): 25–36;

Young, *Juan Ramón Jiménez* (New York: Columbia University Press, 1967);

Young, *The Line in the Margin: Juan Ramón Jiménez and His Readings in Blake, Shelley, and Yeats* (Madison: University of Wisconsin Press, 1980).

Papers:

Juan Ramón Jiménez's manuscripts, letters, memorabilia, and personal library are held in three separate collections: the Archivo Histórico Nacional of Madrid; the Casa Municipal de Cultura "Zenobia y Juan Ramón Jiménez" in Moguer; and the "Sala Zenobia y Juan Ramón Jiménez" in the Biblioteca General, Río Piedras, University of Puerto Rico.

1956 Nobel Prize in Literature Presentation Speech

by Hjalmar Gullberg, Member of the Swedish Academy

A long life consecrated to poetry and to beauty has been honoured this year with the Nobel Prize in Literature. He is an old gardener, this Juan Ramón, who has dedicated half a century to the creation of a new rose, a white mystical rose, which will bear his name.

Jardines lejanos (Distant Gardens), 1904, is one of his books from the beginning of the century. In the southern parts of Andalusia, far off the route from Jerez to Seville well known to Swedish tourists, the poet was born in 1881. But his poetry is not a strong and intoxicating wine, and his work not a grandiose mosque turned into a cathedral. It makes you think, rather, of one of those gardens circled by high, whitewashed walls which you see marking a landscape. He who stops a moment and goes in with his camera runs the risk of being deceived. There is nothing singular or picturesque here, only the usual things: fruit trees and the air which vibrates on passing through them, the pond that reflects the sun and the moon, a bird singing. No small minaret has been transformed into an ivory tower in this fertile garden planted in the soil of Arab culture. But the visitor who lingers will notice that the passivity within the walls is deceiving, that the isolation is only of the circumstantial and transitory, of what pretends to be present. He will not fail to observe that the rose has a radiance which demands sharper senses and a new sensibility. There is a beauty which is more than the play and delight of the senses; in front of the visitor the silent gardener suddenly appears like a strict director of souls. At the entrance of the Juanramonian garden the tourist ought to observe the same rules as on entering a mosque: wash his hands and rinse his mouth in the fountain for ablutions, take off his shoes, etc.

The year in which Ramón Jiménez began to publish his melodious verses was, in the history of Spain, a year for an examination of conscience. On December 10, 1898, in Paris, was signed the treaty with the United States by which Spain lost Cuba, Puerto Rico, and the Philippines, as well as what remained of its navy and its prestige. By a stroke of the pen the remnants of a whole colonial empire were eliminated. In Madrid a group of writers took up the pen to reconquer, in their fashion, the world within the boundaries of Spain. Some of them ultimately attained their goals. The Machado brothers, Valle-Inclán, and Unamuno were among them. The "modernists," as they called themselves, had in turn grouped themselves around their leader, the Nicaraguan Rubén Darío, visiting in Spain. It was Darío also who, at the beginning of the century, sponsored the first book of verses of the new poet, Juan Ramón Jiménez, a book which bore the scarcely martial title, *Almas de violeta* (Souls of Violet), 1900.

He was not an audacious creator who would present himself on stage in full light. His song arrived, timid and intimate, from a penumbral background, and spoke of the moon and of melancholy with echoes of Schumann and Chopin. He wept with Heine and with his countryman, inspired by Heine, Gustavo Adolfo Bécquer, the exquisite poet to whom some short-sighted admirers gave the name, "golden-haired Nordic King." In the manner of Verlaine he murmured his *Arias tristes* (Sad Arias), 1903, in a half-voice. When, little by little but with sure step, he had freed himself from the gentle, captivating arms of French symbolism, the characteristic features of music and intimacy would remain forever impressed on him.

Music and painting—we can note that, in Seville, the young student also studied to be a painter. Just as we speak of the blue and rose periods of Picasso, who was born in the same year, as the historians of literature have called attention to the predominance of different colours in the work of Ramón Jiménez. To the first period belong all the poems in yellow and green—the famous green poem of his disciple García Lorca has its origin here. Later, white predominates, and the nakedness of white characterizes the brilliant, decisive epoch which includes what has been called the second poetic style of Juan Ramón. Here we witness the long period of plenitude of a poet of light. Far off are the melancholy mood-pictures, far off also the anecdotal themes. The poems treat only of poetry and love, and of the landscape and the sea which are identified with poetry and love. A formal asceticism carried to perfection, rejecting every exterior embellishment of the verse, will be the road that will lead to the simplicity that is the supreme form of art, the poetry that the poet calls naked.

This "second style of Juan Ramón" reaches its full development in *Diario de un poeta recién casado* (Diary of a Newly-Wed Poet) in 1917. In this year the newly-wed poet made his first trip to America and his diary is full of an infinite feeling for the sea, full of oceanic poetry. His books *Eternidades* (Eternities), 1918, and *Piedra y cielo* (Stone and Sky), 1919 mark new stages toward the longed-for identification of the "I" with the world; poetry and thought have the purpose of finding "the exact name for things." Gradually the poems become more concise, naked, transparent; they are, in fact, maxims and aphorisms of the mystical poetics of Juan Ramón.

In his constant zeal to surpass previous achievements, Ramón Jiménez has made a clean slate of his earliest production and has radically modified old poems, gathering those meriting his approval into extensive anthologies. After his volumes *Belleza* (Beauty) and *Poesía* (Poetry) in 1923, in his zeal to experiment with new forms, he abandoned the publication of his works in book form and often published without title or author's name, in the form of sheets or leaflets scattered by the wind. In 1936 the civil war interrupted the projected edition of his works in twenty-one volumes. *Animal de fondo* (Animal of Depth), 1949, the last book from his period of exile, is, if read by itself, a sample of a work in progress. Today, therefore, it is still premature to discuss this phase which, in literary history, will perhaps carry the title "the last style of Juan Ramón."

Far away, in what was the colony of Puerto Rico, he is afflicted today by an immense sorrow. It will not be possible for us to see his thin face with its profound eyes and to ask ourselves if it has been taken directly from a painting by El Greco. We find a less solemn self-portrait in the delightful book, *Platero y yo* (Platero and I), 1914. There, dressed in mourning, the poet passes with his Nazarene beard, riding his little donkey while the gypsy children shout at the top of their voices: The madman! The madman! The madman! . . . And in truth it is not always easy to distinguish a madman from a poet. But for like spirits the madness of this man has been eminent wisdom. Rafael Alberti, Jorge Guillén, Pedro Salinas, and others who have written their names in the recent history of Spanish poetry have been his disciples; Federico García Lorca is one of them, and so are the Latin American poets, with Gabriela Mistral at their head. I cite the statement of a Swedish journalist on being informed of the Nobel Prize in Literature for this year: "Juan Ramón Jiménez is a born poet, one of those who are born one day with the same simplicity with which the sun's rays shine, one who purely and simply has been born and has given of himself, unconscious of his natural talents. We do not know when such a poet is born. We know only that one day we find him, we see him, we hear him, just as one day we see a plant flower. We call this a miracle."

In the annals of the Nobel Prize, Spanish literature has been one of the distant gardens. Very rarely have we cast a glance inside. This year's laureate is the last survivor of the famous "generation of 1898." For a generation of poets on both sides of the ocean which separates, and at the same time, unites the Hispanic countries, he has been a master—the master, in effect. When the Swedish Academy renders homage to Juan Ramón Jiménez, it renders homage also to an entire epoch in the glorious Spanish literature.

[© The Nobel Foundation, 1956.]

Jiménez: Banquet Speech

Introductory remarks by R. Granit, Member of the Royal Academy of Sciences, at the Nobel Banquet at the Swedish Academy in Stockholm, 10 December 1956:

Juan Ramón has been called a poet for poets, but the layman can approach him if willing first to partake passively of the sheer visual beauty of his landscape, lovely Andalusia, its birds, its flowers, pomegranates, and oranges. Once inside his world, by leisurely reading and rereading, one gradually awakens to a new "living insight" into it, refreshed by the depth and richness of a rare poetical imagination. While doing so I recalled a conversation between the painter Degas and the poet Mallarmé, as related by Paul Valéry. Degas, struggling with a sonnet, complained of the difficulties, and finally exclaimed: "And yet I do not lack ideas . . ." Mallarmé with great mildness replied: "But Degas, one does not create poetry with ideas. One does it with words." If ever there has been inspired use of words, it is in Juan Ramón Jiménez's poetry, and in this sense he is a poet for poets. This is probably also the reason why, within the whole Spanish-speaking world, he is regarded as the teacher and master.

The literary awards may involve decisions more difficult than the scientific ones. Yet we should be grateful to the founder for having included a literary Prize in his will. It adds dignity to the other awards and to the act itself; it emphasizes the human and cultural element which the two worlds of creative imagination have in common; and perhaps, in the end, it expresses deeper insights than scientists can ever achieve.

As Jiménez was unable to be present, the speech was read by Jaime Benitez, Rector of the University of Puerto Rico

Juan Ramón Jiménez has given me the following message to convey to you:

"I accept with gratitude the undeserved honour which this illustrious Swedish Academy has seen fit to bestow upon me. Besieged by sorrow and sickness, I must remain in Puerto Rico, unable to participate directly in the solemnities. And so that you may have the living testimony of my own intimate feelings gathered in day-by-day association of friendship firmly established in this land of Puerto Rico, I have asked Rector Jaime Benitez of its University, where I am a member of the faculty, to be my personal representative before you in all ceremonies connected with the Nobel Prize awards of 1956."

I have found such affection for Juan Ramón Jiménez and such understanding for his works that I trust you will excuse me if I single out for special thanks one among you so wise and penetrating that I am certain all others will be glad to be recognized in him. I refer to your own great poet Hjalmar Gullberg, whose presentation this afternoon we shall always remember and whose rendition of Juan Ramón Jiménez' poetry has brought to the Scandinavian people the clear purity of our Andalusian master.

Juan Ramón Jiménez has asked me also to say this: "My wife Zenobia is the true winner of this Prize. Her companionship, her help, her inspiration made, for forty years, my work possible. Today, without her, I am desolate and helpless."

I have heard from the trembling lips of Juan Ramón Jiménez some of the most touching expressions of despair. For Juan Ramón is such a poet that his every word reflects his own internal kingdom. We fervently hope that someday his sorrow will be expressed in writing and that the memory of Zenobia will provide renewed and everlasting inspiration to that great master of Hispanic letters, Juan Ramón Jiménez, whom you have honoured so signally today.

[© The Nobel Foundation, 1956.]

Eyvind Johnson
(29 July 1900 – 25 August 1976)

Monica Setterwall Wranne
The Eyvind Johnson Society, Stockholm

This entry was expanded by Wranne from her Johnson entry in *DLB 259: Twentieth-Century Swedish Writers Before World War II.*

BOOKS: *De fyra främlingarna* (Stockholm: Tiden, 1924);
Timans och rättfärdigheten (Stockholm: Bonnier, 1925);
Stad i mörker (Stockholm: Bonnier, 1927);
Lettre recommandée (Paris: Collection européenne, 1927); original Swedish published as *Stad i ljus: En historia från Paris* (Stockholm: Tiden, 1928);
Minnas (Stockholm: Bonnier, 1928); expanded as *Herr Clerk vår mästare: En gruppering,* edited by Örjan Lindberger (Stockholm: Atlantis, 1998);
Kommentar till ett stjärnfall (Stockholm: Bonnier, 1929);
Avsked till Hamlet: En historia om en ungdom (Stockholm: Bonnier, 1930);
Natten är här (Stockholm: Bonnier, 1932);
Bobinack (Stockholm: Bonnier, 1932);
Regn i gryningen (Stockholm: Bonnier, 1933);
Än en gång, kapten! (Stockholm: Bonnier, 1934);
Nu var det 1914 (Stockholm: Bonnier, 1934); translated by Mary Sandbach as *1914* (London: Adam, 1970);
Här har du ditt liv! (Stockholm: Bonnier, 1935);
Se dig inte om! (Stockholm: Bonnier, 1936);
Slutspel i ungdomen (Stockholm: Bonnier, 1937);
Nattövning (Stockholm: Bonnier, 1938);
Den trygga världen (Stockholm: Bonnier, 1940);
Soldatens återkomst (Stockholm: Bonnier, 1940);
Grupp Krilon (Stockholm: Bonnier, 1941);
Krilons resa (Stockholm: Bonnier, 1942);
Krilon själv (Stockholm: Bonnier, 1943);
Sju liv (Stockholm: Bonnier, 1944);
Som en av våra egna: Ett samtal om norska böcker och svenska, by Johnson and Sigurd Hoel (Stockholm: Bonnier, 1944);
Romanen om Olof (Stockholm: Bonnier, 1945)—comprises *Nu var det 1914, Här har du ditt liv!, Se dig inte om!,* and *Slutspel i ungdomen;*

Eyvind Johnson (Hulton Archive/Getty Images)

Pan mot Sparta: Fem noveller med klassiskt motiv (Copenhagen: Folmer Christensen, 1946; Stockholm: Bonnier, 1946);
Strändernas svall: En roman om det närvarande (Stockholm: Bonnier, 1946); translated by M. A. Michael as *Return to Ithaca: The Odyssey Retold as a Modern Novel* (London & New York: Thames & Hudson, 1952);
Krilon: En roman om det sannolika (Stockholm: Bonnier, 1948)—comprises *Grupp Krilon, Krilons resa,* and *Krilon själv;*

Strändernas svall: Ett drama i tre akter och ett antal bilder om den återvändande (Stockholm: Bonnier, 1948);
Dagbok från Schweiz, 1947–1949 (Stockholm: Bonnier, 1949);
Drömmar om rosor och eld (Stockholm: Bonnier, 1949); translated by Erik J. Friis as *Dreams of Roses and Fire* (New York: Hippocrene, 1984);
Lägg undan solen (Stockholm: Bonnier / Helsinki: Schildt, 1951);
Romantisk berättelse (Stockholm: Bonnier, 1953);
Vinterresa i Norrbotten (Stockholm: Bonnier, 1955);
Tidens gång: En romantisk berättelse (Stockholm: Bonnier, 1955);
Molnen över Metapontion (Stockholm: Bonnier, 1957);
Vägar över Metaponto: En resedagbok (Stockholm: Bonnier, 1959);
Hans nådes tid (Stockholm: Bonnier, 1960); translated by Elspeth Harley Schubert as *The Days of His Grace* (London: Chatto & Windus, 1968);
Spår förbi Kolonos: En berättelse (Stockholm: Bonnier, 1961);
Livsdagen lång: En roman, berättad i Rom (Stockholm: Bonnier, 1964);
Stunder, vågor: berättelser från resor (Stockholm: Bonnier, 1964);
Favel ensam (Stockholm: Bonnier, 1968);
Några steg mot tystnaden: En roman om fångna (Stockholm: Bonnier, 1973);
Personligt, Politiskt, Estetiskt, edited by Örjan Lindberger (Stockholm: Bonnier, 1992).

PLAY PRODUCTIONS: *Strändernas svall,* Linköping, Linköpings Stadsteater, 10 November 1948;
Musik för stråkar och Nausikaa ensam, text by Johnson, music by Ingvar Lidholm, Eklidens skola, Nacka, September 1971.

PRODUCED SCRIPTS: *Den respektfulla skökan,* television, translation of Jean-Paul Sartre's *La Putain respectueuse,* Sveriges Radio TV, 7 October 1960;
Smutsiga händer, television, translation of Sartre's *Les Mains sales,* Sveriges Radio TV, 2 September 1963;
Stängda dörrar, television, translation of Sartre's *Huis clos,* Sveriges Television 2, 10 November 1981.

OTHER: *Håndslag: Fakta og orientering for nordmenn,* edited by Johnson (Stockholm, 1942–1945).

SELECTED PERIODICAL PUBLICATION—UNCOLLECTED: Text for *Musik för stråkar och Nausikaa ensam, Prisma,* new series 6 (1948).

Eyvind Johnson's work is central to Swedish fiction of the twentieth century. The richness of his prose, his experiments with narrative form, his erudition in humanist fields, and his aversion to oppression and tyranny made his writings a catalyst of the social and political upheaval in Sweden and in Europe. Many of his novels feature historical settings that depict almost all centuries of European history, including ancient eras of legends and sagas such as that of Odysseus. Yet, whatever the fictional time frame, Johnson is ultimately concerned with the human condition of the narrative present. The trademark of his narrative art is his distinctive mingling of realism with fantasy. The appreciation of Johnson's novels by critics has come about gradually, with their deepening respect and admiration, and over the course of his career he received many literary prizes. In 1974 he and the poet Harry Martinson, a close friend, shared the Nobel Prize in Literature.

Johnson's life and work are the more remarkable because of the modest circumstances of his provenance. Eyvind Olof Verner Johnson was born on 29 July 1900 in the village of Björkelund, just outside the city of Boden, far north in Sweden. (Some sources list his birthplace as Svartbjörnsbyn, but he only went to school there for a few years.) His parents, Olof Petter Johnson and Cevia Gustafsdotter Johnson, had come from southern Sweden, having worked their way north with the construction of the railroad; his father cut stones for the railroad tracks, and his mother baked bread for the navvies. The Johnsons were immigrants, in a sense, to the sparsely populated areas and rugged landscape of Norrbotten. Young Eyvind and his four siblings grew up with tales of wonder about southern Sweden, where apples and pears were said to grow freely and bread was made with wheat flour.

While the family was living in Björkelund, Olof Johnson became ill and unable to work. The family's already strained finances grew desperate, and Johnson soon became the foster child of his mother's sister and her husband, also a quarryman, who had no children of their own. At first they lived in a house across the road from Johnson's mother and father in Björkelund. In 1913, however, the boy and his foster parents moved north with the railroad to Näsberg, a settlement of a few cottages close to a stone quarry. Johnson worked with the grown men in the quarry and also spent time trekking in the wilderness. After a couple of years he left his foster parents' home and started walking south along the railroad tracks, his belongings in a birch-bark backpack.

Johnson spent the next four years doing sundry jobs in the Boden and Luleå areas and experienced hard times. World War I worsened the insecurity of the Swedish economy; the welfare system—for which Sweden was later lauded—was still twenty years away. Johnson worked as a logger, a sawmill worker, a brickyard laborer, a farmhand picking potatoes, and a projectionist in a movie theater, eventually joining the workers' union. He also read voraciously. He first became acquainted with Homer's *Odyssey* (circa 800–700 B.C.) while screening movies in the projection booth. Johnson portrayed this period of social and intellectual discovery, of survival and maturation, in a series of novels he wrote in the the 1930s, beginning with *Nu var det 1914* (1934; translated as *1914*, 1970). Although he did not explicitly call them autobiographical, Johnson nonetheless shared much with their protagonist, a teenager named Olof, such as bouts of hard physical labor, loneliness and wandering, odd jobs, the love of reading, and a growing awareness of the power of words.

In 1919 in Boden, Johnson joined the Young Socialists, a political group that had broken away from the Social Democratic Party in 1908 because of differing attitudes toward social injustice. In his articles that appeared between 1919 and 1924 in the periodical of the Young Socialists, *Brand* (Fire), Johnson's political views and growing social consciousness show the influence of the Russian philosopher Petr Kropotkin's nonviolent anarchism. Kropotkin's belief that society could be changed without violence remained for years a challenge and a central issue for Johnson, who continually sought ways to oppose all forms of tyranny. Indeed, in the early 1920s, Johnson in his writings was already warning against the nascent Nazi movement in Germany.

Johnson's contacts with young anarcho-syndicalists enabled him to move to Stockholm in 1919, and two years later he hid in the cargo hold of a ship on its way to Hamburg; he spent most of the 1920s in Germany and France. While Johnson experienced much material hardship and sometimes verged on starvation in post–World War I Berlin and Paris, he also came of age as a writer during this period. Living in an environment rich in original literary ideas, he often encountered larger-than-life people—many of them survivors from the war who later reappeared as characters in his novels. Yet, a shortage of means prompted Johnson to return to Sweden in 1923. For a year he was politically active as secretary of the Young Socialists in Stockholm. He also published a collection of short stories, *De fyra främlingarna* (1924, The Four Strangers), in which the main character of each story is a misfit in society and lacks the energy necessary to solve his particular dilemma. Some reviewers of the book overemphasized the theme of social outcasts and ridiculed the inability of Johnson's characters to help themselves.

Johnson's first novel, *Timans och rättfärdigheten* (1925, Timans and Righteousness), was written during a return visit to the province of Norrbotten and his foster parents' cottage in Näsberg. The protagonist, Stig Timans, is well-to-do but nevertheless alienated from society. While he feels genuine solidarity with the poor, he cannot engage himself constructively to help them; he is unable to take action against social injustice. One of his father's employees, and a friend of Stig's, struggles for workers' rights and is shot in the process, without Stig coming to his assistance. The themes of guilt, solidarity, and the inability to take decisive action in a postwar world of confusion recall the circumstances of William Shakespeare's Hamlet and recur in several of Johnson's novels of the 1920s and 1930s. A few of the reviewers recognized Johnson's experiences in Berlin and Paris as an extra dimension in the narrative and commended the intensity of his prose. Upon receiving the advance payment for *Timans och rättfärdigheten*, Johnson was able to buy a typewriter and a ticket to return to Berlin and Paris.

Between 1926 and 1930 in France, Johnson's irregular means of subsistence amounted to the meager remunerations he received for articles submitted to Swedish magazines. His increasing knowledge of French language and literature, however, and his contacts with French writers and intellectuals motivated him to experiment with the narrative form. On a tour southwest to the Bay of Biscayne he saw the sea for the first time. Back in Paris he married a young Norwegian girl, Aase Christoffersen, and together they made their home in St. Leu-la-Forêt, just north of Paris, until 1930, when they moved back to Sweden. Despite the couple's financial hardship, these years were relatively calm and full of writing for Johnson. In late 1927, however, he suffered a heavy personal loss when his youngest and closest brother, Tore, died in a hospital in Cassadaga, New York, from tuberculosis. Through their correspondence, Johnson knew that Tore's lungs were afflicted; he took severely to heart the fact that he had not been able to help his brother in time.

Johnson set his next novel, *Stad i mörker* (1927, Town in Darkness), in a small town in northern Sweden, where the freezing winter, the seemingly eternal nights, and the gossip provide the background for the three protagonists. Their lives and reflections represent facets of the writer's own persona in his attempts to come to terms with harsh living conditions. The interlacing of multiple voices also points up Johnson's interest in the instrumentation of music, an early example of a narrative method that he developed in future novels. As in *Stad i mörker,* the act of reconciling oneself with personal hardships is central in *Stad i ljus* (1928, City in Light). Although Johnson submitted the novel in late 1926 for publication, it did not appear in Sweden until 1928. In the meantime, however, *Stad i ljus* was translated into French by Johnson's friend the journalist Victor Vinde and published in Paris as *Lettre recommandée*

(1927, Registered Letter). Johnson presents a dilemma closely modeled on his own: the endless walking of a hungry writer, Torsten, on the streets of Paris, while he awaits a registered letter from Sweden with money for articles submitted. There appear to be two main characters whose voices blend intermittently: Torsten and the city of Paris itself. Johnson's avid reading of Knut Hamsun, Marcel Proust, Henri Bergson, and Sigmund Freud influenced the quality of his prose, his use of psychological time versus physical time, and his portrayal of Torsten as a conglomerate of irrational impulses.

Johnson's next work, the novel *Minnas* (1928, Remembering), was long in the making, since his brother's death in 1927 had delayed the author's writing process. The original title, "Herr Clerk, vår mästare" (Mr. Clerk, Our Master), refers to a double setting: part of the story is set in a small northern town, the other part in Heaven. On Earth, Clerk is the town librarian, and, in Heaven, God is portrayed as a sea captain who tries to keep Earth on a steady course. Clerk in his world of books and God in his supreme position both have an advantageous survey of the human condition and thus a clear view of the desirable outcome of events. Nevertheless, they share the predicament of not being able to avoid disasters. The two parts of Heaven and Earth made the manuscript unwieldy, however, and Johnson eventually deleted all of the heavenly setting, renaming the novel *Minnas*. The deleted parts were later published as part of *Spår förbi Kolonos* (1961, Traces Past Kolonos). Finally, in 1998 the full text of the novel was published under its original title. By the time *Minnas* came out, Johnson was well aware of the stream-of-consciousness technique for which James Joyce was known, although he did not actually read Joyce's novel *Ulysses* (1922) until 1929. In Johnson's novel a character's inner drama is reflected through his or her own turbulent, fragmented thoughts. Early examples of interior monologues, illustrating the psychological probing of a character, also appear in the short story "Svår stund" (1928, Difficult Moment), which was collected later in *Än en gång, kapten!* (1934, Once Again, Captain!), Johnson's third volume of short stories.

Johnson frequently employs interior monologues in his next novel, *Kommentar till ett stjärnfall* (1929, Commentary to a Falling Star). Stormdal, a fruit wholesaler, grows uncontrollably tense to the point of a mental breakdown. His elation at receiving an order—the falling star of the title—stands in vivid contrast to his fixation on bananas. His wife, Laura, brings in a psychiatrist whose questions aggravate rather than help Stormdal, and once his fixation develops into a craze, he is confined to an asylum. The narrative embodies several parallel subplots and characters, such as Stormdal's two sons—Magnus Lyck and Andreas Sonath—by two different mistresses. Magnus and Andreas are in many ways each other's opposites, and, if considered in tandem, they represent various aspects, strengths and weaknesses, of the writer's own persona. Viewing communism as a solution to social injustice, Magnus protests against the bourgeois values of his father; yet, not a committed political activist, he is in search of deeper beliefs. Through childhood memories and, most importantly, a proximity to the primal forces of nature, Magnus eventually finds his source of strength. Andreas, on the other hand, with his good looks and his sense of music (he plays the piano), has no qualms about other people's misfortunes. Sailing through the pleasures of life, he allows women of means to provide for him—Stormdal's own wife being one of them.

Many of the story lines in *Kommentar till ett stjärnfall* intersect with each other; however, although the characters are portrayed with deep psychological insight, they remain essentially apart, disparate, and thus unable to understand one another. The novel represented a breakthrough in terms of critical reception. Reviewers acclaimed the book for Johnson's modern, dynamic characterization of individuals whom the reader sees from inside their thoughts and caprices. Not only was this use of the interior monologue considered a first in Swedish fiction, but also, for the first time in a novel, Stockholm was portrayed as a big city full of lonely people.

Johnson wrote his subsequent work, *Avsked till Hamlet: En historia om en ungdom* (1930, Farewell to Hamlet: A Story of a Youth), in only a couple of months. He considered the novel unfinished but was unable to explore its contents further because they approached too closely his own sorrow and a sense of having failed his brother. The narrative incorporates characters whose relationship as siblings parallels the closeness that Eyvind and Tore Johnson shared. Mårten Torpare cares deeply for his twin sister, Sigrid, who—lacking the education and financial support that her brother received from his wealthy foster parents—has gone on to lead a carefree, somewhat reckless life. When Sigrid dies in childbirth, Torpare blames himself, believing that he neglected to take responsibility for her and to act on behalf of her welfare. His loss also has a bearing on the choices he makes later in his life. He finally takes action, when he prevents his younger sister, Tora, from running off with a revivalist preacher. In this sense, Hamlet's dilemma—the conflict between inaction and action—informs Johnson's narrative, with Torpare serving as the mouthpiece of the writer himself.

Johnson returned to Sweden in the early 1930s and began working on his next novel, but the writing proved slow. In order to provide for his family (which now included a son, Tore, born in 1928) he had to produce short stories continuously; some of these stories were collected for publication in *Natten är här* (1932, Night Is Here). A few of the stories concern Johnson's experiences in France and Germany after World War I and reflect his affinity at that time for the philosophy of Jean-Jacques Rousseau. For Johnson, with the old European culture gone—its monuments and values having been destroyed by the war—the time was ripe for a new individual, a human being unlike any other, to emerge; Rousseau's creative vitality and unbounded appetite for life affirmed this perspective. Johnson's next novel, *Bobinack* (1932), is named after such an experimental human being. Bobinack is a bewildering man, always present in the center of action but not always for clear reasons. At once loved and feared, he laughs loudly and demonically, as if echoing life in its prime. His energy works like an amoral force, for weak and strong characters alike succumb to his power.

Set in Stockholm, the novel starts with a collision. On a busy street in the city a sudden crash occurs between a tram and an automobile. The characters in the book either witness the event from various vantage points or are involved in the collision; Bobinack himself is watching high up on a bridge across the street. The narrative follows the postcollision movements of the characters, who are gradually shown to be interrelated by marriage, money, or mere acquaintance, and through all of them Bobinack works his destabilizing influence. This collision and Bobinack's machinations elicit Johnson's main reason for writing the novel. Influenced by D. H. Lawrence and his emphasis on natural instincts, Johnson uses *Bobinack* to criticize the attack on primitivism by the cultural establishment of the early 1930s.

Johnson resumed the question of how primitivist ideas might revitalize a stifling bourgeois culture in the novel *Regn i gryningen* (1933, Rain at Dawn). The protagonist, Henrik Fax, breaks with his conventional, middle-class life and tests a return to nature by moving back to the rural circumstances of his childhood and engaging in a love affair. In *Regn i gryningen* Henrik Fax, Torpare, and a writer with the initials E. J. try to come to terms with the fluidity of truth and the question of how far one's instincts should be allowed to go in order to break with societal conventions. Through these three different characters embodied in a single narrator, Johnson illuminates the personal dilemma of working through his own unprocessed memories. *Regn i gryningen* was not well received, however; the indignant critics deplored what they considered to be amoral content and subversive tendencies.

Before writing about his childhood in a series of autobiographical novels, Johnson completed the story collection *Än en gång, kapten!* The motifs in most of these stories are based on his home province of Norrbotten, a setting that—with its seemingly endless miles of forests, marshlands, and mosquitoes—marked a first in Swedish fiction at that time. The collection was a success upon publication.

The novels that Johnson based on his life are *Nu var det 1914; Här har du ditt liv!* (1935, Here Is Your Life!); *Se dig inte om!* (1936, Don't Look Back!); and *Slutspel i ungdomen* (1937, Closing Remarks to Youth). All of these works were republished in one volume, titled *Romanen om Olof* (1945, The Novel about Olof). In each of the four books, Johnson inserts a legend, tale, or folk song. In *Nu var det 1914,* the tale of mist and consumption is a poetic rendering of a social disease, tuberculosis, which was rampant in the poverty-stricken areas of Sweden in the early 1900s. In *Här har du ditt liv!* Johnson weaves a folk song of love and betrayal into the narrative, while in *Se dig inte om!* he derives the tale from a true story about people who were lured from Norrbotten to work in Brazil and promised a life of riches and food in abundance but who died there. In the fourth volume, *Slutspel i ungdomen,* a series of imitations of well-known classics, such as Shakespeare's *Hamlet,* the story of Buffalo Bill, and the nineteenth-century Entwicklung novels, appear in Olof's hallucinatory dreams. Reflecting Johnson's experiments in mixing realism with fantasy to convey harsh conditions, the tales of this tetralogy metaphorically illustrate the Norrbotten inheritance that Olof brings with him into the world. The treasure of stories, legends, songs, and books he has read fosters in him a social concern and a sense of responsibility toward his own learning.

Although some critics regarded the interlacing of fictional reality with saga and folk song as an unsuitable mixture of genres, reviewers in general praised Johnson's autobiographical novels as the best works he had yet written. Some critics pointed out his refreshing approach to autobiographical material and his emphasis on words, rather than on deeds, in describing Olof's growth process. In the beginning Olof reflects and ponders more than he speaks. He listens intently to the sounds of words, but only gradually does he begin to communicate. His delirious fantasies in *Slutspel i ungdomen,* the final book of the tetralogy, are those of a verbal equilibrist well acquainted with the classics.

The issues behind the outbreak of the Spanish Civil War in 1936 caused a heated debate among the media in Sweden. Johnson, along with many other writers and intellectuals, expressed his solidarity with the Spanish Republic against Francisco Franco and the military support given him by Adolf Hitler and Benito Mussolini. Johnson's concern in his earlier novels—to ask pertinent questions rather than provide the answers—was now an intellectual luxury that seemed no longer affordable. His support of the Spanish government troops proved a way for him to express in writing his struggle for freedom and democracy. In *Nattövning* (1938, Night Maneuver), his next novel, the narrator—again named Mårten Torpare, who is a pacifist at heart—contemplates how to fight the Fascists in the Spanish Civil War. Although he was slow to finish writing it, Johnson's ideological stand in *Nattövning* is clear and unequivocal. For Torpare, words in the service of humanist values cannot be used as weapons, while words used as weapons run the risk of becoming simplifications or mere antifascist propaganda. The tumult with which the book was received upon its publication showed how divided the ideologies were in political and literary circles at the time in Sweden. Some critics applauded *Nattövning* for its firm stand against Nazism and Fascism; others called it a hateful book; and still others questioned why a writer of Johnson's caliber stooped to the level of propaganda.

On 25 December 1938 Johnson's wife, Aase Johnson, died suddenly and unexpectedly from pneumonia, and in his grief Johnson was unable to resume writing. At the same time, World War II was drawing nearer. On 1 September 1939 Hitler's troops marched into Poland, and on 30 November the Russians detonated bombs in Helsinki. The coalition government in Sweden gave permission to its citizen voluntaries in December 1939 to fight with Finnish troops against the Russians in Finland. In January 1940 Johnson and his close friend Martinson traveled to northern Sweden to persuade the military troops stationed there to enlist as volunteer soldiers in Finland. The two friends themselves left afterward for Finland. Johnson's second wife, Cilla Frankenhaeuser, hailed from Borgå in Finland; she was Finnish but spoke Swedish. The two were married in June 1940 and went on to have two children: Maria, born in 1944, and Anders, born in 1946.

Appropriately for such a war-stricken time, a call for mutual solidarity between Nordic countries in the face of oppression is the guiding motif of Johnson's next novel. In *Soldatens återkomst* (1940, The Soldier's Return) a soldier is killed on a Swedish country road as he returns from fighting in wars on the European continent. His interior monologue, as he lies dying, is intermittently broken by a story of liquor smuggling and by the notes of Torpare—notes assembled as a series of essays on the defense of human decency against all forms of oppression. As the writer's mouthpiece, Torpare conveys a highly personal account of Johnson's own strengths and weaknesses in the manner of Michel Eyquem de Montaigne, whose writings frequently served as a major source of inspiration to Johnson.

As chief editor of the magazine *Håndslag* (Handshake) from 1942 to 1945, Johnson gave moral support to the resistance movement in Norway during the German occupation. Printed on thin paper, measuring only five-by-seven inches, the magazine was small enough to be smuggled in boots across the Swedish-Norwegian border. Johnson began each issue with an editorial, while the news items were written in Norway.

Upon the completion of his autobiographical novels about Olof, Johnson started on a sizable narrative project that reflects the course of events of World War II as they developed and as they influence the fictional characters. The perspective is Swedish, exposing the official government position of neutrality in contrast to a theme of firm resistance against oppression. The Krilon trilogy, which Johnson wrote between 1941 and 1943, consists of *Grupp Krilon* (1941, Group Krilon), *Krilons resa* (1942, Krilon's Journey), and *Krilon själv* (1943, Krilon Himself). The trilogy spans approximately 1,800 pages and was collected in 1948 as *Krilon: En roman om det sannolika* (Krilon: A Novel about the Probable). The subtitle of the 1948 edition indicates Johnson's ambition to go beyond exact realistic detail. True to his opinion that the shortest road to the truth is located in the realm of the fantastic, Johnson presents examples from the borderline area where the expected gives way to fantasy. On such occasions the conventional rules of time and space cease to exist. The figure in a portrait steps out of its frame and begins playing the piano; the emperor of China is crowned while speaking words of wisdom; and an angel with a long, silvery beard reappears at intervals, soothingly directing the course of events.

The Krilon books indeed incorporate accounts of realism—for example, the reports of Germans torturing their Norwegian prisoners. Johnson's characters react to the official Swedish policy of adapting to German demands in funny, rather satirical renderings. With its examples of resistance against tyranny and oppression, this trilogy may be considered Johnson's military service in words, as the writer himself announces toward the end of the third book. Yet, more importantly, the Krilon narratives make up a novel about courage in the face of persecution.

The plot concerns Krilon, a real estate agent, and an assortment of friends: the cabinetmaker Hovall; the carpenter foreman Minning; the building contractor Jonas Frid; the salesman Arpius; the engineer Odenarp; and the surgeon Segel. All of the men meet regularly to speak on elevated subjects. Soon, new competitors in the real estate business, G. Staph and T. Jekau, encroach on Krilon's market shares and eventually bankrupt him. They resort to dirty tricks, discrediting Krilon behind his back—even setting fire to his office and incriminating him in the blaze. They put pressure on Krilon's friends, until all of them turn against him and gradually come under the sway of Staph, Jekau, and their cohorts. Krilon tries at length to unify his friends—as a group they have power, he reminds them, whereas as individuals they are all defenseless—but he fails and is excluded from the group. His friends soon find out, however, that working for Staph means selling one's soul to the devil. Thus, as a call to resistance in the guise of imperial mildness and wisdom, Krilon sends Hovall an eighteenth-century illustration depicting the coronation of the emperor of China. Krilon then sets off in secret for Norway, crossing the border undetected. He meets with the Norwegian resistance movement and receives reports of torture in Norwegian prisons. On his return he discovers that his closest friend, the Polish artist Isabelle Verolyg, has committed suicide. The carrier pigeon, the sign of his safe mission, had not reached her. In spite of this personal tragedy, Krilon is able to instill new courage in his friends, and they reunite around him. Together, they finally oust Staph and his followers.

Johnson weaves allegory into these narratives of oppression and revenge, embedding certain textual clues through the names of the characters. The name of Krilon's nemesis, G. Staph, phonetically signifies the Gestapo. Staph's underlings, Gören, Göllén, and Höllén, stand for Hermann Göring, Joseph Goebbels, and Heinrich Himmler. T. Jekau approximates "Tjekan," the Swedish transcription of the Soviet secret police, the KGB. The American Frank Lind, who becomes Krilon's ally in the struggle against Staph, stands for Franklin Delano Roosevelt. In the third part of the trilogy, *Krilon själv*, they make their treaty—their Mälar-Charta—in a rowboat of a gray battleship color on Lake Mälaren. Johnson implies that Krilon and his friends represent free states fighting for independence against oppression. In this manner the course of events in World War II and the fates of individual states not only provide the backdrop of fictional reality but also are played out on an allegorical level by the characters themselves. Moreover, Krilon fights against evil for the freedom of being human—a freedom that must be won repeatedly. Johnson's depiction of Krilon's struggle displays deep psychological insight, humor, irony, and his distinctive mingling of fantasy and everyday reality.

The effects of war on the individual psyche is a leitmotiv in Johnson's first novel of the postwar era, *Strändernas svall: En roman om det närvarande* (1946; translated as *Return to Ithaca: The Odyssey Retold as a Modern Novel*, 1952). While its subtitle means "a novel about the present," the narrative is set in the ancient period of Homer's epic poem the *Odyssey*, in which the gods command Odysseus to return home to kill the suitors of his queen, Penelope, thereby achieving divine justice and restoring order on the island of Ithaca. In his version of the epic, Johnson questions the authority of the gods and their sense of justice, for his gods are less than divine and his heroes less than heroic. Johnson's Odysseus is a warrior scarred with memories of battle—recollections that he can barely live with and that make him reluctant to kill again. Eumaeus, the swineherd, voices the central idea of the narrative: violence breeds only violence, and killing the suitors will bring further bloodshed from generation to generation unless Odysseus can replace dictatorship with a more humane system.

The novel opens with Odysseus on the island of Calypso, where he has spent the last seven years and from which he departs by raft at the gods' behest. At the same time, in a second narrative thread, Odysseus's wife, Penelope, waits at home on Ithaca for his return. In a third narrative thread, Odysseus's son, Telemachus, visits Nestor and Menelaus and inquires about his father, who has been absent for nineteen years. Barely surviving a storm at sea, Odysseus is thrown up on the Phaeacian beach and is found by Nausikaa. He spends the evening recounting his adventures at her parents' court, and the next day he returns home to Ithaca to resume his rule on the island.

Johnson develops the role of the narrator, a central preoccupation of his writing, much further in *Strändernas svall*. For example, at the Phaeacian court of Nausikaa's parents, Odysseus does not merely report on the horrors of his warrior past. Instead, he strives to make his listeners understand the harsh reality of what he has seen and done. Odysseus's eagerness to convey his experiences in battle in a vivid and palpable way motivates him—and by extension Johnson—to incorporate the supernatural in his account. Johnson suggests that with glittering touches of the fantastic, the unbelievable can better be grasped. He lets his Odysseus develop into a narrator who moves his audience by his use of intense, graphic images of saga-like events. Johnson's characterization of Odysseus as a potent, skillful storyteller helped *Strändernas svall* receive overwhelmingly positive reviews. The book sold well, enabling the writer and his family to move abroad to the canton of Graubünden in southern Switzerland in 1947.

While living in Switzerland, Johnson wrote his first historical novel, *Drömmar om rosor och eld* (1949; translated as *Dreams of Roses and Fire*, 1984). Set in France in the 1600s, a time of religious and political strife between the Catholics and the Huguenots, the book follows the intrigues deftly maneuvered by Cardinal Richelieu and the Paris court of Louis XIII, with the dowager queen, Maria of Medici, in the center. Johnson's novel is based on actual events in the city of Loudun, involving a Catholic priest whose good looks, arrogance, and keen interests in power and in women got him deeply entangled in political intrigues and ultimately aroused the ire of formidable enemies. Witch-hunts were not uncommon at the time, and the priest, accused of being the devil's henchman, was burned at the stake. The case, eventually considered a miscarriage of justice, has since been widely documented.

Among Johnson's sources for *Drömmar om rosor och eld* was a diary, written in the seventeenth century by Marie Aubin, a girl at the Ursuline convent in Loudun; her nephew had the diary published in Amsterdam in 1716. In the diary Aubin gives a detailed account of some of the exorcist séances. The nuns were said to be possessed by shouting devils, and spectators were invited to witness the séances. One spectator, Daniel Drouin, commented caustically on the faulty Latin that one of the devils used, and the crowd laughed. Johnson employs Drouin's remark as the opening paragraph of *Drömmar om rosor och eld*. As is typical of his narratives, the significance of the echo recurs both in the fictional course of events and as a device for injecting a narrator into the text. Mildly satirical, the narrator of *Drömmar om rosor och eld* has Drouin wander about Loudun in search of another caustic remark that will reverberate throughout the city. Mercilessly, as the voice of posterity, the narrator denounces the testimony left behind by the possessed nuns, by the exorcist priests, and—not least—by de Laubardemont, Richelieu's right-hand man and the tormentor behind the scenes.

Although infused with ambiguity, the character of the persecuted priest, Grainier, is the core concern of the novel. Portrayed by Johnson as someone sincerely in search of the truth, Grainier confesses his sins to the lady of his heart, Madeleine de Brone. The accusations against him are absurd; yet, when the screaming, demonized nuns confront him, he admits to hearing a demonic echo inside himself. In essence, Grainier constitutes a person of both strengths and weaknesses, with a demonic potential for both good and evil. Finally, in contrast to Grainier's inner search for truth is Drouin's commentary in his diary on the historical and fictional events. Drouin's diary gives a hilarious account of his self-delusions as an upright citizen, a deputy judge, and as a person who preserves truth for posterity. Drouin's redeeming feature as a character, however, is his loyalty to Grainier as a friend.

Critics received *Drömmar om rosor och eld* with praise for its historical accuracy and the psychological depth of its character portrayals, stressing the significance of the search for truth. Some reviewers drew parallels with contemporary examples of victims of collective hysteria and intolerance, while others recognized the analogy of seventeenth-century devils to contemporary Nazi and Fascist sympathizers. In addition, critics pointed out that while these radical parties no longer posed overt threats after the war, their oppressive tendencies need to be addressed in the context of the human psyche.

For less than a year, in 1949 and 1950, Johnson and his family stayed outside London in Amersham. The novel he wrote at this time, *Lägg undan solen* (1951, Put Away the Sun), tells about a group of fugitives seeking shelter on a mountaintop somewhere in Europe. The geographic area recalls the border between Switzerland and Italy, a region that was previously the Johnsons' home for two years. As European pawns in the power game of neighboring states, the fugitives are led by Gallo, a follower of Peter Kropotkin's antimilitarist philosophy. Gallo is a revolutionary who has had to put aside his pacifist ideals to fight oppression. A central work in Johnson's authorship, *Lägg undan solen* foreshadows *Hans nådes tid* (1960; translated as *The Days of His Grace,* 1968), the historical novel that Johnson set in the time of Charlemagne.

In 1950 Johnson and his family moved back to Sweden for good. From this point on he considered Stockholm his geographical home base, interrupted only by frequent travels in Europe. In 1951, several years into the Cold War, Uppsala University invited him to give the "vårtal," the annual speech given in celebration of spring. Johnson used the occasion to argue in support of Western democratic ideals and the principles of human rights. His speech affirmed that he sided with the West against the Soviet Union and Eastern Europe and continued his struggle for human freedom against oppression—a perspective that he had voiced as early as the 1920s, with his repeated warnings against Nazism. Many intellectuals and writers in Sweden, however, favored a stance of strict neutrality, a position called "tredje ståndpunkten" (third point of view). Protests erupted, and Johnson's speech was hotly debated.

For some time Johnson had contemplated writing a sequel to the Olof tetralogy, placing the main character—a projection of himself—in the 1920s in Berlin and Paris, cities where Johnson spent formative years as a young man. His next two novels, *Romantisk berättelse* (1953, Romantic Tale) and *Tidens gång: En romantisk berättelse* (1955, The Passage of Time: A Romantic Tale), may thus be called autobiographical in that Johnson sought through writing them an answer to the question of how he became an author. Yet, his methods of answering the question hardly follow the typical definition of autobiography. The narrative is not chronological; it refrains from posing questions as to what really took place; and it does not focus on a single, main character. In looking back on his life in the 1920s in these novels, Johnson essentially depicts three selves. One persona is Yngve Garans, a professional author of bourgeois upbringing, who writes in the 1950s about his recollections of the 1920s. To help him, Yngve has a collection of letters written in the 1920s and given to him by his cousin Greger Garans, a journalist of international repute and the second persona of the novels. Yngve also refers to the diary that Greger kept in the 1920s. The third character is Olle Oper, whose background and appearance coincide closely with those of Olof from the tetralogy.

The central features of the novels are music as a leitmotiv and the merging of past and present, as well as of the three personae. Johnson indicates the leitmotiv of music from the opening pages of *Romantisk berättelse*, in which a few bars from Ludwig van Beethoven's *Appassionata* are presented as notes. The act of Olle giving words to music or describing music in words parallels Johnson's own elation and sense of creativity when he himself listened to music, particularly to Beethoven. The other main theme of these novels is that of coalescence. At the end of *Tidens gång* the three characters—Yngve, Greger, and Olle—seem to merge into one, and the different time frames are subsumed in a continuous present that suggests the influence of the French philosopher Henri Bergson on Johnson. The past and present meld together, becoming a part of each other. This revival of Bergson's theories, popular in the 1920s, has a direct bearing on Johnson's subsequent novels.

Johnson composed his next work, *Vinterresa i Norrbotten* (1955, Winter Journey in Norrbotten), in three weeks, following a visit to his home province. He outlines the scenery of the Norrbotten landscape, his characters, and their interactions in precise detail, with the confidence of one revisiting the past, an integral part of himself. While the book is modest in size, it is indispensable for an understanding of Johnson's sense of his origins.

As was his habit, Johnson had begun his next novel, *Molnen över Metapontion* (1957, The Clouds over Metapontion), before completing *Tidens gång*. The narrative of *Molnen över Metapontion* is propelled by two stories of different time periods with many instances of intersecting plot. Xenophon's *Anabasis* and the Persian War of Cyrus against his brother Artaxerxes provide the background of one story, while life in a German concentration camp, where an archeology professor named Lévy is imprisoned, and the subsequent travels of a surviving prisoner, Klemens Decorbie, make up the other. Moreover, ancient Greece, bounded by Magna Graeca in southern Italy to the west and by Persia to the east, in effect parallels the setting of Decorbie's twentieth-century search in southern Italy for traces of Themistogenes, Xenophon's likely comrade in the Persian expedition.

The situation of the prisoners in the concentration camp contrasts with that of the Greek soldiers whom Artaxerxes' troops imprison after the death of Cyrus. In both situations the power of words is decisive. When Lévy entertains the concentration-camp prisoners with stories of the Greek expedition to Persia, his words fortify the prisoners, allowing them to forget for a time their harsh present. Similarly, Xenophon's speech emboldens his Greek soldiers; strengthened and encouraged, they fight their way back to freedom and eventually return to Greece. Their spirit of resistance gives balance to the bleak, unending cycle of human imprisonment. In Johnson's fictional universe, to persevere and maintain hope is always an option.

In 1957 Johnson was elected a member of the Swedish Academy. At the same time, *Molnen över Metapontion* was received with much interest, particularly because of its use of different time levels in an attempt to create simultaneity. It also captures in vivid detail ancient times in Magna Graeca and in Persia, with analogies to the present.

The theme of power is central in Johnson's next novel, *Hans nådes tid*, in which Charlemagne's rise to power and the building of his empire provide the historical frame of the story. With respect to facts and chronology Johnson adheres to standard historical accounts, but his concern lies with the inhabitants of Longobardia, people confronted by Charlemagne's blatant use of power. In *Hans nådes tid* the Lupigis family—a father and his three sons—live in Forojuli, which is present-day Friuli in northern Italy. The sons are all in love with Angila, the daughter of the local duke, but the youngest, Johannes, bonds with her after extinguishing a spark that had fallen on her lap. The Lupigis men join the duke in an uprising against Charlemagne, but the rebels are easily and mercilessly crushed by the emperor's troops. The duke is killed, and Angila is given as part of the plunder to one of Charlemagne's lackeys; abused in body and soul, she is held prisoner for many years. Johannes, who craves revenge, becomes a secretary to Charlemagne. In this position he is now finally able to free Angila, but she dies on their way home.

Johnson intersperses the fictional present, narrated largely by an anonymous speaker, with different historical periods. The narrator is assisted in his account of the events by the notes and reflections of a much older Johannes, who is casting a backward glance on the events that shaped his and his family's life. The frequent quotations in the text from a fictional ninth-century chronicler provide an additional perspective on the central course of events. Furthermore, the fictional characters tell stories and engage in interior monologues, resulting in several levels of narratives: the official language of the chronicles; the careful, semitransparent language of Johannes as loyal secretary to Charlemagne; and the privacy of interior monologues. This intricate pattern of narration has several functions. Narrators with varying distances from the center of action each explore their own interpretations of what actually took place. The many narrative voices help Johnson question the effects of political and military oppression on individuals. Furthermore, the narrative is rich in symbolic language and supernatural characteristics. In his defense of human dignity and of the struggle to persevere against heavy odds, Johnson further develops his narrative methods of mingling saga and realistic detail and of creating a sense of simultaneity in times past and present.

Spår förbi Kolonos was intended as a travel book about Johnson's journey to Greece in 1961. In addition to writing a diary he returned to his own works from the 1920s and 1930s for material. For example, he included chapters on Heaven that were omitted from the novel *Minnas*. Johnson's explorations of Greek geography and history in *Spår förbi Kolonos* gave him an opportunity to retrace his own life and his development as a novelist.

His next novel, *Livsdagen lång: En roman, berättad i Rom* (1964, Life's Long Day: A Novel, Told in Rome), accentuates time as a theme. He shows how different times or moments through history become proximate to each other through the recurrence of certain characters. In each new historical setting a man and a woman reappear. Just as in *Hans nådes tid,* in which Johannes and Angila are separated by her death on their homeward journey, the young couple in *Livsdagen lång* never unite, although they meet in six different narratives from different centuries. While their names might change, there is something about them that always makes them recognize each other as counterparts before they are separated again. As the subtitle implies through the word *berättad* (told), Johnson gives a frame to the six stories with a conversation held intermittently in narrative time. The conversation is between the Narrator and the Historian, both of whom display characteristics of the author himself. The emphasis is as much on the creative process of telling a story as it is on the recurrent meetings of the young couple, who lead a life of growing independence from the Narrator, often evading him. They finally leave him behind in despair of his role as one who mediates reality; he is left with a sense that all of his life has been a dream. If one keeps in mind that all of Johnson's novels are ultimately statements on his own life as a writer, *Livsdagen lång* may be considered a sequel to *Romanen om Olof, Romantisk berättelse,* and *Tidens gång.*

Favel ensam (1968, Favel Alone) represents an isolated narrator's attempt to come to terms with elusive reality. The setting is, alternatively, Amersham, where Johnson lived from 1949 to 1950, and postwar Berlin, which he revisited in 1967. The names of the two main characters, Favel Hyth and Charlon Loday, are references to Raphael Hythloday in Thomas More's *Utopia* (1516), and the meaning of utopia is a leitmotiv in the conversations between Favel and Loday. Johnson suggests in *Favel ensam* that for survivors of the horrors of World War II, the likelihood of creating a better world seems remote. Favel's search for truth and his insistence on revealing family secrets eventually give way to a sort of utopian awareness. He comes to the conclusion that his contribution to a better society is to protect the next generation from the pain of learning the truth about their family relationships.

Johnson further explores the meaning of utopia in relation to the limits of the human condition in his last novel, *Några steg mot tystnaden: En roman om fångna* (1973, Some Steps toward Silence: A Novel about the Imprisoned). This work forms an intricate pattern of narrative voices from different centuries in Europe, interlacing historical events with elements of saga and legend. Robert Guenole is a retired Swedish lawyer who is interested in his family's history, especially in connection with abuses of power by autocratic rulers. He has asked Andreas Fermier to compile and render a narrative out of his extended research on the Colinet-Guenole family. He instructs that Fermier illuminate in particular two ancestors at certain points in their past: the old mercenary soldier Colinet prior to his involvement in the battle at Nancy in 1477 and the deputy judge André-Saturnin Colinet-Guenole at the time he was pleading a case, from 1804 to 1805. The novel also features a future generation of the Guenole family in the personages of Robert's nephew, Thomas, and Thomas's wife, Nina. Thomas and Nina spend their honeymoon in the town of Pontoro on the Swiss-Italian border shortly after the end of World War II.

Political and spiritual imprisonment mark central motifs in *Några steg mot tystnaden*. In Pontoro, Thomas and Nina are shown photographs of victims of Nazi concentration camps. Another case of imprisonment for political reasons is that of the duke of Enghien, who was accused of treason in a sham trial and executed on Napoleon's orders in 1804. At the same time a group of people in Village-des-Lanciers are wrongfully incriminated as murderers. The fictional character André-Saturnin commits himself to pleading their innocence. Strong forces are against him, however, with more than mere indications that Napoleon hides one crime while allowing another. André-Saturnin fails and is dismissed from his position as a deputy judge, and the prisoners are executed. Nevertheless, for the rest of his life André-Saturnin retains his belief in a better world to come.

A third example of political imprisonment, albeit on the periphery of the narrative, is More's confinement in the Tower of London. In his work *Utopia* (1516), he had promoted religious tolerance. Accordingly, he refused to acknowledge Henry VIII's supremacy over the church, and was executed in 1535. A portrait by Hans Holbein the Younger of one of More's daughters, Cecily Heron, assumes special significance in the narrative. Although in the painting Cecily's eyes appear turned away from the viewer on subsequent glances, both Robert and his nephew are convinced that she has looked directly at them. They are also aware of Cecily's strong likeness to the three important women of the narrative: Robert's wife, Lucile; his mistress, Elisabetta; and Thomas's wife, Nina. In this manner and as a contrast to the destructive use of power, Johnson draws a distinct line from the author of *Utopia* to the women of the Colinet-Guenole family.

Colinet appears toward the end of the narrative. His story, or legend, about the student Jean Buridan–who cleverly outwitted the cruel machinations of a noblewoman in Paris in the early 1300s–spreads warmth and satisfaction among his cold and hungry fellow soldiers on the night before the battle at Nancy. Colinet makes explicit an important function of a Johnson narrator: to free his listeners for a moment from their predicament of being human pawns in the power games of rulers.

Några steg mot tystnaden was highly praised by the critics. It was called one of Johnson's greatest, most richly composed works. Shortly after its publication, Johnson was awarded a prestigious literary prize by Litteraturfrämjandet, an association (no longer extant) for the promotion of literature.

In 1974 Eyvind Johnson and Harry Martinson were awarded the Nobel Prize in Literature. The citation for Johnson's award stated that it was "for a narrative art, far-seeing in lands and ages, in the service of freedom." The award brought on a storm of protests in the Swedish press. The immediate background to this reaction was a series of events in January 1974 that had made Johnson resign his membership in the Swedish Writers' Union. These events were related to the activities of the State Intelligence Bureau. Two journalists, members of the Writers' Union, had accused the Intelligence Bureau of espionage in Eastern countries and of keeping under surveillance several leftist organizations in Sweden. Action was brought against the two journalists for having published partly classified material, and they were sentenced to jail. A heated Writers' Union debate followed, centering on the issue of freedom of speech and directed against Swedish authorities in general and the Swedish judicial system in particular. Unwilling to side with political buffeting, Johnson resigned his membership in May 1974. His action drew backbiting comments in the press, somewhat damaging his position as the highly respected writer of *Några steg mot tystnaden* only a few months earlier. Among the critics were also those who, following Johnson's Uppsala "vårtal" in 1951, had chastized Johnson for siding with the United States against the Soviet Union instead of backing a third alternative, Europe free from both East and West.

Several times during his writing career, then, Johnson had appeared as a somewhat politically controversial figure even before the Nobel Prize award was announced on 3 October 1974. The Swedish Academy had chosen two of their own members–Johnson for his prose and Martinson for his poetry. The reaction in the press was immediate and at times vitriolic. Sarcasm was leveled at the Swedish Academy for selecting two of their own members and at the two writers for accepting the prize. Having been publicly berated before, Johnson was less concerned for himself than for Martinson as the more vulnerable of the two. Despite his exposure to criticism, Johnson had plans for new novels, but his health was failing. He died of lung cancer on 25 August 1976.

Of the two writers, Martinson was better known outside of Sweden. Although Johnson's literary texts have been translated into some twenty-six languages, only four of his novels have appeared in English. (One reason may be that the English sentence structure is generally paratactic, making it less readily a vehicle for Johnson's frequently complex sentence structure characterized by subordination and modal phrases.) Despite the criticism, the Swedish Academy had previously shown a willingness to award the prize to its own members, including Verner von Heidenstam in 1916 and Pär Lagerkvist in 1951. A driving force behind the protests in 1974 was the political climate in general. Venerable institutions such as the Swedish Academy were often regarded as old-fashioned and autocratic, and their power to bestow awards to the right persons was held in doubt.

Why did the Swedish Academy make such a controversial decision? The presentation speech at the Nobel Prize festivities stressed a factor largely overlooked by the eager voices of derision. Johnson and Martinson were chosen as the two foremost representatives, in prose and poetry respectively, of a new phenomenon in Swedish literature of the early to mid twentieth century: the so-called proletarian writers, self-taught without means or formal education, who had created a body of literature sprung from the heart of a people hitherto largely anonymous. Furthermore, some of them, and indeed both Johnson and Martinson, had grown beyond their own region, acquiring deep learning in other cultures and literatures.

For Johnson, the act of writing was essential to life itself. In 1927, in his late twenties and at the beginning of his career, Johnson explained the importance of writing in an impassioned letter to his friend Rudolf Värnlund:

> Jag har sagt det förr och säger det tusen gånger tusen: jag lever för att skriva, jag är född till det, det är min instinkt. Jag skulle skriva böcker på näver och med lingonsaft, om det inte funnes andra medel. Jag skulle skriva i mörkret om det inte funnes ljus. Jag är varken proletär eller aristokrat: jag är en som skriver, som är avsedd av sin instinkt, av sitt öde att skriva.

> (I have said it before and will say so thousands of times: I live to write, I was born to write, it is my instinct. I would write books on birch-bark and with the sap of lingon-berries, were there no other means. I would write in the dark, were there no light. I am nei-

ther proletarian, nor aristocrat: I am one who writes, who is intended by instinct, by fate, to write.)

Among Johnson's contributions to the Swedish art of narration are his emphasis on psychological development rather than on the intricacies of a plot, his use of inner monologue to depict a character's conflicts, his self-consciousness as a writer, and the variety of narrators giving a polyphonous character to the text. With increasing complexity a multitude of voices echo throughout the text, as laughter mingles with seriousness, and fantasy meshes with realism–yet always with a sense of responsibility to the story being told and always with an invitation to the reader to participate in the storytelling.

Bibliography:
Per-Olof Mattsson, *Eyvind Johnson: Bibliografi* (Uppsala: Acta Universitatis Upsaliensis, 2000).

Biographies:
Örjan Lindberger, *Norrbottningen som blev europé: Eyvind Johnsons liv och författarskap till och med Romanen om Olof* (Stockholm: Bonnier, 1986);

Lindberger, *Människan i tiden: Eyvind Johnsons liv och författarskap 1938–1976* (Stockholm: Bonnier, 1990).

References:
Stig Bäckman, *Den tidlösa historien: En studie i tre romaner av Eyvind Johnson* (Stockholm: Aldus, 1975);

Sverker Göransson, "Berättartekniken i Eyvind Johnsons roman 'Molnen över Metapontion,'" *Samlaren*, 83 (1962): 67–91;

Elna Hessel, "Så mötte jag författaren Eyvind Johnson: Om Eyvind Johnsons kamp mot nazismen under Andra världskriget, särskilt mot förhållandena i Norge och hur Krilon-romanerna speglar dessa förhållanden," *Parnass*, 2 (1996): 9–13;

Yrjö Hirn, "En fransk häxeriprocess år 1634: några bibliografiska randanteckningar utomkring Eyvind Johnsons senaste roman," in his *Den förgyllda balustraden och andra uppsatser från åren 1949–1952* (Stockholm: Wahlström & Widstrand, 1953);

Bo G. Jansson, *Självironi, självbespegling och självreflexion: Den metafiktiva tendensen i Eyvind Johnsons diktning* (Stockholm: Almquist & Wiksell, 1990);

Mona Kårsnäs, "Eyvind Johnson och djävulen: Människans andra jag och den politiska ondskan: studier kring ett motivkomplex i Eyvind Johnsons romankomst," dissertation, Uppsala University, 1984;

Örjan Lindberger, ed., *Herr Clerk Vår Mästare: En gruppering* (Stockholm: Atlantis, 1998);

Lindberger, ed., *Och så vill jag prata med dig: Brevväxlingen mellan Eyvind Johnson och Elmer Diktonius* (Stockholm: Bonnier, 1997);

Merete Mazzarella, "Myt och verklighet: Berättandets problem i Eyvind Johnsons roman *Strändernas svall*," dissertation, Helsinki University, 1981;

Ole Meyer, *Eyvind Johnsons historiska romaner: Analyser av språksyn och världssyn i fem romaner* (Copenhagen: Akademisk Forlag, 1976);

C. A. Munk-Nielsen, *Eyvind Johnson und Thomas Mann* (Copenhagen: Orbis litterarum, 1958);

Birgit Munkhammar, "30-talets perspektiv: Eyvind Johnson som kritiker i tidningen 'Arbetet,'" *Svensk Litteraturtidskrift*, 3–4 (1977);

Gavin Orton, *Eyvind Johnson* (New York: Twayne, 1972);

Torsten Pettersson, *Att söka sanningen: En grundprincip i Eyvind Johnsons författarskap* (Åbo: Åbo Akademi, 1986);

Nils Schwartz, *Hamlet i klasskampen: En ideologikritisk studie i Eyvind Johnsons 20-talsromaner* (Lund: Liber, 1979);

Monica Setterwall, "The Unwritten Story–A Study of Meta-Form in Three of Eyvind Johnson's Novels," dissertation, University of Wisconsin-Madison, 1980;

Barbro Söderberg, *Flykten mot stjärnorna: struktur och symbol i Eyvind Johnsons* Hans nådes tid (Stockholm: Akademilitteratur, 1980);

Thure Stenström, *Romantikern Eyvind Johnson* (Lund: Ekstrand, 1978);

Gunnar Wiman, "Den inre monologen i Eyvind Johnsons 'Kommentar till ett stjärnfall,'" *Modersmålslärarnas Förenings årsskrift* (1956).

Papers:
The main collection of Eyvind Johnson's papers is housed at the Royal Library in Stockholm.

1974 Nobel Prize in Literature Presentation Speech

by Karl Ragnar Gierow, of the Swedish Academy
(Translation from the Swedish)

Your Majesty, Your Royal Highnesses, Ladies and Gentlemen,

Eyvind Johnson's education–that is, the education provided by society at that time–ended when he was thirteen and was imparted to him at a little village school north of the Arctic Circle. The future awaiting the young Harry Martinson opened up to him when, at the age of six, as a so-called child of the parish, he was sold by auction to the lowest bidder—that is, to the person who took charge of the forsaken boy for the smallest payment out of parochial funds. The fact that, with such a start in life, both of them have their places on this platform today, is the visible testimony to a transformation of society, which, step by step, is still going on all over the world. With us it came unusually early; it is perhaps our country's biggest blessing, perhaps, also, its most remarkable achievement during the last thousand years.

Eyvind Johnson and Harry Martinson did not come alone, nor first. They are representative of the many proletarian writers or working-class poets who, on a wide front, broke into our literature, not to ravage and plunder, but to enrich it with their fortunes. Their arrival meant an influx of experience and creative energy, the value of which can hardly be exaggerated. To that extent they are representative also of the similar breakthrough that has later occurred in the whole of our cultural world. A new class has conquered Parnassus. But if, by a conqueror, we mean the one who gained most from the outcome, then Parnassus has conquered a new class.

To determine an author and his work against the background of his social origin and political environment is, at present, good form. And what is good form is seldom particularly to the point. "Eyvind Johnson's literary achievement is one of the most significant and characteristic of a very fruitful period in the whole of Europe." This last sentence is not mine; it was written thirty years ago by Lucien Maury. Even then, the boy from a primary school in a remote village in the far north of Sweden was an experienced and self-assured European, never forgetful of his origin (of which his autobiographical stories provide a lasting document), but still less bound and inhibited by the environment where he took his first steps. International perspective distinguished Eyvind Johnson's further writings, and it is matched by an equally wide outlook in time, over the destinies and ages of the human race. The renewal of the historical novel which he has carried out on his own, and perhaps exemplified most clearly in great works like *Days of His Grace* and *Steps Towards Silence*, is based not only on extensive research but also on a clear-sightedness which, expressed briefly, sets out to show that everything that happens to us has happened before, and everything that took place once in the world is still taking place, recognizable under changed signs, a constant simultaneity of epochs which may be the only wisdom the past can teach us in our attempts to survey the present and divine an era which we have not yet seen.

If, nevertheless, we are to point to a special phase and one particular mental environment whose traces are ineffaceable in Eyvind Johnson's work with his pen, it is that very period when Lucien Maury discovered that in this Nordic writer, Europe had one of its important intellectuals. The French time analyst described this epoch as very fruitful. What was it that made it so productive? Not favourable conditions, but the indomitable resistance to the conditions that prevailed. D-day had not yet dawned; Nazism still had a stranglehold on Europe. It was in that predicament that Eyvind Johnson spoke out. His attitude was so passionate that its fervour has never since vanished from what he wrote. He retained his European perspective, but, naturally, it was Scandinavia's liberty that was dearest to him just then. He endorsed his conviction with a handshake across the border. Together with a co-editor on the Norwegian side he was responsible during the occupation years for a mouthpiece of the new Scandinavianism, called—*A Handshake*. As from today the two publishers of that little paper are both Nobel Prize winners. The name of Eyvind Johnson's co-editor on the Norwegian side of the frontier was Willy Brandt.

Both Eyvind Johnson and, still more, Harry Martinson have a lot in common with the oldest, and perhaps, greatest of all proletarian writers, the subtly wise and charming author of ingenious fables, Aesop. Like him, they spin webs, capturing you with beguiling words that always contain other, and more, than what they literally say. But the differences between this year's two literary prizewinners are greater than the similarities. Beside Eyvind Johnson, whose writing is based so very much on his fiercely defended citizenship in a free society, Harry Martinson may appear to be almost a purely asocial individual, the incorrigible vagrant in our literature. No one has succeeded in putting him under lock and key. The philosophic tramp, Bolle, in *The Road* is, in many ways, the author's spokesman, and he is not homeless at the gate. He is homeless only when he gets inside four walls. He is the bearer of asocialism as a wish and a principle that brings good luck; he is a vagabond of his own free will, in agreement with life's sound instincts and in spontaneous revolt against what is trying to stifle them—that which is governed by calculation and established by force. He already has his home; it is beyond and outside, and he is always on the way towards it. From this starting point, though in a different key, we can also conceive the tragically beautiful vision of Aniara, of the spaceship which heads away from an increasingly hostile existence on a frozen earth and itself loses its rudder, cut off from its home port and with its destination lost.

"I don't want to have real what most people want to have real," Bolle remarks. In saying this he has also said quite a lot about Harry Martinson's writing. Realism is to be found there to the extent that it can be called elemental: it is based on the closest familiarity with the four elements. Harry Martinson got to know earth and air as a tramp on the roads, fire and water as a stoker at sea. Yet the world of imagination is more important and more real to him than that of reality. Where realism plods methodically along, his imagination races with the swallow-winged glide of the skater. However, it is not a flight from truth; on the contrary. "We must learn the essential difference between what is factual and what is truth," he has said. "We have facts everywhere. They whirl in our eyes like sand." But it is truth we are concerned with, and that is something else. It is a state in nature and in the receptive human being; it is

> the good will with presence and peace of mind to keep watch and to be.

For Harry Martinson fact and fiction are one, and, without any aphoristic hair-splitting, an entire outlook on life is summed up in these pregnant words. The last two, most emphasized, form the simple verb of mere existence: to be. But existence is only fit for human beings if it gives them pleasure, and for that, good will and vigilance are needed. So, in the end, the truth to which this wanderer's path has led him is a gratitude, round-eyed as a child's, for the generous life that has constantly given him trials, riddles and joy in good measure.

After this quickly cut-out silhouette of two remarkable literary profiles, it is my very pleasant duty to express the heartfelt congratulations of the Swedish Academy to Eyvind Johnson and Harry Martinson and to ask them to receive the emblems of the 1974 Nobel Prize for Literature from the hands of His Majesty, the King.

[© The Nobel Foundation, 1974.]

Johnson: Banquet Speech

Eyvind Johnson's speech at the Nobel Banquet at the City Hall in Stockholm, 10 December 1974 (Translation):

On behalf of Harry Martinson and myself I will speak as briefly as possible on the situation in which we now find ourselves.

A poet or prose narrator usually looks back on what he has achieved against a backdrop of the years that have passed, generally finding that some of these achievements are acceptable, while others are less so. Such a form of self-criticism is often valuable in that it lends perspective to our lives. It evokes or fortifies recollections of those teachers who have been important to us. These may be long departed thinkers and poets who nonetheless live on by virtue of their work, or contemporary writers, young and old, who have been a source of gratifying inspiration to us and led us along the paths of promise.

We can recall with profound gratitude the fine teachers of our earliest, important schooldays when as youngsters some of us on slates—we practiced the form and order of letters; in due course to acquire a clearer sense for the better or worse use of the alphabet.

A writer's work often reflects what he or she has been exposed to in life; experiences which are the groundwork of a poem or a story. Poet and storyteller both fabulate in order to produce true pictures of reality—reality as it is, or as it seems to them to be. From the throes of inspiration and the eddies of thought the poet may at last be able to arrive at, and convey the right admixture of words and meaning. And your poet or storyteller may sometimes experience a sense of profound egotistical joy in the function of musing, solving and composing.

And at the centre of all the good writing that has been, and is being created stands Man, in the midst of his own kind and surrounded by the technology, violence and compassion that he may encounter in the suffering and happiness which constitutes his individual or social destiny. In the world of the present, in our time, we feel that suffering, anguish, the torments of body and soul, are greater than ever before in the history of mankind. Many men of science and poets have in their own manner, by various ways and means, and aided by others, sought unceasingly to create a more tolerable world for everyone. And this we should believe: that hope and volition can bring us closer to our ultimate goal: justice for all, injustice for no-one.

Harry Martinson and I would like to thank the Swedish Academy for the honour which it has done us in having the temerity, without consulting us or anyone else, to have placed us in the situation in which we now find ourselves.

At the same time we should like to thank the Foundation which, in the esteemed name of Alfred Nobel, has without protest accepted—indeed been kind enough to approve our presence here today, thereby bestowing upon us something which makes our personal situation—the one to which I have just referred—rather less disagreeable than I have perhaps pretended it to be.

[© The Nobel Foundation, 1974. Eyvind Johnson is the sole author of his speech.]

Erik Axel Karlfeldt
(20 July 1864 – 8 April 1931)

Paul Norlén
University of Washington

BOOKS: *Vildmarks- och kärleksvisor* (Stockholm: Seligmann, 1895);

Fridolins visor och andra dikter (Stockholm: Wahlström & Widstrand, 1898);

Fridolins lustgård och Dalmålningar på rim (Stockholm: Wahlström & Widstrand, 1901);

Fridolins poesi och Dalmålningar på rim (Stockholm: Wahlström & Widstrand, 1902)—includes *Fridolins visor och andra dikter* and *Fridolins lustgård och Dalmålningar på rim;*

Valda stycken (Stockholm: Wahlström & Widstrand, 1904);

Flora och Pomona (Stockholm: Wahlström & Widstrand, 1906);

Vid Gustaf Frödings bår, by Karlfeldt and Nathan Söderbloom (Stockholm: Bonnier, 1911);

Minne af skalden Lars Johanssen (Lucidor) (Stockholm: Norstedt, 1912); republished as *Skalden Lucidor* (Stockholm: Norstedt, 1914);

Flora och Bellona (Stockholm: Wahlström & Widstrand, 1918);

Dalmålningar utlagda på rim (Stockholm: Wahlström & Widstrand, 1920);

Valda dikter tillägnade ungdamen (Stockholm: Wahlström & Widstrand, 1922)—comprises excerpts from *Vildmarks- och kärleksvisor, Fridolins visor, Fridolins lustgård, Flora och Pomona,* and *Flora och Bellona;*

Kärleksdikter i urval (Stockholm: Wahlström & Widstrand, 1923);

Carl Fredrik Dahlgren: En bild ur svensk romantik för hundra år sedan (Stockholm: Wahlström & Widstrand, 1924);

Hösthorn (Stockholm: Wahlström & Widstrand, 1927);

Tankar och tal med ett lyriskt bokslut, edited by Torsten Fogelqvist (Stockholm: Wahlström & Widstrand, 1932);

Karlfeldts ungdomsdiktning, edited by Sven Haglund and Nils Afzelius (Stockholm: Wahlström & Widstrand, 1934);

Henry Fielding: Ett författarporträtt, edited by Sven Stolpe (Borås: Norma, 1985).

Erik Axel Karlfeldt (portrait by Anders Zorn; Zornsamlingarna, Mora, Sweden)

Editions: *De 29 dikterna samt en visbok,* edited by Lars Forssell (Stockholm: Wahlström & Widstrand, 1955);

Samlade dikter (Stockholm: Wahlström & Widstrand, 1981).

Editions in English: *Why Sinclair Lewis Got the Nobel Prize,* translated by Naboth Hedin (New York: Harcourt Brace, 1931);

Arcadia Borealis: Selected Poems of Erik Axel Karlfeldt, translated by Charles Wharton Stork (Minneapolis: University of Minnesota Press, 1938);

Selected poems, in *The North! To the North! Five Swedish Poets of the Nineteenth Century,* edited and translated by Judith Moffett (Carbondale: Southern Illinois University Press, 2001), pp. 165–203.

OTHER: "Minne af Claes Teodor Odhner: Inträdes-tal i Svenska akademien den 20 december 1904," in *Svenska akademiens handlingar: Ifrån år 1886, D. 19, 1904* (Stockholm: Norstedt, 1906).

Erik Axel Karlfeldt was one of several poets who came to prominence in the 1890s in Sweden. Social realism and naturalism, primarily expressed in prose fiction and drama, had been the literary norm in the 1880s. The emphasis was on "putting problems up for debate," in the phrase made famous by the Danish critic Georg Brandes. A reaction against the naturalism of the 1880s was heralded by the young poet Verner von Heidenstam in his programmatic essay "Renässans" (1890, Renaissance). Heidenstam, Oscar Levertin, Gustaf Fröding, and eventually Karlfeldt became the leading figures in the resurgence of Swedish poetry during this time. In certain respects the social concerns of the 1880s did continue into the next decade. However, the new emphasis on imagination, individualism, and aesthetic values was favorable for poetry. The period is often associated with "national Romanticism" in both literature and art, and parallel trends, including the celebration of Swedish provincial life and nature, can be found in the visual arts, in the work of such painters as Carl Larsson and Anders Zorn.

Of the poets of the 1890s, Karlfeldt was the last to make his literary debut, but he continued to write and publish poetry longer than any of his contemporaries. His literary production consists of six volumes of poetry, published between 1895 and 1927, and two monographs of literary history, one on the seventeenth-century Swedish poet Lars Johansson Lucidor (a poet for whom Karlfeldt felt a special affinity) and a second on the Swedish Romantic poet Carl Fredrik Dahlgren. Selected speeches and essays were also collected in a posthumous volume of prose that included his final poems.

Karlfeldt was born Erik Axel Eriksson on 20 July 1864 on the farm "Tolvmansgården" in Karlbo village, Folkärna parish, near the town of Avesta in the southern part of the Swedish province of Dalarna. Centered around Lake Siljan in central and western Sweden, Dalarna was the region where elements of traditional Swedish rural culture persisted the longest. His native region played an important role in Karlfeldt's poetry. His mother, Anna Jansdotter, had a son and two daughters from her first marriage to the farmer and county official Matts Larsson. After her first husband's death, she married her second cousin, Erik Eriksson; Erik Axel was the oldest of their four sons.

A promising student from an early age, Erik Axel enrolled in the secondary school (gymnasium) in Västerås at the age of fourteen, the first person in the family to continue his studies past the elementary-school level. From an early age, he had expressed a desire to become a poet, and as a student he wrote poetry and became involved in student literary societies. Erik Axel completed his *studentexamen* (entry examination for university studies), an important academic milestone in Sweden in 1885. That same year, however, a family crisis altered the promising young student's prospects drastically. Against a backdrop of unwise business speculations and a national crisis in agriculture, his father was accused of forging signatures on financial documents. The charges were especially serious as Erik Eriksson held a position of responsibility in the community as *nämndeman* (analogous to a member of a county board), and he was given a sentence of two years at hard labor. The resulting bankruptcy led to the loss of the family farm at public auction, an event that clearly affected Erik Axel deeply, both by the sudden and irrevocable separation from his childhood environment as well as by the stain on the family's honor. Erik Axel's father died a few years later, in 1889, at the age of fifty-one.

Because of his now financially unstable situation, the first few years of Erik Axel's university studies in Uppsala were frequently interrupted by periods of employment as a private tutor in various places. In 1888 he was employed for a short time as a journalist for the liberal newspaper *Aftonbladet* in Stockholm. The editor of the newspaper, Ernst Beckman, became a friend and mentor. Thanks to a sum of money collected by Beckman (on his own initiative) among his friends and colleagues, Erik Axel was able to pursue a more continuous period of study in Uppsala from 1889 to 1892.

In 1889 Erik Axel changed his surname to "Karlfeldt," a name linked to his home village, Karlbo. In the Swedish countryside, relatively few people had surnames; instead, the patronymic system persisted, in which a person was identified as someone's son or daughter (hence "Eriksson" or "Eriksdotter"). It was becoming more common at this time, however, for a person to choose a surname. After completing his studies, Karlfeldt took a series of positions as a teacher, first in the newly established progressive community of Djursholm, near Stockholm (where he was hired by Beckman, who had left his position as editor of *Aftonbladet* to become president of the development), and then in the town of Molkom in the province of Värmland.

By Swedish standards, Karlfeldt matured slowly as a poet. While at the university in Uppsala, Karlfeldt wrote verse, at first in the prevailing style of the 1880s with its emphasis on social realism. Some of these poems were published in newspapers and student literary journals under various pseudonyms (and collected after his death in *Karlfeldts ungdomsdiktning* [Karlfeldt's Juvenilia], 1934). In the terms of the American poet Richard Hugo, Karlfeldt seems to have found his "triggering subject" in his discovery, or rediscovery, of his home landscape of Dalarna sometime in the early 1890s. This discovery was personal but also in tune with changing trends in literature during that decade. Interest in Swedish rural traditions was also finding popular expression in the *hembygdsrörelsen* (home district movement). The centuries-old rural culture was beginning to disappear; symptoms included mass emigration (especially to North America) as well as a rapid movement within the country from rural villages to cities and towns as industrialization progressed. A notable event in the attempt to preserve remnants of traditional culture was the opening of Skansen, the open-air museum in Stockholm, in 1891.

Karlfeldt's first collection of poems, *Vildmarks- och kärleksvisor* (Songs of Wilderness and Love) was published in 1895. This collection attracted little notice and sold about two hundred copies. While this volume is not as formally accomplished as his subsequent collections, certain themes important to the poet are already apparent. Karlfeldt uses the Swedish word *visa* (meaning song, especially a folk song or ballad; plural *visor*) in the title, rather than the word *dikt* (poem). Earlier in the decade there had been a debate about "art poetry" (*dikt*) and "folk poetry" (*visa*) between the poets Fröding and Levertin. By using the word *visa*, Karlfeldt underscores both the song-like nature of his poems and their connection to his rural heritage.

In the opening poem of the collection, "Fäderna" (The Forefathers), the poet evokes a long line of anonymous ancestors, who lived "i ringhet och frid" (in humbleness and peace). The poet has been torn from his ancestral soil: "Jag är ryckt som en ört ur sin groningsgrund, / halvt nödd, halvt villig er sak jag svek" (I am torn like a plant from its seedling bed, / half in need, half willingly your cause I betrayed). Karlfeldt returns often to this theme of longing for a lost way of life, especially in his early collections. In its celebration of the free and independent Swedish peasant, the poem recalls the early-nineteenth-century Romanticism of Erik Gustaf Geijer and his poem "Odalbonden" (1811, The Yeoman Farmer). Karlfeldt's poem, however, is much more personal in tone; he finds solace and, he hopes, inspiration from the toil of hardworking forebears, along with a sense of guilt for having abandoned their way of life, willingly or not.

The love songs in the collection often depict transitory meetings, while the object of the poems is sometimes nature rather than a human being. In "Bekransa mig!" (Make a Garland for Me!), the poet addresses his "vildmarksbrud" ("wilderness bride," the late-autumn forest) and states that "Jag är den siste, trogne trubaduren / som höjer sång i dina öde salar" (I am the final, faithful troubadour / who raises a song in your desolate halls).

Another noteworthy poem in this first collection, especially from a psychological perspective, is "Avskedssång" (Song of Parting). The poem begins in a moment of departure from an apparent crisis. The time is evening, and a storm approaches that will shake the "arma agnar i ödets såll" (poor husks in fate's sifting sieve). Nature (the storm) and traditional ways (the harvest "sieve") are used as realistic elements with symbolic overtones. Separation (from the family, from familiar surroundings) is imminent, and the poet's mother is addressed; in her eyes, "sorgset fromma" (mournfully pious), he seems to read a "biblisk dikt" (biblical verse). The poem ends with a (Lutheran) hymn-like final verse, suggesting reconciliation and the solace of a traditional faith: "Var jordisk känsla som brutet talar / skall strömma frigjord i evig sång" (Each earthly feeling which brokenly speaks / shall flow, set free, in eternal song). Karlfeldt often adopted this hymn-like tone, perhaps to greatest effect in his final collection, *Hösthorn* (1927, Horn of Autumn), some thirty years later.

In 1896 Karlfeldt returned to Uppsala for further studies in literary and art history. In February 1898 he completed his *licentiatexamen* (doctoral degree) with a thesis on the eighteenth-century English novelist Henry Fielding. While in Uppsala, Karlfeldt became acquainted with Fröding, who had moved to the university town after controversy (including a charge of blasphemy) surrounding his third book of poems. Fröding critiqued many of the poems that appeared in Karlfeldt's second, breakthrough collection, *Fridolins visor och andra dikter* (1898, Fridolin's Songs and Other Poems).

Fridolins visor och andra dikter was the book that established Karlfeldt's reputation. It was generally (though not unanimously) praised by critics in the leading Swedish newspapers and well accepted by the reading public. In this second collection, Karlfeldt has created a character, Fridolin, a university-educated bachelor who has returned to his rural roots. (Correctly or not, Karlfeldt came to be identified with Fridolin for the rest of his life.) Fridolin attempts to bridge the worlds of book learning and peasant knowledge: "och han talar med bönder på böndernas sätt / men med lärde män på latin" (and he speaks with farmers in farmerly ways / but in Latin with learnèd men). The tone of the poems in this collection ranges from sonorously mournful to gently bantering.

Fridolins visor och andra dikter is divided into four parts. The first, "Ur en landtlig ungkarls visbok" (From a Rural Bachelor's Songbook), is most explicitly identified with the Fridolin character. The opening poem, "Rimsmeden" (The Rhymesmith), depicts the poet as a blacksmith, forging his poems "i kvällen då min ungdoms sol gick ned" (at evening as the sun of my youth went down), an example of a persistent theme of decay or mortality in Karlfeldt. His calling as a poet is depicted here in masculine, even muscular, terms that match the physical labors referred to in "Fäderna."

Another theme stands out in the next poem, "Från beväringsåren" (From Years as a Conscript). Starting from a military metaphor of enlistment, the poet is "mönstrad in i Amors här" (recruited into the army of Amor) and "kallad in av sångens gud" (called up by the god of song). The end of the poem suggests a psychological interpretation: "Jag går ut i livets fejder; / om jag ej med ära kommer, kommer aldrig jag igen" (I go out into life's battles; / if I come not back with glory, I will never come back again).

The second section of *Fridolins visor och andra dikter*, "Cecilia Bölljas visbok (fragment)," is, again, presented as a personal collection of songs. The hand-copied *visbok* (*visor*) was popular among the upper classes in seventeenth-century Sweden, a period that greatly interested Karlfeldt. Several of these song collections had been edited, and published, in Sweden in the 1890s. Use of the term lends the collection an archaic quality, emphasizing Karlfeldt's tendency to cultivate the past.

The third section of the book, "Från Folkare-stigar" (From Folkare Paths), depicts the landscape and characters of his home parish. In, for example, the poem "Uppbrott" (Departure), the poet "greedily collects" sensory impressions from his childhood surroundings. The final section, "Liv och död" (Life and Death), offers an alternative to the Fridolin persona in "En löskerkarl" (an archaic-sounding word meaning literally "a loose fellow," a man with no attachments). In contrast to Fridolin, who is a kind of country gentleman, the "löskerkarl" is a homeless, wandering figure, clearly representing another aspect of Karlfeldt's personality. (With its question-and-answer form, this poem also alludes to a well-known seventeenth-century hymn by Lucidor.) In other poems, a similar character is represented by the figure of a *spelman* or wandering musician.

In 1899 Karlfeldt accepted a position as a part-time teacher at a school in Stockholm, where he was employed until 1902. At the end of 1900 he was also granted a position as an assistant librarian at the Royal Library. His third collection, *Fridolins lustgård och Dalmålningar på rim* (1901, Fridolin's Paradise and Dala Paintings in Rhyme), further established his reputation as a major poet in Sweden. The word "lustgård" (literally "pleasure garden") means paradise, with direct reference to the biblical Garden of Eden. The darker tone of this collection, compared to *Fridolins visor och andra dikter,* suggests that the allusion to "paradise" is at least in part meant ironically.

As in Karlfeldt's other books, the first poem sets the tone for the entire collection. The initial poem in *Fridolins lustgård och Dalmålningar på rim* is often quoted as a statement of Karlfeldt's poetic program. The first lines read: "Min sångmö är inte af Pinden, / hon är av Pungmakarbo" (My Muse is not from Pindos, / she is from Pungmakarbo). Clearly the poet's inspiration comes from his native province, but he is far from being a "primitive" or "naive" artist. (Pindos is a mountain chain associated in Greek mythology with Apollo. Pungmakarbo is a village in Dalarna; when he wrote this poem, Karlfeldt had never actually visited the place, but he was struck by the way the name sounded.) One of the strengths of Karlfeldt's poetry stems from his fusion of local, specific traditions with references to European literary tradition. While the musicality and beauty of his lyrics can be enjoyed for their own sake, careful reading reveals Karlfeldt's attention to realistic detail and the sometimes erudite sources for his poems.

In "Lustgården" (Paradise), Fridolin hears a song "att tron är död och kärleken förbrunnen" (that faith is dead and love extinguished). Despite that, "Jag har en sal, mot aftonen belägen, / en lustgård och en borg i ungdomslandet" (I have a hall, toward evening situated, / a paradise and fortress in the land of youth). Rather than abandon his youthful "tjänst i diktens land" (service in the land of poetry), Fridolin has withdrawn to a personal, rural paradise. A parallel to Voltaire's *Candide* (1759) might be drawn; Candide withdrew from public life to cultivate his garden, while Fridolin cuts himself off from the outside world (described as "den borgerliga, stora Staten," the bourgeois, massive State). But Fridolin, and other characters who appear in Karlfeldt's poems, are not meant to represent a philosophy of life. They serve as masks, as Sven Delblanc writes, to "depict his feelings of rootlessness and homesickness." Furthermore, this fictional rural paradise is "without any counterpart in the world" and is "a world which shows nothing of the hardships of work but all the more of play and dance, of holiday and harvest festival."

Several poems in this collection are identified as inspired by a "folk book," *Bondepraktiken* (roughly, "Farmer's Practical Handbook") which had wide distribution in Sweden and other parts of northern Europe. Originally published in Germany in the early 1500s, the book spread first to Denmark, then to Sweden, and was an often-consulted agricultural handbook for several centuries, with information, for example, on when to sow and harvest. One of the poems inspired by *Bondepraktiken,* "Mikrokosmos" (Microcosm), devotes each of its four stanzas to one of the four traditional elements: earth, water, air, and fire.

Several of Karlfeldt's most lyrically evocative love poems are found in this collection, including "Dina ögon äro eldar" (In your eyes a fire is burning) and "Nu öppnar nattglim sin krona" (Now the eye-catch opens its calyx). The latter poem is an excellent example of how specific Karlfeldt is in his depiction of nature, here in reference to particular plants—"nattglim," English "eye-catch"; "ögontröst," English "eyebright"; and "jungfru Marie halm," English "lady's bedstraw"—that bloom in late summer, and whose names in Swedish are themselves allusive: literally night-gleam, eye-solace, and the Virgin Mary's bedstraw. As in other poems, Karlfeldt here shows a remarkable ability to dissolve the boundaries between nature and an individual, human sensibility. The poet becomes submerged in his beloved, not a woman but revealed instead in the last line to be "mörkögda augustinatt" (dark-eyed August night).

"Längtan heter min arvedel" (Longing is my inheritance), which is well-known in Sweden as set to music by Wilhelm Peterson-Berger in 1906, conveys a theme that underscores much of Karlfeldt's production, characterized in one poem as "längtan för längtans skull" (longing for longing's sake). Some critics have detected Nietzschean overtones in several of the poems in *Fridolins lustgård och Dalmålningar på rim,* for example in "Höstens vår" (Autumn's Spring), described as "den vår de svaga kalla höst" (that spring the weak call autumn). The influence of Friedrich Nietzsche, however, especially widespread at this time, can be detected in virtually any writer of the period at one point or another.

"Dalmålningar på rim" is a separate section of eight poems, and these pieces occupy a distinctive and popular place in Karlfeldt's production as well. These poems purport to imitate a type of folk art prevalent in Karlfeldt's home province of Dalarna, especially in the early to mid nineteenth century. Scenes from the Bible or Swedish history, as well as stylized floral patterns, decorated the rooms of houses as well as furniture and trunks. A key element of these paintings is that the biblical figures are depicted as though they were from the province of Dalarna, dressed in provincial costume. While Karlfeldt may have seen such paintings as a child, it is likely that he at least became more closely acquainted with such folk paintings during the years, starting in 1897, when he spent most of his summer and winter vacations in Dalarna. Dala painting was becoming more widely known and appreciated at the end of the nineteenth century. Interest was sparked by reproductions of these paintings published by Ernst Bosæus in the 1870s and 1880s, and collectors, including the recently established Nordiska museet (Nordic Museum) in Stockholm, had begun acquiring and cataloguing them.

Karlfeldt is not describing actual paintings in these poems, and he makes clear in a short preface to this section that some of these "paintings" exist only in the poet's own imagination. He does draw on some particularly popular motifs for the Dala painters, however, such as Elijah's ascent into heaven in "Elie himmelsfärd" (The Assumption of Elijah) and Jonah and the whale in "Jone havsfärd" (Jonah's Sea Journey). "Jungfru Maria" (Virgin Mary) is one of Karlfeldt's most popular poems. Not biblical in reference, the poem describes an ethereal peasant girl with "mandelblommans hy" (almond-flower skin), carrying a rose brought by "en ängel från en salig örtagård" (an angel from a blessed herb garden). This female figure can be seen as an example of a *femme fragile,* in sharp contrast to the many *femmes fatale* of the literature of the period. "Tuna ting" (The Assembly at Tuna), a Dala painting with an historical theme, depicts a gathering of peasants from Dalarna, preparing a letter of protest to King Gustav I Vasa; after they helped him drive out the Danish king and take power, he seems to have forgotten his former allies. Karlfeldt works a variety of registers in these poems, from the humorously ironic to the melancholy. The influence of the great eighteenth-century Swedish poet and troubadour Carl Michael Bellman, who also composed Bible parodies, is apparent in "Jone havsfärd" in particular. Other poems of this type can be found in Karlfeldt's later collections.

Karlfeldt was extremely well-versed in the Bible, and his preferred translation was the so-called Karl XII Bible of 1703, which built upon the earlier Gustav Vasa Bible of 1541. (The Lutheran church was the official, state church in Sweden from the 1520s until the year 2000, and the translation and publication of the Bible was authorized by the king in consultation with church officials.) This translation was the standard version in Sweden for many years and corresponds in importance and literary quality to the King James Bible in English. Several references to the Bible can be found in each of Karlfeldt's books, whether as paraphrase, as allusion, or in the use of particular words that are peculiar to the old Bible translation. As he stated once in an interview, "De gamla uttryckssäten från denna bok ha för mig blivit naturliga" (The old expressions from this book have become natural to me).

The critic Olof Lagercrantz characterized Karlfeldt's poetry in terms of its continuity in his 1938 study, *Jungfrun och demonerna* (The Virgin and the

Demons). The title suggests an ongoing opposition in Karlfeldt's work between purity and passion. Lagercrantz writes:

> There is in Karlfeldt's production a continuity of an almost unbelievable type. The same themes are repeated in poetry collection after poetry collection, are deepened and refined, but nevertheless remain the same. It is the mystery of repetition which often takes hold of us when we read his poems. Like his peasant ancestors, he lived along with the solemn rhythm of the year, marked by the great festivals and by the changes of the seasons.

Lagercrantz also remarks on the specificity of Karlfeldt's poems, "localized and time-specific through allusions to harvest or planting, spring floods or fields of snow, ringing Dalecarlian names, trees, flowers and birds."

Familiarity with the flowers and plants referred to in Karlfeldt's poetry is often beneficial for a complete appreciation of the work. In his study of plants in Karlfeldt's poetry, Thorsten Thunman lists more than 280 names of plants which are specifically mentioned, not including more generic references to parts of plants. As many as seventy trees and bushes are referred to as well. As might be expected, these references are generally quite specific with regard to characteristics such as the time of year a flower blooms, whether the plant is wild or cultivated, or whether it has medicinal or culinary properties.

In 1903 Karlfeldt took a position as librarian at Lantbruksakademien (the Agricultural Academy). It was at about this time that he became more closely acquainted with the painter Zorn, also from Dalarna. Zorn's paintings parallel Karlfeldt's poems in many ways; both, for example, shared an interest in female beauty and in the folkloric traditions of their native province. In a memorial speech given when a monument to Zorn (who died in 1920) was dedicated at the cemetery in the town of Mora, where the artist was buried, Karlfeldt wrote that for him, "the memory of Zorn is illuminated most fully and most beautifully when I see it in connection with his native province." In contrast to Karlfeldt, Zorn acquired an international reputation in his lifetime; painting is not hindered by the need for translation into other languages.

Also in 1903 Karlfeldt was asked to become a member of the Swedish Academy, but he refused. (The Swedish Academy, whose eighteen members are appointed for life, was founded in 1786 by King Gustav III.) In 1904, however, there was another vacancy in the Academy, and this time Karlfeldt was elected without his prior knowledge. The selection was met with general acclaim in the press. Under the leadership of the extremely conservative Carl David af Wirsén, the Academy's permanent secretary since 1884, the Academy had acquired a negative reputation and was perceived as hostile to any new developments in literature. Wirsén viewed the poets of the 1890s with particular suspicion, and Karlfeldt, considered by Wirsén to be the least offensive of the group, was the first writer of that generation to join the Academy.

Despite the continuity in Karlfeldt's production, there is a distinct change between Karlfeldt's first three collections and his next book, *Flora och Pomona* (1906, Flora and Pomona). While the earlier collections frequently dealt with youth and the fear of aging (or at least of leaving youth, "spring" in seasonal terms, behind), beginning with *Flora och Pomona* the poet, now middle-aged, adopts a more consistently autumnal tone. The last two lines of "Augustihymn" (August Hymn) are representative: "Den som bär höstens krona över pannan / drömmer och ler, men skrattar ej som förr" (The one who bears the crown of autumn on his brow / dreams and smiles, but laughs not like before).

Flora and Pomona were the Roman goddesses of flowers and fruit trees, respectively, and references to classical mythology are much more prominent than before in this volume and Karlfeldt's next collection. The opening poem of *Flora och Pomona,* "Tillägnan" (Dedication), announces the contradictions within the poet: "Min mun är full av glädjerop och klagan" (My mouth is full of joyful cries and complaint). A sense of isolation, or of separation from contemporary events, might be read in the line "Jag är den siste riddaren av liljan" (I am the last knight of the lily). Despite the arrival of evening and autumn (suggestions of aging and approaching death), the poet still finds inspiration: "Ur dagens stungna hjärta droppar bloden, / hans bleka mun är varm ännu av sånger" (From the stung heart of day blood is dripping, / his pale mouth is still warm with songs).

A series of poems deals with particular flowers. "Nattyxne" (Night Violet or Butterfly Orchis), described as an "älskogsört" (herb of sexual love), associates this plant with female sexuality. Thunman points out in his study that to "strengthen the poem's erotic mood," Karlfeldt has also used several older names for this flower, such as "Satyrium" (the last word in the poem). "Hjärtstilla" (Motherwort, *Leonurus cardiaca*) is a medicinal plant considered helpful for heart ailments. In this poem, the plant is seen as soothing after "rosornas rus" (the intoxication of roses) of a passionate summer, or youth. By comparision, "höstblommar, / tröstblommar, / armt är ert sånglösa sus" (autumn flowers, / consoling flowers, / poor are your tuneless sighs).

The subject matter of "Häxorna" (The Witches) stands in sharp contrast to "Jungfru Maria." The poem may have been inspired by the witch trials of the 1600s in Sweden, as well as by a well-known case in France from the same period that is also the basis of books by the Swedish novelist and Nobel Prize winner Eyvind Johnson (*Drömmar om rosor och eld,* 1949; translated as *Dreams of Roses and Fire,* 1984) and Aldous Huxley (*The Devils of Loudon,* 1952). The poem is in four parts. In the first part, certain signs on a woman's body witness "att blickens duva / kan lyftas till korpens flykt" (that the glance of the dove / can be raised to the raven's flight), indicating that the young woman is susceptible to temptation. In the second part, the young woman is warned to avoid certain places where demons lurk in wait for young virgins, and instead to "Bed vid din moders grav" (Pray at your mother's grave). The third section describes a witches' sabbath, while the fourth and final section describes how

> Långt, långt
> > bort i kvällarnas kväll
> har skymningsfursten sin boning.
>
> (Far, far
> > away in the evening of evenings
> twilight's prince has his abode.)

A tree grows there, the tree of the knowledge of good and evil from the Book of Genesis:

> Kunskapens frukt av glädje och sorg,
> som Eva blott flyktigt fick smaka,
> flöder ur kvistarnas flätade korg.
>
> (The fruit of knowledge of joy and sorrow,
> which Eve could only taste in passing,
> floods from the woven basket of its twigs.)

"Häxorna" is perhaps Karlfeldt's darkest poem, exemplifying, as Jöran Mjöberg writes, "the antithesis which is the basis of Karlfeldt's concept of woman" as well as his "old-church experience of dualism in the nature of woman."

Upon Wirsén's death in 1912, Karlfeldt became the permanent secretary of the Swedish Academy, a full-time occupation. That same year he completed his study of Lucidor. Karlfeldt had a long-standing interest in the Swedish poets of the seventeenth century, the so-called period of great power, when Swedish military successes gave the country unprecedented status in Europe. Karlfeldt probably began background study for this book while a student in Uppsala in the late 1890s. Lucidor was a François Villon-like figure who traveled widely in Europe, mastered several languages, made his living primarily by writing occasional poems (mainly for weddings and funerals), and was killed in a tavern brawl in 1674 at the age of thirty-six. One of his early wedding poems offended the bridegroom, probably unintentionally, and Lucidor spent time in prison as a result. Lucidor's poems, which embraced both secular and religious themes, were not collected in book form until eighteen years after his death. Several of his hymns were included in the official hymnbook of 1695.

Karlfeldt was drawn to the seventeenth-century Swedish poets in general, and perhaps to Lucidor in particular because of his "outsider" status. (He uses the term *löskerkarl* to describe Lucidor, the term he also used in several of his own poems as a contrast to Fridolin.) Lucidor shared Karlfeldt's knowledge of, and enthusiasm for, botany and the natural world. Karlfeldt's description of Lucidor's depictions of Swedish nature could easily be applied to his own poetry: "Här är ingen idyllens diktskog. Det är den svenska vildmarken med sina djur, svensk folktro, svensk folktron" (This is not the poetic forest of an idyll. This is the Swedish wilderness with its animals, Swedish folk belief, a Swedish folk tone). Karlfeldt's characterization of Lucidor highlights his dual nature: "Han är rusets och ruelsens skald som ingen i hans svenska samtid och som få efter honom" (He is the poet of intoxication and remorse like no other in the Sweden of his time, and like few after him).

Despite the prominence of his position as a cultural figure, both as a poet of growing reputation and as a member, then secretary, of the Swedish Academy, Karlfeldt was extremely guarded about his private life. Even among his acquaintances, few knew, for example, that he was the father of two sons, Folke (born in 1903) and Sune (born in 1907), with Gerda Holmberg, whom he had first met in 1901 and who for a time had been his housekeeper.

In March 1913 Karlfeldt experienced a life-threatening illness. Because he was a public figure, news of his condition and eventual recovery was carried in the press. While ill, Karlfeldt confided to a friend that he had decided to marry Holmberg; this long-considered decision, however, was not carried out until 1916. By then they had another child together, Anna Blanzeflor, born in 1915. Their fourth child, Ulla, was born in 1917.

Karlfeldt was a poet who wrote when he was inspired. Thus, long periods of poetic silence might be followed by a burst of creative activity. Torsten Fogelqvist, Karlfeldt's successor in the Swedish Academy and the author of a biography of the poet, has written that the years 1910 to 1915 were essentially "songless" for Karlfeldt. At the same time, Karlfeldt worked carefully on drafts of poems, often over a period of years, until he felt they were finished, as evidenced by his notebooks. Because he was occupied with other duties, especially involving the Swedish Academy, his next book, *Flora och Bellona* (1918, Flora and Bellona), did not appear until twelve years after *Flora och Pomona*.

Flora och Bellona is in some respects a continuation of themes from the previous book, and it is likely that many of the poems in this collection were written in the years immediately following the publication of *Flora och Pomona*. Bellona was the Roman goddess of war, described as either the wife or sister of Mars. The title poem suggests the range of this collection, from "vårlig dal" (spring valley) to "kala berg" (bare mountain), as well as the poet's greater acceptance of the characteristic oppositions of life.

"Blommornas kärlek" (The Flowers' Love) was written for the 1907 bicentennial celebration of the birth of the great eighteenth-century Swedish naturalist Carl von Linné (Carolus Linnaeus). Besides developing the system of classification of plants (still in use today), Linné attached special importance to the sexual nature of the plant world. Karlfeldt plays on two writings by Linné in this poem, in which Linné is depicted as "en from naturens präst" (a pious priest of nature), who finds that "guden var när" (the god was nearby) in "blommornas kärleksfest" (the flowers' love-feast).

Winter themes are prevalent in this collection, in poems such as "Fjällstorm" (Mountain Storm) and "Mikael," with a patriotic exhortation to youth in "Ny Nord" (New North). Unlike poets such as Heidenstam, Karlfeldt seldom used overtly patriotic or nationalistic tones in his poetry. Themes of passing are seen in poems such as "Klagosång över en landtman" (Lament for a Country Man).

One of Karlfeldt's most personal poems is "Sjukdom" (Sickness). Simple in vocabulary and diction, and speaking in the first person rather than through a third-person mask, the poem describes what would now be called a near-death experience: "Jag seglar till ett fjärran land, / ett fjärran land" (I am sailing to a distant land, / a distant land). He feels an unspecified longing: "Det är en längtan på egen hand, / en längtan för längtans skull" (It is a longing on its own, / a longing for longing's sake). Turning back from "en obeskrivlig port" (an indescribable gate), what he recalls of the "outsägligt ord" (inexpressible word) that he has experienced is "att rösten lät som en väns" (that the voice sounded like a friend's). In part, this poem can be read as a reply to a well-known hymn by J. O. Wallin (number 451 in the 1819 hymnbook). Despite his frequent biblical allusions, this poem is perhaps the closest that Karlfeldt comes to a declaration of faith, and it is characteristically inward and reserved.

In humorous contrast, Karlfeldt pokes gentle fun at his own public persona, and the institution of the Swedish Academy, in "Till en sekreterare" (To a Secretary). His position as permanent secretary of the Swedish Academy involved many public functions with "Kungen själv från bur av guld" (the King himself from a cage of gold) as well as "en strålkrans av prinsar och princessor" (a halo of princes and princesses).

While Karlfeldt is never an overtly political poet and rarely refers to contemporary events, there are political undertones in a few of the poems in *Flora och Bellona*. "I Marsvind" (In the March Wind), for example, sets up a conversation among Fridolin and a group of friends. When the subject of Russia comes up, Fridolin has the last, brief (and perhaps ironic) word: "Hvad bry vi oss om tsaren? / Se staren, se staren!" (What care we about the czar? / See the starling, the starling!). This statement might be read as a quietistic rejection of public involvement on the part of the character Fridolin, or as simple irony, or perhaps as a call to pay attention to the real world of nature ("staren") rather than the abstract world of politics.

"Till en jordförvärvare" (To a Land Acquirer) is directly critical of corporate interests who at the time were buying up farms, and their accompanying forest lands, in rural Sweden. The poem also touches on environmental concerns, including pollution.

World War I is clearly referenced in poems such as "Till Bellona" (To Bellona), which includes an unusually topical reference to "din tjänare Wilson" (your servant Wilson [the American president Woodrow Wilson]); "Svart jul" (Black Christmas), dated 1917 (Irving Berlin's song "White Christmas" had of course not yet been written); or "En pesthymn" (A Plague Hymn). "Det röda korset" (The Red Cross), again with a war theme, is one of a few examples of blank verse (rather than rhymed verse) found in this collection.

"I Fridolins spår" (In Fridolin's Tracks) marks the end of Fridolin's rural world: "O Fridolin, din borg är stängd, / och skum och stum också" (Oh Fridolin, your fortress is closed, / and murky and mute as well). The mood of this poem is in the spirit of the times, as World War I was a pivotal moment in European history; the poem also amplifies Karlfeldt's continual awareness of the passing of traditional ways of life.

In 1916 the family moved to a house on the island of Lidingö, just outside Stockholm, where they lived for two years. However, because of Karlfeldt's official duties and his son's enrollment in a Stockholm gymnasium, the family moved back to Stockholm in the fall of 1918. The last poem in *Flora och Bellona*, "Oktober," expresses Karlfeldt's delight in renting a country house and "för första gången på många år" (for the first time in many years) experiencing "vinter, höst och vår" (winter, fall and spring).

After the death of Alfred Nobel in 1896, his will and testament assigned the role of selecting the recipient of the Nobel Prize in Literature to the Swedish Academy. This charge encountered some resistance within the Academy, but Wirsén, the permanent secretary at the time, saw the chance to administer a literary prize with such a sizable endowment as a unique opportunity. The Academy presented the first Nobel Prize in Literature in 1901. World War I presented problems, however, for the Swedish Academy in this role. Sweden of course remained neutral during that conflict, and the Academy took pains to avoid granting the prize to authors who might offend any of the warring countries. Because of difficulties in shipping and communications, it also became harder for the committee to acquire the materials needed to form a coherent picture of literature from other countries. These wartime conditions thus tended to favor Nordic authors, close neighbors whose work was already known to the Academy.

No prize was awarded in 1914, and the prize for 1915 (which went to the French writer Romain Rolland) was awarded a year late, together with the prize for 1916 (which went to the Swedish author and Academy member Heidenstam). Karlfeldt's name came up at that time as a possible candidate for the award, the proposal being to share the prize with Heidenstam and Per Hallström, another member of the Academy. (Other suggestions involved a shared prize with authors from at least two Nordic countries.) A similar idea emerged in the deliberations for the 1919 award, this time for an award shared between Karlfeldt and Hallström. Karlfeldt, however, refused to be considered, arguing that it would be unseemly for the Academy to grant the prize to its own permanent secretary.

Karlfeldt fulfilled a long-held dream by purchasing an abandoned farm, "Sångs," in the village of Sjugare in Dalarna in 1921. A friend, the painter and book illustrator Gustaf Ankarcrona, helped design the expanded house and adjoining buildings, and in 1922 the family was able to take up part-time residence there. Over the remaining years of his life, Karlfeldt applied his considerable botanical knowledge to designing and planting extensive gardens on the grounds.

A footnote in Karlfeldt's production is his second monograph in literary biography, this time a study of the Lutheran minister, poet, novelist, and humorist Dahlgren. Subtitled *En bild ur svensk romantik för hundra år sedan* (A Picture from Swedish Romanticism One Hundred Years Ago), the book describes Dahlgren as "a forgotten poet, who does not deserve to be thrown onto the scrap heap." Karlfeldt's study, showing positive interest while pointing out Dahlgren's shortcomings as a writer, was not sufficient to reawaken interest in Dahlgren, who is no longer included in anthologies or even mentioned in overviews of the Romantic period in Sweden.

Karlfeldt's final collection, *Hösthorn,* brings together poems written after the publication of *Flora och Bellona* in 1918. The image of the "autumn horn" of the title poem is not a cornucopia but rather a cow's horn, in traditional peasant culture used as a simple musical instrument. The poet uses the instrument to sound the praises of the autumn months, the "princes" of the year, and finds depth in its limited range: "Jag tvingar till andakt dess trotsiga ton" (I force to devotion its contrary tone). *Hösthorn* demonstrates Karlfeldt's continued vitality as a poet, with further refinement of his considerable verbal instrument. On the other hand, the simplicity of a poem such as "Första minnet" (First Memory) suggests a receptivity to new, "modernist" currents in poetry.

Noteworthy in this collection are several poems of a more personal, lyrical nature than in Karlfeldt's previous work. A common theme in these poems is, not surprisingly, death and aging. Several poems in this collection rank among Karlfeldt's best work, including "Sub luna" (Latin for "Under the Moon") and "Vinterorgel" (Winter Organ). Karl-Ivar Hildeman, who wrote extensively about Karlfeldt, often stressing a biographical approach to his poetry, reads "Sub luna" as a retrospective look by the author on both his life and work. "Vinterorgel," which ends the collection, describes a majestic instrument that stands in sharp contrast to the simple peasant horn of the title poem.

The sense of smell was of enormous importance for Karlfeldt, as evidenced by many of his poems. In the opening poem of *Hösthorn,* for example, the poet refers to himself as a servant of "Maj, de ljuva dofters patron" (May, the patron of sweet scents). Karlfeldt's 1930 essay "Lukt och doft" (Smell and Scent), published in the posthumous collection *Tankar och tal med ett lyriskt bokslut* (1932, Thoughts and Speeches with a Lyrical Conclusion), explores the wide variety of aromatic plants that inspired or, much less often, repulsed him.

Although Karlfeldt's health had not been excellent since his serious illness in 1913, his death on 8 April 1931 came suddenly. Earlier that year, he had once again been suggested as a recipient for the Nobel Prize, and in contrast to 1919, he told his wife privately that this time, if it were offered, he would accept the award. He would soon have reached the mandatory retirement age and would be stepping down from his post as permanent secretary (though he would still be a member). Gerda Karlfeldt, however, had no advance knowledge of the Academy's official intentions until the award was announced in October. It was the first, and only, time that the Swedish Academy granted a Nobel Prize in Literature to an author no longer living.

It is also one of the few times that the award has been made to a writer whose work cannot really be appreciated outside its original language. While the considerations of Academy members in this decision were not written down, Karlfeldt's Nobel Prize might be interpreted as a belated recognition of his standing as a "national" poet. This reason, however, would seem to contradict the requirement of "universality" in granting the Nobel Prize. Karlfeldt was not well known outside of Sweden, mainly because of the lack of translations, and the prize was probably a contributing factor in the 1938 publication of the only book-length translation in English.

In formulating the reasons for awarding the prize to Karlfeldt, Swedish poet and Academy member Anders Österling acknowledged that "It is the deliberate self-limitation of lyrical poetry, and at the same time its fate, that its most profound qualities and values are indissolubly connected with the character and rhythm of its original language." He added, "even the treasures of the so-called great literatures have only rarely been enriched by such jewels as Karlfeldt has created in a so-called minor language." The process by which the Swedish Academy has awarded the Nobel Prize in Literature over the years, including Karlfeldt's role during his tenure as permanent secretary, can be followed in Kjell Espmark's 1986 study. *Why Sinclair Lewis Got the Nobel Prize* (1931) is Naboth Hedin's translation of Karlfeldt's presentation speech at the awarding of the 1930 Nobel Prize in Literature to American novelist Sinclair Lewis; it also includes Lewis's Nobel lecture.

Karlfeldt's widow outlived her husband by almost fifty years, carefully preserving their home in Dalarna, and his memory, until her death in 1981. The gardens are open to the public during the summer months.

At the time of his death, Karlfeldt's reputation and popularity were at a high point. While at one time there had been discussion among Swedish critics of the so-called danger of Karlfeldt as a literary model, the fact was that literary norms were rapidly changing, most notably by the introduction of literary modernism, and many of Karlfeldt's concerns were already seen as old-fashioned even at the time of his death. If Karlfeldt did have a successor, however, it would argu-ably be the popular songwriter and troubadour Evert Taube.

Erik Axel Karlfeldt's standing as a poet was revived in the 1950s by a younger generation of poets, among them Lars Forssell, who especially admired his mastery of form and linguistic virtuosity. Although he is no longer a model for younger poets, many of his poems do remain inimitable (and, it might be added, untranslatable) classics of Swedish poetry.

Bibliography:

Nils Afzelius and Arne Bergstrand, *Erik Axel Karlfeldts bibliografi*, 2 volumes (Stockholm: Kungliga biblioteket, 1974, 1989).

Biography:

Torsten Fogelqvist, *Erik Axel Karlfeldt: En minnesteckning* (Stockholm: Norstedt, 1940).

References:

Majt Banck, ed., *Karlfeldt synpunkter och värderingar* (Stockholm: LTs förlag, 1971);

Sven Delblanc, "Karlfeldt–sångare och kyrkvärd," in *Den svenska litteraturen: Den storsvenska generationen 1890–1920,* edited by Lars Lönnroth and Delblanc (Stockholm: Bonnier, 1989), pp. 88–93;

Kjell Espmark, *Det litterära Nobelpriset: Principer och värderingar bakom besluten* (Stockholm: Norstedts, 1986); translated as *The Nobel Prize in Literature: A Study of the Criteria behind the Choices* (Boston: G. K. Hall, 1991);

Ingegerd Fries, *Karlfeldt och dalmålarna* (Falun: Karlfeldt-samfundet, 1996);

Karl-Ivar Hildeman, *En löskekarl: En Karlfeldtsbok* (Stockholm: Wahlström & Widstrand, 1977);

Hildeman, "Erik Axel Karlfeldt: An Evaluation," *Scandinavian Studies,* 40 (1968): 81–94;

Hildeman, *Sub luna och andra Karlfeldtessäer* (Stockholm: Wahlström & Widstrand, 1966);

Olof Lagercrantz, *Jungfrun och demonerna* (Stockholm: Wahlström & Widstrand, 1938);

Jöran Mjöberg, *I Fridolins spår* (Stockholm: Natur och Kultur, 1945);

Thorsten Thunman, *I susande hymner går Flora: Växtmotiv i Karlfeldts diktning* (Falun, Sweden: Karlfeldt-samfundet, 1979);

Carin von Sydow, *Jag ville ha sagt dig det ömmaste ord: Kärleken mellan Gerda och Erik Axel Karlfeldt* (Stockholm: Wahlström & Widstrand, 1999).

Papers:

Collections of Erik Axel Karlfeldt's papers are housed at the Royal Library in Stockholm and at the Nobel Library of the Swedish Academy.

1931 Nobel Prize in Literature Presentation Speech

by Anders Österling, Member of the Nobel Committee of the Swedish Academy

If an interested foreigner were to ask one of Erik Axel Karlfeldt's countrymen what we admire most in this poet and on what qualities his national greatness depends, it would at first seem easy to give an answer. People like to talk of what they love. The Swede would say that we celebrate this poet because he represents our character with a style and a genuineness that we should like to be ours, and because he has sung with singular power and exquisite charm of the tradition of our people, of all the precious features which are the basis for our feeling for home and country in the shadow of the pine-covered mountains.

But the Swede would soon check himself, realizing that such a general explanation is insufficient, that in Karlfeldt there are many things, beloved but difficult to define, which a proper appraisal must take into account but which are inaccessible to the foreigner. Hence we can offer no ready-made expression of our conviction of the high rank of Karlfeldt's poetry, for there are elements of mysticism in it, powers and instincts that elude analysis.

We face a similar difficulty on this occasion when we are to briefly sketch the life-work of the great lyrical poet, since it has now been made the object of a great international award. It is the deliberate self-limitation of lyrical poetry, and at the same time its fate, that its most profound qualities and values are indissolubly connected with the character and rhythm of its original language, with the meaning and weight of every single word. Karlfeldt's individuality may be dimly felt in a translation, but only in Swedish can it be fully comprehended. However, if one attempts to find independent comparative criteria, he is forced to admit that even the treasures of the so-called great literatures have only rarely been enriched by such jewels as Karlfeldt has created in a so-called minor language.

If we look back on Karlfeldt's notable career from its début in 1895 and follow it through the works of three decades, steady though limited in size by his austere standards, we see very clearly how this man used his talents with a rare instinct for the fruitful, the solid, and the genuine. He began as a minstrel and a singer of nature, conscious of his ability but still doubtful of his calling. Was there any use for the dreams that thronged his breast? Could they have a meaning for a whole people? Early in his career, the poet looked for a deputy, an alter ego, an independent figure suited to represent his feelings, his sufferings, and his longing as well as his sarcasm. The famous Fridolin was at first a creation of shyness, for the poet was reluctant to appear in his own person and expose the private life of his soul. Fridolin soon became a classic, and he has his place in the rout of Northern Bacchus, rustic cousin of the characters of Bellman, with a firmer gait, but with flowers on his hat from the harvest festival at Pungmakarebo. Karlfeldt's home became more and more an artistic microcosm in which the universe was mirrored in the same manner as Biblical scenes are mirrored in the baroque fantasies of the frescoes in the farmhouses of Dalekarlia. With his sense of humour, which was often reverence in disguise, he kept his being unstained, and he preserved the magic ring of harmony. But his seemingly peaceful development must have contained many struggles and tensions, just enough to create the necessary pressure for the creative spring. Poetry was for Karlfeldt a continuous test of the strength and substance of his being. Thus he gave a powerful finale to his poetry in *Hösthorn* (1927) [The Horn of Autumn], his epilogue played on a winter organ, whose pipes reach from earth to heaven but at the same time sound a childhood echo of the small white churches in Dalarna.

The unity of his work is a rarity in our time. If one asks about Karlfeldt's main problem, one word may serve as an answer: self-discipline. His originality grew on the soil of a pagan and luxuriant wilderness, and he would not have been drawn so often to witch motifs and the pitchy brew of Uriel if he had not felt the presence of demons. The muffled tumult of nature under the moon of pagan festivals is one of the visions that he evokes. The contrast between the heavy intoxication of the blood and the pure celestial yearnings of the soul recurs constantly in his poetry. Yet the different elements never destroy each other. He tames them as does an artist by remaining faithful to himself and by giving a personal touch even to the smallest detail.

In Karlfeldt we find scarcely a single expression of poetic self-consciousness. The increasing response to his work would have made such an expression superfluous even if his solid peasant blood had not been a protection against aesthetic arrogance. We find everywhere proof of the integrity of professional honour that is revealed in beautiful and permanent work. In an age in which handmade things have become rare, there is a new and almost moral value in the masterly, chiselled, and resonant language of his verse.

Karlfeldt's poetry possesses precisely this stamp of miraculous perfection. Which of us does not remember such stanzas ringing like bells or vibrating like strings, but above all sung with that peculiar and resounding voice that differs from all others? Perhaps we should remember in this context the beautiful song about the old turner, the village craftsman, who played the fiddle for the people on the banks of the Opplimen and made spinning wheels for them. . . .

In all great poetry there is an interrelation between tradition and experiment, and the principles of renewal and conservation are contained in such poetry. The national tradition survives in Karlfeldt because it is renewed personally and has the character of a conquest dearly bought. We may rejoice that this poet, whose inspiration is drawn predominantly from a past that is disappearing or has disappeared, is thoroughly unconventional in his means of expression and shows daring innovations, whereas busy modernists often content themselves with following the latest trends and fads. Nor can there be any doubt that, despite his provincial subject matter, the singer of Dalarna is one of the contemporary poets who have most boldly tried the wings of imagination and experimented with the possibilities of poetic form.

Thus the decision to honour the poetry of Erik Axel Karlfeldt with this year's Nobel Prize is intended as an expression of justice by international standards. Death has stepped between the laureate and his reward; under the circumstances the Prize will be given to his family. He has left us, but his work remains. The tragic world of chance is outshone by the imperishable summer realm of poetry. Before our eyes we see the tomb in the dusk of winter. At the same time we hear the great victorious harmonies sung by the happiness of the creative genius; we feel the scents from the Northern pleasure garden that his poetry created for the comfort and joy of all receptive hearts.

At the banquet, Professor C. W. Oseen spoke about the deceased laureate:

Is there nothing that is only beneficial, to humanity as well as to the individual? Perhaps there is! What the poems of Erik Axel Karlfeldt have meant to the Swedish people, you, honoured guests, cannot know, but for us it remains unforgettable. For thirty-five years they have accompanied the ups and downs of our lives. That nothing may emerge from Karlfeldt's work, this world of beauty, for the benefit of humanity and the individual, I cannot believe, I will not believe. And yet—how far are we from the intentions of Alfred Nobel even here? Out of the prize meant to help a needy artist we have made a wreath, a wreath to adorn the coffin of our most beloved poet.

If today's award does not strictly follow Nobel's intentions, does that mean that the result of this procedure will be less than what Nobel intended? I say not! What we have created is not less but more! This festive ceremony is a tribute to genius. It may not have much in common with Alfred Nobel's dreams but it is akin to his work. He was a genius himself. His work has served humanity, to build and to destroy. It has served and destroyed life. The festive occasion we are celebrating is dedicated to genius with its good and evil faces, with this double significance, because we do not know what humanity needs most and what furthers its prospering most: "good" or "evil." We dedicate this ceremony to genius, brother of madness, to whom we owe everything that makes our lives worthwhile.

[© The Nobel Foundation, 1931.]

Yasunari Kawabata
(14 June 1899 – 16 April 1972)

Van C. Gessel
Brigham Young University

This entry was expanded by Gessel from his Kawabata entry in *DLB 180: Japanese Fiction Writers, 1868–1945*.

BOOKS: *Kanjō sōshoku* (Tokyo: Kinseidō, 1926);
Izu no odoriko (Tokyo: Kinseidō, 1927); translated by Edward G. Seidensticker as *The Izu Dancer* (Tokyo: Hara Shobō, 1964);
Kawabata Yasunari shū, Shinshin Kessaku Shōsetsu Zenshū series (Tokyo: Heibonsha, 1929);
Boku no hyōhonshitsu, Shinkō Geijutsuha Sōsho series (Tokyo: Shinchōsha, 1930);
Hana aru shashin, Shinkō Geijutsuha Sōsho series (Tokyo: Shinchōsha, 1930);
Asakusa kurenaidan (Tokyo: Senshinsha, 1930); translated by Alisa Freedman as *The Scarlet Gang of Asakusa* (Berkeley: University of California Press, 2005);
Keshō to kuchibue (Tokyo: Shinchōsha, 1933);
Suishō gensō, Bungei Fukkō Sōsho series (Tokyo: Kaizōsha, 1934);
Kawabata Yasunari shū (Tokyo: Kaizōsha, 1934);
Jojōka (Tokyo: Takemura Shobō, 1934);
Kinju (Tokyo: Noda Shobō, 1935);
Junsui no koe (Tokyo: Sara Shoten, 1936);
Hana no warutsu (Tokyo: Kaizōsha, 1936);
Yukiguni (Tokyo: Sōgensha, 1937; revised, 1948); translated by Seidensticker as *Snow Country* (New York: Knopf, 1957);
Musumegokoro (Tokyo: Takemura Shobō, 1937);
Josei kaigan (Tokyo: Sōgensha, 1937; revised edition, Tokyo: Eikōsha, 1947);
Kyūchō no tantei (Tokyo: Chūō Kōronsha, 1937);
Otome no minato (Tokyo: Jitsugyō no Nihonsha, 1938);
Tampenshū, Hakushoku Sōsho series (Tokyo: Sunagoya Shobō, 1939);
Kawabata Yasunari shū, Shin Nihon Bungaku Zenshū series (Tokyo: Kaizōsha, 1940);
Shōgatsu sanganichi (Tokyo: Shinseikaku, 1940);
Negao, Yūkō Meisaku Senshū series (Tokyo: Yūkōsha, 1941);
Shōsetsu no kōsei (Tokyo: Mikasa Shobō, 1941);

Aisuru hitotachi (Tokyo: Shinchōsha, 1941);
Bunshō (Tokyo: Tōhō Shobō, 1942);
Kawabata Yasunari shū, Saidai Meisaku Zenshū series (Tokyo: Kawade Shobō, 1942);
Utsukushii tabi (Tokyo: Jitsugyō no Nihonsha, 1942);
Kōgen (Tokyo: Kōchō Shorin, 1942);
Ai (Tokyo: Bitokusha, 1945);
Komadori Onsen (Tokyo: Shōnan Shobō, 1945);
Asagumo (Tokyo: Shinchōsha, 1946);
Hijaku (Tokyo: Shinkigensha, 1946);
Yūbae shōjo (Tokyo: Tanchō Shobō, 1946);
Onsenyado (Tokyo: Jitsugyō no Nihonsha, 1946);
Gakkō no hana (Tokyo: Shōnan Shobō, 1946);
Chirinuru o (Tokyo: Maeda Shuppansha, 1946);
Issō ikka (Tokyo: Seiryusha, 1948);
Kawabata Yasunari shū, 2 volumes (Tokyo: Hosokawa Shoten, 1948);
Shiroi mangetsu (Tokyo: Rotte Shuppansha, 1948);
Aishū (Tokyo: Hosokawa Shoten, 1949);
Nihon shōsetsu daihyōsaku zenshū (Tokyo: Koyama Shoten, 1949);
Asakusa monogatari (Tokyo: Chūō Kōronsha, 1950);
Kageki gakkō (Tokyo: Himawarisha, 1950);
Shin bunshō tokuhon (Tokyo: Akane Shobō, 1951);
Maihime (Tokyo: Asahi Shimbunsha, 1951);
Kawabata Yasunari shū (Tokyo: Shinchōsha, 1951);
Shōsetsu nyūmon (Tokyo: Kaname Shobō, 1952);
Sembazuru (Tokyo: Chikuma Shobō, 1952); translated by Seidensticker as *Thousand Cranes* (New York: Knopf, 1958);
Tenohira no shōsetsu hyappen (Tokyo: Shinchōsha, 1952);
Saikonsha (Tokyo: Mikasa Shobō, 1953);
Kawabata Yasunari shū, Shōwa Bungaku Zenshū series (Tokyo: Kadokawa Shoten, 1953);
Hi mo tsuki mo (Tokyo: Chūō Kōronsha, 1953);
Matsugo no me (Tokyo: Sōgensha, 1953);
Kawabata Yasunari shū, Chōhen Shōsetsu Zenshū series (Tokyo: Shinchōsha, 1953);
Kawa no aru shitamachi no hanashi (Tokyo: Shinchōsha, 1954);

Yasunari Kawabata (right) receiving the 1968 Nobel Prize in Literature from King Gustav VI Adolf of Sweden (Associated Press, Pool)

Kawabata Yasunari shū, Gendai Bungō Meisaku Zenshū series (Tokyo: Kawade Shobō, 1954);

Yama no oto (Tokyo: Chikuma Shobō, 1954); translated by Seidensticker as *The Sound of the Mountain* (New York: Knopf, 1970);

Meijin (Tokyo: Bungei Shunjū Shinsha, 1954); translated by Seidensticker as *The Master of Go* (New York: Knopf, 1972; London: Secker & Warburg, 1973);

Dōyō (Tokyo: Tōhōsha, 1954);

Kawabata Yasunari shū, Nihon Shōnen Shōjo Meisaku Zenshū series (Tokyo: Kawade Shobō, 1954);

Izu no tabi (Tokyo: Chūō Kōronsha, 1954);

Niji ikutabi (Tokyo: Kawade Shobō, 1955);

Shin'yū (Tokyo: Kaiseisha, 1955);

Tōkyō no hito, 4 volumes (Tokyo: Shinchōsha, 1955);

Mizuumi (Tokyo: Shinchōsha, 1955); translated by Reiko Tsukimura as *The Lake* (Tokyo & New York: Kodansha International, 1974; London: Peter Owen, 1977);

Kawabata Yasunari shū (Tokyo: Tōzai Bunmeisha, 1955);

Shōsetsu no kenkyū (Tokyo: Kaname Shobō, 1955);

Tamayura (Tokyo: Kadokawa Shoten, 1955);

Tsubame no dōjo (Tokyo: Chikuma Shobō, 1955);

Kawabata Yasunari shū, Gendai Nihon Bungaku Zenshū series (Tokyo: Chikuma Shobō, 1955);

Onna de aru koto, 2 volumes (Tokyo: Shinchōsha, 1956–1957);

Fuji no hatsuyuki (Tokyo: Shinchōsha, 1958);

Kaze no aru michi (Tokyo: Kadokawa Shoten, 1959);

Nemureru bijo (Tokyo: Shinchōsha, 1961); translated by Seidensticker as "House of the Sleeping Beauties," in *House of the Sleeping Beauties and Other Stories* (Tokyo & New York: Kodansha International, 1969; London: Quadriga, 1969);

Koto (Tokyo: Shinchōsha, 1962); translated by J. Martin Holman as *The Old Capital* (San Francisco: North Point Press, 1987);

Jūnin hyakuwa (Tokyo: Mainichi Shimbunsha, 1963);

Kawabata Yasunari tampen zenshū (Tokyo: Kōdansha, 1964);

Koto no fu (Tokyo: Yuyudō, 1964);

Utsukushisa to kanashimi to (Tokyo: Chūō Kōronsha, 1965); translated by Howard Hibbett as *Beauty and Sadness* (New York: Knopf, 1975; London: Secker & Warburg, 1975);

Kataude (Tokyo: Shinchōsha, 1965); translated by Seidensticker as "One Arm," in *House of the Sleeping Beauties and Other Stories;*

Kawabata Yasunari shū, Nihon Bungaku Zenshū series (Tokyo: Kawade Shobō, 1966);

Kawabata Yasunari jisenshū (Tokyo: Shūeisha, 1966);

Rakka ryūsui (Tokyo: Shinchōsha, 1966);

Kawabata Yasunari shū, Gendai Nihon Bungakukan series (Tokyo: Bungei Shunjū, 1966);

Kawabata Yasunari shū, 2 volumes, Nihon Bungaku Zenshū series (Tokyo: Shūeisha, 1966–1967);

Kawabata Yasunari, 2 volumes, Karāban Nihon Bungaku Zenshū series (Tokyo: Kawade Shobō, 1967–1970);

Gekka no mon (Tokyo: Yamato Shobō, 1967);

Kawabata Yasunari sakuhinshū (Tokyo: Chūō Kōronsha, 1968);

Kawabata Yasunari shū, Gendai Nihon Bungaku series (Tokyo: Chikuma Shobō, 1968);

Kawabata Yasunari shū, Shinchō Nihon Bungaku series (Tokyo: Shinchōsha, 1968);

Kawabata Yasunari shōnen shōjo shōsetsu shū (Tokyo: Shinchōsha, 1968);

Utsukushii Nihon no watakushi–sono josetsu (Tokyo: Kōdansha, 1969); translated by Seidensticker as *Japan, the Beautiful, and Myself: The 1968 Nobel Prize Acceptance Speech* (Tokyo & New York: Kōdansha International, 1969);

Kawabata Yasunari, Gendai Chōhen Bungaku Zenshū series (Tokyo: Kōdansha, 1969);

Kawabata Yasunari, Nihon Bungaku Zenshū series (Tokyo: Shinchōsha, 1969);

Kawabata Yasunari, Gendai Nihon no Bungaku series (Tokyo: Gakushū Kenkyūsha, 1969);

Bi no sonzai to hakken, translated by V. H. Viglielmo as *The Existence and Discovery of Beauty* (Tokyo: Mainichi Shimbunsha, 1969);

Kawabata Yasunari shū, Akatsuki Meisakukan Nihon Bungaku Shiriizu series (Tokyo: Akatsuki Kyōiku Tosho, 1970);

Kawabata Yasunari, Nōberu Bungaku Zenshū series (Tokyo: Shufu no Tomosha, 1971);

Teihon Yukiguni (Tokyo: Bokuyōsha, 1971);

Kawabata Yasunari, Nihon Bungaku Zenshū series (Tokyo: Shūeisha, 1971);

Taidan Nihon no bungaku (Tokyo: Chūō Kōronsha, 1971);

Aru hito no sei no naka ni (Tokyo: Kawada Shobō Shinsha, 1972);

Tampopo (Tokyo: Shinchōsha, 1972);

Nemureru bijo / Yukigunishō (Tokyo: Horupu Shuppan, 1972);

Take no koe momo no hana (Tokyo: Shinchōsha, 1973);

Nihon no bi no kokoro (Tokyo: Kōdansha, 1973);

Kotsuhiroi: Tenohira no shōsetsu (Tokyo: Yumanite, 1975);

Tenju no ko (Tokyo: Shinchōsha, 1975);

Sansai ryokuyū kaiyū, by Kawabata, Tetsuzō Tanikawa, and Shichi Narasaki (Tokyo: Chūō Kōronsha, 1976);

Tokoname atsumi sanage, by Kawabata, Tanikawa, and Narasaki (Tokyo: Chūō Kōronsha, 1976);

Shigaraki bizen tamba, by Kawabata, Tanikawa, and Narasaki (Tokyo: Chūō Kōronsha, 1976);

Seto minō, by Kawabata, Tanikawa, and Narasaki (Tokyo: Chūō Kōronsha, 1976);

Nāshissasu (Tokyo: Tōjusha, 1977);

Konrei to sōrei (Tokyo: Sōgensha, 1978);

Maihime no koyomi (Tokyo: Mainichi Shimbunsha, 1979);

Umi no himatsuri (Tokyo: Mainichi Shimbunsha, 1979).

Collections: *Kawabata Yasunari senshū,* 9 volumes (Tokyo: Kaizōsha, 1938–1939);

Kawabata Yasunari zenshū, 16 volumes (Tokyo: Shinchōsha, 1948–1954);

Kawabata Yasunari zenshū, 10 volumes (Tokyo: Shinchōsha, 1956);

Kawabata Yasunari zenshū, 12 volumes (Tokyo: Shinchōsha, 1959–1961);

Kawabata Yasunari zenshū, 19 volumes (Tokyo: Shinchōsha, 1969–1974);

Bungei jihyō (Tokyo: Kōdansha, 2003).

Editions in English: *Palm-of-the-Hand Stories,* translated by Lane Dunlop and J. Martin Holman (San Francisco: North Point Press, 1988; Tokyo: Tuttle, 1988; London: Picador Classics, 1989);

The Dancing Girl of Izu and Other Stories, translated by Holman (Washington, D.C.: Counterpoint, 1997);

Tales with Two Souls: A Variety in Time and Culture, translated by Peter Metevelis (Pittsburgh: Dorrance, 1999);

First Snow on Fuji, translated by Michael Emmerich (Washington, D.C.: Counterpoint, 1999).

OTHER: *Gendai jidō bungaku jiten,* edited by Kawabata, Mimei Ogawa, and Tsunatake Furuya (Tokyo: Hōbunko, 1955);

Mizuumi, edited by Kawabata (Tokyo: Yuki Shobō, 1961);

Kyōto jiten, edited by Kawabata (Tokyo: Jinbutsu ōraisha, 1967);

Gakushō shin kokugo jiten, edited by Kawabata and Umetomo Saeki (Tokyo: Kōdansha, 1968);

Aesop, *Isoppu,* translated by Kawabata (Tokyo: Fureberu-kan, 1968);

Bunshō no gihō, edited by Kawabata, Sen'ichi Hisamatsu, and Yoshimoto Endō (Tokyo: Meiji Shoin, 1970);

Ōchō monogatarishū, 2 volumes, edited by Kawabata (Tokyo: Kawade Shobō Shinsha, 1971–1972);

The Tale of the Bamboo Cutter / Taketori monogatari, modern retelling by Kawabata, translated by Donald Keene, bilingual edition (Tokyo: Kōdansha International, 1998).

Yasunari Kawabata was the first (and, until 1994, the only) Japanese author to receive the Nobel Prize in Literature, which he won in 1968. His writings attracted a worldwide audience who saw in them expressions of the traditional beauty and aesthetic values of Japan as well as some of the exoticism that was expected in books about the country. Yet, Kawabata's work is much more complex and multidimensional than such a reading suggests. His writings, particularly those of the postwar years, certainly celebrate the rich cultural heritage of Japan, but a careful reading reveals that his preoccupation with the past resulted less from a desire to preserve tradition than from a desire to indulge in the pleasures of the past precisely because they were unattainable. One motif common to most of Kawabata's works is that of distancing: characters rush away from becoming involved with others; men and women, though always attracted to one another, seem like identical magnetic poles in pushing away from those for whom they yearn. Only if one admires beauty from a distance can it remain unspoiled, and both one's appreciation of that remote beauty and one's resignation in recognizing that it can never be intimately embraced can preserve such unspoiled beauty. The intricate, sometimes enigmatic aesthetic values in Kawabata's writings are intriguing, but they, like his characters, are not easily approached and apprehended.

Yasunari Kawabata was born in Osaka on 14 June 1899, the second of two children (Yoshiko, his sister, was four years older than he). His family, while not particularly well-to-do by the time of his birth, could trace its heritage to the third military regent of Japan in the early thirteenth century, and this lineage gave the family some status in the village. His ancestors had erected a temple of the Obaku Zen sect of Buddhism in town, and Yasunari's father, Eikichi Kawabata, had obtained a medical license and become assistant director of a clinic in Osaka. His father had also studied Confucian philosophy, Chinese poetry, and painting in addition to pursuing his medical interests; but he was a man of feeble constitution, and his children inherited his respiratory problems. Kawabata wrote that his family was convinced he would not survive childhood. His father succumbed to tuberculosis when Yasunari was only two years old, and less than a year later his mother, Gen Kawabata, died from the same illness. Yoshiko was taken to live with her maternal aunt, and Yasunari joined his grandparents, Sanpachirō and Kane, in a farming village on the outskirts of Osaka.

Kawabata's grandfather was essentially blind by this time, but he encouraged the boy to pursue his interest in painting. In fall 1906 Kawabata's grandmother died, the third close relative that the boy had lost in five years. Three years later his sister, Yoshiko, died at age fourteen. Kawabata had seen her only twice in the seven years since they had been separated, and he felt detached when the news of her death arrived. Living alone with his blind grandfather, Kawabata developed a lifelong habit of staring mutely, for long periods of time, into the faces of people around him, often to the dismay of those who did not understand the reason for his stares. He also became a voracious reader, even struggling through demanding classics of the Heian period (794–1185) such as Murasaki Shikibu's *The Tale of Genji* and *The Pillow Book of Sei Shōnagon*. Kawabata later claimed that his reading of these ancient texts by women had profoundly influenced his use of language and his literary sensibilities. He had read every volume in the library of his elementary school by his last year there.

Kawabata entered the Ibaraki Middle School in 1912, and before long he decided to become a writer rather than a painter, a shift in career interests that pleased his sightless grandfather. His grandfather soon had him write a letter to an uncle who was providing them with a monthly stipend from the estate: Grandfather, the letter said, was surviving on a few swallows of soup each day, and the boy was contributing to his own sickly nature by eating only pickled plums by day and vegetables before bedtime. Kawabata also began writing essays and poetry, the latter in the new style and colloquial diction made popular by Tōson Shimazaki.

In spring 1914 Kawabata's grandfather, his last surviving relative, was confined to his bed, and during the final month of the old man's life Kawabata began writing a diary recounting his ministrations to the dying man. The toll on the psyche of the sixteen-year-old boy was heavy, and at times he would flee from the house and abandon the old man until after dark. The respite was fleeting, however, for Kawabata then felt guilty that his grandfather might die while he was absent. On the evening of the state funeral for the widow of Emperor Meiji in late May 1914, Kawabata's grandfather died. Following all the deaths of his family members, others began to apply the title "master of funerals" to Kawabata. The boy spent a short time with an uncle and then the following January moved into the middle-school dormitory, where he remained until he graduated.

At school he began to read contemporary Japanese and Russian literature, but he remained under the sway of *The Tale of Genji*. A small local paper published some of his poems, essays, and short pieces of fiction, and after the unexpected death of his English teacher, Kawabata wrote "Shi no hitsugi o kata ni" (With Our Teacher's Casket on Our Shoulders), his first story to be published in a literary journal when it appeared in *Dan'ei* in 1917. During his final year at the school he had a fleeting homosexual affair with another young man in his dormitory, a relationship that Kawabata claimed had "warmed and purified and saved me," presumably from his loneliness.

Partly in the hope that he could at least pursue a career as a literary scholar if he were unable to succeed as a writer, Kawabata applied for admission to and was accepted by the English Literature Department of the First High School in Tokyo, one of the most prestigious public schools in the country. But he paid virtually no attention to the study of his major subject and in fact read mostly the works of Fyodor Dostoevsky and other Russian authors. Lacking confidence in his writing talents, loathing his new dormitory environment in Tokyo, and feeling sorrow at the end of his homosexual affair, Kawabata felt that his personality had been warped by what he called his "orphan's disposition."

To assuage his grief, in late autumn 1918 he set out on a walking tour across the Izu Peninsula, where he encountered a troupe of traveling entertainers and spent several days in their company. Judging from "Izu no odoriko" (1926, The Izu Dancer), the story he eventually wrote about the experience, the time he spent with these simple but honest country folk restored his sense of self-worth and his desire to continue his literary pursuits. The following year Kawabata published an account of his journey in the high-school journal, and he began frequenting a Tokyo restaurant known for its attractive young waitresses. He quickly developed a crush on one waitress, and by 1920, when he moved on to the English Literature Department at Tokyo Imperial University, he had fallen desperately in love with her.

At the university, he and a group of colleagues founded their own literary magazine with the support of Kan Kikuchi, the influential editor of *Bungei Shunjū*. Kikuchi praised highly the first story that Kawabata published in this coterie journal, and the editor continued to be an important literary and personal supporter of the young writer. Kawabata repaid this support by publishing much of his fiction in *Bungei Shunjū*, and Kikuchi also introduced Kawabata to Riichi Yokomitsu and several other writers who became his close friends and literary allies throughout his career.

Although the waitress whom Kawabata was romancing had only recently turned fifteen years old, Kawabata was determined to marry her. Kikuchi promised to provide some financial support; Kawabata visited the father of his fiancée in the "snow country" of northern Japan to gain his permission for the match; and all preparations were completed, but the young woman sent Kawabata a letter announcing that an unspecified "catastrophe" had occurred and that she could never see him again. He was crushed, for through his relationship with her Kawabata had hoped to regain the "heart of a child" that he had lost through the deaths of his family members. He avowed throughout his relationship with the girl that their relations had always been pure, that he had "never laid so much as a finger on the girl"; and one of his closest friends corroborated this claim by insisting that Kawabata "did not have a whit of sexual passion, sensuality, or carnality in him."

Taking refuge in his writing, Kawabata started publishing reviews of contemporary fiction in a well-known monthly magazine, a pursuit that he continued for twenty years. Although other writers were founding and joining ideological and artistic camps and praising only their comrades, Kawabata became one of the most generous, unbiased critics of the modern period. By joining so many diverse artistic groups that none could claim his undivided loyalties, he remained aloof from literary factionalism and wrote his reviews based on what he saw as the intrinsic merits of the writing rather than on any affiliations the author might have.

After a year in the English Literature Department, Kawabata switched his major to Japanese literature—primarily, he claimed, because the Japanese Literature Department required less of its students, and the professors never took roll. By this time he had published translations of some stories by John Galsworthy, Lord Dunsany, and Anton Chekhov. Three years of study was the usual amount of time required to graduate from college, but after four years Kawabata still lacked enough credits in his major field to graduate. His professors took pity on him, and, perhaps hoping that he might develop into a writer, they allowed him to receive a diploma in 1924.

Soon after Kawabata had left the university, he and his friend Yokomitsu launched *Bungei Jidai* (The Age of the Literary Arts), a bold new literary journal that they hoped would be an outlet for a new kind of writing that followed the modernist experiments in Europe. The first issue of the journal appeared in October 1924, and the writing was so fresh and challenging that critics labeled the coterie as members of the *Shinkankaku-ha* (Neo-Perceptionist School). The authors associated with the movement had wearied of the dull, quasi-confessional narratives by writers of the Naturalist School and were yearning for new ways to express feelings and present human interactions. Although the movement was short-lived and produced only a few enduring works (mostly by Yokomitsu), the influence of this movement on Kawabata's work was tremendous.

In the form of what he called "tenohira no shōsetsu" (palm-of-the-hand stories), brief sketches of human experience that he compared to the poetry that most authors produce in their youth, Kawabata published his earliest significant fiction in *Bungei Jidai*. Throughout his career he continued to write these stories, which total more than 140, and he also published a recast version of his account of his grandfather's death as "Jūrokusai no nikki" (1925, Diary of My Sixteenth Year). As his fame increased, Kawabata moved about with great frequency between Tokyo and a hot springs resort on the Izu Peninsula. His literary colleagues, noting his proclivity for spending only a few months in any particular residence, began referring to him as an *eien no tabibito* (eternal traveler), a characterization that also metaphorically describes the fluid relationships between Kawabata's literary characters and between the shapes of his narratives. Stylistically he is known as an elliptical, even surrealistic, writer whose work is governed more by a desire to evoke mood than by an interest in plot, structure, logical development, and so many of the other features often associated with the writing of fiction. Some critics have attributed these stylistic features to his interests in the literature written by women of the court in the tenth century, particularly in the masterpieces such as *The Tale of Genji*, but the influences of European modernistic technique on Kawabata's style and approaches to writing are also of great significance.

In May 1925 Kawabata met Hideko Matsubayashi, a young woman with whom he soon began living in what became a common-law marriage until 1931, when the two finally registered formally as husband and wife. Around this time Kawabata was also writing a script for a motion-picture affiliate of the Neo-Perceptionist School, and critics regard this work, "Kurutta ippeiji" (1926, A Crazy Page), as a landmark in the impressionist motion-picture movement in Japan. The work, which was directed by Teinosuke Kinugasa and follows the actions of a man who has taken a job at an insane asylum so that he can observe the wife whom he has driven to madness, was named one of the best motion pictures of the year.

In 1926 Kawabata also published "Izu no odoriko," the story that is typically regarded as the work that launched his career (and Kawabata once declared any author's "maiden work" to be his masterpiece). While recounting fairly faithfully Kawabata's journey around the Izu Peninsula in search of consolation following the many disappointments and losses of his youth, this story of an intelligent student joining a group of traveling performers regarded as social outcasts seems on the surface to be a straightforward look at youthful love. The reader first sees the student racing up a rain-swept mountain, hoping that he can catch up with the players whom he has seen from a distance in order to get a closer look at the beautiful dancing girl. Kawabata lets the reader think that this young man's aim in pursuing the girl is commonplace—that he is hoping for an opportunity to fulfill his sexual yearning for her.

But the student makes an early discovery in one memorable scene of the story. When the young woman is soaking in an outdoor bath at an inn, she spots the student, leaps from the water, and stretches her naked body to its full length to wave at him and call his name. He quickly realizes that she cannot be more than twelve or thirteen years old, that she has been made up to appear much more mature on previous occasions when he has seen her. Readers might expect the student to feel disappointed and frustrated, but Kawabata surprises them by presenting the joyous relief that this young man feels at no longer finding a barrier of sexual tension separating him from these performers. He can draw emotionally close to them on a level untainted by desire, and they in turn can accept him as a "good person"—words that he hears from the dancing girl and that he had thought he might never hear again.

In representing the intense but passionless purity that becomes the ideal for many of Kawabata's characters, the story gained a wide popular readership and was adapted as a motion picture at least five times following its publication. But the financial success it brought Kawabata was not immediate, and even when *Kanjō sōshoku* (1926, Decorations of Sentiment), his first collection of palm-of-the-hand stories, was published, Kawabata was forced to sell a copy of this collection to a used bookstore in order to have enough money to take a train into town to negotiate with a money lender.

Kawabata's wife gave birth to a daughter in June 1927, but the infant died before she could be named. The couple never again attempted to have children, and Kawabata publicly expressed his fear of taking on the responsibility of parenting, which he described as an "audacious experiment." He distanced himself from the emotions attending family relationships in much the same way that his fictional characters struggle to remain aloof while still participating in life.

After publishing *Izu no odoriko* (1927; translated as *The Izu Dancer*, 1964), another collection of stories, Kawabata, who had been making his home at one of the hot springs resorts on the Izu Peninsula, traveled to Tokyo in April 1927 to attend Yokomitsu's wedding. There he decided that he and his wife should settle permanently in the city, where he could be close to the bustle of literary activity. One of his favorite undertakings was that of serving as a staff member of coterie magazines, and he was probably correct in estimating that he belonged to more editorial staffs at small magazines than any other writer of his day. His involvement in such enterprises widened his circle of contacts among literary figures, further expanded his associations with authors of different camps and persuasions, and gave him a chance to promote the careers of struggling writers who, without his support and encouragement, would have run into barriers of prejudice and disfavor from the establishment. He fostered the careers of writers such as Kanoko Okamoto, a female author, and Tamio Hōjō, a young leper whose stories Kawabata was able to get published and whose collected works Kawabata arranged to have printed after Hōjō's death. The most famous of Kawabata's literary disciples was Yukio Mishima, who survived a couple of scathing reviews of his first collection of stories partly through Kawabata's support.

After settling in Tokyo, Kawabata began to frequent the many cafés and revue theaters in the Asakusa district, where he made friends with dancers and artists who provided him with a wealth of material for journals. He later published these tales in *Asakusa kurenaidan* (1930; translated as *The Scarlet Gang of Asakusa*, 2005), a work that succeeded in putting his favorite nightclub on solid financial ground for the first time. He collected so much material for stories that he attempted several sequels to *Asakusa kurenaidan*, but none was ever completed.

From 1930 to 1934 Kawabata lectured on literature once a week at the Bunka Gakuin school, not because he necessarily enjoyed the classroom but because his friend and mentor Kikuchi had been appointed to head the department of literature there. Visitors to Kawabata's home at this time were astonished at the small menagerie of animals with which he had surrounded himself. Among these were nine dogs and so many birds that he was occasionally seen tossing a dead bird into a cupboard. In 1933 a misanthropic bird lover appeared as the protagonist of his story "Kinju" (translated as "Of Birds and Beasts," 1969).

In the fall of 1933 *Bungakukai*, a literary journal destined to become influential, was launched, and Kawabata joined its staff. *Bungakukai* was especially interesting to Kawabata because it was the first Japanese literary journal to be free of intimate ties to any literary clique, and as such it provided Kawabata and other writers with opportunities to discuss and publish pieces from across the spectrum of literary approaches. His subsequent literary activities reflect some of the difficult choices facing Japanese writers in the mid 1930s. Though Kawabata could not be considered an eager collaborator with the various government agencies that worked to suppress seditious thought and writing as Japan moved closer to world war, he seemed to feel that any responsible writer should try to be involved with those associations that the government was establishing to oversee literary affairs. In January 1934 he joined a literary discussion group organized by a former head of the Public Security Division of the Home Ministry.

A more felicitous endeavor began after Kikuchi used *Bungei Shunjū* to establish a literary prize in honor of his friend Ryūnosuke Akutagawa, a writer who had committed suicide in 1927. The Akutagawa Prize was designed to recognize and encourage the talents of budding writers, and both Kawabata and Yokomitsu were asked to serve on the selection jury for the biannual prize when it was introduced in 1935. This task gave Kawabata yet another opportunity to promote the work of young authors, although in the first year that the prize was to be awarded some fledgling writers may have felt that he was using his position to thwart their ambitions. Osamu Dazai was particularly anxious to receive the first Akutagawa Prize, and he was furious when Kawabata dashed his chances by obliquely suggesting that Dazai's drug addiction hampered his writing abilities. After Dazai had mounted letter-writing campaigns to gain the support of Kawabata and another member of the jury but still failed to win consideration for two subsequent prizes, Dazai stormed over to the house of the other juror and, in an excess of frustration, threw rocks at his house.

In 1935 Kawabata began to write and publish parts of *Yukiguni* (1937; translated as *Snow Country*, 1957), one of his best-known works. He did not conceive of this work as a long, unified narrative, but after having written an initial short story for a magazine, Kawabata felt what he called a "lingering attraction" to the characters and their situation, and he produced a second story for a different magazine with a later publication deadline. The narrative continued in this fashion, with Kawabata adding a new story as the whim struck him, until finally a collection of these connected stories was published as *Yukiguni*. He was never completely satisfied with the way the work ended, and finally, only three months before his death, Kawabata produced a brief palm-of-the-hand condensation of it.

The setting and imagery of *Yukiguni* are ideally suited to the kind of story Kawabata enjoyed relating. His male protagonist, Shimamura, is a critic of Western ballet and a peculiar dilettante who refuses to corrupt his idealized conception of that art form by actually viewing a performance of it. Shimamura is similarly comfortable in his relationship with Komako, the vibrant hot springs geisha, only because he can maintain a geographical (and emotional) distance between himself and her: in order to visit her, Shimamura travels from his home in Tokyo through a long, dark tunnel (like a passageway leading into a fairy-tale land) that crosses the frozen borders of the "snow country" in northern Japan. As the renowned opening passage of the novel presents Shimamura returning through the tunnel to visit Komako, mist from the steam has settled over the windows of the train, and when Shimamura swipes his finger across the glass he is startled to find a female eye appearing on its mirrorlike surface. That disembodied eye represents the only kind of relationship in which Shimamura is comfortable—one in which he is free to sit back and observe without suffering any messy emotional entanglement, to objectify women and other aesthetic pleasures in his life, and to maintain his distance so that he does not have to see all the details that might spoil his fantasies.

Shimamura continues to visit Komako, but when she becomes too real for him to remain comfortable, his mind shifts toward the beautiful, enigmatic Yōko—a woman who has been caring for her terminally ill lover and whom he has seen on the train. The novel ends indeterminately with Yōko critically injured—or perhaps killed—in a fire and with Shimamura convinced that it is time to break off his relationship with Komako.

In 1937 the initial collection of *Yukiguni* stories was published, and Kawabata celebrated its success by purchasing a second home in the resort town of Karuizawa, where he spent his summers throughout the World War II years. He seemed to withdraw more and more from society as the Japanese military tightened its control of the nation by censoring speech and published materials and by interrogating and imprisoning those accused of seditious thoughts. In summer 1938 Kawabata accepted a request from newspapers in Tokyo and Osaka to record the *go* matches in which Shūsai Honnimbō, the master player, was participating. Kawabata revised and restructured these accounts during a period of twelve years throughout and after the war until he finally produced *Meijin* (1954; translated as *The Master of Go,* 1972), which he regarded as his only completed work.

During the war Kawabata also served as a judge of young people's compositions, helped elderly author Shimazaki edit a collection of his writings, and devoted much time to writing stories for children and popular audiences. Another means by which he sought to set aside the unpleasantness of the contemporary period was that of reading and rereading classical Japanese literature. Especially during the last two years of the war, as fire bombings of Tokyo mounted, Kawabata began rereading *The Tale of Genji* at every possible opportunity.

His mind focused upon the days of ancient Japan, and he took pains to preserve and study copies of the tale during the calamitous warfare in the capital. Because *The Tale of Genji* had acquired so much personal significance for him, he began to regard himself as a vessel through which the traditions of the past could be safely preserved during the war and for the future.

In the spring of 1941 a Japanese newspaper that was published in occupied Manchurian territory invited Kawabata to visit. He attended a *go* tournament there and traveled to meet Japanese writers living in the colony. In September of that year he returned, this time under the official sponsorship of the Japanese government, and although he acceded to the request of the military that he deliver some lectures on the superior values of Japanese culture, he was most eager to travel around China and collect folktales. He cut his travels short in late November when rumors of an imminent crisis forced him to return to Japan just a few days before the bombing of Pearl Harbor. The wartime pursuit for which Kawabata is best remembered is his compiling of the writings left by those who had died in battle and the commentary that he provided on them. Published at the end of 1942 and throughout 1944 in serialized form in the newspaper *Tokyo Shimbun,* this series was "Eirei no ibun" (Posthumous Writings of the Spirits of Fallen Heroes).

In spring 1943 Kawabata and his wife adopted a young woman named Masako, the daughter of a maternal cousin. Before long, he dug an air-raid shelter in his garden and spent nights patrolling the neighborhood as part of a fire prevention initiative. In April 1945 he was assigned to visit a naval airbase at the southern tip of the main islands, and there he spent a month with soldiers who were preparing to become kamikaze pilots. Kawabata wrote one story, "Seimei no ki" (1946, The Tree of Life), about his observations there, but generally he seems to have been dispirited by the experience.

Three months before the end of the war, in yet another attempt to preserve something of the culture that he daily saw going up in flames around him, Kawabata contacted many established writers living in Kamakura and asked them to donate books to a lending library he wished to establish. His efforts succeeded, and he was able to set up the Kamakura Bunko library, which quickly moved into publishing after the war and began reprinting affordable editions of some of the best-known works of modern Japanese literature. The rapid resurgence of interest in reading and writing literature after the war, despite all the devastation and poverty, resulted partly from the efforts of the Kamakura Bunko publishers. By January 1946 the firm, which continued to contribute significantly to Japanese literature until it ceased operations in 1950, also launched its own literary magazine, *Ningen* (Humanity), to introduce the work of new writers—and in this journal Kawabata arranged for the publication of a story by an unknown writer, Mishima.

Kawabata's enthusiasm for the publishing operations of Kamakura Bunko was obvious; he contributed his own stories to *Ningen* and published a new story for the *Yukiguni* series in the May 1946 issue of the journal. Beneath his flurry of activity, however, Kawabata clearly mourned the many lives and vestiges of culture that the war had destroyed. As a writer, he felt deeply the need to perpetuate traditions of beauty in Japan that were in danger of being lost. He remarked that what remained for him in the postwar years was to return to the ancient mountains and rivers and to produce elegies for the lost Japan. Mitsuo Nakamura, an astute Japanese critic, has suggested that Kawabata "sensed within the defeated people of Japan the same orphaned condition that had been his own in the past." As if to certify his position as a "master of funerals," Kawabata delivered the eulogies of many of his close literary friends, including Yokomitsu and Kikuchi.

Surrounding himself with cultural relics in the postwar years just as he had cluttered his house with birds and beasts in prewar days, Kawabata became an art collector and built up a reputable collection of eighteenth-century paintings and contemporary works by Japanese as well as Western artists. He attempted to produce modern versions of two works of classical Japanese literature, both *The Tale of Genji* and another Heian tale, *Torikaebaya monogatari,* but he was unable to complete either.

In 1947 the "completed" version of *Yukiguni* was published and received considerable acclaim, although Kawabata maintained reservations about it. Publication of a sixteen-volume set of his collected works began that year, and in June 1948 he was elected fourth president of P.E.N. Japan, a position that enabled him to foster and influence profoundly literary activities in Japan as well as to encourage the translation of Japanese works into other languages so that other people might begin to appreciate them. Kawabata served as president of P.E.N. Japan for seventeen years, through a period in which Japanese literature began to gain international recognition. Because of Kawabata's new stature on the literary committee of this organization, a newspaper invited him to attend a session of the Tokyo War Crimes trials and publish what he observed, and on two subsequent occasions he was invited to Hiroshima to view the atomic bomb destruction. As president of P.E.N. Japan, Kawabata published statements in favor of nuclear disarmament and world peace, and in 1950 he sponsored a P.E.N. conference in Hiroshima on World Peace and Literature.

He also struggled to regain a sense of direction in his writing. Between 1948 and 1952 he wrote *Shōnen* (Boys; first published in the 1948–1954 collected works), a fictional reminiscence of his youthful encounter with the Izu dancer and his homosexual romance during his school days. Despite its direct connection with Kawabata's experience, however, the work lacks the power and grace of his other writings and perhaps suffers from its lack of the "distance" that characterizes his best work.

One of Kawabata's most creative periods was in 1949, when he began to publish serially both *Sembazuru* (1952; translated as *Thousand Cranes,* 1958) and *Yama no oto* (1954; translated as *The Sound of the Mountain,* 1970). Both of these serialized works are similar to *Yukiguni* in their structure and manner of composition, but Kawabata neither took as long to complete them nor continued to expand them later, as he had done with *Yukiguni.* Both *Sembazuru* and *Yama no oto* are not "novels" as much as they are two series of vignettes, each bound by common characters and natural imagery. Some critics have compared Kawabata's mode of composition to that of a master in the *renga,* a medieval poetic form of linked verse in which one verse simultaneously terminates and transmutes the flash of imagistic inspiration in the preceding one—and thereby creates an amorphous form described as a "plotless narrative." In some ways Kawabata's work creates the same kinds of poetic effects and betrays the assumptions of Western readers, who expect something to happen in the way of beginning and ending a story. Kawabata seldom provides such tidy moments for his readers, and in that sense his work is both Japanese in temperament and strikingly modern, or even postmodern, in its literary orientation.

As another indication of Kawabata's concern for the passing of old Japan, *Sembazuru* details what Kawabata saw as the degradation of the tea ceremony in contemporary Japan. Yet, the high point of his late fiction—in the words of Kenkichi Yamamoto, the "very summit of postwar Japanese literature"—was *Yama no oto.* "Izu no odoriko" is unquestionably the purest work of his youth, and *Yukiguni* is the best expression of a middle-aged author contemplating, but not fully resigned to, the distances separating him from others. But *Yama no oto* presents the vision of a wise but wounded man sensing the approach of death, recognizing that he grows increasingly distant from the world around him, and finding a retreat into his memories to be his only solace.

Shingo, the aging protagonist, has begun to forget what has happened recently but recalls the distant past with surprising clarity. Kawabata presents, in a way that Shingo cannot understand, an aging man who in postwar Japan is surrounded by tokens of his failure as a husband, father, and employee, one who can find peace only by hastening into a past that he has idealized as an alternative to this present reality. This character replicates something that Kawabata must have felt as he saw the passing of an ancient culture that he so loved; yet, *Yama no oto* transcends Kawabata's personal recognition by drawing readers into the mind of Shingo as he struggles to prepare for his own death.

Amid all Shingo's disappointments—in his wife, whom he sees as plain and coarse in contrast to her deceased sister, whom he loved in the distant past; in his children, who seem incapable of sustaining relationships with him or with their spouses; and in his work, which is drab and unfulfilling—the only present comfort Shingo can find is in his associations, both real and imagined, with Kikuko, his daughter-in-law. He can sustain an ideal image of her precisely because she is unattainable, as are his memories of the dead sister-in-law whom he had hoped to marry. He thus cherishes the inapproachability of both Kikuko and the dead woman he once loved, and he grows increasingly weary of and removed from the unpleasant realities of the present. Except for Kawabata's depiction of the natural milieu, he presents almost everything about postwar Japanese life as depressing, and from the way Kawabata manipulates imagery, only Shingo and—at least until the end of the novel—Kikuko seem to have any sensitivity to or interest in nature. In the flowers and shrubbery of Shingo's garden Kawabata mirrors the emotions of his characters.

As the novel opens, Shingo hears the sound of the mountain behind his house, a sound that he comprehends as foreshadowing his death. By the end of the work Shingo has decided that he must return to his native Shinshū and see the brilliant reds of the autumn maple leaves that his memories have always associated with his late sister-in-law. But the sound with which the novel ends, as Shingo tries to communicate his feelings to Kikuko, is the sound that she makes in washing the dishes, and she cannot hear his voice. That, perhaps, is as close as Kawabata could come to providing an "ending" for the work: for Kawabata, to kill Shingo might have entailed killing a part of himself.

Having written this exceptional elegy, Kawabata again began to struggle for direction in his writing. Around 1954 he became addicted to sleeping pills, and the quality of his work suffered. Much of his time was devoted to writing serialized novels in newspapers and women's magazines that were aimed at a popular audience. He wrote scripts for two dance dramas, but much of the time that he might have spent on his writing was directed into activities on behalf of his profession, as he continued to labor for P.E.N. This work largely culminated in 1957, when the twenty-ninth international conference of P.E.N. was held in Japan.

The insularity of modern Japanese literature had begun to break down only a few years before, as a handful of Kawabata's works paved the way by being translated into English and several European languages. The extraordinary time and care that Kawabata spent in preparing for the P.E.N. conference did more to open Japanese literature to a world audience than anything else could have done. He spent months jetting to Europe for an executive committee meeting to make the original preparations, contacting writers such as François Mauriac and T. S. Eliot to elicit their support, and traveling throughout Europe, Scandinavia, and Asia to extend personal invitations to the gathering. As a result, the conference prefigured in international cultural affairs what the 1964 Tokyo Olympics did in international relations: it provided the world with a view of a revitalized postwar Japan and attracted a wide assortment of writers, critics, and translators from all over the world.

International contacts were initiated among writers, translators, and publishers, and interest in Japanese literature exploded. Translations of works by Kawabata, Mishima, Jun'ichirō Tanizaki, and other contemporary writers began to appear in many languages, and after Kawabata secured copyrights and intervened with other assistance, Donald Keene published *Modern Japanese Literature: An Anthology* (1956), the first collection of twentieth-century Japanese stories. For his efforts in organizing the conference and for making Japanese literature accessible, Kawabata was awarded the Kikuchi Kan Prize in 1957. He was also elected an international vice president of P.E.N. and was awarded the Goethe Medal at the P.E.N. convention in Frankfurt in 1958.

These activities on behalf of his literary colleagues, combined with a gallstone attack that put Kawabata into a hospital for more than half a year in 1958, reduced the time he spent on his writing; but following his recovery he published a final masterpiece, *Nemureru bijo* (1961; translated as *House of the Sleeping Beauties and Other Stories*, 1969). The implications of the title story are chilling even in simple outline, and they provide a fitting coda to Kawabata's continuing literary depictions of human isolation. The "house" is in fact a peculiar brothel—where physically perfect young women are drugged so that, for a fee, impotent elderly men can lie naked beside them for a night. Bringing together a desire for intimate association and an inability to consummate the yearning, this portrait of pathetic loneliness reiterates a familiar motif of Kawabata's writings, but nowhere else is that desire expressed with such hopeless sorrow. The same longing with no possibility of fulfillment also appears in Kawabata's last story, "Kataude" (1963; translated as "One Arm," 1967). In this surrealistic story a man desires to possess his lover but can approach her only as if she were a physical object; understanding his need and the incapacity he has, she allows him to remove her arm and take it home with him for the night. He embraces it passionately but is filled with horror after he has used only a portion of her body to satisfy his longing for human contact.

While he was still serializing *Koto* (1962; translated as *The Old Capital*, 1987) and *Utsukushisa to kanashimi to* (1965; translated as *Beauty and Sadness*, 1975), Kawabata received yet another honor—the Bunka Kunshō (Medal of Culture), the highest award that the Japanese government confers upon writers. Yet, signs of his physical and creative decline were already appearing. His addiction to sleeping pills marred the writing of *Koto,* and when he once tried to break his dependence on them after he finished the novel, he lapsed into a coma from which he did not emerge for ten days. Most of the rest of the long pieces that he tried to serialize for the next several years remained unfinished. Despite these difficulties Kawabata continued to work on behalf of other writers and in efforts to preserve literary tradition in Japan. In Tokyo he was instrumental in establishing the Nihon Kindai Bungakukan (Museum of Modern Japanese Literature), a library and museum for which he helped design plans and raise construction funds. When the museum was finished in 1967, he became an honorary adviser and later its honorary director.

Kawabata also continued to participate in P.E.N., as he attended its international conferences in São Paolo and Oslo, but in October 1965 he resigned as president of the Japan chapter of the club. Only a month later the people of the Izu Peninsula honored his first work by unveiling a statue depicting the dancing girl and the student at the Yugano hot springs resort.

Early in 1966 Kawabata spent three months in the hospital with a liver disorder. In 1968 he served as campaign chairman for Tōkō Kon, an old school friend and writer who was running for election to the Japanese Diet. That October he was notified that he had been chosen as the first Japanese writer to receive the Nobel Prize in Literature, and Kawabata graciously invited Edward G. Seidensticker, his primary English translator, to join him for the award ceremonies in Stockholm and to translate his acceptance speech, *Utsukushii Nihon no watakushi–sono josetsu* (1969; translated as *Japan, the Beautiful, and Myself,* 1969). In the presentation speech, Anders Österling of the Swedish Academy commented that Kawabata's style displays "a brilliant capacity to illuminate the erotic episode, an exquisite keenness of observation, a whole network of small, mysterious values, which often put the European narrative technique in the shade." Österling compared Kawabata's prose to Japanese painting and to "the genuinely Japanese miniature art of haiku poetry." A surge of acclaim followed the award: Kawabata received a commendation from the Japanese Diet; was elected as an honorary member of the American Academy and Institute of Arts and Letters; received an invitation in spring 1969 to lecture at the University of Hawaii, where he was also given an honorary doctoral degree; and was honored in London by the Japanese consulate, which mounted a public exhibition featuring him and his writings. The Association for the Study of Kawabata Literature was organized in 1970, the same year that a fifth edition of his collected works was published.

Kawabata was doing little writing, however, and in November 1970 he suffered a serious blow to his morale when Mishima, his brightest protégé, committed seppuku at the Tokyo headquarters of the Eastern Command of Japan's Self-Defense Forces. Kawabata was attending funeral services for another friend when the news of Mishima's sensational act reached him, and he rushed to the Self-Defense headquarters but was not permitted to see Mishima's body. When asked to write about Mishima's suicide a couple of months later, Kawabata could not comment. Only thirteen days before his own death could Kawabata write of this event to his publisher in New York: "I am not free for a single moment from the grief and sorrow I feel over Mishima's deplorable death."

Yet, Kawabata continued to pursue nonliterary activities. He campaigned for another friend who was running for election and helped arouse interest in an international conference on Japanese studies, but the only significant writing that he did in the last months of his life was an essay appropriately titled "Yume maboroshi no gotoku nari" (Dreams Are Like Phantoms). It appeared in the journal *Bungei Shunjū* in February 1972.

Kawabata kept an apartment in the Hayama district where he did his writing, and there on 16 April 1972 he was found dead, apparently having taken his own life by gas poisoning. Some of his friends cling to a belief that his death was accidental since he left no suicide note and had given none of them any indication of his intention to die. The Japan P.E.N. Club joined the Japan Writers Association and the Museum of Modern Japanese Literature to sponsor his funeral. His favorite fountain pen, a hundred sheets of blank manuscript paper, his pipe and glasses, a volume of his writings, a kimono, and the purple ceremonial *hakama* he wore to accept the Nobel Prize were placed beside his body in his casket. Exhibitions honoring his work toured the nation for eight months following his death; a memorial society was founded in his honor; and a reading room was named for him in the Museum of Modern Japanese Literature.

Letters:

Kawabata Yasunari–Mishima Yukio: *Ōfuku shokan* (Tokyo: Shinchōsha, 1997).

References:

Tsunatake Furuya, *Hyōden Kawabata Yasunari* (Tokyo: Jitsugyō no Nihonsha, 1960);

Van C. Gessel, *Three Modern Novelists: Sōseki, Tanizaki, Kawabata* (Tokyo: Kōdansha International, 1993);

Izumi Hasegawa, *Kawabata Yasunari ronkō*, third expanded and revised edition (Tokyo: Meiji Shoin, 1984);

Itaru Kawashima, *Kawabata Yasunari no sekai* (Tokyo: Kōdansha, 1969);

Donald Keene, *Dawn to the West,* volume 1 (New York: Holt, Rinehart & Winston, 1984);

Keene, *5 Modern Japanese Novelists* (New York: Columbia University Press, 2003);

Masao Miyoshi, *Accomplices of Silence: The Modern Japanese Novel* (Berkeley: University of California Press, 1974);

Mitsuo Nakamura, *Ronkō Kawabata Yasunari* (Tokyo: Chikuma Shobō, 1978);

Makoto Ōoka, Hideo Takahashi, and Yukio Miyoshi, eds., *Kawabata Yasunari,* Gunzō Nihon no Sakka series, volume 13 (Tokyo: Shōgakkan, 1991);

Gwenn Boardman Petersen, *The Moon in the Water: Understanding Tanizaki, Kawabata, and Mishima* (Honolulu: University Press of Hawaii, 1979);

Junkō Shindō, *Denki Kawabata Yasunari* (Tokyo: Rokkō Shuppan, 1976);

Roy Starrs, *Soundings in Time: The Fictive Art of Kawabata Yasunari* (Richmond, Surrey: Japan Library, 1998);

Hisaaki Yamanouchi, "The Eternal Womanhood: Tanizaki Junichiro and Kawabata Yasunari," in his *The Search for Authenticity in Modern Japanese Literature* (Cambridge & New York: Cambridge University Press, 1978).

Papers:

In addition to papers and memorabilia of Yasunari Kawabata held by the Museum of Modern Japanese Literature in Tokyo, which Kawabata helped found, there are extensive collections of his papers, letters, and personal belongings at the Kawabata Yasunari Kinenkan (Memorial Museum), established at his home in the Hase district of Kamakura City.

1968 Nobel Prize in Literature Presentation Speech

by Anders Österling, Ph.D., of the Swedish Academy
(Translation from the Swedish)

The recipient of this year's Nobel Prize for Literature, the Japanese Yasunari Kawabata, was born in 1899 in the big industrial town of Osaka, where his father was a highly-cultured doctor with literary interests. At an early age, however, he was deprived of this favourable growing-up environment on the sudden death of his parents, and, as an only child, was sent to his blind and ailing grandfather in a remote part of the country. These tragic losses, doubly significant in view of the Japanese people's intense feeling for blood ties, have undoubtedly affected Kawabata's whole outlook on life and has been one of the reasons for his later study of Buddhist philosophy.

As a student at the imperial university in Tokyo, he decided early on a writing career, and he is an example of the kind of restless absorption that is always a condition of the literary calling. In a youthful short story, which first drew attention to him at the age of twenty-seven, he tells of a student who, during lonely autumn walks on the peninsula of Izu, comes across a poor, despised dancing girl, with whom he has a touching love affair; she opens her pure heart and shows the young man a way to deep and genuine feeling. Like a sad refrain in a folksong the theme recurs with many variations in his following works; he presents his own scale of values, and with the years, he has won renown far beyond the borders of Japan. True, of his production only three novels and a few short stories have so far been translated into different languages, evidently because translation in this case offers especially great difficulties and is apt to be far too coarse a filter, in which many finer shades of meaning in his richly expressive language must be lost. But the translated works do give us a sufficiently representative picture of his personality.

In common with his older countryman, Tanizaki, now deceased, he has admittedly been influenced by modern western realism, but, at the same time, he has, with greater fidelity, retained his footing in Japan's classical literature and therefore represents a clear tendency to cherish and preserve a genuinely national tradition of style. In Kawabata's narrative art it is still possible to find a sensitively shaded situation poetry which traces its origin back to Murasaki's vast canvas of life and manners in Japan about the year 1000.

Kawabata has been especially praised as a subtle psychologist of women. He has shown his mastery as such in the two short novels, *The Snow Kingdom* and *A Thousand Cranes*, to use the Swedish titles. In these we see a brilliant capacity to illuminate the erotic episode, an exquisite keenness of observation, a whole network of small, mysterious values, which often put the European narrative technique in the shade. Kawabata's writing is reminiscent of Japanese painting; he is a worshipper of the fragile beauty and melancholy picture language of existence in the life of nature and in man's destiny. If the transience of all outward action can be likened to drifting tufts of grass on the surface of the water, then it is the genuinely Japanese miniature art of haiku poetry which is reflected in Kawabata's prose style.

Even if we feel excluded, as it were, from his writing by a root system, more or less foreign to us, of ancient Japanese ideas and instincts, we may find it tempting in Kawabata to notice certain similarities of temperament with European writers from our own time. Turgeniev is the first to spring to mind, he, too, is a deeply sensitive storyteller and a broadminded painter of the social scene, with pessimistically coloured sympathies within a time of transition between old and new.

Kawabata's most recent work is also his most outstanding, the novel, *The Old Capital*, completed six years ago, and now available in Swedish translation. The story is about the young girl, Chiëko, a foundling exposed by her poverty-stricken parents and adopted into the house of the merchant Takichiro, where she is brought up according to old Japanese principles. She is a sensitive, loyal being, who, only in secret, broods on the riddle of her origin. Popular Japanese belief has it that an exposed child is afflicted with a lifelong curse, in addition to which the condition of being a twin, according to the strange Japanese viewpoint, bears the stigma of shame. One day it happens that she meets a pretty young working girl from a cedar forest near the city and finds that she is her twin sister. They are intimately united beyond the social pale of class—the robust, work-hardened Naëko, and the delicate, anxiously guarded Chiëko, but their bewildering likeness soon gives rise to complications and confusion. The whole story is set against the background of the religious festival year in Kyoto from the cherry-blossom spring to the snow-glittering winter.

The city itself is really the leading character, the capital of the old kingdom, once the seat of the mikado and his court, still a romantic sanctuary after a thousand years, the home of the fine arts and elegant handicraft, nowadays exploited by tourism but still a loved place of pilgrimage. With its Shinto and Buddha temples, its old artisan quarters and botanical gardens, the place possesses a poetry which Kawabata expresses in a tender, courteous manner, with no sentimental overtones, but, naturally, as a moving appeal. He has experienced his country's crushing defeat and no doubt realizes what the future demands in the way of industrial go-ahead spirit, tempo and vitality. But in the postwar wave of violent Americanization, his novel is a gentle reminder of the necessity of trying to save something of the old Japan's beauty and individuality for the new. He describes the religious ceremonies in Kyoto with the same meticulous care as he does the textile trade's choice of patterns in the traditional sashes belonging to the women's dresses. These aspects of the novel may have their documentary worth, but the reader prefers to dwell on such a deeply characteristic passage as when the party of middle-class people from the city visits the botanical garden—which has been closed for a long time because the American occupation troops have had their barracks there—in order to see whether the lovely avenue of camphor trees is still intact and able to delight the connoisseur's eye.

With Kawabata, Japan enters the circle of literary Nobel Prize-winners for the first time. Essential to the forming of the decision is the fact that, as a writer, he imparts a moral-esthetic cultural awareness with unique artistry, thereby, in his way, contributing to the spiritual bridge-building between East and West.

Mr. Kawabata,

The citation speaks of your narrative mastery, which, with great sensibility, expresses the essence of the Japanese mind. With great satisfaction we greet you here in our midst today, an honoured guest from afar, on this platform. On behalf of the Swedish Academy, I beg to express our hearty congratulations, and, at the same time, ask you now to receive this year's Nobel Prize for Literature from the hands of His Majesty, the King.

[© The Nobel Foundation, 1968.]

Kawabata: Banquet Speech

Introductory remarks by M. Zotterman of the Royal Veterinary College at the Nobel Banquet at the City Hall in Stockholm, 10 December 1968:

Yasunari Kawabata—We admire the exquisite artistry and sensibility which you have displayed in your deep analysis of the Japanese character. We offer you, the first Japanese writer to be awarded the Nobel Prize in Literature, our most sincere congratulations. *Kawabata-san, Omedeto gozaimasu!*

Kawabata's speech

Your Majesty, Your Royal Highnesses, Your Excellencies the President and the Trustees of the Nobel Foundation, Members of the Royal Swedish Academy, Excellencies, Ladies and Gentlemen:

It is the great honor of my life to have been proposed by the Swedish Academy for the Nobel Prize for literature for 1968 and to have received the award at Your Majesty's own hands.

The reason for the supreme brilliance of the history of this award is that it is also given to foreigners. It has, so to speak, the breadth of a world award. Two Japanese, Drs. Yukawa and Tomonaga, have in recent years become Nobel Laureates in physics. Alfred Nobel wrote poetry and prose in several languages, and in that spirit the prize for literature has gone to writers in numbers of countries. It is now fifty-five years since it last went to an Oriental, Rabindranath Tagore. In view of the complexities presented by differences in language, and in view of the fact that my works, no doubt more than those of others, have had to be perused in translation, I must indicate my deep and undying gratitude and respect for the resolve shown by Your Excellencies of the Academy. This first award to an Oriental in fifty-five years has I believe made a deep impression upon Japan, and perhaps upon the other countries of Asia as well, and upon all countries whose languages are little known internationally. I do not look upon my happiness and good fortune in having received the award as mine alone. My emotions are yet deeper at the thought that it perhaps has a new and broad significance for the literature of the world.

Such are my feelings, indeed, honored with my fellow laureates by Your Excellencies of the Nobel Foundation upon this grand occasion, and granted the further honor of offering a few words of thanks, that I almost think we have here a symbol of understanding and friendship between East and West, of literature moving from today into tomorrow. I thank you.

[© The Nobel Foundation, 1968. Yasunari Kawabata is the sole author of his speech.]

Kawabata: Nobel Lecture, 12 December 1968

Japan, the Beautiful, and Myself

"In the spring, cherry blossoms, in the summer the cuckoo.
In autumn the moon, and in winter the snow, clear, cold."

"The winter moon comes from the clouds to keep me company.
The wind is piercing, the snow is cold."

The first of these poems is by the priest Dogen (1200–1253) and bears the title "Innate Spirit." The second is by the priest Myoe (1173–1232). When I am asked for specimens of calligraphy, it is these poems that I often choose.

The second poem bears an unusually detailed account of its origins, such as to be an explanation of the heart of its meaning:

> On the night of the twelfth day of the twelfth month of the year 1224, the moon was behind clouds. I sat in Zen meditation in the Kakyu Hall. When the hour of the midnight vigil came, I ceased meditation and descended from the hall on the peak to the lower quarters, and as I did so the moon came from the clouds and set the snow to glowing. The moon was my companion, and not even the wolf howling in the valley brought fear. When, presently, I came out of the lower quarters again, the moon was again behind clouds. As the bell was signalling the late-night vigil, I made my way once more to the peak, and the moon saw me on the way. I entered the meditation hall, and the moon, chasing the clouds, was about to sink behind the peak beyond, and it seemed to me that it was keeping me secret company.

There follows the poem I have quoted, and with the explanation that it was composed as Myoe entered the meditation hall after seeing the moon behind the mountain, there comes yet another poem:

"I shall go behind the mountain. Go there too, O moon.
Night after night we shall keep each other company."

Here is the setting for another poem, after Myoe had spent the rest of the night in the meditation hall, or perhaps gone there again before dawn:

Opening my eyes from my meditations, I saw the moon in the dawn, lighting the window. In a dark place myself, I felt as if my own heart were glowing with light which seemed to be that of the moon:

"My heart shines, a pure expanse of light;
And no doubt the moon will think the light its own."

Because of such a spontaneous and innocent stringing together of mere ejaculations as the following, Myoe has been called the poet of the moon:

"Bright, bright, and bright, bright, bright, and bright, bright.
Bright and bright, bright, and bright, bright moon."

In his three poems on the winter moon, from late night into the dawn, Myoe follows entirely the bent of Saigyo, another poet-priest, who lived from 1118 to 1190: "Though I compose poetry, I do not think of it as composed poetry." The thirty-one syllables of each poem, honest and straightforward as if he were addressing the moon, are not merely to "the moon as my companion." Seeing the moon, he becomes the moon, the moon seen by him becomes him. He sinks into nature, becomes one with nature. The light of the "clear heart" of the priest, seated in the meditation hall in the darkness before the dawn, becomes for the dawn moon its own light.

As we see from the long introduction to the first of Myoe's poems quoted above, in which the winter moon becomes a companion, the heart of the priest, sunk in meditation upon religion and philosophy, there in the mountain hall, is engaged in a delicate interplay and exchange with the moon; and it is this of which the poet sings. My reason for choosing that first poem when asked for a specimen of my calligraphy has to do with its remarkable gentleness and compassion. Winter moon, going behind the clouds and coming forth again, making bright my footsteps as I go to the meditation hall and descend again, making me unafraid of the wolf: does not the wind sink into you, does not the snow, are you not cold? I choose the poem as a poem of warm, deep, delicate compassion, a poem that has in it the deep quiet of the Japanese spirit. Dr. Yashiro Yukio, internationally known as a scholar of Botticelli, a man of great learning in the art of the past and the present, of the East and the West, has summed up one of the special characteristics of Japanese art in a single poetic sentence: "The time of the snows, of the moon, of the blossoms—then more than ever we think of our comrades." When we see the beauty of the snow, when we see the beauty of the full moon, when we see the beauty of the cherries in bloom, when in short we brush against and are awakened by the beauty of the four seasons, it is then that we think most of those close to us, and want them to share the pleasure. The excitement of beauty calls forth strong fellow feelings, yearnings for companionship, and the word "comrade" can be taken to mean "human being." The snow, the moon, the blossoms, words expressive of the seasons as they move one into another, include in the Japanese tradition the beauty of mountains and rivers and grasses and trees, of all the myriad manifestations of nature, of human feelings as well.

That spirit, that feeling for one's comrades in the snow, the moonlight, under the blossoms, is also basic to the tea ceremony. A tea ceremony is a coming together in feeling, a meeting of good comrades in a good season. I may say in passing, that to see my novel *Thousand Cranes* as an evocation of the formal and spiritual beauty of the tea ceremony is a misreading. It is a negative work, an expression of doubt about and warning against the vulgarity into which the tea ceremony has fallen.

"In the spring, cherry blossoms, in the summer the cuckoo.
In autumn the full moon, in winter the snow, clear, cold."

One can, if one chooses, see in Dogen's poem the beauty of the four seasons no more than a conventional, ordinary, mediocre stringing together, in a most awkward form of representative images from the four seasons. One can see it as a poem that is not really a poem at all. And yet very similar is the deathbed poem of the priest Ryokan (1758-1831):

"What shall be my legacy? The blossoms of spring,
The cuckoo in the hills, the leaves of autumn."

In this poem, as in Dogen's, the commonest of figures and the commonest of words are strung together without hesitation—no, to particular effect, rather—and so they transmit the very essence of Japan. And it is Ryokan's last poem that I have quoted.

"A long, misty day in spring:
I saw it to a close, playing ball with the children.

"The breeze is fresh, the moon is clear.
Together let us dance the night away, in what is left of old age."
"It is not that I wish to have none of the world,
It is that I am better at the pleasure enjoyed alone."

Ryokan, who shook off the modern vulgarity of his day, who was immersed in the elegance of earlier centuries, and whose poetry and calligraphy are much admired in Japan today—he lived in the spirit of these poems, a wanderer down country paths, a grass hut for shelter, rags for clothes, farmers to talk to. The profundity of religion and literature was not, for him, in the abstruse. He rather pursued literature and belief in the benign spirit summarized in the Buddhist phrase "a smiling face and gentle words." In his last poem he offered nothing as a legacy. He but hoped that after his death nature would remain beautiful. That could be his bequest. One feels in the poem the emotions of old Japan, and the heart of a religious faith as well.

"I wondered and wondered when she would come.
And now we are together. What thoughts need I have?"

Ryokan wrote love poetry too. This is an example of which I am fond. An old man of sixty-nine (I might point out that at the same age I am the recipient of the Nobel Prize), Ryokan met a twenty-nine-year-old nun named Teishin, and was blessed with love. The poem can be seen as one of happiness at having met the ageless woman, of happiness at having met the one for whom the wait was so long. The last line is simplicity itself.

Ryokan died at the age of seventy-three. He was born in the province of Echigo, the present Niigata Prefecture and the setting of my novel *Snow Country,* a northerly region on what is known as the reverse side of Japan, where cold winds come down across the Japan Sea from Siberia. He lived his whole life in the snow country, and to his "eyes in their last extremity," when he was old and tired and knew that death was near, and had attained enlightenment, the snow country, as we see in his last poem, was yet more beautiful, I should imagine. I have an essay with the title "Eyes in Their Last Extremity."

The title comes from the suicide note of the short-story writer Akutagawa Ryunosuke (1892-1927). It is the phrase that pulls at me with the greatest strength. Akutagawa said that he seemed to be gradually losing the animal something known as the strength to live, and continued:

I am living in a world of morbid nerves, clear and cold as ice. . . . I do not know when I will summon up the resolve to kill myself. But nature is for me more beautiful than it has ever been before. I have no doubt that you will laugh at the contradiction, for here I love nature even when I am contemplating suicide. But nature is beautiful because it comes to my eyes in their last extremity.

Akutagawa committed suicide in 1927, at the age of thirty-five.

In my essay, "Eyes in Their Last Extremity," I had to say: "However alienated one may be from the world, suicide is not a form of enlightenment. However admirable he may be, the man who commits suicide is far from the realm of the saint." I neither admire nor am in sympathy with suicide. I had another friend who died young, an avant-garde painter. He too thought of suicide over the years, and of him I wrote in this same essay: "He seems to have said over and over that there is no art superior to death, that to die is to live," I could see, however, that for him, born in a Buddhist temple and educated in a Buddhist school, the concept of death was very different from that in the West. "Among those who give thoughts to things, is there one who does not think of suicide?" With me was the knowledge that that fellow Ikkyu (1394–1481) twice contemplated suicide. I have "that fellow," because the priest Ikkyu is known even to children as a most amusing person, and because anecdotes about his limitlessly eccentric behavior have come down to us in ample numbers. It is said of him that children climbed his knee to stroke his beard, that wild birds took feed from his hand. It would seem from all this that he was the ultimate in mindlessness, that he was an approachable and gentle sort of priest. As a matter of fact he was the most severe and profound of Zen priests. Said to have been the son of an emperor, he entered a temple at the age of six, and early showed his genius as a poetic prodigy. At the same time he was troubled with the deepest of doubts about religion and life. "If there is a god, let him help me. If there is none, let me throw myself to the bottom of the lake and become food for fishes." Leaving behind these words he sought to throw himself into a lake, but was held back. On another occasion, numbers of his fellows were incriminated when a priest in his Daitokuji Temple committed suicide. Ikkyu went back to the temple, "the burden heavy on my shoulders," and sought to starve himself to death. He gave his collected poetry the title *Collection of the Roiling Clouds,* and himself used the expression "Roiling Clouds" as a pen name. In his collection and its successor are poems quite without parallel in the Chinese and especially the Zen poetry of the Japanese middle ages, erotic poems and poems about the secrets of the bedchamber that leave one in utter astonishment. He sought, by eating fish and drinking spirits and having commerce with women, to go beyond the rules and proscriptions of the Zen of his day, and to seek liberation from them, and thus, turning against established religious forms, he sought in the pursuit of Zen the revival and affirmation of the essence of life, of human existence, in a day of civil war and moral collapse.

His temple, the Daitokuji at Murasakino in Kyoto, remains a center of the tea ceremony, and specimens of his calligraphy are greatly admired as hangings in alcoves of tea rooms.

I myself have two specimens of Ikkyu's calligraphy. One of them is a single line: "It is easy to enter the world of the Buddha, it is hard to enter the world of the devil." Much drawn to these words, I frequently make use of them when asked for a specimen of my own calligraphy. They can be read in any number of ways, as difficult as one chooses, but in that world of the devil added to the world of the Buddha, Ikkyu of Zen comes home to me with great immediacy. The fact that for an artist, seeking truth, good, and beauty, the fear and petition even as a prayer in those words about the world of the devil—the fact that it should be there apparent on the surface, hidden behind, perhaps speaks with the inevitability of fate. There can be no world of the Buddha without the world of the devil. And the world of the devil is the world difficult of entry. It is not for the weak of heart.

"If you meet a Buddha, kill him. If you meet a patriarch of the law,
kill him."

This is a well-known Zen motto. If Buddhism is divided generally into the sects that believe in salvation by faith and those that believe in salvation by one's own efforts, then of course there must be such violent utterances in Zen, which insists upon salvation by one's own efforts. On the other side, the side of salvation by faith, Shinran (1173–1262), the founder of the Shin sect, once said: "The good shall be reborn in paradise, and how much more shall it be so with the bad." This view of things has something in common with Ikkyu's world of the Buddha and world of the devil, and yet at heart the two have their different inclinations. Shinran also said: "I shall not take a single disciple."

"If you meet a Buddha, kill him. If you meet a patriarch of the law, kill him." "I shall not take a single disciple." In these two statements, perhaps, is the rigorous fate of art.

In Zen there is no worship of images. Zen does have images, but in the hall where the regimen of meditation is pursued, there are neither images nor pictures of Buddhas, nor are there scriptures. The Zen disciple sits for long hours silent and motionless, with his eyes closed. Presently he enters a state of impassivity, free from all ideas and all thoughts. He departs from the self and enters the realm of nothingness. This is not the nothingness or the emptiness of the West. It is rather the reverse, a universe of the spirit in which everything communicates freely with everything, transcending bounds, limitless. There are of course masters of Zen, and the disciple is brought toward enlightenment by exchanging questions and answers with his master, and he studies the scriptures. The disciple must, however, always be lord of his own thoughts, and must attain enlightenment through his own efforts. And the emphasis is less upon reason and argument than upon intuition, immediate feeling. Enlightenment comes not from teaching but through the eye awakened inwardly. Truth is in "the discarding of words," it lies "outside words." And so we have the extreme of "silence like thunder," in the Vimalakirti Nirdesa Sutra. Tradition has it that Bodhidharma, a southern Indian prince who lived in about the sixth century and was the founder of Zen in China, sat for nine years in silence facing the wall of a cave, and finally attained enlightenment. The Zen practice of silent meditation in a seated posture derives from Bodhidharma.

Here are two religious poems by Ikkyu:

"Then I ask you answer. When I do not you do not.
What is there then on your heart, O Lord Bodhidharma?"

"And what is it, the heart?
It is the sound of the pine breeze in the ink painting."

Here we have the spirit of Zen in Oriental painting. The heart of the ink painting is in space, abbreviation, what is left undrawn. In the words of the Chinese painter Chin Nung: "You paint the branch well, and you hear the sound of the wind." And the priest Dogen once more: "Are there not these cases? Enlightenment in the voice of the bamboo. Radiance of heart in the peach blossom."

Ikenobo Sen'o, a master of flower arranging, once said (the remark is to be found in his *Sayings*): "With a spray of flowers, a bit of water, one evokes the vastness of rivers and mountains." The Japanese garden too, of course symbolizes the vastness of nature. The Western garden tends to be symmetrical, the Japanese garden asymmetrical, and this is because the asymmetrical has the greater power to symbolize multiplicity and vastness. The asymmetry, of course, rests upon a balance imposed by delicate sensibilities. Nothing is more complicated, varied, attentive to detail, than the Japanese art of landscape gardening. Thus there is the form called the dry landscape, composed entirely of rocks, in which the arrangement of stones gives expression to mountains and rivers that are not present, and even suggests the waves of the great ocean breaking in upon cliffs. Compressed to the ultimate, the Japanese garden becomes the *bonsai* dwarf garden, or the *bonseki,* its dry version.

In the Oriental word for landscape, literally "mountain-water," with its related implications in landscape painting and landscape gardening, there is contained the concept of the sere and wasted, and even of the sad and the threadbare. Yet in the sad, austere, autumnal qualities so valued by the tea ceremony, itself summarized in the expression "gently respectful, cleanly quiet," there lies concealed a great richness of spirit; and the tea room, so rigidly confined and simple, contains boundless space and unlimited elegance. The single flower contains more brightness than a hundred flowers. The great sixteenth-century master of the tea ceremony and flower arranging, Rikyu, taught that it was wrong to use fully opened flowers. Even in the tea ceremony today the general practice is to have in the alcove of the tea room but a single flower, and that a flower in bud. In winter a special flower of winter, let us say a camellia, bearing some such name as White Jewel or Wabisuke, which might be translated literally as "Helpmate in Solitude," is chosen, a camellia remarkable among camellias for its whiteness and the smallness of its blossoms; and but a single bud is set out in the alcove. White is the cleanest of colors, it contains in itself all the other colors. And there must always be dew on the bud. The bud is moistened with a few drops of water. The most splendid of arrangements for the tea ceremony comes in May, when a peony is put out in a celadon vase; but here again there is but a single bud, always with dew upon it. Not only are there drops of water upon the flower, the vase too is frequently moistured.

Among flower vases, the ware that is given the highest rank is old Iga, from the sixteenth and seventeenth centuries, and it commands the highest price. When old Iga has been dampened, its colors and its glow take on a beauty such as to awaken on afresh. Iga was fired at very high temperatures. The straw ash and the smoke from the fuel fell and flowed against the surface, and as the temperature dropped, became a sort of glaze. Because the colors were not fabricated but were rather the result of nature at work in the kiln, color patterns emerged in such varieties as to be called quirks and freaks of the kiln. The rough, austere, strong surfaces of old Iga take on a voluptuous glow when dampened. It breathes to the rhythm of the dew of the flowers.

The taste of the tea ceremony also asks that the tea bowl be moistened before using, to give it its own soft glow.

Ikenobo Sen'o remarked on another occasion (this too is in his *Sayings*) that "the mountains and strands should appear in their own forms." Bringing a new spirit into his school of flower arranging, therefore, he found "flowers" in broken vessels and withered branches, and in them too the enlightenment that comes from flowers. "The ancients arranged flowers and pursued enlightenment." Here we see awakening to the heart of the Japanese spirit, under the influence of Zen. And in it too, perhaps, is the heart of a man living in the devastation of long civil wars.

The Tales of Ise, compiled in the tenth century, is the oldest Japanese collection of lyrical episodes, numbers of which might be called short stories. In one of them we learn that the poet Ariwara no Yukihira, having invited guests, put in flowers:

"Being a man of feeling, he had in a large jar a most unusual wistaria. The trailing spray of flowers was upwards of three and a half feet long."

A spray of wistaria of such length is indeed so unusual as to make one have doubts about the credibility of the writer; and yet I can feel in this great spray a symbol of Heian culture. The wistaria is a very Japanese flower, and it has a feminine elegance. Wistaria sprays, as they trail in the breeze, suggest softness, gentleness, reticence. Disappearing and then appearing again in the early summer greenery, they have in them that feeling for the poignant beauty of things long characterized by the Japanese as *mono no aware*. No doubt there was a particular splendor in that spray upwards of three and a half feet long. The splendors of Heian culture a millennium ago and the emergence of a peculiarly Japanese beauty were as wondrous as this "most unusual wistaria," for the culture of T'ang China had at length been absorbed and Japanized. In poetry there came, early in the tenth century, the first of the imperially commissioned anthologies, the *Kokinshu,* and in fiction, the *Tales of Ise,* followed by the supreme masterpieces of classical Japanese prose, the *Tale of Genji* of Lady Murasaki and the *Pillow Book* of Sei Shonagon, both of whom lived from the late tenth century into the early eleventh. So was established a tradition which influenced and even controlled Japanese literature for eight hundred years. The *Tale of Genji* in particular is the highest pinnacle of Japanese literature. Even down to our day there has not been a piece of fiction to compare with it. That such a modern work should have been written in the eleventh century is a miracle, and as a miracle the work is widely known abroad. Although my grasp of classical Japanese was uncertain, the Heian classics were my principal boyhood reading, and it is the *Genji,* I think, that has meant the most to me. For centuries after it was written, fascination with the *Genji* persisted, and imitations and reworkings did homage to it. The *Genji* was a wide and deep source of nourishment for poetry, of course, and for the fine arts and handicrafts as well, and even for landscape gardening.

Murasaki and Sei Shonagon, and such famous poets as Izumi Shikibu, who probably died early in the eleventh century, and Akazome Emon, who probably died in the mid-eleventh century, were all ladies-in-waiting in the imperial court. Japanese culture was court culture, and court culture was feminine. The day of the *Genji* and the *Pillow Book* was its finest, when ripeness was moving into decay. One feels in it the sadness at the end of glory, the high tide of Japanese court culture. The court went into its decline, power moved from the court nobility to the military aristocracy, in whose hands it remained through almost seven centuries from the founding of the Kamakura Shogunate in 1192 to the Meiji Restoration in 1867 and 1868. It is not to be thought, however, that either the imperial institution or court culture vanished. In the eighth of the imperial anthologies, the *Shinkokinshu* of the early thirteenth century, the technical dexterity of the *Kokinshu* was pushed yet a step further, and sometimes fell into mere verbal dalliance; but there were added elements of the mysterious, the suggestive, the evocative and inferential elements of sensuous fantasy that have something in common with modern symbolist poetry. Saigyo, who has been mentioned earlier, was a representative poet spanning the two ages, Heian and Kamakura.

"I dreamt of him because I was thinking of him.
Had I known it was a dream, I should not have wished to awaken.
"In my dreams I go to him each night without fail.
But this is less than a single glimpse in the waking."

These are by Ono no Komachi, the leading poetess of the *Kokinshu,* who sings of dreams, even, with a straightforward realism. But when we come to the following poems of the Empress Eifuku, who lived at about the same time as Ikkyu, in the Muromachi Period, somewhat later than the *Shinkokinshu,* we have a subtle realism that becomes a melancholy symbolism, delicately Japanese, and seems to me more modern:

"Shining upon the bamboo thicket where the sparrows twitter,
The sunlight takes on the color of the autumn."

"The autumn wind, scattering the bush clover in the garden,
sinks into one's bones.
Upon the wall, the evening sun disappears."

Dogen, whose poem about the clear, cold snow I have quoted, and Myoe, who wrote of the winter moon as his companion, were of generally the *Shinkokinshu* period. Myoe exchanged poems with Saigyo and the two discussed poetry together. The following is from the biography of Myoe by his disciple Kikai:

> Saigyo frequently came and talked of poetry. His own attitude towards poetry, he said, was far from the ordinary. Cherry blossoms, the cuckoo, the moon, snow: confronted with all the manifold forms of nature, his eyes and his ears were filled with emptiness. And were not all the words that came forth true words? When he sang of the blossoms the blossoms were not on his mind, when he sang of the moon he did not think of the moon. As the occasion presented itself, as the urge arose, he wrote poetry. The red rainbow across the sky was as the sky taking on color. The white sunlight was as the sky growing bright. Yet the empty sky, by its nature, was not something to become bright. It was not something to take on color. With a spirit like the empty sky he gives color to all the manifold scenes but not a trace remained. In such poetry was the Buddha, the manifestation of the ultimate truth.

Here we have the emptiness, the nothingness, of the Orient. My own works have been described as works of emptiness, but it is not to be taken for the nihilism of the West. The spiritual foundation would seem to be quite different. Dogen entitled his poem about the seasons, "Innate Reality," and even as he sang of the beauty of the seasons he was deeply immersed in Zen.

[© The Nobel Foundation, 1968. Yasunari Kawabata is the sole author of the text.]

Imre Kertész
(9 November 1929 -   )

Éva Forgács
Art Center College of Design, Pasadena

This entry was expanded by Forgács from her Kertész entry in *DLB Yearbook 2002*. See also the Kertész entry in *DLB 299: Holocaust Novelists*.

BOOKS: *Sorstalanság* (Budapest: Szépirodalmi, 1975); translated by Christopher C. Wilson and Katharina M. Wilson as *Fateless* (Evanston, Ill.: Northwestern University Press, 1992); translated by Tim Wilkinson as *Fatelessness* (New York: Vintage International, 2004);

A nyomkereső (Budapest: Szépirodalmi, 1977);

A kudarc (Budapest: Szépirodalmi, 1988);

Kaddis a meg nem született gyermekért (Budapest: Magvető, 1990); translated by Wilson and Wilson as *Kaddish for a Child Not Born* (Evanston, Ill.: Northwestern University Press, 1997);

Az angol lobogó (Budapest: Holnap, 1991); translated by Wilkinson as *The Union Jack*, in *Hungarian Quarterly*, no. 168 (Winter 2002): 3-28;

Gályanapló (Budapest: Holnap, 1992);

A holocaust mint kultúra (Budapest: Századvég, 1993)—includes "Hosszú, sötét árnyék," translated by Imre Goldstein as "Long, Dark Shadow," in *Contemporary Jewish Writing in Hungary*, edited by Susan Rubin Suleiman and Éva Forgács (Lincoln: University of Nebraska Press, 2003), pp. 171-180;

Jegyzőkönyv, bound with *Élet és irodalom* by Péter Esterházy (Budapest: Magvető-Századvég, 1993), pp. 7-37; translated by Wilkinson as *Sworn Statement*, in *Hungarian Quarterly*, no. 163 (Autumn 2001): 45-58;

Valaki más: A változás krónikája (Budapest: Magvető, 1997);

A gondolatnyi csend, amíg a kivégzőosztag újratölt (Budapest: Magvető, 1998);

Sorstalanság filmforgatókönyv (Budapest: Magvető, 2001);

A száműzött nyelv (Budapest: Magvető, 2001); translated by Ivan Sanders as "The Language of Exile," in *Guardian*, 9 October 2002;

A stockholmi beszéd: Elhangzott 2002 December 7-én a Svéd Akadémia ünnepi ülésén (Budapest: Magvető, 2002);

Felszámolás: Regény (Budapest: Magvető, 2003); translated by Wilkinson as *Liquidation* (New York: Knopf, 2004);

Kalauz, by Kertész, Esterházy, and Péter Nádas (Budapest: Magvető, 2003);

K. dosszié (Budapest: Magvető, 2006).

TRANSLATIONS: Friedrich Nietzsche, *A tragédia születése* (Budapest: Európa Könyvkiadó, 1986);

Sigmund Freud, *Michelangelo Mózese* (Budapest: Európa Könyvkiadó, 1987);

Joseph Roth, *Jób* (Budapest: Európa Könyvkiadó, 1987);

Hugo von Hoffmanstahl, "Az árnyék nélküli asszony," in *Menekülés a homályba: Osztrák elbeszélők* (Budapest: Európa Könyvkiadó, 1988);

Arthur Schnitzler, "Menekülés a homályba," in *Menekülés a homályba: Osztrák elbeszélők* (Budapest: Európa Könyvkiadó, 1988);

Ludwig Wittgenstein, *Észrevételek* (Budapest: Atlantisz, 1993).

The Nobel Prize in Literature was awarded to Hungarian novelist Imre Kertész in 2002 for "writing that upholds the fragile experience of the individual against the barbaric arbitrariness of history," as the citation read. Kertész's writing, although inspired by his experiences in Nazi concentration camps and by living in the totalitarian system in Hungary, addresses more than the political turmoil he had to endure. He examines the threat to the existence of the individual as an historical and cultural construct, a twentieth-century literary theme explored by writers such as Robert Musil in *Der Mann ohne Eigenschaften: Roman* (1930-1943; translated as *The Man without Qualities*, 1955) and Elias Canetti in *Mass und Macht* (1960; translated as *Crowds and Power*, 1962).

Acceptance of the world as an objective reality meant, under the particular circumstances of the regimes Kertész lived in, compliance with totalitarianism. In his essay "Hosszú, sötét árnyék" (1993; trans-

Imre Kertész (left) receiving the 2002 Nobel Prize in Literature from King Carl XVI Gustaf of Sweden (photograph by Henrik Montgomery, Pool, Associated Press, Pressens Bild)

lated as "Long, Dark Shadow," 2003) Kertész writes, "A totalitarizmus, a totalitárius állam, a totalitárius párthatalom—e század minden pusztító hitnél pusztítóbb szörnyetege, ragálya, pestise . . . alapjaiban rendített meg . . . mindent. A totalitarizmus számzi önmagából és törvényen kívül helyezi az *embert*" (Totalitarianism, the totalitarian state, a totalitarian ruling party—this plague, this pestilence, this monster of our century . . . has shaken the foundation of . . . everything. It is *man, the human being,* that totalitarianism banishes, outlaws, puts beyond the pale). As he explained in his Nobel Lecture, however, totalitarianism did not absolve the individual from responsibility:

> Én viszont 1955 egy szép tavaszi napján váratlanul arra a gondolatra jutottam, hogy egyetlen valóság létezik csupán, ez a valóság pedig én magam vagyok, az én életem, ez a törékeny és bizonytalan időre szóló ajándék, amelyet idegen, ismeretlen erők kisajátítottak, államosítottak, meghatározták és megpecsételték, s amelyet az úgynevezett történelemtől, ettől a szörnyűséges Molochtól vissza kell vennem, mert egyedül az enyém, s ekként kell gazdálkodnom vele.

(Whereas I, on a lovely spring day in 1955, suddenly came to the realization that there exists only one reality, and that is me, my own life, this fragile gift bestowed for an uncertain time, which had been seized, expropriated by alien forces, marked up, branded—and which I had to take back from "History," this dreadful Moloch, because it was mine and mine alone, and I had to manage it accordingly.)

Kertész has regarded it as his "egzisztenciális feladat" (existential task) to give as accurate an account of the European catastrophe as possible, as he said in his short after-ceremony talk in Stockholm. He took upon himself the task of not only fathoming the most barbarous event of Christian European civilization, the Nazi Holocaust, but also creating a language in which it could be adequately narrated. The language of literature, he found, could no longer convey what had happened. What he wanted to grasp was the gradual process of disintegration and vanishing of the human being in the totalitarian machinery: the demise of the citizen who had been the bearer of the culture that produced literature. To this end he had to invent a dispassionate language in which he could not only narrate the indifferent universe of the concentration camp with great precision but also offer insight into its very structure, which systematically destroyed the individual. He created a prose that eschews action, character, and expressive language. Alluding to the twelve-tone musical scale pioneered by Arnold Schoenberg, Kertész has said his aim was atonality in the language. He pointed out a coincidence in the word he chose as the title of his first novel, *Sorstalanság* (1975; translated as *Fateless*, 1992): "Sorstalanság: Tizenkét betû. Véletlen ugyan, de jellemző véletlen" (Fateless: twelve letters. It is accidental, but characteristically so).

One of Kertész's central pursuits is his penetrating examination of the fabric of totalitarianism. He scrutinized the smallest details of the deportation process both in his own and many former inmates' memories, and compared them to the photographs taken of deportees arriving at the ramp of the Birkenau extermination camp. As he mentioned in his Nobel lecture, there was a remarkable difference between what he and others remembered, and what the pictures documented. What was erased from memory but is clearly visible in the photographs is the good faith and readiness of most deportees to comply with their captors and executioners:

> Megdöbbenve néztem ezeket a képeket. Szép, mosolygó női arcok, értelmes szemû fiatal emberek, teli jó szándékkal, a közremûködés készségével. Most már megértettem, miért és hogyan mosódhatott el bennük a tétlenségnek és a tehetetlenségnek e megszégyenítő húsz perce. S ha arra gondoltam, hogy mindez ugyanígy ismétlődött, naponta, hetente, havonta, évek hosszú során át, bepillantást nyertem a rettenet technikájába, megtudtam, hogyan lehetséges az ember élete ellen fordítani magát az emberi természetet.

> (I looked at these photographs in utter amazement. I saw lovely, smiling women and bright-eyed young men, all of them well-intentioned, eager to cooperate. Now I understood how and why those humiliating twenty minutes of idleness and helplessness faded from their memories. And when I thought how all this was repeated the same way for days, weeks, months and years on end, I gained an insight into the mechanism of horror; I learned how it became possible to turn human nature against one's own life.)

Kertész examines the Holocaust from the perspective of the entire European historical, philosophical, and literary tradition since the Enlightenment. He regards it as the failure of European culture rather than a particular Jewish catastrophe. His dry and unsentimental prose made him controversial in the eyes of the book publishers and book censors in the Hungary of the 1970s. Not only was he one of the first to break the taboo of writing about the Holocaust, but also he did so from a perspective that fundamentally differed from that sanctioned by officialdom. In Kertész's analysis, looking back from Soviet-dominated Hungary, the Nazi Holocaust was a link in the chain of totalitarian regimes, supported by the education and views of generations of erudite Europeans. He called Auschwitz a "világélmény" (world experience), which revealed the absurd but not quite illogical outcome of the rationalism-based organization of state power. He did not study the particulars of the history of the Jews in Germany and the specifics of that particular country's embracing Nazism, since he was more concerned with the scandalous fact that a European state apparatus came to create a well-oiled mechanism for the ultimate deprivation of a group of individuals of their free will, language, time, and personal characteristics.

Kertész was born on 9 November 1929 in Budapest. He comes from an assimilated middle-class Jewish family. His paternal grandfather, Jakab Klein (who Magyarized the family name to Kertész), having full confidence in his homeland, the dual monarchy of Austria-Hungary, had invested all his fortune in war bonds during World War I; he ended up losing everything. Kertész's father was a timber merchant, and his mother worked as a clerk. He was an only child, and his parents, who divorced around the time of his birth, later sent him to a boarding school. A promising student, Kertész was enrolled in the newly formed "Jewish class" of the Madách Gymnasium in Budapest in 1940. In the summer of 1944, while he was working as a laborer, he was held up in the street and deported to Auschwitz. Selected for work, he was transferred to the Zeitz labor camp and, intermittently, to Buchenwald. A survivor, he had the option to start a new life in another country after the war, but he returned to Hungary in July 1945. Back in Budapest, he became a journalist at *Szikra* (Spark), a publication of the Hungarian Ministry of Heavy Industry, in 1946. He graduated from high school in 1948 and started to work for the Social Democrat journal *Világosság* (Illumination) but was fired in 1950. He became a factory worker, then was drafted and served in the military until 1953. When discharged, he decided he would no longer accept regular employment. He married a woman named Albina in 1953 and co-authored musical comedies, which were produced in various Budapest theaters and paid well enough to give him some financial independence. Later, in the 1960s and 1970s, Kertész translated literary and philosophical works into Hungarian, including books by Sigmund Freud, Friedrich Nietzsche, and Ludwig Wittgenstein.

Kertész lived isolated from the literary community, teaching himself how to write a novel and discovering the writers who had a great impact on his thinking and writing. He was a particularly avid reader of Nietzsche and singled out Albert Camus and Franz Kafka who, both as thinkers and writers, profoundly influenced him. He greatly admired Camus's succinct prose and precision, particularly *L'Etranger* (1942; translated as *The Stranger*, 1946). He read Immanuel Kant, Georg Wilhelm Friedrich Hegel, Blaise Pascal, and Wittgenstein, and was much influenced by German writers from Johann Wolfgang von Goethe to Rainer Maria Rilke, as well as Thomas Mann. He is familiar with the Holocaust literature and is profoundly influenced by those writers who, having survived the catastrophe, later took their own lives: Paul Celan, Jean Améry, Tadeusz Borowski, and Primo Levi. Kertész systematically read documents and memoirs on the Holocaust and studied maps and photographs. He saw Auschwitz as the quintessential twentieth-century catastrophe, and he was prepared to write about his concentration camp experience, but not as his personal history. Rather than making his novel *Sorstalanság* an account of events, he reduced this first book to the bare representation of the totalitarian machinery and its methods to transform the individual into a mere functional entity: a numbered item. On this account *Sorstalanság* was often compared to Levi's *Se questo è un uomo* (1947, If This Is a Man; translated as *Survival in Auschwitz*, 1961).

Kertesz worked on *Sorstalanság* between 1960 and the early 1970s. When he first submitted the manuscript in 1973, the publisher Magvető summarily rejected the book because of its objective stance, which greatly differed from the eloquent tone expected from those who described the sufferings of the Jews during the Holocaust. In communist Hungary, the Holocaust was by and large still a taboo subject. Official politics tried to circumvent the fact that Germany had been one country at the time of the Holocaust and tried to project the political difference between communist East Germany and capitalist West Germany back into the war years, suggesting that the Nazi past belonged to the West only. Discussion of the Holocaust had to condemn that Germany; it had to be "humanist," "anti-fascist," and, most of all, it had to fit into the language that had been created for it within the Hungarian communist cultural context. Moreover, any mention of the Holocaust had to refer to it as a closed chapter of history, hermetically sealed from the present—whereas in Kertész's writing, as he stated in his Nobel lecture, "A Holocaust az én írásaimban sosem tudott múlt idoben megjelenni" (the Holocaust could never be present in the past tense). Such writing as Kertész's was not desirable at a time and place where fathoming the reality of the concentration camps as the epitome of the totalitarian system disagreed with the interests of officialdom.

After the initial refusal from Magvető, Kertész did not believe there was any other forum that would get the book out. However, he was persuaded to approach Szépirodalmi Kiadó, another major literary publishing house, which brought his novel out in 1975.

Sorstalanság is a rigorously constructed novel rather than an autobiography, but it is based on Kertész's actual experience. Fourteen-year-old György Köves, the narrator, is in the midst of adolescence, feeling out of touch with his Jewish middle-class family. His story starts in the spring of 1944, when the wearing of the yellow star and conscription for forced labor service has become the rule for Jews in Budapest, generally accepted as part of "Jewish fate." A whole infrastructure is in place to cater to the particular needs of the draftees, but all the Jews do about it, including the Köves family, is to say prayers. The only character of the novel who sees this situation as nonsense and feels rebellious about it all, while desperately trying to understand the reasons for the discrimination against Jews, is a teenage girl in a neighboring apartment with whom Köves might get involved, were he not propelled into a different orbit. The boy's journey to Auschwitz starts on a bright sunny summer day amid all the good fortune a fourteen-year-old Jewish boy in the Budapest of 1944 could hope for. Not only does he have work, but, more important, as an employee he has a pass that enables him to leave the checkpoints of the capital city at a time when most Jews do not have a presentable ID card.

On this early summer morning a soft-spoken, blue-eyed policeman stops outbound buses at a checkpoint and kindly asks Jewish passengers to get off. The boy follows the order and finds his fellow workers—boys like him—already there, held up from their own respective bus rides. Amid the frequent and random ID controls and unexpected police raids of those times, it is the "natural" course of things for Jews to be held up. The boys almost enjoy having fun in the cool customhouse rather than having to sweat while working. They have the feeling of vacation. After several hours, while the policeman keeps on calling his superiors for further orders, the group is taken to the other end of the city, the premises of a brick factory, where a great number of Jews have already been gathered.

When, after a long, idle time, an official calls for volunteers to work in Germany, young Köves gets almost enthusiastic. He thinks of Germany as a clean, tidy, and well-organized country, where he can do something better than his present lowly work south of Budapest. After all, he has a high-school education and is ready to go abroad. Also, volunteers are promised to fare better than those who do not volunteer, because, as rumor has it, all of them would be taken to Germany anyway. The young boy does not see through the language or the fact that the instructions, which Kertész identifies as a key feature of the Nazi machinery, come in controlled installments. One event leads to the next, and it all seems to him as a chain of serendipitous events rather than a scheme.

After a three-day-and-night train ride in a sealed car, of which Kertész gives a reticent description, the transport arrives in Auschwitz. In a flurry of events and great haste, while he is being advised to declare himself to be sixteen rather than fourteen years old, Köves finds himself in front of a doctor with the other boys. When the doctor has ordered some of the men to go left, and others to go right, the boys are still quite pleased: "Minden mozgott, minden mûködött, mindenki a helyén, s végezte a magáét, pontosn, derûsen, olajozottan. Sok arcon láttam mosolyt, szerényebbet vagy magabiztosabbat" (Everything was working well, everything ran smoothly, everything was in its place and attended to its function, precisely, cheerfully, like a well-oiled machine. On many faces I saw smiles, rather humble but more self-assured). Walking toward the barracks under the supervision of SS soldiers, the boys see a few tidy, well-kept houses and gardens, and a soccer field. "Minden ott volt, hivogatóan, frissen, jó karban, a legnagyobb rendben" (Everything was there, inviting, fresh, in good condition and in the best of order), the protagonist muses. However, on the evening of the same day, already shaved bare, given prisoners' clothes and ill-fitting shoes, he smells the nauseating smoke coming from the Auschwitz crematorium chimneys and knows it all. He understands how those who were sent by the doctor to the other side were processed by the fast and efficiently organized system.

After three days the boy is taken to Buchenwald and then on to a work camp in nearby Zeitz, where the captives slave for a rubber factory. Robotic, they get up at dawn, are minimally nourished, report for work, work all day, then march back, report again, are counted and minimally nourished, and go to sleep. From an older inmate who helps him, the boy learns a few survival skills, which include carefully cleaning himself every day, always putting aside a little food to avoid the feeling of starvation, and opting for minimum visibility in the middle of the row when marching. But he can control all that for only so long. After a few months he is giving up: he develops lesions and is on the verge of dying of sepsis. Useless for work, he is taken back to Buchenwald—"vissza a feladónak" (return to sender)—to die. Reduced to the subhuman, his flickering thoughts of consciousness still propel around his wish to live: "valami halk vágyakozásféle lopott, mintegy az esztelenségtől szégyenkező, s mégiscsak makacskodó szavát: szeretnék kicsit még élni ebben a szép koncentrációs táborban" (senseless, but yet consistently stubborn in their persistence: I would so much like to live a little longer in this beautiful concentration camp).

He is one of the few to be taken to the camp hospital, where doctors and nurses, an international team of captives, work in what appears to be a tacit collaboration against the rationale of the camps, and try to help the sick survive. The boy has the strength that makes recovery possible, and one day, still on his hospital bed, hears an announcement over the megaphone that the camp is liberated. The nightmare is over. He has the option to go to Sweden or some other European country, but he chooses to return home to Hungary, a fatherland that had deported him to die in Auschwitz. He travels home burdened with an experience that he knows will be hard, if not impossible, to share.

Kertész's second volume, *A nyomkereső* (1977, The Path Finder), includes short stories and a short novel titled *Detektívtörténet* (Mystery Story). The title story is the tale of a former concentration camp inmate who revisits the camps and encounters a mysterious, veiled woman who had lost her husband to the Holocaust and, as the narrator learns from the local newspaper while waiting for his outbound train, has taken her own life. This story was one of Kertész's attempts to articulate that Auschwitz was an indelible, irreversible, and insurmountable event.

Detektívtörténet is set in an unidentified state of South America (possibly Chile), where a young, idealist student, Enrique Salinas, scion of one of the country's prominent families, is burning with desire to become an activist against the dictatorship. Unrelated to this wish, the random but ample information gathered by the ubiquitous secret service targets him, as well as his father, among a great number of equally suspect citizens—in fact, everyone is suspect—as potential dangers to the existing order, and both are ground beneath the wheels of the machinery of the totalitarian state. Here Kertész repeats, in a reductive and fictitious form, his quintessential Auschwitz experience: deprivation of a personal fate. A faceless, blind mechanism is at work, operated by the usurpers of power and needing to be fed incessantly. Human personalities are reduced to cases, files, and, according to the system's logic, inevitably, corpses. Innocence—one of Kertész's recurring thoughts—is an anomaly in the system. It irritates the mechanism and challenges its bureaucrats: the innocent, who has ethical power, has to be eliminated.

Throughout the late 1970s Kertész slowly established himself as a writer in Hungary. *Sorstalanság* was increasingly recognized as an important novel, although it received limited attention in literary criticism during the first few years following its 1975 publication. It eventually earned for Kertész the Füst Milán Jutalom (Füst Milán Prize) in 1983 and the Forintos Díj (Forintos Prize) in 1986. In the spring of 1980 Kertész traveled to Germany on a study grant, but in general he supported himself and his wife with translations in the early 1980s.

The title of *A kudarc* (1988, Failure [or Fiasco]) is a key word in Kertész's work. A novel about a novel, this book continues the autobiographical postwar account of György Köves, who, in a slightly Kafkaesque opening, "arrives" by an airplane to exactly where he had set out from: back in Hungary, as if on a trip. His surrealistic arrival is followed by a realistic account of events: he is fired from his job as a journalist and is thrown into the 1950s Budapest nightlife, where the homeless mix with those who do not go home in order to dodge a possible police raid and their evacuation as a "class enemy." He takes up work in a factory, returns to journalism only to be fired again, then is drafted, and after two years of military service he decides to embark on writing a novel. This book is the history of his birth as a writer. Ending at the beginning of the 1956 revolution. *A kudarc* gives a vivid description of the grim Budapest under totalitarian rule during the early 1950s. Clear-cut, impressively described characters populate the cafeterias, restaurants, and apartments. They fear the secret police, try to outsmart them, fall prey to them, kill themselves, lose their minds, struggle to survive, try to take advantage of the few loopholes in the system, or surrender to it. Kertész's descriptions are objective and reticent, but full of life. The individual stories of the appearances, disappearances, and reappearances of some of his characters reflect the whims and turns of political events, and they connect up as the fabric of life under a dictatorial regime. "Failure" is seen as the quintessential experience in Eastern Europe. As Kertész said in a 1991 interview:

> *A kudarc* struktúráját utánozták az események; a nagy öneszmélést és a nagy visszahullást. Ráébredtek a saját egzisztenciájukra, az eleven létükre, tettvágyukra, s aztán az egész visszahanyatlott a káosz örvényébe. . . . Ez így néz ki: trauma, elfojtás—majd a katartikus tisztázás helyett regresszió következik be, visszaesés a trauma által kiváltott tünetekbe.
>
> (Events [in Hungary] imitated, if one can say so, the structure of *Failure*: the cycles of awakening to a new self-consciousness followed by falling back. People came to see their own existence, their real life and desire to act, in a new light, and then reclined back into the fulcrum of chaos. . . . As if obeying the pattern of trauma, suppression, and then, instead of catharsis, regression: a fall back into the syndromes of the original trauma.)

Kertész inserts in *A kudarc* the beginning of a novel written by one of the characters, Berg. Titled "Én, a hóhér" (Me, the Hangman), it is an independent chapter in which Berg, a suffering, idiosyncratic thinker and another alter ego of the author besides the main character, discovers the reservoirs of cruelty and sadism within himself. These ideas square with what Kertész said in an acceptance speech in 1997: "[hogy felfedezzük magunkban] mind az áldozat, mind pedig a hóhér szerepének rémületes lehetőségét" ([we have to discover in ourselves] the horrible potential of the roles of both the victim and the hangman).

Kertész's first postcommunist novel, *Kaddis a meg nem született gyermekért* (1990; translated as *Kaddish for a Child Not Born*, 1997), starts out with the narrator's definitive, emphatic "No" to the idea of having children. Lucid and sad, the novel tells the story of the narrator's marriage, which fails because the narrator (known only as "B"), who had been in Auschwitz, is marked for life by the experience. His young wife, the daughter of Holocaust survivors herself, wants life and a future, to raise a family. The narrator, once again a writer, is in love with his wife and understands her wish, but, with his concentration camp experience haunting him, is unable to participate in the life she desires. The only task he has cut out for himself is to leave testimony of what he had witnessed: "hogy megbélyegzett zsidóként Auschwitzban lehettem, és hogy a zsidóságom révén mégiscsak átéltem valamit, és a szemébe néztem valaminek, és tudok, egyszer s mindenkorra és visszavonhatatlanul tudok valamit, amiből nem engedek, soha nem engedek" (I was allowed to be in Auschwitz and on account of my Jewishness I experienced and survived something and faced something; and now I know something irrevocably, once and for all, something that I won't let go of, will never let go of).

Sorstalanság, *A kudarc,* and *Kaddis a meg nem született gyermekért* have been considered a trilogy, especially in the German literary press. They are connected by autobiographical elements, although each is a work of fiction and a book in its own right. Each of them discusses the horrible enigma of Auschwitz and the Hungary of the 1950s, and each is narrated by a main character that bears many of the author's own characteristics.

Az angol lobogó (1991; translated as *The Union Jack*, 2002) is a brief work, but, as literary critics such as Lajos Márton Varga have observed, a whole life is needed to put those few sentences into context. At the heart of the story is a flash of memory of the sight of a military jeep covered by the Union Jack roaming in the Budapest streets in the days of the revolution in October 1956. People make way for it and applaud it as it passes them, and, in response to the applause, a hand sheathed in a buckskin glove appears from the jeep window and slowly waves to the crowd lining the street:

Integetés volt ez, baráti, üdvözlő, tán egy kissé részvételi mozdulat, mindenesetre fenntartás nélküli helyeslést tartalmazott, és mellesleg a szilárd tudatot is, amivel ez a kesztyus kéz nemsokára a repülőgépről a betonra veuető lépcső korlátját tapintja majd, hazaérkezve a távoli szigetországba. Azután kocsi, kéz, és angol lobogó–minden eltunt a kanyarban, és a tapsok lassan elhaltak.

(It was a friendly, maybe somewhat sympathetic salute, expressing unreserved approval, as well as the firm awareness of soon touching the rail of the stairs leading from the aircraft to the ground after landing in the remote island. Then the hand, the Union Jack–everything vanished in the curve of the street, and the applause slowly subsided.)

But that is not the whole story of the English flag. In a few days, the narrator adds, tanks emerged from the same curve of the same street, albeit from the opposite direction–Russian tanks. The Union Jack, symbol of far-away freedom and civil liberty, is replaced by the monstrous military. This image of October 1956 spells catastrophe and loss of hope for the Hungarian revolutionaries. The fleeting glimpse of the gloved hand stands for the limited, at best moral, support from the West in a curt, single, elusive gesture.

Gályanapló (1992, Galley Diary) includes excerpts of Kertész's diaries written over thirty years, starting in 1961. He recorded reflections on readings, ideas, events, and experiences. The notes reveal a bold, idiosyncratic, sensitive thinker, open to lucid theories as well as to the truths he discovers in sudden moments of inspiration.

Since the early 1990s Kertész often has been invited to participate in and give talks at international conferences on the Holocaust. The substantial essays he wrote for these occasions were published in various periodicals, and then in two volumes: *A holocaust mint kultúra* (1993, Holocaust As Culture), and *A gondolatnyi csend, amíg a kivégzőosztag újratölt* (1998, Moments of Silence While the Execution Squad Reloads). The latter of these collections also includes three interviews with the author.

One of the most significant among the essays, "A holocaust mint kultúra," was written for the Jean Améry Symposium held at the Vienna University in October 1992. Here Kertész defines the Holocaust as an event in European culture ranking with the Crucifixion. An original crime, the killing of the innocent, it has already been processed (in Freudian terms) through the periods of oblivion and suppression and has been saved from oblivion. Erudition and education, he says, referring to both Améry and Borowski, failed to make a difference. The great European culture did not help the camp inmates nor inhibit the perpetrators and murderers. However, bearing witness and creating written monuments will empower the once powerless, he claims. There is power in representation, he asserts, quoting Améry, and continues with a phrase from *A kudarc*: "alannyá változtatni örökös tárgyiságomat, névadónak lenni megnevezett helyett" (which can turn me from eternal object into subject, and into name-giver from the one who is given a name). Kertész poses the question: Can the Holocaust create value? His answer is that "felmérhetetlen szenvedések révén felmérhetetlen tudáshoz vezetett; és ezáltal felmérhetetlen erkölcsi tartalék rejlik benne" (at the price of immeasurable suffering, the Holocaust has opened up immeasurable knowledge, and thus, an immeasurable moral reservoir). And this knowledge, he trusts, may lead to a new catharsis in the future.

The short work *Jegyzőkönyv* (1993; translated as *Sworn Statement,* 2001), published together with a piece by Péter Esterházy, is based on an experience the author had in the early 1990s with duty officers who made him undergo a humiliating bureaucratic process because he had a slightly greater amount of Austrian currency in his pocket than permitted by law when traveling to Vienna. Instead of appearing at a scheduled meeting in the Austrian Ministry of Culture, where he was expected, Kertész was returned to Budapest. His bitter description is an accusation of the mindless, rigid, and unchanged bureaucracy that still complicated the lives of Hungarian citizens after the fall of Communism. Although he does not explicitly mention Auschwitz, Kertész could not help recognizing his archenemy in his treatment. It was the spirit of the camps, the same mindless obedience to rules, and the total and deliberate disregard of the individual. In sympathy with Kertész, Esterházy wrote about a similar experience in his part of the book; another Hungarian writer, Mihály Kornis, demonstrated solidarity and paid tribute to Kertész by performing an adaptation of *Jegyzőkönyv* on stage.

In 1997 Kertész published *Valaki más: A változás krónikája* (Someone Else), a collection of fragmentary essays and diary excerpts in which the author searches for that elusive, familiar stranger that is commonly called the self. In contrast to the closed world of his novels, Kertész now shares his impressions while traveling through Europe. He records his perceptions of the European landscape and cities, discovers Rembrandt's dramatic work, and enjoys the freedom of driving on the freeway with the accompaniment of triumphant music. He commemorates his wife, who died in 1995 of a brain tumor, and their "boldogtalan házasságban élve, oly nagyon szerettük egymást" (unhappy marriage in which we loved each other so much). With his characteristic keen, relentless analysis he explores his past and revisits yet-unanswered questions, the mystery of life and the mystery of his own being above all.

In *Valaki más,* at long last, Kertész finds happiness against the background of the dark years he had been through. Writing about one of his trips with Magda, his new companion (whom he married in 1996), Kertész considers the miracle and enigma of being: "Hannah Arendt állítja, hogy minden írásának egyetlen indítéka: megérteni valamit. De ránk hagyja a 'megérteni' szó homályát" (Hannah Arendt claims that the only motivation of each of her writings was her desire to understand something. But she leaves the fogginess of this word "understand" to us). The unfathomable mystery of existence and of the self humbles Kertész: "'Én': ez egy fikció, amelynek legföljebb a társszerzői lehetünk" ("Me" is a fiction, of which one can be, in the best of cases, a co-author only).

Since the demise of socialism, Kertész has become recognized as one of the most important writers in his own country and has gained international attention since the 1990s as his works have been translated into many languages. His many awards include the Brandenburgischer Literaturpreis (1995) and three prizes in 1997: the Leipziger Buchpreis zur Europäischen Verständigung, the Jeanette-Schocken Preis, and the Friedrich Gundolf Preis. In 1998 he was awarded the Kossuth Díj, the highest cultural prize in Hungary, and the following year Rohwolt Verlag (Reinbek) published a complete edition of his works. He also has won the Herder Preis (2000), the Internazionale Premio Flaiano (2001), the Peter-Chamisso-Preis (2001), the Die Welt Literaturpreis (2002), and the Hans Sahl Prize (2002). In 1998 he was named a member of the Darmstadt-based Deutsche Akademie für Sprache und Dichtung (German Academy of Language and Poetry), and in 2001 he became a member of the Orden pour le Mérite für Wissenschaften und Künste (Order for Merit in Sciences and Arts).

In 2002 Kertész became the first Hungarian writer to be awarded the Nobel Prize in Literature. The news elicited a mixed response in Hungary. There was official jubilation and pride, but also some expression of disappointment that a relatively obscure (in Hungary) writer, and a Jew (whom right-wing nationalists therefore did not accept as "truly" Hungarian), had won this honor. The prize inspired him to reassess his work and to confirm, once again, that writing is a powerful weapon against oppression:

> Tudnunk kell hogy Auschwitz, egy bizonyos értelemben legalábbis–felfüggesztette az irodalmat.... Auschwitz igazi problémája az, hogy megtörtént, és ezen a tényen a legjobb, de a leggonoszabb akarattal sem változtathatunk. E súlyos helyzetnek talán a magyar katolikus költő, Pilinszky János adta a legpontosabb nevet, amikor "botránynak" nevezte; s ezen nyilvánvalóan azt értette, hogy Auschwitz a keresztény kultúrkörben esett meg, s így a metafizikai szellem számára kiheverhetetlen.

(We must know that Auschwitz, in a certain sense at least, suspended literature.... The real problem with Auschwitz is that it happened, and this cannot be altered–not with the best, or worst, will in the world. This gravest of situations was characterized most accurately by the Hungarian Catholic poet János Pilinszky when he called it a "scandal." What he meant by it, clearly, is that Auschwitz occurred in a Christian cultural environment, so for those with a metaphysical turn of mind it can never be overcome.)

Kertész, however, addresses his work to the future as well as dedicating it to the millions who died: "Amikor Auschwitz traumatikus hatásán gondolkodom, ezzel a mai ember vitalitásának és kreativitásának az alapkérdéseihez jutok el; s Auschwitzon gondolkodva így, talán paradox módon, de inkább a jövőn, semmint a múlton gondolkodom" (Whenever I think of the traumatic impact of Auschwitz, I end up dwelling on the vitality and creativity of those living today. Thus, in thinking about Auschwitz, I reflect, paradoxically, not on the past, but the future).

Kertész's first post-Nobel book, *Felszámolás* (2003; translated as *Liquidation,* 2004), is a short novel narrating the last years, love affair, and suicide of a writer, again known only as "B." Reviewing the English translation of the novel, Ruth Franklin observed in *The New York Times Book Review* (19 December 2004): "At times almost playful, at times harrowing, the novel weaves multiple voices and textures into a meditation on reading and writing, activities here inseparable from life itself." Originally intended as a drama, the novel takes place in Hungary after the fall of Communism. It is an addition to the trilogy, turning it to a tetralogy, since it too discusses the ultimate impossibility of life after Auschwitz.

This "B" is younger than the protagonists of the previous novels, since he was born in Auschwitz. He not only takes his own life but also manages to have his former wife execute his spiritual suicide by burning his unpublished work in the fireplace. Through the web of broken friendships and love affairs Kertész once again–as he said in many interviews, for the last time–demonstrates the poisonous legacy of the Holocaust as well as the totalitarian regime in Hungary.

Imre Kertész continues to work and live in Budapest and Berlin. Whether he writes again about the Holocaust, his legacy is clear. His relentless inquiry into that catastrophe and his vision of it as the most formidable lesson that mankind—not solely Jewry—has been taught in the past century makes his writing fundamentally important to the understanding of history and human nature.

Interviews:

Katalin Budai, "'A müvészethez elég az igazság': Beszélgetés Kertész Imrével," *Magyar Napló*, 1 November 1991, pp. 14–17;

Tamás Szőnyei, "'Magyarországot mindenütt szeretik': Intervjú Kertész Imre iróval," *Magyar Narancs*, 12 December 2002, pp. 6–7, 35.

References:

Hans Magnus Enzensberger, "Unerbittlichkeitskünstler. Von Imre Kertész," *Frankfurter Allgemeine Zeitung*, 15 June 2001;

László F. Földényi, "A Large Truth," *Common Knowledge*, 7, no. 1 (Spring 1998): 7–14;

Földényi, "Az erkölcsi magány terhe," *Magyar Lettre Internationale*, no. 25 (1997): 2–3;

Zsuzsanna Gahse, "Das Unerwartete und Imre Kertesz: Eine Laudatio," *Horen: Zeitschrift fur Literatur, Kunst und Kritik*, 42, no. 2 (1997): 67–73;

David Holley, "Hungarian Holocaust Survivor Is Awarded Nobel in Literature," *Los Angeles Times*, 11 October 2002, p. A3;

József Keresztesi, "Leverkühn slágert fütyöl," *Magyar Narancs*, 20 November 2003, pp. 32–33;

Judith Klein, "'. . . als wäre ich selbst der Dichter': Übersetzen als Thema und Metapher literarischer Texte (an Beispielen von Isaak Babel, Aharon Megged und Imre Kertész)," *LiLi: Zeitschrift fur Literaturwissenschaft und Linguistik*, 99 (1995): 155–160;

Péter Nádas, "Kertész munkája és témája," *Élet és irodalom*, 18 October 2002;

Sándor Radnóti, "Auschwitz mint szellemi életforma," *Holmi*, 3 (1991): 372–378;

Ilma Rakusa, "Von Trauma zur Zeugenschaft, Erzählungen und Essays von Imre Kertész," *Neue Züricher Zeitung*, 1 February 2000;

Alan Riding, "Hungarian Holocaust Survivor Is Awarded Nobel in Literature," *New York Times*, 11 October 2002, p. A1;

Tanje Rudtke, "'Eine Kuriose Geschichte': Die Pikara Perspektive im Holocaustroman am Beispiel Von Imre Kertesz' Roman eines Schicksallosen," *Arcadia: Zeitschrift fur Vergleichende Literaturwissenschaft*, 36, no. 1 (2001): 46–57;

Gábor Schein: "Összekötni az összeköthetetlent: Megjegyzések Kertész Imre prózájához," *Jelenkor*, 12 (2002): 1296–1303;

Bernhard Schlink, "Happiness as a Duty: Bernhard Schlink's Eulogy of Imre Kertész during Presentation of the *Die Welt* Literary Prize," *Die Welt*, 9 November 2000, pp. 17–19;

György Spiró, "A hatvan éves Kertész Imre köszöntése," *Élet és irodalom*, 46 (1989): 7;

Péter Szirák, "Emlékezés és példázat: a létezés negatív aspektusa (A Kertész-olvasás)," in his *Folytonosság és változás* (Debrecen: Csokonai, 1998), pp. 82–88;

Steven Totosy de Zepetnek, "And the 2002 Nobel Prize for Literature Goes to Imre Kertész, Jew and Hungarian," *CLCWeb: Comparative Literature and Culture* (2002), <http://clcwebjournal.lib.purdue.edu/library/kertesz2002nobel(totosy02).html>;

Lajos Márton Varga, "A tanúságtétel perspektívái," *Jelenkor*, 12 (1991): 1051–1054;

György Vári, *Kertész Imre: Buchenwald fölött az ég* (Budapest: Kijárat, 2003).

2002 Nobel Prize in Literature Presentation Speech

by Torgny Lindgren, Member of the Swedish Academy

Your Majesties, Your Royal Highnesses, Ladies and Gentlemen,

The realities that are the subject of Imre Kertész's literary production and form its background cannot be understood or described by any of us who have not experienced them. The bestial, systematic evil of Nazism and the bureaucratic, misanthropic stupidity of the socialistic one-party state are hardly comprehensible to minds that have been shaped in civilized societies: nor do they allow themselves to be portrayed in other ways than as crazy paradoxes and absurdities.

Imre Kertész has written about this artistic problem in his *Galley Diary* and in his essay collection *Eine Gedankenlänge Stille*.

It has often been argued that *Fateless* is the hub and center of Kertész's literary production. That may be correct: this ostensibly simple, naked and mundanely unassuming account of a young boy's life and sufferings in Auschwitz, Zeitz and Buchenwald possesses a weightiness and irrefutability that puts it not only at the core of one man's literary production but also of contemporary European prose.

"When you are going to read Kertész, you have to begin with *Fateless!*" is a very common statement. However, it can be called into question.

No matter which Kertész novel or essay we pick up, we soon notice that it is intimately connected to one of the other works in his literary production. In a manner that is hard to explain, the separate parts appear to have grown together, with common root fibers or circulatory systems. *Fiasco,* that many-voiced, off-center account of a system-critical writer's desperate hardships in a totalitarian, anti-educational state, is linked by allusions and thematic details with *The English Flag,* which in turn is intimately connected to the much later book of thoughts *Galley Diary.* From *Kaddish for a Child Not Born,* a mournful and simultaneously ironic requiem for a child who is never allowed to be born, because it would be cruel and criminal to bring it into the world, there are delicate but easily discernible threads that link it to *Fateless* and *Fiasco.*

What finally reveals itself to the reader is a coherent organism, a body or symphonic work in the spirit of Mahler or Webern. Or in a word that borrows its solemn tone from the aging Thomas Mann: Ein WERK. An oeuvre, whose subject is an individual's refusal to abandon his individual will by merging it with a collective identity.

And behind each text, we clearly hear a voice or tone that Kertész himself has formulated this way: In all respects my existence is horrible, except for writing: so I write and write to endure my existence, to justify it.

Kertész approaches tradition in a similar contrapuntal way. In his world, tradition is not a temporal phenomenal, but a spatial one. Tradition is his surroundings, the landscape where he resides and where on his rambles he encounters social companions and conversational companions like Camus, Nietzsche, Schopenhauer, St. John of the Cross, Kafka or Paul Celan.

Sehr verehrter Imre Kertész!

Uns, die wir Ihrer Dichtung begegnet sind und den Vorteil hatten uns in sie zu vertiefen, scheint sie notwendig und unentbehrlich um das "20. Jahrhundert, das wir noch unser eigenes nennen müssen, zu verstehen. Und um so mehr, um auch das Schwanken zwischen Schicksal und Freiheit zu begreifen, welches das Los des preisgegebenen und wehrlosen Menschen während dieses Jahrhunderts gewesen ist. Es war und ist eine Zeit, die scheinbar Ihre Hypothese bestätigt, dass der Affe vom Menschen abstammt und nicht umgekehrt. Hinter diesem Gedanken, der ein wenig misanthropisch vorkommen mag, hört man deutlich den milden und klugen Humor, der Ihr ganzes schriftstellerisches Werk durchströmt.

Sie haben auch einmal geschrieben: Ich werde immer ein zweitrangiger, verkannter und missverstandener ungarischer Schriftsteller sein; die ungarische Sprache wird immer eine zweitrangige, verkannte und missverstandene Sprache sein.

Gegen diese ironische Behauptung möchte die Schwedische Akademie am kräftigsten protestieren und Ihnen gleichzeitig herzlich gratulieren, wenn ich Sie jetzt auffordere, den Nobelpreis für Literatur aus der Hand Seiner Majestät des Königs entgegenzunehmen.

[© The Nobel Foundation, 2002.]

(Translation of German by Philip B. Dematteis)

Greatly admired Imre Kertész!

For those of us who have encountered your fiction and had the benefit of becoming absorbed in it, it seems necessary and indispensable for the understanding of the twentieth century, which we still must call our own. And even more to grasp the oscillation between fate and freedom that has been the lot of the abandoned and defenseless people of this century. It was and is a time that apparently confirms your hypothesis that the ape descended from man and not the reverse. Behind this thought, which might seem a bit misanthropic, one hears distinctly the gentle and wise humor that permeates all of your literary work.

You also once wrote: "I will always be a second-rate, mistaken and misunderstood Hungarian writer; Hungarian will always be a second-rate, mistaken and misunderstood language."

The Swedish Academy would like to protest most strongly against this ironic assertion and at the same time heartily congratulate you, because I now invite you to accept the Nobel Prize in Literature from the hand of His Majesty the King.

Kertész: Banquet Speech

Kertész's speech at the Nobel Banquet, 10 December 2002 (Translation):

Today we are experiencing a globalization, an inflation of the Holocaust. The Holocaust survivor who knows Auschwitz through the experience of suffering, observes it all from the perspective assigned to him. He keeps silent or gives interviews to the Spielberg Foundation, he accepts the compensation payments promised him after a fifty-year delay, or, if he is prominent, he makes a speech in the Swedish Academy.

And he asks the question: what is he bequeathing, what is his spiritual legacy? Has he enriched human knowledge with his tale of suffering? Or has he only born witness to the unimaginable degradation of the human being, in which there is no lesson, and which ought to be forgotten as quickly as possible? I do not see it that way. I have not changed my opinion that the Holocaust is a trauma of European civilization. And it is becoming a life-and-death matter, whether this trauma lives on as culture or neurosis, in a constructive or destructive form in European societies.

However, all that will be a decision of the future, which I can scarcely hope to influence any longer. I have endeavoured—perhaps it is not sheer self-deception—to perform the existential labour that being an Auschwitz-survivor has thrust upon me as a kind of obligation. I realize what a privilege has been bestowed on me. I have seen the true visage of this dreadful century, I have gazed into the eye of the Gorgon, and have been able to keep on living. Yet, I knew I would never be able to free myself from the sight; I knew this visage would always hold me captive. Over the decades and one by one I rejected the misleading slogans of a misleading freedom such as "an inexplicable historical error," "cannot be rationalized," and other tautologies of that kind. They are the gestures of one who wishes to stand above the fray. I have never succumbed to the temptation of self-pity, nor, it may be, to that of true sublimity and divine perspicacity, but I have known from the beginning that my disgrace was not merely a humiliation; it also concealed redemption, if only my heart could be courageous enough to accept this redemption, this peculiarly cruel form of grace, and even to recognize grace at all in such a cruel form. —And if you now ask me what still keeps me here on this earth, what keeps me alive, then, I would answer without any hesitation: love.

[© The Nobel Foundation, 2002. Imre Kertész is the sole author of his speech.]

Press Release: The Nobel Prize in Literature 2002

from the Office of the Permanent Secretary of the Swedish Academy, 10 October 2002

Imre Kertész

The Nobel Prize in Literature for 2002 is awarded to the Hungarian writer Imre Kertész

"for writing that upholds the fragile experience of the individual against the barbaric arbitrariness of history."

In his writing Imre Kertész explores the possibility of continuing to live and think as an individual in an era in which the subjection of human beings to social forces has become increasingly complete. His works return unremittingly to the decisive event in his life: the period spent in Auschwitz, to which he was taken as a teenage boy during the Nazi persecution of Hungary's Jews. For him Auschwitz is not an exceptional occurrence that like an alien body subsists outside the normal history of Western Europe. It is the ultimate truth about human degradation in modern existence.

Kertész's first novel, *Sorstalanság*, 1975 (*Fateless*, 1992), deals with the young Köves, who is arrested and taken to a concentration camp but conforms and survives. The novel uses the alienating device of taking the reality of the camp completely for granted, an everyday existence like any other, admittedly with conditions that are thankless, but not without moments of happiness. Köves regards events like a child without completely understanding them and without finding them unnatural or disquieting—he lacks our ready-made answers. The shocking credibility of the description derives perhaps from this very absence of any element of the moral indignation or metaphysical protest that the subject cries out for. The reader is confronted not only with the cruelty of atrocities but just as much with the thoughtlessness that characterised their execution. Both perpetrators and victims were preoccupied with insistent practical problems, the major questions did not exist. Kertész's message is that *to live is to conform*. The capacity of the captives to come to terms with Auschwitz is one outcome of the same principle that finds expression in everyday human coexistence.

In thinking like this, the author concurs with a philosophical tradition in which life and human spirit are enemies. In *Kaddis a meg nem született gyermekért*, 1990 (*Kaddish for a Child Not Born*, 1997), Kertész presents a consistently negative picture of childhood and from this pre-history derives the paradoxical feeling of being at home in the concentration camp. He completes his implacable existential analysis by depicting love as the highest stage of conformism, total capitulation to the desire to exist at any cost. For Kertész the spiritual dimension of man lies in his inability to adapt to life. Individual experience seems useless as soon as it is considered in the light of the needs and interests of the human collective.

In his collection of fragments *Gályanapló* (Galley Diary), 1992, Kertész demonstrates his full intellectual scope. "Theoretical justifications are merely constructions," he writes, but nevertheless conducts an untiring dialogue with the great tradition of cultural criticism—Pascal, Goethe, Schopenhauer, Nietzsche, Kafka, Camus, Beckett, Bernhard. In essence, Imre Kertész is a minority consisting of one individual. He regards his kinship with the concept of Jew as a definition inflicted on him by the enemy. But through its consequences this arbitrary categorisation has nevertheless been his initiation into the deepest knowledge of humanity and the age in which he lives.

The novels that succeeded *Sorstalanság,* 1975 (*Fateless,* 1992), *A kudarc* (Fiasco), 1988, and *Kaddis a meg nem született gyermekért,* 1990 (*Kaddish for a Child Not Born,* 1997), can almost be characterised as comments and additions to the first and decisive work. This provides the theme of *A kudarc.* While he waits for an expected refusal of his real novel, the one about Auschwitz, the aging author spends his days writing a contemporary novel in the style of Kafka, a claustrophobic description of socialist Eastern Europe. In the end, he is informed that his previous book will, in spite of everything, be published, but all he can feel is emptiness. On display in the literary marketplace, his personality is transformed into an object, his secrets into banalities.

The refusal to compromise in Kertész's stance can be perceived clearly in his style, which is reminiscent of a thickset hawthorn hedge, dense and thorny for unsuspecting visitors. But he relieves his readers of the burden of compulsory emotions and inspires a singular freedom of thought.

[© The Nobel Foundation, 2002.]

Kertész: Nobel Lecture, 7 December 2002

Heureka!
(Translated by Ivan Sanders)

I must begin with a confession, a strange confession perhaps, but a candid one. From the moment I stepped on the airplane to make the journey here and accept this year's Nobel Prize in Literature, I have been feeling the steady, searching gaze of a dispassionate observer on my back. Even at this special moment, when I find myself being the center of attention, I feel I am closer to this cool and detached observer than to the writer whose work, of a sudden, is read around the world. I can only hope that the speech I have the honor to deliver on this occasion will help me dissolve the duality and fuse the two selves within me.

For now, though, I still have trouble understanding the gap that I sense between the high honor and my life and work. Perhaps I lived too long under dictatorships, in a hostile, relentlessly alien intellectual environment, to have developed a distinct literary consciousness; even to contemplate such a thing would have been useless. Besides, all I heard from all sides was that what I gave so much thought to, the "topic" that forever preoccupied me, was neither timely nor very attractive. For this reason, and also because I happen to believe it, I have always considered writing a highly personal, private matter.

Not that such a matter necessarily precludes seriousness—even if this seriousness did seem somewhat ludicrous in a world where only lies were taken seriously. Here the notion that the world is an objective reality existing independently of us was an axiomatic philosophical truth. Whereas I, on a lovely spring day in 1955, suddenly came to the realization that there exists only one reality, and that is me, my own life, this fragile gift bestowed for an uncertain time, which had been seized, expropriated by alien forces, and circumscribed, marked up, branded—and which I had to take back from "History," this dreadful Moloch, because it was mine and mine alone, and I had to manage it accordingly.

Needless to say, all this turned me sharply against everything in that world, which, though not objective, was undeniably a reality. I am speaking of Communist Hungary, of "thriving and flourishing" Socialism. If the world is an objective reality that exists independently of us, then humans themselves, even in their own eyes, are nothing more than objects, and their life stories merely a series of disconnected historical accidents, which they may wonder at, but which they themselves have nothing to do with. It would make no sense to arrange the fragments in a coherent whole, because some of it may be far too objective for the subjective Self to be held responsible for it.

A year later, in 1956, the Hungarian Revolution broke out. For a single moment the country turned subjective. Soviet tanks, however, restored objectivity before long.

I do not mean to be facetious. Consider what happened to language in the twentieth century, what became of words. I daresay that the first and most shocking discovery made by writers in our time was that language, in the form it came down to us, a legacy of some primordial culture, had simply become unsuitable to convey concepts and processes that had once been unambiguous and real. Think of Kafka, think of Orwell, in whose hands the old language simply disintegrated. It was as if they were turning it round and round in an open fire, only to display its ashes afterward, in which new and previously unknown patterns emerged.

But I should like to return to what for me is strictly private—writing. There are a few questions, which someone in my situation will not even ask. Jean-Paul Sartre, for instance, devoted an entire little book to the question: For whom do we write? It is an interesting question, but it can also be dangerous, and I thank my lucky stars that I never had to deal with it. Let us see what the danger consists of. If a writer were to pick a social class or group that he would like, not only to delight but also influence, he would first have to examine his style to see whether it is a suitable means by which to exert influence. He will soon be assailed by doubts, and spend his time watching himself. How can he know for sure what his readers want, what they really like? He cannot very well ask each and every one. And even if he did, it wouldn't do any good. He would have to rely on *his* image of his would-be readers, the expectations *he* ascribed to them, and imagine what would have the effect on *him* that *he* would like to achieve. For whom does a writer write, then? The answer is obvious: he writes for himself.

At least I can say that I have arrived at this answer fairly straightforwardly. Granted, I had it easier—I had no readers and no desire to influence anyone. I did not begin writing for a specific reason, and what I wrote was not addressed to anyone. If I had an aim at all, it was to be faithful, in language and form, to the subject at hand, and nothing more. It was important to make this clear during the ridiculous and sad period when literature was state-controlled and "engagé."

It would be more difficult to answer another, perfectly legitimate though still rather more dubious question: *Why* do we write? Here, too, I was lucky, for it never occurred to me that when it came to this question, one had a choice. I described a relevant incident in my novel *Failure*. I stood in the empty corridor of an office building, and all that happened was that from the direction of another, intersecting corridor I heard echoing footsteps. A strange excitement took hold of me. The sound grew louder and louder, and though they were clearly the steps of a single, unseen person, I suddenly had the feeling that I was hearing the footsteps of thousands. It was as if a huge procession was pounding its way down that corridor. And at that point I perceived the irresistible attraction of those footfalls, that marching multitude. In a single moment I understood the ecstasy of self-abandonment, the intoxicating pleasure of melting into the crowd—what Nietzsche called, in a different context though relevantly for this moment too, a Dionysian experience. It was almost as though some physical force were pushing me, pulling me toward the unseen marching columns. I felt I had to stand back and press against the wall, to keep me from yielding to this magnetic, seductive force.

I have related this intense moment as I (had) experienced it. The source from which it sprang, like a vision, seemed somewhere outside of me, not in me. Every artist is familiar with such moments. At one time they were called sudden inspirations. Still, I wouldn't classify the experience as an artistic revelation, but rather as an existential self-discovery. What I gained from it was not my art—its tools would not be mine for some time—but my life, which I had almost lost. The experience was about solitude, a more difficult life, and the things I have already mentioned—the need to step out of the mesmerizing crowd, out of History, which renders you faceless and fateless. To my horror, I realized that ten years after I had returned from the Nazi concentration camps, and halfway still under the awful spell of Stalinist terror, all that remained of the whole experience were a few muddled impressions, a few anecdotes. Like it didn't even happen to me, as people are wont to say.

It is clear that such visionary moments have a long prehistory. Sigmund Freud would trace them back to a repressed traumatic experience. And he may well be right. I, too, am inclined toward the rational approach; mysticism and unreasoning rapture of all kinds are alien to me. So when I speak of a vision, I must mean something real that assumes a supernatural guise—the sudden, almost violent eruption of a slowly ripening thought within me. Something conveyed in the ancient cry, "Eureka!"—"I've got it!" But what?

I once said that so-called Socialism for me was the petite madeleine cake that, dipped into Proust's tea, evoked in him the flavor of bygone years. For reasons having to do with the language I spoke, I decided, after the suppression of the 1956 revolt, to remain in Hungary. Thus I was able to observe, not as a child this time but as an adult, how a dictatorship functions. I saw how an entire nation could be made to deny its ideals, and watched the early, cautious moves toward accommodation. I understood that hope is an instrument of evil, and the Kantian categorical imperative—ethics in general—is but the pliable handmaiden of self-preservation.

Can one imagine greater freedom than that enjoyed by a writer in a relatively limited, rather tired, even decadent dictatorship? By the nineteen-sixties, the dictatorship in Hungary had reached a state of consolidation that could almost be called a societal consensus. The West later dubbed it, with good-humored forbearance, "goulash Communism." It seemed that after the initial foreign disapproval, Hungary's own version quickly turned into the West's favorite brand of Communism. In the miry depths of this consensus, one either gave up the struggle or found the winding paths to inner freedom. A writer's overhead, after all, is very low; to practice his profession, all he needs are paper and pencil. The nausea and depression to which I awoke each morning led me at once into the world I intended to describe. I had to discover that I had placed a man groaning under the logic of one type of totalitarianism in another totalitarian system, and this turned the language of my novel into a highly allusive medium. If I look back now and size up honestly the situation I was in at the time, I have to conclude that in the West, in a free society, I probably would not have been able to write the novel known by readers today as *Fateless*, the novel singled out by the Swedish Academy for the highest honor.

No, I probably would have aimed at something different. Which is not to say that I would not have tried to get at the truth, but perhaps at a different kind of truth. In the free marketplace of books and ideas, I, too, might have wanted to produce a showier fiction. For example, I might have tried to break up time in my novel, and narrate only the most powerful scenes. But the hero of my novel does not live his own time in the concentration camps, for neither his time nor his language, not even his own person, is really his. He doesn't remember; he exists. So he has to languish, poor boy, in the dreary trap of linearity, and cannot shake off the painful details. Instead of a spectacular series of great and tragic moments, he has to live through everything, which is oppressive and offers little variety, like life itself.

But the method led to remarkable insights. Linearity demanded that each situation that arose be completely filled out. It did not allow me, say, to skip cavalierly over twenty minutes of time, if only because those twenty minutes were there before me, like a gaping, terrifying black hole, like a mass grave. I am speaking of the twenty minutes spent on the arrival platform of the Birkenau extermination camp—the time it took people clambering down from the train to reach the officer doing the selecting. I more or less remembered the twenty minutes, but the novel demanded that I distrust my memory. No matter how many survivors' accounts, reminiscences and confessions I had read, they all agreed that everything proceeded all too quickly and unnoticeably. The doors of the railroad cars were flung open, they heard shouts, the barking of dogs, men and women were abruptly separated, and in the midst of the hubbub, they found themselves in front of an officer. He cast a fleeting glance at them, pointed to something with his outstretched arm, and before they knew it they were wearing prison clothes.

I remembered these twenty minutes differently. Turning to authentic sources, I first read Tadeusz Borowski's stark, unsparing and self-tormenting narratives, among them the story entitled "This Way for the Gas, Ladies and Gentlemen." Later, I came upon a series of photographs of human cargo arriving at the Birkenau railroad platform—photographs taken by an SS soldier and found by American soldiers in a former SS barracks in the already liberated camp at Dachau. I looked at these photographs in utter amazement. I saw lovely, smiling women and bright-eyed young men, all of them well-intentioned, eager to cooperate. Now I understood how and why those humiliating twenty minutes of idleness and helplessness faded from their memories. And when I thought how all this was repeated the same way for days, weeks, months and years on end, I gained an insight into the mechanism of horror; I learned how it became possible to turn human nature against one's own life.

So I proceeded, step by step, on the linear path of discovery; this was my heuristic method, if you will. I realized soon enough that I was not the least bit interested in whom I was writing for and why. One question interested me: What have I still got to do with literature? For it was clear to me that an uncrossable line separated me from literature and the ideals, the spirit associated with the concept of literature. The name of this demarcation line, as of many other things, is Auschwitz. When we write about Auschwitz, we must know that Auschwitz, in a certain sense at least, suspended literature. One can only write a black novel about Auschwitz, or—you should excuse the expression—a cheap serial, which begins in Auschwitz and is still not over. By which I mean that nothing has happened since Auschwitz that could reverse or refute Auschwitz. In my writings the Holocaust could never be present in the past tense.

It is often said of me—some intend it as a compliment, others as a complaint—that I write about a single subject: the Holocaust. I have no quarrel with that. Why shouldn't I accept, with certain qualifications, the place assigned to me on the shelves of libraries? Which writer today is not a writer of the Holocaust? One does not have to choose the Holocaust as one's subject to detect the broken voice that has dominated modern European art for decades. I will go so far as to say that I know of no genuine work of art that does not reflect this break. It is as if, after a night of terrible dreams, one looked around the world, defeated, helpless. I have never tried to see the complex of problems referred to as the Holocaust merely as the insolvable conflict between Germans and Jews. I never believed that it was the latest chapter in the history of Jewish suffering, which followed logically from their earlier trials and tribulations. I never saw it as a one-time aberration, a large-scale pogrom, a precondition for the creation of Israel. What I discovered in Auschwitz is the human condition, the end point of a great adventure, where the European traveler arrived after his two-thousand-year-old moral and cultural history.

Now the only thing to reflect on is where we go from here. The problem of Auschwitz is not whether to draw a line under it, as it were; whether to preserve its memory or slip it into the appropriate pigeonhole of history; whether to erect a monument to the murdered millions, and if so, what kind. The real problem with Auschwitz is that it happened, and this cannot be altered—not with the best, or worst, will in the world. This gravest of situations was characterized most accurately by the Hungarian Catholic poet János Pilinszky when he called it a "scandal." What he meant by it, clearly, is that Auschwitz occurred in a Christian cultural environment, so for those with a metaphysical turn of mind it can never be overcome.

Old prophecies speak of the death of God. Since Auschwitz we are more alone, that much is certain. We must create our values ourselves, day by day, with that persistent though invisible ethical work that will give them life, and perhaps turn them into the foundation of a new European culture. I consider the prize with which the Swedish Academy has seen fit to honor my work as an indication that Europe again needs the experience that witnesses to Auschwitz, to the Holocaust were forced to acquire. The decision—permit me to say this—bespeaks courage, firm resolve even—for those who made it wished me to come here, though they could have easily guessed what they would hear from me. What was revealed in the Final Solution, in *l'univers concentrationnaire,* cannot be misunderstood, and the only way survival is possible, and the preservation of creative power, is if we recognize the zero point that is Auschwitz. Why couldn't this clarity of vision be fruitful? At the bottom of all great realizations, even if they are born of unsurpassed tragedies, there lies the greatest European value of all, the longing for liberty, which suffuses our lives with something more, a richness, making us aware of the positive fact of our existence, and the responsibility we all bear for it.

It makes me especially happy to be expressing these thoughts in my native language: Hungarian. I was born in Budapest, in a Jewish family, whose maternal branch hailed from the Transylvanian city of Kolozsvár (Cluj) and the paternal side from the southwestern corner of the Lake Balaton region. My grandparents still lit the Sabbath candles every Friday night, but they changed their name to a Hungarian one, and it was natural for them to consider Judaism their religion and Hungary their homeland. My maternal grandparents perished in the Holocaust; my paternal grandparents' lives were destroyed by Mátyás Rákosi's Communist rule, when Budapest's Jewish old age home was relocated to the northern border region of the country. I think this brief family history encapsulates and symbolizes this country's modern-day travails. What it teaches me, though, is that there is not only bitterness in grief, but also extraordinary moral potential. Being a Jew to me is once again, first and foremost, a moral challenge. If the Holocaust has by now created a culture, as it undeniably has, its aim must be that an irredeemable reality give rise by way of the spirit to restoration—a catharsis. This desire has inspired me in all my creative endeavors.

Though I am nearing the end of my speech, I must confess I still have not found the reassuring balance between my life, my works and the Nobel Prize. For now I feel profound gratitude—gratitude for the love that saved me and sustains me still. But let us consider that in this difficult-to-follow life journey, in this "career" of mine, if I could so put it, there is something stirring, something absurd, something which cannot be pondered without one being touched by a belief in an otherworldly order, in providence, in metaphysical justice—in other words, without falling into the trap of self-deception, and thus running aground, going under, severing the deep and tortuous ties with the millions who perished and who never knew mercy. It is not so easy to be an exception. But if we were destined to be exceptions, we must make our peace with the absurd order of chance, which reigns over our lives with the whim of a death squad, exposing us to inhuman powers, monstrous tyrannies.

And yet something very special happened while I was preparing this lecture, which in a way reassured me. One day I received a large brown envelope in the mail. It was sent to me by Doctor Volkhard Knigge, the director of the Buchenwald Memorial Center. He enclosed a small envelope with his congratulatory note, and described what was in the envelope, so, in case I didn't have the strength to look, I wouldn't have to. The envelope contained a copy of the original daily report on the camp's prisoners for February 18, 1945. In the "Abgänge," that is, the "Decrement" column, I learned about the death of Prisoner #64,921–Imre Kertész, factory worker, born in 1927. The two false data: the year of my birth and my occupation were entered in the official registry when I was brought to Buchenwald. I had made myself two years older so I wouldn't be classified as a child, and had said worker rather than student to appear more useful to them.

In short, I died once, so I could live. Perhaps that is my real story. If it is, I dedicate this work, born of a child's death, to the millions who died and to those who still remember them. But, since we are talking about literature, after all, the kind of literature that, in the view of your Academy, is also a testimony, my work may yet serve a useful purpose in the future, and—this is my heart's desire—may even speak to the future. Whenever I think of the traumatic impact of Auschwitz, I end up dwelling on the vitality and creativity of those living today. Thus, in thinking about Auschwitz, I reflect, paradoxically, not on the past but the future.

[© The Nobel Foundation, 2002. Imre Kertész is the sole author of the text.]

Rudyard Kipling
(20 December 1865 – 18 January 1936)

Donald Gray
Indiana University

This entry was expanded by Gray from his Kipling entry in *DLB 156: British Short-Fiction Writers, 1880–1914: The Romantic Tradition.* See also the Kipling entries in *DLB 19: British Poets, 1880–1914; DLB 34: British Novelists, 1890–1929: Traditionalists;* and *DLB 141, British Children's Writers, 1880–1914.*

BOOKS: *Schoolboy Lyrics* (Lahore: Privately printed, 1881);

Echoes, by Kipling and Alice Kipling (Lahore: Privately printed, 1884);

Departmental Ditties and Other Verses (Lahore: Privately printed, 1886; enlarged edition, Calcutta: Thacker, Spink, 1886; enlarged edition, Calcutta: Thacker, Spink / London: Thacker, 1888; enlarged edition, Calcutta: Thacker, Spink / London & Bombay: Thacker, 1890); enlarged as *Departmental Ditties, Barrack-Room Ballads and Other Verses* (New York: United States Book Company, 1890); republished as *Departmental Ditties and Ballads and Barrack-Room Ballads* (New York: Doubleday & McClure, 1899);

Plain Tales from the Hills (Calcutta: Thacker, Spink / London: Thacker, 1888; New York: Lovell, 1890; London & New York: Macmillan, 1890);

Soldiers Three: A Collection of Stories Setting Forth Certain Passages in the Lives and Adventures of Privates Terence Mulvaney, Stanley Ortheris, and John Learoyd (Allahabad: Pioneer, 1888; London: Sampson Low, Marston, Searle & Rivington, 1890);

The Story of the Gadsbys: A Tale Without a Plot (Allahabad: Wheeler, 1888; Allahabad: Wheeler / London: Sampson Low, Marston, Searle & Rivington, 1890; New York: Lovell, 1890);

In Black and White (Allahabad: Wheeler, 1888; Allahabad: Wheeler / London: Sampson Low, Marston, Searle & Rivington, 1890);

Under the Deodars (Allahabad: Wheeler, 1888; Allahabad: Wheeler / London: Sampson Low, Marston, Searle & Rivington, 1890; New York: Lovell, 1890);

Rudyard Kipling (George Grantham Bain Collection, Library of Congress Prints and Photographs Division)

The Phantom 'Rickshaw and Other Tales (Allahabad: Wheeler, 1888; Allahabad: Wheeler / London: Sampson Low, Marston, Searle & Rivington, 1890);

Wee Willie Winkie and Other Child Stories (Allahabad: Wheeler, 1888); republished as *Wee Willie Winkie and Other Stories* (Allahabad: Wheeler / London: Sampson Low, Marston, Searle & Rivington, 1890);

"Turnovers," by Kipling and others, 9 volumes (Lahore: Privately printed, 1888–1890);

Soldiers Three [and *In Black and White*] (New York: Lovell, 1890);

Indian Tales (New York: Lovell, 1890);

The Courting of Dinah Shadd and Other Stories (New York: Harper, 1890);

The Light That Failed (London & Melbourne: Ward, Lock, Bowden, 1891; Philadelphia: Lippincott, 1891; revised edition, London & New York: Macmillan, 1891);

The City of Dreadful Night and Other Places (Allahabad: Wheeler, 1891; Allahabad: Wheeler / London: Sampson Low, Marston, 1891);

Letters of Marque (Allahabad: Wheeler, 1891; republished in part, London: Sampson Low, Marston, 1891);

American Notes (New York: Ivers, 1891);

Mine Own People (New York: United States Book Company, 1891);

Life's Handicap: Being Stories of Mine Own People (London & New York: Macmillan, 1891);

The Story of the Gadsbys and Under the Deodars (New York: United States Book Company, 1891);

The Naulahka: A Story of West and East, by Kipling and Wolcott Balestier (London: Heinemann, 1892; New York & London: Macmillan, 1892);

Barrack-Room Ballads and Other Verses (London: Methuen, 1892); republished as *Ballads and Barrack-Room Ballads* (New York & London: Macmillan, 1892; enlarged edition, New York & London: Macmillan, 1893);

Soldiers Three, The Story of the Gadsbys, In Black and White (London: Sampson Low, Marston, 1892; London & New York: Macmillan, 1895; enlarged edition, New York & London: Macmillan, 1895);

Wee Willie Winkie, Under the Deodars, The Phantom 'Rickshaw and Other Stories (London: Sampson Low, Marston, 1892; London & New York: Macmillan, 1895); republished as *Under the Deodars, The Phantom 'Rickshaw, Wee Willie Winkie* (New York & London: Macmillan, 1895);

Many Inventions (London & New York: Macmillan, 1893; New York: Appleton, 1893);

The Jungle Book (London & New York: Macmillan, 1894; New York: Century, 1894);

The Second Jungle Book (London & New York: Macmillan, 1895; enlarged edition, 1895; New York: Century, 1895);

Out of India: Things I Saw, and Failed to See, in Certain Days and Nights at Jeypore and Elsewhere (New York: Dillingham, 1895)—includes *The City of Dreadful Night and Other Places* and *Letters of Marque;*

The Seven Seas (New York: Appleton, 1896; London: Methuen, 1896);

Soldier Tales (London & New York: Macmillan, 1896); republished as *Soldier Stories* (New York & London: Macmillan, 1896);

The Kipling Birthday Book, compiled by Joseph Finn (London & New York: Macmillan, 1896; New York: Doubleday & McClure, 1899);

"Captains Courageous": A Story of the Grand Banks (London & New York: Macmillan, 1897; New York: Century, 1897);

An Almanac of Twelve Sports, text by Kipling, illustrations by William Nicholson (London: Heinemann, 1898; New York: Russell, 1898);

The Day's Work (New York: Doubleday & McClure, 1898; London: Macmillan, 1898);

A Fleet in Being: Notes of Two Trips with the Channel Squadron (London & New York: Macmillan, 1898);

Kipling's Poems, edited by Wallace Rice (Chicago: Star Books, 1899);

Stalky & Co. (London: Macmillan, 1899; New York: Doubleday & McClure, 1899);

From Sea to Sea, 2 volumes (New York: Doubleday & McClure, 1899); republished as *From Sea to Sea and Other Sketches,* 2 volumes (London: Macmillan, 1900);

A Ken of Kipling (New York: New Amsterdam Book Company, 1899);

The Kipling Reader: Selections from the Books of Rudyard Kipling (London & New York: Macmillan, 1900; revised, 1901);

Kim (New York: Doubleday, Page, 1901; London: Macmillan, 1901);

Just So Stories: For Little Children (London: Macmillan, 1902; New York: Doubleday, Page, 1902);

The Five Nations (London: Methuen, 1903; New York: Doubleday, Page, 1903);

Traffics and Discoveries (London: Macmillan, 1904; New York: Doubleday, Page, 1904);

Puck of Pook's Hill (London: Macmillan, 1906; New York: Doubleday, Page, 1906);

Collected Verse (New York: Doubleday, Page, 1907; London: Hodder & Stoughton, 1912);

Letters to the Family: Notes on a Recent Trip to Canada (Toronto: Macmillan, 1908);

Actions and Reactions (London: Macmillan, 1909; New York: Doubleday, Page, 1909);

Abaft the Funnel (New York: Dodge, 1909; authorized edition, New York: Doubleday, Page, 1909);

Kipling Stories and Poems Every Child Should Know, edited by Mary E. Burt and W. T. Chapin (New York: Doubleday, Page, 1909; abridged edition, New York: Garden City, 1938);

Rewards and Fairies (London: Macmillan, 1910; Garden City, N.Y.: Doubleday, Page, 1910);

A History of England, by Kipling and C. R. L. Fletcher (Oxford: Clarendon Press / London: Frowde/Hodder & Stoughton, 1911; Garden City, N.Y.: Doubleday, Page, 1911);

The Kipling Reader for Elementary Grades (New York & Chicago: Appleton, 1912);

The Kipling Reader for Upper Grades (New York & Chicago: Appleton, 1912);

Songs from Books (Garden City, N.Y.: Doubleday, Page, 1912; London: Macmillan, 1913);

The New Army, 6 pamphlets (Garden City, N.Y.: Doubleday, Page, 1914); republished as *The New Army in Training,* 1 volume (London: Macmillan, 1915);

France at War (London: Macmillan, 1915); republished as *France at War on the Frontier of Civilization* (Garden City, N.Y.: Doubleday, Page, 1915);

The Fringes of the Fleet (London: Macmillan, 1915; Garden City, N.Y.: Doubleday, Page, 1915);

Sea Warfare (London: Macmillan, 1916; Garden City, N.Y.: Doubleday, Page, 1917);

A Diversity of Creatures (London: Macmillan, 1917; Garden City, N.Y.: Doubleday, Page, 1917);

The Eyes of Asia (Garden City, N.Y.: Doubleday, Page, 1918);

Twenty Poems (London: Methuen, 1918);

The Graves of the Fallen (London: Imperial War Graves Commission, 1919);

The Years Between (London: Methuen, 1919; Garden City, N.Y.: Doubleday, Page, 1919);

Rudyard Kipling's Verse, Inclusive Edition, 1885–1918 (3 volumes, London: Hodder & Stoughton, 1919; 1 volume, Garden City, N.Y.: Doubleday, Page, 1919);

Letters of Travel (1892–1913) (London: Macmillan, 1920; Garden City, N.Y.: Doubleday, Page, 1920);

Q. Horati Flacci Carminum Librum Quintum a Rudyardo Kipling et Carolo Graves Angelice Redditum et Variorum Notis Adornatum ad Fidem Codicum Mss. Edidit Aluredus D. Godley, by Kipling and others (Oxonii [Oxford]: Blackwell, 1920; Novo Portu [New Haven]: Yalensi [Yale Alumni Association], 1921);

Selected Stories from Kipling, edited by William Lyon Phelps (Garden City, N.Y. & Toronto: Doubleday, Page, 1921);

A Kipling Anthology: Verse (London: Methuen, 1922; Garden City, N.Y.: Doubleday, Page, 1922);

A Kipling Anthology: Prose (London: Macmillan, 1922; Garden City, N.Y.: Doubleday, Page, 1922);

Kipling Calendar (London: Hodder & Stoughton, 1923; Garden City, N.Y.: Doubleday, Page, 1923);

Land and Sea Tales for Scouts and Guides (London: Macmillan, 1923); republished as *Land and Sea Tales for Boys and Girls* (Garden City, N.Y.: Doubleday, Page, 1923); republished as *Land and Sea Tales for Scouts and Scout Masters* (Garden City, N.Y.: Doubleday, Page, 1924);

The Two Jungle Books (London: Macmillan, 1924; Garden City, N.Y.: Doubleday, Page, 1925);

Songs for Youth (London: Hodder & Stoughton, 1924; Garden City, N.Y.: Doubleday, Page, 1925);

A Choice of Songs (London: Methuen, 1925);

Debits and Credits (London: Macmillan, 1926; Garden City, N.Y.: Doubleday, Page, 1926);

Sea and Sussex (London: Macmillan, 1926; Garden City, N.Y.: Doubleday, Page, 1926);

Songs of the Sea (London: Macmillan, 1927; Garden City, N.Y.: Doubleday, Page, 1927);

Rudyard Kipling's Verse, Inclusive Edition, 1885–1926 (London: Hodder & Stoughton, 1927; Garden City, N.Y.: Doubleday, Page, 1927);

A Book of Words: Selections from Speeches and Addresses Delivered Between 1906 and 1927 (London: Macmillan, 1928; Garden City, N.Y.: Doubleday, Page, 1928);

The One Volume Kipling (Garden City, N.Y.: Doubleday, Doran, 1928);

The Complete Stalky & Co. (London: Macmillan, 1929; Garden City, N.Y.: Doubleday, Doran, 1930);

Poems 1886–1929, 3 volumes (London: Macmillan, 1929; Garden City, N.Y.: Doubleday, Doran, 1930);

Selected Stories (London: Macmillan, 1929);

Thy Servant a Dog, Told by Boots (London: Macmillan, 1930; Garden City, N.Y.: Doubleday, Doran, 1930);

Selected Poems (London: Methuen, 1931);

East of Suez (London: Macmillan, 1931);

Humorous Tales (London: Macmillan, 1931); republished as *The Humorous Tales of Rudyard Kipling* (Garden City, N.Y.: Doubleday, Doran, 1931);

Animal Stories (London: Macmillan, 1932; New York: Doubleday, Doran, 1938);

Limits and Renewals (London: Macmillan, 1932; Garden City, N.Y.: Doubleday, Doran, 1932);

Souvenirs of France (London: Macmillan, 1933);

All the Mowgli Stories (London: Macmillan, 1933; Garden City, N.Y.: Doubleday, Doran, 1936);

Rudyard Kipling's Verse, Inclusive Edition, 1885–1932 (London: Hodder & Stoughton, 1933; Garden City, N.Y.: Doubleday, Doran, 1934);

Collected Dog Stories (London: Macmillan, 1934; Garden City, N.Y.: Doubleday, Doran, 1934);

All the Puck Stories (London: Macmillan, 1935);

A Kipling Pageant (Garden City, N.Y.: Doubleday, Doran, 1935);

Something of Myself for My Friends Known and Unknown (London: Macmillan, 1937; Garden City, N.Y.: Doubleday, Doran, 1937);

Rudyard Kipling's Verse, Definitive Edition (London: Hodder & Stoughton, 1940; New York: Doubleday, Doran, 1940);

Kipling's India: Uncollected Sketches, 1884–1888, edited by Thomas Pinney (London: Macmillan, 1985);

Early Verse by Rudyard Kipling 1879–1889: Unpublished, Uncollected, and Rarely Collected Poems, edited by Andrew Rutherford (Oxford & New York: Oxford University Press, 1986);

The Jungle Play, edited by Thomas Pinney (London & New York: Allen Lane, 2000).

Editions and Collections: *The Sussex Edition of the Complete Works of Rudyard Kipling,* 35 volumes (London: Macmillan, 1937–1939); republished as *The Collected Works of Rudyard Kipling, The Burwash Edition,* 28 volumes (Garden City, N.Y.: Doubleday, Doran, 1940);

Something of Myself and Other Autobiographical Writings, edited by Thomas Pinney (Cambridge: Cambridge University Press, 1990);

Writings on Writing by Rudyard Kipling, edited by Sandra Kemp (London & New York: Cambridge University Press, 1996).

OTHER: André Chevrillon, *Britain and the War,* preface by Kipling (London, New York & Toronto: Hodder & Stoughton, 1917); republished as *England and the War* (Garden City, N.Y.: Doubleday, Page, 1917);

The Irish Guards in the Great War, 2 volumes, edited by Kipling (London: Macmillan, 1923; Garden City, N.Y.: Doubleday, Page, 1923).

The first paragraphs of the presentation speech for the award to Rudyard Kipling of the 1907 Nobel Prize in Literature praise his accomplishments as a poet. It is true that the poems collected in *Barrack-Room Ballads and Other Verses* (1892) played an important part in Kipling's rapid emergence during the 1890s as an eminent—perhaps the preeminent—British writer of his generation, and the sounds and themes of some of them still reward attention. But even in many of his poems it is clear that Kipling's principal talent is for narrative. He is best-known now as the fabulist of the *The Jungle Book* (1894), *The Second Jungle Book* (1895), and *Just So Stories: For Little Children* (1902) and as the teller of the episodic adventures of the hero of his novel *Kim* (1901). And his most significant literary achievement lies in a remarkably extensive and varied body of short stories, the form in which he began his career in the 1880s and practiced all through his life.

In his fragmentary autobiography, *Something of Myself for My Friends Known and Unknown* (1937), Kipling wrote, "Everything in my working life has been dealt to me in such a manner that I had just to play it as it came." Certainly one of the strongest influences was his birth and early experience in India. Joseph Rudyard Kipling was born on 30 December 1865 in Bombay. His father, John Lockwood Kipling, who had worked as a sculptor during the construction of the Victoria and Albert Museum in London in the 1860s, had come to India as professor of sculptural history at the University of Bombay. His mother, Alice Macdonald Kipling, had also moved in the company of artists in London. The family was affectionate and interesting, a structure of support and encouragement that Kipling was later to depend on as "the family square."

When Kipling was not yet six years old, he was sent away with his younger sister, Alice (called Trix), to begin his education in England. He and his sister were lodged at Southsea with a religiously Evangelical family who held strict views about the upbringing of children. Kipling perhaps exaggerated the meanness and punitive rigor of this time in his life when he recalled it in his autobiography and in the short story "Baa, Baa Black Sheep," included in *Wee Willie Winkie and Other Child Stories* (1888). He remembered himself as the black sheep. His energy and curiosity about books and almost everything else steadily drew down punishments at home, and undiagnosed problems with his eyesight created difficulties at school. When he was eleven years old his mother came to England, probably summoned by a friend who had discovered Kipling's predicament. She placed her son in the United Services College, a school organized to prepare the sons of military officers and colonial administrators for similar careers.

Kipling flourished in his new school. Here the code of the boys and the rules of the masters made a discipline that was masculine and institutional, its principles and hierarchies clear, its administration consistent. Kipling read widely, learned Latin well enough to amuse himself as an adult by translating and imitating Horace, and wrote for the school paper. He formed the close friendships memorialized in his school novel *Stalky & Co.* (1899) and became what he admired the rest of his life: a capable, knowledgeable member of a group of like-minded males.

At the end of 1882 Kipling returned to India to work as subeditor (the editor was the only other staff member) of the *Civil and Military Gazette,* a daily newspaper in Lahore. He wrote, edited, and translated "scraps" of news: "Wrote in course of year 230 columns matter," he noted in his diary in 1884. He soon began to write stories for the newspaper that had to be fitted into columns of two thousand words, and he also contributed poems and some prose to an all-India newspaper, the *Pioneer,* six hundred miles away in Allahabad; these works, he wrote in a letter to his aunt Edith Macdonald (30 July 1885), "have taken the public's somewhat dense soul and have been widely quoted" in other papers. When in 1887 he moved to a larger paper as a reporter and editor of its supplement, the *Weekly News,* he immediately contracted to supply fiction to the supplement. A collection of his verse, *Departmental Ditties and Other Verses,* was published in India in 1886, and the same Indian publisher collected his short stories in *Plain Tales from the Hills* in 1888.

As a reporter Kipling traveled to public events and the courts of native rulers, and he spent many of his evenings at clubs where, he wrote in his autobiography, he met "none except picked men at their definite tasks." In his poems and stories he characteristically wrote from the perspective of such men, adopting a tone of knowing detachment to tell stories of intrigue, betrayal, ambition, and disillusionment in the garrisons, offices, and bungalows of the British in India. *Departmental Ditties* (three editions in two years) and *Plain Tales from the Hills* were widely read and talked about by the English in India, although the one thousand copies of the latter collection the publisher sent to England were not much noticed. Kipling followed this local success, again in 1888, by collecting some of the stories he had written for the *Weekly News* in six volumes for the Indian Railway Library, published by the proprietors of his newspaper. (Kipling retained the titles of these volumes when they were republished in England and America in 1890 and later in his collected works: *Soldiers Three, In Black and White, The Story of the Gadsbys, Under the Deodars, Wee Willie Winkie and Other Stories,* and *The Phantom 'Rickshaw and Other Stories.*) Then, having completed what he called a seven-year apprenticeship in India, he left in 1889, sailing east to visit China, Japan, and California, then traveling across the United States to sail for England.

Kipling arrived in London in the fall of 1889, three months short of his twenty-fourth birthday. By the end of the next year he was famous. All throughout 1890 he wrote about India in new stories and poems that appeared monthly, sometimes weekly, in British and American periodicals. He collaborated on one novel, *The Naulahka: A Story of West and East* (1892), and completed another, *The Light That Failed* (1891). British and American publishers reprinted the stories of *Plain Tales from the Hills,* which went through three editions in six months in England, and the volumes of the Indian Railway Library. At the end of 1890 Kipling put his new stories together with some unpublished fiction and a dozen stories from Indian newspapers to make his first substantial volume of short stories to be published initially outside India, *Life's Handicap: Being Stories of Mine Own People* (1891). In 1890 his Indian publisher published an edition of *Departmental Ditties* in London, and in 1892 the poems he had been contributing to magazines were published in Britain and America in *Barrack-Room Ballads and Other Verses.*

In the poems he wrote in India and collected in *Departmental Ditties,* Kipling writes of British and Indians who scheme for honors and advancement, of the heat and disease and drink that disable young men, and of the skirmishes and ambushes that kill them: "The flying bullet down the Pass, / That whistles clear: 'All flesh is grass'" ("Arithmetic on the Frontier"). The short lines, easy movement, and steady rhymes and beats of these poems give them a light, sometimes even a breezy tone. But from the start Kipling consciously set himself to write of the costs as well as the material and moral benefits of empire. "I have written the tale of our life / For a sheltered people's mirth / In jesting guise," he writes in a "Prelude" to *Departmental Ditties,* "—but ye are wise, / And ye know what the jest is worth."

In the poems he wrote in England and put into *Barrack-Room Ballads and Other Verses,* Kipling dug more deeply beneath the jest to describe yet more graphically the unsheltered conditions of India and other outposts of the British Empire. Some of the most effective of these poems are ballads written in working-class or Irish dialect, and the freshness of their language and the vigor of their lines and refrains made them stand out amid the subdued tonalities and melancholy themes of *fin-de-siècle* decadence. Each four-line stanza of "The Young British Soldier," for example, moves into a version of its refrain, "Serve, serve, serve as a soldier, / So-oldier *of* the Queen!," and then ends:

> When you're wounded and left on Afghanistan's plains,
> And the women come out to cut up what remains,
> Jest roll to your rifle and blow out your brains
> 'An go to your Gawd like a soldier, . . .
> Go, go, go like a soldier,
> So-oldier *of* the Queen!

"Gentlemen-Rankers" is sung to, and by, "the legion of the lost ones, ... the cohort of the damned," who are "done with Hope and Honour, . . . lost to Love and Truth": "God help us, for we knew the worse too young!"

In this setting of violence and loss, in which youth is wasted and the familiar pieties of home dissolve, the hero is the man who continues to do honest work. Kipling dedicated *Barrack-Room Ballads and Other Verses* to Wolcott Balestier, an American who was his agent and his collaborator on *The Naulahka,* and whose sister Carrie married Kipling in 1892. Balestier died young in 1891, and in the dedication Kipling sends him to heaven where he is welcomed by "the Strong Men" because, like them, he "had done his work and held his peace and had no fear to die." Kipling admired people who do their jobs wherever he found them—Gunga Din, for example, and "Fuzzy-Wuzzy," one of the Africans "with your 'ayrick 'ead of 'air" whose manic courage "broke a British square."

In the stories of *Plain Tales from the Hills* and *Life's Handicap* the name of this hero is Private Terence Mulvaney, described in "The Three Musketeers" (1887, collected in *Plain Tales from the Hills*) as one of "the worst men in the regiment as far as genial blackguardism goes." Mulvaney gets drunk; gets into fights; flirts with other people's wives; and finally loses his corporal's stripes. But when it comes down to it, Mulvaney is capable. He is a brave and effective soldier. In a story that is at once comic and scary he leads a group of naked men in "The Taking of Lungtunphem" (1887, collected in *Plain Tales from the Hills*): 'Twas the Lift'nint got the credit; but 'twas me planned the schame." In "The God from the Machine" (1888, in *Soldiers Three*) he prevents the inappropriate elopement of the Colonel's daughter. In "The Incarnation of Krishna Mulvaney" (1888, collected in *Life's Handicap*) he destroys a scheme in which a contractor is cheating his coolie workers and then, after a farcical sequence created by his drunkenness, impersonates the god Krishna and extorts 434 rupees and a gold necklace from a priest. After he marries and leaves the army, he returns to India in "The Big Drunk Draf" (1888, in *Soldiers Three*) as a civilian, "a great and terrible fall." Even out of uniform he helps to discipline an unruly regiment of men waiting to go home by advising its young officer to tie one of the men spread-eagled to tent pegs and leave him out all one frosty night: "'You look to that little orf'cer bhoy. He has bowils. 'Tis not ivry child that wud chuck the Rig'lations to Flanders an' stretch Peg Barney on a wink from a brokin' an' dilapidated ould carkiss like mesilf'."

Even competent men can be swallowed by the rules and routine of British India, and beneath it, by the strangeness of India itself. Bureaucratic rigidity defeats Dicky Hatt in "In the Pride of His Youth" (1887, included in *Plain Tales from the Hills*), who works "like a horse" to save money to bring his wife and child out from England. But "pay in India is a matter of age, not merit, you see, and if their particular boy wished to work like two boys, Business forbid they should stop him." By the time Dicky is given a salary that will enable him to pay the cost of passage, his child is dead and his wife has divorced him.

Beneath what the British do to one another in India lies what India does to them. Kipling's India is violent, dangerous, and only lightly marked by British rule. When Englishmen cross into this India, even the most compassionate and competent are baffled. Trejago, the hero of "Beyond the Pale" (1888, included in *Plain Tales from the Hills*), is undone just because of his knowledge of India. When he receives a packet of objects from a young woman who has spoken to him from behind a grated window in an alley, his translation of this message begins an affair that lasts until one night, after an interval of three weeks, he knocks at the grating and the girl "held out her arms into the moonlight. Both hands had been cut off at the wrists, and the stumps were nearly healed." Trejago never discovers what has happened.

Kipling's manner in these stories is that of a realist, a devotee of what he calls, in "The Judgment of Dungara" (1888, included in *In Black and White*), "The Great God Dungara, the God of Things as They Are, Most Terrible, One-Eyed, Bearing the Red Elephant Tusk." The world according to Dungara has the glamour of the terrible, and Kipling compounds the thrill by suggesting that he tells the real story beneath the official narrative and superficial glamor of empire. He fills the stories with the place names of India and words from its languages, and with the dialects, jargon, and shoptalk of British soldiers and administrators. His tone, with a few lapses, is matter-of-fact. He wants to shock his readers, but he is not shocked, and some of his most devastating stories concern events that at home would be quite ordinary. In "Bitters Neat" (1887), for example, a story from the *Civil and Military Gazette* that Kipling did not put into *Plain Tales from the Hills* until a collected edition of his writing in 1897, a young woman falls in love with Surrey, an efficient, rather dull man who plods along unaware of her infatuation. She refuses a proposal from another man, goes a little crazy, and is sent home. When Surrey learns why the young woman has gone, he is unstrung: "I didn't see, I didn't see. If I had *only* known." The narrator, who has known the whole story all along, spends no other words of pity or irony on Surrey but cuts directly to what this story is really about: "the hopelessness and tangle of it—the waste and the muddle."

Kipling thus brings to the poems and stories of his first books not only the pleasure he finds in being one of the men who know what they are talking about but also the sense of how things can go suddenly wrong, as he learned at Southsea and wrote about in "Baa, Baa Black Sheep." He makes India into a place that expresses his abiding, although not always paramount, sense of reality as a finally incomprehensible mystery within which humans constructed different codes of belief and conduct, some more honorable and availing than others, but none essentially more true. In some of these stories he makes his skepticism about certainty and permanence into parables about empire itself. The heroes of "The Man Who Would Be King" (1888, in *The Phantom 'Rickshaw*), Peachy Carnahan and Daniel Dravot, are capable soldiers in the style of Terence Mulvaney. They use their knowledge of India to disguise themselves to make a dangerous journey beyond the northern frontier. Then they use their training to drill an army and organize an anarchic region. The region once had been conquered by Alexander, who introduced Masonic rituals, and the two Englishmen use their knowledge of Masonry finally to pass themselves off as gods. The ambitious Dravot has himself crowned king and imagines that he will "make an Empire. . . . Two hundred and fifty thousand men, ready to cut in on Russia's right flank when she tries for India!. . . Oh, it's big! It's big, I tell you." After Dravot is tricked and killed by suspicious priests, Carnahan survives a crucifixion and is set free, maimed and mad, to make his way back to India, carrying Dravot's head and crown in a sack. When Carnahan dies in an asylum, the narrator, who has seen the contents of the sack, asks "'if he had anything upon him by chance when he died?' 'Not to my knowledge,' said the Superintendent. And there the matter rests." Like Alexander yesterday, like England tomorrow, another empire has come to nothing, this time leaving no trace at all on the undisciplined and unprogressive remoteness that absorbs or expels it.

Throughout the 1890s and into the new century, with an energy and fecundity that had not been known in British letters since Charles Dickens, Kipling consolidated his popularity and broadened the range and tactics of his writing. After his marriage to Carrie Balestier in 1892, he moved to Vermont, where he lived for four years. He and his wife had three children: Josephine, born in 1892; Elsie, born in 1896; and John, born in 1897. Kipling's stories and poems were steadily published in magazines and by publishers in Britain and the United States. He wrote two more novels in the realistic manner of many of his stories—*"Captains Courageous"* (1897), a story of fishermen on the Grand Banks off North America, and, more notably, *Kim*. He remembered his school days in *Stalky & Co.* For children he wrote the fables of three of the books for which, with *Kim*, he is principally remembered: *The Jungle Book* and *The Second Jungle Book*, and *Just So Stories*. Two new collections of his stories were published (*Many Inventions*, 1893, and *The Day's Work*, 1898), and two collections of poems (*The Seven Seas*, 1896, and *The Five Nations*, 1903).

When he wrote for children, and when he wrote of his own boyhood in *Stalky & Co.*, Kipling moderated his sense of the fundamental incoherence and incomprehensibility of existence. In the fables of the *Just So Stories* he explains biological adaptations sometimes as sensible mechanisms for survival ("How the Leopard Got His Spots," "The Beginning of the Armadilloes"), and sometimes as just punishments for foolish behavior. "The Elephant's Child" has his nose pulled into a trunk when he gets too close to a crocodile to ask about its eating habits, a punishment that turns into a reward when the child discovers the utility of a trunk in picking fruit, taking baths, and spanking the members of his family who have chided him for his admirable curiosity. Even "The Cat That Walked by Himself" in scornful independence works out a durable contract for fitting harmoniously into domestic society: "He will kill mice, and he will be kind to Babies when he is in the house, just as long as they do not pull his tail too hard. But when he has done that, and between times, and when the moon gets up and the night comes, he is the Cat that walks by himself, and all places are alike to him."

Kipling admits into the stories of *The Jungle Book* and *The Second Jungle Book*, written for older children, much of the violence, loss, and ignorant rigidity that he considered in his first poems and short stories. Mowgli, the principal character of most of the stories, is an abandoned human child adopted into a wolf pack ("Mowgli's Brothers"). He learns the language of animals, successfully negotiates the politics of the pack, acquires enemies and powerful allies (Baloo the bear, Kaa the python), and discovers his own power (no animal can look him in his eyes) to become the master of the jungle. He also learns the Law of the Jungle, which has several clauses (hunt for food and not for pleasure; don't kill men except to demonstrate how to kill, because men have guns) but which comes down to a single injunction: Obey the leader. The Bandar-log, monkeys whose ways closely resemble those of humans, have not learned this law: "They were always just going to have a leader, and laws and customs of their own, but they never did, because their memories would not hold over from day to day, and so they compromised things by making up a saying: 'What the *Bandar-log* think now, the Jungle will think later,' and that comforted them a great deal."

Human society has its own kind of lawlessness. The Monkey-People live near the Cold Lairs, a ruined city that holds a treasure guarded by snakes. In "The King's Ankus," Mowgli and Kaa manage to take a jeweled ankus—a cruel implement used to train and discipline elephants—from the hoard. They return it after six men kill one another in their lust to possess it. "That thing has killed six times in one night," Mowgli tells the old Cobra responsible for its guard. "Let him go out no more."

But Kipling affirms order even in this welter of ignorance and anarchy. In the strongest story in the two collections, "Red Dog," Mowgli saves the wolf pack by using the ferocity of bees to defeat the rapaciousness of wild dogs. Then, in the last story, "The Spring Running," Mowgli obeys the law of his biology and returns to his own kind, eventually, as Kipling has promised, to marry and presumably breed. "But that," Kipling writes, "is a story for grown-ups." In these stories for young readers he allowed the competent leader—here a boy—not simply to fashion a satisfying if temporary structure of useful work in the world, but to organize and prevail in material creation by understanding and directing its powers.

In *Stalky & Co.* the boys who go to school with Stalky and his confederates—M'Turk, the son of an Irish landed family, and the bookish and bespectacled Beetle, Kipling's representation of himself as a schoolboy—are being educated to become officers and colleagues. In "Slaves of the Lamp. Part II," the final story of the collection, M'Turk, Beetle, and others, now graduates of the school, meet at a dinner and hear how the ingenious Stalky, in command of a body of Sikh troops, broke a siege by tricking the besiegers into fighting with one another. "Adequate chap," one of them says, rising to the top of his vocabulary of praise, "Infernally adequate."

But whatever lies ahead, the boyhoods of Stalky and company are safe because the school is commanded by a nearly omniscient and wholly competent Head. The school holds bullies and weak masters who are anxious and arbitrary in their exercise of authority. But Stalky, M'Turk, and Beetle defeat and reform the bullies, consistently frustrate the witless designs of the masters, and turn accusations into triumphs over their adversaries. The Head cannot purge the school of meanness and injustice, nor can he protect the boys from the chances of their futures. But he can create a protected space in which boys like Stalky execute elaborate pranks that teach them later to lead men and save lives, and in which observant boys like Beetle get ready to tell stories about men like Stalky and the Head.

"It will always be one of the darkest mysteries to me," Kipling wrote in a 27 September 1896 letter to the novelist Mary Augusta (Mrs. Humphrey) Ward, "that any human being can make a beginning, end *and* middle to a really long story." Kipling never solved the mystery. The *Jungle Books* and *Stalky & Co.* are made of short narratives connected not by a continuous plot but by the recurring presence of their central characters. That is also how Kipling constructed his novels. The story of Harvey Cheyne, a spoiled rich boy who falls off an ocean liner and is pulled from the sea and put to work on a fishing boat, provides the spine of *"Captains Courageous,"* a simple parable about the redemptive power of learning to do a job in the company of men who know their work. Loaded onto this spine are detailed descriptions of the gear and methods of fishing on the Grand Banks that Kipling gathered from a friend in Vermont, and often engaging appreciations of the variety and color of the dialects, songs, stories, customs, and origins of the people of North America. *The Light That Failed* moves through episodes in the life of Dick Heldar, which for a while is much like that of Kipling: the stringencies of his childhood, his work as a journalist (Dick is a war correspondent who draws rather than writes), and his scramble in the business of journalism and art in London (he does not succeed). When Dick loses his sight as a result of a wound he received in Africa, he schemes and bullies his way back to a battle in the Sudan—at one point he effectively hijacks a camel at gunpoint—where he is killed by "the crowning mercy of a kindly bullet through his head." The principal interests of the book lie in sketches of the bohemian lives of journalists in London and abroad, and in Kipling's judgments of the cold business practices of London agents and editors and the effete work of London artists. Kipling also adds an uncomfortable note of misogyny to his now familiar celebration of the "austere love that springs up between men who have tugged at the same oar together." Maisie, Dick's boyhood love and a technically correct but feeble painter, fails the test of caring for him when he goes blind. Bessie, a waif Dick once used as a model, destroys his masterpiece when he interferes with her hope of being taken care of by one of his friends ("Only a woman would have done that"). One woman does love and would care for him, but she lacks the force to do anything about her feelings except express them in a letter that comes too late.

Kim, Kipling's most popular and best-managed novel, strings its episodes along a story of two connected journeys. Kim—Kimball O'Hara—is the orphaned son of a British nursemaid and a sergeant in an Irish regiment. He has been brought up by a half-caste woman, and he seeks his identity and role in the enormously enjoyable swirl and pageant of Indian life, "wild as that of the Arabian Nights." Early in the book Kim meets a Tibetan lama, who seeks a sacred river that will enable him to get off the wheel of life and its relentless turns from "despair to despair." Kim becomes the lama's *chela,* the boy who begs for him and arranges his travels. Buried beneath anecdotes and descriptions of Indian life is a plot in which Kim and his Indian mentors and allies manage to thwart a couple of threats against British rule in India mounted by treacherous native kings and Russian agents. But the excitement of the story lies in the episodic events, characters, and landscapes of Kim's travels through the streets and roads and wilderness of the India lived in by Indians.

Kim is entirely at home in India. He not only speaks the vernacular but thinks and dreams in Hindi (although when he is in trouble he sometimes thinks in English). After he meets some officers in his father's regiment and is sent by them to an English school in India (the lama pays his tuition), he becomes "blanched like an almond." But he easily passes again as a Hindu boy, even once as a Muslim, when he is artificially darkened and reenters "the roaring whirl of India." None of his important teachers and guides are British Sahibs. Except for the mysterious Lurgan Sahib, a white man adept in the illusions of Indian fakirs, the British officers and clergymen who manipulate Kim stand above and apart from the life in which he grew up. They take him out of that life and then send him back into it as an agent in the Great Game they play to maintain their rule.

"Who is Kim?," the British boy who thinks in Hindi asks himself several times during the novel. "At the Gates of Learning we were taught that to abstain from action was unbefitting a Sahib," he finally answers, "And I am a Sahib." The identity that Kim arrives at and the work that lies before him embody a possibility of union quite different from the idea of the British in India dramatized in many of Kipling's early short stories. Like Trejago in *Plain Tales from the Hills*, and like Mowgli, Kim can live in two cultures. Unlike them, he can make his knowledge of one culture work for the good, as Kipling imagines, of the other. When early in the novel Kim helps the lama onto a railway train to continue his pilgrimage, Kipling remarks on the juncture of "old-world piety and modern progress that is the note of India today." At the end of the novel, Kim peers at the lama, "outlined jet-black against the lemon-colored drift of light," and thinks that he resembles "the stone Bodhisat who looks down on the patent self-registering turnstiles of the Lahore museum." Kim sees, and could be, the future of a British India, a harmony of old gods and modern machines, a hybrid culture more vibrant and exciting than that of England, more coherent and progressive than the ancient and disordered civilization into which the British came.

After Kipling's return to England in 1896 he became an important public figure as well as an extraordinarily popular writer. He corresponded with Theodore Roosevelt, whom he met in America. When Kipling visited Scotland, Andrew Carnegie offered him the use of his house; the writer also spent winters in South Africa in a house provided by Cecil Rhodes. He witnessed some of the South African War (1899–1902), during which he contributed to and helped to edit a newspaper for the troops, established by their commanders. He received honorary degrees from Cambridge and Oxford but refused a knighthood in 1899 and declined to stand as a Conservative for Parliament because he thought that he could better serve his profession and his politics if he worked independently of government and party honors and responsibilities. He bought Bateman's, a seventeenth-century house in Sussex, and knit himself into the life of a member of a high professional caste, exploring the countryside in one or another of the automobiles he enthusiastically acquired and going up to London to associate with other leading men in their professions at clubs and public dinners.

The editorial pages of the London *Times* were open to Kipling whenever he chose to write on current political and social matters. During his lifetime he gave (he took no payment) about twenty poems to the *Times*. In the verse collected in *The Seven Seas* and *The Five Nations*, Kipling used the colloquial diction and thumping beats and rhymes of his early poems to continue to make a poetry that professed to be, and sometimes became, popular song. In "The Song of the Banjo" (1894) he compares his sound to that of a banjo, and "With my '*Pilly-willy-winky-winky popp!*'" and "my '*Tinka-tinka-tinka-tinka-tink!*'" he claims to "draw the world together link by link: / Yea, from Delos up to Limerick and back!" When he wrote in the *Times* on matters of large political moment, however, in poems such as "Recessional" (1897) and "The White Man's Burden" (1899), Kipling chose the vocabulary and cadences of hymn. He warns the Anglo-Saxon people (including Americans) of the transience and the truly sacred responsibilities of empire. This people, he writes in "Recessional," must not forget that they hold "Dominion over palm and pine" by the dispensation of the "God of our fathers, known of old." He angered Americans when he lectured them in "The White Man's Burden" on the proper conduct of the empire they acquired with the Philippines: "Go bind your sons to exile / To serve your captive's needs." In "The Islanders" (1902), another poem published in the *Times,* he came down as hard on the English for grudging their sons to service and depending "on the Younger Nations for the men who could shoot and ride!"

In the stories of *Puck of Pook's Hill* (1906) and *Rewards and Fairies* (1910), written to educate young people in English history, Kipling again imagined, as he had in *Kim,* a whole nation made by the confluence of several cultures. "In God's good time," one of the heroes of "Young Men at the Manor" (from *Puck of Pook's Hill*) predicts, "there will be neither Saxon nor Norman in England"—nor, Kipling suggests, Roman, Pict, Dane, or any of the other peoples who have left their marks on the countryside and in the narratives of what became England. At the same time, the stories recognize that the making of England required the defeat or sublimation of the nations and tribes who fought for dominion.

In some of the short stories written for adults and collected in the four volumes published in the 1890s and the first decade of the new century, Kipling attacked, as he does in his poems, the complacency and enervation that betray empire. "One View of the Ques-

Announcement of an exhibition of Kipling materials (Collection of Matthew J. Bruccoli)

tion" (1890), a story in *Many Inventions,* reverses Kipling's usual perspective and puts an Indian visitor in London so that he could observe, with a smugness that Kipling surely intended as cautionary, that "the fountainhead of power is putrid with long standing still" and predict that "the Sahibs die out at the third generation in our land."

But more usually in the stories of these collections Kipling tends to display not weaknesses at home but the benefits that imperial whites bring to natives. A third-generation Anglo-Indian in "A Tomb of His Ancestors" (1897), published in *The Day's Work,* uses the natives' belief that he is the reincarnation of his grandfather, an administrator of fabled effectiveness, to complete a successful vaccination campaign. In "William the Conqueror" (1895), another story in the same collection, a civil servant alleviates a famine with the help of a British woman, oddly but revealingly named William. Kipling was more than a chauvinist imperialist, but at times he could be just that. By and large in these stories, white people do good for natives, and the British do more good than anyone—certainly more than the engaging American who thinks of war as a game and tries to sell the gun he has invented to the Boers in "A Captive" (1902), or the Boers with their dishonorable guerilla tactics in "A Sahib's War" (1901), both stories collected in *Traffics and Discoveries* (1904).

As he became more explicit than he had previously been about the good that empire can do for lesser breeds, Kipling became more gloomy and conservative about politics at home. He opposed suffrage for women, home rule for Ireland, and the liberal British governments that edged toward these changes. He thought that the United States would be ruined by immigration, and he was deeply hostile to political innovation. In "A Walking Delegate" (1894), collected in *The Day's Work,* a Kansas horse brings the unsettling views of socialism to a Vermont stable: "'As usual,' he said, with an underhung sneer—'bowin' your heads before the Oppressor, that comes to spend his leisure gloatin' over you.'" He is argued down and beaten by the other horses. "'There's jest two kind o' horse in the United States—them ez can an' will do their work after bein' properly broke an' handled, an' them ez won't.'" The lesson of such fables is expressed by the plates and rivets of a ship during its first Atlantic run in "The Ship That Found Herself" (1895, included in *The Day's Work*). Each part must learn its place in the hierarchy of the Design, "how to lock down and lock up on one another," and then "the talking of the separate pieces ceases and melts into one voice, which is the soul of the ship."

Kipling loved the machinery of the modern, the railways and steamships of the old century, the motorcars and wireless and airplanes of the new. When he installed a turbine in an old mill on his property in Sussex, he wrote "Below the Mill Dam" (1902, included in *Traffics and Discoveries*), a fable in which the Waters and the Spirit of the Mill discuss the innovation. All approve, except an old English rat, who is discovered by the electric lights turned on by the turbine and is killed. The speaker of "McAndrew's Hymn" (1893, included in *The Seven Seas*), a dramatic monologue in Scots dialect, finds God and duty in the machinery he tends in the engine room of a ship: "Interdependence, absolute, foreseen, ordained, decreed, / To work, Ye'll note, at ony tilt an' every rate of speed." Design and grandeur in these poems and stories reside in human constructions. But the order of these political and mechanical systems is no less compelling than that of the old gods and heroes. To resist or subvert them is to disintegrate in waste and ruin, like the Bandar-log of the *Jungle Books* and the white men who step into India without the knowledge, discipline, and purpose of Kim.

As his political convictions settled, Kipling's narrative practices became expansive and adventurous. No longer constrained by the limitations of space imposed on his early stories, he constructed elaborate plots, sometimes around nothing more than a practical joke. He often prefaced and concluded his short stories with verses that sometimes enforced, and sometimes complicated, their themes. He occasionally told a story in several voices, giving it the feel, obliqueness, and surprise of conversation. When the stories of the *Jungle Books* and the *Just So Stories* are counted in, he wrote as many fables as realistic short stories in the two decades before World War I.

"The Bridge Builders" (1893, in *The Day's Work*) joins realism and fable to express again Kipling's idea of a British India that harmonizes East and West. It begins as a typical Kipling story about competent men doing good work in India despite the heat, disease, and interference of remote and ignorant superiors. Trying to protect their uncompleted bridge from a flood, the British engineer Findlayson and his Lascar overseer Peroo are swept in their boat into the river, and then into fable. In a trance of weariness smoothed with opium, they witness the gods debate the plea of the river to destroy the bridge that obstructs her. "Be certain that is only for a little," Krishna says, and then tells the gods that except for Brahm, the principle of life, they themselves are only for a time: "The fire-carriages shout the names of new Gods that are *not* the old under new names." When morning comes, the bridge still stands. Findlayson and Peroo are rescued by a Westernized Indian in his steam-launch on his way to the temple "to sanctify some new idol." The realistic part of the story honors Findlayson's work in careful descriptions of it. The fable both subverts and sanctifies it. Although it too will ultimately be washed away, Findlayson's work, like the fire-carriages of the railway, speaks the name of gods. The bridge is an idol rightly to be worshiped, an authentic contemporary expression of reverence for Brahm.

"'They'" (1904, included in *Traffics and Discoveries*) mixes realism and the fantasy of a ghost story to come to a complicated idea about the value and reach of pragmatic knowledge. The narrator clatters in his motorcar through a southern English landscape to find by accident a lovely Elizabethan house behind a lawn full of topiary yew cut as knights and ladies. Gradually, it comes to him that the children he entertains with his motorcar are ghosts summoned by the need of the gracious blind woman who lives alone in the house. Kipling's daughter Josephine had died during his visit to the United States in 1899, and the author's loss underwrites the plangency of the narrator's decision not to return to the house. Kipling prefaced "'They'" with a poem in which the Virgin Mother releases children from heaven so that their spirits will comfort people on earth. The ghostly in this story is not a realist's playful reminder that he does not know everything. It is a possibility of belief, an earthly paradise, from which the narrator is shut out because of his commitment to the valuable, practical work that makes and purchases motorcars.

"Mrs. Bathurst" (1904, included in *Traffics and Discoveries*), one of Kipling's best stories, starts out with its tellers reminiscing about a farcical episode of their youths, turns into something like a ghost story, and ends as a commentary about the difficulty of catching reality in the frame of narrative. Vickers, a naval warrant officer, is haunted by a sequence he sees in a "cinematograph" shown in a carnival at Cape Town. Night after night he takes Pyecroft, the principal teller of the story, to watch this movie clip of a woman stepping out of a train in Paddington Station and walking toward the camera, "lookin' straight at us . . . till she melted out of the picture—like—like a shadow jumpin' over a candle, and as she went I 'eard Dawson in the tickey seats be'ind sing, "Christ! there's Mrs. B!'" Two other people help Pyecroft tell the story. One, like Pyecroft, has known Ada Bathurst as the generous proprietor of a small hotel in Auckland. The other knows what happened to Vickers. None of them know what Mrs. Bathurst was doing in London ("She's lookin' for me," Vickers says), or what Vickers has done to be haunted by her, or what he tells his captain before he is sent upcountry alone on a detail, or why he deserts, or the identity of the other person found with him on a railway track in a teak forest, both "burned to charcoal" by lightning. The artful ramble of the story as its several tellers exchange information and opinions that finally complete without resolving its plot, testify both to the desire of realistic narrative to take in everything, and to the futility of that ambition.

During the last two decades of his life Kipling wrote less prolifically than he had in the years before. The awarding in 1907 of the Nobel Prize—which was "in all ways unexpected," he wrote in his autobiography—certified his eminence. The award surprised and upset some of his contemporaries, who thought his writing vulgar and rowdy and his politics narrow and shrill. Kipling himself was pleased, but characteristically deprecated the grandeur of the ceremony. "It means a gold medal and a parchment certificate and tomorrow they give me a lot of money," he wrote to his children John and Elsie in letters dated 10 December 1907. When he rose to receive the award, he added, "I felt rather like a bad boy up to be caned." But by this time he was accustomed to his role as one of the grand personages of his time and culture, and he continued to address important matters of the moment in his usual venues and styles, from poems in the Times to fables in prose and verse. He spent some of the prize money on improvements to the garden at Bateman's, including the purchase of a sundial that bore the injunction, "It is later than you think."

Kipling's publishers in England and America kept his name before readers with collected editions of his work that periodically added new titles (the first collection was published in 1897), a series of one-volume "Inclusive" editions of his verse (1919, 1927, 1933), reprints of his most popular books, and repackaging of poems and stories into Kipling readers, Kipling pageants, Kipling calendars, and volumes given to stories about animals, dogs, stories for children, and humorous tales. He remained an important public figure. During his cousin Stanley Baldwin's terms as prime minister in the 1920s, Kipling's advice to the Conservative party acquired a quasi-official status, and when he visited Scotland again, he stayed at Balmoral with the king. He suffered a stomach disease that he feared (incorrectly) was cancer, and his wife carefully guarded his privacy at Bateman's. But when (in his opinion) he saw the world going wrong, he used his public presence to try to set it right. With his friend Rider Haggard he founded a short-lived Liberty League to oppose socialism. He bitterly regretted the treaty in 1924 that set Ireland on its way toward independence, and he resigned from the Rhodes Trust in 1925 because he thought its policies encouraged the growth of a commonwealth of autonomous nations to replace an empire ruled by white men from home.

Kipling's most significant publications in the last stage of his career were three collections of short stories: *A Diversity of Creatures* (1917), *Debits and Credits* (1926), and *Limits and Renewals* (1932). In these stories Kipling's conviction that right-minded people knew exactly what to do at least some of the time runs alongside his persistent sense of the uncertainties of knowing and doing. A set of stories about the consequences of World War I shows this mix of skepticism and sometimes belligerent certainty. Like many of his contemporaries, Kipling at first welcomed the war as a bracing occasion to renew and test courage and honor. He enlisted his talent in a series of pamphlets and newspaper articles about the army in France and the work of the navy. When his only son, John, was reported missing in action in France in 1915 (his body was never found), Kipling responded in the manly code in which he had been schooled: in a 12 November 1915 letter he wrote, "it's something to have bred a man." He soon undertook to edit a history of his son's regiment from their letters and journals, *The Irish Guards in the Great War* (1923), and he served on the Imperial War Graves Commission, which established military cemeteries on the Continent and elsewhere.

Some of Kipling's short stories written during the war express a simple patriotic morality. In "Sea Constables" (1915, included in *Debits and Credits*), one of Kipling's competent professional men, serving as a volunteer, forces a neutral vessel trying to run a block into port and lets its captain die unattended of pneumonia. In another, "Mary Postgate," written in the same year and also published in *Debits and Credits,* a child is killed by a bomb dropped from a German airplane. A middle-aged spinster finds the injured German pilot in her garden, and, already grieving over the death of a young friend killed while training to be a pilot, she lets the German die, takes a hot bath, and comes down looking "quite handsome." On the other hand, in some of the poems he wrote during the war Kipling uses quiet ballad measures to express themes of waste and horror common in the poetry of World War I. The speaker of "My Boy Jack" (1918, included in *The Years Between*), Kipling's poem for his son, asks, "'Have you news of my boy Jack?'" When the answer is, *"Not this tide. / For what is sunk will hardly swim, / Not with this wind blowing, and this tide,"* he continues,

> "Oh dear, what comfort can I find?"
> None this tide,
> Nor any tide,
> Except that he did not shame his kind—
> Not even with that wind blowing, and that tide.

After the war Kipling wrote some stories in which he considers its psychic damage and the efforts of friends and small communities to protect or cure its victims. In a story written during the war, "In the Interests of the Brethren" (1918, included in *Debits and Credits*),

Kipling invented Masonic Lodge Faith and Works 5837 E. C., a creation of merchants and professional men to provide food, lodging, and the comforts of ritual to young men on leave from the war. In two later stories, "The Janeites" (1924) and "A Madonna of the Trenches" (1924), both also collected in *Debits and Credits,* the members of the lodge are still in business doing what they can to hold together men who may never recover from the war. Brother Strangeways of the latter story saw an apparition of his recently deceased aunt in the trenches. Literally shocked out of his certainties about life and death, he now refuses to get married and get on with life. Brother Humberstall of "The Janeites," back at the front after the explosion of an ammunition dump "'knocked all 'is Gunnery instruction clean out of 'im'," was sustained by officers who inducted him in a select society who kept the war at bay by testing themselves on the details of Jane Austen's fiction. None of the officers survived the collapse of the front at the Somme, and back home after the war Humberstall gets through his days by trying to play his Janeite game with his sister. Strangeways and Humberstall tell their stories at the lodge, presumably not for the first time, to sympathetic men who hear them through and send them home, only temporarily relieved of the burden of their trouble.

"The Gardener" (1925, in *Debits and Credits*) depicts another kind of war casualty. An unmarried, middle-aged woman goes to a military cemetery in France to visit the grave of a man she has always called her nephew. She is guided by a gardener who may be Christ and who in any event knows her secret and pleases her by referring to the dead man as her son. But the story qualifies this resolution by leaving unexplained a curious episode in which the woman fails to comfort, and even inadvertently insults, another woman who must invent subterfuges to visit the grave of a man who never acknowledged her as her lover when he was living.

"Dayspring Mishandled" (1924, included in *Limits and Renewals*), perhaps the most interesting of Kipling's late short stories, demonstrates how in some of his stories at the end of his career he aimed for clear resolutions that nonetheless drifted toward what he had always known as "the hopelessness and tangle of it." The story is founded on an elaborate hoax, a device of which Kipling was always fond. Castorley, who has risen from writing for a fiction syndicate in the 1890s to become an expert on Geoffrey Chaucer, says something insensitive (readers are never told what) about a paralyzed woman whom Manallace loves and cares for. Manallace, who writes historical novels "in a style that exactly met, but never exceeded, every expectation," spends years fabricating and arranging for the discovery of the manuscript of a supposedly lost tale by Chaucer. Castorley falls into the trap and writes a book on the tale, for which Manallance lies in wait to ambush in a review. But before the book can be published, Castorley dies, perhaps of kidney disease, perhaps at the hands of the physician to whom Lady Castorley turns her eyes as her husband's coffin is moved into the crematorium. Kipling's knowledge of the business of literature, his ingenious plotting, and his parody of Chaucer move this story smartly and lightly through its neat plot. But like Manallace's clever machine of vengeance, the plot pulls up short before, and then tumbles into, troubling matter that readers see at the end was there all along: not just the mystery of Lady Castorley and the possible malignity of her lover but also the unspecified cruelty of her husband, the unexamined affection of Manallace for the sad woman who may never have loved him, and the lost promise of youth and talent–dayspring mishandled–given to hack writing and futile scholarship.

Kipling died on 18 January 1936 of a stroke after he suffered ruptured ulcers. The writer of Kipling's obituary in the 25 January 1936 *Times Literary Supplement,* trying to figure out "Rudyard Kipling's Place in English Literature," acknowledged that by the time of his death "many had lost interest in him and many others had been repelled." What repels readers still is most often the racism and misogyny of Kipling's endorsement of an empire founded on the good work of white men. George Orwell, writing a few years after Kipling's death, judged his politics not only repellant but ignorant in his neglect of the economic basis of empire. But Orwell also thought that because of what Kipling left out as well as what he included, he accurately described the life and attitudes of British colonial administrators and soldiers. Lionel Trilling, who found Kipling unreadable as he grew up into his own liberal politics, nonetheless remained interested in the "anthropological views" that Kipling learned in India: "the perception that another man's idea of virtue and honor may be different from one's own but quite to be respected." Noel Annan has argued that this awareness of the relativity and individual integrity of cultural institutions assures Kipling's place in the history of ideas. This view has also made Kipling interesting to an increasing number of literary and cultural critics and historians who find in his writing not only just a picture of the lives of colonialists but also a sensitive register of the tensions in ideas and attitudes that Kipling only some of the time thought of as valid and valuable.

Other commentators who have sustained or revived interest in Kipling's writing since his death have not troubled so much with his politics but instead honored his craft. Edmund Wilson presented to formalist literary critics in the 1940s a Kipling attractive because of his themes of loneliness and isolation and his accounts of an imperiled fortitude in these conditions. J. M. S. Tompkins has written of the sophisticated use of irony by which Kipling maintained his equilibrium on the edge, and Elliot Gilbert of the tactics that mediate between Kipling's notion of "the irrationality of the universe and man's need to find some order in it." Sandra Kemp has argued that Kipling's recognition of identity as constructed and contingent enabled him to write fictions in which he tries out a repertory of identities to explore the exhilarating possibilities of otherness.

Such attention makes clear the continuity and development of his talent during the half century of his career. He never really learned how to write a novel. As a poet he always had a journalist's, or an adman's, gift for catchy phrases, such as "Oh, East is East, and West is West, and never the twain shall meet" ("The Ballad of East and West," 1889, included in *Barrack-Room Ballads*), and "a woman is only a woman, but a good Cigar is a smoke" ("The Betrothed," 1888, included in *Departmental Ditties*). "If– ," his best-known poem (1910, included in *Rewards and Fairies*), is a string of aphorisms suitable for framing: "If you can fill the unforgiving minute / With sixty seconds' worth of distance run, / Yours is the Earth and everything that's in it, / And–which is more–you'll be a Man, my son!" Like Ernest Hemingway, another master of short narrative with whom he has much in common, Kipling began his trade by writing to specifications in a newspaper office. Revision to him meant taking out, and he edited with a pot of India ink and a brush so that he would not be tempted to restore the words, sentences, and paragraphs he had excised.

If in general Rudyard Kipling traded the colorful stories and tumbling long lines of his early poems for the cocky certainty of editorials and aphorisms, on balance a loss, he did gain a succinctness that gave a quiet power to some of his poems (such as "My Boy Jack"). But the most marked development of his craft shows in his short stories. In them he continually experimented with voices, points of view, and registers that move from realism to fable. He always knew how to suggest that he could not tell the entire story, and by the time he got to his late stories he had learned how to make a controlled, uninflected circumstantial narrative invoke a realm of miracle. He became masterful in his reproduction of a reality in which things would not settle and stay fixed, and in which what was out there beyond what humans usually know was sometimes better, sometimes worse, and always larger than the ordinary conventions of knowing and telling would lead one to expect.

Letters:

Rudyard Kipling to Rider Haggard: The Record of a Friendship, edited by Morton Cohen (London: Hutchinson, 1965; Rutherford, N.J.: Fairleigh Dickinson United Press, 1965);

'O Beloved Kids': Rudyard Kipling's Letters to His Children, edited by Elliot L. Gilbert (London: Weidenfeld & Nicolson, 1983; New York: Harcourt Brace Jovanovich, 1984);

The Letters of Rudyard Kipling, 6 volumes, edited by Thomas Pinney (Basingstoke: Macmillan, 1990–2004; Iowa City: University of Iowa Press, 1990–2004);

Kipling's America: Travel Letters, 1889–1895, edited by D. H. Stewart (Greensboro: ELT Press, University of North Carolina at Greensboro, 2003).

Interviews:

Kipling: Interviews and Recollections, 2 volumes, edited by Harold Orel (Totowa, N.J.: Barnes & Noble, 1983; London: Macmillan, 1983).

Bibliographies:

Flora V. Livingstone, *Bibliography of the Works of Rudyard Kipling* (New York: Wells, 1927); *Supplement* (Cambridge, Mass.: Harvard University Press, 1938; London: Oxford University Press, 1938);

Lloyd H. Chandler, *A Summary of the Work of Rudyard Kipling* (New York: Grolier Club, 1930);

James McG. Stewart, *Kipling: A Bibliographic Catalogue,* edited by A. W. Yeats (Toronto: Dalhousie University Press/University of Toronto Press, 1959);

Helmut E. Gerber and Edward Lauterbach, "Rudyard Kipling: An Annotated Bibliography of Writings About Him," *English Literature in Transition,* 3, nos. 3–5 (1960): 1–235; 8, nos. 3–4 (1965): 136–241;

P. Coustillas, "Bibliographie Selective: Rudyard Kipling: *Kim,*" *Cahiers Victoriens et Edouardiens,* 40 (1994): 163–168.

Biographies:

C. E. Carrington, *The Life of Rudyard Kipling* (London: Macmillan, 1955; Garden City, N.Y.: Doubleday, 1955; revised, 1978);

John Gross, *Rudyard Kipling: The Man, His Work, and His World* (London: Weidenfeld & Nicolson, 1972; New York: Simon & Schuster, 1972);

Martin Fido, *Rudyard Kipling* (London & New York: Hamlyn, 1974);

Philip Mason, *Kipling: The Glass, the Shadow and the Fire* (London: Cape, 1975; New York: Harper & Row, 1975);

Kingsley Amis, *Rudyard Kipling and His World* (London: Thames & Hudson, 1975; New York: Scribners, 1975);

Angus Wilson, *The Strange Ride of Rudyard Kipling: His Life and Work* (London: Secker & Warburg, 1977; New York: Viking, 1978);

Lord Birkenhead, *Rudyard Kipling* (London: Weidenfeld & Nicolson, 1978; New York: Random House, 1978);

Martin Seymour-Smith, *Rudyard Kipling* (London: Macdonald, 1989; New York: St. Martin's Press, 1989);

Harold Orel, *A Kipling Chronology* (Boston: G. K. Hall, 1990; London: Macmillan, 1990);

Andrew Lycett, *Rudyard Kipling* (London: Weidenfeld & Nicolson, 1999; expanded edition, London: Phoenix, 2000);

Harry Ricketts, *The Unforgiving Minute: A Life of Rudyard Kipling* (London: Chatto & Windus, 1999); republished as *Rudyard Kipling: A Life* (New York: Carroll & Graf, 2000);

David Gilmour, *The Long Recessional: The Imperial Life of Rudyard Kipling* (London: Murray, 2002; New York: Farrar, Straus & Giroux, 2002);

Phillip Mallett, *Rudyard Kipling: A Literary Life* (Basingstoke & New York: Palgrave Macmillan, 2003).

References:

Noel Annan, "Kipling's Place in the History of Ideas," *Victorian Studies,* 3 (1960): 323–348;

Stephen Arata, "A Universal Forgiveness: Kipling in the Fin-de-Siècle," *English Literature in Transition,* 36 (1993): 7–38;

Helen Pike Bauer, *Rudyard Kipling: A Study of the Short Fiction* (New York: Twayne, 1994; Oxford & Toronto: Maxwell Macmillan, 1994);

Harold Bloom, ed., *Rudyard Kipling,* second edition (Philadelphia: Chelsea House, 2004; Northam: Roundhouse, 2004);

Bloom, ed., *Rudyard Kipling's Kim* (New York: Chelsea House, 1987);

Christine Bucher, "Envisioning the Imperial Nation in Kipling's *Kim,*" *Journal of Commonwealth and Post-Colonial Studies,* 5 (1998): 7–17;

Terry Caesar, "Suppression, Textuality, Entanglement, and Revenge in Kipling's 'Dayspring Mishandled,'" *English Literature in Transition,* 29 (1986): 54–63;

Children's Literature, special Kipling issue, edited by Judith Plotz, 20 (1992);

Nora Crook, *Kipling's Myths of Love and Death* (London: Macmillan, 1989; New York: St. Martin's Press, 1989);

John deLancey Ferguson, "Kipling's Revision of His Published Works," *Journal of English and Germanic Philology*, 22 (1923): 114–124;

John Derbyshire, "Rudyard Kipling and the God of Things As They Are," *New Criterion*, 18 (2000): 5–13;

Elliot L. Gilbert, *The Good Kipling: Studies in the Short Story* (Athens: Ohio University Press, 1971; Manchester: Manchester University Press, 1971);

Gilbert, "Silence and Survival in Rudyard Kipling's Art and Life," *English Literature in Transition*, 29 (1986): 115–126;

Gilbert, ed., *Kipling and the Critics* (New York: New York University Press, 1965; London: Owen, 1966);

Roger Lancelyn Green, ed., *Kipling: The Critical Heritage* (London: Routledge & Kegan Paul, 1971; New York: Barnes & Noble, 1971);

Ambreen Hai, "On Truth and Lie in a Colonial Sense: Kipling's Tales of Tale-Telling," *ELH*, 64 (1997): 599–625;

James Harrison, *Rudyard Kipling* (Boston: Twayne, 1982);

Christopher Hichens, "Burdens and Songs: The Anglo-American Rudyard Kipling," *Grand Street*, 9 (1990): 203–234;

Peter Hopkirk, *Quest for Kim: In Search of Kipling's Great Game* (London: Murray, 1996; Ann Arbor: University of Michigan Press, 1996);

Jane Hotchkiss, "The Jungle of Eden: Kipling, Wolf-Boys, and the Colonial Imagination," *Victorian Literature and Culture*, 29 (2001): 435–449;

Teresa Hubel, "In Search of the British Indian in British India: White Orphans, Kipling's *Kim*, and Class in Colonial India," *Modern Asian Studies*, 38 (2004): 227–252;

P. J. Keating, *Kipling the Poet* (London: Secker & Warburg, 1994);

Sandra Kemp, *Kipling's Hidden Narratives* (Oxford & New York: Blackwell, 1988);

U. C. Knoepflmacher, "The Chameleon Kipling: His Rise and Fall and Rehabilitation," *Review*, 23 (2001): 1–35;

John Kucich, "Sadomasochism and the Magical Group: Kipling's Middle-Class Imperialism," *Victorian Studies*, 46 (2003): 33–68;

Phillip Mallett, ed., *Kipling Considered* (Basingstoke: Macmillan, 1989; New York: St. Martin's Press, 1989);

John McBratney, *Imperial Subjects, Imperial Space: Rudyard Kipling's Fictions of the Native-Born* (Columbus: Ohio State University Press, 2002);

John A. McClure, *Kipling and Conrad: The Colonial Fiction* (Cambridge, Mass.: Harvard University Press, 1981);

Louis Menand, "Kipling in the History of Forms," in *High and Low Moderns: Literature And Culture, 1889–1939*, edited by Maria DiBattista and Lucy M. Diarmid (New York: Oxford University Press, 1996), pp. 148–165;

Jeffrey Meyers, "Kipling and Hemingway: The Lesson of the Master," *American Literature*, 56 (1984): 87–99;

Harold Orel, ed., *Critical Essays on Rudyard Kipling* (Boston: G. K. Hall, 1989);

George Orwell, "Rudyard Kipling," in his *Dickens, Dali and Others* (London: Secker & Warburg, 1946; New York: Harcourt Brace Jovanovich, 1946), pp. 140–160;

Mark Paffard, *Kipling's Indian Fiction* (Basingstoke: Macmillan, 1989; New York: St. Martin's Press, 1989);

Norman Page, *A Kipling Companion* (London: Macmillan, 1984);

Clara Claiborne Park, "Artist of Empire: Kipling and Kim," *Hudson Review*, 55 (2003): 537–561;

Ann Parry, *The Poetry of Rudyard Kipling: Rousing the Nation* (Buckingham & Philadelphia: Open University Press, 1992);

Parry, "Reading Formations in the Victorian Press: The Reception of Kipling 1888–1891," *Literature and History*, 11 (1985): 254–263;

Don Randall, *Kipling's Imperial Boy: Adolescence and Cultural Hybridity* (Basingstoke & New York: Palgrave Macmillan, 2000);

Randall, "Post-Mutiny Allegories of Empire in Rudyard Kipling's *Jungle Books*," *Texas Studies in Language and Literature*, 41 (1997): 97–120;

Harry Ricketts, "Kipling and the War: A Reading of *Debits and Credits*," *English Literature in Transition*, 29 (1986): 26–39;

Andrew Rutherford, ed., *Kipling's Mind and Art: Selected Critical Essays* (Stanford: Stanford University Press, 1964; Edinburgh & London: Oliver & Boyd, 1964);

David Stewart, "Kipling's Portraits of the Artists," *English Literature in Transition*, 31 (1988): 265–283;

Lionel Trilling, "Kipling," in his *The Liberal Imagination* (New York: Viking, 1950; London: Secker & Warburg, 1951), pp. 118–128;

Edmund Wilson, "The Kipling That Nobody Read," in his *The Wound and the Bow* (Boston: Houghton Mifflin, 1941; London: Secker & Warburg, 1942), pp. 105–181;

Lewis D. Wurgaft, *The Imperial Imagination: Magic and Myth in Kipling's India* (Middletown, Conn.: Wesleyan University Press, 1983);

W. Arthur Young and John H. McGivering, *A Kipling Dictionary* (London: Macmillan, 1967; New York: St. Martin's Press, 1967).

Papers:

The most extensive archive of Rudyard Kipling's letters, manuscripts, and family papers is housed at the University of Sussex Library in Brighton. Other significant collections of letters and manuscripts are in the British Library, the Berg Collection of the New York Public Library, the Library of Congress, the Doubleday Collection of the Princeton University Library, the Bodleian Library, and the university libraries of Syracuse, Harvard, Cornell, and Dalhousie.

1907 Nobel Prize in Literature Presentation Speech

by C. D. af Wirsén, Permanent Secretary of the Swedish Academy, on 10 December 1907 (there was no banquet because of the death of King Oscar II of Sweden on 8 December)

The suggestions for names of suitable recipients of this year's Nobel Prize in Literature have been numerous, and there has been no dearth of exceedingly well-qualified candidates for this honourable and coveted distinction.

From these candidates, the Swedish Academy has selected for this occasion a writer who belongs to Great Britain. For centuries past the literature of England has flourished and blossomed with marvellous luxuriance. When Tennyson's immortal lyre was silenced forever, the cry which is so customary at the passing of literary giants was raised. With him the glorious reign of poetry is over; there is none to take up the mantle. Similar despairing notes were struck in this country on the demise of Tegnér, but it is not so with the fair goddess Poetry. She does not perish, is not deposed from her high estate; she but arrays herself in a fresh garb to suit the altered tastes of a new age.

In the works of Tennyson idealism is so pervasive that it meets the eye in a very palpable and direct form. Traits of idealism, however, may be traced in the conceptions and gifts of writers who differ widely from him, such writers who seem primarily concerned with mere externals and who have won renown especially for their vivid word-picturings of the various phases of the strenuous, pulsating life of our own times, that life which is often chequered and fretted by the painful struggle for existence and by all its concomitant worries and embarrassments. This description applies to Rudyard Kipling, to whom the Swedish Academy has awarded the Nobel Prize in Literature this year. Of him a French author, who has devoted much time and study to English literature, wrote more than six years ago: "He, Kipling, is undoubtedly the most noteworthy figure that has appeared within recent years in the domain of English literature."

Kipling was born in Bombay on December 30, 1865. At the age of six he was placed in the care of some relatives in England, but he returned to India on reaching the age of seventeen. He obtained a position on the staff of *The Civil and Military Gazette,* published at Lahore, and in his early twenties edited *The Pioneer* at Allahabad. In his capacity as a journalist, and for his own purposes, he travelled extensively throughout India. On those journeys he acquired a thorough insight into Hindu conceptions and sentiments and became intimately acquainted with the different Hindu groups, with their varying customs and institutions, and with the special features of English military life in India. This firm grasp of the true inwardness of all things Indian is abundantly reflected in Kipling's writings, so much so that it has even been said that they have brought India nearer home to the English nation than has the construction of the Suez Canal. Of his early works the satirical *Departmental Ditties* (1886) attracted notice by the audacity of the allusions it contained, and by the originality of its tone. Also among the early productions are *Plain Tales from the Hills* (1888) and *Soldiers Three* (1888), collections of stories famous among other things for the three lovingly drawn soldier types: Mulvaney, Ortheris, and Learoyd. Other works in the same category are, for instance, *The Story of the Gadsbys* (1888), *In Black and White* (1888), and *Under the Deodars* (1889), all of which are concerned with society life in Simla. The series entitled *Life's Handicap,* embracing some stories of serious import, appeared in 1891. The same year saw the publication of *The Light that Failed,* a novel somewhat harsh in style but containing some strongly coloured descriptive passages of excellent effect.

As a poet Kipling was already full-fledged at the appearance of *Barrack-Room Ballads* (1892), magnificent soldier-songs brimming over with virile humour and depicting realistically Tommy Atkins in all his phases, valiantly marching onward to encounter dangers and misery wherever it pleases "the Widow of Windsor," or her successor on the throne, to dispatch him. In Kipling the British Army has found a minstrel to interpret in a new, original, and tragicomical manner the toils and deprivations through which it has to pass, and to depict its life and work with abundant acknowledgment of the great qualities it displays, but without the least trace of meretricious embellishment. In his verses descriptive of soldiers and sailors he so happily expresses their own thoughts, often in the very language they themselves employ, that they appreciate him deeply and, as we are told, sing his song whenever they have a pause in the day's occupations. Surely, there is hardly any greater mark of honour that can be given to a poet than to be beloved by the lower orders.

In the cycle entitled *The Seven Seas* (1896) Kipling reveals himself as an imperialist, a citizen of a worldwide empire. He has undoubtedly done more than any other writer of pure literature to draw tighter the bonds of union between England and her colonies.

In Sweden, as elsewhere, "the jungle books" by Kipling, the first of which appeared in 1894, are much admired and beloved. A primordial type of imaginative power inspired the creator of these mythlike tales of the animals in whose midst Mowgli waxed in strength: Bagheera the Black Panther, Baloo the Bear, Kaa the cunning and mighty Rock-Python, Nag the White Cobra, and the chattering, foolish Monkeys. Some of the scenes are simply sublime; for instance, the one where Mowgli is resting in "the living armchair" Kaa, while the latter, who has witnessed so many generations of trees and animals, dreams of bygone ages; or again when Mowgli causes Hathi the Elephant to "let in the jungle" to take over the fields of men. These descriptions display an instinctive feeling for a poetry of nature which is quite phenomenal, and Kipling is far more in his true element in the primeval grandeur of these jungle stories than, for instance, in "The Ship that Found Herself" (in *The Day's Work*, 1898), an interesting though eccentric personification of mechanical inventions. *The Jungle Book* tales have made Kipling a favourite author among children in many countries. Adults share the delight experienced by the young and relive their childhood while perusing these marvellously delightful, wonderfully imaginative fables of animals.

Among the large number of Kipling's creations, *Kim* (1901) deserves special notice, for in the delineation of the Buddhist priest, who goes on a pilgrimage along the banks of the stream that purifies from sin, there is an elevated diction as well as a tenderness and charm which are otherwise unusual traits in this dashing writer's style. There is, too, in the figure of the little rascal Kim, the priest's chela, a thorough type of good-humoured roguishness.

The accusation has occasionally been made against Kipling that his language is at times somewhat coarse and that his use of soldier's slang in some of the broadest of his songs and ballads verges on the vulgar. Though there may be some truth in such remarks, their importance is offset by the invigorating directness and ethical stimulus of Kipling's style. He has won immense popularity, not only in the Anglo-Indian world, which possesses in him a great literary master, but also far beyond the limits of the vast British Empire. During his serious illness in America in 1899, the American newspapers issued daily bulletins regarding his condition, and the German Emperor dispatched a telegram to his wife to express his earnest sympathy.

What is then the cause of this world-wide popularity that Kipling enjoys? Or, rather: In what way has Kipling shown himself to deserve it? How is it, too, that he has been deemed worthy of the Nobel Prize in Literature, for which a writer must especially show an idealism in his conceptions and in his art? The answer follows:

Kipling may not be eminent essentially for the profundity of his thought or for the surpassing wisdom of his meditations. Yet even the most cursory observer sees immediately his absolutely unique power of observation, capable of reproducing with astounding accuracy the minutest detail from real life. However, the gift of observation alone, be it ever so closely true to nature, would not suffice as a qualification in this instance. There is something else by which his poetical gifts are revealed. His marvellous power of imagination enables him to give us not only copies from nature but also visions out of his own inner consciousness. His landscapes appear to the inner vision as sudden apparitions do to the eye. In sketching a personality he makes clear, almost in his first words, the peculiar traits of that person's character and temper. Creativeness which does not rest content with merely photographing the temporary phases of things but desires to penetrate to their inmost kernel and soul, is the basis of his literary activity, as Kipling himself says: "He draws the thing as he sees it for the God of things as they are." In these weighty words lies a real appreciation of the poet's responsibility in the exercise of his calling.

Rudyard Kipling's manly, at times brusque, energy does not preclude tenderness and delicacy of touch, though these qualities never clamour affectedly for recognition in his works. The simple "Story of Muhammad Din" is imbued with the poetry of genuine heartfelt emotion, and who can ever forget the little drummer boys in "The Taking of Lungtumpen" (in *Plain Tales*)?

In the innermost being of this indefatigable observer of life and human nature vibrate strings attuned to a lofty note. His poem "To the True Romance" reveals that yearning for a patiently sought, never to be attained ideal that resides in living form in the breast of every true poet, from where the scenes and impressions of the sensuous world can never dislodge it:

> Enough for me in dreams to see
> And touch thy garment's hem:
> Thy feet have trod so near to God
> I may not follow them!

This writer's philosophy of life is diffused with a piety characteristic of the Old Testament, or rather perhaps of Puritan times, wholly devoid of pretentiousness or wordiness, based upon a conviction that "the fear of the Lord is the beginning of wisdom" and that there exists a

> God of our fathers, known of old,
> Beneath whose awful Hand we hold
> Dominion. . . .

If Kipling is an idealist from an aesthetic point of view by reason of poetical intuition, he is so, too, from an ethical-religious standpoint by virtue of his sense of duty, which has its inspiration in a faith firmly rooted in conviction. He is acutely conscious of the truth that even the mightiest states would perish unless they rested upon the sure foundation in the citizens' hearts of a loyal observance of the law and a reasoned self-restraint. For Kipling, God is first and foremost Almighty Providence, termed in *Life's Handicap* a "Greet Overseer." The English as a nation can well appreciate these conceptions, and Kipling has become the nation's poet, owing not only to his numerous highly prized soldier-songs, but perhaps quite as much to the brief lines of the hymn ("Recessional") which he composed on the occasion of Queen Victoria's Diamond Jubilee in 1897. Especially striking are these words expressing genuine and humble religious feelings:

> The tumult and the shouting dies;
> The Captains and the Kings depart:
> Still stands Thine ancient sacrifice,
> An humble and a contrite heart.

The recessional hymn voices the spirit of national pride, yet it also conveys a warning against the dangers of presumptuous pride. . . .

Quite naturally, during the Boer War Kipling sided with his own nation, the English. He has, however, done full justice to the heroic courage of the Boers, for his imperialism is not of the uncompromising type that pays no regard to the sentiments of others.

Many and varied are the movements that have had their vogue in English literature, a literature unparalleled for wealth of output and adorned to surpass all others by the immortal figure of Shakespeare. In Kipling may be traced perhaps more of Swift and Defoe than of Spenser, Keats, Shelley, or Tennyson. Clearly, however, imagination is as strong in him as empirical observation. Though he does not possess the refined and sensuously beautiful style of Swinburne, yet he escapes, on the other hand, all tendency toward a pagan worship of pleasure for pleasure's sake. He avoids all morbid sentimentality in matter and Alexandrian superflorescence in form.

Kipling favours concreteness and concentration; empty abstractions and circumlocutionary descriptions are wholly absent from his works. He has a knack for finding the telling phrase, the characteristic epithet, with swift accuracy and certainty. He has been compared now to Bret Harte, now to Pierre Loti, now to Dickens; he is, however, always original, and it would seem that his powers of invention are inexhaustible. Nevertheless, the apostle of the imagination is likewise, as stated above, the standard-bearer of law-abidingness and discipline. The Laws of the Jungle are the Laws of the Universe; if we ask what their chief purport is, we shall receive the brief answer: "Struggle, Duty, Obedience." Kipling thus advocates courage, self-sacrifice, and loyalty; unmanliness and lack of self-discipline are abominations to him, and in the world order he perceives a nemesis before which presumption is constrained to surrender.

If Kipling is quite independent as a writer, it does not follow that he has learned nothing from others; even the greatest masters have done so. With Bret Harte, Kipling shares his appreciation of the picturesqueness of vagabond life, and with Defoe his accuracy in depicting every detail and his sense of the values of exactness in the use of terms and phrases. Like Dickens he feels a keen sympathy with those of low degree in the community, and like him he can perceive the humour in trifling traits and acts. But his style is distinctively original and personal. It accomplishes its ends by suggestion rather than by description. It is not quite uniformly brilliant but it is always eminently expressive and picturesque. The series *From Sea to Sea* (1899) is a veritable model of graphic description, whether the scene is laid in the Elephant City governed by the Grand Divinity of Laziness, in Palm Island, or in Singapore, or whether the story deals with manners and customs of Japan. Kipling has at his command a large fund of irony—sometimes highly pungent—but he has abundant resources of sympathy, too, sympathy for the most part extended to those soldiers and sailors who have upheld the honour of England in far-distant lands. He has every right and reason to tell them: "I have eaten your bread and your salt, I have drunk your water and wine, I have lived your life, I have watched o'er your beds of death."

He attained fame and success as a very young man, but he has continued to develop ever since. One of his biographers has stated that there are three "notes" to be traced in his authorship. The satirical note is found in *Departmental Ditties, Plain Tales from the Hills, The Story of the Gadsbys,* with its amusing commendation of single blessedness, and in the much-debated novel, *The Light that Failed.* The second, the note of sympathy and human kindness, is most clearly marked in "The Story of Muhammad Din" and in "Without Benefit of Clergy" (in *Life's Handicap*), a gem of heartfelt emotion. The third, the ethical note, is clearly traceable in *Life's Handicap.* Whether there be much value or not in this classification which, as is usually the case in such matters, cannot be consistently applied to the whole of his production, one thing is certain: Kipling has written and sung of faithful labour, fulfilment of duty, and love of one's country. Love of one's country with Kipling does not mean solely devotion to the island kingdom of England, but rather an enthusiastic affection for the British Empire. The closer uniting of that Empire's separate members is a long and fervently cherished aspiration of the poet's. That is surely clear from his exclamation: "What should they know of England who only England know?"

Kipling has given us descriptions in vivid colours of many different countries. But the picturesque surface of things has not been the principal matter with him; he has always, in all places, had a manly ideal before him: ever to be "ready, ay ready at the call of duty" and then, when the appointed time comes, to "go to God like a soldier."

The Swedish Academy, in awarding the Nobel Prize in Literature this year to Rudyard Kipling, desires to pay a tribute of homage to the literature of England, so rich in manifold glories, and to the greatest genius in the realm of narrative that that country has produced in our times.

[© The Nobel Foundation, 1907.]

Nobel Prize Laureates in Literature, 1901–2005

1901: Sully Prudhomme (France)
1902: Theodor Mommsen (Germany; born Denmark)
1903: Bjørnstjerne Bjørnson (Norway)
1904: Frédéric Mistral (France) and José Echegaray (Spain)
1905: Henryk Sienkiewicz (Poland)
1906: Giosuè Carducci (Italy)
1907: Rudyard Kipling (United Kingdom; born Bombay, British India)
1908: Rudolf Eucken (Germany)
1909: Selma Lagerlöf (Sweden)
1910: Paul Heyse (Germany)
1911: Maurice Maeterlinck (Belgium)
1912: Gerhart Hauptmann (Germany)
1913: Rabindranath Tagore (India)
1914: No prize was awarded
1915: Romain Rolland (France)
1916: Verner von Heidenstam (Sweden)
1917: Karl Gjellerup (Denmark) and Henrik Pontoppidan (Denmark)
1918: No prize was awarded
1919: Carl Spitteler (Switzerland)
1920: Knut Hamsun (Norway)
1921: Anatole France (France)
1922: Jacinto Benavente (Spain)
1923: William Butler Yeats (Ireland)
1924: Władysław Reymont (Poland)
1925: George Bernard Shaw (United Kingdom; born Ireland)
1926: Grazia Deledda (Italy; born Sardinia)
1927: Henri Bergson (France)
1928: Sigrid Undset (Norway; born Denmark)
1929: Thomas Mann (Germany)
1930: Sinclair Lewis (United States)
1931: Erik Axel Karlfeldt (Sweden)
1932: John Galsworthy (United Kingdom)
1933: Ivan Bunin (stateless; domicile in France; born Russia)
1934: Luigi Pirandello (Italy)
1935: No prize was awarded
1936: Eugene O'Neill (United States)
1937: Roger Martin du Gard (France)
1938: Pearl S. Buck (United States)
1939: Frans Eemil Sillanpää (Finland)
1940: No prize was awarded
1941: No prize was awarded
1942: No prize was awarded
1943: No prize was awarded
1944: Johannes V. Jensen (Denmark)
1945: Gabriela Mistral (Chile)
1946: Hermann Hesse (Switzerland; born Germany)
1947: André Gide (France)
1948: T. S. Eliot (United Kingdom; born United States)
1949: William Faulkner (United States)
1950: Bertrand Russell (United Kingdom)
1951: Pär Lagerkvist (Sweden)
1952: François Mauriac (France)
1953: Sir Winston Churchill (United Kingdom)
1954: Ernest Hemingway (United States)
1955: Halldór Laxness (Iceland)
1956: Juan Ramón Jiménez (Spain)
1957: Albert Camus (France; born Algeria)
1958: Boris Pasternak (USSR)
1959: Salvatore Quasimodo (Italy)
1960: Saint-John Perse (France; born Guadeloupe Island)
1961: Ivo Andrić (Yugoslavia; born Bosnia)
1962: John Steinbeck (United States)
1963: Giorgos Seferis (Greece; born Turkey)
1964: Jean-Paul Sartre (France)
1965: Mikhail Sholokhov (USSR)
1966: Shmuel Yosef Agnon (Israel) and Nelly Sachs (Sweden; born Germany)
1967: Miguel Ángel Asturias (Guatemala)
1968: Yasunari Kawabata (Japan)
1969: Samuel Beckett (Ireland)
1970: Aleksandr Solzhenitsyn (USSR)
1971: Pablo Neruda (Chile)
1972: Heinrich Böll (Federal Republic of Germany)
1973: Patrick White (Australia; born United Kingdom)
1974: Eyvind Johnson (Sweden) and Harry Martinson (Sweden)
1975: Eugenio Montale (Italy)
1976: Saul Bellow (United States; born Canada)
1977: Vicente Aleixandre (Spain)
1978: Isaac Bashevis Singer (United States; born Poland)

1979: Odysseus Elytis (Greece)
1980: Czesław Miłosz (Poland/United States)
1981: Elias Canetti (United Kingdom; born Bulgaria)
1982: Gabriel García Márquez (Colombia)
1983: William Golding (United Kingdom)
1984: Jaroslav Seifert (Czechoslovakia)
1985: Claude Simon (France)
1986: Wole Soyinka (Nigeria)
1987: Joseph Brodsky (United States; born USSR)
1988: Najīb Mahfūz (Egypt)
1989: Camilo José Cela (Spain)
1990: Octavio Paz (Mexico)
1991: Nadine Gordimer (South Africa)
1992: Derek Walcott (Saint Lucia)
1993: Toni Morrison (United States)
1994: Kenzaburō Ōe (Japan)
1995: Seamus Heaney (Ireland)
1996: Wisława Szymborska (Poland)
1997: Dario Fo (Italy)
1998: José Saramago (Portugal)
1999: Günter Grass (Federal Republic of Germany)
2000: Gao Xingjian (France; born China)
2001: V. S. Naipaul (United Kingdom; born Trinidad)
2002: Imre Kertész (Hungary)
2003: J. M. Coetzee (South Africa)
2004: Elfriede Jelinek (Austria)
2005: Harold Pinter (United Kingdom)

Contributors

Ann-Charlotte Gavel Adams . . . . *University of Washington*
Andrea Bisicchia . . . . *University of Padua*
Catharine Savage Brosman . . . . *Tulane University*
Brendan Corcoran. . . . . *Indiana State University*
Roy C. Cowen. . . . . *University of Michigan*
Steve Dowden . . . . *Brandeis University*
Éva Forgács . . . . *Art Center College of Design, Pasadena*
Van C. Gessel . . . . *Brigham Young University*
Donald Gray . . . . *Indiana University*
Charles H. Helmetag. . . . . *Villanova University*
Poul Houe . . . . *University of Minnesota*
Mabel Lee . . . . *University of Sydney*
Sigrid Mayer . . . . *University of Wyoming*
Joseph Mileck . . . . *University of California, Berkeley*
Harald Næss . . . . *University of Wisconsin–Madison*
Paul Norlén. . . . . *University of Washington*
Michael C. Prusse . . . . *Pädagogische Hochschule Zürich, Zurich University of Applied Sciences, School of Education*
Sven Hakon Rossel . . . . *University of Vienna*
Hans H. Skei. . . . . *University of Oslo*
Rowland Smith . . . . *University of Calgary*
Sanford Sternlicht . . . . *Syracuse University*
John C. Unrue. . . . .
Raymond Leslie Williams . . . . *University of California, Riverside*
Monica Setterwall Wranne . . . . *The Eyvind Johnson Society, Stockholm*
Howard T. Young . . . . *Pomona College*

Cumulative Index

Dictionary of Literary Biography, Volumes 1-330
Dictionary of Literary Biography Yearbook, 1980-2002
Dictionary of Literary Biography Documentary Series, Volumes 1-19
Concise Dictionary of American Literary Biography, Volumes 1-7
Concise Dictionary of British Literary Biography, Volumes 1-8
Concise Dictionary of World Literary Biography, Volumes 1-4

Cumulative Index

DLB before number: *Dictionary of Literary Biography*, Volumes 1-330
Y before number: *Dictionary of Literary Biography Yearbook*, 1980-2002
DS before number: *Dictionary of Literary Biography Documentary Series*, Volumes 1-19
CDALB before number: *Concise Dictionary of American Literary Biography*, Volumes 1-7
CDBLB before number: *Concise Dictionary of British Literary Biography*, Volumes 1-8
CDWLB before number: *Concise Dictionary of World Literary Biography*, Volumes 1-4

A

Aakjær, Jeppe 1866-1930 ....DLB-214
Aarestrup, Emil 1800-1856 ....DLB-300
Abbey, Edward 1927-1989 ....DLB-256, 275
Abbey, Edwin Austin 1852-1911 ....DLB-188
Abbey, Maj. J. R. 1894-1969 ....DLB-201
Abbey Press DLB-49
The Abbey Theatre and Irish Drama, 1900-1945 ....DLB-10
Abbot, Willis J. 1863-1934............DLB-29
Abbott, Edwin A. 1838-1926 ....DLB-178
Abbott, Jacob 1803-1879 ....DLB-1, 42, 243
Abbott, Lee K. 1947- DLB-130
Abbott, Lyman 1835-1922..............DLB-79
Abbott, Robert S. 1868-1940.........DLB-29, 91
'Abd al-Hamid al-Katib circa 689-750 ....DLB-311
Abe Kōbō 1924-1993.................DLB-182
Abelaira, Augusto 1926- DLB-287
Abelard, Peter circa 1079-1142? DLB-115, 208
Abelard-Schuman.....................DLB-46
Abell, Arunah S. 1806-1888..........DLB-43
Abell, Kjeld 1901-1961 ....DLB-214
Abercrombie, Lascelles 1881-1938........DLB-19
   The Friends of the Dymock Poets........Y-00
Aberdeen University Press Limited DLB-106
Abish, Walter 1931- DLB-130, 227
Ablesimov, Aleksandr Onisimovich 1742-1783........................DLB-150
Abraham à Sancta Clara 1644-1709......DLB-168
Abrahams, Peter 1919- DLB-117, 225; CDWLB-3
Abramov, Fedor Aleksandrovich 1920-1983 ....DLB-302
Abrams, M. H. 1912- DLB-67
Abramson, Jesse 1904-1979 ....DLB-241
Abrogans circa 790-800 ....DLB-148
Abschatz, Hans Aßmann von 1646-1699 ....DLB-168

Abse, Dannie 1923- DLB-27, 245
Abu al-'Atahiyah 748-825?.............DLB-311
Abu Nuwas circa 757-814 or 815 ....DLB-311
Abu Tammam circa 805-845 ....DLB-311
Abutsu-ni 1221-1283 ....DLB-203
Academy Chicago Publishers DLB-46
Accius circa 170 B.C.-circa 80 B.C. DLB-211
"An account of the death of the Chevalier de La Barre," Voltaire DLB-314
Accrocca, Elio Filippo 1923-1996........DLB-128
Ace Books DLB-46
Achebe, Chinua 1930- DLB-117; CDWLB-3
Achtenberg, Herbert 1938- DLB-124
Ackerman, Diane 1948- DLB-120
Ackroyd, Peter 1949- DLB-155, 231
Acorn, Milton 1923-1986..............DLB-53
Acosta, José de 1540-1600 ....DLB-318
Acosta, Oscar Zeta 1935?-1974? DLB-82
Acosta Torres, José 1925- DLB-209
Actors Theatre of Louisville DLB-7
Adair, Gilbert 1944- DLB-194
Adair, James 1709?-1783?.............DLB-30
Aðalsteinn Kristmundsson (see Steinn Steinarr)
Adam, Graeme Mercer 1839-1912 ....DLB-99
Adam, Robert Borthwick, II 1863-1940 ....DLB-187
Adame, Leonard 1947- DLB-82
Adameşteanu, Gabriel 1942- DLB-232
Adamic, Louis 1898-1951 ....DLB-9
Adamov, Arthur Surenovitch 1908-1970 ....DLB-321
Adamovich, Georgii 1894-1972 ....DLB-317
Adams, Abigail 1744-1818 ....DLB-183, 200
Adams, Alice 1926-1999 .... DLB-234; Y-86
Adams, Bertha Leith (Mrs. Leith Adams, Mrs. R. S. de Courcy Laffan) 1837?-1912 ....DLB-240
Adams, Brooks 1848-1927 ....DLB-47
Adams, Charles Francis, Jr. 1835-1915 ....DLB-47

Adams, Douglas 1952-2001........ DLB-261; Y-83
Adams, Franklin P. 1881-1960..........DLB-29
Adams, Glenda 1939- DLB-325
Adams, Hannah 1755-1832 ....DLB-200
Adams, Henry 1838-1918 .... DLB-12, 47, 189
Adams, Herbert Baxter 1850-1901 ....DLB-47
Adams, James Truslow 1878-1949 .... DLB-17; DS-17
Adams, John 1735-1826.............DLB-31, 183
Adams, John Quincy 1767-1848..........DLB-37
Adams, Léonie 1899-1988 ....DLB-48
Adams, Levi 1802-1832................DLB-99
Adams, Richard 1920- DLB-261
Adams, Samuel 1722-1803.............DLB-31, 43
Adams, Sarah Fuller Flower 1805-1848 ....DLB-199
Adams, Thomas 1582/1583-1652 ....DLB-151
Adams, William Taylor 1822-1897 ....DLB-42
J. S. and C. Adams [publishing house].....DLB-49
Adamson, Harold 1906-1980..........DLB-265
Adamson, Sir John 1867-1950 ....DLB-98
Adamson, Robert 1943- DLB-289
Adcock, Arthur St. John 1864-1930 ....DLB-135
Adcock, Betty 1938- DLB-105
   "Certain Gifts" DLB-105
   Tribute to James Dickey Y-97
Adcock, Fleur 1934- DLB-40
Addams, Jane 1860-1935..............DLB-303
Addison, Joseph 1672-1719 ....DLB-101; CDBLB-2
Ade, George 1866-1944.............DLB-11, 25
Adeler, Max (see Clark, Charles Heber)
Adlard, Mark 1932- DLB-261
Adler, Richard 1921- DLB-265
Adonias Filho (Adonias Aguiar Filho) 1915-1990 ....DLB-145, 307
Adorno, Theodor W. 1903-1969........DLB-242
Adoum, Jorge Enrique 1926- DLB-283

Advance Publishing Company DLB-49	Ahlin, Lars 1915-1997 . . . . DLB-257	Alden, Henry Mills 1836-1919 . . . . DLB-79
Ady, Endre 1877-1919 . . . . . . DLB-215; CDWLB-4	Ai 1947- DLB-120	Alden, Isabella 1841-1930 . . . . DLB-42
AE 1867-1935 . . . . DLB-19; CDBLB-5	Ai Wu 1904-1992 . . . . DLB-328	John B. Alden [publishing house] DLB-49
Ælfric circa 955-circa 1010 . . . . DLB-146	Aichinger, Ilse 1921- DLB-85, 299	Alden, Beardsley, and Company DLB-49
Aeschines circa 390 B.C.-circa 320 B.C. DLB-176	Aickman, Robert 1914-1981 . . . . DLB-261	Aldington, Richard 1892-1962 . . . . DLB-20, 36, 100, 149
Aeschylus 525-524 B.C.-456-455 B.C. DLB-176; CDWLB-1	Aidoo, Ama Ata 1942- DLB-117; CDWLB-3	Aldis, Dorothy 1896-1966 . . . . DLB-22
Aesthetic Papers DLB-1	Aiken, Conrad 1889-1973 . . . . DLB-9, 45, 102; CDALB-5	Aldis, H. G. 1863-1919 . . . . DLB-184
Aesthetics Eighteenth-Century Aesthetic Theories DLB-31	Aiken, Joan 1924-2004 . . . . DLB-161	Aldiss, Brian W. 1925- DLB-14, 261, 271
African Literature Letter from Khartoum Y-90	Aikin, Lucy 1781-1864 . . . . DLB-144, 163	Aldrich, Thomas Bailey 1836-1907 . . . . DLB-42, 71, 74, 79
African American Afro-American Literary Critics: An Introduction DLB-33	Ainsworth, William Harrison 1805-1882 . . . . DLB-21	Alegría, Ciro 1909-1967 . . . . DLB-113
	Aïssé, Charlotte-Elizabeth 1694?-1733 . . . DLB-313	Alegría, Claribel 1924- DLB-145, 283
The Black Aesthetic: Background DS-8	Aistis, Jonas 1904-1973 . . . . . DLB-220; CDWLB-4	Aleixandre, Vicente 1898-1984 . . . . . DLB-108, 329
The Black Arts Movement, by Larry Neal DLB-38	Aitken, Adam 1960- DLB-325	Aleksandravičius, Jonas (see Aistis, Jonas)
Black Theaters and Theater Organizations in America, 1961-1982: A Research List DLB-38	Aitken, George A. 1860-1917 . . . . DLB-149	Aleksandrov, Aleksandr Andreevich (see Durova, Nadezhda Andreevna)
	Robert Aitken [publishing house] DLB-49	Alekseeva, Marina Anatol'evna (see Marinina, Aleksandra)
Black Theatre: A Forum [excerpts] . . . DLB-38	Aitmatov, Chingiz 1928- DLB-302	d'Alembert, Jean Le Rond 1717-1783 . . . . DLB-313
Callaloo [journal] Y-87	Akenside, Mark 1721-1770 . . . . DLB-109	Alencar, José de 1829-1877 . . . . DLB-307
Community and Commentators: Black Theatre and Its Critics DLB-38	Akhmatova, Anna Andreevna 1889-1966 . . . . DLB-295	Aleramo, Sibilla (Rena Pierangeli Faccio) 1876-1960 . . . . DLB-114, 264
The Emergence of Black Women Writers DS-8	Akins, Zoë 1886-1958 . . . . DLB-26	Aleshkovsky, Petr Markovich 1957- . . . DLB-285
	Aksakov, Ivan Sergeevich 1823-1826 . . . . . DLB-277	Aleshkovsky, Yuz 1929- DLB-317
The Hatch-Billops Collection DLB-76	Aksakov, Sergei Timofeevich 1791-1859 . . . . DLB-198	Alexander, Cecil Frances 1818-1895 . . . . . DLB-199
A Look at the Contemporary Black Theatre Movement DLB-38	Aksyonov, Vassily 1932- DLB-302	Alexander, Charles 1868-1923 . . . . DLB-91
The Moorland-Spingarn Research Center DLB-76	Akunin, Boris (Grigorii Shalvovich Chkhartishvili) 1956- DLB-285	Charles Wesley Alexander [publishing house] DLB-49
"The Negro as a Writer," by G. M. McClellan DLB-50	Akutagawa Ryūnosuke 1892-1927 . . . . . . DLB-180	Alexander, James 1691-1756 . . . . DLB-24
"Negro Poets and Their Poetry," by Wallace Thurman DLB-50	Alabaster, William 1568-1640 . . . . DLB-132	Alexander, Lloyd 1924- DLB-52
	Alain de Lille circa 1116-1202/1203 . . . . . DLB-208	Alexander, Meena 1951- DLB-323
Olaudah Equiano and Unfinished Journeys: The Slave-Narrative Tradition and Twentieth-Century Continuities, by Paul Edwards and Pauline T. Wangman DLB-117	Alain-Fournier 1886-1914 . . . . DLB-65	Alexander, Sir William, Earl of Stirling 1577?-1640 . . . . DLB-121
	Alanus de Insulis (see Alain de Lille)	
	Alarcón, Francisco X. 1954- DLB-122	Alexie, Sherman 1966- DLB-175, 206, 278
	Alarcón, Justo S. 1930- DLB-209	Alexis, Willibald 1798-1871 . . . . DLB-133
	Alba, Nanina 1915-1968 . . . . DLB-41	Alf laylah wa laylah ninth century onward DLB-311
PHYLON (Fourth Quarter, 1950), The Negro in Literature: The Current Scene DLB-76	Albee, Edward 1928- . . . DLB-7, 266; CDALB-1	Alfred, King 849-899 . . . . DLB-146
	Albert, Octavia 1853-ca. 1889 . . . . DLB-221	Alger, Horatio, Jr. 1832-1899 . . . . DLB-42
The Schomburg Center for Research in Black Culture DLB-76	Albert the Great circa 1200-1280 . . . . DLB-115	Algonquin Books of Chapel Hill DLB-46
	Alberti, Rafael 1902-1999 . . . . DLB-108	Algren, Nelson 1909-1981 . . . . DLB-9; Y-81, 82; CDALB-1
Three Documents [poets], by John Edward Bruce DLB-50	Albertinus, Aegidius circa 1560-1620 . . . . DLB-164	
After Dinner Opera Company Y-92	Alcaeus born circa 620 B.C. DLB-176	Nelson Algren: An International Symposium Y-00
Agassiz, Elizabeth Cary 1822-1907 . . . . . . DLB-189	Alcoforado, Mariana, the Portuguese Nun 1640-1723 . . . . DLB-287	Ali, Agha Shahid 1949-2001 . . . . DLB-323
Agassiz, Louis 1807-1873 . . . . DLB-1, 235	Alcott, Amos Bronson 1799-1888 . . . . DLB-1, 223; DS-5	Ali, Ahmed 1908-1994 . . . . DLB-323
Agee, James 1909-1955 . . . . . . DLB-2, 26, 152; CDALB-1		Ali, Monica 1967- DLB-323
	Alcott, Louisa May 1832-1888 . . . DLB-1, 42, 79, 223, 239; DS-14; CDALB-3	'Ali ibn Abi Talib circa 600-661 . . . . DLB-311
The Agee Legacy: A Conference at the University of Tennessee at Knoxville Y-89		Aljamiado Literature DLB-286
	Alcott, William Andrus 1798-1859 . . . . DLB-1, 243	Allan, Andrew 1907-1974 . . . . DLB-88
Agnon, Shmuel Yosef 1887-1970 . . . . DLB-329	Alcuin circa 732-804 . . . . DLB-148	Allan, Ted 1916-1995 . . . . DLB-68
Aguilera Malta, Demetrio 1909-1981 . . . . DLB-145	Aldana, Francisco de 1537-1578 . . . . DLB-318	
Aguirre, Isidora 1919- DLB-305	Aldanov, Mark (Mark Landau) 1886-1957 . . . . DLB-317	Allbeury, Ted 1917- DLB-87
Agustini, Delmira 1886-1914 . . . . DLB-290		Alldritt, Keith 1935- DLB-14

Allen, Dick 1939- DLB-282

Allen, Ethan 1738-1789 .... DLB-31

Allen, Frederick Lewis 1890-1954 .... DLB-137

Allen, Gay Wilson 1903-1995 ..... DLB-103; Y-95

Allen, George 1808-1876 .... DLB-59

Allen, Grant 1848-1899 .... DLB-70, 92, 178

Allen, Henry W. 1912-1991............... Y-85

Allen, Hervey 1889-1949......... DLB-9, 45, 316

Allen, James 1739-1808 .... DLB-31

Allen, James Lane 1849-1925............ DLB-71

Allen, Jay Presson 1922- DLB-26

John Allen and Company DLB-49

Allen, Paula Gunn 1939- DLB-175

Allen, Samuel W. 1917- DLB-41

Allen, Woody 1935- DLB-44

George Allen [publishing house] DLB-106

George Allen and Unwin Limited DLB-112

Allende, Isabel 1942- DLB-145; CDWLB-3

Alline, Henry 1748-1784 .... DLB-99

Allingham, Margery 1904-1966.......... DLB-77

The Margery Allingham Society........ Y-98

Allingham, William 1824-1889 .... DLB-35

W. L. Allison [publishing house] DLB-49

The *Alliterative Morte Arthure and the Stanzaic Morte Arthur* circa 1350-1400 .... DLB-146

Allott, Kenneth 1912-1973 .... DLB-20

Allston, Washington 1779-1843 .... DLB-1, 235

Almeida, Manuel Antônio de 1831-1861 .... DLB-307

John Almon [publishing house] DLB-154

Alonzo, Dámaso 1898-1990........... DLB-108

Alsop, George 1636-post 1673 .... DLB-24

Alsop, Richard 1761-1815 .... DLB-37

Henry Altemus and Company.......... DLB-49

Altenberg, Peter 1885-1919 .... DLB-81

Althusser, Louis 1918-1990 .... DLB-242

Altolaguirre, Manuel 1905-1959 .... DLB-108

Aluko, T. M. 1918- DLB-117

Alurista 1947- DLB-82

Alvarez, A. 1929- DLB-14, 40

Alvarez, Julia 1950- DLB-282

Alvaro, Corrado 1895-1956............. DLB-264

Alver, Betti 1906-1989 ...... DLB-220; CDWLB-4

Amadi, Elechi 1934- DLB-117

Amado, Jorge 1912-2001 .... DLB-113

Amalrik, Andrei 1938-1980..................... DLB-302

Ambler, Eric 1909-1998................ DLB-77

The Library of America................ DLB-46

The Library of America: An Assessment After Two Decades Y-02

America: or, A Poem on the Settlement of the British Colonies, by Timothy Dwight DLB-37

American Bible Society Department of Library, Archives, and Institutional Research Y-97

American Conservatory Theatre DLB-7

American Culture American Proletarian Culture: The Twenties and Thirties DS-11

Studies in American Jewish Literature........ Y-02

The American Library in Paris Y-93

American Literature The Literary Scene and Situation and . . . (Who Besides Oprah) Really Runs American Literature? Y-99

Who Owns American Literature, by Henry Taylor Y-94

Who Runs American Literature? Y-94

American News Company............. DLB-49

A Century of Poetry, a Lifetime of Collecting: J. M. Edelstein's Collection of Twentieth-Century American Poetry Y-02

The American Poets' Corner: The First Three Years (1983-1986) Y-86

American Publishing Company......... DLB-49

American Spectator [Editorial] Rationale From the Initial Issue of the American Spectator (November 1932)............... DLB-137

American Stationers' Company......... DLB-49

The American Studies Association of Norway...................... Y-00

American Sunday-School Union DLB-49

American Temperance Union DLB-49

American Tract Society............... DLB-49

The American Trust for the British Library ... Y-96

American Writers' Congress 25-27 April 1935 .... DLB-303

American Writers Congress The American Writers Congress (9-12 October 1981) Y-81

The American Writers Congress: A Report on Continuing Business Y-81

Ames, Fisher 1758-1808................ DLB-37

Ames, Mary Clemmer 1831-1884 .... DLB-23

Ames, William 1576-1633 .... DLB-281

Amfiteatrov, Aleksandr 1862-1938 ...... DLB-317

Amiel, Henri-Frédéric 1821-1881........ DLB-217

Amini, Johari M. 1935- DLB-41

Amis, Kingsley 1922-1995 ...DLB-15, 27, 100, 139, 326; Y-96; CDBLB-7

Amis, Martin 1949- DLB-14, 194

Ammianus Marcellinus circa A.D. 330-A.D. 395 .... DLB-211

Ammons, A. R. 1926-2001 .... DLB-5, 165

Amory, Thomas 1691?-1788 .... DLB-39

Amsterdam, 1998 Booker Prize winner, Ian McEwan DLB-326

Amyot, Jacques 1513-1593............. DLB-327

Anand, Mulk Raj 1905-2004 .... DLB-323

Anania, Michael 1939- DLB-193

Anaya, Rudolfo A. 1937- DLB-82, 206, 278

Ancrene Riwle circa 1200-1225........... DLB-146

Andersch, Alfred 1914-1980............. DLB-69

Andersen, Benny 1929- DLB-214

Andersen, Hans Christian 1805-1875 .... DLB-300

Anderson, Alexander 1775-1870 .... DLB-188

Anderson, David 1929- DLB-241

Anderson, Frederick Irving 1877-1947 .... DLB-202

Anderson, Jessica 1916- DLB-325

Anderson, Margaret 1886-1973 .... DLB-4, 91

Anderson, Maxwell 1888-1959 .... DLB-7, 228

Anderson, Patrick 1915-1979........... DLB-68

Anderson, Paul Y. 1893-1938 .... DLB-29

Anderson, Poul 1926-2001 .... DLB-8

Tribute to Isaac Asimov Y-92

Anderson, Robert 1750-1830........... DLB-142

Anderson, Robert 1917- DLB-7

Anderson, Sherwood 1876-1941 .... DLB-4, 9, 86; DS-1; CDALB-4

Andrade, Jorge (Aluísio Jorge Andrade Franco) 1922-1984 .... DLB-307

Andrade, Mario de 1893-1945.......... DLB-307

Andrade, Oswald de (José Oswald de Sousa Andrade) 1890-1954 .... DLB-307

Andreae, Johann Valentin 1586-1654 .... DLB-164

Andreas Capellanus fl. circa 1185 .... DLB-208

Andreas-Salomé, Lou 1861-1937......... DLB-66

Andreev, Leonid Nikolaevich 1871-1919 .... DLB-295

Andres, Stefan 1906-1970 .... DLB-69

Andresen, Sophia de Mello Breyner 1919- DLB-287

Andreu, Blanca 1959- DLB-134

Andrewes, Lancelot 1555-1626 ..... DLB-151, 172

Andrews, Charles M. 1863-1943........ DLB-17

Andrews, Miles Peter ?-1814 .... DLB-89

Andrews, Stephen Pearl 1812-1886...... DLB-250

Andrian, Leopold von 1875-1951 .... DLB-81

Andrić, Ivo 1892-1975 .... DLB-147, 329; CDWLB-4

Andrieux, Louis (see Aragon, Louis)

Andrus, Silas, and Son................ DLB-49

Andrzejewski, Jerzy 1909-1983 .... DLB-215

Angell, James Burrill 1829-1916 .... DLB-64

Angell, Roger 1920- DLB-171, 185

Angelou, Maya 1928- DLB-38; CDALB-7

Tribute to Julian Mayfield............. Y-84

Anger, Jane fl. 1589 .... DLB-136

Angers, Félicité (see Conan, Laure)

The Anglo-Saxon Chronicle
circa 890-1154 .... DLB-146

Angus and Robertson (UK) Limited DLB-112

Anhalt, Edward 1914-2000............. DLB-26

Anissimov, Myriam 1943- DLB-299

Anker, Nini Roll 1873-1942 .... DLB-297

Annenkov, Pavel Vasil'evich
1813?-1887.................... DLB-277

Annensky, Innokentii Fedorovich
1855-1909 .... DLB-295

Henry F. Anners [publishing house]...... DLB-49

Annolied between 1077 and 1081 .... DLB-148

Anouilh, Jean 1910-1987............... DLB-321

Anscombe, G. E. M. 1919-2001 .... DLB-262

Anselm of Canterbury 1033-1109....... DLB-115

Anstey, F. 1856-1934 .... DLB-141, 178

'Antarah ('Antar ibn Shaddad al-'Absi)
?-early seventh century?........... DLB-311

Anthologizing New Formalism DLB-282

Anthony, Michael 1932- DLB-125

Anthony, Piers 1934- DLB-8

Anthony, Susanna 1726-1791 .... DLB-200

Antin, David 1932- DLB-169

Antin, Mary 1881-1949 .... DLB-221; Y-84

Anton Ulrich, Duke of Brunswick-Lüneburg
1633-1714..................... DLB-168

Antschel, Paul (see Celan, Paul)

Antunes, António Lobo 1942- DLB-287

Anyidoho, Kofi 1947- DLB-157

Anzaldúa, Gloria 1942- DLB-122

Anzengruber, Ludwig 1839-1889 .... DLB-129

Apess, William 1798-1839.......... DLB-175, 243

Apodaca, Rudy S. 1939- DLB-82

Apollinaire, Guillaume 1880-1918 .. DLB-258, 321

Apollonius Rhodius third century B.C..... DLB-176

Apple, Max 1941- DLB-130

Appelfeld, Aharon 1932- DLB-299

D. Appleton and Company DLB-49

Appleton-Century-Crofts DLB-46

Applewhite, James 1935- DLB-105

Tribute to James Dickey............... Y-97

Apple-wood Books DLB-46

April, Jean-Pierre 1948- DLB-251

Apukhtin, Aleksei Nikolaevich
1840-1893 .... DLB-277

Apuleius circa A.D. 125-post A.D. 164
.... DLB-211; CDWLB-1

Aquin, Hubert 1929-1977............... DLB-53

Aquinas, Thomas 1224/1225-1274 ...... DLB-115

Aragon, Louis 1897-1982 .... DLB-72, 258

Aragon, Vernacular Translations in the
Crowns of Castile and 1352-1515 ... DLB-286

Aralica, Ivan 1930- DLB-181

Aratus of Soli
circa 315 B.C.-circa 239 B.C. DLB-176

Arbasino, Alberto 1930- DLB-196

Arbor House Publishing Company DLB-46

Arbuthnot, John 1667-1735............. DLB-101

Arcadia House DLB-46

Arce, Julio G. (see Ulica, Jorge)

Archer, William 1856-1924............. DLB-10

Archilochhus
mid seventh century B.C.E..........DLB-176

The Archpoet circa 1130?-? DLB-148

Archpriest Avvakum (Petrovich)
1620?-1682.................... DLB-150

Arden, John 1930- DLB-13, 245

Arden of Faversham DLB-62

Ardis Publishers Y-89

Ardizzone, Edward 1900-1979 .... DLB-160

Arellano, Juan Estevan 1947- DLB-122

The Arena Publishing Company DLB-49

Arena Stage...................... DLB-7

Arenas, Reinaldo 1943-1990............ DLB-145

Arendt, Hannah 1906-1975 .... DLB-242

Arensberg, Ann 1937- Y-82

Arghezi, Tudor 1880-1967 ... DLB-220; CDWLB-4

Arguedas, José María 1911-1969 .... DLB-113

Argüelles, Hugo 1932-2003 .... DLB-305

Argueta, Manlio 1936- DLB-145

'Arib al-Ma'muniyah 797-890 .... DLB-311

Arias, Ron 1941- DLB-82

Arishima Takeo 1878-1923............ DLB-180

Aristophanes circa 446 B.C.-circa 386 B.C.
.... DLB-176; CDWLB-1

Aristotle 384 B.C.-322 B.C.
.... DLB-176; CDWLB-1

Ariyoshi Sawako 1931-1984............ DLB-182

Arland, Marcel 1899-1986 .... DLB-72

Arlen, Michael 1895-1956 ....DLB-36, 77, 162

Arlt, Roberto 1900-1942............. DLB-305

Armah, Ayi Kwei 1939- ...DLB-117; CDWLB-3

Armantrout, Rae 1947- DLB-193

Der arme Hartmann ?-after 1150 .... DLB-148

Armed Services Editions............... DLB-46

Armitage, G. E. (Robert Edric) 1956- .. DLB-267

Armstrong, Martin Donisthorpe
1882-1974.................... DLB-197

Armstrong, Richard 1903-1986 .... DLB-160

Armstrong, Terence Ian Fytton (see Gawsworth, John)

Arnauld, Antoine 1612-1694 .... DLB-268

Arndt, Ernst Moritz 1769-1860......... DLB-90

Arnim, Achim von 1781-1831.......... DLB-90

Arnim, Bettina von 1785-1859 .... DLB-90

Arnim, Elizabeth von (Countess Mary Annette
Beauchamp Russell) 1866-1941 .... DLB-197

Arno Press DLB-46

Arnold, Edwin 1832-1904 .... DLB-35

Arnold, Edwin L. 1857-1935 ....DLB-178

Arnold, Matthew
1822-1888 .... DLB-32, 57; CDBLB-4

Preface to *Poems* (1853) DLB-32

Arnold, Thomas 1795-1842 .... DLB-55

Edward Arnold [publishing house]...... DLB-112

Arnott, Peter 1962- DLB-233

Arnow, Harriette Simpson 1908-1986 ..... DLB-6

Arp, Bill (see Smith, Charles Henry)

Arpino, Giovanni 1927-1987............DLB-177

Arrabal, Fernando 1932- DLB-321

Arrebo, Anders 1587-1637 .... DLB-300

Arreola, Juan José 1918-2001 .... DLB-113

Arrian circa 89-circa 155................DLB-176

J. W. Arrowsmith [publishing house] DLB-106

Arrufat, Antón 1935- DLB-305

Art
John Dos Passos: Artist Y-99

The First Post-Impressionist
Exhibition.....................DS-5

The Omega Workshops..............DS-10

The Second Post-Impressionist
Exhibition DS-5

Artaud, Antonin 1896-1948 .... DLB-258, 321

Artel, Jorge 1909-1994 .... DLB-283

Arthur, Timothy Shay
1809-1885 ....DLB-3, 42, 79, 250; DS-13

Artmann, H. C. 1921-2000............. DLB-85

Artsybashev, Mikhail Petrovich
1878-1927..................... DLB-295

Arvin, Newton 1900-1963 .... DLB-103

Asch, Nathan 1902-1964 .... DLB-4, 28

Nathan Asch Remembers Ford Madox
Ford, Sam Roth, and Hart Crane Y-02

Ascham, Roger 1515/1516-1568......... DLB-236

Aseev, Nikolai Nikolaevich
1889-1963 .... DLB-295

Ash, John 1948- DLB-40

Ashbery, John 1927- DLB-5, 165; Y-81

Ashbridge, Elizabeth 1713-1755 .... DLB-200

Ashburnham, Bertram Lord
1797-1878 .... DLB-184

Ashendene Press..................... DLB-112

Asher, Sandy 1942- Y-83

Ashton, Winifred (see Dane, Clemence)

Asimov, Isaac 1920-1992 ....DLB-8; Y-92

Tribute to John Ciardi Y-86

Askew, Anne circa 1521-1546......... DLB-136

Aspazija 1865-1943........ DLB-220; CDWLB-4

Asselin, Olivar 1874-1937............. DLB-92

The Association of American Publishers Y-99

The Association for Documentary Editing.... Y-00

The Association for the Study of
  Literature and Environment (ASLE)......Y-99
Astell, Mary 1666-1731 ....DLB-252
Astley, Thea 1925- DLB-289
Astley, William (see Warung, Price)
Asturias, Miguel Ángel
  1899-1974 ....DLB-113, 290, 329; CDWLB-3
Atava, S. (see Terpigorev, Sergei Nikolaevich)
Atheneum Publishers..................DLB-46
Atherton, Gertrude 1857-1948.....DLB-9, 78, 186
Athlone Press......................DLB-112
Atkins, Josiah circa 1755-1781 ....DLB-31
Atkins, Russell 1926- DLB-41
Atkinson, Kate 1951- DLB-267
Atkinson, Louisa 1834-1872...........DLB-230
The Atlantic Monthly Press............DLB-46
Attaway, William 1911-1986 ....DLB-76
Atwood, Margaret 1939- DLB-53, 251, 326
Aubert, Alvin 1930- DLB-41
Aub, Max 1903-1972.................DLB-322
Aubert de Gaspé, Phillipe-Ignace-François
  1814-1841 ....DLB-99
Aubert de Gaspé, Phillipe-Joseph
  1786-1871.......................DLB-99
Aubigné, Théodore Agrippa d'
  1552-1630......................DLB-327
Aubin, Napoléon 1812-1890 ....DLB-99
Aubin, Penelope
  1685-circa 1731 ....DLB-39
  Preface to *The Life of Charlotta
    du Pont* (1723) DLB-39
Aubrey-Fletcher, Henry Lancelot (see Wade, Henry)
Auchincloss, Louis 1917- DLB-2, 244; Y-80
Auden, W. H.
  1907-1973...........DLB-10, 20; CDBLB-6
Audiberti, Jacques 1899-1965 ....DLB-321
Audio Art in America: A Personal Memoir....Y-85
Audubon, John James 1785-1851........DLB-248
Audubon, John Woodhouse
  1812-1862 ....DLB-183
Auerbach, Berthold 1812-1882 ....DLB-133
Auernheimer, Raoul 1876-1948 ....DLB-81
Augier, Emile 1820-1889 ....DLB-192
Augustine 354-430...................DLB-115
Aulnoy, Marie-Catherine Le Jumel
  de Barneville, comtesse d'
  1650/1651-1705 ....DLB-268
Aulus Gellius
  circa A.D. 125-circa A.D. 180? DLB-211
Austen, Jane 1775-1817 ......DLB-116; CDBLB-3
Auster, Paul 1947- DLB-227
Austin, Alfred 1835-1913...............DLB-35
Austin, J. L. 1911-1960 ....DLB-262
Austin, Jane Goodwin 1831-1894 ....DLB-202
Austin, John 1790-1859 ....DLB-262

Austin, Mary Hunter
  1868-1934 ....DLB-9, 78, 206, 221, 275
Austin, William 1778-1841..............DLB-74
Australie (Emily Manning)
  1845-1890 ....DLB-230
Authors and Newspapers Association DLB-46
Authors' Publishing Company...........DLB-49
Avallone, Michael 1924-1999 .....DLB-306; Y-99
  Tribute to John D. MacDonald Y-86
  Tribute to Kenneth Millar Y-83
  Tribute to Raymond Chandler Y-88
Avalon Books DLB-46
Avancini, Nicolaus 1611-1686..........DLB-164
Avendaño, Fausto 1941- DLB-82
Averroës 1126-1198..................DLB-115
Avery, Gillian 1926- DLB-161
Avicenna 980-1037 ....DLB-115
Ávila Jiménez, Antonio 1898-1965 .....DLB-283
Avison, Margaret 1918-1987 ....DLB-53
Avon Books........................DLB-46
Avyžius, Jonas 1922-1999 ....DLB-220
Awdry, Wilbert Vere 1911-1997 ....DLB-160
Awoonor, Kofi 1935- DLB-117
Ayala, Francisco 1906- DLB-322
Ayckbourn, Alan 1939- DLB-13, 245
Ayer, A. J. 1910-1989.................DLB-262
Aymé, Marcel 1902-1967...............DLB-72
Aytoun, Sir Robert 1570-1638 ....DLB-121
Aytoun, William Edmondstoune
  1813-1865 ....DLB-32, 159
Azevedo, Aluísio 1857-1913............DLB-307
Azevedo, Manuel Antônio Álvares de
  1831-1852 ....DLB-307
Azorín (José Martínez Ruiz)
  1873-1967 ....DLB-322

B

B.V. (see Thomson, James)
Ba Jin 1904-2005 ....DLB-328
Babbitt, Irving 1865-1933 ....DLB-63
Babbitt, Natalie 1932- DLB-52
John Babcock [publishing house].........DLB-49
Babel, Isaak Emmanuilovich
  1894-1940 ....DLB-272
Babits, Mihály 1883-1941 ...DLB-215; CDWLB-4
Babrius circa 150-200.................DLB-176
Babson, Marian 1929- DLB-276
Baca, Jimmy Santiago 1952- DLB-122
Bacchelli, Riccardo 1891-1985 ....DLB-264
Bache, Benjamin Franklin 1769-1798......DLB-43
Bachelard, Gaston 1884-1962 ....DLB-296
Bacheller, Irving 1859-1950 ....DLB-202
Bachmann, Ingeborg 1926-1973 ....DLB-85

Bačinskaitė-Bučienė, Salomėja (see Nėris, Salomėja)
Bacon, Delia 1811-1859..............DLB-1, 243
Bacon, Francis
  1561-1626 ....DLB-151, 236, 252; CDBLB-1
Bacon, Sir Nicholas circa 1510-1579 .....DLB-132
Bacon, Roger circa 1214/1220-1292 .....DLB-115
Bacon, Thomas circa 1700-1768.........DLB-31
Bacovia, George
  1881-1957 ....DLB-220; CDWLB-4
Richard G. Badger and Company DLB-49
Bagaduce Music Lending Library Y-00
Bage, Robert 1728-1801................DLB-39
Bagehot, Walter 1826-1877 ....DLB-55
Baggesen, Jens 1764-1826 ....DLB-300
Bagley, Desmond 1923-1983 ....DLB-87
Bagley, Sarah G. 1806-1848?...........DLB-239
Bagnold, Enid
  1889-1981 ....DLB-13, 160, 191, 245
Bagryana, Elisaveta
  1893-1991 ....DLB-147; CDWLB-4
Bahr, Hermann 1863-1934 ....DLB-81, 118
Baïf, Jean-Antoine de 1532-1589 ....DLB-327
Bail, Murray 1941- DLB-325
Bailey, Abigail Abbot
  1746-1815 ....DLB-200
Bailey, Alfred Goldsworthy 1905-1997 ....DLB-68
Bailey, H. C. 1878-1961 ....DLB-77
Bailey, Jacob 1731-1808 ....DLB-99
Bailey, Paul 1937- DLB-14, 271
Bailey, Philip James 1816-1902 ....DLB-32
Francis Bailey [publishing house].........DLB-49
Baillargeon, Pierre 1916-1967 ....DLB-88
Baillie, Hugh 1890-1966 ....DLB-29
Baillie, Joanna 1762-1851 ....DLB-93
Bailyn, Bernard 1922- DLB-17
Bain, Alexander
  English Composition and Rhetoric (1866)
    [excerpt] DLB-57
Bainbridge, Beryl 1933- DLB-14, 231
Baird, Irene 1901-1981 ....DLB-68
Baker, Augustine 1575-1641.............DLB-151
Baker, Carlos 1909-1987 ....DLB-103
Baker, David 1954- DLB-120
Baker, George Pierce 1866-1935 ....DLB-266
Baker, Herschel C. 1914-1990...........DLB-111
Baker, Houston A., Jr. 1943- DLB-67
Baker, Howard
  Tribute to Caroline Gordon Y-81
  Tribute to Katherine Anne Porter Y-80
Baker, Nicholson 1957- DLB-227; Y-00
  Review of Nicholson Baker's *Double Fold:
    Libraries and the Assault on Paper* Y-00
Baker, Samuel White 1821-1893 ....DLB-166
Baker, Thomas 1656-1740 ....DLB-213

Walter H. Baker Company ("Baker's Plays") DLB-49

The Baker and Taylor Company DLB-49

Bakhtin, Mikhail Mikhailovich 1895-1975..................... DLB-242

Bakunin, Mikhail Aleksandrovich 1814-1876..................... DLB-277

Balaban, John 1943- DLB-120

Bald, Wambly 1902-1990............... DLB-4

Balde, Jacob 1604-1668............... DLB-164

Balderston, John 1889-1954 .... DLB-26

Baldwin, James 1924-1987 ..... DLB-2, 7, 33, 249, 278; Y-87; CDALB-1

Baldwin, Joseph Glover 1815-1864................ DLB-3, 11, 248

Baldwin, Louisa (Mrs. Alfred Baldwin) 1845-1925..................... DLB-240

Baldwin, William circa 1515-1563 ...... DLB-132

Richard and Anne Baldwin [publishing house] DLB-170

Bale, John 1495-1563 .... DLB-132

Balestrini, Nanni 1935- DLB-128, 196

Balfour, Sir Andrew 1630-1694 .... DLB-213

Balfour, Arthur James 1848-1930 .... DLB-190

Balfour, Sir James 1600-1657 .... DLB-213

Ballantine Books..................... DLB-46

Ballantyne, R. M. 1825-1894 .... DLB-163

Ballard, J. G. 1930- DLB-14, 207, 261, 319

Ballard, Martha Moore 1735-1812 ...... DLB-200

Ballerini, Luigi 1940- DLB-128

Ballou, Maturin Murray (Lieutenant Murray) 1820-1895 .... DLB-79, 189

Robert O. Ballou [publishing house] DLB-46

Bal'mont, Konstantin Dmitrievich 1867-1942..................... DLB-295

Balzac, Guez de 1597?-1654 .... DLB-268

Balzac, Honoré de 1799-1855 .... DLB-119

Bambara, Toni Cade 1939-1995 .... DLB-38, 218; CDALB-7

Bamford, Samuel 1788-1872 .... DLB-190

A. L. Bancroft and Company DLB-49

Bancroft, George 1800-1891... DLB-1, 30, 59, 243

Bancroft, Hubert Howe 1832-1918....DLB-47, 140

Bandeira, Manuel 1886-1968 .... DLB-307

Bandelier, Adolph F. 1840-1914 .... DLB-186

Bang, Herman 1857-1912 .... DLB-300

Bangs, John Kendrick 1862-1922 ...... DLB-11, 79

Banim, John 1798-1842........DLB-116, 158, 159

Banim, Michael 1796-1874 .... DLB-158, 159

Banks, Iain (M.) 1954- DLB-194, 261

Banks, John circa 1653-1706 .... DLB-80

Banks, Russell 1940- DLB-130, 278

Bannerman, Helen 1862-1946 .... DLB-141

Bantam Books........................ DLB-46

Banti, Anna 1895-1985................DLB-177

Banville, John 1945- DLB-14, 271, 326

Banville, Théodore de 1823-1891....... DLB-217

Bao Tianxiao 1876-1973 .... DLB-328

Baraka, Amiri 1934- DLB-5, 7, 16, 38; DS-8; CDALB-1

Barańczak, Stanisław 1946- DLB-232

Baranskaia, Natal'ia Vladimirovna 1908- DLB-302

Baratynsky, Evgenii Abramovich 1800-1844 .... DLB-205

Barba-Jacob, Porfirio 1883-1942........ DLB-283

Barbauld, Anna Laetitia 1743-1825.......... DLB-107, 109, 142, 158

Barbeau, Marius 1883-1969 .... DLB-92

Barber, John Warner 1798-1885 .... DLB-30

Bàrberi Squarotti, Giorgio 1929- DLB-128

Barbey d'Aurevilly, Jules-Amédée 1808-1889 .... DLB-119

Barbier, Auguste 1805-1882 .... DLB-217

Barbilian, Dan (see Barbu, Ion)

Barbour, John circa 1316-1395 .... DLB-146

Barbour, Ralph Henry 1870-1944........ DLB-22

Barbu, Ion 1895-1961...... DLB-220; CDWLB-4

Barbusse, Henri 1873-1935 .... DLB-65

Barclay, Alexander circa 1475-1552 ..... DLB-132

E. E. Barclay and Company DLB-49

C. W. Bardeen [publishing house] DLB-49

Barham, Richard Harris 1788-1845 ..... DLB-159

Barich, Bill 1943- DLB-185

Baring, Maurice 1874-1945............. DLB-34

Baring-Gould, Sabine 1834-1924 ... DLB-156, 190

Barker, A. L. 1918-2002 .... DLB-14, 139

Barker, Clive 1952- DLB-261

Barker, Dudley (see Black, Lionel)

Barker, George 1913-1991 .... DLB-20

Barker, Harley Granville 1877-1946 ...... DLB-10

Barker, Howard 1946- DLB-13, 233

Barker, James Nelson 1784-1858......... DLB-37

Barker, Jane 1652-1727 .... DLB-39, 131

Barker, Lady Mary Anne 1831-1911 .... DLB-166

Barker, Pat 1943- DLB-271, 326

Barker, William circa 1520-after 1576.... DLB-132

Arthur Barker Limited DLB-112

Barkov, Ivan Semenovich 1732-1768..... DLB-150

Barks, Coleman 1937- DLB-5

Barlach, Ernst 1870-1938 .... DLB-56, 118

Barlow, Joel 1754-1812 .... DLB-37

The Prospect of Peace (1778) DLB-37

Barnard, John 1681-1770 .... DLB-24

Barnard, Marjorie (M. Barnard Eldershaw) 1897-1987 ....DLB-260

Barnard, Robert 1936- DLB-276

Barne, Kitty (Mary Catherine Barne) 1883-1957 .... DLB-160

Barnes, Barnabe 1571-1609 .... DLB-132

Barnes, Djuna 1892-1982.... DLB-4, 9, 45; DS-15

Barnes, Jim 1933- DLB-175

Barnes, Julian 1946- DLB-194; Y-93

Notes for a Checklist of Publications Y-01

Barnes, Margaret Ayer 1886-1967 .... DLB-9

Barnes, Peter 1931- DLB-13, 233

Barnes, William 1801-1886 .... DLB-32

A. S. Barnes and Company DLB-49

Barnes and Noble Books DLB-46

Barnet, Miguel 1940- DLB-145

Barney, Natalie 1876-1972 ...... DLB-4; DS-15

Barnfield, Richard 1574-1627............DLB-172

Baroja, Pío 1872-1956............... DLB-322

Richard W. Baron [publishing house]..... DLB-46

Barr, Amelia Edith Huddleston 1831-1919 .... DLB-202, 221

Barr, Robert 1850-1912 ....DLB-70, 92

Barral, Carlos 1928-1989 .... DLB-134

Barrax, Gerald William 1933- DLB-41, 120

Barrès, Maurice 1862-1923............ DLB-123

Barreno, Maria Isabel (see The Three Marias: A Landmark Case in Portuguese Literary History)

Barrett, Eaton Stannard 1786-1820....... DLB-116

Barrie, J. M. 1860-1937 ..... DLB-10, 141, 156; CDBLB-5

Barrie and Jenkins DLB-112

Barrio, Raymond 1921- DLB-82

Barrios, Gregg 1945- DLB-122

Barry, Philip 1896-1949 ....DLB-7, 228

Barry, Robertine (see Françoise)

Barry, Sebastian 1955- DLB-245

Barse and Hopkins.................. DLB-46

Barstow, Stan 1928- DLB-14, 139, 207

Tribute to John Braine Y-86

Barth, John 1930- DLB-2, 227

Barthelme, Donald 1931-1989 ....DLB-2, 234; Y-80, 89

Barthelme, Frederick 1943- DLB-244; Y-85

Barthes, Roland 1915-1980 .... DLB-296

Bartholomew, Frank 1898-1985.........DLB-127

Bartlett, John 1820-1905............. DLB-1, 235

Bartol, Cyrus Augustus 1813-1900.... DLB-1, 235

Barton, Bernard 1784-1849............. DLB-96

Barton, John ca. 1610-1675 .... DLB-236

Barton, Thomas Pennant 1803-1869 .... DLB-140

Bartram, John 1699-1777 .... DLB-31

Bartram, William 1739-1823 .... DLB-37

Barykova, Anna Pavlovna 1839-1893 . . . . DLB-277

Bashshar ibn Burd circa 714-circa 784 . . . . DLB-311

Basic Books DLB-46

Basille, Theodore (see Becon, Thomas)

Bass, Rick 1958- DLB-212, 275

Bass, T. J. 1932- Y-81

Bassani, Giorgio 1916-2000 . . . . DLB-128, 177, 299

Basse, William circa 1583-1653 . . . . DLB-121

Bassett, John Spencer 1867-1928 . . . . DLB-17

Bassler, Thomas Joseph (see Bass, T. J.)

Bate, Walter Jackson 1918-1999. . . . . DLB-67, 103

Bateman, Stephen circa 1510-1584. . . . . . DLB-136

Christopher Bateman
 [publishing house] DLB-170

Bates, H. E. 1905-1974. . . . . DLB-162, 191

Bates, Katharine Lee 1859-1929 . . . . DLB-71

Batiushkov, Konstantin Nikolaevich
 1787-1855. . . . . DLB-205

B. T. Batsford [publishing house]. DLB-106

Batteux, Charles 1713-1780 . . . . DLB-313

Battiscombe, Georgina 1905- DLB-155

The Battle of Maldon circa 1000 . . . . DLB-146

Baudelaire, Charles 1821-1867 . . . . DLB-217

Baudrillard, Jean 1929- DLB-296

Bauer, Bruno 1809-1882 . . . . DLB-133

Bauer, Wolfgang 1941- DLB-124

Baum, L. Frank 1856-1919 . . . . DLB-22

Baum, Vicki 1888-1960 . . . . .DLB-85

Baumbach, Jonathan 1933- Y-80

Bausch, Richard 1945- DLB-130

    Tribute to James Dickey Y-97

    Tribute to Peter Taylor Y-94

Bausch, Robert 1945- DLB-218

Bawden, Nina 1925- DLB-14, 161, 207

Bax, Clifford 1886-1962. . . . . DLB-10, 100

Baxter, Charles 1947- DLB-130

Bayer, Eleanor (see Perry, Eleanor)

Bayer, Konrad 1932-1964 . . . . DLB-85

Bayle, Pierre 1647-1706. . . . . DLB-268, 313

Bayley, Barrington J. 1937- DLB-261

Baynes, Pauline 1922- DLB-160

Baynton, Barbara 1857-1929 . . . . DLB-230

Bazin, Hervé (Jean Pierre Marie Hervé-Bazin)
 1911-1996 . . . . DLB-83

The BBC Four Samuel Johnson Prize
 for Non-fiction Y-02

Beach, Sylvia 1887-1962. . . . . DLB-4; DS-15

Beacon Press DLB-49

Beadle and Adams DLB-49

Beagle, Peter S. 1939- Y-80

Beal, M. F. 1937- Y-81

Beale, Howard K. 1899-1959 . . . . DLB-17

Beard, Charles A. 1874-1948 . . . . DLB-17

Beat Generation (Beats)
    As I See It, by Carolyn Cassady DLB-16
    A Beat Chronology: The First Twenty-five
     Years, 1944-1969 . . . . DLB-16
    The Commercialization of the Image
     of Revolt, by Kenneth Rexroth DLB-16
    Four Essays on the Beat Generation . . . DLB-16
    in New York City DLB-237
    in the West DLB-237
    Outlaw Days DLB-16
    Periodicals of DLB-16

Beattie, Ann 1947- DLB-218, 278; Y-82

Beattie, James 1735-1803 . . . . DLB-109

Beatty, Chester 1875-1968 . . . . DLB-201

Beauchemin, Nérée 1850-1931 . . . . DLB-92

Beauchemin, Yves 1941- DLB-60

Beaugrand, Honoré 1848-1906 . . . . DLB-99

Beaulieu, Victor-Lévy 1945- DLB-53

Beaumarchais, Pierre-Augustin Caron de
 1732-1799 . . . . DLB-313

Beaumer, Mme de ?-1766. . . . . DLB-313

Beaumont, Francis circa 1584-1616
 and Fletcher, John
 1579-1625 . . . . DLB-58; CDBLB-1

Beaumont, Sir John 1583?-1627 . . . . DLB-121

Beaumont, Joseph 1616-1699 . . . . DLB-126

Beauvoir, Simone de 1908-1986 . . . . . DLB-72; Y-86

    Personal Tribute to Simone de Beauvoir Y-86

Beaver, Bruce 1928- DLB-289

Becher, Ulrich 1910-1990 . . . . DLB-69

Becker, Carl 1873-1945 . . . . DLB-17

Becker, Jurek 1937-1997 . . . . DLB-75, 299

Becker, Jurgen 1932- DLB-75

Beckett, Mary 1926- DLB-319

Beckett, Samuel
 1906-1989 . . . . DLB-13, 15, 233, 319,
                              321, 329; Y-90; CDBLB-7

Beckford, William 1760-1844. . . . . . . DLB-39, 213

Beckham, Barry 1944- DLB-33

Bećković, Matija 1939- DLB-181

Becon, Thomas circa 1512-1567 . . . . DLB-136

Becque, Henry 1837-1899 . . . . DLB-192

Beddoes, Thomas 1760-1808 . . . . DLB-158

Beddoes, Thomas Lovell 1803-1849 . . . . . DLB-96

Bede circa 673-735 . . . . DLB-146

Bedford-Jones, H. 1887-1949 . . . . DLB-251

Bedregal, Yolanda 1913-1999 . . . . DLB-283

Beebe, William 1877-1962 . . . . DLB-275

Beecher, Catharine Esther
 1800-1878 . . . . DLB-1, 243

Beecher, Henry Ward
 1813-1887 . . . . DLB-3, 43, 250

Beer, George L. 1872-1920 . . . . DLB-47

Beer, Johann 1655-1700 . . . . DLB-168

Beer, Patricia 1919-1999 . . . . DLB-40

Beerbohm, Max 1872-1956 . . . . DLB-34, 100

Beer-Hofmann, Richard 1866-1945 . . . . . . DLB-81

Beers, Henry A. 1847-1926 . . . . DLB-71

S. O. Beeton [publishing house] DLB-106

Begley, Louis 1933- DLB-299

Bégon, Elisabeth 1696-1755 . . . . DLB-99

Behan, Brendan
 1923-1964 . . . . DLB-13, 233; CDBLB-7

Behn, Aphra 1640?-1689 . . . . DLB-39, 80, 131

Behn, Harry 1898-1973 . . . . DLB-61

Behrman, S. N. 1893-1973 . . . . DLB-7, 44

Beklemishev, Iurii Solomonovich
 (see Krymov, Iurii Solomonovich)

Belaney, Archibald Stansfeld (see Grey Owl)

Belasco, David 1853-1931 . . . . .DLB-7

Clarke Belford and Company DLB-49

Belgian Luxembourg American Studies
 Association Y-01

Belinsky, Vissarion Grigor'evich
 1811-1848 . . . . DLB-198

Belitt, Ben 1911-2003. . . . . DLB-5

Belknap, Jeremy 1744-1798 . . . . DLB-30, 37

Bell, Adrian 1901-1980 . . . . DLB-191

Bell, Clive 1881-1964. . . . . DS-10

Bell, Daniel 1919- DLB-246

Bell, Gertrude Margaret Lowthian
 1868-1926 . . . . DLB-174

Bell, James Madison 1826-1902 . . . . .DLB-50

Bell, Madison Smartt 1957- DLB-218, 278

    Tribute to Andrew Nelson Lytle Y-95

    Tribute to Peter Taylor Y-94

Bell, Marvin 1937- DLB-5

Bell, Millicent 1919- DLB-111

Bell, Quentin 1910-1996 . . . . DLB-155

Bell, Vanessa 1879-1961 . . . . DS-10

George Bell and Sons DLB-106

Robert Bell [publishing house] DLB-49

Bellamy, Edward 1850-1898 . . . . DLB-12

Bellamy, Joseph 1719-1790 . . . . DLB-31

John Bellamy [publishing house] DLB-170

La Belle Assemblée 1806-1837 . . . . DLB-110

Bellezza, Dario 1944-1996 . . . . DLB-128

Belli, Carlos Germán 1927- DLB-290

Belli, Gioconda 1948- DLB-290

Belloc, Hilaire 1870-1953 . . . . DLB-19, 100, 141, 174

Belloc, Madame (see Parkes, Bessie Rayner)

Bellonci, Maria 1902-1986 . . . . DLB-196

Bellow, Saul 1915-2005
 . . . . DLB-2, 28, 299, 329; Y-82;
                                       DS-3; CDALB-1

    Tribute to Isaac Bashevis Singer Y-91

Belmont Productions DLB-46	The Tilling Society................... Y-98	Bernardin de Saint-Pierre 1737-1814..... DLB-313
Belov, Vasilii Ivanovich 1932- DLB-302	Benson, Jackson J. 1930- DLB-111	Bernari, Carlo 1909-1992..............DLB-177
Bels, Alberts 1938- DLB-232	Benson, Robert Hugh 1871-1914 .... DLB-153	Bernhard, Thomas 1931-1989 ....DLB-85, 124; CDWLB-2
Belševica, Vizma 1931- ... DLB-232; CDWLB-4	Benson, Stella 1892-1933 .... DLB-36, 162	Berniéres, Louis de 1954- DLB-271
Bely, Andrei 1880-1934 .... DLB-295	Bent, James Theodore 1852-1897........DLB-174	Bernstein, Charles 1950- DLB-169
Bemelmans, Ludwig 1898-1962 .... DLB-22	Bent, Mabel Virginia Anna ?-? DLB-174	Béroalde de Verville, François 1556-1626 .... DLB-327
Bemis, Samuel Flagg 1891-1973 .... DLB-17	Bentham, Jeremy 1748-1832.... DLB-107, 158, 252	Berriault, Gina 1926-1999 .... DLB-130
William Bemrose [publishing house] DLB-106	Bentley, E. C. 1875-1956................ DLB-70	Berrigan, Daniel 1921- DLB-5
Ben no Naishi 1228?-1271?............ DLB-203	Bentley, Phyllis 1894-1977 .... DLB-191	Berrigan, Ted 1934-1983 .... DLB-5, 169
Benavente, Jacinto 1866-1954.......... DLB-329	Bentley, Richard 1662-1742 .... DLB-252	Berry, Wendell 1934- DLB-5, 6, 234, 275
Benchley, Robert 1889-1945............ DLB-11	Richard Bentley [publishing house] DLB-106	Berryman, John 1914-1972.... DLB-48; CDALB-1
Bencúr, Matej (see Kukučin, Martin)	Benton, Robert 1932- DLB-44	Bersianik, Louky 1930- DLB-60
Benedetti, Mario 1920- DLB-113	Benziger Brothers DLB-49	Berssenbrugge, Mei-mei 1947- DLB-312
Benedict, Pinckney 1964- DLB-244	*Beowulf* circa 900-1000 or 790-825 .... DLB-146; CDBLB-1	Thomas Bertholet [publishing house].....DLB-170
Benedict, Ruth 1887-1948............. DLB-246	Berberova, Nina 1901-1993 .... DLB-317	Berto, Giuseppe 1914-1978.............DLB-177
Benedictus, David 1938- DLB-14	Berent, Wacław 1873-1940............ DLB-215	Bertocci, Peter Anthony 1910-1989 .....DLB-279
Benedikt Gröndal 1826-1907 .... DLB-293	Beresford, Anne 1929- DLB-40	Bertolucci, Attilio 1911-2000 .... DLB-128
Benedikt, Michael 1935- DLB-5	Beresford, John Davys 1873-1947................DLB-162, 178, 197	Berton, Pierre 1920-2004 .... DLB-68
Benediktov, Vladimir Grigor'evich 1807-1873 .... DLB-205	"Experiment in the Novel" (1929) [excerpt].................... DLB-36	Bertrand, Louis "Aloysius" 1807-1841 ....DLB-217
Benét, Stephen Vincent 1898-1943 .... DLB-4, 48, 102, 249	Beresford-Howe, Constance 1922- DLB-88	Besant, Sir Walter 1836-1901 ...... DLB-135, 190
Stephen Vincent Benét Centenary Y-97	R. G. Berford Company............... DLB-49	Bessa-Luís, Agustina 1922- DLB-287
Benét, William Rose 1886-1950 .... DLB-45	Berg, Elizabeth 1948- DLB-292	Bessette, Gerard 1920- DLB-53
Benford, Gregory 1941- Y-82	Berg, Stephen 1934- DLB-5	Bessie, Alvah 1904-1985............... DLB-26
Benítez, Sandra 1941- DLB-292	Bergengruen, Werner 1892-1964 .... DLB-56	Bester, Alfred 1913-1987.............. DLB-8
Benjamin, Park 1809-1864 .... DLB-3, 59, 73, 250	Berger, John 1926- DLB-14, 207, 319, 326	Besterman, Theodore 1904-1976 .... DLB-201
Benjamin, Peter (see Cunningham, Peter)	Berger, Meyer 1898-1959 .... DLB-29	Beston, Henry (Henry Beston Sheahan) 1888-1968 ....DLB-275
Benjamin, S. G. W. 1837-1914 .... DLB-189	Berger, Thomas 1924- DLB-2; Y-80	Best-Seller Lists An Assessment..................... Y-84
Benjamin, Walter 1892-1940 .... DLB-242	A Statement by Thomas Berger Y-80	What's Really Wrong With Bestseller Lists................... Y-84
Benlowes, Edward 1602-1676.......... DLB-126	Bergman, Hjalmar 1883-1931.......... DLB-259	Bestuzhev, Aleksandr Aleksandrovich (Marlinsky) 1797-1837 .... DLB-198
Benn, Gottfried 1886-1956............. DLB-56	Bergman, Ingmar 1918- DLB-257	Bestuzhev, Nikolai Aleksandrovich 1791-1855..................... DLB-198
Benn Brothers Limited DLB-106	Bergson, Henri 1859-1941 .... DLB-329	Betham-Edwards, Matilda Barbara (see Edwards, Matilda Barbara Betham-)
Bennett, Alan 1934- DLB-310	Berkeley, Anthony 1893-1971........... DLB-77	Betjeman, John 1906-1984 ....DLB-20; Y-84; CDBLB-7
Bennett, Arnold 1867-1931.... DLB-10, 34, 98, 135; CDBLB-5	Berkeley, George 1685-1753 .... DLB-31, 101, 252	Betocchi, Carlo 1899-1986............ DLB-128
The Arnold Bennett Society............ Y-98	The Berkley Publishing Corporation DLB-46	Bettarini, Mariella 1942- DLB-128
Bennett, Charles 1899-1995 .... DLB-44	Berkman, Alexander 1870-1936 .... DLB-303	Betts, Doris 1932- DLB-218; Y-82
Bennett, Emerson 1822-1905 .... DLB-202	Berlin, Irving 1888-1989.............. DLB-265	Beveridge, Albert J. 1862-1927...........DLB-17
Bennett, Gwendolyn 1902-1981 .... DLB-51	Berlin, Lucia 1936- DLB-130	Beveridge, Judith 1956- DLB-325
Bennett, Hal 1930- DLB-33	Berman, Marshall 1940- DLB-246	Beverley, Robert circa 1673-1722 ..... DLB-24, 30
Bennett, James Gordon 1795-1872 .... DLB-43	Berman, Sabina 1955- DLB-305	Bevilacqua, Alberto 1934- DLB-196
Bennett, James Gordon, Jr. 1841-1918 .... DLB-23	Bernal, Vicente J. 1888-1915............ DLB-82	Bevington, Louisa Sarah 1845-1895..... DLB-199
Bennett, John 1865-1956 .... DLB-42	Bernanos, Georges 1888-1948 .... DLB-72	Beyle, Marie-Henri (see Stendhal)
Bennett, Louise 1919- DLB-117; CDWLB-3	Bernard, Catherine 1663?-1712 ....DLB-268	Bèze, Théodore de (Theodore Beza) 1519-1605 .... DLB-327
Benni, Stefano 1947- DLB-196	Bernard, Harry 1898-1979 .... DLB-92	Bhatt, Sujata 1956- DLB-323
Benoist, Françoise-Albine Puzin de La Martinière 1731-1809 .... DLB-313	Bernard, John 1756-1828 .... DLB-37	Białoszewski, Miron 1922-1983 .... DLB-232
Benoit, Jacques 1941- DLB-60	Bernard of Chartres circa 1060-1124? ... DLB-115	
Benson, A. C. 1862-1925 .... DLB-98	Bernard of Clairvaux 1090-1153 .... DLB-208	
Benson, E. F. 1867-1940 .... DLB-135, 153	Bernard, Richard 1568-1641/1642 ...... DLB-281	
The E. F. Benson Society Y-98	Bernard Silvestris fl. circa 1130-1160 .... DLB-208	

Bianco, Margery Williams 1881-1944 . . . . DLB-160

Bibaud, Adèle 1854-1941 . . . . DLB-92

Bibaud, Michel 1782-1857 . . . . DLB-99

Bibliography
   Bibliographical and Textual Scholarship Since World War II Y-89
   Center for Bibliographical Studies and Research at the University of California, Riverside Y-91
   The Great Bibliographers Series Y-93
   Primary Bibliography: A Retrospective Y-95

Bichsel, Peter 1935- DLB-75

Bickerstaff, Isaac John 1733-circa 1808 . . . . DLB-89

Drexel Biddle [publishing house] DLB-49

Bidermann, Jacob 1577 or 1578-1639 . . . . DLB-164

Bidwell, Walter Hilliard 1798-1881 . . . . DLB-79

Biehl, Charlotta Dorothea 1731-1788 . . . . . DLB-300

Bienek, Horst 1930-1990 . . . . DLB-75

Bierbaum, Otto Julius 1865-1910 . . . . DLB-66

Bierce, Ambrose 1842-1914? DLB-11, 12, 23, 71, 74, 186; CDALB-3

Bigelow, William F. 1879-1966 . . . . DLB-91

Biggers, Earl Derr 1884-1933 . . . . DLB-306

Biggle, Lloyd, Jr. 1923-2002 . . . . DLB-8

Bigiaretti, Libero 1905-1993 . . . . DLB-177

Bigland, Eileen 1898-1970 . . . . DLB-195

Biglow, Hosea (see Lowell, James Russell)

Bigongiari, Piero 1914-1997 . . . . DLB-128

Bilac, Olavo 1865-1918 . . . . DLB-307

Bilenchi, Romano 1909-1989 . . . . DLB-264

Billinger, Richard 1890-1965 . . . . DLB-124

Billings, Hammatt 1818-1874 . . . . DLB-188

Billings, John Shaw 1898-1975 . . . . DLB-137

Billings, Josh (see Shaw, Henry Wheeler)

Binchy, Maeve 1940- DLB-319

Binding, Rudolf G. 1867-1938 . . . . DLB-66

Bing Xin 1900-1999 . . . . DLB-328

Bingay, Malcolm 1884-1953 . . . . DLB-241

Bingham, Caleb 1757-1817 . . . . DLB-42

Bingham, George Barry 1906-1988 . . . . . . DLB-127

Bingham, Sallie 1937- DLB-234

William Bingley [publishing house] DLB-154

Binyon, Laurence 1869-1943 . . . . DLB-19

Biographia Brittanica DLB-142

Biography
   Biographical Documents Y-84, 85
   A Celebration of Literary Biography Y-98
   Conference on Modern Biography Y-85
   The Cult of Biography
     Excerpts from the Second Folio Debate: "Biographies are generally a disease of English Literature" Y-86
   New Approaches to Biography: Challenges from Critical Theory, USC Conference on Literary Studies, 1990 . . . . Y-90
   "The New Biography," by Virginia Woolf, *New York Herald Tribune*, 30 October 1927 . . . . DLB-149
   "The Practice of Biography," in *The English Sense of Humour and Other Essays*, by Harold Nicolson DLB-149
   "Principles of Biography," in *Elizabethan and Other Essays*, by Sidney Lee . . . DLB-149
   Remarks at the Opening of "The Biographical Part of Literature" Exhibition, by William R. Cagle Y-98
   Survey of Literary Biographies Y-00
   A Transit of Poets and Others: American Biography in 1982 . . . . Y-82
   The Year in Literary Biography Y-83–01

Biography, The Practice of:
   An Interview with B. L. Reid Y-83
   An Interview with David Herbert Donald . . Y-87
   An Interview with Humphrey Carpenter . . . Y-84
   An Interview with Joan Mellen Y-94
   An Interview with John Caldwell Guilds . . . Y-92
   An Interview with William Manchester . . . Y-85

John Bioren [publishing house] DLB-49

Bioy Casares, Adolfo 1914-1999 . . . . DLB-113

Bird, Isabella Lucy 1831-1904 . . . . DLB-166

Bird, Robert Montgomery 1806-1854 . . . . DLB-202

Bird, William 1888-1963 . . . . DLB-4; DS-15
   The Cost of the *Cantos:* William Bird to Ezra Pound Y-01

Birken, Sigmund von 1626-1681 . . . . DLB-164

Birney, Earle 1904-1995 . . . . DLB-88

Birrell, Augustine 1850-1933 . . . . DLB-98

Bisher, Furman 1918- DLB-171

Bishop, Elizabeth 1911-1979 . . . . DLB-5, 169; CDALB-6
   The Elizabeth Bishop Society Y-01

Bishop, John Peale 1892-1944 . . . . . . DLB-4, 9, 45

Bismarck, Otto von 1815-1898 . . . . DLB-129

Bisset, Robert 1759-1805 . . . . DLB-142

Bissett, Bill 1939- DLB-53

Bitov, Andrei Georgievich 1937- DLB-302

Bitzius, Albert (see Gotthelf, Jeremias)

Bjørnboe, Jens 1920-1976 . . . . DLB-297

Bjørnson, Bjørnstjerne 1832-1910 . . . . . . DLB-329

Bjørnvig, Thorkild 1918- DLB-214

Black, David (D. M.) 1941- DLB-40

Black, Gavin (Oswald Morris Wynd) 1913-1998 . . . . DLB-276

Black, Lionel (Dudley Barker) 1910-1980 . . . . DLB-276

Black, Winifred 1863-1936 . . . . DLB-25

Walter J. Black [publishing house] DLB-46

Blackamore, Arthur 1679-? DLB-24, 39

Blackburn, Alexander L. 1929- Y-85

Blackburn, John 1923-1993 . . . . DLB-261

Blackburn, Paul 1926-1971 . . . . DLB-16; Y-81

Blackburn, Thomas 1916-1977 . . . . DLB-27

Blacker, Terence 1948- DLB-271

Blackmore, R. D. 1825-1900 . . . . DLB-18

Blackmore, Sir Richard 1654-1729 . . . . . . DLB-131

Blackmur, R. P. 1904-1965 . . . . DLB-63

Blackwell, Alice Stone 1857-1950 . . . . DLB-303

Basil Blackwell, Publisher DLB-106

Blackwood, Algernon Henry 1869-1951 . . . . DLB-153, 156, 178

Blackwood, Caroline 1931-1996 . . . . . DLB-14, 207

William Blackwood and Sons, Ltd. DLB-154

Blackwood's Edinburgh Magazine 1817-1980 . . . . DLB-110

Blades, William 1824-1890 . . . . DLB-184

Blaga, Lucian 1895-1961 . . . . DLB-220

Blagden, Isabella 1817?-1873 . . . . DLB-199

Blair, Eric Arthur (see Orwell, George)

Blair, Francis Preston 1791-1876 . . . . DLB-43

Blair, Hugh
   Lectures on Rhetoric and Belles Lettres (1783), [excerpts] DLB-31

Blair, James circa 1655-1743 . . . . DLB-24

Blair, John Durburrow 1759-1823 . . . . DLB-37

Blais, Marie-Claire 1939- DLB-53

Blaise, Clark 1940- DLB-53

Blake, George 1893-1961 . . . . DLB-191

Blake, Lillie Devereux 1833-1913 . . . . DLB-202, 221

Blake, Nicholas (C. Day Lewis) 1904-1972 . . . . DLB-77

Blake, William 1757-1827 . . . . DLB-93, 154, 163; CDBLB-3

The Blakiston Company DLB-49

Blanchard, Stephen 1950- DLB-267

Blanchot, Maurice 1907-2003 . . . . DLB-72, 296

Blanckenburg, Christian Friedrich von 1744-1796 . . . . DLB-94

Blandiana, Ana 1942- DLB-232; CDWLB-4

Blanshard, Brand 1892-1987 . . . . DLB-279

Blasco Ibáñez, Vicente 1867-1928 . . . . . . DLB-322

Blaser, Robin 1925- DLB-165

Blaumanis, Rudolfs 1863-1908 . . . . DLB-220

Bleasdale, Alan 1946- DLB-245

Bledsoe, Albert Taylor 1809-1877 . . . . DLB-3, 79, 248

Bleecker, Ann Eliza 1752-1783 . . . . DLB-200

Blelock and Company DLB-49

Blennerhassett, Margaret Agnew 1773-1842 . . . . DLB-99

Geoffrey Bles [publishing house] DLB-112

Blessington, Marguerite, Countess of 1789-1849 . . . . DLB-166

Blew, Mary Clearman 1939- DLB-256

Blicher, Steen Steensen 1782-1848 ...... DLB-300

The Blickling Homilies circa 971 .... DLB-146

Blind, Mathilde 1841-1896 .... DLB-199

The Blind Assassin, 2000 Booker Prize winner, Margaret Atwood. DLB-326

Blish, James 1921-1975 .... DLB-8

E. Bliss and E. White [publishing house] DLB-49

Bliven, Bruce 1889-1977 .... DLB-137

Blixen, Karen 1885-1962 .... DLB-214

Bloch, Ernst 1885-1977 .... DLB-296

Bloch, Robert 1917-1994 .... DLB-44

    Tribute to John D. MacDonald Y-86

Block, Lawrence 1938- DLB-226

Block, Rudolph (see Lessing, Bruno)

Blok, Aleksandr Aleksandrovich 1880-1921 .... DLB-295

Blondal, Patricia 1926-1959 .... DLB-88

Bloom, Harold 1930- DLB-67

Bloomer, Amelia 1818-1894 .... DLB-79

Bloomfield, Robert 1766-1823 .... DLB-93

Bloomsbury Group.................... DS-10

    The *Dreadnought* Hoax DS-10

Bloor, Ella Reeve 1862-1951............. DLB-303

Blotner, Joseph 1923- DLB-111

Blount, Thomas 1618?-1679.......... DLB-236

Bloy, Léon 1846-1917 .... DLB-123

Blume, Judy 1938- DLB-52

    Tribute to Theodor Seuss Geisel Y-91

Blunck, Hans Friedrich 1888-1961 ..... DLB-66

Blunden, Edmund 1896-1974 .... DLB-20, 100, 155

Blundeville, Thomas 1522?-1606 .... DLB-236

Blunt, Lady Anne Isabella Noel 1837-1917 .... DLB-174

Blunt, Wilfrid Scawen 1840-1922 ..... DLB-19, 174

Bly, Nellie (see Cochrane, Elizabeth)

Bly, Robert 1926- DLB-5

Blyton, Enid 1897-1968. .... DLB-160

Boaden, James 1762-1839 .... DLB-89

Boal, Augusto 1931- DLB-307

Boas, Frederick S. 1862-1957 .... DLB-149

The Bobbs-Merrill Company DLB-46, 291

    The Bobbs-Merrill Archive at the Lilly Library, Indiana University..... Y-90

Boborykin, Petr Dmitrievich 1836-1921 .... DLB-238

Bobrov, Semen Sergeevich 1763?-1810 .... DLB-150

Bobrowski, Johannes 1917-1965 .... DLB-75

Bocage, Manuel Maria Barbosa du 1765-1805 .... DLB-287

Bodenheim, Maxwell 1892-1954 ...... DLB-9, 45

Bodenstedt, Friedrich von 1819-1892 ... DLB-129

Bodini, Vittorio 1914-1970 .... DLB-128

Bodkin, M. McDonnell 1850-1933 .... DLB-70

Bodley, Sir Thomas 1545-1613 .... DLB-213

Bodley Head....................... DLB-112

Bodmer, Johann Jakob 1698-1783 .... DLB-97

Bodmershof, Imma von 1895-1982 ..... DLB-85

Bodsworth, Fred 1918- DLB-68

Böðvar Guðmundsson 1939- DLB-293

Boehm, Sydney 1908-1990 .... DLB-44

Boer, Charles 1939- DLB-5

Boethius circa 480-circa 524 .... DLB-115

Boethius of Dacia circa 1240-? DLB-115

Bogan, Louise 1897-1970 .... DLB-45, 169

Bogarde, Dirk 1921-1999 .... DLB-14

Bogdanov, Aleksandr Aleksandrovich 1873-1928...................... DLB-295

Bogdanovich, Ippolit Fedorovich circa 1743-1803 .... DLB-150

David Bogue [publishing house]....... DLB-106

Bohjalian, Chris 1960- DLB-292

Böhme, Jakob 1575-1624 .... DLB-164

H. G. Bohn [publishing house]........ DLB-106

Bohse, August 1661-1742 .... DLB-168

Boie, Heinrich Christian 1744-1806 ...... DLB-94

Boileau-Despréaux, Nicolas 1636-1711.... DLB-268

Bojunga, Lygia 1932- DLB-307

Bok, Edward W. 1863-1930 .... DLB-91; DS-16

Boland, Eavan 1944- DLB-40

Boldrewood, Rolf (Thomas Alexander Browne) 1826?-1915...................... DLB-230

Bolingbroke, Henry St. John, Viscount 1678-1751 .... DLB-101

Böll, Heinrich 1917-1985..... DLB-69, 329; Y-85; CDWLB-2

Bolling, Robert 1738-1775.............. DLB-31

Bolotov, Andrei Timofeevich 1738-1833...................... DLB-150

Bolt, Carol 1941- DLB-60

Bolt, Robert 1924-1995 .... DLB-13, 233

Bolton, Herbert E. 1870-1953........... DLB-17

Bonaventura....................... DLB-90

Bonaventure circa 1217-1274......... DLB-115

Bonaviri, Giuseppe 1924- DLB-177

Bond, Edward 1934- DLB-13, 310

Bond, Michael 1926- DLB-161

Bondarev, Iurii Vasil'evich 1924- DLB-302

The Bone People, 1985 Booker Prize winner, Keri Hulme DLB-326

Albert and Charles Boni [publishing house] DLB-46

Boni and Liveright DLB-46

Bonnefoy, Yves 1923- DLB-258

Bonner, Marita 1899-1971 .... DLB-228

Bonner, Paul Hyde 1893-1968 ....DS-17

Bonner, Sherwood (see McDowell, Katharine Sherwood Bonner)

Robert Bonner's Sons.................. DLB-49

Bonnin, Gertrude Simmons (see Zitkala-Ša)

Bonsanti, Alessandro 1904-1984 ....DLB-177

Bontempelli, Massimo 1878-1960....... DLB-264

Bontemps, Arna 1902-1973 .... DLB-48, 51

The Book Buyer (1867-1880, 1884-1918, 1935-1938.....................DS-13

The Book League of America. DLB-46

Book Reviewing
    The American Book Review: A Sketch ... Y-92

    Book Reviewing and the Literary Scene Y-96, 97

    Book Reviewing in America Y-87–94

    Book Reviewing in America and the Literary Scene Y-95

    Book Reviewing in Texas.............. Y-94

    Book Reviews in Glossy Magazines...... Y-95

    Do They or Don't They? Writers Reading Book Reviews...... Y-01

    The Most Powerful Book Review in America [*New York Times Book Review*] Y-82

    Some Surprises and Universal Truths Y-92

    The Year in Book Reviewing and the Literary Situation Y-98

Book Supply Company DLB-49

The Book Trade History Group........... Y-93

The Booker Prize Y-96–98

    Address by Anthony Thwaite, Chairman of the Booker Prize Judges Comments from Former Booker Prize Winners Y-86

Boorde, Andrew circa 1490-1549 .... DLB-136

Boorstin, Daniel J. 1914- DLB-17

    Tribute to Archibald MacLeish Y-82

    Tribute to Charles Scribner Jr. Y-95

Booth, Franklin 1874-1948 .... DLB-188

Booth, Mary L. 1831-1889 .... DLB-79

Booth, Philip 1925- Y-82

Booth, Wayne C. 1921- DLB-67

Booth, William 1829-1912 .... DLB-190

Bor, Josef 1906-1979 .... DLB-299

Borchardt, Rudolf 1877-1945 .... DLB-66

Borchert, Wolfgang 1921-1947 .... DLB-69, 124

Bording, Anders 1619-1677 .... DLB-300

Borel, Pétrus 1809-1859 .... DLB-119

Borgen, Johan 1902-1979 .... DLB-297

Borges, Jorge Luis 1899-1986 ... DLB-113, 283; Y-86; CDWLB-3

    The Poetry of Jorge Luis Borges Y-86

    A Personal Tribute Y-86

Borgese, Giuseppe Antonio 1882-1952. ... DLB-264

Börne, Ludwig 1786-1837 ....DLB-90	Bove, Emmanuel 1898-1945 ....DLB-72	Bradbury and Evans DLB-106
Bornstein, Miriam 1950- DLB-209	Bowen, Elizabeth 1899-1973 ....DLB-15, 162; CDBLB-7	Braddon, Mary Elizabeth 1835-1915 ....DLB-18, 70, 156
Borowski, Tadeusz 1922-1951 ....DLB-215; CDWLB-4	Bowen, Francis 1811-1890 ....DLB-1, 59, 235	Bradford, Andrew 1686-1742 ....DLB-43, 73
Borrow, George 1803-1881 ....DLB-21, 55, 166	Bowen, John 1924- DLB-13	Bradford, Gamaliel 1863-1932 ....DLB-17
Bosanquet, Bernard 1848-1923 ....DLB-262	Bowen, Marjorie 1886-1952 ....DLB-153	Bradford, John 1749-1830 ....DLB-43
Boscán, Juan circa 1490-1542 ....DLB-318	Bowen-Merrill Company DLB-49	Bradford, Roark 1896-1948 ....DLB-86
Bosch, Juan 1909-2001 ....DLB-145	Bowering, George 1935- DLB-53	Bradford, William 1590-1657 ....DLB-24, 30
Bosco, Henri 1888-1976 ....DLB-72	Bowers, Bathsheba 1671-1718 ....DLB-200	Bradford, William, III 1719-1791 ....DLB-43, 73
Bosco, Monique 1927- DLB-53	Bowers, Claude G. 1878-1958 ....DLB-17	Bradlaugh, Charles 1833-1891 ....DLB-57
Bosman, Herman Charles 1905-1951 ....DLB-225	Bowers, Edgar 1924-2000 ....DLB-5	Bradley, David 1950- DLB-33
Bossuet, Jacques-Bénigne 1627-1704 ....DLB-268	Bowers, Fredson Thayer 1905-1991 ....DLB-140; Y-91	Bradley, F. H. 1846-1924 ....DLB-262
Bostic, Joe 1908-1988 ....DLB-241	The Editorial Style of Fredson Bowers Y-91	Bradley, Katherine Harris (see Field, Michael)
Boston, Lucy M. 1892-1990 ....DLB-161	Fredson Bowers and Studies in Bibliography Y-91	Bradley, Marion Zimmer 1930-1999 ....DLB-8
Boston Quarterly Review DLB-1	Fredson Bowers and the Cambridge Beaumont and Fletcher Y-91	Bradley, William Aspenwall 1878-1939 ....DLB-4
Boston University Editorial Institute at Boston University Y-00	Fredson Bowers as Critic of Renaissance Dramatic Literature Y-91	Ira Bradley and Company DLB-49
Special Collections at Boston University Y-99	Fredson Bowers as Music Critic Y-91	J. W. Bradley and Company DLB-49
Boswell, James 1740-1795 ....DLB-104, 142; CDBLB-2	Fredson Bowers, Master Teacher Y-91	Bradshaw, Henry 1831-1886 ....DLB-184
Boswell, Robert 1953- DLB-234	An Interview [on Nabokov] Y-80	Bradstreet, Anne 1612 or 1613-1672 ....DLB-24; CDALB-2
Bosworth, David Y-82	Working with Fredson Bowers Y-91	Bradūnas, Kazys 1917- DLB-220
Excerpt from "Excerpts from a Report of the Commission," in *The Death of Descartes* Y-82	Bowles, Paul 1910-1999 ....DLB-5, 6, 218; Y-99	Bradwardine, Thomas circa 1295-1349 ....DLB-115
	Bowles, Samuel, III 1826-1878 ....DLB-43	Brady, Frank 1924-1986 ....DLB-111
Bote, Hermann circa 1460-circa 1520 ....DLB-179	Bowles, William Lisle 1762-1850 ....DLB-93	Frederic A. Brady [publishing house] DLB-49
Botev, Khristo 1847-1876 ....DLB-147	Bowman, Louise Morey 1882-1944 ....DLB-68	Braga, Rubem 1913-1990 ....DLB-307
Botkin, Vasilii Petrovich 1811-1869 ....DLB-277	Bowne, Borden Parker 1847-1919 ....DLB-270	Bragg, Melvyn 1939- DLB-14, 271
Botta, Anne C. Lynch 1815-1891 ....DLB-3, 250	Boyd, James 1888-1944 ....DLB-9; DS-16	Brahe, Tycho 1546-1601 ....DLB-300
Botto, Ján (see Krasko, Ivan)	Boyd, John 1912-2002 ....DLB-310	Charles H. Brainard [publishing house] DLB-49
Bottome, Phyllis 1882-1963 ....DLB-197	Boyd, John 1919- DLB-8	Braine, John 1922-1986 ....DLB-15; Y-86; CDBLB-7
Bottomley, Gordon 1874-1948 ....DLB-10	Boyd, Martin 1893-1972 ....DLB-260	Braithwait, Richard 1588-1673 ....DLB-151
Bottoms, David 1949- DLB-120; Y-83	Boyd, Thomas 1898-1935 ....DLB-9, 316; DS-16	Braithwaite, William Stanley 1878-1962 ....DLB-50, 54
Tribute to James Dickey Y-97	Boyd, William 1952- DLB-231	Bräker, Ulrich 1735-1798 ....DLB-94
Bottrall, Ronald 1906-1959 ....DLB-20	Boye, Karin 1900-1941 ....DLB-259	Bramah, Ernest 1868-1942 ....DLB-70
Bouchardy, Joseph 1810-1870 ....DLB-192	Boyesen, Hjalmar Hjorth 1848-1895 ....DLB-12, 71; DS-13	Branagan, Thomas 1774-1843 ....DLB-37
Boucher, Anthony 1911-1968 ....DLB-8	Boylan, Clare 1948- DLB-267	Brancati, Vitaliano 1907-1954 ....DLB-264
Boucher, Jonathan 1738-1804 ....DLB-31	Boyle, Kay 1902-1992 DLB-4, 9, 48, 86; DS-15; Y-93	Branch, William Blackwell 1927- DLB-76
Boucher de Boucherville, Georges 1814-1894 ....DLB-99	Boyle, Roger, Earl of Orrery 1621-1679 ....DLB-80	Brand, Christianna 1907-1988 ....DLB-276
Boudreau, Daniel (see Coste, Donat)	Boyle, T. Coraghessan 1948- DLB-218, 278; Y-86	Brand, Max (see Faust, Frederick Schiller)
Bouhours, Dominique 1628-1702 ....DLB-268	Božić, Mirko 1919- DLB-181	Brandão, Raul 1867-1930 ....DLB-287
Bourassa, Napoléon 1827-1916 ....DLB-99	Brackenbury, Alison 1953- DLB-40	Branden Press DLB-46
Bourget, Paul 1852-1935 ....DLB-123	Brackenridge, Hugh Henry 1748-1816 ....DLB-11, 37	Brandes, Georg 1842-1927 ....DLB-300
Bourinot, John George 1837-1902 ....DLB-99	The Rising Glory of America DLB-37	Branner, H.C. 1903-1966 ....DLB-214
Bourjaily, Vance 1922- DLB-2, 143	Brackett, Charles 1892-1969 ....DLB-26	Brant, Sebastian 1457-1521 ....DLB-179
Bourne, Edward Gaylord 1860-1908 ....DLB-47	Brackett, Leigh 1915-1978 ....DLB-8, 26	Brantôme (Pierre de Bourdeille) 1540?-1614 ....DLB-327
Bourne, Randolph 1886-1918 ....DLB-63	John Bradburn [publishing house] DLB-49	Brassey, Lady Annie (Allnutt) 1839-1887 ....DLB-166
Bousoño, Carlos 1923- DLB-108	Bradbury, Malcolm 1932-2000 ....DLB-14, 207	Brathwaite, Edward Kamau 1930- DLB-125; CDWLB-3
Bousquet, Joë 1897-1950 ....DLB-72	Bradbury, Ray 1920- DLB-2, 8; CDALB-6	Brault, Jacques 1933- DLB-53
Bova, Ben 1932- Y-81		
Bovard, Oliver K. 1872-1945 ....DLB-25		Braun, Matt 1932- DLB-212

Cumulative Index

Braun, Volker 1939- DLB-75, 124

Brautigan, Richard 1935-1984 .... DLB-2, 5, 206; Y-80, 84

Braxton, Joanne M. 1950- DLB-41

Bray, Anne Eliza 1790-1883 .... DLB-116

Bray, Thomas 1656-1730 .... DLB-24

Brazdžionis, Bernardas 1907-2002 .... DLB-220

George Braziller [publishing house] DLB-46

The Bread Loaf Writers' Conference 1983 .... Y-84

Breasted, James Henry 1865-1935 .... DLB-47

Brecht, Bertolt 1898-1956 .... DLB-56, 124; CDWLB-2

Bredel, Willi 1901-1964 .... DLB-56

Bregendahl, Marie 1867-1940 .... DLB-214

Breitinger, Johann Jakob 1701-1776 .... DLB-97

Brekke, Paal 1923-1993 .... DLB-297

Bremser, Bonnie 1939- DLB-16

Bremser, Ray 1934-1998 .... DLB-16

Brennan, Christopher 1870-1932 .... DLB-230

Brentano, Bernard von 1901-1964 .... DLB-56

Brentano, Clemens 1778-1842 .... DLB-90

Brentano, Franz 1838-1917 .... DLB-296

Brentano's DLB-49

Brenton, Howard 1942- DLB-13

Breslin, Jimmy 1929-1996 .... DLB-185

Breton, André 1896-1966 .... DLB-65, 258

Breton, Nicholas circa 1555-circa 1626 .... DLB-136

The Breton Lays 1300-early fifteenth century DLB-146

Brett, Lily 1946- DLB-325

Brett, Simon 1945- DLB-276

Brewer, Gil 1922-1983 .... DLB-306

Brewer, Luther A. 1858-1933 .... DLB-187

Brewer, Warren and Putnam DLB-46

Brewster, Elizabeth 1922- DLB-60

Breytenbach, Breyten 1939- DLB-225

Bridge, Ann (Lady Mary Dolling Sanders O'Malley) 1889-1974 .... DLB-191

Bridge, Horatio 1806-1893 .... DLB-183

Bridgers, Sue Ellen 1942- DLB-52

Bridges, Robert 1844-1930 .... DLB-19, 98; CDBLB-5

The Bridgewater Library DLB-213

Bridie, James 1888-1951 .... DLB-10

Brieux, Eugene 1858-1932 .... DLB-192

Brigadere, Anna 1861-1933 .... DLB-220; CDWLB-4

Briggs, Charles Frederick 1804-1877 .... DLB-3, 250

Brighouse, Harold 1882-1958 .... DLB-10

Bright, Mary Chavelita Dunne (see Egerton, George)

Brightman, Edgar Sheffield 1884-1953 .... DLB-270

B. J. Brimmer Company DLB-46

Brines, Francisco 1932- DLB-134

Brink, André 1935- DLB-225

Brinley, George, Jr. 1817-1875 .... DLB-140

Brinnin, John Malcolm 1916-1998 .... DLB-48

Brisbane, Albert 1809-1890 .... DLB-3, 250

Brisbane, Arthur 1864-1936 .... DLB-25

British Academy DLB-112

The British Critic 1793-1843 .... DLB-110

British Library
   The American Trust for the British Library Y-96
   The British Library and the Regular Readers' Group Y-91
   Building the New British Library at St Pancras Y-94

British Literary Prizes DLB-207; Y-98

British Literature
   The "Angry Young Men" DLB-15
   Author-Printers, 1476-1599 .... DLB-167
   The Comic Tradition Continued DLB-15
   Documents on Sixteenth-Century Literature DLB-167, 172
   Eikon Basilike 1649 .... DLB-151
   Letter from London Y-96
   A Mirror for Magistrates DLB-167
   "Modern English Prose" (1876), by George Saintsbury DLB-57
   Sex, Class, Politics, and Religion [in the British Novel, 1930-1959] DLB-15
   Victorians on Rhetoric and Prose Style DLB-57
   The Year in British Fiction Y-99–01
   "You've Never Had It So Good," Gusted by "Winds of Change": British Fiction in the 1950s, 1960s, and After DLB-14

British Literature, Old and Middle English
   Anglo-Norman Literature in the Development of Middle English Literature DLB-146
   The *Alliterative Morte Arthure and the Stanzaic Morte Arthur* circa 1350-1400 .... DLB-146
   Ancrene Riwle circa 1200-1225 .... DLB-146
   The Anglo-Saxon Chronicle circa 890-1154 .... DLB-146
   The Battle of Maldon circa 1000 .... DLB-146
   Beowulf circa 900-1000 or 790-825 .... DLB-146; CDBLB-1
   The Blickling Homilies circa 971 .... DLB-146
   The Breton Lays 1300-early fifteenth century DLB-146
   The Castle of Perserverance circa 1400-1425 .... DLB-146
   The Celtic Background to Medieval English Literature DLB-146
   The Chester Plays circa 1505-1532; revisions until 1575 .... DLB-146
   Cursor Mundi circa 1300 .... DLB-146
   The English Language: 410 to 1500 .... DLB-146
   The Germanic Epic and Old English Heroic Poetry: *Widsith, Waldere,* and *The Fight at Finnsburg* DLB-146
   Judith circa 930 .... DLB-146
   The Matter of England 1240-1400 .... DLB-146
   The Matter of Rome early twelfth to late fifteenth centuries DLB-146
   Middle English Literature: An Introduction DLB-146
   The Middle English Lyric DLB-146
   Morality Plays: *Mankind* circa 1450-1500 and *Everyman* circa 1500 .... DLB-146
   N-Town Plays circa 1468 to early sixteenth century DLB-146
   Old English Literature: An Introduction DLB-146
   Old English Riddles eighth to tenth centuries DLB-146
   The Owl and the Nightingale circa 1189-1199 .... DLB-146
   The Paston Letters 1422-1509 .... DLB-146
   The Seafarer circa 970 .... DLB-146
   The South English Legendary circa thirteenth to fifteenth centuries DLB-146

The British Review and London Critical Journal 1811-1825 .... DLB-110

Brito, Aristeo 1942- DLB-122

Brittain, Vera 1893-1970 .... DLB-191

Briusov, Valerii Iakovlevich 1873-1924 .... DLB-295

Brizeux, Auguste 1803-1858 .... DLB-217

Broadway Publishing Company DLB-46

Broch, Hermann 1886-1951 .... DLB-85, 124; CDWLB-2

Brochu, André 1942- DLB-53

Brock, Edwin 1927-1997 .... DLB-40

Brockes, Barthold Heinrich 1680-1747 .... DLB-168

Brod, Max 1884-1968 .... DLB-81

Brodber, Erna 1940- DLB-157

Brodhead, John R. 1814-1873 .... DLB-30

Brodkey, Harold 1930-1996 .... DLB-130

Brodsky, Joseph (Iosif Aleksandrovich Brodsky) 1940-1996 .... DLB-285, 329; Y-87

   Nobel Lecture 1987 .... Y-87

Brodsky, Michael 1948- DLB-244

Broeg, Bob 1918- DLB-171

Brøgger, Suzanne 1944- DLB-214

Brome, Richard circa 1590-1652 .... DLB-58

Brome, Vincent 1910-2004 .... DLB-155

Bromfield, Louis 1896-1956 .... DLB-4, 9, 86

Bromige, David 1933- DLB-193

Broner, E. M. 1930- DLB-28

   Tribute to Bernard Malamud Y-86

Bronk, William 1918-1999 .... DLB-165

Bronnen, Arnolt 1895-1959 .... DLB-124

Brontë, Anne 1820-1849 .... DLB-21, 199

Brontë, Charlotte
1816-1855 ...... DLB-21, 159, 199; CDBLB-4

Brontë, Emily
1818-1848 ...... DLB-21, 32, 199; CDBLB-4

The Brontë Society Y-98

Brook, Stephen 1947- DLB-204

Brook Farm 1841-1847 .... DLB-1; 223; DS-5

Brooke, Frances 1724-1789. .... DLB-39, 99

Brooke, Henry 1703?-1783. .... DLB-39

Brooke, L. Leslie 1862-1940 .... DLB-141

Brooke, Margaret, Ranee of Sarawak
1849-1936 .... DLB-174

Brooke, Rupert
1887-1915 .... DLB-19, 216; CDBLB-6

The Friends of the Dymock Poets........ Y-00

Brooker, Bertram 1888-1955 .... DLB-88

Brooke-Rose, Christine 1923- DLB-14, 231

Brookner, Anita 1928- DLB-194, 326; Y-87

Brooks, Charles Timothy 1813-1883... DLB-1, 243

Brooks, Cleanth 1906-1994 .... DLB-63; Y-94

Tribute to Katherine Anne Porter Y-80

Tribute to Walker Percy Y-90

Brooks, Gwendolyn
1917-2000 .... DLB-5, 76, 165; CDALB-1

Tribute to Julian Mayfield Y-84

Brooks, Jeremy 1926-1994............... DLB-14

Brooks, Mel 1926- DLB-26

Brooks, Noah 1830-1903......... DLB-42; DS-13

Brooks, Richard 1912-1992 .... DLB-44

Brooks, Van Wyck 1886-1963 .... DLB-45, 63, 103

Brophy, Brigid 1929-1995 .... DLB-14, 70, 271

Brophy, John 1899-1965 .... DLB-191

Brorson, Hans Adolph 1694-1764 .... DLB-300

Brossard, Chandler 1922-1993 .... DLB-16

Brossard, Nicole 1943- DLB-53

Broster, Dorothy Kathleen 1877-1950 .... DLB-160

Brother Antoninus (see Everson, William)

Brotherton, Lord 1856-1930 .... DLB-184

Brougham, John 1810-1880 .... DLB-11

Brougham and Vaux, Henry Peter
Brougham, Baron 1778-1868.... DLB-110, 158

Broughton, James 1913-1999............. DLB-5

Broughton, Rhoda 1840-1920 .... DLB-18

Broun, Heywood 1888-1939 .... DLB-29, 171

Browder, Earl 1891-1973 .... DLB-303

Brown, Alice 1856-1948. .... DLB-78

Brown, Bob 1886-1959 .... DLB-4, 45; DS-15

Brown, Cecil 1943- DLB-33

Brown, Charles Brockden
1771-1810 .... DLB-37, 59, 73; CDALB-2

Brown, Christy 1932-1981............... DLB-14

Brown, Dee 1908-2002 .... Y-80

Brown, Frank London 1927-1962 .... DLB-76

Brown, Fredric 1906-1972 .... DLB-8

Brown, George Mackay
1921-1996 .... DLB-14, 27, 139, 271

Brown, Harry 1917-1986 .... DLB-26

Brown, Ian 1945- DLB-310

Brown, Larry 1951- DLB-234, 292

Brown, Lew 1893-1958 .... DLB-265

Brown, Marcia 1918- DLB-61

Brown, Margaret Wise 1910-1952........ DLB-22

Brown, Morna Doris (see Ferrars, Elizabeth)

Brown, Oliver Madox 1855-1874........ DLB-21

Brown, Sterling 1901-1989. .... DLB-48, 51, 63

Brown, T. E. 1830-1897................ DLB-35

Brown, Thomas Alexander (see Boldrewood, Rolf)

Brown, Warren 1894-1978 .... DLB-241

Brown, William Hill 1765-1793 .... DLB-37

Brown, William Wells
1815-1884 .... DLB-3, 50, 183, 248

Brown University
The Festival of Vanguard Narrative...... Y-93

Browne, Charles Farrar 1834-1867 .... DLB-11

Browne, Frances 1816-1879 .... DLB-199

Browne, Francis Fisher 1843-1913 .... DLB-79

Browne, Howard 1908-1999 .... DLB-226

Browne, J. Ross 1821-1875. .... DLB-202

Browne, Michael Dennis 1940- DLB-40

Browne, Sir Thomas 1605-1682 .... DLB-151

Browne, William, of Tavistock
1590-1645 .... DLB-121

Browne, Wynyard 1911-1964 .... DLB-13, 233

Browne and Nolan. DLB-106

Brownell, W. C. 1851-1928 .... DLB-71

Browning, Elizabeth Barrett
1806-1861 .... DLB-32, 199; CDBLB-4

Browning, Robert
1812-1889 .... DLB-32, 163; CDBLB-4

Essay on Chatterton DLB-32

Introductory Essay: *Letters of Percy
Bysshe Shelley* (1852) DLB-32

"The Novel in [Robert Browning's]
'The Ring and the Book'" (1912),
by Henry James DLB-32

Brownjohn, Allan 1931- DLB-40

Tribute to John Betjeman Y-84

Brownson, Orestes Augustus
1803-1876 .... DLB-1, 59, 73, 243; DS-5

Bruccoli, Matthew J. 1931- DLB-103

Joseph [Heller] and George [V. Higgins] Y-99

Response [to Busch on Fitzgerald]........ Y-96

Tribute to Albert Erskine Y-93

Tribute to Charles E. Feinberg Y-88

Working with Fredson Bowers Y-91

Bruce, Charles 1906-1971 .... DLB-68

Bruce, John Edward 1856-1924

Three Documents [African American
poets] DLB-50

Bruce, Leo 1903-1979 .... DLB-77

Bruce, Mary Grant 1878-1958.......... DLB-230

Bruce, Philip Alexander 1856-1933....... DLB-47

Bruce-Novoa, Juan 1944- DLB-82

Bruckman, Clyde 1894-1955........... DLB-26

Bruckner, Ferdinand 1891-1958........ DLB-118

Brundage, John Herbert (see Herbert, John)

Brunner, John 1934-1995.............. DLB-261

Tribute to Theodore Sturgeon Y-85

Brutus, Dennis
1924- DLB-117, 225; CDWLB-3

Bryan, C. D. B. 1936- DLB-185

Bryan, William Jennings 1860-1925 ..... DLB-303

Bryant, Arthur 1899-1985 .... DLB-149

Bryant, William Cullen 1794-1878
.... DLB-3, 43, 59, 189, 250; CDALB-2

Bryce, James 1838-1922............ DLB-166, 190

Bryce Echenique, Alfredo
1939- DLB-145; CDWLB-3

Bryden, Bill 1942- DLB-233

Brydges, Sir Samuel Egerton
1762-1837 .... DLB-107, 142

Bryskett, Lodowick 1546?-1612 .... DLB-167

Buchan, John 1875-1940 .... DLB-34, 70, 156

Buchanan, George 1506-1582 .... DLB-132

Buchanan, Robert 1841-1901 .... DLB-18, 35

"The Fleshly School of Poetry and
Other Phenomena of the Day"
(1872) DLB-35

"The Fleshly School of Poetry:
Mr. D. G. Rossetti" (1871),
by Thomas Maitland DLB-35

Buchler, Justus 1914-1991 .... DLB-279

Buchman, Sidney 1902-1975 .... DLB-26

Buchner, Augustus 1591-1661.......... DLB-164

Büchner, Georg
1813-1837 .... DLB-133; CDWLB-2

Bucholtz, Andreas Heinrich 1607-1671..... DLB-168

Buck, Pearl S.
1892-1973 .... DLB-9, 102, 329; CDALB-7

Bucke, Charles 1781-1846 .... DLB-110

Bucke, Richard Maurice 1837-1902....... DLB-99

Buckingham, Edwin 1810-1833.......... DLB-73

Buckingham, Joseph Tinker 1779-1861 .... DLB-73

Buckler, Ernest 1908-1984 .... DLB-68

Buckley, Vincent 1925-1988 .... DLB-289

Buckley, William F., Jr. 1925- DLB-137; Y-80

Publisher's Statement From the
Initial Issue of *National Review*
(19 November 1955)........... DLB-137

Buckminster, Joseph Stevens
1784-1812 .... DLB-37

Buckner, Robert 1906-1989............. DLB-26

Budd, Thomas ?-1698 . . . . DLB-24
Budé, Guillaume 1468-1540 . . . . DLB-327
Budrys, A. J. 1931- DLB-8
Buechner, Frederick 1926- Y-80
Buell, John 1927- DLB-53
Buenaventura, Enrique 1925-2003 . . . . . . DLB-305
Bufalino, Gesualdo 1920-1996 . . . . DLB-196
Buffon, Georges-Louis Leclerc de
   1707-1788 . . . . DLB-313
    "Le Discours sur le style" DLB-314
Job Buffum [publishing house] DLB-49
Bugnet, Georges 1879-1981 . . . . DLB-92
al-Buhturi 821-897 . . . . DLB-311
Buies, Arthur 1840-1901 . . . . DLB-99
Bukiet, Melvin Jules 1953- DLB-299
Bukowski, Charles 1920-1994 . . . DLB-5, 130, 169
Bulatović, Miodrag
   1930-1991 . . . . DLB-181; CDWLB-4
Bulgakov, Mikhail Afanas'evich
   1891-1940 . . . . DLB-272
Bulgarin, Faddei Venediktovich
   1789-1859 . . . . DLB-198
Bulger, Bozeman 1877-1932 . . . . DLB-171
Bull, Olaf 1883-1933 . . . . DLB-297
Bullein, William
   between 1520 and 1530-1576 . . . . DLB-167
Bullins, Ed 1935- DLB-7, 38, 249
Bulosan, Carlos 1911-1956 . . . . DLB-312
Bulwer, John 1606-1656 . . . . DLB-236
Bulwer-Lytton, Edward (also Edward
   Bulwer) 1803-1873 . . . . DLB-21
   "On Art in Fiction" (1838) DLB-21
Bumpus, Jerry 1937- Y-81
Bunce and Brother DLB-49
Bunin, Ivan 1870-1953 . . . . DLB-317, 329
Bunner, H. C. 1855-1896 . . . . DLB-78, 79
Bunting, Basil 1900-1985 . . . . DLB-20
Buntline, Ned (Edward Zane Carroll
   Judson) 1821-1886 . . . . DLB-186
Bunyan, John 1628-1688 . . . . . DLB-39; CDBLB-2
   The Author's Apology for
     His Book DLB-39
Burch, Robert 1925- DLB-52
Burciaga, José Antonio 1940- DLB-82
Burdekin, Katharine (Murray Constantine)
   1896-1963 . . . . DLB-255
Bürger, Gottfried August 1747-1794 . . . . . . DLB-94
Burgess, Anthony (John Anthony Burgess Wilson)
   1917-1993 . . . . . . DLB-14, 194, 261; CDBLB-8
   The Anthony Burgess Archive at
     the Harry Ransom Humanities
     Research Center Y-98
   Anthony Burgess's 99 Novels:
     An Opinion Poll Y-84
Burgess, Gelett 1866-1951 . . . . DLB-11

Burgess, John W. 1844-1931 . . . . DLB-47
Burgess, Thornton W. 1874-1965 . . . . DLB-22
Burgess, Stringer and Company DLB-49
Burgos, Julia de 1914-1953 . . . . DLB-290
Burick, Si 1909-1986 . . . . DLB-171
Burk, John Daly circa 1772-1808 . . . . DLB-37
Burk, Ronnie 1955- DLB-209
Burke, Edmund 1729?-1797 . . . . . . DLB-104, 252
Burke, James Lee 1936- DLB-226
Burke, Johnny 1908-1964 . . . . DLB-265
Burke, Kenneth 1897-1993 . . . . DLB-45, 63
Burke, Thomas 1886-1945 . . . . DLB-197
Burley, Dan 1907-1962 . . . . DLB-241
Burley, W. J. 1914- DLB-276
Burlingame, Edward Livermore
   1848-1922 . . . . DLB-79
Burliuk, David 1882-1967 . . . . DLB-317
Burman, Carina 1960- DLB-257
Burnet, Gilbert 1643-1715 . . . . DLB-101
Burnett, Frances Hodgson
   1849-1924 . . . . DLB-42, 141; DS-13, 14
Burnett, W. R. 1899-1982 . . . . DLB-9, 226
Burnett, Whit 1899-1973 . . . . DLB-137
Burney, Fanny 1752-1840 . . . . DLB-39
   Dedication, The Wanderer (1814) DLB-39
   Preface to Evelina (1778) DLB-39
Burns, Alan 1929- DLB-14, 194
Burns, Joanne 1945- DLB-289
Burns, John Horne 1916-1953 . . . . Y-85
Burns, Robert 1759-1796 . . . . DLB-109; CDBLB-3
Burns and Oates DLB-106
Burnshaw, Stanley 1906- DLB-48; Y-97
   James Dickey and Stanley Burnshaw
     Correspondence Y-02
   Review of Stanley Burnshaw: The
     Collected Poems and Selected
     Prose Y-02
   Tribute to Robert Penn Warren Y-89
Burr, C. Chauncey 1815?-1883 . . . . DLB-79
Burr, Esther Edwards 1732-1758 . . . . DLB-200
Burroughs, Edgar Rice 1875-1950 . . . . DLB-8
   The Burroughs Bibliophiles Y-98
Burroughs, John 1837-1921 . . . . DLB-64, 275
Burroughs, Margaret T. G. 1917- DLB-41
Burroughs, William S., Jr. 1947-1981 . . . . . DLB-16
Burroughs, William Seward 1914-1997
   . . . . DLB-2, 8, 16, 152, 237; Y-81, 97
Burroway, Janet 1936- DLB-6
Burt, Maxwell Struthers
   1882-1954 . . . . DLB-86; DS-16
A. L. Burt and Company DLB-49
Burton, Hester 1913-2000 . . . . DLB-161
Burton, Isabel Arundell 1831-1896 . . . . . . DLB-166

Burton, Miles (see Rhode, John)
Burton, Richard Francis
   1821-1890 . . . . DLB-55, 166, 184
Burton, Robert 1577-1640 . . . . DLB-151
Burton, Virginia Lee 1909-1968 . . . . DLB-22
Burton, William Evans 1804-1860 . . . . DLB-73
Burwell, Adam Hood 1790-1849 . . . . DLB-99
Bury, Lady Charlotte 1775-1861 . . . . DLB-116
Busch, Frederick 1941-2006 . . . . DLB-6, 218
   Excerpts from Frederick Busch's USC
     Remarks [on F. Scott Fitzgerald] Y-96
   Tribute to James Laughlin Y-97
   Tribute to Raymond Carver Y-88
Busch, Niven 1903-1991 . . . . DLB-44
Bushnell, Horace 1802-1876 . . . . DS-13
Business & Literature
   The Claims of Business and Literature:
     An Undergraduate Essay by
     Maxwell Perkins Y-01
Bussières, Arthur de 1877-1913 . . . . DLB-92
Butler, Charles circa 1560-1647 . . . . DLB-236
Butler, Guy 1918- DLB-225
Butler, Joseph 1692-1752 . . . . DLB-252
Butler, Josephine Elizabeth 1828-1906 . . . DLB-190
Butler, Juan 1942-1981 . . . . DLB-53
Butler, Judith 1956- DLB-246
Butler, Octavia E. 1947-2006 . . . . DLB-33
Butler, Pierce 1884-1953 . . . . DLB-187
Butler, Robert Olen 1945- DLB-173
Butler, Samuel 1613-1680 . . . . DLB-101, 126
Butler, Samuel
   1835-1902 . . . . . . DLB-18, 57, 174; CDBLB-5
Butler, William Francis 1838-1910 . . . . . . DLB-166
E. H. Butler and Company DLB-49
Butor, Michel 1926- DLB-83
Nathaniel Butter
   [publishing house] DLB-170
Butterworth, Hezekiah 1839-1905 . . . . DLB-42
Buttitta, Ignazio 1899-1997 . . . . DLB-114
Butts, Mary 1890-1937 . . . . DLB-240
Buzo, Alex 1944- DLB-289
Buzzati, Dino 1906-1972 . . . . DLB-177
Byars, Betsy 1928- DLB-52
Byatt, A. S. 1936- DLB-14, 194, 319, 326
Byles, Mather 1707-1788 . . . . DLB-24
Henry Bynneman
   [publishing house] DLB-170
Bynner, Witter 1881-1968 . . . . DLB-54
Byrd, William circa 1543-1623 . . . . DLB-172
Byrd, William, II 1674-1744 . . . . DLB-24, 140
Byrne, John Keyes (see Leonard, Hugh)
Byron, George Gordon, Lord
   1788-1824 . . . . DLB-96, 110; CDBLB-3
   The Byron Society of America Y-00

Byron, Robert 1905-1941 ....DLB-195

Byzantine Novel, The Spanish DLB-318

C

Caballero Bonald, José Manuel
1926- DLB-108

Cabañero, Eladio 1930- DLB-134

Cabell, James Branch 1879-1958 ....DLB-9, 78

Cabeza de Baca, Manuel 1853-1915 .....DLB-122

Cabeza de Baca Gilbert, Fabiola
1898-1993 ....DLB-122

Cable, George Washington
1844-1925 ....DLB-12, 74; DS-13

Cable, Mildred 1878-1952 ....DLB-195

Cabral, Manuel del 1907-1999 ....DLB-283

Cabral de Melo Neto, João
1920-1999 ....DLB-307

Cabrera, Lydia 1900-1991 ....DLB-145

Cabrera Infante, Guillermo
1929- DLB-113; CDWLB-3

Cabrujas, José Ignacio 1937-1995........DLB-305

Cadell [publishing house]..............DLB-154

Cady, Edwin H. 1917- DLB-103

Caedmon fl. 658-680.................DLB-146

Caedmon School circa 660-899 ....DLB-146

Caesar, Irving 1895-1996..............DLB-265

Cafés, Brasseries, and Bistros...........DS-15

Cage, John 1912-1992 ....DLB-193

Cahan, Abraham 1860-1951 ....DLB-9, 25, 28

Cahn, Sammy 1913-1993...............DLB-265

Cain, George 1943- DLB-33

Cain, James M. 1892-1977.............DLB-226

Cain, Paul (Peter Ruric, George Sims)
1902-1966 ....DLB-306

Caird, Edward 1835-1908 ....DLB-262

Caird, Mona 1854-1932................DLB-197

Čaks, Aleksandrs
1901-1950 ....DLB-220; CDWLB-4

Caldecott, Randolph 1846-1886 ....DLB-163

John Calder Limited
[Publishing house]................DLB-112

Calderón de la Barca, Fanny
1804-1882 ....DLB-183

Caldwell, Ben 1937- DLB-38

Caldwell, Erskine 1903-1987 ....DLB-9, 86

H. M. Caldwell Company DLB-49

Caldwell, Taylor 1900-1985..............DS-17

Calhoun, John C. 1782-1850 ....DLB-3, 248

Călinescu, George 1899-1965 ....DLB-220

Calisher, Hortense 1911- DLB-2, 218

Calkins, Mary Whiton 1863-1930.......DLB-270

Callaghan, Mary Rose 1944- DLB-207

Callaghan, Morley 1903-1990 .....DLB-68; DS-15

Callahan, S. Alice 1868-1894 ....DLB-175, 221

Callaloo [journal].........................Y-87

Callimachus circa 305 B.C.-240 B.C....... DLB-176

Calmer, Edgar 1907-1986.................DLB-4

Calverley, C. S. 1831-1884 ....DLB-35

Calvert, George Henry
1803-1889 ....DLB-1, 64, 248

Calverton, V. F. (George Goetz)
1900-1940 ....DLB-303

Calvin, Jean 1509-1564 ....DLB-327

Calvino, Italo 1923-1985 ....DLB-196

Cambridge, Ada 1844-1926..............DLB-230

Cambridge Press DLB-49

Cambridge Songs (Carmina Cantabrigensia)
circa 1050 ....DLB-148

Cambridge University
Cambridge and the Apostles.......... DS-5

Cambridge University Press DLB-170

Camden, William 1551-1623.............DLB-172

Camden House: An Interview with
James Hardin.......................Y-92

Cameron, Eleanor 1912-2000 ....DLB-52

Cameron, George Frederick
1854-1885 ....DLB-99

Cameron, Lucy Lyttelton 1781-1858......DLB-163

Cameron, Peter 1959- DLB-234

Cameron, William Bleasdell 1862-1951....DLB-99

Camm, John 1718-1778 ....DLB-31

Camões, Luís de 1524-1580.............DLB-287

Camon, Ferdinando 1935- DLB-196

Camp, Walter 1859-1925................DLB-241

Campana, Dino 1885-1932 ....DLB-114

Campbell, Bebe Moore 1950- DLB-227

Campbell, David 1915-1979.............DLB-260

Campbell, Gabrielle Margaret Vere
(see Shearing, Joseph, and Bowen, Marjorie)

Campbell, James Dykes 1838-1895 ......DLB-144

Campbell, James Edwin 1867-1896 ....DLB-50

Campbell, John 1653-1728...............DLB-43

Campbell, John W., Jr. 1910-1971 ....DLB-8

Campbell, Ramsey 1946- DLB-261

Campbell, Robert 1927-2000 ....DLB-306

Campbell, Roy 1901-1957 ....DLB-20, 225

Campbell, Thomas 1777-1844 ....DLB-93, 144

Campbell, William Edward (see March, William)

Campbell, William Wilfred 1858-1918 ....DLB-92

Campion, Edmund 1539-1581 ....DLB-167

Campion, Thomas
1567-1620 ....DLB-58, 172; CDBLB-1

Campo, Rafael 1964- DLB-282

Campton, David 1924- DLB-245

Camus, Albert 1913-1960 ......DLB-72, 321, 329

Camus, Jean-Pierre 1584-1652...........DLB-268

The Canadian Publishers' Records Database ...Y-96

Canby, Henry Seidel 1878-1961.........DLB-91

Cancioneros.........................DLB-286

Candelaria, Cordelia 1943- DLB-82

Candelaria, Nash 1928- DLB-82

Candide, Voltaire DLB-314

Canetti, Elias
1905-1994 ..... DLB-85, 124, 329; CDWLB-2

Canham, Erwin Dain 1904-1982........DLB-127

Canitz, Friedrich Rudolph Ludwig von
1654-1699 ....DLB-168

Cankar, Ivan 1876-1918..... DLB-147; CDWLB-4

Cannan, Gilbert 1884-1955 .... DLB-10, 197

Cannan, Joanna 1896-1961 ....DLB-191

Cannell, Kathleen 1891-1974.............DLB-4

Cannell, Skipwith 1887-1957 ....DLB-45

Canning, George 1770-1827............DLB-158

Cannon, Jimmy 1910-1973 ....DLB-171

Cano, Daniel 1947- DLB-209

Old Dogs / New Tricks? New
Technologies, the Canon, and the
Structure of the Profession Y-02

Cantú, Norma Elia 1947- DLB-209

Cantwell, Robert 1908-1978 ....DLB-9

Jonathan Cape and Harrison Smith
[publishing house]................DLB-46

Jonathan Cape Limited DLB-112

Čapek, Karel 1890-1938 .... DLB-215; CDWLB-4

Capen, Joseph 1658-1725...............DLB-24

Capes, Bernard 1854-1918..............DLB-156

Capote, Truman 1924-1984
.... DLB-2, 185, 227; Y-80, 84; CDALB-1

Capps, Benjamin 1922- DLB-256

Caproni, Giorgio 1912-1990 ....DLB-128

Caragiale, Mateiu Ioan 1885-1936........DLB-220

Carballido, Emilio 1925- DLB-305

Cardarelli, Vincenzo 1887-1959 ....DLB-114

Cardenal, Ernesto 1925- DLB-290

Cárdenas, Reyes 1948- DLB-122

Cardinal, Marie 1929-2001 ....DLB-83

Cardoza y Aragón, Luis 1901-1992......DLB-290

Carducci, Giosuè 1835-1907 ....DLB-329

Carew, Jan 1920- DLB-157

Carew, Thomas 1594 or 1595-1640.....DLB-126

Carey, Henry circa 1687-1689-1743 ....DLB-84

Carey, Mathew 1760-1839 .... DLB-37, 73

M. Carey and Company DLB-49

Carey, Peter 1943- DLB-289, 326

Carey and Hart DLB-49

Carlell, Lodowick 1602-1675............DLB-58

Carleton, William 1794-1869...........DLB-159

G. W. Carleton [publishing house] DLB-49

Carlile, Richard 1790-1843 ....DLB-110, 158

Cumulative Index

Carlson, Ron 1947- DLB-244

Carlyle, Jane Welsh 1801-1866.......... DLB-55

Carlyle, Thomas
1795-1881.......... DLB-55, 144; CDBLB-3

"The Hero as Man of Letters:
Johnson, Rousseau, Burns"
(1841) [excerpt] DLB-57

The Hero as Poet. Dante; Shakspeare
(1841) DLB-32

Carman, Bliss 1861-1929 .... DLB-92

Carmina Burana circa 1230 .... DLB-138

Carnap, Rudolf 1891-1970 .... DLB-270

Carnero, Guillermo 1947- DLB-108

Carossa, Hans 1878-1956 .... DLB-66

Carpenter, Humphrey
1946-2005 .... DLB-155; Y-84, 99

Carpenter, Stephen Cullen ?-1820? DLB-73

Carpentier, Alejo
1904-1980 .... DLB-113; CDWLB-3

Carr, Emily 1871-1945 .... DLB-68

Carr, John Dickson 1906-1977 .... DLB-306

Carr, Marina 1964- DLB-245

Carr, Virginia Spencer 1929- DLB-111; Y-00

Carrera Andrade, Jorge 1903-1978 ..... DLB-283

Carrier, Roch 1937- DLB-53

Carrillo, Adolfo 1855-1926............ DLB-122

Carroll, Gladys Hasty 1904-1999........ DLB-9

Carroll, John 1735-1815 .... DLB-37

Carroll, John 1809-1884 .... DLB-99

Carroll, Lewis
1832-1898 ..... DLB-18, 163, 178; CDBLB-4

The Lewis Carroll Centenary Y-98

The Lewis Carroll Society
of North America Y-00

Carroll, Paul 1927-1996 .... DLB-16

Carroll, Paul Vincent 1900-1968 .... DLB-10

Carroll and Graf Publishers DLB-46

Carruth, Hayden 1921- DLB-5, 165

Tribute to James Dickey............... Y-97

Tribute to Raymond Carver............ Y-88

Carryl, Charles E. 1841-1920............ DLB-42

Carson, Anne 1950- DLB-193

Carson, Rachel 1907-1964 ....DLB-275

Carswell, Catherine 1879-1946.......... DLB-36

Cartagena, Alfonso de circa 1384-1456 .. DLB-286

Cartagena, Teresa de 1425?-? DLB-286

Cărtărescu, Mirea 1956- DLB-232

Carter, Angela
1940-1992 .... DLB-14, 207, 261, 319

Carter, Elizabeth 1717-1806............ DLB-109

Carter, Henry (see Leslie, Frank)

Carter, Hodding, Jr. 1907-1972 .... DLB-127

Carter, Jared 1939- DLB-282

Carter, John 1905-1975................ DLB-201

Carter, Landon 1710-1778.............. DLB-31

Carter, Lin 1930-1988 .... Y-81

Carter, Martin 1927-1997 ....DLB-117; CDWLB-3

Carter, Robert, and Brothers DLB-49

Carter and Hendee.................... DLB-49

Cartwright, Jim 1958- DLB-245

Cartwright, John 1740-1824 .... DLB-158

Cartwright, William circa 1611-1643 .... DLB-126

Caruthers, William Alexander
1802-1846 .... DLB-3, 248

Carver, Jonathan 1710-1780 .... DLB-31

Carver, Raymond 1938-1988 ... DLB-130; Y-83,88

First Strauss "Livings" Awarded to Cynthia
Ozick and Raymond Carver
An Interview with Raymond Carver.... Y-83

Carvic, Heron 1917?-1980 ....DLB-276

Cary, Alice 1820-1871................ DLB-202

Cary, Joyce 1888-1957 ... DLB-15, 100; CDBLB-6

Cary, Patrick 1623?-1657 .... DLB-131

Casal, Julián del 1863-1893 .... DLB-283

Case, John 1540-1600................. DLB-281

Casey, Gavin 1907-1964 .... DLB-260

Casey, Juanita 1925- DLB-14

Casey, Michael 1947- DLB-5

Cassady, Carolyn 1923- DLB-16

"As I See It" DLB-16

Cassady, Neal 1926-1968 ....DLB-16, 237

Cassell and Company................. DLB-106

Cassell Publishing Company DLB-49

Cassill, R. V. 1919-2002 ....DLB-6, 218; Y-02

Tribute to James Dickey............... Y-97

Cassity, Turner 1929- DLB-105; Y-02

Cassius Dio circa 155/164-post 229 .....DLB-176

Cassola, Carlo 1917-1987 ....DLB-177

Castellano, Olivia 1944- DLB-122

Castellanos, Rosario
1925-1974..........DLB-113, 290; CDWLB-3

Castelo Branco, Camilo 1825-1890 ..... DLB-287

Castile, Protest Poetry in.............. DLB-286

Castile and Aragon, Vernacular Translations
in Crowns of 1352-1515........... DLB-286

Castillejo, Cristóbal de 1490?-1550 ..... DLB-318

Castillo, Ana 1953- DLB-122, 227

Castillo, Rafael C. 1950- DLB-209

The Castle of Perserverance
circa 1400-1425 .... DLB-146

Castlemon, Harry (see Fosdick, Charles Austin)

Castro, Brian 1950- DLB-325

Castro, Consuelo de 1946- DLB-307

Castro Alves, Antônio de 1847-1871..... DLB-307

Čašule, Kole 1921- DLB-181

Caswall, Edward 1814-1878 .... DLB-32

Catacalos, Rosemary 1944- DLB-122

Cather, Willa 1873-1947
.... DLB-9, 54, 78, 256; DS-1; CDALB-3

The Willa Cather Pioneer Memorial
and Education Foundation Y-00

Catherine II (Ekaterina Alekseevna), "The Great,"
Empress of Russia 1729-1796....... DLB-150

Catherwood, Mary Hartwell 1847-1902... DLB-78

Catledge, Turner 1901-1983............DLB-127

Catlin, George 1796-1872 .... DLB-186, 189

Cato the Elder 234 B.C.-149 B.C. DLB-211

Cattafi, Bartolo 1922-1979 .... DLB-128

Catton, Bruce 1899-1978 ....DLB-17

Catullus circa 84 B.C.-54 B.C.
....................DLB-211; CDWLB-1

Causley, Charles 1917-2003 .... DLB-27

Caute, David 1936- DLB-14, 231

Cavendish, Duchess of Newcastle,
Margaret Lucas
1623?-1673............. DLB-131, 252, 281

Cawein, Madison 1865-1914 .... DLB-54

William Caxton [publishing house] DLB-170

The Caxton Printers, Limited DLB-46

Caylor, O. P. 1849-1897 .... DLB-241

Caylus, Marthe-Marguerite de
1671-1729..................... DLB-313

Cayrol, Jean 1911-2005 .... DLB-83

Cecil, Lord David 1902-1986.......... DLB-155

Cela, Camilo José
1916-2002 ....DLB-322, 329; Y-89

Nobel Lecture 1989 .... Y-89

Celan, Paul 1920-1970 ...... DLB-69; CDWLB-2

Celati, Gianni 1937- DLB-196

Celaya, Gabriel 1911-1991 .... DLB-108

Céline, Louis-Ferdinand 1894-1961 ...... DLB-72

Celtis, Conrad 1459-1508............. DLB-179

Cendrars, Blaise 1887-1961 .... DLB-258

The Steinbeck Centennial Y-02

Censorship
The Island Trees Case: A Symposium on
School Library Censorship Y-82

Center for Bibliographical Studies and
Research at the University of
California, Riverside Y-91

Center for Book Research Y-84

The Center for the Book in the Library
of Congress Y-93

A New Voice: The Center for the
Book's First Five Years............. Y-83

Centlivre, Susanna 1669?-1723.......... DLB-84

The Centre for Writing, Publishing and
Printing History at the University
of Reading Y-00

The Century Company DLB-49

A Century of Poetry, a Lifetime of Collecting:
J. M. Edelstein's Collection of
Twentieth-Century American Poetry Y-02

Cernuda, Luis 1902-1963 ....DLB-134

Cerruto, Oscar 1912-1981 ....DLB-283

Cervantes, Lorna Dee 1954- DLB-82

Césaire, Aimé 1913- DLB-321

de Céspedes, Alba 1911-1997 ....DLB-264

Cetina, Gutierre de 1514-17?-1556 ......DLB-318

Ch., T. (see Marchenko, Anastasiia Iakovlevna)

Cha, Theresa Hak Kyung 1951-1982 ....DLB-312

Chaadaev, Petr Iakovlevich
   1794-1856 ....DLB-198

Chabon, Michael 1963- DLB-278

Chacel, Rosa 1898-1994 ....DLB-134, 322

Chacón, Eusebio 1869-1948 ....DLB-82

Chacón, Felipe Maximiliano 1873-? DLB-82

Chadwick, Henry 1824-1908 ....DLB-241

Chadwyck-Healey's Full-Text Literary Databases:
   Editing Commercial Databases of
   Primary Literary Texts Y-95

Challans, Eileen Mary (see Renault, Mary)

Chalmers, George 1742-1825............DLB-30

Chaloner, Sir Thomas 1520-1565 ....DLB-167

Chamberlain, Samuel S. 1851-1916.......DLB-25

Chamberland, Paul 1939- DLB-60

Chamberlin, William Henry 1897-1969....DLB-29

Chambers, Charles Haddon 1860-1921 ...DLB-10

Chambers, María Cristina (see Mena, María Cristina)

Chambers, Robert W. 1865-1933 ....DLB-202

W. and R. Chambers
   [publishing house] DLB-106

Chambers, Whittaker 1901-1961 ....DLB-303

Chamfort, Sébastien-Roch Nicolas de
   1740?-1794.....................DLB-313

Chamisso, Adelbert von 1781-1838.......DLB-90

Champfleury 1821-1889 ....DLB-119

Champier, Symphorien 1472?-1539? DLB-327

Chan, Jeffery Paul 1942- DLB-312

Chandler, Harry 1864-1944............DLB-29

Chandler, Norman 1899-1973 ....DLB-127

Chandler, Otis 1927-2006.............DLB-127

Chandler, Raymond
   1888-1959 ....DLB-226, 253; DS-6; CDALB-5
   Raymond Chandler Centenary..........Y-88

Chang, Diana 1934- DLB-312

Channing, Edward 1856-1931............DLB-17

Channing, Edward Tyrrell
   1790-1856 ....DLB-1, 59, 235

Channing, William Ellery
   1780-1842 ....DLB-1, 59, 235

Channing, William Ellery, II
   1817-1901 ....DLB-1, 223

Channing, William Henry
   1810-1884 ....DLB-1, 59, 243

Chapelain, Jean 1595-1674.............DLB-268

Chaplin, Charlie 1889-1977 ....DLB-44

Chapman, George
   1559 or 1560-1634 ....DLB-62, 121

Chapman, Olive Murray 1892-1977 .....DLB-195

Chapman, R. W. 1881-1960 ....DLB-201

Chapman, William 1850-1917 ....DLB-99

John Chapman [publishing house].......DLB-106

Chapman and Hall [publishing house] ...DLB-106

Chappell, Fred 1936- DLB-6, 105
   "A Detail in a Poem" DLB-105
   Tribute to Peter Taylor Y-94

Chappell, William 1582-1649 ....DLB-236

Char, René 1907-1988 ....DLB-258

Charbonneau, Jean 1875-1960..........DLB-92

Charbonneau, Robert 1911-1967 ....DLB-68

Charles, Gerda 1914-1996 ....DLB-14

William Charles [publishing house].......DLB-49

Charles d'Orléans 1394-1465 ....DLB-208

Charley (see Mann, Charles)

Charrière, Isabelle de 1740-1805 ....DLB-313

Charskaia, Lidiia 1875-1937............DLB-295

Charteris, Leslie 1907-1993 ....DLB-77

Chartier, Alain circa 1385-1430 ....DLB-208

Charyn, Jerome 1937- Y-83

Chase, Borden 1900-1971 ....DLB-26

Chase, Edna Woolman 1877-1957 ....DLB-91

Chase, James Hadley (René Raymond)
   1906-1985 ....DLB-276

Chase, Mary Coyle 1907-1981..........DLB-228

Chase-Riboud, Barbara 1936- DLB-33

Chateaubriand, François-René de
   1768-1848 ....DLB-119

Châtelet, Gabrielle-Emilie Du
   1706-1749 ....DLB-313

Chatterjee, Upamanyu 1959- DLB-323

Chatterton, Thomas 1752-1770 ....DLB-109
   Essay on Chatterton (1842), by
   Robert Browning DLB-32

Chatto and Windus..................DLB-106

Chatwin, Bruce 1940-1989 ....DLB-194, 204

Chaucer, Geoffrey
   1340?-1400 ....DLB-146; CDBLB-1
   New Chaucer Society Y-00

Chaudhuri, Amit 1962- DLB-267, 323

Chaudhuri, Nirad C. 1897-1999 ....DLB-323

Chauncy, Charles 1705-1787 ....DLB-24

Chauveau, Pierre-Joseph-Olivier
   1820-1890 ....DLB-99

Chávez, Denise 1948- DLB-122

Chávez, Fray Angélico 1910-1996 ....DLB-82

Chayefsky, Paddy 1923-1981..... DLB-7, 44; Y-81

Cheesman, Evelyn 1881-1969 ....DLB-195

Cheever, Ezekiel 1615-1708 ....DLB-24

Cheever, George Barrell 1807-1890 ....DLB-59

Cheever, John 1912-1982
   .... DLB-2, 102, 227; Y-80, 82; CDALB-1

Cheever, Susan 1943- Y-82

Cheke, Sir John 1514-1557 ....DLB-132

Chekhov, Anton Pavlovich 1860-1904 ...DLB-277

Chelsea House......................DLB-46

Chênedollé, Charles de 1769-1833 ......DLB-217

Cheney, Brainard
   Tribute to Caroline Gordon Y-81

Cheney, Ednah Dow 1824-1904 ......DLB-1, 223

Cheney, Harriet Vaughan 1796-1889......DLB-99

Chénier, Marie-Joseph 1764-1811 ....DLB-192

Cheng Xiaoqing 1893-1976............DLB-328

Cherny, Sasha 1880-1932 ....DLB-317

Chernyshevsky, Nikolai Gavrilovich
   1828-1889 ....DLB-238

Cherry, Kelly 1940 ....Y-83

Cherryh, C. J. 1942- Y-80

Chesebro', Caroline 1825-1873 ....DLB-202

Chesney, Sir George Tomkyns
   1830-1895 ....DLB-190

Chesnut, Mary Boykin 1823-1886.......DLB-239

Chesnutt, Charles Waddell
   1858-1932 .... DLB-12, 50, 78

Chesson, Mrs. Nora (see Hopper, Nora)

Chester, Alfred 1928-1971 ....DLB-130

Chester, George Randolph 1869-1924 ....DLB-78

The Chester Plays circa 1505-1532;
   revisions until 1575 ....DLB-146

Chesterfield, Philip Dormer Stanhope,
   Fourth Earl of 1694-1773...........DLB-104

Chesterton, G. K. 1874-1936
   .. DLB-10, 19, 34, 70, 98, 149, 178; CDBLB-6
   "The Ethics of Elfland" (1908) DLB-178

Chettle, Henry
   circa 1560-circa 1607...............DLB-136

Cheuse, Alan 1940- DLB-244

Chew, Ada Nield 1870-1945 ....DLB-135

Cheyney, Edward P. 1861-1947.........DLB-47

Chiang Yee 1903-1977 ....DLB-312

Chiara, Piero 1913-1986 ....DLB-177

Chicanos
   Chicano History DLB-82
   Chicano Language DLB-82
   Chicano Literature: A Bibliography .. DLB-209
   A Contemporary Flourescence of Chicano
   Literature Y-84
   Literatura Chicanesca: The View From
   Without DLB-82

Child, Francis James 1825-1896....DLB-1, 64, 235

Child, Lydia Maria 1802-1880 ....DLB-1, 74, 243

Child, Philip 1898-1978 ....DLB-68

Childers, Erskine 1870-1922 ....DLB-70

Children's Literature
   Afterword: Propaganda, Namby-Pamby,
   and Some Books of Distinction ...DLB-52

Children's Book Awards and Prizes... DLB-61
Children's Book Illustration in the
   Twentieth Century DLB-61
Children's Illustrators, 1800-1880 ... DLB-163
The Harry Potter Phenomenon Y-99
   Pony Stories, Omnibus
   Essay on DLB-160
The Reality of One Woman's Dream:
   The de Grummond Children's
   Literature Collection Y-99
School Stories, 1914-1960 .... DLB-160
The Year in Children's
   Books................. Y-92–96, 98–01
The Year in Children's Literature Y-97
Childress, Alice 1916-1994 ....DLB-7, 38, 249
Childress, Mark 1957- DLB-292
Childs, George W. 1829-1894 .... DLB-23
Chilton Book Company DLB-46
Chin, Frank 1940- DLB-206, 312
Chin, Justin 1969- DLB-312
Chin, Marilyn 1955- DLB-312
Chinweizu 1943- DLB-157
Chinnov, Igor' 1909-1996............. DLB-317
Chitham, Edward 1932- DLB-155
Chittenden, Hiram Martin 1858-1917 .... DLB-47
Chivers, Thomas Holley 1809-1858... DLB-3, 248
Chkhartishvili, Grigorii Shalvovich
   (see Akunin, Boris)
Chocano, José Santos 1875-1934 .... DLB-290
Cholmondeley, Mary 1859-1925 .... DLB-197
Chomsky, Noam 1928- DLB-246
Chopin, Kate 1850-1904... DLB-12, 78; CDALB-3
Chopin, René 1885-1953 .... DLB-92
Choquette, Adrienne 1915-1973 .... DLB-68
Choquette, Robert 1905-1991 .... DLB-68
Choyce, Lesley 1951- DLB-251
Chrétien de Troyes
   circa 1140-circa 1190 .... DLB-208
Christensen, Inger 1935- DLB-214
Christensen, Lars Saabye 1953- DLB-297
The Christian Examiner DLB-1
The Christian Publishing Company...... DLB-49
Christie, Agatha
   1890-1976........DLB-13, 77, 245; CDBLB-6
Christine de Pizan
   circa 1365-circa 1431 .... DLB-208
Christopher, John (Sam Youd) 1922- .. DLB-255
Christus und die Samariterin circa 950 ..... DLB-148
Christy, Howard Chandler 1873-1952 ... DLB-188
Chu, Louis 1915-1970................ DLB-312
Chukovskaia, Lidiia 1907-1996 .... DLB-302
Chulkov, Mikhail Dmitrievich
   1743?-1792 .... DLB-150
Church, Benjamin 1734-1778 .... DLB-31

Church, Francis Pharcellus 1839-1906 .... DLB-79
Church, Peggy Pond 1903-1986 .... DLB-212
Church, Richard 1893-1972 .... DLB-191
Church, William Conant 1836-1917..... DLB-79
Churchill, Caryl 1938- DLB-13, 310
Churchill, Charles 1731-1764 .... DLB-109
Churchill, Winston 1871-1947 .... DLB-202
Churchill, Sir Winston
   1874-1965... DLB-100, 329; DS-16; CDBLB-5
Churchyard, Thomas 1520?-1604 ...... DLB-132
E. Churton and Company DLB-106
Chute, Marchette 1909-1994 .... DLB-103
Ciardi, John 1916-1986............DLB-5; Y-86
Cibber, Colley 1671-1757 .... DLB-84
Cicero 106 B.C.-43 B.C......DLB-211, CDWLB-1
Cima, Annalisa 1941- DLB-128
Čingo, Živko 1935-1987.............. DLB-181
Cioran, E. M. 1911-1995 .... DLB-220
Čipkus, Alfonsas (see Nyka-Niliūnas, Alfonsas)
Cirese, Eugenio 1884-1955............ DLB-114
Cīrulis, Jānis (see Bels, Alberts)
Cisneros, Antonio 1942- DLB-290
Cisneros, Sandra 1954- DLB-122, 152
City Lights Books................... DLB-46
Civil War (1861–1865)
   Battles and Leaders of the Civil War....DLB-47
   Official Records of the Rebellion DLB-47
   Recording the Civil War DLB-47
Cixous, Hélène 1937- DLB-83, 242
Claire d'Albe, Sophie Cottin DLB-314
Clampitt, Amy 1920-1994 .... DLB-105
   Tribute to Alfred A. Knopf......... Y-84
Clancy, Tom 1947- DLB-227
Clapper, Raymond 1892-1944 .... DLB-29
Clare, John 1793-1864 .... DLB-55, 96
Clarendon, Edward Hyde, Earl of
   1609-1674..................... DLB-101
Clark, Alfred Alexander Gordon
   (see Hare, Cyril)
Clark, Ann Nolan 1896-1995.......... DLB-52
Clark, C. E. Frazer, Jr. 1925-2001... DLB-187; Y-01
   C. E. Frazer Clark Jr. and
   Hawthorne Bibliography......... DLB-269
   The Publications of C. E. Frazer
   Clark Jr.................... DLB-269
Clark, Catherine Anthony 1892-1977..... DLB-68
Clark, Charles Heber 1841-1915 .... DLB-11
Clark, Davis Wasgatt 1812-1871........ DLB-79
Clark, Douglas 1919-1993 ....DLB-276
Clark, Eleanor 1913-1996 .... DLB-6
Clark, J. P. 1935- DLB-117; CDWLB-3
Clark, Lewis Gaylord
   1808-1873..............DLB-3, 64, 73, 250

Clark, Mary Higgins 1929- DLB-306
Clark, Walter Van Tilburg
   1909-1971................. DLB-9, 206
Clark, William 1770-1838......... DLB-183, 186
Clark, William Andrews, Jr.
   1877-1934......................DLB-187
C. M. Clark Publishing Company DLB-46
Clarke, Sir Arthur C. 1917- DLB-261
   Tribute to Theodore Sturgeon Y-85
Clarke, Austin 1896-1974............ DLB-10, 20
Clarke, Austin C. 1934- DLB-53, 125
Clarke, Gillian 1937- DLB-40
Clarke, James Freeman
   1810-1888 .... DLB-1, 59, 235; DS-5
Clarke, John circa 1596-1658 .... DLB-281
Clarke, Lindsay 1939- DLB-231
Clarke, Marcus 1846-1881 .... DLB-230
Clarke, Pauline 1921- DLB-161
Clarke, Rebecca Sophia 1833-1906 ...... DLB-42
Clarke, Samuel 1675-1729 .... DLB-252
Robert Clarke and Company........... DLB-49
Clarkson, Thomas 1760-1846.......... DLB-158
Claudel, Paul 1868-1955 ..... DLB-192, 258, 321
Claudius, Matthias 1740-1815 .... DLB-97
Clausen, Andy 1943- DLB-16
Claussen, Sophus 1865-1931 .... DLB-300
Clawson, John L. 1865-1933 ....DLB-187
Claxton, Remsen and Haffelfinger DLB-49
Clay, Cassius Marcellus 1810-1903 ..... DLB-43
Clayton, Richard (see Haggard, William)
Cleage, Pearl 1948- DLB-228
Cleary, Beverly 1916- DLB-52
Cleary, Kate McPhelim 1863-1905...... DLB-221
Cleaver, Vera 1919-1992 and
   Cleaver, Bill 1920-1981 .... DLB-52
Cleeve, Brian 1921-2003 ....DLB-276
Cleland, John 1710-1789.............. DLB-39
Clemens, Samuel Langhorne (Mark Twain)
   1835-1910 .... DLB-11, 12, 23, 64, 74,
          186, 189; CDALB-3
   Comments From Authors and Scholars on
   their First Reading of Huck Finn Y-85
   Huck at 100: How Old Is
   Huckleberry Finn? Y-85
   Mark Twain on Perpetual Copyright..... Y-92
   A New Edition of Huck Finn............ Y-85
Clement, Hal 1922-2003 .... DLB-8
Clemo, Jack 1916-1994................ DLB-27
Clephane, Elizabeth Cecilia 1830-1869 .. DLB-199
Cleveland, John 1613-1658............ DLB-126
Cliff, Michelle 1946- DLB-157; CDWLB-3
Clifford, Lady Anne 1590-1676 .... DLB-151
Clifford, James L. 1901-1978 .... DLB-103

Clifford, Lucy 1853?-1929..... DLB-135, 141, 197

Clift, Charmian 1923-1969 .... DLB-260

Clifton, Lucille 1936- DLB-5, 41

Clines, Francis X. 1938- DLB-185

Clive, Caroline (V) 1801-1873.......... DLB-199

Edward J. Clode [publishing house]....... DLB-46

Clough, Arthur Hugh 1819-1861 .... DLB-32

Cloutier, Cécile 1930- DLB-60

Clouts, Sidney 1926-1982 .... DLB-225

Clutton-Brock, Arthur 1868-1924 .... DLB-98

Coates, Robert M.
    1897-1973............ DLB-4, 9, 102; DS-15

Coatsworth, Elizabeth 1893-1986 .... DLB-22

Cobb, Charles E., Jr. 1943- DLB-41

Cobb, Frank I. 1869-1923 .... DLB-25

Cobb, Irvin S. 1876-1944.......... DLB-11, 25, 86

Cobbe, Frances Power 1822-1904 .... DLB-190

Cobbett, William 1763-1835 .... DLB-43, 107, 158

Cobbledick, Gordon 1898-1969........ DLB-171

Cochran, Thomas C. 1902-1999 .... DLB-17

Cochrane, Elizabeth 1867-1922 ..... DLB-25, 189

Cockerell, Sir Sydney 1867-1962 .... DLB-201

Cockerill, John A. 1845-1896........... DLB-23

Cocteau, Jean 1889-1963 .... DLB-65, 258, 321

Coderre, Emile (see Jean Narrache)

Cody, Liza 1944- DLB-276

Coe, Jonathan 1961- DLB-231

Coetzee, J. M. 1940- DLB-225, 326, 329

Coffee, Lenore J. 1900?-1984........... DLB-44

Coffin, Robert P. Tristram 1892-1955 ..... DLB-45

Coghill, Mrs. Harry (see Walker, Anna Louisa)

Cogswell, Fred 1917- DLB-60

Cogswell, Mason Fitch 1761-1830 .... DLB-37

Cohan, George M. 1878-1942 .... DLB-249

Cohen, Arthur A. 1928-1986 .... DLB-28

Cohen, Leonard 1934- DLB-53

Cohen, Matt 1942- DLB-53

Cohen, Morris Raphael 1880-1947 ...... DLB-270

Colasanti, Marina 1937- DLB-307

Colbeck, Norman 1903-1987.......... DLB-201

Colden, Cadwallader
    1688-1776 .... DLB-24, 30, 270

Colden, Jane 1724-1766 .... DLB-200

Cole, Barry 1936- DLB-14

Cole, George Watson 1850-1939........ DLB-140

Colegate, Isabel 1931- DLB-14, 231

Coleman, Emily Holmes 1899-1974 .... DLB-4

Coleman, Wanda 1946- DLB-130

Coleridge, Hartley 1796-1849 .... DLB-96

Coleridge, Mary 1861-1907......... DLB-19, 98

Coleridge, Samuel Taylor
    1772-1834 .... DLB-93, 107; CDBLB-3

Coleridge, Sara 1802-1852............ DLB-199

Colet, John 1467-1519 .... DLB-132

Colette 1873-1954 .... DLB-65

Colette, Sidonie Gabrielle (see Colette)

Colinas, Antonio 1946- DLB-134

Coll, Joseph Clement 1881-1921 .... DLB-188

A Century of Poetry, a Lifetime of Collecting:
    J. M. Edelstein's Collection of
    Twentieth-Century American Poetry Y-02

Collier, John 1901-1980 .... DLB-77, 255

Collier, John Payne 1789-1883......... DLB-184

Collier, Mary 1690-1762 .... DLB-95

Collier, Robert J. 1876-1918........... DLB-91

P. F. Collier [publishing house] DLB-49

Collin and Small DLB-49

Collingwood, R. G. 1889-1943 .... DLB-262

Collingwood, W. G. 1854-1932 .... DLB-149

Collins, An floruit circa 1653........... DLB-131

Collins, Anthony 1676-1729........... DLB-252

Collins, Merle 1950- DLB-157

Collins, Michael 1964- DLB-267

Collins, Michael (see Lynds, Dennis)

Collins, Mortimer 1827-1876 .... DLB-21, 35

Collins, Tom (see Furphy, Joseph)

Collins, Wilkie
    1824-1889 ...... DLB-18, 70, 159; CDBLB-4

    "The Unknown Public" (1858)
        [excerpt] DLB-57

    The Wilkie Collins Society Y-98

Collins, William 1721-1759 .... DLB-109

Isaac Collins [publishing house]......... DLB-49

William Collins, Sons and Company..... DLB-154

Collis, Maurice 1889-1973 .... DLB-195

Collyer, Mary 1716?-1763? DLB-39

Colman, Benjamin 1673-1747 .... DLB-24

Colman, George, the Elder 1732-1794..... DLB-89

Colman, George, the Younger
    1762-1836 .... DLB-89

S. Colman [publishing house] DLB-49

Colombo, John Robert 1936- DLB-53

Colonial Literature.................. DLB-307

Colquhoun, Patrick 1745-1820 .... DLB-158

Colter, Cyrus 1910-2002 .... DLB-33

Colum, Padraic 1881-1972 .... DLB-19

The Columbia History of the American Novel
    A Symposium on................... Y-92

Columbus, Christopher 1451-1506....... DLB-318

Columella fl. first century A.D........... DLB-211

Colvin, Sir Sidney 1845-1927 .... DLB-149

Colwin, Laurie 1944-1992 .... DLB-218; Y-80

Comden, Betty 1915- and
    Green, Adolph 1918-2002 ...... DLB-44, 265

Comi, Girolamo 1890-1968........... DLB-114

Comisso, Giovanni 1895-1969.......... DLB-264

Commager, Henry Steele 1902-1998...... DLB-17

Commynes, Philippe de
    circa 1447-1511 .... DLB-208

Compton, D. G. 1930- DLB-261

Compton-Burnett, Ivy 1884?-1969 .... DLB-36

Conan, Laure (Félicité Angers)
    1845-1924 .... DLB-99

Concord, Massachusetts
    Concord History and Life.......... DLB-223

    Concord: Literary History
        of a Town DLB-223

    The Old Manse, by Hawthorne DLB-223

    The Thoreauvian Pilgrimage: The
        Structure of an American Cult ... DLB-223

Concrete Poetry.................... DLB-307

Conde, Carmen 1901-1996........... DLB-108

Condillac, Etienne Bonnot de
    1714-1780 .... DLB-313

Condorcet, Marie-Jean-Antoine-Nicolas Caritat,
    marquis de 1743-1794 .... DLB-313

    "The Tenth Stage"................. DLB-314

Congreve, William
    1670-1729 .... DLB-39, 84; CDBLB-2

    Preface to *Incognita* (1692) DLB-39

W. B. Conkey Company DLB-49

Conlon, Evelyn 1952- DLB-319

Conn, Stewart 1936- DLB-233

Connell, Evan S., Jr. 1924- DLB-2; Y-81

Connelly, Marc 1890-1980 .... DLB-7; Y-80

Connolly, Cyril 1903-1974............ DLB-98

Connolly, James B. 1868-1957 .... DLB-78

Connor, Ralph (Charles William Gordon)
    1860-1937 .... DLB-92

Connor, Tony 1930- DLB-40

Conquest, Robert 1917- DLB-27

Conrad, Joseph
    1857-1924 .... DLB-10, 34, 98, 156; CDBLB-5

John Conrad and Company DLB-49

Conroy, Jack 1899-1990................. Y-81

    A Tribute [to Nelson Algren].......... Y-81

Conroy, Pat 1945- DLB-6

The Conservationist, 1974 Booker Prize winner,
    Nadine Gordimer DLB-326

Considine, Bob 1906-1975............ DLB-241

Consolo, Vincenzo 1933- DLB-196

Constable, Henry 1562-1613 .... DLB-136

Archibald Constable and Company DLB-154

Constable and Company Limited DLB-112

Constant, Benjamin 1767-1830......... DLB-119

Constant de Rebecque, Henri-Benjamin de
    (see Constant, Benjamin)

Constantine, David 1944- DLB-40

Constantine, Murray (see Burdekin, Katharine)

Constantin-Weyer, Maurice 1881-1964.... DLB-92

Contempo (magazine)
    Contempo Caravan:
      Kites in a Windstorm Y-85

The Continental Publishing Company.... DLB-49

A Conversation between William Riggan
    and Janette Turner Hospital............ Y-02

Conversations with Editors Y-95

Conway, Anne 1631-1679.............. DLB-252

Conway, Moncure Daniel
    1832-1907.................... DLB-1, 223

Cook, Ebenezer circa 1667-circa 1732..... DLB-24

Cook, Edward Tyas 1857-1919......... DLB-149

Cook, Eliza 1818-1889 .... DLB-199

Cook, George Cram 1873-1924 .... DLB-266

Cook, Michael 1933-1994 .... DLB-53

David C. Cook Publishing Company..... DLB-49

Cooke, George Willis 1848-1923 .... DLB-71

Cooke, John Esten 1830-1886 .... DLB-3, 248

Cooke, Philip Pendleton
    1816-1850................. DLB-3, 59, 248

Cooke, Rose Terry 1827-1892 ..... DLB-12, 74

Increase Cooke and Company DLB-49

Cook-Lynn, Elizabeth 1930- DLB-175

Coolbrith, Ina 1841-1928......... DLB-54, 186

Cooley, Peter 1940- DLB-105

    "Into the Mirror" DLB-105

Coolidge, Clark 1939- DLB-193

Coolidge, Susan
    (see Woolsey, Sarah Chauncy)

George Coolidge [publishing house]...... DLB-49

Coomaraswamy, Ananda 1877-1947..... DLB-323

Cooper, Anna Julia 1858-1964 .... DLB-221

Cooper, Edith Emma 1862-1913 .... DLB-240

Cooper, Giles 1918-1966 .... DLB-13

Cooper, J. California 19??- DLB-212

Cooper, James Fenimore
    1789-1851....... DLB-3, 183, 250; CDALB-2

    The Bicentennial of James Fenimore Cooper:
      An International Celebration........ Y-89

    The James Fenimore Cooper Society..... Y-01

Cooper, Kent 1880-1965................ DLB-29

Cooper, Susan 1935- DLB-161, 261

Cooper, Susan Fenimore 1813-1894..... DLB-239

William Cooper [publishing house] DLB-170

J. Coote [publishing house]............ DLB-154

Coover, Robert 1932- DLB-2, 227; Y-81

    Tribute to Donald Barthelme Y-89

    Tribute to Theodor Seuss Geisel Y-91

Copeland and Day DLB-49

Ćopić, Branko 1915-1984.............. DLB-181

Copland, Robert 1470?-1548 .... DLB-136

Coppard, A. E. 1878-1957 .... DLB-162

Coppée, François 1842-1908 .... DLB-217

Coppel, Alfred 1921-2004 .... Y-83

    Tribute to Jessamyn West.............. Y-84

Coppola, Francis Ford 1939- DLB-44

Copway, George (Kah-ge-ga-gah-bowh)
    1818-1869 ....DLB-175, 183

Copyright
    The Development of the Author's
      Copyright in Britain DLB-154

    The Digital Millennium Copyright Act:
      Expanding Copyright Protection in
      Cyberspace and Beyond Y-98

    Editorial: The Extension of Copyright ... Y-02

    Mark Twain on Perpetual Copyright Y-92

    Public Domain and the Violation
      of Texts Y-97

    The Question of American Copyright
      in the Nineteenth Century
      Preface, by George Haven Putnam
      The Evolution of Copyright, by
        Brander Matthews
      Summary of Copyright Legislation in
        the United States, by R. R. Bowker
      Analysis of the Provisions of the
        Copyright Law of 1891, by
        George Haven Putnam
      The Contest for International Copyright,
        by George Haven Putnam
      Cheap Books and Good Books,
        by Brander Matthews DLB-49

    Writers and Their Copyright Holders:
      the WATCH Project Y-94

Corazzini, Sergio 1886-1907.......... DLB-114

Corbett, Richard 1582-1635.......... DLB-121

Corbière, Tristan 1845-1875.......... DLB-217

Corcoran, Barbara 1911- DLB-52

Cordelli, Franco 1943- DLB-196

Corelli, Marie 1855-1924 .... DLB-34, 156

Corle, Edwin 1906-1956............... Y-85

Corman, Cid 1924-2004............ DLB-5, 193

Cormier, Robert 1925-2000 ... DLB-52; CDALB-6

    Tribute to Theodor Seuss Geisel Y-91

Corn, Alfred 1943- DLB-120, 282; Y-80

Corneille, Pierre 1606-1684 ....DLB-268

Cornford, Frances 1886-1960.......... DLB-240

Cornish, Sam 1935- DLB-41

Cornish, William
    circa 1465-circa 1524 .... DLB-132

Cornwall, Barry (see Procter, Bryan Waller)

Cornwallis, Sir William, the Younger
    circa 1579-1614.................. DLB-151

Cornwell, David John Moore (see le Carré, John)

Cornwell, Patricia 1956- DLB-306

Coronel Urtecho, José 1906-1994....... DLB-290

Corpi, Lucha 1945- DLB-82

Corrington, John William
    1932-1988 .... DLB-6, 244

Corriveau, Monique 1927-1976 .... DLB-251

Corrothers, James D. 1869-1917......... DLB-50

Corso, Gregory 1930-2001........DLB-5, 16, 237

Cortázar, Julio 1914-1984....DLB-113; CDWLB-3

Cortéz, Carlos 1923-2005............. DLB-209

Cortez, Jayne 1936- DLB-41

Corvinus, Gottlieb Siegmund
    1677-1746 .... DLB-168

Corvo, Baron (see Rolfe, Frederick William)

Cory, Annie Sophie (see Cross, Victoria)

Cory, Desmond (Shaun Lloyd McCarthy)
    1928- DLB-276

Cory, William Johnson 1823-1892....... DLB-35

Coryate, Thomas 1577?-1617........DLB-151, 172

Ćosić, Dobrica 1921- DLB-181; CDWLB-4

Cosin, John 1595-1672........... DLB-151, 213

Cosmopolitan Book Corporation........ DLB-46

Cossa, Roberto 1934- DLB-305

Costa, Maria Velho da (see The Three Marias:
    A Landmark Case in Portuguese
    Literary History)

Costain, Thomas B. 1885-1965 .... DLB-9

Coste, Donat (Daniel Boudreau)
    1912-1957...................... DLB-88

Costello, Louisa Stuart 1799-1870........ DLB-166

Cota-Cárdenas, Margarita 1941- DLB-122

Côté, Denis 1954- DLB-251

Cotten, Bruce 1873-1954 ....DLB-187

Cotter, Joseph Seamon, Jr. 1895-1919..... DLB-50

Cotter, Joseph Seamon, Sr. 1861-1949 ..... DLB-50

Cottin, Sophie 1770-1807 .... DLB-313

    Claire d'Albe..................... DLB-314

Joseph Cottle [publishing house] DLB-154

Cotton, Charles 1630-1687............. DLB-131

Cotton, John 1584-1652................ DLB-24

Cotton, Sir Robert Bruce 1571-1631 .... DLB-213

Couani, Anna 1948- DLB-325

Coulter, John 1888-1980............... DLB-68

Cournos, John 1881-1966............. DLB-54

Courteline, Georges 1858-1929 .... DLB-192

Cousins, Margaret 1905-1996 ....DLB-137

Cousins, Norman 1915-1990 ....DLB-137

Couvreur, Jessie (see Tasma)

Coventry, Francis 1725-1754.......... DLB-39

    Dedication, *The History of Pompey
    the Little* (1751) DLB-39

Coverdale, Miles 1487 or 1488-1569 .... DLB-167

N. Coverly [publishing house] DLB-49

Covici-Friede DLB-46

Cowan, Peter 1914-2002............... DLB-260

Coward, Noel
    1899-1973......... DLB-10, 245; CDBLB-6

Coward, McCann and Geoghegan....... DLB-46

Cowles, Gardner 1861-1946 . . . . .DLB-29

Cowles, Gardner "Mike", Jr.
1903-1985 . . . . DLB-127, 137

Cowley, Abraham 1618-1667. . . . . . .DLB-131, 151

Cowley, Hannah 1743-1809. . . . . .DLB-89

Cowley, Malcolm
1898-1989 . . . . DLB-4, 48; DS-15; Y-81, 89

Cowper, Richard (John Middleton Murry Jr.)
1926-2002 . . . . .DLB-261

Cowper, William 1731-1800. . . . . . . .DLB-104, 109

Cox, A. B. (see Berkeley, Anthony)

Cox, James McMahon 1903-1974 . . . . . . .DLB-127

Cox, James Middleton 1870-1957 . . . . . . .DLB-127

Cox, Leonard circa 1495-circa 1550 . . . . .DLB-281

Cox, Palmer 1840-1924 . . . . .DLB-42

Coxe, Louis 1918-1993 . . . . .DLB-5

Coxe, Tench 1755-1824 . . . . .DLB-37

Cozzens, Frederick S. 1818-1869 . . . . .DLB-202

Cozzens, James Gould 1903-1978 . . . .
. . . . DLB-9, 294; Y-84; DS-2; CDALB-1

   Cozzens's *Michael Scarlett* Y-97

   Ernest Hemingway's Reaction to
      James Gould Cozzens Y-98

   James Gould Cozzens—A View
      from Afar Y-97

   James Gould Cozzens: How to
      Read Him. Y-97

   James Gould Cozzens Symposium and
      Exhibition at the University of
      South Carolina, Columbia Y-00

   Mens Rea (or Something) Y-97

   Novels for Grown-Ups Y-97

Crabbe, George 1754-1832 . . . . .DLB-93

Crace, Jim 1946- DLB-231

Crackanthorpe, Hubert 1870-1896 . . . . . . .DLB-135

Craddock, Charles Egbert (see Murfree, Mary N.)

Cradock, Thomas 1718-1770 . . . . .DLB-31

Craig, Daniel H. 1811-1895. . . . . .DLB-43

Craik, Dinah Maria 1826-1887 . . . . . .DLB-35, 163

Cramer, Richard Ben 1950- DLB-185

Cranch, Christopher Pearse
1813-1892 . . . . .DLB-1, 42, 243; DS-5

Crane, Hart 1899-1932 . . . . .DLB-4, 48; CDALB-4

   Nathan Asch Remembers Ford Madox
      Ford, Sam Roth, and Hart Crane Y-02

Crane, R. S. 1886-1967 . . . . .DLB-63

Crane, Stephen
1871-1900 . . . . . . .DLB-12, 54, 78; CDALB-3

   Stephen Crane: A Revaluation, Virginia
      Tech Conference, 1989. . . . . .Y-89

   The Stephen Crane Society. Y-98, 01

Crane, Walter 1845-1915. . . . . .DLB-163

Cranmer, Thomas 1489-1556 . . . . . .DLB-132, 213

Crapsey, Adelaide 1878-1914. . . . . .DLB-54

Crashaw, Richard 1612/1613-1649 . . . . . .DLB-126

Craven, Avery 1885-1980 . . . . .DLB-17

Crawford, Charles 1752-circa 1815 . . . . . . .DLB-31

Crawford, F. Marion 1854-1909 . . . . .DLB-71

Crawford, Isabel Valancy 1850-1887. . . . . .DLB-92

Crawley, Alan 1887-1975 . . . . .DLB-68

Crayon, Geoffrey (see Irving, Washington)

Crayon, Porte (see Strother, David Hunter)

Creamer, Robert W. 1922- DLB-171

Creasey, John 1908-1973 . . . . .DLB-77

Creative Age Press. DLB-46

Creative Nonfiction .Y-02

Crébillon, Claude-Prosper Jolyot de *fils*
1707-1777 . . . . .DLB-313

Crébillon, Claude-Prosper Jolyot de *père*
1674-1762 . . . . .DLB-313

William Creech [publishing house] DLB-154

Thomas Creede [publishing house] DLB-170

Creel, George 1876-1953 . . . . .DLB-25

Creeley, Robert 1926-2005
. . . . .DLB-5, 16, 169; DS-17

Creelman, James
1859-1915 . . . . .DLB-23

Cregan, David 1931- DLB-13

Creighton, Donald 1902-1979 . . . . .DLB-88

Crémazie, Octave 1827-1879 . . . . .DLB-99

Crémer, Victoriano 1909?- DLB-108

Crenne, Helisenne de (Marguerite de Briet)
1510?-1560? .DLB-327

Crescas, Hasdai circa 1340-1412? DLB-115

Crespo, Angel 1926-1995 . . . . .DLB-134

Cresset Press DLB-112

Cresswell, Helen 1934- DLB-161

Crèvecoeur, Michel Guillaume Jean de
1735-1813 . . . . .DLB-37

Crewe, Candida 1964- DLB-207

Crews, Harry 1935- DLB-6, 143, 185

Crichton, Michael (John Lange, Jeffrey Hudson,
Michael Douglas) 1942- DLB-292; Y-81

Crispin, Edmund (Robert Bruce Montgomery)
1921-1978 . . . . .DLB-87

Cristofer, Michael 1946- DLB-7

Criticism

   Afro-American Literary Critics:
      An Introduction DLB-33

   The Consolidation of Opinion: Critical
      Responses to the Modernists DLB-36

   "Criticism in Relation to Novels"
      (1863), by G. H. Lewes DLB-21

   The Limits of Pluralism DLB-67

   Modern Critical Terms, Schools, and
      Movements. DLB-67

   "Panic Among the Philistines":
      A Postscript, An Interview
      with Bryan Griffin Y-81

   The Recovery of Literature: Criticism
      in the 1990s: A Symposium Y-91

   The Stealthy School of Criticism (1871),
      by Dante Gabriel Rossetti. DLB-35

Crnjanski, Miloš
1893-1977 . . . . .DLB-147; CDWLB-4

Crocker, Hannah Mather 1752-1829 . . . . .DLB-200

Crockett, David (Davy)
1786-1836 . . . . DLB-3, 11, 183, 248

Croft-Cooke, Rupert (see Bruce, Leo)

Crofts, Freeman Wills 1879-1957. . . . . .DLB-77

Croker, John Wilson 1780-1857. . . . . .DLB-110

Croly, George 1780-1860. . . . . .DLB-159

Croly, Herbert 1869-1930 . . . . .DLB-91

Croly, Jane Cunningham 1829-1901 . . . . .DLB-23

Crompton, Richmal 1890-1969 . . . . .DLB-160

Cronin, A. J. 1896-1981. . . . . .DLB-191

Cros, Charles 1842-1888. . . . . .DLB-217

Crosby, Caresse 1892-1970 and
   Crosby, Harry 1898-1929 and . . DLB-4; DS-15

Crosby, Harry 1898-1929 . . . . .DLB-48

Crosland, Camilla Toulmin (Mrs. Newton
   Crosland) 1812-1895. . . . . .DLB-240

Cross, Amanda (Carolyn G. Heilbrun)
1926-2003 . . . . .DLB-306

Cross, Gillian 1945- DLB-161

Cross, Victoria 1868-1952 . . . . .DLB-135, 197

Crossley-Holland, Kevin 1941- DLB-40, 161

Crothers, Rachel 1870-1958. . . . . .DLB-7, 266

Thomas Y. Crowell Company DLB-49

Crowley, John 1942- Y-82

Crowley, Mart 1935- DLB-7, 266

Crown Publishers .DLB-46

Crowne, John 1641-1712 . . . . .DLB-80

Crowninshield, Edward Augustus
1817-1859 . . . . .DLB-140

Crowninshield, Frank 1872-1947 . . . . .DLB-91

Croy, Homer 1883-1965 . . . . .DLB-4

Crumley, James 1939- DLB-226; Y-84

Cruse, Mary Anne 1825?-1910 . . . . .DLB-239

Cruz, Migdalia 1958- DLB-249

Cruz, Sor Juana Inés de la 1651-1695 . . . .DLB-305

Cruz, Victor Hernández 1949- DLB-41

Cruz e Sousa, João 1861-1898. . . . . .DLB-307

Csokor, Franz Theodor 1885-1969 . . . . . . .DLB-81

Csoóri, Sándor 1930- DLB-232; CDWLB-4

Cuadra, Pablo Antonio 1912-2002 . . . . . .DLB-290

Cuala Press DLB-112

Cudworth, Ralph 1617-1688 . . . . .DLB-252

Cueva, Juan de la 1543-1612 . . . . .DLB-318

Cugoano, Quobna Ottabah 1797-?. Y-02

Cullen, Countee
1903-1946 . . . . .DLB-4, 48, 51; CDALB-4

Culler, Jonathan D. 1944- DLB-67, 246

Cullinan, Elizabeth 1933- DLB-234

Culverwel, Nathaniel 1619?-1651? DLB-252

Cumberland, Richard 1732-1811. . . . . .DLB-89

Cummings, Constance Gordon 1837-1924 .... DLB-174

Cummings, E. E. 1894-1962 .... DLB-4, 48; CDALB-5

The E. E. Cummings Society Y-01

Cummings, Ray 1887-1957 .... DLB-8

Cummings and Hilliard DLB-49

Cummins, Maria Susanna 1827-1866 ..... DLB-42

Cumpián, Carlos 1953- DLB-209

Cunard, Nancy 1896-1965 .... DLB-240

Joseph Cundall [publishing house] DLB-106

Cuney, Waring 1906-1976 .... DLB-51

Cuney-Hare, Maude 1874-1936 .... DLB-52

Cunha, Euclides da 1866-1909 .... DLB-307

Cunningham, Allan 1784-1842 .... DLB-116, 144

Cunningham, J. V. 1911-1985 .... DLB-5

Cunningham, Michael 1952- DLB-292

Cunningham, Peter (Peter Lauder, Peter Benjamin) 1947- DLB-267

Peter F. Cunningham [publishing house] DLB-49

Cunqueiro, Alvaro 1911-1981 .... DLB-134

Cuomo, George 1929- Y-80

Cupples, Upham and Company DLB-49

Cupples and Leon DLB-46

Cuppy, Will 1884-1949 .... DLB-11

Curiel, Barbara Brinson 1956- DLB-209

Edmund Curll [publishing house] DLB-154

Currie, James 1756-1805 .... DLB-142

Currie, Mary Montgomerie Lamb Singleton, Lady Currie (see Fane, Violet)

Cursor Mundi circa 1300 .... DLB-146

Curti, Merle E. 1897-1996 .... DLB-17

Curtis, Anthony 1926- DLB-155

Curtis, Cyrus H. K. 1850-1933 .... DLB-91

Curtis, George William 1824-1892 .... DLB-1, 43, 223

Curzon, Robert 1810-1873 .... DLB-166

Curzon, Sarah Anne 1833-1898 .... DLB-99

Cusack, Dymphna 1902-1981 .... DLB-260

Cushing, Eliza Lanesford 1794-1886 .... DLB-99

Cushing, Harvey 1869-1939 .... DLB-187

Custance, Olive (Lady Alfred Douglas) 1874-1944 .... DLB-240

Cynewulf circa 770-840 .... DLB-146

Cyrano de Bergerac, Savinien de 1619-1655 .... DLB-268

Czepko, Daniel 1605-1660 .... DLB-164

Czerniawski, Adam 1934- DLB-232

D

Dabit, Eugène 1898-1936 .... DLB-65

Daborne, Robert circa 1580-1628 .... DLB-58

Dąbrowska, Maria 1889-1965 .... DLB-215; CDWLB-4

Dacey, Philip 1939- DLB-105

"Eyes Across Centuries: Contemporary Poetry and 'That Vision Thing,'" DLB-105

Dach, Simon 1605-1659 .... DLB-164

Dacier, Anne Le Fèvre 1647-1720 .... DLB-313

Dagerman, Stig 1923-1954 .... DLB-259

Daggett, Rollin M. 1831-1901 .... DLB-79

D'Aguiar, Fred 1960- DLB-157

Dahl, Roald 1916-1990 .... DLB-139, 255

Tribute to Alfred A. Knopf Y-84

Dahlberg, Edward 1900-1977 .... DLB-48

Dahn, Felix 1834-1912 .... DLB-129

The Daily Worker DLB-303

Dal', Vladimir Ivanovich (Kazak Vladimir Lugansky) 1801-1872 .... DLB-198

Dale, Peter 1938- DLB-40

Daley, Arthur 1904-1974 .... DLB-171

Dall, Caroline Healey 1822-1912 ..... DLB-1, 235

Dallas, E. S. 1828-1879 .... DLB-55

The Gay Science [excerpt](1866) DLB-21

The Dallas Theater Center DLB-7

D'Alton, Louis 1900-1951 .... DLB-10

Dalton, Roque 1935-1975 .... DLB-283

Daly, Carroll John 1889-1958 .... DLB-226

Daly, T. A. 1871-1948 .... DLB-11

Damon, S. Foster 1893-1971 .... DLB-45

William S. Damrell [publishing house] DLB-49

Dana, Charles A. 1819-1897 ..... DLB-3, 23, 250

Dana, Richard Henry, Jr. 1815-1882 .... DLB-1, 183, 235

Dandridge, Ray Garfield 1882-1930 ...... DLB-51

Dane, Clemence 1887-1965 .... DLB-10, 197

Danforth, John 1660-1730 .... DLB-24

Danforth, Samuel, I 1626-1674 .... DLB-24

Danforth, Samuel, II 1666-1727 .... DLB-24

Dangerous Acquaintances, Pierre-Ambroise-François Choderlos de Laclos DLB-314

Daniel, John M. 1825-1865 .... DLB-43

Daniel, Samuel 1562 or 1563-1619 .... DLB-62

Daniel Press DLB-106

Daniel', Iulii 1925-1988 .... DLB-302

Daniells, Roy 1902-1979 .... DLB-68

Daniels, Jim 1956- DLB-120

Daniels, Jonathan 1902-1981 .... DLB-127

Daniels, Josephus 1862-1948 .... DLB-29

Daniels, Sarah 1957- DLB-245

Danilevsky, Grigorii Petrovich 1829-1890 .... DLB-238

Dannay, Frederic 1905-1982 .... DLB-137

Danner, Margaret Esse 1915- DLB-41

John Danter [publishing house] DLB-170

Dantin, Louis (Eugene Seers) 1865-1945 .... DLB-92

Danto, Arthur C. 1924- DLB-279

Danzig, Allison 1898-1987 .... DLB-171

D'Arcy, Ella circa 1857-1937 .... DLB-135

Darío, Rubén 1867-1916 .... DLB-290

Dark, Eleanor 1901-1985 .... DLB-260

Darke, Nick 1948- DLB-233

Darley, Felix Octavious Carr 1822-1888 .... DLB-188

Darley, George 1795-1846 .... DLB-96

Darmesteter, Madame James (see Robinson, A. Mary F.)

Darrow, Clarence 1857-1938 .... DLB-303

Darwin, Charles 1809-1882 .... DLB-57, 166

Darwin, Erasmus 1731-1802 .... DLB-93

Daryush, Elizabeth 1887-1977 .... DLB-20

Das, Kamala 1934- DLB-323

Dashkova, Ekaterina Romanovna (née Vorontsova) 1743-1810 .... DLB-150

Dashwood, Edmée Elizabeth Monica de la Pasture (see Delafield, E. M.)

Dattani, Mahesh 1958- DLB-323

Daudet, Alphonse 1840-1897 .... DLB-123

d'Aulaire, Edgar Parin 1898-1986 and d'Aulaire, Ingri 1904-1980 .... DLB-22

Davenant, Sir William 1606-1668 .... DLB-58, 126

Davenport, Guy 1927-2005 .... DLB-130

Tribute to John Gardner Y-82

Davenport, Marcia 1903-1996 .... DS-17

Davenport, Robert circa 17th century DLB-58

Daves, Delmer 1904-1977 .... DLB-26

Davey, Frank 1940- DLB-53

Davidson, Avram 1923-1993 .... DLB-8

Davidson, Donald 1893-1968 .... DLB-45

Davidson, Donald 1917-2003 .... DLB-279

Davidson, John 1857-1909 .... DLB-19

Davidson, Lionel 1922- DLB-14, 276

Davidson, Robyn 1950- DLB-204

Davidson, Sara 1943- DLB-185

Davíð Stefánsson frá Fagraskógi 1895-1964 .... DLB-293

Davie, Donald 1922-1995 .... DLB-27

Davie, Elspeth 1919-1995 .... DLB-139

Davies, Sir John 1569-1626 .... DLB-172

Davies, John, of Hereford 1565?-1618 ... DLB-121

Davies, Rhys 1901-1978 .... DLB-139, 191

Davies, Robertson 1913-1995 .... DLB-68

Davies, Samuel 1723-1761 .... DLB-31

Davies, Thomas 1712?-1785 .... DLB-142, 154

Davies, W. H. 1871-1940 . . . . DLB-19, 174	Deacon, William Arthur 1890-1977 . . . . DLB-68	Delany, Martin Robinson 1812-1885 . . . . . . DLB-50
Peter Davies Limited DLB-112	Deal, Borden 1922-1985 . . . . DLB-6	Delany, Samuel R. 1942- DLB-8, 33
Davin, Nicholas Flood 1840?-1901 . . . . DLB-99	de Angeli, Marguerite 1889-1987 . . . . DLB-22	de la Roche, Mazo 1879-1961 . . . . DLB-68
Daviot, Gordon 1896?-1952 . . . . DLB-10 (see also Tey, Josephine)	De Angelis, Milo 1951- DLB-128	Delavigne, Jean François Casimir 1793-1843 . . . . DLB-192
Davis, Arthur Hoey (see Rudd, Steele)	Debord, Guy 1931-1994 . . . . DLB-296	Delbanco, Nicholas 1942- DLB-6, 234
Davis, Benjamin J. 1903-1964 . . . . DLB-303	De Bow, J. D. B. 1820-1867 . . . . . . DLB-3, 79, 248	Delblanc, Sven 1931-1992 . . . . DLB-257
Davis, Charles A. (Major J. Downing) 1795-1867 . . . . DLB-11	Debs, Eugene V. 1855-1926 . . . . DLB-303	Del Castillo, Ramón 1949- DLB-209
Davis, Clyde Brion 1894-1962 . . . . DLB-9	de Bruyn, Günter 1926- DLB-75	Deledda, Grazia 1871-1936 . . . . DLB-264, 329
Davis, Dick 1945- DLB-40, 282	de Camp, L. Sprague 1907-2000 . . . . DLB-8	De León, Nephtal 1945- DLB-82
Davis, Frank Marshall 1905-1987 . . . . DLB-51	De Carlo, Andrea 1952- DLB-196	Deleuze, Gilles 1925-1995 . . . . DLB-296
Davis, H. L. 1894-1960 . . . . DLB-9, 206	De Casas, Celso A. 1944- DLB-209	Delfini, Antonio 1907-1963 . . . . DLB-264
Davis, Jack 1917-2000 . . . . DLB-325	Dechert, Robert 1895-1975 . . . . DLB-187	Delgado, Abelardo Barrientos 1931- DLB-82
Davis, John 1774-1854 . . . . DLB-37	Declaration of the Rights of Man and of the Citizen DLB-314	Del Giudice, Daniele 1949- DLB-196
Davis, Lydia 1947- DLB-130	*Declaration of the Rights of Woman,* Olympe de Gouges DLB-314	De Libero, Libero 1906-1981 . . . . DLB-114
Davis, Margaret Thomson 1926- DLB-14	Dedications, Inscriptions, and Annotations Y-01–02	Delibes, Miguel 1920- DLB-322
Davis, Ossie 1917-2005 . . . . DLB-7, 38, 249	Dee, John 1527-1608 or 1609 . . . . DLB-136, 213	Delicado, Francisco circa 1475-circa 1540? DLB-318
Davis, Owen 1874-1956 . . . . DLB-249	Deeping, George Warwick 1877-1950 . . . . DLB-153	DeLillo, Don 1936- DLB-6, 173
Davis, Paxton 1925-1994 . . . . Y-89	Deffand, Marie de Vichy-Chamrond, marquise Du 1696-1780 . . . . DLB-313	de Lint, Charles 1951- DLB-251
Davis, Rebecca Harding 1831-1910 . . . . DLB-74, 239	Defoe, Daniel 1660-1731 . . . . DLB-39, 95, 101; CDBLB-2	de Lisser H. G. 1878-1944 . . . . DLB-117
Davis, Richard Harding 1864-1916 . . . . DLB-12, 23, 78, 79, 189; DS-13	Preface to *Colonel Jack* (1722) DLB-39	Dell, Floyd 1887-1969 . . . . DLB-9
Davis, Samuel Cole 1764-1809 . . . . DLB-37	Preface to *The Farther Adventures of Robinson Crusoe* (1719) DLB-39	Dell Publishing Company DLB-46
Davis, Samuel Post 1850-1918 . . . . DLB-202	Preface to *Moll Flanders* (1722) DLB-39	delle Grazie, Marie Eugene 1864-1931 . . . . DLB-81
Davison, Frank Dalby 1893-1970 . . . . DLB-260	Preface to *Robinson Crusoe* (1719) DLB-39	Deloney, Thomas died 1600 . . . . DLB-167
Davison, Peter 1928- DLB-5	Preface to *Roxana* (1724) DLB-39	Deloria, Ella C. 1889-1971 . . . . DLB-175
Davydov, Denis Vasil'evich 1784-1839 . . . . DLB-205	de Fontaine, Felix Gregory 1834-1896 . . . . DLB-43	Deloria, Vine, Jr. 1933- DLB-175
Davys, Mary 1674-1732 . . . . DLB-39	De Forest, John William 1826-1906 . . . . DLB-12, 189	del Rey, Lester 1915-1993 . . . . DLB-8
Preface to *The Works of Mrs. Davys* (1725) DLB-39	DeFrees, Madeline 1919- DLB-105	Del Vecchio, John M. 1947- DS-9
DAW Books DLB-46	"The Poet's Kaleidoscope: The Element of Surprise in the Making of the Poem" DLB-105	Del'vig, Anton Antonovich 1798-1831 . . . . DLB-205
Dawe, Bruce 1930- DLB-289	DeGolyer, Everette Lee 1886-1956 . . . . . . DLB-187	de Man, Paul 1919-1983 . . . . DLB-67
Dawson, Ernest 1882-1947 . . . . DLB-140; Y-02	de Graff, Robert 1895-1981 . . . . Y-81	DeMarinis, Rick 1934- DLB-218
Dawson, Fielding 1930- DLB-130	de Graft, Joe 1924-1978 . . . . DLB-117	Demby, William 1922- DLB-33
Dawson, Sarah Morgan 1842-1909 . . . . . . DLB-239	De Groen, Alma 1941- DLB-325	De Mille, James 1833-1880 . . . . DLB-99, 251
Dawson, William 1704-1752 . . . . DLB-31	*De Heinrico* circa 980? DLB-148	de Mille, William 1878-1955 . . . . DLB-266
Day, Angel fl. 1583-1599 . . . . DLB-167, 236	Deighton, Len 1929- DLB-87; CDBLB-8	Deming, Philander 1829-1915 . . . . DLB-74
Day, Benjamin Henry 1810-1889 . . . . DLB-43	DeJong, Meindert 1906-1991 . . . . DLB-52	Deml, Jakub 1878-1961 . . . . DLB-215
Day, Clarence 1874-1935 . . . . DLB-11	Dekker, Thomas circa 1572-1632 . . . . . . DLB-62, 172; CDBLB-1	Demorest, William Jennings 1822-1895 . . . . DLB-79
Day, Dorothy 1897-1980 . . . . DLB-29	Delacorte, George T., Jr. 1894-1991 . . . . . . DLB-91	De Morgan, William 1839-1917 . . . . DLB-153
Day, Frank Parker 1881-1950 . . . . DLB-92	Delafield, E. M. 1890-1943 . . . . DLB-34	Demosthenes 384 B.C.-322 B.C. DLB-176
Day, John circa 1574-circa 1640 . . . . DLB-62	Delahaye, Guy (Guillaume Lahaise) 1888-1969 . . . . DLB-92	Henry Denham [publishing house] DLB-170
Day, Marele 1947- DLB-325	de la Mare, Walter 1873-1956 . . . . DLB-19, 153, 162, 255; CDBLB-6	Denham, Sir John 1615-1669 . . . . DLB-58, 126
Day, Thomas 1748-1789 . . . . DLB-39	Deland, Margaret 1857-1945 . . . . DLB-78	Denison, Merrill 1893-1975 . . . . DLB-92
John Day [publishing house] DLB-170	Delaney, Shelagh 1939- DLB-13; CDBLB-8	T. S. Denison and Company DLB-49
The John Day Company DLB-46	Delano, Amasa 1763-1823 . . . . DLB-183	Dennery, Adolphe Philippe 1811-1899 . . . DLB-192
Mahlon Day [publishing house] DLB-49		Dennie, Joseph 1768-1812 . . . . . DLB-37, 43, 59, 73
Day Lewis, C. (see Blake, Nicholas)		Dennis, C. J. 1876-1938 . . . . DLB-260
Dazai Osamu 1909-1948 . . . . DLB-182		Dennis, John 1658-1734 . . . . DLB-101
		Dennis, Nigel 1912-1989 . . . . DLB-13, 15, 233
		Denslow, W. W. 1856-1915 . . . . DLB-188
		Dent, J. M., and Sons DLB-112

Cumulative Index

Dent, Lester 1904-1959 . . . . DLB-306
Dent, Tom 1932-1998. . . . . DLB-38
Denton, Daniel circa 1626-1703 . . . . DLB-24
DePaola, Tomie 1934- DLB-61
De Quille, Dan 1829-1898 . . . . DLB-186
De Quincey, Thomas
   1785-1859. . . . . DLB-110, 144; CDBLB-3
   "Rhetoric" (1828; revised, 1859)
      [excerpt]. DLB-57
   "Style" (1840; revised, 1859)
      [excerpt]. DLB-57
Derby, George Horatio 1823-1861 . . . . DLB-11
J. C. Derby and Company DLB-49
Derby and Miller DLB-49
De Ricci, Seymour 1881-1942 . . . . DLB-201
Derleth, August 1909-1971 . . . . DLB-9; DS-17
Derrida, Jacques 1930-2004 . . . . DLB-242
The Derrydale Press. DLB-46
Derzhavin, Gavriil Romanovich
   1743-1816. DLB-150
Desai, Anita 1937- DLB-271, 323
Desani, G. V. 1909-2000. . . . . DLB-323
Desaulniers, Gonzalve 1863-1934. . . . . DLB-92
Desbordes-Valmore, Marceline
   1786-1859. DLB-217
Descartes, René 1596-1650 . . . . DLB-268
Deschamps, Emile 1791-1871 . . . . DLB-217
Deschamps, Eustache 1340?-1404 . . . . . . DLB-208
Desbiens, Jean-Paul 1927- DLB-53
des Forêts, Louis-Rene 1918-2001 . . . . DLB-83
Deshpande, Shashi 1938- DLB-323
Desiato, Luca 1941- DLB-196
Desjardins, Marie-Catherine
   (see Villedieu, Madame de)
Desnica, Vladan 1905-1967 . . . . DLB-181
Desnos, Robert 1900-1945 . . . . DLB-258
Des Périers, Bonaventure
   1510?-1543?. DLB-327
Desportes, Philippe 1546-1606 . . . . DLB-327
DesRochers, Alfred 1901-1978 . . . . DLB-68
Des Roches, Madeleine 1520?-1587? and
   Catherine des Roches 1542-1587?. DLB-327
Des Roches, Madeleine
   1520?-1587?. DLB-327
Desrosiers, Léo-Paul 1896-1967 . . . . DLB-68
Dessaulles, Louis-Antoine 1819-1895 . . . . . DLB-99
Dessì, Giuseppe 1909-1977 . . . . .DLB-177
Destouches, Louis-Ferdinand
   (see Céline, Louis-Ferdinand)
Desvignes, Lucette 1926- DLB-321
DeSylva, Buddy 1895-1950 . . . . DLB-265
De Tabley, Lord 1835-1895 . . . . DLB-35
Deutsch, Babette 1895-1982 . . . . DLB-45

Deutsch, Niklaus Manuel
   (see Manuel, Niklaus)
André Deutsch Limited DLB-112
Devanny, Jean 1894-1962. . . . . DLB-260
Deveaux, Alexis 1948- DLB-38
De Vere, Aubrey 1814-1902 . . . . DLB-35
Devereux, second Earl of Essex, Robert
   1565-1601 . . . . DLB-136
The Devin-Adair Company DLB-46
De Vinne, Theodore Low
   1828-1914 . . . . DLB-187
Devlin, Anne 1951- DLB-245
DeVoto, Bernard 1897-1955 . . . . DLB-9, 256
De Vries, Peter 1910-1993 . . . . .DLB-6; Y-82
   Tribute to Albert Erskine Y-93
Dewart, Edward Hartley 1828-1903. . . . . . DLB-99
Dewdney, Christopher 1951- DLB-60
Dewdney, Selwyn 1909-1979 . . . . DLB-68
Dewey, John 1859-1952 . . . . .DLB-246, 270
Dewey, Orville 1794-1882. . . . . DLB-243
Dewey, Thomas B. 1915-1981 . . . . DLB-226
DeWitt, Robert M., Publisher DLB-49
DeWolfe, Fiske and Company DLB-49
Dexter, Colin 1930- DLB-87
de Young, M. H. 1849-1925 . . . . DLB-25
Dhlomo, H. I. E. 1903-1956. . . . . . . .DLB-157, 225
Dhu al-Rummah (Abu al-Harith Ghaylan ibn 'Uqbah)
   circa 696-circa 735 . . . . DLB-311
Dhuoda circa 803-after 843 . . . . DLB-148
The Dial 1840-1844. . . . . DLB-223
The Dial Press DLB-46
"Dialogue entre un prêtre et un moribond,"
   Marquis de Sade. DLB-314
Diamond, I. A. L. 1920-1988 . . . . DLB-26
Dias Gomes, Alfredo 1922-1999. . . . . DLB-307
Díaz del Castillo, Bernal
   circa 1496-1584 . . . . DLB-318
Dibble, L. Grace 1902-1998 . . . . DLB-204
Dibdin, Thomas Frognall
   1776-1847 . . . . DLB-184
Di Cicco, Pier Giorgio 1949- DLB-60
Dick, Philip K. 1928-1982 . . . . DLB-8
Dick and Fitzgerald. DLB-49
Dickens, Charles 1812-1870
   . . . . DLB-21, 55, 70, 159,
              166; DS-5; CDBLB-4
Dickey, Eric Jerome 1961- DLB-292
Dickey, James 1923-1997 . . . . DLB-5, 193;
   Y-82, 93, 96, 97; DS-7, 19; CDALB-6
   James Dickey and Stanley Burnshaw
      Correspondence Y-02
   James Dickey at Seventy–A Tribute Y-93
   James Dickey, American Poet. Y-96
   The James Dickey Society Y-99

   The Life of James Dickey: A Lecture to
      the Friends of the Emory Libraries,
      by Henry Hart. Y-98
   Tribute to Archibald MacLeish Y-82
   Tribute to Malcolm Cowley. Y-89
   Tribute to Truman Capote. Y-84
   Tributes [to Dickey] Y-97
Dickey, William 1928-1994 . . . . DLB-5
Dickinson, Emily
   1830-1886 . . . . DLB-1, 243; CDALB-3
Dickinson, John 1732-1808. . . . . DLB-31
Dickinson, Jonathan 1688-1747 . . . . DLB-24
Dickinson, Patric 1914-1994. . . . . DLB-27
Dickinson, Peter 1927- DLB-87, 161, 276
John Dicks [publishing house] DLB-106
Dickson, Gordon R. 1923-2001 . . . . DLB-8
Dictionary of Literary Biography
   Annual Awards for Dictionary of
   Literary Biography Editors and
   Contributors Y-98-02
Dictionary of Literary Biography
   Yearbook Awards. Y-92-93, 97-02
The Dictionary of National Biography DLB-144
Diderot, Denis 1713-1784 . . . . DLB-313
   "The Encyclopedia". DLB-314
Didion, Joan 1934-
   . . . . DLB-2, 173, 185; Y-81, 86; CDALB-6
Di Donato, Pietro 1911-1992 . . . . DLB-9
Die Fürstliche Bibliothek Corvey Y-96
Diego, Gerardo 1896-1987 . . . . DLB-134
Dietz, Howard 1896-1983. . . . . DLB-265
Díez, Luis Mateo 1942- DLB-322
Digby, Everard 1550?-1605 . . . . DLB-281
Digges, Thomas circa 1546-1595 . . . . DLB-136
The Digital Millennium Copyright Act:
   Expanding Copyright Protection in
   Cyberspace and Beyond Y-98
Diktonius, Elmer 1896-1961. . . . . DLB-259
Dillard, Annie 1945- DLB-275, 278; Y-80
Dillard, R. H. W. 1937- DLB-5, 244
Charles T. Dillingham Company DLB-49
G. W. Dillingham Company DLB-49
Edward and Charles Dilly
   [publishing house] DLB-154
Dilthey, Wilhelm 1833-1911. . . . . DLB-129
Dimitrova, Blaga 1922- DLB-181; CDWLB-4
Dimov, Dimitr 1909-1966. . . . . DLB-181
Dimsdale, Thomas J. 1831?-1866. . . . . DLB-186
Dinescu, Mircea 1950- DLB-232
Dinesen, Isak (see Blixen, Karen)
Ding Ling 1904-1986 . . . . DLB-328
Dingelstedt, Franz von 1814-1881 . . . . . . DLB-133
Dinis, Júlio (Joaquim Guilherme
   Gomes Coelho) 1839-1871. . . . . DLB-287
Dintenfass, Mark 1941- Y-84

Diogenes, Jr. (see Brougham, John)

Diogenes Laertius circa 200 . . . . DLB-176

DiPrima, Diane 1934- DLB-5, 16

Disch, Thomas M. 1940- DLB-8, 282

"Le Discours sur le style," Georges-Louis Leclerc de Buffon. DLB-314

Disgrace, 1999 Booker Prize winner, J. M. Coetzee. DLB-326

Diski, Jenny 1947- DLB-271

Disney, Walt 1901-1966. . . . . DLB-22

Disraeli, Benjamin 1804-1881 . . . . DLB-21, 55

D'Israeli, Isaac 1766-1848 . . . . DLB-107

DLB Award for Distinguished Literary Criticism Y-02

Ditlevsen, Tove 1917-1976 . . . . .DLB-214

Ditzen, Rudolf (see Fallada, Hans)

Divakaruni, Chitra Banerjee 1956- DLB-323

Dix, Dorothea Lynde 1802-1887 . . . . . DLB-1, 235

Dix, Dorothy (see Gilmer, Elizabeth Meriwether)

Dix, Edwards and Company DLB-49

Dix, Gertrude circa 1874-?. DLB-197

Dixie, Florence Douglas 1857-1905 . . . . . DLB-174

Dixon, Ella Hepworth 1855 or 1857-1932. . . . . DLB-197

Dixon, Paige (see Corcoran, Barbara)

Dixon, Richard Watson 1833-1900 . . . . . . .DLB-19

Dixon, Stephen 1936- DLB-130

DLB Award for Distinguished Literary Criticism Y-02

Dmitriev, Andrei Viktorovich 1956- DLB-285

Dmitriev, Ivan Ivanovich 1760-1837. . . . . DLB-150

Dobell, Bertram 1842-1914 . . . . .DLB-184

Dobell, Sydney 1824-1874 . . . . .DLB-32

Dobie, J. Frank 1888-1964. . . . . DLB-212

Dobles Yzaguirre, Julieta 1943- DLB-283

Döblin, Alfred 1878-1957 . . . . . DLB-66; CDWLB-2

Dobroliubov, Nikolai Aleksandrovich 1836-1861 . . . . DLB-277

Dobson, Austin 1840-1921 . . . . DLB-35, 144

Dobson, Rosemary 1920- DLB-260

Doctorow, E. L. 1931- DLB-2, 28, 173; Y-80; CDALB-6

Dodd, Susan M. 1946- DLB-244

Dodd, William E. 1869-1940. . . . . .DLB-17

Anne Dodd [publishing house] DLB-154

Dodd, Mead and Company. DLB-49

Doderer, Heimito von 1896-1966 . . . . DLB-85

B. W. Dodge and Company. DLB-46

Dodge, Mary Abigail 1833-1896 . . . . .DLB-221

Dodge, Mary Mapes 1831?-1905 . . . . DLB-42, 79; DS-13

Dodge Publishing Company DLB-49

Dodgson, Charles Lutwidge (see Carroll, Lewis)

Dodsley, Robert 1703-1764 . . . . .DLB-95

R. Dodsley [publishing house]. DLB-154

Dodson, Owen 1914-1983. . . . . .DLB-76

Dodwell, Christina 1951- DLB-204

Doesticks, Q. K. Philander, P. B. (see Thomson, Mortimer)

Doheny, Carrie Estelle 1875-1958 . . . . DLB-140

Doherty, John 1798?-1854 . . . . DLB-190

Doig, Ivan 1939- DLB-206

Doinaş, Ştefan Augustin 1922- DLB-232

Dolet, Etienne 1509-1546 . . . . .DLB-327

Domínguez, Sylvia Maida 1935- DLB-122

Donaghy, Michael 1954- DLB-282

Patrick Donahoe [publishing house] DLB-49

Donald, David H. 1920- DLB-17; Y-87

Donaldson, Scott 1928- DLB-111

Doni, Rodolfo 1919- DLB-177

Donleavy, J. P. 1926- DLB-6, 173

Donnadieu, Marguerite (see Duras, Marguerite)

Donne, John 1572-1631 . . . . DLB-121, 151; CDBLB-1

Donnelly, Ignatius 1831-1901 . . . . DLB-12

R. R. Donnelley and Sons Company. DLB-49

Donoghue, Emma 1969- DLB-267

Donohue and Henneberry. DLB-49

Donoso, José 1924-1996 . . . . DLB-113; CDWLB-3

M. Doolady [publishing house] DLB-49

Dooley, Ebon (see Ebon)

Doolittle, Hilda 1886-1961 . . . . . DLB-4, 45; DS-15

Doplicher, Fabio 1938- DLB-128

Dor, Milo 1923- DLB-85

George H. Doran Company DLB-46

Dorat, Jean 1508-1588. . . . . DLB-327

Dorcey, Mary 1950- DLB-319

Dorgelès, Roland 1886-1973 . . . . DLB-65

Dorn, Edward 1929-1999 . . . . .DLB-5

Dorr, Rheta Childe 1866-1948. . . . . DLB-25

Dorris, Michael 1945-1997 . . . . DLB-175

Dorset and Middlesex, Charles Sackville, Lord Buckhurst, Earl of 1643-1706 . . . .DLB-131

Dorsey, Candas Jane 1952- DLB-251

Dorst, Tankred 1925- DLB-75, 124

Dos Passos, John 1896-1970 . . . . DLB-4, 9, 316; DS-1, 15; CDALB-5

John Dos Passos: A Centennial Commemoration Y-96

John Dos Passos: Artist Y-99

John Dos Passos Newsletter Y-00

U.S.A. (Documentary). DLB-274

Dostoevsky, Fyodor 1821-1881 . . . . DLB-238

Doubleday and Company DLB-49

Doubrovsky, Serge 1928- DLB-299

Dougall, Lily 1858-1923 . . . . .DLB-92

Doughty, Charles M. 1843-1926. . . . . DLB-19, 57, 174

Douglas, Lady Alfred (see Custance, Olive)

Douglas, Ellen (Josephine Ayres Haxton) 1921- DLB-292

Douglas, Gavin 1476-1522. . . . . DLB-132

Douglas, Keith 1920-1944 . . . . .DLB-27

Douglas, Norman 1868-1952. . . . . DLB-34, 195

Douglass, Frederick 1817-1895 . . . . DLB-1, 43, 50, 79, 243; CDALB-2

Frederick Douglass Creative Arts Center . . . Y-01

Douglass, William circa 1691-1752 . . . . . . .DLB-24

Dourado, Autran 1926- DLB-145, 307

Dove, Arthur G. 1880-1946. . . . . .DLB-188

Dove, Rita 1952- DLB-120; CDALB-7

Dover Publications. DLB-46

Doves Press DLB-112

Dovlatov, Sergei Donatovich 1941-1990 . . . . .DLB-285

Dowden, Edward 1843-1913 . . . . .DLB-35, 149

Dowell, Coleman 1925-1985 . . . . DLB-130

Dowland, John 1563-1626. . . . . DLB-172

Downes, Gwladys 1915- DLB-88

Downing, J., Major (see Davis, Charles A.)

Downing, Major Jack (see Smith, Seba)

Dowriche, Anne before 1560-after 1613 . . . . DLB-172

Dowson, Ernest 1867-1900 . . . . DLB-19, 135

William Doxey [publishing house]. DLB-49

Doyle, Sir Arthur Conan 1859-1930 . . . DLB-18, 70, 156, 178; CDBLB-5

The Priory Scholars of New York Y-99

Doyle, Kirby 1932- DLB-16

Doyle, Roddy 1958- DLB-194, 326

Drabble, Margaret 1939- DLB-14, 155, 231; CDBLB-8

Tribute to Graham Greene Y-91

Drach, Albert 1902-1995 . . . . .DLB-85

Drachmann, Holger 1846-1908. . . . . .DLB-300

Dracula (Documentary) DLB-304

Dragojević, Danijel 1934- DLB-181

Dragún, Osvaldo 1929-1999 . . . . DLB-305

Drake, Samuel Gardner 1798-1875 . . . . . .DLB-187

Drama (*See* Theater)

The Dramatic Publishing Company DLB-49

Dramatists Play Service DLB-46

Drant, Thomas early 1540s?-1578 . . . . DLB-167

Draper, John W. 1811-1882. . . . . .DLB-30

Draper, Lyman C. 1815-1891 . . . . DLB-30

Drayton, Michael 1563-1631. . . . . DLB-121

Dreiser, Theodore 1871-1945 . . . . DLB-9, 12, 102, 137; DS-1; CDALB-3

Cumulative Index

The International Theodore Dreiser Society Y-01

Notes from the Underground of *Sister Carrie* Y-01

Dresser, Davis 1904-1977 .... DLB-226

Drew, Elizabeth A.
"A Note on Technique" [excerpt] (1926) DLB-36

Drewe, Robert 1943- DLB-325

Drewitz, Ingeborg 1923-1986 .... DLB-75

Drieu La Rochelle, Pierre 1893-1945 .... DLB-72

Drinker, Elizabeth 1735-1807 .... DLB-200

Drinkwater, John 1882-1937 .... DLB-10, 19, 149

The Friends of the Dymock Poets Y-00

Droste-Hülshoff, Annette von 1797-1848 .... DLB-133; CDWLB-2

The Drue Heinz Literature Prize
Excerpt from "Excerpts from a Report of the Commission," in David Bosworth's *The Death of Descartes* An Interview with David Bosworth Y-82

Drummond, William, of Hawthornden 1585-1649 .... DLB-121, 213

Drummond, William Henry 1854-1907 .... DLB-92

Drummond de Andrade, Carlos 1902-1987 .... DLB-307

Druzhinin, Aleksandr Vasil'evich 1824-1864 .... DLB-238

Druzhnikov, Yuri 1933- DLB-317

Dryden, Charles 1860?-1931 .... DLB-171

Dryden, John 1631-1700 .... DLB-80, 101, 131; CDBLB-2

Držić, Marin circa 1508-1567 .... DLB-147; CDWLB-4

Duane, William 1760-1835 .... DLB-43

Du Bartas, Guillaume 1544-1590 .... DLB-327

Dubé, Marcel 1930- DLB-53

Dubé, Rodolphe (see Hertel, François)

Du Bellay, Joachim 1522?-1560 .... DLB-327

Dubie, Norman 1945- DLB-120

Dubin, Al 1891-1945 .... DLB-265

Du Boccage, Anne-Marie 1710-1802 .... DLB-313

Dubois, Silvia 1788 or 1789?-1889 .... DLB-239

Du Bois, W. E. B. 1868-1963 .... DLB-47, 50, 91, 246; CDALB-3

Du Bois, William Pène 1916-1993 .... DLB-61

Dubrovina, Ekaterina Oskarovna 1846-1913 .... DLB-238

Dubus, Andre 1936-1999 .... DLB-130

Tribute to Michael M. Rea Y-97

Dubus, Andre, III 1959- DLB-292

Ducange, Victor 1783-1833 .... DLB-192

Du Chaillu, Paul Belloni 1831?-1903 .... DLB-189

Ducharme, Réjean 1941- DLB-60

Dučić, Jovan 1871-1943 .... DLB-147; CDWLB-4

Duck, Stephen 1705?-1756 .... DLB-95

Gerald Duckworth and Company Limited DLB-112

Duclaux, Madame Mary (see Robinson, A. Mary F.)

Dudek, Louis 1918-2001 .... DLB-88

Dudintsev, Vladimir Dmitrievich 1918-1998 .... DLB-302

Dudley-Smith, Trevor (see Hall, Adam)

Duell, Sloan and Pearce DLB-46

Duerer, Albrecht 1471-1528 .... DLB-179

Duff Gordon, Lucie 1821-1869 .... DLB-166

Dufferin, Helen Lady, Countess of Gifford 1807-1867 .... DLB-199

Duffield and Green DLB-46

Duffy, Maureen 1933- DLB-14, 310

Dufief, Nicholas Gouin 1776-1834 .... DLB-187

Dufresne, John 1948- DLB-292

Dugan, Alan 1923-2003 .... DLB-5

Dugard, William 1606-1662 .... DLB-170, 281

William Dugard [publishing house] DLB-170

Dugas, Marcel 1883-1947 .... DLB-92

William Dugdale [publishing house] DLB-106

Du Guillet, Pernette 1520?-1545 .... DLB-327

Duhamel, Georges 1884-1966 .... DLB-65

Dujardin, Edouard 1861-1949 .... DLB-123

Dukes, Ashley 1885-1959 .... DLB-10

Dumas, Alexandre *fils* 1824-1895 .... DLB-192

Dumas, Alexandre *père* 1802-1870 .... DLB-119, 192

Dumas, Henry 1934-1968 .... DLB-41

du Maurier, Daphne 1907-1989 .... DLB-191

Du Maurier, George 1834-1896 .... DLB-153, 178

Dummett, Michael 1925- DLB-262

Dunbar, Paul Laurence 1872-1906 .... DLB-50, 54, 78; CDALB-3

Introduction to *Lyrics of Lowly Life* (1896), by William Dean Howells DLB-50

Dunbar, William circa 1460-circa 1522 .... DLB-132, 146

Duncan, Dave 1933- DLB-251

Duncan, David James 1952- DLB-256

Duncan, Norman 1871-1916 .... DLB-92

Duncan, Quince 1940- DLB-145

Duncan, Robert 1919-1988 .... DLB-5, 16, 193

Duncan, Ronald 1914-1982 .... DLB-13

Duncan, Sara Jeannette 1861-1922 .... DLB-92

Dunigan, Edward, and Brother DLB-49

Dunlap, John 1747-1812 .... DLB-43

Dunlap, William 1766-1839 .... DLB-30, 37, 59

Dunlop, William "Tiger" 1792-1848 .... DLB-99

Dunmore, Helen 1952- DLB-267

Dunn, Douglas 1942- DLB-40

Dunn, Harvey Thomas 1884-1952 .... DLB-188

Dunn, Stephen 1939- DLB-105

"The Good, The Not So Good" DLB-105

Dunne, Dominick 1925- DLB-306

Dunne, Finley Peter 1867-1936 .... DLB-11, 23

Dunne, John Gregory 1932- Y-80

Dunne, Philip 1908-1992 .... DLB-26

Dunning, Ralph Cheever 1878-1930 .... DLB-4

Dunning, William A. 1857-1922 .... DLB-17

Duns Scotus, John circa 1266-1308 .... DLB-115

Dunsany, Lord (Edward John Moreton Drax Plunkett, Baron Dunsany) 1878-1957 .... DLB-10, 77, 153, 156, 255

Dunton, W. Herbert 1878-1936 .... DLB-188

John Dunton [publishing house] DLB-170

Dupin, Amantine-Aurore-Lucile (see Sand, George)

Du Pont de Nemours, Pierre Samuel 1739-1817 .... DLB-313

Dupuy, Eliza Ann 1814-1880 .... DLB-248

Durack, Mary 1913-1994 .... DLB-260

Durand, Lucile (see Bersianik, Louky)

Duranti, Francesca 1935- DLB-196

Duranty, Walter 1884-1957 .... DLB-29

Duras, Marguerite (Marguerite Donnadieu) 1914-1996 .... DLB-83, 321

Durfey, Thomas 1653-1723 .... DLB-80

Durova, Nadezhda Andreevna (Aleksandr Andreevich Aleksandrov) 1783-1866 .... DLB-198

Durrell, Lawrence 1912-1990 .... DLB-15, 27, 204; Y-90; CDBLB-7

William Durrell [publishing house] DLB-49

Dürrenmatt, Friedrich 1921-1990 .... DLB-69, 124; CDWLB-2

Duston, Hannah 1657-1737 .... DLB-200

Dutt, Toru 1856-1877 .... DLB-240

E. P. Dutton and Company DLB-49

Duun, Olav 1876-1939 .... DLB-297

Duvoisin, Roger 1904-1980 .... DLB-61

Duyckinck, Evert Augustus 1816-1878 .... DLB-3, 64, 250

Duyckinck, George L. 1823-1863 .... DLB-3, 250

Duyckinck and Company DLB-49

Dwight, John Sullivan 1813-1893 .... DLB-1, 235

Dwight, Timothy 1752-1817 .... DLB-37

America: or, A Poem on the Settlement of the British Colonies, by Timothy Dwight DLB-37

Dybek, Stuart 1942- DLB-130

Tribute to Michael M. Rea Y-97

Dyer, Charles 1928- DLB-13

Dyer, Sir Edward 1543-1607 .... DLB-136

Dyer, George 1755-1841 .... DLB-93

Dyer, John 1699-1757 .... DLB-95

Dyk, Viktor 1877-1931 .... DLB-215

Dylan, Bob 1941- DLB-16

E

Eager, Edward 1911-1964 . . . . DLB-22

Eagleton, Terry 1943- DLB-242

Eames, Wilberforce
  1855-1937 . . . . DLB-140

Earle, Alice Morse
  1853-1911 . . . . DLB-221

Earle, John 1600 or 1601-1665 . . . . DLB-151

James H. Earle and Company DLB-49

East Europe
  Independence and Destruction,
    1918-1941 . . . . DLB-220
  Social Theory and Ethnography:
    Languageand Ethnicity in
    Western versus Eastern Man DLB-220

Eastlake, William 1917-1997 . . . . DLB-6, 206

Eastman, Carol ?- DLB-44

Eastman, Charles A. (Ohiyesa)
  1858-1939 . . . . DLB-175

Eastman, Max 1883-1969 . . . . DLB-91

Eaton, Daniel Isaac 1753-1814 . . . . DLB-158

Eaton, Edith Maude 1865-1914 . . . . . DLB-221, 312

Eaton, Winnifred 1875-1954 . . . . DLB-221, 312

Eberhart, Richard 1904-2005 . . . DLB-48; CDALB-1
  Tribute to Robert Penn Warren Y-89

Ebner, Jeannie 1918-2004 . . . . DLB-85

Ebner-Eschenbach, Marie von
  1830-1916 . . . . DLB-81

Ebon 1942- DLB-41

E-Books' Second Act in Libraries Y-02

Ecbasis Captivi circa 1045 . . . . DLB-148

Ecco Press DLB-46

Echegaray, José 1832-1916 . . . . DLB-329

Eckhart, Meister circa 1260-circa 1328 . . . DLB-115

The Eclectic Review 1805-1868 . . . . DLB-110

Eco, Umberto 1932- DLB-196, 242

Eddison, E. R. 1882-1945 . . . . DLB-255

Edel, Leon 1907-1997 . . . . DLB-103

Edelfeldt, Inger 1956- DLB-257

J. M. Edelstein's Collection of Twentieth-
  Century American Poetry (A Century of Poetry,
  a Lifetime of Collecting) Y-02

Edes, Benjamin 1732-1803 . . . . DLB-43

Edgar, David 1948- DLB-13, 233
  Viewpoint: Politics and
    Performance DLB-13

Edgerton, Clyde 1944- DLB-278

Edgeworth, Maria
  1768-1849 . . . . DLB-116, 159, 163

The Edinburgh Review 1802-1929 . . . . DLB-110

Edinburgh University Press DLB-112

Editing
  Conversations with Editors Y-95
  Editorial Statements DLB-137
  The Editorial Style of Fredson Bowers Y-91
  Editorial: The Extension of Copyright Y-02
  We See the Editor at Work Y-97
  Whose *Ulysses*? The Function of Editing . . . Y-97

The Editor Publishing Company DLB-49

Editorial Institute at Boston University Y-00

Edmonds, Helen Woods Ferguson
  (see Kavan, Anna)

Edmonds, Randolph 1900-1983 . . . . DLB-51

Edmonds, Walter D. 1903-1998 . . . . DLB-9

Edric, Robert (see Armitage, G. E.)

Edschmid, Kasimir 1890-1966 . . . . DLB-56

Edson, Margaret 1961- DLB-266

Edson, Russell 1935- DLB-244

Edwards, Amelia Anne Blandford
  1831-1892 . . . . DLB-174

Edwards, Dic 1953- DLB-245

Edwards, Edward 1812-1886 . . . . DLB-184

Edwards, Jonathan 1703-1758 . . . . DLB-24, 270

Edwards, Jonathan, Jr. 1745-1801 . . . . DLB-37

Edwards, Junius 1929- DLB-33

Edwards, Matilda Barbara Betham
  1836-1919 . . . . DLB-174

Edwards, Richard 1524-1566 . . . . DLB-62

Edwards, Sarah Pierpont 1710-1758 . . . . . . DLB-200

James Edwards [publishing house] DLB-154

Effinger, George Alec 1947- DLB-8

Egerton, George 1859-1945 . . . . DLB-135

Eggleston, Edward 1837-1902 . . . . DLB-12

Eggleston, Wilfred 1901-1986 . . . . DLB-92

Eglītis, Anšlavs 1906-1993 . . . . DLB-220

Eguren, José María 1874-1942 . . . . DLB-290

Ehrenreich, Barbara 1941- DLB-246

Ehrenstein, Albert 1886-1950 . . . . DLB-81

Ehrhart, W. D. 1948- DS-9

Ehrlich, Gretel 1946- DLB-212, 275

Eich, Günter 1907-1972 . . . . DLB-69, 124

Eichendorff, Joseph Freiherr von
  1788-1857 . . . . DLB-90

Eifukumon'in 1271-1342 . . . . DLB-203

Eigner, Larry 1926-1996 . . . . DLB-5, 193

Eikon Basilike 1649 . . . . DLB-151

Eilhart von Oberge
  circa 1140-circa 1195 . . . . DLB-148

Einar Benediktsson 1864-1940 . . . . DLB-293

Einar Kárason 1955- DLB-293

Einar Már Guðmundsson 1954- DLB-293

Einhard circa 770-840 . . . . DLB-148

Eiseley, Loren 1907-1977 . . . . DLB-275, DS-17

Eisenberg, Deborah 1945- DLB-244

Eisenreich, Herbert 1925-1986 . . . . DLB-85

Eisner, Kurt 1867-1919 . . . . DLB-66

Ekelöf, Gunnar 1907-1968 . . . . DLB-259

Eklund, Gordon 1945- Y-83

Ekman, Kerstin 1933- DLB-257

Ekwensi, Cyprian 1921- . . . DLB-117; CDWLB-3

Elaw, Zilpha circa 1790-? DLB-239

George Eld [publishing house] DLB-170

Elder, Lonne, III 1931- DLB-7, 38, 44

Paul Elder and Company DLB-49

Eldershaw, Flora (M. Barnard Eldershaw)
  1897-1956 . . . . DLB-260

Eldershaw, M. Barnard (see Barnard, Marjorie and
  Eldershaw, Flora)

The Elected Member, 1970 Booker Prize winner,
  Bernice Rubens DLB-326

The Electronic Text Center and the Electronic
  Archive of Early American Fiction at the
  University of Virginia Library Y-98

Eliade, Mircea 1907-1986 . . . . DLB-220; CDWLB-4

Elie, Robert 1915-1973 . . . . DLB-88

Elin Pelin 1877-1949 . . . . DLB-147; CDWLB-4

Eliot, George
  1819-1880 . . . . DLB-21, 35, 55; CDBLB-4
  The George Eliot Fellowship Y-99

Eliot, John 1604-1690 . . . . DLB-24

Eliot, T. S. 1888-1965
  . . . . . . DLB-7, 10, 45, 63, 245, 329; CDALB-5
  T. S. Eliot Centennial: The Return
    of the Old Possum Y-88
  The T. S. Eliot Society: Celebration and
    Scholarship, 1980-1999 . . . . Y-99

Eliot's Court Press DLB-170

Elizabeth I 1533-1603 . . . . DLB-136

Elizabeth von Nassau-Saarbrücken
  after 1393-1456 . . . . DLB-179

Elizondo, Salvador 1932- DLB-145

Elizondo, Sergio 1930- DLB-82

Elkin, Stanley
  1930-1995 . . . . DLB-2, 28, 218, 278; Y-80

Elles, Dora Amy (see Wentworth, Patricia)

Ellet, Elizabeth F. 1818?-1877 . . . . DLB-30

Elliot, Ebenezer 1781-1849 . . . . DLB-96, 190

Elliot, Frances Minto (Dickinson)
  1820-1898 . . . . DLB-166

Elliott, Charlotte 1789-1871 . . . . DLB-199

Elliott, George 1923- DLB-68

Elliott, George P. 1918-1980 . . . . DLB-244

Elliott, Janice 1931-1995 . . . . DLB-14

Elliott, Sarah Barnwell 1848-1928 . . . . DLB-221

Elliott, Sumner Locke 1917-1991 . . . . DLB-289

Elliott, Thomes and Talbot DLB-49

Elliott, William, III 1788-1863 . . . . DLB-3, 248

Ellin, Stanley 1916-1986 . . . . DLB-306

Ellis, Alice Thomas (Anna Margaret Haycraft)
  1932- DLB-194

Ellis, Bret Easton 1964- DLB-292

Ellis, Edward S. 1840-1916 . . . . DLB-42

Cumulative Index

Frederick Staridge Ellis
[publishing house] DLB-106

Ellis, George E.
"The New Controversy Concerning
Miracles DS-5

The George H. Ellis Company DLB-49

Ellis, Havelock 1859-1939 . . . . DLB-190

Ellison, Harlan 1934- DLB-8

    Tribute to Isaac Asimov Y-92

Ellison, Ralph
1914-1994 . . . . DLB-2, 76, 227; Y-94; CDALB-1

Ellmann, Richard 1918-1987 . . . . . . DLB-103; Y-87

Ellroy, James 1948- DLB-226; Y-91

    Tribute to John D. MacDonald Y-86

    Tribute to Raymond Chandler Y-88

Eluard, Paul 1895-1952 . . . . DLB-258

Elyot, Thomas 1490?-1546 . . . . DLB-136

Elytis, Odysseus 1911-1996 . . . . DLB-329

Emanuel, James Andrew 1921- DLB-41

Emecheta, Buchi 1944- DLB-117; CDWLB-3

Emerson, Ralph Waldo
1803-1882 . . . . . DLB-1, 59, 73, 183, 223, 270;
DS-5; CDALB-2

    Ralph Waldo Emerson in 1982 . . . . Y-82

    The Ralph Waldo Emerson Society Y-99

Emerson, William 1769-1811 . . . . DLB-37

Emerson, William R. 1923-1997 . . . . Y-97

Emin, Fedor Aleksandrovich
circa 1735-1770 . . . . DLB-150

Emmanuel, Pierre 1916-1984 . . . . DLB-258

Empedocles fifth century B.C. DLB-176

Empson, William 1906-1984 . . . . DLB-20

Enchi Fumiko 1905-1986 . . . . DLB-182

"The Encyclopedia," Denis Diderot DLB-314

Ende, Michael 1929-1995 . . . . DLB-75

Endō Shūsaku 1923-1996 . . . . DLB-182

Engel, Marian 1933-1985 . . . . DLB-53

Engel'gardt, Sof'ia Vladimirovna
1828-1894 . . . . .DLB-277

Engels, Friedrich 1820-1895 . . . . DLB-129

Engle, Paul 1908-1991 . . . . DLB-48

    Tribute to Robert Penn Warren Y-89

English, Thomas Dunn 1819-1902 . . . . . . DLB-202

The English Patient, 1992 Booker Prize winner,
Michael Ondaatje DLB-326

Ennius 239 B.C.-169 B.C. DLB-211

Enquist, Per Olov 1934- DLB-257

Enright, Anne 1962- DLB-267

Enright, D. J. 1920-2002 . . . . DLB-27

Enright, Elizabeth 1909-1968 . . . . DLB-22

Enright, Nick 1950-2003 . . . . DLB-325

Epic, The Sixteenth-Century Spanish DLB-318

Epictetus circa 55-circa 125-130 . . . . .DLB-176

Epicurus 342/341 B.C.-271/270 B.C. DLB-176

d'Epinay, Louise (Louise-Florence-Pétronille Tardieu
d'Esclavelles, marquise d'Epinay)
1726-1783 . . . . DLB-313

Epps, Bernard 1936- DLB-53

Epshtein, Mikhail Naumovich 1950- . . DLB-285

Epstein, Julius 1909-2000 and
Epstein, Philip 1909-1952 . . . . DLB-26

Epstein, Leslie 1938- DLB-299

Editors, Conversations with Y-95

Equiano, Olaudah
circa 1745-1797 . . . . . . DLB-37, 50; CDWLB-3

    Olaudah Equiano and Unfinished
Journeys: The Slave-Narrative
Tradition and Twentieth-Century
Continuities DLB-117

Eragny Press DLB-112

Erasmus, Desiderius 1467-1536 . . . . DLB-136

Erba, Luciano 1922- DLB-128

Erdman, Nikolai Robertovich
1900-1970 . . . . .DLB-272

Erdrich, Louise
1954- DLB-152, 175, 206; CDALB-7

Erenburg, Il'ia Grigor'evich 1891-1967 . . .DLB-272

Erichsen-Brown, Gwethalyn Graham
(see Graham, Gwethalyn)

Eriugena, John Scottus circa 810-877 . . . . DLB-115

Ernst, Paul 1866-1933 . . . . DLB-66, 118

Erofeev, Venedikt Vasil'evich
1938-1990 . . . . DLB-285

Erofeev, Viktor Vladimirovich 1947- . . . DLB-285

Ershov, Petr Pavlovich 1815-1869 . . . . DLB-205

Erskine, Albert 1911-1993 . . . . Y-93

    At Home with Albert Erskine Y-00

Erskine, John 1879-1951 . . . . DLB-9, 102

Erskine, Mrs. Steuart ?-1948 . . . . DLB-195

Ertel', Aleksandr Ivanovich
1855-1908 . . . . DLB-238

Ervine, St. John Greer 1883-1971 . . . . DLB-10

Eschenburg, Johann Joachim
1743-1820 . . . . DLB-97

Escofet, Cristina 1945- DLB-305

Escoto, Julio 1944- DLB-145

Esdaile, Arundell 1880-1956 . . . . DLB-201

Esenin, Sergei Aleksandrovich
1895-1925 . . . . DLB-295

Eshleman, Clayton 1935- DLB-5

Espaillat, Rhina P. 1932- DLB-282

Espanca, Florbela 1894-1930 . . . . DLB-287

Espriu, Salvador 1913-1985 . . . . DLB-134

Ess Ess Publishing Company DLB-49

Essex House Press DLB-112

Esson, Louis 1878-1943 . . . . DLB-260

Essop, Ahmed 1931- DLB-225

Esterházy, Péter 1950- DLB-232; CDWLB-4

Estes, Eleanor 1906-1988 . . . . DLB-22

Estes and Lauriat DLB-49

Estienne, Henri II (Henricus Stephanus)
1531-1597 . . . . DLB-327

Estleman, Loren D. 1952- DLB-226

Eszterhas, Joe 1944- DLB-185

Etherege, George 1636-circa 1692 . . . . . . DLB-80

Ethridge, Mark, Sr. 1896-1981 . . . . .DLB-127

Ets, Marie Hall 1893-1984 . . . . DLB-22

Etter, David 1928- DLB-105

Ettner, Johann Christoph 1654-1724 . . . . DLB-168

Eucken, Rudolf 1846-1926 . . . . DLB-329

Eudora Welty Remembered in
Two Exhibits Y-02

Eugene Gant's Projected Works Y-01

Eupolemius fl. circa 1095 . . . . DLB-148

Euripides circa 484 B.C.-407/406 B.C.
. . . . .DLB-176; CDWLB-1

Evans, Augusta Jane 1835-1909 . . . . DLB-239

Evans, Caradoc 1878-1945 . . . . DLB-162

Evans, Charles 1850-1935 . . . . .DLB-187

Evans, Donald 1884-1921 . . . . DLB-54

Evans, George Henry 1805-1856 . . . . DLB-43

Evans, Hubert 1892-1986 . . . . DLB-92

Evans, Mari 1923- DLB-41

Evans, Mary Ann (see Eliot, George)

Evans, Nathaniel 1742-1767 . . . . DLB-31

Evans, Sebastian 1830-1909 . . . . DLB-35

Evans, Ray 1915- DLB-265

M. Evans and Company DLB-46

Evaristi, Marcella 1953- DLB-233

Everett, Alexander Hill 1790-1847 . . . . . . DLB-59

Everett, Edward 1794-1865 . . . . DLB-1, 59, 235

Everson, R. G. 1903- DLB-88

Everson, William 1912-1994 . . . . .DLB-5, 16, 212

Evreinov, Nikolai 1879-1953 . . . . .DLB-317

Ewald, Johannes 1743-1781 . . . . DLB-300

Ewart, Gavin 1916-1995 . . . . DLB-40

Ewing, Juliana Horatia 1841-1885 . . . DLB-21, 163

The Examiner 1808-1881 . . . . DLB-110

Exley, Frederick 1929-1992 . . . . . . .DLB-143; Y-81

Editorial: The Extension of Copyright Y-02

von Eyb, Albrecht 1420-1475 . . . . .DLB-179

Eyre and Spottiswoode DLB-106

Ezekiel, Nissim 1924-2004 . . . . DLB-323

Ezera, Regīna 1930- DLB-232

Ezzo ?-after 1065 . . . . DLB-148

F

Faber, Frederick William 1814-1863 . . . . . . DLB-32

Faber and Faber Limited DLB-112

Faccio, Rena (see Aleramo, Sibilla)

Facsimiles
    The Uses of Facsimile: A Symposium.....Y-90

Fadeev, Aleksandr Aleksandrovich
    1901-1956......................DLB-272

Fagundo, Ana María 1938- DLB-134

Fainzil'berg, Il'ia Arnol'dovich
    (see Il'f, Il'ia and Petrov, Evgenii)

Fair, Ronald L. 1932- DLB-33

Fairfax, Beatrice (see Manning, Marie)

Fairlie, Gerard 1899-1983 ....DLB-77

Faldbakken, Knut 1941- DLB-297

Falkberget, Johan (Johan Petter Lillebakken)
    1879-1967......................DLB-297

Fallada, Hans 1893-1947..............DLB-56

The Famished Road, 1991 Booker Prize winner,
    Ben Okri........................DLB-326

Fancher, Betsy 1928- Y-83

Fane, Violet 1843-1905 ....DLB-35

Fanfrolico Press DLB-112

Fanning, Katherine 1927- DLB-127

Fanon, Frantz 1925-1961 ....DLB-296

Fanshawe, Sir Richard 1608-1666 ....DLB-126

Fantasy Press Publishers DLB-46

Fante, John 1909-1983 ....DLB-130; Y-83

Al-Farabi circa 870-950..............DLB-115

Farabough, Laura 1949- DLB-228

Farah, Nuruddin 1945- ...DLB-125; CDWLB-3

Farber, Norma 1909-1984 ....DLB-61

A Farewell to Arms (Documentary)........DLB-308

Fargue, Léon-Paul 1876-1947 ....DLB-258

Farigoule, Louis (see Romains, Jules)

Farjeon, Eleanor 1881-1965............DLB-160

Farley, Harriet 1812-1907...............DLB-239

Farley, Walter 1920-1989................DLB-22

Farmborough, Florence 1887-1978.......DLB-204

Farmer, Beverley 1941-...............DLB-325

Farmer, Penelope 1939- DLB-161

Farmer, Philip José 1918- DLB-8

Farnaby, Thomas 1575?-1647...........DLB-236

Farningham, Marianne (see Hearn, Mary Anne)

Farquhar, George circa 1677-1707........DLB-84

Farquharson, Martha (see Finley, Martha)

Farrar, Frederic William 1831-1903......DLB-163

Farrar, Straus and Giroux DLB-46

Farrar and Rinehart DLB-46

Farrell, J. G. 1935-1979 ..... DLB-14, 271, 326

Farrell, James T. 1904-1979 ....DLB-4, 9, 86; DS-2

Fast, Howard 1914-2003 ....DLB-9

Faulkner, William 1897-1962 ....
    DLB-9, 11, 44, 102, 316, 330; DS-2; Y-86; CDALB-5

    Faulkner and Yoknapatawpha
        Conference, Oxford, Mississippi......Y-97

    Faulkner Centennial Addresses..........Y-97

"Faulkner 100–Celebrating the Work,"
    University of South Carolina,
    Columbia Y-97

Impressions of William Faulkner.........Y-97

William Faulkner and the People-to-People
    Program Y-86

William Faulkner Centenary
    Celebrations Y-97

The William Faulkner Society..........Y-99

George Faulkner [publishing house] DLB-154

Faulks, Sebastian 1953- DLB-207

Fauset, Jessie Redmon 1882-1961 ....DLB-51

Faust, Frederick Schiller (Max Brand)
    1892-1944.....................DLB-256

Faust, Irvin
    1924- DLB-2, 28, 218, 278; Y-80, 00

    I Wake Up Screaming [Response to
        Ken Auletta] Y-97

    Tribute to Bernard Malamud Y-86

    Tribute to Isaac Bashevis Singer Y-91

    Tribute to Meyer Levin................Y-81

Fawcett, Edgar 1847-1904 ....DLB-202

Fawcett, Millicent Garrett 1847-1929 .....DLB-190

Fawcett Books DLB-46

Fay, Theodore Sedgwick 1807-1898......DLB-202

Fearing, Kenneth 1902-1961 ....DLB-9

Federal Writers' Project DLB-46

Federman, Raymond 1928- Y-80

Fedin, Konstantin Aleksandrovich
    1892-1977 ....DLB-272

Fedorov, Innokentii Vasil'evich
    (see Omulevsky, Innokentii Vasil'evich)

Feiffer, Jules 1929- DLB-7, 44

Feinberg, Charles E. 1899-1988.... DLB-187; Y-88

Feind, Barthold 1678-1721 ....DLB-168

Feinstein, Elaine 1930- DLB-14, 40

Feirstein, Frederick 1940- DLB-282

Feiss, Paul Louis 1875-1952 ....DLB-187

Feldman, Irving 1928- DLB-169

Felipe, Carlos 1911-1975 ....DLB-305

Felipe, Léon 1884-1968 ....DLB-108

Fell, Frederick, Publishers DLB-46

Fellowship of Southern Writers Y-98

Felltham, Owen 1602?-1668 ....DLB-126, 151

Felman, Shoshana 1942- DLB-246

Fels, Ludwig 1946- DLB-75

Felton, Cornelius Conway
    1807-1862 ....DLB-1, 235

Fel'zen, Iurii (Nikolai Berngardovich Freidenshtein)
    1894?-1943 ....DLB-317

Mothe-Fénelon, François de Salignac de la
    1651-1715 ....DLB-268

Fenn, Harry 1837-1911 ....DLB-188

Fennario, David 1947- DLB-60

Fenner, Dudley 1558?-1587?...........DLB-236

Fenno, Jenny 1765?-1803..............DLB-200

Fenno, John 1751-1798................DLB-43

R. F. Fenno and Company.............DLB-49

Fenoglio, Beppe 1922-1963 ....DLB-177

Fenton, Geoffrey 1539?-1608..........DLB-136

Fenton, James 1949- DLB-40

    The Hemingway/Fenton
        Correspondence Y-02

Ferber, Edna 1885-1968.......DLB-9, 28, 86, 266

Ferdinand, Vallery, III (see Salaam, Kalamu ya)

Ferguson, Sir Samuel 1810-1886 ....DLB-32

Ferguson, William Scott 1875-1954 .....DLB-47

Fergusson, Robert 1750-1774 ....DLB-109

Ferland, Albert 1872-1943 ....DLB-92

Ferlinghetti, Lawrence
    1919- DLB-5, 16; CDALB-1

    Tribute to Kenneth Rexroth Y-82

Fermor, Patrick Leigh 1915- DLB-204

Fern, Fanny (see Parton, Sara Payson Willis)

Ferrars, Elizabeth (Morna Doris Brown)
    1907-1995 ....DLB-87

Ferré, Rosario 1942- DLB-145

Ferreira, Vergílio 1916-1996............DLB-287

E. Ferret and Company DLB-49

Ferrier, Susan 1782-1854 ....DLB-116

Ferril, Thomas Hornsby 1896-1988......DLB-206

Ferrini, Vincent 1913- DLB-48

Ferron, Jacques 1921-1985.............DLB-60

Ferron, Madeleine 1922- DLB-53

Ferrucci, Franco 1936- DLB-196

Fet, Afanasii Afanas'evich
    1820?-1892 ....DLB-277

Fetridge and Company DLB-49

Feuchtersleben, Ernst Freiherr von
    1806-1849 ....DLB-133

Feuchtwanger, Lion 1884-1958 ....DLB-66

Feuerbach, Ludwig 1804-1872 ....DLB-133

Feuillet, Octave 1821-1890.............DLB-192

Feydeau, Georges 1862-1921 ....DLB-192

Fibiger, Mathilde 1830-1872............DLB-300

Fichte, Johann Gottlieb 1762-1814 ......DLB-90

Ficke, Arthur Davison 1883-1945 ....DLB-54

Fiction
    American Fiction and the 1930s DLB-9

    Fiction Best-Sellers, 1910-1945 ....DLB-9

    Postmodern Holocaust Fiction DLB-299

    The Year in Fiction Y-84, 86, 89, 94–99

    The Year in Fiction: A Biased View Y-83

    The Year in U.S. Fiction Y-00, 01

    The Year's Work in Fiction: A Survey Y-82

Fiedler, Leslie A. 1917-2003 ....DLB-28, 67

    Tribute to Bernard Malamud Y-86

    Tribute to James Dickey Y-97

Field, Barron 1789-1846 . . . . DLB-230
Field, Edward 1924- DLB-105
Field, Eugene 1850-1895. . DLB-23, 42, 140; DS-13
Field, John 1545?-1588 . . . . DLB-167
Field, Joseph M. 1810-1856 . . . . DLB-248
Field, Marshall, III 1893-1956 . . . . DLB-127
Field, Marshall, IV 1916-1965 . . . . DLB-127
Field, Marshall, V 1941- DLB-127
Field, Michael (Katherine Harris Bradley) 1846-1914. . . . . DLB-240
   "The Poetry File" DLB-105
Field, Nathan 1587-1619 or 1620 . . . . DLB-58
Field, Rachel 1894-1942 . . . . DLB-9, 22
Fielding, Helen 1958- DLB-231
Fielding, Henry 1707-1754 . . . . . . DLB-39, 84, 101; CDBLB-2
   "Defense of *Amelia*" (1752) DLB-39
   The History of the Adventures of Joseph Andrews [excerpt] (1742) DLB-39
   Letter to [Samuel] Richardson on *Clarissa* (1748). DLB-39
   Preface to *Joseph Andrews* (1742) DLB-39
   Preface to Sarah Fielding's *Familiar Letters* (1747) [excerpt] DLB-39
   Preface to Sarah Fielding's *The Adventures of David Simple* (1744) . . . DLB-39
   Review of *Clarissa* (1748) DLB-39
   Tom Jones (1749) [excerpt] DLB-39
Fielding, Sarah 1710-1768 . . . . DLB-39
   Preface to *The Cry* (1754) DLB-39
Fields, Annie Adams 1834-1915 . . . . DLB-221
Fields, Dorothy 1905-1974 . . . . DLB-265
Fields, James T. 1817-1881 . . . . DLB-1, 235
Fields, Julia 1938- DLB-41
Fields, Osgood and Company DLB-49
Fields, W. C. 1880-1946 . . . . DLB-44
Fierstein, Harvey 1954- DLB-266
Figes, Eva 1932- DLB-14, 271
Figuera, Angela 1902-1984 . . . . DLB-108
Filmer, Sir Robert 1586-1653 . . . . DLB-151
Filson, John circa 1753-1788 . . . . DLB-37
Finch, Anne, Countess of Winchilsea 1661-1720. . . . . DLB-95
Finch, Annie 1956- DLB-282
Finch, Robert 1900- DLB-88
Findley, Timothy 1930-2002. . . . . DLB-53
Finlay, Ian Hamilton 1925- DLB-40
Finley, Martha 1828-1909. . . . . DLB-42
Finn, Elizabeth Anne (McCaul) 1825-1921 . . . . DLB-166
Finnegan, Seamus 1949- DLB-245
Finney, Jack 1911-1995 . . . . DLB-8
Finney, Walter Braden (see Finney, Jack)
Firbank, Ronald 1886-1926 . . . . DLB-36
Firmin, Giles 1615-1697 . . . . DLB-24
First Edition Library/Collectors' Reprints, Inc. Y-91

Fischart, Johann 1546 or 1547-1590 or 1591 . . . . DLB-179
Fischer, Karoline Auguste Fernandine 1764-1842. . . . . DLB-94
Fischer, Tibor 1959- DLB-231
Fish, Stanley 1938- DLB-67
Fishacre, Richard 1205-1248 . . . . DLB-115
Fisher, Clay (see Allen, Henry W.)
Fisher, Dorothy Canfield 1879-1958 . . . DLB-9, 102
Fisher, Leonard Everett 1924- DLB-61
Fisher, Roy 1930- DLB-40
Fisher, Rudolph 1897-1934 . . . . DLB-51, 102
Fisher, Steve 1913-1980 . . . . DLB-226
Fisher, Sydney George 1856-1927. . . . . . . DLB-47
Fisher, Vardis 1895-1968. . . . . DLB-9, 206
Fiske, John 1608-1677. . . . . DLB-24
Fiske, John 1842-1901 . . . . DLB-47, 64
Fitch, Thomas circa 1700-1774 . . . . DLB-31
Fitch, William Clyde 1865-1909 . . . . DLB-7
FitzGerald, Edward 1809-1883. . . . . DLB-32
Fitzgerald, F. Scott 1896-1940 . . . . DLB-4, 9, 86; Y-81, 92; DS-1, 15, 16; CDALB-4
   F. Scott Fitzgerald: A Descriptive Bibliography, Supplement (2001) Y-01
   F. Scott Fitzgerald Centenary Celebrations Y-96
   F. Scott Fitzgerald Inducted into the American Poets' Corner at St. John the Divine; Ezra Pound Banned Y-99
   "F. Scott Fitzgerald: St. Paul's Native Son and Distinguished American Writer": University of Minnesota Conference, 29-31 October 1982. . . . . Y-82
   First International F. Scott Fitzgerald Conference Y-92
   The Great Gatsby (Documentary) DLB-219
   Tender Is the Night (Documentary) . . . DLB-273
Fitzgerald, Penelope 1916-2000. . . . . DLB-14, 194, 326
Fitzgerald, Robert 1910-1985 . . . . Y-80
FitzGerald, Robert D. 1902-1987 . . . . . . DLB-260
Fitzgerald, Thomas 1819-1891 . . . . DLB-23
Fitzgerald, Zelda Sayre 1900-1948 . . . . Y-84
Fitzhugh, Louise 1928-1974 . . . . DLB-52
Fitzhugh, William circa 1651-1701 . . . . . . DLB-24
Flagg, James Montgomery 1877-1960 . . . . DLB-188
Flanagan, Thomas 1923-2002 . . . . Y-80
Flanner, Hildegarde 1899-1987. . . . . DLB-48
Flanner, Janet 1892-1978. . . . . DLB-4; DS-15
Flannery, Peter 1951- DLB-233
Flaubert, Gustave 1821-1880 . . . . . DLB-119, 301
Flavin, Martin 1883-1967 . . . . DLB-9
Fleck, Konrad (fl. circa 1220) DLB-138
Flecker, James Elroy 1884-1915 . . . . . DLB-10, 19
Fleeson, Doris 1901-1970 . . . . DLB-29
Fleißer, Marieluise 1901-1974 . . . . . . DLB-56, 124

Fleischer, Nat 1887-1972 . . . . DLB-241
Fleming, Abraham 1552?-1607 . . . . DLB-236
Fleming, Ian 1908-1964 . . . DLB-87, 201; CDBLB-7
Fleming, Joan 1908-1980 . . . . DLB-276
Fleming, May Agnes 1840-1880 . . . . DLB-99
Fleming, Paul 1609-1640 . . . . DLB-164
Fleming, Peter 1907-1971 . . . . DLB-195
Fletcher, Giles, the Elder 1546-1611 . . . . DLB-136
Fletcher, Giles, the Younger 1585 or 1586-1623. . . . . DLB-121
Fletcher, J. S. 1863-1935 . . . . DLB-70
Fletcher, John 1579-1625. . . . . DLB-58
Fletcher, John Gould 1886-1950. . . . . . DLB-4, 45
Fletcher, Phineas 1582-1650 . . . . DLB-121
Flieg, Helmut (see Heym, Stefan)
Flint, F. S. 1885-1960 . . . . DLB-19
Flint, Timothy 1780-1840 . . . . DLB-73, 186
Fløgstad, Kjartan 1944- DLB-297
Florensky, Pavel Aleksandrovich 1882-1937 . . . . DLB-295
Flores, Juan de fl. 1470-1500. . . . . DLB-286
Flores-Williams, Jason 1969- DLB-209
Florio, John 1553?-1625 . . . . DLB-172
Fludd, Robert 1574-1637 . . . . DLB-281
Flynn, Elizabeth Gurley 1890-1964 . . . . . DLB-303
Fo, Dario 1926- DLB-330; Y-97
   Nobel Lecture 1997: Contra Jogulatores Obloquentes Y-97
Foden, Giles 1967- DLB-267
Fofanov, Konstantin Mikhailovich 1862-1911 . . . . DLB-277
Foix, J. V. 1893-1987. . . . . DLB-134
Foley, Martha 1897-1977 . . . . DLB-137
Folger, Henry Clay 1857-1930 . . . . DLB-140
Folio Society DLB-112
Follain, Jean 1903-1971 . . . . DLB-258
Follen, Charles 1796-1840. . . . . DLB-235
Follen, Eliza Lee (Cabot) 1787-1860 . . . DLB-1, 235
Follett, Ken 1949- DLB-87; Y-81
Follett Publishing Company DLB-46
John West Folsom [publishing house] DLB-49
Folz, Hans between 1435 and 1440-1513 . . . . DLB-179
Fonseca, Manuel da 1911-1993 . . . . DLB-287
Fonseca, Rubem 1925- DLB-307
Fontane, Theodor 1819-1898 . . . . DLB-129; CDWLB-2
Fontenelle, Bernard Le Bovier de 1657-1757 . . . . DLB-268, 313
Fontes, Montserrat 1940- DLB-209
Fonvisin, Denis Ivanovich 1744 or 1745-1792 . . . . DLB-150
Foote, Horton 1916- DLB-26, 266

Foote, Mary Hallock
  1847-1938 . . . . DLB-186, 188, 202, 221

Foote, Samuel 1721-1777 . . . . DLB-89

Foote, Shelby 1916-2005 . . . . DLB-2, 17

Forbes, Calvin 1945- DLB-41

Forbes, Ester 1891-1967 . . . . DLB-22

Forbes, John 1950-1998 . . . . DLB=325

Forbes, Rosita 1893?-1967 . . . . DLB-195

Forbes and Company DLB-49

Force, Peter 1790-1868 . . . . DLB-30

Forché, Carolyn 1950- DLB-5, 193

Ford, Charles Henri 1913-2002 . . . . DLB-4, 48

Ford, Corey 1902-1969 . . . . DLB-11

Ford, Ford Madox
  1873-1939 . . . . DLB-34, 98, 162; CDBLB-6

Nathan Asch Remembers Ford Madox
  Ford, Sam Roth, and Hart Crane Y-02

J. B. Ford and Company DLB-49

Ford, Jesse Hill 1928-1996 . . . . DLB-6

Ford, John 1586-? DLB-58; CDBLB-1

Ford, R. A. D. 1915-1998 . . . . DLB-88

Ford, Richard 1944- DLB-227

Ford, Worthington C. 1858-1941 . . . . DLB-47

Fords, Howard, and Hulbert DLB-49

Foreman, Carl 1914-1984 . . . . DLB-26

Forester, C. S. 1899-1966 . . . . DLB-191

The C. S. Forester Society Y-00

Forester, Frank (see Herbert, Henry William)

Formalism, New

  Anthologizing New Formalism DLB-282

  The Little Magazines of the
    New Formalism DLB-282

  The New Narrative Poetry DLB-282

  Presses of the New Formalism and
    the New Narrative DLB-282

  The Prosody of the New Formalism . . DLB-282

  Younger Women Poets of the
    New Formalism DLB-282

Forman, Harry Buxton 1842-1917 . . . . . . DLB-184

Fornés, María Irene 1930- DLB-7

Forrest, Leon 1937-1997 . . . . DLB-33

Forsh, Ol'ga Dmitrievna 1873-1961 . . . . . . DLB-272

Forster, E. M. 1879-1970
  . DLB-34, 98, 162, 178, 195; DS-10; CDBLB-6
  "Fantasy," from *Aspects of the Novel*
    (1927) DLB-178

Forster, Georg 1754-1794 . . . . DLB-94

Forster, John 1812-1876 . . . . DLB-144

Forster, Margaret 1938- DLB-155, 271

Forsyth, Frederick 1938- DLB-87

Forsyth, William
  "Literary Style" (1857) [excerpt] DLB-57

Forten, Charlotte L. 1837-1914 . . . . . . DLB-50, 239

  Pages from Her Diary DLB-50

Fortini, Franco 1917-1994 . . . . DLB-128

Fortune, Mary ca. 1833-ca. 1910 . . . . DLB-230

Fortune, T. Thomas 1856-1928 . . . . DLB-23

Fosdick, Charles Austin 1842-1915 . . . . . . DLB-42

Fosse, Jon 1959- DLB-297

Foster, David 1944- DLB-289

Foster, Genevieve 1893-1979 . . . . DLB-61

Foster, Hannah Webster
  1758-1840 . . . . DLB-37, 200

Foster, John 1648-1681 . . . . DLB-24

Foster, Michael 1904-1956 . . . . DLB-9

Foster, Myles Birket 1825-1899 . . . . DLB-184

Foster, William Z. 1881-1961 . . . . DLB-303

Foucault, Michel 1926-1984 . . . . DLB-242

Robert and Andrew Foulis
  [publishing house] DLB-154

Fouqué, Caroline de la Motte 1774-1831 . . . DLB-90

Fouqué, Friedrich de la Motte
  1777-1843 . . . . DLB-90

Four Seas Company DLB-46

Four Winds Press DLB-46

Fournier, Henri Alban (see Alain-Fournier)

Fowler, Christopher 1953- DLB-267

Fowler, Connie May 1958- DLB-292

Fowler and Wells Company DLB-49

Fowles, John
  1926- DLB-14, 139, 207; CDBLB-8

Fox, John 1939- DLB-245

Fox, John, Jr. 1862 or 1863-1919 . . . . DLB-9; DS-13

Fox, Paula 1923- DLB-52

Fox, Richard Kyle 1846-1922 . . . . DLB-79

Fox, William Price 1926- DLB-2; Y-81

  Remembering Joe Heller Y-99

Richard K. Fox [publishing house] DLB-49

Foxe, John 1517-1587 . . . . DLB-132

Fraenkel, Michael 1896-1957 . . . . DLB-4

Frame, Ronald 1953- DLB-319

France, Anatole 1844-1924 . . . . . . DLB-123, 330

France, Richard 1938- DLB-7

Francis, Convers 1795-1863 . . . . DLB-1, 235

Francis, Dick 1920- DLB-87; CDBLB-8

Francis, Sir Frank 1901-1988 . . . . DLB-201

Francis, Jeffrey, Lord 1773-1850 . . . . DLB-107

C. S. Francis [publishing house] DLB-49

Franck, Sebastian 1499-1542 . . . . DLB-179

Francke, Kuno 1855-1930 . . . . DLB-71

Françoise (Robertine Barry) 1863-1910 . . . . DLB-92

François, Louise von 1817-1893 . . . . DLB-129

Frank, Bruno 1887-1945 . . . . DLB-118

Frank, Leonhard 1882-1961 . . . . DLB-56, 118

Frank, Melvin 1913-1988 . . . . DLB-26

Frank, Waldo 1889-1967 . . . . DLB-9, 63

Franken, Rose 1895?-1988 . . . . . . DLB-228, Y-84

Franklin, Benjamin
  1706-1790 . . . . DLB-24, 43, 73, 183; CDALB-2

Franklin, James 1697-1735 . . . . DLB-43

Franklin, John 1786-1847 . . . . DLB-99

Franklin, Miles 1879-1954 . . . . DLB-230

Franklin Library DLB-46

Frantz, Ralph Jules 1902-1979 . . . . DLB-4

Franzos, Karl Emil 1848-1904 . . . . DLB-129

Fraser, Antonia 1932- DLB-276

Fraser, G. S. 1915-1980 . . . . DLB-27

Fraser, Kathleen 1935- DLB-169

Frattini, Alberto 1922- DLB-128

Frau Ava ?-1127 . . . . DLB-148

Fraunce, Abraham 1558?-1592 or 1593 . . DLB-236

Frayn, Michael 1933- DLB-13, 14, 194, 245

Frazier, Charles 1950- DLB-292

Fréchette, Louis-Honoré 1839-1908 . . . . . . DLB-99

Frederic, Harold 1856-1898 . . . . DLB-12, 23; DS-13

Freed, Arthur 1894-1973 . . . . DLB-265

Freeling, Nicolas 1927-2003 . . . . DLB-87

  Tribute to Georges Simenon Y-89

Freeman, Douglas Southall
  1886-1953 . . . . DLB-17; DS-17

Freeman, Joseph 1897-1965 . . . . DLB-303

Freeman, Judith 1946- DLB-256

Freeman, Legh Richmond 1842-1915 . . . . . DLB-23

Freeman, Mary E. Wilkins
  1852-1930 . . . . DLB-12, 78, 221

Freeman, R. Austin 1862-1943 . . . . DLB-70

Freidank circa 1170-circa 1233 . . . . DLB-138

Freiligrath, Ferdinand 1810-1876 . . . . DLB-133

Fremlin, Celia 1914- DLB-276

Frémont, Jessie Benton 1834-1902 . . . . . . DLB-183

Frémont, John Charles
  1813-1890 . . . . DLB-183, 186

French, Alice 1850-1934 . . . . DLB-74; DS-13

French, David 1939- DLB-53

French, Evangeline 1869-1960 . . . . DLB-195

French, Francesca 1871-1960 . . . . DLB-195

James French [publishing house] DLB-49

Samuel French [publishing house] DLB-49

Samuel French, Limited DLB-106

French Literature

  Georges-Louis Leclerc de Buffon, "Le Discours
    sur le style" DLB-314

  Marie-Jean-Antoine-Nicolas Caritat, marquis de
    Condorcet, "The Tenth Stage" . . . DLB-314

  Sophie Cottin, *Claire d'Albe* DLB-314

  Declaration of the Rights of Man and of
    the Citizen DLB-314

  Denis Diderot, "The Encyclopedia" . . DLB-314

  Epic and Beast Epic DLB-208

French Arthurian Literature........ DLB-208

Olympe de Gouges, *Declaration of the Rights of Woman*.................... DLB-314

Françoise d'Issembourg de Graffigny, *Letters from a Peruvian Woman*............. DLB-314

Claude-Adrien Helvétius, *The Spirit of Laws*....................... DLB-314

Paul Henri Thiry, baron d'Holbach (writing as Jean-Baptiste de Mirabaud), *The System of Nature*.................... DLB-314

Pierre-Ambroise-François Choderlos de Laclos, *Dangerous Acquaintances*......... DLB-314

Lyric Poetry..................... DLB-268

Louis-Sébastien Mercier, *Le Tableau de Paris*...................... DLB-314

Charles-Louis de Secondat, baron de Montesquieu, *The Spirit of Laws*.. DLB-314

Other Poets..................... DLB-217

Poetry in Nineteenth-Century France: Cultural Background and Critical Commentary................ DLB-217

Roman de la Rose: Guillaume de Lorris 1200 to 1205-circa 1230, Jean de Meun 1235/1240-circa 1305.... DLB-208

Jean-Jacques Rousseau, *The Social Contract*..................... DLB-314

Marquis de Sade, "Dialogue entre un prêtre et un moribond"................ DLB-314

Saints' Lives.................... DLB-208

Troubadours, *Trobairitz*, and Trouvères.................... DLB-208

Anne-Robert-Jacques Turgot, baron de l'Aulne, "Memorandum on Local Government"................. DLB-314

Voltaire, "An account of the death of the chevalier de La Barre"............. DLB-314

Voltaire, *Candide*.................. DLB-314

Voltaire, *Philosophical Dictionary*...... DLB-314

French Theater
   Medieval French Drama.......... DLB-208

   Parisian Theater, Fall 1984: Toward a New Baroque.................. Y-85

Freneau, Philip 1752-1832...........DLB-37, 43

   The Rising Glory of America........ DLB-37

Freni, Melo 1934-................. DLB-128

Fréron, Elie Catherine 1718-1776....... DLB-313

Freshfield, Douglas W. 1845-1934.......DLB-174

Freud, Sigmund 1856-1939........... DLB-296

Freytag, Gustav 1816-1895............ DLB-129

Frída Á. Sigurðardóttir 1940-........ DLB-293

Fridegård, Jan 1897-1968.............. DLB-259

Fried, Erich 1921-1988................ DLB-85

Friedan, Betty 1921-2006............. DLB-246

Friedman, Bruce Jay 1930-.... DLB-2, 28, 244

Friedman, Carl 1952-................ DLB-299

Friedman, Kinky 1944-.............. DLB-292

Friedrich von Hausen circa 1171-1190... DLB-138

Friel, Brian 1929-............... DLB-13, 319

Friend, Krebs 1895?-1967?............ DLB-4

Fries, Fritz Rudolf 1935-............. DLB-75

Frisch, Max 1911-1991........DLB-69, 124; CDWLB-2

Frischlin, Nicodemus 1547-1590........DLB-179

Frischmuth, Barbara 1941-........... DLB-85

Fritz, Jean 1915-................... DLB-52

Froissart, Jean circa 1337-circa 1404..... DLB-208

Fromm, Erich 1900-1980............. DLB-296

Fromentin, Eugene 1820-1876......... DLB-123

Frontinus circa A.D. 35-A.D. 103/104..... DLB-211

Frost, A. B. 1851-1928......... DLB-188; DS-13

Frost, Robert 1874-1963........ DLB-54; DS-7; CDALB-4

   The Friends of the Dymock Poets....... Y-00

Frostenson, Katarina 1953-........... DLB-257

Frothingham, Octavius Brooks 1822-1895.................... DLB-1, 243

Froude, James Anthony 1818-1894................DLB-18, 57, 144

Fruitlands 1843-1844......... DLB-1, 223; DS-5

Fry, Christopher 1907-2005........... DLB-13

   Tribute to John Betjeman............. Y-84

Fry, Roger 1866-1934.................. DS-10

Fry, Stephen 1957-................. DLB-207

Frye, Northrop 1912-1991.......DLB-67, 68, 246

Fuchs, Daniel 1909-1993.....DLB-9, 26, 28; Y-93

   Tribute to Isaac Bashevis Singer........ Y-91

Fuentes, Carlos 1928-.....DLB-113; CDWLB-3

Fuertes, Gloria 1918-1998............ DLB-108

Fugard, Athol 1932-................ DLB-225

The Fugitives and the Agrarians: The First Exhibition.................. Y-85

Fujiwara no Shunzei 1114-1204........ DLB-203

Fujiwara no Tameaki 1230s?-1290s?.... DLB-203

Fujiwara no Tameie 1198-1275......... DLB-203

Fujiwara no Teika 1162-1241.......... DLB-203

Fuks, Ladislav 1923-1994............. DLB-299

Fulbecke, William 1560-1603?.........DLB-172

Fuller, Charles 1939-............ DLB-38, 266

Fuller, Henry Blake 1857-1929......... DLB-12

Fuller, John 1937-.................. DLB-40

Fuller, Margaret (see Fuller, Sarah)

Fuller, Roy 1912-1991.............. DLB-15, 20

   Tribute to Christopher Isherwood....... Y-86

Fuller, Samuel 1912-1997............. DLB-26

Fuller, Sarah 1810-1850.......... DLB-1, 59, 73, 183, 223, 239; DS-5; CDALB-2

Fuller, Thomas 1608-1661............ DLB-151

Fullerton, Hugh 1873-1945............DLB-171

Fullwood, William fl. 1568........... DLB-236

Fulton, Alice 1952-................. DLB-193

Fulton, Len 1934-.................... Y-86

Fulton, Robin 1937-................. DLB-40

Furbank, P. N. 1920-............... DLB-155

Furetière, Antoine 1619-1688...........DLB-268

Furman, Laura 1945-................. Y-86

Furmanov, Dmitrii Andreevich 1891-1926....................DLB-272

Furness, Horace Howard 1833-1912..... DLB-64

Furness, William Henry 1802-1896................ DLB-1, 235

Furnivall, Frederick James 1825-1910.... DLB-184

Furphy, Joseph (Tom Collins) 1843-1912................... DLB-230

Furthman, Jules 1888-1966............ DLB-26

   Shakespeare and Montaigne: A Symposium by Jules Furthman...... Y-02

Furui Yoshikichi 1937-.............. DLB-182

Fushimi, Emperor 1265-1317.......... DLB-203

Futabatei Shimei (Hasegawa Tatsunosuke) 1864-1909................... DLB-180

Fyleman, Rose 1877-1957............. DLB-160

G

G., 1972 Booker Prize winner, John Berger..................... DLB-326

Gaarder, Jostein 1952-.............. DLB-297

Gadallah, Leslie 1939-............. DLB-251

Gadamer, Hans-Georg 1900-2002...... DLB-296

Gadda, Carlo Emilio 1893-1973.........DLB-177

Gaddis, William 1922-1998.........DLB-2, 278

   William Gaddis: A Tribute............ Y-99

Gág, Wanda 1893-1946.............. DLB-22

Gagarin, Ivan Sergeevich 1814-1882.... DLB-198

Gagnon, Madeleine 1938-........... DLB-60

Gaiman, Neil 1960-................ DLB-261

Gaine, Hugh 1726-1807.............. DLB-43

Hugh Gaine [publishing house]........ DLB-49

Gaines, Ernest J. 1933-.....DLB-2, 33, 152; Y-80; CDALB-6

Gaiser, Gerd 1908-1976.............. DLB-69

Gaitskill, Mary 1954-............... DLB-244

Galarza, Ernesto 1905-1984........... DLB-122

Galaxy Science Fiction Novels.......... DLB-46

Galbraith, Robert (or Caubraith) circa 1483-1544.................. DLB-281

Gale, Zona 1874-1938...........DLB-9, 228, 78

Galen of Pergamon 129-after 210........DLB-176

Gales, Winifred Marshall 1761-1839.... DLB-200

Galich, Aleksandr 1918-1977...........DLB-317

Medieval Galician-Portuguese Poetry.... DLB-287

Gall, Louise von 1815-1855............ DLB-133

Gallagher, Tess 1943-.......DLB-120, 212, 244

Gallagher, Wes 1911-1997............DLB-127

Gallagher, William Davis 1808-1894..... DLB-73

Gallant, Mavis 1922- DLB-53

Gallegos, María Magdalena 1935- DLB-209

Gallico, Paul 1897-1976 ....DLB-9, 171

Gallop, Jane 1952- DLB-246

Galloway, Grace Growden 1727-1782.....DLB-200

Galloway, Janice 1956- DLB-319

Gallup, Donald 1913-2000............DLB-187

Galsworthy, John 1867-1933
..DLB-10, 34, 98, 162, 330; DS-16; CDBLB-5

Galt, John 1779-1839 ....DLB-99, 116, 159

Galton, Sir Francis 1822-1911 ....DLB-166

Galvin, Brendan 1938- DLB-5

Gambaro, Griselda 1928- DLB-305

Gambit................DLB-46

Gamboa, Reymundo 1948- DLB-122

Gammer Gurton's Needle DLB-62

Gan, Elena Andreevna (Zeneida R-va)
1814-1842 ....DLB-198

Gandhi, Mohandas Karamchand
1869-1948 ....DLB-323

Gandlevsky, Sergei Markovich
1952- DLB-285

Gannett, Frank E. 1876-1957 ....DLB-29

Gant, Eugene: Projected Works............Y-01

Gao Xingjian 1940- DLB-330; Y-00

Nobel Lecture 2000: "The Case for
Literature" Y-00

Gaos, Vicente 1919-1980.............DLB-134

García, Andrew 1854?-1943 ....DLB-209

García, Cristina 1958- DLB-292

García, Lionel G. 1935- DLB-82

García, Richard 1941- DLB-209

García, Santiago 1928- DLB-305

García Márquez, Gabriel
1927- DLB-113, 330; Y-82; CDWLB-3

The Magical World of Macondo.........Y-82

Nobel Lecture 1982: The Solitude of
Latin America...................Y-82

A Tribute to Gabriel García Márquez......Y-82

García Marruz, Fina 1923- DLB-283

García-Camarillo, Cecilio 1943- DLB-209

Garcilaso de la Vega circa 1503-1536.....DLB-318

Garcilaso de la Vega, Inca 1539-1616 ....DLB-318

Gardam, Jane 1928- DLB-14, 161, 231

Gardell, Jonas 1963- DLB-257

Garden, Alexander circa 1685-1756......DLB-31

Gardiner, John Rolfe 1936- DLB-244

Gardiner, Margaret Power Farmer
(see Blessington, Marguerite, Countess of)

Gardner, John
1933-1982 ....DLB-2; Y-82; CDALB-7

Garfield, Leon 1921-1996 ....DLB-161

Garis, Howard R. 1873-1962 ....DLB-22

Garland, Hamlin 1860-1940 .. DLB-12, 71, 78, 186

The Hamlin Garland Society Y-01

Garneau, François-Xavier 1809-1866 .....DLB-99

Garneau, Hector de Saint-Denys
1912-1943 ....DLB-88

Garneau, Michel 1939- DLB-53

Garner, Alan 1934- DLB-161, 261

Garner, Helen 1942- DLB-325

Garner, Hugh 1913-1979 ....DLB-68

Garnett, David 1892-1981 ....DLB-34

Garnett, Eve 1900-1991 ....DLB-160

Garnett, Richard 1835-1906 ....DLB-184

Garnier, Robert 1545?-1590 ....DLB-327

Garrard, Lewis H. 1829-1887 ....DLB-186

Garraty, John A. 1920- DLB-17

Garrett, Almeida (João Baptista da Silva
Leitão de Almeida Garrett)
1799-1854 ....DLB-287

Garrett, George
1929- DLB-2, 5, 130, 152; Y-83

Literary Prizes......................Y-00

My Summer Reading Orgy: Reading
for Fun and Games: One Reader's
Report on the Summer of 2001 ......Y-01

A Summing Up at Century's End........Y-99

Tribute to James Dickey Y-97

Tribute to Michael M. Rea Y-97

Tribute to Paxton Davis Y-94

Tribute to Peter Taylor Y-94

Tribute to William Goyen Y-83

A Writer Talking: A Collage...........Y-00

Garrett, John Work 1872-1942.........DLB-187

Garrick, David 1717-1779 ....DLB-84, 213

Garrison, William Lloyd
1805-1879 ....DLB-1, 43, 235; CDALB-2

Garro, Elena 1920-1998..............DLB-145

Garshin, Vsevolod Mikhailovich
1855-1888.....................DLB-277

Garth, Samuel 1661-1719..............DLB-95

Garve, Andrew 1908-2001..............DLB-87

Gary, Romain 1914-1980...........DLB-83, 299

Gascoigne, George 1539?-1577 ....DLB-136

Gascoyne, David 1916-2001 ....DLB-20

Gash, Jonathan (John Grant) 1933- DLB-276

Gaskell, Elizabeth Cleghorn
1810-1865 ......DLB-21, 144, 159; CDBLB-4

The Gaskell Society Y-98

Gaskell, Jane 1941- DLB-261

Gaspey, Thomas 1788-1871 ....DLB-116

Gass, William H. 1924- DLB-2, 227

Gates, Doris 1901-1987 ....DLB-22

Gates, Henry Louis, Jr. 1950- DLB-67

Gates, Lewis E. 1860-1924 ....DLB-71

Gatto, Alfonso 1909-1976 ....DLB-114

Gault, William Campbell 1910-1995 .....DLB-226

Tribute to Kenneth Millar Y-83

Gaunt, Mary 1861-1942 ....DLB-174, 230

Gautier, Théophile 1811-1872 ....DLB-119

Gautreaux, Tim 1947- DLB-292

Gauvreau, Claude 1925-1971 ....DLB-88

The *Gawain*-Poet
fl. circa 1350-1400.................DLB-146

Gawsworth, John (Terence Ian Fytton
Armstrong) 1912-1970..............DLB-255

Gay, Ebenezer 1696-1787..............DLB-24

Gay, John 1685-1732 ....DLB-84, 95

Gayarré, Charles E. A. 1805-1895........DLB-30

Charles Gaylord [publishing house].......DLB-49

Gaylord, Edward King 1873-1974 ....DLB-127

Gaylord, Edward Lewis 1919-2003 ......DLB-127

Gazdanov, Gaito 1903-1971............DLB-317

Gébler, Carlo 1954- DLB-271

Geda, Sigitas 1943- DLB-232

Geddes, Gary 1940- DLB-60

Geddes, Virgil 1897-1989 ....DLB-4

Gedeon (Georgii Andreevich Krinovsky)
circa 1730-1763 ....DLB-150

Gee, Maggie 1948- DLB-207

Gee, Shirley 1932- DLB-245

Geibel, Emanuel 1815-1884............DLB-129

Geiogamah, Hanay 1945- DLB-175

Geis, Bernard, Associates..............DLB-46

Geisel, Theodor Seuss 1904-1991 ... DLB-61; Y-91

Gelb, Arthur 1924- DLB-103

Gelb, Barbara 1926- DLB-103

Gelber, Jack 1932- DLB-7, 228

Gélinas, Gratien 1909-1999 ....DLB-88

Gellert, Christian Füerchtegott
1715-1769 ....DLB-97

Gellhorn, Martha 1908-1998...........Y-82, 98

Gems, Pam 1925- DLB-13

Genet, Jean 1910-1986........ DLB-72, 321; Y-86

Genette, Gérard 1930- DLB-242

Genevoix, Maurice 1890-1980..........DLB-65

Genis, Aleksandr Aleksandrovich
1953- DLB-285

Genlis, Stéphanie-Félicité Ducrest, comtesse de
1746-1830 ....DLB-313

Genovese, Eugene D. 1930- DLB-17

Gent, Peter 1942- Y-82

Geoffrey of Monmouth
circa 1100-1155 ....DLB-146

George, Elizabeth 1949- DLB-306

George, Henry 1839-1897 ....DLB-23

George, Jean Craighead 1919- DLB-52

George, W. L. 1882-1926 ....DLB-197

George III, King of Great Britain
and Ireland 1738-1820 ....DLB-213

Georgslied 896? DLB-148

Gerber, Merrill Joan 1938- DLB-218

Gerhardie, William 1895-1977 . . . . DLB-36

Gerhardt, Paul 1607-1676 . . . . DLB-164

Gérin, Winifred 1901-1981 . . . . DLB-155

Gérin-Lajoie, Antoine 1824-1882 . . . . DLB-99

German Literature
   A Call to Letters and an Invitation
     to the Electric Chair DLB-75

   The Conversion of an Unpolitical
     Man. DLB-66

   The German Radio Play DLB-124

   The German Transformation from the
     Baroque to the Enlightenment. . . . DLB-97

   Germanophilism. DLB-66

   A Letter from a New Germany Y-90

   The Making of a People. DLB-66

   The Novel of Impressionism DLB-66

   Pattern and Paradigm: History as
     Design DLB-75

   Premisses DLB-66

   The 'Twenties and Berlin. DLB-66

   Wolfram von Eschenbach's *Parzival*:
     Prologue and Book 3. . . . . DLB-138

   Writers and Politics: 1871-1918 . . . . . . DLB-66

German Literature, Middle Ages
   Abrogans circa 790-800 . . . . DLB-148

   Annolied between 1077 and 1081. . . . . DLB-148

   The Arthurian Tradition and
     Its European Context DLB-138

   Cambridge Songs (Carmina Cantabrigensia)
     circa 1050 . . . . DLB-148

   Christus und die Samariterin circa 950. . . DLB-148

   De Heinrico circa 980? DLB-148

   Ecbasis Captivi circa 1045 . . . . DLB-148

   Georgslied 896? DLB-148

   German Literature and Culture from
     Charlemagne to the Early Courtly
     Period DLB-148; CDWLB-2

   The Germanic Epic and Old English
     Heroic Poetry: *Widsith, Waldere*,
     and *The Fight at Finnsburg*. DLB-146

   Graf Rudolf between circa
     1170 and circa 1185. . . . . DLB-148

   Heliand circa 850. . . . . DLB-148

   Das Hildesbrandslied
     circa 820 . . . . DLB-148; CDWLB-2

   Kaiserchronik circa 1147 . . . . DLB-148

   The Legends of the Saints and a
     Medieval Christian
     Worldview. DLB-148

   Ludus de Antichristo circa 1160 . . . . DLB-148

   Ludwigslied 881 or 882 . . . . DLB-148

   Muspilli circa 790-circa 850 . . . . DLB-148

   Old German Genesis and *Old German
     Exodus* circa 1050-circa 1130 . . . . DLB-148

   Old High German Charms
     and Blessings. DLB-148; CDWLB-2

   The *Old High German Isidor*
     circa 790-800 . . . . DLB-148

Petruslied circa 854? DLB-148

Physiologus circa 1070-circa 1150 . . . . . DLB-148

Ruodlieb circa 1050-1075 . . . . DLB-148

"*Spielmannsepen*" (circa 1152
   circa 1500) DLB-148

The Strasbourg Oaths 842. . . . . DLB-148

Tatian circa 830. . . . . DLB-148

Waltharius circa 825. . . . . DLB-148

Wessobrunner Gebet circa 787-815 . . . . . DLB-148

German Theater
   German Drama 800-1280 . . . . DLB-138

   German Drama from Naturalism
     to Fascism: 1889-1933 . . . . DLB-118

Gernsback, Hugo 1884-1967 . . . . DLB-8, 137

Gerould, Katharine Fullerton
   1879-1944. DLB-78

Samuel Gerrish [publishing house]. DLB-49

Gerrold, David 1944- DLB-8

Gersão, Teolinda 1940- DLB-287

Gershon, Karen 1923-1993. . . . . DLB-299

Gershwin, Ira 1896-1983 . . . . DLB-265

   The Ira Gershwin Centenary. Y-96

Gerson, Jean 1363-1429 . . . . DLB-208

Gersonides 1288-1344 . . . . DLB-115

Gerstäcker, Friedrich 1816-1872 . . . . DLB-129

Gertsen, Aleksandr Ivanovich
   (see Herzen, Alexander)

Gerstenberg, Heinrich Wilhelm von
   1737-1823 . . . . DLB-97

Gervinus, Georg Gottfried
   1805-1871 . . . . DLB-133

Gery, John 1953- DLB-282

Geßner, Solomon 1730-1788. . . . . DLB-97

Geston, Mark S. 1946- DLB-8

Al-Ghazali 1058-1111 . . . . DLB-115

Ghelderode, Michel de (Adolphe-Adhémar Martens)
   1898-1962 . . . . DLB-321

Ghose, Zulfikar 1935- DLB-323

Ghosh, Amitav 1956- DLB-323

The Ghost Road, 1995 Booker Prize winner,
   Pat Barker DLB-326

Gibbings, Robert 1889-1958. . . . . DLB-195

Gibbon, Edward 1737-1794. . . . . DLB-104

Gibbon, John Murray 1875-1952 . . . . DLB-92

Gibbon, Lewis Grassic (see Mitchell, James Leslie)

Gibbons, Floyd 1887-1939 . . . . DLB-25

Gibbons, Kaye 1960- DLB-292

Gibbons, Reginald 1947- DLB-120

Gibbons, William eighteenth century. DLB-73

Gibson, Charles Dana
   1867-1944. . . . . DLB-188; DS-13

Gibson, Graeme 1934- DLB-53

Gibson, Margaret 1944- DLB-120

Gibson, Margaret Dunlop 1843-1920. . . . .DLB-174

Gibson, Wilfrid 1878-1962 . . . . DLB-19

The Friends of the Dymock Poets Y-00

Gibson, William 1914- DLB-7

Gibson, William 1948- DLB-251

Gide, André 1869-1951 . . . . DLB-65, 321, 330

Giguère, Diane 1937- DLB-53

Giguère, Roland 1929- DLB-60

Gil de Biedma, Jaime 1929-1990 . . . . DLB-108

Gil-Albert, Juan 1906-1994. . . . . DLB-134

Gilbert, Anthony 1899-1973. . . . . DLB-77

Gilbert, Elizabeth 1969- DLB-292

Gilbert, Sir Humphrey 1537-1583 . . . . . . DLB-136

Gilbert, Michael 1912- DLB-87

Gilbert, Sandra M. 1936- DLB-120, 246

Gilchrist, Alexander 1828-1861 . . . . DLB-144

Gilchrist, Ellen 1935- DLB-130

Gilder, Jeannette L. 1849-1916 . . . . DLB-79

Gilder, Richard Watson 1844-1909 . . .DLB-64, 79

Gildersleeve, Basil 1831-1924. . . . . DLB-71

Giles, Henry 1809-1882 . . . . DLB-64

Giles of Rome circa 1243-1316. . . . . DLB-115

Gilfillan, George 1813-1878 . . . . DLB-144

Gill, Eric 1882-1940 . . . . DLB-98

Gill, Sarah Prince 1728-1771 . . . . DLB-200

William F. Gill Company DLB-49

Gillespie, A. Lincoln, Jr. 1895-1950 . . . . . . DLB-4

Gillespie, Haven 1883-1975 . . . . DLB-265

Gilliam, Florence fl. twentieth century DLB-4

Gilliatt, Penelope 1932-1993. . . . . DLB-14

Gillott, Jacky 1939-1980. . . . . DLB-14

Gilman, Caroline H. 1794-1888 . . . . DLB-3, 73

Gilman, Charlotte Perkins 1860-1935 . . . DLB-221

   The Charlotte Perkins Gilman Society . . . Y-99

W. and J. Gilman [publishing house] DLB-49

Gilmer, Elizabeth Meriwether
   1861-1951 . . . . DLB-29

Gilmer, Francis Walker 1790-1826 . . . . DLB-37

Gilmore, Mary 1865-1962 . . . . DLB-260

Gilroy, Frank D. 1925- DLB-7

Gimferrer, Pere (Pedro) 1945- DLB-134

Ginger, Aleksandr S. 1897-1965 . . . . .DLB-317

Gingrich, Arnold 1903-1976. . . . . .DLB-137

   Prospectus From the Initial Issue of
     Esquire (Autumn 1933). DLB-137

   "With the Editorial Ken," Prospectus
     From the Initial Issue of *Ken*
     (7 April 1938) DLB-137

Ginibi, Ruby Langford 1934- DLB-325

Ginsberg, Allen
   1926-1997 . . . .DLB-5, 16, 169, 237; CDALB-1

Ginzburg, Evgeniia
   1904-1977. . . . . DLB-302

Ginzburg, Lidiia Iakovlevna
   1902-1990 . . . . DLB-302

Ginzburg, Natalia 1916-1991..........DLB-177

Ginzkey, Franz Karl 1871-1963..........DLB-81

Gioia, Dana 1950-..........DLB-120, 282

Giono, Jean 1895-1970..........DLB-72, 321

Giotti, Virgilio 1885-1957..........DLB-114

Giovanni, Nikki 1943-....DLB-5, 41; CDALB-7

Giovannitti, Arturo 1884-1959..........DLB-303

Gipson, Lawrence Henry 1880-1971......DLB-17

Girard, Rodolphe 1879-1956..........DLB-92

Giraudoux, Jean 1882-1944..........DLB-65, 321

Girondo, Oliverio 1891-1967..........DLB-283

Gissing, George 1857-1903......DLB-18, 135, 184

   The Place of Realism in Fiction (1895)...DLB-18

Giudici, Giovanni 1924-..........DLB-128

Giuliani, Alfredo 1924-..........DLB-128

Gjellerup, Karl 1857-1919..........DLB-300, 330

Glackens, William J. 1870-1938..........DLB-188

Gladilin, Anatolii Tikhonovich 1935-..........DLB-302

Gladkov, Fedor Vasil'evich 1883-1958....DLB-272

Gladstone, William Ewart 1809-1898..........DLB-57, 184

Glaeser, Ernst 1902-1963..........DLB-69

Glancy, Diane 1941-..........DLB-175

Glanvill, Joseph 1636-1680..........DLB-252

Glanville, Brian 1931-..........DLB-15, 139

Glapthorne, Henry 1610-1643?..........DLB-58

Glasgow, Ellen 1873-1945..........DLB-9, 12

   The Ellen Glasgow Society..........Y-01

Glasier, Katharine Bruce 1867-1950......DLB-190

Glaspell, Susan 1876-1948......DLB-7, 9, 78, 228

Glass, Montague 1877-1934..........DLB-11

Glassco, John 1909-1981..........DLB-68

Glauser, Friedrich 1896-1938..........DLB-56

Glavin, Anthony 1946-..........DLB-319

F. Gleason's Publishing Hall..........DLB-49

Gleim, Johann Wilhelm Ludwig 1719-1803..........DLB-97

Glendinning, Robin 1938-..........DLB-310

Glendinning, Victoria 1937-..........DLB-155

Glidden, Frederick Dilley (Luke Short) 1908-1975..........DLB-256

Glinka, Fedor Nikolaevich 1786-1880....DLB-205

Glover, Keith 1966-..........DLB-249

Glover, Richard 1712-1785..........DLB-95

Glover, Sue 1943-..........DLB-310

Glück, Louise 1943-..........DLB-5

Glyn, Elinor 1864-1943..........DLB-153

Gnedich, Nikolai Ivanovich 1784-1833...DLB-205

Gobineau, Joseph-Arthur de 1816-1882..........DLB-123

The God of Small Things, 1997 Booker Prize winner, Arundhati Roy..........DLB-326

Godber, John 1956-..........DLB-233

Godbout, Jacques 1933-..........DLB-53

Goddard, Morrill 1865-1937..........DLB-25

Goddard, William 1740-1817..........DLB-43

Godden, Rumer 1907-1998..........DLB-161

Godey, Louis A. 1804-1878..........DLB-73

Godey and McMichael..........DLB-49

Godfrey, Dave 1938-..........DLB-60

Godfrey, Thomas 1736-1763..........DLB-31

Godine, David R., Publisher..........DLB-46

Godkin, E. L. 1831-1902..........DLB-79

Godolphin, Sidney 1610-1643..........DLB-126

Godwin, Gail 1937-..........DLB-6, 234

M. J. Godwin and Company..........DLB-154

Godwin, Mary Jane Clairmont 1766-1841..........DLB-163

Godwin, Parke 1816-1904......DLB-3, 64, 250

Godwin, William 1756-1836......DLB-39, 104, 142, 158, 163, 262; CDBLB-3

   Preface to *St. Leon* (1799)..........DLB-39

Goering, Reinhard 1887-1936..........DLB-118

Goes, Albrecht 1908-..........DLB-69

Goethe, Johann Wolfgang von 1749-1832..........DLB-94; CDWLB-2

Goetz, Curt 1888-1960..........DLB-124

Goffe, Thomas circa 1592-1629..........DLB-58

Goffstein, M. B. 1940-..........DLB-61

Gogarty, Oliver St. John 1878-1957....DLB-15, 19

Gogol, Nikolai Vasil'evich 1809-1852....DLB-198

Goines, Donald 1937-1974..........DLB-33

Gold, Herbert 1924-..........DLB-2; Y-81

   Tribute to William Saroyan..........Y-81

Gold, Michael 1893-1967..........DLB-9, 28

Goldbarth, Albert 1948-..........DLB-120

Goldberg, Dick 1947-..........DLB-7

Golden Cockerel Press..........DLB-112

Golding, Arthur 1536-1606..........DLB-136

Golding, Louis 1895-1958..........DLB-195

Golding, William 1911-1993..........DLB-15, 100, 255, 326, 330; Y-83; CDBLB-7

   Nobel Lecture 1993..........Y-83

   The Stature of William Golding..........Y-83

Goldman, Emma 1869-1940..........DLB-221

Goldman, William 1931-..........DLB-44

Goldring, Douglas 1887-1960..........DLB-197

Goldschmidt, Meir Aron 1819-1887.....DLB-300

Goldsmith, Oliver 1730?-1774
   ......DLB-39, 89, 104, 109, 142; CDBLB-2

Goldsmith, Oliver 1794-1861..........DLB-99

Goldsmith Publishing Company..........DLB-46

Goldstein, Richard 1944-..........DLB-185

Goldsworthy, Peter 1951-..........DLB-325

Gollancz, Sir Israel 1864-1930..........DLB-201

Victor Gollancz Limited..........DLB-112

Gomberville, Marin Le Roy, sieur de 1600?-1674..........DLB-268

Gombrowicz, Witold 1904-1969..........DLB-215; CDWLB-4

Gomez, Madeleine-Angélique Poisson de 1684-1770..........DLB-313

Gómez de Ciudad Real, Alvar (Alvar Gómez de Guadalajara) 1488-1538..........DLB-318

Gómez-Quiñones, Juan 1942-..........DLB-122

Laurence James Gomme [publishing house]..........DLB-46

Gompers, Samuel 1850-1924..........DLB-303

Gonçalves Dias, Antônio 1823-1864.....DLB-307

Goncharov, Ivan Aleksandrovich 1812-1891..........DLB-238

Goncourt, Edmond de 1822-1896......DLB-123

Goncourt, Jules de 1830-1870..........DLB-123

Gonzales, Rodolfo "Corky" 1928-......DLB-122

Gonzales-Berry, Erlinda 1942-..........DLB-209

   "Chicano Language"..........DLB-82

González, Angel 1925-..........DLB-108

Gonzalez, Genaro 1949-..........DLB-122

Gonzalez, N. V. M. 1915-1999..........DLB-312

González, Otto-Raúl 1921-..........DLB-290

Gonzalez, Ray 1952-..........DLB-122

González de Mireles, Jovita 1899-1983..........DLB-122

González Martínez, Enrique 1871-1952...DLB-290

González-T., César A. 1931-..........DLB-82

Goodis, David 1917-1967..........DLB-226

Goodison, Lorna 1947-..........DLB-157

Goodman, Allegra 1967-..........DLB-244

Goodman, Nelson 1906-1998..........DLB-279

Goodman, Paul 1911-1972..........DLB-130, 246

The Goodman Theatre..........DLB-7

Goodrich, Frances 1891-1984 and Hackett, Albert 1900-1995..........DLB-26

Goodrich, Samuel Griswold 1793-1860..........DLB-1, 42, 73, 243

S. G. Goodrich [publishing house]..........DLB-49

C. E. Goodspeed and Company..........DLB-49

Goodwin, Stephen 1943-..........Y-82

Googe, Barnabe 1540-1594..........DLB-132

Gookin, Daniel 1612-1687..........DLB-24

Gopegui, Belén 1963-..........DLB-322

Goran, Lester 1928-..........DLB-244

Gordimer, Nadine 1923-..........DLB-225, 326, 330; Y-91

   Nobel Lecture 1991..........Y-91

Gordon, Adam Lindsay 1833-1870......DLB-230

Gordon, Caroline
1895-1981 . . . . DLB-4, 9, 102; DS-17; Y-81

Gordon, Charles F. (see OyamO)

Gordon, Charles William (see Connor, Ralph)

Gordon, Giles 1940- DLB-14, 139, 207

Gordon, Helen Cameron, Lady Russell
1867-1949. . . . . DLB-195

Gordon, Lyndall 1941- DLB-155

Gordon, Mack 1904-1959. . . . . DLB-265

Gordon, Mary 1949- DLB-6; Y-81

Gordone, Charles 1925-1995 . . . . DLB-7

Gore, Catherine 1800-1861 . . . . DLB-116

Gore-Booth, Eva 1870-1926 . . . . DLB-240

Gores, Joe 1931- DLB-226; Y-02

Tribute to Kenneth Millar Y-83

Tribute to Raymond Chandler. Y-88

Gorey, Edward 1925-2000 . . . . DLB-61

Gorgias of Leontini
circa 485 B.C.-376 B.C. DLB-176

Gor'ky, Maksim 1868-1936 . . . . DLB-295

Gorodetsky, Sergei Mitrofanovich
1884-1967. . . . . DLB-295

Gorostiza, José 1901-1979. . . . . DLB-290

Görres, Joseph 1776-1848 . . . . DLB-90

Gosse, Edmund 1849-1928. . . . . .DLB-57, 144, 184

Gosson, Stephen 1554-1624 . . . . .DLB-172

The Schoole of Abuse (1579) DLB-172

Gotanda, Philip Kan 1951- DLB-266

Gotlieb, Phyllis 1926- DLB-88, 251

Go-Toba 1180-1239. . . . . DLB-203

Gottfried von Straßburg
died before 1230 . . . . . . DLB-138; CDWLB-2

Gotthelf, Jeremias 1797-1854. . . . . DLB-133

Gottschalk circa 804/808-869 . . . . DLB-148

Gottsched, Johann Christoph
1700-1766 . . . . DLB-97

Götz, Johann Nikolaus 1721-1781. . . . . DLB-97

Goudge, Elizabeth 1900-1984. . . . . DLB-191

Gouges, Olympe de 1748-1793 . . . . DLB-313

Declaration of the Rights of Woman. DLB-314

Gough, John B. 1817-1886 . . . . DLB-243

Gould, Wallace 1882-1940 . . . . DLB-54

Gournay, Marie de 1565-1645 . . . . DLB-327

Govoni, Corrado 1884-1965. . . . . DLB-114

Govrin, Michal 1950- DLB-299

Gower, John circa 1330-1408 . . . . DLB-146

Goyen, William 1915-1983. . . . . .DLB-2, 218; Y-83

Goytisolo, José Augustín 1928- DLB-134

Goytisolo, Juan 1931- DLB-322

Goytisolo, Luis 1935- DLB-322

Gozzano, Guido 1883-1916 . . . . DLB-114

Grabbe, Christian Dietrich 1801-1836 . . . DLB-133

Gracq, Julien (Louis Poirier) 1910- DLB-83

Grady, Henry W. 1850-1889 . . . . DLB-23

Graf, Oskar Maria 1894-1967 . . . . DLB-56

Graf Rudolf between circa 1170 and
circa 1185. DLB-148

Graff, Gerald 1937- DLB-246

Graffigny, Françoise d'Issembourg de
1695-1758. DLB-313

Letters from a Peruvian Woman DLB-314

Richard Grafton [publishing house] DLB-170

Grafton, Sue 1940- DLB-226

Graham, Frank 1893-1965 . . . . DLB-241

Graham, George Rex 1813-1894 . . . . DLB-73

Graham, Gwethalyn (Gwethalyn Graham
Erichsen-Brown) 1913-1965 . . . . DLB-88

Graham, Jorie 1951- DLB-120

Graham, Katharine 1917-2001 . . . . DLB-127

Graham, Lorenz 1902-1989 . . . . DLB-76

Graham, Philip 1915-1963 . . . . DLB-127

Graham, R. B. Cunninghame
1852-1936 . . . . .DLB-98, 135, 174

Graham, Shirley 1896-1977 . . . . DLB-76

Graham, Stephen 1884-1975. . . . . DLB-195

Graham, W. S. 1918-1986 . . . . DLB-20

William H. Graham [publishing house] . . . DLB-49

Graham, Winston 1910-2003 . . . . DLB-77

Grahame, Kenneth 1859-1932 . . . DLB-34, 141, 178

Grainger, Martin Allerdale 1874-1941 . . . . DLB-92

Gramatky, Hardie 1907-1979 . . . . DLB-22

Gramcko, Ida 1924-1994 . . . . DLB-290

Gramsci, Antonio 1891-1937 . . . . DLB-296

Granada, Fray Luis de 1504-1588 . . . . . . DLB-318

Grand, Sarah 1854-1943. . . . . .DLB-135, 197

Grandbois, Alain 1900-1975 . . . . DLB-92

Grandson, Oton de circa 1345-1397. . . . . DLB-208

Grange, John circa 1556-? DLB-136

Granger, Thomas 1578-1627. . . . . DLB-281

Granich, Irwin (see Gold, Michael)

Granin, Daniil 1918- DLB-302

Granovsky, Timofei Nikolaevich
1813-1855 . . . . DLB-198

Grant, Anne MacVicar 1755-1838 . . . . . . DLB-200

Grant, Duncan 1885-1978 . . . . .DS-10

Grant, George 1918-1988 . . . . DLB-88

Grant, George Monro 1835-1902. . . . . . . DLB-99

Grant, Harry J. 1881-1963 . . . . DLB-29

Grant, James Edward 1905-1966 . . . . DLB-26

Grant, John (see Gash, Jonathan)

War of the Words (and Pictures): The Creation
of a Graphic Novel Y-02

Grass, Günter 1927- DLB-75, 124, 330; CDWLB-2

Nobel Lecture 1999:
"To Be Continued . . ." Y-99

Tribute to Helen Wolff. Y-94

Grasty, Charles H. 1863-1924 . . . . DLB-25

Grau, Shirley Ann 1929- DLB-2, 218

Graves, John 1920- Y-83

Graves, Richard 1715-1804. . . . . DLB-39

Graves, Robert 1895-1985
. . . . DLB-20, 100, 191; DS-18; Y-85; CDBLB-6

The St. John's College
Robert Graves Trust Y-96

Gray, Alasdair 1934- DLB-194, 261, 319

Gray, Asa 1810-1888 . . . . DLB-1, 235

Gray, David 1838-1861 . . . . DLB-32

Gray, Simon 1936- DLB-13

Gray, Robert 1945- DLB-325

Gray, Thomas 1716-1771 . . . . DLB-109; CDBLB-2

Grayson, Richard 1951- DLB-234

Grayson, William J. 1788-1863. . . . DLB-3, 64, 248

The Great Bibliographers Series. Y-93

The Great Gatsby (Documentary) DLB-219

"The Greatness of Southern Literature":
League of the South Institute for the
Study of Southern Culture and History
. . . . Y-02

Grech, Nikolai Ivanovich 1787-1867 . . . . . DLB-198

Greeley, Horace 1811-1872. . . .DLB-3, 43, 189, 250

Green, Adolph 1915-2002 . . . . DLB-44, 265

Green, Anna Katharine
1846-1935 . . . . DLB-202, 221

Green, Duff 1791-1875 . . . . DLB-43

Green, Elizabeth Shippen 1871-1954 . . . . DLB-188

Green, Gerald 1922- DLB-28

Green, Henry 1905-1973 . . . . DLB-15

Green, Jonas 1712-1767 . . . . DLB-31

Green, Joseph 1706-1780. . . . . DLB-31

Green, Julien 1900-1998 . . . . DLB-4, 72

Green, Paul 1894-1981 . . . . DLB-7, 9, 249; Y-81

Green, T. H. 1836-1882 . . . . DLB-190, 262

Green, Terence M. 1947- DLB-251

T. and S. Green [publishing house]. DLB-49

Green Tiger Press DLB-46

Timothy Green [publishing house]. DLB-49

Greenaway, Kate 1846-1901 . . . . DLB-141

Greenberg: Publisher DLB-46

Greene, Asa 1789-1838. . . . . DLB-11

Greene, Belle da Costa 1883-1950 . . . . . .DLB-187

Greene, Graham 1904-1991
. . . . .DLB-13, 15, 77, 100, 162, 201, 204;
Y-85, 91; CDBLB-7

Tribute to Christopher Isherwood Y-86

Greene, Robert 1558-1592 . . . . .DLB-62, 167

Greene, Robert Bernard (Bob), Jr.
1947- DLB-185

Benjamin H Greene [publishing house] . . . DLB-49

Greenfield, George 1917-2000 . . . . Y-91, 00

Derek Robinson's Review of George
    Greenfield's *Rich Dust* Y-02
Greenhow, Robert 1800-1854 . . . . .DLB-30
Greenlee, William B. 1872-1953 . . . . .DLB-187
Greenough, Horatio 1805-1852 . . . . . . .DLB-1, 235
Greenwell, Dora 1821-1882 . . . . .DLB-35, 199
Greenwillow Books DLB-46
Greenwood, Grace (see Lippincott, Sara Jane Clarke)
Greenwood, Walter 1903-1974 . . . . . . .DLB-10, 191
Greer, Ben 1948- DLB-6
Greflinger, Georg 1620?-1677 . . . . .DLB-164
Greg, W. R. 1809-1881 . . . . .DLB-55
Greg, W. W. 1875-1959 . . . . .DLB-201
Gregg, Josiah 1806-1850 . . . . .DLB-183, 186
Gregg Press DLB-46
Gregory, Horace 1898-1982 . . . . .DLB-48
Gregory, Isabella Augusta Persse, Lady
    1852-1932 . . . . .DLB-10
Gregory of Rimini circa 1300-1358 . . . . . .DLB-115
Gregynog Press DLB-112
Greiff, León de 1895-1976 . . . . .DLB-283
Greiffenberg, Catharina Regina von
    1633-1694 . . . . .DLB-168
Greig, Noël 1944- DLB-245
Grekova, Irina (Elena Sergeevna Venttsel')
    1907-2002 . . . . .DLB-302
Grenfell, Wilfred Thomason
    1865-1940 . . . . .DLB-92
Grenville, Kate 1950- DLB-325
Gress, Elsa 1919-1988 . . . . .DLB-214
Greve, Felix Paul (see Grove, Frederick Philip)
Greville, Fulke, First Lord Brooke
    1554-1628 . . . . .DLB-62, 172
Grey, Sir George, K.C.B. 1812-1898 . . . . .DLB-184
Grey, Lady Jane 1537-1554 . . . . .DLB-132
Grey, Zane 1872-1939 . . . . .DLB-9, 212
    Zane Grey's West Society Y-00
Grey Owl (Archibald Stansfeld Belaney)
    1888-1938 . . . . .DLB-92; DS-17
Grey Walls Press DLB-112
Griboedov, Aleksandr Sergeevich
    1795?-1829 . . . . .DLB-205
Grice, Paul 1913-1988 . . . . .DLB-279
Grier, Eldon 1917- DLB-88
Grieve, C. M. (see MacDiarmid, Hugh)
Griffin, Bartholomew fl. 1596 . . . . .DLB-172
Griffin, Bryan
    "Panic Among the Philistines":
    A Postscript, An Interview
    with Bryan Griffin Y-81
Griffin, Gerald 1803-1840 . . . . .DLB-159
The Griffin Poetry Prize Y-00
Griffith, Elizabeth 1727?-1793 . . . . . . .DLB-39, 89
    Preface to *The Delicate Distress* (1769) . . .DLB-39

Griffith, George 1857-1906 . . . . .DLB-178
Ralph Griffiths [publishing house] DLB-154
Griffiths, Trevor 1935- DLB-13, 245
S. C. Griggs and Company DLB-49
Griggs, Sutton Elbert 1872-1930 . . . . .DLB-50
Grignon, Claude-Henri 1894-1976 . . . . . . .DLB-68
Grigor'ev, Apollon Aleksandrovich
    1822-1864 . . . . .DLB-277
Grigorovich, Dmitrii Vasil'evich
    1822-1899 . . . . .DLB-238
Grigson, Geoffrey 1905-1985 . . . . .DLB-27
Grillparzer, Franz
    1791-1872 . . . . .DLB-133; CDWLB-2
Grimald, Nicholas
    circa 1519-circa 1562 . . . . .DLB-136
Grimké, Angelina Weld 1880-1958 . . . .DLB-50, 54
Grimké, Sarah Moore 1792-1873 . . . . . . .DLB-239
Grimm, Frédéric Melchior 1723-1807 . . . .DLB-313
Grimm, Hans 1875-1959 . . . . .DLB-66
Grimm, Jacob 1785-1863 . . . . .DLB-90
Grimm, Wilhelm
    1786-1859 . . . . .DLB-90; CDWLB-2
Grimmelshausen, Johann Jacob Christoffel von
    1621 or 1622-1676 . . . . . .DLB-168; CDWLB-2
Grimshaw, Beatrice Ethel 1871-1953 . . . . .DLB-174
Grímur Thomsen 1820-1896 . . . . .DLB-293
Grin, Aleksandr Stepanovich
    1880-1932 . . . . .DLB-272
Grindal, Edmund 1519 or 1520-1583 . . . .DLB-132
Gripe, Maria (Kristina) 1923- DLB-257
Griswold, Rufus Wilmot
    1815-1857 . . . . .DLB-3, 59, 250
Gronlund, Laurence 1846-1899 . . . . .DLB-303
Grosart, Alexander Balloch 1827-1899 . . .DLB-184
Grosholz, Emily 1950- DLB-282
Gross, Milt 1895-1953 . . . . .DLB-11
Grosset and Dunlap DLB-49
Grosseteste, Robert circa 1160-1253 . . . . .DLB-115
Grossman, Allen 1932- DLB-193
Grossman, David 1954- DLB-299
Grossman, Vasilii Semenovich
    1905-1964 . . . . .DLB-272
Grossman Publishers DLB-46
Grosvenor, Gilbert H. 1875-1966 . . . . .DLB-91
Groth, Klaus 1819-1899 . . . . .DLB-129
Groulx, Lionel 1878-1967 . . . . .DLB-68
Grove, Frederick Philip (Felix Paul Greve)
    1879-1948 . . . . .DLB-92
Grove Press DLB-46
Groys, Boris Efimovich 1947- DLB-285
Grubb, Davis 1919-1980 . . . . .DLB-6
Gruelle, Johnny 1880-1938 . . . . .DLB-22
von Grumbach, Argula
    1492-after 1563? DLB-179

Grundtvig, N. F. S. 1783-1872 . . . . .DLB-300
Grymeston, Elizabeth
    before 1563-before 1604 . . . . .DLB-136
Grynberg, Henryk 1936- DLB-299
Gryphius, Andreas
    1616-1664 . . . . .DLB-164; CDWLB-2
Gryphius, Christian 1649-1706 . . . . .DLB-168
Guare, John 1938- DLB-7, 249
Guarnieri, Gianfrancesco 1934- DLB-307
Guberman, Igor Mironovich 1936- DLB-285
Guðbergur Bergsson 1932- DLB-293
Guðmundur Böðvarsson 1904-1974 . . . . .DLB-293
Guðmundur Gíslason Hagalín
    1898-1985 . . . . .DLB-293
Guðmundur Magnússon (see Jón Trausti)
Guerra, Tonino 1920- DLB-128
Guest, Barbara 1920- DLB-5, 193
Guevara, Fray Antonio de 1480?-1545 . . .DLB-318
Guèvremont, Germaine 1893-1968 . . . . . .DLB-68
Guglielminetti, Amalia 1881-1941 . . . . . .DLB-264
Guidacci, Margherita 1921-1992 . . . . . . .DLB-128
Guillén, Jorge 1893-1984 . . . . .DLB-108
Guillén, Nicolás 1902-1989 . . . . .DLB-283
Guilloux, Louis 1899-1980 . . . . .DLB-72
Guilpin, Everard
    circa 1572-after 1608? DLB-136
Guiney, Louise Imogen 1861-1920 . . . . . . .DLB-54
Guiterman, Arthur 1871-1943 . . . . .DLB-11
Gul', Roman 1896-1986 . . . . .DLB-317
Gumilev, Nikolai Stepanovich
    1886-1921 . . . . .DLB-295
Günderrode, Caroline von
    1780-1806 . . . . .DLB-90
Gundulić, Ivan 1589-1638 . . .DLB-147; CDWLB-4
Gunesekera, Romesh 1954- DLB-267, 323
Gunn, Bill 1934-1989 . . . . .DLB-38
Gunn, James E. 1923- DLB-8
Gunn, Neil M. 1891-1973 . . . . .DLB-15
Gunn, Thom 1929- DLB-27; CDBLB-8
Gunnar Gunnarsson 1889-1975 . . . . .DLB-293
Gunnars, Kristjana 1948- DLB-60
Günther, Johann Christian 1695-1723 . . . .DLB-168
Gupta, Sunetra 1965- DLB-323
Gurik, Robert 1932- DLB-60
Gurney, A. R. 1930- DLB-266
Gurney, Ivor 1890-1937 . . . . .Y-02
    The Ivor Gurney Society Y-98
Guro, Elena Genrikhovna 1877-1913 . . . . .DLB-295
Gustafson, Ralph 1909-1995 . . . . .DLB-88
Gustafsson, Lars 1936- DLB-257
Gütersloh, Albert Paris 1887-1973 . . . . . . .DLB-81
Guterson, David 1956- DLB-292

Cumulative Index

Guthrie, A. B., Jr. 1901-1991 .... DLB-6, 212
Guthrie, Ramon 1896-1973 .... DLB-4
Guthrie, Thomas Anstey (see Anstey, FC)
Guthrie, Woody 1912-1967 .... DLB-303
The Guthrie Theater DLB-7
Gutiérrez Nájera, Manuel 1859-1895 .... DLB-290
Guttormur J. Guttormsson 1878-1966 ... DLB-293
Gutzkow, Karl 1811-1878 .... DLB-133
Guy, Ray 1939- DLB-60
Guy, Rosa 1925- DLB-33
Guyot, Arnold 1807-1884 .... DS-13
Gwynn, R. S. 1948- DLB-282
Gwynne, Erskine 1898-1948 .... DLB-4
Gyles, John 1680-1755 .... DLB-99
Gyllembourg, Thomasine 1773-1856 .... DLB-300
Gyllensten, Lars 1921- DLB-257
Gyrðir Elíasson 1961- DLB-293
Gysin, Brion 1916-1986 .... DLB-16

H

H.D. (see Doolittle, Hilda)
Habermas, Jürgen 1929- DLB-242
Habington, William 1605-1654 .... DLB-126
Hacker, Marilyn 1942- DLB-120, 282
Hackett, Albert 1900-1995 .... DLB-26
Hacks, Peter 1928- DLB-124
Hadas, Rachel 1948- DLB-120, 282
Hadden, Briton 1898-1929 .... DLB-91
Hagedorn, Friedrich von 1708-1754 .... DLB-168
Hagedorn, Jessica Tarahata 1949- DLB-312
Hagelstange, Rudolf 1912-1984 .... DLB-69
Hagerup, Inger 1905-1985 .... DLB-297
Haggard, H. Rider
  1856-1925 .... DLB-70, 156, 174, 178
Haggard, William (Richard Clayton)
  1907-1993 .... DLB-276; Y-93
Hagy, Alyson 1960- DLB-244
Hahn-Hahn, Ida Gräfin von 1805-1880 .. DLB-133
Haig-Brown, Roderick 1908-1976 .... DLB-88
Haight, Gordon S. 1901-1985 .... DLB-103
Hailey, Arthur 1920-2004 .... DLB-88; Y-82
Haines, John 1924- DLB-5, 212
Hake, Edward fl. 1566-1604 .... DLB-136
Hake, Thomas Gordon 1809-1895 .... DLB-32
Hakluyt, Richard 1552?-1616 .... DLB-136
Halas, František 1901-1949 .... DLB-215
Halbe, Max 1865-1944 .... DLB-118
Halberstam, David 1934- DLB-241
Haldane, Charlotte 1894-1969 .... DLB-191
Haldane, J. B. S. 1892-1964 .... DLB-160
Haldeman, Joe 1943- DLB-8

Haldeman-Julius Company DLB-46
Hale, E. J., and Son DLB-49
Hale, Edward Everett
  1822-1909 .... DLB-1, 42, 74, 235
Hale, Janet Campbell 1946- DLB-175
Hale, Kathleen 1898-2000 .... DLB-160
Hale, Leo Thomas (see Ebon)
Hale, Lucretia Peabody 1820-1900 ..... DLB-42
Hale, Nancy
  1908-1988 .... DLB-86; DS-17; Y-80, 88
Hale, Sarah Josepha (Buell)
  1788-1879 .... DLB-1, 42, 73, 243
Hale, Susan 1833-1910 .... DLB-221
Hales, John 1584-1656 .... DLB-151
Halévy, Ludovic 1834-1908 .... DLB-192
Haley, Alex 1921-1992 ...... DLB-38; CDALB-7
Haliburton, Thomas Chandler
  1796-1865 .... DLB-11, 99
Hall, Adam (Trevor Dudley-Smith)
  1920-1995 .... DLB-276
Hall, Anna Maria 1800-1881 .... DLB-159
Hall, Donald 1928- DLB-5
Hall, Edward 1497-1547 .... DLB-132
Hall, Halsey 1898-1977 .... DLB-241
Hall, James 1793-1868 .... DLB-73, 74
Hall, Joseph 1574-1656 .... DLB-121, 151
Hall, Radclyffe 1880-1943 .... DLB-191
Hall, Rodney 1935- DLB-289
Hall, Sarah Ewing 1761-1830 .... DLB-200
Hall, Stuart 1932- DLB-242
Samuel Hall [publishing house] DLB-49
al-Hallaj 857-922 .... DLB-311
Hallam, Arthur Henry 1811-1833 .... DLB-32
  On Some of the Characteristics of
  Modern Poetry and On the
  Lyrical Poems of Alfred
  Tennyson (1831) DLB-32
Halldór Laxness (Halldór Guðjónsson)
  1902-1998 .... DLB-293
Halleck, Fitz-Greene 1790-1867 ..... DLB-3, 250
Haller, Albrecht von 1708-1777 ...... DLB-168
Halliday, Brett (see Dresser, Davis)
Halligan, Marion 1940- DLB-325
Halliwell-Phillipps, James Orchard
  1820-1889 .... DLB-184
Hallmann, Johann Christian
  1640-1704 or 1716? DLB-168
Hallmark Editions DLB-46
Halper, Albert 1904-1984 .... DLB-9
Halperin, John William 1941- DLB-111
Halstead, Murat 1829-1908 .... DLB-23
Hamann, Johann Georg 1730-1788 ...... DLB-97
Hamburger, Michael 1924- DLB-27
Hamilton, Alexander 1712-1756 .... DLB-31

Hamilton, Alexander 1755?-1804 .... DLB-37
Hamilton, Cicely 1872-1952 .... DLB-10, 197
Hamilton, Edmond 1904-1977 .... DLB-8
Hamilton, Elizabeth 1758-1816 .... DLB-116, 158
Hamilton, Gail (see Corcoran, Barbara)
Hamilton, Gail (see Dodge, Mary Abigail)
Hamish Hamilton Limited DLB-112
Hamilton, Hugo 1953- DLB-267
Hamilton, Ian 1938-2001 .... DLB-40, 155
Hamilton, Janet 1795-1873 .... DLB-199
Hamilton, Mary Agnes 1884-1962 ...... DLB-197
Hamilton, Patrick 1904-1962 ..... DLB-10, 191
Hamilton, Virginia 1936-2002 ... DLB-33, 52; Y-01
Hamilton, Sir William 1788-1856 ..... DLB-262
Hamilton-Paterson, James 1941- DLB-267
Hammerstein, Oscar, 2nd 1895-1960 .... DLB-265
Hammett, Dashiell
  1894-1961 .... DLB-226; DS-6; CDALB-5
  An Appeal in TAC Y-91
  The Glass Key and Other Dashiell
    Hammett Mysteries Y-96
  Knopf to Hammett: The Editoral
    Correspondence Y-00
  The Maltese Falcon (Documentary) DLB-280
Hammon, Jupiter 1711-died between
  1790 and 1806 .... DLB-31, 50
Hammond, John ?-1663 .... DLB-24
Hamner, Earl 1923- DLB-6
Hampson, John 1901-1955 .... DLB-191
Hampton, Christopher 1946- DLB-13
Hamsun, Knut 1859-1952 .... DLB-297, 330
Handel-Mazzetti, Enrica von 1871-1955 ... DLB-81
Handke, Peter 1942- DLB-85, 124
Handlin, Oscar 1915- DLB-17
Hankin, St. John 1869-1909 .... DLB-10
Hanley, Clifford 1922- DLB-14
Hanley, James 1901-1985 .... DLB-191
Hannah, Barry 1942- DLB-6, 234
Hannay, James 1827-1873 .... DLB-21
Hannes Hafstein 1861-1922 .... DLB-293
Hano, Arnold 1922- DLB-241
Hanrahan, Barbara 1939-1991 .... DLB-289
Hansberry, Lorraine
  1930-1965 .... DLB-7, 38; CDALB-1
Hansen, Joseph 1923-2004 .... DLB-226
Hansen, Martin A. 1909-1955 .... DLB-214
Hansen, Thorkild 1927-1989 .... DLB-214
Hanson, Elizabeth 1684-1737 .... DLB-200
Hapgood, Norman 1868-1937 .... DLB-91
Happel, Eberhard Werner 1647-1690 ... DLB-168
Haq, Kaiser 1950- DLB-323
Harbach, Otto 1873-1963 .... DLB-265

The Harbinger 1845-1849 . . . . .DLB-1, 223

Harburg, E. Y. "Yip" 1896-1981 . . . . .DLB-265

Harcourt Brace Jovanovich DLB-46

Hardenberg, Friedrich von (see Novalis)

Harding, Walter 1917-1996 . . . . .DLB-111

Hardwick, Elizabeth 1916- DLB-6

Hardy, Alexandre 1572?-1632 . . . . .DLB-268

Hardy, Frank 1917-1994 . . . . .DLB-260

Hardy, Thomas
 1840-1928 . . . . . . .DLB-18, 19, 135; CDBLB-5

 "Candour in English Fiction" (1890) . . .DLB-18

Hare, Cyril 1900-1958 . . . . .DLB-77

Hare, David 1947- DLB-13, 310

Hare, R. M. 1919-2002 . . . . .DLB-262

Hargrove, Marion 1919-2003 . . . . .DLB-11

Häring, Georg Wilhelm Heinrich
 (see Alexis, Willibald)

Harington, Donald 1935- DLB-152

Harington, Sir John 1560-1612 . . . . .DLB-136

Harjo, Joy 1951- DLB-120, 175

Harkness, Margaret (John Law)
 1854-1923 . . . . .DLB-197

Harley, Edward, second Earl of Oxford
 1689-1741 . . . . .DLB-213

Harley, Robert, first Earl of Oxford
 1661-1724 . . . . .DLB-213

Harlow, Robert 1923- DLB-60

Harman, Thomas fl. 1566-1573 . . . . .DLB-136

Harness, Charles L. 1915- DLB-8

Harnett, Cynthia 1893-1981 . . . . .DLB-161

Harnick, Sheldon 1924- DLB-265

 Tribute to Ira Gershwin. Y-96

 Tribute to Lorenz Hart Y-95

Harper, Edith Alice Mary (see Wickham, Anna)

Harper, Fletcher 1806-1877 . . . . .DLB-79

Harper, Frances Ellen Watkins
 1825-1911 . . . . .DLB-50, 221

Harper, Michael S. 1938- DLB-41

Harper and Brothers DLB-49

Harpur, Charles 1813-1868 . . . . .DLB-230

Harraden, Beatrice 1864-1943 . . . . .DLB-153

George G. Harrap and Company
 Limited DLB-112

Harriot, Thomas 1560-1621 . . . . .DLB-136

Harris, Alexander 1805-1874 . . . . .DLB-230

Harris, Benjamin ?-circa 1720 . . . . . .DLB-42, 43

Harris, Christie 1907-2002 . . . . .DLB-88

Harris, Errol E. 1908- DLB-279

Harris, Frank 1856-1931 . . . . .DLB-156, 197

Harris, George Washington
 1814-1869 . . . . .DLB-3, 11, 248

Harris, Joanne 1964- DLB-271

Harris, Joel Chandler
 1848-1908 . . . . .DLB-11, 23, 42, 78, 91

The Joel Chandler Harris Association Y-99

Harris, Mark 1922- DLB-2; Y-80

 Tribute to Frederick A. Pottle Y-87

Harris, William Torrey 1835-1909 . . . . . . .DLB-270

Harris, Wilson 1921- DLB-117; CDWLB-3

Harrison, Mrs. Burton
 (see Harrison, Constance Cary)

Harrison, Charles Yale 1898-1954 . . . . . . .DLB-68

Harrison, Constance Cary 1843-1920 . . . .DLB-221

Harrison, Frederic 1831-1923 . . . . . .DLB-57, 190

 "On Style in English Prose" (1898) DLB-57

Harrison, Harry 1925- DLB-8

James P. Harrison Company DLB-49

Harrison, Jim 1937- Y-82

Harrison, M. John 1945- DLB-261

Harrison, Mary St. Leger Kingsley
 (see Malet, Lucas)

Harrison, Paul Carter 1936- DLB-38

Harrison, Susan Frances 1859-1935 . . . . . .DLB-99

Harrison, Tony 1937- DLB-40, 245

Harrison, William 1535-1593 . . . . .DLB-136

Harrison, William 1933- DLB-234

Harrisse, Henry 1829-1910 . . . . .DLB-47

Harry, J. S. 1939- .DLB-325

The Harry Ransom Humanities Research Center
 at the University of Texas at Austin Y-00

Harryman, Carla 1952- DLB-193

Harsdörffer, Georg Philipp 1607-1658 . . . .DLB-164

Harsent, David 1942- DLB-40

Hart, Albert Bushnell 1854-1943 . . . . .DLB-17

Hart, Anne 1768-1834 . . . . .DLB-200

Hart, Elizabeth 1771-1833 . . . . .DLB-200

Hart, Julia Catherine 1796-1867 . . . . .DLB-99

Hart, Kevin 1954- .DLB-325

Hart, Lorenz 1895-1943 . . . . .DLB-265

 Larry Hart: Still an Influence Y-95

 Lorenz Hart: An American Lyricist Y-95

 The Lorenz Hart Centenary Y-95

Hart, Moss 1904-1961 . . . . .DLB-7, 266

Hart, Oliver 1723-1795 . . . . .DLB-31

Rupert Hart-Davis Limited DLB-112

Harte, Bret 1836-1902
 . . . . DLB-12, 64, 74, 79, 186; CDALB-3

Harte, Edward Holmead 1922- DLB-127

Harte, Houston Harriman 1927- DLB-127

Harte, Jack 1944- .DLB-319

Hartlaub, Felix 1913-1945 . . . . .DLB-56

Hartleben, Otto Erich 1864-1905 . . . . .DLB-118

Hartley, David 1705-1757 . . . . .DLB-252

Hartley, L. P. 1895-1972 . . . . .DLB-15, 139

Hartley, Marsden 1877-1943 . . . . .DLB-54

Hartling, Peter 1933- DLB-75

Hartman, Geoffrey H. 1929- DLB-67

Hartmann, Sadakichi 1867-1944 . . . . .DLB-54

Hartmann von Aue
 circa 1160-circa 1205 . . . .DLB-138; CDWLB-2

Hartshorne, Charles 1897-2000 . . . . .DLB-270

Haruf, Kent 1943- .DLB-292

Harvey, Gabriel 1550?-1631 . . .DLB-167, 213, 281

Harvey, Jack (see Rankin, Ian)

Harvey, Jean-Charles 1891-1967 . . . . .DLB-88

Harvill Press Limited DLB-112

Harwood, Gwen 1920-1995 . . . . .DLB-289

Harwood, Lee 1939- DLB-40

Harwood, Ronald 1934- DLB-13

al-Hasan al-Basri 642-728 . . . . .DLB-311

Hašek, Jaroslav 1883-1923 . . .DLB-215; CDWLB-4

Haskins, Charles Homer 1870-1937 . . . . . .DLB-47

Haslam, Gerald 1937- DLB-212

Hass, Robert 1941- DLB-105, 206

Hasselstrom, Linda M. 1943- DLB-256

Hastings, Michael 1938- DLB-233

Hatar, Győző 1914- DLB-215

The Hatch-Billops Collection DLB-76

Hathaway, William 1944- DLB-120

Hatherly, Ana 1929- DLB-287

Hauch, Carsten 1790-1872 . . . . .DLB-300

Hauff, Wilhelm 1802-1827 . . . . .DLB-90

Hauge, Olav H. 1908-1994 . . . . .DLB-297

Haugen, Paal-Helge 1945- DLB-297

Haugwitz, August Adolph von
 1647-1706 . . . . .DLB-168

Hauptmann, Carl 1858-1921 . . . . . . .DLB-66, 118

Hauptmann, Gerhart
 1862-1946 . . . . .DLB-66, 118, 330; CDWLB-2

Hauser, Marianne 1910- Y-83

Havel, Václav 1936- DLB-232; CDWLB-4

Haven, Alice B. Neal 1827-1863 . . . . .DLB-250

Havergal, Frances Ridley 1836-1879 . . . . .DLB-199

Hawes, Stephen 1475?-before 1529 . . . . . .DLB-132

Hawker, Robert Stephen 1803-1875 . . . . .DLB-32

Hawkes, John
 1925-1998 . . . . .DLB-2, 7, 227; Y-80, Y-98

 John Hawkes: A Tribute Y-98

 Tribute to Donald Barthelme Y-89

Hawkesworth, John 1720-1773 . . . . .DLB-142

Hawkins, Sir Anthony Hope (see Hope, Anthony)

Hawkins, Sir John 1719-1789 . . . . . .DLB-104, 142

Hawkins, Walter Everette 1883-? DLB-50

Hawthorne, Nathaniel 1804-1864
 . . .DLB-1, 74, 183, 223, 269; DS-5; CDALB-2

 The Nathaniel Hawthorne Society Y-00

 The Old Manse DLB-223

Hawthorne, Sophia Peabody 1809-1871 .... DLB-183, 239

Hay, John 1835-1905 .... DLB-12, 47, 189

Hay, John 1915- DLB-275

Hayashi Fumiko 1903-1951 .... DLB-180

Haycox, Ernest 1899-1950 .... DLB-206

Haycraft, Anna Margaret (see Ellis, Alice Thomas)

Hayden, Robert 1913-1980 .... DLB-5, 76; CDALB-1

Haydon, Benjamin Robert 1786-1846 ... DLB-110

Hayes, John Michael 1919- DLB-26

Hayley, William 1745-1820 .... DLB-93, 142

Haym, Rudolf 1821-1901 .... DLB-129

Hayman, Robert 1575-1629 .... DLB-99

Hayman, Ronald 1932- DLB-155

Hayne, Paul Hamilton 1830-1886 .... DLB-3, 64, 79, 248

Hays, Mary 1760-1843 .... DLB-142, 158

Hayslip, Le Ly 1949- DLB-312

Hayward, John 1905-1965 .... DLB-201

Haywood, Eliza 1693?-1756 .... DLB-39

   Dedication of *Lasselia* [excerpt] (1723) DLB-39

   Preface to *The Disguis'd Prince* [excerpt] (1723) DLB-39

   The Tea-Table [excerpt] DLB-39

Haywood, William D. 1869-1928 .... DLB-303

Willis P. Hazard [publishing house] DLB-49

Hazlitt, William 1778-1830 .... DLB-110, 158

Hazzard, Shirley 1931- DLB-289; Y-82

Head, Bessie 1937-1986 .... DLB-117, 225; CDWLB-3

Headley, Joel T. 1813-1897 ... DLB-30, 183; DS-13

Heaney, Seamus 1939- DLB-40, 330; Y-95; CDBLB-8

   Nobel Lecture 1994: Crediting Poetry Y-95

Heard, Nathan C. 1936- DLB-33

Hearn, Lafcadio 1850-1904 ...... DLB-12, 78, 189

Hearn, Mary Anne (Marianne Farningham, Eva Hope) 1834-1909 .... DLB-240

Hearne, John 1926- DLB-117

Hearne, Samuel 1745-1792 .... DLB-99

Hearne, Thomas 1678?-1735 .... DLB-213

Hearst, William Randolph 1863-1951 .... DLB-25

Hearst, William Randolph, Jr. 1908-1993 .... DLB-127

Heartman, Charles Frederick 1883-1953 .... DLB-187

Heat and Dust, 1975 Booker Prize winner, Ruth Prawer Jhabvala DLB-326

Heath, Catherine 1924- DLB-14

Heath, James Ewell 1792-1862 .... DLB-248

Heath, Roy A. K. 1926- DLB-117

Heath-Stubbs, John 1918- DLB-27

Heavysege, Charles 1816-1876 .... DLB-99

Hebbel, Friedrich 1813-1863 .... DLB-129; CDWLB-2

Hebel, Johann Peter 1760-1826 .... DLB-90

Heber, Richard 1774-1833 .... DLB-184

Hébert, Anne 1916-2000 .... DLB-68

Hébert, Jacques 1923- DLB-53

Hebreo, León circa 1460-1520 .... DLB-318

Hecht, Anthony 1923- DLB-5, 169

Hecht, Ben 1894-1964 ....DLB-7, 9, 25, 26, 28, 86

Hecker, Isaac Thomas 1819-1888 ..... DLB-1, 243

Hedge, Frederic Henry 1805-1890 .... DLB-1, 59, 243; DS-5

Hefner, Hugh M. 1926- DLB-137

Hegel, Georg Wilhelm Friedrich 1770-1831 .... DLB-90

Heiberg, Johan Ludvig 1791-1860 ...... DLB-300

Heiberg, Johanne Luise 1812-1890 ...... DLB-300

Heide, Robert 1939- DLB-249

Heidegger, Martin 1889-1976 .... DLB-296

Heidenstam, Verner von 1859-1940 ..... DLB-330

Heidish, Marcy 1947- Y-82

Heißenbüttel, Helmut 1921-1996 .... DLB-75

Heike monogatari DLB-203

Hein, Christoph 1944- ... DLB-124; CDWLB-2

Hein, Piet 1905-1996 .... DLB-214

Heine, Heinrich 1797-1856 ... DLB-90; CDWLB-2

Heinemann, Larry 1944- DS-9

William Heinemann Limited DLB-112

Heinesen, William 1900-1991 .... DLB-214

Heinlein, Robert A. 1907-1988 .... DLB-8

Heinrich, Willi 1920- DLB-75

Heinrich Julius of Brunswick 1564-1613 .... DLB-164

Heinrich von dem Türlîn fl. circa 1230 .... DLB-138

Heinrich von Melk fl. after 1160 .... DLB-148

Heinrich von Veldeke circa 1145-circa 1190 .... DLB-138

Heinse, Wilhelm 1746-1803 .... DLB-94

Heinz, W. C. 1915- DLB-171

Heiskell, John 1872-1972 .... DLB-127

Hejinian, Lyn 1941- DLB-165

Helder, Herberto 1930- DLB-287

Heliand circa 850 .... DLB-148

Heller, Joseph 1923-1999 ...... DLB-2, 28, 227; Y-80, 99, 02

   Excerpts from Joseph Heller's USC Address, "The Literature of Despair" Y-96

   Remembering Joe Heller, by William Price Fox Y-99

   A Tribute to Joseph Heller Y-99

Heller, Michael 1937- DLB-165

Hellman, Lillian 1906-1984 ..... DLB-7, 228; Y-84

Hellwig, Johann 1609-1674 .... DLB-164

Helprin, Mark 1947- Y-85; CDALB-7

Helvétius, Claude-Adrien 1715-1771 ..... DLB-313

   The Spirit of Laws DLB-314

Helwig, David 1938- DLB-60

Hemans, Felicia 1793-1835 .... DLB-96

Hemenway, Abby Maria 1828-1890 ..... DLB-243

Hemingway, Ernest 1899-1961 ...... DLB-4, 9, 102, 210, 316, 330; Y-81, 87, 99; DS-1, 15, 16; CDALB-4

   A Centennial Celebration Y-99

   Come to Papa Y-99

   The Ernest Hemingway Collection at the John F. Kennedy Library Y-99

   Ernest Hemingway Declines to Introduce *War and Peace* Y-01

   Ernest Hemingway's Reaction to James Gould Cozzens Y-98

   Ernest Hemingway's Toronto Journalism Revisited: With Three Previously Unrecorded Stories Y-92

   Falsifying Hemingway Y-96

   A Farewell to Arms (Documentary) DLB-308

   Hemingway Centenary Celebration at the JFK Library Y-99

   The Hemingway/Fenton Correspondence Y-02

   Hemingway in the JFK Y-99

   The Hemingway Letters Project Finds an Editor Y-02

   Hemingway Salesmen's Dummies Y-00

   Hemingway: Twenty-Five Years Later Y-85

   A Literary Archaeologist Digs On: A Brief Interview with Michael Reynolds Y-99

   Not Immediately Discernible . . . but Eventually Quite Clear: The *First Light* and *Final Years* of Hemingway's Centenary Y-99

   Packaging Papa: *The Garden of Eden* Y-86

   Second International Hemingway Colloquium: Cuba Y-98

Hémon, Louis 1880-1913 .... DLB-92

Hempel, Amy 1951- DLB-218

Hempel, Carl G. 1905-1997 .... DLB-279

Hemphill, Paul 1936- Y-87

Hénault, Gilles 1920-1996 .... DLB-88

Henchman, Daniel 1689-1761 .... DLB-24

Henderson, Alice Corbin 1881-1949 ..... DLB-54

Henderson, Archibald 1877-1963 .... DLB-103

Henderson, David 1942- DLB-41

Henderson, George Wylie 1904-1965 .... DLB-51

Henderson, Zenna 1917-1983 .... DLB-8

Henighan, Tom 1934- DLB-251

Henisch, Peter 1943- DLB-85

Henley, Beth 1952- Y-86

Henley, William Ernest 1849-1903 . . . . DLB-19	Hernández, Miguel 1910-1942. . . . . DLB-134	Hickman, William Albert 1877-1957 . . . . . . DLB-92
Henniker, Florence 1855-1923 . . . . DLB-135	Hernton, Calvin C. 1932- DLB-38	Hicks, Granville 1901-1982 . . . . DLB-246
Henning, Rachel 1826-1914 . . . . DLB-230	Herodotus circa 484 B.C.-circa 420 B.C. DLB-176; CDWLB-1	Hidalgo, José Luis 1919-1947 . . . . DLB-108
Henningsen, Agnes 1868-1962 . . . . DLB-214	Héroët, Antoine 1490?-1567? DLB-327	Hiebert, Paul 1892-1987 . . . . DLB-68
Henry, Alexander 1739-1824 . . . . DLB-99	Heron, Robert 1764-1807 . . . . DLB-142	Hieng, Andrej 1925- DLB-181
Henry, Buck 1930- DLB-26	Herr, Michael 1940- DLB-185	Hierro, José 1922-2002 . . . . DLB-108
Henry, Marguerite 1902-1997 . . . . DLB-22	Herrera, Darío 1870-1914 . . . . DLB-290	Higgins, Aidan 1927- DLB-14
Henry, O. (see Porter, William Sydney)	Herrera, Fernando de 1534?-1597 . . . . . . DLB-318	Higgins, Colin 1941-1988 . . . . DLB-26
Henry, Robert Selph 1889-1970 . . . . DLB-17	Herrera, Juan Felipe 1948- DLB-122	Higgins, George V. 1939-1999 . . . . DLB-2; Y-81, 98-99
Henry, Will (see Allen, Henry W.)	E. R. Herrick and Company DLB-49	Afterword [in response to Cozzen's Mens Rea (or Something)] Y-97
Henry VIII of England 1491-1547 . . . . . . DLB-132	Herrick, Robert 1591-1674 . . . . DLB-126	
Henry of Ghent circa 1217-1229 - 1293 . . . . DLB-115	Herrick, Robert 1868-1938 . . . . DLB-9, 12, 78	At End of Day: The Last George V. Higgins Novel Y-99
Henryson, Robert 1420s or 1430s-circa 1505 . . . . DLB-146	Herrick, William 1915-2004 . . . . Y-83	The Books of George V. Higgins: A Checklist of Editions and Printings Y-00
	Herrmann, John 1900-1959 . . . . DLB-4	
Henschke, Alfred (see Klabund)	Hersey, John 1914-1993 . . . DLB-6, 185, 278, 299; CDALB-7	George V. Higgins in Class Y-02
Hensher, Philip 1965- DLB-267		Tribute to Alfred A. Knopf Y-84
Hensley, Sophie Almon 1866-1946 . . . . . . DLB-99	Hertel, François 1905-1985 . . . . DLB-68	Tributes to George V. Higgins Y-99
Henson, Lance 1944- DLB-175	Hervé-Bazin, Jean Pierre Marie (see Bazin, Hervé)	"What You Lose on the Swings You Make Up on the Merry-Go-Round" Y-99
Henty, G. A. 1832-1902 . . . . DLB-18, 141	Hervey, John, Lord 1696-1743 . . . . DLB-101	
The Henty Society Y-98	Herwig, Georg 1817-1875 . . . . DLB-133	Higginson, Thomas Wentworth 1823-1911 . . . . DLB-1, 64, 243
Hentz, Caroline Lee 1800-1856 . . . . . . DLB-3, 248	Herzen, Alexander (Aleksandr Ivanovich Gersten) 1812-1870 . . . . DLB-277	Highsmith, Patricia 1921-1995 . . . . DLB-306
Heraclitus fl. circa 500 B.C. DLB-176		Highwater, Jamake 1942?- DLB-52; Y-85
	Herzog, Emile Salomon Wilhelm (see Maurois, André)	Hijuelos, Oscar 1951- DLB-145
Herbert, Agnes circa 1880-1960 . . . . DLB-174	Hesiod eighth century B.C. DLB-176	Hildegard von Bingen 1098-1179 . . . . DLB-148
Herbert, Alan Patrick 1890-1971 . . . . . DLB-10, 191	Hesse, Hermann 1877-1962 . . . . DLB-66, 330; CDWLB-2	Das Hildesbrandslied circa 820 . . . . DLB-148; CDWLB-2
Herbert, Edward, Lord, of Cherbury 1582-1648 . . . . DLB-121, 151, 252		Hildesheimer, Wolfgang 1916-1991 . . . DLB-69, 124
Herbert, Frank 1920-1986 . . . . . . DLB-8; CDALB-7	Hessus, Eobanus 1488-1540 . . . . DLB-179	Hildreth, Richard 1807-1865 . . . DLB-1, 30, 59, 235
Herbert, George 1593-1633 . . DLB-126; CDBLB-1	Heureka! (see Kertész, Imre and Nobel Prize in Literature: 2002) Y-02	Hill, Aaron 1685-1750 . . . . DLB-84
Herbert, Henry William 1807-1858 . . . . . DLB-3, 73	Hewat, Alexander circa 1743-circa 1824 . . . DLB-30	Hill, Geoffrey 1932- DLB-40; CDBLB-8
Herbert, John 1926-2001 . . . . DLB-53	Hewett, Dorothy 1923-2002 . . . . DLB-289	George M. Hill Company DLB-49
Herbert, Mary Sidney, Countess of Pembroke (see Sidney, Mary)	Hewitt, John 1907-1987 . . . . DLB-27	Hill, "Sir" John 1714?-1775 . . . . DLB-39
	Hewlett, Maurice 1861-1923 . . . . DLB-34, 156	Lawrence Hill and Company, Publishers DLB-46
Herbert, Xavier 1901-1984 . . . . DLB-260	Heyen, William 1940- DLB-5	
Herbert, Zbigniew 1924-1998 . . . . DLB-232; CDWLB-4	Heyer, Georgette 1902-1974 . . . . DLB-77, 191	Hill, Joe 1879-1915 . . . . DLB-303
	Heym, Stefan 1913-2001 . . . . DLB-69	Hill, Leslie 1880-1960 . . . . DLB-51
Herbst, Josephine 1892-1969 . . . . DLB-9	Heyse, Paul 1830-1914 . . . . DLB-129, 330	Hill, Reginald 1936- DLB-276
Herburger, Gunter 1932- DLB-75, 124	Heytesbury, William circa 1310-1372 or 1373 . . . . DLB-115	Hill, Susan 1942- DLB-14, 139
Herculano, Alexandre 1810-1877 . . . . DLB-287		Hill, Walter 1942- DLB-44
Hercules, Frank E. M. 1917-1996 . . . . DLB-33	Heyward, Dorothy 1890-1961 . . . . DLB-7, 249	Hill and Wang DLB-46
Herder, Johann Gottfried 1744-1803 . . . . . DLB-97	Heyward, DuBose 1885-1940 . . . DLB-7, 9, 45, 249	Hillberry, Conrad 1928- DLB-120
B. Herder Book Company DLB-49	Heywood, John 1497?-1580? DLB-136	Hillerman, Tony 1925- DLB-206, 306
Heredia, José-María de 1842-1905 . . . . . . DLB-217	Heywood, Thomas 1573 or 1574-1641 . . . . DLB-62	Hilliard, Gray and Company DLB-49
Herford, Charles Harold 1853-1931 . . . . . DLB-149	Hiaasen, Carl 1953- DLB-292	Hills, Lee 1906-2000 . . . . DLB-127
Hergesheimer, Joseph 1880-1954 . . . . . . DLB-9, 102	Hibberd, Jack 1940- DLB-289	Hillyer, Robert 1895-1961 . . . . DLB-54
Heritage Press DLB-46	Hibbs, Ben 1901-1975 . . . . DLB-137	Hilsenrath, Edgar 1926- DLB-299
Hermann the Lame 1013-1054 . . . . DLB-148	"The Saturday Evening Post reaffirms a policy," Ben Hibb's Statement in The Saturday Evening Post (16 May 1942) DLB-137	Hilton, James 1900-1954 . . . . DLB-34, 77
Hermes, Johann Timotheu 1738-1821 . . . . . DLB-97		Hilton, Walter died 1396 . . . . DLB-146
Hermlin, Stephan 1915-1997 . . . . DLB-69		Hilton and Company DLB-49
Hernández, Alfonso C. 1938- DLB-122	Hichens, Robert S. 1864-1950 . . . . DLB-153	
Hernández, Inés 1947- DLB-122	Hickey, Emily 1845-1924 . . . . DLB-199	Himes, Chester 1909-1984 . . . DLB-2, 76, 143, 226

Joseph Hindmarsh [publishing house] DLB-170

Hine, Daryl 1936- DLB-60

Hingley, Ronald 1920- DLB-155

Hinojosa-Smith, Rolando 1929- DLB-82

Hinton, S. E. 1948- CDALB-7

Hippel, Theodor Gottlieb von
1741-1796 ....DLB-97

Hippius, Zinaida Nikolaevna
1869-1945 ....DLB-295

Hippocrates of Cos fl. circa
425 B.C. DLB-176; CDWLB-1

Hirabayashi Taiko 1905-1972.........DLB-180

Hirsch, E. D., Jr. 1928- DLB-67

Hirsch, Edward 1950- DLB-120

"Historical Novel," The Holocaust......DLB-299

Hoagland, Edward 1932- DLB-6

Hoagland, Everett H., III 1942- DLB-41

Hoban, Russell 1925- DLB-52; Y-90

Hobbes, Thomas 1588-1679... DLB-151, 252, 281

Hobby, Oveta 1905-1995 ....DLB-127

Hobby, William 1878-1964 ....DLB-127

Hobsbaum, Philip 1932- DLB-40

Hobsbawm, Eric (Francis Newton)
1917- DLB-296

Hobson, Laura Z. 1900-1986 ....DLB-28

Hobson, Sarah 1947- DLB-204

Hoby, Thomas 1530-1566 ....DLB-132

Hoccleve, Thomas
circa 1368-circa 1437 ....DLB-146

Hoch, Edward D. 1930- DLB-306

Hochhuth, Rolf 1931- DLB-124

Hochman, Sandra 1936- DLB-5

Hocken, Thomas Morland 1836-1910 ... DLB-184

Hocking, William Ernest 1873-1966......DLB-270

Hodder and Stoughton, Limited........DLB-106

Hodgins, Jack 1938- DLB-60

Hodgman, Helen 1945- DLB-14

Hodgskin, Thomas 1787-1869 ....DLB-158

Hodgson, Ralph 1871-1962 ....DLB-19

Hodgson, William Hope
1877-1918..........DLB-70, 153, 156, 178

Hoe, Robert, III 1839-1909 ....DLB-187

Hoeg, Peter 1957- DLB-214

Hoel, Sigurd 1890-1960 ....DLB-297

Hoem, Edvard 1949- DLB-297

Hoffenstein, Samuel 1890-1947 ....DLB-11

Hoffman, Alice 1952- DLB-292

Hoffman, Charles Fenno 1806-1884... DLB-3, 250

Hoffman, Daniel 1923- DLB-5

Tribute to Robert Graves.............Y-85

Hoffmann, E. T. A.
1776-1822............DLB-90; CDWLB-2

Hoffman, Frank B. 1888-1958 ....DLB-188

Hoffman, William 1925- DLB-234

Tribute to Paxton Davis...............Y-94

Hoffmanswaldau, Christian Hoffman von
1616-1679.....................DLB-168

Hofmann, Michael 1957- DLB-40

Hofmannsthal, Hugo von
1874-1929.........DLB-81, 118; CDWLB-2

Hofmo, Gunvor 1921-1995 ....DLB-297

Hofstadter, Richard 1916-1970.......DLB-17, 246

Hogan, Desmond 1950- DLB-14, 319

Hogan, Linda 1947- DLB-175

Hogan and Thompson................DLB-49

Hogarth Press................DLB-112; DS-10

Hogg, James 1770-1835.........DLB-93, 116, 159

Hohberg, Wolfgang Helmhard Freiherr von
1612-1688 ....DLB-168

von Hohenheim, Philippus Aureolus
Theophrastus Bombastus (see Paracelsus)

Hohl, Ludwig 1904-1980 ....DLB-56

Højholt, Per 1928- DLB-214

Holan, Vladimir 1905-1980 ....DLB-215

d'Holbach, Paul Henri Thiry, baron
1723-1789.....................DLB-313

The System of Nature (as Jean-Baptiste de
Mirabaud)...................DLB-314

Holberg, Ludvig 1684-1754 ....DLB-300

Holbrook, David 1923- DLB-14, 40

Holcroft, Thomas 1745-1809 ... DLB-39, 89, 158

Preface to *Alwyn* (1780)............DLB-39

Holden, Jonathan 1941- DLB-105

"Contemporary Verse Story-telling"... DLB-105

Holden, Molly 1927-1981..............DLB-40

Hölderlin, Friedrich
1770-1843............. DLB-90; CDWLB-2

Holdstock, Robert 1948- DLB-261

Holiday, 1974 Booker Prize winner,
Stanley Middleton DLB-326

Holiday House DLB-46

Holinshed, Raphael died 1580 ....DLB-167

Holland, J. G. 1819-1881 ....DS-13

Holland, Norman N. 1927- DLB-67

Hollander, John 1929- DLB-5

Holley, Marietta 1836-1926 ....DLB-11

Hollinghurst, Alan 1954- DLB-207, 326

Hollingsworth, Margaret 1940- DLB-60

Hollo, Anselm 1934- DLB-40

Holloway, Emory 1885-1977 ....DLB-103

Holloway, John 1920- DLB-27

Holloway House Publishing Company ... DLB-46

Holme, Constance 1880-1955 ....DLB-34

Holmes, Abraham S. 1821?-1908........DLB-99

Holmes, John Clellon 1926-1988 .....DLB-16, 237

"Four Essays on the Beat
Generation"..................DLB-16

Holmes, Mary Jane 1825-1907.....DLB-202, 221

Holmes, Oliver Wendell
1809-1894 ...... DLB-1, 189, 235; CDALB-2

Holmes, Richard 1945- DLB-155

Holmes, Thomas James 1874-1959.......DLB-187

The Holocaust "Historical Novel" DLB-299

Holocaust Fiction, Postmodern.........DLB-299

Holocaust Novel, The "Second-Generation"
..............................DLB-299

Holroyd, Michael 1935- DLB-155; Y-99

Holst, Hermann E. von 1841-1904 ......DLB-47

Holt, John 1721-1784 ....DLB-43

Henry Holt and Company DLB-49, 284

Holt, Rinehart and Winston............DLB-46

Holtby, Winifred 1898-1935...........DLB-191

Holthusen, Hans Egon 1913-1997 ......DLB-69

Hölty, Ludwig Christoph Heinrich
1748-1776 ....DLB-94

Holub, Miroslav
1923-1998 ....DLB-232; CDWLB-4

Holz, Arno 1863-1929 ....DLB-118

Home, Henry, Lord Kames
(see Kames, Henry Home, Lord)

Home, John 1722-1808................DLB-84

Home, William Douglas 1912-1992......DLB-13

Home Publishing Company DLB-49

Homer circa eighth-seventh centuries B.C.
.....................DLB-176; CDWLB-1

Homer, Winslow 1836-1910 ....DLB-188

Homes, Geoffrey (see Mainwaring, Daniel)

Honan, Park 1928- DLB-111

Hone, William 1780-1842..........DLB-110, 158

Hongo, Garrett Kaoru 1951- DLB-120, 312

Honig, Edwin 1919- DLB-5

Hood, Hugh 1928-2000 ....DLB-53

Hood, Mary 1946- DLB-234

Hood, Thomas 1799-1845 ....DLB-96

Hook, Sidney 1902-1989 ....DLB-279

Hook, Theodore 1788-1841 ....DLB-116

Hooker, Jeremy 1941- DLB-40

Hooker, Richard 1554-1600 ....DLB-132

Hooker, Thomas 1586-1647 ....DLB-24

hooks, bell 1952- DLB-246

Hooper, Johnson Jones
1815-1862 ....DLB-3, 11, 248

Hope, A. D. 1907-2000................DLB-289

Hope, Anthony 1863-1933 ....DLB-153, 156

Hope, Christopher 1944- DLB-225

Hope, Eva (see Hearn, Mary Anne)

Hope, Laurence (Adela Florence
Cory Nicolson) 1865-1904..........DLB-240

Hopkins, Ellice 1836-1904 ....DLB-190

Hopkins, Gerard Manley
   1844-1889 . . . . .DLB-35, 57; CDBLB-5

Hopkins, John ?-1570. . . . . .DLB-132

Hopkins, John H., and Son DLB-46

Hopkins, Lemuel 1750-1801 . . . . .DLB-37

Hopkins, Pauline Elizabeth 1859-1930 . . . .DLB-50

Hopkins, Samuel 1721-1803 . . . . .DLB-31

Hopkinson, Francis 1737-1791 . . . . .DLB-31

Hopkinson, Nalo 1960- DLB-251

Hopper, Nora (Mrs. Nora Chesson)
   1871-1906 . . . . .DLB-240

Hoppin, Augustus 1828-1896 . . . . .DLB-188

Hora, Josef 1891-1945 . . . . . .DLB-215; CDWLB-4

Horace 65 B.C.-8 B.C. DLB-211; CDWLB-1

Horgan, Paul 1903-1995 . . . . . DLB-102, 212; Y-85

   Tribute to Alfred A. Knopf Y-84

Horizon Press. DLB-46

Horkheimer, Max 1895-1973 . . . . .DLB-296

Hornby, C. H. St. John 1867-1946. . . . . . .DLB-201

Hornby, Nick 1957- DLB-207

Horne, Frank 1899-1974 . . . . .DLB-51

Horne, Richard Henry (Hengist)
   1802 or 1803-1884 . . . . .DLB-32

Horne, Thomas 1608-1654 . . . . .DLB-281

Horney, Karen 1885-1952 . . . . .DLB-246

Hornung, E. W. 1866-1921 . . . . .DLB-70

Horovitz, Israel 1939- DLB-7

Horta, Maria Teresa (see The Three Marias:
   A Landmark Case in Portuguese
   Literary History)

Horton, George Moses 1797?-1883? DLB-50

   George Moses Horton Society Y-99

Horváth, Ödön von 1901-1938 . . . . . .DLB-85, 124

Horwood, Harold 1923- DLB-60

E. and E. Hosford [publishing house] DLB-49

Hoskens, Jane Fenn 1693-1770? DLB-200

Hoskyns, John circa 1566-1638 . . . .DLB-121, 281

Hosokawa Yūsai 1535-1610. . . . . .DLB-203

Hospers, John 1918- DLB-279

Hospital, Janette Turner 1942- DLB-325

Hostovský, Egon 1908-1973. . . . . .DLB-215

Hotchkiss and Company DLB-49

Hotel du Lac, 1984 Booker Prize winner,
   Anita Brookner DLB-326

Hough, Emerson 1857-1923. . . . . . . .DLB-9, 212

Houghton, Stanley 1881-1913 . . . . .DLB-10

Houghton Mifflin Company DLB-49

Hours at Home DS-13

Household, Geoffrey 1900-1988 . . . . .DLB-87

Housman, A. E. 1859-1936 . . . DLB-19; CDBLB-5

Housman, Laurence 1865-1959. . . . . .DLB-10

Houston, Pam 1962- DLB-244

Houwald, Ernst von 1778-1845 . . . . .DLB-90

Hovey, Richard 1864-1900 . . . . .DLB-54

How Late It Was, How Late, 1994 Booker Prize winner,
   James Kelman DLB-326

Howard, Donald R. 1927-1987 . . . . .DLB-111

Howard, Maureen 1930- Y-83

Howard, Richard 1929- DLB-5

Howard, Roy W. 1883-1964 . . . . .DLB-29

Howard, Sidney 1891-1939 . . . . . . DLB-7, 26, 249

Howard, Thomas, second Earl of Arundel
   1585-1646 . . . . .DLB-213

Howe, E. W. 1853-1937. . . . . .DLB-12, 25

Howe, Henry 1816-1893 . . . . .DLB-30

Howe, Irving 1920-1993 . . . . .DLB-67

Howe, Joseph 1804-1873 . . . . .DLB-99

Howe, Julia Ward 1819-1910. . . . . DLB-1, 189, 235

Howe, Percival Presland 1886-1944. . . . . .DLB-149

Howe, Susan 1937- DLB-120

Howell, Clark, Sr. 1863-1936. . . . . .DLB-25

Howell, Evan P. 1839-1905 . . . . .DLB-23

Howell, James 1594?-1666 . . . . .DLB-151

Howell, Soskin and Company DLB-46

Howell, Warren Richardson
   1912-1984 . . . . .DLB-140

Howells, William Dean 1837-1920
   . . . . DLB-12, 64, 74, 79, 189; CDALB-3

   Introduction to Paul Laurence
   Dunbar's *Lyrics of Lowly Life*
   (1896) DLB-50

   The William Dean Howells Society Y-01

Howitt, Mary 1799-1888 . . . . DLB-110, 199

Howitt, William 1792-1879 . . . . .DLB-110

Hoyem, Andrew 1935- DLB-5

Hoyers, Anna Ovena 1584-1655 . . . . .DLB-164

Hoyle, Fred 1915-2001 . . . . .DLB-261

Hoyos, Angela de 1940- DLB-82

Henry Hoyt [publishing house] DLB-49

Hoyt, Palmer 1897-1979. . . . . .DLB-127

Hrabal, Bohumil 1914-1997 . . . . .DLB-232

Hrabanus Maurus 776?-856. . . . . .DLB-148

Hronský, Josef Cíger 1896-1960 . . . . .DLB-215

Hrotsvit of Gandersheim
   circa 935-circa 1000 . . . . .DLB-148

Hubbard, Elbert 1856-1915 . . . . .DLB-91

Hubbard, Kin 1868-1930. . . . . .DLB-11

Hubbard, William circa 1621-1704 . . . . . . .DLB-24

Huber, Therese 1764-1829. . . . . .DLB-90

Huch, Friedrich 1873-1913 . . . . .DLB-66

Huch, Ricarda 1864-1947 . . . . .DLB-66

Huddle, David 1942- DLB-130

Hudgins, Andrew 1951- DLB-120, 282

Hudson, Henry Norman 1814-1886 . . . . . .DLB-64

Hudson, Stephen 1868?-1944 . . . . .DLB-197

Hudson, W. H. 1841-1922. . . . . . DLB-98, 153, 174

Hudson and Goodwin. DLB-49

Huebsch, B. W., oral history Y-99

B. W. Huebsch [publishing house]. DLB-46

Hueffer, Oliver Madox 1876-1931 . . . . . . .DLB-197

Huet, Pierre Daniel
   Preface to *The History of Romances*
   (1715) DLB-39

Hugh of St. Victor circa 1096-1141 . . . . . .DLB-208

Hughes, David 1930- DLB-14

Hughes, Dusty 1947- DLB-233

Hughes, Hatcher 1881-1945 . . . . .DLB-249

Hughes, John 1677-1720. . . . . .DLB-84

Hughes, Langston 1902-1967 . . . . . . .DLB-4, 7, 48,
   51, 86, 228, 315; DS-15; CDALB-5

Hughes, Richard 1900-1976. . . . . . . .DLB-15, 161

Hughes, Ted 1930-1998. . . . . .DLB-40, 161

Hughes, Thomas 1822-1896 . . . . .DLB-18, 163

Hugo, Richard 1923-1982 . . . . .DLB-5, 206

Hugo, Victor 1802-1885 . . . . . . DLB-119, 192, 217

Hugo Awards and Nebula Awards DLB-8

Huidobro, Vicente 1893-1948 . . . . .DLB-283

Hull, Richard 1896-1973 . . . . .DLB-77

Hulda (Unnur Benediktsdóttir Bjarklind)
   1881-1946 . . . . .DLB-293

Hulme, Keri 1947- DLB-326

Hulme, T. E. 1883-1917. . . . . .DLB-19

Hulton, Anne ?-1779? DLB-200

Humanism, Sixteenth-Century
   Spanish DLB-318

Humboldt, Alexander von 1769-1859 . . . . .DLB-90

Humboldt, Wilhelm von 1767-1835. . . . . . .DLB-90

Hume, David 1711-1776. . . . . .DLB-104, 252

Hume, Fergus 1859-1932 . . . . .DLB-70

Hume, Sophia 1702-1774 . . . . .DLB-200

Hume-Rothery, Mary Catherine
   1824-1885 . . . . .DLB-240

Humishuma
   (see Mourning Dove)

Hummer, T. R. 1950- DLB-120

Humor
   American Humor: A Historical
   Survey DLB-11

   American Humor Studies Association Y-99

   The Comic Tradition Continued
   [in the British Novel]. DLB-15

   Humorous Book Illustration DLB-11

   International Society for Humor Studies. . .Y-99

   Newspaper Syndication of American
   Humor DLB-11

   Selected Humorous Magazines
   (1820-1950) DLB-11

Bruce Humphries [publishing house] DLB-46

Humphrey, Duke of Gloucester
   1391-1447 . . . . .DLB-213

Cumulative Index

Humphrey, William
1924-1997..............DLB-6, 212, 234, 278

Humphreys, David 1752-1818 .... DLB-37

Humphreys, Emyr 1919- DLB-15

Humphreys, Josephine 1945- DLB-292

Hunayn ibn Ishaq 809-873 or 877....... DLB-311

Huncke, Herbert 1915-1996............ DLB-16

Huneker, James Gibbons
1857-1921..................... DLB-71

Hunold, Christian Friedrich
1681-1721..................... DLB-168

Hunt, Irene 1907- DLB-52

Hunt, Leigh 1784-1859..........DLB-96, 110, 144

Hunt, Violet 1862-1942 ....DLB-162, 197

Hunt, William Gibbes 1791-1833........ DLB-73

Hunter, Evan (Ed McBain)
1926-2005 ....DLB-306; Y-82

   Tribute to John D. MacDonald Y-86

Hunter, Jim 1939- DLB-14

Hunter, Kristin 1931- DLB-33

   Tribute to Julian Mayfield Y-84

Hunter, Mollie 1922- DLB-161

Hunter, N. C. 1908-1971 .... DLB-10

Hunter-Duvar, John 1821-1899 .... DLB-99

Huntington, Henry E. 1850-1927....... DLB-140

   The Henry E. Huntington Library Y-92

Huntington, Susan Mansfield
1791-1823..................... DLB-200

Hurd and Houghton................. DLB-49

Hurst, Fannie 1889-1968 .... DLB-86

Hurst and Blackett DLB-106

Hurst and Company.................. DLB-49

Hurston, Zora Neale
1901?-1960......... DLB-51, 86; CDALB-7

Husserl, Edmund 1859-1938 .... DLB-296

Husson, Jules-François-Félix (see Champfleury)

Huston, John 1906-1987................ DLB-26

Hutcheson, Francis 1694-1746 ..... DLB-31, 252

Hutchinson, Ron 1947- DLB-245

Hutchinson, R. C. 1907-1975 .... DLB-191

Hutchinson, Thomas 1711-1780...... DLB-30, 31

Hutchinson and Company
(Publishers) Limited.............. DLB-112

Huth, Angela 1938- DLB-271

Hutton, Richard Holt
1826-1897..................... DLB-57

von Hutten, Ulrich 1488-1523 ....DLB-179

Huxley, Aldous 1894-1963
...... DLB-36, 100, 162, 195, 255; CDBLB-6

Huxley, Elspeth Josceline
1907-1997....................DLB-77, 204

Huxley, T. H. 1825-1895 .... DLB-57

Huyghue, Douglas Smith 1816-1891 ..... DLB-99

Huysmans, Joris-Karl 1848-1907 .... DLB-123

Hwang, David Henry
1957- DLB-212, 228, 312

Hyde, Donald 1909-1966............ DLB-187

Hyde, Mary 1912-2003................ DLB-187

Hyman, Trina Schart 1939- DLB-61

I

Iavorsky, Stefan 1658-1722............ DLB-150

Iazykov, Nikolai Mikhailovich
1803-1846 .... DLB-205

Ibáñez, Armando P. 1949- DLB-209

Ibáñez, Sara de 1909-1971 .... DLB-290

Ibarbourou, Juana de 1892-1979....... DLB-290

Ibn Abi Tahir Tayfur 820-893 .... DLB-311

Ibn Qutaybah 828-889 .... DLB-311

Ibn al-Rumi 836-896................. DLB-311

Ibn Sa'd 784-845.................... DLB-311

Ibrahim al-Mawsili 742 or 743-803 or 804 DLB-311

Ibn Bajja circa 1077-1138............. DLB-115

Ibn Gabirol, Solomon
circa 1021-circa 1058 .... DLB-115

Ibn al-Muqaffa' circa 723-759 .... DLB-311

Ibn al-Mu'tazz 861-908 .... DLB-311

Ibuse Masuji 1898-1993 .... DLB-180

Ichijō Kanera
(see Ichijō Kaneyoshi)

Ichijō Kaneyoshi (Ichijō Kanera)
1402-1481 .... DLB-203

Iffland, August Wilhelm
1759-1814...................... DLB-94

Iggulden, John 1917- DLB-289

Ignatieff, Michael 1947- DLB-267

Ignatow, David 1914-1997 .... DLB-5

Ike, Chukwuemeka 1931- DLB-157

Ikkyū Sōjun 1394-1481............... DLB-203

Iles, Francis
(see Berkeley, Anthony)

Il'f, Il'ia (Il'ia Arnol'dovich Fainzil'berg)
1897-1937......................DLB-272

Illich, Ivan 1926-2002................ DLB-242

Illustration
   Children's Book Illustration in the
      Twentieth Century DLB-61

   Children's Illustrators, 1800-1880 ... DLB-163

   Early American Book Illustration DLB-49

   The Iconography of Science-Fiction
      Art......................... DLB-8

   The Illustration of Early German
      Literary Manuscripts, circa
      1150-circa 1300 .... DLB-148

   Minor Illustrators, 1880-1914 ...... DLB-141

Illyés, Gyula 1902-1983 .... DLB-215; CDWLB-4

Imbs, Bravig 1904-1946 .... DLB-4; DS-15

Imbuga, Francis D. 1947- DLB-157

Immermann, Karl 1796-1840 .... DLB-133

Imru' al-Qays circa 526-circa 565 .... DLB-311

In a Free State, 1971 Booker Prize winner,
V. S. Naipaul DLB-326

Inchbald, Elizabeth 1753-1821 .... DLB-39, 89

Indiana University Press................ Y-02

Ingamells, Rex 1913-1955 .... DLB-260

Inge, William 1913-1973....DLB-7, 249; CDALB-1

Ingelow, Jean 1820-1897............ DLB-35, 163

Ingemann, B. S. 1789-1862............ DLB-300

Ingersoll, Ralph 1900-1985..............DLB-127

The Ingersoll Prizes Y-84

Ingoldsby, Thomas (see Barham, Richard Harris)

Ingraham, Joseph Holt 1809-1860 .... DLB-3, 248

Inman, John 1805-1850 .... DLB-73

Innerhofer, Franz 1944- DLB-85

Innes, Michael (J. I. M. Stewart)
1906-1994 ....DLB-276

Innis, Harold Adams 1894-1952........ DLB-88

Innis, Mary Quayle 1899-1972 .... DLB-88

Inō Sōgi 1421-1502................... DLB-203

Inoue Yasushi 1907-1991 .... DLB-182

"The Greatness of Southern Literature":
League of the South Institute for the
Study of Southern Culture and History
.... Y-02

International Publishers Company....... DLB-46

Internet (publishing and commerce)
   Author Websites................... Y-97

   The Book Trade and the Internet Y-00

   E-Books Turn the Corner Y-98

   The E-Researcher: Possibilities
      and Pitfalls Y-00

   Interviews on E-publishing............ Y-00

   John Updike on the Internet Y-97

   LitCheck Website.................. Y-01

   Virtual Books and Enemies of Books..... Y-00

Interviews
   Adoff, Arnold..................... Y-01

   Aldridge, John W. Y-91

   Anastas, Benjamin Y-98

   Baker, Nicholson Y-00

   Bank, Melissa Y-98

   Bass, T. J. Y-80

   Bernstein, Harriet................. Y-82

   Betts, Doris Y-82

   Bosworth, David Y-82

   Bottoms, David Y-83

   Bowers, Fredson................... Y-80

   Burnshaw, Stanley Y-97

   Carpenter, Humphrey Y-84, 99

   Carr, Virginia Spencer Y-00

   Carver, Raymond Y-83

   Cherry, Kelly Y-83

   Conroy, Jack Y-81

   Coppel, Alfred Y-83

   Cowley, Malcolm................... Y-81

Davis, Paxton Y-89	Pennington, Lee Y-82	An Interview with Edward B. Jenkinson An Interview with Lamarr Mooneyham An Interview with Harriet Bernstein...... Y-82
Devito, Carlo Y-94	Penzler, Otto Y-96	
De Vries, Peter Y-82	Plimpton, George Y-99	Islas, Arturo 1938-1991 .... DLB-122
Dickey, James Y-82	Potok, Chaim Y-84	
Donald, David Herbert Y-87	Powell, Padgett Y-01	Issit, Debbie 1966- DLB-233
Editors, Conversations with Y-95	Prescott, Peter S. Y-86	Ivanišević, Drago 1907-1981 .... DLB-181
Ellroy, James Y-91	Rabe, David Y-91	Ivanov, Georgii 1894-1954 .... DLB-317
Fancher, Betsy Y-83	Rechy, John Y-82	Ivanov, Viacheslav Ivanovich 1866-1949 .... DLB-295
Faust, Irvin Y-00	Reid, B. L. Y-83	
Fulton, Len Y-86	Reynolds, Michael Y-95, 99	Ivanov, Vsevolod Viacheslavovich 1895-1963 .... DLB-272
Furst, Alan Y-01	Robinson, Derek Y-02	
Garrett, George Y-83	Rollyson, Carl Y-97	Ivask, Yuri 1907-1986 .... DLB-317
Gelfman, Jane Y-93	Rosset, Barney Y-02	Ivaska, Astrīde 1926- DLB-232
Goldwater, Walter Y-93	Schlafly, Phyllis Y-82	M. J. Ivers and Company DLB-49
Gores, Joe Y-02	Schroeder, Patricia Y-99	Iwaniuk, Wacław 1915-2001 .... DLB-215
Greenfield, George Y-91	Schulberg, Budd Y-81, 01	Iwano Hōmei 1873-1920 .... DLB-180
Griffin, Bryan Y-81	Scribner, Charles, III Y-94	Iwaszkiewicz, Jarosław 1894-1980 ...... DLB-215
Groom, Winston Y-01	Sipper, Ralph Y-94	Iyayi, Festus 1947- DLB-157
Guilds, John Caldwell Y-92	Smith, Cork Y-95	Izumi Kyōka 1873-1939 .... DLB-180
Hamilton, Virginia Y-01	Staley, Thomas F. Y-00	
Hardin, James Y-92	Styron, William Y-80	# J
Harris, Mark Y-80	Talese, Nan Y-94	
Harrison, Jim Y-82	Thornton, John Y-94	Jackmon, Marvin E. (see Marvin X)
Hazzard, Shirley Y-82	Toth, Susan Allen Y-86	Jacks, L. P. 1860-1955 .... DLB-135
Herrick, William Y-01	Tyler, Anne Y-82	Jackson, Angela 1951- DLB-41
Higgins, George V. Y-98	Vaughan, Samuel Y-97	Jackson, Charles 1903-1968 .... DLB-234
Hoban, Russell Y-90	Von Ogtrop, Kristin Y-92	Jackson, Helen Hunt 1830-1885 .... DLB-42, 47, 186, 189
Holroyd, Michael Y-99	Wallenstein, Barry Y-92	
Horowitz, Glen Y-90	Weintraub, Stanley Y-82	Jackson, Holbrook 1874-1948 .... DLB-98
Iggulden, John Y-01	Williams, J. Chamberlain Y-84	Jackson, Laura Riding 1901-1991 ...... DLB-48
Jakes, John Y-83	Into the Past: William Jovanovich's Reflections in Publishing Y-02	Jackson, Shirley 1916-1965 .... DLB-6, 234; CDALB-1
Jenkinson, Edward B. Y-82		
Jenks, Tom Y-86	Ionesco, Eugène 1909-1994 .... DLB-321	Jacob, Max 1876-1944 .... DLB-258
Kaplan, Justin Y-86	Ireland, David 1927- DLB-289	Jacob, Naomi 1884?-1964 .... DLB-191
King, Florence Y-85	The National Library of Ireland's New James Joyce Manuscripts Y-02	Jacob, Piers Anthony Dillingham (see Anthony, Piers)
Klopfer, Donald S. Y-97		
Krug, Judith Y-82	Irigaray, Luce 1930- DLB-296	Jacob, Violet 1863-1946 .... DLB-240
Lamm, Donald Y-95	Irving, John 1942- DLB-6, 278; Y-82	Jacobi, Friedrich Heinrich 1743-1819 .... DLB-94
Laughlin, James Y-96	Irving, Washington 1783-1859 .... DLB-3, 11, 30, 59, 73, 74, 183, 186, 250; CDALB-2	Jacobi, Johann Georg 1740-1841 .... DLB-97
Lawrence, Starling Y-95		George W. Jacobs and Company DLB-49
Lindsay, Jack Y-84	Irwin, Grace 1907- DLB-68	Jacobs, Harriet 1813-1897 .... DLB-239
Mailer, Norman Y-97	Irwin, Will 1873-1948 .... DLB-25	Jacobs, Joseph 1854-1916 .... DLB-141
Manchester, William Y-85	Isaksson, Ulla 1916-2000 .... DLB-257	Jacobs, W. W. 1863-1943 .... DLB-135
Max, D. T. Y-94	Iser, Wolfgang 1926- DLB-242	The W. W. Jacobs Appreciation Society ... Y-98
McCormack, Thomas Y-98	Isherwood, Christopher 1904-1986 .... DLB-15, 195; Y-86	Jacobsen, J. P. 1847-1885 .... DLB-300
McNamara, Katherine Y-97		Jacobsen, Jørgen-Frantz 1900-1938 ..... DLB-214
Mellen, Joan Y-94	The Christopher Isherwood Archive, The Huntington Library Y-99	Jacobsen, Josephine 1908- DLB-244
Menaker, Daniel Y-97		Jacobsen, Rolf 1907-1994 .... DLB-297
Mooneyham, Lamarr Y-82	Ishiguro, Kazuo 1954- DLB-194, 326	Jacobson, Dan 1929- DLB-14, 207, 225, 319
Murray, Les Y-01	Ishikawa Jun 1899-1987 .... DLB-182	Jacobson, Howard 1942- DLB-207
Nosworth, David Y-82	Iskander, Fazil' Abdulevich 1929- DLB-302	Jacques de Vitry circa 1160/1170-1240 ... DLB-208
O'Connor, Patrick Y-84, 99	The Island Trees Case: A Symposium on School Library Censorship An Interview with Judith Krug An Interview with Phyllis Schlafly	Jæger, Frank 1926-1977 .... DLB-214
Ozick, Cynthia Y-83		Ja'far al-Sadiq circa 702-765 .... DLB-311
Penner, Jonathan Y-83		

Cumulative Index

William Jaggard [publishing house] DLB-170

Jahier, Piero 1884-1966........... DLB-114, 264

al-Jahiz circa 776-868 or 869 .... DLB-311

Jahnn, Hans Henny 1894-1959 ..... DLB-56, 124

Jaimes, Freyre, Ricardo 1866?-1933 ..... DLB-283

Jakes, John 1932- DLB-278; Y-83

    Tribute to John Gardner Y-82

    Tribute to John D. MacDonald Y-86

Jakobína Johnson (Jakobína Sigurbjarnardóttir)
1883-1977.................... DLB-293

Jakobson, Roman 1896-1982 .... DLB-242

James, Alice 1848-1892................ DLB-221

James, C. L. R. 1901-1989 .... DLB-125

James, Clive 1939- DLB-325

James, George P. R. 1801-1860 .... DLB-116

James, Henry 1843-1916
......DLB-12, 71, 74, 189; DS-13; CDALB-3

    "The Future of the Novel" (1899) DLB-18

    "The Novel in [Robert Browning's]
'The Ring and the Book'"
(1912) DLB-32

James, John circa 1633-1729 .... DLB-24

James, M. R. 1862-1936.......... DLB-156, 201

James, Naomi 1949- DLB-204

James, P. D. (Phyllis Dorothy James White)
1920- DLB-87, 276; DS-17; CDBLB-8

    Tribute to Charles Scribner Jr. Y-95

James, Thomas 1572?-1629 .... DLB-213

U. P. James [publishing house] DLB-49

James, Will 1892-1942.................DS-16

James, William 1842-1910 ....DLB-270

James VI of Scotland, I of England
1566-1625 ....DLB-151, 172

    *Ane Schort Treatise Conteining Some Revlis
and Cautelis to Be Obseruit and
Eschewit in Scottis Poesi* (1584)......DLB-172

Jameson, Anna 1794-1860.......... DLB-99, 166

Jameson, Fredric 1934- DLB-67

Jameson, J. Franklin 1859-1937 .... DLB-17

Jameson, Storm 1891-1986............ DLB-36

Jančar, Drago 1948- DLB-181

Janés, Clara 1940- DLB-134

Janevski, Slavko 1920-2000 . DLB-181; CDWLB-4

Janowitz, Tama 1957- DLB-292

Jansson, Tove 1914-2001 .... DLB-257

Janvier, Thomas 1849-1913 .... DLB-202

Japan

    "The Development of Meiji Japan" .. DLB-180

    "Encounter with the West"......... DLB-180

Japanese Literature

    Letter from Japan................. Y-94, 98

    Medieval Travel Diaries DLB-203

    Surveys: 1987-1995 .... DLB-182

Jaramillo, Cleofas M. 1878-1956........ DLB-122

Jaramillo Levi, Enrique 1944- DLB-290

Jarir after 650-circa 730............... DLB-311

Jarman, Mark 1952- DLB-120, 282

Jarrell, Randall
1914-1965 .... DLB-48, 52; CDALB-1

Jarrold and Sons.................... DLB-106

Jarry, Alfred 1873-1907.......... DLB-192, 258

Jarves, James Jackson 1818-1888 .... DLB-189

Jasmin, Claude 1930- DLB-60

Jaunsudrabiņš, Jānis 1877-1962......... DLB-220

Jay, John 1745-1829................. DLB-31

Jean de Garlande (see John of Garland)

Jefferies, Richard 1848-1887 .... DLB-98, 141

    The Richard Jefferies Society........... Y-98

Jeffers, Lance 1919-1985............... DLB-41

Jeffers, Robinson
1887-1962.......... DLB-45, 212; CDALB-4

Jefferson, Thomas
1743-1826.......... DLB-31, 183; CDALB-2

Jégé 1866-1940 .... DLB-215

Jelinek, Elfriede 1946- DLB-85, 330

Jellicoe, Ann 1927- DLB-13, 233

Jemison, Mary circa 1742-1833.......... DLB-239

Jen, Gish 1955- DLB-312

Jenkins, Dan 1929- DLB-241

Jenkins, Elizabeth 1905- DLB-155

Jenkins, Robin 1912-2005...........DLB-14, 271

Jenkins, William Fitzgerald (see Leinster, Murray)

Herbert Jenkins Limited.............. DLB-112

Jennings, Elizabeth 1926- DLB-27

Jens, Walter 1923- DLB-69

Jensen, Axel 1932-2003 .... DLB-297

Jensen, Johannes V. 1873-1950 ..... DLB-214, 330

Jensen, Merrill 1905-1980............. DLB-17

Jensen, Thit 1876-1957 .... DLB-214

Jephson, Robert 1736-1803............ DLB-89

Jerome, Jerome K. 1859-1927 .....DLB-10, 34, 135

    The Jerome K. Jerome Society.......... Y-98

Jerome, Judson 1927-1991............. DLB-105

    "Reflections: After a Tornado"...... DLB-105

Jerrold, Douglas 1803-1857 .... DLB-158, 159

Jersild, Per Christian 1935- DLB-257

Jesse, F. Tennyson 1888-1958........... DLB-77

Jewel, John 1522-1571................ DLB-236

John P. Jewett and Company DLB-49

Jewett, Sarah Orne 1849-1909 ...DLB-12, 74, 221

The Jewish Publication Society........... DLB-49

Studies in American Jewish Literature Y-02

Jewitt, John Rodgers 1783-1821 .... DLB-99

Jewsbury, Geraldine 1812-1880 .... DLB-21

Jewsbury, Maria Jane 1800-1833 .... DLB-199

Jhabvala, Ruth Prawer
1927- DLB-139, 194, 323, 326

Jiang Guangci 1901-1931 .... DLB-328

Jiménez, Juan Ramón 1881-1958 ... DLB-134, 330

Jin, Ha 1956- DLB-244, 292

Joans, Ted 1928-2003 .... DLB-16, 41

Jodelle, Estienne 1532?-1573........... DLB-327

Jōha 1525-1602.................... DLB-203

Jóhann Sigurjónsson 1880-1919 .... DLB-293

Jóhannes úr Kötlum 1899-1972 .... DLB-293

Johannis de Garlandia (see John of Garland)

John, Errol 1924-1988 .... DLB-233

John, Eugenie (see Marlitt, E.)

John of Dumbleton
circa 1310-circa 1349 .... DLB-115

John of Garland (Jean de Garlande,
Johannis de Garlandia)
circa 1195-circa 1272 .... DLB-208

The John Reed Clubs................. DLB-303

Johns, Captain W. E. 1893-1968 .... DLB-160

Johnson, Mrs. A. E. ca. 1858-1922...... DLB-221

Johnson, Amelia (see Johnson, Mrs. A. E.)

Johnson, B. S. 1933-1973 .... DLB-14, 40

Johnson, Charles 1679-1748 .... DLB-84

Johnson, Charles 1948- DLB-33, 278

Johnson, Charles S. 1893-1956........ DLB-51, 91

Johnson, Colin (Mudrooroo) 1938- ... DLB-289

Johnson, Denis 1949- DLB-120

Johnson, Diane 1934- Y-80

Johnson, Dorothy M. 1905–1984....... DLB-206

Johnson, E. Pauline (Tekahionwake)
1861-1913 ....DLB-175

Johnson, Edgar 1901-1995 .... DLB-103

Johnson, Edward 1598-1672 .... DLB-24

Johnson, Eyvind 1900-1976 .... DLB-259, 330

Johnson, Fenton 1888-1958 .... DLB-45, 50

Johnson, Georgia Douglas
1877?-1966................. DLB-51, 249

Johnson, Gerald W. 1890-1980 .... DLB-29

Johnson, Greg 1953- DLB-234

Johnson, Helene 1907-1995 .... DLB-51

Jacob Johnson and Company DLB-49

Johnson, James Weldon
1871-1938.............. DLB-51; CDALB-4

Johnson, John H. 1918-2005...........DLB-137

    "Backstage," Statement From the
Initial Issue of *Ebony*
(November 1945 ....DLB-137

Johnson, Joseph [publishing house] DLB-154

Johnson, Linton Kwesi 1952- DLB-157

Johnson, Lionel 1867-1902 .... DLB-19

Johnson, Nunnally 1897-1977........... DLB-26

Johnson, Owen 1878-1952 .... Y-87

Johnson, Pamela Hansford 1912-1981 .... DLB-15

Johnson, Pauline 1861-1913 .... DLB-92

Johnson, Ronald 1935-1998............DLB-169

Johnson, Samuel 1696-1772... DLB-24; CDBLB-2

Johnson, Samuel
 1709-1784.........DLB-39, 95, 104, 142, 213

 Rambler, no. 4 (1750) [excerpt].........DLB-39

The BBC Four Samuel Johnson Prize
 for Non-fiction......................Y-02

Johnson, Samuel 1822-1882..........DLB-1, 243

Johnson, Susanna 1730-1810............DLB-200

Johnson, Terry 1955-................DLB-233

Johnson, Uwe 1934-1984.....DLB-75; CDWLB-2

Benjamin Johnson [publishing house].....DLB-49

Benjamin, Jacob, and Robert Johnson
 [publishing house].................DLB-49

Johnston, Annie Fellows 1863-1931.......DLB-42

Johnston, Basil H. 1929-..............DLB-60

Johnston, David Claypole 1798?-1865....DLB-188

Johnston, Denis 1901-1984.............DLB-10

Johnston, Ellen 1835-1873.............DLB-199

Johnston, George 1912-1970............DLB-260

Johnston, George 1913-1970............DLB-88

Johnston, Sir Harry 1858-1927.........DLB-174

Johnston, Jennifer 1930-..............DLB-14

Johnston, Mary 1870-1936..............DLB-9

Johnston, Richard Malcolm 1822-1898....DLB-74

Johnstone, Charles 1719?-1800?.........DLB-39

Johst, Hanns 1890-1978................DLB-124

Jökull Jakobsson 1933-1978............DLB-293

Jolas, Eugene 1894-1952..............DLB-4, 45

Jolley, Elizabeth 1923-...............DLB-325

Jón Stefán Sveinsson or Svensson (see Nonni)

Jón Trausti (Guðmundur Magnússon)
 1873-1918........................DLB-293

Jón úr Vör (Jón Jónsson) 1917-2000.....DLB-293

Jónas Hallgrímsson 1807-1845..........DLB-293

Jones, Alice C. 1853-1933.............DLB-92

Jones, Charles C., Jr. 1831-1893........DLB-30

Jones, D. G. 1929-....................DLB-53

Jones, David 1895-1974...DLB-20, 100; CDBLB-7

Jones, Diana Wynne 1934-..............DLB-161

Jones, Ebenezer 1820-1860.............DLB-32

Jones, Ernest 1819-1868...............DLB-32

Jones, Gayl 1949-...................DLB-33, 278

Jones, George 1800-1870...............DLB-183

Jones, Glyn 1905-1995.................DLB-15

Jones, Gwyn 1907-..................DLB-15, 139

Jones, Henry Arthur 1851-1929..........DLB-10

Jones, Hugh circa 1692-1760............DLB-24

Jones, James 1921-1977.......DLB-2, 143; DS-17

 James Jones Papers in the Handy
 Writers' Colony Collection at
 the University of Illinois at
 Springfield......................Y-98

The James Jones Society...............Y-92

Jones, Jenkin Lloyd 1911-2004..........DLB-127

Jones, John Beauchamp 1810-1866........DLB-202

Jones, Joseph, Major
 (see Thompson, William Tappan)

Jones, LeRoi (see Baraka, Amiri)

Jones, Lewis 1897-1939.................DLB-15

Jones, Madison 1925-..................DLB-152

Jones, Marie 1951-....................DLB-233

Jones, Preston 1936-1979...............DLB-7

Jones, Rodney 1950-..................DLB-120

Jones, Thom 1945-....................DLB-244

Jones, Sir William 1746-1794..........DLB-109

Jones, William Alfred 1817-1900........DLB-59

Jones's Publishing House..............DLB-49

Jong, Erica 1942-............DLB-2, 5, 28, 152

Jonke, Gert F. 1946-..................DLB-85

Jonson, Ben
 1572?-1637.........DLB-62, 121; CDBLB-1

Jonsson, Tor 1916-1951................DLB-297

Jordan, June 1936-....................DLB-38

Jorgensen, Johannes 1866-1956..........DLB-300

Jose, Nicholas 1952-..................DLB-325

Joseph, Jenny 1932-...................DLB-40

Joseph and George.....................Y-99

Michael Joseph Limited................DLB-112

Josephson, Matthew 1899-1978...........DLB-4

Josephus, Flavius 37-100..............DLB-176

Josephy, Alvin M., Jr.
 Tribute to Alfred A. Knopf..........Y-84

Josiah Allen's Wife (see Holley, Marietta)

Josipovici, Gabriel 1940-.........DLB-14, 319

Josselyn, John ?-1675.................DLB-24

Joudry, Patricia 1921-2000.............DLB-88

Jouve, Pierre Jean 1887-1976..........DLB-258

Jovanovich, William 1920-2001..........Y-01

 Into the Past: William Jovanovich's
  Reflections on Publishing..........Y-02

 [Response to Ken Auletta]............Y-97

 The Temper of the West: William
  Jovanovich.......................Y-02

 Tribute to Charles Scribner Jr........Y-95

Jovine, Francesco 1902-1950...........DLB-264

Jovine, Giuseppe 1922-................DLB-128

Joyaux, Philippe (see Sollers, Philippe)

Joyce, Adrien (see Eastman, Carol)

Joyce, James 1882-1941
 ....DLB-10, 19, 36, 162, 247; CDBLB-6

 Danis Rose and the Rendering of *Ulysses*....Y-97

 James Joyce Centenary: Dublin, 1982.....Y-82

 James Joyce Conference...............Y-85

 A Joyce (Con)Text: Danis Rose and the
  Remaking of *Ulysses*.............Y-97

The National Library of Ireland's
 New James Joyce Manuscripts.......Y-02

The New *Ulysses*.....................Y-84

Public Domain and the Violation of
 Texts............................Y-97

The Quinn Draft of James Joyce's
 Circe Manuscript..................Y-00

Stephen Joyce's Letter to the Editor of
 The Irish Times..................Y-97

Ulysses, Reader's Edition: First Reactions...Y-97

We See the Editor at Work.............Y-97

Whose *Ulysses?* The Function of Editing...Y-97

Jozsef, Attila 1905-1937......DLB-215; CDWLB-4

San Juan de la Cruz 1542-1591.........DLB-318

Juarroz, Roberto 1925-1995............DLB-283

Orange Judd Publishing Company........DLB-49

Judd, Sylvester 1813-1853...........DLB-1, 243

Judith circa 930....................DLB-146

Juel-Hansen, Erna 1845-1922...........DLB-300

Julian of Norwich 1342-circa 1420......DLB-1146

Julius Caesar
 100 B.C.-44 B.C.........DLB-211; CDWLB-1

June, Jennie
 (see Croly, Jane Cunningham)

Jung, Carl Gustav 1875-1961...........DLB-296

Jung, Franz 1888-1963.................DLB-118

Jünger, Ernst 1895-1998......DLB-56; CDWLB-2

Der jüngere Titurel circa 1275......DLB-138

Jung-Stilling, Johann Heinrich
 1740-1817.......................DLB-94

Junqueiro, Abílio Manuel Guerra
 1850-1923.......................DLB-287

Justice, Donald 1925-................Y-83

Juvenal circa A.D. 60-circa A.D. 130
 ....DLB-211; CDWLB-1

The Juvenile Library
 (see M. J. Godwin and Company)

K

Kacew, Romain (see Gary, Romain)

Kafka, Franz 1883-1924........DLB-81; CDWLB-2

Kahn, Gus 1886-1941..................DLB-265

Kahn, Roger 1927-....................DLB-171

Kaikō Takeshi 1939-1989...............DLB-182

Káinn (Kristján Níels Jónsson/Kristjan
 Niels Julius) 1860-1936...........DLB-293

Kaiser, Georg 1878-1945.....DLB-124; CDWLB-2

Kaiserchronik circa 1147............DLB-148

Kaleb, Vjekoslav 1905-................DLB-181

Kalechofsky, Roberta 1931-............DLB-28

Kaler, James Otis 1848-1912.........DLB-12, 42

Kalmar, Bert 1884-1947................DLB-265

Kamensky, Vasilii Vasil'evich
 1884-1961......................DLB-295

Kames, Henry Home, Lord
 1696-1782......................DLB-31, 104

Cumulative Index

Kamo no Chōmei (Kamo no Nagaakira)
  1153 or 1155-1216 . . . . DLB-203
Kamo no Nagaakira (see Kamo no Chōmei)
Kampmann, Christian 1939-1988 . . . . DLB-214
Kandel, Lenore 1932- DLB-16
Kane, Sarah 1971-1999 . . . . DLB-310
Kaneko, Lonny 1939- DLB-312
Kang, Younghill 1903-1972 . . . . DLB-312
Kanin, Garson 1912-1999 . . . . DLB-7
  A Tribute (to Marc Connelly) Y-80
Kaniuk, Yoram 1930- DLB-299
Kant, Hermann 1926- DLB-75
Kant, Immanuel 1724-1804 . . . . DLB-94
Kantemir, Antiokh Dmitrievich
  1708-1744 . . . . DLB-150
Kantor, MacKinlay 1904-1977 . . . . DLB-9, 102
Kanze Kōjirō Nobumitsu 1435-1516 . . . . DLB-203
Kanze Motokiyo (see Zeami)
Kaplan, Fred 1937- DLB-111
Kaplan, Johanna 1942- DLB-28
Kaplan, Justin 1925- DLB-111; Y-86
Kaplinski, Jaan 1941- DLB-232
Kapnist, Vasilii Vasilevich 1758?-1823 . . . DLB-150
Karadžić, Vuk Stefanović
  1787-1864 . . . . DLB-147; CDWLB-4
Karamzin, Nikolai Mikhailovich
  1766-1826 . . . . DLB-150
Karinthy, Frigyes 1887-1938 . . . . DLB-215
Karlfeldt, Erik Axel 1864-1931 . . . . DLB-330
Karmel, Ilona 1925-2000 . . . . DLB-299
Karnad, Girish 1938- DLB-323
Karsch, Anna Louisa 1722-1791 . . . . DLB-97
Kasack, Hermann 1896-1966 . . . . DLB-69
Kasai Zenzō 1887-1927 . . . . DLB-180
Kaschnitz, Marie Luise 1901-1974 . . . . . . DLB-69
Kassák, Lajos 1887-1967 . . . . DLB-215
Kaštelan, Jure 1919-1990 . . . . DLB-147
Kästner, Erich 1899-1974 . . . . DLB-56
Kataev, Evgenii Petrovich
  (see Il'f, Il'ia and Petrov, Evgenii)
Kataev, Valentin Petrovich 1897-1986 . . . . DLB-272
Katenin, Pavel Aleksandrovich
  1792-1853 . . . . DLB-205
Kattan, Naim 1928- DLB-53
Katz, Steve 1935- Y-83
Ka-Tzetnik 135633 (Yehiel Dinur)
  1909-2001 . . . . DLB-299
Kauffman, Janet 1945- DLB-218; Y-86
Kauffmann, Samuel 1898-1971 . . . . DLB-127
Kaufman, Bob 1925-1986 . . . . DLB-16, 41
Kaufman, George S. 1889-1961 . . . . DLB-7
Kaufmann, Walter 1921-1980 . . . . DLB-279

Kavan, Anna (Helen Woods Ferguson
  Edmonds) 1901-1968 . . . . DLB-255
Kavanagh, P. J. 1931- DLB-40
Kavanagh, Patrick 1904-1967 . . . . DLB-15, 20
Kaverin, Veniamin Aleksandrovich
  (Veniamin Aleksandrovich Zil'ber)
  1902-1989 . . . . DLB-272
Kawabata Yasunari 1899-1972 . . . . . DLB-180, 330
Kay, Guy Gavriel 1954- DLB-251
Kaye-Smith, Sheila 1887-1956 . . . . DLB-36
Kazakov, Iurii Pavlovich 1927-1982 . . . . . DLB-302
Kazin, Alfred 1915-1998 . . . . DLB-67
Keane, John B. 1928-2002 . . . . DLB-13
Keary, Annie 1825-1879 . . . . DLB-163
Keary, Eliza 1827-1918 . . . . DLB-240
Keating, H. R. F. 1926- DLB-87
Keatley, Charlotte 1960- DLB-245
Keats, Ezra Jack 1916-1983 . . . . DLB-61
Keats, John 1795-1821 . . . DLB-96, 110; CDBLB-3
Keble, John 1792-1866 . . . . DLB-32, 55
Keckley, Elizabeth 1818?-1907 . . . . DLB-239
Keeble, John 1944- Y-83
Keeffe, Barrie 1945- DLB-13, 245
Keeley, James 1867-1934 . . . . DLB-25
W. B. Keen, Cooke and Company DLB-49
The Mystery of Carolyn Keene Y-02
Kefala, Antigone 1935- DLB-289
Keillor, Garrison 1942- Y-87
Keith, Marian (Mary Esther MacGregor)
  1874?-1961 . . . . DLB-92
Keller, Gary D. 1943- DLB-82
Keller, Gottfried
  1819-1890 . . . . DLB-129; CDWLB-2
Keller, Helen 1880-1968 . . . . DLB-303
Kelley, Edith Summers 1884-1956 . . . . DLB-9
Kelley, Emma Dunham ?-? DLB-221
Kelley, Florence 1859-1932 . . . . DLB-303
Kelley, William Melvin 1937- DLB-33
Kellogg, Ansel Nash 1832-1886 . . . . DLB-23
Kellogg, Steven 1941- DLB-61
Kelly, George E. 1887-1974 . . . . DLB-7, 249
Kelly, Hugh 1739-1777 . . . . DLB-89
Kelly, Piet and Company DLB-49
Kelly, Robert 1935- DLB-5, 130, 165
Kelman, James 1946- DLB-194, 319, 326
Kelmscott Press DLB-112
Kelton, Elmer 1926- DLB-256
Kemble, E. W. 1861-1933 . . . . DLB-188
Kemble, Fanny 1809-1893 . . . . DLB-32
Kemelman, Harry 1908-1996 . . . . DLB-28
Kempe, Margery circa 1373-1438 . . . . DLB-146
Kempinski, Tom 1938- DLB-310

Kempner, Friederike 1836-1904 . . . . DLB-129
Kempowski, Walter 1929- DLB-75
Kenan, Randall 1963- DLB-292
Claude Kendall [publishing company] DLB-46
Kendall, Henry 1839-1882 . . . . DLB-230
Kendall, May 1861-1943 . . . . DLB-240
Kendell, George 1809-1867 . . . . DLB-43
Keneally, Thomas 1935- DLB-289, 299, 326
Kenedy, P. J., and Sons DLB-49
Kenkō circa 1283-circa 1352 . . . . DLB-203
Kenna, Peter 1930-1987 . . . . DLB-289
Kennan, George 1845-1924 . . . . DLB-189
Kennedy, A. L. 1965- DLB-271
Kennedy, Adrienne 1931- DLB-38
Kennedy, John Pendleton 1795-1870 . . . DLB-3, 248
Kennedy, Leo 1907-2000 . . . . DLB-88
Kennedy, Margaret 1896-1967 . . . . DLB-36
Kennedy, Patrick 1801-1873 . . . . DLB-159
Kennedy, Richard S. 1920- DLB-111; Y-02
Kennedy, William 1928- DLB-143; Y-85
Kennedy, X. J. 1929- DLB-5
  Tribute to John Ciardi Y-86
Kennelly, Brendan 1936- DLB-40
Kenner, Hugh 1923-2003 . . . . DLB-67
  Tribute to Cleanth Brooks Y-80
Mitchell Kennerley [publishing house] DLB-46
Kenny, Maurice 1929- DLB-175
Kent, Frank R. 1877-1958 . . . . DLB-29
Kenyon, Jane 1947-1995 . . . . DLB-120
Kenzheev, Bakhyt Shkurullaevich
  1950- DLB-285
Keough, Hugh Edmund 1864-1912 . . . . . . DLB-171
Keppler and Schwartzmann DLB-49
Ker, John, third Duke of Roxburghe
  1740-1804 . . . . DLB-213
Ker, N. R. 1908-1982 . . . . DLB-201
Keralio-Robert, Louise-Félicité de
  1758-1822 . . . . DLB-313
Kerlan, Irvin 1912-1963 . . . . DLB-187
Kermode, Frank 1919- DLB-242
Kern, Jerome 1885-1945 . . . . DLB-187
Kernaghan, Eileen 1939- DLB-251
Kerner, Justinus 1786-1862 . . . . DLB-90
Kerouac, Jack
  1922-1969 . . DLB-2, 16, 237; DS-3; CDALB-1
  Auction of Jack Kerouac's
    On the Road Scroll Y-01
  The Jack Kerouac Revival Y-95
  "Re-meeting of Old Friends":
    The Jack Kerouac Conference Y-82
  Statement of Correction to "The Jack
    Kerouac Revival" Y-96
Kerouac, Jan 1952-1996 . . . . DLB-16

Charles H. Kerr and Company DLB-49	Killigrew, Anne 1660-1685 . . . . .DLB-131	Kirkland, Caroline M. 1801-1864 . . . . DLB-3, 73, 74, 250; DS-13
Kerr, Orpheus C. (see Newell, Robert Henry)	Killigrew, Thomas 1612-1683 . . . . .DLB-58	Kirkland, Joseph 1830-1893. . . . . DLB-12
Kersh, Gerald 1911-1968. . . . . .DLB-255	Kilmer, Joyce 1886-1918 . . . . .DLB-45	Francis Kirkman [publishing house] DLB-170
Kertész, Imre DLB-299, 330; Y-02	Kilroy, Thomas 1934- DLB-233	Kirkpatrick, Clayton 1915-2004 . . . . . . .DLB-127
Kesey, Ken 1935-2001 . . . . .DLB-2, 16, 206; CDALB-6	Kilwardby, Robert circa 1215-1279 . . . . . .DLB-115	Kirkup, James 1918- DLB-27
Kessel, Joseph 1898-1979 . . . . .DLB-72	Kilworth, Garry 1941- DLB-261	Kirouac, Conrad (see Marie-Victorin, Frère)
Kessel, Martin 1901-1990 . . . . .DLB-56	Kim, Anatolii Andreevich 1939- DLB-285	Kirsch, Sarah 1935- DLB-75
Kesten, Hermann 1900-1996 . . . . .DLB-56	Kimball, Richard Burleigh 1816-1892 . . . .DLB-202	Kirst, Hans Hellmut 1914-1989. . . . . .DLB-69
Keun, Irmgard 1905-1982 . . . . .DLB-69	Kincaid, Jamaica 1949- DLB-157, 227; CDALB-7; CDWLB-3	Kiš, Danilo 1935-1989. . . . . . DLB-181; CDWLB-4
Key, Ellen 1849-1926. . . . . .DLB-259	Kinck, Hans Ernst 1865-1926 . . . . .DLB-297	Kita Morio 1927- DLB-182
Key and Biddle DLB-49	King, Charles 1844-1933 . . . . .DLB-186	Kitcat, Mabel Greenhow 1859-1922 . . . . .DLB-135
Keynes, Sir Geoffrey 1887-1982. . . . . . . .DLB-201	King, Clarence 1842-1901 . . . . .DLB-12	Kitchin, C. H. B. 1895-1967 . . . . .DLB-77
Keynes, John Maynard 1883-1946. . . . . DS-10	King, Florence 1936- Y-85	Kittredge, William 1932- DLB-212, 244
Keyserling, Eduard von 1855-1918 . . . . . . .DLB-66	King, Francis 1923- DLB-15, 139	Kiukhel'beker, Vil'gel'm Karlovich 1797-1846. . . . . .DLB-205
al-Khalil ibn Ahmad circa 718-791 . . . . . .DLB-311	King, Grace 1852-1932 . . . . .DLB-12, 78	Kizer, Carolyn 1925- DLB-5, 169
Khan, Adib 1949- DLB-323	King, Harriet Hamilton 1840-1920 . . . . . .DLB-199	Kjaerstad, Jan 1953- DLB-297
Khan, Ismith 1925-2002 . . . . .DLB-125	King, Henry 1592-1669 . . . . .DLB-126	Klabund 1890-1928. . . . . .DLB-66
al-Khansa' fl. late sixth-mid seventh centuries DLB-311	Solomon King [publishing house] DLB-49	Klaj, Johann 1616-1656 . . . . .DLB-164
	King, Stephen 1947- DLB-143; Y-80	Klappert, Peter 1942- DLB-5
Kharitonov, Evgenii Vladimirovich 1941-1981 . . . . .DLB-285	King, Susan Petigru 1824-1875 . . . . .DLB-239	Klass, Philip (see Tenn, William)
Kharitonov, Mark Sergeevich 1937- . . .DLB-285	King, Thomas 1943- DLB-175	Klein, A. M. 1909-1972 . . . . .DLB-68
Khaytov, Nikolay 1919- DLB-181	King, Woodie, Jr. 1937- DLB-38	Kleist, Ewald von 1715-1759 . . . . .DLB-97
Khemnitser, Ivan Ivanovich 1745-1784. . . . . .DLB-150	Kinglake, Alexander William 1809-1891 . . . . .DLB-55, 166	Kleist, Heinrich von 1777-1811. . . . . .DLB-90; CDWLB-2
Kheraskov, Mikhail Matveevich 1733-1807 . . . . .DLB-150	Kingo, Thomas 1634-1703. . . . . .DLB-300	Klíma, Ivan 1931- DLB-232; CDWLB-4
Khlebnikov, Velimir 1885-1922 . . . . .DLB-295	Kingsbury, Donald 1929- DLB-251	Klimentev, Andrei Platonovic (see Platonov, Andrei Platonovich)
Khodasevich, Vladislav 1886-1939 . . . . . .DLB-317	Kingsley, Charles 1819-1875 . . . . .DLB-21, 32, 163, 178, 190	Klinger, Friedrich Maximilian 1752-1831 . . . . .DLB-94
Khomiakov, Aleksei Stepanovich 1804-1860 . . . . .DLB-205	Kingsley, Henry 1830-1876 . . . . .DLB-21, 230	Kliuev, Nikolai Alekseevich 1884-1937 . . .DLB-295
Khristov, Boris 1945- DLB-181	Kingsley, Mary Henrietta 1862-1900. . . . .DLB-174	Kliushnikov, Viktor Petrovich 1841-1892. . . . . .DLB-238
Khvoshchinskaia, Nadezhda Dmitrievna 1824-1889 . . . . .DLB-238	Kingsley, Sidney 1906-1995. . . . . .DLB-7	Klopfer, Donald S. Impressions of William Faulkner Y-97
	Kingsmill, Hugh 1889-1949. . . . . .DLB-149	
Khvostov, Dmitrii Ivanovich 1757-1835. . . . . .DLB-150	Kingsolver, Barbara 1955- DLB-206; CDALB-7	Oral History Interview with Donald S. Klopfer Y-97
Kibirov, Timur Iur'evich (Timur Iur'evich Zapoev) 1955- DLB-285	Kingston, Maxine Hong 1940- . . DLB-173, 212, 312; Y-80; CDALB-7	Tribute to Alfred A. Knopf Y-84
Kidd, Adam 1802?-1831 . . . . .DLB-99	Kingston, William Henry Giles 1814-1880 . . . . .DLB-163	Klopstock, Friedrich Gottlieb 1724-1803 . . . . .DLB-97
William Kidd [publishing house] DLB-106	Kinnan, Mary Lewis 1763-1848. . . . . .DLB-200	Klopstock, Meta 1728-1758 . . . . .DLB-97
Kidde, Harald 1878-1918. . . . . .DLB-300	Kinnell, Galway 1927- DLB-5; Y-87	Kluge, Alexander 1932- DLB-75
Kidder, Tracy 1945- DLB-185	Kinsella, John 1963- DLB-325	Kluge, P. F. 1942- .Y-02
Kiely, Benedict 1919- DLB-15, 319	Kinsella, Thomas 1928- DLB-27	Knapp, Joseph Palmer 1864-1951 . . . . . . .DLB-91
Kieran, John 1892-1981 . . . . .DLB-171	Kipling, Rudyard 1865-1936 . . . . .DLB-19, 34, 141, 156, 330; CDBLB-5	Knapp, Samuel Lorenzo 1783-1838 . . . . . . .DLB-59
Kierkegaard, Søren 1813-1855 . . . . .DLB-300	Kipphardt, Heinar 1922-1982 . . . . .DLB-124	J. J. and P. Knapton [publishing house] . . .DLB-154
Kies, Marietta 1853-1899. . . . . .DLB-270	Kirby, William 1817-1906 . . . . .DLB-99	Kniazhnin, Iakov Borisovich 1740-1791 . . . . .DLB-150
Kiggins and Kellogg. DLB-49	Kircher, Athanasius 1602-1680 . . . . .DLB-164	
Kiley, Jed 1889-1962 . . . . .DLB-4	Kireevsky, Ivan Vasil'evich 1806-1856. . . .DLB-198	Knickerbocker, Diedrich (see Irving, Washington)
Kilgore, Bernard 1908-1967 . . . . .DLB-127	Kireevsky, Petr Vasil'evich 1808-1856 . . . .DLB-205	Knigge, Adolph Franz Friedrich Ludwig, Freiherr von 1752-1796 . . . . .DLB-94
Kilian, Crawford 1941- DLB-251	Kirk, Hans 1898-1962 . . . . .DLB-214	
Killens, John Oliver 1916-1987 . . . . .DLB-33	Kirk, John Foster 1824-1904 . . . . .DLB-79	Charles Knight and Company. DLB-106
Tribute to Julian Mayfield Y-84	Kirkconnell, Watson 1895-1977. . . . . .DLB-68	Knight, Damon 1922-2002 . . . . .DLB-8

Cumulative Index

Knight, Etheridge 1931-1992 . . . . DLB-41

Knight, John S. 1894-1981 . . . . DLB-29

Knight, Sarah Kemble 1666-1727 . . . . DLB-24, 200

Knight-Bruce, G. W. H. 1852-1896 . . . . . .DLB-174

Knister, Raymond 1899-1932 . . . . DLB-68

Knoblock, Edward 1874-1945. . . . . DLB-10

Knopf, Alfred A. 1892-1984 . . . . Y-84

    Knopf to Hammett: The Editoral
        Correspondence Y-00

Alfred A. Knopf [publishing house] DLB-46

Knorr von Rosenroth, Christian
    1636-1689 . . . . DLB-168

Knowles, John 1926-2001 . . . . . . DLB-6; CDALB-6

Knox, Frank 1874-1944 . . . . DLB-29

Knox, John circa 1514-1572 . . . . DLB-132

Knox, John Armoy 1850-1906 . . . . DLB-23

Knox, Lucy 1845-1884. . . . . DLB-240

Knox, Ronald Arbuthnott 1888-1957 . . . . . DLB-77

Knox, Thomas Wallace 1835-1896. . . . . . DLB-189

Knudsen, Jakob 1858-1917 . . . . DLB-300

Knut, Dovid 1900-1955 . . . . DLB-317

Kobayashi Takiji 1903-1933 . . . . DLB-180

Kober, Arthur 1900-1975 . . . . DLB-11

Kobiakova, Aleksandra Petrovna
    1823-1892 . . . . DLB-238

Kocbek, Edvard 1904-1981 . . .DLB-147; CDWLB-4

Koch, C. J. 1932- DLB-289

Koch, Howard 1902-1995. . . . . DLB-26

Koch, Kenneth 1925-2002 . . . . DLB-5

Kōda Rohan 1867-1947 . . . . DLB-180

Koehler, Ted 1894-1973 . . . . DLB-265

Koenigsberg, Moses 1879-1945. . . . . DLB-25

Koeppen, Wolfgang 1906-1996. . . . . DLB-69

Koertge, Ronald 1940- DLB-105

Koestler, Arthur 1905-1983 . . . . . . Y-83; CDBLB-7

Kohn, John S. Van E. 1906-1976. . . . . DLB-187

Kokhanovskaia
    (see Sokhanskaia, Nadezhda Stepanova)

Kokoschka, Oskar 1886-1980. . . . . DLB-124

Kolatkar, Arun 1932-2004 . . . . DLB-323

Kolb, Annette 1870-1967. . . . . DLB-66

Kolbenheyer, Erwin Guido
    1878-1962. . . . . DLB-66, 124

Kolleritsch, Alfred 1931- DLB-85

Kolodny, Annette 1941- DLB-67

Koltès, Bernard-Marie 1948-1989. . . . . . . DLB-321

Kol'tsov, Aleksei Vasil'evich
    1809-1842 . . . . DLB-205

Komarov, Matvei circa 1730-1812. . . . . . . DLB-150

Komroff, Manuel 1890-1974. . . . . DLB-4

Komunyakaa, Yusef 1947- DLB-120

Kondoleon, Harry 1955-1994. . . . . DLB-266

Koneski, Blaže 1921-1993. . . DLB-181; CDWLB-4

Konigsburg, E. L. 1930- DLB-52

Konparu Zenchiku 1405-1468? DLB-203

Konrád, György 1933- DLB-232; CDWLB-4

Konrad von Würzburg
    circa 1230-1287 . . . . DLB-138

Konstantinov, Aleko 1863-1897 . . . . DLB-147

Konwicki, Tadeusz 1926- DLB-232

Koontz, Dean 1945- DLB-292

Kooser, Ted 1939- DLB-105

Kopit, Arthur 1937- DLB-7

Kops, Bernard 1926?- DLB-13

Kornbluth, C. M. 1923-1958 . . . . DLB-8

Körner, Theodor 1791-1813 . . . . DLB-90

Kornfeld, Paul 1889-1942. . . . . DLB-118

Korolenko, Vladimir Galaktionovich
    1853-1921 . . . . .DLB-277

Kosinski, Jerzy 1933-1991. . . . . . .DLB-2, 299; Y-82

Kosmač, Ciril 1910-1980 . . . . DLB-181

Kosovel, Srečko 1904-1926. . . . . DLB-147

Kostrov, Ermil Ivanovich 1755-1796 . . . . . DLB-150

Kotzebue, August von 1761-1819 . . . . DLB-94

Kotzwinkle, William 1938- DLB-173

Kovačić, Ante 1854-1889 . . . . DLB-147

Kovalevskaia, Sof'ia Vasil'evna
    1850-1891 . . . . .DLB-277

Kovič, Kajetan 1931- DLB-181

Kozlov, Ivan Ivanovich 1779-1840. . . . . . . DLB-205

Kracauer, Siegfried 1889-1966 . . . . DLB-296

Kraf, Elaine 1946- Y-81

Kramer, Jane 1938- DLB-185

Kramer, Larry 1935- DLB-249

Kramer, Mark 1944- DLB-185

Kranjčević, Silvije Strahimir 1865-1908 . . DLB-147

Krasko, Ivan 1876-1958 . . . . DLB-215

Krasna, Norman 1909-1984 . . . . DLB-26

Kraus, Hans Peter 1907-1988 . . . . DLB-187

Kraus, Karl 1874-1936 . . . . DLB-118

Krause, Herbert 1905-1976. . . . . DLB-256

Krauss, Ruth 1911-1993 . . . . DLB-52

Krauth, Nigel 1949- DLB-325

Kreisel, Henry 1922-1991. . . . . DLB-88

Krestovsky V.
    (see Khvoshchinskaia, Nadezhda Dmitrievna)

Krestovsky, Vsevolod Vladimirovich
    1839-1895 . . . . DLB-238

Kreuder, Ernst 1903-1972 . . . . DLB-69

Krėvė-Mickevičius, Vincas 1882-1954 . . . DLB-220

Kreymborg, Alfred 1883-1966 . . . . DLB-4, 54

Krieger, Murray 1923-2000 . . . . DLB-67

Krim, Seymour 1922-1989 . . . . DLB-16

Kripke, Saul 1940- DLB-279

Kristensen, Tom 1893-1974 . . . . DLB-214

Kristeva, Julia 1941- DLB-242

Kristján Níels Jónsson/Kristjan Niels Julius
    (see Káinn)

Kritzer, Hyman W. 1918-2002 . . . . Y-02

Krivulin, Viktor Borisovich 1944-2001. . . DLB-285

Krleža, Miroslav
    1893-1981 . . . . .DLB-147; CDWLB-4

Krock, Arthur 1886-1974 . . . . DLB-29

Kroetsch, Robert 1927- DLB-53

Kropotkin, Petr Alekseevich 1842-1921 . . .DLB-277

Kross, Jaan 1920- DLB-232

Kruchenykh, Aleksei Eliseevich
    1886-1968 . . . . DLB-295

Krúdy, Gyula 1878-1933. . . . . DLB-215

Krutch, Joseph Wood
    1893-1970. . . . . .DLB-63, 206, 275

Krylov, Ivan Andreevich 1769-1844 . . . . . DLB-150

Krymov, Iurii Solomonovich
    (Iurii Solomonovich Beklemishev)
    1908-1941 . . . . .DLB-272

Kubin, Alfred 1877-1959. . . . . DLB-81

Kubrick, Stanley 1928-1999 . . . . DLB-26

Kudrun circa 1230-1240. . . . . DLB-138

Kuffstein, Hans Ludwig von 1582-1656. . DLB-164

Kuhlmann, Quirinus 1651-1689. . . . . DLB-168

Kuhn, Thomas S. 1922-1996 . . . . .DLB-279

Kuhnau, Johann 1660-1722 . . . . DLB-168

Kukol'nik, Nestor Vasil'evich
    1809-1868 . . . . DLB-205

Kukučín, Martin
    1860-1928 . . . . .DLB-215; CDWLB-4

Kumin, Maxine 1925- DLB-5

Kuncewicz, Maria 1895-1989 . . . . DLB-215

Kundera, Milan 1929- DLB-232; CDWLB-4

Kunene, Mazisi 1930- DLB-117

Kunikida Doppo 1869-1908 . . . . DLB-180

Kunitz, Stanley 1905-2006 . . . . DLB-48

Kunjufu, Johari M. (see Amini, Johari M.)

Kunnert, Gunter 1929- DLB-75

Kunze, Reiner 1933- DLB-75

Kuo, Helena 1911-1999 . . . . DLB-312

Kupferberg, Tuli 1923- DLB-16

Kuprin, Aleksandr Ivanovich
    1870-1938. . . . . DLB-295

Kuraev, Mikhail Nikolaevich 1939- . . . DLB-285

Kurahashi Yumiko 1935- DLB-182

Kureishi, Hanif 1954- DLB-194, 245

Kürnberger, Ferdinand 1821-1879 . . . . . . DLB-129

Kurz, Isolde 1853-1944 . . . . DLB-66

Kusenberg, Kurt 1904-1983 . . . . DLB-69

Kushchevsky, Ivan Afanas'evich
    1847-1876 . . . . DLB-238

Kushner, Tony 1956- DLB-228

Kuttner, Henry 1915-1958................DLB-8

Kuzmin, Mikhail Alekseevich
   1872-1936.....................DLB-295

Kuznetsov, Anatoli
   1929-1979.................DLB-299, 302

Kyd, Thomas 1558-1594...............DLB-62

Kyffin, Maurice circa 1560?-1598.......DLB-136

Kyger, Joanne 1934-....................DLB-16

Kyne, Peter B. 1880-1957................DLB-78

Kyōgoku Tamekane 1254-1332.........DLB-203

Kyrklund, Willy 1921-.................DLB-257

L

L. E. L. (see Landon, Letitia Elizabeth)

Labé, Louise 1520?-1566...............DLB-327

Laberge, Albert 1871-1960.............DLB-68

Laberge, Marie 1950-..................DLB-60

Labiche, Eugène 1815-1888............DLB-192

Labrunie, Gerard (see Nerval, Gerard de)

La Bruyère, Jean de 1645-1696.........DLB-268

La Calprenède 1609?-1663.............DLB-268

Lacan, Jacques 1901-1981..............DLB-296

La Capria, Raffaele 1922-..............DLB-196

La Ceppède, Jean de 1550?-1623........DLB-327

La Chaussée, Pierre-Claude Nivelle de
   1692-1754.....................DLB-313

Laclos, Pierre-Ambroise-François Choderlos de
   1741-1803.....................DLB-313

Dangerous Acquaintances............DLB-314

Lacombe, Patrice
   (see Trullier-Lacombe, Joseph Patrice)

Lacretelle, Jacques de 1888-1985........DLB-65

Lacy, Ed 1911-1968...................DLB-226

Lacy, Sam 1903-......................DLB-171

Ladd, Joseph Brown 1764-1786.........DLB-37

La Farge, Oliver 1901-1963..............DLB-9

Lafayette, Marie-Madeleine, comtesse de
   1634-1693.....................DLB-268

Laffan, Mrs. R. S. de Courcy
   (see Adams, Bertha Leith)

Lafferty, R. A. 1914-2002................DLB-8

La Flesche, Francis 1857-1932..........DLB-175

La Fontaine, Jean de 1621-1695........DLB-268

Laforet, Carmen 1921-2004............DLB-322

Laforge, Jules 1860-1887...............DLB-217

Lagerkvist, Pär 1891-1974..............DLB-259

Lagerlöf, Selma
   1858-1940.....................DLB-259

Lagorio, Gina 1922-..................DLB-196

La Guma, Alex
   1925-1985........DLB-117, 225; CDWLB-3

Lahaise, Guillaume (see Delahaye, Guy)

La Harpe, Jean-François de 1739-1803....DLB-313

Lahiri, Jhumpa 1967-.................DLB-323

Lahontan, Louis-Armand de Lom d'Arce,
   Baron de 1666-1715?.............DLB-99

Lai He 1894-1943....................DLB-328

Laing, Kojo 1946-....................DLB-157

Laird, Carobeth 1895-1983..............Y-82

Laird and Lee.......................DLB-49

Lake, Paul 1951-....................DLB-282

Lalić, Ivan V. 1931-1996...............DLB-181

Lalić, Mihailo 1914-1992...............DLB-181

Lalonde, Michèle 1937-................DLB-60

Lamantia, Philip 1927-.................DLB-16

Lamartine, Alphonse de
   1790-1869.....................DLB-217

Lamb, Lady Caroline
   1785-1828.....................DLB-116

Lamb, Charles
   1775-1834......DLB-93, 107, 163; CDBLB-3

Lamb, Mary 1764-1874...............DLB-163

Lambert, Angela 1940-................DLB-271

Lambert, Anne-Thérèse de (Anne-Thérèse de
   Marguenat de Courcelles, marquise de Lambert)
   1647-1733.....................DLB-313

Lambert, Betty 1933-1983..............DLB-60

La Mettrie, Julien Offroy de
   1709-1751.....................DLB-313

Lamm, Donald
   Goodbye, Gutenberg? A Lecture at
   the New York Public Library,
   18 April 1995...................Y-95

Lamming, George
   1927-..................DLB-125; CDWLB-3

La Mothe Le Vayer, François de
   1588-1672.....................DLB-268

L'Amour, Louis 1908-1988........DLB-206; Y-80

Lampman, Archibald 1861-1899........DLB-92

Lamson, Wolffe and Company..........DLB-49

Lancer Books........................DLB-46

Lanchester, John 1962-................DLB-267

Lander, Peter (see Cunningham, Peter)

Landesman, Jay 1919- and
   Landesman, Fran 1927-...........DLB-16

Landolfi, Tommaso 1908-1979.........DLB-177

Landon, Letitia Elizabeth 1802-1838.....DLB-96

Landor, Walter Savage 1775-1864....DLB-93, 107

Landry, Napoléon-P. 1884-1956........DLB-92

Landvik, Lorna 1954-.................DLB-292

Lane, Charles 1800-1870.......DLB-1, 223; DS-5

Lane, F. C. 1885-1984.................DLB-241

Lane, Laurence W. 1890-1967..........DLB-91

Lane, M. Travis 1934-.................DLB-60

Lane, Patrick 1939-...................DLB-53

Lane, Pinkie Gordon 1923-............DLB-41

John Lane Company..................DLB-49

Laney, Al 1896-1988...............DLB-4, 171

Lang, Andrew 1844-1912.......DLB-98, 141, 184

Langer, Susanne K. 1895-1985.........DLB-270

Langevin, André 1927-.................DLB-60

Langford, David 1953-................DLB-261

Langgässer, Elisabeth 1899-1950........DLB-69

Langhorne, John 1735-1779...........DLB-109

Langland, William circa 1330-circa 1400..DLB-146

Langton, Anna 1804-1893..............DLB-99

Lanham, Edwin 1904-1979..............DLB-4

Lanier, Sidney 1842-1881.........DLB-64; DS-13

Lanyer, Aemilia 1569-1645............DLB-121

Lao She 1899-1966...................DLB-328

Lapointe, Gatien 1931-1983............DLB-88

Lapointe, Paul-Marie 1929-............DLB-88

La Ramée, Pierre de (Petrus Ramus, Peter Ramus)
   1515-1572.....................DLB-327

Larcom, Lucy 1824-1893.........DLB-221, 243

Lardner, John 1912-1960..............DLB-171

Lardner, Ring 1885-1933
   ....DLB-11, 25, 86, 171; DS-16; CDALB-4

Lardner 100: Ring Lardner
   Centennial Symposium.............Y-85

Lardner, Ring, Jr. 1915-2000........DLB-26, Y-00

Larivey, Pierre de 1541-1619............DLB-327

Larkin, Philip 1922-1985.......DLB-27; CDBLB-8

The Philip Larkin Society..............Y-99

La Roche, Sophie von 1730-1807........DLB-94

La Rochefoucauld, François duc de
   1613-1680.....................DLB-268

La Rocque, Gilbert 1943-1984..........DLB-60

Laroque de Roquebrune, Robert
   (see Roquebrune, Robert de)

Larrick, Nancy 1910-2004..............DLB-61

Lars, Claudia 1899-1974...............DLB-283

Larsen, Nella 1893-1964...............DLB-51

Larsen, Thøger 1875-1928.............DLB-300

Larson, Clinton F. 1919-1994..........DLB-256

La Sale, Antoine de
   circa 1386-1460/1467............DLB-208

Las Casas, Fray Bartolomé de
   1474-1566.....................DLB-318

Lasch, Christopher 1932-1994.........DLB-246

Lasdun, James 1958-.................DLB-319

Lasker-Schüler, Else 1869-1945......DLB-66, 124

Lasnier, Rina 1915-1997................DLB-88

Lassalle, Ferdinand 1825-1864.........DLB-129

Last Orders, 1996 Booker Prize winner,
   Graham Swift..................DLB-326

La Taille, Jean de 1534?-1611?.........DLB-327

Late-Medieval Castilian Theater........DLB-286

Latham, Robert 1912-1995............DLB-201

Lathan, Emma (Mary Jane Latsis [1927-1997] and
   Martha Henissart [1929-]).........DLB-306

Lathrop, Dorothy P. 1891-1980..........DLB-22

Lathrop, George Parsons 1851-1898.....DLB-71

Lathrop, John, Jr. 1772-1820 . . . . DLB-37	Lazarević, Laza K. 1851-1890. . . . . DLB-147	"Principles of Biography," in *Elizabethan and Other Essays* DLB-149
Latimer, Hugh 1492?-1555. . . . . DLB-136	Lazarus, George 1904-1997 . . . . DLB-201	Lee, Tanith 1947- DLB-261
Latimore, Jewel Christine McLawler (see Amini, Johari M.)	Lazhechnikov, Ivan Ivanovich 1792-1869. . . . . DLB-198	Lee, Vernon 1856-1935 . . . . .DLB-57, 153, 156, 174, 178
Latin Literature, The Uniqueness of DLB-211	Lea, Henry Charles 1825-1909 . . . . DLB-47	Lee and Shepard. DLB-49
La Tour du Pin, Patrice de 1911-1975. . . . DLB-258	Lea, Sydney 1942- DLB-120, 282	Le Fanu, Joseph Sheridan 1814-1873. . . . . DLB-21, 70, 159, 178
Latymer, William 1498-1583 . . . . DLB-132	Lea, Tom 1907-2001 . . . . DLB-6	Lefèvre d'Etaples, Jacques 1460?-1536. . . . . DLB-327
Laube, Heinrich 1806-1884 . . . . DLB-133	Leacock, John 1729-1802 . . . . DLB-31	Leffland, Ella 1931- Y-84
Laud, William 1573-1645 . . . . DLB-213	Leacock, Stephen 1869-1944 . . . . DLB-92	le Fort, Gertrud von 1876-1971. . . . . DLB-66
Laughlin, James 1914-1997. . . . . . DLB-48; Y-96, 97	Lead, Jane Ward 1623-1704 . . . . DLB-131	Le Gallienne, Richard 1866-1947 . . . . DLB-4
A Tribute [to Henry Miller] Y-80	Leadenhall Press. DLB-106	Legaré, Hugh Swinton 1797-1843 . . . . .DLB-3, 59, 73, 248
Tribute to Albert Erskine Y-93	"The Greatness of Southern Literature": League of the South Institute for the Study of Southern Culture and History Y-02	
Tribute to Kenneth Rexroth. Y-82		Legaré, James Mathewes 1823-1859. . . . DLB-3, 248
Tribute to Malcolm Cowley. Y-89		Léger, Antoine-J. 1880-1950 . . . . DLB-88
Laumer, Keith 1925-1993 . . . . DLB-8	Leakey, Caroline Woolmer 1827-1881 . . . . DLB-230	Leggett, William 1801-1839 . . . . DLB-250
Lauremberg, Johann 1590-1658 . . . . DLB-164	Leapor, Mary 1722-1746. . . . . DLB-109	Le Guin, Ursula K. 1929- DLB-8, 52, 256, 275; CDALB-6
Laurence, Margaret 1926-1987. . . . . DLB-53	Lear, Edward 1812-1888. . . . . . . DLB-32, 163, 166	
Laurentius von Schnüffis 1633-1702. . . . . DLB-168	Leary, Timothy 1920-1996. . . . . DLB-16	Lehman, Ernest 1920- DLB-44
Laurents, Arthur 1918- DLB-26	W. A. Leary and Company DLB-49	Lehmann, John 1907-1989 . . . . .DLB-27, 100
Laurie, Annie (see Black, Winifred)	Léautaud, Paul 1872-1956 . . . . DLB-65	John Lehmann Limited. DLB-112
Laut, Agnes Christiana 1871-1936 . . . . . . DLB-92	Leavis, F. R. 1895-1978 . . . . DLB-242	Lehmann, Rosamond 1901-1990 . . . . DLB-15
Lauterbach, Ann 1942- DLB-193	Leavitt, David 1961- DLB-130	Lehmann, Wilhelm 1882-1968 . . . . DLB-56
Lautréamont, Isidore Lucien Ducasse, Comte de 1846-1870 . . . . DLB-217	Leavitt and Allen DLB-49	Leiber, Fritz 1910-1992. . . . . DLB-8
	Le Blond, Mrs. Aubrey 1861-1934. . . . . . .DLB-174	Leibniz, Gottfried Wilhelm 1646-1716 . . . DLB-168
Lavater, Johann Kaspar 1741-1801 . . . . . . DLB-97	le Carré, John (David John Moore Cornwell) 1931- DLB-87; CDBLB-8	Leicester University Press. DLB-112
Lavin, Mary 1912-1996 . . . . DLB-15, 319		Leigh, Carolyn 1926-1983 . . . . DLB-265
Law, John (see Harkness, Margaret)	Tribute to Graham Greene. Y-91	Leigh, W. R. 1866-1955 . . . . DLB-188
Lawes, Henry 1596-1662 . . . . DLB-126	Tribute to George Greenfield. Y-00	Leinster, Murray 1896-1975 . . . . DLB-8
Lawler, Ray 1922- DLB-289	Lécavelé, Roland (see Dorgeles, Roland)	Leiser, Bill 1898-1965 . . . . DLB-241
Lawless, Anthony (see MacDonald, Philip)	Lechlitner, Ruth 1901- DLB-48	Leisewitz, Johann Anton 1752-1806 . . . . . DLB-94
Lawless, Emily (The Hon. Emily Lawless) 1845-1913. . . . . DLB-240	Leclerc, Félix 1914-1988. . . . . DLB-60	Leitch, Maurice 1933- DLB-14
	Le Clézio, J. M. G. 1940- DLB-83	Leithauser, Brad 1943- DLB-120, 282
Lawrence, D. H. 1885-1930 . . . . . DLB-10, 19, 36, 98, 162, 195; CDBLB-6	Leder, Rudolf (see Hermlin, Stephan)	Leland, Charles G. 1824-1903 . . . . DLB-11
	Lederer, Charles 1910-1976 . . . . DLB-26	
The D. H. Lawrence Society of North America. Y-00	Ledwidge, Francis 1887-1917 . . . . DLB-20	Leland, John 1503?-1552 . . . . DLB-136
	Lee, Chang-rae 1965- DLB-312	Lemaire de Belges, Jean 1473-? DLB-327
Lawrence, David 1888-1973 . . . . DLB-29	Lee, Cherylene 1953- DLB-312	Lemay, Pamphile 1837-1918 . . . . DLB-99
Lawrence, Jerome 1915-2004 . . . . DLB-228	Lee, Dennis 1939- DLB-53	Lemelin, Roger 1919-1992 . . . . DLB-88
Lawrence, Seymour 1926-1994 . . . . Y-94	Lee, Don L. (see Madhubuti, Haki R.)	Lemercier, Louis-Jean-Népomucène 1771-1840. . . . . DLB-192
Tribute to Richard Yates. Y-92	Lee, George W. 1894-1976 . . . . DLB-51	
Lawrence, T. E. 1888-1935. . . . . DLB-195	Lee, Gus 1946- DLB-312	Le Moine, James MacPherson 1825-1912 . DLB-99
The T. E. Lawrence Society. Y-98	Lee, Harper 1926- DLB-6; CDALB-1	Lemon, Mark 1809-1870 . . . . DLB-163
Lawson, George 1598-1678 . . . . DLB-213	Lee, Harriet 1757-1851 and Lee, Sophia 1750-1824 . . . . DLB-39	Le Moyne, Jean 1913-1996 . . . . DLB-88
Lawson, Henry 1867-1922 . . . . DLB-230		Lemperly, Paul 1858-1939 . . . . .DLB-187
Lawson, John ?-1711. . . . . DLB-24	Lee, Laurie 1914-1997 . . . . DLB-27	Leñero, Vicente 1933- DLB-305
Lawson, John Howard 1894-1977. . . . . . DLB-228	Lee, Leslie 1935- DLB-266	L'Engle, Madeleine 1918- DLB-52
Lawson, Louisa Albury 1848-1920. . . . . . DLB-230	Lee, Li-Young 1957- DLB-165, 312	Lennart, Isobel 1915-1971 . . . . DLB-44
Lawson, Robert 1892-1957. . . . . DLB-22	Lee, Manfred B. 1905-1971. . . . . DLB-137	Lennox, Charlotte 1729 or 1730-1804 . . . . DLB-39
Lawson, Victor F. 1850-1925 . . . . DLB-25	Lee, Nathaniel circa 1645-1692 . . . . DLB-80	Lenox, James 1800-1880. . . . . DLB-140
Layard, Austen Henry 1817-1894 . . . . . . DLB-166	Lee, Robert E. 1918-1994 . . . . DLB-228	Lenski, Lois 1893-1974 . . . . DLB-22
Layton, Irving 1912- DLB-88	Lee, Sir Sidney 1859-1926 . . . . DLB-149, 184	Lentricchia, Frank 1940- DLB-246
LaZamon fl. circa 1200. . . . . DLB-146		

Lenz, Hermann 1913-1998 . . . . .DLB-69

Lenz, J. M. R. 1751-1792 . . . . .DLB-94

Lenz, Siegfried 1926- DLB-75

León, Fray Luis de 1527-1591 . . . . .DLB-318

Leonard, Elmore 1925- DLB-173, 226

Leonard, Hugh 1926- DLB-13

Leonard, William Ellery 1876-1944 . . . . . . .DLB-54

Leong, Russell C. 1950- DLB-312

Leonov, Leonid Maksimovich
 1899-1994 . . . . .DLB-272

Leonowens, Anna 1834-1914 . . . . . . .DLB-99, 166

Leont'ev, Konstantin Nikolaevich
 1831-1891 . . . . .DLB-277

Leopold, Aldo 1887-1948 . . . . .DLB-275

LePan, Douglas 1914-1998 . . . . .DLB-88

Lepik, Kalju 1920-1999 . . . . .DLB-232

Leprohon, Rosanna Eleanor 1829-1879 . . . .DLB-99

Le Queux, William 1864-1927 . . . . .DLB-70

Lermontov, Mikhail Iur'evich
 1814-1841 . . . . .DLB-205

Lerner, Alan Jay 1918-1986 . . . . .DLB-265

Lerner, Max 1902-1992 . . . . .DLB-29

Lernet-Holenia, Alexander 1897-1976 . . . . .DLB-85

Le Rossignol, James 1866-1969 . . . . .DLB-92

Lesage, Alain-René 1668-1747 . . . . .DLB-313

Lescarbot, Marc circa 1570-1642 . . . . .DLB-99

LeSeur, William Dawson 1840-1917 . . . . . .DLB-92

LeSieg, Theo. (see Geisel, Theodor Seuss)

Leskov, Nikolai Semenovich
 1831-1895 . . . . .DLB-238

Leslie, Doris before 1902-1982 . . . . .DLB-191

Leslie, Eliza 1787-1858 . . . . .DLB-202

Leslie, Frank (Henry Carter)
 1821-1880 . . . . .DLB-43, 79

Frank Leslie [publishing house] DLB-49

Leśmian, Bolesław 1878-1937 . . . . .DLB-215

Lesperance, John 1835?-1891 . . . . .DLB-99

Lespinasse, Julie de 1732-1776 . . . . .DLB-313

Lessing, Bruno 1870-1940 . . . . .DLB-28

Lessing, Doris
 1919- DLB-15, 139; Y-85; CDBLB-8

Lessing, Gotthold Ephraim
 1729-1781 . . . . .DLB-97; CDWLB-2

The Lessing Society Y-00

L'Estoile, Pierre de 1546-1611 . . . . .DLB-327

Le Sueur, Meridel 1900-1996 . . . . .DLB-303

Lettau, Reinhard 1929-1996 . . . . .DLB-75

Letters from a Peruvian Woman, Françoise d'Issembourg
 de Graffigny .DLB-314

The Hemingway Letters Project Finds
 an Editor Y-02

Lever, Charles 1806-1872 . . . . .DLB-21

Lever, Ralph ca. 1527-1585 . . . . .DLB-236

Leverson, Ada 1862-1933 . . . . .DLB-153

Levertov, Denise
 1923-1997 . . . . .DLB-5, 165; CDALB-7

Levi, Peter 1931-2000 . . . . .DLB-40

Levi, Primo 1919-1987 . . . . DLB-177, 299

Levien, Sonya 1888-1960 . . . . .DLB-44

Levin, Meyer 1905-1981 . . . . DLB-9, 28; Y-81

Levin, Phillis 1954- DLB-282

Lévinas, Emmanuel 1906-1995 . . . . .DLB-296

Levine, Norman 1923- DLB-88

Levine, Philip 1928- DLB-5

Levis, Larry 1946- DLB-120

Lévi-Strauss, Claude 1908- DLB-242

Levitov, Aleksandr Ivanovich
 1835?-1877 .DLB-277

Levy, Amy 1861-1889 . . . . .DLB-156, 240

Levy, Benn Wolfe 1900-1973 . . . . . . DLB-13; Y-81

Levy, Deborah 1959- DLB-310

Lewald, Fanny 1811-1889 . . . . .DLB-129

Lewes, George Henry 1817-1878 . . . . .DLB-55, 144

 "Criticism in Relation to Novels"
  (1863) DLB-21

 The Principles of Success in Literature
  (1865) [excerpt] DLB-57

Lewis, Agnes Smith 1843-1926 . . . . .DLB-174

Lewis, Alfred H. 1857-1914 . . . . .DLB-25, 186

Lewis, Alun 1915-1944 . . . . .DLB-20, 162

Lewis, C. Day (see Day Lewis, C.)

Lewis, C. I. 1883-1964 . . . . .DLB-270

Lewis, C. S. 1898-1963
 . . . . DLB-15, 100, 160, 255; CDBLB-7

 The New York C. S. Lewis Society Y-99

Lewis, Charles B. 1842-1924 . . . . .DLB-11

Lewis, David 1941-2001 . . . . .DLB-279

Lewis, Henry Clay 1825-1850 . . . . .DLB-3, 248

Lewis, Janet 1899-1999 . . . . .Y-87

 Tribute to Katherine Anne Porter Y-80

Lewis, Matthew Gregory
 1775-1818 . . . . .DLB-39, 158, 178

Lewis, Meriwether 1774-1809 . . . . . .DLB-183, 186

Lewis, Norman 1908-2003 . . . . .DLB-204

Lewis, R. W. B. 1917-2002 . . . . .DLB-111

Lewis, Richard circa 1700-1734 . . . . .DLB-24

Lewis, Saunders 1893-1985 . . . . .DLB-310

Lewis, Sinclair
 1885-1951 . . . . . .DLB-9, 102; DS-1; CDALB-4

 Sinclair Lewis Centennial Conference Y-85

 The Sinclair Lewis Society Y-99

Lewis, Wilmarth Sheldon 1895-1979 . . . . .DLB-140

Lewis, Wyndham 1882-1957 . . . . .DLB-15

 Time and Western Man
  [excerpt] (1927) DLB-36

Lewisohn, Ludwig 1882-1955 . . . DLB-4, 9, 28, 102

Leyendecker, J. C. 1874-1951 . . . . .DLB-188

Leyner, Mark 1956- DLB-292

Lezama Lima, José 1910-1976 . . . . . .DLB-113, 283

Lézardière, Marie-Charlotte-Pauline Robert de
 1754-1835 . . . . .DLB-313

L'Heureux, John 1934- DLB-244

Libbey, Laura Jean 1862-1924 . . . . .DLB-221

Libedinsky, Iurii Nikolaevich
 1898-1959 . . . . .DLB-272

The Liberator DLB-303

Library History Group Y-01

E-Books' Second Act in Libraries Y-02

The Library of America DLB-46

The Library of America: An Assessment
 After Two Decades Y-02

Licensing Act of 1737 . . . . .DLB-84

Leonard Lichfield I [publishing house] . . .DLB-170

Lichtenberg, Georg Christoph
 1742-1799 . . . . .DLB-94

The Liddle Collection Y-97

Lidman, Sara 1923-2004 . . . . .DLB-257

Lieb, Fred 1888-1980 . . . . .DLB-171

Liebling, A. J. 1904-1963 . . . . .DLB-4, 171

Lieutenant Murray (see Ballou, Maturin Murray)

Life and Times of Michael K, 1983 Booker Prize winner,
 J. M. Coetzee DLB-326

Life of Pi, 2002 Booker Prize winner,
 Yann Martel .DLB-326

Lighthall, William Douw 1857-1954 . . . . . .DLB-92

Lihn, Enrique 1929-1988 . . . . .DLB-283

Lilar, Françoise (see Mallet-Joris, Françoise)

Lili'uokalani, Queen 1838-1917 . . . . .DLB-221

Lillo, George 1691-1739 . . . . .DLB-84

Lilly, J. K., Jr. 1893-1966 . . . . .DLB-140

Lilly, Wait and Company DLB-49

Lily, William circa 1468-1522 . . . . .DLB-132

Lim, Shirley Geok-lin 1944- DLB-312

Lima, Jorge de 1893-1953 . . . . .DLB-307

Lima Barreto, Afonso Henriques de
 1881-1922 . . . . .DLB-307

Limited Editions Club DLB-46

Limón, Graciela 1938- DLB-209

Limonov, Eduard 1943- DLB-317

Lincoln and Edmands DLB-49

Lind, Jakov 1927- DLB-299

Linda Vilhjálmsdóttir 1958- DLB-293

Lindesay, Ethel Forence
 (see Richardson, Henry Handel)

Lindgren, Astrid 1907-2002 . . . . .DLB-257

Lindgren, Torgny 1938- DLB-257

Lindsay, Alexander William, Twenty-fifth
 Earl of Crawford 1812-1880 . . . . .DLB-184

Lindsay, Sir David circa 1485-1555 . . . . . .DLB-132

Lindsay, David 1878-1945........... DLB-255	Callaloo............................. Y-87	The James Fenimore Cooper Society..... Y-01
Lindsay, Jack 1900-1990............... Y-84	Expatriates in Paris................. DS-15	The Stephen Crane Society......... Y-98, 01
Lindsay, Lady (Caroline Blanche Elizabeth Fitzroy Lindsay) 1844-1912.................... DLB-199	New Literary Periodicals: A Report for 1987............... Y-87	The E. E. Cummings Society.......... Y-01
	A Report for 1988............... Y-88	The James Dickey Society........... Y-99
Lindsay, Norman 1879-1969.......... DLB-260	A Report for 1989............... Y-89	John Dos Passos Newsletter.......... Y-00
Lindsay, Vachel 1879-1931............. DLB-54; CDALB-3	A Report for 1990............... Y-90	The Priory Scholars [Sir Arthur Conan Doyle] of New York............. Y-99
	A Report for 1991............... Y-91	
The Line of Beauty, 2004 Booker Prize winner, Alan Hollinghurst.............. DLB-326	A Report for 1992............... Y-92	The International Theodore Dreiser Society....................... Y-01
	A Report for 1993............... Y-93	The Friends of the Dymock Poets....... Y-00
Linebarger, Paul Myron Anthony (see Smith, Cordwainer)	Literary Research Archives The Anthony Burgess Archive at the Harry Ransom Humanities Research Center................ Y-98	The George Eliot Fellowship.......... Y-99
Ling Shuhua 1900-1990............. DLB-328		The T. S. Eliot Society: Celebration and Scholarship, 1980-1999............ Y-99
Link, Arthur S. 1920-1998............ DLB-17		
Linn, Ed 1922-2000................ DLB-241	Archives of Charles Scribner's Sons..... DS-17	The Ralph Waldo Emerson Society...... Y-99
Linn, John Blair 1777-1804............ DLB-37	Berg Collection of English and American Literature of the New York Public Library.......... Y-83	The William Faulkner Society......... Y-99
Lins, Osman 1924-1978.......... DLB-145, 307		The C. S. Forester Society............ Y-00
Linton, Eliza Lynn 1822-1898.......... DLB-18		The Hamlin Garland Society.......... Y-01
Linton, William James 1812-1897....... DLB-32	The Bobbs-Merrill Archive at the Lilly Library, Indiana University..... Y-90	The [Elizabeth] Gaskell Society......... Y-98
Barnaby Bernard Lintot [publishing house]............. DLB-170		The Charlotte Perkins Gilman Society.... Y-99
	Die Fürstliche Bibliothek Corvey....... Y-96	The Ellen Glasgow Society........... Y-01
Lion Books....................... DLB-46	Guide to the Archives of Publishers, Journals, and Literary Agents in North American Libraries......... Y-93	Zane Grey's West Society............ Y-00
Lionni, Leo 1910-1999............... DLB-61		The Ivor Gurney Society............ Y-98
Lippard, George 1822-1854........... DLB-202		The Joel Chandler Harris Association.... Y-99
Lippincott, Sara Jane Clarke 1823-1904.................... DLB-43	The Henry E. Huntington Library...... Y-92	The Nathaniel Hawthorne Society....... Y-00
	The Humanities Research Center, University of Texas.............. Y-82	The [George Alfred] Henty Society...... Y-98
J. B. Lippincott Company............ DLB-49		George Moses Horton Society......... Y-99
Lippmann, Walter 1889-1974.......... DLB-29	The John Carter Brown Library....... Y-85	The William Dean Howells Society...... Y-01
Lipton, Lawrence 1898-1975........... DLB-16	Kent State Special Collections......... Y-86	WW2 HMSO Paperbacks Society....... Y-98
Lisboa, Irene 1892-1958............. DLB-287	The Lilly Library.................. Y-84	American Humor Studies Association.... Y-99
Liscow, Christian Ludwig 1701-1760.................... DLB-97	The Modern Literary Manuscripts Collection in the Special Collections of the Washington University Libraries............. Y-87	International Society for Humor Studies... Y-99
		The W. W. Jacobs Appreciation Society.. Y-98
Lish, Gordon 1934-................ DLB-130		The Richard Jefferies Society.......... Y-98
Tribute to Donald Barthelme.......... Y-89	A Publisher's Archives: G. P. Putnam.... Y-92	The Jerome K. Jerome Society......... Y-98
Tribute to James Dickey............. Y-97	Special Collections at Boston University.................... Y-99	The D. H. Lawrence Society of North America................. Y-00
Lisle, Charles-Marie-René Leconte de 1818-1894.................... DLB-217	The University of Virginia Libraries..... Y-91	The T. E. Lawrence Society........... Y-98
	The William Charvat American Fiction Collection at the Ohio State University Libraries............... Y-92	The [Gotthold] Lessing Society......... Y-00
Lispector, Clarice 1925?-1977......... DLB-113, 307; CDWLB-3		The New York C. S. Lewis Society...... Y-99
		The Sinclair Lewis Society............ Y-99
LitCheck Website.................. Y-01	Literary Societies.................. Y-98–02	The Jack London Research Center....... Y-00
Literary Awards and Honors........... Y-81–02	The Margery Allingham Society....... Y-98	The Jack London Society............ Y-99
Booker Prize................... Y-86, 96–98	The American Studies Association of Norway..................... Y-00	The Cormac McCarthy Society........ Y-99
The Drue Heinz Literature Prize........ Y-82		The Melville Society................ Y-01
The Elmer Holmes Bobst Awards in Arts and Letters................ Y-87	The Arnold Bennett Society.......... Y-98	The Arthur Miller Society............ Y-01
	The Association for the Study of Literature and Environment (ASLE)...................... Y-99	The Milton Society of America......... Y-00
The Griffin Poetry Prize............. Y-00		International Marianne Moore Society... Y-98
Literary Prizes [British]......... DLB-15, 207		International Nabokov Society......... Y-99
National Book Critics Circle Awards...................... Y-00–01	Belgian Luxembourg American Studies Association.................... Y-01	The Vladimir Nabokov Society........ Y-01
	The E. F. Benson Society............ Y-98	The Flannery O'Connor Society....... Y-99
The National Jewish Book Awards.................. Y-85	The Elizabeth Bishop Society.......... Y-01	The Wilfred Owen Association........ Y-98
	The [Edgar Rice] Burroughs Bibliophiles.................... Y-98	Penguin Collectors' Society.......... Y-98
Nobel Prize.................... Y-80–02		The [E. A.] Poe Studies Association...... Y-99
Winning an Edgar................ Y-98	The Byron Society of America......... Y-00	The Katherine Anne Porter Society...... Y-01
The Literary Chronicle and Weekly Review 1819-1828................... DLB-110	The Lewis Carroll Society of North America................ Y-00	The Beatrix Potter Society............ Y-98
	The Willa Cather Pioneer Memorial and Education Foundation......... Y-00	The Ezra Pound Society............. Y-01
Literary Periodicals:		
	New Chaucer Society.............. Y-00	
	The Wilkie Collins Society.......... Y-98	

564

The Powys Society Y-98
Proust Society of America Y-00
The Dorothy L. Sayers Society Y-98
The Bernard Shaw Society Y-99
The Society for the Study of
   Southern Literature................Y-00
The Wallace Stevens Society Y-99
The Harriet Beecher Stowe Center Y-00
The R. S. Surtees Society Y-98
The Thoreau Society..................Y-99
The Tilling [E. F. Benson] Society.......Y-98
The Trollope Societies................Y-00
H. G. Wells Society Y-98
The Western Literature Association Y-99
The William Carlos Williams Society Y-99
The Henry Williamson Society.........Y-98
The [Nero] Wolfe Pack Y-99
The Thomas Wolfe Society............Y-99
Worldwide Wodehouse Societies........Y-98
The W. B. Yeats Society of N.Y. Y-99
The Charlotte M. Yonge Fellowship Y-98
Literary Theory
   The Year in Literary Theory....... Y-92–Y-93
Literature at Nurse, or Circulating Morals (1885),
   by George Moore DLB-18
Litt, Toby 1968- DLB-267, 319
Littell, Eliakim 1797-1870 ....DLB-79
Littell, Robert S. 1831-1896..............DLB-79
Little, Brown and Company DLB-49
Little Magazines and Newspapers DS-15
   Selected English-Language Little
     Magazines and Newspapers
     [France, 1920-1939] DLB-4
   The Little Magazines of the
     New Formalism.................DLB-282
The Little Review 1914-1929 .... DS-15
Littlewood, Joan 1914-2002.............DLB-13
Liu, Aimee E. 1953- DLB-312
Liu E 1857-1909......................DLB-328
Lively, Penelope 1933- ... DLB-14, 161, 207, 326
Liverpool University Press.............DLB-112
The Lives of the Poets (1753) DLB-142
Livesay, Dorothy 1909-1996 ....DLB-68
Livesay, Florence Randal 1874-1953 ......DLB-92
Livings, Henry 1929-1998 ....DLB-13
Livingston, Anne Howe 1763-1841 ... DLB-37, 200
Livingston, Jay 1915-2001 ....DLB-265
Livingston, Myra Cohn 1926-1996 ....DLB-61
Livingston, William 1723-1790...........DLB-31
Livingstone, David 1813-1873 ....DLB-166
Livingstone, Douglas 1932-1996 ....DLB-225
Livshits, Benedikt Konstantinovich
   1886-1938 or 1939 ....DLB-295
Livy 59 B.C.-A.D. 17 ....DLB-211; CDWLB-1

Liyong, Taban lo (see Taban lo Liyong)
Lizárraga, Sylvia S. 1925- DLB-82
Llamazares, Julio 1955- DLB-322
Llewellyn, Kate 1936- DLB-325
Llewellyn, Richard 1906-1983..........DLB-15
Lloréns Torres, Luis 1876-1944 ....DLB-290
Edward Lloyd [publishing house] DLB-106
Lobato, José Bento Monteiro
   1882-1948 ....DLB-307
Lobel, Arnold 1933- DLB-61
Lochhead, Liz 1947- DLB-310
Lochridge, Betsy Hopkins (see Fancher, Betsy)
Locke, Alain 1886-1954...............DLB-51
Locke, David Ross 1833-1888........DLB-11, 23
Locke, John 1632-1704..... DLB-31, 101, 213, 252
Locke, Richard Adams 1800-1871 ....DLB-43
Locker-Lampson, Frederick
   1821-1895 ....DLB-35, 184
Lockhart, John Gibson
   1794-1854 ....DLB-110, 116 144
Lockridge, Francis 1896-1963 ....DLB-306
Lockridge, Richard 1898-1982...........DLB-306
Lockridge, Ross, Jr. 1914-1948 .... DLB-143; Y-80
Locrine and Selimus....................DLB-62
Lodge, David 1935- DLB-14, 194
Lodge, George Cabot 1873-1909........DLB-54
Lodge, Henry Cabot 1850-1924 ....DLB-47
Lodge, Thomas 1558-1625 ....DLB-172
   Defence of Poetry (1579) [excerpt] DLB-172
Loeb, Harold 1891-1974 ....DLB-4; DS-15
Loeb, William 1905-1981 ....DLB-127
Loesser, Frank 1910-1969 ....DLB-265
Lofting, Hugh 1886-1947..............DLB-160
Logan, Deborah Norris 1761-1839 ......DLB-200
Logan, James 1674-1751............DLB-24, 140
Logan, John 1923-1987 ....DLB-5
Logan, Martha Daniell 1704?-1779 ....DLB-200
Logan, William 1950- DLB-120
Logau, Friedrich von 1605-1655 ....DLB-164
Logue, Christopher 1926- DLB-27
Lohenstein, Daniel Casper von
   1635-1683 ....DLB-168
Lohrey, Amanda 1947- DLB-325
Lo-Johansson, Ivar 1901-1990 ....DLB-259
Lokert, George (or Lockhart)
   circa 1485-1547 ....DLB-281
Lomonosov, Mikhail Vasil'evich
   1711-1765.....................DLB-150
London, Jack
   1876-1916 ..... DLB-8, 12, 78, 212; CDALB-3
   The Jack London Research Center......Y-00
   The Jack London Society Y-99
The London Magazine 1820-1829 ....DLB-110

Long, David 1948- DLB-244
Long, H., and Brother DLB-49
Long, Haniel 1888-1956 ....DLB-45
Long, Ray 1878-1935..................DLB-137
Longfellow, Henry Wadsworth
   1807-1882 ....DLB-1, 59, 235; CDALB-2
Longfellow, Samuel 1819-1892 ....DLB-1
Longford, Elizabeth 1906-2002 ....DLB-155
   Tribute to Alfred A. Knopf Y-84
Longinus circa first century DLB-176
Longley, Michael 1939- DLB-40
T. Longman [publishing house] DLB-154
Longmans, Green and Company DLB-49
Longmore, George 1793?-1867 ....DLB-99
Longstreet, Augustus Baldwin
   1790-1870 ....DLB-3, 11, 74, 248
D. Longworth [publishing house] DLB-49
Lønn, Øystein 1936- DLB-297
Lonsdale, Frederick 1881-1954 ....DLB-10
Loos, Anita 1893-1981..... DLB-11, 26, 228; Y-81
Lopate, Phillip 1943- Y-80
Lope de Rueda 1510?-1565? DLB-318
Lopes, Fernão 1380/1390?-1460? DLB-287
Lopez, Barry 1945- DLB-256, 275
López, Diana (see Isabella, Ríos)
López, Josefina 1969- DLB-209
López de Mendoza, Íñigo
   (see Santillana, Marqués de)
López Velarde, Ramón 1888-1921.......DLB-290
Loranger, Jean-Aubert 1896-1942 ....DLB-92
Lorca, Federico García 1898-1936 ....DLB-108
Lord, John Keast 1818-1872 ....DLB-99
Lorde, Audre 1934-1992 ....DLB-41
Lorimer, George Horace 1867-1937.......DLB-91
A. K. Loring [publishing house]..........DLB-49
Loring and Mussey DLB-46
Lorris, Guillaume de (see *Roman de la Rose*)
Lossing, Benson J. 1813-1891 ....DLB-30
Lothar, Ernst 1890-1974...............DLB-81
D. Lothrop and Company..............DLB-49
Lothrop, Harriet M. 1844-1924..........DLB-42
Loti, Pierre 1850-1923 ....DLB-123
Lotichius Secundus, Petrus 1528-1560.... DLB-179
Lott, Emmeline fl. nineteenth century DLB-166
Louisiana State University Press Y-97
Lounsbury, Thomas R. 1838-1915 ....DLB-71
Louÿs, Pierre 1870-1925 ....DLB-123
Løveid, Cecilie 1951- DLB-297
Lovejoy, Arthur O. 1873-1962..........DLB-270
Lovelace, Earl 1935- DLB-125; CDWLB-3
Lovelace, Richard 1618-1657...........DLB-131

John W. Lovell Company............DLB-49

Lovell, Coryell and Company..........DLB-49

Lover, Samuel 1797-1868..........DLB-159, 190

Lovesey, Peter 1936- DLB-87

    Tribute to Georges Simenon...........Y-89

Lovinescu, Eugen
1881-1943...........DLB-220; CDWLB-4

Lovingood, Sut
(see Harris, George Washington)

Low, Samuel 1765-? DLB-37

Lowell, Amy 1874-1925...........DLB-54, 140

Lowell, James Russell 1819-1891
.......DLB-1, 11, 64, 79, 189, 235; CDALB-2

Lowell, Robert
1917-1977..........DLB-5, 169; CDALB-7

Lowenfels, Walter 1897-1976..............DLB-4

Lowndes, Marie Belloc 1868-1947.......DLB-70

Lowndes, William Thomas 1798-1843...DLB-184

Humphrey Lownes [publishing house]....DLB-170

Lowry, Lois 1937- DLB-52

Lowry, Malcolm 1909-1957 ...DLB-15; CDBLB-7

Lowther, Pat 1935-1975 ....DLB-53

Loy, Mina 1882-1966...............DLB-4, 54

Loynaz, Dulce María 1902-1997.......DLB-283

Lozeau, Albert 1878-1924.............DLB-92

Lu Ling 1923-1994..................DLB-328

Lu Xun 1881-1936...................DLB-328

Lu Yin 1898?-1934..................DLB-328

Lubbock, Percy 1879-1965............DLB-149

Lucan A.D. 39-A.D. 65..............DLB-211

Lucas, E. V. 1868-1938........DLB-98, 149, 153

Fielding Lucas Jr. [publishing house]......DLB-49

Luce, Clare Booth 1903-1987........DLB-228

Luce, Henry R. 1898-1967.............DLB-91

John W. Luce and Company DLB-46

Lucena, Juan de ca. 1430-1501........DLB-286

Lucian circa 120-180.................DLB-176

Lucie-Smith, Edward 1933- DLB-40

Lucilius circa 180 B.C.-102/101 B.C......DLB-211

Lucini, Gian Pietro 1867-1914........DLB-114

Luco Cruchaga, Germán 1894-1936....DLB-305

Lucretius circa 94 B.C.-circa 49 B.C.
..................DLB-211; CDWLB-1

Luder, Peter circa 1415-1472...........DLB-179

Ludlam, Charles 1943-1987..........DLB-266

Ludlum, Robert 1927-2001..............Y-82

Ludus de Antichristo circa 1160...........DLB-148

Ludvigson, Susan 1942- DLB-120

Ludwig, Jack 1922- DLB-60

Ludwig, Otto 1813-1865..............DLB-129

Ludwigslied 881 or 882...............DLB-148

Luera, Yolanda 1953- DLB-122

Luft, Lya 1938- DLB-145

Lugansky, Kazak Vladimir
(see Dal', Vladimir Ivanovich)

Lugn, Kristina 1948- DLB-257

Lugones, Leopoldo 1874-1938........DLB-283

Luhan, Mabel Dodge 1879-1962.......DLB-303

Lukács, Georg (see Lukács, György)

Lukács, György
1885-1971........DLB-215, 242; CDWLB-4

Luke, Peter 1919-1995 ....DLB-13

Lummis, Charles F. 1859-1928........DLB-186

Lundkvist, Artur 1906-1991..........DLB-259

Lunts, Lev Natanovich
1901-1924....................DLB-272

F. M. Lupton Company DLB-49

Lupus of Ferrières
circa 805-circa 862................DLB-148

Lurie, Alison 1926- DLB-2

Lussu, Emilio 1890-1975.............DLB-264

Lustig, Arnošt 1926- DLB-232, 299

Luther, Martin
1483-1546..........DLB-179; CDWLB-2

Luzi, Mario 1914-2005...............DLB-128

L'vov, Nikolai Aleksandrovich
1751-1803....................DLB-150

Lyall, Gavin 1932-2003 ....DLB-87

Lydgate, John circa 1370-1450.........DLB-146

Lyly, John circa 1554-1606........DLB-62, 167

Lynch, Martin 1950- DLB-310

Lynch, Patricia 1898-1972............DLB-160

Lynch, Richard fl. 1596-1601..........DLB-172

Lynd, Robert 1879-1949..............DLB-98

Lynds, Dennis (Michael Collins)
1924- DLB-306

    Tribute to John D. MacDonald.........Y-86

    Tribute to Kenneth Millar.............Y-83

    Why I Write Mysteries: Night and Day...Y-85

Lyon, Matthew 1749-1822.............DLB-43

Lyotard, Jean-François 1924-1998......DLB-242

Lyricists
    Additional Lyricists: 1920-1960.....DLB-265

Lysias circa 459 B.C.-circa 380 B.C........DLB-176

Lytle, Andrew 1902-1995..........DLB-6; Y-95

    Tribute to Caroline Gordon............Y-81

    Tribute to Katherine Anne Porter Y-80

Lytton, Edward
(see Bulwer-Lytton, Edward)

Lytton, Edward Robert Bulwer
1831-1891......................DLB-32

M

Maass, Joachim 1901-1972.............DLB-69

Mabie, Hamilton Wright 1845-1916......DLB-71

Mac A'Ghobhainn, Iain (see Smith, Iain Crichton)

MacArthur, Charles 1895-1956.....DLB-7, 25, 44

Macaulay, Catherine 1731-1791........DLB-104

Macaulay, David 1945- DLB-61

Macaulay, Rose 1881-1958............DLB-36

Macaulay, Thomas Babington
1800-1859..........DLB-32, 55; CDBLB-4

Macaulay Company DLB-46

MacBeth, George 1932-1992...........DLB-40

Macbeth, Madge 1880-1965...........DLB-92

MacCaig, Norman 1910-1996..........DLB-27

MacDiarmid, Hugh
1892-1978...............DLB-20; CDBLB-7

MacDonald, Cynthia 1928- DLB-105

MacDonald, George 1824-1905....DLB-18, 163, 178

MacDonald, John D.
1916-1986.............DLB-8, 306; Y-86

MacDonald, Philip 1899?-1980 ....DLB-77

Macdonald, Ross (see Millar, Kenneth)

Macdonald, Sharman 1951- DLB-245

MacDonald, Wilson 1880-1967 ....DLB-92

Macdonald and Company (Publishers) ..DLB-112

MacEwen, Gwendolyn 1941-1987 ...DLB-53, 251

Macfadden, Bernarr 1868-1955.......DLB-25, 91

MacGregor, John 1825-1892..........DLB-166

MacGregor, Mary Esther (see Keith, Marian)

Macherey, Pierre 1938- DLB-296

Machado, Antonio 1875-1939.........DLB-108

Machado, Manuel 1874-1947..........DLB-108

Machado de Assis, Joaquim Maria
1839-1908.....................DLB-307

Machar, Agnes Maule 1837-1927........DLB-92

Machaut, Guillaume de
circa 1300-1377..................DLB-208

Machen, Arthur Llewelyn Jones
1863-1947..............DLB-36, 156, 178

MacIlmaine, Roland fl. 1574...........DLB-281

MacInnes, Colin 1914-1976............DLB-14

MacInnes, Helen 1907-1985............DLB-87

Mac Intyre, Tom 1931- DLB-245

Mačiulis, Jonas (see Maironis, Jonas)

Mack, Maynard 1909-2001 ....DLB-111

Mackall, Leonard L. 1879-1937........DLB-140

MacKay, Isabel Ecclestone 1875-1928.....DLB-92

Mackay, Shena 1944- DLB-231, 319

MacKaye, Percy 1875-1956............DLB-54

Macken, Walter 1915-1967.............DLB-13

MacKenna, John 1952- DLB-319

Mackenzie, Alexander 1763-1820......DLB-99

Mackenzie, Alexander Slidell
1803-1848....................DLB-183

Mackenzie, Compton 1883-1972.....DLB-34, 100

Mackenzie, Henry 1745-1831..........DLB-39

    The Lounger, no. 20 (1785) DLB-39

Mackenzie, Kenneth (Seaforth Mackenzie) 1913-1955...DLB-260

Mackenzie, William 1758-1828...DLB-187

Mackey, Nathaniel 1947-...DLB-169

Mackey, William Wellington 1937-...DLB-38

Mackintosh, Elizabeth (see Tey, Josephine)

Mackintosh, Sir James 1765-1832...DLB-158

Macklin, Charles 1699-1797...DLB-89

Maclaren, Ian (see Watson, John)

Maclaren-Ross, Julian 1912-1964...DLB-319

MacLaverty, Bernard 1942-...DLB-267

MacLean, Alistair 1922-1987...DLB-276

MacLean, Katherine Anne 1925-...DLB-8

Maclean, Norman 1902-1990...DLB-206

MacLeish, Archibald 1892-1982...DLB-4, 7, 45; Y-82; DS-15; CDALB-7

MacLennan, Hugh 1907-1990...DLB-68

MacLeod, Alistair 1936-...DLB-60

Macleod, Fiona (see Sharp, William)

Macleod, Norman 1906-1985...DLB-4

Mac Low, Jackson 1922-2004...DLB-193

MacMahon, Bryan 1909-1998...DLB-319

Macmillan and Company...DLB-106

The Macmillan Company...DLB-49

Macmillan's English Men of Letters, First Series (1878-1892)...DLB-144

MacNamara, Brinsley 1890-1963...DLB-10

MacNeice, Louis 1907-1963...DLB-10, 20

Macphail, Andrew 1864-1938...DLB-92

Macpherson, James 1736-1796...DLB-109

Macpherson, Jay 1931-...DLB-53

Macpherson, Jeanie 1884-1946...DLB-44

Macrae Smith Company...DLB-46

MacRaye, Lucy Betty (see Webling, Lucy)

John Macrone [publishing house]...DLB-106

MacShane, Frank 1927-1999...DLB-111

Macy-Masius...DLB-46

Madden, David 1933-...DLB-6

Madden, Sir Frederic 1801-1873...DLB-184

Maddow, Ben 1909-1992...DLB-44

Maddux, Rachel 1912-1983...DLB-234; Y-93

Madgett, Naomi Long 1923-...DLB-76

Madhubuti, Haki R. 1942-...DLB-5, 41; DS-8

Madison, James 1751-1836...DLB-37

Madsen, Svend Åge 1939-...DLB-214

Madrigal, Alfonso Fernández de (El Tostado) ca. 1405-1455...DLB-286

Maeterlinck, Maurice 1862-1949...DLB-192

Mafūz, Najīb 1911-...Y-88

Nobel Lecture 1988...Y-88

The Little Magazines of the New Formalism...DLB-282

Magee, David 1905-1977...DLB-187

Maginn, William 1794-1842...DLB-110, 159

Magoffin, Susan Shelby 1827-1855...DLB-239

Mahan, Alfred Thayer 1840-1914...DLB-47

Mahapatra, Jayanta 1928-...DLB-323

Maheux-Forcier, Louise 1929-...DLB-60

Mahin, John Lee 1902-1984...DLB-44

Mahon, Derek 1941-...DLB-40

Maiakovsky, Vladimir Vladimirovich 1893-1930...DLB-295

Maikov, Apollon Nikolaevich 1821-1897...DLB-277

Maikov, Vasilii Ivanovich 1728-1778...DLB-150

Mailer, Norman 1923-...DLB-2, 16, 28, 185, 278; Y-80, 83, 97; DS-3; CDALB-6

Tribute to Isaac Bashevis Singer...Y-91

Tribute to Meyer Levin...Y-81

Maillart, Ella 1903-1997...DLB-195

Maillet, Adrienne 1885-1963...DLB-68

Maillet, Antonine 1929-...DLB-60

Maillu, David G. 1939-...DLB-157

Maimonides, Moses 1138-1204...DLB-115

Main Selections of the Book-of-the-Month Club, 1926-1945...DLB-9

Mainwaring, Daniel 1902-1977...DLB-44

Mair, Charles 1838-1927...DLB-99

Mair, John circa 1467-1550...DLB-281

Maironis, Jonas 1862-1932...DLB-220; CDWLB-4

Mais, Roger 1905-1955...DLB-125; CDWLB-3

Maitland, Sara 1950-...DLB-271

Major, Andre 1942-...DLB-60

Major, Charles 1856-1913...DLB-202

Major, Clarence 1936-...DLB-33

Major, Kevin 1949-...DLB-60

Major Books...DLB-46

Makanin, Vladimir Semenovich 1937-...DLB-285

Makarenko, Anton Semenovich 1888-1939...DLB-272

Makemie, Francis circa 1658-1708...DLB-24

The Making of Americans Contract...Y-98

Makovsky, Sergei 1877-1962...DLB-317

Maksimov, Vladimir Emel'ianovich 1930-1995...DLB-302

Maksimović, Desanka 1898-1993...DLB-147; CDWLB-4

Malamud, Bernard 1914-1986...DLB-2, 28, 152; Y-80, 86; CDALB-1

Bernard Malamud Archive at the Harry Ransom Humanities Research Center...Y-00

Mălăncioiu, Ileana 1940-...DLB-232

Malaparte, Curzio (Kurt Erich Suckert) 1898-1957...DLB-264

Malerba, Luigi 1927-...DLB-196

Malet, Lucas 1852-1931...DLB-153

Malherbe, François de 1555-1628...DLB-327

Mallarmé, Stéphane 1842-1898...DLB-217

Malleson, Lucy Beatrice (see Gilbert, Anthony)

Mallet-Joris, Françoise (Françoise Lilar) 1930-...DLB-83

Mallock, W. H. 1849-1923...DLB-18, 57

"Every Man His Own Poet; or, The Inspired Singer's Recipe Book" (1877)...DLB-35

"Le Style c'est l'homme" (1892)...DLB-57

Memoirs of Life and Literature (1920), [excerpt]...DLB-57

Malone, Dumas 1892-1986...DLB-17

Malone, Edmond 1741-1812...DLB-142

Malory, Sir Thomas circa 1400-1410 - 1471...DLB-146; CDBLB-1

Malouf, David 1934-...DLB-289

Malpede, Karen 1945-...DLB-249

Malraux, André 1901-1976...DLB-72

The Maltese Falcon (Documentary)...DLB-280

Malthus, Thomas Robert 1766-1834...DLB-107, 158

Maltz, Albert 1908-1985...DLB-102

Malzberg, Barry N. 1939-...DLB-8

Mamet, David 1947-...DLB-7

Mamin, Dmitrii Narkisovich 1852-1912...DLB-238

Manaka, Matsemela 1956-...DLB-157

Mañas, José Ángel 1971-...DLB-322

Manchester University Press...DLB-112

Mandel, Eli 1922-1992...DLB-53

Mandel'shtam, Nadezhda Iakovlevna 1899-1980...DLB-302

Mandel'shtam, Osip Emil'evich 1891-1938...DLB-295

Mandeville, Bernard 1670-1733...DLB-101

Mandeville, Sir John mid fourteenth century...DLB-146

Mandiargues, André Pieyre de 1909-1991...DLB-83

Manea, Norman 1936-...DLB-232

Manfred, Frederick 1912-1994...DLB-6, 212, 227

Manfredi, Gianfranco 1948-...DLB-196

Mangan, Sherry 1904-1961...DLB-4

Manganelli, Giorgio 1922-1990...DLB-196

Manilius fl. first century A.D...DLB-211

Mankiewicz, Herman 1897-1953...DLB-26

Mankiewicz, Joseph L. 1909-1993...DLB-44

Mankowitz, Wolf 1924-1998...DLB-15

Manley, Delarivière 1672?-1724...DLB-39, 80

Preface to The Secret History, of Queen Zarah, and the Zarazians (1705)...DLB-39

Mann, Abby 1927-...DLB-44

Cumulative Index

Mann, Charles 1929-1998 . . . . Y-98
Mann, Emily 1952- DLB-266
Mann, Heinrich 1871-1950 . . . . DLB-66, 118
Mann, Horace 1796-1859 . . . . DLB-1, 235
Mann, Klaus 1906-1949 . . . . DLB-56
Mann, Mary Peabody 1806-1887 . . . . DLB-239
Mann, Thomas 1875-1955 . . . DLB-66; CDWLB-2
Mann, William D'Alton 1839-1920 . . . . . DLB-137
Mannin, Ethel 1900-1984 . . . . DLB-191, 195
Manning, Emily (see Australie)
Manning, Frederic 1882-1935 . . . . DLB-260
Manning, Laurence 1899-1972 . . . . DLB-251
Manning, Marie 1873?-1945 . . . . DLB-29
Manning and Loring DLB-49
Mannyng, Robert fl. 1303-1338 . . . . DLB-146
Mano, D. Keith 1942- DLB-6
Manor Books DLB-46
Manrique, Gómez 1412?-1490 . . . . DLB-286
Manrique, Jorge ca. 1440-1479 . . . . DLB-286
Mansfield, Katherine 1888-1923 . . . . DLB-162
Mantel, Hilary 1952- DLB-271
Manuel, Niklaus circa 1484-1530 . . . . DLB-179
Manzini, Gianna 1896-1974 . . . . DLB-177
Mao Dun 1896-1981 . . . . DLB-328
Mapanje, Jack 1944- DLB-157
Maraini, Dacia 1936- DLB-196
Maraise, Marie-Catherine-Renée Darcel de 1737-1822 . . . . DLB-314
Maramzin, Vladimir Rafailovich 1934- DLB-302
March, William (William Edward Campbell) 1893-1954 . . . . DLB-9, 86, 316
Marchand, Leslie A. 1900-1999 . . . . DLB-103
Marchant, Bessie 1862-1941 . . . . DLB-160
Marchant, Tony 1959- DLB-245
Marchenko, Anastasiia Iakovlevna 1830-1880 . . . . DLB-238
Marchessault, Jovette 1938- DLB-60
Marcinkevičius, Justinas 1930- DLB-232
Marcos, Plínio (Plínio Marcos de Barros) 1935-1999 . . . . DLB-307
Marcus, Frank 1928- DLB-13
Marcuse, Herbert 1898-1979 . . . . DLB-242
Marden, Orison Swett 1850-1924 . . . . DLB-137
Marechera, Dambudzo 1952-1987 . . . . . . DLB-157
Marek, Richard, Books DLB-46
Mares, E. A. 1938- DLB-122
Marguerite de Navarre 1492-1549 . . . . . . DLB-327
Margulies, Donald 1954- DLB-228
Mariana, Juan de 1535 or 1536-1624 . . . . DLB-318
Mariani, Paul 1940- DLB-111

Marías, Javier 1951- DLB-322
Marie de France fl. 1160-1178 . . . . DLB-208
Marie-Victorin, Frère (Conrad Kirouac) 1885-1944 . . . . DLB-92
Marin, Biagio 1891-1985 . . . . DLB-128
Marinetti, Filippo Tommaso 1876-1944 . . . . DLB-114, 264
Marinina, Aleksandra (Marina Anatol'evna Alekseeva) 1957- DLB-285
Marinković, Ranko 1913-2001 . . . . DLB-147; CDWLB-4
Marion, Frances 1886-1973 . . . . DLB-44
Marius, Richard C. 1933-1999 . . . . Y-85
Marivaux, Pierre Carlet de Chamblain de 1688-1763 . . . . DLB-314
Markandaya, Kamala 1924-2004 . . . . DLB-323
Markevich, Boleslav Mikhailovich 1822-1884 . . . . DLB-238
Markfield, Wallace 1926-2002 . . . . DLB-2, 28
Markham, E. A. 1939- DLB-319
Markham, Edwin 1852-1940 . . . . DLB-54, 186
Markish, David 1938- DLB-317
Markle, Fletcher 1921-1991 . . . . DLB-68; Y-91
Marlatt, Daphne 1942- DLB-60
Marlitt, E. 1825-1887 . . . . DLB-129
Marlowe, Christopher 1564-1593 . . . . DLB-62; CDBLB-1
Marlyn, John 1912-1985 . . . . DLB-88
Marmion, Shakerley 1603-1639 . . . . DLB-58
Marmontel, Jean-François 1723-1799 . . . . DLB-314
Der Marner before 1230-circa 1287 . . . . . DLB-138
Marnham, Patrick 1943- DLB-204
Marot, Clément 1496-1544 . . . . DLB-327
The *Marprelate Tracts* 1588-1589 . . . . DLB-132
Marquand, John P. 1893-1960 . . . . DLB-9, 102
Marques, Helena 1935- DLB-287
Marqués, René 1919-1979 . . . . DLB-113, 305
Marquis, Don 1878-1937 . . . . DLB-11, 25
Marriott, Anne 1913-1997 . . . . DLB-68
Marryat, Frederick 1792-1848 . . . . DLB-21, 163
Marsé, Juan 1933- DLB-322
Marsh, Capen, Lyon and Webb DLB-49
Marsh, George Perkins 1801-1882 . . . . DLB-1, 64, 243
Marsh, James 1794-1842 . . . . DLB-1, 59
Marsh, Narcissus 1638-1713 . . . . DLB-213
Marsh, Ngaio 1899-1982 . . . . DLB-77
Marshall, Alan 1902-1984 . . . . DLB-260
Marshall, Edison 1894-1967 . . . . DLB-102
Marshall, Edward 1932- DLB-16
Marshall, Emma 1828-1899 . . . . DLB-163
Marshall, James 1942-1992 . . . . DLB-61
Marshall, Joyce 1913- DLB-88

Marshall, Paule 1929- DLB-33, 157, 227
Marshall, Tom 1938-1993 . . . . DLB-60
Marsilius of Padua circa 1275-circa 1342 . . . . DLB-115
Mars-Jones, Adam 1954- DLB-207, 319
Marson, Una 1905-1965 . . . . DLB-157
Marston, John 1576-1634 . . . . DLB-58, 172
Marston, Philip Bourke 1850-1887 . . . . . . DLB-35
Martel, Yann 1963- DLB-326
Martens, Kurt 1870-1945 . . . . DLB-66
Martí, José 1853-1895 . . . . DLB-290
Martial circa A.D. 40-circa A.D. 103 . . . . DLB-211; CDWLB-1
William S. Martien [publishing house] . . . DLB-49
Martin, Abe (see Hubbard, Kin)
Martin, Catherine ca. 1847-1937 . . . . DLB-230
Martin, Charles 1942- DLB-120, 282
Martin, Claire 1914- DLB-60
Martin, David 1915-1997 . . . . DLB-260
Martin, Jay 1935- DLB-111
Martin, Johann (see Laurentius von Schnüffis)
Martin, Thomas 1696-1771 . . . . DLB-213
Martin, Violet Florence (see Ross, Martin)
Martin du Gard, Roger 1881-1958 . . . . . . DLB-65
Martineau, Harriet 1802-1876 . . . . . DLB-21, 55, 159, 163, 166, 190
Martínez, Demetria 1960- DLB-209
Martínez de Toledo, Alfonso 1398?-1468 . . . . DLB-286
Martínez, Eliud 1935- DLB-122
Martínez, Max 1943- DLB-82
Martínez, Rubén 1962- DLB-209
Martín Gaite, Carmen 1925-2000 . . . . . . DLB-322
Martín-Santos, Luis 1924-1964 . . . . DLB-322
Martinson, Harry 1904-1978 . . . . DLB-259
Martinson, Moa 1890-1964 . . . . DLB-259
Martone, Michael 1955- DLB-218
Martyn, Edward 1859-1923 . . . . DLB-10
Marvell, Andrew 1621-1678 . . . . DLB-131; CDBLB-2
Marvin X 1944- DLB-38
Marx, Karl 1818-1883 . . . . DLB-129
Marzials, Theo 1850-1920 . . . . DLB-35
Masefield, John 1878-1967 . . . . DLB-10, 19, 153, 160; CDBLB-5
Masham, Damaris Cudworth, Lady 1659-1708 . . . . DLB-252
Masino, Paola 1908-1989 . . . . DLB-264
Mason, A. E. W. 1865-1948 . . . . DLB-70
Mason, Bobbie Ann 1940- DLB-173; Y-87; CDALB-7
Mason, F. van Wyck (Geoffrey Coffin, Frank W. Mason, Ward Weaver) 1901-1978 . . . . DLB-306

Mason, William 1725-1797............DLB-142

Mason Brothers....................DLB-49

The Massachusetts Quarterly Review
1847-1850......................DLB-1

The Masses......................DLB-303

Massey, Gerald 1828-1907............DLB-32

Massey, Linton R. 1900-1974..........DLB-187

Massie, Allan 1938-................DLB-271

Massinger, Philip 1583-1640.........DLB-58

Masson, David 1822-1907............DLB-144

Masters, Edgar Lee
1868-1950.............DLB-54; CDALB-3

Masters, Hilary 1928-..............DLB-244

Masters, Olga 1919-1986.............DLB-325

Mastronardi, Lucio 1930-1979.........DLB-177

Mat' Maria (Elizaveta Kuz'mina-Karavdeva
Skobtsova, née Pilenko) 1891-1945....DLB-317

Matevski, Mateja 1929-...DLB-181; CDWLB-4

Mather, Cotton
1663-1728.......DLB-24, 30, 140; CDALB-2

Mather, Increase 1639-1723...........DLB-24

Mather, Richard 1596-1669...........DLB-24

Matheson, Annie 1853-1924...........DLB-240

Matheson, Richard 1926-..........DLB-8, 44

Matheus, John F. 1887-1986...........DLB-51

Mathews, Aidan 1956-...............DLB-319

Mathews, Cornelius 1817?-1889...DLB-3, 64, 250

Elkin Mathews [publishing house].......DLB-112

Mathews, John Joseph 1894-1979.......DLB-175

Mathias, Roland 1915-..............DLB-27

Mathis, June 1892-1927..............DLB-44

Mathis, Sharon Bell 1937-..........DLB-33

Matković, Marijan 1915-1985..........DLB-181

Matoš, Antun Gustav 1873-1914.......DLB-147

Matos Paoli, Francisco 1915-2000......DLB-290

Matsumoto Seichō 1909-1992..........DLB-182

The Matter of England 1240-1400......DLB-146

The Matter of Rome early twelfth to late
fifteenth century................DLB-146

Matthew of Vendôme
circa 1130-circa 1200..............DLB-208

Matthews, Brander 1852-1929..DLB-71, 78; DS-13

Matthews, Brian 1936-..............DLB-325

Matthews, Jack 1925-...............DLB-6

Matthews, Victoria Earle 1861-1907....DLB-221

Matthews, William 1942-1997..........DLB-5

Matthías Jochumsson 1835-1920........DLB-293

Matthías Johannessen 1930-..........DLB-293

Matthiessen, F. O. 1902-1950.........DLB-63

Matthiessen, Peter 1927-......DLB-6, 173, 275

Maturin, Charles Robert 1780-1824.....DLB-178

Matute, Ana María 1926-.............DLB-322

Maugham, W. Somerset 1874-1965
....DLB-10, 36, 77, 100, 162, 195; CDBLB-6

Maupassant, Guy de 1850-1893........DLB-123

Maupertuis, Pierre-Louis Moreau de
1698-1759....................DLB-314

Maupin, Armistead 1944-............DLB-278

Mauriac, Claude 1914-1996...........DLB-83

Mauriac, François 1885-1970..........DLB-65

Maurice, Frederick Denison 1805-1872....DLB-55

Maurois, André 1885-1967............DLB-65

Maury, James 1718-1769..............DLB-31

Mavor, Elizabeth 1927-.............DLB-14

Mavor, Osborne Henry (see Bridie, James)

Maxwell, Gavin 1914-1969............DLB-204

Maxwell, William
1908-2000............DLB-218, 278; Y-80

Tribute to Nancy Hale...............Y-88

H. Maxwell [publishing house].........DLB-49

John Maxwell [publishing house].......DLB-106

May, Elaine 1932-..................DLB-44

May, Karl 1842-1912................DLB-129

May, Thomas 1595/1596-1650..........DLB-58

Mayer, Bernadette 1945-............DLB-165

Mayer, Mercer 1943-................DLB-61

Mayer, O. B. 1818-1891.............DLB-3, 248

Mayes, Herbert R. 1900-1987.........DLB-137

Mayes, Wendell 1919-1992............DLB-26

Mayfield, Julian 1928-1984......DLB-33; Y-84

Mayhew, Henry 1812-1887.....DLB-18, 55, 190

Mayhew, Jonathan 1720-1766..........DLB-31

Mayne, Ethel Colburn 1865-1941.......DLB-197

Mayne, Jasper 1604-1672.............DLB-126

Mayne, Seymour 1944-...............DLB-60

Mayor, Flora Macdonald 1872-1932.....DLB-36

Mayröcker, Friederike 1924-..........DLB-85

Mazrui, Ali A. 1933-................DLB-125

Mažuranić, Ivan 1814-1890...........DLB-147

Mazursky, Paul 1930-................DLB-44

McAlmon, Robert 1896-1956...DLB-4, 45; DS-15

"A Night at Bricktop's"..............Y-01

McArthur, Peter 1866-1924...........DLB-92

McAuley, James 1917-1976...........DLB-260

Robert M. McBride and Company........DLB-46

McCabe, Patrick 1955-..............DLB-194

McCafferty, Owen 1961-.............DLB-310

McCaffrey, Anne 1926-..............DLB-8

McCann, Colum 1965-................DLB-267

McCarthy, Cormac 1933-.....DLB-6, 143, 256

The Cormac McCarthy Society..........Y-99

McCarthy, Mary 1912-1989........DLB-2; Y-81

McCarthy, Shaun Lloyd (see Cory, Desmond)

McCay, Winsor 1871-1934.............DLB-22

McClane, Albert Jules 1922-1991.......DLB-171

McClatchy, C. K. 1858-1936...........DLB-25

McClellan, George Marion 1860-1934....DLB-50

"The Negro as a Writer"............DLB-50

McCloskey, Robert 1914-2003.........DLB-22

McCloy, Helen 1904-1992............DLB-306

McClung, Nellie Letitia 1873-1951.....DLB-92

McClure, James 1939-...............DLB-276

McClure, Joanna 1930-..............DLB-16

McClure, Michael 1932-.............DLB-16

McClure, Phillips and Company........DLB-46

McClure, S. S. 1857-1949............DLB-91

A. C. McClurg and Company..........DLB-49

McCluskey, John A., Jr. 1944-........DLB-33

McCollum, Michael A. 1946-..........Y-87

McConnell, William C. 1917-.........DLB-88

McCord, David 1897-1997............DLB-61

McCord, Louisa S. 1810-1879.........DLB-248

McCorkle, Jill 1958-..........DLB-234; Y-87

McCorkle, Samuel Eusebius 1746-1811....DLB-37

McCormick, Anne O'Hare 1880-1954....DLB-29

McCormick, Kenneth Dale 1906-1997....Y-97

McCormick, Robert R. 1880-1955......DLB-29

McCourt, Edward 1907-1972...........DLB-88

McCoy, Horace 1897-1955............DLB-9

McCrae, Hugh 1876-1958............DLB-260

McCrae, John 1872-1918.............DLB-92

McCrumb, Sharyn 1948-.............DLB-306

McCullagh, Joseph B. 1842-1896......DLB-23

McCullers, Carson
1917-1967.....DLB-2, 7, 173, 228; CDALB-1

McCulloch, Thomas 1776-1843.........DLB-99

McCunn, Ruthanne Lum 1946-.........DLB-312

McDermott, Alice 1953-.............DLB-292

McDonald, Forrest 1927-............DLB-17

McDonald, Walter 1934-.......DLB-105, DS-9

"Getting Started: Accepting the
Regions You Own—or Which
Own You"....................DLB-105

Tribute to James Dickey..............Y-97

McDougall, Colin 1917-1984..........DLB-68

McDowell, Katharine Sherwood Bonner
1849-1883..................DLB-202, 239

Obolensky McDowell
[publishing house]................DLB-46

McEwan, Ian 1948-......DLB-14, 194, 319, 326

McFadden, David 1940-..............DLB-60

McFall, Frances Elizabeth Clarke
(see Grand, Sarah)

McFarland, Ron 1942-...............DLB-256

McFarlane, Leslie 1902-1977..........DLB-88

McFee, William 1881-1966............ DLB-153

McGahan, Andrew 1966-........... DLB-325

McGahern, John 1934-...... DLB-14, 231, 319

McGee, Thomas D'Arcy 1825-1868...... DLB-99

McGeehan, W. O. 1879-1933........DLB-25, 171

McGill, Ralph 1898-1969............. DLB-29

McGinley, Phyllis 1905-1978........ DLB-11, 48

McGinniss, Joe 1942-............... DLB-185

McGirt, James E. 1874-1930........... DLB-50

McGlashan and Gill................. DLB-106

McGough, Roger 1937-.............. DLB-40

McGrath, John 1935-............... DLB-233

McGrath, Patrick 1950-............ DLB-231

McGraw-Hill...................... DLB-46

McGuane, Thomas 1939-..... DLB-2, 212; Y-80

    Tribute to Seymour Lawrence.......... Y-94

McGuckian, Medbh 1950-........... DLB-40

McGuffey, William Holmes 1800-1873.... DLB-42

McGuinness, Frank 1953-............ DLB-245

McHenry, James 1785-1845........... DLB-202

McIlvanney, William 1936-....... DLB-14, 207

McIlwraith, Jean Newton 1859-1938..... DLB-92

McInerney, Jay 1955-............... DLB-292

McInerny, Ralph 1929-............. DLB-306

McIntosh, Maria Jane 1803-1878... DLB-239, 248

McIntyre, James 1827-1906.......... DLB-99

McIntyre, O. O. 1884-1938........... DLB-25

McKay, Claude 1889-1948..... DLB-4, 45, 51, 117

The David McKay Company.......... DLB-49

McKean, William V. 1820-1903........ DLB-23

McKenna, Stephen 1888-1967........ DLB-197

The McKenzie Trust.................. Y-96

McKerrow, R. B. 1872-1940........... DLB-201

McKinley, Robin 1952-.............. DLB-52

McKnight, Reginald 1956-.......... DLB-234

McLachlan, Alexander 1818-1896....... DLB-99

McLaren, Floris Clark 1904-1978........ DLB-68

McLaverty, Michael 1907-1992.......... DLB-15

McLean, Duncan 1964-............. DLB-267

McLean, John R. 1848-1916............ DLB-23

McLean, William L. 1852-1931........ DLB-25

McLennan, William 1856-1904......... DLB-92

McLoughlin Brothers................ DLB-49

McLuhan, Marshall 1911-1980......... DLB-88

McMaster, John Bach 1852-1932........ DLB-47

McMillan, Terri 1951-............... DLB-292

McMurtry, Larry 1936-
    ....DLB-2, 143, 256; Y-80, 87; CDALB-6

McNally, Terrence 1939-.........DLB-7, 249

McNeil, Florence 1937-............. DLB-60

McNeile, Herman Cyril 1888-1937...... DLB-77

McNickle, D'Arcy 1904-1977.......DLB-175, 212

McPhee, John 1931-............DLB-185, 275

McPherson, James Alan 1943-..... DLB-38, 244

McPherson, Sandra 1943-.............. Y-86

McTaggart, J. M. E. 1866-1925......... DLB-262

McWhirter, George 1939-........... DLB-60

McWilliam, Candia 1955-........... DLB-267

McWilliams, Carey 1905-1980......... DLB-137

    "*The Nation's* Future." Carey
    McWilliams's Editorial Policy
    in *Nation*.................... DLB-137

Mda, Zakes 1948-................. DLB-225

Mead, George Herbert 1863-1931.......DLB-270

Mead, L. T. 1844-1914.............. DLB-141

Mead, Matthew 1924-.............. DLB-40

Mead, Taylor circa 1931-............ DLB-16

Meany, Tom 1903-1964..............DLB-171

Mears, Gillian 1964-................ DLB-325

Mechthild von Magdeburg
    circa 1207-circa 1282............. DLB-138

Medieval Galician-Portuguese Poetry.... DLB-287

Medill, Joseph 1823-1899............. DLB-43

Medoff, Mark 1940-................. DLB-7

Meek, Alexander Beaufort
    1814-1865.................. DLB-3, 248

Meeke, Mary ?-1816................ DLB-116

Mehta, Ved 1934-................. DLB-323

Mei, Lev Aleksandrovich 1822-1862.....DLB-277

Meinke, Peter 1932-................. DLB-5

Meireles, Cecília 1901-1964.......... DLB-307

Mejía, Pedro 1497-1551............. DLB-318

Mejia Vallejo, Manuel 1923-......... DLB-113

Melanchthon, Philipp 1497-1560.......DLB-179

Melançon, Robert 1947-............. DLB-60

Mell, Max 1882-1971............. DLB-81, 124

Mellow, James R. 1926-1997.......... DLB-111

Mel'nikov, Pavel Ivanovich 1818-1883... DLB-238

Meltzer, David 1937-................ DLB-16

Meltzer, Milton 1915-............... DLB-61

Melville, Elizabeth, Lady Culross
    circa 1585-1640.................DLB-172

Melville, Herman
    1819-1891....... DLB-3, 74, 250; CDALB-2

    The Melville Society................ Y-01

Melville, James
    (Roy Peter Martin) 1931-........DLB-276

"Memorandum on Local Government," Anne-
    Robert-Jacques Turgot, bacon de
    l'Aulne...................... DLB-314

Mena, Juan de 1411-1456............ DLB-286

Mena, María Cristina 1893-1965... DLB-209, 221

Menander 342-341 B.C.-circa 292-291 B.C.
    ....DLB-176; CDWLB-1

Menantes (see Hunold, Christian Friedrich)

Mencke, Johann Burckhard 1674-1732... DLB-168

Mencken, H. L. 1880-1956
    ....DLB-11, 29, 63, 137, 222; CDALB-4

    "Berlin, February, 1917"............... Y-00

    From the Initial Issue of *American Mercury*
    (January 1924)................DLB-137

    Mencken and Nietzsche: An
    Unpublished Excerpt from H. L.
    Mencken's *My Life as Author and
    Editor*...................... Y-93

Mendelssohn, Moses 1729-1786........ DLB-97

Mendes, Catulle 1841-1909............DLB-217

Méndez M., Miguel 1930-........... DLB-82

Mendoza, Diego Hurtado de
    1504-1575.................... DLB-318

Mendoza, Eduardo 1943-........... DLB-322

The Mercantile Library of New York........ Y-96

Mercer, Cecil William (see Yates, Dornford)

Mercer, David 1928-1980..........DLB-13, 310

Mercer, John 1704-1768............. DLB-31

Mercer, Johnny 1909-1976........... DLB-265

Mercier, Louis-Sébastien 1740-1814..... DLB-314

    Le Tableau de Paris............... DLB-314

Meredith, George
    1828-1909....DLB-18, 35, 57, 159; CDBLB-4

Meredith, Louisa Anne 1812-1895.. DLB-166, 230

Meredith, Owen
    (see Lytton, Edward Robert Bulwer)

Meredith, William 1919-.............. DLB-5

Meres, Francis
    Palladis Tamia, Wits Treasurie (1598)
    [excerpt].....................DLB-172

Merezhkovsky, Dmitrii Sergeevich
    1865-1941.................... DLB-295

Mergerle, Johann Ulrich
    (see Abraham ä Sancta Clara)

Mérimée, Prosper 1803-1870.......DLB-119, 192

Merino, José María 1941-........... DLB-322

Merivale, John Herman 1779-1844....... DLB-96

Meriwether, Louise 1923-............ DLB-33

Merleau-Ponty, Maurice 1908-1961.... DLB-296

Merlin Press....................... DLB-112

Merriam, Eve 1916-1992............. DLB-61

The Merriam Company............... DLB-49

Merril, Judith 1923-1997............. DLB-251

    Tribute to Theodore Sturgeon......... Y-85

Merrill, James 1926-1995.......DLB-5, 165; Y-85

Merrill and Baker................... DLB-49

The Mershon Company............... DLB-49

Merton, Thomas 1915-1968........DLB-48; Y-81

Merwin, W. S. 1927-............. DLB-5, 169

Julian Messner [publishing house]....... DLB-46

Mészöly, Miklós 1921-.............. DLB-232

J. Metcalf [publishing house]........... DLB-49

Metcalf, John 1938- DLB-60

The Methodist Book Concern..........DLB-49

Methuen and Company...............DLB-112

Meun, Jean de (see *Roman de la Rose*)

Mew, Charlotte 1869-1928 ....DLB-19, 135

Mewshaw, Michael 1943- Y-80

    Tribute to Albert Erskine Y-93

Meyer, Conrad Ferdinand 1825-1898 ....DLB-129

Meyer, E. Y. 1946- DLB-75

Meyer, Eugene 1875-1959 ....DLB-29

Meyer, Michael 1921-2000............DLB-155

Meyers, Jeffrey 1939- DLB-111

Meynell, Alice 1847-1922...........DLB-19, 98

Meynell, Viola 1885-1956 ....DLB-153

Meyrink, Gustav 1868-1932 ....DLB-81

Mézières, Philipe de circa 1327-1405 .....DLB-208

Michael, Ib 1945- DLB-214

Michael, Livi 1960- DLB-267

Michaëlis, Karen 1872-1950 ....DLB-214

Michaels, Anne 1958- DLB-299

Michaels, Leonard 1933-2003 ....DLB-130

Michaux, Henri 1899-1984 ....DLB-258

Micheaux, Oscar 1884-1951 ....DLB-50

Michel of Northgate, Dan
    circa 1265-circa 1340...............DLB-146

Micheline, Jack 1929-1998..............DLB-16

Michener, James A. 1907?-1997 ....DLB-6

Micklejohn, George circa 1717-1818.......DLB-31

Middle Hill Press DLB-106

Middleton, Christopher 1926- DLB-40

Middleton, Richard 1882-1911 ....DLB-156

Middleton, Stanley 1919- DLB-14, 326

Middleton, Thomas 1580-1627 ....DLB-58

Midnight's Children, 1981 Booker Prize winner,
    Salman Rushdie..................DLB-326

Miegel, Agnes 1879-1964 ....DLB-56

Miežėlaitis, Eduardas 1919-1997 ....DLB-220

Miguéis, José Rodrigues 1901-1980......DLB-287

Mihailović, Dragoslav 1930- DLB-181

Mihalić, Slavko 1928- DLB-181

Mikhailov, A.
    (see Sheller, Aleksandr Konstantinovich)

Mikhailov, Mikhail Larionovich
    1829-1865 ....DLB-238

Mikhailovsky, Nikolai Konstantinovich
    1842-1904.....................DLB-277

Miles, Josephine 1911-1985 ....DLB-48

Miles, Susan (Ursula Wyllie Roberts)
    1888-1975 ....DLB-240

Miliković, Branko 1934-1961............DLB-181

Milius, John 1944- DLB-44

Mill, James 1773-1836 .... DLB-107, 158, 262

Mill, John Stuart
    1806-1873 ......DLB-55, 190, 262; CDBLB-4

    Thoughts on Poetry and Its Varieties
    (1833) DLB-32

Andrew Millar [publishing house] DLB-154

Millar, Kenneth
    1915-1983 .... DLB-2, 226; Y-83; DS-6

Millás, Juan José 1946- DLB-322

Millay, Edna St. Vincent
    1892-1950 ....DLB-45, 249; CDALB-4

Millen, Sarah Gertrude 1888-1968 ......DLB-225

Miller, Andrew 1960- DLB-267

Miller, Arthur 1915-2005... DLB-7, 266; CDALB-1

    The Arthur Miller Society...............Y-01

Miller, Caroline 1903-1992 ....DLB-9

Miller, Eugene Ethelbert 1950- DLB-41

    Tribute to Julian Mayfield Y-84

Miller, Heather Ross 1939- DLB-120

Miller, Henry
    1891-1980 .... DLB-4, 9; Y-80; CDALB-5

Miller, Hugh 1802-1856................DLB-190

Miller, J. Hillis 1928- DLB-67

Miller, Jason 1939- DLB-7

Miller, Joaquin 1839-1913 ....DLB-186

Miller, May 1899-1995.................DLB-41

Miller, Paul 1906-1991 ....DLB-127

Miller, Perry 1905-1963 .... DLB-17, 63

Miller, Sue 1943- DLB-143

Miller, Vassar 1924-1998 ....DLB-105

Miller, Walter M., Jr. 1923-1996 ....DLB-8

Miller, Webb 1892-1940................DLB-29

James Miller [publishing house] DLB-49

Millett, Kate 1934- DLB-246

Millhauser, Steven 1943- DLB-2

Millican, Arthenia J. Bates 1920- DLB-38

Milligan, Alice 1866-1953 ....DLB-240

Mills, Magnus 1954- DLB-267

Mills and Boon DLB-112

Milman, Henry Hart 1796-1868 ....DLB-96

Milne, A. A. 1882-1956 ..... DLB-10, 77, 100, 160

Milner, Ron 1938- DLB-38

William Milner [publishing house].......DLB-106

Milnes, Richard Monckton (Lord Houghton)
    1809-1885 ....DLB-32, 184

Milton, John
    1608-1674 .....DLB-131, 151, 281; CDBLB-2

    The Milton Society of America..........Y-00

Miłosz, Czesław
    1911-2004.............DLB-215; CDWLB-4

Minakami Tsutomu 1919- DLB-182

Minamoto no Sanetomo 1192-1219......DLB-203

Minco, Marga 1920- DLB-299

The Minerva Press....................DLB-154

Minnesang circa 1150-1280 ....DLB-138

    The Music of *Minnesang* DLB-138

Minns, Susan 1839-1938 ....DLB-140

Minsky, Nikolai 1855-1937 ....DLB-317

Minton, Balch and Company DLB-46

Minyana, Philippe 1946- DLB-321

Mirbeau, Octave 1848-1917........DLB-123, 192

Mirikitani, Janice 1941- DLB-312

Mirk, John died after 1414?............DLB-146

Miró, Gabriel 1879-1930 ....DLB-322

Miró, Ricardo 1883-1940...............DLB-290

Miron, Gaston 1928-1996 ....DLB-60

A Mirror for Magistrates DLB-167

Mirsky, D. S. 1890-1939 ....DLB-317

Mishima Yukio 1925-1970 ....DLB-182

Mistral, Gabriela 1889-1957 ....DLB-283

Mitchel, Jonathan 1624-1668............DLB-24

Mitchell, Adrian 1932- DLB-40

Mitchell, Donald Grant
    1822-1908 ....DLB-1, 243; DS-13

Mitchell, Gladys 1901-1983.............DLB-77

Mitchell, James Leslie 1901-1935.........DLB-15

Mitchell, John (see Slater, Patrick)

Mitchell, John Ames 1845-1918..........DLB-79

Mitchell, Joseph 1908-1996 .... DLB-185; Y-96

Mitchell, Julian 1935- DLB-14

Mitchell, Ken 1940- DLB-60

Mitchell, Langdon 1862-1935 ....DLB-7

Mitchell, Loften 1919-2001 ....DLB-38

Mitchell, Margaret 1900-1949 ...DLB-9; CDALB-7

Mitchell, S. Weir 1829-1914............DLB-202

Mitchell, Sue 1943- (see Miller)

Mitchell, W. J. T. 1942- DLB-246

Mitchell, W. O. 1914-1998 ....DLB-88

Mitchison, Naomi Margaret (Haldane)
    1897-1999 .... DLB-160, 191, 255, 319

Mitford, Mary Russell 1787-1855.... DLB-110, 116

Mitford, Nancy 1904-1973..............DLB-191

Mittelholzer, Edgar
    1909-1965 ....DLB-117; CDWLB-3

Mitterer, Erika 1906-2001 ....DLB-85

Mitterer, Felix 1948- DLB-124

Mitternacht, Johann Sebastian
    1613-1679 ....DLB-168

Miyamoto Yuriko 1899-1951 ....DLB-180

Mizener, Arthur 1907-1988 ....DLB-103

Mo, Timothy 1950- DLB-194

Moberg, Vilhelm 1898-1973 ....DLB-259

Modern Age Books DLB-46

Modern Language Association of America
    The Modern Language Association of
    America Celebrates Its Centennial ...Y-84

The Modern Library DLB-46

Modiano, Patrick 1945- DLB-83, 299

Modjeska, Drusilla 1946- DLB-325

Moffat, Yard and Company DLB-46

Moffet, Thomas 1553-1604 .... DLB-136

Mofolo, Thomas 1876-1948 .... DLB-225

Mohr, Nicholasa 1938- DLB-145

Moix, Ana María 1947- DLB-134

Molesworth, Louisa 1839-1921 .... DLB-135

Molière (Jean-Baptiste Poquelin)
1622-1673 .... DLB-268

Møller, Poul Martin 1794-1838 .... DLB-300

Möllhausen, Balduin 1825-1905 .... DLB-129

Molnár, Ferenc 1878-1952 ... DLB-215; CDWLB-4

Molnár, Miklós (see Mészöly, Miklós)

Momaday, N. Scott
1934- DLB-143, 175, 256; CDALB-7

Monkhouse, Allan 1858-1936 .... DLB-10

Monro, Harold 1879-1932 .... DLB-19

Monroe, Harriet 1860-1936 .... DLB-54, 91

Monsarrat, Nicholas 1910-1979 .... DLB-15

Montagu, Lady Mary Wortley
1689-1762 .... DLB-95, 101

Montague, C. E. 1867-1928 .... DLB-197

Montague, John 1929- DLB-40

Montaigne, Michel de 1533-1592 .... DLB-327

Montale, Eugenio 1896-1981 .... DLB-114

Montalvo, Garci Rodríguez de
ca. 1450?-before 1505 .... DLB-286

Montalvo, José 1946-1994 .... DLB-209

Montemayor, Jorge de 1521?-1561? DLB-318

Montero, Rosa 1951- DLB-322

Monterroso, Augusto 1921-2003 .... DLB-145

Montesquieu, Charles-Louis de Secondat, baron de
1689-1755 .... DLB-314

The Spirit of Laws DLB-314

Montesquiou, Robert de 1855-1921 ..... DLB-217

Montgomerie, Alexander
circa 1550?-1598 .... DLB-167

Montgomery, James 1771-1854 ...... DLB-93, 158

Montgomery, John 1919- DLB-16

Montgomery, Lucy Maud
1874-1942 .... DLB-92; DS-14

Montgomery, Marion 1925- DLB-6

Montgomery, Robert Bruce (see Crispin, Edmund)

Montherlant, Henry de 1896-1972 ... DLB-72, 321

The Monthly Review 1749-1844 .... DLB-110

Monti, Ricardo 1944- DLB-305

Montigny, Louvigny de 1876-1955 .... DLB-92

Montoya, José 1932- DLB-122

Moodie, John Wedderburn Dunbar
1797-1869 .... DLB-99

Moodie, Susanna 1803-1885 .... DLB-99

Moody, Joshua circa 1633-1697 .... DLB-24

Moody, William Vaughn 1869-1910 ..... DLB-7, 54

Moon Tiger, 1987 Booker Prize winner,
Penelope Lively DLB-326

Moorcock, Michael 1939- ... DLB-14, 231, 261, 319

Moore, Alan 1953- DLB-261

Moore, Brian 1921-1999 .... DLB-251

Moore, Catherine L. 1911-1987 .... DLB-8

Moore, Clement Clarke 1779-1863 .... DLB-42

Moore, Dora Mavor 1888-1979 .... DLB-92

Moore, G. E. 1873-1958 .... DLB-262

Moore, George 1852-1933 .... DLB-10, 18, 57, 135

Literature at Nurse, or Circulating Morals
(1885) DLB-18

Moore, Lorrie 1957- DLB-234

Moore, Marianne
1887-1972 .... DLB-45; DS-7; CDALB-5

International Marianne Moore Society ... Y-98

Moore, Mavor 1919- DLB-88

Moore, Richard 1927- DLB-105

"The No Self, the Little Self, and
the Poets" DLB-105

Moore, T. Sturge 1870-1944 .... DLB-19

Moore, Thomas 1779-1852 .... DLB-96, 144

Moore, Ward 1903-1978 .... DLB-8

Moore, Wilstach, Keys and Company DLB-49

Moorehead, Alan 1901-1983 .... DLB-204

Moorhouse, Frank 1938- DLB-289

Moorhouse, Geoffrey 1931- DLB-204

Moorish Novel of the Sixteenth
Century, The DLB-318

The Moorland-Spingarn Research
Center DLB-76

Moorman, Mary C. 1905-1994 .... DLB-155

Mora, Pat 1942- DLB-209

Moraes, Dom 1938-2004 .... DLB-323

Moraes, Vinicius de 1913-1980 .... DLB-307

Moraga, Cherríe 1952- DLB-82, 249

Morales, Alejandro 1944- DLB-82

Morales, Mario Roberto 1947- DLB-145

Morales, Rafael 1919- DLB-108

Morality Plays: Mankind circa 1450-1500
and Everyman circa 1500 .... DLB-146

Morand, Paul (1888-1976) DLB-65

Morante, Elsa 1912-1985 .... DLB-177

Morata, Olympia Fulvia 1526-1555 ..... DLB-179

Moravia, Alberto 1907-1990 .... DLB-177

Mordaunt, Elinor 1872-1942 .... DLB-174

Mordovtsev, Daniil Lukich 1830-1905 ... DLB-238

More, Hannah
1745-1833 .... DLB-107, 109, 116, 158

More, Henry 1614-1687 .... DLB-126, 252

More, Sir Thomas
1477/1478-1535 .... DLB-136, 281

Morejón, Nancy 1944- DLB-283

Morellet, André 1727-1819 .... DLB-314

Morency, Pierre 1942- DLB-60

Moreno, Dorinda 1939- DLB-122

Moretti, Marino 1885-1979 .... DLB-114, 264

Morgan, Berry 1919-2002 .... DLB-6

Morgan, Charles 1894-1958 .... DLB-34, 100

Morgan, Edmund S. 1916- DLB-17

Morgan, Edwin 1920- DLB-27

Morgan, John Pierpont 1837-1913 ...... DLB-140

Morgan, John Pierpont, Jr. 1867-1943 ... DLB-140

Morgan, Robert 1944- DLB-120, 292

Morgan, Sally 1951- DLB-325

Morgan, Sydney Owenson, Lady
1776?-1859 .... DLB-116, 158

Morgner, Irmtraud 1933-1990 .... DLB-75

Morhof, Daniel Georg 1639-1691 .... DLB-164

Mori, Kyoko 1957- DLB-312

Mori Ōgai 1862-1922 .... DLB-180

Mori, Toshio 1910-1980 .... DLB-312

Móricz, Zsigmond 1879-1942 .... DLB-215

Morier, James Justinian
1782 or 1783?-1849 .... DLB-116

Mörike, Eduard 1804-1875 .... DLB-133

Morin, Paul 1889-1963 .... DLB-92

Morison, Richard 1514?-1556 .... DLB-136

Morison, Samuel Eliot 1887-1976 .... DLB-17

Morison, Stanley 1889-1967 .... DLB-201

Moritz, Karl Philipp 1756-1793 .... DLB-94

Moriz von Craûn circa 1220-1230 .... DLB-138

Morley, Christopher 1890-1957 .... DLB-9

Morley, John 1838-1923 .... DLB-57, 144, 190

Moro, César 1903-1956 .... DLB-290

Morris, George Pope 1802-1864 .... DLB-73

Morris, James Humphrey (see Morris, Jan)

Morris, Jan 1926- DLB-204

Morris, Lewis 1833-1907 .... DLB-35

Morris, Margaret 1737-1816 .... DLB-200

Morris, Mary McGarry 1943- DLB-292

Morris, Richard B. 1904-1989 .... DLB-17

Morris, William 1834-1896
..... DLB-18, 35, 57, 156, 178, 184; CDBLB-4

Morris, Willie 1934-1999 .... Y-80

Tribute to Irwin Shaw Y-84

Tribute to James Dickey Y-97

Morris, Wright
1910-1998 .... DLB-2, 206, 218; Y-81

Morrison, Arthur 1863-1945 .... DLB-70, 135, 197

Morrison, Charles Clayton 1874-1966 .... DLB-91

Morrison, John 1904-1998 .... DLB-260

Morrison, Toni 1931-
.... DLB-6, 33, 143; Y-81, 93; CDALB-6

Nobel Lecture 1993 .... Y-93

Morrissy, Mary 1957- DLB-267

William Morrow and Company DLB-46

Morse, James Herbert 1841-1923 ....DLB-71

Morse, Jedidiah 1761-1826...............DLB-37

Morse, John T., Jr. 1840-1937 ....DLB-47

Morselli, Guido 1912-1973..............DLB-177

Morte Arthure, the *Alliterative* and the *Stanzaic* circa 1350-1400............DLB-146

Mortimer, Favell Lee 1802-1878.........DLB-163

Mortimer, John 1923- DLB-13, 245, 271; CDBLB-8

Morton, Carlos 1942- DLB-122

Morton, H. V. 1892-1979..............DLB-195

John P. Morton and Company DLB-49

Morton, Nathaniel 1613-1685 ....DLB-24

Morton, Sarah Wentworth 1759-1846 .....DLB-37

Morton, Thomas circa 1579-circa 1647 ....DLB-24

Moscherosch, Johann Michael 1601-1669 ....DLB-164

Humphrey Moseley [publishing house]................DLB-170

Möser, Justus 1720-1794................DLB-97

Mosley, Nicholas 1923- DLB-14, 207

Mosley, Walter 1952- DLB-306

Moss, Arthur 1889-1969 ....DLB-4

Moss, Howard 1922-1987 ....DLB-5

Moss, Thylias 1954- DLB-120

Motion, Andrew 1952- DLB-40

Motley, John Lothrop 1814-1877.............DLB-1, 30, 59, 235

Motley, Willard 1909-1965 ....DLB-76, 143

Mott, Lucretia 1793-1880..............DLB-239

Benjamin Motte Jr. [publishing house]................DLB-154

Motteux, Peter Anthony 1663-1718.......DLB-80

Mottram, R. H. 1883-1971...............DLB-36

Mount, Ferdinand 1939- DLB-231

Mouré, Erin 1955- DLB-60

Mourning Dove (Humishuma) between 1882 and 1888?-1936 ....DLB-175, 221

Movies Fiction into Film, 1928-1975: A List of Movies Based on the Works of Authors in British Novelists, 1930-1959..................DLB-15

Movies from Books, 1920-1974........DLB-9

Mowat, Farley 1921- DLB-68

A. R. Mowbray and Company, Limited DLB-106

Mowrer, Edgar Ansel 1892-1977 ....DLB-29

Mowrer, Paul Scott 1887-1971 ....DLB-29

Edward Moxon [publishing house]......DLB-106

Joseph Moxon [publishing house].......DLB-170

Moyes, Patricia 1923-2000.............DLB-276

Mphahlele, Es'kia (Ezekiel) 1919- DLB-125, 225; CDWLB-3

Mrożek, Sławomir 1930- ..DLB-232; CDWLB-4

Mtshali, Oswald Mbuyiseni 1940- DLB-125, 225

Mu Shiying 1912-1940.................DLB-328

al-Mubarrad 826-898 or 899 ....DLB-311

Mucedorus........................DLB-62

Mudford, William 1782-1848..........DLB-159

Mudrooroo (see Johnson, Colin)

Mueller, Lisel 1924- DLB-105

Muhajir, El (see Marvin X)

Muhajir, Nazzam Al Fitnah (see Marvin X)

Muhammad the Prophet circa 570-632 ...DLB-311

Mühlbach, Luise 1814-1873............DLB-133

Muir, Edwin 1887-1959 ....DLB-20, 100, 191

Muir, Helen 1937- DLB-14

Muir, John 1838-1914 ....DLB-186, 275

Muir, Percy 1894-1979................DLB-201

Mujū Ichien 1226-1312 ....DLB-203

Mukherjee, Bharati 1940- DLB-60, 218, 323

Mulcaster, Richard 1531 or 1532-1611 ...DLB-167

Muldoon, Paul 1951- DLB-40

Mulisch, Harry 1927- DLB-299

Mulkerns, Val 1925- DLB-319

Müller, Friedrich (see Müller, Maler)

Müller, Heiner 1929-1995 ....DLB-124

Müller, Maler 1749-1825 ....DLB-94

Muller, Marcia 1944- DLB-226

Müller, Wilhelm 1794-1827 ....DLB-90

Mumford, Lewis 1895-1990 ....DLB-63

Munby, A. N. L. 1913-1974...........DLB-201

Munby, Arthur Joseph 1828-1910 ....DLB-35

Munday, Anthony 1560-1633 ......DLB-62, 172

Mundt, Clara (see Mühlbach, Luise)

Mundt, Theodore 1808-1861 ....DLB-133

Munford, Robert circa 1737-1783........DLB-31

Mungoshi, Charles 1947- DLB-157

Munk, Kaj 1898-1944 ....DLB-214

Munonye, John 1929- DLB-117

Muñoz Molina, Antonio 1956- DLB-322

Munro, Alice 1931- DLB-53

George Munro [publishing house].......DLB-49

Munro, H. H. 1870-1916 ....DLB-34, 162; CDBLB-5

Munro, Neil 1864-1930 ....DLB-156

Norman L. Munro [publishing house].....DLB-49

Munroe, Kirk 1850-1930 ....DLB-42

Munroe and Francis...................DLB-49

James Munroe and Company DLB-49

Joel Munsell [publishing house].........DLB-49

Munsey, Frank A. 1854-1925 ....DLB-25, 91

Frank A. Munsey and Company.........DLB-49

Mura, David 1952- DLB-312

Murakami Haruki 1949- DLB-182

Muratov, Pavel 1881-1950.............DLB-317

Murayama, Milton 1923- DLB-312

Murav'ev, Mikhail Nikitich 1757-1807....DLB-150

Murdoch, Iris 1919-1999 ....DLB-14, 194, 233, 326; CDBLB-8

Murdock, James From *Sketches of Modern Philosophy*........ DS-5

Murdoch, Rupert 1931- DLB-127

Murfree, Mary N. 1850-1922 ....DLB-12, 74

Murger, Henry 1822-1861............DLB-119

Murger, Louis-Henri (see Murger, Henry)

Murnane, Gerald 1939- DLB-289

Murner, Thomas 1475-1537.............DLB-179

Muro, Amado 1915-1971...............DLB-82

Murphy, Arthur 1727-1805 ....DLB-89, 142

Murphy, Beatrice M. 1908-1992 ....DLB-76

Murphy, Dervla 1931- DLB-204

Murphy, Emily 1868-1933..............DLB-99

Murphy, Jack 1923-1980 ....DLB-241

John Murphy and Company DLB-49

Murphy, John H., III 1916- DLB-127

Murphy, Richard 1927-1993 ....DLB-40

Murphy, Tom 1935- DLB-310

Murray, Albert L. 1916- DLB-38

Murray, Gilbert 1866-1957 ....DLB-10

Murray, Jim 1919-1998 ....DLB-241

John Murray [publishing house] DLB-154

Murray, Judith Sargent 1751-1820 .... DLB-37, 200

Murray, Les 1938- DLB-289

Murray, Pauli 1910-1985 ....DLB-41

Murry, John Middleton 1889-1957 .....DLB-149

"The Break-Up of the Novel" (1922)....................DLB-36

Murry, John Middleton, Jr. (see Cowper, Richard)

Musäus, Johann Karl August 1735-1787......................DLB-97

Muschg, Adolf 1934- DLB-75

Musil, Robert 1880-1942........DLB-81, 124; CDWLB-2

Muspilli circa 790-circa 850.............DLB-148

Musset, Alfred de 1810-1857 .... DLB-192, 217

Benjamin B. Mussey and Company...................DLB-49

Muste, A. J. 1885-1967 ....DLB-303

Mutafchieva, Vera 1929- DLB-181

Mutis, Alvaro 1923- DLB-283

Mwangi, Meja 1948- DLB-125

Myers, Frederic W. H. 1843-1901 . . . . DLB-190

Myers, Gustavus 1872-1942 . . . . DLB-47

Myers, L. H. 1881-1944 . . . . DLB-15

Myers, Walter Dean 1937- DLB-33

Myerson, Julie 1960- DLB-267

Mykle, Agnar 1915-1994 . . . . DLB-297

Mykolaitis-Putinas, Vincas 1893-1967 . . . . DLB-220

Myles, Eileen 1949- DLB-193

Myrdal, Jan 1927- DLB-257

Mystery
    1985: The Year of the Mystery: A Symposium Y-85

    Comments from Other Writers Y-85

    The Second Annual New York Festival of Mystery Y-00

    Why I Read Mysteries Y-85

    Why I Write Mysteries: Night and Day, by Michael Collins Y-85

N

Na Prous Boneta circa 1296-1328 . . . . DLB-208

Nabl, Franz 1883-1974 . . . . DLB-81

Nabakov, Véra 1902-1991 . . . . Y-91

Nabokov, Vladimir 1899-1977 . . . . DLB-2, 244, 278, 317; Y-80, 91; DS-3; CDALB-1
    International Nabokov Society Y-99

    An Interview [On Nabokov], by Fredson Bowers Y-80

    Nabokov Festival at Cornell Y-83

    The Vladimir Nabokov Archive in the Berg Collection of the New York Public Library: An Overview Y-91

    The Vladimir Nabokov Society Y-01

Nádaši, Ladislav (see Jégé)

Naden, Constance 1858-1889 . . . . DLB-199

Nadezhdin, Nikolai Ivanovich 1804-1856 . . . . DLB-198

Nadson, Semen Iakovlevich 1862-1887 . . . DLB-277

Naevius circa 265 B.C.-201 B.C. DLB-211

Nafis and Cornish DLB-49

Nagai Kafū 1879-1959 . . . . DLB-180

Nagel, Ernest 1901-1985 . . . . DLB-279

Nagibin, Iurii Markovich 1920-1994 . . . . DLB-302

Nagrodskaia, Evdokiia Apollonovna 1866-1930 . . . . DLB-295

Naipaul, Shiva 1945-1985 . . . . DLB-157; Y-85

Naipaul, V. S. 1932- . . . DLB-125, 204, 207, 326; Y-85, Y-01; CDBLB-8; CDWLB-3

    Nobel Lecture 2001: "Two Worlds" Y-01

Nakagami Kenji 1946-1992 . . . . DLB-182

Nakano-in Masatada no Musume (see Nijō, Lady)

Nałkowska, Zofia 1884-1954 . . . . DLB-215

Namora, Fernando 1919-1989 . . . . DLB-287

Joseph Nancrede [publishing house] DLB-49

Naranjo, Carmen 1930- DLB-145

Narayan, R. K. 1906-2001 . . . . DLB-323

Narbikova, Valeriia Spartakovna 1958- DLB-285

Narezhny, Vasilii Trofimovich 1780-1825 . . . . DLB-198

Narrache, Jean (Emile Coderre) 1893-1970 . . . . DLB-92

Nasby, Petroleum Vesuvius (see Locke, David Ross)

Eveleigh Nash [publishing house] DLB-112

Nash, Ogden 1902-1971 . . . . DLB-11

Nashe, Thomas 1567-1601? DLB-167

Nason, Jerry 1910-1986 . . . . DLB-241

Nasr, Seyyed Hossein 1933- DLB-279

Nast, Condé 1873-1942 . . . . DLB-91

Nast, Thomas 1840-1902 . . . . DLB-188

Nastasijević, Momčilo 1894-1938 . . . . DLB-147

Nathan, George Jean 1882-1958 . . . . DLB-137

Nathan, Robert 1894-1985 . . . . DLB-9

Nation, Carry A. 1846-1911 . . . . DLB-303

National Book Critics Circle Awards Y-00-01

The National Jewish Book Awards Y-85

Natsume Sōseki 1867-1916 . . . . DLB-180

Naughton, Bill 1910-1992 . . . . DLB-13

Nava, Michael 1954- DLB-306

Navarro, Joe 1953- DLB-209

Naylor, Gloria 1950- DLB-173

Nazor, Vladimir 1876-1949 . . . . DLB-147

Ndebele, Njabulo 1948- DLB-157, 225

Neagoe, Peter 1881-1960 . . . . DLB-4

Neal, John 1793-1876 . . . . DLB-1, 59, 243

Neal, Joseph C. 1807-1847 . . . . DLB-11

Neal, Larry 1937-1981 . . . . DLB-38

The Neale Publishing Company DLB-49

Nearing, Scott 1883-1983 . . . . DLB-303

Nebel, Frederick 1903-1967 . . . . DLB-226

Nebrija, Antonio de 1442 or 1444-1522 . . DLB-286

Nedreaas, Torborg 1906-1987 . . . . DLB-297

F. Tennyson Neely [publishing house] DLB-49

Negoițescu, Ion 1921-1993 . . . . DLB-220

Negri, Ada 1870-1945 . . . . DLB-114

Nehru, Pandit Jawaharlal 1889-1964 . . . . DLB-323

Neihardt, John G. 1881-1973 . . . . . DLB-9, 54, 256

Neidhart von Reuental circa 1185-circa 1240 . . . . DLB-138

Neilson, John Shaw 1872-1942 . . . . DLB-230

Nekrasov, Nikolai Alekseevich 1821-1877 . . . . DLB-277

Nekrasov, Viktor Platonovich 1911-1987 . . . . DLB-302

Neledinsky-Meletsky, Iurii Aleksandrovich 1752-1828 . . . . DLB-150

Nelligan, Emile 1879-1941 . . . . DLB-92

Nelson, Alice Moore Dunbar 1875-1935 . . DLB-50

Nelson, Antonya 1961- DLB-244

Nelson, Kent 1943- DLB-234

Nelson, Richard K. 1941- DLB-275

Nelson, Thomas, and Sons [U.K.] DLB-106

Nelson, Thomas, and Sons [U.S.] DLB-49

Nelson, William 1908-1978 . . . . DLB-103

Nelson, William Rockhill 1841-1915 . . . . . DLB-23

Nemerov, Howard 1920-1991 . . . . . DLB-5, 6; Y-83

Németh, László 1901-1975 . . . . DLB-215

Nepos circa 100 B.C.-post 27 B.C. DLB-211

Nèris, Salomėja 1904-1945 . . DLB-220; CDWLB-4

Neruda, Pablo 1904-1973 . . . . DLB-283

Nerval, Gérard de 1808-1855 . . . . DLB-217

Nervo, Amado 1870-1919 . . . . DLB-290

Nesbit, E. 1858-1924 . . . . DLB-141, 153, 178

Ness, Evaline 1911-1986 . . . . DLB-61

Nestroy, Johann 1801-1862 . . . . DLB-133

Nettleship, R. L. 1846-1892 . . . . DLB-262

Neugeboren, Jay 1938- DLB-28

Neukirch, Benjamin 1655-1729 . . . . DLB-168

Neumann, Alfred 1895-1952 . . . . DLB-56

Neumann, Ferenc (see Molnár, Ferenc)

Neumark, Georg 1621-1681 . . . . DLB-164

Neumeister, Erdmann 1671-1756 . . . . DLB-168

Nevins, Allan 1890-1971 . . . . DLB-17; DS-17

Nevinson, Henry Woodd 1856-1941 . . . . DLB-135

The New American Library DLB-46

New Directions Publishing Corporation . . . DLB-46

The New Monthly Magazine 1814-1884 . . . . DLB-110

New York Times Book Review Y-82

John Newbery [publishing house] DLB-154

Newbolt, Henry 1862-1938 . . . . DLB-19

Newbound, Bernard Slade (see Slade, Bernard)

Newby, Eric 1919- DLB-204

Newby, P. H. 1918-1997 . . . . DLB-15, 326

Thomas Cautley Newby [publishing house] DLB-106

Newcomb, Charles King 1820-1894 . . . DLB-1, 223

Newell, Peter 1862-1924 . . . . DLB-42

Newell, Robert Henry 1836-1901 . . . . DLB-11

Newhouse, Samuel I. 1895-1979 . . . . DLB-127

Newman, Cecil Earl 1903-1976 . . . . DLB-127

Newman, David 1937- DLB-44

Newman, Frances 1883-1928 . . . . Y-80

Newman, Francis William 1805-1897 . . . . DLB-190

Newman, G. F. 1946- DLB-310

Newman, John Henry 1801-1890 . . . . DLB-18, 32, 55

Mark Newman [publishing house] DLB-49

Newmarch, Rosa Harriet 1857-1940 . . . . . DLB-240

George Newnes Limited DLB-112
Newsome, Effie Lee 1885-1979 . . . . DLB-76
Newton, A. Edward 1864-1940 . . . . DLB-140
Newton, Sir Isaac 1642-1727 . . . . DLB-252
Nexø, Martin Andersen 1869-1954 . . . . . . DLB-214
Nezval, Vítěslav
  1900-1958 . . . . DLB-215; CDWLB-4
Ngugi wa Thiong'o
  1938- DLB-125; CDWLB-3
Niatum, Duane 1938- DLB-175
The *Nibelungenlied* and the *Klage*
  circa 1200 . . . . DLB-138
Nichol, B. P. 1944-1988 . . . . DLB-53
Nicholas of Cusa 1401-1464 . . . . DLB-115
Nichols, Ann 1891?-1966. . . . . DLB-249
Nichols, Beverly 1898-1983 . . . . DLB-191
Nichols, Dudley 1895-1960 . . . . DLB-26
Nichols, Grace 1950- DLB-157
Nichols, John 1940- Y-82
Nichols, Mary Sargeant (Neal) Gove
  1810-1884 . . . . DLB-1, 243
Nichols, Peter 1927- DLB-13, 245
Nichols, Roy F. 1896-1973 . . . . DLB-17
Nichols, Ruth 1948- DLB-60
Nicholson, Edward Williams Byron
  1849-1912 . . . . DLB-184
Nicholson, Geoff 1953- DLB-271
Nicholson, Norman 1914-1987 . . . . DLB-27
Nicholson, William 1872-1949 . . . . DLB-141
Ní Chuilleanáin, Eiléan 1942- DLB-40
Nicol, Eric 1919- DLB-68
Nicolai, Friedrich 1733-1811 . . . . DLB-97
Nicolas de Clamanges circa 1363-1437 . . . DLB-208
Nicolay, John G. 1832-1901 and
  Hay, John 1838-1905 . . . . DLB-47
Nicole, Pierre 1625-1695 . . . . DLB-268
Nicolson, Adela Florence Cory (see Hope, Laurence)
Nicolson, Harold 1886-1968 . . . . . . DLB-100, 149
  "The Practice of Biography," in
    *The English Sense of Humour and
    Other Essays* DLB-149
Nicolson, Nigel 1917-2004 . . . . DLB-155
Ní Dhuibhne, Éilís 1954- DLB-319
Niebuhr, Reinhold 1892-1971 . . . . . DLB-17; DS-17
Niedecker, Lorine 1903-1970 . . . . DLB-48
Nieman, Lucius W. 1857-1935 . . . . DLB-25
Nietzsche, Friedrich
  1844-1900 . . . . DLB-129; CDWLB-2
  Mencken and Nietzsche: An Unpublished
    Excerpt from H. L. Mencken's *My Life
    as Author and Editor* Y-93
Nievo, Stanislao 1928- DLB-196
Niggli, Josefina 1910-1983 . . . . Y-80
Nightingale, Florence 1820-1910 . . . . . . DLB-166

Nijō, Lady (Nakano-in Masatada no Musume)
  1258-after 1306 . . . . DLB-203
Nijō Yoshimoto 1320-1388. . . . . DLB-203
Nikitin, Ivan Savvich 1824-1861 . . . . DLB-277
Nikitin, Nikolai Nikolaevich 1895-1963 . . DLB-272
Nikolev, Nikolai Petrovich 1758-1815 . . . . DLB-150
Niles, Hezekiah 1777-1839 . . . . DLB-43
Nims, John Frederick 1913-1999 . . . . DLB-5
  Tribute to Nancy Hale Y-88
Nin, Anaïs 1903-1977 . . . . DLB-2, 4, 152
Nína Björk Árnadóttir 1941-2000 . . . . . . DLB-293
Niño, Raúl 1961- DLB-209
Nissenson, Hugh 1933- DLB-28
Niven, Frederick John 1878-1944 . . . . DLB-92
Niven, Larry 1938- DLB-8
Nixon, Howard M. 1909-1983 . . . . DLB-201
Nizan, Paul 1905-1940 . . . . DLB-72
Njegoš, Petar II Petrović
  1813-1851 . . . . DLB-147; CDWLB-4
Nkosi, Lewis 1936- DLB-157, 225
Noah, Mordecai M. 1785-1851 . . . . DLB-250
Noailles, Anna de 1876-1933 . . . . DLB-258
Nobel Peace Prize
  The Nobel Prize and Literary Politics Y-88
  Elie Wiesel Y-86
Nobel Prize in Literature
  Shmuel Yosef Agnon DLB-329
  Vicente Aleixandre DLB-108, 329
  Ivo Andrić DLB-147, 329; CDWLB-4
  Miguel Ángel Asturias DLB-113, 290,
    329; CDWLB-3
  Samuel Beckett DLB-13, 15, 233, 319,
    321, 329; Y-90; CDBLB-7
  Saul Bellow DLB-2, 28, 299, 329;
    Y-82; DS-3; CDALB-1
  Jacinto Benavente DLB-329
  Henri Bergson DLB-329
  Bjørnstjerne Bjørnson DLB-329
  Heinrich Böll . . . DLB-69, 329; Y-85; CDWLB-2
  Joseph Brodsky DLB-285, 329; Y-87
  Pearl S. Buck DLB-9, 102, 329; CDALB-7
  Ivan Bunin. DLB-317, 329
  Albert Camus DLB-72, 321, 329
  Elias Canetti . . . DLB-85, 124, 329; CDWLB-2
  Giosuè Carducci DLB-329
  Camilo José Cela. DLB-322, 329; Y-89
  Sir Winston Churchill DLB-100, 329;
    DS-16; CDBLB-5
  J. M. Coetzee DLB-225, 326, 329
  Grazia Deledda DLB-264, 329
  Jose Echegaray DLB-329
  T. S. Eliot DLB-7, 10, 45, 63, 245, 329;
    Y-88, 99; CDALB-5
  Odysseus Elytis DLB-329
  Rudolf Eucken DLB-329

  William Faulkner DLB-9, 11, 44, 102, 316,
    330; DS-2; Y-86; CDALB-5
  Dario Fo DLB-330; Y-97
  Anatole France DLB-123, 330
  John Galsworthy DLB-10, 34, 98, 162,
    330; DS-16; CDBLB-5
  Gao Xingjian. DLB-330; Y-00
  Gabriel García Márquez DLB-13,
    330; Y-82; CDWLB-3
  André Gide DLB-65, 321, 330
  Karl Gjellerup DLB-300, 330
  William Golding DLB-15, 100, 255,
    326, 330; Y-83; CDBLB-7
  Nadine Gordimer DLB-225, 326, 330;
    Y-91
  Günter Grass. DLB-75, 124, 330; Y-99
  Knut Hamsun DLB-297, 330
  Gerhart Hauptmann DLB-66, 118,
    330; CDWLB-2
  Seamus Heaney. DLB-40, 330; Y-95;
    CDBLB-8
  Verner von Heidenstam DLB-330
  Ernest Hemingway DLB-4, 9, 102,
    210, 316, 330; Y-81, 87, 99; DS-1, 15, 16;
    CDALB-4
  Hermann Hesse DLB-66, 330; CDWLB-2
  Paul Heyse DLB-129, 330
  Elfriede Jelinek DLB-85, 330
  Johannes V. Jensen DLB-330
  Juan Ramón Jiménez DLB-134, 330
  Eyvind Johnson DLB-259, 330
  Erik Axel Karlfeldt DLB-330
  Yasunari Kawabata DLB-180, 330
  Imre Kertész DLB-299, 330; Y-02
  Rudyard Kipling DLB-19, 34, 141, 156,
    330; CDBLB-5
  Najīb Mahfūz Y-88
  Toni Morrison Y-93
  V. S. Naipaul Y-01
  Kenzaburō Ōe Y-94
  Octavio Paz Y-90
  José Saramago Y-98
  Jaroslav Seifert Y-84
  Claude Simon Y-85
  Wole Soyinka Y-86
  Wisława Szymborska Y-96
  Derek Walcott Y-92
Nobre, António 1867-1900. . . . . DLB-287
Nodier, Charles 1780-1844 . . . . DLB-119
Noël, Marie (Marie Mélanie Rouget)
  1883-1967 . . . . DLB-258
Noel, Roden 1834-1894. . . . . DLB-35
Nogami Yaeko 1885-1985 . . . . DLB-180
Nogo, Rajko Petrov 1945- DLB-181
Nolan, William F. 1928- DLB-8
  Tribute to Raymond Chandler Y-88
Noland, C. F. M. 1810?-1858 . . . . DLB-11

Noma Hiroshi 1915-1991 .... DLB-182

Nonesuch Press.................... DLB-112

Creative Nonfiction Y-02

Nonni (Jón Stefán Sveinsson or Svensson)
1857-1944..................... DLB-293

Noon, Jeff 1957- DLB-267

Noonan, Robert Phillipe (see Tressell, Robert)

Noonday Press DLB-46

Noone, John 1936- DLB-14

Nora, Eugenio de 1923- DLB-134

Nordan, Lewis 1939- DLB-234

Nordbrandt, Henrik 1945- DLB-214

Nordhoff, Charles 1887-1947 .... DLB-9

Norén, Lars 1944- DLB-257

Norfolk, Lawrence 1963- DLB-267

Norman, Charles 1904-1996 .... DLB-111

Norman, Marsha 1947- DLB-266; Y-84

Norris, Charles G. 1881-1945............ DLB-9

Norris, Frank
1870-1902....... DLB-12, 71, 186; CDALB-3

Norris, Helen 1916- DLB-292

Norris, John 1657-1712 .... DLB-252

Norris, Leslie 1921- DLB-27, 256

Norse, Harold 1916- DLB-16

Norte, Marisela 1955- DLB-209

North, Marianne 1830-1890............DLB-174

North Point Press DLB-46

Nortje, Arthur 1942-1970 .... DLB-125, 225

Norton, Alice Mary (see Norton, Andre)

Norton, Andre 1912-2005............. DLB-8, 52

Norton, Andrews 1786-1853.... DLB-1, 235; DS-5

Norton, Caroline 1808-1877 ... DLB-21, 159, 199

Norton, Charles Eliot 1827-1908 .. DLB-1, 64, 235

Norton, John 1606-1663................ DLB-24

Norton, Mary 1903-1992 .... DLB-160

Norton, Thomas 1532-1584............ DLB-62

W. W. Norton and Company........... DLB-46

Norwood, Robert 1874-1932 .... DLB-92

Nosaka Akiyuki 1930- DLB-182

Nossack, Hans Erich 1901-1977 .... DLB-69

Notker Balbulus circa 840-912 .... DLB-148

Notker III of Saint Gall
circa 950-1022 .... DLB-148

Notker von Zweifalten ?-1095......... DLB-148

Nourse, Alan E. 1928-1992 .... DLB-8

Novak, Slobodan 1924- DLB-181

Novak, Vjenceslav 1859-1905 .... DLB-147

Novakovich, Josip 1956- DLB-244

Novalis 1772-1801.......... DLB-90; CDWLB-2

Novaro, Mario 1868-1944 .... DLB-114

Novás Calvo, Lino 1903-1983 .... DLB-145

Novelists
Library Journal Statements and
Questionnaires from First Novelists Y-87

Novels
The Columbia History of the American Novel
A Symposium on................. Y-92

The Great Modern Library Scam Y-98

Novels for Grown-Ups................ Y-97

The Proletarian Novel DLB-9

Novel, The "Second-Generation" Holocaust
.... DLB-299

The Year in the Novel Y-87–88, Y-90–93

Novels, British
"The Break-Up of the Novel" (1922),
by John Middleton Murry....... DLB-36

The Consolidation of Opinion: Critical
Responses to the Modernists..... DLB-36

"Criticism in Relation to Novels"
(1863), by G. H. Lewes DLB-21

"Experiment in the Novel" (1929)
[excerpt], by John D. Beresford ... DLB-36

"The Future of the Novel" (1899), by
Henry James DLB-18

The Gay Science (1866), by E. S. Dallas
[excerpt]..................... DLB-21

A Haughty and Proud Generation
(1922), by Ford Madox Hueffer .. DLB-36

Literary Effects of World War II DLB-15

"Modern Novelists –Great and Small"
(1855), by Margaret Oliphant DLB-21

The Modernists (1932),
by Joseph Warren Beach DLB-36

A Note on Technique (1926), by
Elizabeth A. Drew [excerpts]..... DLB-36

Novel-Reading: *The Works of Charles
Dickens; The Works of W. Makepeace
Thackeray* (1879),
by Anthony Trollope........... DLB-21

Novels with a Purpose (1864), by
Justin M'Carthy............... DLB-21

"On Art in Fiction" (1838),
by Edward Bulwer............. DLB-21

The Present State of the English Novel
(1892), by George Saintsbury DLB-18

Representative Men and Women:
A Historical Perspective on
the British Novel, 1930-1960..... DLB-15

"The Revolt" (1937), by Mary Colum
[excerpts] DLB-36

"Sensation Novels" (1863), by
H. L. Manse DLB-21

Sex, Class, Politics, and Religion [in
the British Novel, 1930-1959] DLB-15

Time and Western Man (1927),
by Wyndham Lewis [excerpts] ... DLB-36

Noventa, Giacomo 1898-1960 .... DLB-114

Novikov, Nikolai Ivanovich
1744-1818..................... DLB-150

Novomeský, Laco 1904-1976 .... DLB-215

Nowlan, Alden 1933-1983 .... DLB-53

Nowra, Louis 1950- DLB-325

Noyes, Alfred 1880-1958 .... DLB-20

Noyes, Crosby S. 1825-1908........... DLB-23

Noyes, Nicholas 1647-1717 .... DLB-24

Noyes, Theodore W. 1858-1946......... DLB-29

Nozick, Robert 1938-2002 ....DLB-279

N-Town Plays circa 1468 to early
sixteenth century................ DLB-146

Nugent, Frank 1908-1965.............. DLB-44

Nunez, Sigrid 1951- DLB-312

Nušić, Branislav
1864-1938 ....DLB-147; CDWLB-4

David Nutt [publishing house] DLB-106

Nwapa, Flora
1931-1993 ....DLB-125; CDWLB-3

Nye, Edgar Wilson (Bill)
1850-1896 ....DLB-11, 23, 186

Nye, Naomi Shihab 1952- DLB-120

Nye, Robert 1939- DLB-14, 271

Nyka-Niliūnas, Alfonsas 1919- DLB-220

O

Oakes, Urian circa 1631-1681 .... DLB-24

Oakes Smith, Elizabeth
1806-1893 .... DLB-1, 239, 243

Oakley, Violet 1874-1961 .... DLB-188

Oates, Joyce Carol 1938-
.............DLB-2, 5, 130; Y-81; CDALB-6

Tribute to Michael M. Rea............ Y-97

Ōba Minako 1930- DLB-182

Ober, Frederick Albion 1849-1913 ...... DLB-189

Ober, William 1920-1993 .... Y-93

Oberholtzer, Ellis Paxson 1868-1936 ..... DLB-47

The Obituary as Literary Form Y-02

Obradović, Dositej 1740?-1811..........DLB-147

O'Brien, Charlotte Grace 1845-1909 .... DLB-240

O'Brien, Edna 1932- DLB-14, 231, 319; CDBLB-8

O'Brien, Fitz-James 1828-1862 .... DLB-74

O'Brien, Flann (see O'Nolan, Brian)

O'Brien, Kate 1897-1974 .... DLB-15

O'Brien, Tim
1946- DLB-152; Y-80; DS-9; CDALB-7

Ó Cadhain, Máirtín 1905-1970......... DLB-319

O'Casey, Sean 1880-1964..... DLB-10; CDBLB-6

Occom, Samson 1723-1792 ....DLB-175

Occomy, Marita Bonner 1899-1971 ...... DLB-51

Ochs, Adolph S. 1858-1935 .... DLB-25

Ochs-Oakes, George Washington
1861-1931 ....DLB-137

O'Connor, Flannery 1925-1964
.........DLB-2, 152; Y-80; DS-12; CDALB-1

The Flannery O'Connor Society Y-99

O'Connor, Frank 1903-1966 .... DLB-162

O'Connor, Joseph 1963- DLB-267

Octopus Publishing Group........... DLB-112

Oda Sakunosuke 1913-1947 .... DLB-182

Odell, Jonathan 1737-1818 .... DLB-31, 99

O'Dell, Scott 1903-1989.................DLB-52

Odets, Clifford 1906-1963............DLB-7, 26

Odhams Press Limited.................DLB-112

Odio, Eunice 1922-1974.................DLB-283

Odoevsky, Aleksandr Ivanovich
  1802-1839......................DLB-205

Odoevsky, Vladimir Fedorovich
  1804 or 1803-1869................DLB-198

Odoevtseva, Irina 1895-1990............DLB-317

O'Donnell, Peter 1920-.................DLB-87

O'Donovan, Michael (see O'Connor, Frank)

O'Dowd, Bernard 1866-1953............DLB-230

Ōe, Kenzaburō 1935-..............DLB-182; Y-94

  Nobel Lecture 1994: Japan, the
    Ambiguous, and Myself.............Y-94

Oehlenschläger, Adam 1779-1850........DLB-300

O'Faolain, Julia 1932-........DLB-14, 231, 319

O'Faolain, Sean 1900-1991..........DLB-15, 162

Off-Loop Theatres......................DLB-7

Offord, Carl Ruthven 1910-1990.........DLB-76

Offshore, 1979 Booker Prize winner,
  Penelope Fitzgerald.................DLB-326

O'Flaherty, Liam 1896-1984....DLB-36, 162; Y-84

Ogarev, Nikolai Platonovich 1813-1877...DLB-277

J. S. Ogilvie and Company..............DLB-49

Ogilvy, Eliza 1822-1912.................DLB-199

Ogot, Grace 1930-......................DLB-125

O'Grady, Desmond 1935-.................DLB-40

Ogunyemi, Wale 1939-...................DLB-157

O'Hagan, Howard 1902-1982..............DLB-68

O'Hara, Frank 1926-1966..........DLB-5, 16, 193

O'Hara, John
  1905-1970.....DLB-9, 86, 324; DS-2; CDALB-5

  John O'Hara's Pottsville Journalism......Y-88

O'Hare, Kate Richards 1876-1948........DLB-303

O'Hegarty, P. S. 1879-1955..............DLB-201

Ohio State University
  The William Charvat American Fiction
    Collection at the Ohio State
    University Libraries...............Y-92

Okada, John 1923-1971..................DLB-312

Okara, Gabriel 1921-.......DLB-125; CDWLB-3

O'Keeffe, John 1747-1833................DLB-89

Nicholas Okes [publishing house]........DLB-170

Okigbo, Christopher
  1930-1967.............DLB-125; CDWLB-3

Okot p'Bitek 1931-1982......DLB-125; CDWLB-3

Okpewho, Isidore 1941-..................DLB-157

Okri, Ben 1959-........DLB-157, 231, 319, 326

Ólafur Jóhann Sigurðsson 1918-1988....DLB-293

The Old Devils, 1986 Booker Prize winner,
  Kingsley Amis......................DLB-326

Old Dogs / New Tricks? New Technologies,
  the Canon, and the Structure of
  the Profession......................Y-02

Old Franklin Publishing House..........DLB-49

Old German Genesis and *Old German Exodus*
  circa 1050-circa 1130...............DLB-148

The *Old High German Isidor*
  circa 790-800......................DLB-148

Older, Fremont 1856-1935................DLB-25

Oldham, John 1653-1683.................DLB-131

Oldman, C. B. 1894-1969................DLB-201

Olds, Sharon 1942-.....................DLB-120

Olearius, Adam 1599-1671...............DLB-164

O'Leary, Ellen 1831-1889...............DLB-240

O'Leary, Juan E. 1879-1969.............DLB-290

Olesha, Iurii Karlovich 1899-1960......DLB-272

Oliphant, Laurence 1829?-1888......DLB-18, 166

Oliphant, Margaret 1828-1897...DLB-18, 159, 190

  "Modern Novelists–Great and Small"
    (1855).........................DLB-21

Oliveira, Carlos de 1921-1981..........DLB-287

Oliver, Chad 1928-1993..................DLB-8

Oliver, Mary 1935-....................DLB-5, 193

Ollier, Claude 1922-...................DLB-83

Olsen, Tillie 1912/1913-
  ....DLB-28, 206; Y-80; CDALB-7

Olson, Charles 1910-1970........DLB-5, 16, 193

Olson, Elder 1909-1992.............DLB-48, 63

Olson, Sigurd F. 1899-1982.............DLB-275

The Omega Workshops...................DS-10

Omotoso, Kole 1943-...................DLB-125

Omulevsky, Innokentii Vasil'evich
  1836 [or 1837]-1883...............DLB-238

Ondaatje, Michael 1943-.....DLB-60, 323, 326

O'Neill, Eugene 1888-1953......DLB-7; CDALB-5

  Eugene O'Neill Memorial Theater
    Center..........................DLB-7

  Eugene O'Neill's Letters: A Review......Y-88

Onetti, Juan Carlos
  1909-1994............DLB-113; CDWLB-3

Onions, George Oliver 1872-1961........DLB-153

Onofri, Arturo 1885-1928...............DLB-114

O'Nolan, Brian 1911-1966...............DLB-231

Oodgeroo of the Tribe Noonuccal
  (Kath Walker) 1920-1993............DLB-289

Opie, Amelia 1769-1853............DLB-116, 159

Opitz, Martin 1597-1639................DLB-164

Oppen, George 1908-1984............DLB-5, 165

Oppenheim, E. Phillips 1866-1946.......DLB-70

Oppenheim, James 1882-1932.............DLB-28

Oppenheimer, Joel 1930-1988.........DLB-5, 193

Optic, Oliver (see Adams, William Taylor)

Orczy, Emma, Baroness 1865-1947........DLB-70

Oregon Shakespeare Festival...........Y-00

Origo, Iris 1902-1988...................DLB-155

O'Riordan, Kate 1960-..................DLB-267

Orlovitz, Gil 1918-1973................DLB-2, 5

Orlovsky, Peter 1933-..................DLB-16

Ormond, John 1923-......................DLB-27

Ornitz, Samuel 1890-1957...........DLB-28, 44

O'Rourke, P. J. 1947-..................DLB-185

Orozco, Olga 1920-1999.................DLB-283

Orten, Jiří 1919-1941..................DLB-215

Ortese, Anna Maria 1914-...............DLB-177

Ortiz, Lourdes 1943-...................DLB-322

Ortiz, Simon J. 1941-.......DLB-120, 175, 256

Ortnit and *Wolfdietrich* circa 1225-1250....DLB-138

Orton, Joe 1933-1967......DLB-13, 310; CDBLB-8

Orwell, George (Eric Arthur Blair)
  1903-1950...DLB-15, 98, 195, 255; CDBLB-7

  The Orwell Year.....................Y-84

  (Re-)Publishing Orwell..............Y-86

Ory, Carlos Edmundo de 1923-..........DLB-134

Osbey, Brenda Marie 1957-.............DLB-120

Osbon, B. S. 1827-1912.................DLB-43

Osborn, Sarah 1714-1796................DLB-200

Osborne, John 1929-1994.....DLB-13; CDBLB-7

Oscar and Lucinda, 1988 Booker Prize winner,
  Peter Carey......................DLB-326

Osgood, Frances Sargent 1811-1850.....DLB-250

Osgood, Herbert L. 1855-1918...........DLB-47

James R. Osgood and Company...........DLB-49

Osgood, McIlvaine and Company........DLB-112

O'Shaughnessy, Arthur 1844-1881........DLB-35

Patrick O'Shea [publishing house].......DLB-49

Osipov, Nikolai Petrovich 1751-1799....DLB-150

Oskison, John Milton 1879-1947........DLB-175

Osler, Sir William 1849-1919..........DLB-184

Osofisan, Femi 1946-.......DLB-125; CDWLB-3

Ostenso, Martha 1900-1963..............DLB-92

Ostrauskas, Kostas 1926-..............DLB-232

Ostriker, Alicia 1937-.................DLB-120

Ostrovsky, Aleksandr Nikolaevich
  1823-1886........................DLB-277

Ostrovsky, Nikolai Alekseevich
  1904-1936........................DLB-272

Osundare, Niyi 1947-......DLB-157; CDWLB-3

Oswald, Eleazer 1755-1795..............DLB-43

Oswald von Wolkenstein
  1376 or 1377-1445.................DLB-179

Otero, Blas de 1916-1979...............DLB-134

Otero, Miguel Antonio 1859-1944........DLB-82

Otero, Nina 1881-1965..................DLB-209

Otero Silva, Miguel 1908-1985.........DLB-145

Otfried von Weißenburg
  circa 800-circa 875?..............DLB-148

Otis, Broaders and Company.............DLB-49

Otis, James (see Kaler, James Otis)

Cumulative Index

Otis, James, Jr. 1725-1783 . . . . DLB-31

Otsup, Nikolai 1894-1958. . . . . DLB-317

Ottaway, James 1911-2000 . . . . DLB-127

Ottendorfer, Oswald 1826-1900 . . . . DLB-23

Ottieri, Ottiero 1924-2002 . . . . DLB-177

Otto-Peters, Louise 1819-1895 . . . . DLB-129

Otway, Thomas 1652-1685 . . . . DLB-80

Ouellette, Fernand 1930- DLB-60

Ouida 1839-1908 . . . . DLB-18, 156

Outing Publishing Company DLB-46

Overbury, Sir Thomas
  circa 1581-1613 . . . . DLB-151

The Overlook Press DLB-46

Ovid 43 B.C.-A.D. 17 . . . . . . DLB-211; CDWLB-1

Oviedo, Gonzalo Fernández de
  1478-1557 . . . . DLB-318

Owen, Guy 1925-1981 . . . . DLB-5

Owen, John 1564-1622 . . . . DLB-121

John Owen [publishing house] DLB-49

Peter Owen Limited DLB-112

Owen, Robert 1771-1858 . . . . DLB-107, 158

Owen, Wilfred
  1893-1918 . . . . DLB-20; DS-18; CDBLB-6
  A Centenary Celebration Y-93
  The Wilfred Owen Association Y-98

The Owl and the Nightingale
  circa 1189-1199 . . . . DLB-146

Owsley, Frank L. 1890-1956 . . . . DLB-17

Oxford, Seventeenth Earl of, Edward
  de Vere 1550-1604 . . . . DLB-172

OyamO (Charles F. Gordon)
  1943- DLB-266

Ozerov, Vladislav Aleksandrovich
  1769-1816 . . . . DLB-150

Ozick, Cynthia 1928- . . . DLB-28, 152, 299; Y-82
  First Strauss "Livings" Awarded
    to Cynthia Ozick and
    Raymond Carver
    An Interview with Cynthia Ozick Y-83
  Tribute to Michael M. Rea Y-97

P

Pace, Richard 1482?-1536 . . . . DLB-167

Pacey, Desmond 1917-1975 . . . . DLB-88

Pacheco, José Emilio 1939- DLB-290

Pack, Robert 1929- DLB-5

Paddy Clarke Ha Ha Ha, 1993 Booker Prize winner,
  Roddy Doyle DLB-326

Padell Publishing Company DLB-46

Padgett, Ron 1942- DLB-5

Padilla, Ernesto Chávez 1944- DLB-122

L. C. Page and Company DLB-49

Page, Louise 1955- DLB-233

Page, P. K. 1916- DLB-68

Page, Thomas Nelson
  1853-1922 . . . . DLB-12, 78; DS-13

Page, Walter Hines 1855-1918 . . . . DLB-71, 91

Paget, Francis Edward 1806-1882 . . . . DLB-163

Paget, Violet (see Lee, Vernon)

Pagliarani, Elio 1927- DLB-128

Pagnol, Marcel 1895-1974 . . . . DLB-321

Pain, Barry 1864-1928 . . . . DLB-135, 197

Pain, Philip ?-circa 1666 . . . . DLB-24

Paine, Robert Treat, Jr. 1773-1811 . . . . . . DLB-37

Paine, Thomas
  1737-1809 . . . . DLB-31, 43, 73, 158; CDALB-2

Painter, George D. 1914- DLB-155

Painter, William 1540?-1594 . . . . DLB-136

Palazzeschi, Aldo 1885-1974 . . . . DLB-114, 264

Palei, Marina Anatol'evna 1955- DLB-285

Palencia, Alfonso de 1424-1492 . . . . DLB-286

Palés Matos, Luis 1898-1959 . . . . DLB-290

Paley, Grace 1922- DLB-28, 218

Paley, William 1743-1805 . . . . DLB-252

Palfrey, John Gorham
  1796-1881 . . . . DLB-1, 30, 235

Palgrave, Francis Turner 1824-1897 . . . . . DLB-35

Palissy, Bernard 1510?-1590? DLB-327

Palmer, Joe H. 1904-1952 . . . . DLB-171

Palmer, Michael 1943- DLB-169

Palmer, Nettie 1885-1964 . . . . DLB-260

Palmer, Vance 1885-1959 . . . . DLB-260

Paltock, Robert 1697-1767 . . . . DLB-39

Paludan, Jacob 1896-1975 . . . . DLB-214

Paludin-Müller, Frederik 1809-1876 . . . . . DLB-300

Pan Books Limited DLB-112

Panaev, Ivan Ivanovich 1812-1862 . . . . . . DLB-198

Panaeva, Avdot'ia Iakovlevna
  1820-1893 . . . . DLB-238

Panama, Norman 1914-2003 and
  Frank, Melvin 1913-1988 . . . . DLB-26

Pancake, Breece D'J 1952-1979 . . . . DLB-130

Panduro, Leif 1923-1977 . . . . DLB-214

Panero, Leopoldo 1909-1962 . . . . DLB-108

Pangborn, Edgar 1909-1976 . . . . DLB-8

Panizzi, Sir Anthony 1797-1879 . . . . DLB-184

Panneton, Philippe (see Ringuet)

Panova, Vera Fedorovna 1905-1973 . . . . . DLB-302

Panshin, Alexei 1940- DLB-8

Pansy (see Alden, Isabella)

Pantheon Books DLB-46

Papadat-Bengescu, Hortensia
  1876-1955 . . . . DLB-220

Papantonio, Michael 1907-1976 . . . . DLB-187

Paperback Library DLB-46

Paperback Science Fiction DLB-8

Papini, Giovanni 1881-1956 . . . . DLB-264

Paquet, Alfons 1881-1944 . . . . DLB-66

Paracelsus 1493-1541 . . . . DLB-179

Paradis, Suzanne 1936- DLB-53

Páral, Vladimír, 1932- DLB-232

Pardoe, Julia 1804-1862 . . . . DLB-166

Paré, Ambroise 1510 or 1517?-1590 . . . . . DLB-327

Paredes, Américo 1915-1999 . . . . DLB-209

Pareja Diezcanseco, Alfredo 1908-1993 . . DLB-145

Parents' Magazine Press DLB-46

Paretsky, Sara 1947- DLB-306

Parfit, Derek 1942- DLB-262

Parise, Goffredo 1929-1986 . . . . DLB-177

Parish, Mitchell 1900-1993 . . . . DLB-265

Parizeau, Alice 1930-1990 . . . . DLB-60

Park, Ruth 1923?- DLB-260

Parke, John 1754-1789 . . . . DLB-31

Parker, Dan 1893-1967 . . . . DLB-241

Parker, Dorothy 1893-1967 . . . . . . DLB-11, 45, 86

Parker, Gilbert 1860-1932 . . . . DLB-99

Parker, James 1714-1770 . . . . DLB-43

Parker, John [publishing house] DLB-106

Parker, Matthew 1504-1575 . . . . DLB-213

Parker, Robert B. 1932- DLB-306

Parker, Stewart 1941-1988 . . . . DLB-245

Parker, Theodore 1810-1860 . . . DLB-1, 235; DS-5

Parker, William Riley 1906-1968 . . . . DLB-103

J. H. Parker [publishing house] DLB-106

Parkes, Bessie Rayner (Madame Belloc)
  1829-1925 . . . . DLB-240

Parkman, Francis
  1823-1893 . . . . DLB-1, 30, 183, 186, 235

Parks, Gordon 1912- DLB-33

Parks, Tim 1954- DLB-231

Parks, William 1698-1750 . . . . DLB-43

William Parks [publishing house] DLB-49

Parley, Peter (see Goodrich, Samuel Griswold)

Parmenides late sixth-fifth century B.C. . . DLB-176

Parnell, Thomas 1679-1718 . . . . DLB-95

Parnicki, Teodor 1908-1988 . . . . DLB-215

Parnok, Sofiia Iakovlevna (Parnokh)
  1885-1933 . . . . DLB-295

Parr, Catherine 1513?-1548 . . . . DLB-136

Parra, Nicanor 1914- DLB-283

Parrington, Vernon L. 1871-1929 . . . . . DLB-17, 63

Parrish, Maxfield 1870-1966 . . . . DLB-188

Parronchi, Alessandro 1914- DLB-128

Parshchikov, Aleksei Maksimovich
  (Raiderman) 1954- DLB-285

Partisan Review DLB-303

Parton, James 1822-1891 . . . . DLB-30

Parton, Sara Payson Willis
   1811-1872 . . . . DLB-43, 74, 239

S. W. Partridge and Company DLB-106

Parun, Vesna 1922- DLB-181; CDWLB-4

Pascal, Blaise 1623-1662. . . . . DLB-268

Pasinetti, Pier Maria 1913- DLB-177

   Tribute to Albert Erskine Y-93

Pasolini, Pier Paolo 1922-1975 . . . . . DLB-128, 177

Pastan, Linda 1932- DLB-5

Pasternak, Boris
   1890-1960 . . . . DLB-302

Paston, George (Emily Morse Symonds)
   1860-1936 . . . . DLB-149, 197

The Paston Letters 1422-1509 . . . . DLB-146

Pastoral Novel of the Sixteenth
   Century, The DLB-318

Pastorius, Francis Daniel
   1651-circa 1720 . . . . DLB-24

Patchen, Kenneth 1911-1972 . . . . DLB-16, 48

Pater, Walter 1839-1894. . . DLB-57, 156; CDBLB-4

   Aesthetic Poetry (1873) DLB-35

   "Style" (1888) [excerpt] DLB-57

Paterson, A. B. "Banjo" 1864-1941 . . . . . . DLB-230

Paterson, Katherine 1932- DLB-52

Patmore, Coventry 1823-1896 . . . . DLB-35, 98

Paton, Alan 1903-1988 . . . . DLB-225; DS-17

Paton, Joseph Noel 1821-1901 . . . . DLB-35

Paton Walsh, Jill 1937- DLB-161

Patrick, Edwin Hill ("Ted") 1901-1964 . . . DLB-137

Patrick, John 1906-1995 . . . . DLB-7

Pattee, Fred Lewis 1863-1950 . . . . DLB-71

Patterson, Alicia 1906-1963 . . . . DLB-127

Patterson, Eleanor Medill 1881-1948 . . . . . DLB-29

Patterson, Eugene 1923- DLB-127

Patterson, Joseph Medill 1879-1946 . . . . . . DLB-29

Pattillo, Henry 1726-1801 . . . . DLB-37

Paul, Elliot 1891-1958 . . . . DLB-4; DS-15

Paul, Jean (see Richter, Johann Paul Friedrich)

Paul, Kegan, Trench, Trubner and
   Company Limited DLB-106

Peter Paul Book Company DLB-49

Stanley Paul and Company Limited DLB-112

Paulding, James Kirke
   1778-1860 . . . . DLB-3, 59, 74, 250

Paulin, Tom 1949- DLB-40

Pauper, Peter, Press DLB-46

Paustovsky, Konstantin Georgievich
   1892-1968 . . . . DLB-272

Pavese, Cesare 1908-1950 . . . . DLB-128, 177

Pavić, Milorad 1929- DLB-181; CDWLB-4

Pavlov, Konstantin 1933- DLB-181

Pavlov, Nikolai Filippovich 1803-1864 . . . . DLB-198

Pavlova, Karolina Karlovna 1807-1893 . . . . DLB-205

Pavlović, Miodrag
   1928- DLB-181; CDWLB-4

Pavlovsky, Eduardo 1933- DLB-305

Paxton, John 1911-1985 . . . . DLB-44

Payn, James 1830-1898 . . . . DLB-18

Payne, John 1842-1916 . . . . DLB-35

Payne, John Howard 1791-1852 . . . . DLB-37

Payson and Clarke DLB-46

Paz, Octavio 1914-1998 . . . . DLB-290; Y-90, 98

   Nobel Lecture 1990 . . . . Y-90

Pazzi, Roberto 1946- DLB-196

Pea, Enrico 1881-1958 . . . . DLB-264

Peabody, Elizabeth Palmer
   1804-1894 . . . . DLB-1, 223

   Preface to *Record of a School:
   Exemplifying the General Principles
   of Spiritual Culture* DS-5

Elizabeth Palmer Peabody
   [publishing house] DLB-49

Peabody, Josephine Preston 1874-1922 . . . DLB-249

Peabody, Oliver William Bourn
   1799-1848 . . . . DLB-59

Peace, Roger 1899-1968 . . . . DLB-127

Peacham, Henry 1578-1644? DLB-151

Peacham, Henry, the Elder
   1547-1634 . . . . DLB-172, 236

Peachtree Publishers, Limited DLB-46

Peacock, Molly 1947- DLB-120

Peacock, Thomas Love 1785-1866 . . . DLB-96, 116

Pead, Deuel ?-1727 . . . . DLB-24

Peake, Mervyn 1911-1968 . . . . . . DLB-15, 160, 255

Peale, Rembrandt 1778-1860 . . . . DLB-183

Pear Tree Press DLB-112

Pearce, Philippa 1920- DLB-161

H. B. Pearson [publishing house] DLB-49

Pearson, Hesketh 1887-1964 . . . . DLB-149

Peattie, Donald Culross 1898-1964 . . . . . . DLB-275

Pechersky, Andrei (see Mel'nikov, Pavel Ivanovich)

Peck, George W. 1840-1916 . . . . DLB-23, 42

H. C. Peck and Theo. Bliss
   [publishing house] DLB-49

Peck, Harry Thurston 1856-1914 . . . . . DLB-71, 91

Peden, William 1913-1999 . . . . DLB-234

   Tribute to William Goyen Y-83

Peele, George 1556-1596 . . . . DLB-62, 167

Pegler, Westbrook 1894-1969 . . . . DLB-171

Péguy, Charles 1873-1914 . . . . DLB-258

Peirce, Charles Sanders 1839-1914 . . . . . . DLB-270

Pekić, Borislav 1930-1992 . . . DLB-181; CDWLB-4

Pelecanos, George P. 1957- DLB-306

Peletier du Mans, Jacques 1517-1582 . . . . DLB-327

Pelevin, Viktor Olegovich 1962- DLB-285

Pellegrini and Cudahy DLB-46

Pelletier, Aimé (see Vac, Bertrand)

Pelletier, Francine 1959- DLB-251

Pellicer, Carlos 1897?-1977 . . . . DLB-290

Pemberton, Sir Max 1863-1950 . . . . DLB-70

de la Peña, Terri 1947- DLB-209

Penfield, Edward 1866-1925 . . . . DLB-188

Penguin Books [U.K.] DLB-112

   Fifty Penguin Years Y-85

   Penguin Collectors' Society Y-98

Penguin Books [U.S.] DLB-46

Penn, William 1644-1718 . . . . DLB-24

Penn Publishing Company DLB-49

Penna, Sandro 1906-1977 . . . . DLB-114

Pennell, Joseph 1857-1926 . . . . DLB-188

Penner, Jonathan 1940- Y-83

Pennington, Lee 1939- Y-82

Penton, Brian 1904-1951 . . . . DLB-260

Pepper, Stephen C. 1891-1972 . . . . DLB-270

Pepys, Samuel
   1633-1703 . . . . DLB-101, 213; CDBLB-2

Percy, Thomas 1729-1811 . . . . DLB-104

Percy, Walker 1916-1990 . . . . DLB-2; Y-80, 90

   Tribute to Caroline Gordon Y-81

Percy, William 1575-1648 . . . . DLB-172

Perec, Georges 1936-1982 . . . . DLB-83, 299

Perelman, Bob 1947- DLB-193

Perelman, S. J. 1904-1979 . . . . DLB-11, 44

Perez, Raymundo "Tigre"
   1946- DLB-122

Pérez de Ayala, Ramón 1880-1962 . . . . . DLB-322

Pérez de Guzmán, Fernán
   ca. 1377-ca. 1460 . . . . DLB-286

Pérez-Reverte, Arturo 1951- DLB-322

Peri Rossi, Cristina 1941- DLB-145, 290

Perkins, Eugene 1932- DLB-41

Perkins, Maxwell
   The Claims of Business and Literature:
   An Undergraduate Essay Y-01

Perkins, William 1558-1602 . . . . DLB-281

Perkoff, Stuart Z. 1930-1974 . . . . DLB-16

Perley, Moses Henry 1804-1862 . . . . DLB-99

Permabooks DLB-46

Perovsky, Aleksei Alekseevich
   (Antonii Pogorel'sky) 1787-1836 . . . . . DLB-198

Perrault, Charles 1628-1703 . . . . DLB-268

Perri, Henry 1561-1617 . . . . DLB-236

Perrin, Alice 1867-1934 . . . . DLB-156

Perry, Anne 1938- DLB-276

Perry, Bliss 1860-1954 . . . . DLB-71

Perry, Eleanor 1915-1981 . . . . DLB-44

Perry, Henry (see Perri, Henry)

Perry, Matthew 1794-1858 . . . . DLB-183

Cumulative Index

Perry, Sampson 1747-1823............ DLB-158

Perse, Saint-John 1887-1975........... DLB-258

Persius A.D. 34-A.D. 62............... DLB-211

Perutz, Leo 1882-1957................ DLB-81

Pesetsky, Bette 1932-................ DLB-130

Pessanha, Camilo 1867-1926.......... DLB-287

Pessoa, Fernando 1888-1935.......... DLB-287

Pestalozzi, Johann Heinrich 1746-1827.... DLB-94

Peter, Laurence J. 1919-1990........... DLB-53

Peter of Spain circa 1205-1277......... DLB-115

Peterkin, Julia 1880-1961............. DLB-9

Peters, Ellis (Edith Pargeter)
1913-1995......................DLB-276

Peters, Lenrie 1932-................ DLB-117

Peters, Robert 1924-................ DLB-105

    "Foreword to *Ludwig of Baviria*"..... DLB-105

Petersham, Maud 1889-1971 and
Petersham, Miska 1888-1960......... DLB-22

Peterson, Charles Jacobs 1819-1887...... DLB-79

Peterson, Len 1917-................. DLB-88

Peterson, Levi S. 1933-.............. DLB-206

Peterson, Louis 1922-1998............ DLB-76

Peterson, T. B., and Brothers.......... DLB-49

Petitclair, Pierre 1813-1860........... DLB-99

Petrescu, Camil 1894-1957............ DLB-220

Petronius circa A.D. 20-A.D. 66
.... DLB-211; CDWLB-1

Petrov, Aleksandar 1938-............ DLB-181

Petrov, Evgenii (Evgenii Petrovich Kataev)
1903-1942...................... DLB-272

Petrov, Gavriil 1730-1801............ DLB-150

Petrov, Valeri 1920-................ DLB-181

Petrov, Vasilii Petrovich 1736-1799...... DLB-150

Petrović, Rastko
1898-1949.............DLB-147; CDWLB-4

Petrushevskaia, Liudmila Stefanovna
1938-........................... DLB-285

Petruslied circa 854?................ DLB-148

Petry, Ann 1908-1997................ DLB-76

Pettie, George circa 1548-1589........ DLB-136

Pétur Gunnarsson 1947-............. DLB-293

Peyton, K. M. 1929-................ DLB-161

Pfaffe Konrad fl. circa 1172........... DLB-148

Pfaffe Lamprecht fl. circa 1150......... DLB-148

Pfeiffer, Emily 1827-1890............. DLB-199

Pforzheimer, Carl H. 1879-1957........ DLB-140

Phaedrus circa 18 B.C.-circa A.D. 50..... DLB-211

Phaer, Thomas 1510?-1560........... DLB-167

Phaidon Press Limited............... DLB-112

Pharr, Robert Deane 1916-1992........ DLB-33

Phelps, Elizabeth Stuart 1815-1852...... DLB-202

Phelps, Elizabeth Stuart 1844-1911... DLB-74, 221

Philander von der Linde
  (see Mencke, Johann Burckhard)

Philby, H. St. John B. 1885-1960...... DLB-195

Philip, Marlene Nourbese 1947-...... DLB-157

Philippe, Charles-Louis 1874-1909....... DLB-65

Philips, John 1676-1708............... DLB-95

Philips, Katherine 1632-1664.......... DLB-131

Phillipps, Sir Thomas 1792-1872........ DLB-184

Phillips, Caryl 1958-............... DLB-157

Phillips, David Graham
1867-1911................ DLB-9, 12, 303

Phillips, Jayne Anne 1952-......DLB-292; Y-80

    Tribute to Seymour Lawrence.......... Y-94

Phillips, Robert 1938-............... DLB-105

    "Finding, Losing, Reclaiming: A Note
on My Poems"............... DLB-105

    Tribute to William Goyen............ Y-83

Phillips, Stephen 1864-1915........... DLB-10

Phillips, Ulrich B. 1877-1934.......... DLB-17

Phillips, Wendell 1811-1884.......... DLB-235

Phillips, Willard 1784-1873............ DLB-59

Phillips, William 1907-2002........... DLB-137

Phillips, Sampson and Company........ DLB-49

Phillpotts, Adelaide Eden (Adelaide Ross)
1896-1993..................... DLB-191

Phillpotts, Eden 1862-1960...DLB-10, 70, 135, 153

Philo circa 20-15 B.C.-circa A.D. 50.......DLB-176

Philosophical Dictionary, Voltaire.......... DLB-314

Philosophical Library................. DLB-46

Philosophy

    Eighteenth-Century Philosophical
Background................... DLB-31

    Philosophic Thought in Boston..... DLB-235

    Translators of the Twelfth Century:
Literary Issues Raised and
Impact Created.............. DLB-115

Elihu Phinney [publishing house]........ DLB-49

Phoenix, John (see Derby, George Horatio)

PHYLON (Fourth Quarter, 1950),
The Negro in Literature:
The Current Scene................ DLB-76

Physiologus circa 1070-circa 1150........ DLB-148

Π.O. (Pi O, Peter Oustabasides)
1951-........................... DLB-325

Piccolo, Lucio 1903-1969............ DLB-114

Pichette, Henri 1924-2000............ DLB-321

Pickard, Tom 1946-................. DLB-40

William Pickering [publishing house].... DLB-106

Pickthall, Marjorie 1883-1922.......... DLB-92

Picoult, Jodi 1966-................. DLB-292

Pictorial Printing Company............ DLB-49

Piel, Gerard 1915-2004............... DLB-137

    "An Announcement to Our Readers,"
Gerard Piel's Statement in *Scientific
American* (April 1948).......... DLB-137

Pielmeier, John 1949-............... DLB-266

Piercy, Marge 1936-............DLB-120, 227

Pierre, DBC 1961-................. DLB-326

Pierro, Albino 1916-1995............. DLB-128

Pignotti, Lamberto 1926-............ DLB-128

Pike, Albert 1809-1891................ DLB-74

Pike, Zebulon Montgomery 1779-1813... DLB-183

Pillat, Ion 1891-1945................. DLB-220

Pil'niak, Boris Andreevich (Boris Andreevich
Vogau) 1894-1938..............DLB-272

Pilon, Jean-Guy 1930-............... DLB-60

Pinar, Florencia fl. ca. late
fifteenth century................. DLB-286

Pinckney, Eliza Lucas 1722-1793....... DLB-200

Pinckney, Josephine 1895-1957.......... DLB-6

Pindar circa 518 B.C.-circa 438 B.C.
.....................DLB-176; CDWLB-1

Pindar, Peter (see Wolcot, John)

Pineda, Cecile 1942-................ DLB-209

Pinero, Arthur Wing 1855-1934........ DLB-10

Piñero, Miguel 1946-1988............ DLB-266

Pinget, Robert 1919-1997............. DLB-83

Pinkney, Edward Coote
1802-1828...................... DLB-248

Pinnacle Books..................... DLB-46

Piñon, Nélida 1935-.............DLB-145, 307

Pinsky, Robert 1940-................. Y-82

    Reappointed Poet Laureate............ Y-98

Pinter, Harold 1930-.... DLB-13, 310; CDBLB-8

    Writing for the Theatre............ DLB-13

Pinto, Fernão Mendes 1509/1511?-1583.. DLB-287

Piontek, Heinz 1925-................ DLB-75

Piozzi, Hester Lynch [Thrale]
1741-1821..................DLB-104, 142

Piper, H. Beam 1904-1964............. DLB-8

Piper, Watty...................... DLB-22

Pirandello, Luigi 1867-1936........... DLB-264

Pirckheimer, Caritas 1467-1532.........DLB-179

Pirckheimer, Willibald 1470-1530.......DLB-179

Pires, José Cardoso 1925-1998......... DLB-287

Pisar, Samuel 1929-................. Y-83

Pisarev, Dmitrii Ivanovich 1840-1868.....DLB-277

Pisemsky, Aleksei Feofilaktovich
1821-1881..................... DLB-238

Pitkin, Timothy 1766-1847............ DLB-30

Pitter, Ruth 1897-1992............... DLB-20

Pix, Mary 1666-1709................. DLB-80

Pixerécourt, René Charles Guilbert de
1773-1844..................... DLB-192

Pizarnik, Alejandra 1936-1972......... DLB-283

Plá, Josefina 1909-1999.............. DLB-290

Plaatje, Sol T. 1876-1932..........DLB-125, 225

Planchon, Roger 1931-............. DLB-321

Plante, David 1940- Y-83

Plantinga, Alvin 1932- DLB-279

Platen, August von 1796-1835 ....DLB-90

Plath, Sylvia
    1932-1963 ....DLB-5, 6, 152; CDALB-1

Plato circa 428 B.C.-348-347 B.C.
    .... DLB-176; CDWLB-1

Plato, Ann 1824-? DLB-239

Platon 1737-1812 ....DLB-150

Platonov, Andrei Platonovich (Andrei
    Platonovich Klimentev)
    1899-1951 ....DLB-272

Platt, Charles 1945- DLB-261

Platt and Munk Company DLB-46

Plautus circa 254 B.C.-184 B.C.
    .... DLB-211; CDWLB-1

Playboy Press........................DLB-46

John Playford [publishing house] DLB-170

Der Pleier fl. circa 1250 ....DLB-138

Pleijel, Agneta 1940- DLB-257

Plenzdorf, Ulrich 1934- DLB-75

Pleshcheev, Aleksei Nikolaevich
    1825?-1893 ....DLB-277

Plessen, Elizabeth 1944- DLB-75

Pletnev, Petr Aleksandrovich
    1792-1865 ....DLB-205

Pliekšāne, Elza Rozenberga (see Aspazija)

Pliekšāns, Jānis (see Rainis, Jānis)

Plievier, Theodor 1892-1955 ....DLB-69

Plimpton, George 1927-2003 .. DLB-185, 241; Y-99

Pliny the Elder A.D. 23/24-A.D. 79 ....DLB-211

Pliny the Younger
    circa A.D. 61-A.D. 112 ....DLB-211

Plomer, William
    1903-1973 ....DLB-20, 162, 191, 225

Plotinus 204-270.......... DLB-176; CDWLB-1

Plowright, Teresa 1952- DLB-251

Plume, Thomas 1630-1704 ....DLB-213

Plumly, Stanley 1939- DLB-5, 193

Plumpp, Sterling D. 1940- DLB-41

Plunkett, James 1920-2003................DLB-14

Plutarch
    circa 46-circa 120........ DLB-176; CDWLB-1

Plymell, Charles 1935- DLB-16

Pocket Books........................DLB-46

Podestá, José J. 1858-1937 ....DLB-305

Poe, Edgar Allan 1809-1849
    ....DLB-3, 59, 73, 74, 248; CDALB-2

    The Poe Studies Association Y-99

Poe, James 1921-1980 ....DLB-44

The Poet Laureate of the United States Y-86

    Statements from Former Consultants
    in Poetry......................Y-86

Poetry
    Aesthetic Poetry (1873) DLB-35

A Century of Poetry, a Lifetime of
    Collecting: J. M. Edelstein's
    Collection of Twentieth-
    Century American Poetry..........Y-02

"Certain Gifts," by Betty Adcock DLB-105

Concrete Poetry DLB-307

Contempo Caravan: Kites in a
    Windstorm.....................Y-85

"Contemporary Verse Story-telling,"
    by Jonathan Holden DLB-105

"A Detail in a Poem," by Fred
    Chappell....................DLB-105

"The English Renaissance of Art"
    (1908), by Oscar Wilde DLB-35

"Every Man His Own Poet; or,
    The Inspired Singer's Recipe
    Book" (1877), by
    H. W. Mallock DLB-35

"Eyes Across Centuries: Contemporary
    Poetry and 'That Vision Thing,'"
    by Philip Dacey...............DLB-105

A Field Guide to Recent Schools
    of American Poetry................Y-86

"Finding, Losing, Reclaiming:
    A Note on My Poems,
    by Robert Phillips" DLB-105

"The Fleshly School of Poetry and Other
    Phenomena of the Day" (1872)....DLB-35

"The Fleshly School of Poetry:
    Mr. D. G. Rossetti" (1871) DLB-35

The G. Ross Roy Scottish Poetry Collection
    at the University of South Carolina ...Y-89

"Getting Started: Accepting the Regions
    You Own—or Which Own You,"
    by Walter McDonald DLB-105

"The Good, The Not So Good," by
    Stephen Dunn................DLB-105

The Griffin Poetry Prize Y-00

The Hero as Poet. Dante; Shakspeare
    (1841), by Thomas Carlyle.......DLB-32

"Images and 'Images,'" by Charles
    Simic.......................DLB-105

"Into the Mirror," by Peter Cooley ...DLB-105

"Knots into Webs: Some Autobiographical
    Sources," by Dabney Stuart DLB-105

"L'Envoi" (1882), by Oscar Wilde DLB-35

"Living in Ruin," by Gerald Stern....DLB-105

Looking for the Golden Mountain:
    Poetry Reviewing Y-89

Lyric Poetry (French)..............DLB-268

Medieval Galician-Portuguese
    Poetry......................DLB-287

"The No Self, the Little Self, and the
    Poets," by Richard Moore........DLB-105

On Some of the Characteristics of Modern
    Poetry and On the Lyrical Poems of
    Alfred Tennyson (1831) DLB-32

The Pitt Poetry Series: Poetry Publishing
    Today Y-85

"The Poetry File," by Edward
    Field DLB-105

Poetry in Nineteenth-Century France:
    Cultural Background and Critical
    Commentary DLB-217

The Poetry of Jorge Luis Borges Y-86

"The Poet's Kaleidoscope: The Element
    of Surprise in the Making of the
    Poem" by Madeline DeFrees DLB-105

The Pre-Raphaelite Controversy......DLB-35

Protest Poetry in Castile DLB-286

"Reflections: After a Tornado,"
    by Judson Jerome DLB-105

Statements from Former Consultants
    in Poetry......................Y-86

Statements on the Art of Poetry DLB-54

The Study of Poetry (1880), by
    Matthew Arnold...............DLB-35

A Survey of Poetry Anthologies,
    1879-1960 ....DLB-54

Thoughts on Poetry and Its Varieties
    (1833), by John Stuart Mill.......DLB-32

Under the Microscope (1872), by
    A. C. Swinburne...............DLB-35

The Unterberg Poetry Center of the
    92nd Street Y Y-98

Victorian Poetry: Five Critical
    Views DLBV-35

Year in Poetry Y-83–92, 94–01

Year's Work in American Poetry.........Y-82

Poets
    The Lives of the Poets (1753) DLB-142

    Minor Poets of the Earlier
    Seventeenth Century DLB-121

    Other British Poets Who Fell
    in the Great War.............DLB-216

    Other Poets [French] DLB-217

    Second-Generation Minor Poets of
    the Seventeenth Century DLB-126

    Third-Generation Minor Poets of
    the Seventeenth Century DLB-131

Pogodin, Mikhail Petrovich 1800-1875....DLB-198

Pogorel'sky, Antonii
    (see Perovsky, Aleksei Alekseevich)

Pohl, Frederik 1919- DLB-8

    Tribute to Isaac Asimov Y-92

    Tribute to Theodore Sturgeon Y-85

Poirier, Louis (see Gracq, Julien)

Poláček, Karel 1892-1945 ... DLB-215; CDWLB-4

Polanyi, Michael 1891-1976...........DLB-100

Pole, Reginald 1500-1558 ....DLB-132

Polevoi, Nikolai Alekseevich 1796-1846...DLB-198

Polezhaev, Aleksandr Ivanovich
    1804-1838 ....DLB-205

Poliakoff, Stephen 1952- DLB-13

Polidori, John William 1795-1821 ....DLB-116

Polite, Carlene Hatcher 1932- DLB-33

Pollard, Alfred W. 1859-1944 ....DLB-201

Pollard, Edward A. 1832-1872 ....DLB-30

Pollard, Graham 1903-1976............DLB-201

Pollard, Percival 1869-1911 ....DLB-71

Pollard and Moss....................DLB-49

Pollock, Sharon 1936- DLB-60

Polonsky, Abraham 1910-1999 ....DLB-26

Polonsky, Iakov Petrovich 1819-1898 . . . . . DLB-277

Polotsky, Simeon 1629-1680 . . . . DLB-150

Polybius circa 200 B.C.-118 B.C. DLB-176

Pomialovsky, Nikolai Gerasimovich
1835-1863 . . . . DLB-238

Pomilio, Mario 1921-1990 . . . . .DLB-177

Pompéia, Raul (Raul d'Avila Pompéia)
1863-1895 . . . . DLB-307

Ponce, Mary Helen 1938- DLB-122

Ponce-Montoya, Juanita 1949- DLB-122

Ponet, John 1516?-1556 . . . . DLB-132

Ponge, Francis 1899-1988 . . . . .DLB-258; Y-02

Poniatowska, Elena
1933- DLB-113; CDWLB-3

Ponsard, François 1814-1867 . . . . DLB-192

William Ponsonby [publishing house] DLB-170

Pontiggia, Giuseppe 1934- DLB-196

Pontoppidan, Henrik 1857-1943 . . . . DLB-300

Pony Stories, Omnibus Essay on DLB-160

Poole, Ernest 1880-1950 . . . . DLB-9

Poole, Sophia 1804-1891 . . . . DLB-166

Poore, Benjamin Perley 1820-1887 . . . . DLB-23

Popa, Vasko 1922-1991 . . . . . DLB-181; CDWLB-4

Pope, Abbie Hanscom 1858-1894 . . . . DLB-140

Pope, Alexander
1688-1744 . . . . . . DLB-95, 101, 213; CDBLB-2

Poplavsky, Boris 1903-1935 . . . . DLB-317

Popov, Aleksandr Serafimovich
(see Serafimovich, Aleksandr Serafimovich)

Popov, Evgenii Anatol'evich 1946- DLB-285

Popov, Mikhail Ivanovich
1742-circa 1790 . . . . DLB-150

Popović, Aleksandar 1929-1996 . . . . DLB-181

Popper, Karl 1902-1994 . . . . DLB-262

Popular Culture Association/
American Culture Association Y-99

Popular Library DLB-46

Poquelin, Jean-Baptiste (see Molière)

Porete, Marguerite ?-1310 . . . . DLB-208

Porlock, Martin (see MacDonald, Philip)

Porpoise Press DLB-112

Porta, Antonio 1935-1989 . . . . DLB-128

Porter, Anna Maria 1780-1832 . . . . . DLB-116, 159

Porter, Cole 1891-1964 . . . . DLB-265

Porter, David 1780-1843 . . . . DLB-183

Porter, Dorothy 1954- DLB-325

Porter, Eleanor H. 1868-1920 . . . . DLB-9

Porter, Gene Stratton (see Stratton-Porter, Gene)

Porter, Hal 1911-1984 . . . . DLB-260

Porter, Henry circa sixteenth century DLB-62

Porter, Jane 1776-1850 . . . . DLB-116, 159

Porter, Katherine Anne 1890-1980
. . . . . . .DLB-4, 9, 102; Y-80; DS-12; CDALB-7

The Katherine Anne Porter Society Y-01

Porter, Peter 1929- DLB-40, 289

Porter, William Sydney (O. Henry)
1862-1910 . . . . DLB-12, 78, 79; CDALB-3

Porter, William T. 1809-1858 . . . . . DLB-3, 43, 250

Porter and Coates DLB-49

Portillo Trambley, Estela 1927-1998 . . . . . DLB-209

Portis, Charles 1933- DLB-6

Medieval Galician-Portuguese Poetry DLB-287

Posey, Alexander 1873-1908 . . . . .DLB-175

Possession, 1990 Booker Prize winner,
A. S. Byatt DLB-326

Postans, Marianne circa 1810-1865 . . . . . . DLB-166

Postgate, Raymond 1896-1971 . . . . .DLB-276

Postl, Carl (see Sealsfield, Carl)

Postmodern Holocaust Fiction DLB-299

Poston, Ted 1906-1974 . . . . DLB-51

Potekhin, Aleksei Antipovich
1829-1908 . . . . DLB-238

Potok, Chaim 1929-2002 . . . . DLB-28, 152

A Conversation with Chaim Potok Y-84

Tribute to Bernard Malamud Y-86

Potter, Beatrix 1866-1943 . . . . DLB-141

The Beatrix Potter Society Y-98

Potter, David M. 1910-1971 . . . . DLB-17

Potter, Dennis 1935-1994 . . . . DLB-233

John E. Potter and Company DLB-49

Pottle, Frederick A. 1897-1987 . . . . . DLB-103; Y-87

Poulin, Jacques 1937- DLB-60

Pound, Ezra 1885-1972
. . . . DLB-4, 45, 63; DS-15; CDALB-4

The Cost of the Cantos: William Bird
to Ezra Pound Y-01

The Ezra Pound Society Y-01

Poverman, C. E. 1944- DLB-234

Povey, Meic 1950- DLB-310

Povich, Shirley 1905-1998 . . . . .DLB-171

Powell, Anthony 1905-2000 . . . DLB-15; CDBLB-7

The Anthony Powell Society: Powell and
the First Biennial Conference Y-01

Powell, Dawn 1897-1965
Dawn Powell, Where Have You Been
All Our Lives? Y-97

Powell, John Wesley 1834-1902 . . . . DLB-186

Powell, Padgett 1952- DLB-234

Powers, J. F. 1917-1999 . . . . DLB-130

Powers, Jimmy 1903-1995 . . . . DLB-241

Pownall, David 1938- DLB-14

Powys, John Cowper 1872-1963 . . . . . DLB-15, 255

Powys, Llewelyn 1884-1939 . . . . DLB-98

Powys, T. F. 1875-1953 . . . . DLB-36, 162

The Powys Society Y-98

Poynter, Nelson 1903-1978 . . . . DLB-127

Prada, Juan Manuel de 1970- DLB-322

Prado, Adélia 1935- DLB-307

Prado, Pedro 1886-1952 . . . . DLB-283

Prados, Emilio 1899-1962 . . . . DLB-134

Praed, Mrs. Caroline (see Praed, Rosa)

Praed, Rosa (Mrs. Caroline Praed)
1851-1935 . . . . DLB-230

Praed, Winthrop Mackworth 1802-1839 . . DLB-96

Praeger Publishers DLB-46

Praetorius, Johannes 1630-1680 . . . . DLB-168

Pratolini, Vasco 1913-1991 . . . . .DLB-177

Pratt, E. J. 1882-1964 . . . . DLB-92

Pratt, Samuel Jackson 1749-1814 . . . . DLB-39

Preciado Martin, Patricia 1939- DLB-209

Préfontaine, Yves 1937- DLB-53

Prelutsky, Jack 1940- DLB-61

Prentice, George D. 1802-1870 . . . . DLB-43

Prentice-Hall DLB-46

Prescott, Orville 1906-1996 . . . . Y-96

Prescott, William Hickling
1796-1859 . . . . DLB-1, 30, 59, 235

Prešeren, France
1800-1849 . . . . DLB-147; CDWLB-4

Presses (See also Publishing)
Small Presses in Great Britain and
Ireland, 1960-1985 . . . . DLB-40

Small Presses I: Jargon Society Y-84

Small Presses II: The Spirit That Moves
Us Press Y-85

Small Presses III: Pushcart Press Y-87

Preston, Margaret Junkin
1820-1897 . . . . DLB-239, 248

Preston, May Wilson 1873-1949 . . . . DLB-188

Preston, Thomas 1537-1598 . . . . DLB-62

Prévert, Jacques 1900-1977 . . . . DLB-258

Prévost d'Exiles, Antoine François
1697-1763 . . . . DLB-314

Price, Anthony 1928- DLB-276

Price, Reynolds 1933- DLB-2, 218, 278

Price, Richard 1723-1791 . . . . DLB-158

Price, Richard 1949- Y-81

Prichard, Katharine Susannah
1883-1969 . . . . DLB-260

Prideaux, John 1578-1650 . . . . DLB-236

Priest, Christopher 1943- DLB-14, 207, 261

Priestley, J. B. 1894-1984
. . . . DLB-10, 34, 77, 100, 139; Y-84; CDBLB-6

Priestley, Joseph 1733-1804 . . . . DLB-252

Prigov, Dmitrii Aleksandrovich 1940- . . DLB-285

Prime, Benjamin Young 1733-1791 . . . . . . DLB-31

Primrose, Diana floruit circa 1630 . . . . . . DLB-126

Prince, F. T. 1912-2003 . . . . DLB-20

Prince, Nancy Gardner
1799-circa 1856 . . . . DLB-239

Prince, Thomas 1687-1758 . . . . DLB-24, 140

Pringle, Thomas 1789-1834 . . . . .DLB-225

Printz, Wolfgang Casper 1641-1717 . . . . . .DLB-168

Prior, Matthew 1664-1721 . . . . .DLB-95

Prisco, Michele 1920-2003 . . . . .DLB-177

Prishvin, Mikhail Mikhailovich
  1873-1954 . . . . .DLB-272

Pritchard, William H. 1932- DLB-111

Pritchett, V. S. 1900-1997 . . . . .DLB-15, 139

Probyn, May 1856 or 1857-1909 . . . . .DLB-199

Procter, Adelaide Anne 1825-1864 . . . .DLB-32, 199

Procter, Bryan Waller 1787-1874 . . . . . .DLB-96, 144

Proctor, Robert 1868-1903 . . . . .DLB-184

Prokopovich, Feofan 1681?-1736 . . . . .DLB-150

Prokosch, Frederic 1906-1989 . . . . .DLB-48

Pronzini, Bill 1943- DLB-226

Propertius circa 50 B.C.-post 16 B.C.
  . . . . .DLB-211; CDWLB-1

Propper, Dan 1937- DLB-16

Prose, Francine 1947- DLB-234

Protagoras circa 490 B.C.-420 B.C. DLB-176

Protest Poetry in Castile
  ca. 1445-ca. 1506 . . . . .DLB-286

Proud, Robert 1728-1813 . . . . .DLB-30

Proust, Marcel 1871-1922 . . . . .DLB-65

 Marcel Proust at 129 and the Proust
   Society of America Y-00

 Marcel Proust's *Remembrance of Things Past*:
   The Rediscovered Galley Proofs Y-00

Prutkov, Koz'ma Petrovich
  1803-1863 . . . . .DLB-277

Prynne, J. H. 1936- DLB-40

Przybyszewski, Stanislaw 1868-1927 . . . . . .DLB-66

Pseudo-Dionysius the Areopagite floruit
  circa 500 . . . . .DLB-115

Public Lending Right in America
 PLR and the Meaning of Literary
   Property Y-83

 Statement by Sen. Charles
   McC. Mathias, Jr. PLR Y-83

 Statements on PLR by American Writers . . .Y-83

Public Lending Right in the United Kingdom
 The First Year in the United Kingdom Y-83

Publishers [listed by individual names]
 Publishers, Conversations with:
   An Interview with Charles Scribner III . . .Y-94

 An Interview with Donald Lamm Y-95

 An Interview with James Laughlin Y-96

 An Interview with Patrick O'Connor Y-84

Publishing
 The Art and Mystery of Publishing:
   Interviews Y-97

 Book Publishing Accounting: Some Basic
   Concepts Y-98

 1873 Publishers' Catalogues DLB-49

 The Literary Scene 2002: Publishing, Book
   Reviewing, and Literary Journalism . . .Y-02

 Main Trends in Twentieth-Century
   Book Clubs .DLB-46

 Overview of U.S. Book Publishing,
   1910-1945 . . . . .DLB-9

 The Pitt Poetry Series: Poetry Publishing
   Today Y-85

 Publishing Fiction at LSU Press Y-87

 The Publishing Industry in 1998:
   Sturm-und-drang.com Y-98

 The Publishing Industry in 1999 . . . . . . .Y-99

 Publishers and Agents: The Columbia
   Connection Y-87

 Responses to Ken Auletta Y-97

 Southern Writers Between the Wars DLB-9

 The State of Publishing Y-97

 Trends in Twentieth-Century
   Mass Market Publishing DLB-46

 The Year in Book Publishing Y-86

Pückler-Muskau, Hermann von
  1785-1871 . . . . DLB-133

Puértolas, Soledad 1947- DLB-322

Pufendorf, Samuel von 1632-1694 . . . . . . .DLB-168

Pugh, Edwin William 1874-1930 . . . . .DLB-135

Pugin, A. Welby 1812-1852 . . . . .DLB-55

Puig, Manuel 1932-1990 . . . .DLB-113; CDWLB-3

Puisieux, Madeleine d'Arsant de
  1720-1798 . . . . .DLB-314

Pulgar, Hernando del (Fernando del Pulgar)
  ca. 1436-ca. 1492 . . . . .DLB-286

Pulitzer, Joseph 1847-1911 . . . . .DLB-23

Pulitzer, Joseph, Jr. 1885-1955 . . . . .DLB-29

Pulitzer Prizes for the Novel, 1917-1945 . . . . .DLB-9

Pulliam, Eugene 1889-1975 . . . . .DLB-127

Purcell, Deirdre 1945- DLB-267

Purchas, Samuel 1577?-1626 . . . . .DLB-151

Purdy, Al 1918-2000 . . . . .DLB-88

Purdy, James 1923- DLB-2, 218

Purdy, Ken W. 1913-1972 . . . . .DLB-137

Pusey, Edward Bouverie 1800-1882 . . . . . .DLB-55

Pushkin, Aleksandr Sergeevich
  1799-1837 . . . . .DLB-205

Pushkin, Vasilii L'vovich
  1766-1830 . . . . .DLB-205

Putnam, George Palmer
  1814-1872 . . . . .DLB-3, 79, 250, 254

G. P. Putnam [publishing house] DLB-254

G. P. Putnam's Sons [U.K.] DLB-106

G. P. Putnam's Sons [U.S.] DLB-49

 A Publisher's Archives: G. P. Putnam Y-92

Putnam, Hilary 1926- DLB-279

Putnam, Samuel 1892-1950 . . . . .DLB-4; DS-15

Puttenham, George 1529?-1590 . . . . .DLB-281

Puzo, Mario 1920-1999 . . . . .DLB-6

Pyle, Ernie 1900-1945 . . . . .DLB-29

Pyle, Howard
  1853-1911 . . . . .DLB-42, 188; DS-13

Pyle, Robert Michael 1947- DLB-275

Pym, Barbara 1913-1980 . . . . . . DLB-14, 207; Y-87

Pynchon, Thomas 1937- DLB-2, 173

Pyramid Books DLB-46

Pyrnelle, Louise-Clarke 1850-1907 . . . . . . .DLB-42

Pythagoras circa 570 B.C.-? DLB-176

Q

Qays ibn al-Mulawwah circa 680-710 . . . .DLB-311

Qian Zhongshu 1910-1998 . . . . .DLB-328

Quad, M. (see Lewis, Charles B.)

Quaritch, Bernard 1819-1899 . . . . .DLB-184

Quarles, Francis 1592-1644 . . . . .DLB-126

The Quarterly Review 1809-1967 . . . . .DLB-110

Quasimodo, Salvatore 1901-1968 . . . . . . .DLB-114

Queen, Ellery (see Dannay, Frederic, and
  Manfred B. Lee)

Queen, Frank 1822-1882 . . . . .DLB-241

The Queen City Publishing House DLB-49

Queirós, Eça de 1845-1900 . . . . .DLB-287

Queneau, Raymond 1903-1976 . . . . . .DLB-72, 258

Quennell, Peter 1905-1993 . . . . .DLB-155, 195

Quental, Antero de
  1842-1891 . . . . .DLB-287

Quesada, José Luis 1948- DLB-290

Quesnel, Joseph 1746-1809 . . . . .DLB-99

Quiller-Couch, Sir Arthur Thomas
  1863-1944 . . . . .DLB-135, 153, 190

Quin, Ann 1936-1973 . . . . .DLB-14, 231

Quinault, Philippe 1635-1688 . . . . .DLB-268

Quincy, Samuel, of Georgia
  fl. eighteenth century DLB-31

Quincy, Samuel, of Massachusetts
  1734-1789 . . . . .DLB-31

Quindlen, Anna 1952- DLB-292

Quine, W. V. 1908-2000 . . . . .DLB-279

Quinn, Anthony 1915-2001 . . . . .DLB-122

Quinn, John 1870-1924 . . . . .DLB-187

Quiñónez, Naomi 1951- DLB-209

Quintana, Leroy V. 1944- DLB-82

Quintana, Miguel de 1671-1748
 A Forerunner of Chicano
   Literature DLB-122

Quintilian circa A.D. 40-circa A.D. 96 . . . . .DLB-211

Quintus Curtius Rufus
  fl. A.D. 35 . . . . .DLB-211

Harlin Quist Books DLB-46

Quoirez, Françoise (see Sagan, Françoise)

R

Raabe, Wilhelm 1831-1910 . . . . .DLB-129

Raban, Jonathan 1942- DLB-204

Rabe, David 1940- DLB-7, 228; Y-91

Rabelais, François 1494?-1593 . . . . .DLB-327

Cumulative Index

Rabi'ah al-'Adawiyyah circa 720-801 .... DLB-311
Raboni, Giovanni 1932- DLB-128
Rachilde 1860-1953 .... DLB-123, 192
Racin, Kočo 1908-1943................ DLB-147
Racine, Jean 1639-1699 .... DLB-268
Rackham, Arthur 1867-1939........... DLB-141
Raczymow, Henri 1948- DLB-299
Radauskas, Henrikas
 1910-1970............ DLB-220; CDWLB-4
Radcliffe, Ann 1764-1823 ....DLB-39, 178
Raddall, Thomas 1903-1994 .... DLB-68
Radford, Dollie 1858-1920 .... DLB-240
Radichkov, Yordan 1929-2004 .... DLB-181
Radiguet, Raymond 1903-1923 .... DLB-65
Radishchev, Aleksandr Nikolaevich
 1749-1802...................... DLB-150
Radnóti, Miklós
 1909-1944 .... DLB-215; CDWLB-4
Radrigán, Juan 1937- DLB-305
Radványi, Netty Reiling (see Seghers, Anna)
Rafat, Taufiq 1927-1998 .... DLB-323
Rahv, Philip 1908-1973................ DLB-137
Raich, Semen Egorovich 1792-1855 ..... DLB-205
Raičković, Stevan 1928- DLB-181
Raiderman (see Parshchikov, Aleksei Maksimovich)
Raimund, Ferdinand Jakob 1790-1836 .... DLB-90
Raine, Craig 1944- DLB-40
Raine, Kathleen 1908-2003............. DLB-20
Rainis, Jānis 1865-1929..... DLB-220; CDWLB-4
Rainolde, Richard
 circa 1530-1606 .... DLB-136, 236
Rainolds, John 1549-1607............. DLB-281
Rakić, Milan 1876-1938 .....DLB-147; CDWLB-4
Rakosi, Carl 1903-2004 .... DLB-193
Ralegh, Sir Walter
 1554?-1618............ DLB-172; CDBLB-1
Raleigh, Walter
 Style (1897) [excerpt]................ DLB-57
Ralin, Radoy 1923-2004............... DLB-181
Ralph, Julian 1853-1903 .... DLB-23
Ramanujan, A. K. 1929-1993 .... DLB-323
Ramat, Silvio 1939- DLB-128
Ramée, Marie Louise de la (see Ouida)
Ramírez, Sergío 1942- DLB-145
Ramke, Bin 1947- DLB-120
Ramler, Karl Wilhelm 1725-1798 .... DLB-97
Ramon Ribeyro, Julio 1929-1994 .... DLB-145
Ramos, Graciliano 1892-1953 .... DLB-307
Ramos, Manuel 1948- DLB-209
Ramos Sucre, José Antonio 1890-1930... DLB-290
Ramous, Mario 1924- DLB-128
Rampersad, Arnold 1941- DLB-111

Ramsay, Allan 1684 or 1685-1758 .... DLB-95
Ramsay, David 1749-1815 .... DLB-30
Ramsay, Martha Laurens 1759-1811..... DLB-200
Ramsey, Frank P. 1903-1930 .... DLB-262
Ranch, Hieronimus Justesen
 1539-1607..................... DLB-300
Ranck, Katherine Quintana 1942- DLB-122
Rand, Avery and Company DLB-49
Rand, Ayn 1905-1982 ...DLB-227, 279; CDALB-7
Rand McNally and Company DLB-49
Randall, David Anton 1905-1975 .... DLB-140
Randall, Dudley 1914-2000 .... DLB-41
Randall, Henry S. 1811-1876 .... DLB-30
Randall, James G. 1881-1953 .... DLB-17
The Randall Jarrell Symposium: A Small
 Collection of Randall Jarrells........ Y-86
Excerpts From Papers Delivered at the
 Randall Jarrel Symposium.......... Y-86
Randall, John Herman, Jr. 1899-1980.....DLB-279
Randolph, A. Philip 1889-1979.......... DLB-91
Anson D. F. Randolph
 [publishing house] DLB-49
Randolph, Thomas 1605-1635...... DLB-58, 126
Random House DLB-46
Rankin, Ian (Jack Harvey) 1960- DLB-267
Henry Ranlet [publishing house] DLB-49
Ransom, Harry 1908-1976 .... DLB-187
Ransom, John Crowe
 1888-1974.......... DLB-45, 63; CDALB-7
Ransome, Arthur 1884-1967 .... DLB-160
Rao, Raja 1908- DLB-323
Raphael, Frederic 1931- DLB-14, 319
Raphaelson, Samson 1896-1983 .... DLB-44
Rare Book Dealers
 Bertram Rota and His Bookshop........ Y-91
 An Interview with Glenn Horowitz Y-90
 An Interview with Otto Penzler Y-96
 An Interview with Ralph Sipper........ Y-94
 New York City Bookshops in the
  1930s and 1940s: The Recollections
  of Walter Goldwater Y-93
Rare Books
 Research in the American Antiquarian
  Book Trade Y-97
 Two Hundred Years of Rare Books and
  Literary Collections at the
  University of South Carolina Y-00
Rascón Banda, Víctor Hugo 1948- DLB-305
Rashi circa 1040-1105................ DLB-208
Raskin, Ellen 1928-1984................ DLB-52
Rasputin, Valentin Grigor'evich
 1937- DLB-302
Rastell, John 1475?-1536..........DLB-136, 170
Rattigan, Terence
 1911-1977............. DLB-13; CDBLB-7
Raven, Simon 1927-2001 ....DLB-271

Ravenhill, Mark 1966- DLB-310
Ravnkilde, Adda 1862-1883........... DLB-300
Rawicz, Piotr 1919-1982............... DLB-299
Rawlings, Marjorie Kinnan 1896-1953
 ....DLB-9, 22, 102; DS-17; CDALB-7
Rawlinson, Richard 1690-1755 .... DLB-213
Rawlinson, Thomas 1681-1725 .... DLB-213
Rawls, John 1921-2002................DLB-279
Raworth, Tom 1938- DLB-40
Ray, David 1932- DLB-5
Ray, Gordon Norton 1915-1986.....DLB-103, 140
Ray, Henrietta Cordelia 1849-1916 ...... DLB-50
Raymond, Ernest 1888-1974........... DLB-191
Raymond, Henry J. 1820-1869........DLB-43, 79
Raymond, René (see Chase, James Hadley)
Razaf, Andy 1895-1973 .... DLB-265
al-Razi 865?-925? DLB-311
Rea, Michael 1927-1996 .... Y-97
 Michael M. Rea and the Rea Award for
  the Short Story Y-97
Reach, Angus 1821-1856 .... DLB-70
Read, Herbert 1893-1968 .... DLB-20, 149
Read, Martha Meredith
 fl. nineteenth century DLB-200
Read, Opie 1852-1939 .... DLB-23
Read, Piers Paul 1941- DLB-14
Reade, Charles 1814-1884 .... DLB-21
Reader's Digest Condensed Books....... DLB-46
Readers Ulysses Symposium................ Y-97
Reading, Peter 1946- DLB-40
Reading Series in New York City Y-96
Reaney, James 1926- DLB-68
Rebhun, Paul 1500?-1546................DLB-179
Rèbora, Clemente 1885-1957 .... DLB-114
Rebreanu, Liviu 1885-1944 .... DLB-220
Rechy, John 1934- DLB-122, 278; Y-82
Redding, J. Saunders 1906-1988.......DLB-63, 76
J. S. Redfield [publishing house] DLB-49
Redgrove, Peter 1932-2003............. DLB-40
Redmon, Anne 1943- Y-86
Redmond, Eugene B. 1937- DLB-41
Redol, Alves 1911-1969 .... DLB-287
James Redpath [publishing house] DLB-49
Reed, Henry 1808-1854................ DLB-59
Reed, Henry 1914-1986 .... DLB-27
Reed, Ishmael
 1938- DLB-2, 5, 33, 169, 227; DS-8
Reed, Rex 1938- DLB-185
Reed, Sampson 1800-1880 .... DLB-1, 235
Reed, Talbot Baines 1852-1893 .... DLB-141
Reedy, William Marion 1862-1920 ...... DLB-91

584

Reese, Lizette Woodworth 1856-1935 . . . . . DLB-54

Reese, Thomas 1742-1796 . . . . DLB-37

Reeve, Clara 1729-1807 . . . . DLB-39

   Preface to *The Old English Baron*
   (1778) DLB-39

   The Progress of Romance (1785)
   [excerpt] DLB-39

Reeves, James 1909-1978 . . . . DLB-161

Reeves, John 1926- DLB-88

Reeves-Stevens, Garfield 1953- DLB-251

Régio, José (José Maria dos Reis Pereira)
   1901-1969 . . . . DLB-287

Henry Regnery Company DLB-46

Rêgo, José Lins do 1901-1957 . . . . DLB-307

Rehberg, Hans 1901-1963 . . . . DLB-124

Rehfisch, Hans José 1891-1960 . . . . DLB-124

Reich, Ebbe Kløvedal 1940- DLB-214

Reid, Alastair 1926- DLB-27

Reid, B. L. 1918-1990 . . . . DLB-111

Reid, Christopher 1949- DLB-40

Reid, Forrest 1875-1947 . . . . DLB-153

Reid, Helen Rogers 1882-1970. . . . . DLB-29

Reid, James fl. eighteenth century DLB-31

Reid, Mayne 1818-1883. . . . . DLB-21, 163

Reid, Thomas 1710-1796 . . . . DLB-31, 252

Reid, V. S. (Vic) 1913-1987 . . . . DLB-125

Reid, Whitelaw 1837-1912 . . . . DLB-23

Reilly and Lee Publishing Company DLB-46

Reimann, Brigitte 1933-1973 . . . . DLB-75

Reinmar der Alte circa 1165-circa 1205 . . . DLB-138

Reinmar von Zweter
   circa 1200-circa 1250. . . . . DLB-138

Reisch, Walter 1903-1983 . . . . DLB-44

Reizei Family DLB-203

Religion
   A Crisis of Culture: The Changing
   Role of Religion in the
   New Republic. DLB-37

The Remains of the Day, 1989 Booker Prize winner,
   Kazuo Ishiguro DLB-326

Remarque, Erich Maria
   1898-1970 . . . . DLB-56; CDWLB-2

Remington, Frederic
   1861-1909 . . . . DLB-12, 186, 188

Remizov, Aleksei Mikhailovich
   1877-1957. . . . . DLB-295

Renaud, Jacques 1943- DLB-60

Renault, Mary 1905-1983 . . . . Y-83

Rendell, Ruth (Barbara Vine)
   1930- DLB-87, 276

Rensselaer, Maria van Cortlandt van
   1645-1689 . . . . DLB-200

Repplier, Agnes 1855-1950 . . . . DLB-221

Reshetnikov, Fedor Mikhailovich
   1841-1871 . . . . DLB-238

Restif (Rétif) de La Bretonne, Nicolas-Edme
   1734-1806 . . . . DLB-314

Rettenbacher, Simon 1634-1706 . . . . DLB-168

Retz, Jean-François-Paul de Gondi,
   cardinal de 1613-1679 . . . . DLB-268

Reuchlin, Johannes 1455-1522. . . . . DLB-179

Reuter, Christian 1665-after 1712 . . . . . . DLB-168

Fleming H. Revell Company DLB-49

Reverdy, Pierre 1889-1960. . . . . DLB-258

Reuter, Fritz 1810-1874 . . . . DLB-129

Reuter, Gabriele 1859-1941 . . . . DLB-66

Reventlow, Franziska Gräfin zu
   1871-1918 . . . . DLB-66

Review of Reviews Office DLB-112

Rexroth, Kenneth 1905-1982
    . . . . . . DLB-16, 48, 165, 212; Y-82; CDALB-1

   The Commercialization of the Image
   of Revolt DLB-16

Rey, H. A. 1898-1977. . . . . DLB-22

Reyes, Carlos José 1941- DLB-305

Reynal and Hitchcock DLB-46

Reynolds, G. W. M. 1814-1879 . . . . DLB-21

Reynolds, John Hamilton
   1794-1852 . . . . DLB-96

Reynolds, Sir Joshua 1723-1792 . . . . DLB-104

Reynolds, Mack 1917-1983 . . . . DLB-8

Reza, Yazmina 1959- DLB-321

Reznikoff, Charles 1894-1976 . . . . DLB-28, 45

Rhetoric
   Continental European Rhetoricians,
   1400-1600, and Their Influence
   in Reaissance England DLB-236

   A Finding Guide to Key Works on
   Microfilm DLB-236

   Glossary of Terms and Definitions of
   Rhetoic and Logic DLB-236

Rhett, Robert Barnwell 1800-1876 . . . . DLB-43

Rhode, John 1884-1964 . . . . DLB-77

Rhodes, Eugene Manlove 1869-1934 . . . . DLB-256

Rhodes, James Ford 1848-1927 . . . . DLB-47

Rhodes, Richard 1937- DLB-185

Rhys, Jean 1890-1979
    . . . . DLB-36, 117, 162; CDBLB-7; CDWLB-3

Ribeiro, Bernadim
   fl. ca. 1475/1482-1526/1544 . . . . DLB-287

Ricardo, David 1772-1823 . . . . DLB-107, 158

Ricardou, Jean 1932- DLB-83

Riccoboni, Marie-Jeanne (Marie-Jeanne de
   Heurles Laboras de Mézières Riccoboni)
   1713-1792 . . . . DLB-314

Rice, Anne (A. N. Roquelare, Anne Rampling)
   1941- DLB-292

Rice, Christopher 1978- DLB-292

Rice, Elmer 1892-1967. . . . . DLB-4, 7

Rice, Grantland 1880-1954 . . . . DLB-29, 171

Rich, Adrienne 1929- DLB-5, 67; CDALB-7

Richard, Mark 1955- DLB-234

Richard de Fournival
   1201-1259 or 1260 . . . . DLB-208

Richards, David Adams 1950- DLB-53

Richards, George circa 1760-1814 . . . . DLB-37

Richards, I. A. 1893-1979. . . . . DLB-27

Richards, Laura E. 1850-1943 . . . . DLB-42

Richards, William Carey 1818-1892 . . . . . DLB-73

Grant Richards [publishing house] DLB-112

Richardson, Charles F. 1851-1913 . . . . DLB-71

Richardson, Dorothy M. 1873-1957 . . . . . DLB-36

   The Novels of Dorothy Richardson
   (1918), by May Sinclair DLB-36

Richardson, Henry Handel
   (Ethel Florence Lindesay Robertson)
   1870-1946 . . . . DLB-197, 230

Richardson, Jack 1935- DLB-7

Richardson, John 1796-1852 . . . . DLB-99

Richardson, Samuel
   1689-1761 . . . . DLB-39, 154; CDBLB-2

   Introductory Letters from the Second
   Edition of *Pamela* (1741) DLB-39

   Postscript to [the Third Edition of]
   Clarissa (1751) DLB-39

   Preface to the First Edition of
   Pamela (1740) DLB-39

   Preface to the Third Edition of
   Clarissa (1751) [excerpt] DLB-39

   Preface to Volume 1 of *Clarissa*
   (1747) DLB-39

   Preface to Volume 3 of *Clarissa*
   (1748) DLB-39

Richardson, Willis 1889-1977 . . . . DLB-51

Riche, Barnabe 1542-1617 . . . . DLB-136

Richepin, Jean 1849-1926 . . . . DLB-192

Richler, Mordecai 1931-2001 . . . . DLB-53

Richter, Conrad 1890-1968 . . . . DLB-9, 212

Richter, Hans Werner 1908-1993 . . . . DLB-69

Richter, Johann Paul Friedrich
   1763-1825 . . . . DLB-94; CDWLB-2

Joseph Rickerby [publishing house] DLB-106

Rickword, Edgell 1898-1982 . . . . DLB-20

Riddell, Charlotte 1832-1906. . . . . DLB-156

Riddell, John (see Ford, Corey)

Ridge, John Rollin 1827-1867 . . . . DLB-175

Ridge, Lola 1873-1941 . . . . DLB-54

Ridge, William Pett 1859-1930 . . . . DLB-135

Riding, Laura (see Jackson, Laura Riding)

Ridler, Anne 1912-2001 . . . . DLB-27

Ridruego, Dionisio 1912-1975 . . . . DLB-108

Riel, Louis 1844-1885 . . . . DLB-99

Riemer, Johannes 1648-1714 . . . . DLB-168

Riera, Carme 1948- DLB-322

Rifbjerg, Klaus 1931- DLB-214

Riffaterre, Michael 1924- DLB-67

A Conversation between William Riggan
  and Janette Turner Hospital............ Y-02
Riggs, Lynn 1899-1954................DLB-175
Riis, Jacob 1849-1914................. DLB-23
John C. Riker [publishing house]........ DLB-49
Riley, James 1777-1840................ DLB-183
Riley, John 1938-1978................. DLB-40
Rilke, Rainer Maria
  1875-1926............. DLB-81; CDWLB-2
Rimanelli, Giose 1926- DLB-177
Rimbaud, Jean-Nicolas-Arthur
  1854-1891 .... DLB-217
Rinehart and Company DLB-46
Ringuet 1895-1960.................... DLB-68
Ringwood, Gwen Pharis 1910-1984...... DLB-88
Rinser, Luise 1911-2002................ DLB-69
Ríos, Alberto 1952- DLB-122
Ríos, Isabella 1948- DLB-82
Ripley, Arthur 1895-1961............... DLB-44
Ripley, George 1802-1880 .... DLB-1, 64, 73, 235
The Rising Glory of America:
  Three Poems DLB-37
The Rising Glory of America: Written in 1771
  (1786), by Hugh Henry Brackenridge
  and Philip Freneau DLB-37
Riskin, Robert 1897-1955 .... DLB-26
Risse, Heinz 1898-1989 .... DLB-69
Rist, Johann 1607-1667................ DLB-164
Ristikivi, Karl 1912-1977................ DLB-220
Ritchie, Anna Mowatt 1819-1870 ..... DLB-3, 250
Ritchie, Anne Thackeray 1837-1919...... DLB-18
Ritchie, Thomas 1778-1854 .... DLB-43
Rites of Passage, 1980 Booker Prize winner,
  William Golding................. DLB-326
The Ritz Paris Hemingway Award.......... Y-85
  Mario Varga Llosa's Acceptance Speech .. Y-85
Rivard, Adjutor 1868-1945.............. DLB-92
Rive, Richard 1931-1989 .... DLB-125, 225
Rivera, José 1955- DLB-249
Rivera, Marina 1942- DLB-122
Rivera, Tomás 1935-1984................ DLB-82
Rivers, Conrad Kent 1933-1968......... DLB-41
Riverside Press DLB-49
Rivington, James circa 1724-1802........ DLB-43
Charles Rivington [publishing house].... DLB-154
Rivkin, Allen 1903-1990................ DLB-26
Roa Bastos, Augusto 1917-2005 .... DLB-113
Robbe-Grillet, Alain 1922- DLB-83
Robbins, Tom 1936- Y-80
Roberts, Charles G. D. 1860-1943....... DLB-92
Roberts, Dorothy 1906-1993 .... DLB-88
Roberts, Elizabeth Madox
  1881-1941 .... DLB-9, 54, 102

Roberts, John (see Swynnerton, Thomas)
Roberts, Kate 1891-1985 .... DLB-319
Roberts, Keith 1935-2000............. DLB-261
Roberts, Kenneth 1885-1957 .... DLB-9
Roberts, Michèle 1949- DLB-231
Roberts, Theodore Goodridge
  1877-1953..................... DLB-92
Roberts, Ursula Wyllie (see Miles, Susan)
Roberts, William 1767-1849 .... DLB-142
James Roberts [publishing house]....... DLB-154
Roberts Brothers.................... DLB-49
A. M. Robertson and Company........ DLB-49
Robertson, Ethel Florence Lindesay
  (see Richardson, Henry Handel)
Robertson, William 1721-1793 .... DLB-104
Robin, Leo 1895-1984 .... DLB-265
Robins, Elizabeth 1862-1952 .... DLB-197
Robinson, A. Mary F. (Madame James
  Darmesteter, Madame Mary
  Duclaux) 1857-1944............... DLB-240
Robinson, Casey 1903-1979 .... DLB-44
Robinson, Derek 1932- Y-02
Robinson, Edwin Arlington
  1869-1935 .... DLB-54; CDALB-3
  Review by Derek Robinson of George
  Greenfield's *Rich Dust*............. Y-02
Robinson, Henry Crabb 1775-1867 ......DLB-107
Robinson, James Harvey 1863-1936 ..... DLB-47
Robinson, Lennox 1886-1958 .... DLB-10
Robinson, Mabel Louise 1874-1962 ...... DLB-22
Robinson, Marilynne 1943- DLB-206
Robinson, Mary 1758-1800 .... DLB-158
Robinson, Richard circa 1545-1607 ..... DLB-167
Robinson, Therese 1797-1870 .... DLB-59, 133
Robison, Mary 1949- DLB-130
Roblès, Emmanuel 1914-1995 .... DLB-83
Roccatagliata Ceccardi, Ceccardo
  1871-1919..................... DLB-114
Rocha, Adolfo Correira da (see Torga, Miguel)
Roche, Billy 1949- DLB-233
Rochester, John Wilmot, Earl of
  1647-1680..................... DLB-131
Rochon, Esther 1948- DLB-251
Rock, Howard 1911-1976............. DLB-127
Rockwell, Norman Perceval 1894-1978 .. DLB-188
Rodgers, Carolyn M. 1945- DLB-41
Rodgers, W. R. 1909-1969 .... DLB-20
Rodney, Lester 1911- DLB-241
Rodoreda, Mercé 1908-1983 .... DLB-322
Rodrigues, Nelson 1912-1980.......... DLB-307
Rodríguez, Claudio 1934-1999......... DLB-134
Rodríguez, Joe D. 1943- DLB-209
Rodriguez, Judith 1936- DLB-325

Rodríguez, Luis J. 1954- DLB-209
Rodriguez, Richard 1944- DLB-82, 256
Rodríguez Julia, Edgardo 1946- DLB-145
Roe, E. P. 1838-1888 .... DLB-202
Roethke, Theodore
  1908-1963 .... DLB-5, 206; CDALB-1
Rogers, Jane 1952- DLB-194
Rogers, Pattiann 1940- DLB-105
Rogers, Samuel 1763-1855............. DLB-93
Rogers, Will 1879-1935 .... DLB-11
Rohmer, Sax 1883-1959 .... DLB-70
Roig, Montserrat 1946-1991........... DLB-322
Roiphe, Anne 1935- Y-80
Rojas, Arnold R. 1896-1988........... DLB-82
Rojas, Fernando de ca. 1475-1541 ...... DLB-286
Roland de la Platière, Marie-Jeanne
  (Madame Roland) 1754-1793........ DLB-314
Rolfe, Edwin (Solomon Fishman)
  1909-1954 .... DLB-303
Rolfe, Frederick William
  1860-1913 .... DLB-34, 156
Rolland, Romain 1866-1944............ DLB-65
Rolle, Richard circa 1290-1300 - 1349 ... DLB-146
Rölvaag, O. E. 1876-1931.......... DLB-9, 212
Romains, Jules 1885-1972.......... DLB-65, 321
A. Roman and Company DLB-49
Roman de la Rose: Guillaume de Lorris
  1200/1205-circa 1230, Jean de
  Meun 1235-1240-circa 1305........ DLB-208
Romano, Lalla 1906-2001 ....DLB-177
Romano, Octavio 1923- DLB-122
Rome, Harold 1908-1993 .... DLB-265
Romero, Leo 1950- DLB-122
Romero, Lin 1947- DLB-122
Romero, Orlando 1945- DLB-82
Ronsard, Pierre de 1524-1585 .... DLB-327
Rook, Clarence 1863-1915............ DLB-135
Roosevelt, Theodore
  1858-1919 .... DLB-47, 186, 275
Root, Waverley 1903-1982.............. DLB-4
Root, William Pitt 1941- DLB-120
Roquebrune, Robert de 1889-1978....... DLB-68
Rorty, Richard 1931- DLB-246, 279
Rosa, João Guimarães 1908-1967 ...DLB-113, 307
Rosales, Luis 1910-1992 .... DLB-134
Roscoe, William 1753-1831 .... DLB-163
Rose, Dilys 1954- DLB-319
Rose, Reginald 1920-2002 .... DLB-26
Rose, Wendy 1948- DLB-175
Rosegger, Peter 1843-1918 .... DLB-129
Rosei, Peter 1946- DLB-85
Rosen, Norma 1925- DLB-28
Rosenbach, A. S. W. 1876-1952 .... DLB-140

Rosenbaum, Ron 1946- DLB-185

Rosenbaum, Thane 1960- DLB-299

Rosenberg, Isaac 1890-1918 . . . . . . .DLB-20, 216

Rosenfeld, Isaac 1918-1956 . . . . .DLB-28

Rosenthal, Harold 1914-1999 . . . . .DLB-241

    Jimmy, Red, and Others: Harold
    Rosenthal Remembers the Stars of
    the Press Box Y-01

Rosenthal, M. L. 1917-1996. . . . . .DLB-5

Rosenwald, Lessing J. 1891-1979 . . . . .DLB-187

Ross, Alexander 1591-1654 . . . . .DLB-151

Ross, Harold 1892-1951 . . . . .DLB-137

Ross, Jerry 1926-1955 . . . . .DLB-265

Ross, Leonard Q. (see Rosten, Leo)

Ross, Lillian 1927- DLB-185

Ross, Martin 1862-1915. . . . . .DLB-135

Ross, Sinclair 1908-1996 . . . . .DLB-88

Ross, W. W. E. 1894-1966. . . . . .DLB-88

Rosselli, Amelia 1930-1996 . . . . .DLB-128

Rossen, Robert 1908-1966. . . . . .DLB-26

Rosset, Barney 1922- Y-02

Rossetti, Christina 1830-1894 . . .DLB-35, 163, 240

Rossetti, Dante Gabriel
    1828-1882 . . . . DLB-35; CDBLB-4

    The Stealthy School of
    Criticism (1871) DLB-35

Rossner, Judith 1935- DLB-6

Rostand, Edmond 1868-1918 . . . . .DLB-192

Rosten, Leo 1908-1997 . . . . .DLB-11

Rostenberg, Leona 1908-2005 . . . . .DLB-140

Rostopchina, Evdokiia Petrovna
    1811-1858 . . . . .DLB-205

Rostovsky, Dimitrii 1651-1709. . . . . .DLB-150

Rota, Bertram 1903-1966. . . . . .DLB-201

    Bertram Rota and His Bookshop Y-91

Roth, Gerhard 1942- DLB-85, 124

Roth, Henry 1906?-1995. . . . . .DLB-28

Roth, Joseph 1894-1939. . . . . .DLB-85

Roth, Philip
    1933- DLB-2, 28, 173; Y-82; CDALB-6

Rothenberg, Jerome 1931- DLB-5, 193

Rothschild Family DLB-184

Rotimi, Ola 1938- DLB-125

Rotrou, Jean 1609-1650 . . . . .DLB-268

Rousseau, Jean-Jacques 1712-1778 . . . . . .DLB-314

    The Social Contract DLB-314

Routhier, Adolphe-Basile 1839-1920 . . . . . .DLB-99

Routier, Simone 1901-1987 . . . . .DLB-88

George Routledge and Sons. DLB-106

Roversi, Roberto 1923- DLB-128

Rowe, Elizabeth Singer 1674-1737 . . . . .DLB-39, 95

Rowe, Nicholas 1674-1718 . . . . .DLB-84

Rowlands, Ian 1964- DLB-310

Rowlands, Samuel circa 1570-1630 . . . . . .DLB-121

Rowlandson, Mary
    circa 1637-circa 1711 . . . . .DLB-24, 200

Rowley, William circa 1585-1626 . . . . .DLB-58

Rowling, J. K.
    The Harry Potter Phenomenon Y-99

Rowse, A. L. 1903-1997. . . . . .DLB-155

Rowson, Susanna Haswell
    circa 1762-1824 . . . . DLB-37, 200

Roy, Arundhati 1961- DLB-323, 326

Roy, Camille 1870-1943. . . . . .DLB-92

The G. Ross Roy Scottish Poetry Collection
    at the University of South Carolina Y-89

Roy, Gabrielle 1909-1983 . . . . .DLB-68

Roy, Jules 1907-2000 . . . . .DLB-83

The Royal Court Theatre and the English
    Stage Company. DLB-13

The Royal Court Theatre and the New
    Drama DLB-10

The Royal Shakespeare Company
    at the Swan .Y-88

Royall, Anne Newport 1769-1854 . . . .DLB-43, 248

Royce, Josiah 1855-1916 . . . . .DLB-270

The Roycroft Printing Shop. DLB-49

Royde-Smith, Naomi 1875-1964 . . . . . . .DLB-191

Royster, Vermont 1914-1996 . . . . .DLB-127

Richard Royston [publishing house] DLB-170

Rozanov, Vasilii Vasil'evich
    1856-1919 . . . . .DLB-295

Różewicz, Tadeusz 1921- DLB-232

Ruark, Gibbons 1941- DLB-120

Ruban, Vasilii Grigorevich 1742-1795 . . . .DLB-150

Rubens, Bernice 1928-2004 . . . . . DLB-14, 207, 326

Rubião, Murilo 1916-1991. . . . . .DLB-307

Rubina, Dina Il'inichna 1953- DLB-285

Rubinshtein, Lev Semenovich 1947- . . .DLB-285

Rudd and Carleton DLB-49

Rudd, Steele (Arthur Hoey Davis). DLB-230

Rudkin, David 1936- DLB-13

Rudnick, Paul 1957- DLB-266

Rudnicki, Adolf 1909-1990 . . . . .DLB-299

Rudolf von Ems circa 1200-circa 1254. . . .DLB-138

Ruffin, Josephine St. Pierre 1842-1924. . . . .DLB-79

Rufo, Juan Gutiérrez 1547?-1620? DLB-318

Ruganda, John 1941- DLB-157

Ruggles, Henry Joseph 1813-1906. . . . . . . .DLB-64

Ruiz de Burton, María Amparo
    1832-1895 . . . . .DLB-209, 221

Rukeyser, Muriel 1913-1980 . . . . .DLB-48

Rule, Jane 1931- DLB-60

Rulfo, Juan 1918-1986 . . . . . .DLB-113; CDWLB-3

Rumaker, Michael 1932- DLB-16

Rumens, Carol 1944- DLB-40

Rummo, Paul-Eerik 1942- DLB-232

Runyon, Damon
    1880-1946. . . . . DLB-11, 86, 171

Ruodlieb circa 1050-1075 . . . . .DLB-148

Rush, Benjamin 1746-1813 . . . . .DLB-37

Rush, Rebecca 1779-? DLB-200

Rushdie, Salman 1947- DLB-194, 323, 326

Rusk, Ralph L. 1888-1962. . . . . .DLB-103

Ruskin, John
    1819-1900 . . . . . .DLB-55, 163, 190; CDBLB-4

Russ, Joanna 1937- DLB-8

Russell, Benjamin 1761-1845 . . . . .DLB-43

Russell, Bertrand 1872-1970. . . . . . . .DLB-100, 262

Russell, Charles Edward 1860-1941 . . . . . .DLB-25

Russell, Charles M. 1864-1926 . . . . .DLB-188

Russell, Eric Frank 1905-1978 . . . . .DLB-255

Russell, Fred 1906-2003. . . . . .DLB-241

Russell, George William (see AE)

Russell, Countess Mary Annette Beauchamp
    (see Arnim, Elizabeth von)

Russell, Willy 1947- DLB-233

B. B. Russell and Company. DLB-49

R. H. Russell and Son DLB-49

Rutebeuf fl.1249-1277 . . . . .DLB-208

Rutherford, Mark 1831-1913. . . . . .DLB-18

Ruxton, George Frederick
    1821-1848 . . . . .DLB-186

R-va, Zeneida (see Gan, Elena Andreevna)

Ryan, Gig 1956- DLB-325

Ryan, James 1952- DLB-267

Ryan, Michael 1946- Y-82

Ryan, Oscar 1904- DLB-68

Rybakov, Anatolii Naumovich
    1911-1994 . . . . .DLB-302

Ryder, Jack 1871-1936 . . . . .DLB-241

Ryga, George 1932-1987 . . . . .DLB-60

Rylands, Enriqueta Augustina Tennant
    1843-1908 . . . . .DLB-184

Rylands, John 1801-1888. . . . . .DLB-184

Ryle, Gilbert 1900-1976. . . . . .DLB-262

Ryleev, Kondratii Fedorovich
    1795-1826 . . . . .DLB-205

Rymer, Thomas 1643?-1713 . . . . .DLB-101

Ryskind, Morrie 1895-1985. . . . . .DLB-26

Rzhevsky, Aleksei Andreevich
    1737-1804 . . . . .DLB-150

S

The Saalfield Publishing Company DLB-46

Saba, Umberto 1883-1957 . . . . .DLB-114

Sábato, Ernesto 1911- DLB-145; CDWLB-3

Saberhagen, Fred 1930- DLB-8

Cumulative Index

Sabin, Joseph 1821-1881............. DLB-187
Sabino, Fernando (Fernando Tavares Sabino) 1923-2004.................... DLB-307
Sacer, Gottfried Wilhelm 1635-1699..... DLB-168
Sachs, Hans 1494-1576...... DLB-179; CDWLB-2
Sá-Carneiro, Mário de 1890-1916....... DLB-287
Sack, John 1930-2004................ DLB-185
Sackler, Howard 1929-1982............ DLB-7
Sackville, Lady Margaret 1881-1963.... DLB-240
Sackville, Thomas 1536-1608 and Norton, Thomas 1532-1584......... DLB-62
Sackville, Thomas 1536-1608........... DLB-132
Sackville-West, Edward 1901-1965...... DLB-191
Sackville-West, Vita 1892-1962...... DLB-34, 195
Sacred Hunger, 1992 Booker Prize winner, Barry Unsworth................ DLB-326
Sá de Miranda, Francisco de 1481-1588?.................... DLB-287
Sade, Marquis de (Donatien-Alphonse-François, comte de Sade) 1740-1814......... DLB-314
    "Dialogue entre un prêtre et un moribond".................. DLB-314
Sadlier, Mary Anne 1820-1903.......... DLB-99
D. and J. Sadlier and Company......... DLB-49
Sadoff, Ira 1945-................... DLB-120
Sadoveanu, Mihail 1880-1961.......... DLB-220
Sadur, Nina Nikolaevna 1950-....... DLB-285
Sáenz, Benjamin Alire 1954-......... DLB-209
Saenz, Jaime 1921-1986.......... DLB-145, 283
Saffin, John circa 1626-1710........... DLB-24
Sagan, Françoise 1935-............. DLB-83
Sage, Robert 1899-1962................ DLB-4
Sagel, Jim 1947-................... DLB-82
Sagendorph, Robb Hansell 1900-1970... DLB-137
Sahagún, Carlos 1938-.............. DLB-108
Sahgal, Nayantara 1927-............ DLB-323
Sahkomaapii, Piitai (see Highwater, Jamake)
Sahl, Hans 1902-1993................ DLB-69
Said, Edward W. 1935-.............. DLB-67
Saigyō 1118-1190................... DLB-203
Saijo, Albert 1926-................ DLB-312
Saiko, George 1892-1962............. DLB-85
Sainte-Beuve, Charles-Augustin 1804-1869.................... DLB-217
Saint-Exupéry, Antoine de 1900-1944..... DLB-72
Saint-Gelais, Mellin de 1490?-1558...... DLB-327
St. John, J. Allen 1872-1957............ DLB-188
St John, Madeleine 1942-........... DLB-267
St. Johns, Adela Rogers 1894-1988....... DLB-29
St. Omer, Garth 1931-.............. DLB-117
Saint Pierre, Michel de 1916-1987...... DLB-83
Saintsbury, George 1845-1933....... DLB-57, 149
    "Modern English Prose" (1876)...... DLB-57

The Present State of the English Novel (1892),................ DLB-18
Saint-Simon, Louis de Rouvroy, duc de 1675-1755..................... DLB-314
St. Dominic's Press.................. DLB-112
The St. John's College Robert Graves Trust.. Y-96
St. Martin's Press................... DLB-46
St. Nicholas 1873-1881............... DS-13
Saiokuken Sōchō 1448-1532........... DLB-203
Saki (see Munro, H. H.)
Salaam, Kalamu ya 1947-............ DLB-38
Salacrou, Armand 1899-1989.......... DLB-321
Šalamun, Tomaž 1941-..... DLB-181; CDWLB-4
Salas, Floyd 1931-.................. DLB-82
Sálaz-Marquez, Rubén 1935-........ DLB-122
Salcedo, Hugo 1964-................ DLB-305
Salemson, Harold J. 1910-1988.......... DLB-4
Salesbury, William 1520?-1584?........ DLB-281
Salinas, Luis Omar 1937-............ DLB-82
Salinas, Pedro 1891-1951............. DLB-134
Salinger, J. D. 1919-......... DLB-2, 102, 173; CDALB-1
Salkey, Andrew 1928-1995........... DLB-125
Sallust circa 86 B.C.-35 B.C. DLB-211; CDWLB-1
Salt, Waldo 1914-1987................ DLB-44
Salter, James 1925-................. DLB-130
Salter, Mary Jo 1954-............... DLB-120
Saltus, Edgar 1855-1921.............. DLB-202
Saltykov, Mikhail Evgrafovich 1826-1889.................... DLB-238
Salustri, Carlo Alberto (see Trilussa)
Salverson, Laura Goodman 1890-1970.... DLB-92
Samain, Albert 1858-1900............. DLB-217
Sampson, Richard Henry (see Hull, Richard)
Samuels, Ernest 1903-1996............ DLB-111
Sanborn, Franklin Benjamin 1831-1917................... DLB-1, 223
Sánchez, Florencio 1875-1910......... DLB-305
Sánchez, Luis Rafael 1936-...... DLB-145, 305
Sánchez, Philomeno "Phil" 1917-..... DLB-122
Sánchez, Ricardo 1941-1995........... DLB-82
Sánchez, Saúl 1943-................. DLB-209
Sanchez, Sonia 1934-............ DLB-41; DS-8
Sánchez de Arévalo, Rodrigo 1404-1470.................... DLB-286
Sánchez de Badajoz, Diego ?-1552?..... DLB-318
Sánchez Ferlosio, Rafael 1927-....... DLB-322
Sand, George 1804-1876.......... DLB-119, 192
Sandburg, Carl 1878-1967.......... DLB-17, 54; CDALB-3
Sandel, Cora (Sara Fabricius) 1880-1974.................... DLB-297

Sandemose, Aksel 1899-1965.......... DLB-297
Sanders, Edward 1939-......... DLB-16, 244
Sanderson, Robert 1587-1663.......... DLB-281
Sandoz, Mari 1896-1966........... DLB-9, 212
Sandwell, B. K. 1876-1954............ DLB-92
Sandy, Stephen 1934-............... DLB-165
Sandys, George 1578-1644......... DLB-24, 121
Sangster, Charles 1822-1893........... DLB-99
Sanguineti, Edoardo 1930-......... DLB-128
Sanjōnishi Sanetaka 1455-1537......... DLB-203
San Pedro, Diego de fl. ca. 1492........ DLB-286
Sansay, Leonora ?-after 1823.......... DLB-200
Sansom, William 1912-1976........... DLB-139
Sant'Anna, Affonso Romano de 1937-...................... DLB-307
Santayana, George 1863-1952...... DLB-54, 71, 246, 270; DS-13
Santiago, Danny 1911-1988........... DLB-122
Santillana, Marqués de (Íñigo López de Mendoza) 1398-1458.................... DLB-286
Santmyer, Helen Hooven 1895-1986........ Y-84
Santos, Bienvenido 1911-1996......... DLB-312
Sanvitale, Francesca 1928-......... DLB-196
Sapidus, Joannes 1490-1561............DLB-179
Sapir, Edward 1884-1939............. DLB-92
Sapper (see McNeile, Herman Cyril)
Sappho circa 620 B.C.-circa 550 B.C. DLB-176; CDWLB-1
Saramago, José 1922-......... DLB-287; Y-98
    Nobel Lecture 1998: How Characters Became the Masters and the Author Their Apprentice................ Y-98
Sarban (John W. Wall) 1910-1989...... DLB-255
Sardou, Victorien 1831-1908.......... DLB-192
Sarduy, Severo 1937-1993............. DLB-113
Sargent, Pamela 1948-............... DLB-8
Saro-Wiwa, Ken 1941-...............DLB-157
Saroyan, Aram   Rites of Passage [on William Saroyan].... Y-83
Saroyan, William 1908-1981...... DLB-7, 9, 86; Y-81; CDALB-7
Sarraute, Nathalie 1900-1999....... DLB-83, 321
Sarrazin, Albertine 1937-1967............ DLB-83
Sarris, Greg 1952-.................DLB-175
Sarton, May 1912-1995............DLB-48; Y-81
Sartre, Jean-Paul 1905-1980...... DLB-72, 296, 321
Sassoon, Siegfried 1886-1967............ DLB-20, 191; DS-18
    A Centenary Essay.................. Y-86
    Tributes from Vivien F. Clarke and Michael Thorpe................. Y-86
Sata Ineko 1904-1998............... DLB-180
Saturday Review Press................ DLB-46
Saunders, James 1925-2004............ DLB-13

Saunders, John Monk 1897-1940 . . . . DLB-26

Saunders, Margaret Marshall
   1861-1947 . . . . DLB-92

Saunders and Otley DLB-106

Saussure, Ferdinand de 1857-1913 . . . . . . DLB-242

Savage, James 1784-1873 . . . . DLB-30

Savage, Marmion W. 1803?-1872 . . . . DLB-21

Savage, Richard 1697?-1743 . . . . DLB-95

Savard, Félix-Antoine 1896-1982 . . . . DLB-68

Savery, Henry 1791-1842 . . . . DLB-230

Saville, (Leonard) Malcolm 1901-1982 . . . DLB-160

Saville, 1976 Booker Prize winner,
   David Storey DLB-326

Savinio, Alberto 1891-1952 . . . . DLB-264

Sawyer, Robert J. 1960- DLB-251

Sawyer, Ruth 1880-1970 . . . . DLB-22

Sayer, Mandy 1963- DLB-325

Sayers, Dorothy L.
   1893-1957 . . . . DLB-10, 36, 77, 100; CDBLB-6

   The Dorothy L. Sayers Society Y-98

Sayle, Charles Edward 1864-1924 . . . . DLB-184

Sayles, John Thomas 1950- DLB-44

Sbarbaro, Camillo 1888-1967 . . . . DLB-114

Scalapino, Leslie 1947- DLB-193

Scannell, Vernon 1922- DLB-27

Scarry, Richard 1919-1994 . . . . DLB-61

Scève, Maurice circa 1502-circa 1564 . . . . . DLB-327

Schack, Hans Egede 1820-1859 . . . . DLB-300

Schaefer, Jack 1907-1991 . . . . DLB-212

Schaeffer, Albrecht 1885-1950 . . . . DLB-66

Schaeffer, Susan Fromberg 1941- . . . DLB-28, 299

Schaff, Philip 1819-1893 . . . . DS-13

Schaper, Edzard 1908-1984 . . . . DLB-69

Scharf, J. Thomas 1843-1898 . . . . DLB-47

Schede, Paul Melissus 1539-1602 . . . . DLB-179

Scheffel, Joseph Viktor von 1826-1886 . . . DLB-129

Scheffler, Johann 1624-1677 . . . . DLB-164

Schéhadé, Georges 1905-1999 . . . . DLB-321

Schelling, Friedrich Wilhelm Joseph von
   1775-1854 . . . . DLB-90

Scherer, Wilhelm 1841-1886 . . . . DLB-129

Scherfig, Hans 1905-1979 . . . . DLB-214

Schickele, René 1883-1940 . . . . DLB-66

Schiff, Dorothy 1903-1989 . . . . DLB-127

Schiller, Friedrich
   1759-1805 . . . . DLB-94; CDWLB-2

Schindler's Ark, 1982 Booker Prize winner,
   Thomas Keneally DLB-326

Schirmer, David 1623-1687 . . . . DLB-164

Schlaf, Johannes 1862-1941 . . . . DLB-118

Schlegel, August Wilhelm 1767-1845 . . . . . DLB-94

Schlegel, Dorothea 1763-1839 . . . . DLB-90

Schlegel, Friedrich 1772-1829 . . . . DLB-90

Schleiermacher, Friedrich 1768-1834 . . . . . DLB-90

Schlesinger, Arthur M., Jr. 1917- DLB-17

Schlumberger, Jean 1877-1968 . . . . DLB-65

Schmid, Eduard Hermann Wilhelm
   (see Edschmid, Kasimir)

Schmidt, Arno 1914-1979 . . . . DLB-69

Schmidt, Johann Kaspar (see Stirner, Max)

Schmidt, Michael 1947- DLB-40

Schmidtbonn, Wilhelm August
   1876-1952 . . . . DLB-118

Schmitz, Aron Hector (see Svevo, Italo)

Schmitz, James H. 1911-1981 . . . . DLB-8

Schnabel, Johann Gottfried 1692-1760 . . . DLB-168

Schnackenberg, Gjertrud 1953- DLB-120

Schnitzler, Arthur
   1862-1931 . . . . DLB-81, 118; CDWLB-2

Schnurre, Wolfdietrich 1920-1989 . . . . DLB-69

Schocken Books DLB-46

Scholartis Press DLB-112

Scholderer, Victor 1880-1971 . . . . DLB-201

The Schomburg Center for Research
   in Black Culture DLB-76

Schönbeck, Virgilio (see Giotti, Virgilio)

Schönherr, Karl 1867-1943 . . . . DLB-118

Schoolcraft, Jane Johnston 1800-1841 . . . . DLB-175

School Stories, 1914-1960 . . . . DLB-160

Schopenhauer, Arthur 1788-1860 . . . . DLB-90

Schopenhauer, Johanna 1766-1838 . . . . . . DLB-90

Schorer, Mark 1908-1977 . . . . DLB-103

Schottelius, Justus Georg 1612-1676 . . . . . DLB-164

Schouler, James 1839-1920 . . . . DLB-47

Schoultz, Solveig von 1907-1996 . . . . DLB-259

Schrader, Paul 1946- DLB-44

Schreiner, Olive
   1855-1920 . . . . DLB-18, 156, 190, 225

Schroeder, Andreas 1946- DLB-53

Schubart, Christian Friedrich Daniel
   1739-1791 . . . . DLB-97

Schubert, Gotthilf Heinrich 1780-1860 . . . . DLB-90

Schücking, Levin 1814-1883 . . . . DLB-133

Schulberg, Budd 1914- DLB-6, 26, 28; Y-81

   Excerpts from USC Presentation
   [on F. Scott Fitzgerald] Y-96

F. J. Schulte and Company DLB-49

Schulz, Bruno 1892-1942 . . . . DLB-215; CDWLB-4

Schulze, Hans (see Praetorius, Johannes)

Schupp, Johann Balthasar 1610-1661 . . . . . DLB-164

Schurz, Carl 1829-1906 . . . . DLB-23

Schuyler, George S. 1895-1977 . . . . DLB-29, 51

Schuyler, James 1923-1991 . . . . DLB-5, 169

Schwartz, Delmore 1913-1966 . . . . DLB-28, 48

Schwartz, Jonathan 1938- Y-82

Schwartz, Lynne Sharon 1939- DLB-218

Schwarz, Sibylle 1621-1638 . . . . DLB-164

Schwarz-Bart, Andre 1928- DLB-299

Schwerner, Armand 1927-1999 . . . . DLB-165

Schwob, Marcel 1867-1905 . . . . DLB-123

Sciascia, Leonardo 1921-1989 . . . . DLB-177

Science Fiction and Fantasy
   Documents in British Fantasy and
     Science Fiction DLB-178

   Hugo Awards and Nebula Awards DLB-8

   The Iconography of Science-Fiction
     Art DLB-8

   The New Wave DLB-8

   Paperback Science Fiction DLB-8

   Science Fantasy DLB-8

   Science-Fiction Fandom and
     Conventions DLB-8

   Science-Fiction Fanzines: The Time
     Binders DLB-8

   Science-Fiction Films DLB-8

   Science Fiction Writers of America
     and the Nebula Award DLB-8

   Selected Science-Fiction Magazines and
     Anthologies DLB-8

   A World Chronology of Important Science
     Fiction Works (1818-1979) DLB-8

   The Year in Science Fiction
     and Fantasy Y-00, 01

Scot, Reginald circa 1538-1599 . . . . DLB-136

Scotellaro, Rocco 1923-1953 . . . . DLB-128

Scott, Alicia Anne (Lady John Scott)
   1810-1900 . . . . DLB-240

Scott, Catharine Amy Dawson
   1865-1934 . . . . DLB-240

Scott, Dennis 1939-1991 . . . . DLB-125

Scott, Dixon 1881-1915 . . . . DLB-98

Scott, Duncan Campbell 1862-1947 . . . . . . DLB-92

Scott, Evelyn 1893-1963 . . . . DLB-9, 48

Scott, F. R. 1899-1985 . . . . DLB-88

Scott, Frederick George 1861-1944 . . . . . . DLB-92

Scott, Geoffrey 1884-1929 . . . . DLB-149

Scott, Harvey W. 1838-1910 . . . . DLB-23

Scott, John 1948- DLB-325

Scott, Lady Jane (see Scott, Alicia Anne)

Scott, Paul 1920-1978 . . . . DLB-14, 207, 326

Scott, Sarah 1723-1795 . . . . DLB-39

Scott, Tom 1918-1995 . . . . DLB-27

Scott, Sir Walter 1771-1832
   . . . . . . DLB-93, 107, 116, 144, 159; CDBLB-3

Scott, William Bell 1811-1890 . . . . DLB-32

Walter Scott Publishing Company
   Limited DLB-112

William R. Scott [publishing house] DLB-46

Scott-Heron, Gil 1949- DLB-41

Scribe, Eugene 1791-1861 . . . . DLB-192

Scribner, Arthur Hawley 1859-1932 . . . . DS-13, 16

Scribner, Charles 1854-1930..........DS-13, 16
Scribner, Charles, Jr. 1921-1995 .... Y-95
    Reminiscences DS-17
Charles Scribner's Sons DLB-49; DS-13, 16, 17
    Archives of Charles Scribner's Sons.....DS-17
Scribner's Magazine DS-13
Scribner's Monthly DS-13
Scripps, E. W. 1854-1926 .... DLB-25
Scudder, Horace Elisha 1838-1902.... DLB-42, 71
Scudder, Vida Dutton 1861-1954 .... DLB-71
Scudéry, Madeleine de 1607-1701 .... DLB-268
Scupham, Peter 1933- DLB-40
The Sea, 2005 Booker Prize winner,
    John Banville DLB-326
The Sea, The Sea, 1978 Booker Prize winner,
    Iris Murdoch DLB-326
Seabrook, William 1886-1945........... DLB-4
Seabury, Samuel 1729-1796.............. DLB-31
Seacole, Mary Jane Grant 1805-1881 .... DLB-166
The Seafarer circa 970................. DLB-146
Sealsfield, Charles (Carl Postl)
    1793-1864.................. DLB-133, 186
Searle, John R. 1932- DLB-279
Sears, Edward I. 1819?-1876............. DLB-79
Sears Publishing Company............. DLB-46
Seaton, George 1911-1979 .... DLB-44
Seaton, William Winston 1785-1866...... DLB-43
Sebillet, Thomas 1512-1589 .... DLB-327
Martin Secker [publishing house] DLB-112
Martin Secker, and Warburg Limited.... DLB-112
The "Second Generation" Holocaust
    Novel DLB-299
Sedgwick, Arthur George 1844-1915 ..... DLB-64
Sedgwick, Catharine Maria
    1789-1867..........DLB-1, 74, 183, 239, 243
Sedgwick, Ellery 1872-1960 .... DLB-91
Sedgwick, Eve Kosofsky 1950- DLB-246
Sedley, Sir Charles 1639-1701 .... DLB-131
Seeberg, Peter 1925-1999 .... DLB-214
Seeger, Alan 1888-1916................ DLB-45
Seers, Eugene (see Dantin, Louis)
Segal, Erich 1937- Y-86
Segal, Lore 1928- DLB-299
Šegedin, Petar 1909-1998 .... DLB-181
Seghers, Anna 1900-1983 .... DLB-69; CDWLB-2
Seid, Ruth (see Sinclair, Jo)
Seidel, Frederick Lewis 1936- Y-84
Seidel, Ina 1885-1974 .... DLB-56
Seifert, Jaroslav
    1901-1986 ....DLB-215; Y-84; CDWLB-4
    Jaroslav Seifert Through the Eyes of
    the English-Speaking Reader Y-84
    Three Poems by Jaroslav Seifert......... Y-84

Seifullina, Lidiia Nikolaevna 1889-1954...DLB-272
Seigenthaler, John 1927- DLB-127
Seizin Press....................... DLB-112
Séjour, Victor 1817-1874 .... DLB-50
Séjour Marcou et Ferrand, Juan Victor
    (see Séjour, Victor)
Sekowski, Józef-Julian, Baron Brambeus
    (see Senkovsky, Osip Ivanovich)
Selby, Bettina 1934- DLB-204
Selby, Hubert Jr. 1928-2004 .... DLB-2, 227
Selden, George 1929-1989 .... DLB-52
Selden, John 1584-1654 .... DLB-213
Selenić, Slobodan 1933-1995 .... DLB-181
Self, Edwin F. 1920- DLB-137
Self, Will 1961- DLB-207
Seligman, Edwin R. A. 1861-1939 .... DLB-47
Selimović, Meša
    1910-1982 .... DLB-181; CDWLB-4
Sellars, Wilfrid 1912-1989 ....DLB-279
Sellings, Arthur (Arthur Gordon Ley)
    1911-1968 .... DLB-261
Selous, Frederick Courteney 1851-1917 ...DLB-174
Seltzer, Chester E. (see Muro, Amado)
Thomas Seltzer [publishing house] DLB-46
Selvadurai, Shyam 1965- DLB-323
Selvon, Sam 1923-1994..... DLB-125; CDWLB-3
Semel, Nava 1954- DLB-299
Semmes, Raphael 1809-1877 .... DLB-189
Senancour, Etienne de 1770-1846 .... DLB-119
Sena, Jorge de 1919-1978 .... DLB-287
Sendak, Maurice 1928- DLB-61
Sender, Ramón J. 1901-1982 .... DLB-322
Seneca the Elder
    circa 54 B.C.-circa A.D. 40 .... DLB-211
Seneca the Younger
    circa 1 B.C.-A.D. 65..... DLB-211; CDWLB-1
Senécal, Eva 1905-1988 .... DLB-92
Sengstacke, John 1912-1997 .... DLB-127
Senior, Olive 1941- DLB-157
Senkovsky, Osip Ivanovich
    (Józef-Julian Sekowski, Baron Brambeus)
    1800-1858 .... DLB-198
Šenoa, August 1838-1881....DLB-147; CDWLB-4
Sentimental Fiction of the Sixteenth
    Century DLB-318
Sepamla, Sipho 1932- DLB-157, 225
Serafimovich, Aleksandr Serafimovich
    (Aleksandr Serafimovich Popov)
    1863-1949 ....DLB-272
Serao, Matilde 1856-1927 .... DLB-264
Seredy, Kate 1899-1975................ DLB-22
Sereni, Vittorio 1913-1983 .... DLB-128
William Seres [publishing house] DLB-170

Sergeev-Tsensky, Sergei Nikolaevich (Sergei
    Nikolaevich Sergeev) 1875-1958.....DLB-272
Serling, Rod 1924-1975............... DLB-26
Sernine, Daniel 1955- DLB-251
Serote, Mongane Wally 1944- DLB-125, 225
Serraillier, Ian 1912-1994 .... DLB-161
Serrano, Nina 1934- DLB-122
Service, Robert 1874-1958 .... DLB-92
Sessler, Charles 1854-1935 ....DLB-187
Seth, Vikram 1952- DLB-120, 271, 323
Seton, Elizabeth Ann 1774-1821 .... DLB-200
Seton, Ernest Thompson
    1860-1942 .... DLB-92; DS-13
Seton, John circa 1509-1567 .... DLB-281
Setouchi Harumi 1922- DLB-182
Settle, Mary Lee 1918- DLB-6
Seume, Johann Gottfried 1763-1810...... DLB-94
Seuse, Heinrich 1295?-1366 ....DLB-179
Seuss, Dr. (see Geisel, Theodor Seuss)
Severianin, Igor' 1887-1941 .... DLB-295
Severin, Timothy 1940- DLB-204
Sévigné, Marie de Rabutin Chantal,
    Madame de 1626-1696 ....DLB-268
Sewall, Joseph 1688-1769 .... DLB-24
Sewall, Richard B. 1908-2003.......... DLB-111
Sewall, Samuel 1652-1730.............. DLB-24
Sewell, Anna 1820-1878 .... DLB-163
Sewell, Stephen 1953- DLB-325
Sexton, Anne 1928-1974... DLB-5, 169; CDALB-1
Seymour-Smith, Martin 1928-1998 ..... DLB-155
Sgorlon, Carlo 1930- DLB-196
Shaara, Michael 1929-1988 .... Y-83
Shabel'skaia, Aleksandra Stanislavovna
    1845-1921 .... DLB-238
Shadwell, Thomas 1641?-1692.......... DLB-80
Shaffer, Anthony 1926-2001 .... DLB-13
Shaffer, Peter 1926- DLB-13, 233; CDBLB-8
Muhammad ibn Idris al-Shafi'i 767-820 .. DLB-311
Shaftesbury, Anthony Ashley Cooper,
    Third Earl of 1671-1713 .... DLB-101
Shaginian, Marietta Sergeevna
    1888-1982 ....DLB-272
Shairp, Mordaunt 1887-1939 .... DLB-10
Shakespeare, Nicholas 1957- DLB-231
Shakespeare, William
    1564-1616 ..... DLB-62, 172, 263; CDBLB-1
    The New Variorum Shakespeare Y-85
    Shakespeare and Montaigne: A Symposium
    by Jules Furthman Y-02
    $6,166,000 for a *Book!* Observations on
    *The Shakespeare First Folio: The History
    of the Book* Y-01
    Taylor-Made Shakespeare? Or Is
    "Shall I Die?" the Long-Lost Text
    of Bottom's Dream? Y-85

The Shakespeare Globe Trust Y-93

Shakespeare Head Press. DLB-112

Shakhova, Elisaveta Nikitichna
   1822-1899 . . . . .DLB-277

Shakhovskoi, Aleksandr Aleksandrovich
   1777-1846. . . . . .DLB-150

Shalamov, Varlam Tikhonovich
   1907-1982 . . . . .DLB-302

al-Shanfara fl. sixth century DLB-311

Shange, Ntozake 1948- DLB-38, 249

Shapcott, Thomas W. 1935- DLB-289

Shapir, Ol'ga Andreevna 1850-1916 . . . . .DLB-295

Shapiro, Karl 1913-2000 . . . . .DLB-48

Sharon Publications DLB-46

Sharov, Vladimir Aleksandrovich
   1952- DLB-285

Sharp, Margery 1905-1991 . . . . .DLB-161

Sharp, William 1855-1905 . . . . .DLB-156

Sharpe, Tom 1928- DLB-14, 231

Shaw, Albert 1857-1947 . . . . .DLB-91

Shaw, George Bernard
   1856-1950 . . . . DLB-10, 57, 190, CDBLB-6

   The Bernard Shaw Society Y-99

   "Stage Censorship: The Rejected
     Statement" (1911) [excerpts] DLB-10

Shaw, Henry Wheeler 1818-1885 . . . . .DLB-11

Shaw, Irwin
   1913-1984 . . . . . . DLB-6, 102; Y-84; CDALB-1

Shaw, Joseph T. 1874-1952. . . . . .DLB-137

   "As I Was Saying," Joseph T. Shaw's
     Editorial Rationale in Black Mask
     (January 1927) DLB-137

Shaw, Mary 1854-1929 . . . . .DLB-228

Shaw, Robert 1927-1978 . . . . .DLB-13, 14

Shaw, Robert B. 1947- DLB-120

Shawn, Wallace 1943- DLB-266

Shawn, William 1907-1992 . . . . .DLB-137

Frank Shay [publishing house] DLB-46

Shchedrin, N. (see Saltykov, Mikhail Evgrafovich)

Shcherbakova, Galina Nikolaevna
   1932- DLB-285

Shcherbina, Nikolai Fedorovich
   1821-1869 . . . . .DLB-277

Shea, John Gilmary 1824-1892 . . . . .DLB-30

Sheaffer, Louis 1912-1993 . . . . .DLB-103

Sheahan, Henry Beston (see Beston, Henry)

Shearing, Joseph 1886-1952 . . . . .DLB-70

Shebbeare, John 1709-1788 . . . . .DLB-39

Sheckley, Robert 1928- DLB-8

Shedd, William G. T. 1820-1894 . . . . .DLB-64

Sheed, Wilfrid 1930- DLB-6

Sheed and Ward [U.S.] DLB-46

Sheed and Ward Limited [U.K.] DLB-112

Sheldon, Alice B. (see Tiptree, James, Jr.)

Sheldon, Edward 1886-1946 . . . . .DLB-7

Sheldon and Company DLB-49

Sheller, Aleksandr Konstantinovich
   1838-1900 . . . . .DLB-238

Shelley, Mary Wollstonecraft 1797-1851
   . . . . DLB-110, 116, 159, 178; CDBLB-3

   Preface to Frankenstein; or, The
     Modern Prometheus (1818) DLB-178

Shelley, Percy Bysshe
   1792-1822 . . . . . .DLB-96, 110, 158; CDBLB-3

Shelnutt, Eve 1941- DLB-130

Shen Congwen 1902-1988. . . . . .DLB-328

Shenshin (see Fet, Afanasii Afanas'evich)

Shenstone, William 1714-1763 . . . . .DLB-95

Shepard, Clark and Brown DLB-49

Shepard, Ernest Howard 1879-1976 . . . . .DLB-160

Shepard, Sam 1943- DLB-7, 212

Shepard, Thomas I, 1604 or 1605-1649 . . .DLB-24

Shepard, Thomas, II, 1635-1677 . . . . .DLB-24

Shepherd, Luke fl. 1547-1554. . . . . .DLB-136

Sherburne, Edward 1616-1702 . . . . .DLB-131

Sheridan, Frances 1724-1766 . . . . .DLB-39, 84

Sheridan, Richard Brinsley
   1751-1816 . . . . DLB-89; CDBLB-2

Sherman, Francis 1871-1926 . . . . .DLB-92

Sherman, Martin 1938- DLB-228

Sherriff, R. C. 1896-1975 . . . . . . .DLB-10, 191, 233

Sherrod, Blackie 1919- DLB-241

Sherry, Norman 1935- DLB-155

   Tribute to Graham Greene Y-91

Sherry, Richard 1506-1551 or 1555 . . . . . .DLB-236

Sherwood, Mary Martha 1775-1851 . . . . .DLB-163

Sherwood, Robert E. 1896-1955 . . .DLB-7, 26, 249

Shevyrev, Stepan Petrovich
   1806-1864 . . . . .DLB-205

Shi Tuo (Lu Fen) 1910-1988 . . . . .DLB-328

Shiel, M. P. 1865-1947 . . . . .DLB-153

Shiels, George 1886-1949 . . . . .DLB-10

Shiga Naoya 1883-1971 . . . . .DLB-180

Shiina Rinzō 1911-1973 . . . . .DLB-182

Shikishi Naishinnō 1153?-1201 . . . . .DLB-203

Shillaber, Benjamin Penhallow
   1814-1890 . . . . .DLB-1, 11, 235

Shimao Toshio 1917-1986 . . . . .DLB-182

Shimazaki Tōson 1872-1943 . . . . .DLB-180

Shimose, Pedro 1940- DLB-283

Shine, Ted 1931- DLB-38

Shinkei 1406-1475 . . . . .DLB-203

Ship, Reuben 1915-1975 . . . . .DLB-88

Shirer, William L. 1904-1993 . . . . .DLB-4

Shirinsky-Shikhmatov, Sergii Aleksandrovich
   1783-1837 . . . . .DLB-150

Shirley, James 1596-1666 . . . . .DLB-58

Shishkov, Aleksandr Semenovich
   1753-1841 . . . . .DLB-150

Shmelev, I. S. 1873-1950 . . . . .DLB-317

Shockley, Ann Allen 1927- DLB-33

Sholokhov, Mikhail Aleksandrovich
   1905-1984 . . . . .DLB-272

Shōno Junzō 1921- DLB-182

Shore, Arabella 1820?-1901. . . . . .DLB-199

Shore, Louisa 1824-1895 . . . . .DLB-199

Short, Luke (see Glidden, Frederick Dilley)

Peter Short [publishing house] DLB-170

Shorter, Dora Sigerson 1866-1918 . . . . . . .DLB-240

Shorthouse, Joseph Henry 1834-1903 . . . . .DLB-18

Short Stories
   Michael M. Rea and the Rea Award
     for the Short Story Y-97

   The Year in Short Stories Y-87

   The Year in the Short Story. Y-88, 90–93

Shōtetsu 1381-1459 . . . . .DLB-203

Showalter, Elaine 1941- DLB-67

Shreve, Anita 1946- DLB-292

Shteiger, Anatolii 1907-1944. . . . . .DLB-317

Shukshin, Vasilii Makarovich
   1929-1974 . . . . .DLB-302

Shulevitz, Uri 1935- DLB-61

Shulman, Max 1919-1988 . . . . .DLB-11

Shute, Henry A. 1856-1943 . . . . .DLB-9

Shute, Nevil (Nevil Shute Norway)
   1899-1960 . . . . .DLB-255

Shuttle, Penelope 1947- DLB-14, 40

Shvarts, Evgenii L'vovich 1896-1958 . . . . .DLB-272

Sibawayhi circa 750-circa 795. . . . . .DLB-311

Sibbes, Richard 1577-1635 . . . . .DLB-151

Sibiriak, D. (see Mamin, Dmitrii Narkisovich)

Siddal, Elizabeth Eleanor 1829-1862 . . . . .DLB-199

Sidgwick, Ethel 1877-1970 . . . . .DLB-197

Sidgwick, Henry 1838-1900. . . . . .DLB-262

Sidgwick and Jackson Limited DLB-112

Sidhwa, Bapsi 1939- DLB-323

Sidney, Margaret (see Lothrop, Harriet M.)

Sidney, Mary 1561-1621 . . . . .DLB-167

Sidney, Sir Philip
   1554-1586 . . . . .DLB-167; CDBLB-1

   An Apologie for Poetrie (the Olney edition,
     1595, of Defence of Poesie) DLB-167

Sidney's Press. DLB-49

The Siege of Krishnapur, 1973 Booker Prize winner,
   J. G. Farrell DLB-326

Sierra, Rubén 1946- DLB-122

Sierra Club Books DLB-49

Siger of Brabant circa 1240-circa 1284 . . . .DLB-115

Sigourney, Lydia Huntley
   1791-1865 . . . . . . DLB-1, 42, 73, 183, 239, 243

Silkin, Jon 1930-1997 . . . . .DLB-27

Silko, Leslie Marmon 1948- DLB-143, 175, 256, 275
Silliman, Benjamin 1779-1864 ..... DLB-183
Silliman, Ron 1946- DLB-169
Silliphant, Stirling 1918-1996 ..... DLB-26
Sillitoe, Alan 1928- DLB-14, 139; CDBLB-8
   Tribute to J. B. Priestly Y-84
Silman, Roberta 1934- DLB-28
Silone, Ignazio (Secondino Tranquilli) 1900-1978 ..... DLB-264
Silva, Beverly 1930- DLB-122
Silva, Clara 1905-1976 ..... DLB-290
Silva, José Asunció 1865-1896 ..... DLB-283
Silverberg, Robert 1935- DLB-8
Silverman, Kaja 1947- DLB-246
Silverman, Kenneth 1936- DLB-111
Simak, Clifford D. 1904-1988 ..... DLB-8
Simcoe, Elizabeth 1762-1850 ..... DLB-99
Simcox, Edith Jemima 1844-1901 ..... DLB-190
Simcox, George Augustus 1841-1905 ..... DLB-35
Sime, Jessie Georgina 1868-1958 ..... DLB-92
Simenon, Georges 1903-1989 ..... DLB-72; Y-89
Simic, Charles 1938- DLB-105
   "Images and 'Images'" DLB-105
Simionescu, Mircea Horia 1928- DLB-232
Simmel, Georg 1858-1918 ..... DLB-296
Simmel, Johannes Mario 1924- DLB-69
Valentine Simmes [publishing house] DLB-170
Simmons, Ernest J. 1903-1972 ..... DLB-103
Simmons, Herbert Alfred 1930- DLB-33
Simmons, James 1933- DLB-40
Simms, William Gilmore 1806-1870 ..... DLB-3, 30, 59, 73, 248
Simms and M'Intyre DLB-106
Simon, Claude 1913-2005 ..... DLB-83; Y-85
   Nobel Lecture Y-85
Simon, Neil 1927- DLB-7, 266
Simon and Schuster DLB-46
Simonov, Konstantin Mikhailovich 1915-1979 ..... DLB-302
Simons, Katherine Drayton Mayrant 1890-1969 ..... Y-83
Simović, Ljubomir 1935- DLB-181
Simpkin and Marshall [publishing house] DLB-154
Simpson, Helen 1897-1940 ..... DLB-77
Simpson, Louis 1923- DLB-5
Simpson, N. F. 1919- DLB-13
Sims, George 1923-1999 ..... DLB-87; Y-99
Sims, George Robert 1847-1922 ..... DLB-35, 70, 135
Sinán, Rogelio 1902-1994 ..... DLB-145, 290
Sinclair, Andrew 1935- DLB-14

Sinclair, Bertrand William 1881-1972 ..... DLB-92
Sinclair, Catherine 1800-1864 ..... DLB-163
Sinclair, Clive 1948- DLB-319
Sinclair, Jo 1913-1995 ..... DLB-28
Sinclair, Lister 1921- DLB-88
Sinclair, May 1863-1946 ..... DLB-36, 135
   The Novels of Dorothy Richardson (1918) DLB-36
Sinclair, Upton 1878-1968 ..... DLB-9; CDALB-5
Upton Sinclair [publishing house] DLB-46
Singer, Isaac Bashevis 1904-1991 ..... DLB-6, 28, 52, 278; Y-91; CDALB-1
Singer, Mark 1950- DLB-185
Singh, Khushwant 1915- DLB-323
Singmaster, Elsie 1879-1958 ..... DLB-9
Siniavsky, Andrei (Abram Tertz) 1925-1997 ..... DLB-302
Sinisgalli, Leonardo 1908-1981 ..... DLB-114
Siodmak, Curt 1902-2000 ..... DLB-44
Sîrbu, Ion D. 1919-1989 ..... DLB-232
Siringo, Charles A. 1855-1928 ..... DLB-186
Sissman, L. E. 1928-1976 ..... DLB-5
Sisson, C. H. 1914-2003 ..... DLB-27
Sitwell, Edith 1887-1964 ..... DLB-20; CDBLB-7
Sitwell, Osbert 1892-1969 ..... DLB-100, 195
Sivanandan, Ambalavaner 1923- DLB-323
Sixteenth-Century Spanish Epic, The DLB-318
Skácel, Jan 1922-1989 ..... DLB-232
Skalbe, Kārlis 1879-1945 ..... DLB-220
Skármeta, Antonio 1940- DLB-145; CDWLB-3
Skavronsky, A. (see Danilevsky, Grigorii Petrovich)
Skeat, Walter W. 1835-1912 ..... DLB-184
William Skeffington [publishing house] DLB-106
Skelton, John 1463-1529 ..... DLB-136
Skelton, Robin 1925-1997 ..... DLB-27, 53
Škėma, Antanas 1910-1961 ..... DLB-220
Skinner, Constance Lindsay 1877-1939 ..... DLB-92
Skinner, John Stuart 1788-1851 ..... DLB-73
Skipsey, Joseph 1832-1903 ..... DLB-35
Skou-Hansen, Tage 1925- DLB-214
Skrzynecki, Peter 1945- DLB-289
Škvorecký, Josef 1924- DLB-232; CDWLB-4
Slade, Bernard 1930- DLB-53
Slamnig, Ivan 1930- DLB-181
Slančeková, Božena (see Timrava)
Slataper, Scipio 1888-1915 ..... DLB-264
Slater, Patrick 1880-1951 ..... DLB-68
Slaveykov, Pencho 1866-1912 ..... DLB-147
Slaviček, Milivoj 1929- DLB-181
Slavitt, David 1935- DLB-5, 6

Sleigh, Burrows Willcocks Arthur 1821-1869 ..... DLB-99
Sleptsov, Vasilii Alekseevich 1836-1878 ..... DLB-277
Slesinger, Tess 1905-1945 ..... DLB-102
Slessor, Kenneth 1901-1971 ..... DLB-260
Slick, Sam (see Haliburton, Thomas Chandler)
Sloan, John 1871-1951 ..... DLB-188
Sloane, William, Associates DLB-46
Slonimsky, Mikhail Leonidovich 1897-1972 ..... DLB-272
Sluchevsky, Konstantin Konstantinovich 1837-1904 ..... DLB-277
Small, Maynard and Company DLB-49
Smart, Christopher 1722-1771 ..... DLB-109
Smart, David A. 1892-1957 ..... DLB-137
Smart, Elizabeth 1913-1986 ..... DLB-88
Smart, J. J. C. 1920- DLB-262
Smedley, Menella Bute 1820?-1877 ..... DLB-199
William Smellie [publishing house] DLB-154
Smiles, Samuel 1812-1904 ..... DLB-55
Smiley, Jane 1949- DLB-227, 234
Smith, A. J. M. 1902-1980 ..... DLB-88
Smith, Adam 1723-1790 ..... DLB-104, 252
Smith, Adam (George Jerome Waldo Goodman) 1930- DLB-185
Smith, Alexander 1829-1867 ..... DLB-32, 55
   "On the Writing of Essays" (1862) DLB-57
Smith, Amanda 1837-1915 ..... DLB-221
Smith, Betty 1896-1972 ..... Y-82
Smith, Carol Sturm 1938- Y-81
Smith, Charles Henry 1826-1903 ..... DLB-11
Smith, Charlotte 1749-1806 ..... DLB-39, 109
Smith, Chet 1899-1973 ..... DLB-171
Smith, Cordwainer 1913-1966 ..... DLB-8
Smith, Dave 1942- DLB-5
   Tribute to James Dickey Y-97
   Tribute to John Gardner Y-82
Smith, Dodie 1896-1990 ..... DLB-10
Smith, Doris Buchanan 1934-2002 ..... DLB-52
Smith, E. E. 1890-1965 ..... DLB-8
Smith, Elihu Hubbard 1771-1798 ..... DLB-37
Smith, Elizabeth Oakes (Prince) (see Oakes Smith, Elizabeth)
Smith, Eunice 1757-1823 ..... DLB-200
Smith, F. Hopkinson 1838-1915 ..... DS-13
Smith, George D. 1870-1920 ..... DLB-140
Smith, George O. 1911-1981 ..... DLB-8
Smith, Goldwin 1823-1910 ..... DLB-99
Smith, H. Allen 1907-1976 ..... DLB-11, 29
Smith, Harry B. 1860-1936 ..... DLB-187
Smith, Hazel Brannon 1914-1994 ..... DLB-127
Smith, Henry circa 1560-circa 1591 ..... DLB-136

Smith, Horatio (Horace)
1779-1849 . . . . DLB-96, 116

Smith, Iain Crichton (Iain Mac A'Ghobhainn)
1928-1998 . . . . DLB-40, 139, 319

Smith, J. Allen 1860-1924 . . . . DLB-47

Smith, James 1775-1839 . . . . DLB-96

Smith, Jessie Willcox 1863-1935 . . . . DLB-188

Smith, John 1580-1631 . . . . DLB-24, 30

Smith, John 1618-1652 . . . . DLB-252

Smith, Josiah 1704-1781 . . . . DLB-24

Smith, Ken 1938- DLB-40

Smith, Lee 1944- DLB-143; Y-83

Smith, Logan Pearsall 1865-1946 . . . . DLB-98

Smith, Margaret Bayard 1778-1844 . . . . . DLB-248

Smith, Mark 1935- Y-82

Smith, Michael 1698-circa 1771 . . . . DLB-31

Smith, Pauline 1882-1959 . . . . DLB-225

Smith, Red 1905-1982 . . . . DLB-29, 171

Smith, Roswell 1829-1892 . . . . DLB-79

Smith, Samuel Harrison 1772-1845 . . . . . . DLB-43

Smith, Samuel Stanhope 1751-1819 . . . . . . DLB-37

Smith, Sarah (see Stretton, Hesba)

Smith, Sarah Pogson 1774-1870 . . . . DLB-200

Smith, Seba 1792-1868 . . . . DLB-1, 11, 243

Smith, Stevie 1902-1971 . . . . DLB-20

Smith, Sydney 1771-1845 . . . . DLB-107

Smith, Sydney Goodsir 1915-1975 . . . . DLB-27

Smith, Sir Thomas 1513-1577 . . . . DLB-132

Smith, Vivian 1933- DLB-325

Smith, W. Gordon 1928-1996 . . . . DLB-310

Smith, Wendell 1914-1972 . . . . DLB-171

Smith, William fl. 1595-1597 . . . . DLB-136

Smith, William 1727-1803 . . . . DLB-31

A General Idea of the College of Mirania
(1753) [excerpts] DLB-31

Smith, William 1728-1793 . . . . DLB-30

Smith, William Gardner 1927-1974 . . . . . . DLB-76

Smith, William Henry 1808-1872 . . . . DLB-159

Smith, William Jay 1918- DLB-5

Smith, Elder and Company DLB-154

Harrison Smith and Robert Haas
[publishing house] DLB-46

J. Stilman Smith and Company DLB-49

W. B. Smith and Company DLB-49

W. H. Smith and Son DLB-106

Leonard Smithers [publishing house] DLB-112

Smollett, Tobias
1721-1771 . . . . DLB-39, 104; CDBLB-2

Dedication to *Ferdinand Count Fathom*
(1753) DLB-39

Preface to *Ferdinand Count Fathom*
(1753) DLB-39

Preface to *Roderick Random* (1748) DLB-39

Smythe, Francis Sydney 1900-1949 . . . . . . DLB-195

Snelling, William Joseph 1804-1848 . . . . . DLB-202

Snellings, Rolland (see Touré, Askia Muhammad)

Snodgrass, W. D. 1926- DLB-5

Snorri Hjartarson 1906-1986 . . . . DLB-293

Snow, C. P.
1905-1980 . . . . . DLB-15, 77; DS-17; CDBLB-7

Snyder, Gary
1930- DLB-5, 16, 165, 212, 237, 275

Sobiloff, Hy 1912-1970 . . . . DLB-48

The Social Contract, Jean-Jacques
Rousseau DLB-314

The Society for Textual Scholarship and
TEXT Y-87

The Society for the History of Authorship,
Reading and Publishing Y-92

Söderberg, Hjalmar 1869-1941 . . . . DLB-259

Södergran, Edith 1892-1923 . . . . DLB-259

Soffici, Ardengo 1879-1964 . . . . DLB-114, 264

Sofola, 'Zulu 1938- DLB-157

Sokhanskaia, Nadezhda Stepanovna
(Kokhanovskaia) 1823?-1884 . . . . DLB-277

Sokolov, Sasha (Aleksandr Vsevolodovich
Sokolov) 1943- DLB-285

Solano, Solita 1888-1975 . . . . DLB-4

Soldati, Mario 1906-1999 . . . . DLB-177

Soledad (see Zamudio, Adela)

Šoljan, Antun 1932-1993 . . . . DLB-181

Sollers, Philippe (Philippe Joyaux)
1936- DLB-83

Sollogub, Vladimir Aleksandrovich
1813-1882 . . . . DLB-198

Sollors, Werner 1943- DBL-246

Solmi, Sergio 1899-1981 . . . . DLB-114

Sologub, Fedor 1863-1927 . . . . DLB-295

Solomon, Carl 1928- DLB-16

Solórzano, Carlos 1922- DLB-305

Soloukhin, Vladimir Alekseevich
1924-1997 . . . . DLB-302

Solov'ev, Sergei Mikhailovich
1885-1942 . . . . DLB-295

Solov'ev, Vladimir Sergeevich
1853-1900 . . . . DLB-295

Solstad, Dag 1941- DLB-297

Solway, David 1941- DLB-53

Solzhenitsyn, Aleksandr
1918- DLB-302
Solzhenitsyn and America Y-85

Some Basic Notes on Three Modern Genres:
Interview, Blurb, and Obituary Y-02

Somerville, Edith Œnone 1858-1949 . . . . . DLB-135

Something to Answer For, 1969 Booker Prize winner,
P. H. Newby DLB-326

Somov, Orest Mikhailovich 1793-1833 . . . DLB-198

Sønderby, Knud 1909-1966 . . . . DLB-214

Sone, Monica 1919- DLB-312

Song, Cathy 1955- DLB-169, 312

Sonnevi, Göran 1939- DLB-257

Sono Ayako 1931- DLB-182

Sontag, Susan 1933-2004 . . . . DLB-2, 67

Sophocles 497/496 B.C.-406/405 B.C.
. . . . DLB-176; CDWLB-1

Šopov, Aco 1923-1982 . . . . DLB-181

Sorel, Charles ca.1600-1674 . . . . DLB-268

Sørensen, Villy 1929- DLB-214

Sorensen, Virginia 1912-1991 . . . . DLB-206

Sorge, Reinhard Johannes 1892-1916 . . . . DLB-118

Sorokin, Vladimir Georgievich
1955- DLB-285

Sorrentino, Gilbert 1929- DLB-5, 173; Y-80

Sosa, Roberto 1930- DLB-290

Sotheby, James 1682-1742 . . . . DLB-213

Sotheby, John 1740-1807 . . . . DLB-213

Sotheby, Samuel 1771-1842 . . . . DLB-213

Sotheby, Samuel Leigh 1805-1861 . . . . . . DLB-213

Sotheby, William 1757-1833 . . . . DLB-93, 213

Soto, Gary 1952- DLB-82

Soueif, Ahdaf 1950- DLB-267

Souster, Raymond 1921- DLB-88

The *South English Legendary* circa
thirteenth-fifteenth centuries DLB-146

Southerland, Ellease 1943- DLB-33

Southern, Terry 1924-1995 . . . . DLB-2

Southern Illinois University Press Y-95

Southern Literature
Fellowship of Southern Writers Y-98

The Fugitives and the Agrarians:
The First Exhibition Y-85

"The Greatness of Southern Literature":
League of the South Institute for the
Study of Southern Culture and
History Y-02

The Society for the Study of
Southern Literature Y-00

Southern Writers Between the Wars DLB-9

Southerne, Thomas 1659-1746 . . . . DLB-80

Southey, Caroline Anne Bowles
1786-1854 . . . . DLB-116

Southey, Robert 1774-1843 . . . . . DLB-93, 107, 142

Southwell, Robert 1561?-1595 . . . . DLB-167

Southworth, E. D. E. N. 1819-1899 . . . . . DLB-239

Sowande, Bode 1948- DLB-157

Tace Sowle [publishing house] DLB-170

Soyfer, Jura 1912-1939 . . . . DLB-124

Soyinka, Wole
1934- DLB-125; Y-86, Y-87; CDWLB-3

Nobel Lecture 1986: This Past Must
Address Its Present Y-86

Spacks, Barry 1931- DLB-105

Spalding, Frances 1950- DLB-155

Spanish Byzantine Novel, The DLB-318

Spanish Travel Writers of the
    Late Middle Ages...............DLB-286

Spark, Muriel 1918- ... DLB-15, 139; CDBLB-7

Michael Sparke [publishing house].......DLB-170

Sparks, Jared 1789-1866 .... DLB-1, 30, 235

Sparshott, Francis 1926- DLB-60

Späth, Gerold 1939- DLB-75

Spatola, Adriano 1941-1988 .... DLB-128

Spaziani, Maria Luisa 1924- DLB-128

Specimens of Foreign Standard Literature
    1838-1842 .... DLB-1

The Spectator 1828- DLB-110

Spedding, James 1808-1881 .... DLB-144

Spee von Langenfeld, Friedrich
    1591-1635 .... DLB-164

Speght, Rachel 1597-after 1630 .... DLB-126

Speke, John Hanning 1827-1864........ DLB-166

Spellman, A. B. 1935- DLB-41

Spence, Catherine Helen 1825-1910..... DLB-230

Spence, Thomas 1750-1814 .... DLB-158

Spencer, Anne 1882-1975 .... DLB-51, 54

Spencer, Charles, third Earl of Sunderland
    1674-1722..................... DLB-213

Spencer, Elizabeth 1921- DLB-6, 218

Spencer, George John, Second Earl Spencer
    1758-1834..................... DLB-184

Spencer, Herbert 1820-1903 ....DLB-57, 262

    "The Philosophy of Style" (1852) DLB-57

Spencer, Scott 1945- Y-86

Spender, J. A. 1862-1942............. DLB-98

Spender, Stephen 1909-1995 ... DLB-20; CDBLB-7

Spener, Philipp Jakob 1635-1705 .... DLB-164

Spenser, Edmund
    circa 1552-1599 .... DLB-167; CDBLB-1

    Envoy from *The Shepheardes Calender*.... DLB-167

    "The Generall Argument of the
    Whole Booke," from
    The Shepheardes Calender DLB-167

    "A Letter of the Authors Expounding
    His Whole Intention in the Course
    of this Worke: Which for that It
    Giueth Great Light to the Reader,
    for the Better Vnderstanding
    Is Hereunto Annexed,"
    from *The Faerie Queene* (1590) DLB-167

    "To His Booke," from
    The Shepheardes Calender (1579) ... DLB-167

    "To the Most Excellent and Learned
    Both Orator and Poete, Mayster
    Gabriell Haruey, His Verie Special
    and Singular Good Frend E. K.
    Commendeth the Good Lyking of
    This His Labour, and the Patronage
    of the New Poete," from
    The Shepheardes Calender DLB-167

Sperr, Martin 1944- DLB-124

Spewack, Bella Cowen 1899-1990 ...... DLB-266

Spewack, Samuel 1899-1971 .... DLB-266

Spicer, Jack 1925-1965 .... DLB-5, 16, 193

Spiegelman, Art 1948- DLB-299

Spielberg, Peter 1929- Y-81

Spielhagen, Friedrich 1829-1911........ DLB-129

"*Spielmannsepen*" (circa 1152-circa 1500)... DLB-148

Spier, Peter 1927- DLB-61

Spillane, Mickey 1918-2006 .... DLB-226

Spink, J. G. Taylor 1888-1962 .... DLB-241

Spinrad, Norman 1940- DLB-8

    Tribute to Isaac Asimov............... Y-92

Spires, Elizabeth 1952- DLB-120

The Spirit of Laws, Claude-Adrien
    Helvétius DLB-314

The Spirit of Laws, Charles-Louis de Secondat, baron
    de Montesquieu DLB-314

Spitteler, Carl 1845-1924 .... DLB-129

Spivak, Lawrence E. 1900-1994 .... DLB-137

Spofford, Harriet Prescott
    1835-1921 .... DLB-74, 221

Sponde, Jean de 1557-1595 .... DLB-327

Sports

    Jimmy, Red, and Others: Harold
    Rosenthal Remembers the Stars
    of the Press Box Y-01

    The Literature of Boxing in England
    through Arthur Conan Doyle Y-01

    Notable Twentieth-Century Books
    about Sports DLB-241

Sprigge, Timothy L. S. 1932- DLB-262

Spring, Howard 1889-1965............ DLB-191

Springs, Elliott White 1896-1959 .... DLB-316

Squibob (see Derby, George Horatio)

Squier, E. G. 1821-1888 .... DLB-189

Staal-Delaunay, Marguerite-Jeanne Cordier de
    1684-1750..................... DLB-314

Stableford, Brian 1948- DLB-261

Stacpoole, H. de Vere 1863-1951 .... DLB-153

Staël, Germaine de 1766-1817...... DLB-119, 192

Staël-Holstein, Anne-Louise Germaine de
    (see Staël, Germaine de)

Staffeldt, Schack 1769-1826............ DLB-300

Stafford, Jean 1915-1979 ....DLB-2, 173

Stafford, William 1914-1993 .... DLB-5, 206

Stallings, Laurence 1894-1968 .....DLB-7, 44, 316

Stallworthy, Jon 1935- DLB-40

Stampp, Kenneth M. 1912- DLB-17

Stănescu, Nichita 1933-1983 .... DLB-232

Stanev, Emiliyan 1907-1979........... DLB-181

Stanford, Ann 1916-1987 .... DLB-5

Stangerup, Henrik 1937-1998 .... DLB-214

Stanihurst, Richard 1547-1618 .... DLB-281

Stanitsky, N. (see Panaeva, Avdot'ia Iakovlevna)

Stankevich, Nikolai Vladimirovich
    1813-1840 .... DLB-198

Stanković, Borisav ("Bora")
    1876-1927............DLB-147; CDWLB-4

Stanley, Henry M. 1841-1904.... DLB-189; DS-13

Stanley, Thomas 1625-1678 .... DLB-131

Stannard, Martin 1947- DLB-155

William Stansby [publishing house] DLB-170

Stanton, Elizabeth Cady 1815-1902 ...... DLB-79

Stanton, Frank L. 1857-1927............ DLB-25

Stanton, Maura 1946- DLB-120

Stapledon, Olaf 1886-1950 .... DLB-15, 255

Star Spangled Banner Office............ DLB-49

Stark, Freya 1893-1993............... DLB-195

Starkey, Thomas circa 1499-1538....... DLB-132

Starkie, Walter 1894-1976............. DLB-195

Starkweather, David 1935- DLB-7

Starrett, Vincent 1886-1974 ....DLB-187

Stationers' Company of London, The DLB-170

Statius circa A.D. 45-A.D. 96 .... DLB-211

Staying On, 1977 Booker Prize winner,
    Paul Scott...................... DLB-326

Stead, Christina 1902-1983............ DLB-260

Stead, Robert J. C. 1880-1959 .... DLB-92

Steadman, Mark 1930- DLB-6

Stearns, Harold E. 1891-1943...... DLB-4; DS-15

Stebnitsky, M. (see Leskov, Nikolai Semenovich)

Stedman, Edmund Clarence 1833-1908... DLB-64

Steegmuller, Francis 1906-1994 .... DLB-111

Steel, Flora Annie 1847-1929 ...... DLB-153, 156

Steele, Max 1922-2005 .... Y-80

Steele, Richard
    1672-1729.......... DLB-84, 101; CDBLB-2

Steele, Timothy 1948- DLB-120

Steele, Wilbur Daniel 1886-1970 .... DLB-86

Wallace Markfield's "Steeplechase" Y-02

Steere, Richard circa 1643-1721 .... DLB-24

Stefán frá Hvítadal (Stefán Sigurðsson)
    1887-1933..................... DLB-293

Stefán Guðmundsson (see Stephan G. Stephansson)

Stefán Hörður Grímsson
    1919 or 1920-2002............... DLB-293

Steffens, Lincoln 1866-1936 .... DLB-303

Stefanovski, Goran 1952- DLB-181

Stegner, Wallace
    1909-1993 .... DLB-9, 206, 275; Y-93

Stehr, Hermann 1864-1940............. DLB-66

Steig, William 1907-2003 .... DLB-61

Stein, Gertrude 1874-1946
    .... DLB-4, 54, 86, 228; DS-15; CDALB-4

Stein, Leo 1872-1947.................. DLB-4

Stein and Day Publishers DLB-46

Steinbeck, John 1902-1968
    .... DLB-7, 9, 212, 275, 309; DS-2; CDALB-5

    John Steinbeck Research Center,
    San Jose State University........... Y-85

    The Steinbeck Centennial Y-02

Steinem, Gloria 1934- DLB-246

Steiner, George 1929- DLB-67, 299

Steinhoewel, Heinrich 1411/1412-1479 ...DLB-179

Steinn Steinarr (Aðalsteinn Kristmundsson)
1908-1958 ....DLB-293

Steinunn Sigurðardóttir 1950- DLB-293

Steloff, Ida Frances 1887-1989 ....DLB-187

Stendhal 1783-1842 ....DLB-119

Stephan G. Stephansson (Stefán Guðmundsson)
1853-1927 ....DLB-293

Stephen, Leslie 1832-1904 ...... DLB-57, 144, 190

Stephen Family (Bloomsbury Group) DS-10

Stephens, A. G. 1865-1933. ....DLB-230

Stephens, Alexander H. 1812-1883 ....DLB-47

Stephens, Alice Barber 1858-1932 ....DLB-188

Stephens, Ann 1810-1886 ....DLB-3, 73, 250

Stephens, Charles Asbury 1844?-1931. ....DLB-42

Stephens, James 1882?-1950 ....DLB-19, 153, 162

Stephens, John Lloyd 1805-1852 ....DLB-183, 250

Stephens, Michael 1946- DLB-234

Stephensen, P. R. 1901-1965 ....DLB-260

Sterling, George 1869-1926 ....DLB-54

Sterling, James 1701-1763. ....DLB-24

Sterling, John 1806-1844 ....DLB-116

Stern, Gerald 1925- DLB-105

"Living in Ruin" DLB-105

Stern, Gladys B. 1890-1973 ....DLB-197

Stern, Madeleine B. 1912- DLB-111, 140

Stern, Richard 1928- DLB-218; Y-87

Stern, Stewart 1922- DLB-26

Sterne, Laurence 1713-1768 ...DLB-39; CDBLB-2

Sternheim, Carl 1878-1942. ....DLB-56, 118

Sternhold, Thomas ?-1549. ....DLB-132

Steuart, David 1747-1824 ....DLB-213

Stevens, Henry 1819-1886. ....DLB-140

Stevens, Wallace 1879-1955 ....DLB-54; CDALB-5

The Wallace Stevens Society. Y-99

Stevenson, Anne 1933- DLB-40

Stevenson, D. E. 1892-1973 ....DLB-191

Stevenson, Lionel 1902-1973 ....DLB-155

Stevenson, Robert Louis
1850-1894 .... DLB-18, 57, 141, 156, 174;
DS-13; CDBLB-5
"On Style in Literature:
Its Technical Elements" (1885) DLB-57

Stewart, Donald Ogden
1894-1980 ....DLB-4, 11, 26; DS-15

Stewart, Douglas 1913-1985 ....DLB-260

Stewart, Dugald 1753-1828 ....DLB-31

Stewart, George, Jr. 1848-1906 ....DLB-99

Stewart, George R. 1895-1980 ....DLB-8

Stewart, Harold 1916-1995 ....DLB-260

Stewart, J. I. M. (see Innes, Michael)

Stewart, Maria W. 1803?-1879..........DLB-239

Stewart, Randall 1896-1964............DLB-103

Stewart, Sean 1965- DLB-251

Stewart and Kidd Company DLB-46

Sthen, Hans Christensen 1544-1610 ....DLB-300

Stickney, Trumbull 1874-1904 ....DLB-54

Stieler, Caspar 1632-1707..............DLB-164

Stifter, Adalbert
1805-1868 ....DLB-133; CDWLB-2

Stiles, Ezra 1727-1795 ....DLB-31

Still, James 1906-2001 .... DLB-9; Y-01

Stirling, S. M. 1953- DLB-251

Stirner, Max 1806-1856 ....DLB-129

Stith, William 1707-1755................DLB-31

Stivens, Dal 1911-1997.................DLB-260

Elliot Stock [publishing house]..........DLB-106

Stockton, Annis Boudinot 1736-1801.....DLB-200

Stockton, Frank R.
1834-1902 ....DLB-42, 74; DS-13

Stockton, J. Roy 1892-1972 ....DLB-241

Ashbel Stoddard [publishing house].......DLB-49

Stoddard, Charles Warren 1843-1909 ....DLB-186

Stoddard, Elizabeth 1823-1902 ....DLB-202

Stoddard, Richard Henry
1825-1903 ....DLB-3, 64, 250; DS-13

Stoddard, Solomon 1643-1729...........DLB-24

Stoker, Bram
1847-1912 .... DLB-36, 70, 178; CDBLB-5

On Writing Dracula, from the
Introduction to Dracula (1897) ...DLB-178

Dracula (Documentary) DLB-304

Frederick A. Stokes Company DLB-49

Stokes, Thomas L. 1898-1958 ....DLB-29

Stokesbury, Leon 1945- DLB-120

Stolberg, Christian Graf zu 1748-1821.....DLB-94

Stolberg, Friedrich Leopold Graf zu
1750-1819 ....DLB-94

Stone, Lucy 1818-1893 ....DLB-79, 239

Stone, Melville 1848-1929 ....DLB-25

Stone, Robert 1937- DLB-152

Stone, Ruth 1915- DLB-105

Stone, Samuel 1602-1663 ....DLB-24

Stone, William Leete 1792-1844 ....DLB-202

Herbert S. Stone and Company..........DLB-49

Stone and Kimball DLB-49

Stoppard, Tom
1937- DLB-13, 233; Y-85; CDBLB-8

Playwrights and Professors DLB-13

Storey, Anthony 1928- DLB-14

Storey, David 1933- .. DLB-13, 14, 207, 245, 326

Storm, Theodor
1817-1888 ....DLB-129; CDWLB-2

Storni, Alfonsina 1892-1938 ....DLB-283

Story, Thomas circa 1670-1742 ....DLB-31

Story, William Wetmore 1819-1895....DLB-1, 235

Storytelling: A Contemporary Renaissance....Y-84

Stoughton, William 1631-1701...........DLB-24

Stout, Rex 1886-1975..................DLB-306

Stow, John 1525-1605 ....DLB-132

Stow, Randolph 1935- DLB-260

Stowe, Harriet Beecher 1811-1896......DLB-1,12,
42, 74, 189, 239, 243; CDALB-3

The Harriet Beecher Stowe Center.......Y-00

Stowe, Leland 1899-1994................DLB-29

Stoyanov, Dimitr Ivanov (see Elin Pelin)

Strabo 64/63 B.C.-circa A.D. 25..........DLB-176

Strachey, Lytton 1880-1932......DLB-149; DS-10

Preface to Eminent Victorians DLB-149

William Strahan [publishing house]......DLB-154

Strahan and Company.................DLB-106

Strand, Mark 1934- DLB-5

The Strasbourg Oaths 842 ....DLB-148

Stratemeyer, Edward 1862-1930 ....DLB-42

Strati, Saverio 1924- DLB-177

Stratton and Barnard.................DLB-49

Stratton-Porter, Gene
1863-1924 ....DLB-221; DS-14

Straub, Peter 1943- Y-84

Strauß, Botho 1944- DLB-124

Strauß, David Friedrich 1808-1874 ......DLB-133

Strauss, Jennifer 1933- DLB-325

The Strawberry Hill Press DLB-154

Strawson, P. F. 1919- DLB-262

Streatfeild, Noel 1895-1986 ....DLB-160

Street, Cecil John Charles (see Rhode, John)

Street, G. S. 1867-1936.................DLB-135

Street and Smith.....................DLB-49

Streeter, Edward 1891-1976 ....DLB-11

Streeter, Thomas Winthrop 1883-1965 ...DLB-140

Stretton, Hesba 1832-1911..........DLB-163, 190

Stribling, T. S. 1881-1965 ....DLB-9

Der Stricker circa 1190-circa 1250.......DLB-138

Strickland, Samuel 1804-1867 ....DLB-99

Strindberg, August 1849-1912..........DLB-259

Stringer, Arthur 1874-1950 ....DLB-92

Stringer and Townsend DLB-49

Strittmatter, Erwin 1912-1994 ....DLB-69

Strniša, Gregor 1930-1987 ....DLB-181

Strode, William 1630-1645 ....DLB-126

Strong, L. A. G. 1896-1958 ....DLB-191

Strother, David Hunter (Porte Crayon)
1816-1888 ....DLB-3, 248

Strouse, Jean 1945- DLB-111

Strugatsky, Arkadii Natanovich
1925- DLB-302

Strugatsky, Boris Natanovich 1933- . . . DLB-302

Stuart, Dabney 1937- DLB-105

   "Knots into Webs: Some
Autobiographical Sources" DLB-105

Stuart, Jesse 1906-1984 . . . . . . DLB-9, 48, 102; Y-84

Lyle Stuart [publishing house] DLB-46

Stuart, Ruth McEnery 1849?-1917 . . . . . . DLB-202

Stub, Ambrosius 1705-1758 . . . . DLB-300

Stubbs, Harry Clement (see Clement, Hal)

Stubenberg, Johann Wilhelm von
1619-1663 . . . . DLB-164

Stuckenberg, Viggo 1763-1905 . . . . DLB-300

Studebaker, William V. 1947- DLB-256

Studies in American Jewish Literature Y-02

Studio DLB-112

Stump, Al 1916-1995 . . . . DLB-241

Sturgeon, Theodore
1918-1985 . . . . DLB-8; Y-85

Sturges, Preston 1898-1959 . . . . DLB-26

Styron, William
1925- DLB-2, 143, 299; Y-80; CDALB-6

   Tribute to James Dickey Y-97

Suard, Jean-Baptiste-Antoine
1732-1817 . . . . DLB-314

Suárez, Clementina 1902-1991 . . . . DLB-290

Suárez, Mario 1925- DLB-82

Suassuna, Ariano 1927- DLB-307

Such, Peter 1939- DLB-60

Suckling, Sir John 1609-1641? DLB-58, 126

Suckow, Ruth 1892-1960 . . . . DLB-9, 102

Sudermann, Hermann 1857-1928 . . . . DLB-118

Sue, Eugène 1804-1857 . . . . DLB-119

Sue, Marie-Joseph (see Sue, Eugène)

Suetonius circa A.D. 69-post A.D. 122 . . . . DLB-211

Suggs, Simon (see Hooper, Johnson Jones)

Sui Sin Far (see Eaton, Edith Maude)

Suits, Gustav 1883-1956 . . . . DLB-220; CDWLB-4

Sukenick, Ronald 1932-2004 . . . . . . DLB-173; Y-81

   An Author's Response Y-82

Sukhovo-Kobylin, Aleksandr Vasil'evich
1817-1903 . . . . DLB-277

Suknaski, Andrew 1942- DLB-53

Sullivan, Alan 1868-1947 . . . . DLB-92

Sullivan, C. Gardner 1886-1965 . . . . DLB-26

Sullivan, Frank 1892-1976 . . . . DLB-11

Sulte, Benjamin 1841-1923 . . . . DLB-99

Sulzberger, Arthur Hays 1891-1968 . . . . . DLB-127

Sulzberger, Arthur Ochs 1926- DLB-127

Sulzer, Johann Georg 1720-1779 . . . . DLB-97

Sumarokov, Aleksandr Petrovich
1717-1777 . . . . DLB-150

Summers, Hollis 1916-1987 . . . . DLB-6

Sumner, Charles 1811-1874 . . . . DLB-235

Sumner, William Graham 1840-1910 . . . . . DLB-270

Henry A. Sumner
[publishing house] DLB-49

Sundman, Per Olof 1922-1992 . . . . DLB-257

Supervielle, Jules 1884-1960 . . . . DLB-258

Surtees, Robert Smith 1803-1864 . . . . DLB-21

   The R. S. Surtees Society Y-98

Sutcliffe, Matthew 1550?-1629 . . . . DLB-281

Sutcliffe, William 1971- DLB-271

Sutherland, Efua Theodora 1924-1996 . . . DLB-117

Sutherland, John 1919-1956 . . . . DLB-68

Sutro, Alfred 1863-1933 . . . . DLB-10

Svava Jakobsdóttir 1930- DLB-293

Svendsen, Hanne Marie 1933- DLB-214

Svevo, Italo (Ettore Schmitz)
1861-1928 . . . . DLB-264

Swados, Harvey 1920-1972 . . . . DLB-2

Swain, Charles 1801-1874 . . . . DLB-32

Swallow Press DLB-46

Swan Sonnenschein Limited DLB-106

Swanberg, W. A. 1907-1992 . . . . DLB-103

Swedish Literature
   The Literature of the Modern
   Breakthrough DLB-259

Swenson, May 1919-1989 . . . . DLB-5

Swerling, Jo 1897-1964 . . . . DLB-44

Swift, Graham 1949- DLB-194, 326

Swift, Jonathan
1667-1745 . . . . . . DLB-39, 95, 101; CDBLB-2

Swinburne, A. C.
1837-1909 . . . . DLB-35, 57; CDBLB-4

   Under the Microscope (1872) DLB-35

Swineshead, Richard floruit circa 1350 . . . DLB-115

Swinnerton, Frank 1884-1982 . . . . DLB-34

Swisshelm, Jane Grey 1815-1884 . . . . DLB-43

Swope, Herbert Bayard 1882-1958 . . . . . . DLB-25

Swords, James ?-1844 . . . . DLB-73

Swords, Thomas 1763-1843 . . . . DLB-73

T. and J. Swords and Company DLB-49

Swynnerton, Thomas (John Roberts)
circa 1500-1554 . . . . DLB-281

Sykes, Ella C. ?-1939 . . . . DLB-174

Sylvester, Josuah 1562 or 1563-1618 . . . . DLB-121

Symonds, Emily Morse (see Paston, George)

Symonds, John Addington
1840-1893 . . . . DLB-57, 144

   "Personal Style" (1890) DLB-57

Symons, A. J. A. 1900-1941 . . . . DLB-149

Symons, Arthur 1865-1945 . . . . . . DLB-19, 57, 149

Symons, Julian 1912-1994 . . . . . . DLB-87, 155; Y-92

   Julian Symons at Eighty Y-92

Symons, Scott 1933- DLB-53

Synge, John Millington
1871-1909 . . . . DLB-10, 19; CDBLB-5

Synge Summer School: J. M. Synge
and the Irish Theater, Rathdrum,
County Wiclow, Ireland Y-93

Syrett, Netta 1865-1943 . . . . DLB-135, 197

The System of Nature, Paul Henri Thiry,
baron d'Holbach (as Jean-Baptiste
de Mirabaud) DLB-314

Szabó, Lőrinc 1900-1957 . . . . DLB-215

Szabó, Magda 1917- DLB-215

Szymborska, Wisława
1923- DLB-232, Y-96; CDWLB-4

   Nobel Lecture 1996:
   The Poet and the World Y-96

T

Taban lo Liyong 1939?- DLB-125

al-Tabari 839-923 . . . . DLB-311

Tablada, José Juan 1871-1945 . . . . DLB-290

Le Tableau de Paris, Louis-Sébastien
Mercier DLB-314

Tabori, George 1914- DLB-245

Tabucchi, Antonio 1943- DLB-196

Taché, Joseph-Charles 1820-1894 . . . . DLB-99

Tachihara Masaaki 1926-1980 . . . . DLB-182

Tacitus circa A.D. 55-circa A.D. 117
. . . . DLB-211; CDWLB-1

Tadijanović, Dragutin 1905- DLB-181

Tafdrup, Pia 1952- DLB-214

Tafolla, Carmen 1951- DLB-82

Taggard, Genevieve 1894-1948 . . . . DLB-45

Taggart, John 1942- DLB-193

Tagger, Theodor (see Bruckner, Ferdinand)

Tagore, Rabindranath 1861-1941 . . . . DLB-323

Taiheiki late fourteenth century DLB-203

Tait, J. Selwin, and Sons DLB-49

Tait's Edinburgh Magazine 1832-1861 . . . . . . DLB-110

The Takarazaka Revue Company Y-91

Talander (see Bohse, August)

Talese, Gay 1932- DLB-185

   Tribute to Irwin Shaw Y-84

Talev, Dimitr 1898-1966 . . . . DLB-181

Taliaferro, H. E. 1811-1875 . . . . DLB-202

Tallent, Elizabeth 1954- DLB-130

TallMountain, Mary 1918-1994 . . . . DLB-193

Talvj 1797-1870 . . . . DLB-59, 133

Tamási, Áron 1897-1966 . . . . DLB-215

Tammsaare, A. H.
1878-1940 . . . . DLB-220; CDWLB-4

Tan, Amy 1952- DLB-173, 312; CDALB-7

Tandori, Dezső 1938- DLB-232

Tanner, Thomas 1673/1674-1735 . . . . DLB-213

Tanizaki Jun'ichirō 1886-1965 . . . . DLB-180

Tapahonso, Luci 1953- DLB-175

The Mark Taper Forum DLB-7

Taradash, Daniel 1913-2003 . . . . DLB-44

Tarasov-Rodionov, Aleksandr Ignat'evich
1885-1938 . . . . DLB-272

Tarbell, Ida M. 1857-1944 . . . . DLB-47

Tardieu, Jean 1903-1995 . . . . DLB-321

Tardivel, Jules-Paul 1851-1905 . . . . DLB-99

Targan, Barry 1932- DLB-130

 Tribute to John Gardner Y-82

Tarkington, Booth 1869-1946 . . . . DLB-9, 102

Tashlin, Frank 1913-1972 . . . . DLB-44

Tasma (Jessie Couvreur) 1848-1897 . . . . . DLB-230

Tate, Allen 1899-1979 . . . . . . DLB-4, 45, 63; DS-17

Tate, James 1943- DLB-5, 169

Tate, Nahum circa 1652-1715 . . . . DLB-80

Tatian circa 830 . . . . DLB-148

Taufer, Veno 1933- DLB-181

Tauler, Johannes circa 1300-1361 . . . . DLB-179

Tavares, Salette 1922-1994 . . . . DLB-287

Tavčar, Ivan 1851-1923 . . . . DLB-147

Taverner, Richard ca. 1505-1575 . . . . DLB-236

Taylor, Ann 1782-1866 . . . . DLB-163

Taylor, Bayard 1825-1878 . . . . DLB-3, 189, 250

Taylor, Bert Leston 1866-1921 . . . . DLB-25

Taylor, Charles H. 1846-1921 . . . . DLB-25

Taylor, Edward circa 1642-1729 . . . . DLB-24

Taylor, Elizabeth 1912-1975 . . . . DLB-139

Taylor, Sir Henry 1800-1886 . . . . DLB-32

Taylor, Henry 1942- DLB-5

 Who Owns American Literature Y-94

Taylor, Jane 1783-1824 . . . . DLB-163

Taylor, Jeremy circa 1613-1667 . . . . DLB-151

Taylor, John 1577 or 1578 - 1653 . . . . DLB-121

Taylor, Mildred D. 1943- DLB-52

Taylor, Peter 1917-1994 . . . DLB-218, 278; Y-81, 94

Taylor, Susie King 1848-1912 . . . . DLB-221

Taylor, William Howland 1901-1966 . . . . . DLB-241

William Taylor and Company DLB-49

Teale, Edwin Way 1899-1980 . . . . DLB-275

Teasdale, Sara 1884-1933 . . . . DLB-45

Teffi, Nadezhda 1872-1952 . . . . DLB-317

Teillier, Jorge 1935-1996 . . . . DLB-283

Telles, Lygia Fagundes 1924- DLB-113, 307

The Temper of the West: William Jovanovich Y-02

Temple, Sir William 1555?-1627 . . . . DLB-281

Temple, Sir William 1628-1699 . . . . DLB-101

Temple, William F. 1914-1989 . . . . DLB-255

Temrizov, A. (see Marchenko, Anastasia Iakovlevna)

Tench, Watkin ca. 1758-1833 . . . . DLB-230

Tencin, Alexandrine-Claude Guérin de
1682-1749 . . . . DLB-314

Tender Is the Night (Documentary) DLB-273

Tendriakov, Vladimir Fedorovich
1923-1984 . . . . DLB-302

Tenn, William 1919- DLB-8

Tennant, Emma 1937- DLB-14

Tenney, Tabitha Gilman 1762-1837 . . . DLB-37, 200

Tennyson, Alfred 1809-1892 . . DLB-32; CDBLB-4

 On Some of the Characteristics of
 Modern Poetry and On the Lyrical
 Poems of Alfred Tennyson
 (1831) DLB-32

Tennyson, Frederick 1807-1898 . . . . DLB-32

Tenorio, Arthur 1924- DLB-209

"The Tenth Stage," Marie-Jean-Antoine-Nicolas
Caritat, marquis de Condorcet DLB-314

Tepl, Johannes von
circa 1350-1414/1415 . . . . DLB-179

Tepliakov, Viktor Grigor'evich
1804-1842 . . . . DLB-205

Terence circa 184 B.C.-159 B.C. or after
. . . . DLB-211; CDWLB-1

St. Teresa of Ávila 1515-1582 . . . . DLB-318

Terhune, Albert Payson 1872-1942 . . . . DLB-9

Terhune, Mary Virginia 1830-1922 . . . . DS-13

Terpigorev, Sergei Nikolaevich (S. Atava)
1841-1895 . . . . DLB-277

Terry, Megan 1932- DLB-7, 249

Terson, Peter 1932- DLB-13

Tesich, Steve 1943-1996 . . . . Y-83

Tessa, Delio 1886-1939 . . . . DLB-114

Testori, Giovanni 1923-1993
. . . . DLB-128, 177

Texas
 The Year in Texas Literature Y-98

Tey, Josephine 1896?-1952 . . . . DLB-77

Thacher, James 1754-1844 . . . . DLB-37

Thacher, John Boyd 1847-1909 . . . . DLB-187

Thackeray, William Makepeace
1811-1863 . . . DLB-21, 55, 159, 163; CDBLB-4

Thames and Hudson Limited DLB-112

Thanet, Octave (see French, Alice)

Thaxter, Celia Laighton
1835-1894 . . . . DLB-239

Thayer, Caroline Matilda Warren
1785-1844 . . . . DLB-200

Thayer, Douglas H. 1929- DLB-256

Theater
 Black Theatre: A Forum [excerpts] DLB-38

 Community and Commentators:
 Black Theatre and Its Critics DLB-38

 German Drama from Naturalism
 to Fascism: 1889-1933 . . . . DLB-118

 A Look at the Contemporary Black
 Theatre Movement DLB-38

 The Lord Chamberlain's Office and
 Stage Censorship in England DLB-10

 New Forces at Work in the American
 Theatre: 1915-1925 . . . . DLB-7

 Off Broadway and Off-Off Broadway . . . DLB-7

 Oregon Shakespeare Festival Y-00

 Plays, Playwrights, and Playgoers DLB-84

 Playwrights on the Theater DLB-80

 Playwrights and Professors DLB-13

 Producing *Dear Bunny, Dear Volodya:*
 The Friendship and the Feud Y-97

 Viewpoint: Politics and Performance,
 by David Edgar DLB-13

 Writing for the Theatre,
 by Harold Pinter DLB-13

 The Year in Drama Y-82–85, 87–98

 The Year in U.S. Drama Y-00

Theater, English and Irish
 Anti-Theatrical Tracts DLB-263

 The Chester Plays circa 1505-1532;
 revisions until 1575 . . . . DLB-146

 Dangerous Years: London Theater,
 1939-1945 . . . . DLB-10

 A Defense of Actors DLB-263

 The Development of Lighting in the
 Staging of Drama, 1900-1945 . . . . DLB-10

 Education DLB-263

 The End of English Stage Censorship,
 1945-1968 . . . . DLB-13

 Epigrams and Satires DLB-263

 Eyewitnesses and Historians DLB-263

 Fringe and Alternative Theater in
 Great Britain DLB-13

 The Great War and the Theater,
 1914-1918 [Great Britain] DLB-10

 Licensing Act of 1737 . . . . DLB-84

 Morality Plays: *Mankind* circa 1450-1500
 and *Everyman* circa 1500 . . . . DLB-146

 The New Variorum Shakespeare Y-85

 N-Town Plays circa 1468 to early
 sixteenth century DLB-146

 Politics and the Theater DLB-263

 Practical Matters DLB-263

 Prologues, Epilogues, Epistles to Readers,
 and Excerpts from Plays DLB-263

 The Publication of English
 Renaissance Plays DLB-62

 Regulations for the Theater DLB-263

 Sources for the Study of Tudor and
 Stuart Drama DLB-62

 Stage Censorship: "The Rejected Statement"
 (1911), by Bernard Shaw
 [excerpts] DLB-10

 Synge Summer School: J. M. Synge and
 the Irish Theater, Rathdrum,
 County Wiclow, Ireland Y-93

 The Theater in Shakespeare's Time . . . DLB-62

 The Theatre Guild DLB-7

 The Townely Plays fifteenth and
 sixteenth centuries DLB-146

 The Year in British Drama Y-99–01

 The Year in Drama: London Y-90

 The Year in London Theatre Y-92

A Yorkshire Tragedy DLB-58

Theaters
- The Abbey Theatre and Irish Drama, 1900-1945 .... DLB-10
- Actors Theatre of Louisville............ DLB-7
- American Conservatory Theatre DLB-7
- Arena Stage DLB-7
- Black Theaters and Theater Organizations in America, 1961-1982: A Research List...... DLB-38
- The Dallas Theater Center DLB-7
- Eugene O'Neill Memorial Theater Center DLB-7
- The Goodman Theatre DLB-7
- The Guthrie Theater DLB-7
- The Mark Taper Forum............. DLB-7
- The National Theatre and the Royal Shakespeare Company: The National Companies DLB-13
- Off-Loop Theatres DLB-7
- The Royal Court Theatre and the English Stage Company......... DLB-13
- The Royal Court Theatre and the New Drama.................. DLB-10
- The Takarazaka Revue Company Y-91

Thegan and the Astronomer fl. circa 850..................... DLB-148

Thelwall, John 1764-1834.......... DLB-93, 158

Theocritus circa 300 B.C.-260 B.C. DLB-176

Theodorescu, Ion N. (see Arghezi, Tudor)

Theodulf circa 760-circa 821............ DLB-148

Theophrastus circa 371 B.C.-287 B.C. DLB-176

Thériault, Yves 1915-1983 .... DLB-88

Thério, Adrien 1925- DLB-53

Theroux, Paul 1941- DLB-2, 218; CDALB-7

Thesiger, Wilfred 1910-2003 .... DLB-204

They All Came to Paris DS-15

Thibaudeau, Colleen 1925- DLB-88

Thiele, Colin 1920- DLB-289

Thielen, Benedict 1903-1965 .... DLB-102

Thiong'o Ngugi wa (see Ngugi wa Thiong'o)

Thiroux d'Arconville, Marie-Geneviève 1720-1805..................... DLB-314

This Quarter 1925-1927, 1929-1932 ....DS-15

Thoma, Ludwig 1867-1921............. DLB-66

Thoma, Richard 1902-1974 .... DLB-4

Thomas, Audrey 1935- DLB-60

Thomas, D. M. 1935- ...DLB-40, 207, 299; Y-82; CDBLB-8

The Plagiarism Controversy Y-82

Thomas, Dylan 1914-1953....... DLB-13, 20, 139; CDBLB-7

The Dylan Thomas Celebration Y-99

Thomas, Ed 1961- DLB-310

Thomas, Edward 1878-1917............DLB-19, 98, 156, 216

The Friends of the Dymock Poets Y-00

Thomas, Frederick William 1806-1866 .. DLB-202

Thomas, Gwyn 1913-1981......... DLB-15, 245

Thomas, Isaiah 1750-1831 ....DLB-43, 73, 187

Thomas, Johann 1624-1679 .... DLB-168

Thomas, John 1900-1932............... DLB-4

Thomas, Joyce Carol 1938- DLB-33

Thomas, Lewis 1913-1993 ....DLB-275

Thomas, Lorenzo 1944- DLB-41

Thomas, Norman 1884-1968 .... DLB-303

Thomas, R. S. 1915-2000..... DLB-27; CDBLB-8

Isaiah Thomas [publishing house] DLB-49

Thomasîn von Zerclære circa 1186-circa 1259 .... DLB-138

Thomason, George 1602?-1666........ DLB-213

Thomasius, Christian 1655-1728 .... DLB-168

Thompson, Daniel Pierce 1795-1868 .... DLB-202

Thompson, David 1770-1857 .... DLB-99

Thompson, Dorothy 1893-1961......... DLB-29

Thompson, E. P. 1924-1993........... DLB-242

Thompson, Flora 1876-1947.......... DLB-240

Thompson, Francis 1859-1907.............. DLB-19; CDBLB-5

Thompson, George Selden (see Selden, George)

Thompson, Henry Yates 1838-1928..... DLB-184

Thompson, Hunter S. 1939-2005....... DLB-185

Thompson, Jim 1906-1977............ DLB-226

Thompson, John 1938-1976 .... DLB-60

Thompson, John R. 1823-1873.... DLB-3, 73, 248

Thompson, Lawrance 1906-1973 .... DLB-103

Thompson, Maurice 1844-1901.......DLB-71, 74

Thompson, Ruth Plumly 1891-1976...... DLB-22

Thompson, Thomas Phillips 1843-1933... DLB-99

Thompson, William 1775-1833 .... DLB-158

Thompson, William Tappan 1812-1882 .... DLB-3, 11, 248

Thomson, Cockburn "Modern Style" (1857) [excerpt] DLB-57

Thomson, Edward William 1849-1924 ... DLB-92

Thomson, James 1700-1748 .... DLB-95

Thomson, James 1834-1882 .... DLB-35

Thomson, Joseph 1858-1895 ....DLB-174

Thomson, Mortimer 1831-1875 .... DLB-11

Thomson, Rupert 1955- DLB-267

Thon, Melanie Rae 1957- DLB-244

Thor Vilhjálmsson 1925- DLB-293

Þórarinn Eldjárn 1949- DLB-293

Þórbergur Þórðarson 1888-1974......... DLB-293

Thoreau, Henry David 1817-1862 .... DLB-1, 183, 223, 270, 298; DS-5; CDALB-2

The Thoreau Society Y-99

The Thoreauvian Pilgrimage: The Structure of an American Cult .. DLB-223

Thorne, William 1568?-1630 .... DLB-281

Thornton, John F. [Repsonse to Ken Auletta] Y-97

Thorpe, Adam 1956- DLB-231

Thorpe, Thomas Bangs 1815-1878................. DLB-3, 11, 248

Thorup, Kirsten 1942- DLB-214

Thotl, Birgitte 1610-1662 .... DLB-300

Thrale, Hester Lynch (see Piozzi, Hester Lynch [Thrale])

The Three Marias: A Landmark Case in Portuguese Literary History (Maria Isabel Barreno, 1939- ; Maria Teresa Horta, 1937- ; Maria Velho da Costa, 1938-) DLB-287

Thubron, Colin 1939- DLB-204, 231

Thucydides circa 455 B.C.-circa 395 B.C..........DLB-176

Thulstrup, Thure de 1848-1930........ DLB-188

Thümmel, Moritz August von 1738-1817...................... DLB-97

Thurber, James 1894-1961 .... DLB-4, 11, 22, 102; CDALB-5

Thurman, Wallace 1902-1934 .... DLB-51

"Negro Poets and Their Poetry" DLB-50

Thwaite, Anthony 1930- DLB-40

The Booker Prize, Address Y-86

Thwaites, Reuben Gold 1853-1913 ...... DLB-47

Tibullus circa 54 B.C.-circa 19 B.C. DLB-211

Ticknor, George 1791-1871.... DLB-1, 59, 140, 235

Ticknor and Fields DLB-49

Ticknor and Fields (revived)........... DLB-46

Tieck, Ludwig 1773-1853 .... DLB-90; CDWLB-2

Tietjens, Eunice 1884-1944............. DLB-54

Tikkanen, Märta 1935- DLB-257

Tilghman, Christopher circa 1948 ...... DLB-244

Tilney, Edmund circa 1536-1610 .... DLB-136

Charles Tilt [publishing house]......... DLB-106

J. E. Tilton and Company DLB-49

Time-Life Books..................... DLB-46

Times Books...................... DLB-46

Timothy, Peter circa 1725-1782.......... DLB-43

Timrava 1867-1951................. DLB-215

Timrod, Henry 1828-1867 .... DLB-3, 248

Tindal, Henrietta 1818?-1879 .... DLB-199

Tinker, Chauncey Brewster 1876-1963.... DLB-140

Tinsley Brothers.................... DLB-106

Tiptree, James, Jr. 1915-1987 .... DLB-8

Tišma, Aleksandar 1924-2003 .... DLB-181

Titus, Edward William 1870-1952................. DLB-4; DS-15

Tiutchev, Fedor Ivanovich 1803-1873.... DLB-205

Tlali, Miriam 1933- DLB-157, 225

Todd, Barbara Euphan 1890-1976 ...... DLB-160

Todorov, Tzvetan 1939- DLB-242

Tofte, Robert
   1561 or 1562-1619 or 1620.........DLB-172

Tóibín, Colm 1955- DLB-271

Toklas, Alice B. 1877-1967 ....DLB-4; DS-15

Tokuda Shūsei 1872-1943 ....DLB-180

Toland, John 1670-1722 ....DLB-252

Tolkien, J. R. R.
   1892-1973 ......DLB-15, 160, 255; CDBLB-6

Toller, Ernst 1893-1939 ....DLB-124

Tollet, Elizabeth 1694-1754 ....DLB-95

Tolson, Melvin B. 1898-1966.........DLB-48, 76

Tolstaya, Tatyana 1951- DLB-285

Tolstoy, Aleksei Konstantinovich
   1817-1875..................DLB-238

Tolstoy, Aleksei Nikolaevich 1883-1945...DLB-272

Tolstoy, Leo 1828-1910 ....DLB-238

Tomalin, Claire 1933- DLB-155

Tómas Guðmundsson 1901-1983 ....DLB-293

Tomasi di Lampedusa, Giuseppe
   1896-1957 ....DLB-177

Tomlinson, Charles 1927- DLB-40

Tomlinson, H. M. 1873-1958....DLB-36, 100, 195

Abel Tompkins [publishing house].......DLB-49

Tompson, Benjamin 1642-1714 ....DLB-24

Tomson, Graham R.
   (see Watson, Rosamund Marriott)

Ton'a 1289-1372.....................DLB-203

Tondelli, Pier Vittorio 1955-1991........DLB-196

Tonks, Rosemary 1932- DLB-14, 207

Tonna, Charlotte Elizabeth 1790-1846....DLB-163

Jacob Tonson the Elder
   [publishing house] DLB-170

Toole, John Kennedy 1937-1969 ....Y-81

Toomer, Jean
   1894-1967 ....DLB-45, 51; CDALB-4

Topsoe, Vilhelm 1840-1881 ....DLB-300

Tor Books DLB-46

Torberg, Friedrich 1908-1979............DLB-85

Torga, Miguel (Adolfo Correira da Rocha)
   1907-1995 ....DLB-287

Torre, Francisco de la ?-? DLB-318

Torrence, Ridgely 1874-1950 ....DLB-54, 249

Torrente Ballester, Gonzalo
   1910-1999 ....DLB-322

Torres-Metzger, Joseph V. 1933- DLB-122

Torres Naharro, Bartolomé de
   1485?-1523? DLB-318

El Tostado (see Madrigal, Alfonso Fernández de)

Toth, Susan Allen 1940- Y-86

Richard Tottell [publishing house] DLB-170

   "The Printer to the Reader,"
   (1557) DLB-167

Tough-Guy Literature DLB-9

Touré, Askia Muhammad 1938- DLB-41

Tourgée, Albion W. 1838-1905 ....DLB-79

Tournemir, Elizaveta Sailhas de (see Tur, Evgeniia)

Tourneur, Cyril circa 1580-1626 ....DLB-58

Tournier, Michel 1924- DLB-83

Frank Tousey [publishing house].......DLB-49

Tower Publications....................DLB-46

Towne, Benjamin circa 1740-1793 ....DLB-43

Towne, Robert 1936- DLB-44

The Townely Plays fifteenth and sixteenth
   centuries DLB-146

Townsend, Sue 1946- DLB-271

Townshend, Aurelian
   by 1583-circa 1651 ....DLB-121

Toy, Barbara 1908-2001................DLB-204

Tozzi, Federigo 1883-1920 ....DLB-264

Tracy, Honor 1913-1989 ....DLB-15

Traherne, Thomas 1637?-1674 ....DLB-131

Traill, Catharine Parr 1802-1899........DLB-99

Train, Arthur 1875-1945 ....DLB-86; DS-16

Tranquilli, Secondino (see Silone, Ignazio)

The Transatlantic Publishing Company ...DLB-49

The Transatlantic Review 1924-1925 ....DS-15

The Transcendental Club
   1836-1840 ....DLB-1; DLB-223

Transcendentalism........DLB-1; DLB-223; DS-5

   "A Response from America," by
   John A. Heraud DS-5

   Publications and Social Movements DLB-1

   The Rise of Transcendentalism,
   1815-1860....................DS-5

   Transcendentalists, American DS-5

   "What Is Transcendentalism? By a
   Thinking Man," by James
   Kinnard Jr. DS-5

transition 1927-1938.....................DS-15

Translations (Vernacular) in the Crowns of
   Castile and Aragon 1352-1515 ......DLB-286

Tranströmer, Tomas 1931- DLB-257

Tranter, John 1943- DLB-289

Travel Writing
   American Travel Writing, 1776-1864
   (checklist) DLB-183

   British Travel Writing, 1940-1997
   (checklist) DLB-204

   Travel Writers of the Late
   Middle Ages DLB-286

   (1876-1909.....................DLB-174

   (1837-1875 ....DLB-166

   (1910-1939 ....DLB-195

Traven, B. 1882?/1890?-1969?.........DLB-9, 56

Travers, Ben 1886-1980.........DLB-10, 233

Travers, P. L. (Pamela Lyndon)
   1899-1996 ....DLB-160

Trediakovsky, Vasilii Kirillovich
   1703-1769 ....DLB-150

Treece, Henry 1911-1966 ....DLB-160

Treitel, Jonathan 1959- DLB-267

Trejo, Ernesto 1950-1991..............DLB-122

Trelawny, Edward John
   1792-1881 ....DLB-110, 116, 144

Tremain, Rose 1943- DLB-14, 271

Tremblay, Michel 1942- DLB-60

Trent, William P. 1862-1939 ......DLB-47, 71

Trescot, William Henry 1822-1898.......DLB-30

Tressell, Robert (Robert Phillipe Noonan)
   1870-1911 ....DLB-197

Trevelyan, Sir George Otto
   1838-1928 ....DLB-144

Trevisa, John circa 1342-circa 1402 ......DLB-146

Trevisan, Dalton 1925- DLB-307

Trevor, William 1928- DLB-14, 139

Triana, José 1931- DLB-305

Trierer Floyris circa 1170-1180 ....DLB-138

Trifonov, Iurii Valentinovich
   1925-1981 ....DLB-302

Trillin, Calvin 1935- DLB-185

Trilling, Lionel 1905-1975 ....DLB-28, 63

Trilussa 1871-1950....................DLB-114

Trimmer, Sarah 1741-1810 ....DLB-158

Triolet, Elsa 1896-1970 ....DLB-72

Tripp, John 1927- DLB-40

Trocchi, Alexander 1925-1984..........DLB-15

Troisi, Dante 1920-1989 ....DLB-196

Trollope, Anthony
   1815-1882 ......DLB-21, 57, 159; CDBLB-4

   Novel-Reading: *The Works of Charles
   Dickens; The Works of W. Makepeace
   Thackeray* (1879) DLB-21

   The Trollope Societies..................Y-00

Trollope, Frances 1779-1863 ....DLB-21, 166

Trollope, Joanna 1943- DLB-207

Troop, Elizabeth 1931- DLB-14

Tropicália.........................DLB-307

Trotter, Catharine 1679-1749 ....DLB-84, 252

Trotti, Lamar 1898-1952 ....DLB-44

Trottier, Pierre 1925- DLB-60

Trotzig, Birgitta 1929- DLB-257

Troupe, Quincy Thomas, Jr. 1943- DLB-41

John F. Trow and Company DLB-49

Trowbridge, John Townsend 1827-1916...DLB-202

Trudel, Jean-Louis 1967- DLB-251

True History of the Kelly Gang, 2001 Booker Prize winner,
   Peter Carey DLB-326

Truillier-Lacombe, Joseph-Patrice
   1807-1863 ....DLB-99

Trumbo, Dalton 1905-1976 ....DLB-26

Trumbull, Benjamin 1735-1820 ....DLB-30

Trumbull, John 1750-1831 ....DLB-31

Trumbull, John 1756-1843.............DLB-183

Cumulative Index

Truth, Sojourner 1797?-1883 .... DLB-239

Tscherning, Andreas 1611-1659 .... DLB-164

Tsubouchi Shōyō 1859-1935 .... DLB-180

Tsvetaeva, Marina Ivanovna
1892-1941..................... DLB-295

Tuchman, Barbara W.
Tribute to Alfred A. Knopf............. Y-84

Tucholsky, Kurt 1890-1935 .... DLB-56

Tucker, Charlotte Maria
1821-1893 .... DLB-163, 190

Tucker, George 1775-1861 .... DLB-3, 30, 248

Tucker, James 1808?-1866?............ DLB-230

Tucker, Nathaniel Beverley
1784-1851................... DLB-3, 248

Tucker, St. George 1752-1827 .... DLB-37

Tuckerman, Frederick Goddard
1821-1873..................... DLB-243

Tuckerman, Henry Theodore 1813-1871 .... DLB-64

Tumas, Juozas (see Vaizgantas)

Tunis, John R. 1889-1975 .... DLB-22, 171

Tunstall, Cuthbert 1474-1559 .... DLB-132

Tunström, Göran 1937-2000........... DLB-257

Tuohy, Frank 1925- DLB-14, 139

Tupper, Martin F. 1810-1889 .... DLB-32

Tur, Evgeniia 1815-1892.............. DLB-238

Turbyfill, Mark 1896-1991 .... DLB-45

Turco, Lewis 1934- Y-84

Tribute to John Ciardi Y-86

Turgenev, Aleksandr Ivanovich
1784-1845..................... DLB-198

Turgenev, Ivan Sergeevich
1818-1883..................... DLB-238

Turgot, baron de l'Aulne, Anne-Robert-Jacques
1727-1781 .... DLB-314

"Memorandum on Local
Government"................. DLB-314

Turnbull, Alexander H. 1868-1918...... DLB-184

Turnbull, Andrew 1921-1970 .... DLB-103

Turnbull, Gael 1928- DLB-40

Turnèbe, Odet de 1552-1581 .... DLB-327

Turner, Arlin 1909-1980.............. DLB-103

Turner, Charles (Tennyson)
1808-1879..................... DLB-32

Turner, Ethel 1872-1958 .... DLB-230

Turner, Frederick 1943- DLB-40

Turner, Frederick Jackson
1861-1932 .... DLB-17, 186

A Conversation between William Riggan
and Janette Turner Hospital............ Y-02

Turner, Joseph Addison 1826-1868 ...... DLB-79

Turpin, Waters Edward 1910-1968....... DLB-51

Turrini, Peter 1944- DLB-124

Tusquets, Esther 1936- DLB-322

Tutuola, Amos 1920-1997... DLB-125; CDWLB-3

Twain, Mark (see Clemens, Samuel Langhorne)

Tweedie, Ethel Brilliana
circa 1860-1940 ....DLB-174

A Century of Poetry, a Lifetime of
Collecting: J. M. Edelstein's
Collection of Twentieth-
Century American Poetry YB-02

Twombly, Wells 1935-1977............ DLB-241

Twysden, Sir Roger 1597-1672 .... DLB-213

Tyard, Pontus de 1521?-1605.......... DLB-327

Ty-Casper, Linda 1931- DLB-312

Tyler, Anne 1941- DLB-6, 143; Y-82; CDALB-7

Tyler, Mary Palmer 1775-1866 .... DLB-200

Tyler, Moses Coit 1835-1900 ....DLB-47, 64

Tyler, Royall 1757-1826................ DLB-37

Tylor, Edward Burnett 1832-1917 .... DLB-57

Tynan, Katharine 1861-1931 ...... DLB-153, 240

Tyndale, William circa 1494-1536 ...... DLB-132

Tyree, Omar 1969- DLB-292

U

Uchida, Yoshiko 1921-1992 .. DLB-312; CDALB-7

Udall, Nicholas 1504-1556............. DLB-62

Ugrêsić, Dubravka 1949- DLB-181

Uhland, Ludwig 1787-1862............. DLB-90

Uhse, Bodo 1904-1963.. .... DLB-69

Ujević, Augustin "Tin"
1891-1955 .... DLB-147

Ulenhart, Niclas fl. circa 1600 .... DLB-164

Ulfeldt, Leonora Christina 1621-1698 ... DLB-300

Ulibarrí, Sabine R. 1919-2003 .... DLB-82

Ulica, Jorge 1870-1926 .... DLB-82

Ulitskaya, Liudmila Evgen'evna
1943- DLB-285

Ulivi, Ferruccio 1912- DLB-196

Ulizio, B. George 1889-1969 .... DLB-140

Ulrich von Liechtenstein
circa 1200-circa 1275 .... DLB-138

Ulrich von Zatzikhoven
before 1194-after 1214............ DLB-138

'Umar ibn Abi Rabi'ah 644-712 or 721 .. DLB-311

Unaipon, David 1872-1967............ DLB-230

Unamuno, Miguel de 1864-1936 ... DLB-108, 322

Under, Marie 1883-1980 ... DLB-220; CDWLB-4

Underhill, Evelyn 1875-1941 .... DLB-240

Undset, Sigrid 1882-1949............. DLB-297

Ungaretti, Giuseppe 1888-1970 .... DLB-114

Unger, Friederike Helene
1741-1813..................... DLB-94

United States Book Company DLB-49

Universal Publishing and Distributing
Corporation..................... DLB-46

University of Colorado
Special Collections at the University of
Colorado at Boulder Y-98

Indiana University Press................. Y-02

The University of Iowa
Writers' Workshop Golden Jubilee Y-86

University of Missouri Press.............. Y-01

University of South Carolina
The G. Ross Roy Scottish
Poetry Collection Y-89

Two Hundred Years of Rare Books and
Literary Collections at the
University of South Carolina Y-00

The University of South Carolina Press...... Y-94

University of Virginia
The Book Arts Press at the University
of Virginia..................... Y-96

The Electronic Text Center and the
Electronic Archive of Early American
Fiction at the University of Virginia
Library Y-98

University of Virginia Libraries......... Y-91

University of Wales Press............. DLB-112

University Press of Florida Y-00

University Press of Kansas.............. Y-98

University Press of Mississippi............ Y-99

Unnur Benediktsdóttir Bjarklind (see Hulda)

Uno Chiyo 1897-1996 .... DLB-180

Unruh, Fritz von 1885-1970 .... DLB-56, 118

Unsworth, Barry 1930- DLB-194, 326

Unt, Mati 1944- DLB-232

The Unterberg Poetry Center of the
92nd Street Y..................... Y-98

Untermeyer, Louis 1885-1977 .... DLB-303

T. Fisher Unwin [publishing house] DLB-106

Upchurch, Boyd B. (see Boyd, John)

Updike, John 1932- DLB-2, 5, 143, 218, 227;
Y-80, 82; DS-3; CDALB-6

John Updike on the Internet Y-97

Tribute to Alfred A. Knopf Y-84

Tribute to John Ciardi Y-86

Upīts, Andrejs 1877-1970 .... DLB-220

Uppdal, Kristofer 1878-1961 .... DLB-297

Upton, Bertha 1849-1912............. DLB-141

Upton, Charles 1948- DLB-16

Upton, Florence K. 1873-1922 .... DLB-141

Upward, Allen 1863-1926 .... DLB-36

Urban, Milo 1904-1982 .... DLB-215

Ureña de Henríquez, Salomé 1850-1897 . DLB-283

Urfé, Honoré d' 1567-1625 ....DLB-268

Urista, Alberto Baltazar (see Alurista)

Urquhart, Fred 1912-1995 .... DLB-139

Urrea, Luis Alberto 1955- DLB-209

Urzidil, Johannes 1896-1970........... DLB-85

U.S.A. (Documentary) DLB-274

Usigli, Rodolfo 1905-1979 .... DLB-305

Usk, Thomas died 1388.............. DLB-146

Uslar Pietri, Arturo 1906-2001........ DLB-113

Uspensky, Gleb Ivanovich
1843-1902 . . . . DLB-277

Ussher, James 1581-1656. . . . . .DLB-213

Ustinov, Peter 1921-2004 . . . . DLB-13

Uttley, Alison 1884-1976 . . . . DLB-160

Uz, Johann Peter 1720-1796 . . . . DLB-97

V

Vadianus, Joachim 1484-1551 . . . . DLB-179

Vac, Bertrand (Aimé Pelletier) 1914- DLB-88

Vācietis, Ojārs 1933-1983 . . . . .DLB-232

Vaculík, Ludvík 1926- DLB-232

Vaičiulaitis, Antanas 1906-1992. . . . . .DLB-220

Vaičiūnaite, Judita 1937- DLB-232

Vail, Laurence 1891-1968 . . . . .DLB-4

Vail, Petr L'vovich 1949- DLB-285

Vailland, Roger 1907-1965 . . . . .DLB-83

Vaižgantas 1869-1933 . . . . .DLB-220

Vajda, Ernest 1887-1954. . . . . .DLB-44

Valdés, Alfonso de circa 1490?-1532 . . . . .DLB-318

Valdés, Gina 1943- DLB-122

Valdes, Juan de 1508-1541. . . . . .DLB-318

Valdez, Luis Miguel 1940- DLB-122

Valduga, Patrizia 1953- DLB-128

Vale Press. DLB-112

Valente, José Angel 1929-2000. . . . . .DLB-108

Valenzuela, Luisa 1938- . . . DLB-113; CDWLB-3

Valera, Diego de 1412-1488. . . . . .DLB-286

Valeri, Diego 1887-1976 . . . . .DLB-128

Valerius Flaccus fl. circa A.D. 92. . . . . . . .DLB-211

Valerius Maximus fl. circa A.D. 31 . . . . . .DLB-211

Valéry, Paul 1871-1945. . . . . .DLB-258

Valesio, Paolo 1939- DLB-196

Valgardson, W. D. 1939- DLB-60

Valle, Luz 1899-1971 . . . . .DLB-290

Valle, Víctor Manuel 1950- DLB-122

Valle-Inclán, Ramón del
1866-1936 . . . . DLB-134, 322

Vallejo, Armando 1949- DLB-122

Vallejo, César Abraham 1892-1938. . . . . .DLB-290

Vallès, Jules 1832-1885. . . . . .DLB-123

Vallette, Marguerite Eymery (see Rachilde)

Valverde, José María 1926-1996 . . . . . . .DLB-108

Vampilov, Aleksandr Valentinovich (A. Sanin)
1937-1972. .DLB-302

Van Allsburg, Chris 1949- DLB-61

Van Anda, Carr 1864-1945 . . . . .DLB-25

Vanbrugh, Sir John 1664-1726. . . . . .DLB-80

Vance, Jack 1916?- DLB-8

Vančura, Vladislav
1891-1942 . . . . DLB-215; CDWLB-4

van der Post, Laurens 1906-1996. . . . . . .DLB-204

Van Dine, S. S. (see Wright, Willard Huntington)

Van Doren, Mark 1894-1972. . . . . .DLB-45

van Druten, John 1901-1957 . . . . .DLB-10

Van Duyn, Mona 1921-2004 . . . . .DLB-5

Tribute to James Dickey Y-97

Van Dyke, Henry 1852-1933. . . . . .DLB-71; DS-13

Van Dyke, Henry 1928- DLB-33

Van Dyke, John C. 1856-1932. . . . . .DLB-186

Vane, Sutton 1888-1963. . . . . .DLB-10

Van Gieson, Judith 1941- DLB-306

Vanguard Press DLB-46

van Gulik, Robert Hans 1910-1967. . . . . . . DS-17

van Itallie, Jean-Claude 1936- DLB-7

Van Loan, Charles E. 1876-1919 . . . . .DLB-171

Vann, Robert L. 1879-1940 . . . . .DLB-29

Van Rensselaer, Mariana Griswold
1851-1934 . . . . DLB-47

Van Rensselaer, Mrs. Schuyler
(see Van Rensselaer, Mariana Griswold)

Van Vechten, Carl 1880-1964 . . . . DLB-4, 9, 51

van Vogt, A. E. 1912-2000. . . . . .DLB-8, 251

Varela, Blanca 1926- DLB-290

Vargas Llosa, Mario
1936- DLB-145; CDWLB-3

Acceptance Speech for the Ritz Paris
Hemingway Award. Y-85

Varley, John 1947- Y-81

Varnhagen von Ense, Karl August
1785-1858 . . . . .DLB-90

Varnhagen von Ense, Rahel
1771-1833 . . . . .DLB-90

Varro 116 B.C.-27 B.C. DLB-211

Vasilenko, Svetlana Vladimirovna
1956- DLB-285

Vasiliu, George (see Bacovia, George)

Vásquez, Richard 1928- DLB-209

Vassa, Gustavus (see Equiano, Olaudah)

Vassalli, Sebastiano 1941- DLB-128, 196

Vaugelas, Claude Favre de 1585-1650 . . . .DLB-268

Vaughan, Henry 1621-1695. . . . . .DLB-131

Vaughan, Thomas 1621-1666 . . . . .DLB-131

Vaughn, Robert 1592?-1667 . . . . .DLB-213

Vaux, Thomas, Lord 1509-1556 . . . . .DLB-132

Vazov, Ivan 1850-1921. . . . . . DLB-147; CDWLB-4

Vázquez Montalbán, Manuel
1939- DLB-134, 322

Véa, Alfredo, Jr. 1950- DLB-209

Veblen, Thorstein 1857-1929 . . . . .DLB-246

Vedel, Anders Sørensen 1542-1616 . . . . . .DLB-300

Vega, Janine Pommy 1942- DLB-16

Veiller, Anthony 1903-1965 . . . . .DLB-44

Velásquez-Trevino, Gloria 1949- DLB-122

Veley, Margaret 1843-1887 . . . . .DLB-199

Velleius Paterculus
circa 20 B.C.-circa A.D. 30 . . . . .DLB-211

Veloz Maggiolo, Marcio 1936- DLB-145

Vel'tman, Aleksandr Fomich
1800-1870 . . . . .DLB-198

Venegas, Daniel ?-? DLB-82

Venevitinov, Dmitrii Vladimirovich
1805-1827 . . . . .DLB-205

Verbitskaia, Anastasiia Alekseevna
1861-1928 . . . . .DLB-295

Verde, Cesário 1855-1886 . . . . .DLB-287

Vergil, Polydore circa 1470-1555 . . . . .DLB-132

Veríssimo, Erico 1905-1975 . . . . DLB-145, 307

Verlaine, Paul 1844-1896. . . . . .DLB-217

Vernacular Translations in the Crowns of
Castile and Aragon 1352-1515 . . . . . .DLB-286

Verne, Jules 1828-1905 . . . . .DLB-123

Vernon God Little, 2003 Booker Prize winner,
DBC Pierre .DLB-326

Verplanck, Gulian C. 1786-1870 . . . . .DLB-59

Vertinsky, Aleksandr 1889-1957 . . . . .DLB-317

Very, Jones 1813-1880 . . . . DLB-1, 243; DS-5

Vesaas, Halldis Moren 1907-1995 . . . . . .DLB-297

Vesaas, Tarjei 1897-1970. . . . . .DLB-297

Vian, Boris 1920-1959 . . . . DLB-72, 321

Viazemsky, Petr Andreevich
1792-1878 . . . . .DLB-205

Vicars, Thomas 1591-1638 . . . . .DLB-236

Vicente, Gil 1465-1536/1540? DLB-287, 318

Vickers, Roy 1888?-1965. . . . . .DLB-77

Vickery, Sukey 1779-1821 . . . . .DLB-200

Victoria 1819-1901 . . . . .DLB-55

Victoria Press. DLB-106

La vida de Lazarillo de Tormes DLB-318

Vidal, Gore 1925- DLB-6, 152; CDALB-7

Vidal, Mary Theresa 1815-1873 . . . . .DLB-230

Vidmer, Richards 1898-1978 . . . . .DLB-241

Viebig, Clara 1860-1952 . . . . .DLB-66

Vieira, António, S. J. (Antonio Vieyra)
1608-1697 . . . . .DLB-307

Viereck, George Sylvester 1884-1962 . . . . .DLB-54

Viereck, Peter 1916- DLB-5

Vietnam War (ended 1975)
Resources for the Study of Vietnam War
Literature DLB-9

Viets, Roger 1738-1811 . . . . .DLB-99

Vigil-Piñon, Evangelina 1949- DLB-122

Vigneault, Gilles 1928- DLB-60

Vigny, Alfred de 1797-1863 . . . . DLB-119, 192, 217

Vigolo, Giorgio 1894-1983 . . . . .DLB-114

Vik, Bjorg 1935- DLB-297

The Viking Press .DLB-46

Vila-Matas, Enrique 1948- DLB-322

Vilde, Eduard 1865-1933. . . . . .DLB-220

Cumulative Index

Vilinskaia, Mariia Aleksandrovna
 (see Vovchok, Marko)

Villa, José García 1908-1997 . . . . DLB-312

Villanueva, Alma Luz 1944- DLB-122

Villanueva, Tino 1941- DLB-82

Villard, Henry 1835-1900 . . . . DLB-23

Villard, Oswald Garrison 1872-1949 . . DLB-25, 91

Villarreal, Edit 1944- DLB-209

Villarreal, José Antonio 1924- DLB-82

Villaseñor, Victor 1940- DLB-209

Villedieu, Madame de (Marie-Catherine
 Desjardins) 1640?-1683 . . . . DLB-268

Villegas, Antonio de ?-? DLB-318

Villegas de Magnón, Leonor
 1876-1955 . . . . DLB-122

Villehardouin, Geoffroi de
 circa 1150-1215 . . . . DLB-208

Villemaire, Yolande 1949- DLB-60

Villena, Enrique de
 ca. 1382/84-1432 . . . . DLB-286

Villena, Luis Antonio de 1951- DLB-134

Villiers, George, Second Duke
 of Buckingham 1628-1687 . . . . DLB-80

Villiers de l'Isle-Adam, Jean-Marie
 Mathias Philippe-Auguste,
 Comte de 1838-1889 . . . . DLB-123, 192

Villon, François 1431-circa 1463? DLB-208

Vinaver, Michel (Michel Grinberg)
 1927- DLB-321

Vine Press DLB-112

Viorst, Judith 1931- DLB-52

Vipont, Elfrida (Elfrida Vipont Foulds,
 Charles Vipont) 1902-1992 . . . . DLB-160

Viramontes, Helena María 1954- DLB-122

Virgil 70 B.C.-19 B.C. DLB-211; CDWLB-1

Vischer, Friedrich Theodor 1807-1887 . . . DLB-133

Vitier, Cintio 1921- DLB-283

Vitrac, Roger 1899-1952 . . . . DLB-321

Vitruvius circa 85 B.C.-circa 15 B.C. DLB-211

Vitry, Philippe de 1291-1361 . . . . DLB-208

Vittorini, Elio 1908-1966 . . . . DLB-264

Vivanco, Luis Felipe 1907-1975 . . . . DLB-108

Vives, Juan Luis 1493-1540 . . . . DLB-318

Vivian, E. Charles (Charles Henry Cannell,
 Charles Henry Vivian, Jack Mann,
 Barry Lynd) 1882-1947 . . . . DLB-255

Viviani, Cesare 1947- DLB-128

Vivien, Renée 1877-1909 . . . . DLB-217

Vizenor, Gerald 1934- DLB-175, 227

Vizetelly and Company DLB-106

Vladimov, Georgii
 1931-2003 . . . . DLB-302

Voaden, Herman 1903-1991 . . . . DLB-88

Voß, Johann Heinrich 1751-1826 . . . . DLB-90

Vogau, Boris Andreevich
 (see Pil'niak, Boris Andreevich)

Voigt, Ellen Bryant 1943- DLB-120

Voinovich, Vladimir Nikolaevich
 1932- DLB-302

Vojnović, Ivo 1857-1929 . . . . . DLB-147; CDWLB-4

Vold, Jan Erik 1939- DLB-297

Volkoff, Vladimir 1932- DLB-83

P. F. Volland Company DLB-46

Vollbehr, Otto H. F.
 1872?-1945 or 1946 . . . . DLB-187

Vologdin (see Zasodimsky, Pavel Vladimirovich)

Voloshin, Maksimilian Aleksandrovich
 1877-1932 . . . . DLB-295

Volponi, Paolo 1924-1994 . . . . DLB-177

Voltaire (François-Marie Arouet)
 1694-1778 . . . . DLB-314

 "An account of the death of the chevalier de
  La Barre" DLB-314

 Candide DLB-314

 Philosophical Dictionary DLB-314

Vonarburg, Élisabeth 1947- DLB-251

von der Grün, Max 1926- DLB-75

Vonnegut, Kurt 1922- DLB-2, 8, 152;
  Y-80; DS-3; CDALB-6

 Tribute to Isaac Asimov Y-92

 Tribute to Richard Brautigan Y-84

Voranc, Prežihov 1893-1950 . . . . DLB-147

Voronsky, Aleksandr Konstantinovich
 1884-1937 . . . . DLB-272

Vorse, Mary Heaton 1874-1966 . . . . DLB-303

Vovchok, Marko 1833-1907 . . . . DLB-238

Voynich, E. L. 1864-1960 . . . . DLB-197

Vroman, Mary Elizabeth
 circa 1924-1967 . . . . DLB-33

W

Wace, Robert ("Maistre")
 circa 1100-circa 1175 . . . . DLB-146

Wackenroder, Wilhelm Heinrich
 1773-1798 . . . . DLB-90

Wackernagel, Wilhelm 1806-1869 . . . . . DLB-133

Waddell, Helen 1889-1965 . . . . DLB-240

Waddington, Miriam 1917-2004 . . . . DLB-68

Wade, Henry 1887-1969 . . . . DLB-77

Wagenknecht, Edward 1900-2004 . . . . . DLB-103

Wägner, Elin 1882-1949 . . . . DLB-259

Wagner, Heinrich Leopold 1747-1779 . . . . DLB-94

Wagner, Henry R. 1862-1957 . . . . DLB-140

Wagner, Richard 1813-1883 . . . . DLB-129

Wagoner, David 1926- DLB-5, 256

Wah, Fred 1939- DLB-60

Waiblinger, Wilhelm 1804-1830 . . . . DLB-90

Wain, John
 1925-1994 . . . DLB-15, 27, 139, 155; CDBLB-8

 Tribute to J. B. Priestly Y-84

Wainwright, Jeffrey 1944- DLB-40

Waite, Peirce and Company DLB-49

Wakeman, Stephen H. 1859-1924 . . . . . . DLB-187

Wakoski, Diane 1937- DLB-5

Walahfrid Strabo circa 808-849 . . . . DLB-148

Henry Z. Walck [publishing house] DLB-46

Walcott, Derek
 1930- DLB-117; Y-81, 92; CDWLB-3

 Nobel Lecture 1992: The Antilles:
  Fragments of Epic Memory Y-92

Robert Waldegrave [publishing house] DLB-170

Waldis, Burkhard circa 1490-1556? DLB-178

Waldman, Anne 1945- DLB-16

Waldrop, Rosmarie 1935- DLB-169

Walker, Alice 1900-1982 . . . . DLB-201

Walker, Alice
 1944- DLB-6, 33, 143; CDALB-6

Walker, Annie Louisa (Mrs. Harry Coghill)
 circa 1836-1907 . . . . DLB-240

Walker, George F. 1947- DLB-60

Walker, John Brisben 1847-1931 . . . . DLB-79

Walker, Joseph A. 1935- DLB-38

Walker, Kath (see Oodgeroo of the Tribe Noonuccal)

Walker, Margaret 1915-1998 . . . . DLB-76, 152

Walker, Obadiah 1616-1699 . . . . DLB-281

Walker, Ted 1934- DLB-40

Walker, Evans and Cogswell Company . . . DLB-49

Wall, John F. (see Sarban)

Wallace, Alfred Russel 1823-1913 . . . . . . DLB-190

Wallace, Dewitt 1889-1981 . . . . DLB-137

Wallace, Edgar 1875-1932 . . . . DLB-70

Wallace, Lew 1827-1905 . . . . DLB-202

Wallace, Lila Acheson 1889-1984 . . . . . . DLB-137

 "A Word of Thanks," From the Initial
  Issue of Reader's Digest
  (February 1922) DLB-137

Wallace, Naomi 1960- DLB-249

Wallace Markfield's "Steeplechase" Y-02

Wallace-Crabbe, Chris 1934- DLB-289

Wallant, Edward Lewis
 1926-1962 . . . . DLB-2, 28, 143, 299

Waller, Edmund 1606-1687 . . . . DLB-126

Walpole, Horace 1717-1797 . . . . . DLB-39, 104, 213

 Preface to the First Edition of
  The Castle of Otranto (1764) DLB-39, 178

 Preface to the Second Edition of
  The Castle of Otranto (1765) DLB-39, 178

Walpole, Hugh 1884-1941 . . . . DLB-34

Walrond, Eric 1898-1966 . . . . DLB-51

Walser, Martin 1927- DLB-75, 124

Walser, Robert 1878-1956 . . . . DLB-66

Walsh, Ernest 1895-1926 . . . . DLB-4, 45

Walsh, Robert 1784-1859 . . . . DLB-59

Walters, Henry 1848-1931 . . . . DLB-140

Waltharius circa 825. . . . . DLB-148

Walther von der Vogelweide
circa 1170-circa 1230 . . . . DLB-138

Walton, Izaak
1593-1683 . . . . DLB-151, 213; CDBLB-1

Walwicz, Ania 1951- DLB-325

Wambaugh, Joseph 1937- DLB-6; Y-83

Wand, Alfred Rudolph 1828-1891. . . . . . . DLB-188

Wandor, Michelene 1940- DLB-310

Waniek, Marilyn Nelson 1946- DLB-120

Wanley, Humphrey 1672-1726. . . . . DLB-213

War of the Words (and Pictures):
The Creation of a Graphic Novel Y-02

Warburton, William 1698-1779 . . . . DLB-104

Ward, Aileen 1919- DLB-111

Ward, Artemus (see Browne, Charles Farrar)

Ward, Arthur Henry Sarsfield (see Rohmer, Sax)

Ward, Douglas Turner 1930- DLB-7, 38

Ward, Mrs. Humphry 1851-1920 . . . . DLB-18

Ward, James 1843-1925. . . . . DLB-262

Ward, Lynd 1905-1985 . . . . DLB-22

Ward, Lock and Company DLB-106

Ward, Nathaniel circa 1578-1652 . . . . DLB-24

Ward, Theodore 1902-1983. . . . . DLB-76

Wardle, Ralph 1909-1988 . . . . DLB-103

Ware, Henry, Jr. 1794-1843 . . . . DLB-235

Ware, William 1797-1852. . . . . DLB-1, 235

Warfield, Catherine Ann 1816-1877 . . . . . DLB-248

Waring, Anna Letitia 1823-1910 . . . . DLB-240

Frederick Warne and Company [U.K.] DLB-106

Frederick Warne and Company [U.S.] DLB-49

Warner, Anne 1869-1913. . . . . DLB-202

Warner, Charles Dudley 1829-1900 . . . . . . DLB-64

Warner, Marina 1946- DLB-194

Warner, Rex 1905-1986. . . . . DLB-15

Warner, Susan 1819-1885 . . . . DLB-3, 42, 239, 250

Warner, Sylvia Townsend
1893-1978 . . . . DLB-34, 139

Warner, William 1558-1609. . . . . DLB-172

Warner Books DLB-46

Warr, Bertram 1917-1943. . . . . DLB-88

Warren, John Byrne Leicester
(see De Tabley, Lord)

Warren, Lella 1899-1982 . . . . Y-83

Warren, Mercy Otis 1728-1814 . . . . . . DLB-31, 200

Warren, Robert Penn 1905-1989 . . . . . DLB-2, 48,
152, 320; Y-80, 89; CDALB-6

Tribute to Katherine Anne Porter Y-80

Warren, Samuel 1807-1877. . . . . DLB-190

Die Wartburgkrieg circa 1230-circa 1280. . . . DLB-138

Warton, Joseph 1722-1800 . . . . DLB-104, 109

Warton, Thomas 1728-1790 . . . . DLB-104, 109

Warung, Price (William Astley)
1855-1911 . . . . DLB-230

Washington, George 1732-1799 . . . . DLB-31

Washington, Ned 1901-1976 . . . . DLB-265

Wassermann, Jakob 1873-1934 . . . . DLB-66

Wasserstein, Wendy 1950-2006. . . . . DLB-228

Wassmo, Herbjørg 1942- DLB-297

Wasson, David Atwood 1823-1887 . . . . DLB-1, 223

Watanna, Onoto (see Eaton, Winnifred)

Waten, Judah 1911?-1985 . . . . DLB-289

Waterhouse, Keith 1929- DLB-13, 15

Waterman, Andrew 1940- DLB-40

Waters, Frank 1902-1995. . . . . DLB-212; Y-86

Waters, Michael 1949- DLB-120

Watkins, Tobias 1780-1855 . . . . DLB-73

Watkins, Vernon 1906-1967. . . . . DLB-20

Watmough, David 1926- DLB-53

Watson, Colin 1920-1983 . . . . DLB-276

Watson, Ian 1943- DLB-261

Watson, James Wreford (see Wreford, James)

Watson, John 1850-1907 . . . . DLB-156

Watson, Rosamund Marriott
(Graham R. Tomson) 1860-1911 . . . . DLB-240

Watson, Sheila 1909-1998 . . . . DLB-60

Watson, Thomas 1545?-1592 . . . . DLB-132

Watson, Wilfred 1911-1998. . . . . DLB-60

W. J. Watt and Company. DLB-46

Watten, Barrett 1948- DLB-193

Watterson, Henry 1840-1921 . . . . DLB-25

Watts, Alan 1915-1973 . . . . DLB-16

Watts, Isaac 1674-1748. . . . . DLB-95

Franklin Watts [publishing house] DLB-46

Waugh, Alec 1898-1981. . . . . DLB-191

Waugh, Auberon 1939-2000 . . . DLB-14, 194; Y-00

Waugh, Evelyn 1903-1966
. . . . DLB-15, 162, 195; CDBLB-6

Way and Williams DLB-49

Wayman, Tom 1945- DLB-53

Wearne, Alan 1948- DLB-325

Weatherly, Tom 1942- DLB-41

Weaver, Gordon 1937- DLB-130

Weaver, Robert 1921- DLB-88

Webb, Beatrice 1858-1943 . . . . DLB-190

Webb, Francis 1925-1973 . . . . DLB-260

Webb, Frank J. fl. 1857 . . . . DLB-50

Webb, James Watson 1802-1884 . . . . DLB-43

Webb, Mary 1881-1927 . . . . DLB-34

Webb, Phyllis 1927- DLB-53

Webb, Sidney 1859-1947 . . . . DLB-190

Webb, Walter Prescott 1888-1963 . . . . DLB-17

Webbe, William ?-1591 . . . . DLB-132

Webber, Charles Wilkins
1819-1856? DLB-202

Weber, Max 1864-1920 . . . . DLB-296

Webling, Lucy (Lucy Betty MacRaye)
1877-1952 . . . . DLB-240

Webling, Peggy (Arthur Weston)
1871-1949 . . . . DLB-240

Webster, Augusta 1837-1894 . . . . DLB-35, 240

Webster, John
1579 or 1580-1634?. DLB-58; CDBLB-1

The Melbourne Manuscript Y-86

Webster, Noah
1758-1843 . . . . DLB-1, 37, 42, 43, 73, 243

Webster, Paul Francis 1907-1984 . . . . DLB-265

Charles L. Webster and Company DLB-49

Weckherlin, Georg Rodolf 1584-1653 . . . . DLB-164

Wedekind, Frank
1864-1918 . . . . DLB-118; CDWLB-2

Weeks, Edward Augustus, Jr.
1898-1989 . . . . DLB-137

Weeks, Stephen B. 1865-1918 . . . . DLB-187

Weems, Mason Locke 1759-1825 . . DLB-30, 37, 42

Weerth, Georg 1822-1856 . . . . DLB-129

Weidenfeld and Nicolson. DLB-112

Weidman, Jerome 1913-1998 . . . . DLB-28

Weigl, Bruce 1949- DLB-120

Weil, Jiří 1900-1959 . . . . DLB-299

Weinbaum, Stanley Grauman
1902-1935 . . . . DLB-8

Weiner, Andrew 1949- DLB-251

Weintraub, Stanley 1929- DLB-111; Y82

Weise, Christian 1642-1708 . . . . DLB-168

Weisenborn, Gunther 1902-1969. . . . . DLB-69, 124

Weiss, John 1818-1879 . . . . DLB-1, 243

Weiss, Paul 1901-2002 . . . . DLB-279

Weiss, Peter 1916-1982 . . . . DLB-69, 124

Weiss, Theodore 1916-2003 . . . . DLB-5

Weiß, Ernst 1882-1940 . . . . DLB-81

Weiße, Christian Felix 1726-1804 . . . . DLB-97

Weitling, Wilhelm 1808-1871. . . . . DLB-129

Welch, Denton 1915-1948 . . . . DLB-319

Welch, James 1940- DLB-175, 256

Welch, Lew 1926-1971? DLB-16

Weldon, Fay 1931- . DLB-14, 194, 319; CDBLB-8

Wellek, René 1903-1995 . . . . DLB-63

Weller, Archie 1957- DLB-325

Wells, Carolyn 1862-1942 . . . . DLB-11

Wells, Charles Jeremiah
circa 1800-1879 . . . . DLB-32

Wells, Gabriel 1862-1946. . . . . DLB-140

Wells, H. G. 1866-1946
. . . . DLB-34, 70, 156, 178; CDBLB-6

H. G. Wells Society Y-98

Preface to *The Scientific Romances of
H. G. Wells* (1933) DLB-178

Wells, Helena 1758?-1824 .... DLB-200

Wells, Rebecca 1952- DLB-292

Wells, Robert 1947- DLB-40

Wells-Barnett, Ida B. 1862-1931 ..... DLB-23, 221

Welsh, Irvine 1958- DLB-271

Welty, Eudora 1909-2001 .... DLB-2, 102, 143; Y-87, 01; DS-12; CDALB-1

   Eudora Welty: Eye of the Storyteller Y-87

   Eudora Welty Newsletter Y-99

   Eudora Welty's Funeral Y-01

   Eudora Welty's Ninetieth Birthday Y-99

   Eudora Welty Remembered in Two Exhibits Y-02

Wendell, Barrett 1855-1921 .... DLB-71

Wentworth, Patricia 1878-1961 .... DLB-77

Wentworth, William Charles 1790-1872 .... DLB-230

Wenzel, Jean-Paul 1947- DLB-321

Werder, Diederich von dem 1584-1657 .. DLB-164

Werfel, Franz 1890-1945 .... DLB-81, 124

Werner, Zacharias 1768-1823 .... DLB-94

The Werner Company DLB-49

Wersba, Barbara 1932- DLB-52

Wescott, Glenway 1901-1987 .... DLB-4, 9, 102; DS-15

Wesker, Arnold 1932- DLB-13, 310, 319; CDBLB-8

Wesley, Charles 1707-1788 .... DLB-95

Wesley, John 1703-1791 .... DLB-104

Wesley, Mary 1912-2002 .... DLB-231

Wesley, Richard 1945- DLB-38

Wessel, Johan Herman 1742-1785 .... DLB-300

A. Wessels and Company DLB-46

Wessobrunner Gebet circa 787-815 .... DLB-148

West, Anthony 1914-1988 .... DLB-15

   Tribute to Liam O'Flaherty Y-84

West, Cheryl L. 1957- DLB-266

West, Cornel 1953- DLB-246

West, Dorothy 1907-1998 .... DLB-76

West, Jessamyn 1902-1984 .... DLB-6; Y-84

West, Mae 1892-1980 .... DLB-44

West, Michael Lee 1953- DLB-292

West, Michelle Sagara 1963- DLB-251

West, Morris 1916-1999 .... DLB-289

West, Nathanael 1903-1940 .... DLB-4, 9, 28; CDALB-5

West, Paul 1930- DLB-14

West, Rebecca 1892-1983 .... DLB-36; Y-83

West, Richard 1941- DLB-185

West and Johnson DLB-49

Westcott, Edward Noyes 1846-1898 ..... DLB-202

The Western Literature Association Y-99

The Western Messenger 1835-1841 .... DLB-1; DLB-223

Western Publishing Company DLB-46

Western Writers of America Y-99

The Westminster Review 1824-1914 .... DLB-110

Weston, Arthur (see Webling, Peggy)

Weston, Elizabeth Jane circa 1582-1612 ... DLB-172

Wetherald, Agnes Ethelwyn 1857-1940 ... DLB-99

Wetherell, Elizabeth (see Warner, Susan)

Wetherell, W. D. 1948- DLB-234

Wetzel, Friedrich Gottlob 1779-1819 ...... DLB-90

Weyman, Stanley J. 1855-1928 ..... DLB-141, 156

Wezel, Johann Karl 1747-1819 .... DLB-94

Whalen, Philip 1923-2002 .... DLB-16

Whalley, George 1915-1983 .... DLB-88

Wharton, Edith 1862-1937 .... DLB-4, 9, 12, 78, 189; DS-13; CDALB-3

Wharton, William 1925- Y-80

Whately, Mary Louisa 1824-1889 ...... DLB-166

Whately, Richard 1787-1863 .... DLB-190

   Elements of Rhetoric (1828; revised, 1846) [excerpt] DLB-57

Wheatley, Dennis 1897-1977 .... DLB-77, 255

Wheatley, Phillis circa 1754-1784 .... DLB-31, 50; CDALB-2

Wheeler, Anna Doyle 1785-1848? DLB-158

Wheeler, Charles Stearns 1816-1843 .. DLB-1, 223

Wheeler, Monroe 1900-1988 .... DLB-4

Wheelock, John Hall 1886-1978 .... DLB-45

   From John Hall Wheelock's Oral Memoir Y-01

Wheelwright, J. B. 1897-1940 .... DLB-45

Wheelwright, John circa 1592-1679 ...... DLB-24

Whetstone, George 1550-1587 .... DLB-136

Whetstone, Colonel Pete (see Noland, C. F. M.)

Whewell, William 1794-1866 .... DLB-262

Whichcote, Benjamin 1609?-1683 ...... DLB-252

Whicher, Stephen E. 1915-1961 .... DLB-111

Whipple, Edwin Percy 1819-1886 ..... DLB-1, 64

Whitaker, Alexander 1585-1617 .... DLB-24

Whitaker, Daniel K. 1801-1881 .... DLB-73

Whitcher, Frances Miriam 1812-1852 .... DLB-11, 202

White, Andrew 1579-1656 .... DLB-24

White, Andrew Dickson 1832-1918 ...... DLB-47

White, E. B. 1899-1985 ... DLB-11, 22; CDALB-7

White, Edgar B. 1947- DLB-38

White, Edmund 1940- DLB-227

White, Ethel Lina 1887-1944 .... DLB-77

White, Hayden V. 1928- DLB-246

White, Henry Kirke 1785-1806 .... DLB-96

White, Horace 1834-1916 .... DLB-23

White, James 1928-1999 .... DLB-261

White, Patrick 1912-1990 .... DLB-260

White, Phyllis Dorothy James (see James, P. D.)

White, Richard Grant 1821-1885 .... DLB-64

White, T. H. 1906-1964 .... DLB-160, 255

White, Walter 1893-1955 .... DLB-51

Wilcox, James 1949- DLB-292

William White and Company DLB-49

White, William Allen 1868-1944 .... DLB-9, 25

White, William Anthony Parker (see Boucher, Anthony)

White, William Hale (see Rutherford, Mark)

Whitechurch, Victor L. 1868-1933 .... DLB-70

Whitehead, Alfred North 1861-1947 .... DLB-100, 262

Whitehead, E. A. (Ted Whitehead) 1933- DLB-310

Whitehead, James 1936- Y-81

Whitehead, William 1715-1785 ...... DLB-84, 109

Whitfield, James Monroe 1822-1871 ..... DLB-50

Whitfield, Raoul 1898-1945 .... DLB-226

Whitgift, John circa 1533-1604 .... DLB-132

Whiting, John 1917-1963 .... DLB-13

Whiting, Samuel 1597-1679 .... DLB-24

Whitlock, Brand 1869-1934 .... DLB-12

Whitman, Albery Allson 1851-1901 ..... DLB-50

Whitman, Alden 1913-1990 .... Y-91

Whitman, Sarah Helen (Power) 1803-1878 .... DLB-1, 243

Whitman, Walt 1819-1892 ... DLB-3, 64, 224, 250; CDALB-2

Albert Whitman and Company DLB-46

Whitman Publishing Company DLB-46

Whitney, Geoffrey 1548 or 1552?-1601 .... DLB-136

Whitney, Isabella fl. 1566-1573 .... DLB-136

Whitney, John Hay 1904-1982 .... DLB-127

Whittemore, Reed 1919-1995 .... DLB-5

Whittier, John Greenleaf 1807-1892 .... DLB-1, 243; CDALB-2

Whittlesey House DLB-46

Wickham, Anna (Edith Alice Mary Harper) 1884-1947 .... DLB-240

Wickram, Georg circa 1505-circa 1561 ... DLB-179

Wicomb, Zoë 1948- DLB-225

Wideman, John Edgar 1941- DLB-33, 143

Widener, Harry Elkins 1885-1912 ...... DLB-140

Wiebe, Rudy 1934- DLB-60

Wiechert, Ernst 1887-1950 .... DLB-56

Wied, Gustav 1858-1914 .... DLB-300

Wied, Martina 1882-1957 .... DLB-85

Wiehe, Evelyn May Clowes (see Mordaunt, Elinor)

Wieland, Christoph Martin 1733-1813 .... DLB-97

Wienbarg, Ludolf 1802-1872 .... DLB-133

Wieners, John 1934- DLB-16

Wier, Ester 1910-2000 . . . . DLB-52

Wiesel, Elie
1928- DLB-83, 299; Y-86, 87; CDALB-7

    Nobel Lecture 1986: Hope, Despair and Memory Y-86

Wiggin, Kate Douglas 1856-1923 . . . . DLB-42

Wigglesworth, Michael 1631-1705 . . . . DLB-24

Wilberforce, William 1759-1833 . . . . DLB-158

Wilbrandt, Adolf 1837-1911 . . . . DLB-129

Wilbur, Richard 1921- . . . DLB-5, 169; CDALB-7

    Tribute to Robert Penn Warren Y-89

Wilcox, James 1949- DLB-292

Wild, Peter 1940- DLB-5

Wilde, Lady Jane Francesca Elgee
1821?-1896 . . . . DLB-199

Wilde, Oscar 1854-1900
. DLB-10, 19, 34, 57, 141, 156, 190; CDBLB-5
    "The Critic as Artist" (1891) DLB-57
    "The Decay of Lying" (1889) DLB-18
    "The English Renaissance of
    Art" (1908) DLB-35
    "L'Envoi" (1882) DLB-35

    Oscar Wilde Conference at Hofstra University Y-00

Wilde, Richard Henry 1789-1847 . . . . . . DLB-3, 59

W. A. Wilde Company DLB-49

Wilder, Billy 1906-2002 . . . . DLB-26

Wilder, Laura Ingalls 1867-1957 . . . . . DLB-22, 256

Wilder, Thornton
1897-1975 . . . . DLB-4, 7, 9, 228; CDALB-7

    Thornton Wilder Centenary at Yale Y-97

Wildgans, Anton 1881-1932 . . . . DLB-118

Wilding, Michael 1942- DLB-325

Wiley, Bell Irvin 1906-1980 . . . . DLB-17

John Wiley and Sons DLB-49

Wilhelm, Kate 1928- DLB-8

Wilkes, Charles 1798-1877 . . . . DLB-183

Wilkes, George 1817-1885 . . . . DLB-79

Wilkins, John 1614-1672 . . . . DLB-236

Wilkinson, Anne 1910-1961 . . . . DLB-88

Wilkinson, Christopher 1941- DLB-310

Wilkinson, Eliza Yonge
1757-circa 1813 . . . . DLB-200

Wilkinson, Sylvia 1940- Y-86

Wilkinson, William Cleaver 1833-1920 . . . . DLB-71

Willard, Barbara 1909-1994 . . . . DLB-161

Willard, Emma 1787-1870 . . . . DLB-239

Willard, Frances E. 1839-1898 . . . . DLB-221

Willard, Nancy 1936- DLB-5, 52

Willard, Samuel 1640-1707 . . . . DLB-24

L. Willard [publishing house] DLB-49

Willeford, Charles 1919-1988 . . . . DLB-226

William of Auvergne 1190-1249 . . . . DLB-115

William of Conches
circa 1090-circa 1154 . . . . DLB-115

William of Ockham circa 1285-1347 . . . . . DLB-115

William of Sherwood
1200/1205-1266/1271 . . . . DLB-115

The William Charvat American Fiction
Collection at the Ohio State
University Libraries Y-92

Williams, Ben Ames 1889-1953 . . . . DLB-102

Williams, C. K. 1936- DLB-5

Williams, Chancellor 1905-1992 . . . . DLB-76

Williams, Charles 1886-1945 . . . DLB-100, 153, 255

Williams, Denis 1923-1998 . . . . DLB-117

Williams, Emlyn 1905-1987 . . . . DLB-10, 77

Williams, Garth 1912-1996 . . . . DLB-22

Williams, George Washington
1849-1891 . . . . DLB-47

Williams, Heathcote 1941- DLB-13

Williams, Helen Maria 1761-1827 . . . . . . DLB-158

Williams, Hugo 1942- DLB-40

Williams, Isaac 1802-1865 . . . . DLB-32

Williams, Joan 1928- DLB-6

Williams, Joe 1889-1972 . . . . DLB-241

Williams, John A. 1925- DLB-2, 33

Williams, John E. 1922-1994 . . . . DLB-6

Williams, Jonathan 1929- DLB-5

Williams, Miller 1930- DLB-105

Williams, Nigel 1948- DLB-231

Williams, Raymond
1921-1988 . . . . DLB-14, 231, 242

Williams, Roger circa 1603-1683 . . . . DLB-24

Williams, Rowland 1817-1870 . . . . DLB-184

Williams, Samm-Art 1946- DLB-38

Williams, Sherley Anne 1944-1999 . . . . DLB-41

Williams, T. Harry 1909-1979 . . . . DLB-17

Williams, Tennessee
1911-1983 . . . . . DLB-7; Y-83; DS-4; CDALB-1

Williams, Terry Tempest 1955- . . . DLB-206, 275

Williams, Ursula Moray 1911- DLB-160

Williams, Valentine 1883-1946 . . . . DLB-77

Williams, William Appleman 1921-1990 . . . DLB-17

Williams, William Carlos
1883-1963 . . . . . . DLB-4, 16, 54, 86; CDALB-4

    The William Carlos Williams Society Y-99

Williams, Wirt 1921-1986 . . . . DLB-6

A. Williams and Company DLB-49

Williams Brothers DLB-49

Williamson, David 1942- DLB-289

Williamson, Henry 1895-1977 . . . . DLB-191

    The Henry Williamson Society Y-98

Williamson, Jack 1908- DLB-8

Willingham, Calder Baynard, Jr.
1922-1995 . . . . DLB-2, 44

Williram of Ebersberg circa 1020-1085 . . . DLB-148

Willis, John circa 1572-1625 . . . . DLB-281

Willis, Nathaniel Parker 1806-1867
. . . . DLB-3, 59, 73, 74, 183, 250; DS-13

Willis, Ted 1918-1992 . . . . DLB-310

Willkomm, Ernst 1810-1886 . . . . DLB-133

Wills, Garry 1934- DLB-246

    Tribute to Kenneth Dale McCormick Y-97

Willson, Meredith 1902-1984 . . . . DLB-265

Willumsen, Dorrit 1940- DLB-214

Wilmer, Clive 1945- DLB-40

Wilson, A. N. 1950- DLB-14, 155, 194

Wilson, Angus 1913-1991 . . . . . . DLB-15, 139, 155

Wilson, Arthur 1595-1652 . . . . DLB-58

Wilson, August 1945-2005 . . . . DLB-228

Wilson, Augusta Jane Evans 1835-1909 . . . DLB-42

Wilson, Colin 1931- DLB-14, 194

    Tribute to J. B. Priestly Y-84

Wilson, Edmund 1895-1972 . . . . DLB-63

Wilson, Ethel 1888-1980 . . . . DLB-68

Wilson, F. P. 1889-1963 . . . . DLB-201

Wilson, Harriet E.
1827/1828?-1863? DLB-50, 239, 243

Wilson, Harry Leon 1867-1939 . . . . DLB-9

Wilson, John 1588-1667 . . . . DLB-24

Wilson, John 1785-1854 . . . . DLB-110

Wilson, John Anthony Burgess
(see Burgess, Anthony)

Wilson, John Dover 1881-1969 . . . . DLB-201

Wilson, Lanford 1937- DLB-7

Wilson, Margaret 1882-1973 . . . . DLB-9

Wilson, Michael 1914-1978 . . . . DLB-44

Wilson, Mona 1872-1954 . . . . DLB-149

Wilson, Robert Charles 1953- DLB-251

Wilson, Robert McLiam 1964- DLB-267

Wilson, Robley 1930- DLB-218

Wilson, Romer 1891-1930 . . . . DLB-191

Wilson, Thomas 1524-1581 . . . . DLB-132, 236

Wilson, Woodrow 1856-1924 . . . . DLB-47

Effingham Wilson [publishing house] DLB-154

Wimpfeling, Jakob 1450-1528 . . . . DLB-179

Wimsatt, William K., Jr. 1907-1975 . . . . . . DLB-63

Winchell, Walter 1897-1972 . . . . DLB-29

J. Winchester [publishing house] DLB-49

Winckelmann, Johann Joachim
1717-1768 . . . . DLB-97

Winckler, Paul 1630-1686 . . . . DLB-164

Wind, Herbert Warren 1916-2005 . . . . . . DLB-171

John Windet [publishing house] DLB-170

Windham, Donald 1920- DLB-6

Windsor, Gerard 1944- DLB-325

Wing, Donald Goddard 1904-1972 . . . . . . DLB-187

Wing, John M. 1844-1917 . . . . DLB-187

Allan Wingate [publishing house] DLB-112

Winnemucca, Sarah 1844-1921 . . . . DLB-175

Winnifrith, Tom 1938- DLB-155

Winsloe, Christa 1888-1944 . . . . DLB-124

Winslow, Anna Green 1759-1780 . . . . DLB-200

Cumulative Index

Winsor, Justin 1831-1897 .... DLB-47

John C. Winston Company DLB-49

Winters, Yvor 1900-1968 .... DLB-48

Winterson, Jeanette 1959- DLB-207, 261

Winther, Christian 1796-1876 .... DLB-300

Winthrop, John 1588-1649 .... DLB-24, 30

Winthrop, John, Jr. 1606-1676 .... DLB-24

Winthrop, Margaret Tyndal
  1591-1647 .... DLB-200

Winthrop, Theodore
  1828-1861 .... DLB-202

Winton, Tim 1960- DLB-325

Wirt, William 1772-1834 .... DLB-37

Wise, John 1652-1725 .... DLB-24

Wise, Thomas James 1859-1937 .... DLB-184

Wiseman, Adele 1928-1992 .... DLB-88

Wishart and Company DLB-112

Wisner, George 1812-1849 .... DLB-43

Wister, Owen 1860-1938 .... DLB-9, 78, 186

Wister, Sarah 1761-1804 .... DLB-200

Wither, George 1588-1667 .... DLB-121

Witherspoon, John 1723-1794 .... DLB-31

The Works of the Rev. John Witherspoon
  (1800-1801) [excerpts] DLB-31

Withrow, William Henry 1839-1908 ..... DLB-99

Witkacy (see Witkiewicz, Stanisław Ignacy)

Witkiewicz, Stanisław Ignacy
  1885-1939 .... DLB-215; CDWLB-4

Wittenwiler, Heinrich before 1387-
  circa 1414? DLB-179

Wittgenstein, Ludwig 1889-1951 .... DLB-262

Wittig, Monique 1935- DLB-83

Witting, Amy (Joan Austral Levick, née Fraser)
  1918-2001 .... DLB-325

Wodehouse, P. G.
  1881-1975 .... DLB-34, 162; CDBLB-6

  Worldwide Wodehouse Societies Y-98

Wohmann, Gabriele 1932- DLB-75

Woiwode, Larry 1941- DLB-6

  Tribute to John Gardner Y-82

Wolcot, John 1738-1819 .... DLB-109

Wolcott, Roger 1679-1767 .... DLB-24

Wolf, Christa 1929- DLB-75; CDWLB-2

Wolf, Friedrich 1888-1953 .... DLB-124

Wolfe, Gene 1931- DLB-8

Wolfe, Thomas 1900-1938 ....
  DLB-9, 102, 229; Y-85; DS-2, DS-16; CDALB-5
  "All the Faults of Youth and Inexperience":
    A Reader's Report on
    Thomas Wolfe's *O Lost* Y-01

  Emendations for *Look Homeward, Angel* Y-00

  Eugene Gant's Projected Works Y-01

  Fire at the Old Kentucky Home
    [Thomas Wolfe Memorial] Y-98

  Thomas Wolfe Centennial
    Celebration in Asheville Y-00

  The Thomas Wolfe Collection at
    the University of North Carolina
    at Chapel Hill Y-97

  The Thomas Wolfe Society Y-97, 99

Wolfe, Tom 1931- DLB-152, 185

John Wolfe [publishing house] DLB-170

Reyner (Reginald) Wolfe
  [publishing house] DLB-170

Wolfenstein, Martha 1869-1906 .... DLB-221

Wolff, David (see Maddow, Ben)

Wolff, Egon 1926- DLB-305

Wolff, Helen 1906-1994 .... Y-94

Wolff, Tobias 1945- DLB-130

  Tribute to Michael M. Rea Y-97

  Tribute to Raymond Carver Y-88

Wolfram von Eschenbach
  circa 1170-after 1220 ... DLB-138; CDWLB-2

  Wolfram von Eschenbach's *Parzival*:
    Prologue and Book 3 .... DLB-138

Wolker, Jiří 1900-1924 .... DLB-215

Wollstonecraft, Mary 1759-1797
  .... DLB-39, 104, 158, 252; CDBLB-3

Women
  Women's Work, Women's Sphere:
    Selected Comments from Women
    Writers DLB-200

Women Writers in Sixteenth-Century
  Spain DLB-318

Wondratschek, Wolf 1943- DLB-75

Wong, Elizabeth 1958- DLB-266

Wong, Nellie 1934- DLB-312

Wong, Shawn 1949- DLB-312

Wongar, B. (Sreten Bozic) 1932- DLB-325

Wood, Anthony à 1632-1695 .... DLB-213

Wood, Benjamin 1820-1900 .... DLB-23

Wood, Charles 1932-1980 .... DLB-13

  The Charles Wood Affair:
    A Playwright Revived Y-83

Wood, Mrs. Henry 1814-1887 .... DLB-18

Wood, Joanna E. 1867-1927 .... DLB-92

Wood, Sally Sayward Barrell Keating
  1759-1855 .... DLB-200

Wood, William fl. seventeenth century DLB-24

Samuel Wood [publishing house] DLB-49

Woodberry, George Edward
  1855-1930 .... DLB-71, 103

Woodbridge, Benjamin 1622-1684 .... DLB-24

Woodbridge, Frederick J. E. 1867-1940 ...DLB-270

Woodcock, George 1912-1995 .... DLB-88

Woodhull, Victoria C. 1838-1927 .... DLB-79

Woodmason, Charles circa 1720-? DLB-31

Woodress, James Leslie, Jr. 1916- DLB-111

Woods, Margaret L. 1855-1945 .... DLB-240

Woodson, Carter G. 1875-1950 .... DLB-17

Woodward, C. Vann 1908-1999 .... DLB-17

Woodward, Stanley 1895-1965 .... DLB-171

Woodworth, Samuel 1785-1842 .... DLB-250

Wooler, Thomas 1785 or 1786-1853 ..... DLB-158

Woolf, David (see Maddow, Ben)

Woolf, Douglas 1922-1992 .... DLB-244

Woolf, Leonard 1880-1969 .... DLB-100; DS-10

Woolf, Virginia 1882-1941
  .... DLB-36, 100, 162; DS-10; CDBLB-6
  "The New Biography," *New York Herald
    Tribune*, 30 October 1927 .... DLB-149

Woollcott, Alexander 1887-1943 .... DLB-29

Woolman, John 1720-1772 .... DLB-31

Woolner, Thomas 1825-1892 .... DLB-35

Woolrich, Cornell 1903-1968 .... DLB-226

Woolsey, Sarah Chauncy 1835-1905 ..... DLB-42

Woolson, Constance Fenimore
  1840-1894 .... DLB-12, 74, 189, 221

Worcester, Joseph Emerson
  1784-1865 .... DLB-1, 235

Wynkyn de Worde [publishing house] DLB-170

Wordsworth, Christopher 1807-1885 .... DLB-166

Wordsworth, Dorothy 1771-1855 ....DLB-107

Wordsworth, Elizabeth
  1840-1932 .... DLB-98

Wordsworth, William
  1770-1850 .... DLB-93, 107; CDBLB-3

Workman, Fanny Bullock
  1859-1925 .... DLB-189

World Literatue Today: A Journal for the
  New Millennium Y-01

World Publishing Company DLB-46

World War I (1914-1918) DS-18

  The Great War Exhibit and Symposium
    at the University of South Carolina ... Y-97

  The Liddle Collection and First World
    War Research Y-97

  Other British Poets Who Fell
    in the Great War DLB-216

  The Seventy-Fifth Anniversary of
    the Armistice: The Wilfred Owen
    Centenary and the Great War Exhibit
    at the University of Virginia Y-93

World War II (1939–1945)
  Literary Effects of World War II DLB-15

  World War II Writers Symposium
    at the University of South Carolina,
    12–14 April 1995 .... Y-95

  WW2 HMSO Paperbacks Society Y-98

R. Worthington and Company DLB-49

Wotton, Sir Henry 1568-1639 .... DLB-121

Wouk, Herman 1915- Y-82; CDALB-7

  Tribute to James Dickey Y-97

Wreford, James 1915-1990 .... DLB-88

Wren, Sir Christopher 1632-1723 .... DLB-213

Wren, Percival Christopher 1885-1941 .. DLB-153

Wrenn, John Henry 1841-1911 .... DLB-140

Wright, C. D. 1949- DLB-120

Wright, Charles 1935- DLB-165; Y-82

Wright, Charles Stevenson 1932- DLB-33

Wright, Chauncey 1830-1875 ....DLB-270

Wright, Frances 1795-1852 ....DLB-73

Wright, Harold Bell 1872-1944 ....DLB-9

Wright, James 1927-1980
..................DLB-5, 169; CDALB-7

Wright, Jay 1935- DLB-41

Wright, Judith 1915-2000............DLB-260

Wright, Louis B. 1899-1984............DLB-17

Wright, Richard
  1908-1960 .... DLB-76, 102; DS-2; CDALB-5

Wright, Richard B. 1937- DLB-53

Wright, S. Fowler 1874-1965 ....DLB-255

Wright, Sarah Elizabeth 1928- DLB-33

Wright, T. H. "Style" (1877) [excerpt] DLB-57

Wright, Willard Huntington (S. S. Van Dine)
  1887-1939 ....DLB-306; DS-16

Wrightson, Patricia 1921- DLB-289

Wrigley, Robert 1951- DLB-256

Writers' Forum Y-85

Writing
  A Writing Life....................Y-02
  On Learning to Write Y-88
  The Profession of Authorship:
    Scribblers for Bread Y-89
  A Writer Talking: A Collage.........Y-00

Wroth, Lawrence C. 1884-1970 ....DLB-187

Wroth, Lady Mary 1587-1653 ....DLB-121

Wu Jianren (Wo Foshanren)
  1866-1910 ....DLB-328

Wu Zuxiang 1908-1994...............DLB-328

Wumingshi (Bu Baonan) 1917-2002.....DLB-328

Wurlitzer, Rudolph 1937- DLB-173

Wyatt, Sir Thomas circa 1503-1542.....DLB-132

Wycherley, William
  1641-1715 .... DLB-80; CDBLB-2

Wyclif, John circa 1335-1384 ....DLB-146

Wyeth, N. C. 1882-1945 ....DLB-188; DS-16

Wyle, Niklas von circa 1415-1479 ....DLB-179

Wylie, Elinor 1885-1928 ....DLB-9, 45

Wylie, Philip 1902-1971................DLB-9

Wyllie, John Cook 1908-1968 ....DLB-140

Wyman, Lillie Buffum Chace
  1847-1929 ....DLB-202

Wymark, Olwen 1934- DLB-233

Wynd, Oswald Morris (see Black, Gavin)

Wyndham, John (John Wyndham Parkes
  Lucas Beynon Harris) 1903-1969 ....DLB-255

Wynne-Tyson, Esmé 1898-1972.........DLB-191

X

Xenophon circa 430 B.C.-circa 356 B.C. DLB-176

Xiang Kairan (Pingjiang Buxiaoshengj Buxiaosheng)
  1890-1957 ....DLB-328

Xiao Hong 1911-1942................DLB-328

Xu Dishan (Luo Huasheng)
  1893-1941 ....DLB-328

Xu Zhenya 1889-1937................DLB-328

Y

Yahp, Beth 1964- DLB-325

Yamamoto, Hisaye 1921- DLB-312

Yamanaka, Lois-Ann 1961- DLB-312

Yamashita, Karen Tei 1951- DLB-312

Yamauchi, Wakako 1924- DLB-312

Yang Kui 1905-1985.................DLB-328

Yasuoka Shōtarō 1920- DLB-182

Yates, Dornford 1885-1960 .... DLB-77, 153

Yates, J. Michael 1938- DLB-60

Yates, Richard 1926-1992 ... DLB-2, 234; Y-81, 92

Yau, John 1950- DLB-234, 312

Yavorov, Peyo 1878-1914 ....DLB-147

Ye Shaojun (Ye Shengtao) 1894-1988.....DLB-328

Yearsley, Ann 1753-1806 ....DLB-109

Yeats, William Butler
  1865-1939 ....DLB-10, 19, 98, 156; CDBLB-5
  The W. B. Yeats Society of N.Y. Y-99

Yellen, Jack 1892-1991................DLB-265

Yep, Laurence 1948- DLB-52, 312

Yerby, Frank 1916-1991 ....DLB-76

Yezierska, Anzia 1880-1970 ....DLB-28, 221

Yolen, Jane 1939- DLB-52

Yonge, Charlotte Mary 1823-1901....DLB-18, 163
  The Charlotte M. Yonge Fellowship Y-98

The York Cycle circa 1376-circa 1569 ....DLB-146

A Yorkshire Tragedy....................DLB-58

Thomas Yoseloff [publishing house] DLB-46

Youd, Sam (see Christopher, John)

Young, A. S. "Doc" 1919-1996.........DLB-241

Young, Al 1939- DLB-33

Young, Arthur 1741-1820..............DLB-158

Young, Dick 1917 or 1918-1987........DLB-171

Young, Edward 1683-1765.............DLB-95

Young, Frank A. "Fay" 1884-1957 ....DLB-241

Young, Francis Brett 1884-1954.........DLB-191

Young, Gavin 1928- DLB-204

Young, Stark 1881-1963........DLB-9, 102; DS-16

Young, Waldeman 1880-1938 ....DLB-26

William Young [publishing house] DLB-49

Young Bear, Ray A. 1950- DLB-175

Yourcenar, Marguerite 1903-1987 ... DLB-72; Y-88

Yovkov, Yordan 1880-1937 ....DLB-147; CDWLB-4

Yu Dafu 1896-1945..................DLB-328

Yushkevich, Semen 1868-1927 ....DLB-317

Yver, Jacques 1520?-1570? DLB-327

Z

Zachariä, Friedrich Wilhelm 1726-1777 ....DLB-97

Zagajewski, Adam 1945- DLB-232

Zagoskin, Mikhail Nikolaevich
  1789-1852 ....DLB-198

Zaitsev, Boris 1881-1972 ....DLB-317

Zajc, Dane 1929- DLB-181

Zālīte, Māra 1952- DLB-232

Zalygin, Sergei Pavlovich 1913-2000.....DLB-302

Zamiatin, Evgenii Ivanovich 1884-1937... DLB-272

Zamora, Bernice 1938- DLB-82

Zamudio, Adela (Soledad) 1854-1928....DLB-283

Zand, Herbert 1923-1970...............DLB-85

Zangwill, Israel 1864-1926...... DLB-10, 135, 197

Zanzotto, Andrea 1921- DLB-128

Zapata Olivella, Manuel 1920- DLB-113

Zapoev, Timur Iur'evich
  (see Kibirov, Timur Iur'evich)

Zasodimsky, Pavel Vladimirovich
  1843-1912 ....DLB-238

Zebra Books........................DLB-46

Zebrowski, George 1945- DLB-8

Zech, Paul 1881-1946 ....DLB-56

Zeidner, Lisa 1955- DLB-120

Zeidonis, Imants 1933- DLB-232

Zeimi (Kanze Motokiyo) 1363-1443 .....DLB-203

Zelazny, Roger 1937-1995 ....DLB-8

Zeng Pu 1872-1935 ....DLB-328

Zenger, John Peter 1697-1746.........DLB-24, 43

Zepheria...........................DLB-172

Zernova, Ruf' 1919-2004 ....DLB-317

Zesen, Philipp von 1619-1689 ....DLB-164

Zhadovskaia, Iuliia Valerianovna
  1824-1883 .... DLB-277

Zhang Ailing (Eileen Chang)
  1920-1995 ....DLB-328

Zhang Henshui 1895-1967 ....DLB-328

Zhang Tianyi 1906-1985...............DLB-328

Zhao Shuli 1906-1970 ....DLB-328

Zhukova, Mar'ia Semenovna
  1805-1855 .... DLB-277

Zhukovsky, Vasilii Andreevich
  1783-1852 ....DLB-205

Zhvanetsky, Mikhail Mikhailovich
  1934- DLB-285

G. B. Zieber and Company DLB-49

Ziedonis, Imants 1933- CDWLB-4

Zieroth, Dale 1946- DLB-60

Zigler und Kliphausen, Heinrich
  Anshelm von 1663-1697 ....DLB-168

Zil'ber, Veniamin Aleksandrovich
  (see Kaverin, Veniamin Aleksandrovich)

Zimmer, Paul 1934- DLB-5

Zinberg, Len (see Lacy, Ed)

Zincgref, Julius Wilhelm 1591-1635 .....DLB-164

Zindel, Paul 1936- DLB-7, 52; CDALB-7

Zinnes, Harriet 1919- DLB-193

Zinov'ev, Aleksandr Aleksandrovich
  1922- DLB-302

Zinov'eva-Annibal, Lidiia Dmitrievna
  1865 or 1866-1907 ....DLB-295

Zinzendorf, Nikolaus Ludwig von
  1700-1760 ....DLB-168

Zitkala-Ša 1876-1938................DLB-175	Zschokke, Heinrich 1771-1848.........DLB-94	Zweig, Arnold 1887-1968.............DLB-66
Zīverts, Mārtiņš 1903-1990...........DLB-220	Zubly, John Joachim 1724-1781.........DLB-31	Zweig, Stefan 1881-1942...........DLB-81, 118
Zlatovratsky, Nikolai Nikolaevich 1845-1911....................DLB-238	Zu-Bolton, Ahmos, II 1936-.........DLB-41	Zwicky, Fay 1933-................DLB-325
Zola, Emile 1840-1902..............DLB-123	Zuckmayer, Carl 1896-1977........DLB-56, 124	Zwinger, Ann 1925-................DLB-275
Zolla, Elémire 1926-...............DLB-196	Zukofsky, Louis 1904-1978..........DLB-5, 165	Zwingli, Huldrych 1484-1531..........DLB-179
Zolotow, Charlotte 1915-...........DLB-52	Zupan, Vitomil 1914-1987...........DLB-181	**Ø**
Zoshchenko, Mikhail Mikhailovich 1895-1958...................DLB-272	Župančič, Oton 1878-1949...DLB-147; CDWLB-4	Øverland, Arnulf 1889-1968.........DLB-297
	zur Mühlen, Hermynia 1883-1951.......DLB-56	

ISBN-13: 978-0-7876-8148-7
ISBN-10: 0-7876-8148-2

PN
171
.P75
N58

2007
pt.2